W0013364

To Carolina wrestling fans
past, present and future

TABLE OF CONTENTS

Graham Cawthon is one of a small but dedicated group of journalists who is keeping pro wrestling history alive, keeping it from fading into distant memory like the heat in a Southern arena or the glory of Bruno in the Garden. I'd like to think I'm another, getting most of my enjoyment from wrestling these days from either reading or writing one of these books about the "good old days".

In this magnificent reference book, Graham recalls nearly every show from Jim Crockett Promotions during a very transformative period, but also tracks the greatest percentage of NWA World Heavyweight Championship defenses outside the territory in the process. There are newspaper clippings and photo illustrations of some of the great cards and moments, to help you visualize the time period, to lose yourself in a memory. And it's a book that, if you're a fan of the glory days of "pro rasslin", you can lean back in the recliner with and kill however much time you have.

There's still a bunch of this sport's history to be documented. But books like this make us all want to continue to try!

Jim Cornette
Louisville, Ky.
December 2013

CONTRIBUTORS

I would like to thank each and every person that has helped in making the site what it is today. Without their support, this book would not exist.

Financial Contributers:

Jared Hawkins
Jim Zordani
Andrew Calvert
John Lister
Richard Rollock
Casey Tomten
Gregory Mosorjak
Dante Ramirez
Sean Oliver
Robert Kleeman
Scotty Wampler
Chris Lesinsky
Joseph Hamdan
Alan Complitano
Mike Abitabile
Michael Shoopman
William Newton
Oswald Jackson
Andy Jackson
Patrick A. Riley
Craig Benee
Cherish Wilson
www.profightdb.com
Mike Levay
Grand National Media
Josh Almas
David Colvin
Ryan Schmauch
Bjoern Schnelle
Jason Bishop
Joseph Sauber
Chip Bland
Jonathan McLarty
Danny Bazarsky
Sean Breazeal
Jason Hunsicker
Aaron Smetlzer
Daniel Quinones
Daniele Fusetto
Dale Hicks
Matt Peddycord

Mike Sernoski
Nicholas Morris
John D'Amato
Damon Campagna
Anthony Fullbrook
Gary Merrithew
Angele Cyr
Michael Wilkinson
Chris Harrington
Anthony Miletic
Gregory Leobilla
Ashley Cox
Michael Sempervive

Individuals:

Aaron Cushman
Adam Firestorm
Adam Martin
Adam Roy
Adam Sanders
Adrián Valdivia
Akeem Parsons
Alan Keiper
Alan Timper
Alex Ho
Alex Josephs aka atox
Alex Padrino
Alex Sarti
Allan Robinson
Andrew Calvert
Andrew Christeson
Andrew Gardner
Andrew McRae
Andrew Mollon
Andrew Pritchard
Andy Roberts
Antoine Cagne
Art Jonathan
Ash Purkiss
Becky Taylor
Ben Ivanson
Ben LeDoux
Ben Martin
Ben Temples
Benjamin Puttmann
Bill Wilson
Blackjack Parsons
Bob Johnson
Bobby Adkins
Brad MacDonald
Brad Stutts
Bradley Owen
Brandon Baker
Brett Morgenheim
Brett Wolverton
Brent Hawryluk

Brian Beasley
Brian Dixon
Brian Bingman
Brian Henke
Brian Matheson
Brian Paige
Brian Pickering
Brian Scala
Brock Moore
Candace Hinchey
Carl Campbell
Casey Tomten
Charles Jean
Charles Martin
Charles Short
Charles Wheeler
Cherish Wilson
Chris Berube
Chris Bradshaw
Chris Corridan
Chris Cushman
Chris Dean
Chris Owens
Chris Putro
Chris Skolds
Chris Smith
Chris Tabar
Christian Heintz
Christian Rhode
Christophe Simon
Christopher Fabris
Clayton Carvalho
Clint Halford
Cory Wiatrek
Craig Skennard
Dan Feriolo
Daniel Clemens
Daniel Hill
Daniel Whitehead
Darren Wyse
Dave DeRobbio
Dave Greiser
Dave Layne
David Andre
David Emmell
David Frederick
David Gochenour
David Grebenc
David Grenier
David Hunter
David James
David Taub
David Wallace
Dennis Jackson
Denny Burkholder
Derek Bedard
Derek Bush

Derek Sabato
Derrick Leroux
Devin Cutting
Devin Kelly
Don R. Willhite Jr.
Doug Garrison
Dustin Robinson
Earl Shelley
Ed Demko
Ed Stylc
Eric Cohen
Eric Denton
Eric Ehrhardt
Eric Foster
Eric Larson
Eric Walker
Erik Carlson
Erik Gerlach
Francesco Casto
Fraser Coffeen
Gareth Reed
Gary Robinson
Gary Will
Gerard Bowes
Glenn Newsome
Gordon
Graham Reynolds
Grant Sawyer
Greg Bernard
Greg Houde
Greg Mosorjak
Greg Nugent
Greg Parks
Greg Rufolo
Guillermo Monti
Houston Mitchell
Issacc Cearc
J Michael Kenyon
Jack Van Dyke
Jake Oresick
Jaime Gonzalez
Jake Pappalardo
James Linnebur
James Maxwell
James Trepanier
Jamie Johnson
Jared Hawkins
Jared Insell
Jared Oloffson
Jason Bishop
Jason Dickinson
Jason Kreitzer
Jason Ouimette
Jason Satterfield
Jed Highum
Jeff Barberi
Jeff Bradley

CONTRIBUTORS

Jeff Fong
Jeffrey Barberi
Jeffrey Jacobson
Jeremy Miles
Jeremy Morgan
Jesse Richardson
Jessica Bullion
Jessica Kuter
Jim Frisk
Jim Zordani
JJ
Joe Jones
Joe Super
Joel Kolsrud
Jon Herman
John Corcoran
John Culbert
John English
John Preston
John Sturm
Johnathan Barton
Jonathan McLarty
Jonathan Raines
Joe Jones
Jordan Claridge
Jose Perez
Joseph Klunk
Josh Eanes
Josh Gaby
Josh Watko
Joshua Morales
JR Jackson
Justin Bailey
Justin Ballard
Justin Domenicucci
Justin Henry
Justin Lijoi
Kavan Hashemian
Keith Brookes
Keith Drabik
Kelly Fairbee
Kenneth McMahon
Kevin Moss
Kevin Barry
Kevin LeClair
Kevin Perry
Kody Hawes
Kris Alvarenga
Kris Levin
Kriss Knights
Kurt Killberg
Kurtis Williams
Larry Stoy
Luis Morales
Luke Hixon
Madison Carter
Maik Burhenne
Mark Davis

Mark Eastridge
Mark Tomol
Mary Blair
Matt Coyle
Matt Davis
Matt Farmer
Matt Henstock
Matt Hern
Matt Jones
Matt Langley
Matt Mattsey
Matt Mauler
Matt Mitchell
Matt O'Brien
Matt Reischl
Matt Wingblad
Matthew Cagle
Max Levy
Michael Bahn
Michael Chilson
Michael Cline
Michael Danilowicz
Michael DeCarolis
Michael Hicks
Michael Rodgers
Michael Motley
Michael Radtke
Michael Schmidt
Michael Silvers
Mike Abitabile
Mike Farro
Mike Labbe
Mike Minadeo
Mike Nice
Mike Noland
Mike DuPree
Mike Sweet
Mister Saint Laurent
Napoleon Santucci
Nick Burgard
Nick Kudreyko
Nick Taylor
Nick West
Noel O'Connor
Pablo Ricca
Pasquale Rulli
Patrick Conkling
Patrick Dailey
Paul Nemer
Paul Zimmerman Jr.
Peter Baird
Peter Tavares
Phil Stenger
Philip Smeltzer
Ramiro Jesus
Escamilla Islas
Raul Garcia
Ray Smith

Ric Gillespie
Ric Smith
Rich Abbott
Rich Jones
Rich Miller
Richard Boscia
Richard Land
Richard J Palladino
Rick Baptist
Rob den Hertog
Rob Thompson
Robert Becker
Robert Hawkins
Robert Portillo
Robert Sandholzer
Robert Sayers
Robert Welch
Robert Wojnarowski
Ron Witmer
Ronald Love
Ronny Kerk
Ross Harris
Rusty Beames
Ryan Droste
Ryan Martinez
Ryan Niemiller
Sam Finley
Sandra Diaz
Scott Douglas
Scott Gold
Scott Thomason
Scott Wojcicki
Sean Watts
Simon Rowley
Stephen Dame
Stephen Gray
Steven Frye
Steve Breech
Steve Dolgosh
Steve Hourdakis
Steve Johnson
Steve Mas
Steve Mueller
Steve Perkins
Steve Nichols
Stephen Lyon
Steven Schera
Steven Smith
Struan Mackenzie
Ted Oliver
Terry Canova
Terry Wall
Thorsten Hogrefe
Tim Johnson
Tim Moysey
Tim Noel
Tim Taylor
Tim Walker

Todd Smith
Tony Bouin
Tom Srbinovski
Trae Wisecarver
Travis Banks
Troy Higgenbotham
Vance Nevada
Wes Kinley
West Potter
Will Bartley
Yair Grinblat
Yasuhiko Morozumi
Anonymous; In memory
of a good friend
MidAtlanticGateway.com

INTRODUCTION

In many ways, it's still 1985 in the Carolinas.

The 2014 infrastructure is all there. But get around the right crowd, and it's like nothing has happened in the pro wrestling world since the heyday of the Horsemen.

Having been a Carolina resident for nearly a decade, I've seen it firsthand.

Go to a pro sporting event -- doesn't matter what kind -- and see if you don't hear a "Woooo" to rival that of Ric Flair's. Go to the right game, and the Nature Boy is liable to make a cameo on the big screen.

The fans are still there. Well, they may not be fans of "sports entertainment" but they remember the days of their youth when they would drive to see Flair, Blackjack Mulligan, Dusty Rhodes, Ricky Steamboat and Ivan Koloff battle it out at the local armory or high school gym.

If they were lucky, they made regular trips to the Dorton Arena, Spartanburg Memorial Auditorium or -- the mecca -- the Greensboro Coliseum.

They can tell you stories about seeing Andre the Giant when he would make his occasional stop through town. Or how Wahoo McDaniel would stitch up his weathered forehead backstage after a bloody brawl, noting it was cheaper than a trip to the emergency room. Or what the atmosphere was like at the first Great American Bash supercard, held at the Charlotte Memorial Stadium.

And then there is the nostalgia scene.

Though they get only periodic stops by nationally recognized groups, wrestling fans in the Carolinas have their pick of numerous independent organizations and conventions to support. And many of these shows successfully rely on the continued drawing power of such names as Ricky Morton, Tully Blanchard, JJ Dillon, Magnum TA, and Nikita Koloff to fill the seats.

This project is two-fold. It's not just the story of Jim Crockett Promotions, following the company from the year of the inaugural Starrcade supercard, the westward expansion into the Georgia, Florida, and Mid-South territories and to the eventual sale to Ted Turner. It's also the story of the NWA World Title.

For many, the NWA championship is synonymous with Crockett and the WCW moniker. But that wasn't always the case. Champions like the Funks, Lou Thesz, and Harley Race certainly defended their heavyweight crown when they came through the Carolinas but their international schedule didn't keep them in town long.

In 1983, the championship was defended throughout multiple territories around the world. From World Class Championship Wrestling in Texas to the Central States territory to Florida, Toronto, Portland and Japan. But in the years that followed, as Jim Crockett Jr. plotted his own westward expansion akin to that of Vince McMahon's, the champion and his belt slowly became the almost exclusive property of Jim Crockett Promotions. Now you can see for yourself how busy the national and international schedule was for the reigning champion, and how his path crisscrossed the feuds and rivalries in the Carolinas before eventually becoming a permanent fixture under the Crockett banner.

In the pages ahead, you will learn the story -- on almost a day-by-day basis -- of JCP's success and eventual downfall in the 1980s. There have already been countless documentaries and interviews conducted on the subject. But there has never before been a study of the schedule, of the spot shows and TV tapings, of the attendance or lack thereof or of Crockett's own national expansion efforts to compete with the growing World Wrestling Federation.

And so this is my love letter to my fellow Carolina residents. The ones that look back fondly on wrestling in the 1980s, years before there was a Monday Night War. The ones that made sure they had front row seats every time their idols came to town. And the ones that will never have a connection to the wrestling world as strong as that provided by Jim Crockett Promotions.

For those that still see Ric Flair as the champ, the Horsemen as the symbol of excellence, the Rock 'n' Roll Express and Midnight Express as tag teams extraordinaire and love the vocal tones of Bob Caudle, David Crockett, et. al., this book is for you.

Didn't grow up at the right time or place? Then this book will, hopefully, show you why so many fans cling to this era and regard it as the standard for what pro wrestling should be.

-- Graham Cawthon

1983.

Hulk Hogan, fresh off the popularity of "Rocky 3," chased AWA champ Nick Bockwinkel across the Twin Cities.

The legendary team of the Road Warriors formed in Georgia.

Jimmy Snuka surpassed champ Bob Backlund as the top fan favorite in the northeast. But the controversial death of Snuka's girlfriend would ultimately hinder his main event potential in the WWF.

Southwest Championship Wrestling, one of the first territories to reach a national audience through cable TV, lost its spot on the USA Network.

Vince McMahon began his plans for national domination.

And, in the Carolinas, Jim Crockett Promotions found itself on the verge of reaching new found heights in popularity.

Spurred on by the business leadership of Jim Crockett Jr. and creative input from Dusty Rhodes, JCP would end up being one of the most talked about promotions not only of the year but of the decade.

At the beginning of 1983, JCP taped their weekly broadcasts in a quaint Charlotte TV studio. A few months later, they upgraded to arenas throughout the territory, increasing production value and attendance.

The blood feud between Ricky Steamboat & Jay Youngblood and Sgt. Slaughter & Don Kernodle culminated that March with a steel cage match that drew more than 15,000 fans to the Greensboro Coliseum, turned thousands away and backed up traffic for miles on I-85.

No doubt inspired by the turnout for "The Final Conflict" cage match, JCP devised a plan to host its traditional Thanksgiving supercard from Greensboro and make it available to more fans than what the arena could accomodate.

The inaugural "Starrcade," centered on Ric Flair's quest to regain the NWA crown from Harley Race, took place that Thanksgiving and was one of the early successes of closed-circuit TV, a precursor to pay-per-view. Fans throughout the Carolinas (as well as Puerto Rico) could travel to their local arena to see an exclusive feed of the action in Greensboro. And despite a winter storm, more than 50,000 fans saw the action live that night.

Closed-circuit was an ever-evolving experiment for the wrestling industry. The WWF saw regular successes by airing a closed-circuit feed of MSG action at the adjacent MSG Theater. But the widely promoted 1976 Muhammad Ali vs. Antonio Inoki battle in Tokyo, backed by Vince McMahon Sr. (who even featured Ali in a confrontation on WWWF TV against Gorilla Monsoon leading into the event), was a disaster. Ticket sales moved so slowly for the closed-circuit show at Shea Stadium that McMahon was forced to bring in a recovering Bruno Sammartino, who suffered a broken neck just months earlier.

It would be years before pay-per-view offerings would become commonplace.

By the end of the year, with JCP as the leading promotion behind the National Wrestling Alliance, plans were already set for Starrcade '84. And with it, a counter to McMahon's national expansion.

But McMahon would leave his own mark on the promotion. Andre the Giant and Women's Champion the Fabulous Moolah, who regularly traveled across various territories including the Carolinas, signed exclusive contracts with the WWF. Additionally, Crockett stars Roddy Piper, Greg Valentine, and Bob Orton Jr. would join the McMahon fold during "The War of '84."

1983

Mid-Atlantic Championship Wrestling - 1/1/83:
Paul Jones & the One Man Gang defeated Mid-Atlantic TV Champion Mike Rotundo & Jimmy Valiant
Bruiser Brody defeated Vinnie Valentino
Tommy Gilbert defeated NWA Tag Team Champion Don Kernodle via disqualification
Mid-Atlantic Heavyweight Champion Jack Brisco & Jerry Brisco defeated Jim Dalton & Ken Timbs
Ricky Steamboat defeated Masa Fuchi

Worldwide - 1/1/83:
Ricky Steamboat defeated Frank Monte
Tommy Gilbert defeated Ken Timbs
Mid-Atlantic TV Champion Mike Rotundo defeated Masa Fuchi
Bruiser Brody defeated Mark Fleming
Mid-Atlantic Heavyweight Champion Jack Brisco & Jerry Brisco defeated Ben Alexander & Jim Dalton

JCP @ Charlotte, NC - Coliseum - January 1, 1983
Sweet Brown Sugar defeated Dory Funk Jr.
NWA US Champion Greg Valentine defeated Bob Orton Jr.
NWA Tag Team Champions Sgt. Slaughter & Don Kernodle defeated Ricky Steamboat & Jay Youngblood
NWA World Champion Ric Flair defeated Roddy Piper

Central States @ St. Louis, MO - January 1, 1983
Butch Reed fought NWA World Champion Ric Flair to a draw in a Best 2 out of 3 falls match; fall #3: the 60-minute time limit expired

JCP @ Roanoke, VA - Civic Center - January 2, 1983
Frank Monte defeated Mark Fleming
Tommy Gilbert defeated Ricky Harris
Iceman King Parsons & Porkchop Cash defeated Masa Fuchi & Gene Anderson
Jimmy Valiant, Sweet Brown Sugar, & Abdullah the Butcher defeated Dory Funk Jr., Paul Jones, & the One Man Gang
Roddy Piper & Bob Orton Jr. defeated NWA World Champion Ric Flair & NWA US Champion Greg Valentine

JCP @ Asheville, NC - Civic Center - January 2, 1983
Mike Davis defeated Ken Timbs
Johnny Weaver & Jerry Brisco defeated Jim Nelson & Jim Dalton
Mid-Atlantic TV Champion Mike Rotundo defeated Dizzy Hogan
Mid-Atlantic Heavyweight Champion Jack Brisco defeated Paul Jones
Jay Youngblood defeated NWA Tag Team Champion Don Kernodle
Ricky Steamboat defeated NWA Tag Team Champion Sgt. Slaughter via disqualification

JCP @ Greensboro, NC - Coliseum - January 2, 1983
Frank Monte defeated Ricky Harris
Vinnie Valentino defeated Bill White
Tommy Gilbert defeated Masa Fuchi
Jimmy Valiant & Abdullah the Butcher defeated Gene Anderson & the One Man Gang
NWA US Champion Greg Valentine defeated Bob Orton Jr.
Ricky Steamboat & Jay Youngblood defeated NWA Tag Team Champions Sgt. Slaughter & Don Kernodle via disqualification
Roddy Piper fought NWA World Champion Ric Flair to a double disqualification

JCP @ Fayetteville, NC - January 3, 1983
Roddy Piper defeated NWA US Champion Greg Valentine

CWF @ West Palm Beach, FL - January 3, 1983
Barry Windham defeated NWA World Champion Ric Flair via disqualification

JCP @ Raleigh, NC - Dorton Arena - January 4, 1983
Vinnie Valentino defeated Ken Timbs
Sweet Brown Sugar defeated Jim Nelson
Mid-Atlantic TV Champion Mike Rotundo defeated Jim Dalton
Jimmy Valiant, Mid-Atlantic Heavyweight Champion Jack Brisco & Jerry Brisco defeated Dory Funk Jr., Paul Jones, & the One Man Gang
Roddy Piper defeated NWA US Champion Greg Valentine

JCP @ Columbia, SC - Township Auditorium - January 4, 1983
Dizzy Hogan defeated Mike Davis
Porkchop Cash & Iceman King Parsons defeated Masa Fuchi & Frank Monte
Gene Anderson defeated Tommy Gilbert
Bob Orton Jr. defeated Bruiser Brody via disqualification
Abdullah the Butcher defeated Jos LeDuc
Ricky Steamboat & Jay Youngblood defeated NWA Tag Team Champions Sgt. Slaughter & Don Kernodle in a non-title match

CWF @ Tampa, FL - January 4, 1983
Kevin Sullivan defeated Brian Blair
Terry Allen & Scott McGhee defeated the Kangaroos
The Midnight Rider defeated the Texan
Mike Graham, Ron Bass, & Rufus R. Jones defeated Jake Roberts, Angelo Mosca, & Jimmy Garvin
Barry Windham defeated NWA World Champion Ric Flair via disqualification

JCP @ Charlotte, NC - January 5, 1983
TV taping:
Ricky Steamboat & Jay Youngblood defeated Ricky Harris & Masa Fuchi

CWF @ Miami Beach, FL - Convention Center - January 5, 1983 (3,284)
Scott McGhee fought Jimmy Garvin to a draw
Jake Roberts defeated Terry Allen
Angelo Mosca defeated the Midnight Rider via disqualification
Mike Graham defeated Kevin Sullivan
The Fabulous Kangaroos defeated Barry Windham & Ron Bass
NWA World Champion Ric Flair defeated Rufus R. Jones via disqualification

JCP @ Sumter, SC - Sumter County Exhibition Center - January 5, 1983
Vinnie Valentino vs. Bill White
Jim Dalton vs. Iceman King Parsons
Larry Lane vs. Mike Davis
Mid-Atlantic Heavyweight Champion Jack Brisco vs. Jim Nelson
Abdullah the Butcher, Jimmy Valiant, & Sweet Brown Sugar vs. Johnny Gray, Paul Jones, & Brusier Brody

WWC @ San Juan, Puerto Rico - January 6, 1983
WWC World Champion Carlos Colon pinned NWA World Champion Ric Flair in a non-title match with a backslide (or via submission?)

JCP @ Norfolk, VA - Scope - January 6, 1983
Jim Nelson defeated Vinnie Valentino
The One Man Gang defeated Mike Davis
Johnny Weaver & Tommy Gilbert defeated Red Dog Lane & Ken Timbs
NWA US Champion Greg Valentine, Gene Anderson, & Dory Funk Jr. defeated Abdullah the Butcher, Jimmy Valiant, & Sweet Brown Sugar in a steel cage match
Mid-Atlantic TV Champion Mike Rotundo defeated Paul Jones
Ricky Steamboat & Jay Youngblood fought NWA Tag Team Champions Sgt. Slaughter & Don Kernodle to a double count-out

WWC @ Caguas, Puerto Rico - January 7, 1983
Ric Flair defeated Hercules Ayala

JCP @ Richmond, VA - Coliseum - January 7, 1983
Mike Davis defeated Masa Fuchi
Jim Nelson defeated King Parsons
Johnny Weaver & Vinnie Valentino defeated Gene Anderson & Red Dog Lane
Abdullah the Butcher & Bob Orton Jr. defeated Jos LeDuc & One Man Gang
Jimmy Valiant defeated NWA US Champion Greg Valentine
Ricky Steamboat & Jay Youngblood fought NWA Tag Team Champions Sgt. Slaughter & Don Kernodle to a double count-out

JCP @ Charleston, SC - County Hall - January 7, 1983
Brickhouse Brown defeated Ali Bey
Mark Fleming defeated Hans Schroeder
Penny Mitchell & Peggy Patterson defeated Donna Christanello & Leilani Kai
Don Kernodle & Ernie Ladd defeated Angelo Mosca Sr. & Jr.

Mid-Atlantic Championship Wrestling - 1/8/83:
Mid-Atlantic TV Champion Mike Rotundo defeated Ken Timbs
Jerry Brisco, Bob Orton Jr., & Dick Slater fought Dory Funk Jr., Red Dog Lane, & NWA US Champion Greg Valentine to a double disqualification after Slater turned on his team
Jay Youngblood defeated Ricky Harris
Johnny Weaver defeated NWA Tag Team Champion Don Kernodle via disqualification
Tommy Gilbert defeated Ben Alexander

Worldwide - 1/8/83:
Roddy Piper defeated Ken Timbs
Ricky Steamboat & Jay Youngblood defeated Ricky Harris & Masa Fuchi
NWA US Champion Greg Valentine & Dick Slater defeated Tommy Gilbert & Mark Fleming
Bob Orton Jr. defeated Frank Monte
Mid-Atlantic TV Champion Mike Rotundo defeated Red Dog Lane

WWC @ San Juan, Puerto Rico - January 8, 1983
Carlos Colon & the Invader defeated NWA World Champion Ric Flair & Terry Funk

Toronto, Ontario - Maple Leaf Gardens - January 9, 1983
King Parsons defeated Jerry Bryant at 8:12
Jim Nelson defeated Nick DeCarlo at 9:56
Rudy & Terry Kay defeated Ken Timbs & Frank Monte at 16:04
Salvatore Bellomo defeated Buddy Rose via disqualification at 14:06
North American Champion Leo Burke defeated Johnny Weaver at 13:36
Ray Stevens defeated Jimmy Snuka via count-out at 10:24
Canadian Champion Angelo Mosca defeated Leroy Brown in a steel cage match at 7:17

JCP @ Hampton, VA - Coliseum - January 9, 1983
Bob Orton Jr. defeated NWA US Champion Greg Valentine via disqualification

JCP @ Savannah, GA - Civic Center - January 9, 1983
Abe Jacobs defeated Bill White
Larry Lane defeated Mike Davis
Porkchop Cash defeated Ricky Harris via disqualification
Mid-Atlantic Heavyweight Champion Jack Brisco, Mid-Atlantic TV Champion Mike Rotundo, & Abdullah the Butcher defeated Larry Lane, Gene Anderson, & Paul Jones

Ricky Steamboat & Jay Youngblood defeated NWA Tag Team Champions Sgt. Slaughter & Don Kernodle

WWC @ Santo Domingo, Dominican Republic - January 9, 1983
Victor Jovica defeated Roddy Piper via disqualification
Jack Veneno pinned NWA World Champion Ric Flair to win the title; the decision was later reversed

CWF @ West Palm Beach, FL - January 10, 1983
NWA World Champion Ric Flair defeated Barry Windham

JCP @ Greenville, SC - January 10, 1983
Abe Jacobs defeated Ben Alexander
Dizzy Hogan defeated Porkchop Cash
Mid-Atlantic TV Champion Mike Rotundo defeated Paul Jones
Mid-Atlantic Heavyweight Champion Jack Brisco defeated Dory Funk Jr. ($100,000 challenge)
Jerry Brisco defeated NWA US Champion Greg Valentine
Ricky Steamboat & Jay Youngblood defeated NWA Tag Team Champions Sgt. Slaughter & Don Kernodle in a non-title match

JCP @ Columbia, SC - January 11, 1983
Vinnie Valentino defeated Jim Dalton
Johnny Weaver defeated Masa Fuchi
Tommy Gilbert defeated Bill White
Bob Orton Jr., Mid-Atlantic Heavyweight Champion Jack Brisco & Jerry Brisco defeated Gene Anderson, Jim Nelson, & Larry Lane
NWA US Champion Greg Valentine defeated Roddy Piper
Jimmy Valiant defeated the One Man Gang via disqualification

JCP @ Raleigh, NC - January 11, 1983
Mike Davis defeated Frank Monte
Sweet Brown Sugar defeated Dizzy Hogan
Ricky Harris & Ken Timbs defeated Porkchop Cash & Iceman King Parsons
Mid-Atlantic TV Champion Mike Rotundo defeated Paul Jones
Abdullah the Butcher defeated Dory Funk Jr. via disqualification
Ricky Steamboat & Jay Youngblood defeated NWA Tag Team Champions Sgt. Slaughter & Don Kernodle via count-out

CWF @ Tampa, FL - Ft. Hesterly Armory - January 11, 1983
Leroy Brown defeated Ron Bass
The Kangaroos defeated Scott McGhee & Terry Allen
Charlie Cook defeated Jimmy Garvin via disqualification when JJ Dillon interfered
Rufus R. Jones defeated Jake Roberts via disqualification
The Midnight Rider & Barry Windham defeated NWA World Champion Ric Flair & Kevin Sullivan at the 10-minute mark in a mask vs. money match when the Rider pinned Flair

JCP @ Charlotte, NC - January 12, 1983
TV taping:
Ricky Steamboat & Jay Youngblood defeated Larry Lane & Ken Timbs

CWF @ Miami, FL - Baseball Stadium - January 12, 1983 (4,625)
Scott McGhee fought Kangaroo #2 to a draw
Terry Allen defeated Kangaroo #1 via disqualification
Charlie Cook defeated Jimmy Garvin via disqualification
Barry Windham, Rufus R. Jones, & Mike Graham defeated Kevin Sullivan, Leroy Brown, & Angelo Mosca
NWA World Champion Ric Flair pinned Ron Bass
The Midnight Rider defeated Jake Roberts in a lights out $10,000 vs. mask match

JCP @ York, SC - York Comprehensive High School - January 13, 1983
Tommy Gilbert vs. Jim Nelson
Mid-Atlantic TV Champion Mike Rotundo vs. Larry Lane
Sweet Brown Sugar vs. Dick Slater
Jimmy Valiant, Bob Orton Jr., & Jay Youngblood vs. Jos LeDuc, Paul Jones, & the One Man Gang (w/ Oliver Humperdink)
Mid-Atlantic Heavyweight Champion Jack Brisco vs. NWA US Champion Greg Valentine

JCP @ Charleston, SC - January 14, 1983
Dizzy Hogan defeated Ricky Harris
Sweet Brown Sugar defeated Jim Nelson
The One Man Gang defeated Tommy Gilbert
Dory Funk Jr. defeated Mid-Atlantic TV Champion Mike Rotundo
Roddy Piper defeated NWA US Champion Greg Valentine

CWF @ Orlando, FL - January 14, 1983
The Midnight Rider defeated NWA World Champion Ric Flair

Mid-Atlantic Championship Wrestling - 1/15/83:
NWA Tag Team Champions Sgt. Slaughter & Don Kernodle defeated Tommy Gilbert & Vinnie Valentino
Jimmy Valiant, Mid-Atlantic TV Champion Mike Rotundo, & Bob Orton Jr. defeated Bill White, Jim Nelson, & Ricky Harris
Jerry Brisco & Sweet Brown Sugar defeated Dory Funk Jr. & Dick Slater
Johnny Weaver defeated Ken Timbs
Dick Slater defeated Mike Davis

Worldwide - 1/15/83:
Ricky Steamboat & Jay Youngblood defeated Red Dog Lane & Ken Timbs
NWA US Champion Greg Valentine, Dory Funk Jr., & Dick Slater defeated King Parsons, Tommy Gilbert, & Vinnie Valentino
Mid-Atlantic TV Champion Mike Rotundo defeated Ricky Harris

Bob Orton Jr. defeated Bill White
Johnny Weaver & Sweet Brown Sugar defeated Jim Dalton & Masa Fuchi

CWF @ Tampa, FL - January 15, 1983
Charlie Cook & Scott McGhee fought the Kangaroos to a draw
Kevin Sullivan defeated Terry Allen
Ron Bass defeated Jake Roberts
Rufus R. Jones defeated Angelo Mosca via disqualification
Mike Graham defeated Jimmy Garvin
The Midnight Rider fought Leroy Brown to a draw
NWA World Champion Ric Flair defeated Barry Windham

GCW @ Atlanta, GA - WTBS Studios - January 15, 1983
TV taping:
NWA World Champion Ric Flair defeated Pat Rose

JCP @ Spartanburg, SC - Memorial Auditorium - January 15, 1983
Red Dog Lane pinned Tommy Gilbert
Dizzy Hogan defeated Ken Timbs
Johnny Weaver & Mike Davis defeated Bill White & Gene Anderson
Dory Funk Jr. fought Sweet Brown Sugar to a draw
Jimmy Valiant, Jerry Brisco, & Bob Orton Jr. defeated NWA US Champion Greg Valentine, Dick Slater, & the One Man Gang (sub. for Sir Oliver Humperdink)

JCP @ Kingston, NC - January 15, 1983
Ricky Harris defeated Vinnie Valentino
Porkchop Cash & Iceman King Parsons defeated Masa Fuchi & Jim Dalton
Mid-Atlantic TV Champion Mike Rotundo defeated Jim Nelson
Mid-Atlantic TV Champion Mike Rotundo defeated Paul Jones via disqualification
NWA Tag Team Champions Sgt. Slaughter & Don Kernodle defeated Porkchop Cash & Iceman King Parsons

JCP @ Asheville, NC - Civic Center - January 16, 1983
Tiny Tom defeated Little Tokyo
Mark Fleming defeated Ken Timbs
Tommy Gilbert defeated Larry Lane
Johnny Weaver defeated Gene Anderson
Mid-Atlantic Heavyweight Champion Jack Brisco defeated Paul Jones
NWA US Champion Greg Valentine & Dick Slater defeated Bob Orton Jr. & Jerry Brisco
Ricky Steamboat & Jay Youngblood defeated NWA Tag Team Champions Sgt. Slaughter & Don Kernodle via count-out

JCP @ Hampton, VA - January 16, 1983
Sweet Brown Sugar defeated Dizzy Hogan
Jimmy Valiant defeated the One Man Gang
Dory Funk Jr. defeated Mid-Atlantic Heavyweight Champion

Jack Brisco
NWA US Champion Greg Valentine defeated Bob Orton Jr.

Central States @ Wichita, KS - January 17, 1983
NWA World Champion Ric Flair vs. Harley Race

JCP @ Iva, NC - January 17, 1983
Ricky Harris defeated Frank Monte
Iceman King Parsons defeated Bill White
Johnny Weaver & Tommy Gilbert defeated Larry Lane & Gene Anderson
Jerry Brisco defeated NWA Tag Team Champion Sgt. Slaughter via disqualification
Ricky Steamboat defeated NWA US Champion Greg Valentine

JCP @ Columbia, SC - January 18, 1983
Vinnie Valentino defeated Frank Monte
Bill White defeated Mike Davis
Sweet Brown Sugar defeated Paul Jones
Jimmy Valiant defeated the One Man Gang
Dick Slater defeated Bob Orton Jr.
Mid-Atlantic Heavyweight Champion Jack Brisco defeated Dory Funk Jr.
Tiny Tom defeated Little Tokyo
Ricky Steamboat & Jay Youngblood defeated NWA Tag Team Champions Sgt. Slaughter & Don Kernodle via disqualification

Central States @ Joplin, MO - January 18, 1983
NWA World Champion Ric Flair fought Harley Race to a double disqualification

Central States @ Decatur, IL - January 19, 1983
NWA World Champion Ric Flair defeated Harley Race via disqualification

Central States @ Kansas City, KS - January 20, 1983
Bruiser Brody fought NWA World Champion Ric Flair to a draw

JCP @ Norfolk, VA - January 20, 1983
Tiny Tom defeated Little Tokyo
Tommy Gilbert defeated Larry Lane
Mid-Atlantic Heavyweight Champion Jack Brisco defeated Paul Jones
Dick Slater defeated Jerry Brisco
Johnny Weaver, Jimmy Valiant, & Sweet Brown Sugar defeated NWA US Champion Greg Valentine, Dory Funk Jr., & Sir Oliver Humperdink
Ricky Steamboat & Jay Youngblood defeated NWA Tag Team Champions Sgt. Slaughter & Don Kernodle

JCP @ Richmond, VA - Coliseum - January 21, 1983
Mid-Atlantic TV Champion Mike Rotundo defeated Dizzy Hogan
Tiny Tom defeated Little Tokyo

18

Roddy Piper fought Dick Slater to a no contest
Jimmy Valiant defeated Sir Oliver Humperdink
Ricky Steamboat & Jay Youngblood defeated NWA Tag Team
Champions Sgt. Slaughter & Don Kernodle

Central States @ Chillicothe, MO - Fieldhouse - January 21, 1983
Buzz Tyler vs. NWA World Champion Ric Flair

Worldwide - 1/22/83:
NWA Tag Team Champions Sgt. Slaughter & Don Kernodle
defeated Iceman King Parsons & Mark Fleming
Jimmy Valiant, Bob Orton Jr., & Mid-Atlantic TV Champion
Mike Rotundo defeated Bill White, Private Nelson, & Ricky
Harris
Jerry Brisco & Sweet Brown Sugar defeated Dick Slater & Dory
Funk Jr.
Johnny Weaver defeated Ken Timbs
Dick Slater defeated Mike Davis

GCW @ Atlanta, GA - WTBS Studios - January 22, 1983
TV taping:
Butch Reed defeated NWA World Champion Ric Flair

JCP @ Greensboro, NC - Coliseum - January 23, 1983 (matinee)
The One Man Gang defeated Jimmy Valiant
Tiny Tom defeated Little Tokyo
Mid-Atlantic Heavyweight Champion Jack Brisco, Sweet Sugar
Brown, & Mid-Atlantic TV Champion Mike Rotundo defeated
Dory Funk Jr., Paul Jones, & Larry Lane
Roddy Piper & Jerry Brisco defeated NWA US Champion Greg
Valentine & Dick Slater
NWA Tag Team Champions Sgt. Slaughter & Don Kernodle
defeated Ricky Steamboat & Jay Youngblood

Toronto, Ontario - Maple Leaf Gardens - January 23, 1983
Billy Red Lyons defeated Jerry Bryant at 13:52
Johnny Weaver defeated Tim Gerard at 10:21
The Destroyer & Bobby Bass defeated Rudy & Terry Kay at
22:46
Leo Burke fought Tony Parisi to a 20-minute draw
Big John Studd defeated Tony Garea at 15:02
Ricky Steamboat & Jay Youngbloow defeated NWA Tag Team
Champions Sgt. Slaughter & Don Kernodle via disqualification
Jimmy Snuka defeated Ray Stevens at 8:56

JCP @ Charlotte, NC - January 23, 1983
Dory Funk Jr. defeated Mid-Atlantic Heavyweight Champion
Jack Brisco to win the title

GCW @ Atlanta, GA - Omni - January 23, 1983
Brad Armstrong defeated Chick Donovan
The Moondogs (w/ JJ Dillon) defeated Tom Prichard & Joe
Lightfoot
Paul Ellering defeated Johnny Rich
Ray Candy fought the Super Destroyer to a draw
Bruiser Brody defeated Tito Santana
NWA National Heavyweight Champion Paul Orndorff defeated
Ivan Koloff
Ole Anderson & Buzz Sawyer defeated Stan Hansen & Tommy
Rich
Butch Reed defeated NWA World Champion Ric Flair in a
$5,000 challenge match

GCW @ Charleston, WV - January 24, 1983
Butch Reed defeated NWA World Champion Ric Flair via
disqualification

JCP @ Fayetteville, NC - January 24, 1983
Masa Fuchi defeated Vinnie Valentino
Iceman King Parsons defeated Ricky Harris
Johnny Weaver defeated Paul Jones
Gene Anderson & Larry Lane defeated Tommy Gilbert &
Sweet Brown Sugar
Jack Brisco defeated Mid-Atlantic Heavyweight Champion
Dory Funk Jr.
Ricky Steamboat & Jay Youngbloow defeated NWA Tag Team
Champions Sgt. Slaughter & Don Kernodle

JCP @ Greenville, SC - Memorial Auditorium - January 24, 1983
Mike Davis defeated Ken Timbs
Dizzy Hogan defeated Porkchop Cash
Tiny Tom defeated Little Tokyo
Mid-Atlantic TV Champion Mike Rotundo defeated Jim Nelson
(sub. for Jos LeDuc)
Jimmy Valiant defeated the One Man Gang via disqualification
Roddy Piper & Jack Brisco defeated NWA US Champion Greg
Valentine & Dick Slater

JCP @ Columbia, SC - January 25, 1983
Iceman King Parsons defeated Jim Dalton
Gene Anderson & Jim Nelson defeated Mike Davis & Tommy
Gilbert
Jack Brisco defeated Larry Lane
Jimmy Valiant defeated the One Man Gang
Roddy Piper, Jerry Brisco, & Johnny Weaver defeated NWA
US Champion Greg Valentine, Mid-Atlantic Heavyweight
Champion Dory Funk Jr., & Dick Slater

GCW @ Charleston, WV - Civic Center - January 25, 1983
Brad Armstrong fought Chick Donovan to a draw
The Super Destroyer defeated Johnny Rich
Bruiser Brody defeated Tito Santana
Stan Hansen defeated Ole Anderson via disqualification
Ivan Koloff & Buzz Sawyer defeated Tommy Rich & Paul
Orndorff

NWA World Champion Ric Flair defeated Butch Reed via disqualification

GCW @ Canton, OH - January 25, 1983
NWA World Champion Ric Flair defeated Paul Orndorff

JCP @ Charlotte, NC - January 26, 1983
TV taping:
Ricky Steamboat & Jay Youngblood defeated Frank Monte & Jim Dalton
NWA World Champion Ric Flair defeated Pat Rose

JCP @ Sumter, SC - Sumter County Exhibition Center - January 26, 1983
Tiny Tom defeated Little Tokyo
Porkchop Cash defeated Masa Fuchi
Tommy Gilbert defeated Larry Lane
Mid-Atlantic TV Champion Mike Rotundo defeated Paul Jones
Ricky Steamboat & Jay Youngbloow defeated NWA Tag Team Champions Sgt. Slaughter & Don Kernodle

JCP @ Harrisonburg, VA - High School - January 27, 1983
Jerry Brisco, Johnny Weaver, & Abdullah the Butcher vs. Paul Jones, Jos LeDuc, & Sir Oliver Humperdink
Bob Orton Jr. vs. Dick Slater
Roddy Piper vs. NWA US Champion Greg Valentine

Worldwide - 1/29/83:
Jerry Brisco defeated Frank Monte
NWA US Champion Greg Valentine & Dick Slater defeated King Parsons & Mike Davis
Mid-Atlantic Heavyweight Champion Dory Funk Jr. defeated Vinnie Valentino
The One Man Gang defeated Rick Benfield
Sweet Brown Sugar, Jimmy Valiant, & Dizzy Hogan defeated Ricky Harris, Ken Timbs, & Ben Alexander
Ricky Steamboat & Jay Youngblood defeated Jim Dalton & Frank Monte

GCW @ Columbus, OH - Ohio Center - January 29, 1983
The Iron Sheik defeated Tito Santana
Dick Murdoch defeated the Super Destroyer
Bruiser Brody defeated Brad Armstrong
Paul Orndorff defeated Ivan Koloff
Stan Hansen & Tommy Rich defeated Ole Anderson & Buzz Sawyer via disqualification
NWA World Champion Ric Flair defeated Butch Reed via disqualification

JCP @ Charleston, SC - January 28, 1983
Tiny Tom defeated Little Tokyo
Ken Timbs defeated Iceman King Parsons
Jim Nelson defeated Mike Davis
Sweet Brown Sugar defeated Larry Lane

The One Man Gang defeated Jimmy Valiant via disqualification
Jack Brisco defeated Mid-Atlantic Heavyweight Champion Dory Funk Jr.
Ricky Steamboat & Jay Youngbloow defeated NWA Tag Team Champions Sgt. Slaughter & Don Kernodle

Mid-Atlantic Championship Wrestling - 1/29/83:
NWA US Champion Greg Valentine defeated Mike Davis
Dick Slater defeated Rick Benfield
NWA Tag Team Champions Sgt. Slaughter & Don Kernodle defeated Gary Black & Ken Hall
Dizzy Hogan & Sweet Sugar Brown defeated Ricky Harris & Ken Timbs

JCP @ Charlotte, NC - Coliseum - January 30, 1983
Mid-Atlantic TV Champion Mike Rotundo won an 18-man battle royal
Dick Slater defeated Jerry Brisco via disqualification
Jimmy Valiant defeated the One Man Gang
Roddy Piper & Dusty Rhodes defeated Paul Jones & Red Dog Lane
Mid-Atlantic Heavyweight Champion Dory Funk Jr. defeated Jack Brisco
NWA US Champion Greg Valentine vs. ?
Ricky Steamboat & Jay Youngblood fought NWA Tag Team Champions Sgt. Slaughter & Don Kernodle to a double disqualification

JCP @ Greenville, SC - Memorial Auditorium - January 31, 1983
Porkchop Cash & Iceman King Parsons defeated Ken Timbs (sub. for Ricky Harris) & Jim Dalton
Dizzy Hogan defeated Ricky Harris
Johnny Weaver defeated Gene Anderson
Jimmy Valiant defeated the One Man Gang in a No DQ match
Jack Brisco defeated Dick Slater via disqualification
NWA Tag Team Champions Sgt. Slaughter & Don Kernodle defeated Ricky Steamboat & Jay Youngblood in a lumberjack match

JCP @ Lumberton, NC - February 1983
Mid-Atlantic Heavyweight Champion Dory Funk Jr. vs. Jack Brisco

JCP @ Columbia, SC - February 1, 1983
Bill White defeated Mike Davis
Vinnie Valentino defeated Ken Timbs
Johnny Weaver & Tommy Gilbert defeated Gene Anderson & Larry Lane
Jerry Brisco fought Mid-Atlantic Heavyweight Champion Dory Funk Jr. to a draw
Roddy Piper defeated Dick Slater via disqualification
Ricky Steamboat & Jay Youngblood defeated NWA Tag Team Champions Sgt. Slaughter & Don Kernodle in a non-title bootcamp match

JCP @ Raleigh, NC - Dorton Arena - February 1, 1983
Porkchop Cash & Iceman King Parsons defeated Masa Fuchi & Ricky Harris
Dizzy Hogan defeated the Champ (Brian Blair)
Sweet Brown Sugar defeated Paul Jones
Mid-Atlantic TV Champion Mike Rotundo defeated Jim Nelson
Jack Brisco defeated NWA US Champion Greg Valentine
The One Man Gang defeated Jimmy Valiant via disqualification

JCP @ Charlotte, NC - February 2, 1983
TV taping:
Ricky Steamboat & Jay Youngblood defeated Ricky Harris & Ken Timbs

WCCW @ Lawton, OK - February 2, 1983
NWA World Champion Ric Flair defeated David Von Erich via disqualification

GCW @ Dayton, OH - Hara Arena - February 3, 1983
Johnny Rich defeated Chick Donovan
Tito Santana fought the Super Destroyer to a draw
Bruiser Brody defeated Brad Armstrong
Ivan Koloff, Ole Anderson, & Buzz Sawyer defeated Butch Reed, Tommy Rich, & Stan Hansen
NWA World Champion Ric Flair defeated Paul Orndorff

JCP @ Sumter, SC - February 3, 1983
Abe Jacobs defeated Ken Timbs
Ricky Harris defeated Mike Davis
Mid-Atlantic TV Champion Mike Rotundo defeated Dizzy Hogan
Jack Brisco defeated Paul Jones
Ricky Steamboat & Jay Youngblood defeated NWA Tag Team Champions Sgt. Slaughter & Don Kernodle via disqualification

JCP @ Norfolk, VA - Febraury 3, 1983
Frank Monte defeated Mark Fleming
Porkchop Cash defeated Masa Fuchi
Johnny Weaver, Tommy Gilbert, & Iceman King Parsons defeated Jim Nelson, Gene Anderson, & Larry Lane
Mid-Atlantic Heavyweight Champion Dory Funk Jr. defeated Sweet Brown Sugar Jimmy Valiant defeated the One Man Gang
NWA US Champion Greg Valentine defeated the Champ
Roddy Piper defeated Dick Slater

WCCW @ Dallas, TX - Sportatorium - February 4, 1983
TV taping:
Brian Adias & Velvet McIntyre defeated Magic Dragon & Judy Martin
King Kong Bundy defeated Sal Olivares
Texas Heavyweight Champion David Von Erich defeated Bill Irwin
Jose Lothario & Al Madril defeated Michael Hayes & Buddy Roberts via disqualification

The Great Kabuki defeated Checkmate via disqualification
NWA World Champion Ric Flair defeated Terry Gordy

JCP @ Richmond, VA - Coliseum - February 4, 1983
Abe Jacobs & Mark Fleming defeated Frank Monte & Jim Dalton
Johnny Weaver defeated Paul Jones via disqualification
The One Man Gang defeated Jimmy Valiant via disqualification
Mid-Atlantic TV Champion Mike Rotundo defeated Mid-Atlantic Heavyweight Champion Dory Funk Jr.
Roddy Piper & the Champ defeated NWA US Champion Greg Valentine & Dick Slater

JCP @ Charleston, SC - February 4, 1983
Porkchop Cash & Iceman King Parsons vs. Ken Timbs & Masa Fuchi
Jim Nelson vs. Mike Davis
Sweet Brown Sugar vs. Ricky Harris
Mid-Atlantic Heavyweight Champion Jack Brisco vs. Dizzy Hogan
NWA Tag Team Champions Sgt. Slaughter & Don Kernodle vs. Ricky Steamboat & Jay Youngblood (lumerjack match)

Mid-Atlantic Championship Wrestling - 2/5/83:
Ricky Steamboat & Jay Youngblood defeated Ricky Harris & Ken Timbs
Mid-Atlantic Heavyweight Champion Dory Funk Jr. defeated Tommy Gilbert
The One Man Gang defeated Mike Davis
Mid-Atlantic TV Champion Mike Rotundo defeated Frank Monte

Worldwide - 2/5/83:
NWA Tag Team Champions Sgt. Slaughter & Don Kernodle defeated Dizzy Hogan & Mike Davis
The Champ defeated Ricky Harris
Mid-Atlantic TV Champion Mike Rotundo defeated Ken Timbs
Sweet Brown Sugar defeated Frank Monte

JCP @ Greensboro, NC - Coliseum - February 5, 1983
NWA US Champion Greg Valentine & Iceman King Parsons defeated Masa Fuchi & Ken Timbs
Dizzy Hogan defeated Bill White
Dusty Rhodes defeated Gene Anderson
Jimmy Valiant defeated the One Man Gang
Dick Slater defeated Jerry Brisco
Ricky Steamboat & Jay Youngblood fought NWA Tag Team Champions Sgt. Slaughter & Don Kernodle to a no contest when Steamboat and Slaughter became physical with the two referees used for the match; after the bout, Steamboat used a steel chair on the champions and the brawl continued between the two teams for several minutes; eventually, Steamboat & Youngblood gained the upper hand over Slaughter & Kernodle until referees and other wrestlers came out to break up the fight

WCCW @ Seagoville, TX - February 5, 1983
NWA World Champion Ric Flair fought Kevin Von Erich to a double disqualification

JCP @ Fayetteville, NC - Cumberland County Civic Center - February 6, 1983
Tommy Gilbert defeated the Champ
Mid-Atlantic TV Champion Mike Rotundo defeated Larry Lane
Jimmy Valiant defeated the One Man Gang
NWA Tag Team Champions Sgt. Slaughter & Don Kernodle defeated Dizzy Hogan & Sweet Brown Sugar
Jay Youngblood defeated Mid-Atlantic Heavyweight Champion Dory Funk Jr. in a bounty match
NWA US Champion Greg Valentine & Dick Slater defeated Mid-Atlantic TV Champion Mike Rotundo & Jack Brisco
NWA World Champion Ric Flair defeated Ricky Steamboat

JCP @ Greenville, SC - Memorial Auditorium - February 7, 1983
Vinnie Valentino defeated Frank Monte
Jack Brisco defeated Mid-Atlantic Heavyweight Champion Dory Funk Jr.
Johnny Weaver & Jerry Brisco defeated Gene Anderson & Masa Fuchi
Dick Slater defeated ?
Ricky Steamboat & Jay Youngblood defeated NWA Tag Team Champions Sgt. Slaughter & Don Kernodle in a non-title bootcamp match
NWA World Champion Ric Flair defeated Mid-Atlantic TV Champion Mike Rotundo

JCP @ Columbia, SC - February 8, 1983
Porkchop Cash & Vinnie Valentino defeated Ken Timbs & Jim Dalton
Johnny Weaver defeated Gene Anderson
Jay Youngblood defeated Mid-Atlantic Heavyweight Champion Dory Funk Jr.
Dick Slater defeated the Champ
Jack & Jerry Brisco defeated NWA Tag Team Champions Sgt. Slaughter & Don Kernodle via disqualification
NWA World Champion Ric Flair defeated Ricky Steamboat

CWF @ Miami, FL - February 9, 1983 (6,196)
Scott McGhee & Terry Allen fought the Kangaroos to a draw
Charlie Cook defeated Cyclone Negro
Rufus R. Jones & Ron Bass defeated Angelo Mosca & Leroy Brown via disqualification
Roddy Piper defeated Mr. NY; after the match, Piper unmasked him to be Chic Donovan
Mike Graham defeated Don Kent
Andre the Giant & Barry Windham defeated Kevin Sullivan & Jake Roberts
The Midnight Rider defeated NWA World Champion Ric Flair to win the title

JCP @ Norfolk, VA - February 10, 1983
Dizzy Hogan defeated Ricky Harris
Mid-Atlantic TV Champion Mike Rotundo defeated Larry Lane
Roddy Piper & Jerry Brisco defeated NWA US Champion Greg Valentine & Dick Slater
Jack Brisco won a battle royal
NWA World Champion Ric Flair defeated Ricky Steamboat

JCP @ Charleston, SC - County Hall - February 11, 1983
Frank Monte defeated Ricky Harris
Tommy Gilbert fought Larry Lane to a draw
Sweet Brown Sugar defeated the Ninja
Dick Slater defeated Jerry Brisco
Jack Brisco defeated Mid-Atlantic Heavyweight Champion Dory Funk Jr. via disqualification

Central States @ St. Louis, MO - Kiel Auditorium - February 11, 1983 (19,819)
Shown on Japan TV:
Roger Kirby defeated Manny Fernandez at 12:11
Bill Cody, Buzz Tyler, & Rick Martel defeated Crusher Ayala, Dewey Robertson, & Kim Duk at 10:08
Ken Patera defeated Ox Baker at 7:28
Butch Reed defeated Bobby Duncum at 19:04
Bob Orton Jr. & Dick Murdoch defeated Bob Brown & Dick the Bruiser at 15:41
Missouri Heavyweight Champion Kerry Von Erich defeated Greg Valentine at 22:04
NWA World Champion Ric Flair fought Bruiser Brody to a draw in a Best 2 out of 3 falls match; fall #1: Brody pinned Flair at 21:04; fall #2: Brody was disqualified at 43:44; fall #3: the 60-minute time limit expired
Giant Baba defeated PWF Heavyweight Champion Harley Race to win the title at 13:04

CWF @ Miami, FL - February 11, 1983
NWA World Champion Ric Flair defeated the Midnight Rider via disqualification

Mid-Atlantic Championship Wrestling - 2/12/83:
Jack Brisco defeated Ricky Harris
Jerry Brisco & Mid-Atlantic TV Champion Mike Rotundo defeated Mid-Atlantic Heavyweight Champion Dory Funk Jr. & Dick Slater via disqualification
Dizzy Hogan & Sweet Brown Sugar defeated Jim Dalton & Ken Timbs

Worldwide - 2/12/83:
Dizzy Hogan & Sweet Brown Sugar defeated Ricky Harris & Red Dog Lane
Mid-Atlantic Heavyweight Champion Dory Funk Jr. defeated Frank Monte Dick Slater defeated Mike Thompson
Mid-Atlantic TV Champion Mike Rotundo defeated Ken Timbs

JCP @ Sumter, SC - February 12, 1983
Frank Monte & Vinnie Valentino defeated Ken Timbs & Masa Fuchi
Sweet Brown Sugar defeated the One Man Gang
NWA Tag Team Champions Sgt. Slaughter & Don Kernodle defeated Mid-Atlantic TV Champion Mike Rotundo & Jerry Brisco
NWA World Champion Ric Flair defeated Jimmy Valiant

CWF @ Sarasota, FL - February 12, 1983
The Midnight Rider defeated NWA World Champion Ric Flair

JCP @ Asheville, NC - Civic Center - February 13, 1983
Bill White defeated Masa Fuchi
The Ninja defeated Vinnie Valentino
The One Man Gang defeated Dizzy Hogan
Ricky Steamboat & Jay Youngblood defeated NWA US Champion Greg Valentine & Dick Slater
Jimmy Valiant defeated Terry Funk
Jack & Jerry Brisco defeated NWA Tag Team Champions Sgt. Slaughter & Don Kernodle via disqualification

CWF @ Orlando, FL - February 13, 1983
Charlie Cook defeated Ciclone Negro
Scott McGhee defeated Don Kent
Terry Allen defeated John Heffernan
Kevin Sullivan & Leroy Brown defeated Rufus R. Jones & Barry Windham
Ron Bass defeated Angelo Mosca
The Midnight Rider fought Roddy Piper to a draw
Andre the Giant fought NWA World Champion Ric Flair to a double count-out at the 24-minute mark

CWF @ West Palm Beach, FL - February 14, 1983
Terry Allen defeated Don Kent
John Heffernan defeated Raul Mata
Angelo Mosca, Roddy Piper, & Jake Roberts defeated Rufus R. Jones, Ron Bass, & Charlie Cook
Andre the Giant & the Midnight Rider defeated Kevin Sullivan & Leroy Brown in a lights out match
NWA World Champion Ric Flair defeated Barry Windham in a steel cage match

JCP @ Piedmont, SC - February 14, 1983
Jim Dalton vs. Frank Monte
Dizzy Hogan vs. Ricky Harris
Jay Youngblood vs. Red Dog Lane
Ricky Steamboat vs. NWA US Champion Greg Valentine
Mid-Atlantic TV Champion Mike Rotundo & Sweet Brown Sugar vs. NWA Tag Team Champions Sgt. Slaughter & Don Kernodle

CWF @ Tampa, FL - Ft. Homer Hesterly Armory - February 15, 1983
Charlie Cook defeated Jake Roberts

Ron Bass defeated Kevin Sullivan via disqualification
Charlie Cook (sub. for Mike Graham) & Barry Windham defeated Angelo Mosca & Roddy Piper via disqualification
The Midnight Rider & Terry Allen defeated Global Tag Team Champions the Fabulous Kangaroos to win the titles
Rufus R. Jones fought Leroy Brown to a double count-out in a lights out match
NWA World Champion Ric Flair defeated Scott McGhee at 24:03

CWF @ Ocala, FL - Jai Alai Fronton - February 17, 1983
Ron Bass & Charlie Cook defeated the Texan & Angelo Mosca
Terry Allen defeated Don Kent
Scott McGhee defeated John Heffernan
The Midnight Rider & Rufus R. Jones defeated Kevin Sullivan & Leroy Brown
NWA World Champion Ric Flair defeated Barry Windham

CWF @ Hollywood, FL - February 18, 1983
The Kangaroos vs. Ron Bass & Mike Graham
NWA World Champion Ric Flair vs. Barry Windham
The Midnight Rider vs. Kevin Sullivan (Lights out, I quit match)
Also included 2 more matches, including a 6 man tag team match

JCP @ Richmond, VA - Coliseum - February 18, 1983
The Ninja defeated Ricky Morton
Jim Nelson defeated Jim Dalton
Jack & Jerry Brisco defeated NWA Tag Team Champions Sgt. Slaughter & Don Kernodle via disqualification
Jimmy Valiant defeated the One Man Gang
Roddy Piper defeated Dick Slater

JCP @ Charleston, SC - County Hall - February 18, 1983
Frank Monte defeated Ken Timbs
Johnny Weaver & Tommy Gilbert defeated Gene Anderson & Larry Lane
Mid-Atlantic Heavyweight Champion Dory Funk Jr. fought Sweet Brown Sugar to a no contest
Ricky Steamboat & Jay Youngblood defeated NWA US Champion Greg Valentine & Terry Funk

Worldwide - 2/19/83:
The One Man Gang defeated Frank Monte
Jack Brisco defeated Bill White
Mid-Atlantic TV Champion Mike Rotundo defeated Johnny Weaver
Dick Slater & Mid-Atlantic Heavyweight Champion Dory Funk Jr. defeated Ricky Morton & Ron Rossi

CWF @ Sarasota, FL - February 19, 1983
NWA World Champion Ric Flair vs. the Midnight Rider

Mid-Atlantic Championship Wrestling - 2/19/83:
Jack Brisco defeated Ken Timbs
Mid-Atlantic TV Champion Mike Rotundo defeated Ricky Harris
Dick Slater & Mid-Atlantic Heavyweight Champion Dory Funk Jr. defeated Frank Monte & Ricky Morton
Mid-Atlantic Heavyweight Champion Dory Funk Jr. fought Ricky Morton to a draw

JCP @ Greensboro, NC - Coliseum - February 20, 1983
Red Dog Lane defeated Ricky Morton
Dizzy Hogan & Sweet Brown Sugar defeated Ricky Harris & Bill White
Jack Brisco defeated Paul Jones
Dick Slater defeated Jerry Brisco
Jimmy Valiant defeated the One Man Gang in a New York Streetfight
Ricky Steamboat & Jay Youngblood defeated NWA World Champion Ric Flair & NWA US Champion Greg Valentine when Steamboat pinned Flair
NWA Tag Team Champions Sgt. Slaughter & Don Kernodle defeated Terry Funk & Mid-Atlantic Heavyweight Champion Dory Funk Jr.

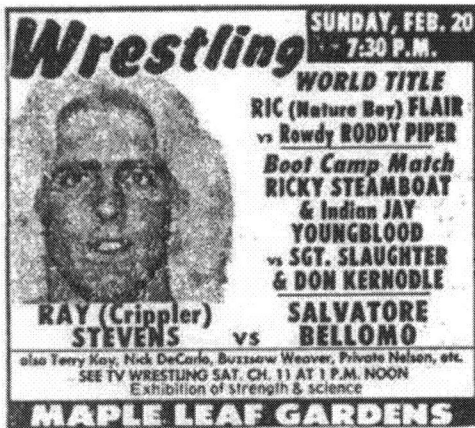

Toronto, Ontario - Maple Leaf Gardens - February 20, 1983
Rudy Kay & Nick DeCarlo fought Jim Nelson & Tim Gerrard to a draw
Johnny Weaver defeated Bobby Bass
The Destroyer defeated Terry Kay
Leo Burke fought Tony Parisi to a no contest
Salvatore Bellomo defeated Ray Stevens via disqualification
Ricky Steamboat & Jay Youngblood defeated NWA Tag Team Champions Sgt. Slaughter & Don Kernodle in a bootcamp match
NWA World Champion Ric Flair pinned Terry Funk (sub. for Roddy Piper) at 17:28

JCP @ Woodlawn - February 21, 1983
Abe Jacobs defeated Masa Fuchi

Tommy Gilbert defeated the Ninja
Dizzy Hogan & Johnny Weaver defeated Gene Anderson & Larry Lane
Mid-Atlantic Heavyweight Champion Dory Funk Jr. defeated Sweet Brown Sugar
NWA US Champion Greg Valentine defeated Mid-Atlantic TV Champion Mike Rotundo

JCP @ Columbia, SC - Township Auditorium - February 22, 1983
Mid-Atlantic Championship Wrestling - 2/26/83:
NWA US Champion Greg Valentine defeated Vinnie Valentino
NWA Tag Team Champions Sgt. Slaughter & Don Kernodle defeated Frank Monte & Dizzy Hogan
Sweet Brown Sugar defeated Ricky Harris
Jack Brisco defeated Red Dog Lane
Dick Slater defeated Mid-Atlantic TV Champion Mike Rotundo to win the title

Auckland, New Zealand - February 24, 1983
NWA World Champion Ric Flair defeated Mark Lewin

JCP @ Harrisonburg, VA - High School - February 24, 1983
Jimmy Valiant vs. the One Man Gang
Jack Brisco vs. Mid-Atlantic Heavyweight Champion Dory Funk Jr.

New Plymouth, New Zealand - February 25, 1983
Mark Lewin vs. NWA World Champion Ric Flair

JCP @ Charleston, SC - County Hall - February 25, 1983
Bill White defeated Frank Monte
Mike George defeated Ken Timbs
Jay Youngblood defeated the Ninja
Ricky Steamboat defeated Mid-Atlantic TV Champion Dick Slater
Sweet Brown Sugar defeated Mid-Atlantic Heavyweight Champion Dory Funk Jr. via disqualification; there were two referees for the match

Worldwide - 2/26/83:
Jack & Jerry Brisco defeated Ricky Harris & Masa Fuchi
Mid-Atlantic Heavyweight Champion Dory Funk Jr. defeated Bill White
The One Man Gang defeated Vinnie Valentino
NWA Tag Team Champions Sgt. Slaughter & Don Kernodle defeated Frank Monte & Ben Alexander
NWA US Champion Greg Valentine defeated Dizzy Hogan
Mid-Atlantic TV Champion Dick Slater defeated Ron Rossi
Sweet Brown Sugar defeated Ken Timbs

JCP @ Spartanburg, SC - Memorial Auditorium - February 26, 1983
Masa Fuchi defeated Vinnie Valentino

Mike George defeated Ricky Harris
Dizzy Hogan defeated Jim Nelson
NWA Tag Team Champions Sgt. Slaughter & Don Kernodle defeated Mike Rotundo & Jerry Brisco
Jimmy Valiant defeated the One Man Gang

Christchurch, New Zealand - February 26, 1983
Mark Lewin vs. NWA World Champion Ric Flair

JCP @ Winston Salem, NC - February 27, 1983
Mike George defeated Frank Monte
Johnny Weaver & Nelson Royal defeated Gene Anderson & Larry Lane
Ricky Steamboat & Jay Youngblood defeated Mid-Atlantic TV Champion Dick Slater & the One Man Gang
NWA Tag Team Champions Sgt. Slaughter & Don Kernodle defeated Mike Rotundo & Jerry Brisco

Dunedin, New Zealand - February 27, 1983
Mark Lewin vs. NWA World Champion Ric Flair

JCP @ Greenville, SC - February 28, 1983
Masa Fuchi defeated Vinnie Valentino
Mid-Atlantic Heavyweight Champion Dory Funk Jr. defeated Mike Rotundo
The One Man Gang defeated Johnny Weaver
Gene Anderson & Red Dog Lane defeated Dizzy Hogan & Mike George
NWA US Champion Greg Valentine defeated Jimmy Valiant; Roddy Piper was the guest referee for the match

Invercargill, New Zealand - February 28, 1983
Mark Lewin vs. NWA World Champion Ric Flair

JCP @ Columbia, SC - February 1983
Jack Brisco defeated Mid-Atlantic Heavyweight Champion Dory Funk Jr. in a Texas Death Match

JCP @ Columbia, SC - March 1, 1983
Gene Anderson & Larry Lane defeated Tom Prichard & Joe Lightfoot
Sweet Brown Sugar & Dizzy Hogan defeated the Moondogs
Mid-Atlantic Heavyweight Champion Dory Funk Jr. defeated Jack Brisco
Jimmy Valiant defeated NWA US Champion Greg Valentine via disqualification

JCP @ Charlotte, NC - March 2, 1983
TV taping:
Ricky Steamobat & Jay Youngblood defeated Ben Alexander & Ken Timbs
Ricky Steamobat & Jay Youngblood defeated Ben Alexander & Masa Fuchi

JCP @ Sumter, SC - Sumter County Exhibition Center - March 3, 1983
Joe Lightfoot defeated Ricky Harris
Velvet McIntyre defeated Donna Christanello
Mike George & Chick Donovan defeated the Moondogs
Mid-Atlantic Heavyweight Champion Dory Funk Jr. defeated Sweet Brown Sugar
Jimmy Valiant defeated the One Man Gang in a New York Streetfight

Auckland, New Zealand - YMCA - March 3, 1983
NWA World Champion Ric Flair defeated Mark Lewin in a Best 2 out of 3 falls match; fall #1: Flair won; fall #2: Lewin defeated Flair via submission with a sleeper; fall #3: Flair defeated Lewin via reverse decision at 3:05; Lewin originally won the match and title following a delayed suplex into the ring but the call was changed because Lewin threw Flair over the top moments earlier, as the referee was knocked down on the floor; after the bout, Lewin hit Flair with the title belt and left ringside with it

Hamilton, New Zealand - March 4, 1983
Steve Rickard vs. NWA World Champion Ric Flair

JCP @ Charleston, SC - County Hall - March 4, 1983
Ricky Harris defeated Vinnie Valentino
Dizzy Hogan defeated Ken Timbs (sub. for Bill White)
Jimmy Valiant defeated NWA US Champion Greg Valentine in a non-title match
Ricky Steamboat & Jay Youngblood defeated Mid-Atlantic TV Champion Dick Slater & the One Man Gang
Sweet Brown Sugar defeated Mid-Atlantic Heavyweight Champion Dory Funk Jr. in a Texas Death Match

Worldwide - 3/5/83:
Ricky Steamobat & Jay Youngblood defeated Ben Alexander & Masa Fuchi
NWA Tag Team Champions Sgt. Slaughter & Don Kernodle defeated Vinnie Valentino & Ron Rossi
The One Man Gang defeated Ken Timbs
NWA US Champion Greg Valentine defeated Joe Lightfoot
Mid-Atlantic Heavyweight Champion Dory Funk Jr. defeated Tom Prichard
Jack & Jerry Brisco defeated Red Dog Lane & Ricky Harris

Mid-Atlantic Championship Wrestling - 3/5/83:
Mike Rotundo defeated Mid-Atlantic TV Champion Dick Slater via disqualification
Johnny Weaver & Jim Nelson defeated Masa Fuchi & Ricky Harris
The One Man Gang defeated Joe Lightfoot
NWA US Champion Greg Valentine defeated Tom Prichard
Ricky Steamboat & Jay Youngblood defeated Ben Alexander & Ken Timbs
NWA Tag Team Champions Sgt. Slaughter & Don Kernodle defeated Ron Rossi & Mark Fleming

GCW @ Atlanta, GA - WTBS Studios - March 5, 1983
TV taping:
NWA World Champion Ric Flair defeated Denny Brown

Continental @ Birmingham, AL - March 5, 1983
NWA World Champion Ric Flair defeated Jimmy Golden

JCP @ Charleston, SC - County Hall - March 5, 1983
Pretty Boy Fergie defeated Ron Ritchie (sub. for Keith Larson)
Velvet McIntyre won a 6-women battle royal; stipulations stated the winner would challenge Women's Champion the Fabulous Moolah
Women's Champion the Fabulous Moolah defeated Velvet McIntyre
The Ninja defeated Porkchop Cash via disqualification when Cash hit the referee

JCP @ Charlotte, NC - Coliseum - March 5, 1983
Masa Fuchi defeated Bill White
Sweet Brown Sugar defeated the Ninja
Mike George defeated Ricky Harris

Jim Nelson defeated NWA Tag Team Champion Sgt. Slaughter via disqualification
Mid-Atlantic Heavyweight Champion Dory Funk Jr. defeated Jack Brisco
Ricky Steamboat, Jay Youngblood, & Jimmy Valiant defeated NWA US Champion Greg Valentine, Terry Funk, & Sir Oliver Humperdink

JCP @ Savannah, GA - Civic Center - March 6, 1983
Gene Anderson defeated Dizzy Hogan
Mike George defeated Masa Fuchi
The One Man Gang defeated Sweet Brown Sugar
NWA US Champion Greg Valentine defeated Mike Rotundo
Jimmy Valiant defeated Mid-Atlantic TV Champion Dick Slater via disqualification
Jack & Jerry Brisco defeated Terry Funk & Mid-Atlantic Heavyweight Champion Dory Funk Jr.

Toronto, Ontario - Maple Leaf Gardens - March 6, 1983
Billy Red Lyons defeated Bobby Bass
Johnny Weaver & Terry Kay defeated the Destroyer & Red Dog Lane
Jim Nelson pinned Rudy Kay
Leo Burke defeated Vinnie Valentino
Tiger Jeet Singh defeated Kurt Von Hess
Big John Studd defeated Salvatore Bellomo
Ricky Steamboat & Jay Youngblood defeated NWA Tag Team Champions Sgt. Slaughter & Don Kernodle via count-out

JCP @ Greenville, SC - March 7, 1983
Gene Anderson & Masa Fuchi defeated Mike Davis & Mike George
Bugsy McGraw defeated the Ninja
Jimmy Valiant defeated Sir Oliver Humperdink
Jimmy Valiant defeated the One Man Gang; due to stipulations, Valiant earned a lights out match against Sir Oliver Humperdink
Roddy Piper defeated Mid-Atlantic TV Champion Dick Slater

JCP @ Columbia, SC - March 8, 1983
Bill White defeated Dale Barnett
Johnny Weaver defeated Chick Donovan
Ricky Steamboat & Jay Youngblood defeated Gene Anderson & Larry Lane
Jimmy Valiant & Bugsy McGraw defeated Mid-Atlantic TV Champion Dick Slater & the One Man Gang
Jack Brisco defeated Mid-Atlantic Heavyweight Champion Dory Funk Jr. via disqualification

JCP @ Charlotte, NC - March 9, 1983
NWA World Champion Ric Flair defeated Ron Rossi
Championship Wrestling - 3/9/83:
NWA US Champion Greg Valentine vs. Jim Burnette
The One Man Gang & Mid-Atlantic TV Champion Dick Slater vs. Ron Rossi & Vinnie Valentino

Mike Rotundo & Sweet Sugar Brown vs. Bill White & Rick Harris
Johnny Weaver & Jim Nelson vs. Chic Donovan & Ben Alexander
Mid-Atlantic Heavyweight Champion Dory Funk Jr. vs. Ken Timbs
NWA World Champion Ric Flair defeated Masa Fuchi
Roddy Piper vs. NWA US Champion Greg Valentine

JCP @ Sumter, SC - Sumter County Exhibition Center - March 9, 1983
Masa Fuchi vs. Mike Davis
Dizzy Hogan vs. the Ninja
Ricky Steamboat & Jay Youngblood vs. Jack & Jerry Brisco
Jimmy Valient & Bugsy McGraw vs. NWA Tag Team Champions Sgt. Slaughter & Don Kernodle

JCP @ Fisherville, VA - March 9, 1983
Tommy Gilbert defeated Bill White
Frank Monte defeated Ken Timbs
Masa Fuchi defeated Mark Fleming
Johnny Weaver & Jim Nelson defeated Larry Lane & Gene Anderson
Sweet Brown Sugar defeated the Ninja via disqualification
Mid-Atlantic TV Champion Dick Slater defeated Jerry Brisco
Jimmy Valiant defeated NWA US Champion Greg Valentine

JCP @ Hampton, VA - March 11, 1983
Terri Shane & Joyce Grable defeated Judy Martin & Liz Chapman
Mike George defeated Ken Timbs
Mike Rotundo defeated Mark Fleming
Ricky Steamboat & Jay Youngblood defeated the One Man Gang & Red Dog Lane
Roddy Piper defeated Mid-Atlantic TV Champion Dick Slater
NWA World Champion Ric Flair defeated Mid-Atlantic Heavyweight Champion Dory Funk Jr.

JCP @ Charleston, SC - County Hall - March 11, 1983
Bugsy McGraw defeated Masa Fuchi
Sweet Brown Sugar defeated Ricky Harris
NWA Tag Team Champions Sgt. Slaughter & Don Kernodle defeated Johnny Weaver & Jim Nelson via disqualification
Jimmy Valiant defeated Gene Anderson; stipulations stated Valiant would face Sir Oliver Humperdink if he won
Jimmy Valiant defeated Sir Oliver Humperdink in a lights out match

Mid-Atlantic Championship Wrestling - 3/12/83:
Jim Nelson & Johnny Weaver defeated Ben Alexander & Chick Donovan
Mid-Atlantic Heavyweight Champion Dory Funk Jr. defeated Ken Timbs
NWA World Champion Ric Flair defeated Masa Fuchi
NWA US Champion Greg Valentine defeated Jim Burnett

The One Man Gang & Mid-Atlantic TV Champion Dick Slater defeated Ron Rossi & Vinnie Valentino
Mike Rotundo & Sweet Brown Sugar defeated Bill White & Ricky Harris

Worldwide - 3/12/83:
NWA US Champion Greg Valentine defeated Ken Timbs
Mid-Atlantic TV Champion Dick Slater & the One Man Gang defeated Mike George & Vinnie Valentino
Mid-Atlantic Heavyweight Champion Dory Funk Jr. defeated Jim Burnett
NWA World Champion Ric Flair defeated Ron Rossi
Johnny Weaver, Jim Nelson, & Sweet Brown Sugar defeated Ben Alexander, Bill White, & Masa Fuchi
Mike Rotundo defeated Chick Donovan

JCP @ Greensboro, NC - Coliseum - March 12, 1983
Featured Bob Caudle on commentary, with David Crockett joining in begining with the Roddy Piper vs. Mid-Atlantic TV Champion Dick Slater match:
Jerry Brisco defeated Ken Timbs via submission with the figure-4 at 3:55 following a butterfly suplex
Mike Rotundo pinned Rick Harris following the airplane spin at 4:46
Jim Nelson & Johnny Weaver defeated Red Dog Lane & Gene Anderson at 6:30 when Nelson pinned Lane with an inside cradle
Roddy Piper pinned Mid-Atlantic TV Champion Dick Slater (w/ Gary Hart) at 17:24 with a fist drop; the title was only at stake for the first 15 minutes of the match; after the contest, Piper left ringside with the title belt
NWA World Champion Ric Flair fought NWA US Champion Greg Valentine to a 60-minute time-limit draw
Ricky Steamobat & Jay Youngblood defeated NWA Tag Team Champions Sgt. Slaughter & Don Kernodle in a no time limit steel cage match to win the titles at around the 33-minute mark when Youngblood pinned Kernodle after Steamboat put his partner on top of Kernodle behind the referee's back, moments after Slaughter had done the same to put Kernodle on Youngblood; prior to the bout, the champions came out to Bill Conti's "Gonna Fly Now" and Kernodle wore a T-shirt which read "Greensboro March 13" on the front and "Slaughter Kernodle World Champs" on the back; Sandy Scott was the guest referee for the match; stipulations stated Steamboat & Youngblood would have to break up if they didn't win the titles

JCP @ Roanoke, VA - Civic Center - March 13, 1983
Mike George defeated Bill White
Liz Chase defeated Judy Martin
Sweet Brown Sugar & Dizzy Hogan defeated Masa Fuchi & Jos LeDuc
Jimmy Valiant defeated the One Man Gang in a chain match
Bugsy McGraw defeated Mid-Atlantic TV Champion Dick Slater
Jimmy Valiant defeated Sir Oliver Humperdink in a lights out match

CWF @ Pensacola, FL - March 13, 1983
NWA World Champion Ric Flair defeated Ken Lucas via disqualification

JCP @ Greenville, SC - Memorial Auditorium - March 13, 1983
Gene Anderson defeated Vinnie Valentino
Jerry Brisco defeated Lenny Lane
Sgt. Slaughter & Don Kernodle defeated Johnny Weaver & Jim Nelson
Jack Brisco defeated Mid-Atlantic Heavyweight Champion Dory Funk Jr. via disqualification
NWA US Champion Greg Valentine defeated Roddy Piper

Continental @ Birmingham, AL - March 14, 1983
NWA World Champion Ric Flair fought Mr. Olympia to a double disqualification

JCP @ Newton - March 14, 1983
Mike Rotundo defeated Ken Timbs
Liz Chase defeated Judy Martin
NWA Tag Team Champions Ricky Steamboat & Jay Youngblood defeated Gene Anderson & Larry Lane
Jerry Brisco defeated Mid-Atlantic Heavyweight Champion Dory Funk Jr. via disqualification

JCP @ Raleigh, NC - Dorton Arena - March 15, 1983
Dizzy Hogan defeated Bill White
Jos LeDuc defeated Ricky Harris
Bugsy McGraw defeated Masa Fuchi
Jimmy Valiant defeated the One Man Gang in a streetfight
NWA US Champion Greg Valentine defeated Sweet Brown Sugar

JCP @ Richmond, VA - Coliseum - March 15, 1983
NWA World Champion Ric Flair fought NWA US Champion Greg Valentine to a draw

JCP @ Columbia, SC - March 15, 1983
Mike George defeated Ken Timbs
Mike Rotundo defeated Larry Lane
Jerry Brisco defeated Gene Anderson
Sgt. Slaughter & Don Kernodle defeated Jim Nelson & Johnny Weaver
Jack Brisco defeated Mid-Atlantic Heavyweight Champion Dory Funk Jr.

Continental @ Mobile, AL - March 16, 1983
NWA World Champion Ric Flair fought Ron Fuller to a no contest

GCW @ Dayton, OH - March 17, 1983
NWA World Champion Ric Flair defeated Paul Orndorff

JCP @ Norfolk, VA - March 17, 1983
Vinnie Valentino defeated Mark Fleming
Jerry Brisco defeated Masa Fuchi
NWA US Champion Greg Valentine & Mid-Atlantic TV Champion Dick Slater defeated Mike Rotundo & Bugsy McGraw
Mid-Atlantic Heavyweight Champion Dory Funk Jr. defeated Jack Brisco
Jimmy Valiant defeated the One Man Gang in a No DQ match
Jimmy Valiant defeated Sir Oliver Humperdink in a lights out match

JCP @ Richmond, VA - Coliseum - March 18, 1983
Mike George defeafted Mark Fleming
Mike Rotundo defeated Masa Fuchi
Jack & Jerry Brisco defeated Gene Anderson & Larry Lane
Mike Rotundo won a battle royal
Jimmy Valiant, NWA Tag Team Champion Ricky Steamboat, & Bugsy McGraw defeated Mid-Atlantic TV Champion Dick Slater, the One Man Gang, & Sir Oliver Humperdink
NWA World Champion Ric Flair fought NWA US Champion Greg Valentine to a draw

JCP @ Charleston, SC - County Hall - March 18, 1983
Wayne Jones defeated Bill White
Mike Davis defeated Ken Timbs
Jos LeDuc defeated Ricky Harris
Sgt. Slaughter & Don Kernodle defeated Johnny Weaver & Jim Nelson
Mid-Atlantic Heavyweight Champion Dory Funk Jr. defeated Sweet Brown Sugar in a Texas Death match

Mid-Atlantic Championship Wrestling - 3/19/83:
The Great Kabuki defeated Mike Davis
The One Man Gang defeated Ken Timbs
Mid-Atlantic Heavyweight Champion Dory Funk Jr. defeated Masa Fuchi
Sgt. Slaughter & Don Kernodle defeated Ron Rossi & Vinnie Valentino
Mike Rotundo, Sweet Brown Sugar, & Wayne Jones defeated Ricky Harris, Ben Alexander, & Red Dog Lane
NWA US Champion Greg Valentine defeated Bill White

Worldwide - 3/19/83:
NWA US Champion Greg Valentine defeated Mike Davis
The One Man Gang defeated Ron Rossi
Mid-Atlantic Heavyweight Champion Dory Funk Jr. defeated Ben Alexander
The Great Kabuki defeated Vinnie Valentino
Sweet Brown Sugar & Wayne Jones defeated Masa Fuchi & Ricky Harris
Sgt. Slaughter & Don Kernodle defeated Bill White & Ken Timbs

JCP @ Spartanburg, SC - March 19, 1983
Bugsy McGraw defeated Ricky Harris
Dizzy Hogan defeated Bill White
Jake Roberts defeated Mike Davis
Sgt. Slaughter & Don Kernodle defeated Johnny Weaver & Jim Nelson
Jimmy Valiant defeated NWA US Champion Greg Valentine via disqualification

JCP @ Savannah, GA - Civic Center - March 20, 1983
Jerry Brisco defeated Ken Timbs
Jos LeDuc defeated Ricky Harris
Mike George & Mike Davis defeated Bill White & Masa Fuchi
Jimmy Valiant defeated Sir Oliver Humperdink
Sweet Brown Sugar defeated Jake Roberts via disqualification
Jimmy Valiant & Bugsy McGraw defeated NWA US Champion Greg Valentine & Mid-Atlantic TV Champion Dick Slater

JCP @ Asheville, NC - Civic Center - March 20, 1983
Ben Alexander defeated Wayne Jones
Mike Rotundo defeated Red Dog Lane
Johnny Weaver defeated Gene Anderson
Sgt. Slaughter, Don Kernodle, & the One Man Gang defeated Jim Nelson, NWA Tag Team Champions Ricky Steamboat & Jay Youngblood
Jack Brisco defeated Mid-Atlantic Heavyweight Champion Dory Funk Jr. via disqualification

WCCW @ San Antonio, TX - March 20, 1983
Jimmy Garvin defeated Ken Mantell
Jose Lothario defeated Michael Hayes via disqualification
Iceman King Parsons defeated Terry Gordy
David Von Erich defeated the Great Kabuki
King Kong Bundy defeated Tola Yatsu via disqualification
NWA World Champion Ric Flair defeated Kerry Von Erich via disqualification in a steel cage match

JCP @ Greenville, SC - Memorial Auditorium - March 21, 1983
Ricky Harris vs. Mike George
Jerry Brisco vs. Gene Anderson
Sweet Sugar Brown vs. Red Dog Lane
Johnny Weaver & Jim Nelson defeated Jake Roberts & the One Man Gang
NWA Tag Team Champions Ricky Steamboat & Jay Youngblood vs. Sgt. Slaughter & Don Kernodle (steel cage match)

Central States @ Wichita, KS - March 21, 1983
NWA World Champion Ric Flair defeated Harley Race

Central States @ Topeka, KS - March 22, 1983
NWA World Champion Ric Flair defeated Manny Fernandez

JCP @ Columbia, SC - March 22, 1983
Ken Timbs defeated Paul Jones
Vinnie Valentino defeated Masa Fuchi
Gene Anderson defeated Mike Davis
Jos LeDuc defeated Mid-Atlantic TV Champion Dick Slater
Sgt. Slaughter & Don Kernodle defeated NWA Tag Team Champions Ricky Steamboat & Jay Youngblood

JCP @ Winston-Salem, NC - Coliseum - March 24, 1983

JCP @ Harrisonburg, VA - High School - March 24, 1983
Jos LeDuc vs. Rick Harris
Bugsy McGraw vs. the Ninja
Mid-Atlantic Heavyweight Champion Dory Funk Jr. vs. Jack Brisco
NWA US Champion Greg Valentine vs. Mike Rotundo
Mid-Atlantic TV Champion Dick Slater vs. Jimmy Valiant
(Valiant faces Sir Oliver Humperdink in a lights out match if he wins)

Central States @ Kansas City, MO - March 24, 1983
NWA World Champion Ric Flair defeated Bruiser Brody via disqualification

Central States @ St. Louis, MO - March 25, 1983
NWA World Champion Ric Flair defeated Kerry Von Erich in a Best 2 out of 3 falls match

JCP @ Charleston, SC - County Hall - March 25, 1983
Bill White defeated Mike Davis
Sweet Brown Sugar defeated Ken Timbs
Johnny Weaver defeated Ricky Harris
Jim Nelson, NWA Tag Team Champions Ricky Steamboat & Jay Youngblood defeated the Great Kabuki, Sgt. Slaughter & Don Kernodle

Mid-Atlantic Championship Wrestling - 3/26/83:
Sgt. Slaughter & Don Kernodle defeated Mike George & Mike Davis
Mid-Atlantic Heavyweight Champion Dory Funk Jr. & Jake Roberts defeated Vinnie Valentino & Sweet Brown Sugar
Jos LeDuc defeated Mid-Atlantic TV Champion Dick Slater via disqualification
Jack & Jerry Brisco defeated Masa Fuchi & Ricky Harris

Worldwide - 3/26/83:
Sgt. Slaughter & Don Kernodle defeated Bill White & Mike Davis
Mid-Atlantic Heavyweight Champion Dory Funk Jr. & Jake Roberts defeated Mike Rotundo & Vinnie Valentino
Jack & Jerry Brisco defeated Red Dog Lane & Ken Timbs

JCP @ Charlotte, NC - Coliseum - March 26, 1983
Mike Davis defeated Ken Timbs

Bill White fought Abe Jacobs to a draw
Wayne Jones defeated Ben Alexander
Mid-Atlantic TV Champion Dick Slater vs. Jos LeDuc
Jack & Jerry Brisco defeated Mid-Atlantic Heavyweight
Champion Dory Funk Jr. & Paul Jones
NWA US Champion Greg Valentine, Sgt. Slaughter, & Don
Kernodle vs. Jim Nelson, NWA Tag Team Champions Ricky
Steamboat & Jay Youngblood

**JCP @ Asheville, NC - Civic Center - March 27, 1983
(matinee)**
Roddy Piper defeated Mid-Atlantic TV Champion Dick Slater to
win the title

JCP @ Roanoke, VA - Civic Center - March 27, 1983
Jake Roberts & Gene Anderson defeated Mike Davis & Mark
Fleming
Bugsy McGraw defeated Ricky Harris
Mid-Atlantic TV Champion Roddy Piper defeated Dick Slater
Sgt. Slaughter & Don Kernodle defeated NWA Tag Team
Champions Ricky Steamboat & Jay Youngblood
Jimmy Valiant defeated NWA US Champion Greg Valentine
via disqualification

Toronto, Ontario - Maple Leaf Gardens - March 27, 1983
Rudy Kay fought Billy Red Lyons to a draw
The Destroyer defeated Nick DeCarlo
Tony Parisi defeated Kurt Von Hess
Bobby Bass defeated Brian Mackney
Tiger Jeet Singh defeated Frankie Lane
Jim Nelson defeated Canadian TV Champion Terry Kay at
13:31 to win the title
Mike Rotundo defeated Leo Burke via disqualification
NWA Tag Team Champions Ricky Steamboat & Jay
Youngblood defeated Sgt. Slaughter & Don Kernodle in a steel
cage match
NWA World Champion Ric Flair defeated Mid-Atlantic TV
Champion Roddy Piper at 19:26

**JCP @ Greenville, SC - Memorial Auditorium - March 28,
1983**
Ben Alexander defeated Vinnie Valentino
Ricky Harris defeated Wayne Jones
Dick Slater defeated Jos LeDuc in a taped fist match
NWA Tag Team Champions Ricky Steamboat & Jay
Youngblood defeated Mid-Atlantic Heavyweight Champion
Dory Funk Jr. & Jake Roberts
NWA US Champion Greg Valentine defeated Mid-Atlantic TV
Champion Roddy Piper; only the US title was at stake; there
were two referees for the bout

WCCW @ Ft. Worth, TX - March 28, 1983
Chavo Guerrero defeated the Magic Dragon
Ken Mantell defeated Killer Karl Krupp via disqualification
Kamala defeated Mike Bond

Jimmy Garvin fought Jose Lotharlo to a draw
Iceman King Parsons defeated WCCW TV Champion Tola
Yatsu to win the title
Michael Hayes, Terry Gordy, & Buddy Roberts defeated NWA
World Champion Ric Flair, King Kong Bundy, & the Great
Kabuki; David Von Erich was the guest referee for the match

JCP @ Columbia, SC - March 29, 1983
Vinnie Valentino defeated Ben Alexander
Masa Fuchi defeated Wayne Jones
Bill White defeated Mark Fleming
The Great Kaubki defeated Sweet Brown Sugar
Dick Slater defeated Jos LeDuc via disqualification
Mid-Atlantic TV Champion Roddy Piper defeated NWA US
Champion Greg Valentine via disqualification

JCP @ Waytheville, VA - March 29, 1983
Abe Jacobs defeated Ricky Harris
Johnny Weaver defeated Gene Anderson
Don Kernodle defeated Jim Nelson
Jimmy Valiant defeated the One Man Gang
Jimmy Valiant defeated Sir Oliver Humperdink

WCCW @ Dallas, TX - State Fair Coliseum - April 1, 1983
Killer Karl Krupp defeated the Magic Dragon
Jimmy Garvin defeated Mike Bond
Jose Lotharlo defeated King Kong Bundy
Michael Hayes defeated Iceman King Parsons via count-out
Tola Yatsu defeated the Great Kabuki via count-out
NWA World Champion Ric Flair defeated Kevin Von Erich via
disqualification
David Von Erich defeated Terry Gordy in a handcuff match

JCP @ Charleston, SC - County Hall - April 1, 1983
Johnny Weaver defeated Bill White
Mike Rotundo defeated Gene Anderson
Mid-Atlantic Heavyweight Champion Dory Funk Jr. & Jake
Roberts defeated Sweet Brown Sugar & Wayne Jones
Mid-Atlantic TV Champion Roddy Piper defeated NWA US
Champion Greg Valentine via disqualification

Mid-Atlantic Championship Wrestling - 4/2/83:
Mid-Atlantic TV Champion Roddy Piper defeated Ricky Harris
The Great Kabuki defeated Bill White
Jos LeDuc, Jimmy Valiant, & Bugsy McGraw defeated Masa
Fuchi, Ben Alexander, & Ken Timbs
Mid-Atlantic Heavyweight Champion Dory Funk Jr. & Jake
Roberts defeated Mike Davis & Johnny Weaver
Mike Rotundo & Sweet Brown Sugar defeated Bill White & Red
Dog Lane

Worldwide - 4/2/83:
Mid-Atlantic Heavyweight Champion Dory Funk Jr. & Jake
Roberts defeated Mike Davis & Vinnie Valentino
Mid-Atlantic TV Champion Roddy Piper defeated Ken

30

TimbsB Jos LeDuc, Jimmy Valiant, & Bugsy McGraw defeated Ben Alexander, Bill White, & Ricky Harris
The One Man Gang defeated Ron Rossi

JCP @ Charlottesville, VA - University Hall - April 2, 1983 (2,500)
Included NWA Tag Team Champions Ricky Steamboat & Jay Youngblood, Sgt. Slaughter, Don Kernodle, Bugsy McGraw, and the Great Kabuki

GCW @ Atlanta, GA - Omni - April 3, 1983
Paul Ellering defeated Joe Lightfoot
Arn Anderson & Matt Borne (w/ Paul Ellering) defeated Brian Blair & Tito Santana
Killer Brooks defeated Brett Wayne
The Masked Superstar defeated Buzz Sawyer via disqualification
National Heavyweight Champion Larry Zbyszko defeated Tommy Rich
Dusty Rhodes & Dick Murdoch defeated Ivan Koloff & the Iron Sheik (w/ Homer O'Dell)
Tony Atlas fought NWA World Champion Ric Flair to a no contest

JCP @ Greensboro, NC - Coliseum - April 3, 1983
Easter Sunday
Red Dog Lane defeated Mike Davis
Jake Roberts defeated Vinnie Valentino
Mike Rotundo defeated Gene Anderson
The Great Kabuki, Sgt. Slaughter, & Don Kernodle defeated Jim Nelson, NWA Tag Team Champions Ricky Steamboat & Jay Youngblood
Jack & Jerry Brisco defeated Mid-Atlantic Heavyweight Champion Dory Funk Jr. & Paul Jones
Dick Slater defeated Mid-Atlantic TV Champion Roddy Piper to win the title
Andre the Giant, Jimmy Valiant, & Bugsy McGraw defeated NWA US Champion Greg Valentine, the One Man Gang, & Sir Oliver Humperdink

JCP @ Greenville, SC - Memorial Auditorium - April 4, 1983
Mike Davis defeated Masa Fuchi
The Great Kabuki defeated Jim Nelson
Jake Roberts defeated Johnny Weaver
Jack Brisco defeated Red Dog Lane
Andre the Giant, Jimmy Valiant, & Bugsy McGraw defeated NWA US Champion Greg Valentine, the One Man Gang, & Sir Oliver Humperdink

GCW @ Huntington, WV - Memorial Fieldhouse - April 7, 1983
NWA World Champion Ric Flair defeated Tony Atlas

JCP @ Sumter, SC - April 7, 1983
Jos LeDuc vs. Ricky Harris

Mike Rotundo vs. Paul Ellering
Jake Roberts vs. Sweet Brown Sugar
The Great Kabuki vs. Johnny Weaver
Jack & Jerry Brisco vs. Mid-Atlantic Heavyweight Champion Dory Funk Jr. & Paul Jones

JCP @ Charlotte, NC - Coliseum - April 8, 1983
Mike Rotundo defeated Masa Fuchi
Red Dog Lane defeated Sweet Sugar Brown
Jos LeDuc defeated Gene Anderson
Jack & Jerry Brisco defeated Jake Roberts & the Great Kabuki
NWA US Champion Greg Valentine fought Roddy Piper to a draw
Andre the Giant, Jimmy Valiant, & Bugsy McGraw defeated Mid-Atlantic TV Champion Dick Slater, the One Man Gang, & Sir Oliver Humperdink
Sgt. Slaughter & Don Kernodle defeated NWA Tag Team Champions Ricky Steamboat & Jay Youngblood in a non-title steel cage match

GCW @ Dayton, OH - Hara Arena - April 8, 1983
Killer Brooks defeated Brett Wayne
Matt Borne & Arn Anderson (w/ Paul Ellering) defeated Brian Blair & Joe Lightfoot
Tito Santana fought Ivan Koloff (w/ Homer O'Dell) to a double count-out
Tommy Rich defeated Larry Zbyszko
Dick Murdoch fought Buzz Sawyer to a no contest
Tony Atlas defeated NWA World Champion Ric Flair

Mid-Atlantic Championship Wrestling - 4/9/83:
Jack Brisco defeated Ken Timbs
Mike Rotundo & Jim Nelson defeated Sgt. Slaughter & Don Kernodle via disqualification
Jake Roberts defeated Vinnie Valentino
The Great Kabuki defeated Mike Davis & Abe Jacobs in a handicap match
NWA Tag Team Champions Ricky Steamboat & Jay Youngblood defeated Ben Alexander & Masa Fuchi

GCW @ Atlanta, GA - WTBS Studios - April 9, 1983 (matinee)
World Championship Wrestling - 4/9/83 - hosted by Gordon Solie; included interviews with Tommy Rich, Tony Atlas, Killer Brooks & Buzz Sawyer, NWA National Heavyweight Champion Larry Zybszko, Dick Murdoch, Paul Ellering & Gen. Homer O'Dell, Rich & Murdoch, and live event news from Freddie Miller; featured a pre recorded promo by Dusty Rhodes & Murdoch in which they said the Texas Outlaws were back together and going after the Iron Sheik & Ivan Koloff in a double bullrope match; included a promo by NWA World Champion Ric Flair & Sawyer in which Flair said Sawyer was his close, personal friend and would be soon facing Tony Atlas: Tony Atlas pinned Deke Rivers with the gorilla press / splash combo
Brett Wayne defeated Jim Smith via submission with the

figure-4
Arn Anderson & Matt Borne (w/ Paul Ellering) defeated Tony Zane & Mike Starbuck when Borne pinned Starbuck with a sit-down splash off the top
Tommy Rich defeated Killer Brooks via disqualification when NWA National Heavyweight Champion Larry Zbyszko attempted to interfere and was brought into the ring by Rich
Pat Rose pinned Mike Jackson with a cradle
NWA World Champion Ric Flair defeated David Jones via submission with the figure-4 in a non-title match

GCW @ Cincinnati, OH - Riverfront Coliseum - April 9, 1983
Arn Anderson & Matt Borne (w/ Paul Ellering) defeated Brett Wayne & Joe Lightfoot
Killer Brooks defeated Brian Blair
Larry Zbyszko defeated Tito Santana
Buzz Sawyer defeated Dick Murdoch
Tony Atlas defeated Ivan Koloff (w/ Homer O'Dell)
Tommy Rich defeated NWA World Champion Ric Flair

JCP @ Asheville, NC - Civic Center - April 10, 1983
Red Dog Lane defeated Bill White
Jerry Brisco defeated Ricky Harris
The Great Kabuki defeated Mike Rotundo
Jake Roberts defeated Jack Brisco
Jos LeDuc defeated Mid-Atlantic TV Champion Dick Slater
NWA Tag Team Champions Ricky Steamboat & Jay Youngblood defeated Sgt. Slaughter & Don Kernodle

JCP @ Fayetteville, NC - April 10, 1983
Mike Davis defeated Masa Fuchi
Vinnie Valentino defeated Gene Anderson
Bugsy McGraw defeated Ken Timbs
Jimmy Valiant defeated Sir Oliver Humperdink
Roddy Piper defeated Mid-Atlantic TV Champion Dick Slater
Sgt. Slaughter & Don Kernodle defeated NWA Tag Team Champions Ricky Steamboat & Jay Youngblood
NWA World Champion Ric Flair defeated NWA US Champion Greg Valentine

Toronto, Ontario - Maple Leaf Gardens - April 10, 1983
Nick DeCarlo & Bob Marcus defeated Kurt Von Hess & Bobby Bass
Canadian TV Champion Jim Nelson fought Sweet Sugar Brown to a draw
Johnny Weaver defeated North American Champion Leo Burke to win the title
Jimmy Valiant & Tony Parisi defeated the One Man Gang & Sir Oliver Humperdink
Andre the Giant defeated the Destroyer & the Executioner in a handicap match
Jimmy Snuka defeated Ray Stevens via count-out in a Texas Death Match
NWA World Champion Ric Flair defeated Roddy Piper via

disqualification at 19:48; Sandy Scott was the guest referee for the match

JCP @ Greenville, SC - April 11, 1983
Keith Larsen defeated Ken Timbs
Gene Anderson defeated Vinnie Valentino
The Great Kabuki defeated Mike Davis
Roddy Piper defeated NWA US Champion Greg Valentine
Mid-Atlantic TV Champion Dick Slater defeated Jos LeDuc in a taped fist match
Sgt. Slaughter & Don Kernodle defeated NWA Tag Team Champions Ricky Steamboat & Jay Youngblood via disqualification

CWF @ Tampa, FL - Ft. Homer Hesterly Armory - April 12, 1983
The Professional defeated Rufus R. Jones
Charlie Cook defeated Adrian Street via disqualification
Florida Heavyweight Champion Scott McGhee defeated Kevin Sullivan via disqualification
Brad Armstrong & Terry Allen defeated Global Tag Team Champions the Kangaroos to win the titles
Southern Champion Barry Windham defeated Frank Dusek
NWA World Champion Ric Flair defeated Big Daddy via disqualification at the 8-minute mark
Dusty Rhodes & Blackjack Mulligan defeated Angelo Mosca & Purple Haze via disqualification at 7:48

CWF @ Miami Beach, FL - Convention Center - April 13, 1983 (6,271)
Charlie Cook defeated Frank Dusek via disqualification
Terry Allen & Brad Armstrong defeated the Fabulous Kangaroos
Adrian Street defeated Scott McGhee
Dusty Rhodes, Blackjack Mulligan, & Big Daddy defeated Angelo Mosca, Kevin Sullivan, & Purple Haze
NWA World Champion Ric Flair fought Barry Windham to a 60-minute time-limit draw

JCP @ Charleston, SC - County Hall - April 15, 1983
Mike Davis defeated Vinnie Valentino
Ken Timbs defeated Wayne Jones
Jim Nelson defeated Bill White
Johnny Weaver defeated Ricky Harris
Liz Chase defeated Leilani Kai
Sgt. Slaughter & Don Kernodle defeated NWA Tag Team Champions Ricky Steamboat & Jay Youngblood in a non-title steel cage match

Mid-Atlantic Championship Wrestling - 4/16/83:
Mike Rotundo defeated Masa Fuchi
Jimmy Valiant defeated the Great Kabuki
Jos LeDuc defeated Ricky Harris
The One Man Gang defeated Wayne Jones
NWA US Champion Greg Valentine & Mid-Atlantic TV

Champion Dick Slater defeated Keith Larsen & Sweet Brown Sugar
Jack & Jerry Brisco defeated Bill White & Ben Alexander

Worldwide - 4/16/83:
Jos LeDuc defeated Ken Timbs
The One Man Gang defeated Mike Davis
Bugsy McGraw defeated Bill White
Mike Rotundo defeated Red Dog Lane
Jake Roberts defeated Wayne Jones
NWA US Champion Greg Valentine & Mid-Atlantic TV Champion Dick Slater defeated Sweet Brown Sugar & Vinnie Valentino

JCP @ Greensboro, NC - Coliseum - April 16, 1983
Bill White defeated Wayne Jones
Jim Nelson defeated Ken Timbs
Gene Anderson defeated Mike Davis
Jack & Jerry Brisco defeated Red Dog Lane & Masa Fuchi
Jimmy Valiant defeated the Great Kabuki
Roddy Piper defeated NWA US Champion Greg Valentine to win the title
Sgt. Slaughter & Don Kernodle defeated NWA Tag Team Champions Ricky Steamboat & Jay Youngblood via disqualification

CWF @ St. Petersburg, FL - Bayfront Center - April 16, 1983
Charlie Cook fought the Professional to a draw
Big Daddy & Rufus R. Jones defeated the Kangaroos
Brad Armstrong defeated Adrian Street via disqualification
The Purple Haze defeated Terry Allen
Scott McGhee defeated Florida Heavyweight Champion Kevin Sullivan to win the title
Blackjack Mulligan & Barry Windham defeated Angelo Mosca & Frank Dusek in a bunkhouse match
NWA World Champion Ric Flair defeated Dusty Rhodes (w/ the Midnight Rider - Blackjack Mulligan) via disqualification at the 13-minute mark; Rhodes originally won the match and title when the Rider made the pinfall after Rhodes hit the Bionic Elbow; after the bout, Flair fought with the Rider as Kevin Sullivan came out and fought with Rhodes; because no official counted the pinfall, Flair retained the title

CWF @ Orlando, FL - April 17, 1983
Rufus R. Jones & Charlie Cook defeated the Kangaroos
Big Daddy fought Leroy Brown to a draw
Scott McGhee defeated Adrian Street
Kevin Sullivan & Purple Haze defeated Terry Allen & Brad Armstrong
Blackjack Mulligan defeated Angelo Mosca
NWA World Champion Ric Flair fought Barry Windham to a draw

JCP @ Greenville, SC - April 18, 1983
Sweet Brown Sugar defeated Rene Goulet
Keith Larsen defeated Bill White
Don Kernodle defeated Jim Nelson in a bootcamp match
Jack & Jerry Brisco defeated Paul Jones & Jake Roberts
Jimmy Valiant defeated NWA US Champion Greg Valentine

JCP @ Charlotte, NC - WPCQ Studios - 1983
Jimmy Valiant pinned the Great Kabuki (w/ Gary Hart) at the 23-second mark in an impromptu match after throwing Kabuki off the top and hitting an elbow drop; prior to the bout, Hart, with Kabuki, cut a promo in which he said no American wanted a piece of Kabuki; moments later, Valiant answered, grabbed Hart by the tie, punched him, and climbed in the ring; after the match, Kabuki sprayed red mist into Valiant's eyes, causing Valiant to fall into the audience

Following week:
Featured David Crockett conducting an interview with Gary Hart regarding Valiant's injury, with Hart saying Valiant answered the challenge but only the Great Kabuki walked away from the battle

JCP @ Charlotte, NC - WPCQ Studio - 1983
Jos LeDuc vs. Mid-Atlantic TV Champion Dick Slater (impromptu match); prior to the bout, Bob Caudle conducting an interview with LeDuc in which he said he was back from his injury sustained at the hands of Jimmy Valiant and then threatened former manager Sir Oliver Humperdink; LeDuc then challenged NWA TV Champion Dick Slater and noted no one beat him for the belt; Slater then appeared, with the two agreeing to an impromptu match; NWA US Champion Greg Valentine provided guest commentary for the match

JCP @ Charlotte, NC - WPCQ Studio - 1983
Jos LeDuc defeated Mid-Atlantic TV Champion Dick Slater via disqualification at 9:25 when NWA US Champion Greg Valentine appeared on the ring apron, with LeDuc dragging him into the ring and brawling with him; moments later, Slater and Valentine double teamed LeDuc

JCP @ Columbia, SC - April 20, 1983
Jake Roberts defeated Sweet Brown Sugar
NWA Tag Team Champions Ricky Steamboat & Jay Youngblood defeated Jake Roberts & Larry Lane

JCP @ Harrisonburg, VA - High School - April 21, 1983
The Magic Dragon vs. Keith Larsen
Red Dog Lane vs. Mike Davis
Jos LeDuc vs. Ken Timbs
The Great Kabuki vs. Mike Rotunda
NWA Tag Team Champions Ricky Steamboat & Jay Youngblood vs. Sgt. Slaughter & the One Man Gang

Central States @ St. Louis, MO - April 22, 1983
NWA World Champion Ric Flair defeated Jerry Blackwell

JCP @ Charleston, SC - County Hall - April 22, 1983
Johnny Weaver vs. the Magic Dragon
Sgt. Slaughter vs. Jim Nelson (bootcamp match)
Mike Rotundo vs. the Great Kabuki (kendo stick match)

Mid-Atlantic Championship Wrestling - 4/23/83:
Mike Rotundo defeated Ken Timbs
Jake Roberts defeated Wayne Jones
The One Man Gang defeated Ron Rossi
The Great Kabuki & Magic Dragon defeated Mark Fleming & Keith Larsen
NWA Tag Team Champions Ricky Steamboat & Jay Youngblood defeated Bill White & Red Dog Lane

JCP @ Greenville, SC - April 23, 1983
Dusty Rhodes defeated Adrian Street via disqualification
Sam Houston defeated Bobby Bass
Don Kernodle defeated Johnny Weaver
Pez Whatley defeated Kurt Von Hess
Tully Blanchard defeated Brian Adias
NWA World Champion Ric Flair fought NWA Tag Team Champion Ricky Steamboat to a draw
Jack & Jerry Brisco defeated Mark & NWA Tag Team Champion Jay Youngblood via disqualification

JCP @ Asheville, NC - Civic Center - April 24, 1983
Mike Davis defeated Bill White
Rene Goulet defeated Vinnie Valentino
Jack & Jerry Brisco defeated Gene Anderson & Red Dog Lane
Jos LeDuc defeated the One Man Gang
Jimmy Valiant & Bugsy McGraw defeated the Great Kabuki & the Magic Dragon
NWA US Champion Roddy Piper defeated Mid-Atlantic TV Champion Dick Slater
NWA World Champion Ric Flair defeated Greg Valentine

JCP @ Charlotte, NC - Coliseum - April 24, 1983
Ricky Harris defeated Keith Larsen
Johnny Weaver defeated Masa Fuchi
The Magic Dragon defeated Jim Nelson
Jake Roberts defeated Sweet Brown Sugar
Jimmy Valiant defeated the Great Kabuki
NWA US Champion Roddy Piper defeated Mid-Atlantic TV Champion Dick Slater
Sgt. Slaughter & Don Kernodle defeated NWA Tag Team Champions Ricky Steamboat & Jay Youngblood via disqualification
NWA World Champion Ric Flair defeated Greg Valentine via disqualification

JCP @ Greenville, SC - April 25, 1983
Vinnie Valentino defeated Masa Fuchi

Johnny Weaver defeated Ricky Harris
Jake Roberts defeated Sweet Brown Sugar
Jack & Jerry Brisco defeated the Great Kabuki & the Magic Dragon
NWA US Champion Roddy Piper defeated Greg Valentine in a No DQ match
NWA World Champion Ric Flair defeated Mid-Atlantic TV Champion Dick Slater via disqualification

JCP @ Columbia, SC - April 26, 1983
NWA US Champion Roddy Piper, Jos Leduc, & Bugsy McGraw defeated Greg Valentine, the One Man Gang, & Sir Oliver Humperdink
NWA World Champion Ric Flair fought Jimmy Valiant to a no contest

JCP @ Norfolk, VA - April 28, 1983
Jack & Jerry Brisco defeated Jake Roberts & the Magic Dragon
NWA World Champion Ric Flair defeated Mid-Atlantic TV Champion Dick Slater

JCP @ Charleston, SC - County Hall - April 29, 1983
Vinnie Valentino defeated Ken Timbs
Jim Nelson defeated Bill White
Jimmy Valiant, Bugsy McGraw, & Mike Rotundo defeated the One Man Gang, Jake Roberts, & Sir Oliver Humperdink
Jos LeDuc defeated Mid-Atlantic TV Champion Dick Slater; Slater retained the title since the decision came after the first 15 minutes of the match

JCP @ Wilmington, NC - Legion Stadium - April 29, 1983
Wayne Jones vs. Masa Fuchi
Mike Davis vs. Keith Larsen
Johnny Weaver vs. Ricky Harris
Red Dog Lane vs. Sweet Brown Sugar
The Great Kabuki & Magic Dragon vs. Jack & Jerry Brisco
NWA Tag Team Champions Ricky Steamboat & Jay Youngblood vs. Sgt. Slaughter & Don Kernodle (steel cage match)

CHAMPIONSHIP WRESTLING

LEGION STADIUM

● FRIDAY, APRIL 29 ● 8:15 P.M.

Tickets: Adults-$8   Children-$4

Sponsored By New Hanover Youth Baseball!

● WORLD TAG TEAM MATCH ●

10 FOOT CAGE

Sgt. Slaughter
Don Kernodle

Vs.

Ricky Steamboat
Jay Youngblood

● TAG MATCH ●

Kabuki
Magic Dragon

Vs.

Jack Brisco
Gerald Brisco

Red Dog Lane Vs. Sweet Brown Sugar

Johnny Weaver Vs. Ricky Harris

Mike Davis Vs. Keith Larson

Wayne Jones Vs. Masa Fuchi

35

Central States @ St. Louis, MO - Kiel Auditorium - April 29, 1983
Liz Chase, Manny Fernandez, & Mark Romero defeated Bill Cody, Leilani Kai, & Ray Hernandez
Bob Orton Jr. defeated Dewey Robertson
George Wells fought NWA US Champion Roddy Piper to a draw
NWA US Champion Greg Valentine defeated Buzz Tyler
Bob Brown & Rick Martel defeated Grizzly Adams & Kim Duk
Harley Race defeated David Von Erich
NWA World Champion Ric Flair defeated Jerry Blackwell via count-out

Mid-Atlantic Championship Wrestling - 4/30/83:
Johnny Weaver & Mike Rotundo defeated Red Dog Lane & Masa Fuchi
NWA US Champion Roddy Piper defeated Ben Alexander
Rufus R. Jones defeated Bill White
Jos LeDuc defeated Snake Brown
The Great Kabuki & Magic Dragon defeated Vinnie Valentino & Ron Rossi

Worldwide - 4/30/83:
Johnny Weaver & Mike Rotundo defeated Ben Alexander & Snake Brown
Rufus R. Jones defeated Masa Fuchi
NWA US Champion Roddy Piper defeated Red Dog Lane
Jack & Jerry Brisco defeated Bill White & Gene Anderson
The Great Kabuki & Magic Dragon defeated Jim Nelson & Keith Larsen

GCW @ Atlanta, GA - WTBS Studios - April 30, 1983 (matinee)
World Championship Wrestling - 4/30/83 - 2-hour edition; hosted by Gordon Solie; featured a promo by NWA World Champion Ric Flair in which he said he isn't happy with being ordered to defend the title against Tony Atlas within 30 days; included a pre-taped special report with NWA President Bob Geigel who claimed that, due to a controversial finish to their last title match, Flair must defend the title against Atlas in Atlanta on May 1 with a special referee named by GCW; Geigel then appeared in person on set, confronted Flair, and told Flair to sign the contract or he would take the title with him to the NWA offices; Flair later reluctantly signed the contract for Geigel which brought out an excited Atlas; featured promos with NWA National Champion Larry Zbyszko & Killer Brooks, the Iron Sheik & Buzz Sawyer, Dick Murdoch & Ron Garvin, and Tommy Rich & Paul Orndorff; included a feature on the recent professional boxing match with Ernie Shavers facing Ken Norton, Sr. and the arrival of Shavers in a referee's shirt, confronting Flair and saying he'd make sure Flair & Atlas' title bout in Atlanta would be a fair one; featured Mike Jackson commenting on how excited the fans and Atlas are that Flair signed for a title match; included Pro Wrestling Illustrated's Bill Apter & Craig Peters hosting a Q&A with Zbyszko answering questions from the fans; featured the previous week's Atlas Vs.

Rose match; included Zbyszko asking Geigel to ban Rich from challenging him for the NWA National Heavyweight Title and footage from their recent Omni title bout being shown; Geigel replied by stripping Zbyszko of the title because he purchased it from Brooks; featured Sheik yelling threats at Dusty Rhodes & Tommy Rich:
Brian Blair defeated Ron Rossie via submission with the sleeper
Killer Brooks pinned Bobby Scott with the legdrop off the middle turnbuckle; Buzz Sawyer provided guest commentary for the match
Chic Donovan pinned Mike Starbuck with a neckbreaker
Ron Garvin pinned Ron Horn after two knee smashes to the chest
Arn Anderson & Matt Bourne (w/ Paul Ellering) defeated Joe Lightfoot & Zane Smith when Anderson pinned Smith with the gourdbuster; Ellering provided guest commentary for the match
The Iron Sheik (w/ Gen. Homer O'Dell) pinned Zane Smith after a back suplex and elbow drop
Paul Orndorff & Tommy Rich defeated two unknowns when Rich scored the pin after a double-team back suplex / clothesline combo
Mike Jackson pinned Ron Horn after a pair of dropkicks
Ron Garvin pinned Bobby Scott after a knee smash to the chest; the bottom ring rope broke as Garvin jumped off it for the finish

JCP @ Richmond, VA - Coliseum - April 30, 1983
Mike Rotundo defeated Bill White
Rufus R Jones defeated Ricky Harris
Jack & Jerry Brisco defeated Gene Anderson & Angelo Mosca
Bugsy McGraw defeated the One Man Gang
Jake Roberts defeated Mike Graham
Jos LeDuc defeated Mid-Atlantic TV Champion Dick Slater to win the title
Jimmy Valiant defeated the Great Kabuki in a New York Streetfight
NWA US Champion Roddy Piper defeated Greg Valentine
NWA Tag Team Champions Ricky Steamboat & Jay Youngblood defeated Sgt. Slaughter & Don Kernodle

JCP @ Greensboro, NC - Coliseum - May 1, 1983
Keith Larsen defeated Ken Timbs
Mid-Atlantic TV Champion Jos LeDuc defeated Rick Harris
Bugsy McGraw defeated the One Man Gang
Jake Roberts defeated Mike Graham
Dick Slater defeated Sweet Brown Sugar
Jack & Jerry Brisco defeated Angelo Mosca & Gene Anderson
Jimmy Valiant defeated the Great Kabuki in a New York Streetfight
Greg Valentine defeated NWA US Champion Roddy Piper to win the title
NWA Tag Team Champions Ricky Steamboat & Jay Youngblood defeated Sgt. Slaughter & Don Kernodle

GCW @ Atlanta, GA - Omni - May 1, 1983
Bob Roop defeated Joe Lightfoot
Ray Candy defeated Chick Donovan
Arn Anderson & Matt Borne (w/ Paul Ellering) defeated Brian Blair & Tito Santana
Ron Garvin defeated the Iron Sheik (w/ Paul Ellering)
Dick Murdoch defeated Buzz Sawyer via count-out
Tommy Rich & Paul Orndorff defeated Larry Zbyszko & Killer Brooks
Tony Atlas defeated NWA World Champion Ric Flair via disqualification

JCP @ Greenville, SC - Memorial Auditorium - May 2, 1983
The Magic Dragon defeated Mike Davis
Kelly Kiniski defeated Keith Larsen
Mike Rotundo defeated Jake Roberts
NWA US Champion Greg Valentine defeated Rufus R. Jones
Jimmy Valiant defeated the Great Kabuki
NWA Tag Team Champions Ricky Steamboat & Jay Youngblood fought Jack & Jerry Brisco to a double disqualification

GCW @ Beckley, WV - May 2, 1983
Tony Atlas defeated NWA World Champion Ric Flair via disqualification

GCW @ Williamson, WV - Fieldhouse - May 3, 1983
Matt Borne & Arn Anderson vs. Brett Wayne & Buddy Lane
Brian Blair vs. Paul Ellering
Ron Garvin vs. the Iron Sheik
Buzz Sawyer vs. Dick Murdoch
National Heavyweight Champion Larry Zbyszko vs. Tony Atlas
NWA World Champion Ric Flair vs. Tommy Rich

JCP @ Columbia, SC - May 3, 1983
Vinnie Valentino defeated Ken Timbs
Kelly Kiniski defeated Keith Larsen
Johnny Weaver defeated NWA TV Champion Dick Slater via disqualification
Don Kernodle defeated Jim Nelson in a bootcamp match
NWA US Champion Greg Valentine defeated Rufus R. Jones
NWA Tag Team Champions Ricky Steamboat & Jay Youngblood fought Jack & Jerry Brisco to a double disqualification

JCP @ Raleigh, NC - May 3, 1983
Vinnie Valentino defeated Ken Timbs
Kelly Kiniski defeated Keith Larsen
Don Kernodle defeated Jim Nelson in a bootcamp match
Johnny Weaver defeated NWA TV Champion Dick Slater via disqualification
NWA US Champion Greg Valentine defeated Rufus R. Jones
NWA Tag Team Champions Ricky Steamboat & Jay Youngblood fought Jack & Jerry Brisco to a no contest

GCW @ Akron, OH - The Breakaway - May 4, 1983
Matt Borne & Arn Anderson (w/ Paul Ellering) defeated Tito Santana & Brian Blair
Paul Ellering defeated Joe Lightfoot
Ron Garvin defeated the Iron Sheik (w/ Paul Ellering)
Dick Murdoch defeated Killer Brooks
Tommy Rich defeated Larry Zbyszko
Tony Atlas defeated NWA World Champion Ric Flair

JCP @ Sumter, SC - Sumter County Exhibition Center - May 5, 1983
Wayne Jones vs. Masa Fuchi
Rufus R. Jones vs. Rick Harris
Jake Roberts vs. Mike Rotundo
Mid-Atlantic TV Champion Jos LeDuc vs. the One Man Gang
NWA Tag Team Champions Ricky Steamobat & Jay Youngblood vs. NWA US Champion Greg Valentine & Dick Slater

GCW @ Toledo, OH - May 5, 1983
Tony Atlas defeated NWA World Champion Ric Flair

JCP @ Lenoir, NC - May 6, 1983
Ben Alexander defeated Mike Davis
Masa Fuchi defeated Abe Jacobs
Mike Rotundo fought Johnny Weaver to a draw
Jimmy Valiant, Mid-Atlantic TV Champion Jos LeDuc, & Bugsy McGraw defeated the One Man Gang, Gene Anderson, & Sir Oliver Humperdink

JCP @ Charleston, SC - County Hall - May 6, 1983
Ricky Harris defeated Vinnie Valentino
Susan Starr & Liz Chase defeated Lailiani Kai & Donna Christianello
Nelson Royal defeated Jake Roberts
NWA Tag Team Champions Ricky Steamboat & Jay Youngblood defeated NWA US Champion Greg Valentine & Dick Slater

GCW @ Atlanta, GA - WTBS Studios - May 7, 1983
NWA World Champion Ric Flair defeated Mike Starbuck

GCW @ Cincinnati, OH - Riverfront Coliseum - May 7, 1983
Bob Roop defeated Joe Lightfoot
Ron Garvin defeated the Iron Sheik (w/ Paul Ellering)
Matt Borne & Arn Anderson (w/ Paul Ellering) defeated Tito Santana & Brian Blair
Tony Atlas defeated Larry Zbyszko
Dusty Rhodes & Dick Murdoch defeated Buzz Sawyer & Killer Brooks
NWA World Champion Ric Flair defeated Tommy Rich

JCP @ Hampton, VA - May 7, 1983
Mid-Atlantic Heavyweight Champion Dory Funk Jr. & Jake

Roberts defeated NWA US Champion Greg Valentine & Dick Slater

PNW @ Centralia, WA - May 8, 1983
NWA World Champion Ric Flair defeated Billy Jack Haynes via disqualification

JCP @ Savannah, GA - Civic Center - May 8, 1983
Tag Team Tournament Quarter-Finals: Jack & Jerry Brisco defeated the One Man Gang & Kelly Kiniski
Tag Team Tournament Quarter-Finals: The Great Kabuki & the Magic Dragon defeated Jimmy Valiant & Bugsy McGraw
Tag Team Tournament Quarter-Finals: Mike Rotundo & Rufus R. Jones defeated NWA US Champion Greg Valentine & Gene Anderson
Tag Team Tournament Quarter-Finals: Mid-Atlantic Heavyweight Champion Dory Funk Jr. & Jake Roberts defeated Johnny Weaver & Nelson Royal
Tag Team Tournament Semi-Finals: Jack & Jerry Brisco defeated the Great Kabuki & the Magic Dragon
Tag Team Tournament Semi-Finals: Jake Roberts & Mid-Atlantic Heavyweight Champion Dory Funk Jr. defeated Mike Rotundo & Rufus R. Jones
Tag Team Tournament Finals: Jack & Jerry Brisco defeated Jake Roberts & Mid-Atlantic Heavyweight Champion Dory Funk Jr.; stipulations stated the winning team would earn a NWA Tag Team Title shot

JCP @ Greenville, SC - Memorial Coliseum - May 9, 1983
Vinnie Valentino defeated Bill White
Nelson Royal defeated Ken Timbs
Mid-Atlantic Heavyweight Champion Dory Funk Jr. & Jake Roberts defeated Mike Rotundo & Johnny Weaver
The One Man Gang defeated Mid-Atlantic TV Champion Jos LeDuc
NWA Tag Team Champions Ricky Steamboat & Jay Youngblood fought Jack & Jerry Brisco to a double count-out

PNW @ Longview, WA - May 9, 1983
NWA World Champion Ric Flair defeated Buddy Rose via count-out

PNW @ Portland, OR - May 10, 1983
Roddy Piper fought NWA World Champion Ric Flair to a draw in a Best 2 out of 3 falls match; fall #3: the 60-minute time-limit expired

JCP @ Columbia, SC - Township Auditorium - May 10, 1983
Kelly Kiniski defeated Keith Larson
The Magic Dragon defeated Mark Fleming
Bugsy McGraw defeated NWA US Champion Greg Valentine via count-out
Mid-Atlantic TV Champion Jos LeDuc defeated the One Man Gang
Jimmy Valiant defeated the Great Kabuki

PNW @ Seattle, WA - May 11, 1983
NWA World Champion Ric Flair defeated Roddy Piper via reverse decision

PNW @ Yakima, WA - May 12, 1983
NWA World Champion Ric Flair defeated Billy Jack Haynes via disqualification

JCP @ Norfolk, VA - Scope - May 12, 1983
The Magic Dragon defeated Keith Larson
Gene Anderson defeated Rick McCord
Mike Rotundo & Rufus R. Jones defeated Mid-Atlantic Heavyweight Champion Dory Funk Jr. & Jake Roberts
NWA US Champion Greg Valentine defeated Johnny Weaver
Jimmy Valiant defeated the Great Kabuki
NWA Tag Team Champions Ricky Steamboat & Jay Youngblood defeated Jack & Jerry Brisco

PNW @ Eugene, OR - May 13, 1983
NWA World Champion Ric Flair defeated Billy Jack Haynes via disqualification

JCP @ Charleston, SC - County Hall - May 13, 1983
Vinnie Valentino defeated Ken Timbs
Kelly Kiniski defeated Abe Jacobs
Rufus R. Jones defeated Larry Cheatam
Jimmy Valiant & Bugsy McGraw defeated the Great Kabuki & the Magic Dragon
The One Man Gang defeated Mid-Atlantic TV Champion Jos LeDuc; the title was only at stake for the first 15 minutes of the bout, thus LeDuc retained the title

Mid-Atlantic Championship Wrestling - 5/14/83:
The Great Kabuki & Magic Dragon defeated Keith Larsen & Rick McCord
Mike Rotundo & Rufus R. Jones defeated Jake Roberts & Mid-Atlantic Heavyweight Champion Dory Funk Jr.

PNW @ Portland, OR - May 14, 1983
Roddy Piper & Billy Jack Haynes defeated NWA World Champion Ric Flair & Rip Oliver

JCP @ Wilmington, NC - Legion Stadium - May 14, 1983
Masa Fuchi vs. Abe Jacobs
Ken Timbs vs. Wayne Jones
Gene Anderson vs. Vinnie Valentino
Mid-Atlantic TV Champion Jos LeDuc vs. the One Man Gang
The Great Kabuki & Magic Dragon vs. Buggsy McGraw & Rufus R. Jones
NWA US Champion Greg Valentine vs. Jimmy Valiant

CHAMPIONSHIP WRESTLING

LEGION STADIUM

• SATURDAY, MAY 14, • 8:15 P.M.

Tickets: Adults-$6   Children-$3

Sponsored By New Hanover Youth Baseball

GREG VALENTINE   **Vs.**   **JIMMY VALIANT**

• TAG MATCH •

KABUKI and **MAGIC DRAGON** (With Gary Hart)   **Vs.**   **BUGSEY MCGRAW** and **RUFUS R. JONES**

JOS LEDUC Vs. ONE MAN GANG

GENE ANDERSON Vs. VINNIE VALENTINO

KEN TIMBS Vs. WAYNE JONES

MASA FUCHI Vs. ABE JACOBS

39

Worldwide - 5/14/83:
Mike Rotundo & Rufus R. Jones defeated Masa Fuchi & Ricky Harris
Mid-Atlantic Heavyweight Champion Dory Funk Jr. & Jake Roberts defeated Rick McCord & Keith Larsen

JCP @ Roanoke, VA - Civic Center - May 14, 1983
Mid-Atlantic Heavyweight Champion Dory Funk Jr. & Jake Roberts defeated Mike Rotundo & Johnny Weaver

JCP @ Charlotte, NC - Coliseum - May 15, 1983
Kelly Kiniski & the One Man Gang defeated Rick McCord & Vinnie Valentino
Mid-Atlantic Heavyweight Champion Dory Funk Jr. defeated Mike Rotundo
Jimmy Valiant, Rufus R. Jones, & Bugsy McGraw defeated the Great Kabuki, Gary Hart, & the Magic Dragon
NWA US Champion Greg Valentine defeated Mid-Atlantic TV Champion Jos LeDuc
Jack & Jerry Brisco defeated NWA Tag Team Champions Ricky Steamboat & Jay Youngblood and Sgt. Slaughter & Don Kernodle in a round robin tournament; the Briscos defeated Steamboat & Youngblood via disqualification in the final match

JCP @ Asheville, NC - Civic Center - May 15, 1983
Bill White defeated Ken Timbs
Kelly Kiniski defeated Abe Jacobs
Mid-Atlantic TV Champion Jos LeDuc & Rufus R. Jones defeated Kelly Kiniski & the One Man Gang
Mid-Atlantic Heavyweight Champion Dory Funk Jr. defeated Mike Rotundo
NWA US Champion Greg Valentine defeated Bugsy McGraw
Jack & Jerry Brisco defeated NWA Tag Team Champions Ricky Steamboat & Jay Youngblood

Toronto, Ontario - Maple Leaf Garden - May 15, 1983
Bob Marcus pinned Ricky Harris at 9:21
Iron Mike Sharpe pinned Joe Marcus at 8:09
Gene Kiniski & the Executioner defeated Salvatore Bellomo & Nick DeCarlo at 15:04
Canadian TV Champion Pvt. Nelson pinned Keith Larsen at 14:06
North American Champion Johnny Weaver defeated Leo Burke at 18:52
Rocky Johnson defeated WWF IC Champion Don Muraco via count-out at 11:21
Roddy Piper defeated Terry Funk via count-out at 11:14
Canadian Champion Angelo Mosca defeated Bob Orton Jr. at 10:12

JCP @ Fayetteville, NC - May 16, 1983
Mike Rotundo fought Jake Roberts to a draw

JCP @ Greenville, SC - May 16, 1983
Kelly Kiniski defeated Vinnie Valentino

Rufus R. Jones defeated the Magic Dragon
Jimmy Valiant defeated the Great Kabuki
NWA US Champion Greg Valentine defeated Dory Funk Jr.
Mid-Atlantic TV Champion Jos LeDuc defeated the One Man Gang

Central States @ Wichita, KS - May 16, 1983
NWA World Champion Ric Flair defeated Buzz Tyler via disqualification

JCP @ Raleigh, NC - May 17, 1983
Rick McCord defeated Masa Fuchi
Mike Rotundo defeated Gene Anderson
Jimmy Valiant & Bugsy McGraw defeated the Great Kabuki & the Magic Dragon
Rufus R. Jones defeated Jake Roberts via disqualification
NWA US Champion Greg Valentine defeated Dory Funk Jr.

Central States @ Kansas City, MO - May 19, 1983
NWA World Champion Ric Flair defeated Missouri Heavyweight Champion Harley Race

Central States @ St. Joseph, MO - May 20, 1983
NWA World Champion Ric Flair defeated Dewey Robertson

JCP @ Charleston, SC - County Hall - May 20, 1983
Jake Roberts defeated Chuck Connors
Dory Funk Jr. defeated Jack Brown
Rick Harris defeated Ken Hall
Vinnie Valentino defeated Glenn Lane
Jack & Jerry Brisco defeated NWA Tag Team Champions Ricky Steamboat & Jay Youngblood via disqualification when one of the champions struck the referee

Mid-Atlantic Championship Wrestling - 5/21/83:
NWA US Champion Greg Valentine defeated Ken Hall
The One Man Gang & Kelly Kiniski defeated Rick McCord & Vinnie Valentino
Jim Nelson defeated Jack Brisco via disqualification
Mid-Atlantic TV Champion Jos LeDuc defeated Rick Connors
Dory Funk Jr. & Jake Roberts defeated Keith Larsen & Masa Fuchi

JCP @ Greensboro, NC - Coliseum - May 21, 1983
Keith Larsen defeated Masa Fuchi
Bill White defeated Ken Hall
Gene Anderson & the Magic Dragon defeated Rick Connors & Vinnie Valentino
Johnny Weaver defeated Ricky Harris
Rufus R. Jones defeated Jake Roberts
The Great Kabuki defeated Jimmy Valiant
NWA US Champion Greg Valentine defeated Mid-Atlantic TV Champion Jos LeDuc

Jack & Jerry Brisco defeated NWA Tag Team Champions Ricky Steamboat & Jay Youngblood via disqualification

JCP @ Spartanburg, SC - Memorial Auditorium - May 21, 1983
Ken Timbs defeated Ben Alexander
Abe Jacobs defeated Rick Harris
Liz Chase defeated Peggy Lee
Johnny Weaver & Rick McCord defeated Kelly Kiniski & Jack Brown
Bugsy McGraw defeated the One Man Gang
NWA Mid-Atlantic Heavyweight Champion Dory Funk Jr. defeated Mike Rotundo

JCP @ Greenville, SC - Memorial Auditorium - May 23, 1983
Mid-Atlantic Tag Team Championship Tournament Semi Finals: The One Man Gang & Kelly Kiniski defeated Jimmy Valiant & Bugsy McGraw
Mid-Atlantic Tag Team Championship Tournament Semi Finals: Mike Rotundo & Rufus R. Jones defeated Dory Funk Jr. & Jake Roberts
Keith Larsen defeated Rene Goulet
Rick McCord defeated the Magic Dragon
The Great Kabuki defeated Mid-Atlantic TV Champion Jos LeDuc to win the title
Mid-Atlantic Tag Team Championship Tournament Finals: The One Man Gang & Kelly Kiniski defeated Mike Rotundo & Rufus R. Jones
Jack & Jerry Brisco defeated NWA Tag Team Champions Ricky Steamboat & Jay Youngblood via disqualification

Continental @ Birmingham, AL - May 23, 1983
NWA World Champion Ric Flair defeated Austin Idol

JCP @ Columbia, SC - May 24, 1983
Dory Funk Jr. & Jake Roberts defeated Mike Rotundo & SD Jones

JCP @ Raleigh, NC - Dorton Arena - May 24, 1983
Masa Fuchi & Ricky Harris defeated Glen Lane & Abe Jacobs
Vinnie Valentino defeated Bill White
Rene Goulet defeated Ken Hall
Rick McCord defeated Gene Anderson
Mid-Atlantic Tag Team Champion the One Man Gang defeated Jos LeDuc
Jack & Jerry Brisco defeated NWA Tag Team Champions Ricky Steamboat & Jay Youngblood via disqualification

JCP @ Norfolk, VA - May 26, 1983
Rufus R. Jones defeated Jake Roberts
NWA World Champion Ric Flair defeated NWA US Champion Greg Valentine

JCP @ Charleston, SC - County Hall - May 27, 1983
Vinnie Valentino fought Keith Larson to a draw
Masa Fuchi & Rick Harris defeated Abe Jacobs & Glenn Lane
Bugsy McGraw defeated the Magic Dragon
Rufus R. Jones defeated Jake Roberts
Jimmy Valiant defeated Mid-Atlantic TV Champion the Great Kabuki

JCP @ Richmond, VA - Coliseum - May 27, 1983
Johnny Weaver vs. Rene Goulet
Mike Rotundo vs. Mid-Atlantic Tag Team Champion Kelly Kiniski
Bob Orton Jr. vs. Gene Anderson
Jos LeDuc vs. Mid-Atlantic Tag Team Champion the One Man Gang; stipulations stated LeDuc would get 5 minutes in the ring with Sir Oliver Humperdink if he won
NWA Tag Team Champions Ricky Steamobat & Jay Youngblood vs. Jack & Jerry Brisco
NWA World Champion Ric Flair defeated NWA US Champion Greg Valentine

Mid-Atlantic Championship Wrestling - 5/28/83:
Bob Orton Jr. defeated Ricky Harris
NWA US Champion Greg Valentine defeated Keith Larsen
Mid-Atlantic Tag Team Champions the One Man Gang & Kelly Kiniski defeated Vinnie Valentino & Ken Hall
Jimmy Valiant & Rufus R. Jones defeated Jack & Jerry Brisco
Jake Roberts defeated Rick McCord

JCP @ Charlotte, NC - May 28, 1983 (4,114)
Gene Anderson & Rene Goulet defeated Mike Davis & Keith Larsen
Vinnie Valentino defeated Masa Fuchi
Bob Orton Jr. defeated Bill White
Wahoo McDaniel defeated the Magic Dragon
Mid-Atlantic TV Champion the Great Kabuki defeated Jimmy Valiant via count-out
NWA Tag Team Champions Ricky Steamobat & Jay Youngblood defeated Jack & Jerry Brisco
NWA US Champion Greg Valentine defeated NWA World Champion Ric Flair via disqualification

JCP @ Asheville, NC - Civic Center - May 29, 1983
Vinnie Valentino defeated Bill White
Keith Larsen & Mike Davis defeated Rene Goulet & Rick Harris
Wahoo McDaniel defeated Jake Roberts
Dory Funk Jr. defeated Mike Rotundo
NWA Tag Team Champions Ricky Steamboat & Jay Youngblood defeated Jack & Jerry Brisco
NWA US Champion Greg Valentine defeated NWA World Champion Ric Flair; only the US title was at stake

Wrestling

World title
RIC (Nature Boy) FLAIR
vs GREG VALENTINE

Inter-Continental title
MAGNIFICENT MURACO
vs ROCKY JOHNSON

$100,000 challenge
DORY FUNK
vs MIKE ROTUNDO

also . . . . Weaver, Leo Burke,
K. Kiniski, Marcus Bros. etc.

SEE TV WRESTLING SAT. CH. 11 @ 1 P.M. noon
exhibition of strength & science

SUNDAY, MAY 29th. 8 P.M

MAPLE LEAF GARDENS

CHAMPIONSHIP WRESTLING

LEGION STADIUM

MONDAY, MAY 30 ● 8:15 P.M.

Tickets: Adults-$6   Children -$3
Sponsored By New Hanover Youth Baseball

● **U. S. TITLE MATCH** ●

WAHOO McDANIEL   **Vs.**   **GREG VALENTINE**

● **WORLD'S TAG TEAM TITLE MATCH** ●

RICKY STEAMBOAT and **JAY YOUNGBLOOD**   **Vs.**   **JACK BRISCO** and **GERALD BRISCO**

● **TV TITLE MATCH** ●

JOS LEDUC   Vs.   **KABUKI**

MAGIC DRAGON VS. MIKE DAVIS
RICKY HARRIS VS. VINNIE VALENTINO

Toronto, Ontario - Maple Leaf Garden - May 29, 1983
Bob Marcus defeated Alec Gerard at 14:26
Billy Red Lyons defeated Tim Gerard at 15:38
The Executioner defeated Joe Marcus at 14:56
Mid-Atlantic Tag Team Champion Kelly Kiniski defeated Nick DeCarlo at 11:12
Mike Rotundo defeated Dory Funk Jr. at 13:48 in a $100,000 challenge match
Leo Burke defeated North American Champion Johnny Weaver to win the title at 14:40
WWF IC Champion Don Muraco defeated Rocky Johnson at 15:18
NWA World Champion Ric Flair pinned NWA US Champion Greg Valentine at 19:31

JCP @ Wilmington, NC - Legion Stadium - May 30, 1983
Ricky Harris vs. Vinnie Valentino
Magic Dragon vs. Mike Davis
Mid-Atlantic TV Champion the Great Kabuki vs. Jos LeDuc
NWA Tag Team Champions Ricky Steamboat & Jay Youngblood vs. Jack & Jerry Brisco
NWA US Champion Greg Valentine vs. Wahoo McDaniel

JCP @ Columbia, SC - May 31, 1983
Mike Rotundo & Rufus R. Jones defeated Dory Funk Jr. & Jake Roberts

WCCW @ Del Rio, TX - Civic Center - June 2, 1983
Armand Hussein vs. Ken Johnson
Chris Adams vs. Tora Yatsu
Jose Lothario vs. Michael Hayes
Bill Rathe vs. Kamala
NWA World Champion Ric Flair vs. American Heavyweight Champion Kevin Von Erich

JCP @ Sumter, SC - June 2, 1983
Bill White defeated Sgt. Jacques Goulet
The Magic Dragon defeated Abe Jacobs
Bob Orton Jr. & Bugsy McGraw defeated Gene Anderson & Mid-Atlantic Tag Team Champion Kelly Kiniski
Rufus R. Jones defeated Mid-Atlantic TV Champion the Great Kabuki
NWA US Champion Greg Valentine defeated Wahoo McDaniel

JCP @ Charleston, SC - County Hall - June 3, 1983
Jacques Goulet defeated Bill White
Gene Anderson defeated Brett Hart
Bob Orton Jr. defeated Mid-Atlantic Tag Team Champion Kelly Kiniski
Jimmy Valiant, Johnny Weaver (sub. for Bugsy McGraw), & Rufus R. Jones defeated Mid-Atlantic TV Champion the Great Kabuki, Magic Dragon, & Gary Hart
NWA US Champion Greg Valentine defeated Wahoo McDaniel

Jimmy Valiant & Rufus R. Jones defeated Sgt. Jacques Goulet & Bill White
NWA US Champion Greg Valentine defeated Vinnie Valentino
Dory Funk Jr. defeated Brett Hart (Barry Horowitz)
Mid-Atlantic TV Champion the Great Kabuki defeated Keith Larsen

Worldwide - 6/4/83:
NWA US Champion Greg Valentine defeated Brett Hart
Bob Orton Jr. defeated Bill White
Bugsy McGraw defeated Ben Alexander
Dory Funk Jr. defeated Vinnie Valentino
Keith Larsen defeated Mid-Atlantic TV Chapion the Great Kabuki via disqualification

JCP @ Greensboro, NC - Coliseum - June 4, 1983
NWA Tag Team Champions Ricky Steamboat & Jay Youngblood defetaed Jack & Jerry Brisco
Jimmy Valiant vs. Mid-Atlantic TV Champion the Great Kabuki (Gary Hart handcuffed to Rufus R. Jones at ringside; if Valiant wins, he gets 5 minutes with Hart)
Wahoo McDaniel vs. NWA US Champion Greg Valentine

AJPW @ Japan - June 4, 1983
NWA World Champion Ric Flair pinned NWA Tag Team Champion Ricky Steamboat at 16:19 when the momentum of a crossbody off the top by Steamboat put Flair on top for the win; after the bout, Steamboat handed Flair the title belt and shook his hand

AJPW @ Kisarasu, Japan - June 5, 1983
Genichiro Tenryu & Jumbo Tsuruta defeated NWA World Champion Ric Flair & Dick Slater

JCP @ Hampton, VA - Coliseum - June 5, 1983
Wahoo McDaniel defeated NWA US Champion Greg Valentine via disqualification

JCP @ Greenville, SC - Memorial Auditorium - June 6, 1983
Abe Jacobs defeated Ben Alexander
Gene Anderson defeated Brett Hart
The Magic Dragon defeated Vinnie Valentino
Jimmy Valiant & Johnny Weaver defeated Mid-Atlantic Tag Team Champions the One Man Gang & Kelly Kiniski via disqualification
Mid-Atlantic TV Champion thc Grcat Kabuki defeated Jos LeDuc
NWA US Champion Greg Valentine defeated Bob Orton Jr.

AJPW @ Otsu, Japan - June 6, 1983
NWA World Champion Ric Flair fought Bruiser Brody to a double count-out

AJPW @ Kifu, Japan - June 7, 1983
NWA World Champion Ric Flair & Roddy Piper defeated
Jumbo Tsuruta & Ashura Hara

AJPW @ Tokyo, Japan - June 8, 1983
NWA World Champion Ric Flair fought Jumbo Tsuruta to a
draw in a Best 2 out of 3 falls match

Central States @ St. Louis, MO - June 10, 1983
Missouri Heavyweight Champion & Central States Champion
Harley Race pinned NWA World Champion Ric Flair to win the
title in a Best 2 out of 3 falls match; fall #3: Race pinned Flair
by lifting his shoulder out of a back suplex, with Flair pinning
himself

JCP @ Charleston, SC - County Hall - June 10, 1983
Masa Fuchi defeated Abe Jacobs
Bill White defeated Brett Hart
The Magic Dragon defeated Rick McCord
Jake Roberts defeated Mike Rotunda
Dory Funk Jr. fought Mid-Atlantic TV Champion the Great
Kabuki to a double disqualification

Mid-Atlantic Championship Wrestling - 6/11/83:
NWA Tag Team Champions Ricky Steamboat & Jay
Youngblood defeated Bill White & Masa Fuchi
NWA US Champion Greg Valentine defeated Mark Fleming
Mid-Atlantic TV Champion the Great Kabuki & Mid-Atlantic Tag
Team Champion the One Man Gang defeated Brett Hart &
Rick McCord
Jake Roberts defeated Mike Davis
Bob Orton Jr. defeated Ben Alexander

Worldwide - 6/11/83:
NWA Tag Team Champions Ricky Steamboat & Jay
Youngblood defeated Brett Hart & Rick McCord
NWA US Champion Greg Valentine defeated Mike Davis
Bob Orton Jr. defeated Masa Fuchi
Jake Roberts defeated Vinnie Valentino
Mid-Atlantic TV Champion & Magic Dragon defeated Keith
Larsen & Mark Fleming

JCP @ Spartanburg, SC - Memorial Auditorium - June 11, 1983
Keith Larsen & Rick McCord defeated Masa Fuchi & Bill White
Jos LeDuc defeated Mid-Atlantic Tag Team Champion Kelly
Kiniski
Johnny Weaver defeated the Magic Dragon
Rufus R. Jones defeated Mid-Atlantic TV Champion the Great
Kabuki

JCP @ Roanoke, VA - Civic Center - June 11, 1983
NWA US Champion Greg Valentine defeated Ric Flair via
disqualification

JCP @ Columbia, SC - Township Auditorium - June 12, 1983
Vinnie Valentino defeated Abe Jacobs
The Magic Dragon defeated Brett Hart
Keith Larson & Rick McCord defeated Gene Anderson & Ben
Alexander
Jake Roberts defeated Mike Davis
Jimmy Valiant & Rufus R. Jones defeated Jack & Jerry Brisco
NWA US Champion Greg Valentine defeated Ric Flair via
disqualification

Toronto, Ontario - Maple Leaf Gardens - June 12, 1983
Mid-Atlantic Tag Team Champion Kelly Kiniski & Rene Goulet
defeated John Bonello & Don Kolov
Bob Marcus defeated Bill White
Nick DeCarlo defeated Joe Marcus
Dick Slater defeated Jos LeDuc
Johnny Weaver defeated Leo Burke
Mid-Atlantic TV Champion the Great Kabuki defeated Mike
Rotundo
Sgt. Slaughter defeated NWA Tag Team Champion Jay
Youngblood
WWF IC Champion Don Muraco defeated Canadian
Heavyweight Champion Angelo Mosca via disqualification

JCP @ Savannah, GA - June 12, 1983
NWA US Champion Greg Valentine defeated Ric Flair via
disqualification at 12:17

JCP @ Greenville, SC - June 13, 1983
Vinnie Valentino vs. Masa Fuchi
Mid-Atlantic Tag Team Champion the One Man Gang vs. ?
Rick McCord vs. the Magic Dragon
Jack & Jerry Brisco vs. Jimmy Valiant & Bob Orton Jr.
Ric Flair defeated NWA US Champion Greg Valentine

JCP @ Raleigh, NC - June 14, 1983
Ric Flair defeated NWA US Champion Greg Valentine via
disqualification

JCP @ Sumter, SC - June 15, 1983
Bill White vs. Rick McCord
Abe Jacobs vs. Jacques Goulet
Kim Duk vs. Cy Jernigan
Jack & Jerry Brisco vs. Jimmy Valiant & Rufus R. Jones
Ric Flair vs. NWA US Champion Greg Valentine

JCP @ Norfolk, VA - June 16, 1983
Ric Flair defeated NWA US Champion Greg Valentine via
disqualification

Central States @ Kansas City, KS - June 16, 1983
NWA World Champion Harley Race defeated Dewey
Robertson

WRESTLING

FRIDAY, JUNE 17

CHARLESTON COUNTY HALL 8:15 P.M.

U.S. TITLE MATCH

Champion GREG VALENTINE
-VS-
RUFUS R. JONES

SPECIAL! RODDY PIPER WILL BE AT RINGSIDE

& 4 OTHER BOUTS

TICKETS ON SALE

MILLER DRUG	COUNTY
REYNOLDS AVENUE	HALL
NORTH CHARLESTON	1000 KING ST.

JCP @ Charleston, SC - County Hall - June 17, 1983
Golden Boy Gray defeated Vinnie Valentino
Bill White defeated Glenn Lane
Mid-Atlantic Tag Team Champion Kelly Kiniski defeated Rick McCord
Jacques Goulet defeated Brett Hart
Dick Slater defeated Johnny Weaver
NWA US Champion Greg Valentine defeated Rufus R. Jones

WCCW Star Wars - Dallas, TX - Reunion Arena - June 17, 1983 (21,000)
Genichiro Tenryu pinned Johnny Mantell
Vickie Carranza pinned Lola Gonzales
Jose Lothario, Chris Adams, & Chavo Guerrero defeated Bill Irwin, Fishman, & the Mongol when Guerrero pinned the Mongol
Buddy Roberts pinned Iceman King Parsons in a hair vs. hair match at around the 5:20 mark with a roll over and grabbing the tights for leverage, pulling them up so far that it was censored on the screen; after the bout, Roberts argued with referee David Manning over whether he did pull the tights before then attacking Parsons; Parsons eventually fought Roberts off and then rubbed shaving cream all over his head; moments later, Michael Hayes appeared and briefly fought with Parsons until Parsons gained the advantage, with Hayes then helping Roberts backstage (*The Triumph & Tragedy of World Class Championship Wrestling*)
David Von Erich defeated Jimmy Garvin via disqualification; due to stipulations, Garvin & Sunshine became Von Erich's valets for a day
All Japan United National Champion Jumbo Tsuruta pinned Ted DiBiase
All Japan PWF Champion the Giant Baba pinned King Kong Bundy
Kamala defeated Armand Hussein, Tola Yatsu, & Mike Bond in a handicap match by pinning Yatsu and Bond; stipulations stated the loser of the fall would leave WCCW
NWA World Champion Harley Race defeated Kevin Von Erich via disqualification at 14:00 when David Von Erich, who came ringside late in the bout after Kevin appeared to have suffered a serious shoulder injury, attacked the champion after Race kicked him; stipulations stated it was legal to throw your opponent over the top rope
Kerry Von Erich & Bruiser Brody defeated American Tag Team Champions Michael Hayes & Terry Gordy when Von Erich pinned Hayes to win the titles

Mid-Atlantic Championship Wrestling - 6/18/83:
Bob Orton Jr. defeafed Bill Howard
Dory Funk Jr. & Jake Roberts defeated Mark Fleming & Mike Davis
Mid-Atlantic TV Champion the Great Kabuki defeated John Bonello
Dick Slater defeated Keith Larsen

Worldwide - 6/18/83:
Bob Orton Jr. defeated Golden Boy Gray
Dory Funk Jr. & Jake Roberts defeated Mark Fleming & Brett Hart
Mid-Atlantic TV Champion the Great Kabuki defeated Keith Larsen
Dick Slater defeated Mike Davis

JCP @ Greenville, SC - June 18, 1983
Vinnie Valentino defeated Bill White
Mid-Atlantic Tag Team Champion Kelly Kiniski defeated Brett Hart
Bob Orton Jr. defeated Kim Duk
Dick Slater defeated Johnny Weaver
Jack & Jerry Brisco defeated NWA Tag Team Champions Ricky Steamboat & Jay Youngblood to win the titles
NWA US Champion Greg Valentine & Mid-Atlantic Heavyweight Champion Dory Funk Jr. defeated Ric Flair & Roddy Piper via disqualification

CHAMPIONSHIP WRESTLING
LEGION STADIUM
SUNDAY, JUNE 19 • 7:30 P.M.
Tickets: Adults-$6   Children -$3
Sponsored By New Hanover Youth Baseball

RIC FLAIR and RODDY PIPER **Vs.** GREG VALENTINE and DICK SLATER

JACK BRISCO and GERALD BRISCO **Vs.** RUFUS R. JONES and JIMMY VALIANT

• MID ATLANTIC TAG ACTION •
ONE MAN GANG and KELLY KINISKI **Vs.** BOB ORTON and JOS LE DUC

BUGSY McGRAW Vs. MAGIC DRAGON
PLUS OTHERS!

JCP @ Wilmington, NC - Legion Stadium - June 19, 1983
Bugsy McGraw vs. Magic Dragon
Bob Orton Jr. & Jos LeDuc vs. Mid-Atlantic Tag Team Champions the One Man Gang & Kelly Kiniski
NWA Tag Team Champions Jack & Jerry Brisco vs. Rufus R. Jones & Jimmy Valiant
Ric Flair & Roddy Piper vs. NWA US Champion Greg Valentine & Dick Slater

CWF @ Gainesville, FL - June 19, 1983
Barry Windham vs. NWA World Champion Harley Race

CWF @ Orlando, FL - June 19, 1983
NWA World Champion Harley Race defeated Dusty Rhodes

CWF @ Tampa, FL - June 21, 1983
NWA World Champion Harley Race defeated Scott McGhee at the 30-minute mark

JCP @ Columbia, SC - June 21, 1983
Ric Flair defeated NWA US Champion Greg Valentine via disqualification

CWF @ Miami, FL - Convention Hall - June 22, 1983
Charlie Cook defeated Mr. Olympia
Bobby Duncum defeated Brad Armstrong
Scott McGhee defeated Adrian Street
Kevin Sullivan & Purple Haze defeated Barry Windham & Ron Bass in a taped fist match
Blackjack Mulligan defeated Angelo Mosca
NWA World Champion Harley Race defeated Dusty Rhodes via count-out

JCP @ Richmond, VA - June 24, 1983
Bob Orton Jr. vs. Jake Roberts
Rufus R. Jones vs. Dick Slater
Dick Slater vs. Jos LeDuc
NWA Tag Team Champions Jack & Jerry Brisco vs. Ricky Steamboat & Jay Youngblood
Ric Flair defeated NWA US Champion Greg Valentine via disqualification

Toronto, Ontario - Maple Leaf Gardens - June 24, 1983
NWA World Champion Harley Race defeated Ric Flair via disqualification

JCP @ Charleston, SC - County Hall - June 24, 1983
Bill Howard defeated John Bonello
Rick McCord defeated Kim Duk
Gene Anderson defeated Keith Larsen
The Magic Dragon defeated Mike Davis
Mike Rotundo defeated Mid-Atlantic Tag Team Champion Kelly Kiniski
Ric Flair & Roddy Piper defeated NWA US Champion Greg Valentine & Mid-Atlantic Tag Team Champion the One Man Gang

JCP @ Charlotte, NC - Coliseum - June 25, 1983
Rick McCord defeated Masa Fuchi
Mike Rotundo defeated Mid-Atlantic Tag Team Champion Kelly Kiniski
Jos LeDuc defeated Mid-Atlantic Tag Team Champion the One Man Gang
Jake Roberts defeated Bob Orton Jr.
Rufus R. Jones defeated the Magic Dragon
Mid-Atlantic TV Champion the Great Kabuki defeated Jimmy Valiant
Ric Flair & Roddy Piper defeated NWA US Champion Greg Valentine & Mid-Atlantic Heavyweight Champion Dory Funk Jr.

NWA Tag Team Champions Jack & Jerry Brisco defeated Ricky Steamboat & Jay Youngblood

CWF @ Orlando, FL - June 25, 1983
NWA World Champion Harley Race defeated Barry Windham

JCP @ Asheville, NC - Civic Center - June 26, 1983
Masa Fuchi defeated Mark Fleming
Rene Goulet defeated Rick McCord
Gene Anderson defeated John Bonello
Keith Larsen defeated Ben Alexander
Ric Flair & Roddy Piper defeated NWA US Champion Greg Valentine & Jake Roberts
NWA Tag Team Champions Jack & Jerry Brisco defeated Ricky Steamboat & Jay Youngblood

JCP @ Greenville, SC - Memorial Auditorium - June 27, 1983
Gene Anderson defeated Rene Goulet
Keith Larsen defeated Rick McCord
Mid-Atlantic Tag Team Champion Kelly Kiniski defeated John Bonello
Bob Orton Jr. defeated the Magic Dragon
Rufus R. Jones defeated Bill White
Ric Flair defeated Mid-Atlantic Heavyweight Champion Dory Funk Jr.
NWA Tag Team Champions Jack & Jerry Brisco defeated Ricky Steamboat & Jay Youngblood

JCP @ Columbia, SC - June 28, 1983
Ric Flair & Roddy Piper defeated NWA US Champion Greg Valentine & Mid-Atlantic Heavyweight Champion Dory Funk Jr.

GCW @ Cleveland, OH - Richfield Convention Center - June 30, 1983
Bob Roop defeated Killer Brooks
Pez Whatley defeated Buzz Sawyer (w/ Paul Ellering)
The Road Warriors (w/ Paul Ellering) defeated Rick Rood & Joe Lightfoot
Tommy Rich defeated Larry Zbyszko
Ole Anderson defeated Paul Ellering via disqualification
Ron Garvin defeated the Iron Sheik (w/ Paul Ellering)
NWA World Champion Harley Race fought Stan Hansen to a double count-out

JCP @ Charleston, SC - County Hall - July 1, 1983
Mike Davis defeated Glenn Lane
Mark Fleming defeated Bill Howard
Johnny Weaver defeated Bill White
Mike Rotundo defeated Mid-Atlantic Tag Team Champion Kelly Kiniski
Ric Flair & Roddy Piper defeated NWA US Champion Greg Valentine & Mid-Atlantic Tag Team Champion the One Man Gang

GCW @ Dayton, OH - Hara Arena - July 1, 1983
The Road Warriors (w/ Paul Ellering) defeated Rick Rood & Joe Lightfoot
Ole Anderson defeated Paul Ellering via disqualification
Ron Garvin defeated the Iron Sheik (w/ Paul Ellering)
Tommy Rich fought Buzz Sawyer (w/ Paul Ellering) to a double count-out
Larry Zbyszko defeated Pez Whatley via count-out
Stan Hansen fought NWA World Champion Harley Race to a double count-out

JCP @ Greensboro, NC - Coliseum - July 2, 1983
Gene Anderson defeated Joel Deaton
Susan Starr defeated Leilani Kai
Dick Slater defeated John Bonello
Jimmy Valiant & Rufus R. Jones defeated Mid-Atlantic TV Champion the Great Kabuki & Gary Hart
Wahoo McDaniel & Roddy Piper fought NWA US Champion Greg Valentine & Dory Funk Jr. to a no contest
NWA Tag Team Champions Jack & Jerry Brisco defeated Ricky Steamboat & Jay Youngblood
NWA World Champion Harley Race defeated Ric Flair via disqualification

CHAMPIONSHIP WRESTLING
LEGION STADIUM
SUNDAY, JULY 3 • 8:00 P.M.
Tickets: Adults-$6   Children-$3
Sponsored By New Hanover Youth Baseball
• THE MATCH •
JACK BRISCO and GERALD BRISCO **Vs.** RICKY STEAMBOAT and JAY YOUNGBLOOD
JIMMY VALIANT **Vs.** THE GREAT KABUKI With Manager Gary Hart
JAKE ROBERTS VS. MIKE ROTUNDO
BOB ORTON VS. KELLY KINISKI
MASA FUCHI VS. VINNIE VALENTINO
MARK FLEMING VS. GOLDEN BOY GRAY

JCP @ Wilmington, NC - Legion Stadium - July 3, 1983
Mark Fleming vs. Golden Boy Gray
Masa Fuchi vs. Vinnie Valentino
Bob Orton Jr. vs. Mid-Atlantic Tag Team Champion Kelly Kiniski
Jake Roberts vs. Mike Rotundo
Jimmy Valiant vs. Mid-Atlantic TV Champion the Great Kabuki
NWA Tag Team Champions Jack & Jerry Brisco vs. Ricky Steamboat & Jay Youngblood

JCP @ Savannah, GA - Civic Center - July 3, 1983
John Bonello defeated Bill Howard

Keith Larson & Ric McCord defeated Bill White & Jacques Goulet

Dick Slater defeated Johnny Weaver

Mid-Atlantic Tag Team Champion the One Man Gang defeated Jos LeDuc

Roddy Piper & Wahoo McDaniel defeated NWA US Champion Greg Valentine & Mid-Atlantic Heavyweight Champion Dory Funk Jr.

NWA World Champion Harley Race defeated Ric Flair via disqualification

JCP @ Greenville, SC - Memorial Auditorium - July 4, 1983
TV taping:
Dark match after the taping: Ric Flair fought NWA World Champion Harley Race to a double disqualification

JCP @ Raleigh, NC - Dorton Arena - July 5, 1983
Jos LeDuc defeated Armand Hussein

Bugsy McGraw defeated the Magic Dragon

Mid-Atlantic Tag Team Champion the One Man Gang defeated Mike Rotundo

Jake Roberts defeated Rufus R. Jones

Roddy Piper & Jimmy Valiant vs. Mid-Atlantic Heavyweight Champion Dory Funk Jr. & NWA US Champion Greg Valentine

NWA World Champion Harley Race fought Ric Flair to a double count-out

JCP @ Sumter, SC - July 6, 1983
NWA World Champion Harley Race fought Ric Flair to a double disqualification

JCP @ Greenville, SC - Memorial Auditorium - July 6, 1983
Ric Flair defeated NWA World Champion Harley Race via disqualification

JCP @ Norfolk, VA - Scope - July 7, 1983
NWA US Champion Greg Valentine & Jake Roberts defeated Ric Flair & Roddy Piper via disqualification

NWA World Champion Harley Race defeated Wahoo McDaniel

JCP @ Charleston, SC - County Hall - July 8, 1983
Keith Larsen vs. Golden Boy Grey

Jacques Goulet vs. John Bonello

Johnny Weaver defeated Armand Hussein

Bugsy McGraw vs. the Magic Dragon

Jimmy Valiant & Rufus R. Jones vs. Mid-Atlantic TV Champion the Great Kabuki & Gary Hart

JCP @ Richmond, VA - Coliseum - July 8, 1983
Mid-Atlantic Tag Team Champion the One Man Gang defeated Mike Rotundo

Bob Orton Jr. defeated Jake Roberts

Roddy Piper & Wahoo McDaniel defeated NWA US Champion Greg Valentine & Mid-Atlantic Heavyweight Champion Dory Funk Jr.

NWA Tag Team Champions Jack & Jerry Brisco defeated Ricky Steamboat & Jay Youngblood

Ric Flair defeated NWA World Champion Harley Race via disqualification

JCP @ Charlotte, NC - Coliseum - July 9, 1983
Keith Larsen & Rick McCord defeated Gene Anderson & Bill Howard

Assassin #1 defeated John Bonello

Jake Roberts defeated Mike Davis

Dick Slater defeated Jos LeDuc

NWA US Champion Greg Valentine defeated Roddy Piper via disqualification

NWA Tag Team Champions Jack & Jerry Brisco defeated Ricky Steamboat & Jay Youngblood

Ric Flair defeated NWA World Champion Harley Race via disqualification

JCP @ Asheville, NC - Civic Center - July 10, 1983
Rick McCord & Keith Larsen defeated Gene Anderson & Bill White

Keith Larsen defeated Golden Boy Grey

The Assassin defeated Brett Hart

Wahoo McDaniel defeated the Magic Dragon

NWA US Champion Greg Valentine defeated Roddy Piper via disqualification

NWA World Champion Harley Race fought Ric Flair to a no contest

NWA Tag Team Champions Jack & Jerry Brisco defeated Bob Orton Jr. & Rufus R. Jones

Toronto, Ontario - Exhibition Stadium - July 10, 1983 (20,703)
Nick DeCarlo & Billy Red Lyons defeated the Executioner & Bill Armstrong at 5:06

Mid-Atlantic Tag Team Champion Kelly Kiniski & Rene Goulet defeated Bob & Joe Marcus at 6:22

Johnny Weaver & Mike Rotunda defeated Alec & Tim Gerrard at 5:35

Women's Champion the Fabulous Moolah pinned Princess Victoria at 11:28

Dick Slater defeated Nick DeCarlo (sub. for Jos LeDuc)

Mid-Atlantic TV Champion the Great Kabuki pinned Jimmy Valiant at 14:31

Ricky Steamboat & Jay Youngblood defeated Jake Roberts & Dory Funk Jr. at 21:55

Canadian Heavyweight Champion Angelo Mosca pinned Mid-Atlantic Tag Team Champion the One Man Gang at 7:27

NWA US Champion Greg Valentine fought Wahoo McDaniel to a double count-out at 8:09

Ric Flair defeated NWA World Champion Harley Race via disqualification at 17:21

Wrestling SUNDAY, JULY 10th, 8 PM
NIGHT OF CHAMPIONS

WORLD TITLE
RIC (Nature Boy) FLAIR vs HARLEY RACE

NWA TV TITLE
HANDSOME JIMMY (Boogie-Woogie man) vs THE GREAT KABUKI

CANADIAN TITLE
ANGELO (King Kong) MOSCA vs ONE MAN GANG

U.S. TITLE
GREG VALENTINE vs WAHOO McDANIELS

LADY'S WORLD TITLE
THE FABULOUS MOOLAH vs PRINCESS VICTORIA

SPECIAL
Dick Slater vs Big Joe LeDuc

WORLD TAG TEAM TITLE
RICKY STEAMBOAT & INDIAN JAY YOUNGBLOOD vs DORY FUNK JR. & JAKE THE SNAKE ROBERTS

PLUS 3 MORE TAG TEAM BOUTS

Championship prices $15.00, $12.00, $10.00 & $7.00
Advance tickets available Maple Leaf Gardens 12 to 6 daily

Info 977-1093

SEE TV WRESTLING SAT. CH. 11 AT 1 PM   EXHIBITION OF STRENGTH and SCIENCE

EXHIBITION STADIUM

49

JCP @ Greenville, SC - Memorial Auditorium - July 11, 1983
Brett Hart defeated Joel Deaton
John Bonello defeated Gary Royal
Bugsy McGraw defeated the Magic Dragon
Mike Rotundo defeated Jake Roberts
Dory Funk Jr. defeated Rufus R. Jones
Roddy Piper defeated NWA US Champion Greg Valentine via disqualification

JCP @ Raleigh, NC - Dorton Arena - July 12, 1983
Ric Flair & Rufus R. Jones defeated Dory Funk Jr. & Jake Roberts

JCP @ Harrisonburg, VA - High School - July 14, 1983
Cy Jernigan defeated Tom Lentz
Masa Fuchi defeated Golden Boy Gray
The Assassin defeated Keith Larsen
Mike Davis defeated Jake Roberts
NWA Tag Team Champions Jack & Jerry Brisco defeated Ricky Steamboat & Jay Youngblood

Central States @ Kansas City, MO - July 14, 1983
Ric Flair fought NWA World Champion Harley Race to a no contest

Central States @ St. Louis, MO - July 15, 1983
Missouri State Title Championship Tournament:
Opening Round:
Bob Orton Jr. defeated Manny Fernandez
Jesse Ventura defeated Emile Vachon
Blackjack Lanza defeated Jerry Ho
Butch Reed defeated Baron Von Raschke
Jerry Blackwell defeated Buzz Tyler
Dick the Bruiser defeated Bobby Duncum
Ric Flair defeated Bob Brown
Dewey Robertson defeated George Wells
Hulk Hogan defeated Kortsia Korchenko
Quarter Finals:
David Von Erich defeated Bob Orton Jr.
Butch Reed defeated Jesse Ventura
Blackjack Lanza defeated Dick the Bruiser via disqualification
Ric Flair defeated George Wells
Hulk Hogan fought Jerry Blackwell to a no contest
Semi Finals: David Von Erich defeated Butch Reed
Semi Finals: Ric Flair defeated Butch Reed
Finals: Ric Flair defeated David Von Erich

Worldwide - 7/83 - hosted by David Crockett; included comments from Ric Flair and Roddy Piper, with Flair stating he would take the NWA World Title from Harley Race, and Piper, wielding a pipe and trash can, promising revenge on NWA US Champion Greg Valentine for the damage done to his ear; featured Crockett interviewing Arman Hussein & Gary Hart, who discussed Hussein's parents and origins, with Hussein then insulting Rufus R. Jones, calling him an uneducated black man who was like the others in the country, trying to "overcome" political persecution, while Hussein stated he and Hart faced no such obstacles; included Crockett interviewing Hart, along with Hussein, who mocked Jimmy Valiant's face being burned and claimed Valiant would have to come through Hussein, the Magic Dragon, and Mid-Atlantic TV Champion Great Kabuki to get to him; featured Crockett interviewing Jones, who wished to find a partner and get revenge on Paul Jones, Jake Roberts, & Dory Funk Jr; included Crockett interviewing Valiant, with his face badly burned, who stated he would leave town if he couldn't rid the area of Hart, Oliver Humperdink, Mid-Atlantic Tag Team Champion the One Man Gang, and Kabuki, and that he wanted them in steel cage and loser leaves town matches; featured Crockett interviewing Jones, who stated, as a well-dressed man, he expected a fine woman from Florida and not some redneck dressed up like Dusty Rhodes:
Jimmy Valiant pinned Bill White at 1:53 after an elbow drop
Rufus R. Jones pinned Bill Howard at 4:48 after a headbutt
The Assassin pinned Keith Larson at 3:06 with a powerslam
Arman Hussein (w/ Gary Hart) pinned Mike Davis at 3:46 after two knee smashes to the chest
Bugsy McGraw pinned Ben Alexander at 2:08 with a splash
Mike Rotundo pinned Rick McCord at 5:26 after an airplane spin
Dick Slater & Mid-Atlantic Heavyweight Champion Dory Funk Jr (w/ Paul Jones) defeated Gary Royal & John Bonello at 8:09 when Slater pinned Bonello after a running kick to the head; after the match, David Crockett interviewed Jones, Funk, & Slater, with Jones stating no one could defeat Funk in their $100,000 open challenge, with Slater thanking Jones for getting him out of suspensions, and Jones asking for some competition before telling Rufus R. Jones to prove himself and earn a title shot

JCP @ Hampton, VA - Coliseum - July 15, 1983
The Assassin defeated Masa Fuchi
Keith Larson defeated Gene Anderson
Jake Roberts & Armand Hussein defeated Mike Davis & Vinnie Valentino
Dory Funk Jr. defeated Johnny Weaver
Roddy Piper defeated NWA US Champion Greg Valentine
NWA Tag Team Champions Jack & Jerry Brisco defeated Ricky steamboat & Jay Youngblood

JCP @ Charleston, SC - County Hall - July 15, 1983
Glenn Lane vs. Golden Boy Grey
Joel Deaton vs. Abe Jacobs
Dick Slater vs. Rick McCord
Jimmy Valiant & Rufus R. Jones vs. Mid-Atlantic TV Champion the Great Kabuki & Gary Hart (steel cage match)

JCP @ Spartanburg, SC - Memorial Auditorium - July 16, 1983
Bill Howard defeated Mark Fleming

Mid-Atlantic Tag Team Champion Kelly Kiniski defeated Mike Davis

Bugsy McGraw defeated Mid-Atlantic Tag Team Champion One Man Gang

Jimmy Valiant, Bob Orton Jr., & Johnny Weaver defeated Mid-Atlantic TV Champion the Great Kabuki, Magic Dragon, & Gart Hart

JCP @ Greensboro, NC - Coliseum - July 17, 1983
Ric Flair defeated NWA World Champion Harley Race via disqualification

JCP @ Greenville, SC - Memorial Auditorium - July 18, 1983
Bugsy McGraw defeated Mid-Atlantic Tag Team Champion One Man Gang

Keith Larsen & Rick McCord defeated the Magic Dragon & Masa Fuchi

Mike Davis defeated Tom Lintz

Jimmy Valiant & Bob Orton Jr. defeated Mid-Atlantic TV Champion the Great Kabuki & Gary Hart via count-out

Ricky Steamboat & Jay Youngblood defeated NWA Tag Team Champions Jack & Jerry Brisco

JCP @ Emporia, VA - July 20, 1983
Rufus R. Jones & Bugsy McGraw defeated Mid-Atlantic Tag Team Champions the One Man Gang & Kelly Kiniski to win the titles

JCP @ Winston-Salem, NC - July 20, 1983
Mid-Atlantic Heavyweight Champion Dory Funk Jr. vs. Mid-Atlantic Tag Team Champion Rufus R Jones ($100,000 challenge)

Ric Flair defeated NWA World Champion Harley Race via disqualification in a Best 2 out of 3 falls match

Also included Jimmy Valiant, NWA US Champion Greg Valentine, Roddy Piper, Ricky Steamboat & Jay Youngblood, NWA Tag Team Champions Jack & Jerry Brisco, and Jos LeDuc

JCP @ Norfolk, VA - Scope - July 21, 1983
Keith Larson defeated Bill Howard

Mike Davis defeated Gene Anderson

Dick Slater defeated Cy Jernigan

The Assassin defeated Barry Hart

Ric Flair & Paul Jones defeated Mid-Atlantic Heavyweight Champion Dory Funk Jr. & Jake Roberts

NWA Tag Team Champions Jack & Jerry Brisco defeated Ricky Steamboat & Jay Youngblood

NWA World Champion Harley Race defeated Bob Orton Jr.

JCP @ Sumter, SC - July 21, 1983
Kelly Kiniski defeated John Bonello

Armand Hussein defeated Rick McCord

Joel Deaton vs. Jacques Goulet

Jimmy Valiant, Johnny Weaver, & Mid-Atlantic Tag Team Champion Bugsy McGraw defeated Gary Hart, Mid-Atlantic TV Champion the Great Kabuki, & the Magic Dragon

Roddy Piper defeated NWA US Champion Greg Valentine via disqualification

JCP @ Richmond, VA - Coliseum - July 22, 1983
Keith Larsen & Cy Jernigan defeated Gene Anderson & Bill Howard

Assassin #1 defeated Mike Davis

Dick Slater fought Bob Orton Jr. to a double count-out

Mid-Atlantic TV Champion the Great Kabuki defeated Mike Rotundo

Mid-Atlantic Heavyweight Champion Dory Funk Jr. defeated Mid-Atlantic Tag Team Champion Rufus R Jones

Roddy Piper defeated NWA US Champion Greg Valentine via disqualification

NWA World Champion Harley Race defeated Ric Flair via disqualification; Sandy Scott was the guest referee

Jimmy Valiant defeated the One Man Gang & Sir Oliver Humperdink in a handicap hair vs. hair loser leaves town steel cage match

JCP @ Charleston, SC - County Hall - July 22, 1983
Tom Lintz defeated John Bonello

Vinnie Valentino & Brett Hart defeated the Magic Dragon & Masa Fuchi

Kelly Kiniski defeated Rick McCord (sub. for Johnny Weaver)

Mid-Atlantic Tag Team Champion Bugsy McGraw defeated Jake Roberts

NWA Tag Team Champion Jack & Jerry Brisco defeated Johnny Weaver (sub. for injured Ricky Steamboat) & Jay Youngblood

JCP @ Charlotte, NC - Coliseum - July 23, 1983
Rene Goulet defeated John Bonello

Vinnie Valentino defeated Golden Boy Grey

Dick Slater & Jake Roberts defeated Johnny Weaver & Brett Hart

Mid-Atlantic Heavyweight Champion Dory Funk Jr. defeated Mid-Atlantic Tag Team Champion Rufus R Jones

Jimmy Valiant & Bob Orton Jr. defeated Mid-Atlantic TV Champion the Great Kabuki & Gary Hart in a steel cage match

Ric Flair defeated NWA World Champion Harley Race via disqualification; Sandy Scott was the guest referee

JCP @ Asheville, NC - Civic Center - July 24, 1983
Brett Hart defeated Tom Lentz

The Assassin defeated Keith Larsen

The Magic Dragon defeated John Bonello

Dick Slater defeated Mid-Atlantic Tag Team Champion Bugsy McGraw

NWA Tag Team Champions Jack & Jerry Brisco defeated Ric Flair & Roddy Piper

NWA World Champion Harley Race defeated Ricky Steamboat via disqualification

Toronto, Ontario - Exhibition Stadium - July 24, 1983 (11,000)
NWA US Champion Greg Valentine defeated Cy Jernigan at 9:16
The One Man Gang defeated Mike Davis
Jacques Goulet & Kelly Kiniski defeated Nick DeCarlo & Vinnie Valentino
Bob Marcus defeated Masa Fuchi
Mid-Atlantic Tag Team Champion Rufus R. Jones defeated Jake Roberts
Mid-Atlantic Heavyweight Champion Dory Funk Jr. pinned Mike Rotundo at 23:04
Jimmy Valiant & Bob Orton Jr. defeated Mid-Atlantic TV Champion the Great Kabuki & Gary Hart in a steel cage match at 7:05
NWA Tag Team Champions Jack & Jerry Brisco defeated Ricky Steamboat & Jay Youngblood via disqualification at 18:22
Sgt. Slaughter defeated Canadian Heavyweight Champion Angelo Mosca to win the title at 22:18
NWA World Champion Harley Race defeated Ric Flair via disqualification at 16:42 when Flair accidentally punched guest referee Johnny Weaver after Race moved out of the way; after the bout, Weaver punched Flair as payback

JCP @ Greenville, SC - July 25, 1983
Ric Flair defeated Dick Slater

JCP @ Sumter, SC - July 25, 1983
Keith Larsen defeated Joel Deaton
The Magic Dragon defeated Brett Hart
Jimmy Valiant & Bob Orton Jr. defeated Mid-Atlantic TV Champion the Great Kabuki & Gary Hart
Roddy Piper defeated NWA US Champion Greg Valentine
Ric Flair defeated Dick Slater

JCP @ Columbia, SC - July 26, 1983
Roddy Piper defeated NWA US Champion Greg Valentine
Ric Flair & Ricky Steamboat defeated NWA Tag Team Champions Jack & Jerry Brisco via disqualification

JCP @ Spartanburg, SC - Memorial Auditorium - July 27, 1983
TV taping:
NWA Tag Team Champions Jack & Jerry Brisco defeated Ric Flair & Roddy Piper via disqualification

JCP @ Charleston, SC - County Hall - July 29, 1983
Abe Jacobs defeated Masa Fuchi
Gene Anderson defeated Vinnie Valentino
Jake Roberts defeated Brett Hart
Mike Rotundo defeated Kelly Kiniski
The One Man Gang defeated Mid-Atlantic Tag Team Champion Bugsy McGraw
Mid-Atlantic Tag Team Champion Rufus R. Jones defeated

Mid-Atlantic Heavyweight Champion Dory Funk Jr. via disqualification

JCP @ Culpeper, VA - Junior High School - July 29, 1983
Jimmy Valiant & Bob Orton Jr. defeated Mid-Atlantic TV Champion the Great Kabuki & Gary Hart

WCCW @ San Juan, Puerto Rico - July 30, 1983
NWA World Champion Harley Race vs. Gran Apolo

CHAMPIONSHIP WRESTLING
LEGION STADIUM,
SUNDAY, JULY 30 ● 8:15 P.M.
Tickets: Adults $8   Children $4
Sponsored By New Hanover Youth Baseball
● 10 FOOT FENCE ●
Jimmy Valiant and Bobby Orton VS. Kabuki and Gary Hart
Greg Valentine VS. Roddy Piper
Keith Larson and Rick McCord VS. Bill Howard and Sgt. Jacque Goulet
Vinnie Valentino VS. Gene Anderson
Mike Davis VS. Joe Deaton

JCP @ Wilmington, NC - Legion Stadium - July 30, 1983
Mike Davis & Vinnie Valentino vs. Gene Anderson & Joe Deaton
Keith Larsen & Rick McCord vs. Bill Howard & Sgt. Jacques Goulet
NWA US Champion Greg Valentine vs. Roddy Piper
Jimmy Valiant & Bob Orton Jr. vs. Mid-Atlantic TV Champion the Great Kabuki & Gary Hart (steel cage match)

CWF @ Orlando, FL - July 31, 1983
Charlie Cook defeated the Great Yatsu
Les Thornton defeated Ox Baker via disqualification
Kareem Muhammad & Elijah Akeem defeated Global Tag Team Champions Scott McGhee & Mike Graham to win the titles
Barry Windham defeated Jos LeDuc
Blackjack Mulligan, Angelo Mosca Sr. & Jr. defeated Kevin Sullivan, Ron Bass, & Purple Haze
NWA World Champion Harley Race defeated Dusty Rhodes via disqualification

JCP @ Greenville, SC - August 1, 1983
Vinnie Valentino defeated Tom Lintz
Gene Anderson defeated Mike Davis
Mike Rotundo defeated the Assassin
Jake Roberts defeated Mid-Atlantic Tag Team Champion Rufus R. Jones
Bob Orton Jr. defeated Mid-Atlantic Heavyweight Champion Dory Funk Jr.
Ric Flair & Ricky Steamboat defeated NWA Tag Team Champions Jack & Jerry Brisco via disqualification

JCP @ Tampa, FL - August 2, 1983
Dusty Rhodes vs. NWA World Champion Harley Race

JCP @ Columbia, SC - August 2, 1983
Ric Flair & Roddy Piper defeated NWA Tag Team Champions Jack & Jerry Brisco via disqualification

JCP @ Miami, FL - August 3, 1983 (7,881)
Charlie Cook fought Les Thornton to a draw
Mike Graham defeated Ox Baker
Jos LeDuc defeated Scott McGhee
Mil Mascaras defeated the Masked Texan
Angelo Mosca defeated Purple Haze
The Junkyard Dog defeated Ron Bass
Dusty Rhodes & Blackjack Mulligan defeated Elijah Akeem & Kareem Muhammad in a lights out match
NWA World Champion Harley Race defeated Barry Windham via disqualification

JCP @ Spartanburg, SC - Memorial Auditorium - August 3, 1983
TV taping:
NWA US Champion Greg Valentine defeated Brett Hart
Mid-Atlantic TV Champion the Great Kabuki & the Magic Dragon defeated John Bonello & Ric McCord
The Assassins defeated Mike Rotundo & Mike Davis
Bob Orton Jr. defeated Ben Alexander
Bugsy McGraw defeated Golden Boy Grey
The Assassins defeated Brett Hart & John Bonello
Mid-Atlantic TV Champion the Great Kabuki defeated Ric McCord
Roddy Piper defeated Masa Fuchi
Bob Orton Jr. defeated Golden Boy Grey
Ric Flair, Roddy Piper, & Jimmy Valiant vs. NWA US Champion Greg Valentine, Dick Slater, & Mid-Atlantic TV Champion the Great Kabuki

JCP @ Sumter, SC - Sumter County Exhibition Center - August 4, 1983
Keith Larsen vs. Joel Deaton
Rick McCord vs. Jacques Goulet
The Assassin vs. Brett Hart
Mike Rotundo vs. Dick Slater

Ric Flair & Ricky Steamboat defeated NWA Tag Team Champions Jack & Jerry Brisco via disqualification

Central States @ St. Louis, MO - August 5, 1983
Ron Ritchie defeated Steve Hall
Bob Brown & Princess Victoria defeated Roger Kirby & Leilani Kai
Barry Windham defeated Tonga John
The Super Destroyer defeated George Wells
Bob Orton Jr. defeated Rick Martel
Hulk Hogan, Dick the Bruiser, & Ron Ritchie (sub. for David Von Erich) defeated Jerry Blackwell, Blackjack Mulligan, & Baron Von Raschke
NWA World Champion Harley Race defeated Missouri Heavyweight Champion Ric Flair in a Best 2 out of 3 falls match

JCP @ Charleston, SC - County Hall - August 5, 1983
Kelly Kiniski vs. Joel Deaton
Jacques Goulet vs. Brett Hart
Assassin #1 vs. Keith Larsen
Mid-Atlantic TV Champion the Great Kabuki vs. Bugsy McGraw
Jimmy Valiant vs. the One Man Gang & Sir Oliver Humperdink (loser leaves town match)

JCP @ Richmond, VA - Coliseum - August 5, 1983
Rufus R Jones defeated Mid-Atlantic Heavyweight Champion Dory Funk Jr. to win the title
Roddy Piper & Wahoo McDaniel defeated NWA Tag Team Champions Jack & Jerry Brisco

Championship Wrestling - 8/6/83:
Ric Flair vs. NWA World Champion Harley Race (Best 2 out of 3 falls)
Roddy Piper vs. Mr. Fuchi
Mid-Atlantic TV Champion the Great Kabuki vs. Rick McCord

CWF @ Ft. Pierce, FL - August 6, 1983
Blackjack Mulligan vs. NWA World Champion Harley Race

JCP @ Charlotte, NC - Coliseum - August 6, 1983
Assassin #1 defeated Golden Boy Grey
Gene Anderson defeated Vinnie Valentino
The One Man Gang & Kelly Kiniski defeated Johnny Weaver & Mike Davis
Bob Orton Jr., Mid-Atlantic Heavyweight Champion Rufus R. Jones, & Bugsy McGraw defeated Dory Funk Jr., Paul Jones, & Jake Roberts
Wahoo McDaniel defeated Dick Slater via count-out
Ric Flair & Ricky Steamboat defeated NWA Tag Team Champions Jack & Jerry Brisco via disqualification

JCP @ Asheville, NC - Civic Center - August 7, 1983
Vinnie Valentino defeated Tom Lentz
Brett Hart defeated Golden Boy Grey
Joel Deaton defeated Cy Jernigan
Ric Flair, Roddy Piper, & Ricky Steamboat defeated Dick
Slater, NWA Tag Team Champions Jack & Jerry Brisco
NWA World Champion Harley Race defeated Wahoo McDaniel
via disqualification

JCP @ Greensboro, NC - Coliseum - August 7, 1983
Rick McGraw defeated Billy Howard
Gene Anderson defeated Keith Larsen
The Assassin defeated Steve Muslin
Jimmy Valiant defeated Mid-Atlantic TV Champion the Great
Kabuki
Mid-Atlantic Heavyweight Champion Rufus R. Jones & Bugsy
McGraw defeated Dory Funk Jr. & Jake Roberts
Roddy Piper & Wahoo McDaniel defeated NWA US Champion
Greg Valentine & Dick Slater in an Indian strap match
NWA World Champion Harley Race defeated Bob Orton Jr.
Ric Flair & Ricky Steamboat defeated NWA Tag Team
Champions Jack & Jerry Brisco via disqualification

Toronto, Ontario - Maple Leaf Gardens - August 7, 1983
Canadian TV Championship Tournament Quarter-Finals: Don
Kernodle defeated Joe Marcus
Canadian TV Championship Tournament Quarter-Finals:
Johnny Weaver fought Kelly Kiniski to a double count-out
Canadian TV Championship Tournament Quarter-Finals: Sgt.
Jacques Goulet defeated Nick DeCarlo
Canadian TV Championship Tournament Quarter-Finals: Mike
Rotundo defeated the Magic Dragon
Canadian TV Championship Tournament Semi-Finals: Mike
Rotundo defeated Sgt. Jacques Goulet
Canadian TV Championship Tournament Finals: Mike Rotundo
defeated Don Kernodle
Little Beaver defeated Little Brutus
Andre the Giant defeated the One Man Gang
Sgt. Slaughter fought Angelo Mosca to a no contest

JCP @ Greenville, SC - August 8, 1983
Ric Flair & Ricky Steamboat defeated NWA Tag Team
Champions Jack & Jerry Brisco via disqualification

JCP @ Raleigh, NC - August 9, 1983
Ric Flair & Ricky Steamboat defeated NWA Tag Team
Champions Jack & Jerry Brisco via disqualification

JCP @ ? - August 10, 1983
TV taping:
Mid-Atlantic TV Champion the Great Kabuki defeated Tracy
Store
Mike Rotundo & Mid-Atlantic Heavyweight Champion Rufus R.
Jones defeated Ben Alexander & Bill Howard
Dick Slater defeated Glen Lane

Jake Roberts defeated Brett Hart
Assassin #2 defeated Vinnie Valentino
Jimmy Valiant defeated Bob Brown
Mid-Atlantic TV Champion the Great Kabuki defeated Joel
Deaton
Championship Wrestling - 8/13/83:
Jimmy Valiant defeated Bill Howard
Ricky Steamboat & Jay Youngblood vs. NWA Tag Team
Champions Jack & Jerry Brisco Jake Roberts defeated Tracy
Store
Dick Slater defeated Keith Larsen
Mike Rotundo & Mid-Atlantic Heavyweight Champion Rufus R.
Jones defeated Golden Boy Grey & Bob Brown
Assassin #2 defeated Mike Davis

Central States @ Kansas City, MO - August 11, 1983
Manny Fernandez, Jerry Ho, & Mark Romero defeated Jerry
Brown, Steve Sybert, & Mike Pagel
Buck Robley defeated Kortsia Korchenko
George Wells defeated Tonga John
George Wells & Ron Ritchie defeated Sheik Abdullah & Roger
Kirby
NWA World Champion Harley Race defeated the Super
Destroyer

JCP @ Stafford, VA - High School - August 11, 1983 (1,800)
Mike Davis defeated Golden Boy Gray
The Assassin defeated Mike Davis
Jacques Goulet defeated Mark Fleming
Bugsy McGraw defeated the One Man Gang
Ric Flair & Ricky Steamboat defeated NWA Tag Team
Champions Jack & Jerry Brisco

JCP @ Hampton, VA - August 12, 1983
Ric Flair defeated Dick Slater

JCP @ Charleston, SC - County Hall - August 12, 1983
Gene Anderson vs. Brett Hart
Keith Larsen & Rick McCord vs. Bill Howard & Tom Lintz
Peggy Lee vs. Princess Victoria
Bob Orton Jr. vs. Jake Roberts
Roddy Piper vs. NWA US Champion Greg Valentine

JCP @ Roanoke, VA - Civic Center - August 13, 1983
Ric Flair & Ricky Steamboat defeated NWA Tag Team
Champions Jack & Jerry Brisco via disqualification

CWF @ West Palm Beach, FL - Auditorium - August 15, 1983
Les Thornton vs. the Great Yatsu
Jos LeDuc vs. Charlie Cook
Southern Champion Ron Bass vs. Scott McGhee
Mike Graham vs. Purple Haze
Barry Windham & Angelo Mosca vs. Elijah Akeem & Kareem

Muhammad
NWA World Champion Harley Race vs. Dusty Rhodes

JCP @ Greenville, SC - August 15, 1983
Jacques Goulet defeated Cy Jernigan
Gene Anderson defeated Keith Larsen
Dick Slater defeated Bugsy McGraw
Mid-Atlantic Heavyweight Champion Rufus R. Jones defeated Jake Roberts
The Assassins defeated Johnny Weaver & Mike Rotundo
Roddy Piper defeated NWA US Champion Greg Valentine via reverse decision

JCP @ Raleigh, NC - August 16, 1983
NWA Tag Team Champions Jack & Jerry Brisco defeated Ric Flair & Ricky Steamboat

CWF @ Tampa, FL - August 16, 1983
Dusty Rhodes vs. NWA World Champion Harley Race

JCP @ Winston-Salem, NC - Memorial Coliseum - August 17, 1983
Worldwide taping:
Johnny Weaver & Mike Rotundo vs. the Assassins
Ric Flair, Roddy Piper, & Ricky Steamboat vs. Dick Slater, NWA Tag Team Champions Jack & Jerry Brisco
Also included: NWA US Champion Greg Valentine, Bugsy McGraw, Paul Jones, Bob Orton Jr., Jake Roberts, and Mid-Atlantic Heavyweight Champion Rufus R. Jones

CWF @ Sunrise, FL - August 17, 1983
Charlie Cook vs. Kareem Muhammad
Scott McGhee vs. Elijah Akeem
Angelo Mosca Sr. & Jr. vs. Kevin Sullivan & Purple Haze
Mike Graham vs. NWA World Champion Harley Race
Barry Windham vs. Jos LeDuc (Texas Death Match)
Dusty Rhodes vs. Ron Bass (Texas Death Match)

JCP @ Sumter, SC - Sumter County Exhibition Center - August 18, 1983
Joel Deaton vs. Mike Davis
Golden Boy Grey vs. Mike Davis
Jacques Goulet & Bill Howard vs. Rick McCord & Steve Muslin
The Magic Dragon vs. Brett Hart
Jake Roberts vs. Bob Orton Jr.
Mid-Atlantic TV Champion the Great Kabuki vs. Jimmy Valiant

JCP @ Richmond, VA - Coliseum - August 19, 1983
Mark Fleming defeated Tom Lentz
Gene Anderson & Kelly Kiniski defeated Johnny Weaver & Cy Journigan
Dick Slater defeated Bugsy McGraw
Dory Funk Jr. defeated Mid-Atlantic Heavyweight Champion Rufus R. Jones
Jimmy Valiant defeated Mid-Atlantic TV Champion the Great Kabuki
NWA Tag Team Champions Jack & Jerry Brisco defeated Ric Flair & Ricky Steamboat
Ric Flair defeated NWA World Champion Harley Race via disqualification at 21:30

JCP @ Charleston, SC - County Hall - August 19, 1983
Brett Hart defeated Bill Howard
Jacques Goulet defeated Vinnie Valentino
Mike Davis defeated the Magic Dragon
Bob Orton Jr. & Mike Rotundo fought the Assassins to a 30-minute time-limit draw
NWA US Champion Greg Valentine pinned Roddy Piper

CWF @ Sarasota, FL - Robarts Sports Arena - August 20, 1983
Les Thornton fought Yoshi Yatsu to a 20-minute time-limit draw
Jos LeDuc pinned Charlie Cook at 14:40
The Purple Haze defeated Scott McGhee at the 10-minute mark

Angelo Mosca defeated Southern Heavyweight Champion Ron Bass via disqualification

NWA World Champion Harley Race defeated Barry Windham via disqualification at 21:04

Dusty Rhodes & Blackjack Mulligan defeated Elijah Akeem & Kareem Muhammed in a lights out steel cage match

JCP @ Greensboro, NC - Coliseum - August 21, 1983
The Assassins defeated Mike Rotundo & Bob Orton Jr.

Mid-Atlantic Heavyweight Champion Rufus R. Jones defeated Jake Roberts

Gene Anderson defeated Cy Jernigan

Bugsy McGraw defeated Golden Boy Grey

Roddy Piper defeated NWA US Champion Greg Valentine

Mid-Atlantic TV Champion the Great Kabuki defeated Jimmy Valiant in a loser leaves town match

NWA Tag Team Champions Jack & Jerry Brisco defeated Ricky Steamboat & Wahoo McDaniel via disqualification when the challengers struck the official

JCP @ Asheville, NC - Civic Center - August 21, 1983
Mike Davis defeated Billy Howard

The Magic Dragon defeated Vinnie Valentino

Johnny Weaver defeated Kelly Kiniski

Wahoo McDaniel & Roddy Piper defeated NWA US Champion Greg Valentine & Dick Slater in a double Indian strap match

NWA Tag Team Champions Jack & Jerry Brisco defeated Ric Flair & Ricky Steamboat

JCP @ Greenville, SC - August 22, 1983
Vinnie Valentino defeated Golden Boy Grey

Brett Hart defeated Bill Howard

Mike Davis defeated Kelly Kiniski

Dick Slater defeated Johnny Weaver

Roddy Piper defeated NWA US Champion Greg Valentine

NWA Tag Team Champions Jack & Jerry Brisco defeated Ricky Steamboat & Wahoo McDaniel via disqualification

CWF @ Miami, FL - August 24, 1983
Dusty Rhodes vs. NWA World Champion Harley Race

JCP @ ? - August 24, 1983
TV taping:

Ric Flair defeated Golden Boy Grey

The Assassins defeated Ric McCord & Steve Muslim

Bugsy McGraw defeated Ben Alexander

NWA US Champion Greg Valentine defeated Vinnie Valentino

Roddy Piper & Bob Orton Jr. defeated Bill Howard & Kelly Kiniski

Dick Slater & Jake Roberts defeated Steve Muslim & Vinnie Valentino

The Assassins defeated Gene Ligon & Keith Larsen

Ric Flair defeated Ben Alexander

Ricky Steamboat & Jay Youngblood defeated Bill Howard & Golden Boy Grey

CWF @ Ft. Myers, FL - August 25, 1983
Barry Windham vs. NWA World Champion Harley Race

JCP @ Harrisonburg, VA - High School - August 25, 1983
Golden Boy Gray vs. Cy Jernigan

Joel Deaton vs. Vinnie Valentino

Kelly Kiniski vs. Mike Davis

Dick Slater vs. Bugsy McGraw

Roddy Piper vs. NWA US Champion Greg Valentine

Central States @ Kansas City, MO - August 25, 1983
George Wells & Jerry Ho defeated Kortsia Korchenko & Tonga John

Mike Pagel defeated Steve Sybert via disqualification

Ron Ritchie & Buck Robley defeated Sheik Abdullah & Roger Kirby via disqualification

Jerry Brown defeated Mark Romero

NWA World Champion Harley Race defeated the Super Destroyer

JCP @ Charleston, SC - County Hall - August 26, 1983
Keith Larsen defeated Tom Lintz

Jacques Goulet defeated Rick McCord

Jay Youngblood defeated Mid-Atlantic TV Champion the Great Kabuki

The Assassins defeated Mike Rotundo & Johnny Weaver

Jake Roberts defeated Mid-Atlantic Heavyweight Champion Rufus R. Jones

JCP @ Charlottesville, VA - August 27, 1983
Vinnie Valentino defeated Bill Howard

Mike Davis defeated Tom Lintz

Kelly Kiniski defeated Brett Hart

The Assassins defeated Bugsy McGraw & Cy Jernigan

Dick Slater defeated Jay Youngblood

Jimmy Valiant & Mid-Atlantic Heavyweight Champion Rufus R. Jones defeated Mid-Atlantic TV Champion the Great Kabuki & Gary Hart in a steel cage match

Toronto, Ontario - Maple Leaf Gardens - August 28, 1983
Nick DeCarlo defeated Tim Gerrard

Bob Marcus defeated Golden Boy Grey

Rene Goulet defeated Brett Hart

Billy Red Lyons defeated Bill Howard

Johnny Weaver defeated Kelly Kiniski

Mike Rotundo defeated Don Kernodle

NWA US Champion Greg Valentine & Jake Roberts defeated Roddy Piper & Jimmy Valiant via disqualification

Sgt. Slaughter defeated Angelo Mosca via count-out

GCW @ Atlanta, GA - Omni - August 28, 1983
Mr. Wrestling I pinned Joe Lightfoot with a bridge following a running knee lift

Brett Wayne pinned Bob Roop with an inside cradle

Bruno Sammartino Jr. defeated Paul Ellering via count-out

when Ellering left the ring after sustaining a press slam
NWA Tag Team Champions Jack & Jerry Brisco defeated
NWA National Tag Team Champions the Road Warriors via
count-out in a No DQ match after the Briscos used steel chairs
on the Road Warriors and prevented them from getting back in
the ring
Tommy Rich pinned Bill Irwin in a whipping match with an
inside cradle; after the bout, Rich began lashing Irwin until Mid-
Atlantic TV Champion the Great Kabuki, along with Gary Hart,
attacked him; moments later, Ole Anderson and Pez Whatley
made the save
Pez Whatley pinned Mid-Atlantic TV Champion the Great
Kabuki (w/ Gary Hart) with a flying headbutt after Ole Anderson
came ringside and tripped Kabuki; after the match, Whatley
and Anderson celebrated in the crowd as Hart cut a promo in
the ring
Buzz Sawyer (w/ Paul Ellering) defeated Dick Slater via
disqualification when referee Nick Patrick caught Slater
wearing brass knuckles as he had Sawyer covered following a
punch; the weapon was originally used by Sawyer after the
referee had been knocked down by Ellering; after the bout,
Sawyer & Ellering attacked Slater and dropped him with a
spike piledriver

JCP @ Greenville, SC - August 29, 1983

The Magic Dragon defeated Rick McCord
Gene Anderson defeated Steve Muslim
The Assassins defeated Mike Rotundo & Johnny Weaver
Bob Orton Jr. defeated Mid-Atlantic TV Champion the Great
Kabuki via disqualification
Ric Flair & Roddy Piper defeated NWA US Champion Greg
Valentine & Dick Slater

JCP @ Columbia, SC - August 30, 1983

Ric Flair defeated Dick Slater via disqualification

JCP @ ? - August 1983

Mid Atlantic Championship Wrestling - 8/31/83:
Ric Flair defeated NWA World Champion Harley Race via
disqualification at around the 22-minute mark when, as Flair
had Race in the figure-4, Bob Orton Jr. appeared and held off
an interfering Dick Slater until Orton and Slater both attacked
Flair, hit a spike piledriver, and wrenched Flair's neck;
moments later, Roddy Piper and Wahoo McDaniel came out to
clear the ring and check on Flair (*Nature Boy Ric Flair: The
Definitive Collection*)

JCP @ Sumter, SC - September 1, 1983

Kelly Kiniski vs. Steve Muslim
The Magic Dragon vs. Vinnie Valentino
Brett Hart vs. Bill Howard
The Assassins vs. Mike Rotundo & Johnny Weaver
Charlie Brown & Bugsy McGraw vs. Mid-Atlantic TV Champion
the Great Kabuki & Gary Hart (steel cage match)

JCP @ Norfolk, VA - September 1, 1983

Keith Larsen defeated Tom Lintz
Ric McCord defeated Jacques Goulet
Gene Anderson defeated Mike Davis
Wahoo McDaniel & Bob Orton Jr. defeated Dick Slater & Jake
Roberts
NWA US Champion Greg Valentine defeated Mid-Atlantic
Heavyweight Champion Rufus R. Jones
NWA Tag Team Champions Jack & Jerry Brisco defeated
Roddy Piper & Ricky Steamboat

WCCW @ Dallas, TX - September 1983

NWA World Champion Harley Race defeated Iceman King
Parsons via disqualification

CWF @ St. Petersburg, FL - September 1983

NWA World Champion Harley Race fought Dusty Rhodes to a
draw

JCP @ Charleston, SC - County Hall - September 2, 1983

Bill Howard defeated Vinnie Valentino
The Magic Dragon defeated Golden Boy Grey
Brett Hart defeated Kelly Kiniski
The Assassins defeated Mike Rotundo & Johnny Weaver
Charlie Brown & Bugsy McGraw defeated Mid-Atlantic TV
Champion the Great Kabuki & Gary Hart

JCP @ Richmond, VA - September 2, 1983

Tom Lintz defeated Mike Davis
Keith Larsen defeated Steve Muslim
Gene Anderson defeated Ric McCord
Bob Orton Jr. defeated Jacques Goulet
Mid-Atlantic Heavyweight Champion Rufus R. Jones defeated
Jake Roberts
Wahoo McDaniel & Roddy Piper defeated NWA US Champion
Greg Valentine & Dick Slater
Ricky Steamboat & Jay Youngblood defeated NWA Tag Team
Champions Jack & Jerry Brisco in a non-title match

Mid-Atlantic Championship Wrestling - 9/3/83:
Ric Flair & Wahoo McDaniel vs. Ron Rossi & Bill Howard

Worldwide - 9/3/83:
WWF All American Wrestling - 10/9/83: Ric Flair & Wahoo
McDaniel defeated Tom Lintz & Jerry Grey when McDaniel
pinned Lintz

CWF @ Ocala, FL - Jai Alai Fronton - September 4, 1983 (matinee)

Les Thornton vs. Kareem Muhammad
Charlie Cook vs. Kevin Sullivan
Scott McGhee vs. Jos LeDuc
Angelo Mosca vs. Purple Haze (Canadian death match)

Blackjack Mulligan vs. Elijah Akeem
NWA World Champion Harley Race vs. Barry Windham

JCP @ Asheville, NC - Civic Center - September 4, 1983
Keith Larsen defeated Tom Lentz
Billy Howard defeated Mark Fleming
Bugsy McGraw defeated Rene Goulet
Wahoo McDaniel fought Dick Slater to a no contest
Charlie Brown & Mid-Atlantic Heavyweight Champion Rufus R. Jones defeated Mid-Atlantic TV Champion the Great Kabuki & Gary Hart
Roddy Piper defeated NWA US Champion Greg Valentine

JCP @ Savannah, GA - Civic Center - September 4, 1983
Brett Hart defeated Golden Boy Grey
Magic Dragon defeated Ric McCord
The Assassins defeated Mike Rotundo & Johnny Weaver
Charlie Brown & Mid-Atlantic Heavyweight Champion Rufus R. Jones defeated Mid-Atlantic TV Champion the Great Kabuki & Gary Hart in a steel cage match
NWA US Champion Greg Valentine defeated Roddy Piper via disqualification
Wahoo McDaniel defeated Dick Slater in a lumberjack match

JCP @ Greenville, SC - September 5, 1983
Brett Hart defeated Bill White
The Magic Dragon defeated Mike Davis
The Assassins defeated Johnny Weaver & Mike Rotundo
Charlie Brown defeated Mid-Atlantic TV Champion the Great Kabuki
Ricky Steamboat & Jay Youngblood defeated NWA Tag Team Champions Jack & Jerry Brisco

CWF @ Tampa, FL - Ft. Homer Hesterly Armory - September 6, 1983
Les Thornton defeated Angelo Mosca Jr.
Charlie Cook defeated the Great Yatsu
Southern Champion Ron Bass defeated Scott McGhee
Mike Graham & Angelo Mosca defeated Kareem Muhammad & Elijah Akeem via disqualification
Blackjack Mulligan defeated NWA World Champion Harley Race
Jos LeDuc defeated Barry Windham in a lumberjack match
Dusty Rhodes defeated Purple Haze at 13:41 in a lights out, taped fist match

CWF @ Miami Beach, FL - Convention Center - September 7, 1983 (5,675)
Les Thornton vs. Charlie Cook
Scott McGhee defeated Kevin Sullivan via disqualification
Mike Graham defeated Ron Bass via disqualification
Jos LeDuc defeated Barry Windham in a lumberjack match
Blackjack Mulligan & Angelo Mosca defeated Elijah Akeem & Kareem Muhammed via disqualification

NWA World Champion Harley Race defeated Ric Flair
Dusty Rhodes defeated Purple Haze in a chain match

CWF @ Daytona Beach, FL - Spruce Creek High School - September 9, 1983
Charlie Cook vs. Kareem Muhammad
Scott McGhee vs. Elijah Akeem
Ric Flair vs. Mike Graham
Blackjack Mulligan & Barry Windham vs. Ron Bass & Jos LeDuc
NWA World Champion Harley Race vs. Angelo Mosca

JCP @ Charleston, SC - County Hall - September 9, 1983
Keith Larsen defeated Golden Boy Grey
Mark Youngblood & Rick McCord defeated Jacques Goulet & Bill Howard
Wahoo McDaniel defeated Dick Slater
Ricky Steamboat & Jay Youngblood defeated NWA Tag Team Champions Jack & Jerry Brisco

Mid-Atlantic Championship Wrestling - 9/10/83:
Wahoo McDaniel & Mid-Atlantic Heavyweight Champion Rufus R. Jones defeated Bill White & Ben Alexander

CWF @ Lakeland, FL - Civic Center - September 10, 1983
Ric Flair vs. Mike Graham; stipulations stated the winner would earn a future NWA World Title shot
Blackjack Mulligan & Angelo Mosca vs. Ron Bass & Jos LeDuc (bunkhouse match)
Dusty Rhodes defeated Kevin Sullivan in a loser leaves town for 60 days steel cage match
NWA World Champion Harley Race vs. Barry Windham (Best 2 out of 3 falls match)
Also included 3 other matches

JCP @ Greensboro, NC - Coliseum - September 10, 1983
Steve Muslin vs. Golden Boy Grey
Vinnie Valentino vs. Magic Dragon
Rick McCord vs. Gene Anderson
Johnny Weaver & Gene Anderson vs. the Assassins
Wahoo McDaniel vs. Dick Slater
Charlie Brown vs. Mid-Atlantic TV Champion the Great Kabuki
Ricky Steamboat & Jay Youngblood vs. NWA Tag Team Champions Jack & Jerry Brisco

CWF @ Miami, FL - Convention Hall - September 14, 1983
Angelo Mosca Jr. vs. Sam Houston
Mike Davis vs. Yatsu
Charlie Cook vs. Elijah Akeem
Mike Graham vs. Kareem Muhammed
Angelo Mosca & Barry Windham vs. Jos LeDuc & Ron Bass
Dusty Rhodes defeated Ric Flair via disqualification in a $10,000 bounty match

JCP @ Spartanburg, SC - Memorial Auditorium - September 14, 1983
TV taping:
Wahoo McDaniel, Charlie Brown, & Mark Youngblood defeated NWA US Champion Greg Valentine, Jake Roberts, & Mid-Atlantic TV Champion the Great Kabuki
Also included NWA Tag Team Champions Jack & Jerry Brisco, Ricky Steamboat & Jay Youngblood, Mike Rotundo, Mid-Atlantic Heavyweight Champion Rufus R. Jones, and Bugsy McGraw

JCP @ Sumter, SC - Sumter County Exhibition Center - September 15, 1983
The Magic Dragon defeated Vinnie Valentino
Kelly Kiniski defeated John Bonello
Scott McGhee defeated Bill Howard
The Assassins defeated Johnny Weaver (sub. for Bugsy McGraw) & Mike Rotundo
Mid-Atlantic Heavyweight Champion Rufus R. Jones & Charlie Brown defeated Jake Roberts & Mid-Atlantic TV Champion the Great Kabuki
NWA US Champion Greg Valentine defeated Mark Youngblood (sub. for Roddy Piper)

JCP @ Hampton, VA - September 15, 1983
TV taping:
Wahoo McDaniel & Mark Youngblood defeated NWA US Champion Greg Valentine & Dick Slater via disqualification
Wahoo McDaniel & Roddy Piper defeated Kelly Kiniski & Ben Alexander

Central States @ St. Louis, MO - September 16, 1983
George Wells & Bob Brown defeated Jerry Brown & Sheik Abdullah
Buck Robley defeated Ron Ritchie
Blackjack Mulligan defeated Jerry Ho
Iceman King Parsons defeated Roger Kirby
Barry Windham & Austin Idol (sub. for Dick the Bruiser) defeated the Super Destroyer & Bob Orton Jr.
Hulk Hogan defeated Jerry Blackwell
David Von Erich defeated Missouri State Champion Ric Flair to win the title via submission

JCP @ Charleston, SC - County Hall - September 16, 1983
Rick McCord defeated Golden Boy Grey
John Bonello defeated Tom Lintz
Gene Anderson defeated Keith Larsen
The Magic Dragon defeated Vinnie Valentino
Charlie Brown defeated Mid-Atlantic TV Champion the Great Kabuki; the title was only at stake for the first 15 minutes of the bout, thus Kabuki retained the belt
Ricky Steamboat & Jay Youngblood defeated NWA Tag Team Champions Jack & Jerry Brisco via disqualification

WWC @ San Juan, Puerto Rico - September 17, 1983
Pedro Morales defeated Ric Flair via disqualification at 11:28
NWA World Champion Harley Race fought Carlos Colon to a draw

JCP @ Conway, SC - September 17, 1983
The Ninja defeated Mark Fleming
John Bonello defeated Tom Lintz
Vinnie Valentino defeated Bill Howard
Dory Funk Jr. defeated Bugsy McGraw
Mid-Atlantic Heavyweight Champion Rufus R. Jones defeated Jake Roberts
Wahoo McDaniel defeated Dick Slater

JCP @ Charlotte, NC - Coliseum - September 17, 1983
Brett Hart defeated Golden Boy Grey
Scott McGhee defeated Kelly Kiniski
The Assassins defeated Ric McCord & Keith Larsen
Bob Orton Jr. defeated Johnny Weaver
Charlie Brown defeated Mid-Atlantic TV Champion the Great Kabuki
NWA US Champion Greg Valentine defeated Mark Youngblood
Ricky Steamboat & Jay Youngblood defeated NWA Tag Team Champions Jack & Jerry Brisco

WCCW @ Dallas, TX - September 17, 1983
Kevin Von Erich vs. NWA World Champion Harley Race

JCP @ Greensboro, NC - Coliseum - September 18, 1983
The Ninja defeated Brett Hart
Gene Anderson defeated Vinnie Valentino
Bugsy McGraw & Charlie Brown defeated Mid-Atlantic TV Champion the Great Kabuki & Dick Slater
Wahoo McDaniel defeated NWA US Champion Greg Valentine in a lumberjack match
Ricky Steamboat & Jay Youngblood defeated NWA Tag Team Champions Jack & Jerry Brisco

JCP @ Asheville, NC - Civic Center - September 18, 1983
The Magic Dragon defeated Brett Hart
Gene Anderson defeaed Vinnie Valentino
Bugsy McGraw defeated Dory Funk Jr.
Wahoo McDaniel & Charlie Brown defeated Dick Slater & Mid-Atlantic TV Champion the Great Kabuki
NWA Tag Team Champions Jack & Jerry Brisco defeated Ricky Steamboat & Jay Youngblood
Roddy Piper fought NWA US Champion Greg Valentine to a double disqualification in a lumberjack match

Toronto, Ontario - Maple Leaf Gardens - September 18, 1983
Don Kernodle defeated Rick McCord
Johnny Weaver & Keith Larsen defeated Kelly Kiniski & the Executioner

NWA US Champion Greg Valentine defeated Bob Orton Jr.
Angelo Mosca defeated Sgt. Slaughter via count-out
NWA World Champion Harley Race defeated Mike Rotundo

JCP @ Greenville, SC - Memorial Auditorium - September 19, 1983
John Bonello defeated Abe Jacobs
Mid-Atlantic Heavyweight Champion Rufus R. Jones defeated Jake Roberts
Bob Orton Jr. defeated Bugsy McGraw
Vinnie Valentino & Scott McGhee defeated Gene Anderson & the Ninja
NWA Mid-Atlantic Tag Team Champions Wahoo McDaniel & Mark Youngblood defeated NWA US Champion Greg Valentine & Dick Slater via disqualification

JCP @ Columbia, SC - September 19, 1983 Gene Anderson & Kelly Kiniski defeated Scott McGhee & John Bonello
Mid-Atlantic Heavyweight Champion Rufus R. Jones defeated Jake Roberts in a Texas Death Match
Charlie Brown defeated Baron Von Raschke
Ricky Steamboat & Jay Youngblood defeated NWA Tag Team Champions Jack & Jerry Brisco

JCP @ Fayetteville, NC - September 19, 1983
The Assassins defeated Mark Fleming & Steve Muslim
Charlie Brown defeated Mid-Atlantic TV Champion the Great Kabuki in a bounty match
Ricky Steamboat & Jay Youngblood defeated NWA Tag Team Champions Jack & Jerry Brisco

Mid-Atlantic Wrestling

Harrisonburg High School
September 22, 8:15 P.M.
Main Event
Jack & Jerry Brisco & Dick Slater
vs.
Rick Steamboat, Jay Youngblood &
Wahoo McDaniels
Bob Orton, Jr. vs. Johnny Weaver
Gene Anderson vs. Bret Hast
Kelly Kiniski vs. Vinnie Valentino

Tickets on sale at Charles Mathias
& Harrisonburg High School

JCP @ Harrisonburg, VA - High School - September 22, 1983
Kelly Kiniski vs. Vinnie Valentino
Gene Anderson vs. Brett Hart
Bob Orton Jr. vs. Johnny Weaver
Dick Slater, NWA Tag Team Champions Jack & Jerry Brisco vs. Wahoo McDaniel, Ricky Steamboat & Jay Youngblood

Central States @ Kansas City, KS - September 22, 1983
Ted DiBiase defeated NWA World Champion Harley Race via disqualification

JCP @ Charleston, SC - County Hall - September 23, 1983
John Bonello defeated Golden Boy Grey
Gene Ligon defeated Tom Lintz
Mark Youngblood & Scott McGhee defeated the Magic Dragon & the Ninja
Baron Von Raschke defeated Charlie Brown in a bounty match
Mid-Atlantic Heavyweight Champion Rufus R. Jones & Bugsy McGraw defeated Dory Funk Jr. & Jake Roberts

JCP @ Richmond, VA - Coliseum - September 23, 1983
Brett Hart defeated Kelly Kiniski
Gene Anderson defeated Vinnie Valentino
The Assassins defeated Keith Larson & Rick McCord
Bob Orton Jr. defeated Johnny Weaver
Wahoo McDaniel defeated Dick Slater
Wahoo McDaniel (sub. for Roddy Piper) defeated NWA US Champion Greg Valentine; the original match was scheduled as a lumberjack match
Ricky Steamboat & Jay Youngblood defeated NWA Tag Team Champions Jack & Jerry Brisco via disqualification

JCP @ ? - September 1983
TV taping:
Worldwide:

Worldwide - 9/24/83:
Wahoo McDaniel defeated Bill Howard

JCP @ Greensboro, NC - September 24, 1983
Brett Hart defeated ?
Gene Anderson defeated John Bonello
The Assassins defeated Scott McGhee & Steve Muslim
Bob Orton Jr. defeated Johnny Weaver
Wahoo McDaniel defeated Dick Slater in a taped fist match
Baron Von Raschke defeated Charlie Brown in a bounty match
Ricky Steamboat & Jay Youngblood defeated NWA Tag Team Champions Jack & Jerry Brisco

JCP @ ? - September 1983
TV taping:
Bob Orton Jr. & Dick Slater defeated Rick McCord & Gene Ligon at around the 6:15 mark when Orton pinned McCord with

a powerslam from the middle turnbuckle (*All Star Wrestling Vol. 2*)

JCP @ Hampton, VA - September 25, 1983
Brett Hart defeated Golden Boy Grey
Dory Funk Jr. defeated Scott McGhee
Mid-Atlantic Heavyweight Champion Rufus R. Jones defeated Jake Roberts
The Assassins defeated Bugsy McGraw & Johnny Weaver
Baron Von Raschke defeated Charlie Brown
Wahoo McDaniel & Mark Youngblood defeated NWA US Champion Greg Valentine & Dick Slater

JCP @ Roanoke, VA - Civic Center - September 25, 1983
Gene Anderson defeated Ric McCord
Vinnie Valentino & John Bonello defeated Kelly Kiniski & Tom Lintz
Bob Orton Jr. defeated Steve Muslim
Baron Von Raschke defeated Charlie Brown
Wahoo McDaniel defeated NWA US Champion Greg Valentine in a lumberjack match
NWA Tag Team Champions Jack & Jerry Brisco fought Ricky Steamboat & Jay Youngblood to a double disqualification

JCP @ Greenville, SC - September 26, 1983
Kelly Kiniski defeated Golden Boy Grey
Gene Anderson defeated Vinnie Valentino
Scott McGhee defeated the Magic Dragon
Bob Orton Jr. defeated Steve Muslim
Baron Von Raschke defeated Charlie Brown
Wahoo McDaniel & Mark Youngblood defeated NWA US Champion Greg Valentine & Dick Slater in a double Indian strap match

JCP @ Raleigh, NC - Dorton Arena - September 27, 1983
John Bonello defeated Tom Lintz
Ric McCord defeated the Ninja
The Magic Dragon defeated Brett Hart
Bob Orton Jr. defeated Johnny Weaver
Baron Von Raschke defeated Charlie Brown
Wahoo McDaniel & Mark Youngblood defeated NWA US Champion Greg Valentine & Dick Slater in a double Indian strap match

CWF @ Tampa, FL - September 27, 1983
NWA World Champion Harley Race & Ron Bass vs. Barry Windham & Blackjack Mulligan

CWF @ Miami Beach, FL - Convention Hall - September 28, 1983
Hector Guerrero defeated Sam Houston
Kareem Muhammad defeated Mike Davis
Angelo Mosca & Mike Rotundo defeated Jos LeDuc & Elijah Akeem via disqualification
Blackjack Mulligan fought Abdullah the Butcher to a no contest

in a $10,000 challenge match
Barry Windham defeated NWA World Champion Harley Race in a Best 2 out of 3 falls match; fall #1: Windham won; fall #2: Race won; fall #3: Race was disqualified
Dusty Rhodes defeated Ron Bass in a death match; fall #1: Rhodes won; fall #2: Bass won; fall #3: Bass was disqualified

JCP @ Roswell, VA - September 29, 1983
Vinnie Valentino defeated Cy Jernigan
Brett Hart defeated the Ninja
Bob Orton Jr. defeated Steve Muslim
NWA Tag Team Champion Ricky Steamboat defeated Dick Slater via disqualification
Mark & Jay Youngblood defeated NWA Tag Team Champions Jack & Jerry Brisco

JCP @ Charleston, SC - County Hall - September 30, 1983
Tom Lintz defeated Gene Ligon
Kevin Sullivan defeated Mark Fleming
Mark Lewin defeated John Bonello
The Assassins defeated Johnny Weaver & Scott McGhee
Charlie Brown defeated Baron Von Raschke in a steel cage bounty match

JCP @ Charlottesville, VA - September 30, 1983
The Magic Dragon defeated Cy Jernigan
Vinnie Valentino defeated the Ninja
Bob Orton Jr. defeated Brett Hart
NWA US Champion Greg Valentine & Dick Slater defeated Wahoo McDaniel & Mark Youngblood
Ricky Steamboat & Jay Youngblood defeated NWA Tag Team Champions Jack & Jerry Brisco

CWF @ Ocala, FL - Central Florida Community College - September 30, 1983
Hector Guerrero vs. Elijah Akeem
Kareem Muhammad vs. Mike Davis
Mike Rotundo vs. Jos LeDuc
Blackjack Mulligan vs. Ron Bass
NWA World Champion Harley Race vs. Barry Windham (Best 2 out of 3 falls)

CWF @ St. Petersburg, FL - Bayfront Arena - October 1, 1983
Sam Houston defeated Dennis Brown
Hector Guerrero defeated Mr. Fever
James J. Dillon defeated Mike Davis in a New Jersey streetfight
Jos LeDuc defeated Mike Graham via disqualification
Blackjack Mulligan & Barry Windham defeated Global Tag Team Champions Elijah Akeem & Kareem Muhammed via disqualification
Southern Heavyweight Champion Ron Bass fought Mike Rotundo to a draw

NWA World Champion Harley Race fought Dusty Rhodes to a double count-out at 20:05

JCP @ Morgantown, NC - October 1, 1983
Ric McCord defeated Kelly Kiniski
The Assassins defeated Bugsy McGraw & Johnny Weaver
Baron Von Raschke defeated Charlie Brown in a bounty match

JCP @ Conway, SC - October 1, 1983
Liz Chase defeated Donna Christanello
Joel Deaton defeated Abe Jacobs
Vinnie Valentino defeated Golden Boy Grey
Scott McGhee defeated Tom Lintz
Mid-Atlantic Heavyweight Champion Rufus R. Jones defeated Dory Funk Jr.
Wahoo McDaniel defeated Dick Slater in a lumberjack match

Worldwide - 10/1/83:
Wahoo McDaniel & Chavo Guerrero defeated the Magic Dragon & Jerry Grey

JCP @ Charlotte, NC - Coliseum - October 2, 1983
Vinnie Valentino defeated Tom Lintz
Scott McGhee defeated Golden Boy Grey
Mark Youngblood defeated the Magic Dragon
Gene Anderson defeated Mid-Atlantic Heavyweight Champion Rufus R. Jones
Baron Von Raschke defeated Charlie Brown
Bob Orton Jr. & Dick Slater defeated Ric Flair & Wahoo McDaniel via disqualification

JCP @ Asheville, NC - Civic Center - October 2, 1983
Terry Gibbs defeated the Magic Dragon
Kevin Sullivan defeated Rick McCord
Mark Lewin defeated John Bonello
Ric Flair & Wahoo McDaniel fought Bob Orton Jr. & Dick Slater to a double disqualification
NWA Tag Team Champions Jack & Jerry Brisco defeated Ricky Steamboat & Jay Youngblood

WCCW @ San Antonio, TX - October 2, 1983
Chris Adams & Iceman King Parsons defeated Terry Gordy & Buddy Roberts
Jose Lothario defeated Cocoa Samoa
Kerry Von Erich defeated Boris Zhukov
David Von Erich defeated Jimmy Garvin
Kevin Von Erich defeated NWA World Champion Harley Race via disqualification

WCCW @ Ft. Worth, TX - October 3, 1983
Boris Zhukov defeated Mike Reed
Boris Zhukov defeated Mike Reed
Chris Adams defeated Black Gordman
Iceman King Parsons defeated the Mongol

Michael Hayes defeated Johnny Mantell
Buddy Roberts defeated Art Crews
NWA World Champion Harley Race defeated Kamala via disqualification

JCP @ Greenville, SC - October 3, 1983
Brickhouse Brown defeated Bill Howard
Scott McGhee defeated Kelly Kiniski
The Assassins defeated Bugsy McGraw & Mark Youngblood
Charlie Brown defeated Baron Von Raschke
Ricky Steamboat & Jay Youngblood defeated NWA Tag Team Champions Jack & Jerry Brisco to win the titles

JCP @ Fayetteville, NC - October 3, 1983
Terry Gibbs defeated Golden Boy Grey
Kevin Sullivan & Mark Lewin defeated Keith Larsen & Ric McCord
Dory Funk Jr. defeated Mid-Atlantic Heavyweight Champion Rufus R. Jones
Roddy Piper defeated NWA US Champion Greg Valentine
Dick Slater & Bob Orton Jr. defeated Ric Flair & Wahoo McDaniel via disqualification

JCP @ Columbia, SC - Township Auditorium - October 4, 1983
Vinnie Valentino defeated the Magic Dragon
Terry Gibbs defeated Tom Lintz
Gene Anderson defeated John Bonello
Kevin Sullivan defeated Brett Hart
NWA US Champion Greg Valentine defeated Bugsy McGraw
Bob Orton Jr. & Dick Slater defeated Ric Flair & Wahoo McDaniel via disqualification

JCP @ Raleigh, NC - Dorton Arena - October 4, 1983
Kelly Kiniski defeated Mark Fleming
Ric McCord defeated Gene Ligon
Brickhouse Brown defeated Bill Howard
Johnny Weaver defeated Steve Muslim
Charlie Brown defeated Baron Von Raschke in a steel cage bounty match
NWA Tag Team Champions Ricky Steamboat & Jay Youngblood defeated Jack & Jerry Brisco

WCCW @ Lawton, OK - October 5, 1983
Buddy Roberts defeated Mike Bond
Johnny Mantell defeated Boris Zhukov
Iceman King Parsons defeated Michael Hayes
Chris Adams fought Jimmy Garvin to a no contest
David Von Erich defeated NWA World Champion Harley Race

JCP @ Winston-Salem, NC - Memorial Coliseum - October 5, 1983
TV taping:
The Assassins defeated Mark Youngblood & Scott McGhee
Kevin Sullivan & Mark Lewin defeated Brett Hart & Steve

Muslim
NWA Tag Team Champions Ricky Steamboat & Jay
Youngblood defeated Kelly Kiniski & Ben Alexander
The Assassins vs. Mark Youngblood & Scott McGhee
Kevin Sullivan & Mark Lewin vs. Steve Travis & Brett Hart
NWA Tag Team Champions Ricky Steamboat & Jay
Youngblood defeated Ben Alexander & Kelly Kiniski
Scott McGhee & Mark Youngblood vs. the Ninja & Kelly Kiniski
NWA US Champion Greg Valentine vs. Brett Hart
Bugsy McGraw & Mid-Atlantic Heavyweight Champion Rufus
R. Jones vs. Tom Lentz & Jerry Grey
Baron Von Raschke vs. John Bonello
Mid-Atlantic Championship Wrestling - 10/8/83:
Wahoo McDaniel defeated the Ninja

JCP @ Norfolk, VA - Scope - October 6, 1983
Brickhouse Brown defeated Bill Howard
Gene Anderson defeated Terry Gibbs
Mark Lewin defeated Brett Hart
Kevin Sullivan defeated Johnny Weaver
NWA Tag Team Champions Ricky Steamboat & Jay
Youngblood defeated Jack & Jerry Brisco
Roddy Piper defeated NWA US Champion Greg Valentine in a
lumberjack match
Ric Flair & Wahoo McDaniel defeated Bob Orton Jr. & Dick
Slater via disqualification

JCP @ Sumter, SC - Exhibition Center - October 6, 1983
Scott McGhee defeated Kelly Kiniski
Mark Youngblood defeated the Magic Dragon
Mid-Atlantic Heavyweight Champion Rufus R. Jones defeated
Dory Funk Jr. via disqualification
Andre the Giant, Charlie Brown, & Bugsy McGraw defeated
Baron Von Raschke & the Assassins

JCP @ Richmond, VA - Coliseum - October 7, 1983
Brickhouse Brown defeated Golden Boy Grey
Terry Gibbs defeated Tom Lintz
Kevin Sullivan & Mark Lewin defeated Vinnie Valentino & John
Bonello
Dory Funk Jr. defeated Johnny Weaver
Baron Von Raschke defeated Charlie Brown in a steel cage
bounty match
Johnny Weaver won a 2-ring battle royal by last eliminating
Dory Funk Jr.

JCP @ Charleston, SC - County Hall - October 7, 1983
Kelly Kiniski vs. Rick McCord
Scott McGhee vs. Assassin #2
Mark Youngblood vs. Assassin #1
Roddy Piper defeated NWA US Champion Greg Valentine in a
non-title lumberjack strap match
NWA Tag Team Champions Ricky Steamboat & Jay
Youngblood defeated Jack & Jerry Brisco in a No DQ match

WCCW @ Dallas, TX - Sportatorium - October 7, 1983
TV taping:
Boris Zhukov defeated Mike Reed
Jose Lothario defeated the Mongol via disqualification
Chris Adams & Johnny Mantell defeated Michael Hayes &
Buddy Roberts
Kamala defeated Art Crews
David Von Erich defeated Jimmy Garvin via disqualification
NWA World Champion Harley Race defeated Iceman King
Parsons via disqualification

JCP @ Burlington, NC - October 8, 1983
Brickhouse Brown defeated Golden Boy Grey
Kelly Kiniski defeated Steve Muslim
Scott McGhee defeated the Magic Dragon
NWA US Champion Greg Valentine defeated Johnny Weaver
NWA Tag Team Champions Ricky Steamboat & Jay
Youngblood defeated Jack & Jerry Brisco

JCP @ Greensboro, NC - Coliseum - October 8, 1983
Rick McCord defeated Tom Lintz
Mark Lewin & Kevin Sullivan defeated Vinnie Valentino & John
Bonello
Mid-Atlantic Heavyweight Champion Rufus R. Jones pinned
Dory Funk Jr.
Bugsy McGraw & Mark Youngblood defeated the Assassins
Roddy Piper & Charlie Brown defeated Baron Von Raschke &
Gary Hart
Ric Flair & Wahoo McDaniel fought Bob Orton Jr. & Dick Slater
to a double disqualification

Central States @ St. Louis, MO - October 8, 1983 (6,000)
Ron Ritchie, Bob Brown, & Angelo Mosca Jr. defeated Roger
Kirby, Jerry Brown, & Sheik Abdullah
Buck Robley defeated Jerry Ho
Iceman King Parsons defeated Tonga John
Blackjack Mulligan defeated Buzz Tyler
Barry Windham & David Von Erich defeated Jerry Blackwell &
the Super Destroyer
Hulk Hogan defeated NWA World Champion Harley Race via
disqualification when Race threw the challenger over the top
rope

**CWF @ Ocala, FL - Jai Alai Fronton - October 9, 1983
(matinee)**
Mike Davis vs. Elijah Akeem
Mike Rotundo & Big Daddy vs. Ron Bass & Jos LeDuc
Blackjack Mulligan vs. Kareem Muhammad (brass knuckles
match)
NWA World Champion Harley Race vs. Barry Windham (Best
2 out of 3 falls match)

**JCP @ Greenville, SC - Memorial Auditorium - October 10,
1983**
Gene Anderson defeated Keith Larsen

Chavo Guerrero defeated the Ninja
Kevin Sullivan & Mark Lewin defeated Johnny Weaver & Rick McCord
Wahoo McDaniel defeated NWA US Champion Greg Valentine via count-out
Ric Flair & Roddy Piper defeated Bob Orton Jr. & Dick Slater via disqualification

JCP @ Columbia, SC - Township Auditorium - October 11, 1983
The Magic Dragon defeated Brickhouse Brown
Mark Lewin defeated Brett Hart
Kevin Sullivan defeated Steve Muslim
The Assassins defeated Mid-Atlantic Heavyweight Champion Rufus R. Jones & Mark Youngblood
Charlie Brown defeated Baron Von Raschke in a steel cage bounty match
Ric Flair & Wahoo McDaniel defeated Bob Orton Jr. & Dick Slater

JCP @ Spartanburg, SC - Memorial Auditorium - October 12, 1983
TV taping:
Kevin Sullivan & Mark Lewin defeated Mark Fleming & Vinnie Valentino
The Assassins defeated Steve Muslim & John Bonello
Chavo Guerrero defeated Ben Alexander
Jack & Jerry Brisco defeated Brett Hart & Gene Ligon
Charlie Brown, Brickhouse Brown, & Terry Gibbs defeated Kelly Kiniski, Golden Boy Grey, & Tom Lintz
Bob Orton Jr. & Dick Slater fought Keith Larsen & Ric McCord to a no contest at around the 1:30 mark when Ric Flair ran into the ring and began brawling with both Orton & Slater; moments later, Wahoo McDaniel came out to fight with Slater as Flair went after Orton
The Assassins defeated Mark Youngblood & Scott McGhee
Jack & Jerry Brisco defeated Vinnie Valentino & John Bonello
NWA US Champion Greg Valentine defeated Steve Muslim
Ric Flair, Wahoo McDaniel, & Mark Youngblood defeated Dick Slater, Dory Funk Jr. (w/ Paul Jones), & Mark Lewin when Flair pinned Funk; after the bout, Jones yelled at Funk for losing the match
Mid-Atlantic Championship Wrestling - 10/15/83:
Wahoo McDaniel & Chavo Guerrero defeated the Magic Dragon & Jerry Grey

JCP @ Marion, NC - October 13, 1983
Scott McGhee defeated Bill White
The Assassins defeated Mark Youngblood & Bugsy McGraw
Wahoo McDaniel defeated Dick Slater via count-out

JCP @ Orange, VA - October 13, 1983
Kevin Sullivan defeated Vinnie Valentino
Mark Lewin defeated Steve Muslim
Chavo Guerrero defeated the Ninja
Charlie Brown & Johnny Weaver defeated Bob Orton Jr. &

Baron Von Raschke via disqualification
Ric Flair defeated Dory Funk Jr.

Central States @ Kansas City, MO - October 13, 1983
Hulk Hogan fought NWA World Champion Harley Race to a no contest

JCP @ Hampton, VA - Coliseum - October 14, 1983
Vinnie Valentino defeated Golden Boy Grey
The Magic Dragon defeated Brett Hart
Chavo Guerrero defeated the Ninja
Kevin Sullivan & Mark Lewin defeated Johnny Weaver & Terry Gibbs
Charlie Brown defeated Baron Von Raschke
Ric Flair & Roddy Piper defeated Bob Orton Jr. & Dick Slater

JCP @ Charleston, SC - County Hall - October 14, 1983
Brickhouse Brown and Gene Anderson did not appear as scheduled
Keith Larsen defeated Tom Lintz
Scott McGhee defeated Bill Howard (sub. for Gene Anderson)
The Assassins defeated Mark Youngblood & Bugsy McGraw
Wahoo McDaniel defeated Dick Slater

JCP @ Culpeper, VA - Junior High School - October 15, 1983
Vinnie Valentino defeated the Ninja
Brett Hart defeated Golden Boy Grey
Chavo Guerrero defeated the Magic Dragon
Kevin Sullivan & Mark Lewin defeated Johnny Weaver & Terry Gibbs
Ric Flair defeated Bob Orton Jr. via count-out

JCP @ Roanoke, VA - Civic Center - October 15, 1983
Gene Anderson defeated Keith Larsen
Scott McGhee defeated Kelly Kiniski
The Assassins defeated Bugsy McGraw & Brickhouse Brown
Dick Slater defeated Dory Funk Jr.
Charlie Brown & Mark Youngblood defeated Baron Von Raschke & Gary Hart

Toronto, Ontario - Maple Leaf Gardens - October 16, 1983
Nick DeCarlo defeated Scrap Iron Sheppard
Rudy & Terry Kay defeated Bob & Joe Marcus
Kelly Kiniski defeated Big Mac
Johnny Weaver defeated Bill Howard
Leo Burke defeated Bret Hart
Don Kernodle defeated Canadian TV Champion Mike Rotundo to win the title at 13:02
Angelo Mosca defeated Sgt. Slaughter
Roddy Piper defeated NWA US Champion Greg Valentine

JCP @ Greensboro, NC - Coliseum - October 16, 1983
Dory Funk Jr., Bugsy McGraw, & Mark Youngblood defeated

Paul Jones & the Assassins
Scott McGhee defeated the Magic Dragon
Terry Gibbs defeated Tom Lintz
Gene Anderson defeated Keith Larsen
Jack & Jerry Brisco vs. NWA Tag Team Champions Ricky Steamboat & Jay Youngblood
Wahoo McDaniel defeated Dick Slater via disqualification
Baron Von Raschke vs. Charlie Brown
Ric Flair defeated Bob Orton Jr. in a steel cage match

PNW @ Centralia, WA - October 16, 1983
Rip Oliver defeated Buddy Rose
Jules Strongbow defeated Mike Miller
Siva Afi defeated Scott Ferris
Al Madril fought Ali Hassan to a draw
The Assassin & the Dynamite Kid defeated Curt Hennig & Brian Adidas
NWA World Champion Harley Race defeated Billy Jack

JCP @ Fayetteville, NC - October 16, 1983
Vinnie Valentino defeated the Ninja
Kevin Sullivan & Mark Lewin defeated Scott McGhee & John Bonello
Dory Funk Jr. defeated Chavo Guerrero
Charlie Brown defeated Baron Von Raschke
Ric Flair & Wahoo McDaniel defeated Bob Orton Jr. & Dick Slater

PNW @ Yakima, WA - October 17, 1983
NWA World Champion Harley Race defeated Billy Jack

JCP @ Greenville, SC - Memorial Auditorium - October 17, 1983
John Bonello defeated Golden Boy Grey
Mark Lewin defeated Vinnie Valentino
Chavo Guerrero defeated the Magic Dragon
The Assassins defeated Mark Youngblood & Terry Gibbs
Jerry Brisco defeated NWA Tag Team Champion Ricky Steamboat
Bob Orton Jr. & Dick Slater defeated Ric Flair & Wahoo McDaniel

JCP @ Columbia, SC - Township Auditorium - October 18, 1983
Gene Anderson defeated Steve Muslim
Keith Larsen defeated Bill Howard
Kevin Sullivan defeated Terry Gibbs
The Assassins defeated Charlie Brown & Mark Youngblood
NWA Tag Team Champions Ricky Steamboat & Jay Youngblood defeated Jack & Jerry Brisco

PNW @ Portland, OR - October 18, 1983
Billy Jack defeated Scott Ferris
Al Madril fought Curt Hennig to a time-limit draw
The Assassin & the Dynamite Kid defeated Brian Adidas &

Jules Strongbow
Rip Oliver defeated Ali Hassan
NWA World Champion Harley Race defeated Buddy Rose

JCP @ Shelby, NC - Rec Center - October 19, 1983
TV taping:
Dick Slater defeated Steve Muslim
Kevin Sullivan & Mark Lewin defeated Brett Hart & Vinnie Valentino
Charlie Brown & Bugsy McGraw defeated Kelly Kiniski & Tom Lintz
Mark Youngblood & Scott McGhee defeated the Assassins
Chavo Guerrero defeated the Magic Dragon
Kevin Sullivan & Mark Lewin defeated Brett Hart & John Bonello
Dick Slater defeated Keith Larsen
NWA Tag Team Champions Ricky Steamboat & Jay Youngblood defeated Bill Howard & Tom Lintz
The Assassins defeated Terry Gibbs & Steve Muslim
Mid-Atlantic Championship Wrestling - 10/22/83:
WWF All American Wrestling - 10/30/83: NWA Tag Team Champions Ricky Steamboat & Jay Youngblood defeated Bill Howard & the Magic Dragon when Steamboat pinned Howard with the crossbody off the top

PNW @ Seattle, WA - October 19, 1983
Billy Jack defeated NWA World Champion Harley Race via disqualification

PNW @ Salem, OR - October 20, 1983
NWA World Champion Harley Race fought Billy Jack to a draw

JCP @ Norfolk, VA - Scope - October 20, 1983
Scott McGhee defeated Kelly Kiniski
Mark Youngblood defeated Gene Anderson
Mark Lewin defeated Bugsy McGraw
The Assassins defeated Johnny Weaver & Terry Gibbs
Charlie Brown defeated Mid-Atlantic TV Champion the Great Kabuki
Ric Flair & Wahoo McDaniel fought Bob Orton Jr. & Dick Slater to a double disqualification

JCP @ Sumter, SC - Exhibition Center - October 20, 1983
Vinnie Valentino defeated Tim Gerrard
Gary Royal defeated Ric McCord
Chavo Guerrero defeated the Ninja
Kevin Sullivan defeated Keith Larsen
Mid-Atlantic Heavyweight Champion Rufus R. Jones defeated Dory Funk Jr.
NWA Tag Team Champions Ricky Steamboat & Jay Youngblood defeated Jack & Jerry Brisco

JCP @ Richmond, VA - Coliseum - October 21, 1983
Terry Gibbs defeated Kelly Kiniski
Mark Lewin defeated Johnny Weaver

Bugsy McGraw defeated Gene Anderson
Mid-Atlantic TV Champion the Great Kabuki defeated Scott McGhee
The Assassins defeated Charlie Brown & Mark Youngblood
Jack & Jerry Brisco defeated NWA Tag Team Champions Ricky Steamboat & Jay Youngblood to win the titles
Ric Flair & Wahoo McDaniel defeated Bob Orton Jr. & Dick Slater

JCP @ Charleston, SC - County Hall - October 21, 1983
Brett Hart defeated Tom Lintz
The Magic Dragon defeated John Bonello
Chavo Guerrero defeated the Ninja
Kevin Sullivan defeated Keith Larsen
Dory Funk Jr. defeated Mid-Atlantic Heavyweight Champion Rufus R. Jones
NWA US Champion Greg Valentine defeated Roddy Piper

PNW @ Eugene, OR - Lane County Fairgrounds - October 21, 1983
Buddy Rose & Jules Strongbow defeated The Assassin & the Dynamite Kid
Curt Hennig defeated Scott Farris
Jerry O defeated Matt Borne
Rip Oliver defeated The Sheik
NWA World Champion Harley Race defeated Billy Jack

PNW @ Portland, OR - October 22, 1983
Billy Jack fought NWA World Champion Harley Race to a draw

JCP @ Roanoke, VA - Civic Center - October 23, 1983 (matinee)
Ric McCord defeated ?
Keith Larsen defeated Tim Gerard
Brett Hart defeated Tom Lintz
Mark Lewin & Kevin Sullivan defeated Terry Gibbs & Johnny Weaver
Wahoo McDaniel defeated NWA US Champion Greg Valentine via count-out
Ric Flair & Roddy Piper defeated Bob Orton Jr. & Dick Slater

JCP @ Asheville, NC - Civic Center - October 23, 1983
Kelly Kiniski defeated John Bonello
Vinnie Valentino defeated Golden Boy Gray
Bugsy McGraw defeated the Magic Dragon
The Assassins defeated Mid-Atlantic Heavyweight Champion Rufus R. Jones & Mark Youngblood
Charlie Brown defeated Mid-Atlantic TV Champion the Great Kabuki
NWA Tag Team Champions Jack & Jerry Brisco defeated Ricky Steamboat & Jay Youngblood via disqualification

JCP @ Charlotte, NC - Coliseum - October 23, 1983
Brickhouse Brown defeated Gary Royal
Scott McGhee defeated the Ninja

Angelo Mosca defeated Gene Anderson
Dory Funk Jr. defeated Mark Youngblood
Mid-Atlantic Heavyweight Champion Rufus R. Jones & Bugsy McGraw defeated the Assassins
NWA US Champion Greg Valentine defeated Roddy Piper
NWA Tag Team Champions Jack & Jerry Brisco defeated Ricky Steamboat & Jay Youngblood
Ric Flair & Wahoo McDaniel fought Bob Orton Jr. & Dick Slater to a no contest in a No DQ match

AJPW @ Kitami, Japan - October 24, 1983
NWA World Champion Harley Race vs. Jumbo Tsuruta

JCP @ Greenville, SC - Memorial Auditorium - October 24, 1983
Vinnie Valentino vs. Tom Lintz
Scott McGhee vs. the Ninja
Angelo Mosca vs. Gene Anderson
Mark Lewin vs. Johnny Weaver
Ricky Steamboat & Jay Youngblood vs. NWA Tag Team Champions Jack & Jerry Brisco
Ric Flair & Wahoo McDaniel fought Bob Orton Jr. & Dick Slater to a draw

JCP @ Columbia, SC - Township Auditorium - October 25, 1983
Vinnie Valentino defeated the Magic Dragon
Angelo Mosca defeated Tom Lintz
Mark Lewin & Kevin Sullivan defeated Johnny Weaver & Terry Gibbs
Dory Funk Jr. defeated Scott McGhee
Ric Flair, Roddy Piper, & Wahoo McDaniel defeated NWA US Champion Greg Valentine, Bob Orton Jr., & Dick Slater when Piper pinned Valentine with a neckbreaker

AJPW @ Morioka, Japan - October 26, 1983
NWA World Champion Harley Race fought Jumbo Tsuruta to a draw

JCP @ Winston-Salem, NC - Memorial Coliseum - October 26, 1983
TV taping:
The Assassins defeated Steve Muslim & Tim Gerrard
Mark Youngblood & Mid-Atlantic Heavyweight Champion Rufus R. Jones defeated Bill Howard & Gary Royal
Mid-Atlantic TV Champion the Great Kabuki defeated Keith Larsen
Kevin Sullivan defeated Tim Gerrard
Bob Orton Jr. defeated Ric McCord
Mid-Atlantic TV Champion the Great Kabuki defeated Steve Muslim
The Assassins fought Charlie Brown & Bugsy McGraw to a double disqualification
Chavo Guerrero defeated Gary Royal
Ric Flair, Roddy Piper, & Wahoo McDaniel vs. Dory Funk Jr.,

Bob Orton Jr., & Dick Slater
Worldwide - 10/29/83:
Wahoo McDaniel & Chavo Guerrero defeated Tom Lintz & Kelly Kiniski

JCP @ Charleston, SC - County Hall - October 28, 1983
Gene Anderson defeated Keith Larson
Dory Funk Jr. defeated Steve Muslin
Brickhouse Brown defeated Gary Royal
The Assassins defeated Scott McGhee & Mark Youngblood
Ric Flair & Wahoo McDaniel fought Bob Orton Jr. & Dick Slater to a double disqualification

JCP @ Charlotte, NC - Coliseum - October 30, 1983
Ric Flair defeated Bob Orton Jr.

Toronto, Ontario - Maple Leaf Gardens - October 30, 1983
Joe Marcus defeated Tom Lentz
Kurt Von Hess fought Bob Marcus to a draw
Kelly Kiniski defeated Vinnie Valentino at 7:06
Rudy & Terry Kay defeated Nick DeCarlo & Mark Fleming
Don Kernodle defeated Johnny Weaver
Tito Santana defeated Leo Burke
Charlie Brown defeated Baron Von Raschke
Blackjack Mulligan defeated Sgt. Slaughter via disqualification

AJPW @ Wakamatsu, Japan - October 31, 1983
NWA World Champion Harley Race defeated Ted DiBiase

JCP @ Greenville, SC - Memorial Auditorium - October 31, 1983
Terry Gibbs defeated Bill Howard
Brickhouse Brown defeated the Magic Dragon
John Bonello defeated Gary Royal
NWA TV Champion the Great Kabuki defeated Mark Youngblood
Mid-Atlantic Heavyweight Champion Rufus R. Jones, Dory Funk Jr., & Bugsy McGraw defeated Paul Jones & the Assassins

JCP @ Raleigh, NC - Dorton Arena - November 1, 1983
John Bonello defeated Tom Lintz
Johnny Weaver defeated Gary Royal
Dory Funk Jr. defeated Scott McGhee
NWA US Champion Greg Valentine & Mark Lewin defeated Roddy Piper & Mark Youngblood
Ric Flair & Wahoo McDaniel defeated Dick Slater & Bob Orton Jr. via count-out

JCP @ Spartanburg, SC - Memorial Auditorium - November 2, 1983
TV taping:
Greg Valentine defeated Gary Royal
Dick Slater & Bob Orton, Jr. defeated Scott McGee & Steve Muslin
Mid-Atlantic TV Champion the Great Kabuki defeated John Bonello
Charlie Brown, Mid-Atlantic Heavyweight Champion Rufus R. Jones & Dory Funk Jr. defeated Bill Howard, Kelly Kiniski & Tom Lentz
Wahoo McDaniel defeated Magic Dragon
Dick Slater & Bob Orton Jr. defeated John Bonello & Vinnie Valentino
Mid-Atlantic TV Champion the Great Kabuki defeated Gary Royal
Kevin Sullivan & Mark Lewin defeated Brett Hart & Steve Muslin
Charlie Brown, Bugsy McGraw, & Mid-Atlantic Heavyweight Champion Rufus R. Jones defeated Jerry Gray, Bill Howard, & Ben Alexander

JCP @ Norfolk, VA - Scope - November 3, 1983
Scott McGhee defeated Magic Dragon
Kevin Sullivan defeated Vinnie Valentino
Mark Lewin defeated Mid-Atlantic Heavyweight Champion Rufus R. Jones
Angelo Mosca defeated Gene Anderson
NWA Tag Team Champions Jack & Jerry Brisco defeated Ricky Steamboat & Jay Youngblood
Ric Flair, Roddy Piper, & Wahoo McDaniel defeated NWA US Champion Greg Valentine, Bob Orton Jr., & Dick Slater

Central States @ St. Louis, MO - November 4, 1983
Missouri Heavyweight Champion David Von Erich defeated Ric Flair in a Best 2 out of 3 falls match

JCP @ Charleston, SC - County Hall - November 4, 1983
Terry Gibbs defeated Keith Larsen
John Bonello defeated Tom Lintz
Johnny Weaver defeated the Ninja
Roddy Piper & Angelo Mosca defeated NWA US Champion Greg Valentine & Dory Funk Jr.
Wahoo McDaniel defeated Dick Slater in a taped fist match

JCP @ Spotsylvania, VA - High School - November 4, 1983
Magic Dragon vs. Mark Fleming
Mid-Atlantic Heavyweight Champion Rufus R. Jones vs. Gene Anderson
Mark Lewin vs. Vinnie Valentino
Kevin Sullivan vs. Scott McGhee
Ricky Steamboat & Jay Youngblood vs. NWA Tag Team Champions Jack & Jerry Brisco

JCP @ Rock Hill, SC - Winthrop Coliseum - November 6, 1983 (matinee)
TV taping:
Dick Slater & Bob Orton Jr. defeated Vinnie Valentino & Gene Ligon
Mid-Atlantic TV Champion the Great Kabuki defeated Steve

Muslim
Ricky Steamboat & Jay Youngblood defeated Gary Royal & Bill Howard
The Cobra defeated the Magic Dragon
NWA Tag Team Champions Jack & Jerry Brisco defeated Brett Hart & Rick McCord
Wahoo McDaniel defeated Gary Royal
John Bonello & Steve Muslim defeated Dick Slater & Bob Orton Jr. via disqualification
The Assassins & Paul Jones defeated Charlie Brown, Dory Funk Jr., & Bugsy McGraw
NWA Tag Team Champions Jack & Jerry Brisco defeated Roddy Piper & Wahoo McDaniel
Ric Flair defeated Bob Orton Jr. in a lumberjack match

JCP @ Columbia, SC - Township Auditorium - November 6, 1983
Dory Funk Jr. defeated Scott McGhee
Ric Flair defeated Bob Orton Jr. via disqualification

JCP @ Greenville, SC - Memorial Auditorium - November 7, 1983
Brett Hart defeated Tom Lintz
Keith Larsen & Rick McCord defeated Gary Royal & Golden Boy Grey
Mark Youngblood defeated Kelly Kiniski
Dory Funk Jr. & Mid-Atlantic Heavyweight Champion Rufus R. Jones defeated the Assassins
Mid-Atlantic TV Champion the Great Kabuki defeated Charlie Brown

JCP @ Spartanburg, SC - Memorial Auditorium - November 9, 1983
TV taping:
Kevin Sullivan & Mark Lewin defeated Scott McGee & Terry Gibbs
NWA US Champion Greg Valentine defeated John Bonello
The Assassins fought Charlie Brown & Wahoo McDaniel to a double disqualification
Ricky Steamboat & Jay Youngblood defeated Ben Alexander & Jerry Gray
Dick Slater & Bob Orton Jr. defeated Terry Gibbs & Brett Hart
Angelo Mosca defeated Bill Howard
Kevin Sullivan & Mark Lewin defeated Scott McGee & Rick McCord
Mid-Atlantic TV Champion the Great Kabuki defeated John Bonello
Mark Youngblood defeated Gary Royal
Mid-Atlantic Championship Wrestling - 11/12/83:
Wahoo McDaniel & Charlie Brown defeated Tom Lintz & Kelly Kiniski

Central States @ Kansas City, MO - November 10, 1983
Ric Flair & Kamala fought Bruiser Brody & Mr. Wrestling II to a no contest

JCP @ Richmond, VA - Coliseum - November 11, 1983
Johnny Weaver defeated Gary Royal
Scott McGhee defeated Gene Anderson
Kevin Sullivan defeated Keith Larson
Angelo Mosca defeated Kelly Kiniski
Ricky Steamboat defeated Mark Lewin
NWA US Champion Greg Valentine & Dick Slater defeated Roddy Piper & Wahoo McDaniel
Ric Flair defeated Bob Orton Jr.

JCP @ Charleston, SC - County Hall - November 11, 1983
Terry Gibbs defeated the Magic Dragon
John Bonello defeated Golden Boy Grey
Vinnie Valentino defeated Bill Howard
Mid-Atlantic Heavyweight Champion Rufus R. Jones defeated Mid-Atlantic TV Champion the Great Kabuki; the title was only at stake for the first 15 minutes of the bout, thus Kabuki retained the belt
The Assassins & Paul Jones defeated Charlie Brown, Dory Funk Jr., & Bugsy McGraw

JCP @ Hampton, VA - Coliseum - November 12, 1983
Ric Flair defeated Bob Orton Jr.

CWF @ Ocala, FL - Jai Alai Fronton - November 13, 1983 (matinee)
Sam Houston vs. Dr. X
Big Daddy vs. JJ Dillon
Mike Graham & Mike Davis vs. the One Man Gang & Kareem Muhammad
Barry Windham vs. Ron Bass
NWA World Champion Harley Race vs. Mike Rotundo

JCP @ Asheville, NC - Civic Center - November 13, 1983
John Bonello defeated Tom Lintz
Vinnie Valentino defeated Keith Larsen
The Magic Dragon defeated Bret Hart
Brickhouse Brown defeated Gene Anderson
Mark Lewin & Kevin Sullivan defeated Mark & Jay Youngblood
Ricky Steamboat defeated Mid-Atlantic TV Champion the Great Kabuki
Ric Flair & Wahoo McDaniel defeated Bob Orton Jr. & Dick Slater in a steel cage match

Toronto, Ontario - Maple Leaf Gardens - November 13, 1983
Bob Marcus defeated Tim Gerrard
Nick DeCarlo defeated Scrap Iron Sheppard
Leo Burke defeated Herb Gallant
The Destroyer & Kurt Von Hess defeated Johnny Weaver & Billy Red Lyons
Angelo Mosca & Jimmy Valiant defeated Leo Burke & the Destroyer (sub. for NWA Tag Team Champions Jack & Jerry Brisco)
Blackjack Mulligan fought the Masked Superstar to a no

contest
Roddy Piper defeated NWA US Champion Greg Valentine via disqualification

JCP @ Columbia, SC - Township Auditorium - November 13, 1983
Ric Flair defeated Bob Orton Jr. in a steel cage match

CWF @ Orlando, FL - November 13, 1983
NWA World Champion Harley Race vs. Dusty Rhodes

JCP @ Greenville, SC - Memorial Auditorium - November 14, 1983
John Bonello defeated Bill Howard
Terry Gibbs defeated the Magic Dragon
Vinnie Valentino defeated Gene Anderson
Kevin Sullivan & Mark Lewin defeated Bugsy McGraw & Johnny Weaver
Wahoo McDaniel & Roddy Piper defeated NWA US Champion Greg Valentine & Dick Slater
Ric Flair defeated Bob Orton Jr.

CWF @ Tampa, FL - Sun Dome - November 15, 1983
NWA World Champion Harley Race vs. Mike Rotundo

JCP @ Hampton, VA - Coliseum - November 15, 1983
Bill Howard defeated Ric McCord
Keith Larsen defeated Golden Boy Grey
Johnny Weaver & Mark Fleming defeated Tom Lintz & Kelly Kiniski
Angelo Mosca defeated Gene Anderson
Mid-Atlantic TV Champion the Great Kabuki defeated Scott McGhee
Roddy Piper defeated Dick Slater
Wahoo McDaniel defeated NWA US Champion Wahoo McDaniel via disqualification
Ric Flair defeated Bob Orton Jr.

CWF @ Miami Beach, FL - Convention Center - November 16, 1983 (3,805)
Hector Guerrero defeated Sam Houston
Mike Davis defeated JJ Dillon
Big Daddy defeated Man Mountain Mark at 5:05
Ron Bass defeated Mike Graham at 9:57
Dusty Rhodes, Blackjack Mulligan, & Barry Windham defeated the One Man Gang, Elijah Akeem, & Abdullah the Butcher via disqualification
NWA World Champion Harley Race defeated Mike Rotundo via disqualification at 22:12 when Rotundo threw Race over the top rope

JCP @ Spartanburg, SC - Memorial Auditorium - November 16, 1983
TV taping:

Angelo Mosca defeated Tom Lentz
King Cobra defeated Magic DragonB NWA Tag Team Champions Jack & Jerry Brisco defeated Brett Hart & Rick McCord
Dick Slater & Bob Orton Jr. defeated John Bonello & Steve Muslin
Mid-Atlantic Championship Wrestling - 11/19/83:
Wahoo McDaniel defeated Gary Royal

JCP @ Sumter, SC - November 17, 1983
Ric Flair defeated Bob Orton Jr. in a lumberjack match

JCP @ Stafford, VA - High Scool - November 17, 1983
The Ninja vs. Binnie Valentino
Bill Howard vs. Scott McGhee
The Magic Dragon vs. Terry Gibbs
Dick Slater vs. Jay Youngblood
Wahoo McDaniel & Roddy Piper vs. NWA Tag Team Champions Jack & Jerry Brisco

JCP @ Charlotte, NC - Coliseum - November 17, 1983
Brett Hart defeated Golden Boy Grey
Kelly Kiniski defeated Scott McGhee
Bob Orton Jr. defeated Johnny Weaver
The Assassins defeated Keith Larsen & Rick McCord
Jimmy Valiant defeated Mid-Atlantic TV Champion the Great Kabuki after the 15-minute mark
NWA US Champion Greg Valentine defeated Mark Youngblood (sub. for Roddy Piper)
Ricky Steamboat & Jay Youngblood defeated NWA Tag Team Champions Jack & Jerry Brisco in a non-title No DQ match

JCP @ Charleston, SC - County Hall - November 18, 1983
Brickhouse Brown defeated Golden Boy Grey
Angelo Mosca defeated Gene Anderson
Kevin Sullivan & Mark Lewin defeated Johnny Weaver & Rick McGraw
NWA US Champion Greg Valentine defeated Ricky Steamboat
Ric Flair defeated Bob Orton Jr. in a steel cage match

JCP @ Colonial Heights, VA - High School Gym - November 18, 1983
Sponsored by the Colonial Heights Jaycees
Magic Dragon vs. Scott McGhee
The Ninja vs. Terry Gibbs
Bill Howard vs. Vinnie Valentino
Dick Slater vs. Jay Youngblood
Roddy Piper & Wahoo McDaniel vs. NWA Tag Team Champions Jack & Jerry Brisco

CWF @ Daytona Beach, FL - Spruce Creek High School - November 18, 1983
Southern Champion Mike Rotundo vs. Ron Bass
NWA World Champion Harley Race vs. Barry Windham
Also included 3 other matches

MID ATLANTIC CHAMPIONSHIP WRESTLING

MID ATLANTIC CHAMPIONSHIP WRESTLING
HENDERSONVILLE JAYCEE'S SPON.
SATURDAY, NOVEMBER 19th. 8:15 P.M.
WEST HENDERSON HIGH SCHOOL GYM

SIX MAN TAG TEAM MATCH

MID ATLANTIC CHAMPION
RUFUS R. JONES
AND
CHARLIE BROWN
AND
RICKY STEAMBOAT

VS

ASSASSIN #1
AND
ASSASSIN #2
AND
#1 PAUL JONES

ADVISED BY GARY HART
MANIAC MARK LEWIN   VS   MARK YOUNGBLOOD

ADVISED BY GARY HART
KEVIN SULLIVAN   VS   KEITH LARSON

TOM LINTZ   VS   BRETT HART

GOLDEN BOY GRAY   VS   JOHN BENELLO

TICKETS ON SALE AT THESE LOCATIONS:
WHITLEY DRUGS   RINGSIDE $6.00
CLINTS AMOCO   ADULT GEN. ADMISSION $5.00
THE OPTICAL SHOP   CHILDREN UNDER 10 YRS. $3.00
N W A SUBJECT TO CHANGE

MID ATLANTIC CHAMPIONSHIP WRESTLING

JCP @ Hendersonville, NC - West Henderson High School - November 19, 1983
Jerry Grey vs. John Bonello
Tom Lentz vs. Brett Hart
Kevin Sullivan vs. Keith Larson
Mark Lewin vs. Mark Youngblood
Ricky Steamboat, Charlie Brown, & Mid-Atlantic Heavyweight Champion Rufus R. Jones vs. Paul Jones & the Assassins

JCP @ Front Royal, VA - November 19, 1983
Vinnie Valentino defeated Bill Howard
Scott McGhee defeated Mark Fleming
Terry Gibbs defeated Magic Dragon
Ric Flair & Wahoo McDaniel defeated Bob Orton Jr. & Dick Slater at the 15-minute mark

JCP @ Charlotte, NC - Coliseum - November 19, 1983
Brett Hart defeated Jerry Gray
Kelly Kiniski defeated Scott McGhee
Bob Orton Jr. defeated Johnny Weaver
The Assassins defeated Keith Larson & Rick McCord
Charlie Brown defeated Mid-Atlantic TV Champion the Great Kabuki
NWA US Champion Greg Valentine defeated Mark Youngblood (sub. for Roddy Piper)
Ricky Steamboat & Jay Youngblood defeated NWA Tag Team Champions Jack Brisco & Jerry Brisco in a No DQ match

CWF @ St. Petersburg, FL - Bayfront Center - November 19, 1983
Hector Guerrero & Sam Houston defeated Dr. X & Mr. Olympia
Big Daddy defeated JJ Dillon
The One Man Gang defeated Mike Davis
Barry Windham & Mike Rotundo defeated Elijah Akeem & Kareem Muhammad
NWA World Champion Harley Race defeated Ron Bass via disqualification at 19:10
Brass Knuckles Champion Blackjack Mulligan defeated Abdullah the Butcher via disqualification in a steel cage match

Kitchener, Ontario - November 20, 1983
Nick DeCarlo defeated Kurt Von Hess
Kelly Kiniski defeated Tim Gerrard
Billy Red Lyons fought the Destroyer to a draw
Ric Flair & Angelo Mosca defeated Bob Orton Jr. & Dick Slater via disqualification
Leo Burke defeated Johnny Weaver
Jimmy Valiant defeated Mid-Atlantic TV Champion the Great Kabuki

JCP @ Greenville, SC - Memorial Auditorium - November 21, 1983
Tommy Rich defeated the Magic Dragon
The Assassins defeated Jay Youngblood & Mid-Atlantic Heavyweight Champion Rufus R. Jones
NWA US Champion Greg Valentine defeated Ricky Steamboat
Dick Slater defeated Roddy Piper

Kingston, Ontario - November 21, 1983
Kelly Kiniski defeated Tim Gerrard
Nick DeCarlo defeated Kurt Von Hess
The Destroyer fought Billy Red Lyons to a draw
Johnny Weaver defeated Leo Burke via disqualification

Jimmy Valiant defeated Mid-Atlantic TV Champion the Great Kabuki

JCP @ Goldsboro, NC - November 22, 1983
John Bonello defeated Magic Dragon
Bill Howard defeated Vinnie Valentino
Kelly Kiniski defeated Terry Gibbs
Mid-Atlantic Heavyweight Champion Rufus R. Jones & Mark Youngblood defeated Paul Jones & the Assassin
Charlie Brown & Angelo Mosca defeated Kevin Sullivan & Mark Lewin

JCP @ Winston-Salem, NC - Memorial Coliseum - November 23, 1983
TV taping:
Worldwide - 11/26/83 - featured David Crockett on commentary; included a Jimmy Valiant music video set to the tune of Manhattan Transfer's "Boy from New York City;" included Tony Schiavone conducting an interview with Wahoo McDaniel regarding Paul Jones & the Assassins, during which McDaniel said Jimmy Valiant would be his partner against Jones' men; Valiant then appeared with the American flag, said he was glad to be back in Mid Atlantic, and then kissed Schiavone; featured an ad for the Starrcade 83 t-shirt and photo album; included Crockett conducting an interview with Paul Jones & the Assassins regarding the challenge of McDaniel & Valiant, during which Jones mentioned his men's recent attack on Dory Funk Jr.; featured footage from a recent bout between Funk and Assassin #1 in which Funk took down Jones before Assassin #2 came out, double teamed Funk, and let Jones land several swipes to Funk; included Crockett conducting an interview with Tommy Rich, regarding his return to Mid Atlantic, Angelo Mosca, regarding the attack Angelo Mosca Jr. sustained at the hands of Kevin Sullivan & Mark Lewin, and Mid-Atlantic Heavyweight Champion Rufus R. Jones, regarding the challenge of Dick Slater, and McDaniel, regarding the return of Rich to the territory; during Wahoo's comments, a few of his words were bleeped out; featured Gordon Solie, Jim Crockett, Bob Caudle, and Barbara Clary discussing Starrcade 83; highlights from the event then aired to an instrumental version of Frank Stallone's "Far From Over":
Tommy Rich pinned Jerry Gray with the Thesz Press at 2:46
Mid-Atlantic Heavyweight Champion Rufus R. Jones pinned Bill Howard at 3:23 with a headbutt
Dick Slater pinned John Bonello with a gordbuster at 2:59
Kevin Sullivan & Mark Lewin (w/ Gary Hart) defeated Vinnie Valentino & Rick McCord at 5:04 when Valentino submitted to an arm bar from Lewin
Bob Orton Jr. pinned Brett Hart (Barry Horowitz) with the superplex at 4:38
Wahoo McDaniel pinned Tom Lintz with a chop and elbow drop at 4:22

Starrcade 83 - Greensboro, NC - Coliseum - November 24, 1983 (15,447; announced at over 16,000)
Shown on closed circuit   featured Gordon Solie & Bob Caudle on commentary; following the opening bout, Solie noted Ric Flair was a 2-time former world champion; featured Tony Schiavone backstage with Ric Flair, Roddy Piper, Ricky Steamboat, Jay Youngblood, and Charlie Brown, with Schiavone stating he would be conducting backstage interviews throughout the night; included Barbara Clarey conducting an interview with the Estes family from Gaffney, SC who all agreed Flair would win the main event; featured

71

Schiavone conducting a backstage interview with NWA World Champion Harley Race, alongside NWA US Champion Greg Valentine and NWA Tag Team Champion Jerry Brisco, in which Race said he had been informed of where Flair was hurting and he would target those places; included Schiavone conducting a backstage interview with Angelo Mosca - alongside a bloody Scott McGhee - regarding the injury he sustained earlier in the night and whether he would still be able to referee the tag team title match; featured Clarey conducting an interview with Anne and Jean from Raleigh regarding their favorite wrestlers and who they thought would win the main event; included Schiavone conducting a backstage interview with Flair, Steamboat & Youngblood regarding their respective title matches; featured Clarey conducting an interview in the crowd with Dusty Rhodes, during which the audio repeatedly cut in and out, regarding his challenge to the winner of the Flair / Race match; included Caudle & Solie speaking with radio personality Duke Walker of Durham, NC about Flair's quest for the title; featured Schiavone conducting a backstage interview with Race, Bob Orton Jr., and Dick Slater regarding Flair's return from injury; included Clarey conducting a backstage interview with Rhodes in which he again challenged the winner of the Flair / Race match; featured Schiavone conducting a backstage interview with Flair and Wahoo McDaniel regarding the comments from Race, Orton, and Slater; included Clarey conducting an interview in the crowd with Don Kernodle in which he wished the best of luck to both teams in the tag team title match and said he hoped to see Flair take the title; featured Schiavone conducting a backstage interview with Charlie Brown regarding his title win, Piper regarding his win over Valentine, and Steamboat & Youngblood regarding their title win; featured Clarey conducting an interview with Rhodes, alongside several women who all picked Flair to win the main event; included James "Tiny" Weeks performing the National Anthem immediately before the main event; featured Schiavone conducting a backstage interview with a bloody Flair regarding his title win, during which he was congratulated by Steamboat, Youngblood, Charlie Brown, and others and had champagne poured on him; Rhodes then appeared, shook Flair's hand, and said he would soon see Rhodes in the ring; included Clarey conducting a backstage interview with Race regarding his title loss, during which Race said he would hound Flair until he got the belt back; featured Schiavone conducting a backstage interview with Flair, Steamboat & Youngblood regarding their respective title wins:

The Assassins (w/ Paul Jones) defeated Mid Atlantic Heavyweight Champion Rufus R. Jones & Bugsy McGraw at 8:12 when McGraw was pinned with a roll up after fighting off the other Assassin

Kevin Sullivan & Mark Lewin (w/ Gary Hart) defeated Scott McGhee & Johnny Weaver at 6:42 when Lewin pinned Weaver after hitting a kneedrop off the top onto Weaver's arm, as Sullivan held the arm, behind the referee's back; after the contest, McGhee fought off Sullivan & Lewin and dropkicked Hart into the corner; moments later, Hart pulled a foreign object out of his pant leg, with Sullivan & Lewin then assaulting McGhee with the weapon, busting him open; Angelo Mosca attempted to make the save but was beaten down as well;

moments later, Mosca cleared the ring and carried McGhee backstage

Abdullah the Butcher pinned Carlos Colon at 4:29 after Hugo Savinovich came out after the referee had been knocked down and hit Colon with a foreign object as Abdullah was caught in a figure-4

Dick Slater & Bob Orton Jr. defeated Wahoo McDaniel & Mark Youngblood at 14:46 when Orton pinned Youngblood with the superplex; prior to the bout, ring announcer Tom Miller introduced Dusty Rhodes who was in attendance; after the bout, McDaniel attempted to clear the ring but Slater & Orton double teamed McDaniel's arm on the ring apron

Charlie Brown pinned Mid-Atlantic TV Champion the Great Kabuki (w/ Gary Hart) in a No DQ, no time limit match to win the title at 10:35 with an elbow drop after the champion missed a charge in the corner; stipulations stated that both Brown's mask and the title were only at stake for the first 15 minutes of the match

Ricky Steamboat & Jay Youngblood defeated NWA Tag Team Champions Jack & Jerry Brisco to win the titles at 12:59 when Youngblood pinned Jerry after Steamboat press slammed his partner onto Brisco; Angelo Mosca was the guest referee for the bout; after the bout, the Briscos threw Youngblood to the floor and assaulted Steamboat and Mosca until the new champions eventually cleared the ring (*The Best of Starrcade: 1983-1987, The Most Powerful Families of Wrestling, Starrcade: The Essential Collection, Ricky Steamboat: The Life of the Dragon*)

Roddy Piper defeated NWA US Champion Greg Valentine in a non-title dog collar match at 16:08 by pulling Valentine off the top with the chain, repeatedly punching him, and tying him up to score the win; during the match, Gordon Solie repeatedly said the title was on the line, which was incorrect; after the bout, Valentine attacked Piper and choked him with the chain before leaving the ring (*The Best of Starrcade: 1983-1987, Greatest Wrestling Stars of the 80s, Born to Controversy: The Roddy Piper Story*)

Ric Flair pinned NWA World Champion Harley Race in a steel cage match to win the title at 23:49 with a flying bodypress off the top; Gene Kiniski was the special referee for the match; after the contest, Flair was congratulated in the ring by a number of individuals including Ricky Steamboat, Angelo Mosca, Jay Youngblood, Johnny Weaver, Mid-Atlantic Heavyweight Champion Rufus R. Jones, and Flair's wife Beth; moments thereafter, Beth entered the ring to hug Flair before he took a microphone and thanked all on hand for their support (voted Match of the Year by the Wrestling Observer Newsletter) (*The Best of Starrcade: 1983-1987, The Ultimate Ric Flair Collection, Starrcade: The Essential Collection*)

Central States @ St. Louis, MO - November 25, 1983

Paul Kelly & Velvet McIntyre defeated Scott Farris & Peggy Lee

666 defeated Ron Ritchie

Tiger Mask (sub. for Buck Robley) defeated Angelo Mosca Jr.

Paul Orndorff defeated Steve O (sub. for Rick Martel)

Iceman Parsons defeated Blackjack Lanza

Austin Idol defeated Denny Brown

AWA Tag Team Champions Ken Patera & Jerry Blackwell defeated Dick the Bruiser & Bob Brown
NWA World Champion Ric Flair defeated David Von Erich in a Best 2 out of 3 falls match

GCW @ Atlanta, GA - WTBS Studios - November 26, 1983
NWA World Champion Ric Flair defeated Pat Rose

WCCW @ San Antonio, TX - November 27, 1983
Kevin Von Erich defeated NWA World Champion Ric Flair in a non-title match

WCCW @ Ft. Worth, TX - November 28, 1983
The Missing Link defeated Mike Reed
The Super Destroyer defeated WCCW TV Champion Johnny Mantell to win the title
Buddy Roberts fought Jose Lothario to a draw
Kerry Von Erich & Chris Adams defeated Terry Gordy & Jimmy Garvin via disqualification
David Von Erich defeated NWA World Champion Ric Flair in a non-title match at 23:47

Houston, TX - November 29, 1983
Mr. Wrestling II vs. NWA World Champion Ric Flair

JCP @ Spartanburg, SC - Memorial Auditorium - November 30, 1983
TV taping:
Mid-Atlantic TV Champion Charlie Brown defeated Magic Dragon
Kevin Sullivan & Mark Lewin defeated Rick McCord & John Bonello
NWA Tag Team Champions Ricky Steamboat & Jay Youngblood defeated Gary Royal & Kelly Kiniski
NWA US Champion Greg Valentine defeated Keith Larsen
Mark Youngblood defeated Bill Howard
Dick Slater defeated Vinnie Valentino
Roddy Piper defeated Dick Slater
NWA Tag Team Champions Ricky Steamboat & Jay Youngblood defeated NWA US Champion Greg Valentine & Bob Orton Jr.
Worldwide - 12/3/83:
NWA Tag Team Champions Ricky Steamobat & Jay Youngblood defeated Bill Howard & Jerry Gray
Dick Slater defeated Keith Larsen
Mid-Atlantic TV Champion Charlie Brown defeated Ben Alexander
The Assassins defeated John Bonello & Gene Ligon
Mark Youngblood defeated Magic Dragon
Bob Orton Jr. defeated Vinnie Valentino

JCP @ Sumter, SC - Exhibition Center - December 1, 1983
Kelly Kiniski defeated Rick McCord
Brickhouse Brown defeated Magic Dragon
Bugsy McGraw defeated Terry Gibbs

Bob Orton Jr. defeated Johnny Weaver
NWA US Champion Greg Valentine defeated NWA Tag Team Champion Ricky Steamboat
Wahoo McDaniel defeated Dick Slater

JCP @ Chester, SC - December 1, 1983
Vinnie Valentino vs. Bill Howard
John Bonello vs. Golden Boy Grey
Angelo Mosca vs. Gene Anderson
Mark Youngblood vs. Mark Lewin
Jay Youngblood vs. Mid-Atlantic TV Champion the Great Kabuki
Jimmy Valiant & Mid-Atlantic Heavyweight Champion Rufus R. Jones vs. the Assassins

JCP @ Charleston, SC - County Hall - December 2, 1983
Brett Hart vs. Golden Boy Gray
Angelo Mosca vs. Kelly Kiniski
Mark Youngblood & Bugsy McGraw vs. Mark Lewin & Kevin Sullivan
Wahoo McDaniel vs. the Great Kabuki
NWA Tag Team Champions Ricky Steamboat & Jay Youngblood vs. Dick Slater & Bob Orton Jr.

JCP @ Lynchburg, VA - Armory - December 2, 1983
Roddy Piper & Jimmy Valiant vs. the Assassins
Mid-Atlantic Heavyweight Champion Rufus R. Jones vs. NWA
US Champion Greg Valentine

WCCW @ Dallas, TX - December 2, 1983
Super Destroyer #1 defeated Jose Lothario
Chris Adams fought Super Destroyer #2 to a draw
The Missing Link defeated Johnny Mantell
Cocoa Samoa defeated Boris Zhukov
David, Kevin, & Kerry Von Erich defeated NWA World
Champion Ric Flair, Terry Gordy, & Buddy Roberts

GCW @ Atlanta, GA - WTBS Studios - December 3, 1983
NWA World Champion Ric Flair defeated Mike Starbuck

Cleveland, OH - December 3, 1983
Pez Whatley fought NWA World Champion Ric Flair to a 60-
minute time-limit draw

JCP @ Newton, NC - December 3, 1983
Rick McCord defeated Gary Royal
Brett Hart defeated Jerry Grey
Kelly Kiniski defeated Vinnie Valentino
Johnny Weaver defeated Gene Anderson
Mark Youngblood defeated Great Kabuki
Wahoo McDaniel & Roddy Piper defeated NWA US Champion
Greg Valentine & Bob Orton Jr.

JCP @ Hampton, VA - Coliseum - December 3, 1983
The Assassins defeated Jimmy Valiant & Brickhouse Brown
Keith Larsen defeated Bill Howard
John Bonello defeated Steve Muslin
Terry Gibbs defeated Mark Fleming
Angelo Mosca defeated Don Kernodle
Dick Slater defeated Mid-Atlantic Heavyweight Champion
Rufus R. Jones to win the title
NWA Tag Team Champions Ricky Steamboat & Jay
Youngblood defeated Jack Brisco & Jerry Brisco in a steel
cage match

GCW @ Columbus, GA - December 4, 1983 (matinee)
Pez Whatley fought NWA World Champion Ric Flair to a 60-
minute time-limit draw

**JCP @ Roanoke, VA - Civic Center - December 4, 1983
(matinee)**
John Bonello defeated Bill Howard
Terry Gibbs defeated Rick McCord
Jerry Grey defeated Brickhouse Brown
Gene Anderson defeated Vinnie Valentino
The Assassins defeated Jimmy Valiant & Wahoo McDaniel
NWA Tag Team Champions Ricky Steamboat & Jay
Youngblood defeated Jack Brisco & Jerry Brisco in a cage
match

GCW @ Atlanta, GA - Omni - December 4, 1983 (1,950)
Bob Roop vs. Mike Jackson
Johnny Rich vs. Chick Donovan
Cy Jernigan vs. King Kong Bundy
National TV Champion Jake Roberts (w/ Paul Ellering)
defeated Pez Whatley
Buzz Sawyer (mystery partner) & Brett Sawyer defeated
National Tag Team Champions the Road Warriors (w/ Paul
Ellering) to win the titles
Ted DiBiase fought Buzz Sawyer to a no contest
NWA World Champion Ric Flair defeated Tommy Rich

Toronto, Ontario - Maple Leaf Gardens - December 4, 1983
Rudy Kay defeated Nick DeCarlo
Terry Kay fought Billy Red Lyons to a draw
The Destroyer defeated Joe Marcus
Johnny Weaver defeated Kelly Kiniski
Leo Burke defeated Keith Larsen
Buddy Hart (Bret Hart) defeated the Great Kabuki
Angelo Mosca & Blackjack Mulligan defeated Sgt. Slaughter &
Don Kernodle
Roddy Piper defeated Greg Valentine in a dog collar match

**GCW @ Augusta, GA - Richmond County Civic Center -
December 5, 1983**
Ron Garvin vs. King Kong Bundy
National TV Champion Jake Roberts (w/ Paul Ellering) vs. Pez
Whatley
Buzz & Brett Sawyer vs. the Road Warriors (w/ Paul Ellering)
NWA World Champion Ric Flair defeated Tommy Rich

**JCP @ Greenville, SC - Memorial Auditorium - December 5,
1983**
Terry Gibbs defeated Gary Royal
Kelly Kiniski defeated John Bonello
Bob Orton Jr. defeated Johnny Weaver
The Assassins defeated Jimmy Valiant & Wahoo McDaniel
Angelo Mosca defeated Don Kernodle via disqualification

**JCP @ Fayetteville, NC - Cumberland County Civic Center
- December 5, 1983**
Brickhouse Brown defeated Jerry Grey
Vinnie Valentino defeated Bill Howard
Mark Youngblood defeated Gene Anderson
Rufus R. Jones defeated Mid-Atlantic Heavyweight Champion
Dick Slater via disqualification
Roddy Piper defeated NWA US Champion Greg Valentine
NWA Tag Team Champions Ricky Steamboat & Jay
Youngblood defeated Jack Brisco & Jerry Brisco

JCP @ Raleigh, NC - Dorton Arena - December 6, 1983
John Bonello defeated Jerry Grey
Keith Larsen defeated Brett Hart
Terry Gibbs defeated Rick McCord
NWA US Champion Greg Valentine & Bob Orton Jr. defeated

NWA Tag Team Champions Ricky Steamboat & Jay Youngblood
The Assassins defeated Jimmy Valiant & Mark Youngblood

GCW @ Macon, GA - Coliseum - December 6, 1983
Johnny Rich defeated Chick Donovan
Jake Roberts (w/ Paul Ellering) defeated National TV Champion Ron Garvin to win the title; in actuality, Roberts won the title 11/6/83 in Atlanta
Ted DiBiase defeated Tommy Rich
Buzz & Brett Sawyer fought the Road Warriors (w/ Paul Ellering) to a no contest
NWA World Champion Ric Flair defeated Pez Whatley

JCP @ Columbia, SC - Township Auditorium - December 6, 1983
Vinnie Valentino defeated Bill Howard
Brickhouse Brown defeated Kelly Kiniski
Johnny Weaver defeated Gene Anderson
Roddy Piper defeated Mid-Atlantic Heavyweight Champion Dick Slater
Angelo Mosca & Rufus R. Jones defeated Gary Hart & Don Kernodle

JCP @ Spartanburg, SC - Memorial Auditorium - December 7, 1983
Roddy Piper defeated Mid-Atlantic Heavyweight Champion Dick Slater
NWA Tag Team Champions Ricky Steamboat & Jay Youngblood defeated NWA US Champion Greg Valentine & Bob Orton Jr.
Worldwide - 12/10/83:
Mid-Atlantic TV Champion Charlie Brown & Rufus R. Jones defeated Ben Alexander & Kelly Kiniski
The Great Kabuki defeated Rick McCord
Tommy Rich & Mark Youngblood defeated Jerry Gray & Bill Howard when Rich pinned Grey with the Thesz Press
The Assassins defeated Vinnie Valentino & Keith Larsen
Ricky Steamobat & Jay Youngblood defeated Terry Gibbs & Magic Dragon
The Road Warriors vs. Rick McCord & Steve Mulim (Steve Travis)

JCP @ Norfolk, VA - Scope - December 8, 1983
Mark Fleming defeated Kelly Kiniski
Brett Hart defeated Jerry Grey
Johnny Weaver defeated Gene Anderson
Angelo Mosca defeated Don Kernodle
The Assassins defeated Jimmy Valiant & Rufus R. Jones
Mid-Atlantic Heavyweight Champion Dick Slater & Bob Orton, Jr. defeated NWA Tag Team Champions Ricky Steamboat & Jay Youngblood
Roddy Piper defeated NWA US Champion Greg Valentine

JCP @ Charleston, SC - County Hall - December 9, 1983
John Bonello defeated Ben Alexander
Brickhouse Brown defeated Gary Royal
Keith Larsen defeated Vinnie Valentino
Mark Youngblood & Abe Jacobs defeated Terry Gibbs & Bill Howard
Roddy Piper defeated NWA US Champion Greg Valentine in a non-title dog collar match

JCP @ Richmond, VA - Coliseum - December 9, 1983
Jerry Grey defeated Mark Fleming
Kelly Kiniski defeated Brett Hart
Gene Anderson defeated Ric McCord
Mid-Atlantic Heavyweight Champion Dick Slater defeated Johnny Weaver
The Assassins defeated Jimmy Valiant & Jay Youngblood
Angelo Mosca & NWA Tag Team Champions Ricky Steamboat defeated Don Kernodle & Gary Hart via disqualification

Nagoya, Japan - December 10, 1983
Jumbo Tsuruta fought NWA World Champion Ric Flair to a 60-minute time-limit draw

Yokosuka, Japan - December 11, 1983
Giant Baba, the Great Kabuki, & Dory Funk Jr. defeated NWA World Champion Ric Flair, Barry Windham, & Ron Fuller

Tokyo, Japan - December 12, 1983
The Great Kabuki defeated NWA World Champion Ric Flair via disqualification at 24:24

JCP @ Asheville, NC - Civic Center - December 12, 1983
Rick McCord defeated Golden Boy Grey
Gene Anderson defeated John Bonello
Bob Orton Jr. defeated Johnny Weaver
Mid-Atlantic Heavyweight Champion Dick Slater defeated Rufus R. Jones
Jimmy Valiant & Mark Youngblood defeated the Assassins
Angelo Mosca defeated Don Kernodle via disqualification
NWA Tag Team Champions Ricky Steamboat & Jay Youngblood defeated Jack & Jerry Brisco

JCP @ Shelby, NC - Rec Center - December 13, 1983
TV taping:
Rufus R. Jones & Mark Youngblood defeated Bill Howard & Tony Russo
Don Kernodle defeated Rick McCord
The Assassins defeated Keith Larson & John Bonello
Mid-Atlantic Heavyweight Champion Dick Slater defeated Mark Fleming
NWA Tag Team Champions Ricky Steamboat & Jay Youngblood defeated Hans Schroeder & Gary Royal
Roddy Piper vs. NWA US Champion Greg Valentine; after the bout, Mid-Atlantic Heavyweight Champion Dick Slater attacked Piper and threw him to the floor; moments later, Slater and Bob Orton Jr. double teamed and bloodied Valentine in the ring
Mid-Atlantic Heavyweight Champion Dick Slater pinned NWA US Champion Greg Valentine to win the title in a No DQ match with a knee to the back and back suplex into a bridge after Valentine began fighting Bob Orton Jr., who appeared during the final moments, on the ring apron
Worldwide - 12/24/83:
NWA Tag Team Champions Ricky Steamboat & Jay Youngblood defeated Kelly Kiniski & Bill Howard

Don Kernodle defeated Mark Fleming
Bob Orton Jr. defeated Vinnie Valentino
Tommy Rich defeated Jerry Gray
Angelo Mosca defeated Ben Alexander
Rufus R. Jones & Mark Youngblood defeated Gary Royal & Terry Gibbs

JCP @ Charlotte, NC - Coliseum - December 14, 1983
TV taping:
Featured NWA US Champion Dick Slater giving up his Mid-Atlantic Heavyweight Title and giving it to Ivan Koloff
Don Kernodle defeated Pete Martin
Tommy Rich defeated Magic Dragon
Mid-Atlantic Heavyweight Champion Ivan Koloff defeated Brett Hart
The Road Warriors defeated Rick McCord & Keith Larson
NWA Tag Team Champions Ricky Steamboat & Jay Youngblood defeated Ben Alexander & Kelly Kiniski
NWA Tag Team Champions Ricky Steamboat & Jay Youngblood defeated Terry Gibbs & Gary Royal
The Road Warriors defeated Rick McCord & Keith Larson
Mid-Atlantic Heavyweight Champion Ivan Koloff defeated Gene Ligon
Dick Slater & Bob Orton Jr. defeated John Bonello & Brickhouse Brown
Angelo Mosca & Rufus R. Jones defeated Bill Howard & Kelly Kiniski

WCCW @ Dallas, TX - December 15, 1983
Kerry Von Erich vs. NWA World Champion Ric Flair

Continental @ Birmingham, AL - December 16, 1983
NWA World Champion Ric Flair defeated Bob Armstrong

Worldwide - 12/17/83:
Don Kernodle vs. an unknown
Tommy Rich vs. Magic Dragon
Mid-Atlantic Heavyweight Champion Ivan Koloff vs. Gene Ligon
Bob Orton Jr. & Dick Slater vs. Brickhouse Brown & John Bonello
Angelo Mosca & Rufus R. Jones vs. Kelly Kiniski & Bill Howard

WWC @ Bayamon, Pueto Rico - December 18, 1983
Carlos Colon defeated NWA World Champion Ric Flair in a No DQ steel cage match

WCCW @ San Antonio, TX - December 24, 1983
Kevin Von Erich defeated NWA World Champion Ric Flair

JCP @ Greenville, SC - December 25, 1983
Johnny Weaver won a battle royal
Wahoo McDaniel, Jimmy Valiant, & Rufus R. Jones defeated Paul Jones & the Assassins

Greg Valentine defeated Roddy Piper
NWA Tag Team Champions Ricky Steamboat & Jay Youngblood defeated NWA US Champion Dick Slater & Bob Orton Jr.

JCP @ Charlotte, NC - Coliseum - December 25, 1983
John Bonello defeated Tony Russo
Vinnie Valentino defeated Gene Anderson
Wahoo McDaniel defeated Barry Orton
Bob Orton Jr. defeated Mark Youngblood
Angelo Mosca defeated Don Kernodle
The Assassins defeated Dory Funk Jr. & Rufus R. Jones via disqualification
Jimmy Valiant defeated the Great Kabuki
Roddy Piper defeated Greg Valentine in a dog collar match
NWA Tag Team Champions Ricky Steamboat & Jay Youngblood defeated Jack & Jerry Brisco in a steel cage match

WCCW Star Wars - Dallas, TX - Reunion Arena - December 25, 1983 (19,675)
The Missing Link pinned Johnny Mantell at 6:05
Iceman King Parsons & Brian Adidas defeated American Tag Team Champions the Super Destroyers at 15:35 to win the titles
Kerry Von Erich defeated Kamala via disqualification at 5:12
Mike Reed pinned the Mongol at 13:49
David Von Erich defeated NWA World Champion Ric Flair via disqualification at 23:48 when Flair took one of the microphones from the commentary table and struck the challenger in the face with it as he was caught in the claw; after the bout, Kerry and Kevin Von Erich came out to tend to the bloody David
Jose Lothario pinned Black Gordman at 8:13
Jimmy Garvin pinned American Heavyweight Champion Chris Adams at 14:58 to win the title
Kevin & Mike Von Erich defeated Terry Gordy & Buddy Roberts in a No DQ loser leaves town match at 12:10 when Kevin pinned Gordy; stipulations stated the loser would have to leave the territory for 1 year

JCP @ Greensboro, NC - Coliseum - December 26, 1983
Keith Larsen defeated Golden Boy Grey
Gene Anderson defeated John Bonello
The Assassins defeated Dory Funk Jr. & Johnny Weaver
Wahoo McDaniel & Angelo Mosca defeated Bob Orton Jr. & Don Kernodle
NWA US Champion Dick Slater defeated Rufus R. Jones
Jimmy Valiant defeated the Great Kabuki
Roddy Piper defeated Greg Valentine in a dog collar match
NWA Tag Team Champions Ricky Steamboat & Jay Youngblood defeated Jack & Jerry Brisco in a steel cage match

Toronto, Ontario - Maple Leaf Gardens - December 26, 1983
Terry Kay defeated Nick DeCarlo
Rudy Kay defeated Joe Marcus
Billy Red Lyons defeated the Destroyer via disqualification
Leo Burke defeated Bob Marcus
Little Beaver defeated Pancho Boy
Women's Champion the Fabulous Moolah defeated Leilani Kai
Jimmy Valiant & Johnny Weaver defeated Baron Von Raschke & Gary Hart
Roddy Piper & Dory Funk Jr. defeated the Assassins

JCP @ Raleigh, NC - Dorton Arena - December 27, 1983
Rick McCord defeated Tony Russo
Vinnie Valentino defeated Hans Schroeder
The Assassins defeated Rufus R. Jones & Dory Funk Jr.
Wahoo McDaniel & Angelo Mosca defeated Don Kernodle & Gary Hart
Mid-Atlantic TV Champion Charlie Brown defeated the Great Kabuki via forfeit
NWA US Champion Dick Slater defeated Mark Youngblood

JCP @ Columbia, SC - Township Auditorium - December 27, 1983
John Bonello defeated Gary Royal
Brickhouse Brown defeated Jerry Grey
Gene Anderson defeated Barry Hart
Roddy Piper defeated Greg Valentine in a dog collar match
Johnny Weaver (sub. for NWA Tag Team Champion Jay Youngblood) & NWA Tag Team Champion Ricky Steamboat defeated Jack & Jerry Brisco in a steel cage match

JCP @ Charlotte, NC - Coliseum - December 28, 1983
TV taping:
Rufus R. Jones defeated Jerry Grey
Jimmy Valiant defeated Don Herbert
Bob Orton Jr. defeated Brett Hart
Mid-Atlantic Heavyweight Champion Ivan Koloff defeated Vinnie Valentino
The Road Warriors defeated Rick McCord & Steve Muslin
Mark Youngblood & Dory Funk Jr. defeated Bill Howard & Terry Gibbs
Worldwide - 12/31/83:
Jay Youngblood & Mark Youngblood defeated Hans Schroeder & Russo
Angelo Mosca defeated Mid-Atlantic Heavyweight Champion Ivan Koloff via disqualification
The Road Warriors defeated Keith Larsen & Gene Ligon
NWA US Champion Dick Slater defeated Mark Fleming
Dory Funk Jr. defeated Bill Howard

JCP @ Lynchburg, VA - December 29, 1983
NWA Tag Team Champions Ricky Steamboat & Jay Youngblood vs. Jack & Jerry Brisco (lumberjack match)
Roddy Piper vs. Greg Valentine (dog collar match)

Central States @ Kansas City, MO - December 29, 1983
Bruiser Brody defeated NWA World Champion Ric Flair via disqualification

JCP @ Charleston, SC - County Hall - December 30, 1983
Brickhouse Brown & Keith Larsen defeated Gary Royal & Tony Russo
Brett Hart defeated Don Herbert
Glenn Lane defeated Golden Boy Gray
Barry Odum defeated John Bonello
Angelo Mosca defeated Don Kernodle

JCP @ Richmond, VA - Coliseum - December 30, 1983
Hans Schroeder defeated Barry Buckley
Johnny Weaver defeaetd Gene Anderson
Bob Orton Jr. defeated Mark Youngblood
The Assassins defeated Dory Funk Jr. & Rufus R. Jones
NWA US Champion Dick Slater defeated Wahoo McDaniel
Roddy Piper defeated Greg Valentine in a dog collar match
Jimmy Valiant (sub. for NWA Tag Team Champion Jay Youngblood) & NWA Tag Team Champion Ricky Steamboat defeated Jack & Jerry Brisco in a steel cage match

1984.

With the NWA World Title back around the waist of Carolina favorite Ric Flair, Jim Crockett Promotions and Dusty Rhodes saw the new year as an opportunity for new talent.

Ivan Koloff and Don Kernodle returned from stints in the World Wrestling Federation and quickly had gold around their waists. Dusty was on the road as a full-time member of the roster. Newcomers like Tully Blanchard and Nikita Koloff arrived and immediately made an impact. And fresh faces like Barry Windham, the Junkyard Dog, Adrian Street, and Buzz Sawyer saw brief runs.

But maybe most notable in 1984 was the group that formed in opposition of Vince McMahon's growing WWF. Crockett lost its hold in Toronto following the death of promoter Frank Tunney. Meanwhile, the WWF had taken the WTBS timeslot of Georgia Championship Wrestling and began running regular cards at the Omni in Atlanta. Add to that, the company was enjoying national exposure through the USA Network and MTV.

Crockett and the National Wrestling Alliance fought back by creating partnerships and sending its talent into traditional WWF venues, like the Meadowlands and the Baltimore Civic Center.

By the fall, the NWA and American Wrestling Association partnered to form Pro Wrestling USA – a showcase of nearly every big name in the country that wasn't under contract to McMahon. That meant joint shows and television tapings that featured names like Flair, Rhodes, Sgt. Slaughter, the Road Warriors, Bob Backlund, Superstar Billy Graham, Jerry Lawler, Tommy Rich, Carlos Colon, Tully Blanchard, Harley Race, and many more.

Pro Wrestling USA broadcasts included blatant verbal assaults on the WWF by the likes of Lawler, who accused the wrestlers "up north" of using steroids and relying on rock music. And Backlund was hailed as an uncrowned world champion who never "really" lost his title.

The year also saw an influx of talent from Championship Wrestling from Florida, where Rhodes previously served as booker. By the end of '84, such names as Scott Hall, Dan Spivey, Black Bart, Ron Bass, Brian Adidas, Scott McGhee, the Zimbabwe Express, and JJ Dillon were Crockett stars. And the collaboration with CWF even saw the Florida Heavyweight Title defended as part of that year's Starrcade.

By the end of the year, JCP was a far different promotion than when '84 began. Dusty was positioned as the top babyface in the Carolinas, with the likes of Jimmy Valiant, Dick Slater, Manny Fernandez, Ricky Steamboat, and a fresh-faced Magnum TA standing behind him. On the other side there was a heel Wahoo McDaniel, upstart Blanchard, Bass & Bart, and the uncle and nephew pairing of Ivan & Nikita Koloff. And Flair, the champ, could work on either side, depending on the need each night.

While "The War of '84" forced JCP to retaliate against the WWF, 1985 would see the company recruit even more young talent, find its own spot on cable TV, expand on its supercard concept, and carve its national niche.

1984

Continental @ Birmingham, AL - January 2, 1984
Ric McCord fought the Superstar to a draw
Boris Zhukov defeated Larry Hamilton
Ken Lucas defeated Rip Rogers via disqualification
Wayne Farris & Boris Zhukov defeated Brad & Scott Armstrong
Robert Fuller, Jacques Rougeau, & Ric McCord defeated Jerry Stubbs, Super Olympia, & the Superstar
NWA World Champion Ric Flair defeated Bob Armstrong in a No DQ match

JCP @ Greenville, SC - Memorial Auditorium - January 2, 1984
Bubba Smith defeated Tony Russo
Brickhouse Brown defeated Barry Orton
Mark Youngblood defeated Gene Anderson
Angelo Mosca Sr. & Jr. defeated Don Kernodle & Gary Hart
Roddy Piper defeated Bob Orton Jr.
Ricky Steamboat defeated Mid-Atlantic Heavyweight Champion Ivan Koloff

JCP @ Fayetteville, NC - Cumberland County Civic Center - January 2, 1984
John Bonello defeated Gary Royal
Johnny Weaver defeated Hans Schroeder
The Assassins & Paul Jones defeated Jimmy Valiant, Dory Funk Jr., & Rufus R. Jones
NWA US Champion Dick Slater defeated Wahoo McDaniel

JCP @ Raleigh, NC - Dorton Arena - January 3, 1984
Johnny Weaver & Bubba Smith defeated Hans Schroeder & Don Herbert
Rufus R. Jones defeated Gene Anderson
Ricky Steamboat defeated Mid Atlantic Heavyweight Champion Ivan Koloff in a non-title match
The Assassins defeated Jimmy Valiant & Dory Funk Jr.

JCP @ Columbia, SC - Township Auditorium - January 3, 1984
Sam Houston defeated Tony Russo
Barry Orton defeated Keith Larsen
Angelo Mosca Sr. & Jr. defeated Don Kernodle & Gary Hart
Bob Orton Jr. defeated Wahoo McDaniel via disqualification
NWA World Champion Ric Flair defeated NWA US Champion Dick Slater

JCP @ Spartanburg, SC - Memorial Auditorium - January 4, 1984
NWA World Champion Ric Flair defeated NWA US Champion Dick Slater via disqualification

Worldwide - 1/7/84:
Angelo Mosca Jr. defeated John Bonello
Wahoo McDaniel & Dory Funk Jr. defeated Hans Schroeder & Jerry Gray
Rufus R. Jones defeated Tony Russo
Mid-Atlantic Heavyweight Champion Ivan Koloff & Don Kernodle defeated Vinnie Valentino & Rick McCord

JCP @ Sumter, SC - Exhibition Center - January 5, 1984
Keith Larsen defeated Gary Royal
John Bonello defeated Ali Bey
Barry Orton defeated Sam Houston
Roddy Piper & Mark Youngblood defeated the Assassins
NWA World Champion Ric Flair defeated Bob Orton Jr.

JCP @ Charleston, SC - County Hall - January 6, 1984
Brickhouse Brown defeated Ali Bey
Mark Fleming defeated Hans Schroeder
Peggy Patterson & Penny Mitchell defeated Donna Christianello & Leilani Kai
Ernie Ladd & Don Kernodle defeated Angelo Mosca Sr. & Jr.

Central States @ St. Louis, MO - January 6, 1984 (10,752)
King Cobra & Tiger Mask defeated Roger Kirby & Scott Farris
Tully Blanchard (sub. for Buck Robley) defeated Buzz Tyler
Ron Ritchie defeated 666 (sub. for Buddy Landell)
Dory Funk Jr. fought Bob Orton Jr. to a draw
AWA Tag Team Champions Ken Patera & Jerry Blackwell defeated Dick the Bruiser & Gene Kiniski (sub. for Ted DiBiase)
Harley Race defeated Missouri Heavyweight Champion David Von Erich to win the title
NWA World Champion Ric Flair defeated Bruiser Brody via disqualification at the 24-minute mark

JCP @ Newberry, SC - January 6, 1984
Barry Hart defeated Ben Alexander
Bubba Smith defeated Gary Royal
Women's Champion the Fabulous Moolah defeated Princess Victoria
Mark Youngblood defeated Gene Anderson
Rufus R. Jones & Jimmy Valiant defeated the Assassins

JCP @ Jacksonville, NC - White Oak High School - January 7, 1984
Brickhouse Brown & Bubba Smith vs. Barry Orton & Hans Schroeder
Jeff Sword vs. Sam Houston
Ali Bey vs. Brett Hart
Rufus R. Jones vs. Don Kernodle
NWA US Champion Dick Slater vs. Greg Valentine
NWA World Champion Ric Flair vs. Dory Funk Jr.

JCP @ Charlotte, NC - Coliseum - January 8, 1984
NWA Tag Team Championship Tournament Opening Round:
The Assassins defeated Mark & Jay Youngblood
NWA Tag Team Championship Tournament Opening Round:
Dory Funk Jr. & Jimmy Valiant defeated Ivan Koloff & Ernie
Ladd
NWA Tag Team Championship Tournament Opening Round:
The Road Warriors fought Wahoo McDaniel & NWA National
Tag Team Champion Buzz Sawyer to a double disqualification
at around the 8-minute mark when McDaniel hit the referee
moments after the Road Warriors double teamed Sawyer in
their corner; after the contest, McDaniel & Sawyer cleared the
Road Warriors from the ring before McDaniel attempted to go
after the referee a second time
NWA Tag Team Championship Tournament Opening Round:
David & Kevin Von Erich defeated Rufus R. Jones & Bubba
Smith
NWA Tag Team Championship Tournament Quarter Finals:
The Assassins defeated Angelo Mosca Sr. & Jr.
NWA Tag Team Championship Tournament Quarter Finals:
Bob Orton Jr. & Don Kernodle defeated David & Kevin Von
Erich
NWA Tag Team Championship Tournament Semi Finals: Dory
Funk Jr. & Jimmy Valiant defeated the Assassins
Greg Valentine defeated NWA US Champion Dick Slater via
disqualification
NWA Tag Team Championship Tournament Finals: Bob Orton
Jr. & Don Kernodle (w/ Gary Hart) defeated Dory Funk Jr. &
Jimmy Valiant
Ricky Steamboat defeated Sgt. Slaughter (Steamboat's
retirement match)

Toronto, Ontario - Maple Leaf Gardens - January 8, 1984
The Destroyer fought Billy Red Lyons to a draw
Nick DeCarlo & Brickhouse Brown defeated Gary Royal & Tim
Gerard
Vic Rossetani defeated John Bonello
Rudy & Terry Kay defeated Johnny Weaver & Sam Houston
Roddy Piper defeated Kurt Von Hess (sub. for Buzz Sawyer) in
a dog collar match
Tito Santana defeated Leo Burke
Angelo Mosca Sr. defeated Sgt. Slaughter via count-out

JCP @ Asheville, NC - Civic Center - January 8, 1984
Bubba Smith defeated Ali Bey
Gene Anderson & Hans Schroeder defeated Brett Hart & Keith
Larson
Greg Valentine defeated Bob Orton Jr.
Wahoo McDaniel & Jimmy Valiant defeated the Assassins
NWA US Champion Dick Slater defeated Mark Youngblood
Ricky Steamboat defeated Dory Funk Jr.

**JCP @ Greenville, SC - Memorial Auditorium - January 9,
1984**
Brett Hart defeated Ali Bey
Angelo Mosca Jr. defeated Gene Anderson

Jimmy Valiant & Baron Von Raschke defeated the Assassins
Greg Valentine defeated NWA US Champion Dick Slater via
disqualification
NWA World Champion Ric Flair & Angelo Mosca defeated
NWA Tag Team Champions Bob Orton Jr. & Don Kernodle

JCP @ Raleigh, NC - Dorton Arena - January 10, 1984
Keith Larson defeated Bill White
Rufus R. Jones defeated Ali Bey
Angelo Mosca Sr. & Jr. defeated Ernie Ladd & Don Kernodle
Jimmy Valiant, Dory Funk Jr., & Baron Von Raschke defeated
Paul Jones & the Assassins

JCP @ Columbia, SC - January 10, 1984
Sam Houston & Bubba Smith defeated Barry Orton & Hans
Schroeder
Brett Hart defeated Gary Royal
Ivan Koloff defeated Mark Youngblood
Wahoo McDaniel defeated Bob Orton Jr.
Greg Valentine defeated NWA US Champion Dick Slater via
disqualification

**JCP @ Spartanburg, SC - Memorial Auditorium - January
11, 1984**
TV taping:
Worldwide - 1/14/84:
NWA US Champion Dick Slater defeated Keith Larson
Mid-Atlantic Heavyweight Champion Ivan Koloff defeated
Bubba Smith
Greg Valentine defeated John Bonello
The Assassins defeated Bubba Smith & Sam Houston
Angelo Mosca Jr. defeated Tony Russo
Wahoo McDaniel defeated Ben Alexander

JCP @ Norfolk, VA - Scope - January 12, 1984
Mid-Atlantic Heavyweight Champion Ivan Koloff defeated
Johnny Weaver
Gene Anderson defeated Sam Houston
John Bonello defeated Ali Bey
Johnny Weaver defeated Hans Schroeder
Dory Funk Jr. defeated NWA US Champion Dick Slater via
disqualification
Dusty Rhodes, Jimmy Valiant, & Rufus R. Jones defeated Paul
Jones & the Assassins

JCP @ Charleston, SC - County Hall - January 13, 1984
Baron Von Raschke, Angelo Mosca Sr. & Jr. vs. Ernie Ladd,
Don Kernodle, & Gary Hart

JCP @ North Wilkesboro, NC - January 14, 1984
Brickhouse Brown defeated John Bonello
Barry Orton defeated Sam Houston
Gene Anderson defeated John Bonello
Greg Valentine defeated Bob Orton Jr.

Jimmy Valiant, Dory Funk Jr., & Baron Von Raschke defeated the Assassins & Paul Jones

GCW @ Atlanta, GA - WTBS Studios - January 14, 1984
TV taping:
NWA World Champion Ric Flair defeated Zane Smith

CWF @ Orlando, FL - January 15, 1984
Black Bart defeated Anthony Charles
Mike Graham defeated Kendo Nagasaki via disqualification
Yellow Dog defeated Ron Bass in a bunkhouse match
Kharma defeated Mike Davis
Joe Lightfoot defeated Hector Guerrero
Mike Rotundo fought NWA World Champion Ric Flair to a 60-minute time-limit draw
Billy Jack defeated the One Man Gang via disqualification

JCP @ Fayetteville, NC - Cumberland County Civic Center - January 15, 1984
Keith Larson defeated Ali Bey
Vinnie Valentino defeated Bill White
Wahoo McDaniel & Dory Funk Jr. defeated NWA Tag Team Champions Bob Orton Jr. & Don Kernodle
Greg Valentine defeated NWA US Champion Dick Slater via disqualification
Dusty Rhodes & Jimmy Valiant defeated the Assassins
Rufus R. Jones won a battle royal

JCP @ Greensboro, NC - Coliseum - January 15, 1984
Barry Orton defeated Sam Houston
Angelo Mosca Jr. defeated Gene Anderson
Ernie Ladd defeated Angelo Mosca Sr.
NWA Tag Team Champions Bob Orton Jr. & Don Kernodle defeated Wahoo McDaniel & Mark Youngblood,BR> Ricky Steamboat defeated Ivan Koloff
Dusty Rhodes, Jimmy Valiant & Baron Von Raschke defeated Paul Jones & the Assassins
Greg Valentine defeated NWA US Champion Dick Slater

JCP @ Greenville, SC - Memorial Auditorium - January 16, 1984
Dory Funk Jr. defeated Bob Orton Jr.
Rufus R. Jones defeated Gene Anderson
Johnny Weaver defeated Hans Schroder
Vinnie Valentino defeated Gary Royal
Dusty Rhodes, Jimmy Valiant, & Baron Von Raschke defeated Paul Jones & the Assassins

JCP @ Raleigh, NC - Dorton Arena - January 17, 1984
Bubba Smith defeated Gary Royal
Sam Houston defeated John Bonello
Greg Valentine defeated Bob Orton Jr.
NWA US Champion Dick Slater fought Wahoo McDaniel to a double count-out

Ivan Koloff defeated Dory Funk Jr.
Angelo Mosca Sr. & Jr. defeated Ernie Ladd & Don Kernodle

CWF @ St. Augustine, FL - January 17, 1984
Hector Guerrero defeated Anthony Charles
Joe Lightfoot defeated Black Bart
Kevin Sullivan defeated Mike Davis
Kendo Nagasaki defeated Mike Rotundo via count-out
Yellow Dog & Billy Jack defeated Ron Bass & the One Man Gang
Dusty Rhodes defeated NWA World Champion Ric Flair via disqualification

JCP @ Spartanburg, SC - Memorial Auditorium - January 18, 1984
TV taping:
Worldwide - 1/21/84 - featured David Crockett & Johnny Weaver on commentary:
Baron Von Raschke defeated Gary Royal
NWA World Champion Ric Flair defeated NWA US Champion Dick Slater via reverse decision; Slater originally won the match and title with an elbow to the back of the head and elbow drop, with NWA Tag Team Champion Bob Orton Jr. - who appeared late in the bout - then holding down Flair's foot from the floor; moments later, referee Tommy Young came out and told the initial referee what happened; Jay Youngblood then came out to help Flair but was beaten down as well; moments later, Wahoo McDaniel helped clear the ring for Flair and Youngblood
NWA Tag Team Champions Bob Orton Jr. & Don Kernodle defeated Brett Hart & Brickhouse Brown
Ernie Ladd defeated Sam Houston
The Assassins defeated Dory Funk Jr. & Rufus R. Jones via disqualification
Angelo Mosca Sr. & Jr. defeated Bill White & Tony Russo

JCP @ Harrisonburg, VA - High School - January 19, 1984
Gary Royal vs. Keith Larson
Sam Houston & Johnny Weaver vs. Barry O & Gene Anderson
Ivan Koloff vs. Mark Youngblood
Wahoo McDaniel vs. NWA US Champion Dick Slater
NWA Tag Team Champion Bob Orton Jr. vs. Greg Valentine

JCP @ Sumter, SC - Exhibition Center - January 19, 1984
Bubba Douglas vs. Hans Schroeder
Buddy Landell vs. Brett Hart
Rufus R. Jones vs. Ali Bey
Angelo Mosca Sr. & Jr. vs. Ernie Ladd & Don Kernodle
Jimmy Valiant, Dory Funk Jr., & Baron Von Raschke vs. the Assassins & Paul Jones

JCP @ Charleston, SC - County Hall - January 20, 1984
Vinnie Valentino defeated Ali Bey
Brett Hart fought Bubba Smith to a draw
John Bonello defeated Tony Russo

Rufus R. Jones defeated Hans Schroeder

Baron Von Raschke, Angelo Mosca Sr. & Jr. defeated Ernie Ladd, Don Kernodle, & Gary Hart in a steel cage match

JCP @ Winston-Salem, NC - Memorial Coliseum - January 20, 1984
NWA World Champion Ric Flair defeated NWA US Champion Dick Slater in a non-title match via reverse decision at 3:26

JCP @ Richmond, VA - Coliseum - January 20, 1984
Sam Houston defeated Gary Royal
Johnny Weaver defeated Barry Orton
Gene Anderson defeated Keith Larsen
NWA Tag Team Champion Ivan Koloff defeated Mark Youngblood
The Assassins defeated Dusty Rhodes & Jimmy Valiant
Ricky Steamboat defeated Dory Funk Jr.
Wahoo McDaniel defeated NWA Tag Team Champion Bob Orton Jr.
Greg Valentine defeated NWA US Champion Dick Slater via disqualification

CWF @ Sarasota, FL - January 21, 1984
NWA World Champion Ric Flair defeated Dusty Rhodes via disqualification

JCP @ Rock Hill, SC - Winthrop Coliseum - January 21, 1984
Buddy Landell vs. John Bonello
Brickhouse Brown vs. Vinnie Valentino
Johnny Weaver vs. Gene Anderson
Rufus R. Jones vs. Ernie Ladd
NWA US Champion Dick Slater vs. Greg Valentine
Jimmy Valiant & Dory Funk Jr. vs. the Assassins

CWF @ Sarasota, FL - January 21, 1984
Dusty Rhodes defeated NWA World Champion Ric Flair via disqualification

Toronto, Ontario - Maple Leaf Gardens - January 22, 1984
Bob & Joe Marcus defeated Bobby Bass & Ben Alexander
Keith Larson defeated Kurt Von Hess
Len Denton defeated Nick DeCarlo
Rudy & Terry Kay defeated Johnny Weaver & Keith Larson
Tito Santana defeated Don Kernodle
Leo Burke defeated Roddy Piper via disqualification
Angelo Mosca Sr. defeated Canadian Heavyweight Champion Sgt. Slaughter to win the title at 8:09

JCP @ Roanoke, VA - Civic Center - January 22, 1984
Vinnie Valentino defeated Ali Bey
Paul Jones defeated Jimmy Valiant
Wahoo McDaniel & Jimmy Valiant defeated the Assassins; as a result of the win, Valiant earned 5 minutes in the ring with

Paul Jones
Jimmy Valiant defeated Paul Jones via disqualification
Greg Valentine defeated NWA US Champion Dick Slater via disqualification
Ricky Steamboat defeated Ivan Koloff
Ernie Ladd won a battle royal

Central States @ Wichita, KS - January 23, 1984
Bruiser Brody fought NWA World Champion Ric Flair to a draw

JCP @ Greenville, SC - Memorial Auditorium - January 23, 1984
Sam Houston defeated Tony Russo
Brickhouse Brown fought Bill White to a draw
Johnny Weaver & Tim Horner defeated Len Denton & Tony Anthony
Ivan Koloff defeated Angelo Mosca Jr.
NWA Tag Team Champion Bob Orton Jr. & NWA US Champion Greg Valentine defeated Wahoo McDaniel & Greg Valentine via disqualification

JCP @ Raleigh, NC - Dorton Arena - January 24, 1984
Mark Fleming defeated Ben Alexander
Vinnie Valentino & Tim Horner defeated Len Denton & Tony Anthony
Mid-Atlantic Heavyweight Champion Ivan Koloff defeated Johnny Weaver
NWA US Champion Dick Slater defeated Wahoo McDaniel

Central States @ Tulsa, OK - January 24, 1984
Bruiser Brody fought NWA World Champion Ric Flair to a double disqualification

JCP @ Shelby, NC - Rec Center - January 25, 1984
1/28/84:
Jimmy Valiant & Dory Funk Jr. defeated Bill White & Ben Alexander
The Assassins defeated Brickhouse Brown & Sam Houston
Angelo Mosca Jr. fought Mid-Atlantic Heavyweigght Champion Ivan Koloff to a draw
Rufus R. Jones defeated Gary Royal
Mark Youngblood defeated Tony Russo
Ernie Ladd defeated John Bonello
Worldwide - 2/4/84 - included David Crockett & Johnny Weaver on commentary; featured a promo by Dusty Rhodes regarding the Assassins & Paul Jones; included Crockett conducting an interview with NWA Tag Team Champion Don Kernodle in which he questioned where all the competition was; NWA US Champion Dick Slater then appeared and cut a promo on NWA World Champion Ric Flair, claiming he was the real world champion; footage was then shown of Slater recently pinning Flair while Bob Orton Jr. held Flair's foot down from the floor; featured Crockett conducting a closing interview with NWA Mid Atlantic Heavyweight Champion Angelo Mosca Sr. & Angelo Mosca Sr. regarding Jr.'s title win earlier in the show; moments

later, Crockett conducted an interview with Wahoo McDaniel & Mark Youngblood regarding Youngblood's win earlier in the show and Slater's comments about Flair:
Wahoo McDaniel, Dory Funk Jr., & Rufus R. Jones defeated Bill White, Gary Royal, & Hans Schroeder at around the 2-minute mark when Jones scored the pin following a headbutt
Angelo Mosca Jr. pinned Mid-Atlantic Heavyweight Champion Ivan Koloff (w/ Gary Hart) to win the title at 11:53 with a crossbody off the top; during the bout, it was announced Greg Valentine would face Ernie Ladd the following week in a quarter final match in the NWA TV Title tournament; after the bout, Angelo Mosca Sr. - who provided commentary for the bout with Bob Caudle - left the broadcast area to celebrate with his son in the ring
The Assassins (w/ Paul Jones) defeated Mark Fleming & Brett Hart (Barry Horowitz) at around the 5-minute mark when Hart was pinned following a powerslam / kneedrop off the top double team
NWA TV Championship Quarter Finals: Mark Youngblood pinned Barry Orton with a crossbody at 5:36
The Junkyard Dog pinned Mr. Olympia with an uppercut after avoiding a dropkick off the top at 2:09 (*Mid South Wrestling*)
Tim Horner pinned Tony Russo with a Thesz Press at 5:36
NWA US Champion Dick Slater pinned Vinnie Valentino with a standing elbow off the top at the 5-minute mark

Central States @ Topeka, KS - January 25, 1984
Bruiser Brody fought NWA World Champion Ric Flair to a no contest

Central States @ Kansas City, MO - January 26, 1984
NWA World Champion Ric Flair defeated Harley Race

Central States @ Ft. Scott, KS - January 28, 1984
NWA World Champion Ric Flair vs. Ron Ritchie

WCCW @ San Antonio, TX - Freeman Coliseum - January 29, 1984
Kevin Von Erich vs. NWA World Champion Ric Flair

JCP @ Spencer, NC - January 30, 1984
Mid-Atlantic Heavyweight Champion Angelo Mosca Jr. defeated Ivan Koloff

WCCW Star Wars - Ft. Worth, TX - Tarrant County Civic Center - January 30, 1984
The Junkyard Dog defeated Kamala via disqualification
The Super Destroyers defeated American Tag Team Champions Iceman King Parsons & Brian Adidas to win the titles
The Freebirds defeated David & Kerry Von Erich
Mike Von Erich fought NWA World Champion Ric Flair to a 10-minute draw; stipulations stated if Mike could last the time limit, he would earn a future world title match for David Von Erich

Chris Adams defeated American Heavyweight Champion Jimmy Garvin to win the title

JCP @ Spartanburg, SC - Memorial Auditorium - February 1, 1984
TV taping:
Angelo Mosca Sr. & Jr. vs. NWA Tag Team Champions Don Kernodle & Bob Orton Jr.
Wahoo McDaniel vs. NWA US Champion Dick Slater

JCP @ Norfolk, VA - Scope - February 2, 1984
Tim Horner defeated ?
Keith Larsen defeated Jeff Brower
Vinnie Valentino defeated Gary Royal
Bob Orton Jr. defeated Brickhouse Brown
Ivan Koloff defeated Rufus R. Jones
The Assassins defeated Wahoo McDaniel & Jimmy Valiant
NWA US Champion Dick Slater defeated Greg Valentine

JCP @ Sumter, SC - Sumter County Exhibition Center - February 2, 1984
Bubba Smith vs. Ben Alexander
Sam Houston vs. Tony Russo
Johnny Weaver vs. Gene Anderson
Ernie Ladd vs. Dory Funk Jr.
NWA World Tag Team Champions Don Kernodle & Bob Orton Jr vs. Angelo Mosca Sr. & Jr.

WCCW @ Dallas, TX - Sportatorium - February 3, 1984
TV taping:
Perro Aguayo defeated Fishman
Super Destroyer #1 fought Johnny Mantell to a draw
Iceman King Parsons defeated Super Destroyer #2
The Missing Link defeated Mike Reed (sub. for George Weingeroff)
Mike Von Erich defeated Buddy Roberts
David Von Erich (sub. for Kevin Von Erich) defeated Terry Gordy (sub. for Buddy Roberts) via disqualification
David Von Erich defeated United National Champion Michael Hayes to win the title
NWA World Champion Ric Flair defeated Chris Adams at 15:58

JCP @ Charleston, SC - County Hall - February 3, 1984
Ernie Ladd defeated Johnny Weaver
Ivan Koloff vs. Mid-Atlantic Heavyweight Champion Angelo Mosca Jr.
Jimmy Valiant & Rufus R. Jones vs. the Assassins

WCCW @ San Antonio, TX - February 4, 1984
Perro Aguayo defeated Fishman
The Junkyard Dog defeated Kamala via disqualification
Iceman King Parsons defeated Skandor Akbar via count-out
Iceman King Parsons defeated Super Destroyer #2
Kevin & Kerry Von Erich defeated Michael Hayes & Terry

Gordy in a Texas Tornado match
NWA World Champion Ric Flair defeated David Von Erich in a No DQ match

JCP @ Greenville, SC - Memorial Auditorium - February 5, 1984
NWA US Champion Dick Slater pinned NWA World Champion Ric Flair in a non-title match with a Russian leg sweep

JCP @ Greensboro, NC - Coliseum - February 5, 1984
Bruiser Brody & Stan Hansen defeated Dory Funk Jr. & Terry Gibbs

JCP @ Newberry, SC - February 6, 1984
Brett Hart defeated Ben Alexander
Bubba Smith defeated Nelson Royal
Women's Champion the Fabulous Moolah defeated Princess Victoria
Mark Youngblood defeated Gene Anderson
Jimmy Valiant & Rufus R. Jones defeated the Assassins

JCP @ Columbia, SC - Township Auditorium - February 7, 1984
Vinnie Valentino defeated Tony Russo
Tim Horner defeated Gary Royal
Mark Youngblood defeated Hans Schroeder
Johnny Weaver defeated Ernie Ladd
The Assassins defeated Dory Funk Jr. & Jimmy Valiant via disqualification

JCP @ Raleigh, NC - Dorton Arena - February 7, 1984
Mark Fleming defeated Jeff Sowrd
Keith Larson defeated Ali Bey
Angelo Mosca Jr. defeated Bill White
Jay Youngblood defeated the Great Kabuki via disqualification
Mid Atlantic Heavyweight Champion Angelo Mosca Jr. defeated Ivan Koloff
NWA World Champion Ric Flair & Wahoo McDaniel defeated NWA Tag Team Champions Bob Orton Jr. & Don Kernodle

JCP @ Spartanburg, SC - Memorial Auditorium - February 8, 1984
TV taping:
Worldwide - 2/11/84:
Wahoo McDaniel & Mark Youngblood defeated Tony Russo & Bill White
NWA US Champion Dick Slater defeated Tim Horner
Jimmy Valiant & Dory Funk Jr. defeated the Assassins
Rufus R. Jones defeated Jeff Sword
NWA TV Championship Tournament Quarter Finals: Greg Valentine defeated Ernie Ladd
Angelo Mosca Sr. & Jr. defeated Hans Schroeder & Gary Royal

JCP @ Fishersville, VA - Augusta Expo - February 9, 1984
Included Barry Orton, the Assassins, Jimmy Valiant, Paul Jones, Wahoo McDaniel, Dory Funk Jr., Johnny Weaver, and women wrestlers

JCP @ Lynchburg, VA - Armory - February 9, 1984
NWA Mid Atlantic Heavyweight Champion Angelo Mosca Jr. vs. Ivan Koloff
Greg Valentine vs. NWA US Champion Dick Slater
Also included Rufus R. Jones and Angelo Mosca Sr.

JCP @ Charleston, SC - County Hall - February 10, 1984
Sam Houston defeated Danny Brower
Tim Horner defeated Ali Bey
Vinnie Valentino defeated Tony Russo
Jay & Mark Youngblood defeated Barry O & Gene Anderson
Greg Valentine fought Ernie Ladd to a double disqualification
NWA US Champion Dick Slater defeated NWA World Champion Ric Flair in a non-title lights out match

JCP @ Richmond, VA - Coliseum - February 10, 1984
Ben Alexander defeated Bubba Smith
Brett Hart defeated Jeff Sword
Keith Larson defeated Bill White
Donna Christanello defeated Peggy Patterson
Rufus R. Jones defeated the Great Kabuki via disqualification
NWA Mid Atlantic Heavyweight Champion Angelo Mosca Jr. defeated Ivan Koloff
NWA Tag Team Champions Bob Orton Jr. & Don Kernodle defeated Angelo Mosca Sr. & Wahoo McDaniel
Jimmy Valiant & Angelo Mosca defeated the Assassins

JCP @ Hampton, VA - Coliseum - February 11, 1984
Ali Bey defeated Bubba Smith
Rufus R. Jones defeated Gary Royal
Brickhouse Brown defeated Mark Fleming
NWA Tag Team Champions Bob Orton Jr. & Don Kernodle defeated Wahoo McDaniel & Greg Valentine
Ivan Koloff defeated Angelo Mosca Jr.
NWA US Champion Dick Slater defeated NWA World Champion Ric Flair

Toronto, Ontario - Maple Leaf Gardens - February 12, 1984 (17,087)
Kurt Von Hess fought Joe Marcus to a draw
Swede Hanson defeated John Bonello
Terry & Rudy Kay defeated Johnny Weaver & Billy Red Lyons
Bret Hart defeated JJ Dillon
Leo Burke defeated Vinnie Valentino
Dusty Rhodes & Jimmy Valiant defeated the Assassins via count-out
NWA World Champion Ric Flair defeated Harley Race in a steel cage match

JCP @ Greenville, SC - Memorial Auditorium - February 12, 1984
Bill White defeated Ali Bey
Keith Larson defeated Dan Brower
Gene Anderson defeated Bubba Smith
Tim Horner defeated Ben Alexander
Dory Funk Jr. defeated Ernie Ladd
Mark & Jay Youngblood defeated NWA Tag Team Champions Don Kernodle & Bob Orton Jr. via disqualification
Greg Valentine defeated NWA US Champion Dick Slater in a taped fist match

JCP @ Roanoke, VA - Civic Center - February 12, 1984
Sam Houston fought Gary Royal to a draw
Rufus R. Jones defeated Mark Fleming
Barry Hart defeated Brickhouse Brown
NWA Mid Atlantic Heavyweight Champion Angelo Mosca Jr. defeated Hans Schroeder
Dusty Rhodes, Wahoo McDaniel, & Jimmy Valiant defeated Paul Jones & the Assassins
Angelo Mosca Sr. defeated Ivan Koloff via disqualification

JCP @ Asheville, NC - Civic Center - February 13, 1984
Bubba Smith defeated Tony Russo
Vinnie Valentino defeated Gary Royal
Johnny Weaver defeated Hans Schroeder
Rufus R. Jones defeated Gene Anderson
Jimmy Valiant, Jay & Mark Youngblood defeated Paul Jones & the Assassins
NWA US Champion Dick Slater defeated Greg Valentine

JCP @ Fayetteville, NC - Cumberland County Civic Center - February 13, 1984
Ivan Koloff defeated Angelo Mosca Sr.
Angelo Mosca Jr. defeated Bill White
Keith Larson fought Barry Orton to a draw
Tim Horner defeated Ali Bey
Denny Brown defeated Mark Fleming
NWA Tag Team Champions Bob Orton Jr. & Don Kernodle defeated Dory Funk Jr. & Wahoo McDaniel

CWF @ West Palm Beach, FL - Auditorium - February 13, 1984
Les Thornton pinned Hector Guerrero at 12:38
Kendo Nagasaki pinned Denny Brown at 4:56
Mike Davis defeated the One Man Gang via disqualification at 3:28
Barry Windham, Billy Jack Haynes, & Joe Lightfoot defeated Jim Duggan, Ron Bass, & Black Bart
Dusty Rhodes pinned Kharma
Mike Rotundo fought NWA World Champion Ric Flair to a 60-minute time-limit draw

JCP @ Columbia, SC - Township Auditorium - February 14, 1984
Brett Hart defeated Gary Royal
Sam Houston defeated Tony Russo
Tim Horner defeated Barry O
The Assassins defeated Jimmy Valiant & Dory Funk Jr.
Mark Youngblood defeated Ernie Ladd
Wahoo McDaniel defeated NWA US Champion Dick Slater

CWF @ Ft. Myers, FL - February 14, 1984
NWA World Champion Ric Flair fought Barry Windham to a draw

JCP @ Rockingham, NC - Richmond High School - February 15, 1984
TV taping:
Championship Wrestling - 2/18/84:
NWA TV Tournament Quarter Finals: Assassin #2 (w/ Paul Jones) defeated Johnny Weaver at 8:41 when, as Jones distracted the referee, Assassin #1 - who came ringside late in the bout - interfered, hit a headbutt on Weaver, and scored the pin himself
Ernie Ladd vs. Keith Larson
Angelo Mosca Sr. & Mid-Atlantic Heavyweight Champion Angelo Mosca Jr. vs. two unknowns
Worldwide - 2/18/84:
Mark Youngblood, Angelo Mosca Jr., & Tim Horner vs. Russo, Gary Royal, & Bill White
Ivan Koloff defeated Dave McCoy
NWA TV Championship Tournament Quarter Finals: NWA US Champion Dick Slater pinned Dory Funk Jr.
Ernie Ladd defeated Bubba Smith
Tully Blanchard defeated Vinnie Valentino

- 2/15/84: David Von Erich's funeral was held in Denton, TX. NWA World Champion Ric Flair was among those in attendance.

CWF @ Miami Beach, FL - Convention Hall - February 15, 1984 (4,937)
Denny Brown defeated Anthony Charles
Les Thornton defeated Hector Guerrero
Mike Graham, Mike Davis, & Joe Lightfoot defeated the One Man Gang, Black Bart, & Jim Duggan
Ron Bass defeated Mike Rotundo
Dusty Rhodes & Billy Jack Haynes defeated Kevin Sullivan & Kharma in a Texas Tornado match
NWA World Champion Ric Flair defeated Barry Windham via disqualification

CWF @ Ocala, FL - February 16, 1984
Jim Duggan & the One Man Gang defeated Mike Davis & Joe Lightfoot
Hector Guerrero defeated Anthony Charles
Les Thornton defeated Denny Brown
Mike Graham defeated Kendo Nagasaki via disqualification
Dusty Rhodes defeated Kharma via disqualification

Barry Windham & Billy Jack Haynes defeated Ron Bass & Black Bart via disqualification
NWA World Champion Ric Flair defeated Mike Rotundo

JCP @ Sumter, SC - Exhibition Center - February 16, 1984
Ivan Koloff defeated Keith Larson
Vinnie Valentino defeated Jeff Sword
Tim Horner defeated Ali Bey
Ernie Ladd defeated Denny Brown
Greg Valentine defeated NWA US Champion Dick Slater in a taped fist match
NWA Tag Team Champions Bob Orton Jr. & Don Kernodle defeated Angelo Mosca Sr. & Jr.

JCP @ Powhatan, VA - High School - February 16, 1984

JCP @ Charleston, SC - County Hall - February 17, 1984
Greg Valentine defeated Ernie Ladd
NWA Tag Team Champions Bob Orton Jr. & Don Kernodle defeated Angelo Mosca Sr. & Jr.

JCP @ Lynchburg, VA - City Armory - February 17, 1984
Hans Schroder defeated Sam Houston
Mark Fleming defeated Tony Russo
Tully Blanchard defeated Brett Hart
Johnny Weaver defeated Barry Orton
The Assassins defeated Dory Funk Jr. & Rufus R. Jones
Jimmy Valiant defeated Ivan Koloff

Central States @ St. Louis, MO - Kiel Auditorium - February 17, 1984 (5,000)
The Grapplers defeated Jay & Mark Youngblood
Blackjack Mulligan defeated Bob Brown
Dick Slater defeated King Cobra
AWA Tag Team Champions Ken Patera & Jerry Blackwell defeated Buck Robley & Ron Ritchie
Dusty Rhodes defeated Luke Graham
Wahoo McDaniel defeated Harley Race via disqualification
NWA World Champion Ric Flair defeated Barry Windham via submission

CWF @ Sarasota, FL - February 18, 1984
Les Thornton defeated Hector Guerrero
Jim Duggan & Kharma defeated Denny Brown & Mike Davis
Black Bart defeated Joe Lightfoot in a taped fist match
The One Man Gang defeated Anthony Charles
Mike Rotundo defeated Kendo Nagasaki via disqualification
Billy Jack Haynes defeated Black Bart
NWA World Champion Ric Flair defeated Barry Windham

GCW @ Atlanta, GA - WTBS Studios - February 18, 1984
TV taping:
NWA World Champion Ric Flair pinned Jesse Barr

JCP @ Greensboro, NC - Coliseum - February 18, 1984
Barry Orton defeated Keith Larson
Tim Horner defeated Bill White
Tully Blanchard defeated Mark Fleming
Bubba Smith defeated Tony Russo
Angelo Mosca Jr. defeated Ivan Koloff
Wahoo McDaniel & Mark Youngblood defeated NWA Tag Team Champions Bob Orton Jr. & Don Kernodle via disqualification
Greg Valentine defeated NWA US Champion Dick Slater via disqualification
Dusty Rhodes & Jimmy Valiant defeated the Assassins

CWF @ Orlando, FL - February 19, 1984
Jim Duggan defeated Mike Davis
Kendo Nagasaki defeated Denny Brown
Hector Guerrero defeated Anthony Charles
Joe Lightfoot defeated the One Man Gang via count-out
Billy Jack Haynes & Barry Windham defeated Black Bart & Ron Bass via disqualification
Dusty Rhodes defeated Kharma
Mike Rotundo fought NWA World Champion Ric Flair to a time-limit draw at the 47-minute mark

JCP @ Fayetteville, NC - Cumberland County Civic Center - February 19, 1984
Tully Blanchard defeated Sam Houston
Barry Hart defeated Gary Royal
Greg Valentine & Wahoo McDaniel defeated NWA Tag Team Champion Bob Orton Jr. & NWA US Champion Dick Slater in a Texas Tornado match
Jimmy Valiant, Rufus R. Jones, & Dory Funk Jr. defeated Paul Jones & the Assassins
Angelo Mosca Jr. defeated the Great Kabuki

JCP @ Charlotte, NC - Coliseum - February 19, 1984
Angelo Mosca Sr. & NWA Mid Atlantic Heavyweight Champion Angelo Mosca Jr. defeated Ivan Koloff & Ernie Ladd
Jay & Mark Youngblood defeated Jack & Jerry Brisco
Tim Horner defeated Barry O
Johnny Weaver defeated Jeff Sword
Wahoo McDaniel defeated NWA US Champion Dick Slater via count-out
Greg Valentine, Jimmy Valiant, & Dory Funk Jr. defeated Paul Jones & the Assassins

JCP @ Greenville, SC - Memorial Auditorium - February 20, 1984
Vinnie Valentino defeated Bobby Bass
Tim Horner defeated Gary Royal
Angelo Mosca Jr. defeated Ernie Ladd
Wahoo McDaniel & Jimmy Valiant defeated the Assassins
Jay & Mark Youngblood defeated Jack & Jerry Brisco

Central States @ Topeka, KS - February 21, 1984
NWA World Champion Ric Flair defeated Buzz Tyler

JCP @ Raleigh, NC - Dorton Arena - February 21, 1984
NWA Tag Team Champions Bob Orton Jr. & Don Kernodle
defeated Angelo Mosca Sr. & NWA Mid Atlantic Heavyweight
Champion Angelo Mosca Jr.
Barry Hart defeated Gary Royal
Sam Houston defeated Hans Schroeder
Johnny Weaver defeated Ben Alexander
Ivan Koloff defeated Rufus R. Jones
Greg Valentine defeated the Great Kabuki

JCP @ Columbia, SC - Township Auditorium - February 21, 1984
Tim Horner defeated Bobby Bass
Jay & Mark Youngblood defeated Jack & Jerry Brisco
NWA US Champion Dick Slater defeated Wahoo McDaniel
Paul Jones & the Assassins defeated Jimmy Valiant, Tully
Blanchard, & Dory Funk Jr. in an elimination match
Keith Larson defeated Ali Bey

JCP @ Spartanburg, SC - Memorial Auditorium - February 22, 1984
TV taping:
Worldwide - 2/25/84:
The Assassins defeated Keith Larson & Barry Horowitz
NWA TV Championship Semi Finals: NWA US Champion Dick
Slater defeated Greg Valentine via disqualification at 7:29 after
Valentine shoved the referee while trying to get at Slater; the
bell rang moments before, implying Slater had won via count-
out, but the referee raised Slater's hand immediately after
being shoved
NWA Tag Team Champions Bob Orton Jr. & Don Kernodle
defeated Tim Horner & Vinnie Valentino
The Great Kabuki defeated Brickhouse Brown
Tully Blanchard defeated Sam Houston

Central States @ Kansas City, MO - February 23, 1984
The Junkyard Dog fought NWA World Champion Ric Flair to a
double count-out

JCP @ Elizabethtown, NC - East Bladen High School - February 23, 1984
Buddy Lane vs. Hans Schroeder
Brickhouse Brown vs. Jeff Sword
Tully Blanchard vs. Johnny Weaver
NWA US Champion Dick Slater vs. Dory Funk Jr.
Jimmy Valiant, Rufus R. Jones, & Jay Youngblood vs. the
Assassins & Paul Jones

Central States @ St. Joseph, MO - February 24, 1984
NWA World Champion Ric Flair defeated Bob Brown

JCP @ Richmond, VA - Coliseum - February 24, 1984
Sam Houston defeated Ben Alexander
Brickhouse Brown defeated Gary Royal
Tully Blanchard defeated Johnny Weaver
Dusty Rhodes, Angelo Mosca Sr., & Jimmy Valiant defeated
Paul Jones & the Assassins in an elimination match
Greg Valentine defeated NWA US Champion Dick Slater via
disqualification
NWA Tag Team Champions Bob Orton Jr. & Don Kernodle
defeated Wahoo McDaniel & Mark Youngblood

MID-ATLANTIC CHAMPIONSHIP
WRESTLING SAT., FEB. 25th
8:15 p.m. 8:15 p.m. 8:15 p.m. 8:15 p.m.
STAFFORD SR. H.S. GYM
SPONSORED BY THE BOOSTER CLUB
WAHOO McDANIEL
AND
GREG VALENTINE
• VERSUS •
DICK SLATER AND
BOB ORTON, JR.

DON KERNODLE	v s.	KING KONG MOSCA

| GENE ANDERSON | v s. | JOHNNY WEAVER | TULLY BLANCHARD | v s. | BRICKHOUSE BROWN | GARY ROYAL vs. SAM HOUSTON |

ADULTS: $6.00   CHILDREN UNDER 12: $3.00
Tickets are available at Ross Music, Footlocker, State Farm Insurance at Stafford Courthouse and Stafford High School

JCP @ Fredericksburg, VA - Stafford Senior High School Gym - February 25, 1984
Sam Houston vs. Gary Royal
Johnny Weaver vs. Gene Anderson
Brickhouse Brown vs. Tully Blanchard
Angelo Mosca Sr. vs. Don Kernodle
Wahoo McDaniel & Greg Valentine vs. NWA US Champion Dick Slater & Bob Orton Jr.

JCP @ Conway, SC - February 25, 1984
Barry Hart defeated Ali Bey
Tim Horner defeated Bill White
The Great Kabuki defeated Rufus R. Jones
NWA Mid Atlantic Heavyweight Champion Angelo Mosca Jr. defeated Ivan Koloff
Paul Jones & the Assassins defeated Jimmy Valiant, Dory Funk Jr., & Mark Youngblood

JCP @ Asheville, NC - Civic Center - February 26, 1984
Greg Valentine defeated Jeff Sword
Mark Fleming defeated Bobby Bass
The Great Kabuki defeated Tim Horner
Jay Youngblood defeated Ivan Koloff
NWA Tag Team Champions Bob Orton Jr. & Don Kernodle defeated NWA Mid Atlantic Heavyweight Champion Angelo Mosca Jr. & Mark Youngblood
The Road Warriors fought Angelo Mosca Sr. & Wahoo McDaniel to a no contest

GCW @ Atlanta, GA - Omni - February 26, 1984
NWA World Champion Ric Flair defeated Brad Armstrong

JCP @ Savannah, GA - Civic Center - February 26, 1984
Keith Larson defeated Ali Bey
Sam Houston defeated Ben Alexander
Tully Blanchard defeated Barry Hart
Denny Brown defeated Hans Schroeder
Rufus R. Jones defeated Ernie Ladd
Dory Funk Jr. & Jimmy Valiant defeated the Assassins

JCP @ Columbia, SC - Township Auditorium - February 26, 1984
The Assassins defeated Dory Funk Jr. & Rufus R. Jones
Jimmy Valiant defeated Tully Blanchard
Ernie Ladd defeated Johnny Weaver
Barry O defeated Gene Ligon
Barry Hart defeated Gary Royal
NWA US Champion Dick Slater defeated Greg Valentine

JCP @ Fayetteville, NC - Cumberland County Civic Center - February 27, 1984
Mark Fleming defeated Bobby Bass
Keith Larson defeated Ali Bey
Tully Blanchard defeated Johnny Weaver
Angelo Mosca Sr. & NWA Mid Atlantic Heavyweight Champion Angelo Mosca Jr. defeated Ivan Koloff & the Great Kabuki
The Road Warriors defeated Greg Valentine & Wahoo McDaniel
NWA World Champion Ric Flair defeated NWA US Champion Dick Slater

JCP @ Greenville, SC - Memorial Auditorium - February 27, 1984
Ernie Ladd defeated Brickhouse Brown
Tim Horner defeated Jeff Sword
Barry Orton defeated Sam Houston
Jay & Mark Youngblood fought NWA Tag Team Champions Bob Orton Jr. & Don Kernodle to a 60-minute time-limit draw
Jimmy Valiant, Dory Funk Jr., & Rufus R. Jones defeated Paul Jones & the Assassins

MID ATLANTIC CHAMPIONSHIP WRESTLING

YORK COMPREHENSIVE HIGH SCHOOL GYM
TUESDAY, FEBRUARY 28
8:15 P.M.
SPONSORED BY THE BOOSTER CLUB

TAG TEAM MAIN EVENT

ASSASSINS
NO. 1 and NO. 2
Advised by
No. 1 Paul Jones

vs.

BOOGIE WOOGIE MAN
JIMMY VALIANT
AND
DORY FUNK, JR.

U.S. CHAMPION
DICK SLATER vs. **RUFUS R. JONES**

(THE CAT) ERNIE LADD VS. CHIEF WAHOO McDANIEL

TULLY BLANCHARD vs. VINNIE VALENTINO	GARY ROYAL vs. TIM HORNER	JEFF SWORDS vs. BRETT HART

TICKET LOCATIONS
BOYD TIRE & APPLIANCE
THE MEN'S SHOP
DAVIS SPORTS
NEELY DRUG STORE

PRICES
Ringside $6
Gen. Admission
Adults $5
Children $3

MID ATLANTIC CHAMPIONSHIP WRESTLING

Winston-Salem
MEMORIAL COLISEUM
WEDNESDAY, FEBRUARY 29, 1984 7:30 pm

WORLD HEAVYWEIGHT TITLE MATCH
RICK FLAIR vs DICK SLATER

TAG TEAM MATCH
GREG VALENTINE WAHOO McDANIEL vs. THE ROAD WARRIORS

JIMMY VALIENT vs THE GREAT KABUKI

Plus 8 Big Matches with Such Stars as:

ASSASSIN #1	TULLY BLANCHARD
ASSASSIN #2	DON KERNODLE
DICK SLATER	RUFUS R. JONES
BOB ORTON	MARK YOUNGBLOOD
IVAN KOLOFF	JAY YOUNGBLOOD
ERNIE LADD	ANGELO MOSCA
TIM HORNER	ANGELO MOSCA, JR.

Come Out and Watch Mid Atlantic World Wide Wrestling Being Taped Live!
SUBJECT TO CHANGE

JCP @ York, SC - High School - February 28, 1984
Jeff Sword vs. Brett Hart
Gary Royal vs. Tim Horner
Tully Blanchard vs. Vinnie Valentino
Ernie Ladd vs. Wahoo McDaniel
NWA US Champion Dick Slater vs. Rufus R. Jones
Jimmy Valiant & Dory Funk Jr. vs. the Assassins

JCP @ Winston-Salem, NC - Memorial Coliseum - February 29, 1984
Worldwide taping:
Jimmy Valiant vs. the Great Kabuki
Wahoo McDaniel & Greg Valentine vs. the Road Warriors
NWA World Champion Ric Flair vs. NWA US Champion Dick Slater
Worldwide - 3/3/84:
Jay & Mark Youngblood defeated Barry Orton & Gary Royal when Jay pinned Royal
Angelo Mosca Jr. defeated Ivan Koloff via disqualification when the Great Kabuki & Gary Hart interfered
Brickhouse Brown defeated Ernie Ladd after Rufus R. Jones distracted Ladd
Dick Slater pinned Gene Ligon with a Russian legsweep
Stan Hansen defeated Brett Hart via submission with an armbar
Tully Blanchard pinned Keith Larson with the slingshot suplex

JCP @ Norfolk, VA - Scope - March 1, 1984
Rufus R. Jones & Jimmy Valiant defeated the Assassins
Jimmy Valiant defeated Paul Jones via disqualification
Angelo Mosca Sr. defeated the Great Kabuki
Tully Blanchard defeated Denny Brown
Johnny Weaver defeated Barry O

Mark Fleming defeated Bobby Bass
Greg Valentine & Wahoo McDaniel defeated NWA Tag Team
Champions Bob Orton Jr. & Don Kernodle
NWA World Champion Ric Flair defeated Angelo Mosca Jr.

JCP @ Manning, SC - High School - March 1, 1984
Bill White vs. Tim Horner
Ali Bey vs. Vinnie Valentino
Gary Royal vs. Sam Houston
Angelo Mosca Jr. vs. Tully Blanchard
Mark & Jay Youngblood vs. Ivan Koloff & Ernie Ladd
Dory Funk Jr. vs. NWA US Champion Dick Slater

JCP @ Charleston, SC - County Hall - March 2, 1984
Brett Hart defeated Ali Bey
Tully Blanchard defeated Sam Houston
The Great Kabuki defeated Jay Youngblood
Jimmy Valiant, Rufus R. Jones, & Mark Youngblood defeated
Paul Jones & the Assassins in an elimination match
NWA World Champion Ric Flair defeated Dory Funk Jr.

JCP @ Lynchburg, VA - Armory - March 2, 1984
Wahoo McDaniel & Greg Valentine vs. NWA Tag Team
Champions Bob Orton Jr. & Don Kernodle

Central States @ Kansas City, MO - Kemper Arena - March 4, 1984 (10,123)
NWA World Champion Ric Flair fought Harley Race to a 60-minute time-limit draw

JCP @ Charlotte, NC - Coliseum - March 4, 1984
Keith Larson defeated Gary Royal
Denny Brown defeated Ali Bey
Angelo Mosca Sr. & Jr. defeated Ivan Koloff & the Great
Kabuki
NWA US Champion Dick Slater defeated Greg Valentine in a
taped fist match
Wahoo McDaniel & Mark Youngblood defeated NWA Tag
Team Champions Bob Orton Jr. & Don Kernodle to win the
titles
Jimmy Valiant, Dory Funk Jr., & Rufus R. Jones defeated Paul
Jones & the Assassins in a steel cage match

Continental @ Birmingham, AL - March 5, 1984
Roy Lee Welch defeated Ric McCord
Rip Rogers defeated US Jr. Heavyweight Champion Larry
Hamilton to win the title
Charlie Cook defeated the New Guinea Man Eater
Boris Zhukov defeated Jacques Rougeau via count-out in a
Texas Death Match
Ron & Robert Fuller defeated Jerry Stubbs & Arn Anderson via
disqualification
NWA World Champion Ric Flair defeated Jimmy Golden via
disqualification

JCP @ Greenville, SC - Memorial Auditorium - March 5, 1984
Keith Larson defeated Doug Vines
Brickhouse Brown defeated Hans Schroeder
Ernie Ladd defeated Rufus R. Jones via disqualification
Angelo Mosca Sr. & Jr. defeated Ivan Koloff & the Great
Kabuki
Wahoo McDaniel defeated NWA US Champion Dick Slater in a
non-title Indian Strap Match
Jay & Mark Youngblood defeated Bob Orton Jr. & Don
Kernodle

JCP @ Columbia, SC - Township Auditorium - March 6, 1984
Keith larson defeated Doug Vines
Barry Hart defeated Ben Alexander
Ernie Ladd defeated Denny Brown
Jimmy Valiant defeated Paul Jones
The Assassins defeated Jimmy Valiant & Rufus R. Jones
Jay Youngblood defeated Tully Blanchard

JCP @ Raleigh, NC - Dorton Arena - March 6, 1984
Jeff Sword defeated Mark Fleming
Sam Houston defeated Bobby Bass
Johnny Weaver defeated Barry Orton
The Great Kabuki defeated Tim Horner
Angelo Mosca Jr. defeated Dory Funk Jr.
Angelo Mosca Sr. defeated Ivan Koloff
Bob Orton Jr. & Don Kernodle defeated NWA Tag Team Champions Wahoo McDaniel & Mark Youngblood via disqualification

JCP @ Spartanburg, SC - Memorial Auditorium - March 7, 1984
Ernie Ladd defeated Wahoo McDaniel
Jimmy Valiant & Rufus R. Jones defeated the Assassins
Worldwide - 3/10/84:
The Assassins defeated Tim Horner & Keith Larson when Assassin #2 pinned Larson with a powerslam
Dory Funk Jr. & Angelo Mosca defeated Doug Vines & Kurt Von Hess when Funk pinned Bass
Stan Hansen pinned Steve Brinson with the lariat
NWA TV Championship Finals: Mark Youngblood pinned NWA US Champion Dick Slater at around the 7-minute mark by lifting his shoulder out of a back suplex into a bridge; prior to the bout, Slater attacked Youngblood and Youngblood was helped out of the ring by Tim Horner; moments later, Youngblood brushed off the injury and returned to the ring
Tully Blanchard pinned Mark Fleming with the slingshot suplex

JCP @ Rocky Mount, VA - Franklin City Gym - March 8, 1984
Included Wahoo McDaniel, Tully Blanchard, NWA Tag Team Champion Bob Orton Jr., and NWA US Champion Dick Slater

JCP @ Richmond, VA - Coliseum - March 9, 1984
Bobby Bass defeated Keith Larson
Barry O defeated Denny Brown
Tim Horner defeated Jeff Sword
Dory Funk Jr. defeated Tully Blanchard
Jimmy Valiant defeated Paul Jones
Assassin #1 & #2 defeated Jimmy Valiant & Jay Youngblood
Greg Valentine defeated NWA US Champion Dick Slater in a non-title taped fist match
Wahoo McDaniel & Mark Youngblood defeated Don Kernodle & Bob Orton Jr.

Continental @ Panama City, FL - March 9, 1984
NWA World Champion Ric Flair defeated Charlie Cook

JCP @ Charleston, SC - County Hall - March 9, 1984
Angelo Mosca Sr. & Jr. defeated Ivan Koloff & the Great Kabuki
Rufus R. Jones defeated Ernie Ladd
Included 3 other matches

Central States @ St. Louis, MO - Kiel Auditorium - March 10, 1984 (10,752)
Buzz Tyler & Ron Ritchie vs. the Grapplers
Luke Graham vs. Jay Wolfe
Blackjack Lanza vs. Roger Kirby
Blackjack Mulligan vs. Ox Baker
Greg Gagne & Ted Oates vs. AWA World Champion Jumbo Tsuruta & Genichiro Tenryu
Kamala vs. Bob Brown & Buck Zumhoffe (handicap match)
Wahoo McDaniel defeated Missouri Heavyweight Champion Harley Race in a non-title Indian strap match
Bruiser Brody fought NWA World Champion Ric Flair to a double disqualification at the 20-minute mark

JCP @ Roanoke, VA - Civic Center - March 10, 1984
Doug Vines defeated Gary Hart
Mark Fleming defeated Ali Bey
Gary Royal defeated Sam Houston
The Great Kabuki defeated Johnny Weaver
Angelo Mosca Jr. defeated Tully Blanchard via disqualification
NWA US Champion Dick Slater defeated Greg Valentine
Bob Orton Jr. & Don Kernodle defeated Jay & Mark Youngblood

JCP @ Sumter, SC - Exhibition Center - March 11, 1984
Barry Hart defeated Jeff Sword
Barry O defeated Hans Schroeder
Denny Brown defeated Gary Royal
NWA US Champion Dick Slater defeated Greg Valentine
Angelo Mosca Sr., Jimmy Valiant, & Rufus R. Jones defeated Paul Jones & the Assassins
Angelo Mosca Jr. defeated the Great Kabuki

WCCW @ San Antonio, TX - March 11, 1984
Kelly Kiniski defeated El Bracero
Super Destroyer #2 defeated Chick Donovan
Iceman King Parsons & the Junkyard Dog defeated Kamala & the Missing Link via disqualification
Kerry & Mike Von Erich defeated Terry Gordy & Buddy Roberts
NWA World Champion Ric Flair defeated Kevin Von Erich

JCP @ Savannah, GA - Civic Center - March 11, 1984
Keith Larson defeated Ben Alexander
Vinnie Valentino defeated Bobby Bass
Ernie Ladd defeated Rufus R. Jones via disqualification
Bob Orton Jr. & Don Kernodle defeated Johnny Weaver &

Mark Youngblood
NWA US Champion Dick Slater defeated Greg Valentine in a steel cage match
Jimmy Valiant defeated Assassin #2 in a hair vs. mask match

JCP @ Fayetteville, NC - Cumberland County Civic Center - March 12, 1984
Tully Blanchard defeated Jeff Sword
Gary Royal defeated Sam Houston
Wahoo McDaniel & Mark Youngblood defeated Bob Orton Jr. & Don Kernodle
Ivan Koloff defeated Dory Funk Jr.
The Great Kabuki defeated Angelo Mosca Jr. via count-out
Jimmy Valiant defeated Paul Jones
The Assassins defeated Jay Youngblood & Jimmy Valiant

WCCW @ Ft. Worth, TX - March 12, 1984
Kelly Kiniski defeated El Bracero
Chris Adams fought Michael Hayes to a draw
The Super Destroyers defeated Iceman King Parsons & Johnny Mantell
The Missing Link fought Kerry Von Erich to a draw
NWA World Champion Ric Flair defeated Terry Gordy

JCP @ Greenville, SC - Memorial Auditorium - March 12, 1984
Brickhouse Brown defeated Bobby Bass
Barry O defeated Tim Horner
Johnny Weaver defeated Doug Vines
Rufus R. Jones defeated Ernie Ladd
Angelo Mosca Sr. & King Kong Bundy defeated the Road Warriors
NWA US Champion Dick Slater defeated Greg Valentine

JCP @ Columbia, SC - Township Auditorium - March 13, 1984
Kurt Von Hess defeated Vinnie Valentino
Denny Brown defeated Doug Vines
Keith Larson defeated Barry O
Ernie Ladd defeated Rufus R. Jones via disqualification
Tully Blanchard defeated Johnny Weaver
Ivan Koloff & the Great Kabuki defeated Angelo Mosca Sr. & Jr.
NWA US Champion Dick Slater defeated Greg Valentine in a steel cage match

JCP @ Raliegh, NC - Dorton Arena - March 13, 1984
Tim Horner defeated Bobby Bass
Tim Horner defeated Barry Hart
Jay Youngblood, Jimmy Valiant, & Dory Funk Jr. defeated Paul Jones & the Assassins
Wahoo McDaniel & Mark Youngblood defeated Bob Orton Jr. & Don Kernodle in a Texas Tornado match

JCP @ Norfolk, VA - Scope - March 15, 1984
Mark Fleming defeated Ali Bey
Denny Brown defeated Gary Royal
The Great Kaubki defeated Angelo Mosca Jr.
Tully Blanchard defeated Johnny Weaver
Angelo Mosca Sr. defeated Ivan Koloff
Jimmy Valiant defeated Paul Jones
Wahoo McDaniel & Mark Youngblood defeated Bob Orton Jr. & Don Kernodle

JCP @ Charleston, SC - County Hall - March 16, 1984
Keith Larson defeated Jeff Sword
Bobby Bass defeated Gene Ligon
Kurt Von Hess defeated Tim Horner
Peggy Patterson defeated Peggy Lee
Rufus R. Jones defeated Ernie Ladd
NWA US Champion Dick Slater defeated Greg Valentine in a No DQ steel cage match

JCP @ Lynchburg, VA - Armory - March 16, 1984
Johnny Weaver vs. Doug Vines
Wahoo McDaniel & Mark Youngblood vs. NWA Tag Team Champions Bob Orton Jr. & Don Kernodle

GCW @ Atlanta, GA - WTBS Studios - March 17, 1984
TV taping:
NWA World Champion Ric Flair vs. Pat Rose

JCP @ Greensboro, NC - Coliseum - March 17, 1984
Boogie Jam 84
Tully Blanchard defeated Dory Funk Jr.
Rufus R. Jones defeated Ernie Ladd
NWA Tag Team Champions Wahoo McDaniel & Mark Youngblood defeated Don Kernodle & Bob Orton Jr. in a non-title match
Angelo Mosca Sr., Angelo Mosca Jr., & the Junkyard Dog defeated Gary Hart, the Great Kabuki, & Ivan Koloff
NWA US Champion Dick Slater defeated Greg Valentine in a No DQ steel cage match
NWA World Champion Ric Flair fought Ricky Steamboat to a 60-minute time-limit draw; prior to the bout, the two men shook hands (*Ricky Steamboat: The Life of the Dragon*)
Jimmy Valiant defeated Assassin #2 in a hair vs. mask match; Dusty Rhodes and Paul Jones were tied together at ringside with a bullrope for the match

JCP @ Columbia, SC - Township Auditorium - March 18, 1984
Denny Brown defeated Hans Schroeder
Doug Vines defeated Sam Houston
Tully Blanchard defeated Dory Funk Jr.
Kurt Von Hess defeated Tim Horner
Rufus R. Jones defeated Ernie Ladd
The Junkyard Dog, Angelo Mosca Sr. & Jr. defeated Ivan Koloff, the Great Kabuki, & Gary Hart

JCP @ Asheville, NC - Civic Center - March 18, 1984
Keith Larson defeated Barry O
Johnny Weaver defeated Barry Hart
Vinnie Valentino defeated Ali Bey
Don Kernodle defeated Mark Youngblood
Jimmy Valiant defeated Assassin #2 in a hair vs. mask match
Greg Valentine & Wahoo McDaniel defeated Tully Blanchard &
Don Kernodle in a Texas Tornado match

JCP @ Charlotte, NC - Coliseum - March 18, 1984
Mark Fleming defeated Bobby Bass
Keith Larson defeated Jeff Sword
Gary Royal defeated Barry Hart
Angelo Mosca Sr. defeated the Great Kabuki
Ivan Koloff defeated Mid-Atlantic Heavyweight Champion
Angelo Mosca Jr. to win the title
Greg Valentine & Wahoo McDaniel defeated Tully Blanchard &
NWA Tag Team Champion Don Kernodle in a Texas Tornado
match
Jimmy Valiant, the Junkyard Dog, & Dory Funk Jr. defeated
Paul Jones & the Assassins in an elimination match

Christchurch, New Zealand - March 19, 1984
Harley Race vs. Gerry Morrow (sub. for NWA World Champion
Ric Flair)

JCP @ Appomattox, VA - High School - March 19, 1984
Included Ernie Ladd, the Assassins, Paul Jones, Jimmy
Valiant, Dory Funk Jr., and Rufus R. Jones

Wellington, New Zealand - March 20, 1984
Harley Race defeated NWA World Champion Ric Flair to win
the title in a Best 2 out of 3 falls match

**JCP @ Greenville, SC - Municipal Auditorium - March 20,
1984**
Vinnie Valentino defeated Bobby Bass
Tim Horner defeated Gary Royal
Angelo Mosca Jr. defeated Ernie Ladd
Jimmy Valiant & Wahoo McDaniel defeated Assassin #1 & #2
Jay & Mark Youngblood defeated Jack & Jerry Brisco

JCP @ Raleigh, NC - Dorton Arena - March 20, 1984
Tully Blanchard defeated Johnny Weaver
Mark Fleming defeated Kurt Von Hess
Barry O defeated Barry Hart
Jimmy Valiant defeated Paul Jones
NWA Mid Atlantic Heavyweight Champion Ivan Koloff & the
Great Kabuki defeated Angelo Mosca Sr. & Jr.
Jimmy Valiant & Dory Funk Jr. defeated the Assassins

**JCP @ Spartanburg, SC - Memorial Auditorium - March 21,
1984**
Worldwide - 3/24/84 - featured Johnny Weaver on

*commentary, with Don Kernodle joining him for the first two
matches; included Weaver conducting an interview with Paul
Jones & the Assassins regarding Jimmy Valiant, with the three
saying they would end Valiant's career; after they left, NWA US
Champion Dick Slater walked in, claimed he was both the US
champion and NWA World champion; Slater then said
everyone was gunning for him, including the Junkyard Dog;
Slater then threatened to run a 2x4 down JYD's throat should
he ever be able to beat Slater; featured footage of how NWA
Tag Team Champion Mark Youngblood defeated Slater in the
finals of the NWA TV Championship Tournament; included
Weaver conducting a closing interview with Rufus R. Jones
about his feud with Ernie Ladd, with Jones offering Ladd
$1,000 to get in the ring with him; moments later, Jimmy
Valiant & the Junkyard Dog appeared and discussed their
feuds with Paul Jones' men and JYD facing Slater; Weaver
then brought up the names of Adrian Street & Miss Linda, with
a photo of the two appearing on screen and Valiant saying,
"What is that, a UFO?"; Valiant then said it didn't matter what
they were because he and JYD would take care of them:*
The Great Kabuki (w/ Gary Hart) pinned Tim Horner at 3:49
with a falling fist drop off the top
The Assassin (w/ Paul Jones) pinned Vinnie Valentino with a
standing headbutt at around the 4:20 mark; late in the match, it
was implied Jones gave the Assassin a weapon, which the
Assassin stuffed into his mask leading to the finish
Ivan Koloff & Don Kernodle (w/ Gary Hart) defeated Gene
Ligon & Brickhouse Brown at 6:18 when Kernodle pinned
Ligon with a clothesline
The Junkyard Dog & Jimmy Valiant defeated Gary Royal &
Barry O at 1:16 when JYD pinned Royal with the powerslam
Jay Youngblood & NWA TV Champion & NWA Tag Team
Champion Mark Youngblood defeated Jack & Jerry Briscoe via
disqualification when Mark was thrown over the top rope; after
the bout, the Briscoes dropped Mark across the guardrail on
the floor, with Jack then appplying the figure-4 on the floor as
Jay twice came off the apron with kneedrops onto Mark;
moments later, the Briscos celebrated in the ring (the match
was joined in progress)
Brian Adias pinned Ali Bey with an inside cradle at 4:28
Tully Blanchard (w/ Gary Hart) pinned Brett Hart with the
slingshot suplex at 8:24

Auckland, New Zealand - March 21, 1984
NWA World Champion Harley Race defeated Ric Flair

JCP @ Harrisonburg, VA - High School - March 22, 1984
Barry O & Doug Vines vs. Vinnie Valentino & Mark Fleming
Assassin #1 vs. Tony Charles
Tully Blanchard vs. Johnny Weaver
Assassin #2 vs. Mark Youngblood (Youngblood gets 5 minutes
with Paul Jones if he wins)
NWA US Champion Dick Slater vs. Dory Funk Jr.

Kallang, Singapore - March 23, 1984
Ric Flair defeated NWA World Champion Harley Race to win the title

JCP @ Hampton, VA - Coliseum - March 23, 1984
Don Kernodle & Barry O defeated Larry Hamilton & Vinnie Valentino
Rufus R. Jones defeated Ernie Ladd
Sam Houston defeated Ali Bey
Keith Larson defeated Gary Royal
Jimmy Valiant, Mark Youngblood, & the Junkyard Dog defeated Paul Jones & the Assassins
NWA US Champion Dick Slater defeated Greg Valentine

JCP @ Charleston, SC - County Hall - March 23, 1984
Tully Blanchard defeated Johnny Weaver
Barry O defeated Denny Brown
Brian Adidas defeated Doug Vines
Barry Hart defeated Bobby Bass
Dory Funk Jr., Angelo Mosca Sr. & Jr. defeated NWA Mid Atlantic Heavyweight Champion Ivan Koloff, the Great Kabuki, & Gary Hart

JCP @ Lenoir, NC - March 24, 1984
Sam Houston defeated Ali Bey
Jeff Sword defeated Denny Brown
Angelo Mosca Jr. defeated Tully Blanchard
Assassin #1 defeated Johnny Weaver
Dory Funk Jr. & Jay Youngblood defeated Bob Orton Jr. & Don Kernodle
Rufus R. Jones defeated Ernie Ladd

JCP @ Richmond, VA - Coliseum - March 24, 1984
Larry Hamilton defeated Bobby Bass
Vinnie Valentino defeated Kurt Von Hess
Brian Adidas defeated Barry O
The Junkyard Dog defeated the Great Kabuki
Ivan Koloff defeated Angelo Mosca Sr. in a chain match
Wahoo McDaniel & Mark Youngblood defeated the Road Warriors
NWA US Champion Dick Slater defeated Greg Valentine in a steel cage match
Jimmy Valiant defeated Assassin #2 in a hair vs. mask match

Kallang, Singapore - March 25, 1984
Ric Flair defeated NWA World Champion Harley Race to win the title

JCP @ Roanoke, VA - Civic Center - March 25, 1984 (matinee)
Boogie Jam 84
Jeff Sword defeated Keith Larson
Kurt Von Hess & Hans Schroeder defeated Keith Larson & Denny Brown
Rufus R. Jones defeated Ernie Ladd

Jimmy Valiant defeated Assassin #2
The Junkyard Dog, Angelo Mosca Sr. & Jr. defeated Ivan Koloff, the Great Kabuki, & Gary Hart

JCP @ Greensboro, NC - Coliseum - March 25, 1984
Barry Hart defeated Ali Bey
Brian Adidas defeated Bobby Bass
Johnny Weaver defeated Doug Vines
Jay Youngblood defeated Tully Blanchard
Angelo Mosca Jr. defeated the Great Kabuki
Angelo Mosca Sr. defeated Ivan Koloff
Assassin #1 defeated Jimmy Valiant
Paul Jones defeated Jimmy Valiant
Wahoo McDaniel & Mark Youngblood defeated Bob Orton Jr. & Don Kernodle
NWA US Champion Dick Slater defeated the Junkyard Dog

JCP @ Greenville, SC - Memorial Auditorium - March 26, 1984
Vinnie Valentino & Larry Hamilton defeated Kurt Von Hess & Hans Schroeder
Barry Hart defeated Bob Bass
Dory Funk Jr. fought Brian Adidas to a draw
Jimmy Valiant defeated Paul Jones
Rufus R. Jones & Jimmy Valiant defeated the Assassins
The Junkyard Dog defeated NWA US Champion Dick Slater via count-out

JCP @ Fayetteville, NC - Cumberland County Civic Center - March 26, 1984
Mark Fleming defeated Ali Bey
Johnny Weaver defeated Doug Vines
Wahoo McDaniel & Mark Youngblood defeated Tully Blanchard & Don Kernodle
Ernie Ladd defeated Jay Youngblood
Angelo Mosca Jr. defeated the Great Kabuki
Ivan Koloff defeated Angelo Mosca Sr.

JCP @ Raleigh, NC - Dorton Arena - March 27, 1984
Brian Adidas fought Dory Funk Jr. to a draw
Jeff Sword defeated Denny Brown
Sam Houston defeated Gary Royal
NWA TV Champion Mark Youngblood defeated Tully Blanchard
Wahoo McDaniel defeated Don Kernodle
Angelo Mosca Sr. & Jr. defeated NWA Mid Atlantic Heavyweight Champion Ivan Koloff & the Great Kabuki

JCP @ Columbia, SC - Township Auditorium - March 27, 1984
Doug Vines defeated Mark Fleming
Barry O defeated Barry Hart
Keith Larson defeated Kurt Von Hess
Rufus R. Jones & Jay Youngblood defeated Ernie Ladd & Assassin #1

The Junkyard Dog defeated NWA US Champion Dick Slater via disqualification

Jimmy Valiant defeated Assassin #2; stipulations stated Valiant would have his head shaved if he lost and the Assassin would be unmasked if he lost

JCP @ ? - March / April 1984

Jimmy Valiant pinned Assassin #2 in a hair vs. mask match with the elbow drop after Dusty Rhodes, who was tied to Paul Jones at ringside, hit the Assassin from the ring apron; after the bout, Valiant unmasked the Assassin (Hercules Hernandez) (unsure as to if this is the Columbia or Charlotte match)

JCP @ Spartanburg, SC - Memorial Auditorium - March 28, 1984

Worldwide - 3/31/84 - featured David Crockett & Johnny Weaver on commentary; included Crockett announcing Tully Blanchard would challenge for the NWA TV Title, the Junkyard Dog would face NWA US Champion Dick Slater, Angelo Mosca Sr. & Jr. would be in action, and Adrian Street would appear; featured Crockett conducting an interview with Brian Adias, with Adias discussing his tag team match earlier with Jimmy Valiant; Valiant then walked in and said he and Adias would be after Paul Jones' men; the Junkyard Dog then joined them and talked about his fight earlier against both NWA US Champion Dick Slater and NWA TV Champion Tully Blanchard; included footage of Mark & Jay Youngblood vs. Jack & Jerry Brisco from a recent house show, with the Youngbloods defeating the Briscos via crucifix by Jay to Jack; after the bout, the Briscos double teamed Jay in the ring, with NWA Tag Team Champion Wahoo McDaniel coming out to make the save; moments later, Slater came out and helped in attacking McDaniel and the Youngbloods; featured a music video on Adrian Street, with the song entitled "Imagine What I Could Do To You;" included a vignette showing the Great Kabuki outside wearing a headdress, then a kabuki mask, and finally showing his painted face; featured Crockett conducting a closing interview with Rufus R. Jones in which he said he had his $1,000 to give Ernie Ladd to face him in the ring; moments later, Ladd and Gary Hart came out, demanding the money; Jones and ladd then went out to the ring, with NWA Tag Team Champions Mark Youngblood & Wahoo McDaniel joined Crockett, with Youngblood saying he wasn't done with Blanchard and McDaniel discussing their feud against the Briscos:

Jimmy Valiant & Brian Adias defeated Jeff Sword & Kurt Von Hess at 4:06 when Adias pinned Sword with a modified airplane spin into a Samoan Drop

Tully Blanchard (w/ Paul Jones) pinned NWA TV Champion & NWA Tag Team Champion Mark Youngblood to win the TV title at around the 6:30 mark with a knee to the back; Youngblood's foot was on the bottom rope during the cover but the referee didn't notice it; Jones attempted to push it off the ropes but was too late; during the match, it was noted Ivan Koloff recently regained the Mid-Atlantic Heavyweight Title

The Junkyard Dog defeated NWA US Champion Dick Slater

via disqualification at around the 3:30 mark when JYD began brawling in the ring with NWA TV Champion Tully Blanchard; Blanchard, wearing street clothes, came out during the opening moments of the match and was assaulted in the ring by JYD, with JYD tearing up Blanchard's dress shirt in the process; the bell rang without reason at around the 2-minute mark; late in the match, Blanchard returned ringside, with JYD chasing him around the ring and then back into the ring; after the bout, referee Sonny Fargo was punched by Slater and JYD was double teamed before he eventually fought off both Slater and Blanchard

Angelo Mosca Sr. & Jr. defeated Gary Royal & Bobby Bass at 10:54 when Jr. pinned Royal with a crossbody off the top

Rufus R. Jones (sub. for Mark Fleming) fought Ernie Ladd (w/ Gary Hart) to a no contest at around the 10-second mark; prior to the bout, Ladd agreed to face Jones after Jones paid him $1,000; after taking the money in the ring, Ladd and Hart immediately left ringside with the cash; moments later, Ladd and Hart gloated about taking the money to David Crockett, with Ladd calling Jones "Capt. Nappy Head" and the dumbest man he's ever seen; eventually, Jones came running after them, clearing them from the interview area; Ladd and Jones then began brawling in the ring, with Jones fighting off both Ladd and Hart as the show ended

JCP @ Sumter, SC - Exhibition Center - March 29, 1984

Brian Adidas defeated Ali Bey
Doug Vines defeated Barry Hart
Keith Larson defeated Jeff Sword
Rufus R. Jones defeated Ernie Ladd
Jimmy Valiant defeated Paul Jones
Jimmy Valiant & the Junkyard Dog defeated the Assassins

Central States @ St. Louis, MO - March 29, 1984

NWA World Champion Ric Flair vs. Kerry Von Erich

JCP @ Lynchburg, VA - Armory - March 30, 1984

Tully Blanchard vs. Jay Youngblood
Don Kerndole vs. Mark Youngblood
Rufus R. Jones vs. Ernie Ladd

CWF @ Miami, FL - March 30, 1984

NWA World Champion Ric Flair defeated Barry Windham via disqualification

JCP @ Charleston, SC - County Hall - March 30, 1984

Larry Hamilton defeated Ben Alexander
Jeff Sword defeated Vinnie Valentino
Barry Hart defeated Gary Royal
Brian Adidas defeated Hans Schroeder
Jimmy Valiant & the Junkyard Dog defeated the Assassins; Paul Jones was placed in a cage at ringside for the duration of the bout

WWC @ Bayamon, Puerto Rico - March 31, 1984
NWA World Champion Ric Flair fought King Tonga to a no contest

JCP @ Hickory, NC - March 31, 1984
The Greek Goddess defeated Donna Christanello
Gene Ligon defeated Jeff Sword
Keith Larson defeated Gary Royal
Keith Larson defeated Hans Schroeder
The Junkyard Dog, Angelo Mosca Sr. & Jr. defeated NWA Mid Atlantic Heavyweight Champion Ivan Koloff, the Great Kabuki, & Gary Hart

JCP @ Fayetteville, NC - Cumberland County Civic Center - April 1, 1984
Barry Hart defeated Ali Bey
Ben Alexander defeated Kurt Von Hess
Adrian Street defeated Brian Adidas
Tully Blanchard defeated Larry Hamilton
The Junkyard Dog defeated Ernie Ladd
Angelo Mosca Sr. & Jr. defeated Ivan Koloff & Gary Hart
Jack & Jerry Brisco defeated the Junkyard Dog & Mark Youngblood

St. Thomas, Virgin Island - April 1, 1984
Carlos Colon defeated NWA World Champion Ric Flair

JCP @ Greensboro, NC - Coliseum - April 1, 1984
Larry Hamilton defeated Jeff Sword
Doug Vines defeated Sam Houston
Barry O defeated Mark Fleming
Adrian Street defeated Keith Larson
Tully Blanchard defeated Brian Adidas
Tully Blanchard defeated Larry Hamilton
The Junkyard Dog defeated Ernie Ladd
Angelo Mosca defeated NWA Mid Atlantic Heavyweight Champion Ivan Koloff & Gary Hart
Jack & Jerry Brisco defeated the Junkyard Dog & NWA Tag Team Champion Mark Youngblood

Toronto, Ontario - Maple Leaf Gardens - April 1, 1984
The Destroyer defeated Goldie Rogers
Pez Whatley defeated Gary Royal
The Grapplers defeated Bob Marcus & Vinnie Valentino
The Great Kabuki defeated Brickhouse Brown
Jay Youngblood & Johnny Weaver defeated Terry & Rudy Kay via count-out
Bret Hart defeated Leo Burke via disqualification
Jimmy Valiant, Dory Funk Jr., & Rufus R. Jones defeated Paul Jones & the Assassins

WCCW @ San Antonio, TX - April 2, 1984
Kerry Von Erich defeated NWA World Champion Ric Flair via disqualification

JCP @ Harrisonburg, VA - High School Gym - April 1984
Keith Larson vs. Jeff Sword
Larry Hamilton & Johnny Weaver vs. Bobby Bass & Doug Vines
Angelo Mosca & the Assassin vs. Ernie Ladd & Brian Adias
Jimmy Valiant vs. Paul Jones (New York streetfight)

JCP @ Greenville, SC - Memorial Auditorium - April 2, 1984
Keith Larson defeated Doug Vines
Kurt Von Hess defeated Barry Hart
Tully Blanchard defeated Sam Houston
Adrian Street defeated Hamilton
Ivan Koloff defeated Angelo Mosca Jr.
The Junkyard Dog defeated Dick Slater in a lumberjack match
Jack & Jerry Brisco defeated Wahoo McDaniel & Mark Youngblood

JCP @ Natural Bridge, VA - High School Gym - April 3, 1984
Keith Larson defeated Bobby Bass
Barry Orton defeated Barry Hart
Mark Fleming defeated Jeff Sword
Brian Adidas defeated Bob Orton Jr.
Wahoo McDaniel, Jimmy Valiant, & Angelo Mosca Jr. defeated Paul Jones, Ron Bass, & Assassin #1

Port of Spain, Trinidad - April 3, 1984
NWA World Champion Ric Flair vs. Ray Apollon

JCP @ Raliegh, NC - Dorton Arena - April 3, 1984
Pez Whatley defeated Adrian Street via disqualification
The Great Kabuki defeated Rufus R. Jones
Tully Blanchard defeated Larry Hamilton
Vinnie Valentino defeated Kurt Von Hess
Jay & Mark Youngblood defeated Jack & Jerry Brisco
Ivan Koloff defeated Angelo Mosca Sr. in a Russian chain match

JCP @ Spartanburg, SC - Memorial Auditorium - April 4, 1984
TV taping:
Jack & Jerry Brisco defeated NWA Tag Team Champions Wahoo McDaniel & Mark Youngblood to win the titles
The Junkyard Dog vs. NWA TV Champion Tully Blanchard
Worldwide - 4/7/84:
Wahoo McDaniel & Mark Youngblood defeated Jeff Sword & Hess
NWA TV Champion Tully Blanchard defeated Larry Hamilton
Ivan Koloff & Don Kernodle defeated Vinnie Valentino & Barry Horowitz
The Junkyard Dog vs. the Great Kabuki
Angelo Mosca Jr. defeated Ben Alexander

JCP @ Charleston - County Hall - April 6, 1984
Doug Vines defeated Mark Fleming

Vinnie Valentino defeated Bobby Bass
Rufus R. Jones defeated Bob Orton Jr.
Don Kernodle defeated Pez Whatley
Tully Blanchard defeated Brian Adidas
Jimmy Valiant defeated Paul Jones
Assassin #1 defeated Jimmy Valiant

JCP @ Norfolk, VA - Scope - April 6, 1984

Jeff Sword defeated Keith Larson
Sam Houston defeated Gary Royal
Kurt Von Hess defeated Barry Hart
Angelo Mosca Sr. & Jr. defeated Ivan Koloff & the Great Kabuki
Wahoo McDaniel defeated Adrian Street
Mark & Jay Youngblood defeated Jack & Jerry Brisco
NWA US Champion Dick Slater defeated the Junkyard Dog

GCW @ Baltimore, MD - Civic Center - April 7, 1984

Ernie Ladd defeated the Mystery Man
Tim Horner defeated NWA Tag Team Champion Jerry Brisco
Sweet Brown Sugar defeated the Spoiler
Brad Armstrong defeated Larry Zbyszko
Wahoo McDaniel & King Kong Bundy defeated the Road Warriors via disqualification
Ron Garvin defeated GCW TV Champion Jake Roberts to win the title
NWA World Champion Ric Flair defeated NWA Tag Team Champion Jack Brisco

JCP @ Roanoke, VA - Civic Center - April 8, 1984 (matinee)

Keith Larson defeated Gary Royal
Kurt Von Hess defeated Gary Quartinelli
NWA TV Champion Tully Blanchard & Don Kernodle defeated Pez Whatley & Vinnie Valentino
Brian Adidas defeated NWA TV Champion Tully Blanchard
Jimmy Valiant defeated Paul Jones; the match had a 5-minute time limit; stipulations stated the Assassins were banned from ringside for the match
Assassin #1 defeated Jimmy Valiant
NWA Tag Team Champions Jack & Jerry Brisco defeated Wahoo McDaniel & Mark Youngblood

CWF @ Orlando, FL - April 8, 1984

Kharma defeated Denny Brown
Mike Davis defeated Black Bart
Joe Lightfoot defeated the One Man Gang in a strap match
Florida Heavyweight Champion Billy Jack defeated Kendo Nagasaki
Barry Windham & Mike Rotundo defeated Hector & Chavo Guerrero
Andre the Giant & Mike Graham defeated Kevin Sullivan & Buzz Sawyer in a bunkhouse match
NWA World Champion Ric Flair defeated Dusty Rhodes in a lights out steel cage match

JCP @ Savannah, GA - Civic Center - April 8, 1984

Mark Fleming defeated Ali Bey
Gene Ligon defeated Ben Alexander
Barry Hart defeated Doug Vines
Adrian Street defeated Jay Youngblood
Rufus R. Jones defeated Ernie Ladd
Angelo Mosca Sr. & Jr. defeated Ivan Koloff & the Great Kabuki
NWA US Champion Dick Slater defeated the Junkyard Dog

JCP @ Charlotte, NC - Coliseum - April 8, 1984

Larry Hamilton defeated Bob Bass
Sam Houston defeated Hans Schroeder
Cowboy Lang defeated Little Tokyo
NWA Tag Team Champions Jack & Jerry Brisco defeated Mark & Jay Youngblood
Ivan Koloff defeated Angelo Mosca Jr.
Wahoo McDaniel defeated Adrian Street
NWA US Champion Dick Slater defeated the Junkyard Dog
Jimmy Valiant defeated Assassin #2 in a hair vs. mask match

CWF @ West Palm Beach, FL - April 9, 1984

Black Bart defeated Denny Brown
Mike Davis defeated the One Man Gang
Mike Rotundo & Joe Lightfoot defeated Hector & Chavo Guerrero
Florida Heavyweight Champion Billy Jack defeated Kendo Nagasaki
Buzz Sawyer defeated Mike Graham in a taped fist Texas Death Match
Andre the Giant & Dusty Rhodes defeated Kevin Sullivan & Kharma in a bunkhouse match
NWA World Champion Ric Flair defeated Barry Windham via disqualification

JCP @ Greenville, SC - Memorial Auditorium - April 9, 1984

Adrian Street defeated Sam Houston
Angelo Mosca defeated the Great Kabuki via disqualification
Brian Adidas defeated Kurt Von Hess
Wahoo McDaniel & Mark Youngblood defeated Ivan Koloff & Don Kernodle
The Junkyard Dog & Jay Youngblood defeated NWA US Champion Dick Slater & NWA TV Champion Tully Blanchard

CWF @ Tampa, FL - Sun Dome - April 10, 1984

Black Bart defeated Denny Brown
Mike Davis fought Kendo Nagasaki to a draw
Joe Lightfoot defeated the One Man Gang in a strap match
Mike Davis (sub. for Mike Graham) defeated Kharma
US Tag Team Champions Barry Windham & Mike Rotundo fought Hector & Chavo Guerrero to a double disqualification
NWA World Champion Ric Flair defeated Florida Heavyweight Champion Billy Jack via disqualification
Andre the Giant & Dusty Rhodes defeated Kevin Sullivan & Buzz Sawyer at the 6-minute mark in a lights out bunkhouse match

JCP @ Raleigh, NC - Dorton Arena - April 10, 1984
Keith Larson defeated Kurt Von Hess
Doug Vines defeated Barry Hart
Cowboy Lang defeated Little Tokyo
Adrian Street defeated Sam Houston
The Great Kabuki defeated Brian Adidas
Angelo Mosca Sr. & Jr. defeated Ivan Koloff & Gary Hart in a
double Russian chain match
Angelo Mosca Jr. defeated Ivan Koloff in a Russian chain
match

**JCP @ Columbia, SC - Township Auditorium - April 10,
1984**
Mark Fleming defeated Ali Bey
Pez Whatley defeated Bobby Bass
Assassin #1 defeated Larry Hamilton
Ernie Ladd defeated Rufus R. Jones via disqualification
NWA TV Champion Tully Blanchard & Don Kernodle defeated
Wahoo McDaniel & Mark Youngblood
Jimmy Valiant defeated Paul Jones in a streetfight

**CWF @ Miami Beach, FL - Convention Hall - April 11, 1984
(5,201)**
Denny Brown defeated Inferno #1
Joe Lightfoot defeated JJ Dillon
Mike Rotundo & Mike Davis defeated Hector & Chavo
Guerrero via disqualification
Billy Jack fought Buzz Sawyer to a draw
Barry Windham defeated Black Bart in a brass knuckles taped
fist match
NWA World Champion Ric Flair defeated Dusty Rhodes via
disqualification in a lights out steel cage match
Andre the Giant & Mike Rotundo defeated Kevin Sullivan, the
One Man Gang, & Kharma in a lights out handicap match

JCP @ ? - April 11, 1984
TV taping:

Worldwide - 4/14/84:
Brian Adidas & Pez Whatley defeated Ali Bey & Kurt Von Hess
Ivan Koloff & Don Kernodle defeated Gene Ligon & Vinnie
Valentino
Adrian Street defeated Keith Larson
Angelo Mosca Jr. defeated Barry Orton
The Great Kabuki defeated Brett Hart
Mark & Jay Youngblood defeated Jeff Sword & Doug Vines

CWF @ Tampa, FL - April 12, 1984
TV taping:
NWA World Champion Ric Flair vs. Mike Davis

**JCP @ Amherst, VA - County High School Gym - April 12,
1984**
Included the Assassins, Paul Jones, Wahoo McDaniel, NWA

US Champion Dick Slater, Angelo Mosca Jr., Brian Adias, and
Jimmy Valiant

CWF @ Homestead, FL - April 12, 1984
Mike Rotundo defeated Kharma
Joe Lightfoot fought Hector Guerrero to a draw
Black Bart defeated Barry Windham in a brass knuckles match
Andre the Giant defeated the One Man Gang
Dusty Rhodes defeated NWA World Champion Ric Flair in a
non-title Texas Death Match
Andre the Giant won a battle royal

JCP @ Sumter, SC - Exhibition Center - April 12, 1984
Jeff Sword defeated Sam Houston
Ben Alexander defeated Ali Bey
Larry Hamilton defeated Hans Schroeder
Brian Adidas defeated Jeff Sword
Ernie Ladd & the Assassin defeated Jimmy Valiant & Jay
Youngblood via disqualification

Central States @ St. Louis, MO - April 13, 1984
Jerry & Ted Oates defeated Scott Farris & TG Stone
Ron Ritchie defeated Roger Kirby
Dick the Bruiser defeated Luke Graham
The Grapplers defeated Jim Brunzell & Steve O
Blackjack Lanza fought Ken Patera to a no contest
Chris Adams defeated Jimmy Garvin
NWA World Champion Ric Flair defeated Harley Race

JCP @ Charleston, SC - County Hall - April 13, 1984
Gary Quartenelli defeated Bobby Bass
Jeff Sword defeated Gary Royal
Kurt Von Hess fought Sam Houston to a draw
Hans Schroeder (sub. for Barry Orton) & Don Kernodle
defeated Johnny Weaver & Larry Hamilton
Ernie Ladd defeated Jay Youngblood
Mark Youngblood defeated NWA TV Champion Tully
Blanchard

JCP @ Richmond, VA - Coliseum - April 13, 1984
Barry Hart defeated Ali Bey
Gene Ligon defeated Ben Alexander
Mark Fleming defeated Doug Vines
Cowboy Lang defeated Little Tokyo
Adrian Street defeated Brian Adidas
Pez Whatley defeated the Great Kabuki via disqualification
Dick Slater defeated Jimmy Valiant
Angelo Mosca Sr. & Jr. defeated Ivan Koloff & Gary Hart in a
double chain match

GCW @ Atlanta, GA - WTBS Studios - April 14, 1984
TV taping:
NWA World Champion Ric Flair vs. Pat Rose

JCP @ Fredericksburg, VA - Stafford High School - April 14, 1984
Adrian Street vs. Brian Adidas
Little Tokyo vs. Cowboy Lang
Angelo Mosca Jr. vs. Ivan Koloff
Jimmy Valiant vs. the Assassin
Jimmy Valiant vs. Paul Jones (5-minute challenge)

Nassau, Bahamas - April 14, 1984
NWA World Champion Ric Flair vs. Barry Windham

JCP @ Conway, SC - April 14, 1984
Keith Larson defeated Gary Royal
Sam Houston defeated Kurt Von Hess
Mark & Jay Youngblood defeated Ernie Ladd & Don Kernodle
Angelo Mosca & Pez Whatley defeated the Great Kabuki & Gary Hart
NWA US Champion Dick Slater defeated Pez Whatley

Toronto, Ontario - Maple Leaf Gardens - April 15, 1984
Nick DeCarlo fought Bob Marcus to a draw
The Destroyer & Goldie Rogers defeated Sam Houston & John Bonello
Pez Whatley defeated Ben Alexander
The Great Kabuki defeated Keith Larson
North American Heavyweight Champion Leo Burke defeated Buddy (Bret) Hart
Jay Youngblood & Johnny Weaver defeated Rudy & Terry Kay in a lumberjack match
Jimmy Valiant defeated Assassin #2 in a hair vs. mask match; after the bout, Valiant unmasked Assassin #2 to be Ray Hernandez

JCP @ Asheville, NC - Civic Center - April 15, 1984
Larry Hamilton defeated Kurt Von Hess
Don Kernodle defeated Gene Ligon
Cowboy Lang defeated Little Tokyo
Dick Slater defeated Wahoo McDaniel
Adrian Street defeated Brian Adidas
Angelo Mosca Sr. defeated Ernie Ladd
Angelo Mosca Jr. defeated NWA Mid Atlantic Heavyweight Champion Ivan Koloff via disqualification
Mark Youngblood defeated NWA TV Champion Tully Blanchard

JCP @ Greenville, SC - Memorial Auditorium - April 16, 1984
Gary Royal defeated Ali Bey
Ernie Ladd defeated Jay Youngblood via disqualification
Barry Hart defeated Jeff Sword
Mark Fleming defeated Gary Royal
The Road Warriors defeated Wahoo McDaniel & King Kong Bundy

Continental @ Birmingham, AL - April 16, 1984
NWA World Champion Ric Flair defeated Jimmy Golden via disqualification

JCP @ Fayetteville, NC - Cumberland County Civic Center - April 16, 1984
Cowboy Lang defeated Little Tokyo
Brian Adidas defeated Doug Vines
Kurt Von Hess defeated Gene Ligon
Don Kernodle defeated Larry Hamilton
Mark Youngblood defeated Adrian Street
Ivan Koloff defeated Angelo Mosca Jr.
Angelo Mosca Sr. defeated NWA TV Champion Tully Blanchard

JCP @ Raliegh, NC - Dorton Arena - April 17, 1984
Brian Adidas & Larry Hamilton defeated Gary Royal & Doug Vines
Pez Whatley defeated the Great Kabuki via disqualification
The Assassin defeated Angelo Mosca Sr.
Keith Larson defeated Ali Bey
Mark Fleming defeated Bobby Bass
Jimmy Valiant defeated Paul Jones in a New York Streetfight

Central States @ Rogers, AR - April 17, 1984
NWA World Champion Ric Flair defeated Buzz Tyler

JCP @ Columbia, SC - Township Auditorium - April 17, 1984
Cowboy Lang defeated Little Tokyo
Jeff Sword defeated Barry Hart
Sam Houston defeated Kurt Von Hess
Adrian Street defeated Jay Youngblood via disqualification
Ivan Koloff defeated Angelo Mosca Jr.
Wahoo McDaniel & Mark Youngblood defeated NWA TV Champion Tully Blanchard & Don Kernodle in a Texas Tornado match

JCP @ Spartanburg, SC - Memorial Auditorium - April 18, 1984
TV taping:
Worldwide - 4/21/84:
Jimmy Valiant & Brian Adidas defeated Gary Royal & Doug Vines
Rufus R. Jones defeated Jeff Sword
Adrian Street defeated Pez Whatley
NWA US Champion Dick Slater defeated Sam Houston
Wahoo McDaniel & Mark Youngblood defeated Ben Alexander & Kurt Von Hess
Ivan Koloff & Don Kernodle defeated Larry Hamilton & Brett Hart

Worldwide - 4/28/84:
Pez Whatley defeated Jeff Sword
Brian Adidas defeated Ben Alexander

Little Tokyo defeated Cowboy Lang
Ernie Ladd defeaetd Sam Houston
Mark & Jay Youngblood defeated Gary Royal & Kurt Von Hess

JCP @ Hampton, VA - Coliseum - April 19, 1984
Barry Hart defeated Ali Bey
Sam Houston defeated Kurt Von Hess
Cowboy Lang defeated Little Tokyo
Pez Whatley defeated the Great Kabuki
Angelo Mosca Jr. defeated Adrian Street
NWA TV Champion Tully Blanchard defeated Jay Youngblood
Wahoo McDaniel & Mark Youngblood defeated Ivan Koloff & Don Kernodle

Central States @ Kansas City, KS - April 19, 1984
NWA World Champion Ric Flair defeated Buzz Tyler at the 32-minute mark

JCP @ Harrisonburg, VA - High School - April 19, 1984
Keith Larson vs. Jeff Sword
Larry Hamilton & Johnny Weaver vs. Doug Vines & Bobby Bass
Ernie Ladd vs. Brian Adidas
Angelo Mosca Jr. vs. the Assassin
Jimmy Valiant vs. Paul Jones

JCP @ Lynchburg, VA - Armory - April 20, 1984
Gary Royal defeated Barry Hart
Dick Slater defeated Jay Youngblood
Ivan Koloff & Don Kernodle defeated Wahoo McDaniel & Mark Youngblood
Larry Hamilton defeated Ali Bey
Brian Adidas defeated Kurt Von Hess
Pez Whatley defeated Doug Vines

Central States @ Lincoln, NE - April 20, 1984
NWA World Champion Ric Flair defeated Brad Armstrong

GCW @ Atlanta, GA - WTBS Studios - April 21, 1984
TV taping:
NWA World Champion Ric Flair defeated Tommy Rogers

Central States @ Ft. Scott, KS - April 21, 1984
NWA World Champion Ric Flair defeated Ted Oates

JCP @ Greensboro, NC - Coliseum - April 21, 1984
Larry Hamilton & Sam Houston defeated Gary Royal & Doug Vines
Brian Adidas defeated Kurt Von Hess
The Great Kabuki defeated Johnny Weaver
Assassin #1 defeated Angelo Mosca
Dusty Rhodes defeated Adrian Street via disqualification
NWA Tag Team Champions Jack & Jerry Brisco defeated Pez Whatley & Jay Youngblood

Jimmy Valiant defeated Paul Jones in a steel cage match
Ricky Steamboat defeated NWA US Champion Dick Slater to win the title

JCP @ Charleston, SC - County Hall - April 21, 1984
Keith Larson defeated Ali Bey
Barry Hart defeated Jeff Sword
Angelo Mosca Jr. defeated Bobby Bass
Cowboy Long defeated Little Tokyo
Ernie Ladd defeated Rufus R. Jones
Wahoo McDaniel & Mark Youngblood defeated Ivan Koloff & Don Kernodle

JCP @ Savannah, GA - Civic Center - April 22, 1984
Sam Houston defeated Ali Bey
Barry Hart defeated Gene Ligon
Gary Royal defeated Gary Quartenelli
Johnny Weaver & Brian Adidas defeated the Great Kabuki & Don Kernodle
Assassin #1 defeated Angelo Mosca Sr.
Jimmy Valiant defeated Paul Jones in a steel cage match
NWA World Champion Ric Flair defeated Dick Slater

JCP @ Roanoke, VA - Civic Center - April 22, 1984
Keith Larson defeated Bobby Bass
Larry Hamilton defeated Ben Alexander
Pez Whatley defeated Kurt Von Hess
Cowboy Lang defeated Little Tokyo
Ernie Ladd defeated Rufus R. Jones
Adrian Street defeated Jay Youngblood via disqualification
Jack & Jerry Brisco defeated Wahoo McDaniel & Jay Youngblood

JCP @ Charlotte, NC - Coliseum - April 22, 1984
Doug Vines defeated Mark Fleming
Vinnie Valentino defeated Jeff Sword
Dick Slater defeated Johnny Weaver
Angelo Mosca Sr. defeated Assassin #1
Dusty Rhodes defeated Adrian Street
Angelo Mosca Jr. defeated Mid-Atlantic Heavyweight Champion Ivan Koloff to win the title
Wahoo McDaniel & Mark Youngblood defeated NWA Tag Team Champions Jack & Jerry Brisco via disqualification
Jimmy Valiant defeated Paul Jones
NWA World Champion Ric Flair fought NWA US Champion Ricky Steamboat to a 60-minute time-limit draw

JCP @ Greenville, SC - Memorial Auditorium - April 23, 1984
Sam Houston defeated Bobby Bass
Pez Whatley defeated Kurt Von Hess
Don Kernodle defeated Johnny Weaver
NWA TV Champion Tully Blanchard defeated Brian Adidas
Dusty Rhodes defeated Adrian Street via disqualification
Jack & Jerry Brisco defeated Mark & Jay Youngblood via

disqualification
NWA World Champion Ric Flair fought NWA US Champion Ricky Steamboat to a 60-minute time-limit draw

JCP @ Columbia, SC - Township Auditorium - April 24, 1984
Vinnie Valentino defeated Gary Royal
Barry Hart defeated Ben Alexander
Don Kernodle defeated Johnny Weaver
Adrian Street defeated Pez Whatley
Jimmy Valiant defeated the Assassin
Jack & Jerry Brisco defeated Wahoo McDaniel & Mark Youngblood via disqualification
NWA World Champion Ric Flair defeated Dick Slater

JCP @ Myrtle Beach, SC - April 25, 1984
TV taping:
Ivan Koloff & Don Kernodle defeated Mark Fleming & Vinnie Valentino
Jimmy Valiant & Rufus R. Jones defeated Kurt Von Hess & Gary Royal
Brian Adidas defeated Jeff Sword
Pez Whatley defeated Don Kernodle via disqualification
Angelo Mosca Jr. defeated Doug Vines
Wahoo McDaniel defeated Barry Orton
Dusty Rhodes defeated Adrian Street
NWA Tag Team Champions Jack & Jerry Brisco defeated Mark & Jay Youngblood
NWA World Champion Ric Flair defeated Dick Slater

Worldwide - 5/5/84:
Wahoo McDaniel & Brian Adidas defeated Gary Royal & Bobby Bass
Vinnie Valentino defeated Ernie Ladd via disqualification
Penny Mitchell defeated Leilani Kai
Angelo Mosca Jr. defeated Barry Orton
Ivan Koloff & Don Kernodle defeated Sam Houston & Cortinelli
Jimmy Valiant, Rufus R. Jones, & Pez Whatley vs. Doug Vines, Ben Alexander, & Kurt Von Hess

JCP @ Norfolk, VA - Scope - April 26, 1984
Vinnie Valentino defeated Ben Alexander
Keith Larson defeated Kurt Von Hess
Don Kernodle defeated Johnny Weaver
Dusty Rhodes defeated Adrian Street via disqualification
Wahoo McDaniel defeated NWA TV Champion Tully Blanchard
Jimmy Valiant defeated Paul Jones
Jack & Jerry Brisco defeated Wahoo MCDaniel & Mark Youngblood
NWA World Champion Ric Flair defeated Dick Slater

JCP @ Richmond, VA - Coliseum - April 27, 1984
Keith Larson defeated Ben Alexander
Vinnie Valentino defeated Kurt Von Hess
Ivan Koloff & Don Kernodle defeated Johnny Weaver & Larry

Hamilton
The Assassin defeated Angelo Mosca Sr.
Dick Slater defeated Angelo Mosca Jr.
Wahoo McDaniel & Mark Youngblood defeated Jack & Jerry Brisco
Jimmy Valiant defeated Paul Jones
NWA World Champion Ric Flair fought NWA US Champion Ricky Steamboat to a draw

GCW @ Atlanta, GA - WTBS Studios - April 28, 1984
TV taping:
NWA World Champion Ric Flair vs. Joe Turner

JCP @ Bassett, VA - High School - April 28, 1984

JCP @ Rock Hill, SC - Winthrop Coliseum - April 29, 1984
Keith Larson defeated Gary Royal
Don Kernodle & Kurt Von Hess defeated Larry Hamilton & Sam Houston
Wahoo McDaniel & Brad Armstrong defeated Jack & Jerry Brisco
Ernie Ladd defeated Rufus R. Jones
Adrian Street defeated Jimmy Valiant via disqualification
The Greek Goddess defeated Leilani Kai

Toronto, Ontario - Maple Leaf Gardens - April 29, 1984
Canadian Heavyweight Title Tournament
First Round:
Dick Slater defeated Johnny Weaver
Buddy (Bret) Hart defeated Leo Burke; after the bout, Burke attacked Hart, causing him to be eliminated from the tournament
Brian Adidas defeated NWA TV Champion Tully Blanchard via referee's decision
The Great Kabuki defeated Carlos Colon
Angelo Mosca Jr. defeated Terry Kay
Grappler #1 defeated Jay Youngblood
Mark Youngblood defeated Grappler #2
Pez Whatley defeated Jake Roberts via referee's decision
Ivan Koloff defeated Vinnie Valentino
Quarter-Finals:
Brian Adidas defeated Dick Slater via disqualification
Angelo Mosca Jr. defeated the Great Kabuki at the 38-second mark; after the bout, Kabuki sprayed Mosca in the face with mist, causing him to be eliminated from the tournament
Mark Youngblood fought Grappler #2 to a double disqualification
Ivan Koloff defeated Pez Whatley
Finals: Ivan Koloff defeated Brian Adidas

JCP @ Fayetteville, NC - Cumberland County Civic Center - April 30, 1984
Larry Hamilton fought Gary Royal to a draw
Mark Fleming defeated Ali Bey
Jay Youngblood defeated Kurt Von Hess

Jimmy Valiant defeated Adrian Street
Dick Slater defeated Mark Youngblood

PNW @ Bellingham, WA - April 30, 1984
NWA World Champion Ric Flair defeated Brett Sawyer

JCP @ Greenville, SC - Memorial Auditorium - April 30, 1984
Keith Larson defeated Ben Alexander
Jesse Barr defeated Doug Vines
Ernie Ladd defeated Rufus R. Jones
Wahoo McDaniel defeated NWA TV Champion Tully Blanchard
Ivan Koloff & Don Kernodle defeated Angelo Mosca Sr. & Jr.

PNW @ Portland, OR - May 1, 1984
NWA World Champion Ric Flair fought Billy Jack Haynes to a 60-minute time-limit draw

JCP @ Raleigh, NC - Dorton Arena - May 1, 1984
Jesse Barr defeated Jeff Sword
Keith Larson defeated Doug Vines
Brian Adidas defeated Kurt Von Hess
Ernie Ladd defeated Rufus R. Jones
Dick Slater defeated Jay Youngblood via disqualification
Wahoo McDaniel defeated NWA TV Champion Tully Blanchard

JCP @ Columbia, SC - Township Auditorium - May 1, 1984
Barry Hart defeated Ali Bey
Larry Hamilton defeated Bob Orton Jr.
NWA Tag Team Champions Ivan Koloff & Don Kernodle defeated Angelo Mosca Sr. & Jr.
Pez Whatley defeated the Great Kabuki
Jimmy Valiant defeated Adrian Street

PNW @ Seattle, WA - May 2, 1984
NWA World Champion Ric Flair defeated Billy Jack Haynes

PNW @ Cheney, WA - Eastern Washington University - May 3, 1984
NWA World Champion Ric Flair vs. Billy Jack Haynes
Also included 5 other matches

JCP @ Hampton, VA - Coliseum - May 4, 1984
Barry Hart defeated Jeff Sword
Jesse Barr defeated Bobby Bass
Brian Adidas defeated Doug Vines
The Junkyard Dog defeated Gary Hart
Ernie Ladd defeated Rufus R. Jones
The Junkyard Dog defeated Adrian Street
Dick Slater defeated Jay Youngblood
Wahoo McDaniel & Mark Youngblood defeated Jack & Jerry Brisco

PNW @ Eugene, OR - May 4, 1984
NWA World Champion Ric Flair defeated Brett Sawyer

JCP @ Lynchburg, VA - Armory - May 4, 1984
Judy Martin vs. Desiree Peterson
Ivan Koloff & Don Kernodle vs. Angelo Mosca Sr. & Jr.
Jimmy Valiant vs. NWA TV Champion Tully Blanchard

PNW @ Portland, OR - May 5, 1984
NWA World Champion Ric Flair & Rip Oliver defeated Matt Borne & Buddy Rose

JCP @ Greensboro, NC - Coliseum - May 5, 1984
Mark Fleming defeated Bob Bass
Johnny Weaver defeated Bob Orton Jr.
Brian Adidas defeated Doug Vines
Pez Whatley defeated Jeff Sword
Ernie Ladd defeated Rufus R. Jones
Wahoo McDaniel defeated Tully Blanchard
NWA US Champion Ricky Steamboat defeated Dick Slater
Wahoo McDaniel & Mark Youngblood defeated NWA Tag Team Champions Jack & Jerry Brisco to win the titles

JCP @ Savannah, GA - Civic Center - May 6, 1984
Ben Alexander defeated Gary Quartenelli
Mark Fleming defeated Chuck Marbary
Jeff Sword defeated Gene Ligon
Johnny Weaver & Larry Hamilton defeated Kurt Von Hess & Bobby Bass
Pez Whatley defeated NWA TV Champion Tully Blanchard
Ernie Ladd defeated Rufus R. Jones
Jimmy Valiant defeated Adrian Street

JCP @ Asheville, NC - Civic Center - May 6, 1984
Vinnie Valentino defeated Doug Vines
Sam Houston defeated Ali Bey
Jesse Barr defeated Barry Orton
Ivan Koloff & Don Kernodle defeated Angelo Mosca Sr. & Jr.
Dick Slater defeated Brian Adidas
NWA Tag Team Champions Wahoo McDaniel & Mark Youngblood defeated Jack & Jerry Brisco

JCP @ Charlotte, NC - Coliseum - May 6, 1984
Sam Houston defeated Barry Orton
Doug Vines defeated Barry Hart
Keith Larson defeated Gary Royal
Adrian Street defeated Brian Adidas
Jim Valiant defeated Tully Blanchard
Angelo Mosca Jr. defeated Ivan Koloff
NWA US Champion Ricky Steamboat defeated Dick Slater
NWA Tag Team Champions Wahoo McDaniel & Mark Youngblood defeated Jack & Jerry Brisco

WCCW @ Parade of Champions - Irving, TX - Texas Stadium - May 6, 1984 (32,123)
Chris Adams & Sunshine defeated Jimmy Garvin & Precious
The Junkyard Dog defeated the Missing Link via disqualification
Kamala (w/ Gen. Skandar Akbar & Friday) fought the Great Kabuki (w/ Gary Hart) to a double disqualification at 8:05 when Hart chased Akbar into the ring, with Hart attacking Akbar as Kabuki fought off Kamala (*The Triumph & Tragedy of World Class Championship Wrestling*)
Butch Reed defeated Chick Donovan
Kelly Kinsiki fought Johnny Mantell to a draw
Buck Zumhofe & Iceman King Parsons defeated American Tag Team Champions the Super Destroyers (w/ Skandar Akbar) to win the titles
Fritz, Kevin, & Mike Von Erich defeated WCCW Six-Man Tag Team Champions Michael Hayes, Terry Gordy, & Buddy Roberts in a Badstreet match to win the titles at 6:49 when Kevin pinned Roberts with a crossbody off the top; prior to the bout, Kerry Von Erich escorted his father and brothers out into the stadium; pre-match stipulations stated Kerry would take Fritz' spot on the team if they won the titles; after the match, the Freebirds and Killer Khan attacked the Von Erichs until Kerry made the save (Fritz' last match) (*The Triumph & Tragedy of World Class Championship Wrestling*)
Kerry Von Erich pinned NWA World Champion Ric Flair to win the title with a backslide; stipulations stated Von Erich would win the title if Flair was disqualified; after the bout, Von Erich celebrated in the ring with his family, with Flair telling Von Erich that he would be back

WCCW @ Ft. Worth, TX - May 7, 1984
Buck Zumhofe fought Buddy Roberts to a draw
NWA World Champion Kerry Von Erich pinned Terry Gordy at 16:17 when the momentum of a crossbody off the top by the challenger put Von Erich on top for the win
Jimmy Garvin defeated Chick Donovan
Ric Flair fought Michael Hayes to a double disqualification at 7:26
The Great Kabuki defeated the Missing Link via disqualification
Killer Khan (sub. for WCCW TV Champion Johnny Mantell) defeated Johnny Mantell; Khan won the title as a result of the win

JCP @ South Hill, VA - Parkview High School - March 7, 1984
Included Ernie Ladd, Ivan Koloff, Don Kernodle, Rufus R. Jones, and Brian Adidas

JCP @ Kingston, NC - May 7, 1984
Kurt Von Hess fought Doug Vines to a draw
Jesse Barr defeated Vinnie Valentino
Pez Whatley defeated Barry O
NWA Tag Team Champions Wahoo McDaniel & Mark Youngblood defeated NWA TV Champion Tully Blanchard & Jesse Barr
Jimmy Valiant defeated Adrian Street

WCCW @ Muskogee, OK - May 8, 1984
Buck Zumhofe fought Super Destroyer #2 to a draw
The Great Kabuki fought Kamala to a draw
Kevin Von Erich defeated Terry Gordy
NWA World Champion Kerry Von Erich defeated Ric Flair in a non-title match

JCP @ Raleigh, NC - Dorton Arena - May 8, 1984
Sam Houston defeated Ben Alexander
Brian Adidas defeated Barry O
Adrian Street defeated Rufus R. Jones
Jimmy Valiant defeated Tully Blanchard via disqualification
Ivan Koloff & Don Kernolde defeated NWA Tag Team Champions Wahoo McDaniel & Mark Youngblood to win the titles

JCP @ Columbia, SC - Township Auditorium - May 8, 1984
Vinnie Valentino defeated Jeff Sword
Gary Royal defeated Doug Vines
Jesse Barr defeated Barry Hart
Johnny Weaver defeated Kurt Von Hess
Wahoo McDaniel defeated Ernie Ladd
Ricky Steamboat defeated Dick Slater via disqualification

WCCW @ Corpus Christi, TX - May 9, 1984
NWA World Champion Kerry Von Erich vs. Ric Flair

JCP @ Spencer, NC - North Rowan High School - May 9, 1984
TV taping:
Worldwide - 5/12/84 - featured Johnny Weaver & Mid Atlantic TV Champion Tully Blanchard on commentary:
Jimmy Valiant & King Kong Bundy vs. Doug Vines & Randy Barber
Mark & Jay Youngblood defeated NWA Tag Team Champions Ivan Koloff & Don Kernodle (w/ Gary Hart) via disqualification at around the 7:40 mark after Kernodle struck Jay with a clothesline using a loaded forearm pad; after the bout, Wahoo McDaniel and Pez Whatley ran out to make the save
The Road Warriors vs. Mike Jackson & Steve Brinson
NWA US Champion Ricky Steamboat vs. Barry Orton
The Masked Outlaw (Dory Funk Jr.) defeated Mid-Atlantic Heavyweight Champion Angelo Mosca Jr. to win the title

JCP @ Norfolk, VA - Scope - May 10, 1984
Keith Larson defeated Gary Royal
Jesse Barr defeated Kurt Von Hess
Mark Fleming defeated Jeff Sword
Mark Youngblood defeated NWA TV Champion Tully Blanchard
NWA US Champion Dick Slater defeated Jimmy Valiant

Rufus R. Jones defeated Ernie Ladd
Dusty Rhodes defeated Adrian Street

JCP @ Sumter, SC - Exhibition Center - May 10, 1984
Johnny Weaver defeated Doug Vines
Vinnie Valentino defeated Bobby Bass via disqualification
Brian Adidas defeated Bobby Bass
Pez Whatley defeated Barry O
NWA Tag Team Champions Ivan Koloff & Don Kernodle defeated Angelo Mosca Sr. & Jr.

WCCW @ Dallas, TX - Sportatorium - May 11, 1984
TV taping:
Jules Strongbow defeated Kelly Kiniski
Buck Zumhofe defeated Black Gordman
Super Destroyer #2 defeated Rick Hazzard
NWA World Champion Kerry Von Erich pinned Ric Flair in a non-title match at around the 11:30 mark with an abdominal stretch into a roll up; after the bout, Flair attacked Von Erich but the champion eventually gained the upper hand and cleared Flair from the ring
Michael Hayes, Terry Gordy, Buddy Roberts, & Killer Khan fought the Missing Link, the Great Kabuki, & the Super Destroyers to a double disqualification

WCCW @ San Antonio, TX - May 12, 1984
NWA World Champion Kerry Von Erich defeated Ric Flair

JCP @ Charleston, SC - County Hall - May 12, 1984
Sam Houston defeated Pinky Graham
Doug Vines defeated David Dillon
Jesse Barr defeated Glenn Lane
Pez Whatley defeated Kurt Von Hess
Jimmy Valiant defeated NWA TV Champion Tully Blanchard via disqualification
Rufus R. Jones defeated Ernie Ladd in a lights out match

JCP @ Winchester, VA - James Wood High School - May 12, 1984
The Italian Stallion vs. Ali Bey
Mark Fleming vs. Ben Alexander
Bobby Bass vs. Vinnie Valentino
Johnny Weaver vs. Gary Royal
Mark & Jay Youngblood vs. Dick Slater & Mid-Atlantic Heavyweight Champion the Masked Outlaw

CWF @ Ocala, FL - May 13, 1984 (matinee)
NWA World Champion Kerry Von Erich defeated Mike Rotundo

JCP @ Roanoke, VA - Civic Center - May 13, 1984
Barry Hart defeated Barry O
Ben Alexander defeated Gary Quartinelli
The Junkyard Dog defeated Mid Atlantic TV Champion Tully Blanchard

Assassin #1 defeated Jimmy Valiant
Mark Youngblood defeated Adrian Street
Rufus R. Jones defeated Ernie Ladd

Toronto, Ontario - Maple Leaf Gardens - May 13, 1984
Don Kolov defeated Goldie Rogers
Brian Adidas defeated Terry Kay
Pez Whatley & Vinnie Valentino defeated the Destroyer & Doug Vines
Tony Parisi defeated Canadian TV Champion Don Kernodle via disqualification
North American Heavyweight Champion Leo Burke defeated Buddy (Bret) Hart
Angelo Mosca Sr. & Jr. defeated Ivan Koloff & the Great Kabuki

JCP @ Richmond, VA - Coliseum - May 13, 1984
Gary Royal defeated Jeff Sword
Jesse Barr defeated Kurt Von Hess
The Masked Outlaw defeated Keith Larson
Adrian Street defeated Sam Houston
Rufus R. Jones defeated Ernie Ladd
Jimmy Valiant defeated Assassin #1 via disqualification
The Junkyard Dog defeated Mid Atlantic TV Champion Tully Blanchard
NWA US Champion Ricky Steamboat defeated Dick Slater via disqualification

CWF @ Orlando, FL - Eddie Graham Sports Stadium - May 13, 1984
Roses were given to the first 200 mothers that came in the door
Denny Brown fought Mike Fever to a draw
Chief Joe Lightfoot & Mike Davis defeated Hector & Chavo Guerrero in a No DQ match
Billy Jack defeated Molokai via disqualification (Florida Heavyweight Title)
Barry Windham & Mike Rotundo fought Ron Bass & Black Bart to a no contest (US Tag Team Titles)
NWA World Champion Kerry Von Erich defeated Superstar Billy Graham
Dusty Rhodes defeated Kevin Sullivan in a lights out, pole hangman's noose match

JCP @ Greenville, SC - Memorial Auditorium - May 14, 1984
Brett Hart defeated Gary Royal
Mid-Atlantic Heavyweight Champion the Masked Outlaw defeated Vinnie Valentino
Jimmy Valiant defeated Adrian Street
Ron Garvin defeated Jake Roberts
Don Kernodle & Ivan Koloff fought Pez Whatley & Mark Youngblood to a double disqualification

CWF @ West Palm Beach, FL - City Auditorium - May 14, 1984
Mike Fever fought Denny Brown to a draw
Mike Davis vs. Black Bart
Chief Joe Lightfoot vs. Molokai
Billy Jack & Mike Rotundo vs. Black Bart (sub. for Hector Guerrero) & Chavo Guerrero
Barry Windham vs. Superstar Billy Graham
NWA World Champion Kerry Von Erich vs. Ron Bass
Dusty Rhodes vs. Kevin Sullivan (lights out, pole hangman's noose match)

CWF @ Ft. Myers, FL - May 14, 1984
NWA World Champion Kerry Von Erich defeated Superstar Billy Graham

JCP @ Columbia, SC - Township Auditorium - May 15, 1984
Barry Hart fought Jeff Sword to a draw
Keith Larson defeated Doug Vines
Rufus R. Jones defeated the Great Kabuki
Ron Garvin defeated Jake Roberts
NWA Tag Team Champions Don Kernodle & Ivan Koloff defeated Pez Whatley & Mark Youngblood

JCP @ Raleigh, NC - Dorton Arena - May 15, 1984
NWA TV Champion Tully Blanchard defeated Vinnie Valentino
Dick Slater defeated Brian Adidas
The Outlaw fought Angelo Mosca Jr. to a draw
Adrian Street defeated Jimmy Valiant

CWF @ Miami Beach, FL - Convention Center - May 15, 1984
Chief Joe Lightfoot vs. Hector Guerrero
Florida Heavyweight Champion Billy Jack vs. Molokai
Mike Rotundo vs. Kevin Sullivan
Dusty Rhodes & Barry Windham vs. US Tag Team Champions Ron Bass & Black Bart
NWA World Champion Kerry Von Erich defeated Superstar Billy Graham via disqualification

JCP @ ? - May 16, 1984
TV taping:

Worldwide - 5/19/84:
Mid-Atlantic Heavyweight Champion the Masked Outlaw vs. Keith Larson
Angelo Mosca Jr. vs. Bob Brown
Dick Slater vs. Jason Walker
Wahoo McDaniel vs. Randy Barber
Rufus R. Jones vs. Barry Orton

CWF @ Melbourne, FL - May 17, 1984
NWA World Champion Kerry Von Erich vs. Black Bart

JCP @ Sumter, SC - May 17, 1984
Kurt Von Hess defeated Keith Larson
Brian Adidas defeated Jeff Sword
Rufus R. Jones & Pez Whatley defeated Ernie Ladd & Jesse Barr
Angelo Mosca Jr. defeated the Outlaw
Jimmy Valiant defeated Adrian Street

JCP @ Chester, SC - High School - May 17, 1984
Jeff Sword vs. Brett Hart
Ali Bey vs. Keith Larson
Kurt Von Hess vs. Pinky Graham
Johnny Weaver vs. Adrian Street
Wahoo McDaniel vs. NWA TV Champion Tully Blanchard
Ernie Ladd vs. Rufus R. Jones

JCP @ Roxboro, NC - Optimist Park - May 17, 1984

JCP @ Fisherville, VA - Augusta Expo - May 17, 1984
Included NWA Tag Team Champions Ivan Koloff & Don Kernodle, Mark & Jay Youngblood, Assassin #1, Paul Jones, and Angelo Mosca Jr.

CWF @ Lake City, FL - May 18, 1984
NWA World Champion Kerry Von Erich defeated Superstar Billy Graham

CWF @ Tampa, FL - Sun Dome - May 19, 1984
Denny Brown defeated Inferno #2
Chief Joe Lightfoot fought Mike Davis to a time-limit draw
Mike Rotundo defeated Hector Guerrero
Florida Heavyweight Champion Billy Jack defeated Black Bart
Barry Windham defeated Superstar Billy Graham in an arm wrestling contest via disqualification when Graham hit Windham with a karate chop; Windham won $1,000 of Graham's money as a result of the win
NWA World Champion Kerry Von Erich defeated Ron Bass via disqualification at 16:10
Dusty Rhodes & Blackjack Mulligan defeated Kevin Sullivan & Molokai via disqualification in a lights out, pole hangman's noose match after interference from Mike Rotundo, Denny Brown, Mike Davis, and Chief Joe Lightfoot interfered

JCP @ Greensboro, NC - Coliseum - May 19, 1984
Doug Vines defeated Keith Larson
Kurt Von Hess defeated Gary Royal
Paul Kelly defeated Sam Houston
Dick Slater defeated Barry Hart
Angelo Mosca Sr. defeated Assassin #1
Jimmy Valiant defeated Adrian Street
Tully Blanchard defeated Wahoo McDaniel
Ivan Koloff & Don Kernodle defeated Mark Youngblood & Pez Whatley

JCP @ Charlotte, NC - Coliseum - May 20, 1984
Vinnie Valentino defeated Jeff Sword
Johnny Weaver defeated Bob Bass
Rufus R. Jones & Mark Youngblood defeated Ernie Ladd & Jesse Barr
Assassin #1 defeated Angelo Mosca Sr.
Jimmy Valiant defeated Adrian Street
NWA US Champion Ricky Steamboat defeated Dick Slater
Dusty Rhodes & Wahoo McDaniel defeated NWA Tag Team Champions Ivan Koloff & Don Kernodle via disqualification

JCP @ Greenville, SC - Memorial Auditorium - May 21, 1984
Brett Hart defeated Bobby Bass
Keith Larsen defeated Paul Kelly
Angelo Mosca defeated Assassin #1
Angelo Mosca, Jr. defeated Mid-Atlantic Heavyweight Champion the Masked Outlaw via referee's decision
NWA Tag Team Champions Ivan Koloff & Don Kernodle defeated Pez Whatley & Mark Youngblood

JCP @ Columbia, SC - Township Auditorium - May 22, 1984
Keith Larson defeated Kurt Von Hess
The Great Kabuki defeated Mark Fleming
Ernie Ladd defeated Brett Hart
Angelo Mosca Jr. defeated Assassin #1
NWA Tag Team Champions Ivan Koloff & Don Kernodle defeated Pez Whatley & Mark Youngblood

AJPW @ Tokyo, Japan - May 22, 1984
Harley Race defeated Ric Flair
NWA World Champion Kerry Von Erich fought Jumbo Tsuruta to a double count-out at 30:47 after Tsuruta dropped the champion with a back suplex on the floor as Von Erich had the claw applied, with Tsuruta rolling back into the ring just as the bell rang; prior to and after the match, the two men shook hands

JCP @ Raleigh, NC - Dorton Arena - May 22, 1984
Sam Houston defeated Gary Royal
Vinnie Valentino defeated Doug Vines
Brian Adidas defeated Jesse Barr
Rufus R. Jones defeated Adrian Street
Dick Slater & the Outlaw defeated Johnny Weaver & Angelo Mosca Jr.
Wahoo McDaniel defeated NWA TV Champion Tully Blanchard

JCP @ Spartanburg, SC - Memorial Auditorium - May 23, 1984
TV taping:
Worldwide - 5/26/84:
Angelo Mosca Jr. defeated Gary Royal
NWA Tag Team Champions Ivan Koloff & Don Kernodle defeated Sam Houston & Mark Fleming

Pez Whatley defeated Kurt Von Hess
Jesse Barr defeated Brett Hart
Rufus R. Jones defeated Assassin #1 via disqualification
Mark Youngblood & Brian Adidas defated Doug Vines & Jeff Sword
Worldwide - 6/2/84 - featured David Crockett on commentary; included Crockett conducting an interview with NWA TV Champion Tully Blanchard in which Crockett reviewed footage of Blanchard recently attacking Johnny Weaver at the commentary table, with Blanchard eventually beating Weaver with the TV title belt; Blanchard then said a lot of people were upset that he shortened the TV title time-limit to 10 minutes and then extended it to 20 minutes and then poured $10,000 into a fish bowl and said any man that could beat him would win the belt and the money; featured Crockett conducting an interview with Dick Slater, in possession of the NWA US Title, in which he called Ricky Steamboat a sissy and NWA World Champion Ric Flair a woman; included Crockett conducting an interview with Jimmy Valiant & Pez Whatley in which they brought out a female manequin with a wig, calling it Adrian Street; Valiant eventually said he would put the manequin's dress on Street; featured Crockett conducting an interview with Dusty Rhodes regarding his chase for the NWA World Title; featured Crockett conducting an interview with Paul Jones & the Assassin regarding Valiant; included Crockett conducting a closing interview with NWA Tag Team Champions Don Kernodle & Ivan Koloff regarding them putting Jay Youngblood in the hospital; during the interview, it was noted Koloff was wearing a new USSR headband sent to him by his nephew:
Mark Youngblood pinned Bob Owens at around the 4:11 mark with a double axe handle off the top
NWA Mid Atlantic Heavyweight Champion the Outlaw (w/ Gary Hart) fought Mark Fleming to a no contest at the 2-minute mark when Angelo Mosca Sr., who was watching the match from the aisle, climbed in the ring and told Fleming that he wanted to face the Outlaw; when Fleming objected, Mosca threw him to the floor and brawled with the Outlaw; as Mosca tried to unmask the champion, Hart attacked Mosca from behind and both men choked him with the Outlaw's bullrope; Angelo Mosca Jr. eventually came out to make the save
Wahoo McDaniel pinned Ben Alexander at 4:09 with a chop and forearm to the head; NWA TV Champion Tully Blanchard provided guest commentary for the match
Adrian Street (w/ Ms. Linda) pinned Keith Larson with a reverse splash off the middle turnbuckle at 3:49
The Assassin (w/ Paul Jones) pinned Al Scott at 3:07 after hitting him with a loaded headbutt
NWA Tag Team Campions Ivan Koloff & Don Kernodle (w/ Gary Hart) defeated Randy Barber & Gerald Finley at 4:07 when Kernodle scored the pin with a dropklck from the middle turnbuckle; NWA TV Champion Tully Blanchard provided guest commentary for the bout

JCP @ Norfolk, VA - Scope - May 24, 1984
Vinnie Valentino defeated Doug Vines
Johnny Weaver defeated Jeff Sword
The Junkyard Dog defeated the Great Kabuki
Assassin #1 defeated Angelo Mosca Sr.

NWA TV Champion Tully Blanchard defeated Mark Youngblood
NWA US Champion Ricky Steamboat defeated Dick Slater
Dusty Rhodes & Wahoo McDaniel defeated NWA Tag Team Champions Ivan Koloff & Don Kernodle via disqualification

JCP @ Sumter, SC - Exhibition Center - May 24, 1984
Keith Larson defeated Kurt Von Hess
Brian Adidas defeated Paul Kelly
Angelo Mosca Sr. fought the Outlaw to a draw
Pez Whatley & Rufus R. Jones defeated Ernie Ladd & Jesse Barr
Jimmy Valiant defeated Adrian Street

AJPW @ Yokosuka, Japan - May 24, 1984
Ric Flair defeated NWA World Champion Kerry Von Erich in a Best 2 out of 3 falls match to win the title, 2-1; fall #2: Flair defeated Von Erich via submission with the figure-4; fall #3: Flair pinned Von Erich with a roll over

AJPW @ Funabashi, Japan - May 25, 1984
NWA World Champion Ric Flair fought Harley Race to a draw in a Best 2 out of 3 falls match; fall #3: the two fought to a double count-out

JCP @ Charleston, SC - County Hall - May 25, 1984
Brett Hart defeated Gary Royal
The Outlaw defeated Angelo Mosca Jr.
NWA TV Champion Tully Blanchard defeated Mark Youngblood
Rufus R. Jones & Brian Adidas defeated Ernie Ladd & Sandy Barr
Adrian Street defeated Pez Whatley

JCP @ Richmond, VA - Coliseum - May 25, 1984
Keith Larson defeated Kurt Von Hess
Ron Bass defeated Jeff Sword
Vinnie Valentino defeated Doug Vines
Johnny Weaver defeated Paul Kelly
The Assassin defeated Angelo Mosca Sr.
NWA US Champion Ricky Steamboat fought Dick Slater to a double count-out
Dusty Rhodes & Wahoo McDaniel defeated Ivan Koloff & Don Kernodle

JCP @ Greenville, SC - Memorial Auditorium - May 26, 1984
The Assassin defeated Angelo Mosca Sr.
NWA TV Champion Tully Blanchard defeated Dusty Rhodes
Jimmy Valiant defeated Adrian Street
NWA US Champion Ricky Steamboat defeated Dick Slater

JCP @ Roanoke, VA - Civic Center - May 27, 1984
Mark Youngblood vs. the Outlaw

Rufus R. Jones vs. the Assassin
Jimmy Valiant vs. Adrian Street
The Junkyard Dog & Wahoo McDaniel vs. Ivan Koloff & NWA TV Champion Tully Blanchard (strap/chain match)

Toronto, Ontario - Maple Leaf Gardens - May 27, 1984
Tony Parisi defeated Jeff Sword
Brian Adidas defeated Doug Vines
Terry Kay defeated Don Kolov
Buddy (Bret) Hart & Johnny Weaver defeated Leo Burke & Rudy Kay
The Grapplers defeated Pez Whatley & Vinnie Valentino
Angelo Mosca Jr. defeated the Great Kabuki (w/ Bobby Bass)
Angelo Mosca Sr. defeated Ivan Koloff (w/ Bobby Bass) in a Russian Chain Match
NWA World Champion Ric Flair defeated Dick Slater at 16:38

JCP @ Fayetteville, NC - Cumberland County Civic Center - May 28, 1984
Jesse Barr defeated Keith Larson
Angelo Mosca Jr. defeated the Outlaw
Jimmy Valiant defeated Adrian Street
Ron Garvin defeated Jake Roberts
NWA Tag Team Champions Ivan Koloff & Don Kernodle defeated Mark Youngblood & Rufus R. Jones
Wahoo McDaniel defeated NWA TV Champion Tully Blanchard

AWA @ St. Paul, MN - May 28, 1984
NWA World Champion Ric Flair fought Bruiser Brody to a double disqualification

JCP @ East Rutherford, NJ - Meadowlands - May 29, 1984
Invader #1 (Jose Gonzalez) pinned the Great Kabuki
National TV Champion Ron Garvin pinned Jake Roberts
NWA Jr. Heavyweight Champion Les Thornton defeated El Gran Apollo via count-out
Dusty Rhodes pinned the Assassin (Jesse Barr) at 1:30

NWA Tag Team Champions Ivan Koloff & Don Kernodle defeated Pez Whatley & Mark Youngblood when Whatley was pinned

Wahoo McDaniel fought All Japan PWF Champion Stan Hansen to a double disqualification

NWA National Tag Team Champions the Road Warriors defeated Jimmy Valiant & King Kong Bundy when Road Warrior Hawk pinned Bundy

WWC Universal Heavyweight Champion Carlos Colon pinned NWA TV Champion Tully Blanchard

NWA World Champion Ric Flair pinned NWA US Champion Ricky Steamboat at 32:00 with a roll over and grabbing the tights for leverage

JCP @ Emporia, VA - May 31, 1984
NWA World Champion Ric Flair defeated Dick Slater
Also included NWA TV Champion Tully Blanchard, Adrian Street, Wahoo McDaniel, and Brian Adidas

JCP @ Charlotte Courthouse, VA - Randolph Henry Field - May 31, 1984
Included NWA Tag Team Champions Ivan Koloff & Don Kernodle, Mark Youngblood, Rufus R. Jones, and Johnny Weaver

Central States @ St. Louis, MO - Kiel Auditorium - June 1, 1984
Marty Jannetty defeated Roger Kirby
Tommy Rogers defeated TD Stone
The Masked Grapplers defeated Ted Oates & Thomas Ivey (sub. for Jerry Oates)
Jim Duggan defeated Luke Graham
Wahoo McDaniel defeated Kamala via disqualification
Blackjack Mulligan & Blackjack Lanza defeated Jerry Blackwell & Sheik Adnan Al Kaissie
NWA World Champion Ric Flair fought Kerry Von Erich to a 60-minute time-limit draw

JCP @ Roanoke, VA - Civic Center - June 2, 1984
Mark Fleming defeated Bobby Bass
Keith Larson defeated Gary Quarternelli
Barry Hart defeated Paul Kelly
Mark Youngblood defeated Kurt Von Hess
Pez Whatley defeated Jeff Sword
Angelo Mosca Jr. fought the Outlaw to a draw
National Tag Team Champions the Road Warriors fought NWA Tag Team Champions Ivan Koloff & Don Kernodle to a no contest
NWA World Champion Ric Flair defeated Dick Slater

JCP @ Asheville, NC - Civic Center - June 3, 1984
Keith Larson defeated Doug Vines
The Assassin defeated Mark Fleming
Jesse Barr defeated Sam Houston
NWA World Champion Ric Flair defeated Dick Slater via

disqualification
Jimmy Valiant defeated Adrian Street
NWA TV Champion Tully Blanchard defeated Ron Garvin

JCP @ Savannah, GA - Civic Center - June 3, 1984
Gene Ligon defeated Ben Alexander
Sam Houston defeated Gary Royal
Barry Hart defeated Kurt Von Hess
Angelo Mosca Jr. defeated the Outlaw
NWA Tag Team Champions Ivan Koloff & Don Kernodle defeated Pez Whatley & Mark Youngblood

JCP @ Greenville, SC - Memorial Auditorium - June 4, 1984
Keith Larson defeated Doug Vines
Barry Hart defeated Paul Kelly
Sam Houston defeated Kurt Von Hess
Jimmy Valiant defeated Adrian Street
Angelo Mosca Jr. defeated the Outlaw
NWA Tag Team Champions Ivan Koloff & Don Kernodle defeated Wahoo McDaniel & Brian Adidas
NWA US Champion Ricky Steamboat defeated Dick Slater in a falls count anywhere match
NWA World Champion Ric Flair defeated NWA TV Champion Tully Blanchard

JCP @ Columbia, SC - Township Auditorium - June 5, 1984
Ivan Koloff & Don Kernodle defeated Pez Whatley & Mark Youngblood
Wahoo McDaniel fought NWA TV Champion Tully Blanchard to a draw
Kamala won a battle royal
Angelo Mosca Jr. defeated the Outlaw
Brian Adidas defeated Paul Kelly
Sam Houston defeated Kurt Von Hess
NWA World Champion Ric Flair fought NWA US Champion Ricky Steamboat to a draw

JCP @ Raleigh, NC - Dorton Arena - June 6, 1984
TV taping:
Michael Hayes & Terry Gordy defeated Doug Vines & an unknown
King Kong Bundy defeated Dale Veasey
Rufus R. Jones defeated Assassin #1
Michael Hayes & Buddy Roberts defeated Paul Kelly & Doug Vines
Terry Gordy & Buddy Roberts defeated Jeff Sword & Ben Alexander
Nikita Koloff defeated Brett Hart
King Kong Bundy defeated Paul Kelly
National Tag Team Champions the Road Warriors defeated Keith Larsen & an unknown
Michael Hayes, Terry Gordy, & Buddy Roberts defeated Paul Ellering & National Tag Team Champions the Road Warriors
Wahoo McDaniel defeated NWA TV Champion Tully Blanchard via disqualification

NWA World Champion Ric Flair fought Harley Race to a no contest in a steel cage match

JCP @ Norfolk, VA - Scope - June 7, 1984
Paul Kelly defeated Keith Larson
Johnny Weaver defeated Bob Bass
Pez Whatley defeated Kurt Von Hess
Kamala defeated Barry Hart
Stan Hansen defeated Jesse Barr
Rufus R. Jones defeated the Assassin
Harley Race defeated Angelo Mosca Jr.
The Road Warriors fought the Junkyard Dog & King Kong Bundy to a no contest
Wahoo McDaniel defeated NWA TV Champion Tully Blanchard
The Freebirds defeated Ivan Koloff & Don Kernodle via disqualification
NWA US Champion Ricky Steamboat fought NWA World Champion Ric Flair to a draw

JCP @ Richmond, VA - Coliseum - June 8, 1984
Pez Whatley defeated Doug Vines
Vinnie Valentino defeated Paul Kelly
Sam Houston defeated Gary Royal
Angelo Mosca Jr. won a battle royal
Rufus R. Jones & the Junkyard Dog defeated Assassin #1 & Paul Jones via disqualification
Jimmy Valiant defeated Adrian Street
NWA TV Champion Tully Blanchard defeated Wahoo McDaniel
NWA US Champion Ricky Steamboat defeated Dick Slater in a falls count anywhere match
NWA World Champion Ric Flair defeated Harley Race in a steel cage match

Worldwide - 6/9/84 - featured David Crockett on commentary; included Crockett conducting an interview with NWA TV Champion Tully Blanchard in which he said everyone was complaining about the time limit of his title matches, then said he had extended the time limit to 20 minutes and would continue to put up his $10,000 in title matches; featured Crockett conducting an interview with Dusty Rhodes regarding wanting a title shot with NWA World Champion Ric Flair and that Harley Race wanted back in the title picture as well; Rhodes then noted Blanchard's comments earlier in the show, saying he would take Blanchard's money if he got the chance and then cut a promo on Paul Jones; included Crockett conducting an interview with the Assassin & Jones in which Jones spoke about Valiant and Rhodes being on his registry; featured Crockett conducting an interview with Hart & NWA Mid Atlantic Heavyweight Champion the Outlaw regarding the attack on Gene Ligon earlier in the show and the challenge of Angelo Mosca Jr.:
Angelo Mosca Jr. pinned Ben Alexander at 3:36 with a flying forearm and crossbody off the top
The Assassin (w/ Paul Jones) pinned Gary Cornelli at the 5-minute mark after Jones hit the opponent with his cane behind the referee's back

Pez Whatley & Brian Adidas defeated Doug Vines & Kelly Kiniski at the 6:30 mark when Whatley scored the pin following a flying headbutt; NWA TV Champion Tully Blanchard provided guest commentary for the bout; during the match, it was noted the Road Warriors, Freebirds, and King Kong Bundy were just some of the names coming to the NWA
King Kong Bundy & Wahoo McDaniel defeated Dale Veasy & Carpenter at around the 1:30 mark when Bundy scored the pin following an elbow drop (*unknown location*)
NWA Mid Atlantic Heavyweight Champion the Masked Outlaw (w/ Gary Hart) pinned Gene Ligon at the 6-minute mark with a knee to the head; after the bout, Ligion tried to get at Jones but was attacked from behind by the Outlaw and whipped; NWA TV Champion Tully Blanchard provided guest commentary for the match
Jimmy Valiant pinned Adrian Street (w/ Miss Linda) at 4:53 after applying the sleeper; prior to the bout, Valiant came out with one of Street's dresses; after the match, Valiant tried to put the dress on Street but Linda attacked him from behind, with Street then putting the dress on Valiant; moments later, Valiant knocked Street to the floor and ripped off the dress

JCP @ Greensboro, NC - Coliseum - June 9, 1984
Jesse Barr defeated Keith Larson
Rufus R. Jones & Pez Whatley defeated Paul Jones & the Assassin via disqualification
Doug Vines defeated Mark Fleming
Jeff Sword defeated Sam Houston
Barry Hart defeated Bobby Bass
The Outlaw defeated Angelo Mosca Jr.
Ricky Steamboat defeated the Outlaw
Ivan Koloff & Don Kernodle defeated Mark Youngblood & the Renegade

GCW @ Baltimore, MD - Civic Center - June 9, 1984
Jake Roberts defeated King Konga
Ole Anderson defeated Paul Ellering via disqualification
Nikolai Volkoff defeated King Kong Bundy
The Road Warriors defeated Jerry Lawler & Austin Idol
Harley Race fought Wahoo McDaniel to a draw
The Junkyard Dog & Brad Armstrong defeated Ted DiBiase & the Spoiler
NWA World Champion Ric Flair defeated Ron Garvin

Toronto, Ontario - Maple Leaf Gardens - June 10, 1984
Terry Kay defeated Nick DeCarlo
The Grapplers defeated Buddy (Bret) Hart & Johnny Weaver
Pez Whatley defeated North American Heavyweight Champion Leo Burke via disqualification
Brian Adidas defeated Canadian TV Champion Don Kernodle to win the title
Angelo Mosca Sr. defeated Assassin #1 via disqualification
Angelo Mosca Jr. defeated Canadian Heavyweight Champion Ivan Koloff to win the title

JCP @ Greenville, SC - Memorial Auditorium - June 11, 1984
Mark Fleming fought Kurt Von Hess to a draw
Sam Houston defeated Doug Vines
Kamala defeated Gary Quartinelli
Paul Jones & the Assassin defeated Jimmy Valiant & Rufus R. Jones via disqualification
NWA Tag Team Champions Ivan Koloff & Don Kernodle defeated Mark Youngblood & the Renegade via disqualification

Continental @ Birmingham, AL - June 11, 1984
NWA World Champion Ric Flair defeated Jimmy Golden

Continental @ Pensacola, FL - June 12, 1984
NWA World Champion Ric Flair vs. Bob Armstrong

JCP @ Raleigh, NC - Dorton Arena - June 12, 1984
Barry Hart defeated Kurt Von Hess
Wahoo McDaniel defeated Ernie Ladd
Jimmy Valiant defeated Adrian Street
Don Kernodle & Ivan Koloff defeated Mark Youngblood & the Renegade via disqualification
NWA TV Champion Tully Blanchard defeated Johnny Weaver

JCP @ ? - June 13, 1984
TV taping:
Angelo Mosca Jr. defeated Ben Alexander
The Assassin defeated the Italian Stallion
Pez Whatley & Brian Adidas defeated Doug Vines & Paul Kelly
King Kong Bundy & Wahoo McDaniel defeated Dale Veasey & an unknown
The Masked Outlaw defeated Gene Ligon
Jimmy Valiant defeated Adrian Street via count-out
Worldwide - 6/16/84:
Jimmy Valiant defeated Doug Vines
The Assassin defeated Keith Larson
The Road Warriors defeated Dale Veasy & Sam Houston
NWA US Champion Ricky Steamboat fought Dick Slater to a double count-out
Jesse Barr defeated Paul Kelly

JCP @ Harrisonburg, VA - High School Gym - June 14, 1984
Paul Kelly vs. Keith Larson
Pez Whatley & Brian Adias vs. Ernie Ladd & Jesse Barr
NWA Mid-Atlantic Heavyweight Champion the Outlaw vs. Angelo Mosca Jr.
Jimmy Valiant vs. Adrian Street
Also included Johnny Weaver and Doug Vines

JCP @ Hampton, VA - Coliseum - June 14, 1984
Vinnie Valentino fought Bobby Bass to a draw
Mark Fleming defeated Gary Royal
Kamala defeated Barry Hart
The Junkyard Dog & Rufus R. Jones defeated Assassin #1 &

Paul Jones
Ivan Koloff & Don Kernodle defeated Mark Youngblood & the Renegade via disqualification
NWA TV Champion Tully Blanchard defeated Wahoo McDaniel

JCP @ Reidsville, NC - Diamond I Arena - June 15, 1984

JCP @ Charleston, SC - County Hall - June 15, 1984
Bobby Bass defeated Sam Houston
Barry Hart defeated Jeff Sword
Vinnie Valentino defeated Kurt Von Hess
NWA Tag Team Champions Ivan Koloff & Don Kernodle defeated Mark Youngblood & the Renegade via disqualification
Jimmy Valiant defeated Adrian Street

JCP @ Roanoke, VA - Civic Center - June 15, 1984
Keith Larson defeated Ali Bey
Barry Hart defeated Mark Fleming
Nikita Koloff defeated Paul Kelly
Assassins #1 & #3 defeated Brian Adidas & Keith Larson
Jimmy Valiant defeated Buzz Sawyer via disqualification
NWA TV Champion Tully Blanchard defeated Johnny Weaver
Adrian Street defeated Paul Jones via disqualification

JCP @ Lynchburg, VA - Armory - June 15, 1984 Pez Whatley, Johnny Weaver, & Brian Adidas vs. Jesse Barr, Paul Kelly, & Ernie Ladd
NWA Mid Atlantic Heavyweight Champion the Outlaw vs. Angelo Mosca Jr. Wahoo McDaniel vs. NWA TV Champion Tully Blanchard

JCP @ Conway, SC - June 16, 1984
Vinnie Valentino defeated Doug Vines
Johnny Weaver defeated Jesse Barr
Pez Whatley defeated Ernie Ladd via disqualification
The Outlaw defeated Angelo Mosca Jr.
The Renegade & Mark Youngblood defeated Nikita Koloff & Don Kernodle

JCP @ Charlotte, NC - Coliseum - June 16, 1984
Paul Kelly defeated Barry Hart
Brian Adidas defeated Kurt Von Hess
Sam Houston & Keith Larson defeated Jeff Sword & Gary Royal
Kamala defeated Mark Fleming
Jimmy Valiant defeated Adrian Street
Jimmy Valiant & Rufus R. Jones defeated the Assassin & Paul Jones
Tully Blanchard defeated Wahoo McDaniel
NWA US Champion Ricky Steamboat defeated Ivan Koloff

Totowa, NJ - June 17, 1984
Bobby Bass defeated Terry Dunne
Jesse Barr defeated Paul Kelly

Invader #1 defeated Doug Vines
Ted DiBiase defeated Vinnie Valentino
Wahoo McDaniel & Pez Whatley defeated Stan Hansen & Les Thornton via disqualification
Carlos Colon defeated NWA TV Champion Tully Blanchard

JCP @ Columbia, SC - Township Auditorium - June 17, 1984
Keith Larson defeated the Turk
Sam Houston defeated Mark Fleming
Nikita Koloff defeated Gene Ligon
Ivan Koloff & Don Kernodle defeated the Renegade & Mark Youngblood via disqualification
King Kong Bundy, Rufus R. Jones, & Sweet Brown Sugar defeated Kamala, Paul Jones, & the Assassin

JCP @ Greenville, SC - June 18, 1984
Keith Larson defeated Jeff Sword
Gary Royal defeated Mark Fleming
Brickhouse Brown defeated Kurt Von Hess
Jimmy Valiant, Rufus R. Jones, & Brian Adidas defeated Kamala, Paul Jones, & the Assassin

WCCW @ Ft. Worth, TX - June 18, 1984
Chris Adams defeated George Weingeroff
Jules Strongbow defeated John Tatum
Iceman King Parsons fought Bill Irwin to a draw
The Junkyard Dog defeated Michael Hayes via disqualification
NWA World Champion Ric Flair defeated Mike Von Erich via disqualification

Morristown, NJ - June 18, 1984
Bobby Bass defeated Angelo Gomez
Jody Sheilds defeated Lady Adonis
Jesse Barr defeated Doug Vines
Invader #1 defeated Paul Kelly
Carlos Colon defeated Les Thornton
Stan Hansen defeated Vinnie Valentino
Wahoo McDaniel & Pez Whatley defeated the Road Warriors via disqualification

JCP @ Danville, VA - Tunstall High School - June 19, 1984
Johnny Weaver & Pez Whatley vs. Ernie Ladd & Jesse Barr
Jimmy Valiant vs. Adrian Street

JCP @ Raliegh, NC - Dorton Arena - June 19, 1984
Keith Larson defeated Paul Kelly
Nikita Koloff defeated Barry Hart
The Outlaw defeated Angelo Mosca Jr.
Wahoo McDaniel & Rufus R. Jones defeated Kamala & the Assassin
Mark Youngblood & the Renegade defeated NWA Tag Team Champions Ivan Koloff & Don Kernodle via disqualification

JCP @ Spartanburg, SC - Memorial Auditorium - June 20, 1984
TV taping:
Worldwide - 6/23/84:
Brian Adidas & Pez Whatley defeated Gary Royal & Doug Vines
Angelo Mosca Jr. defeated Paul Kelly
Kamala defeated the Italian Stallion
Nikita Koloff, NWA Tag Team Champions Ivan Koloff & Don Kernodle defeated Sam Houston, Brett Hart, & Mark Fleming

JCP @ Norfolk, VA - Scope - June 21, 1984
Vinnie Valentino defeated Bobby Bass
Keith Larson defeated Gary Royal
Nikita Koloff defeated Sam Houston
Jimmy Valiant defeated the Assassin
Angelo Mosca Jr. defeated Mid-Atlantic Heavyweight Champion the Outlaw to win the title
Paul Jones & Kamala defeated Mid-Atlantic Heavyweight Champion Angelo Mosca Jr. & Rufus R. Jones
NWA Tag Team Champions Ivan Koloff & Don Kernodle defeated Mark Youngblood & the Renegade

JCP @ Sumter, SC - Exhibition Center - June 21, 1984
Mark Fleming defeated Paul Kelly
Kurt Von Hess defeated Gary Quartanelli
Ernie Ladd & Jesse Barr defeated Johnny Weaver & Brian Adidas
Adrian Street defeated Pez Whatley
Wahoo McDaniel defeated NWA TV Champion Tully Blanchard via disqualification

Central States @ St. Louis, MO - June 22, 1984
NWA World Champion Ric Flair defeated Wahoo McDaniel

JCP @ Richmond, VA - Coliseum - June 22, 1984
Keith Larsen defeated Bobby Bass
Nikita Koloff defeated Vinnie Valentino
Angelo Mosca Jr. defeated the Outlaw
Pez Whatley & Brian Adidas defeated Jesse Barr & Paul Kelly
Rufus R. Jones, Jimmy Valiant, & Adrian Street defeated the Assassin, Kamala, & Paul Jones
Mark Youngblood & the Renegade defeated NWA Tag Team Champions Ivan Koloff & Don Kernodle via disqualification

JCP @ Charleston, SC - County Hall - June 22, 1984
Gary Quartanelli defeated Ali Bey
Mark Fleming defeated Jeff Sword
Barry Hart & Sam Houston defeated Gary Royal & Doug Vines
Kurt Von Hess defeated Gene Ligon
NWA TV Champion Tully Blanchard defeated Johnny Weaver

WCCW @ San Antonio, TX - June 23, 1984
Texas Heavyweight Championship Tournament:
Opening round:

Kerry Von Erich defeated Johnny Mantell
Terry Gordy defeated Black Gordman
Gino Hernandez defeated George Weingeroff
Bill Irwin fought Jose Lothario to a draw; Lothario advanced in the tournament
Jules Strongbow defeated John Tatum
Buck Zumhofe defeated Michael Hayes via forfeit
Kevin Von Erich fought Killer Khan to a double disqualification
Quarter-Finals:
Kerry Von Erich defeated Terry Gordy
Gino Hernandez defeated Jose Lothario
Jules Strongbow defeated Buck Zumhofe
Semi-Finals:
Kerry Von Erich defeated Gino Hernandez; Hernandez advanced due to an injury to Von Erich
NWA World Champion Ric Flair defeated Jules Strongbow
Finals: Gino Hernandez defeated NWA World Champion Ric Flair to win the Texas Heavyweight Title

JCP @ Fredericksburg, VA - Stafford Senior High School Gym - June 23, 1984
Nikita Koloff defeated Mark Fleming
Vinnie Valentino & Keith Larsen (sub. for Mark Youngblood & the Renegade) defeated Jesse Barr & Paul Kelly
Adrian Street defeated Brickhouse Brown (sub. for Rufus R. Jones)
NWA Tag Team Champions Ivan Koloff & Don Kernodle defeated Angelo Mosca Jr. & Rufus R. Jones (sub. for King Kong Bundy)

JCP @ Asheville, NC - Civic Center - June 24, 1984
Barry Hart defeated Ali Bey
Keith Larson defeated Jeff Sword
Doug Vines defeated Sam Houston
Gene Ligon defeated Gary Quartanelli
NWA TV Champion Tully Blanchard defeated Wahoo McDaniel
The Outlaw defeated Angelo Mosca Jr.
Ivan Koloff & Don Kernodle defeated Mark Youngblood & the Renegade via disqualification

JCP @ Greensboro, NC - Coliseum - June 24, 1984
Mark Fleming defeated Paul Kelly
Keith Larson defeated Kurt Von Hess
Nikita Koloff defeated Barry Hart
Johnny Weaver defeated Tully Blanchard
NWA Mid Atlantic Heavyweight Champion the Outlaw & Gary Hart defeated Angelo Mosca Jr. & Rufus R. Jones
NWA Tag Team Champions Ivan Koloff & Don Kernodle defeated Mark Youngblood & the Renegade
Wahoo McDaniel pinned NWA US Champion Ricky Steamboat to win the title after NWA TV Champion Tully Blanchard ran out with a steel chair, swung at McDaniel, with McDaniel ducking and Blanchard hitting Steamboat instead; McDaniel then cleared Blanchard from the ring and made the cover

Toronto, Ontario - Maple Leaf Gardens - June 24, 1984
Jesse Barr defeated John Bonello
Nick Decarlo defeated Bob Marcus
Tony Parisi defeated Gary Royal
Canadian TV Champion Brian Adidas defeated Bobby Bass
Pez Whatley & Vinnie Valentino defeated the Grapplers via count-out
Jimmy Valiant, Angelo Mosca Sr., & Buzz Sawyer defeated Kamala, Assassin #1, & Paul Jones

CWF @ Orlando, FL - June 24, 1984
Hector Guerrero defeated Denny Brown
Chavo Guerrero defeated Mike Davis
Ron Bass & Black Bart defeated Mike Graham & Joe Lightfoot
Billy Jack Haynes defeated Superstar Billy Graham via disqualification
Mike Rotundo defeated the One Man Gang via disqualificaion
Blackjack Mulligan defeated Kevin Sullivan in a lumberjack match
NWA World Champion Ric Flair fought Dusty Rhodes to a double disqualification

CWF @ West Palm Beach, FL - June 25, 1984 (2,999)
Dick Slater defeated Mike Graham
Black Bart defeated Denny Brown
Hector & Chavo Guerrero defeated Big Daddy & Mike Fever
Velvet McIntyre & Princess Victoria defeated Peggy Lee & Judy Martin
Billy Jack & Mike Rotundo defeated Superstar Billy Graham & Kevin Sullivan
Blackjack Mulligan defeated the One Man Gang via disqualification in a steel cage match
NWA World Champion Ric Flair fought Barry Windham to a double disqualification

JCP @ Greenville, SC - Memorial Auditorium - June 25, 1984
Nikita Koloff defeated Barry Hart
Sam Houston defeated Paul Kelly
Jeff Sword defeated Gene Ligon
Wahoo McDaniel fought NWA TV champion Tully Blanchard to a draw
The Renegade & Mark Youngblood defeated NWA Tag Team Champions Ivan Koloff & Don Kernodle

JCP @ Fayetteville, NC - Cumberland County Civic Center - June 25, 1984
Kurt Von Hess defeated Ben Alexander
Mark Fleming defeated Ali Bey
Gary Quartanelli defeated Kurt Von Hess
The Outlaw defeated Keith Larson
The Assassin & Kamala defeated Rufus R. Jones & Angelo Mosca

JCP @ Raleigh, NC - Dorton Arena - June 26, 1984
Vinnie Valentino defeated Doug Vines
Kamala defeated Barry Hart
Adrian Street defeated Johnny Weaver
Ron Garvin defeated Jake Roberts
Pez Whatley defeated the Assassin via disqualification
Rufus R. Jones & Angelo Mosca Jr. defeated the Outlaw & Gary Hart via count-out

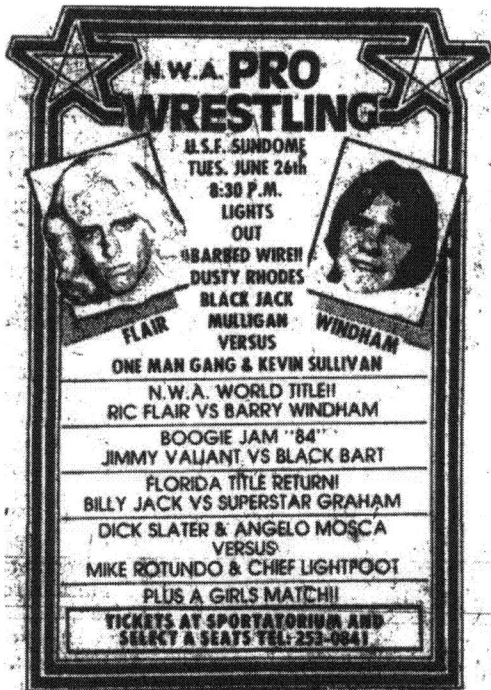

CWF @ Tampa, FL - Sun Dome - June 26, 1984
Velvet McIntyre & Princess Victoria defeated Judy Martin & Peggy Lee
Jimmy Valiant defeated Black Bart
Billy Jack defeated Superstar Billy Graham via disqualification
Dick Slater & Angelo Mosca defeated Mike Rotundo & Chief Joe Lightfoot
NWA World Champion Ric Flair fought Barry Windham to a 60-minute time-limit draw
Dusty Rhodes & Blackjack Mulligan defeated Kevin Sullivan & the One Man Gang in a barbed wire match

JCP @ Columbia, SC - Township Auditorium - June 26, 1984
Paul Kelly defeated Gary Quartenelli
Brian Adidas fought Jesse Barr to a draw
Nikita Koloff defeated Keith Larsen
NWA TV Champion Tully Blanchard defeated Wahoo McDaniel
The Renegade & Mark Youngblood defeated NWA Tag Team Champions Ivan Koloff & Don Kernodle via count-out

WCCW @ ? - June 27, 1984
George Weingeroff defeated Mike Gallagher
Jules Strongbow defeated Krusher Kruschev
Kerry Von Erich & Iceman King Parsons defeated Bill & Scott Irwin
Kevin Von Erich defeated Terry Gordy via disqualification
NWA World Champion Ric Flair defeated Chris Adams

CWF @ Punta Gorda, FL - June 27, 1984
Princess Victoria & Velvet McIntyre defeated Judy Martin & Peggy Lee
Dick Slater defeated Mike Graham
Ron Bass defeated Joe Lightfoot
Billy Jack Haynes defeated Superstar Billy Graham via disqualification
NWA World Champion Ric Flair fought Mike Rotundo to a draw

JCP @ Shelby, NC - Rec Center - June 27, 1984
TV taping:
Brian Adidas, Pez Whatley, & Angelo Mosca Jr. defeated Mike Starbuck, Ron Bass, & Kurt Von Hess
Kamala defeated the Italian Stallion & Jason Walker
Mid-Atlantic Heavyweight Champion the Masked Outlaw defeated Keith Larson
Nikita Koloff defeated Mike Jackson
Terry Gordy & Buddy Roberts defeated Mike Bond & Gary Royal
Wahoo McDaniel pinned Brett Hart with the slingshot suplex at 5:10; Tully Blanchard joined Bob Caudle on commentary for the bout; after the match, McDaniel continued to assault his opponent and fought off two preliminary wrestlers that tried to stop him
Angelo Mosca Jr. defeated Mid-Atlantic Heavyweight Champion the Masked Outlaw to win the title
Worldwide - 6/30/84:

116

Pez Whatley defeated Mike Jackson
Terry Gordy & Buddy Roberts defeated Kurt Von Hess & Mike Bond
Kamala defeated Keith Larson & Roger Bond in a handicap match
Nikita Koloff defeated Paul Kelly
Angelo Mosca Jr. defeated Doug Vines

CWF @ Ocala, FL - June 28, 1984
Hector & Chavo Guerrero defeated Big Daddy & Mike Fever
Princess Victoria & Velvet McIntyre defeated Judy Martin & Peggy Lee
Mike Rotundo fought Angelo Mosca to a draw
Barry Windham fought Dick Slater to a draw
Dusty Rhodes & Jimmy Valiant defeated the One Man Gang & Superstar Billy Graham
NWA World Champion Ric Flair defeated Billy Jack Haynes via disqualification

JCP @ Charleston, SC - June 29, 1984
Paul Kelly defeated Mark Fleming
Keith Larson defeated Ben Alexander
Kurt Von Hess & Bobby Bass defeated Keith Larson & Barry Hart
NWA Mid Atlantic Heavyweight Champion the Outlaw defeated Angelo Mosca Jr.
Wahoo McDaniel defeated NWA TV Champion Tully Blanchard

JCP @ Charleston, SC - County Hall - June 29, 1984
Keith Larsen (sub. for Ken Dillinger) defeated Ben Alexander
Paul Kelly defeated Mark Fleming
Bobby Bass & Kurt Von Hess defeated Brett Hart & Keith Larson
Mid-Atlantic Heavyweight Champion the Outlaw defeated Angelo Mosca Jr. in a Best 2 out of 3 falls match
NWA US Champion Wahoo McDaniel defeated NWA TV Champion Tully Blanchard ($10,000 challenge; only the TV title at stake)

JCP @ Lynchburg, VA - Armory - June 29, 1984
Included NWA Tag Team Champions Ivan Koloff Don Kernodle, Mark Youngblood, the Renegade, Adrian Street, and Pez Whatley

CWF @ Daytona Beach, FL - Spruce Creek High School - June 29, 1984
Princess Victoria & Velvet McIntyre vs. Judy Martin & Peggy Lee
Mike Rotundo vs. Ron Bass
Blackjack Mulligan vs. Angelo Mosca
Barry Windham vs. Dick Slater
NWA World Champion Ric Flair vs. Dusty Rhodes (bunkhouse match)

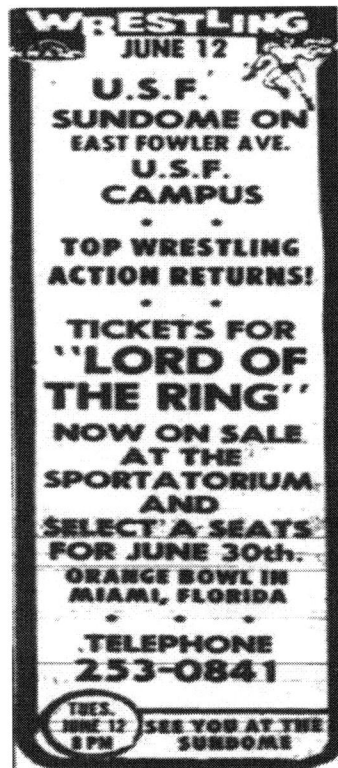

CWF Lords of the Ring - Miami, FL - Orange Bowl - June 30, 1984 (10,000)
Velvet McIntyre & Princess Victoria defeated Judy Martin & Peggy Lee Leather
Mike Graham pinned Chavo Guerrero; stipulations stated the winner would earn a $5,000 bonus
Blackjack Mulligan pinned Kevin Sullivan in a Hangman's Noose match
The Junkyard Dog, Wahoo McDaniel, & Jimmy Valiant defeated Angelo Mosca, Black Bart, & Ron Bass at the 7-minute mark
Hector Guerrero pinned Denny Brown
Dick Slater pinned Joe Lightfoot
Jerry Lawler defeated the One Man Gang via disqualification
Billy Jack Haynes defeated Superstar Billy Graham via submission in a $50,000 full nelson challenge
US Tag Team Champions Barry Windham & Mike Rotunda defeated the Road Warriors via disqualification
Dusty Rhodes defeated NWA World Champion Ric Flair in a non-title Best 2 out of 3 falls match; fall #1: Flair defeated Rhodes via disqualification; fall #2: Rhodes pinned Flair; fall #3: Rhodes defeated Flair via disqualification; the winner won a Lord of the Ring ring and $100,000

WRESTLING

OCALA JAI ALAI FRONTON

NWA

WORLD TITLE

RIC FLAIR
VERSUS
BILLY JACK

DUSTY RHODES AND BOOGIE WOOGIE VALIANT
VERSUS
SUPERSTAR GRAHAM ONE MAN GANG

RIC FLAIR

'GRAHAM

BARRY WINDHAM VS DICK SLATER

MIKE ROTUNDO VS ANGELO MOSCA

PLUS 2 MORE INC. GIRLS

THURS. JUNE 28th 8 PM

ADVANCE TICKETS ARE AVAILABLE AT THE JAI ALAI FRONTON BOX OFFICE

JCP @ Sumter, SC - Sumter County Exhibition Center - July 1, 1984
Jeff Sword defeated Sam Houston
Johnny Weaver defeated Doug Vines
Brian Adidas defeated Kurt Von Hess
NWA Mid Atlantic Heavyweight Champion Angelo Mosca Jr. & Pez Whatley defeated the Outlaw & Gary Hart
Mark Youngblood & the Renegade defeated Ivan Koloff & Don Kernodle
NWA World Champion Ric Flair defeated Wahoo McDaniel

JCP @ Charlotte, NC - Coliseum - July 1, 1984
The Dargon Brothers defeated Jesse Barr & Paul Kelly
Vinnie Valentino defeated Gary Royal
Nikita Koloff defeated Mark Fleming
Buzz Sawyer defeated Barry Hart
Kamala defeated Gary Quartanelli
Mark Youngblood & the Renegade defeated Ivan Koloff & Don Kernodle
Adrian Street defeated Paul Jones via disqualification
Wahoo McDaniel defeated Ricky Steamboat
NWA TV Champion Tully Blanchard defeated NWA World Champion Ric Flair via disqualification

GCW @ Atlanta, GA - July 1, 1984
Ron Garvin defeated GCW TV Champion Jake Roberts to win the title
Dusty Rhodes & Jimmy Valiant vs. the Road Warriors

JCP @ Fayetteville, NC - Cumberland County War Memorial Arena - July 2, 1984
NWA Mid Atlantic Heavyweight Champion Angelo Mosca Jr. & Johnny Weaver defeated the Outlaw & Gary Hart
Nikita Koloff defeated Gary Royal
Brian Adidas defeated Paul Kelly
Buzz Sawyer defeated Gary Quartanelli
NWA TV Champion Tully Blanchard fought Jimmy Valiant to a no contest
Ivan Koloff & Don Kernodle defeated Mark Youngblood & the Renegade via disqualification

JCP @ Greenville, SC - July 2, 1984
Vinnie Valentino defeated Bobby Bass
The Assassins defeated Rufus R. Jones & Pez Whatley
Adrian Street defeated Paul Jones via disqualification
Dusty Rhodes defeated Kamala via disqualification
NWA World Champion Ric Flair defeated Wahoo McDaniel

JCP @ Raleigh, NC - Dorton Arena - July 3, 1984
The Outlaw & Gary Hart defeated Buzz Sawyer & Angelo Mosca Jr.
Rufus R. Jones defeated Jesse Barr
Ricky Steamboat fought NWA TV Champion Tully Blanchard to a no contest
NWA World Champion Ric Flair defeated Wahoo McDaniel

JCP @ Columbia, SC - Township Auditorium - July 3, 1984
Keith Larson defeated Ali Bey
Assassin #3 defeated Sam Houston
Nikita Koloff defeated Barry Hart
Johnny Weaver defeated Kurt Von Hess
Adrian Street defeated Assassin #1
Ivan Koloff & Don Kernodle defeated the Renegade & Mark Youngblood in a lumberjack match
Jimmy Valiant defeated Kamala via disqualification

JCP @ Myrtle Beach, SC - July 4, 1984
NWA World Champion Ric Flair defeated Gary Royal
NWA World Champion Ric Flair defeated Wahoo McDaniel via disqualification

JCP @ Norfolk, VA - Scope - July 5, 1984
Tom Shaft defeated Paul Kelly
Assassin #3 defeated Vinnie Valentino
Mr. Olympia defeated Gary Royal
Buzz Sawyer defeated Keith Larson
NWA TV Champion Tully Blanchard defeated Johnny Weaver
Dusty Rhodes, Adrian Street, & Jimmy Valiant defeated Kamala, Paul Jones, & Assassin #1
NWA World Champion Ric Flair defeated Wahoo McDaniel

JCP @ Charleston, SC - County Hall - July 6, 1984
Barry Hart defeated Doug Vines
Rufus R. Jones defeated Bobby Bass
Angelo Mosca Jr. & Johnny Weaver defeated the Outlaw & Gary Hart
NWA TV Champion Tully Blanchard fought Pez Whatley to a draw

JCP @ Richmond, VA - Coliseum - July 6, 1984
Tom Shaft defeated Gary Royal
Buzz Sawyer defeated Mark Fleming
Nikita Koloff defeated Vinnie Valentino
Assassin #1 defeated Keith Larson
Mr. Olympia defeated Paul Kelly
Adrian Street defeated Paul Jones via disqualification
Jimmy Valiant defeated Assassin #3
NWA Tag Team Champions Ivan Koloff & Don Kernodle defeated Mark Youngblood & the Renegade
Dusty Rhodes defeated Kamala
NWA World Champion Ric Flair defeated Ricky Steamboat

Worldwide - 7/7/84

JCP @ Greensboro, NC - Coliseum - July 7, 1984
Sam Houston defeated Ali Bey
Tom Shaft defeated Kurt Von Hess
Buzz Sawyer defeated Johnny Weaver
Rufus R. Jones defeated Jesse Barr
Adrian Street defeated Paul Jones via disqualification
Jimmy Valiant defeated Kamala

Tully Blanchard defeated Ricky Steamboat via disqualification
NWA World Champion Ric Flair defeated Wahoo McDaniel

JCP @ Asheville, NC - Civic Center - July 8, 1984
Barry Hart defeated Bobby Bass
Mark Fleming defeated Ali Bey
Vinnie Valentino defeated Gary Quartanelli
Nikita Koloff defeated Gary Royal
The Assassins defeated Buzz Sawyer & Adrian Street
Gene & Ole Anderson defeated NWA Tag Team Champions
Ivan Koloff & Don Kernodle via disqualification

JCP @ Greenville, SC - July 9, 1984
Sam Houston defeated Bobby Bass
Jesse Barr defeated Jeff Sword
Buzz Sawyer defeated Vinnie Valentino
Johnny Weaver & Angelo Mosca Jr. defeated the Outlaw &
Gary Hart
Dusty Rhodes, Jimmy Valiant, & Adrian Street defeated Paul
Jones & the Assassins

JCP @ Raleigh, NC - Dorton Arena - July 10, 1984
Pez Whatley, Angelo Mosca Jr., & Brian Adidas defeated Gary
Hart, Buzz Sawyer, & the Outlaw
Nikita Koloff defeated Gary Royal
Keith Larsen defeated Ali Bey
The Renegade & Mark Young defeated NWA Tag Team
Champions Ivan Koloff & Don Kernodle via count-out

**JCP @ Columbia, SC - Township Auditorium - July 10,
1984**
Vinnie Valentino defeated Bobby Bass
Sam Houston defeated Jeff Sword
Tom Shaft defeated Paul Kelly
NWA TV Champion Tully Blanchard defeated Dusty Rhodes
Wahoo McDaniel, Jimmy Valiant, & Adrian Street defeated
Paul Jones, Assassin #1 & #3

Central States @ Lincoln, NE - July 11, 1984
Harley Race defeated NWA World Champion Ric Flair via
disqualification

JCP @ Harrisonburg, VA - High School - July 12, 1984
NWA Tag Team Champions Ivan Koloff & Don Kernodle vs.
Mark Youngblood & the Renegade

Central States @ Springfield, IL - July 12, 1984
Harley Race vs. NWA World Champion Ric Flair

**Central States @ St. Louis, MO - Kiel Auditorium - July 13,
1984**
Ted Oates defeated TG Stone
Grappler #2 defeated Tommy Rogers
Marty Jannetty defeated Grappler #1

The Fabulous Moolah & Peggy Lee defeated Desiree Peterson
& Winona Little Heart
The Missing Link defeated Rufus R. Jones
Missouri Heavyweight Champion Harley Race fought Wahoo
McDaniel to a no contest
Kerry Von Erich & Barry Windham defeated NWA World
Champion Ric Flair & Jerry Blackwell

JCP @ Charleston, SC - County Hall - July 13, 1984
Sam Houston defeated Ali Bey
Mark Fleming defeated Gene Ligon
Brian Adidas fought Jesse Barr to a draw
Angelo Mosca Jr. & Johnny Weaver defeated the Outlaw &
Gary Hart in a lumberjack match
Dusty Rhodes defeated Buzz Sawyer

Worldwide - 7/14/84:
Wahoo McDaniel vs. Ben Alexander
Brian Adidas & Pez Whatley vs. Doug Vines & Kelly
Buzz Sawyer vs. the Italian Stallion
NWA Tag Team Champions Ivan Koloff & Don Kernodle vs.
the Dragon Twins
Nikita Koloff vs. Mark Fleming
Jimmy Valiant vs. Bob Bass

JCP @ Charlotte, NC - Coliseum - July 14, 1984
Sam Houston defeated Doug Vines
Gary Quartanelli defeated Jeff Sword
Nikita Koloff defeated Vinnie Valentino
Brian Adidas fought Buzz Sawyer to a draw
Jimmy Valiant & Adrian Street defeated the Assassins
Ricky Steamboat defeated Wahoo McDaniel via
disqualification
The Renegade & Mark Youngblood defeated NWA Tag Team
Champions Ivan Koloff & Don Kernodle via disqualification

JCP @ Roanoke, VA - Civic Center - July 15, 1984
Barry Hart defeated Mark Fleming
Keith Larson defeated Ali Bey
The Assassins defeated Brian Adidas & Keith Larson
Nikita Koloff defeated Paul Kelly
NWA TV Champion Tully Blanchard defeated Johnny Weaver
Jimmy Valiant defeated Buzz Sawyer via disqualification
Adrian Street defeated Paul Jones via disqualification

JCP @ Savannah, GA - Civic Center - July 15, 1984
Sam Houston defeated Jeff Sword
Bobby Bass defeated Dave Dillenger
Tom Shaft defeated Jesse Barr
Vinnie Valentino defeated Kurt Von Hess
Pez Whatley & Angelo Mosca Jr. defeated the Outlaw & Gary
Hart
NWA Tag Team Champions Ivan Koloff & Don Kerodle
defeated the Renegade & Pez Whatley via disqualification

JCP @ Greenville, SC - July 16, 1984
Rufus R. Jones defeated Kurt Von Hess
NWA TV Champion Tully Blanchard defeated Johnny Weaver
Angelo Mosca Jr. defeated the Outlaw
Nikita Koloff defeated Gary Royal
Barry Hart defeated Paul Kelly
The Renegade & Pez Whatley defeated Ivan Koloff & Don Kernodle in a lumberjack match

JCP @ Fayetteville, NC - July 16, 1984
Vinnie Valentino defeated Jeff Sword
Brian Adidas defeated Doug Vines
Jesse Barr defeated Tom Shaft
Jimmy Valiant defeated Buzz Sawyer via disqualification
The Assassins defeated Wahoo McDaniel & Adrian Street

JCP @ Raliegh, NC - Dorton Arena - July 17, 1984
Keith Larson defeated Kurt Von Hess
Angelo Mosca Jr. defeated the Outlaw
Buzz Sawyer defeated Barry Hart
Nikita Koloff defeated Paul Kelly
The Renegade & Pez Whatley defeated Ivan Koloff & Don Kernodle in a lumberjack match

JCP @ Columbia, SC - Township Auditorium - July 17, 1984
Tom Shaft defeated Bobby Bass
Rufus R. Jones defeated Jesse Barr
Jimmy Valiant defeated NWA TV Champion Tully Blanchard via disqualification
Adrian Street fought Paul Jones to a draw
The Assassins defeated Johnny Weaver & Brian Adidas

JCP @ Winston-Salem, NC - Memorial Coliseum - July 18, 1984
TV taping:
The Outlaw vs. Angelo Mosca Jr. (winner gets to use a whip on his opponent)
Jimmy Valiant, Gene & Ole Anderson vs. Paul Jones & the Assassins
Worldwide - 7/21/84:
Mark & Jay Youngblood vs. Gary Royal & Doug Vines
Buzz Sawyer vs. Keith Larson
The Assassins vs. Vinnie Valentino & Mark Fleming
NWA Tag Team Champions Ivan Koloff & Don Kernodle vs. Barry Horowitz & Sam Houston
Brian Adidas vs. Jeff Sword
Jimmy Valiant & Adrian Street vs. Bob Bass & Turk

Central States @ Kansas City, KS - July 19, 1984
Harley Race defeated NWA World Champion Ric Flair via count-out

JCP @ Norfolk, VA - July 19, 1984
Nikita Koloff defeated Vinnie Valentino

Tom Shaft defeated Ali Bey
Barry Hart & Sam Houston defeated Bobby Bass & Jeff Sword
Angelo Mosca Jr. defeated the Outlaw
Buzz Sawyer defeated Jimmy Valiant
NWA TV Champion Tully Blanchard defeated Brian Adidas
NWA Tag Team Champions Ivan Koloff & Don Kernodle defeated the Renegade & Mark Youngblood

JCP @ Sumter, SC - July 19, 1984
Keith Larson defeated Gary Royal
Paul Kelly defeated Doug Vines
Johnny Weaver defeated Kurt Von Hess
Jesse Barr defeated Mark Fleming
Adrian Street, Rufus R. Jones, & Pez Whatley defeated Paul Jones & the Assassins

JCP @ Charleston, SC - County Hall - July 20, 1984
Ben Alexander defeated Gary Quartenelli
Johnny Weaver defeated Paul Kelly
Jesse Barr defeated Ken Dillinger
Rufus R. Jones defeated Kurt Von Hess
Assassin #1 & #3 defeated Pez Whatley & Adrian Street
Angelo Mosca Jr. defeated the Outlaw in a whip match

JCP @ Greensboro, NC - Coliseum - July 21, 1984
Sam Houston defeated Jesse Barr
Buzz Sawyer defeated Barry Hart
Nikita Koloff defeated Vinnie Valentino
NWA Mid-Atlantic TV Champion Tully Blanchard defeated Pez Whatley
Ivan Koloff & Don Kernodle defeated Jay & Mark Youngblood
Wahoo McDaniel defeated Ricky Steamboat via disqualification
Jimmy Valiant, Rufus R. Jones, & Adrian Street defeated Paul Jones & the Assassins

WCCW @ Austin, TX - July 22, 1984 (5,000)
George Weingeroff defeated Kelly Kiniski
Iceman King Parsons defeated Scott Irwin
Michael Hayes defeated Jules Strongbow
Kerry Von Erich & Chris Adams defeated Jimmy Garvin & the Missing Link
NWA World Champion Ric Flair defeated Kevin Von Erich

WCCW @ San Antonio, TX - July 22, 1984
Buck Zumhofe defeated Kelly Kiniski
Jose Lothario defeated Scott Irwin
Killer Khan defeated Buck Zumhofe
Chris Adams & Stella Mae French defeated Jimmy Garvin & Precious in a loser leaves Texas steel cage match
Gino Hernandez defeated Iceman King Parsons
NWA World Champion Ric Flair fought Kerry Von Erich to a draw

WCCW @ Ft. Worth, TX - July 23, 1984
George Weingeroff defeated Buddy Roberts
Chris Adams defeated Terry Gordy via disqualification
Mike Von Erich defeated Jimmy Garvin
Kelly Kiniski fought Jules Strongbow to a draw
Kerry Von Erich defeated Michael Hayes
NWA World Champion Ric Flair defeated Gino Hernandez

JCP @ Columbia, SC - July 24, 1984
Tom Shaft defeated Doug Vines
Brian Adidas defeated Jeff Sword
NWA TV Champion Tully Blanchard defeated Johnny Weaver
The Renegade & Mark Youngblood fought NWA Tag Team
Champions Don Kernodle & Ivan Koloff to a double
disqualification
The Junkyard Dog defeated Wahoo McDaniel via
disqualification

JCP @ Wilson, NC - July 26, 1984
Jeff Sword defeated Gary Quartanelli
Sam Houston defeated Barry Hart
Nikita Koloff defeated Gary Royal
NWA Tag Team Champions Ivan Koloff & Don Kernodle
defeated the Renegade & Mark Youngblood
Angelo Mosca Jr. defeated Wahoo McDaniel via
disqualification

JCP @ Hampton, VA - Coliseum - July 27, 1984
Sam Houston defeated Paul Kelly
Brian Adidas defeated Jeff Sword
NWA TV Champion Tully Blanchard defeated Johnny Weaver
Pez Whatley defeated Kurt Von Hess
Adrian Street defeated Paul Jones
Angelo Mosca Jr. defeated Buzz Sawyer
Dusty Rhodes & Jimmy Valiant defeated the Assassins

WCCW @ Dallas, TX - July 27, 1984
George weingeroff defeated Mike Gallagher
Jules Strongbow defeated Krusher Krushev
Kevin Von Erich defeated Terry Gordy via disqualification
NWA World Champion Ric Flair defeated Chris Adams
Mike Von Erich & Iceman King Parsons defeated Bill & Scott
Irwin

JCP @ Charleston, SC - County Hall - July 27, 1984
Tom Shaft defeated Jeff Sword
Vinnie Valentino defeated Bobby Bass
Nikita Koloff defeated Brett Hart
The Junkyard Dog & Rufus R. Jones defeated Gary Royal &
Jesse Barr
NWA Tag Team Champions Ivan Koloff & Don Kernodle
defeated Mark Youngblood & the Renegade

Worldwide - 7/28/84:
Brian Adidas vs. Paul Kelly

NWA Tag Team Champions Ivan Koloff & Don Kernodle vs.
the Italian Stallion & Mark Fleming
NWA World Champion Ric Flair vs. Gary Royal
Jimmy Valiant vs. Kurt Von Hess
Jay Youngblood vs. Jeff Sword
Buzz Sawyer vs. Sam Houston

JCP @ Charlotte, NC - Coliseum - July 28, 1984
Brian Adidas defeated Paul Kelly
Pez Whatley defeated Gary Royal
Angelo Mosca Jr. defeated Buzz Sawyer
Dusty Rhodes defeated the Outlaw
The Junkyard Dog defeated Wahoo McDaniel
Ricky Steamboat defeated NWA TV Champion Tully Blanchard
via disqualification
NWA Tag Team Champions Ivan Koloff & Don Kernodle
defeated Mark Youngblood & the Renegade

CWF @ Ocala, FL - Jai Alai Fronton - July 29, 1984
Scott McGhee vs. the Saint
The Break Dancers vs. Hector & Chavo Guerrero
Chief Joe Lightfoot vs. the Dream
Superstar Billy Graham vs. Billy Jack Haynes
Blackjack Mulligan & Barry Windham vs. NWA World
Champion Ric Flair & Angelo Mosca
The One Man Gang vs. Ron Bass (chain match)

CWF @ West Palm Beach, FL - Auditorium - July 30, 1984
Breakdancer #1 defeated Shotgun Willie
Black Bart defeated Dennis Brown
The Dream defeated Breakdancer #2
The Saint defeated Joe Lightfoot
Hector & Chavo Guerrero defeated Mike Rotundo & Scott
McGhee
Scott McGhee defeated Superstar Billy Graham
Dory Funk Jr. defeated Billy Jack
Kevin Sullivan & Ron Bass defeated Blackjack Mulligan & the
One Man Gang in a bunkhouse match
Dusty Rhodes defeated NWA World Champion Ric Flair via
disqualification

JCP @ Raleigh, NC - Dorton Arena - July 31, 1984
Tom Shaft defeated Doug Vines
Johnny Weaver defeated Bobby Bass
Rufus R. Jones defeated Jesse Barr
Brian Adidas defeated Buzz Sawyer
Assassin #3 defeated Adrian Street
Jimmy Valiant defeated Assassin #1 in a lumberjack match

CWF @ Tampa, FL - Sun Dome – July 31, 1984
One Mang Gang & Blackjack Mulligan vs. Ron Bass & Angelo
Mosca
Barry Windham vs. Superstar Billy Graham
NWA World Champion Ric Flair vs. Dusty Rhodes

N.W.A. PRO WRESTLING

WORLD TITLE
RIC FLAIR
VERSUS
DUSTY RHODES

FLORIDA TITLE
BARRY WINDHAM VS SUPERSTAR GRAHAM

ONE MAN GANG & BLACKJACK MULLIGAN
VERSUS
COWBOY RON BASS & ANGELO MOSCA

PLUS FIVE MORE BIG MATCHES!!

FLAIR   RHODES

TUESDAY JULY 31st, 8:30 P.M.
U.S.F. SUNDOME - EAST FOWER AVE.
TEL: 253-0841 FOR RESERVATIONS SPORTATORIUM

MID-ATLANTIC CHAMPIONSHIP

WRESTLING

SATURDAY
AUGUST 11th
8:15 P.M. ● 8:15 P.M. ● 8:15 P.M.

WILMINGTON LEGION STADIUM

Tickets On Sale at FASTOP #1 & FASTOP #2
FOR WORLD'S CHAMPIONSHIP

RIC FLAIR **Vs.** **WAHOO McDANIEL**

TV CHAMPIONSHIP MATCH

TULLY BLANCHARD Vs. **ANGELO MOSCO JR.**

GRUDGE MATCH

RUFUS R. JONES **Vs.** **ASSASSIAN #1**
With PAUL JONES

THE
ASSASSIAN #3 **Vs.** EXOTIC ADRIAN **STREET**
With PAUL JONES   With MISS LINDA

| JESSE BARR Vs. PISTOL PEZ WHATLEY | GARY ROYAL vs. VINNIE VALENTINO | DOUG VINE vs. KEITH LARSON |

JCP @ Columbia, SC - August 1, 1984
Vinnie Valentino defeated Kurt Von Hess
Nikita Koloff defeated Barry Hart
NWA TV Champion Tully Blanchard defeated Pez Whatley
NWA Tag Team Champions Don Kernodle & Ivan Koloff defeated the Renegade & Mark Youngblood
Ricky Steamboat defeated Wahoo McDaniel via disqualification

CWF @ Miami, FL - August 1, 1984
Hector & Chavo Guerrero defeated Joe Lightfoot & Scott McGhee
The Saint defeated Mike Rotundo
Dory Funk Jr. fought Mike Graham to a draw
Scott McGhee defeated Superstar Billy Graham
Blackjack Mulligan & the One Man Gang defeated Ron Bass & Kevin Sullivan
NWA World Champion Ric Flair defeated Billy Jack Haynes via disqualification

CWF @ Lake City, FL - Community College - August 2, 1984
The Break Dancers vs. Hector & Chavo Guerrero
Scott McGhee vs. Black Bart
Mike Rotundo & Chief Joe Lightfoot vs. Superstar Billy Graham & Kevin Sullivan
Billy Jack vs. Angelo Mosca
The One Man Gang vs. Ron Bass
NWA World Champion Ric Flair vs. Barry Windham

JCP @ Norfolk, VA - August 2, 1984
Dusty Rhodes defeated Tully Blanchard

JCP @ Richmond, VA - Coliseum - August 3, 1984
Dusty Rhodes defeated Assassin #1

Worldwide - 8/4/84 - included David Crockett & Johnny Weaver on commentary; Crockett conducting an interview with Dusty Rhodes in which Rhodes challenged Mid-Atlantic TV Champion Tully Blanchard to a 60-minute time-limit match, said he also wanted a shot at NWA US Champion Wahoo McDaniel, and mentioned Barry Windham's arrival to JCP; Bob Seger's "Old Time Rock 'n' Roll" played in the background during the interview; included Bob Caudle conducting an interview with Crockett in which he introduced footage of Jim Crockett Jr. and Barry Windham, with Jim saying he signed Windham to the most lucrative contract in professional sports and gave him the keys to a custom Z28 convertable; Windham then said he was happy to wrestle under the Crockett banner and was looking forward to being part of Starrcade 84; Jim then said Windham would make his debut at the Greensboro Coliseum on Aug. 18 against NWA Tag Team Champion Ivan Koloff; footage then aired of Windham beating then-NWA World Champion Harley Race during a Championship Wrestling from Florida taping; featured Crockett conducting an interview with Wahoo McDaniel regarding the NWA US Title being held up and challenging NWA World Champion Ric Flair; included a vignette of Flair meeting Blackjack Mulligan at a campfire, trying to convince Mulligan to help him against McDaniel & Blanchard; Rhodes stood behind Mulligan during the segment; Mulligan eventually said he wanted to think about it and invited Flair to sit with his other friends and share a beer.
Rufus R. Jones pinned Kurt Von Hess with a headbutt at 2:57
Mark Youngblood (w/ the Renegade) pinned Doug Vines at 3:36 with a double chop
Assassin #1 (w/ Paul Jones) pinned Sam Houston with a right hand punch at 4:20
Jimmy Valiant defeated Jeff Sword via submission with the sleeper at 4:23
NWA Six Man Tag Team Champion Nikita Koloff (w/ NWA Tag Team Champions & NWA Six Man Tag Team Champions Ivan Koloff & Don Kernodle) defeated Gary Royal at 2:52 via submission with the cobra clutch
Wahoo McDaniel & NWA TV Champion Tully Blanchard defeated Brian Adidas & Pez Whatley at 5:37 when McDaniel pinned Whatley with a chop after Blanchard tripped Whatley from the floor; Dusty Rhodes joined David Crockett on commentary for the match; after the match, Adidas made the save

CWF @ Tallahassee, FL - August 4, 1984
NWA World Champion Ric Flair defeated Dusty Rhodes via disqualification

CWF @ Lakeland, FL - August 4, 1984
NWA World Champion Ric Flair defeated Superstar Billy Graham

JCP @ Greensboro, NC - Coliseum - August 4, 1984 (4,231)
Sam Houston defeated Gary Royal
Brian Adidas defeated Jeff Sword
Nikita Koloff defeated Johnny Weaver
Assassin #1 defeated Rufus R. Jones
Mark Youngblood & the Renegade defeated NWA Tag Team Champions Ivan Koloff & Don Kernodle via disqualification when Koloff threw Youngblood over the top rope
NWA TV Champion Tully Blanchard fought Jimmy Valiant to a 20-minute time-limit draw
Wahoo McDaniel pinned Ricky Steamboat at the 23-minute mark

JCP @ Charlotte, NC - Coliseum - August 5, 1984
Dusty Rhodes, Mark & Jay Youngblood defeated Don Kernodle, Ivan & Nikita Koloff

JCP @ Sumter, SC - Sumter County Exhibition Center - August 5, 1984
Buzz Sawyer vs. Sam Houston
Johnny Weaver vs. Don Kernodle
NWA Mid-Atlantic Heavyweight Champion Angelo Mosca Jr.

vs. Ivan Koloff
Jimmy Valiant & Adrian Street vs. the Assassins
NWA TV Champion Tully Blanchard vs. Dusty Rhodes
NWA World Champion Ric Flair vs. Wahoo McDaniel

JCP @ Charleston, SC - County Hall - August 10, 1984
Keith Larson vs. Jeff Sword
Pez Whatley vs. Jesse Barr
Johnny Weaver vs. Buzz Sawyer
NWA TV Champion Tully Blanchard vs. Angelo Mosca Jr.
NWA World Champion Ric Flair vs. Wahoo McDaniel

Worldwide - 8/11/84:
NWA Mid Atlantic Heavyweight Champion Angelo Mosca Jr.
vs. Gary Royal
Brian Adidas vs. Bob Bass
The Assassin vs. Doug Vines
Mark Youngblood & the Renegade vs. Jesse Barr & Jeff Sword
Nikita Koloff & NWA Tag Team Champion Ivan Koloff vs. Sam
Houston & Brett Hart (Barry Horowitz)

JCP @ Wilmington, NC - Legion Stadium - August 11, 1984
Jesse Barr vs. Pez Whatley
Gary Royal vs. Vinnie Valentino
Doug Vines vs. Keith Larson
Assassin #3 vs. Adrian Street
Rufus R. Jones vs. Assassin #1
NWA TV Champion Tully Blanchard vs. Angelo Mosca Jr.
NWA World Champion Ric Flair vs. Wahoo McDaniel

JCP @ Richmond, VA - Coliseum - August 17, 1984
NWA Tag Team Champions Ivan Koloff & Don Kernodle vs.
the Renegade & Brian Adidas
Rufus R. Jones vs. Assassin #1
Jimmy Valiant vs. NWA TV Champion Tully Blanchard (falls
count anywhere, 20-minute time-limit)
NWA World Champion Ric Flair vs. Wahoo McDaniel

JCP @ Shelby, NC - Rec Center - August 1984
*Worldwide - 8/18/84 - featured David Crockett & Johnny
Weaver on commentary; included Crockett conducting an
interview with Paul Jones & JJ Dillon in which Jones said Dillon
and he had monopolized the talent across the country but now
they were in the same territory; Dillon then said Jimmy Valiant
had become a thorn in the side of Jones and he would help his
friend take care of the problem; featured Crockett conducting
an interview with Wahoo McDaniel & NWA TV Champion Tully
Blanchard regarding their partnership; moments later, footage
was shown of Blanchard's recent match with Dusty Rhodes,
during which McDaniel interfered to double team Rhodes;
footage was then shown of Blanchard coming out at the
Charlotte Coliseum as NWA World Champion Ric Flair was
wrestling McDaniel, with the two then dropping Flair with a
spike piledriver; Rhodes, Jimmy Valiant, Ricky Steamboat,
NWA Mid Atlantic Heavyweight Champion Angelo Mosca Jr.,*

*and others then came out to tend to Flair and helped him from
the ring; McDaniel then discussed Flair turning to Blackjack
Mulligan for help against himself and Blanchard; included
Crockett conducting an interview with Jones & Assassin #1
regarding Valiant and Assassin's taped fists; featured Crockett
conducting an interview with Flair regarding McDaniel &
Blanchard and finding Mulligan in Florida to help him out; Flair
then showed footage of Mulligan by a fireside in which he said
he would be coming back to Mid Atlantic after a 3-year
absence to help Flair; Flair then said Blanchard's girlfriends all
ask him "Where's the beef?":*
Brian Adidas pinned Kurt Von Hess at around the 3-minute
mark with an airplane spin
NWA Mid Atlantic Heavyweight Champion Angelo Mosca Jr.
pinned Doug Vines with a crossbody off the top at 5:07
Rufus R. Jones pinned Gary Royal with a headbutt at 5:00
JJ Dillon pinned Sam Houston with a bodyslam and elbowdrop
after avoiding a running knee in the corner
Barry Windham pinned an unknown with a lariat at the 30-
second mark; after the bout, footage was also shown of Mike
Rotundo pinning an unknown in Florida following an airplane
spin (*Championship Wrestling from Florida*)
Wahoo McDaniel pinned Keith Larson with a slingshot suplex
at 5:52; NWA TV Champion Tully Blanchard provided guest
commentary for the match; after the bout, Blanchard cut a
promo on NWA World Champion Ric Flair & Blackjack Mulligan

JCP @ Greensboro, NC - Coliseum - August 18, 1984
Denny Brown defeated Paul Kelly
Ron Bass & Black Bart defeated Rufus R. Jones & Brian
Adidas
Dusty Rhodes defeated Assassin #3 (Hercules)
The Renegade defeated Don Kernodle via disqualification
Barry Windham defeated Ivan Koloff (Windham's debut)
Assassin #1 defeated Jimmy Valiant in a taped fist match
Ricky Steamboat fought NWA TV Champion Tully Blanchard to
a draw
NWA World Champion Ric Flair defeated Wahoo McDaniel via
disqualification

JCP @ Asheville, NC - Civic Center - August 19, 1984
Keith Larson defeated Mike Fever
Keith Larson defeated Jeff Sword
JJ Dillon defeated Denny Brown
Mark Youngblood, Angelo Mosca, & the Renegade defeated
Don Kernodle, Ivan & Nikita Koloff
Assassin #1 defeated Jimmy Valiant in a taped fist match
Dusty Rhodes & Blackjack Mulligan fought NWA US Champion
Wahoo McDaniel & NWA TV Champion Tully Blanchard to a
no contest

JCP @ Charlotte, NC - Coliseum - August 19, 1984
Dusty Rhodes defeated Don Kernodle via disqualification

GCW @ Atlanta, GA - Omni - August 21, 1984
Ivan Koloff defeated Tim Horner

Brad Armstrong defeated NWA TV Champion Tully Blanchard via disqualification
Tommy Rich & Tony Atlas fought Rip Rogers & Ted Oates to a draw
National Tag Team Champion Ron Garvin won a battle royal
Bob Armstrong defeated National Heavyweight Champion Ted DiBiase in a lumberjack match

JCP @ Winston-Salem, NC - Memorial Coliseum - August 22, 1984
TV taping:
NWA World Champion Ric Flair vs. Assassin #1
Wahoo McDaniel vs. Jimmy Valiant
Worldwide - 8/25/84:
Brian Adidas vs. Paul Barnett
JJ Dillon vs. Brett Hart
NWA World Champion Ric Flair vs. Kurt Von Hess
Wahoo McDaniel & NWA TV Champion Tully Blanchard vs. Randy Barber & Horton
NWA Tag Team Champions Ivan Koloff & Don Kernodle vs. Mark & Jay Youngblood

JCP @ Fredericksburg, VA - Stafford Senior High School Gym - August 23, 1984
Bobby Bass defeated Brett Hart
Brett Hart defeated Paul Kelly
Brian Adias defeated Jeff Sword
Mike Rotundo defeated Assassin #3
Jimmy Valiant defeated Assassin #1

Mid South @ New Orleans, LA - Superdome - August 24, 1984 (21,000)
Jim Duggan vs. Hercules
Magnum TA vs. Butch Reed
Dusty Rhodes & Sonny King (sub. for the Junkyard Dog) defeated Bobby Eaton & Dennis Condrey
Kerry Von Erich fought NWA World Champion Ric Flair to a double disqualification

JCP @ Hampton, VA - Coliseum - August 24, 1984
Denny Brown defeated Paul Kelly
JJ Dillon defeated Barry Hart
NWA TV Champion Tully Blanchard defeated Johnny Weaver
Black Bart & Ron Bass defeated Brian Adidas & Sam Houston
Mike Rotundo defeated Nikita Koloff via disqualification
NWA Tag Team Champions Ivan Koloff & Don Kernodle defeated Mark Youngblood & the Renegade

GCW @ Atlanta, GA - August 25, 1984
NWA World Champion Ric Flair defeated Randy Barber

JCP @ Roanoke, VA - Civic Center - August 25, 1984
Denny Brown fought Barry Hart to a draw
Nikita Koloff defeated Mike Fever
Black Bart defeated Johnny Weaver

Ron Bass defeated Rufus R. Jones
NWA Tag Team Champions Ivan Koloff & Don Kernodle vs. Mark Youngblood & the Renegade in a No DQ, Best 2 out of 3 falls match

Mid South @ Oklahoma City, OK - August 26, 1984 (16,000)
Kerry Von Erich fought NWA World Champion Ric Flair to a draw

JCP @ Sumter, SC - August 26, 1984
Keith Larson fought Black Bart to a draw
Ron Bass & Black Bart defeated Denny Brown & Mike Fever
Johnny Weaver defeated JJ Dillon
Angelo Mosca defeated Nikita Koloff via disqualification
Ivan Koloff & Don Kernodle defeated Mark Youngblood & the Renegade

JCP @ Kingston - August 27, 1984
Rufus R. Jones defeated Nikita Koloff via disqualification
Angelo Mosca defeated Assassin #3
NWA Tag Team Champions Ivan Koloff & Don Kernodle defeated Angelo Mosca & Jay Youngblood
Assassin #1 defeated Jimmy Valiant in a taped fist match

JCP @ Greenville, SC - August 27, 1984
Tom Shaft defeated Doug Vines
Mike Rotundo defeated Jeff Sword
Ron Bass & Black Bart defeated Johnny Weaver & Denny Brown
Brian Adidas defeated Ben Alexander
Barry Windham defeated Wahoo McDaniel
NWA TV Champion Tully Blanchard defeated Dusty Rhodes

JCP @ Raleigh, NC - Dorton Arena - August 28, 1984
Barry Hart defeated Doug Vines
Assassin #3 defeated Keith Larson
Nikita Koloff defeated Sam Houston
Angelo Mosca defeated Jeff Sword
Jay Youngblood & the Renegade defeated Ivan Koloff & Don Kernoodle via disqualification
Assassin #1 defeated Jimmy Valiant in a Texas Death Match

JCP @ Columbia, SC - Township Auditorium - August 28, 1984
Mike Fever defeated Denny Brown
Brian Adidas defeated Ben Alexander
Mike Rotundo defeated JJ Dillon
Ron Bass & Black Bart defeated Johnny Weaver & Rufus R. Jones
NWA TV Champion Tully Blanchard fought Barry Windham to a draw
Wahoo McDaniel defeated Dusty Rhodes via disqualification

JCP @ Spartanburg, SC - Memorial Auditorium - August 29, 1984
Worldwide - 9/8/84:
Barry Windham & Mike Rotunda vs. Jeff Sword & Kelly
Black Bart vs. Mike Fever
The Zambuie Express vs. Mark Fleming & Barry Horowitz
Ron Bass defeated NWA Mid Atlantic Heavyweight Champion Angelo Mosca Jr. to win the title
The Assassin vs. Ron Rossi

Dartmouth, Nova Scotia - Sportsplex - August 30, 1984
NWA World Champion Ric Flair vs. Stephen Pettipas

Bridgewater, Nova Scotia - August 31, 1984
NWA World Champion Ric Flair vs. Stephen Pettipas

JCP @ Charleston, SC - County Hall - August 31, 1984
Gene Ligon vs. Ben Alexander
Denny Brown vs. Paul Kelly
Sam Houston & Angelo Mosca Jr. vs. the Zambouie Express
Wahoo McDaniel vs. Mike Rotundo
NWA TV Champion Tully Blanchard vs. Barry Windham

JCP @ Lynchburg, VA - Armory - August 31, 1984

Worldwide - 9/1/84:
Angelo Mosca Jr. & Brian Adidas vs. Jeff Sword & Doug Vines
NWA Tag Team Champion Ivan Koloff vs. Mike Fever
Barry Windham vs. Gary Royal
Ron Bass & Black Bart vs. Gene Ligon & Shaft
Mike Rotunda vs. Paul Kelly
The Zambuie Express vs. Sam Houston & Brown

JCP @ Greensboro, NC - Coliseum - September 1, 1984
Ron Bass & Black Bart defeated Angelo Mosca & Brian Adidas
Barry Windham & Mike Rotunda defeated Nikita Koloff & NWA Tag Team Champion Ivan Koloff via disqualification
Assassin #1 defeated Jimmy Valiant
Dusty Rhodes defeated NWA Tag Team Champion Don Kernodle
NWA World Champion Ric Flair & Blackjack Mulligan fought Wahoo McDaniel & NWA TV Champion Tully Blanchard to a double disqualification

JCP @ Asheville, NC - Civic Center - September 2, 1984 (1,000)
NWA World Champion Ric Flair defeated Wahoo McDaniel

JCP @ Greenville, SC - September 3, 1984
JJ Dillon defeated Denny Brown
Mark Youngblood defeated Paul Kelly
The Renegade defeated Jeff Sword
Black Bart defeated Brian Adidas
Ron Bass defeated Angelo Mosca Jr.

Dusty Rhodes & Ricky Steamboat defeated Wahoo McDaniel & NWA TV Champion Tully Blanchard

JCP @ Raleigh, NC - Dorton Arena - September 4, 1984
Mike Fever defeated Doug Vines
Nikita Koloff defeated Rufus R. Jones
Mike Rotundo defeated Assassin #1
The Zambouie Express defeated Mark Youngblood & the Renegade
Barry Windham defeated NWA Tag Team Champion Ivan Koloff via disqualification

JCP @ Norfolk, VA - September 6, 1984
Keith Larson defeated Gary Royal
Nikita Koloff defeated Johnny Weaver
Wahoo McDaniel & NWA TV Champion Tully Blanchard fought NWA World Champion Ric Flair & Dusty Rhodes via disqualification
Barry Windham defeated Ivan Koloff
Mike Rotundo defeated Don Kernodle
Black Bart & Ron Bass defeated Denny Brown & Sam Houston

JCP @ Harrisonburg, VA - High School - September 6, 1984
Mike Fever vs. Jeff Sword
Brett Hart vs. Doug Lyons
Denny Brown vs. Paul Kelly
Mark Youngblood vs. Assassin #3
Rufus R. Jones vs. Assassin #1
NWA Tag Team Champions Ivan Koloff & Don Kernodle vs. Mark Youngblood & the Renegade

JCP @ Charleston, SC - County Hall - September 7, 1984
Doug Vines defeated Brett Hart
Mike Fever fought Jeff Sword to a draw
Johnny Weaver defeated Assassin #3
The Zambouie Express defeated Mark & Jay Youngblood
Assassin #1 defeated Jimmy Valiant in a taped fist match

JCP @ Richmond, VA - Coliseum - September 7, 1984
Denny Brown defeated Gary Royal
Nikita Koloff defeated Sam Houston
Rufus R. Jones defeated Paul Kelly
Don Kernodle defeated Angelo Mosca
Blackjack Mulligan defeated Wahoo McDaniel via disqualification
Black Bart & Ron Bass defeated Brian Adidas & Mike Rotundo
Barry Windham defeated Ivan Koloff
Dusty Rhodes defeated NWA TV Champion Tully Blanchard

MID-ATLANTIC CHAMPIONSHIP
WRESTLING · SAT. SEPT. 8TH
8:15 P.M. 8:15 P.M. 8:15 P.M.
WILMINGTON LEGION STADIUM
SPONSORED BY YOUTH BASEBALL
SPECIAL CHALLENGE MATCH
WAHOO McDANIEL
· VERSUS ·
BLACKJACK MULLIGAN
20 MINUTE MATCH FOR TV TITLE & $10,000.00
TULLY BLANCHARD
· VERSUS ·
DUSTY RHODES
NEW YORK STREET FIGHT
JIMMY VALIANT
· VERSUS ·
THE ASSASSIN #1

| BRIAN ADIDAS & ANGELO MOSCA, JR. | V S. | THE ZAMBUI EXPRESS | ASSASSIN #3 VS DENNY BROWN | PLUS OTHER MATCHES |

JCP @ Wilmington, NC - Legion Stadium - September 8, 1984
Assassin #3 vs. Denny Brown
Brian Adidas & Angelo Mosca Jr. vs. the Zambuie Express
Jimmy Valiant vs. Assassin #1 (streetfight)
Dusty Rhodes vs. NWA TV Champion Tully Blanchard
Wahoo McDaniel vs. Blackjack Mulligan

JCP @ Charlotte, NC - September 9, 1984
Nikita Koloff defeated Sam Houston & Barry Hart in a handicap match
Black Bart & Ron Bass defeated Brian Adidas & Denny Brown
Gary Royal defeated Doug Vines
Mike Rotundo defeated Don Kernodle
NWA TV Champion Tully Blanchard defeated Ricky Steamboat
Barry Windham defeated Ivan Koloff
Barry Windham defeated Wahoo McDaniel in a Texas Death Match

JCP @ Greenville, SC - September 10, 1984 (800)
The Zambuie Express defeated Angelo Mosca Jr. & Brian Adidas
Mike Rotundo defeated Mid Atlantic Heavyweight Champion Ron Bass via disqualification

Tully Blanchard fought Barry Windham to a 20-minute time-limit draw
Dusty Rhodes pinned Wahoo McDaniel

Montreal, Quebec - Paul Sauve Centre - September 10, 1984
John White defeated yvon Laverdure at 5:51
Gino Brito Jr. & Denis Goulet defeated Tito Senza & Claude Gosselin at 13:58
Armand Rougeau fought Rick Valentine to a draw
Ray Rougeau defeated Sailor White at the 36-second mark
NWA World Champion Ric Flair defeated Gino Brito at the 22-minute mark
Dino Bravo & Rick Martel defeated the Masked Superstar & King Tonga at 15:17
Jos LeDuc defeated Abdullah the Butcher in a Texas Death Match at 4:52

JCP @ Columbia, SC - Township Auditorium - September 11, 1984
Paul Kelly defeated Mike Fever
Denny Brown defeated Gary Royal
Black Bart defeated Rufus R. Jones
Don Kernodle defeated Brian Adidas
Mike Rotundo defeated Ron Bass via disqualification
Ricky Steamboat defeated Wahoo McDaniel

JCP @ Charleston, SC - September 14, 1994
Kareem Muhammad defeated Denny Brown
Elijah Akeem defeated Sam Houston
Nikita Koloff defeated Johnny Weaver
Rufus R. Jones defeated Doug Vines
Ron Bass & Black Bart defeated Mike Rotundo & Brian Adidas
Ivan Koloff & Don Kernodle fought Ricky Steamboat & Barry Windham to a draw
Assassin #1 defeated Jimmy Valiant in a taped fist match
Dusty Rhodes & Ole Anderson defeated NWA US Champion Wahoo McDaniel & NWA TV champion Tully Blanchard

Central States @ St. Louis, MO - September 14, 1984
NWA World Champion Ric Flair defeated Harley Race

Worldwide - 9/15/84:
Mark Youngblood vs. Doug Vines
The Assassin vs. Mike Fever
Barry Windham & Mike Rotunda vs. Kelly & Gary Royal
The Zambuie Express vs. Barry Horowitz & Keith Larson
NWA Tag Team Champion Don Kernodle vs. Denny Brown
Black Bart vs. Sam Houston

JCP @ Greenville, SC - September 15, 1984
Keith Larson defeated Gary Royal
Doug Vines defeated Denny Brown
Rufus R. Jones defeated Paul Kelly
Brian Adidas defeated the Assassin

Mike Rotundo defeated Nikita Koloff
Dusty Rhodes & Barry Windham defeated Ivan Koloff & Don Kernodle via disqualification
NWA TV Champion Tully Blanchard defeated Ricky Steamboat

JCP @ Asheville, NC - Civic Center - September 16, 1984
Sam Houston defeated Doug Vines
Elijah Akeem defeated Denny Brown
Rufus R. Jones defeated Paul Kelly
Ron Bass & Black Bart defeated Mike Rotundo & Angelo Mosca Jr.
Jimmy Valiant defeated the Assassin in a New York Streetfight
Dusty Rhodes & Barry Windham defeated Ivan Koloff & Don Kernodle via disqualification
Ricky Steamboat fought NWA TV Champion Tully Blanchard to a draw

WCCW @ Ft. Worth, TX - September 17, 1984
Koko Ware defeated Mike Reed
El Diablo Grande defeated George Weingeroff
Iceman King Parsons & Mike Von Erich defeated Bill & Scott Irwin
Buck Zumhofe defeated Norvell Austin
The Missing Link defeated Jules Strongbow
NWA World Champion Ric Flair defeated Chris Adams

JCP @ Raleigh, NC - Dorton Arena - September 18, 1984
Elijah Akeem defeated Sam Houston
Kareem Muhammad defeated Denny Brown
Mike Davis defeated Jeff Sword
NWA World Champion Ric Flair & Dusty Rhodes fought NWA US Champion Wahoo McDaniel & NWA TV Champion Tully Blanchard to a no contest
The Ultimate Assassin (Johnny Weaver) defeated the Assassin via disqualification

JCP @ Columbia, SC - September 18, 1984
Gary Royal defeated Mike Fever
Barry Hart defeated Doug Vines
Black Bart defeated Keith Larson
Brian Adidas defeated Nikita Koloff via disqualification
Ron Bass defeated Angelo Mosca
Barry Windham & Mike Rotundo defeated Ivan Koloff & Don Kernodle via disqualification

Memphis, TN - Mid-South Coliseum - September 18, 1984 (3,000)
Pro Wrestling USA taping:
Ricky Morton & Robert Gibson defeated Phil Hickerson & Lanny Poffo
Larry Zbyszko defeated Keith Eric
Harley Race & Dory Funk Jr. defeated Tracey Smothers & Mark Regan
Jerry Lawler defeated Eddie Gilbert
AWA Tag Team Champions the Road Warriors defeated Ken Raper & Craig Carson
Tony Atlas & Butch Reed defeated the Masked Spoiler & Keith Roberson
Tony Atlas & Butch Reed defeated the Dirty White Boys
AWA World Champion Rick Martel defeated the Masked Spoiler
Mr. Saito defeated Keith Eric
Dory Funk Jr. defeated Dutch Mantell
Superstar Billy Graham defeated Craig Carson
Stan Lane & Steve Keirn defeated the Nightmares
10/6/84 - featured Jack Reynolds on commentary; included Lance Russell as the ring announcer; featured a music video on Ricky Morton & Robert Gibson to the tune of Van Halen's "Jump;" included Reynolds conducting an interview with Bob Backlund in which he referred to Backlund as "the champ," with Backlund saying he was still the champion because he wasn't pinned or made to submit and that "they" wanted him out of wrestling; Backlund said he would keep the title until he was pinned or made to submit and spoke of getting letters from fans saying they thought he was still the champion; he then said no one would make him change his ways or lower his standards because he was proud; after Backlund left, Reynolds said Backlund was still recognized by many as the WWF World Champion; featured Reynolds conducting an interview with AWA Tag Team Champions the Road Warriors & Paul Ellering in which they said there was no one from New York that could beat them because they were from Chicago, with Road Warrior Hawk saying he would spit in Al Capone's face if he were still alive; included a closing announcement that Superstar Billy Graham, Stan Lane & Steve Keirn, Dory Funk Jr., AWA World Champion Rick Martel, Mr. Saito, and more would be part of the following week's show:
Ricky Morton & Robert Gibson defeated the Nightmares at 3:59 when Gibson scored the pin following the double dropkick; only the closing moments of the match were shown
Tony Atlas & Butch Reed defeated Kurt Von Hess & Keith Roberson at 3:53 when Reed pinned Roberson after simultaneous gorilla press slams
Dusty Rhodes defeated an unknown via submission with the figure-4 at the 31-second mark (*Carolinas*)
AWA Tag Team Champions the Road Warriors (w/ Paul Ellering) defeated Ken Raper & Mark Regan at 3:06 when Road Warrior Hawk scored the pin following the clothesline off the top; during the bout, Sheik Adnan Al-Kaissie was shown walking around ringside
Nick Bockwinkel pinned Lanny Poffo at 7:17 with a piledriver after lifting his knees to block a moonsault; during the bout, Sheik Adnan Al-Kaissie joined Jack Reynolds on commentary to say he was looking for talent; Reynolds referred to Bockwinkel's piledriver as a suplex until Al-Kaissie corrected him
Jerry Lawler & Tommy Rich defeated Tony Anthony & Len Denton at 4:01 when Rich pinned Anthony with the Thesz Press; Lawler & Rich used Survivor's "Eye of the Tiger" as their entrance music; Terry Funk joined Reynolds on commentary for the bout, during which they discussed Funk's role in 'Paradise Alley'
Mr. Saito (w/ Jimmy Hart) pinned Tracy Smothers at 1:00 with

a back suplex; prior to the bout, Reynolds conducted a ringside interview with Saito & Hart in which Hart offered one million yen to anyone who could beat Saito; Funk provided guest commentary for the match

AWA World Champion Rick Martel pinned Eddie Gilbert in a non-title match at 3:32 with an abdominal stretch into a roll up; prior to the bout, both men shook hands

10/13/84 - featured Jack Reynolds on commentary, with Terry Funk joining him beginning with the second match; included Reynolds conducting an interview with Bob Backlund, who he referred to as the world champion, who said he wasn't there because "they" took the belt from him but because they wanted to lower his standards; Backlund then said no one would tell him to lower his standards or do something he couldn't be proud of; he then said he wouldn't tell the kids not to take a pill but then sneak around and do it himself, like others do; featured Lance Russell as the ring announcer; included a music video on Jimmy Valiant to the tune of Joe Walsh's "Life's Been Good;" featured Reynolds conducting an interview with Ricky Morton & Robert Gibson in which they said they were looking forward to coming to the east coast; included Reynolds conducting an interview with Tony Atlas in which he talked about his poor background, how proud he was to be a pro wrestler in the AWA, and that it didn't matter who they put him in the ring with, even if it was Willie B, the gorilla from the Atlanta zoo:

Stan Lane & Steve Keirn defeated the Masked Spoiler & Phil Hickerson at 6:10 when Keirn pinned Hickerson following a double DDT

AWA Tag Team Champions the Road Warriors (w/ Paul Ellering) defeated Tracy Smothers & Keith Eric at 3:09 when Road Warrior Animal pinned Smohters with a clothesline; Ellering provided guest commentary for the match

Superstar Billy Graham (w/ Jimmy Hart) defeated Ken Raper via submission with the full nelson at 2:21; after the bout, Graham refused to break the hold until Hart climbed in the ring and told him to

Jerry Lawler & Tommy Rich defeated the Nightmares at 6:21 when Lawler scored the pin following the piledriver; prior to the bout, Reynolds conducted a ringside interview with Lawler & Rich in which they cut a promo on AWA Tag Team Champions the Road Warriors

Mr. Saito (w/ Jimmy Hart) defeated Craig Carson via submission with a Scorpion Deathlock at 2:31; prior to the bout, Reynolds conducted a ringside interview with Saito & Hart, during which Hart said he would up his challenge from one million yen to four million to any man who could face and defeat Saito

Harley Race pinned Dutch Mantel following a delayed suplex at 2:06; during the bout, Sheik Adnan Al-Kaissie appeared ringside

JCP @ Norfolk, VA - September 20, 1984
Nikita Koloff defeated Denny Brown
Keith Larson defeated Jeff Sword
Black Bart defeated Mike Davis
Ron Bass defeated Sam Houston
Mike Rotundo defeated Ivan Koloff

Barry Windham defeated Don Kernodle
NWA World Champion Ric Flair & Dusty Rhodes defeated NWA US Champion Wahoo McDaniel & NWA TV Champion Tully Blanchard

JCP @ Orangeburg, SC - September 20, 1984
Mark Fleming fought Paul Kelly to a draw
Mike Fever defeated Gary Royal
Johnny Weaver defeated Doug Vines
The Zambuie Express defeated Keith Larson & Barry Hart
The Assassin defeated Jimmy Valiant in a taped fist match

JCP @ Richmond, VA - September 21, 1984
Nikita Koloff defeated Denny Brown
Sam Houston defeated Jeff Sword
Black Bart defeated Keith Larson
Ron Bass defeated Mike Davis
Dusty Rhodes & Mike Rotundo defeated Ivan Koloff & Don Kernodle via disqualification
Barry Windham defeated NWA US Champion Wahoo McDaniel
Ricky Steamboat fought NWA TV Champion Tully Blanchard to a draw

WCCW @ Dallas, TX - September 21, 1984
Jules Strongbow fought Scott Irwin to a draw
Jake Roberts defeated Buck Zumhofe
Jose Lotharip defeated Killer Khan via disqualification
Kevin Von Erich & Skip Young defeated Koko Ware & Norvell Austin
NWA World Champion Ric Flair defeated Gino Hernandez

JCP @ Charleston, SC - County Hall - September 21, 1984
Paul Kelly defeated Joel Deaton
Kareem Muhammad defeated Barry Hart
The Ultimate Assassin defeated Mike Fever
Mark Youngblood defeated Elijah Akeem
Jimmy Valiant defeated the Assassin in a New York Streetfight

Worldwide - 9/22/84:
Manny Fernandez vs. Gary Royal

JCP @ Greensboro, NC - Coliseum - September 22, 1984
Johnny Weaver & Denny Brown defeated the Zambuie Express
Jay Youngblood & Mike Davis defeated Ron Bass & Black Bart
Mike Rotundo defeated Don Kernodle
Brian Adidas defeated Mike Fever
Barry Windham defeated NWA US Champion Wahoo McDaniel
Jimmy Valiant defeated the Assassin in a New York Streetfight
Ricky Steamboat fought NWA TV Champion Tully Blanchard to a draw

CWF @ Miami Beach, FL - Convention Center - September 22, 1984 (8,000)
Pez Whatley defeated Kevin Sullivan
The One Man Gang defeated Sir Oliver Humperdrink
The One Man Gang defeated the Saint
Scott McGhee defeated Dick Slater
Billy Jack Haynes & Mike Graham fought Dory Funk Jr. & Jesse Barr to a double disqualification
Ricky Morton & Robert Gibson defeated the Road Warriors and Ivan & Nikita Koloff
NWA World Champion Ric Flair defeated Dusty Rhodes via count-out

JCP @ Sumter, SC - September 23, 1984
Denny Brown defeated Paul Kelly
Black Bart & Ron Bass defeated Brian Adidas & Mike Davis
Mike Rotundo defeated Don Kernodle via disqualification
Ivan Koloff defeated Brian Adidas
Jimmy Valiant defeated Assassin #1 in a streetfight
Dusty Rhodes & Barry Windham defeated Wahoo McDaniel & NWA TV Champion Tully Blanchard via disqualification

CWF @ Sarasota, FL - September 23, 1984
The Saint defeated Larry Hamilton
Scott McGhee fought Dick Slater to a draw
Dory Funk Jr. & Jesse Barr defeated Mike Graham & Pez Whatley
Pez Whatley defeated Jim Neidhart
Ricky Morton & Robert Gibson defeated Ken Timbs & Dusty Wolfe
The One Man Gang defeated Kevin Sullivan
NWA World Champion Ric Flair defeated Billy Jack Haynes

JCP @ Greenville, SC - September 24, 1984
Jeff Sword defeated Joel Deaton
Denny Brown defeated Paul Kelly
JJ Dillon defeated Keith Larson
Barry Windham defeated Jeff Sword
Ron Bass & Black Bart defeated Sam Houston & Brian Adidas
Dusty Rhodes defeated Nikita Koloff via disqualification
Wahoo McDaniel defeated Ricky Steamboat

JCP @ Columbia, SC - September 25, 1984
Barry Hart defeated Doug Vines
Jeff Sword defeated Mike Fever
Black Bart defeated Mike Davis
The Zambouie Express defeated Keith Larson & Sam Houston
The Ultimate Assassin defeated Assassin #1 via disqualification
Wahoo McDaniel defeated Barry Windham

CWF @ Tampa, FL - Spartan Sports Center - September 25, 1984
Larry Hamilton defeated Joe Lightfoot
Krusher Kruschev & Jim Neidhart defeated Raul Mata & John King
Ricky Morton & Robert Gibson defeated Ken Timbs & Dusty Wolfe
Chavo & Hector Guerrero defeated the Saint & Buck Robley
Florida Heavyweight Champion Scott McGhee defeated Dick Slater via disqualification
Pez Whatley defeated Kevin Sullivan via disqualification in a Prince of Darkness death match
Dory Funk Jr. & Jesse Barr fought Harley Race & Mike Graham to a double disqualification
Billy Jack Haynes defeated NWA World Champion Ric Flair via disqualification at 31:09 when Flair threw the champion over the top rope

CWF @ Gainesville, FL - O'Connell Center - September 26, 1984
Dick Slater defeated Larry Hamilton
Hector & Chavo Guerrero defeated Ken Timbs & Dusty Wolfe
Scott McGhee fought the Saint to a draw
One Man Gang defeated Kevin Sullivan via disqualification
Jesse Barr & Dory Funk Jr. defeated Harley Race & Mike Graham
NWA World Champion Ric Flair defeated Billy Jack Haynes via disqualification

JCP @ Raleigh, NC - Dorton Arena - September 26, 1984
Ron Bass defeated Mike Rotundo
Black Bart defeated Barry Hart
The Zambouie Express defeated Keith Larson & Denny Brown
Manny Fernandez defeated Mike Fever
Nikita Koloff, NWA Tag Team Champions Ivan Koloff & Don Kernodle defeated Brian Adidas, Mike Davis, & Sam Houston
Assassin #1 defeated the Ultimate Assassin
NWA TV Champion Tully Blanchard defeated Barry Windham via disqualification
Wahoo McDaniel defeated Dusty Rhodes

CWF @ Jacksonville, FL - September 27, 1984
NWA World Champion Ric Flair defeated Scott McGhee

JCP @ Hampton, VA - September 28, 1984
Manny Fernandez defeated Gary Royal
The Zambouie Express defeated Brian Adidas & Keith Larsen
Black Bart defeated Mark Youngblood
The Ultimate Assassin defeated Assassin #1 via disqualification
Wahoo McDaniel fought Barry Windham to a no contest
Dusty Rhodes defeated NWA TV Champion Tully Blanchard via disqualification

Worldwide - 9/29/84 - included Tony Schiavone & Mid-Atlantic TV Champion Tully Blanchard on commentary; featured Schiavone conducting an interview with NWA Tag Team Champions & NWA Six-Man Tag Team Champions Ivan Koloff, Don Kernodle, & Nikita Koloff in which they reviewed

footage of Nikita, with Ivan, facing Dusty Rhodes, Barry Windham beside him, in an arm wrestling contest, with Nikita eventually winning; included Schiavone speaking with Blanchard in which Blanchard said he was searching for the perfect 10 woman; featured Schiavone conducting an interview with Rhodes & Manny Fernandez in which they said they were going after the NWA Tag Team Titles, with the three then reviewing footage of Wahoo McDaniel walking out during a recent match with Fernandez; included Schiavone conducting an interview with JJ Dillon regarding Starrcade Rally 84:
Mike Rotundo pinned Paul Kelly at around 3:45 following the airplane spin
NWA Six-Man Tag Team Champion Nikita Koloff (w/ NWA Tag Team Champion & NWA Six-Man Tag Team Champion Ivan Koloff) defeated Mark Fleming at 2:28 via submission with the Cobra Clutch
Barry Windham pinned an unknown at the 40-second mark with a flying clothesline (taped at another location)
Barry Windham pinned Jeff Sword at the 22-second mark with a flying clothesline (taped another location)
Brian Adidas pinned Mike Jackson at 7:47 with an abdominal stretch into a roll up; prior to the bout, the two shook hands
Dusty Rhodes & Manny Fernandez defeated Steve Grism & Randy Barber at 2:04 when Rhodes pinned Grism following the Bionic Elbow; during the final moments of the match, NWA Tag Team Champions & NWA Six-Man Tag Team Champions Ivan Koloff, Don Kernodle, & Nikita Koloff attacked Fernandez at ringside and bloodied him with their chain until Rhodes made the save
Wahoo McDaniel & Mid-Atlantic TV Champion Tully Blanchard defeated Don Sanders & Steve Miller at 5:37 when Blanchard pinned Sanders with the slingshot suplex; during the bout, it was announced Ole Anderson was heading back to the territory (taped at another location)
Mark Youngblood pinned Joel Deaton at around the 5-minute mark with a tomahawk chop to the chest (the match was joined in progress)

JCP @ Asheville, NC - Civic Center - September 30, 1984
Black Bart defeated Denny Brown
Manny Fernandez defeated Doug Vines
The Zambouie Express defeated Keith Larsen & Barry Hart
Ron Bass defeated Mark Youngblood
The Ultimate Assassin defeated Assassin #1 via disqualification
NWA World Champion Ric Flair & Dusty Rhodes defeated Wahoo McDaniel & NWA TV Champion Tully Blanchard

CWF @ West Palm Beach, FL - WPB Auditorium - October 1, 1984 (2,761)
Jay Youngblood & Angelo Mosca Jr. defeated Ken Timbs & Dusty Wolfe
Buck Robley defeated Hector Guerrero
Larry Hamilton & Pez Whatley defeated Jim Neidhart & Krusher Kruschev
Florida Heavyweight Champion Scott McGhee defeated Jesse Barr

Superstar Billy Graham & the One Man Gang defeated Kevin Sullivan & the Saint
NWA World Champion Ric Flair defeated Billy Jack Haynes

JCP @ Greenwood, SC - Memorial Auditorium - October 1, 1984
Denny Brown defeated Jeff Sword
The Zambuie Express defeated Sam Houston & Joel Deaton
Manny Fernandez defeated Don Kernodle
Assassin #1 defeated the Ultimate Assassin
Barry Windham defeated Nikita Koloff via disqualification
Dusty Rhodes defeated Ivan Koloff

JCP @ Spartanburg, SC - Memorial Auditorium - October 2, 1984
Barry Windham vs. NWA TV Champion Tully Blanchard
Dusty Rhodes vs. Nikita Koloff
Also included Brian Adidas, Mike Rotundo, NWA Tag Team Champions Ivan Koloff & Don Kernodle
Worldwide - 10/6/84:
Mike Rotundo vs. Mike Jackson
Mid-Atlantic Tag Team Champions Ron Bass & Black Bart vs. Sam Houston & Rocky King
Scott Hall & Dan Spivey vs. Gary Royal & Don Sanders
Manny Fernandez vs. Jeff Sword
Barry Windham vs. Paul Kelly
Ivan Koloff vs. Bob Owens
MACW - 10/6/84

JCP @ Columbia, SC - October 2, 1984
Wahoo McDaniel fought NWA World Champion Ric Flair to a double disqualification

JCP @ Raleigh, NC - Dorton Arena - October 3, 1984
Wahoo McDaniel fought NWA World Champion Ric Flair to a double disqualification

JCP @ Richmond, VA - Coliseum - October 5, 1984
Black Bart defeated Mike Davis
Sam Houston defeated Jeff Sword
NWA Tag Team Champions Ivan Koloff & Don Kernodle defeated Manny Fernandez & Brian Adidas
NWA TV Champion Tully Blanchard defeated Ricky Steamboat
Ron Bass defeated Mark Youngblood
NWA World Champion Ric Flair defeated Wahoo McDaniel
Dusty Rhodes defeated Nikita Koloff

JCP @ Charleston, SC - County Hall - October 5, 1984
Mike Fever defeated Joel Deaton
Paul Kelly defeated Brett Hart
Keith Larson defeated Gary Royal
The Ultimate Assassin defeated Paul Jones
Jimmy Valiant defeated Assassin #1 in a death match

JCP @ Greensboro, NC - Coliseum - October 6, 1984
Starrcade Rally 84 - featured a performance from the Gator Tail Band, free T-shirts, an autograph session, and the announcement of who would be part of Starrcade 84; included a segment in which Jim Crockett introduced the two participants in the main event of Starrcade's $1 million match, NWA World Champion Ric Flair and Dusty Rhodes; Flair and Rhodes were then driven into the arena in seperate limos, with Rhodes cutting a promo on the stage and confronting Flair
Nikita Koloff defeated Mike Davis
NWA Mid-Atlantic Heavyweight Champion & NWA Mid-Atlantic Tag Team Champion Ron Bass defeated Mark Youngblood
Manny Fernandez defeated Wahoo McDaniel via count-out
NWA Tag Team Champions Ivan Koloff & Don Kernodle defeated Ole Anderson & Brian Adidas (sub. for Barry Windham)
NWA TV Champion Tully Blanchard defeated Ricky Steamboat via disqualification; there was a 50-minute time-limit for the match

JCP @ Charlotte, NC - October 7, 1984
NWA US Championship Tournament Opening Round: Mike Rotundo defeated Assassin #1 via disqualification
NWA US Championship Tournament Opening Round: Ivan Koloff defeated Brian Adidas
NWA US Championship Tournament Opening Round: Dusty Rhodes defeated Don Kernodle
NWA US Championship Tournament Opening Round: Ricky Steamboat fought Ron Bass to a draw
NWA US Championship Tournament Opening Round: Superstar Billy Graham defeated Carlos Colon via count-out
NWA US Championship Tournament Opening Round: Wahoo McDaniel defeated Mark Youngblood
NWA US Championship Tournament Opening Round: NWA TV Champion Tully Blanchard defeated Jimmy Valiant
NWA US Championship Tournament Quarter Finals: Manny Fernandez defeated Superstar Billy Graham via disqualification
NWA US Championship Tournament Quarter Finals: Dusty Rhodes fought Ivan Koloff to a no contest
NWA US Championship Tournament Quarter Finals: Wahoo McDaniel defeated Mike Rotundo
NWA US Championship Tournament Semi Finals: Manny Fernandez defeated NWA TV Champion Tully Blanchard
NWA US Championship Tournament Finals: Wahoo McDaniel defeated Manny Fernandez

Central States @ Bethalto, IL - Civic Memorial High School Gym - October 7, 1984
Gypsy Joe vs. Tommy Rogers
Marty Jannetty vs. the Animal
The Grapplers vs. Bob Brown & Buzz Tyler
Harley Race vs. Hacksaw Higgins
Ted DiBiase defeated NWA World Champion Ric Flair via disqualification

JCP @ Greenville, SC - October 8, 1984
Sam Bowie defeated Mike Davis
Black Bart defeated Sam Houston
Sam Houston defeated Denny Brown
The Ultimate Assassin defeated Assassin #1
Ivan & Nikita Koloff defeated Brian Adidas & Mark Youngblood
Brian Adidas defeated Don Kernodle via disqualification
Ron Bass defeated Mike Rotundo via disqualification
Dusty Rhodes & Manny Fernandez defeated NWA US Champion Wahoo McDaniel & NWA TV Champion Tully Blanchard in a lights out Texas Tornado match

JCP @ Keanansville - October 11, 1984
Sam Houston defeated Jeff Sword
Nikita Koloff defeated Mike Fever
The Zambouie Express defeated Mike Davis & Keith Larson
Brian Adidas defeated Don Kernodle via disqualification
Manny Fernandez defeated Ivan Koloff

GCW @ Baltimore, MD - Civic Center - October 11, 1984
National TV Champion Bob Roop defeated Jerry Oates
National Tag Team Champions Rip Rogers & Ted Oates defeated Brad Armstrong & Tim Horner
Tommy Rich defeated Mr. Ito
AWA Tag Team Champions the Road Warriors fought Dusty Rhodes & Ole Anderson to a double disqualification
Ron Garvin defeated National Heavyweight Champion Ted DiBiase to win the title
NWA World Champion Ric Flair pinned Harley Race in a steel cage match

JCP @ Hampton, VA - October 12, 1984
Joel Deaton defeated Paul Kelly
The Zambouie Express defeated Sam Houston & Denny Brown
The Assassin defeated Jimmy Valiant
Ron Bass & Black Bart defeated Manny Fernandez & Mike Rotundo
Don Kernodle defeated Brian Adidas
NWA TV Champion Tully Blanchard fought Manny Fernandez to a draw
Dusty Rhodes defeated Ivan Koloff

Worldwide - 10/13/83:
Brian Adidas vs. Jason Walker
Mike Rotundo vs. Rocky King
Scott Hall & Dan Spivey vs. Sanders & Barber
Manny Fernandez vs. Doug Vines
The Zambuie Express vs. Mike Jackson & Miller

STARRCADE 84

RALLY

FREE WRESTLING T-SHIRTS TO FIRST 1,000 FANS IN ATTENDANCE

SATURDAY — OCTOBER 6 — 8:00 PM

FIVE BIG MAIN EVENT MATCHES

TV CHAMPIONSHIP — 50 MINUTES (TV TITLE & $10,000)

TULLY BLANCHARD VS RICKY STEAMBOAT

WORLD TAG TEAM TITLE MATCH

IVAN KOLOFF

and

DON KERNODLE

VS

BARRY WINDHAM

and

OLE' ANDERSON

THE RAGIN' BULL VS WAHOO MCDANIEL

MARK YOUNGBLOOD VS COWBOY RON BASS

BRIAN ADIDAS VS NIKITA KOLOFF

RIC FLAIR

RICKY STEAMBOAT

—ALSO FEATURING
LIVE ENTERTAINMENT
"STARRCADE" RALLY
THE HOTTEST NEW
COUNTRY ROCK BAND
THE GATOR TAIL BAND
FROM FLORIDA
LIVE!!!

—PLUS—
AUTOGRAPH SESSION
WITH SENSATIONAL
BARRY WINDHAM

IN PERSON ... DUSTY RHODES, RIC FLAIR,
JIMMY VALIANT AND OTHERS !!!
TICKETS — $10 - $8 - $5
On sale at Greensboro Coliseum Box Office and all Ticketron outlets

Greensboro
Coliseum

JCP @ Richmond, VA - October 13, 1984
Denny Brown defeated Jeff Sword
The Zambouie Express defeated Joel Deaton & Keith Larson
Black Bart defeated Sam Houston
Ron Bass defeated Mike Davis
Ivan Koloff & Don Kernodle defeated Brian Adidas & the Ultimate Assassin
Dusty Rhodes defeated Nikita Koloff via disqualification in a lumberjack match
NWA TV Champion Tully Blanchard defeated Mike Rotundo
NWA US Champion Wahoo McDaniel fought Manny Fernandez to a no contest in a Texas Death Match
Jimmy Valiant defeated the Assassin in a lights out taped fist steel cage match

JCP @ Asheville, NC - Civic Center - October 14, 1984
Denny Brown defeated Doug Vines
JJ Dillon defeated Keith Larson
The Zambouie Express defeated Sam Houston & Joel Deaton
Don Kernodle defeated Mike Davis
The Assassin defeated Johnny Weaver
Nikita Koloff defeated Brett Hart & Mike Fever
Mike Rotundo & Brian Adidas defeated Ron Bass & Black Bart via disqualification
NWA US Champion Wahoo McDaniel fought Manny Fernandez to a no contest

GCW @ Atlanta, GA - Omni - October 14, 1984
The Italian Stallion defeated Ted Allen
Ox Baker defeated Frankie Lane
Jerry Oates defeated Mr. Ito
Ivan Koloff defeated Tim Horner
Brad Armstrong defeated NWA TV Champion Tully Blanchard via disqualification
Ron Garvin defeated GCW TV Champion Bob Roop via disqualification
NWA National Tag Team Champions Ted Oates & Rip Rogers fought Tony Atlas & Tommy Rich to a no contest
Bob Armstrong defeated Ted DiBiase in a Canadian lumberjack match

JCP @ Fayetteville, NC - Cumberland County War Memorial - October 15, 1984
Joel Deaton defeated Mike Fever
Denny Brown defeated Paul Kelly
Sam Houston defeated Jeff Sword
Ron Bass & Black Bart defeated Keith Larson & Mike Davis
NWA Tag Team Champion Don Kernodle defeated the Ultimate Assassin
Manny Fernandez defeated NWA Tag Team Champion Ivan Koloff
Dusty Rhodes defeated Nikita Koloff via disqualification

Worldwide - 10/20/84:
Mike Rotundo vs. Mark Fleming
Manny Fernandez vs. Jeff Sword

Ron Bass & Black Bart vs. Brown & Keith Larsen
Scott Hall & Dan Spivey vs. Doug Vines & Joel Deaton
Wahoo McDaniel vs. Barry Horowitz
The Zambuie Express vs. Mike Davis & Houston

JCP @ Greensboro, NC - Coliseum - October 20, 1984
Joel Deaton defeated Jeff Sword
Black Bart defeated Keith Larson
The Zambuie Express defeated Mike Davis & Sam Houston
Nikita Koloff defeated Barry Hart & Mark Fleming in a handicap match
Tully Blanchard defeated Brian Adidas
NWA US Champion Wahoo McDaniel defeated Jimmy Valiant
Dusty Rhodes & Manny Fernandez defeated NWA Tag Team Champions Ivan Koloff & Don Kernodle (w/ Nikita Koloff) to win the titles in a steel cage match when Fernandez pinned Koloff after Rhodes hit Koloff in the back of the head with the champions' own foreign object as Koloff had a sleeper applied, with Fernandez then falling on top for the win; late in the match, Fernandez hit a splash off the top of the cage onto Koloff; after the contest, Ivan & Nikita attacked Kernodle and double teamed him for several minutes until other wrestlers and officials pulled them away; eventually, EMTs and Kernodle's parents climbed in the ring to check on him and Kerndole was taken backstage on a stretcher

JCP @ Charlotte, NC - Coliseum - October 21, 1984
Black Bart defeated Mike Davis
American Starship defeated Gary Royal & Jeff Sword
Ron Bass defeated Brian Adidas
The Ultimate Assassin defeated Assassin #1 via count-out
Ivan Koloff defeated Mike Rotundo
NWA Tag Team Champion Dusty Rhodes defeated Nikita Koloff via disqualification in a Texas Bullrope match
NWA Tag Team Champion Manny Fernandez fought NWA US Champion Wahoo McDaniel to a no contest
Ron Garvin fought NWA TV Champion Tully Blanchard to a draw

JCP @ Sumter, SC - October 21, 1984
Denny Brown defeated Gary Royal
Black Bart defeated Joel Deaton
American Starship defeated Doug Vines & Mark Fleming
Ron Bass defeated Brian Adidas
Jimmy Valiant & the Ultimate Assassin fought Assassin #1 & Paul Jones to a draw
NWA Tag Team Champion Manny Fernandez fought NWA TV Champion Tully Blanchard to a draw

JCP @ Spartanburg, SC - Memorial Auditorium - October 23, 1984
Pro Wrestling USA taping:
10/27/84 - featured Gordon Solie on commentary; included Tony Schiavone as the ring announcer; featured Solie conducting an interview with Dusty Rhodes regarding Ivan & Nikita Koloff; included Solie conducting an interview with

135

Rhodes & wrestling coach John Heath, during which it was noted Heath would join Solie on commentary for the next several weeks; featured Doug McCloud conducting an interview with Nick Bockwinkel regarding AWA World Champion Rick Martel and NWA World Champion Ric Flair, other challengers like Dusty Rhodes, and wanting to again be world champion; included a closing announcement that Tommy Rich & Jerry Lawler would be in tag team action the next week:

Jerry Lawler pinned Randy Barber with a fistdrop off the middle turnbuckle at 3:25

Nikita Koloff & NWA Tag Team Champion Ivan Koloff defeated Rocky King & Doug Sanders at 4:51 when Ivan pinned King with the knee off the top to the back; during the bout, Sheik Adnan Al-Kaissie appeared ringside

Mr. Saito pinned Jason Walker at 6:13 with a back suplex; during the ring announcing, Tony Schiavone pronounced Saito as "Siato;" Dusty Rhodes joined Gordon Solie & John Heath on commentary for the match; Adnan Al Kaissie remained ringside for the bout

Bob Backlund pinned Mike Jackson with a reversal into a bridge at 7:55

Ricky Steamboat pinned Gary Royal with a splash off the top at 2:46

AWA Tag Team Champions the Road Warriors (w/ Paul Ellering) defeated Steve Miller & Mark Fleming at 3:11 when Road Warrior Hawk forced a submission with an overhead backbreaker; during the bout, it was noted Universal Heavyweight Champion Carlos Colon and Tommy Rich would be on the following week's show

11/3/84 - featured Gordon Solie & John Heath on commentary; included Solie conducting an interview with NWA Tag Team Champion Ivan Koloff & Nikita Koloff in which Ivan bragged about Nikita learning the English language within a matter of months and then cut a promo on Dusty Rhodes; Nikita then said he would crush Rhodes' unity tour; featured Tony Schiavone as the ring announcer; featured Solie conducting an interview with Tommy Rich regarding his upcoming match with Jerry Lawler against the Road Warriors; included highlights from the Charlie Brown vs. Great Kabuki and Ric Flair vs. NWA World Champion Harley Race matches from Starrcade 83, which Solie said was the most attended wrestling show in history, to promote the upcoming Starrcade 84; featured Solie conducting a ringside interview with AWA Tag Team Champions the Road Warriors & Paul Ellering, following a match, in which they discussed their dominance in wrestling; included a music video of Jimmy Valiant in and out of the ring to Manhattan Transfer's "Boy from New York City;" featured Solie conducting an interview with Bob Backlund in which he said he was going after AWA World Champion Rick Martel and NWA World Champion Ric Flair and wanted it at Madison Square Garden, the Philadelphia Spectrum, Boston Garden, or Hartford Civic Center:

Ricky Steamboat defeated Bobby Bass via submission with the figure-4 at 1:47

Bob Backlund defeated Gary Royal via submission with the Crossface Chicken Wing at 8:01

Nikita Koloff (w/ NWA Tag Team Champion Ivan Koloff) defeated Mark Fleming via submission with a Cobra Clutch at

2:26; during the bout, Dusty Rhodes joined the commentary team to discuss his feud with the Russians, during which it was noted Jimmy Valiant and NWA World Champion Ric Flair would appear on the following week's show; after the match, Nikita continued to attack Fleming until Rhodes ran out and cleared the Koloffs from the ring

Mr. Saito (w/ Sheik Adnan Al-Kaissie) pinned Gene Ligon with a back suplex at 4:43; following the ring introductions, Al-Kaissie grabbed the mic and said he searched for a man to bring the world title to the Arab world and that man was Saito (Al-Kaissie's debut with Saito)

Jerry Lawler & Tommy Rich defeated Randy Barber & Don Sanders at 4:08 when Rich pinned Sanders with the Thesz Press after a double flying fist drop; Sanders was announced as "Sander" before the match and on commentary; late in the bout, Paul Ellering came ringside, distracting Lawler & Rich as well as the referee; after the bout, Ellering confronted Lawler & Rich with a contract until Rich shoved Ellering to the mat and they left with the contract

WWC Universal Heavyweight Champion Carlos Colon pinned Mike Jackson at 5:09 with a sunset flip as Jackson ran the ropes

JCP @ Norfolk, VA - October 25, 1984

Dick Slater defeated Jeff Sword

Black Bart defeated Denny Brown

Ron Bass defeated Mike Davis

American Starship defeated the Zambouie Express via disqualification

The Ultimate Assassin defeated Assassin #1

Ivan Koloff defeated Brian Adidas

Ole Anderson defeated NWA TV Champion Tully Blanchard via disqualification

NWA Tag Team Champion Manny Fernandez fought NWA US Champion Wahoo McDaniel to a no contest

NWA Tag Team Champion Dusty Rhodes defeated Nikita Koloff in a Texas bullrope match

JCP @ Charleston, SC - County Hall - October 26, 1984

Denny Deaton defeated Doug Vines

Gene Ligon defeated Dave Deaton

Mike Davis defeated Joel Deaton

American Starship defeated the Zambouie Express

Mid-Atlantic Tag Team Champions Ron Bass & Black Bart defeated Brian Adidas & Keith Larson

NWA US Champion Wahoo McDaniel fought NWA Tag Team Champion Manny Fernandez to a double disqualification

Worldwide - 10/27/84 - featured David Crockett conducting an interview with NWA Tag Team Champions Manny Fernandez & Dusty Rhodes regarding their recent title victory, with Rhodes bringing two young fans into the shot to wave the American flag; moments later, they reviewed footage of how they won the titles on 10/20/84 in Greensboro by beating Ivan Koloff & Don Kernodle in a steel cage match; included comments from Kyle Petty regarding his being one of the *judges for the Starrcade 84 match between Rhodes and NWA World Champion Ric Flair; featured the announcement the Zambuie Express & Superstar Billy Graham would face American Starship & Buzz Tyler in an elimination match and Paul Jones would face Jimmy Valiant in a tuxedo streetfight at Starrcade; included footage of Bob Caudle speaking with Jones about the upcoming match with Valiant at Starrcade; featured a promo by Valiant, taped in Memphis, TN, regarding the upcoming match; included the announcement that the Starrcade challenger for NWA US Champion Wahoo McDaniel would be announced the following week; featured Crockett conducting an interview with Brian Adidas regarding the leg injury he sustained at the hands of NWA TV Champion Tully Blanchard; moments later, Dick Slater appeared with Adidas thanking him for his help and Slater saying he wanted a shot at Blanchard's $10,000 as well; footage was then shown of how Blanchard injured Adidas until Slater threw in the towel for him, with Blanchard then jumping Slater from behind before Slater threw Blanchard to the floor and assaulted him at ringside; included Crockett conducting an interview with JJ Dillon, NWA Mid Atlantic Tag Team Champions - NWA Mid Atlantic Heavyweight Champion Ron Bass & Black Bart regarding them challenging Rhodes & Fernandez; featured Crockett conducting an interview with Ivan & Nikita Koloff regarding them turning on Kernodle after the loss of the tag team titles in Greensboro, with footage being shown of them double teaming him after the title loss and EMTs tending to Kernodle; moments later, Kernodle's parents were shown climbing in the ring to check on him as well; included Crockett conducting another interview with the Koloffs in which Crockett showed them footage of Kernodle having to be taken out of the ring in Greensboro on a stretcher; featured footage of Dillon outside Ricky Steamboat's gym to see whether it would be a good training ground for his men for Starrcade; moments later, Bass & Bart arrived with the three then checking out the gym and accidentally breaking one of Steamboat's trophies before making a mess at the juice bar; moments later, Dillon had the footage cut off and yelled at Crockett for showing it in the first place:*

Buzz Tyler pinned Gary Royal with a running powerslam at the 52-second mark

NWA Mid Atlantic Tag Team Champion Black Bart (w/ JJ Dillon) pinned Gene Ligon at 3:59 with a boot to the face and elbow drop

Dick Slater pinned Mike Fever at 2:20 with a neckbreaker

Mike Rotundo pinned Joel Deaton with the airplane spin at 1:14

NWA Mid Atlantic Heavyweight Champion & NWA Mid Atlantic Tag Team Champion Ron Bass (w/ JJ Dillon & NWA Mid Atlantic Tag Team Champion Black Bart) pinned Brett Hart (Barry Horowitz) with the running powerslam at the 42-second mark

Nikita Koloff (w/ Ivan Koloff) defeated an unknown via submission with a cobra clutch at the 38-second mark

CWF @ Miami, FL - Baseball Stadium - October 27, 1984
Jay Youngblood defeated the Red Raider; the match was advertised as Jay & Mark Youngblood vs. Buck Robley &

Dutch Mantell

Jesse Barr defeated Scott McGhee in a No DQ, no time limit match

Larry Hamilton defeated the Saint

Krusher Kruschev & Jim Neidhart defeated Pez Whatley & the One Man Gang

Dory Funk Jr. defeated Mike Graham (sub. for Rick McGraw) in a loser is tarred and feathered match

Dusty Rhodes & Jerry Lawler defeated Kevin Sullivan & Purple Haze

NWA World Champion Ric Flair defeated Superstar Billy Graham via disqualification

CWF @ Ocala, FL - Jai Alai Fronton - October 28, 1984 (matinee)
Krusher Kruschev & Jim Neidhart vs. Jay & Mark Youngblood

Superstar Billy Graham vs. Dory Funk Jr.

Florida Heavyweight Champion Jesse Barr vs. Southern Champion Pez Whatley

Dusty Rhodes & Mike Graham vs. Kevin Sullivan & Purple Haze

NWA World Champion Ric Flair vs. Scott McGhee

CWF @ Orlando, FL - October 28, 1984
Jay Youngblood defeated the Red Raider

Jay Youngblood defeated Cocoa Samoa

Krusher Kruschev, the Saint, & Jim Neidhart defeated Pez Whatley, One Man Gang, & Larry Hamilton

Mike Graham defeated Jesse Barr

Dusty Rhodes & Superstar Billy Graham defeated Kevin Sullivan & Purple Haze

Dory Funk Jr. defeated NWA World Champion Ric Flair via disqualification

CWF @ Tampa, FL - October 30, 1984
Mark Youngblood defeated Red Raider

Jay Youngblood defeated Cocoa Samoa

Krusher Kruschev, the Saint, & Jim Neidhart defeated Larry Hamilton, the One Man Gang, & Pez Whatley

Scott McGhee defeated Jesse Barr via disqualification

Mike Graham & Superstar Billy Graham defeated Kevin Sullivan & Purple Haze

Jay Youngblood defeated NWA World Champion Ric Flair

CWF @ Ft. Lauderdale, FL - October 31, 1984
The Saint fought Mark Youngblood to a draw

Jay Youngblood defeated Cocoa Samoa

Krusher Kruschev, Jim Neidhart, & the Saint defeated the One Man Gang, Larry Hamilton, & Pez Whatley

Mike Graham & Superstar Billy Graham defeated Kevin Sullivan & Purple Haze

Jesse Barr defeated Scott McGhee

Dory Funk Jr. defeated NWA World Champion Ric Flair via disqualification

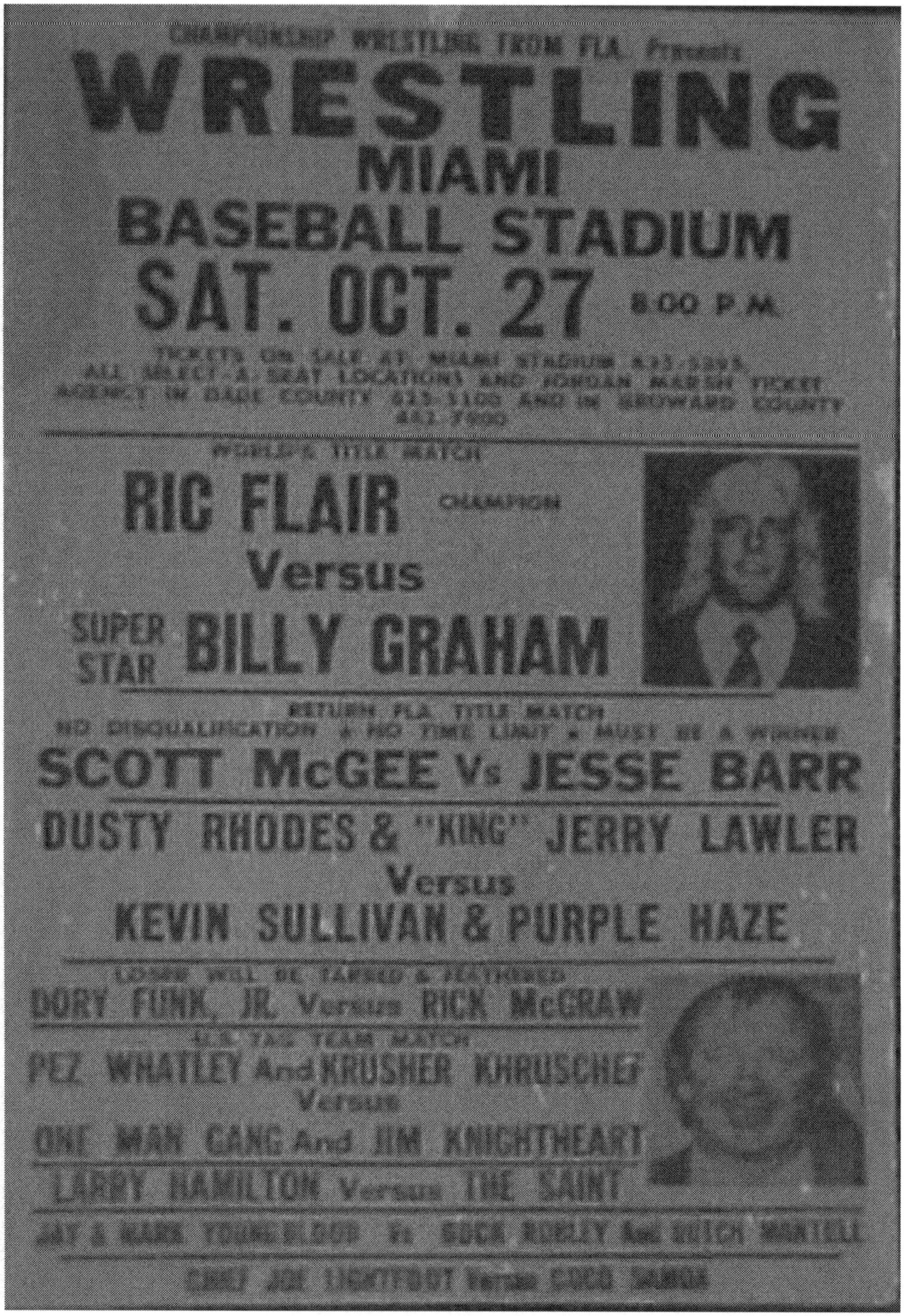
CHAMPIONSHIP WRESTLING FROM FLA. Presents
WRESTLING
MIAMI
BASEBALL STADIUM
SAT. OCT. 27 8:00 P.M.
WORLD'S TITLE MATCH
RIC FLAIR CHAMPION
Versus
SUPER STAR BILLY GRAHAM
RETURN FLA. TITLE MATCH
NO DISQUALIFICATION • NO TIME LIMIT • MUST BE A WINNER
SCOTT McGEE Vs JESSE BARR
DUSTY RHODES & "KING" JERRY LAWLER
Versus
KEVIN SULLIVAN & PURPLE HAZE
LOSER WILL BE TARRED & FEATHERED
DORY FUNK, JR. Versus RICK McGRAW
U.S. TAG TEAM MATCH
PEZ WHATLEY And KRUSHER KHRUSCHEF
Versus
ONE MAN GANG And JIM KNIGHTHEART
LARRY HAMILTON Versus THE SAINT

N.W.A. PRO WRESTLING

FLAIR

GRAHAM

TOMORROW AFTERNOON 3:00 P.M.
OCALA JAI ALAI FRONTON
WORLD CHAMPIONSHIP
RIC FLAIR VS SCOTT McGHEE

KEVIN SULLIVAN & THE PURPLE HAZE
VS
DUSTY RHODES & MIKE GRAHAM

FLORIDA TITLE VS SOUTHERN TITLE
JESSIE BARR VS PEZ WHATLEY

PLUS 2 MORE BIG MATCHES

N.W.A. PRO WRESTLING

TUES. 8 P.M.
SPARTAN SPORTS CENTER
312 N. BOULEVARD AVE.
WORLD TITLE!!
RIC FLAIR VS DORY FUNK JR.

FLAIR

FUNK

KEVIN SULLIVAN & THE PURPLE HAZE
VERSUS
MIKE GRAHAM & SUPERSTAR GRAHAM

PLUS THREE MORE BIG MATCHES!!

FLORIDA TITLE - TO A FINISH!!
JESSIE BARR VS SCOTT McGHEE

TELE: 253-0841 FOR RESV.

139

JCP @ Richmond, VA - Coliseum - November 2, 1984
Black Bart defeated Tommy Kay
American Starship defeated Paul Kelly & Jeff Sword
Buzz Tyler defeated Ivan Koloff
NWA US Champion Wahoo McDaniel & NWA TV Champion Tully Blanchard defeated Dick Slater & Brian Adidas
The Assassin defeated Paul Jones
Ricky Steamboat defeated Ron Bass via disqualification
NWA Tag Team Champions Dusty Rhodes & Manny Fernandez defeated the Zambouie Express

Worldwide - 11/3/84:
Buzz Tyler vs. Ben Alexander
Elijah Akeem vs. Tommy Lee
Mike Davis vs. Gene Ligon
Ivan Koloff vs. Lee Ramsey
Ron Bass vs. Gerald Finley

JCP @ Asheville, NC - Civic Center - November 4, 1984
Denny Brown defeated Gary Royal
Buzz Tyler defeated Black Bart
American Starship defeated the Zambouie Express via disqualification
Ivan Koloff defeated Brian Adidas
The Assassin defeated Paul Jones via disqualification
Ricky Steamboat defeated Ron Bass via disqualification
Dick Slater & NWA Tag Team Champion Manny Fernandez defeated NWA US Champion Wahoo McDaniel & NWA TV Champion Tully Blanchard

WCCW @ San Antonio, TX - November 4, 1984
NWA World Champion Ric Flair defeated Kerry Von Erich in a steel cage match

JCP @ Greenville, SC - November 5, 1984
Tommy Lane defeated Joel Deaton
Keith Larson defeated Mike Fever
Nikita Koloff defeated Buzz Tyler
The Assassin defeated Ivan Koloff via disqualification
Dick Slater defeated NWA US Champion Wahoo McDaniel
NWA Tag Team Champions Dusty Rhodes & Manny Fernandez defeated the Zambouie Express

JCP @ Natural Bridge, VA - High School - November 5, 1984
American Starship vs. JJ Dillon & NWA Mid Atlantic Tag Team Champion Black Bart
Mark Youngblood vs. NWA Mid Atlantic Heavyweight Champion & NWA Mid Atlantic Tag Team Champion Ron Bass

JCP @ Columbia, SC - Township Auditorium - November 6, 1984
Tommy Lane defeated Jeff Sword
Buzz Tyler defeated Kareem Muhammad
American Starship defeated Black Bart & JJ Dillon

Ron Bass defeated Brian Adidas
The Assassin defeated Elijah Akeem via disqualification
NWA TV Champion Tully Blanchard fought Dick Slater to a draw
Ricky Steamboat defeated Wahoo McDaniel via disqualification
NWA Tag Team Champions Dusty Rhodes & Manny Fernandez defeated Ivan & Nikita Koloff in a steel cage match

JCP @ Raleigh, NC - Dorton Arena - November 7, 1984
American Starship defeated Doug Vines & Joel Deaton
Ricky Steamboat defeated Ron Bass via disqualification
The Assassin defeated Ivan Koloff
Nikita Koloff defeated Brian Adidas
Dick Slater defeated Black Bart
Buzz Tyler defeated Jeff Sword
NWA Tag Team Champions Dusty Rhodes & Manny Fernandez defeated NWA US Champion Wahoo McDaniel & NWA TV Champion Tully Blanchard

JCP @ Norfolk, VA - November 8, 1984
Jeff Sword defeated Denny Brown
Keith Larson defeated Gary Royal
Buzz Tyler defeated Mike Fever
The Assassin & American Starship defeated Paul Jones, Jeff Sword, & Kareem Muhammad
NWA World Champion Ric Flair & Dick Slater defeated NWA US Champion Wahoo McDaniel & NWA TV Champion Tully Blanchard
NWA Tag Team Champions Dusty Rhodes & Manny Fernandez defeated Ivan & Nikita Koloff in a steel cage match

WCCW @ Dallas, TX - Sportatorium - November 9, 1984
TV taping:
Iceman King Parsons defeated Kelly Kiniski
Jake Roberts defeated Buck Zumhofe
Bobby Fulton & Tommy Rogers defeated El Diablo Grande & Dale Veasey
Kerry & Mike Von Erich fought Killer Khan & the Missing Link to a draw
NWA World Champion Ric Flair defeated Chris Adams via disqualification
Buddy Roberts defeated Dale Veasey

JCP @ Huntington, WV - November 9, 1984
American Starship defeated JJ Dillon & Joel Deaton
Buzz Tyler defeated Black Bart
Nikita Koloff defeated Brian Adidas
Dick Slater & the Assassin defeated the Zambouie Express
Ivan Koloff defeated Johnny Weaver
Ricky Steamboat defeated Ron Bass via disqualification
NWA Tag Team Champions Dusty Rhodes & Manny Fernandez defeated NWA US Champion Wahoo McDaniel & NWA TV Champion Tully Blanchard

Pro Wrestling USA - 11/10/84 - featured Tony Schiavone as the ring announcer; included Gordon Solie & John Heath on commentary; featured Solie conducting a ringside interview with Jerry Lawler & Tommy Rich in which Lawler said the contract had been signed for he and Rich to face AWA Tag Team Champions the Road Warriors the following week on TV; Rich then commented on the attack he recently sustained from the Road Warriors and comments made by Paul Ellering; Lawler then noted that the Road Warriors do get some cheers but they don't deserve anyone's respect for the way they handle themselves; included a vignette of NWA World Champion Ric Flair in which he was shown pulling up to a private jet in a limo; featured Solie conducting a ringside interview with the Road Warriors & Ellering regarding the comments made earlier in the show from Lawler & Rich and facing them the following week; included Solie conducting an interview with Rich in the studio regarding the upcoming match against the Road Warriors; featured Solie conducting an interview in the studio with Dusty Rhodes regarding Ivan & Nikita Koloff; included a vignette of Jimmy Valiant to the tune of Manhattan Transfer's "Boy from New York City;" moments later, another video of Valiant aired in which he was shown sitting on a street curb, with Valiant then cutting a promo on Paul Jones and the Assassins cutting his beard; Valiant then said he would put the rest of his hair on the line against the masks of the Assassins in what he would call Boogie Jam 84; moments later, a car pulled up with the chauffer telling Valiant that it was time to go, with Valiant climbing inside; a woman looking like a prostitute then walked down the street to the tune of Michael Jackson's "Beat It" and got in the car with Valiant:
Nikita Koloff & NWA Tag Team Champion Ivan Koloff defeated Mike Jackson & Jason Walker at 5:10 when Walker submitted to Nikita's Cobra Clutch
Bob Backlund defeated Randy Barber via submission with the Crossface Chicken Wing at 6:56
Mr. Saito (w/ Adnan) defeated Steve Miller via submission with a Scorpion Deathlock at 3:42
AWA Tag Team Champions the Road Warriors (w/ Paul Ellering) defeated Gene Ligon & Lee Ramsey at 1:31 when Road Warrior Hawk pinned Ramsey following the clothesline off the top

Worldwide - 11/10/84 - featured David Crockett & Johnny Weaver on commentary; included Crockett conducting an interview with Don Kernodle, on crutches and alongside his mother and brother, regarding the attack he sustained from Ivan & Nikita Koloff and the support he has received from the fans; Kernodle then said he didn't know when or if he would be able to return to the ring but said he is thankful for the fans; footage then aired of Kernodle's father sitting at home and saying the family would stand by him whatever comes; Don followed by saying he went out to find a man to face the Koloffs at Starrcade, Ole Anderson; a pre-taped promo then aired in which Ole discussed his history with Ivan Koloff and said he helped get Kernodle into wrestling and while the two haven't always seen eye-to-eye, he had his back against the Russians; Ole then said he would reveal his tag team partner the following week to face the Koloffs; after the promo, Kernodle

said he would be in the corner against the Russians at Starrcade; featured comments from Joe Frazier regarding his being the guest referee for NWA Tag Team Champion Dusty Rhodes vs. NWA World Champion Ric Flair at Starrcade; included a Starrcade update in which it was announced Jimmy Valiant would face Paul Jones in a loser leaves town tuxedo street fight and NWA TV Champion Tully Blanchard would face Ricky Steamboat with a 60-minute time-limit, the disqualification rule would be waived, and each man would put up $10,000; featured the announcement that NWA Brass Knux Champion Black Bart would face NWA Tag Team Champion Manny Fernandez, Dick Slater would challenge Mid-Atlantic Heavyweight Champion Ron Bass, the Zambouie Express would face Buzz Tyler & Assassin #1 in an elimination match, NWA US Champion Wahoo McDaniel vs. Superstar Billy Graham at Starrcade; included a segment in which Bob Caudle spoke with Crockett about new matches signed for Starrcade, which included Brian Adidas vs. Mr. Ito, Florida Heavyweight Champion Jesse Barr vs. Mike Graham, and Denny Brown vs. NWA Jr. Heavyweight Champion Mike Davis, and that Duke Keomuka would join Petty as a judge for the main event; moments later, Steamboat joined the broadcasters to discuss his upcoming match with Blanchard under the stipulations he wanted and putting up his own $10,000 to get that match; Steamboat then signed the contract to face Blanchard, with Blanchard then appearing, saying he would leave Greensboro with his title and $20,000; Steamboat then challenged Blanchard to a match then and there, with Blanchard saying he wasn't dressed for a match, and Steamboat replying by saying Blanchard's mother sucks eggs and his father eats refried beans; moments later, Steamboat went out to the ring and dared Blanchard to follow him; Blanchard eventually followed and took his shirt off before hitting Steamboat with the title belt and following with the slingshot suplex; Blanchard continued to assault Steamboat until Brian Adidas, Fernandez, Brown, and others made the save; included Crockett conducting an interview with Fernandez regarding his upcoming match with Black Bart at Starrcade; moments later, McDaniel walked in to discuss his title defense against Graham in Greensboro; a pre-taped promo from Graham then aired in which he talked about challenging for the US title; featured Crockett conducting an interview with Flair regarding his $1 million title defense against Rhodes at Starrcade; included Crockett conducting an interview with Steamboat regarding the earlier incident with Blanchard; moments later, Steamboat introduced footage of JJ Dillon, Bass, & Bart arriving at Steamboat's gym in Charlotte and injuring his brother before challenging them to a match; featured Crockett conducting an interview with Paul Jones & the Zambouie Express regarding his loser leaves town tuxedo street fight against Valiant at Starrcade; moments later, Assassin #1 walked out to say he would be in Valiant's corner for the match; included pre-taped footage of David Crockett & Bob Caudle speaking with Sandy Scott and Jim Crockett about the card for Starrcade, with Flair then coming out and talking about his upcoming match with Rhodes; Rhodes then walked out and threw Flair's driving hat into the crowd, with Flair then having to be held back as he tried to get at Rhodes; after Rhodes left the interview stage, Flair took the mic and said the *fans were begging him for a handshake last year because he was the man and he would remain the man after Starrcade; moments later, Flair said he's been around the world slaying dragons and would slay the biggest of them all Thanksgiving night*:

Brian Adidas pinned Mark Fleming with the airplane spin at the 58-second mark

NWA US Champion Wahoo McDaniel & NWA TV Champion Tully Blanchard defeated Sam Houston & Brett Hart (Barry Horowitz) at 2:41 when McDaniel pinned Hart with a chop and elbow drop; it was announced during the bout that Kyle Petty would be one of the judges for the main event of Starrcade

Nikita Koloff (w/ Ivan Koloff) defeated Joel Deaton via submission with the Cobra Clutch at 1:15

The Zambuie Express (w/ Paul Jones) defeated Tommy Lee & Gary Royal at 1:13 when Royal was pinned after a slam and elbow drop

Dick Slater pinned an unknown with the neckbreaker; JJ Dillon & Mid-Atlantic Heavyweight Champion Ron Bass provided guest commentary for the bout

JCP @ Fayetteville, NC - Cumberland County War Memorial Arena - November 12, 1984
Denny Brown defeated Barry Hart
Keith Larson defeated Sean Royal
Sam Houston defeated Paul Kelly
Black Bart defeated Mike Davis
Buzz Tyler defeated NWA US Champion Wahoo McDaniel via disqualification
NWA Tag Team Champions Dusty Rhodes & Manny Fernandez defeated Ivan & Nikita Koloff

JCP @ Greenville, SC - November 12, 1984
American Starship defeated Doug Vines & Joel Deaton
Tommy Lane defeated Jeff Sword
Brian Adidas defeated the Inferno
Elijah Akeem defeated Johnny Weaver
The Assassin defeated Kareem Muhammad
Ricky Steamboat defeated Ron Bass via disqualification
Dick Slater defeated NWA TV Champion Tully Blanchard

CWF @ Tampa, FL - Spartan Sports Center - November 13, 1984
Dutch Mantell defeated Jim Neidhart
George Weingeroff defeated Larry Hamilton
Bob Backlund defeated Kendo Nagasaki
Brian Blair defeated Jesse Barr
The Warlord defeated Barber & Owen in a handicap match
Sweet Brown Sugar & Pez Whatley defeated Krusher Kruschev & the Saint
NWA World Champion Ric Flair defeated Jay Youngblood

JCP @ Sumter, SC - Sumter County Exhibition Center - November 15, 1984
Pro Wrestling USA taping:
Dick Slater defeated Gary Royal
Southern Heavyweight Champion Jerry Lawler defeated Mike Fever
Superstar Billy Graham defeated Joel Deaton
NWA Mid Atlantic Tag Team Champions Black Bart & Ron Bass defeated Jerry Lawler & Brian Adidas
NWA Mid Atlantic Tag Team Champions Black Bart & Ron Bass defeated Sam Houston & Brett Hart
Mr. Saito defeated Bob Backlund via disqualification
11/17/84:
Ivan & Nikita Koloff defeated Sam Houston & Brett Hart
NWA Tag Team Champion Manny Fernandez defeated Paul Kelly
Brian Adidas defeated Gary Royal
Harley Race defeated Tommy Lane

Dick Slater defeated Mike Fever
NWA Mid Atlantic Heavyweight Champion Ron Bass vs. Joel Deaton
11/24/84 - included Tony Schiavone as the ring announcer; featured Gordon Solie on commentary; included Solie conducting an interview with NWA Tag Team Champion Dusty Rhodes in which he referenced Bob Backlund's challenge the previous week to both AWA World Champion Rick Martel and NWA World Champion Ric Flair with Rhodes then challenging them both himself; Rhodes also challenged Ivan & Nikita Koloff and AWA Tag Team Champions the Road Warriors to face he and tag team partner Manny Fernandez; featured a segment of Pro Wrestling Illustrated's Press Conference in which Bill Apter conducted an interview with Flair in which Flair commented on his lifestyle and said he would be glad to face and beat Martel and Backlund; Flair then said no one taught him the figure-4 but he perfected the hold; included Solie conducting an interview with Blanchard regarding his putting up $10,000 and his title but then setting the time limit for his title defenses; Solie then conducted an interview with McDaniel regarding facing the likes of Backlund, Martel, and Flair:
NWA World Champion Ric Flair pinned NWA Jr. Heavyweight Champion Mike Davis in a non-title match with a reversal into a backslide at 7:36; Verne Gagne provided guest commentary for the match
Superstar Billy Graham defeated Brett Hart (Barry Horowitz) via submission with the full nelson at 1:26
NWA US Champion Wahoo McDaniel pinned Joel Deaton with a chop to the chest an elbow drop at 4:57
NWA TV Champion Tully Blanchard defeated Sam Houston at 2:02 with the slingshot suplex; $10,000 of Blanchard's money was also on the line in the match
Ivan & Nikita Koloff defeated Tommy Lane & Denny Brown at 3:37 when Lane submitted to Ivan's Cobra Clutch
NWA Mid Atlantic Heavyweight Champion & NWA Mid Atlantic Tag Team Champion Ron Bass (w/ JJ Dillon) defeated Bob Backlund via disqualification at 7:54 when Backlund threw referee Sonny Fargo out of the ring; moments later, Backlund fought off an interfering Dillon and then powerslammed Bass, with Fargo then getting back in the ring and calling for the bell; after the match, Bass attacked Backlund and left the ring
11/31/84 - featured Gordon Solie on commentary; Tony Schiavone was the ring announcer; included Solie conducting an interview with JJ Dillon, Mid-Atlantic Tag Team Champions - Mid-Atlantic Heavyweight Champion Ron Bass & Black Bart regarding Bass's match the previous week against Bob Backlund, during which Dillon said he wanted Bass to get a rematch and prove that his win wasn't a fluke and to get payback for Backlund putting his hands on Dillon; featured Solie conducting an interview with Dick Slater in which he said he doesn't choose sides and was unpredictable; included Solie conducting an interview with Bob Backlund regarding his recent match with Bass, and said he would have to beat the likes of Harley Race, Terry Funk, and NWA Tag Team Champion Dusty Rhodes in order to get him a title shot; featured Solie conducting a closing interview with NWA Tag Team Champions Rhodes & Manny Fernandez in which they discussed the challenges of Ivan & Nikita Koloff and the Road

Warriors:
Superstar Billy Graham defeated Sam Houston via submission with the full nelson at 2:59; during the bout, it was noted the following week's show - called the Class of the 80s - would be loaded with champions
Mr. Saito pinned Lee Ramsey with a back suplex at 3:39
Missouri Heavyweight Champion Harley Race pinned NWA Jr. Heavyweight Champion Mike Davis at 8:48 with a delayed suplex after blocking a headscissors attempt and dropping Davis face-first across the top rope; neither title was at stake
WWC Universal Champion Carlos Colon defeated Ben Alexander via submission with the figure-4 at 3:55
Ivan & Nikita Koloff defeated Gene Ligon & Mike Fever at 4:28 when Fever submitted to Nikita's Cobra Clutch
Southern Heavyweight Champion Jerry Lawler & Brian Adias defeated Joel Deaton & Paul Kelly at 4:01 when Lawler pinned Kelly with a fistdrop off the middle turnbuckle
12/15/84 - featured Gordon Solie on commentary; included Tony Schiavone as the ring announcer; featured a segment of Pro Wrestling Illustrated's Press Conference in which Bill Apter conducted an interview with Ivan & Nikita Koloff regarding why they insult America and yet work for American money; included a music video promoting the debut of Magnum TA set to Steppenwolf's "Born to Be Wild;" featured Solie conducting an interview with Dick Slater and Bob Backlund in which Slater said he had held every regional title but never the world belt, like Backlund, and then shook his hand; Slater then said he was also looking for the world title and might have to face Backlund at some point; Backlund then said he wanted to be champion again; included Solie conducting a closing interview with NWA Tag Team Champion Dusty Rhodes regarding his quest to win the NWA World Title from Ric Flair and defending the tag team belts with Manny Fernandez against such teams as Ivan & Nikita Koloff:
NWA Tag Team Champions Dusty Rhodes & Manny Fernandez defeated Jeff Sword & Doug Vines when Rhodes scored the pin following the Bionic Elbow at 1:12
AWA World Champion Rick Martel pinned Joel Deaton with a slingshot splash into the ring at 5:20
NWA US Champion Wahoo McDaniel pinned Lee Ramsey with a chop and elbow drop at 2:46
NWA World Champion Ric Flair defeated Tommy Lane via submission with the figure-4 at 5:57
NWA Mid Atlantic Tag Team Champions - NWA Mid Atlantic Heavyweight Champion Ron Bass & Black Bart (w/ JJ Dillon) vs. Sam Houston & Brett Hart (Barry Horowitz) at 2:53 when Bass pinned Hart following the running powerslam
NWA TV Champion Tully Blanchard pinned WWC Universal Champion Carlos Colon at 8:29 following a Hot Shot and then grabbing the rope for leverage; only the TV title was at stake; Blanchard's $10,000 was also on the line; after the bout, Colon assaulted Blanchard in and out of the ring; Gordon Solie said Colon won the match via disqualification because Blanchard grabbed the rope but no announcement was made by the ring announcer

JCP @ Appomattox, VA - High School Gym - November 16, 1984

JCP @ Charleston, SC - County Hall - November 16, 1984
Tommy Lane defeated Paul Kelly
Black Bart defeated Brian Adidas
American Starship defeated Joel Deaton & Mike Fever
Ricky Steamboat defeafed Ron Bass via disqualification
Ivan & Nikita Koloff defeated NWA Tag Team Champions
Dusty Rhodes & Manny Fernandez

*Worldwide - 11/17/84 - featured Johnny Weaver & David
Crockett on commentary; included Crockett conducting an
interview with Don Kernodle in which Kernodle, on crutches,
discussed the fact his brother, Keith Larson, would be teaming
with Ole Anderson at Starrcade to face Ivan & Nikita Koloff;
moments later, footage was shown of Crockett announcing
Larson as the mystery partner, with Larson then coming out
and Kernodle appearing, yelling at his brother for taking the
match, and said he would wrestle the Russians himself if he
had to in order to prevent his brother from risking his body;
during the segment, some of Kernodle's comments were
bleeped out; after the video went back to Crockett's initial
interview with Kernodle, Kernodle said he would be at
Starrcade; featured a Starrcade 84 ad to the tune of Frank
Stallone's "Far From Over;" included Crockett conducting a sit-
down interview with NWA World Champion Ric Flair in his
home regarding the previous week's altercation between he
and NWA Tag Team Champion Dusty Rhodes and facing
Rhodes at Starrcade, with Flair saying he was the greatest
wrestler alive today and Rhodes wanted to take that spot from
him; featured Crockett conducting an interview with Dick Slater
and NWA Tag Team Chapions Manny Fernandez regarding
their respective matches at Starrcade against Mid-Atlantic Tag
Team Champions - Mid-Atlantic Heavyweight Champion Ron
Bass & NWA Brass Knux Champion Black Bart, during which
some of Slater's comments were bleeped out; included pre-
taped comments from Kyle Petty regarding his participation in
Starrcade; featured pre-taped comments from Joe Frazier
regarding his participation in Starrcade; included Crockett
conducting an interview with NWA TV Champion Tully
Blanchard regarding his upcoming Starrcade title defense
against Ricky Steamboat and NWA US Champion Wahoo
McDaniel regarding his title defense against Superstar Billy
Graham; featured Crockett conducting an interview with
Rhodes regarding his upcoming title match with Flair.*
The Assassin & Brian Adidas defeated Gary Royal & Paul
Kelly at 3:21 when Adidas pinned Kelly following the airplane
spin; during the bout, it was noted the following week's episode
would feature a video look at Magnum TA, who was on his way
to Jim Crockett Promotions
NWA Tag Team Champion Manny Fernandez pinned Jeff
Sword with the flying forearm at the 57-second mark
NWA Brass Knux Champion & Mid-Atlantic Tag Team
Champion Black Bart (w/ Mid-Atlantic Heavyweight Champion
& Mid-Atlantic Tag Team Champion Black Bart & JJ Dillon)
pinned Joel Deaton at 6:21 with a senton after Deaton missed
a charge in the corner
Buzz Tyler pinned Mark Fleming with the running powerslam at
3:49
Ivan & Nikita Koloff defeated Denny Brown & Tommy Lane at

2:46 when Nikita pinned Lane following the modified
Doomsday Device
Elijah Akeem (w/ Kareem Muhammad) pinned Sam Houston
with an elbow drop at 3:18

CWF @ Sarasota, FL - November 17, 1984
Pez Whatley defeated the Saint via disqualification
Superstar Billy Graham defeated the Red Raider
Mark & Jay Youngblood defeated Kevin Sullivan & King Cobra
Jesse Barr defeated Mike Graham
Dusty Rhodes & Dutch Mantell defeated Jim Neidhart &
Krusher Kruschev
NWA World Champion Ric Flair defeated Sweet Brown Sugar

WCCW @ San Marcos, TX - November 18, 1984
Mike Von Erich & Stella Mae French defeated Nickla Roberts &
Buddy Roberts
Terry Gordy defeated the Missing Link
Kevin Von Erich defeated NWA World Champion Ric Flair via
disqualification

JCP @ Greenville, SC - November 19, 1984
Tommy Lane defeated Paul Kelly
Denny Brown defeated Gary Royal
Ron Bass & Black Bart defeated Buzz Tyler & the Assassin
Ivan Koloff defeated NWA Tag Team Champion Manny
Fernandez in a Texas Death Match
Ricky Steamboat & Dick Slater defeated NWA US Champion
Wahoo McDaniel & NWA TV Champion Tully Blanchard

Starrcade 84 - Greensboro, NC - Coliseum - November 22, 1984 (16,000)
Shown on closed circuit - featured Gordon Solie & Bob Caudle on commentary:
Denny Brown pinned NWA Jr. Heavyweight Champion Mike Davis to win the title
Brian Adidas pinned Mr. Ito
Florida Heavyweight Champion Jesse Barr pinned Mike Graham
The Assassin & Buzz Tyler defeated Muhammad & Akeem in an elimination match
Manny Fernandez defeated Mid Atlantic Brass Knuckles Champion Black Bart to win the title
Paul Jones pinned Jimmy Valiant in a loser leaves town tuxedo street fight
Mid-Atlantic Champion Ron Bass defeated Dick Slater via disqualification
Ivan & Nikita Koloff defeated Ole Anderson & Keith Larson
NWA TV Champion Tully Blanchard pinned Ricky Steamboat at 13:15 after hitting the challenger with a foreign object as Steamboat attempted a sunset flip; each man put up $10,000 for the match, with the winner walking away with $20,000 (*The Best of Starrcade: 1983-1987*)
JCP US Champion Wahoo McDaniel pinned Superstar Billy Graham
NWA World Champion Ric Flair defeated Dusty Rhodes via referee's decision at 12:09 when guest referee Joe Frazier stopped the bout due to a cut over the challenger's right eye, sustained moments earlier after Rhodes was sent into the post head-first; in the event of a draw, Kyle Petty, Duke Keomuka, and Frazier would have served as judges; after the bout, Rhodes was restrained from getting at Frazier by a number of wrestlers and later had his head bandaged before leaving the ring; due to pre-match stipulations, Flair won the $1 million winner's purse (*The Best of Starrcade: 1983-1987, Greatest Wrestling Stars of the 80s*)

Worldwide - 11/24/84 - featured Tony Schiavone & Johnny Weaver on commentary; included Schiavone conducting an interview with NWA TV Champion Tully Blanchard, dressed as a cowboy, in which he responded to comments from NWA Tag Team Champion Dusty Rhodes, Dick Slater, and Ricky Steamboat; Schiavone then brought up North American Heavyweight Champion Magnum TA, on his way to the NWA, as another potential challenger; a music video then aired of Magnum set to Steppenwolf's "Born to be Wild;" following the video, Blanchard cut a promo on Magnum, saying pretty girls and working out in the gym don't win matches; featured Schiavone conducting an interview with Slater & Steamboat in which they reviewed video of Slater & Steamboat beating Mid-Atlantic Tag Team Champions - Mid-Atlantic Heavyweight Champion Ron Bass & Black Bart; after the bout, the champions assaulted Slater & Steamboat with the help of Blanchard, who was dressed in his cowboy garb; Steamboat then cut a promo on Bart, Bass, Blanchard, and JJ Dillon; included Schiavone conducting an interview with NWA Tag Team Champion Manny Fernandez regarding the challenge of Ivan & Nikita Koloff, during which Fernandez spoke about the

injury they gave Don Kernodle, with Kernodle then appearing on a crutch and in a neckbrace; Kernodle then said he apologized to the fans for his actions in the past and now would be defending America each time he's in the ring; featured a segment hosted by Gordon Solie in which he discussed Starrcade 84 and said highlights would air the following week; included Schiavone conducting an interview with NWA US Champion Wahoo McDaniel regarding a recent match with Buzz Tyler; video then aired of the match in which McDaniel left ringside after Tyler got the best of him; later in the bout, McDaniel threw Tyler over the top rope, resulting in a disqualification; after the match, the two men continued to brawl until Tyler cleared the champion from the ring; McDaniel then cut a promo on Tyler being the top contender for his belt:
NWA Tag Team Champion Manny Fernandez pinned Paul Kelly at 3:45 with the flying forearm
Assassin #1 pinned Jeff Sword with a right hand punch at 5:54
Buzz Tyler pinned Joel Deaton with the running powerslam at 2:31
Ivan Koloff pinned Mike Fever at 5:08 with a clothesline off the top; Don Kernodle joined Tony Schiavone on commentary for the bout
Mid-Atlantic Heavyweight Champion & Mid-Atlantic Tag Team Champion Ron Bass (w/ JJ Dillon & Mid-Atlantic Tag Team Champion Black Bart) pinned Tommy Lane with the running powerslam at 4:40; Dillon joined Schiavone & Johnny Weaver on commentary during the match

JCP @ Greenville, SC - November 26, 1984
Buzz Tyler defeated Elijah Akeem
Mike Davis & Tommy Lane defeated Jeff Sword & Paul Kelly
The Assassin defeated Kareem Muhammad in a taped fist match
Denny Brown defeated Sam Houston
Ole Anderson & Keith Larson fought Ivan & Nikita Koloff to a draw
NWA TV Champion Tully Blanchard defeated Brian Adidas
Dick Slater fought NWA US Champion Wahoo McDaniel to a draw
NWA Tag Team Champions Dusty Rhodes & Manny Fernandez defeated Ron Bass & Black Bart

JCP @ Misenheimer, NC - Pfeiffer College Gym - November 27, 1984
TV taping:
Buzz Tyler pinned George South with the Avalanche running powerslam at 1:47
Ron Bass & Black Bart vs. two unknowns

MID-ATLANTIC CHAMPIONSHIP WRESTLING

CUMBERLAND COUNTY MEMORIAL ARENA

THURS. NOV. 22nd

"STARRCADE '84"

DIRECT FROM THE GREENSBORO COLISEUM IN COLOR ON THE

GIANT CLOSED CIRCUIT SCREEN

MILLION DOLLAR CHALLENGE MATCH FOR WORLD'S CHAMPIONSHIP

SPECIAL REFEREE... SMOKIN' JOE FRAZIER
SPECIAL JUDGES... KYLE PETTY AND DUKE KEOMUKA

DUSTY RHODES vs RIC FLAIR

FOR UNITED STATES CHAMPIONSHIP
WAHOO McDANIEL vs SUPERSTAR GRAHAM

WINNER TAKES ALL MATCH
TV TITLE & $10,000.00 vs $10,000.00
NO RUN RULE... DISQUALIFICATION RULE HAS BEEN WAIVED...
TULLY BLANCHARD vs RICKY STEAMBOAT

GRUDGE MATCH
IVAN KOLOFF & NIKITA KOLOFF
* VERSUS *
OLE ANDERSON & KEITH LARSON
DON KERNODLE WILL BE IN THE CORNER

FOR MID-ATLANTIC TITLE
COWBOY RON BASS
WITH JAMES J. DILLON
* VERSUS *
DICK SLATER

TUXEDO STREET FIGHT
LOSER MUST LEAVE TOWN
JIMMY VALIANT vs PAUL JONES
SECONDED BY THE ASSASSIN

FOR BRASS KNUCKS TITLE
BLACK BART
WITH JAMES J. DILLON
* VERSUS *
RAGIN' BULL

ELIMINATION MATCH
THE ZAMBUI EXPRESS vs **THE ASSASSIN # 1 & BUZZ TYLER**

FOR FLORIDA STATE TITLE
BARR vs GRAHAM

ADIDAS vs ITO

FOR WORLD'S JR. HVYWT. TITLE
MIKE DAVIS vs DENNY BROWN

CWF @ Miami Beach, FL - Convention Hall - November 27, 1984
Jesse Barr defeated Sweet Brown Sugar
Brian Blair defeated Rick McCord
Mike Graham defeated King Cobra
Pez Whatley defeated King Cobra
The Saint defeated Dutch Mantell
Jim Neidhart & Krusher Kruschev defeated Jay & Mark Youngblood
NWA World Champion Ric Flair defeated Billy Jack Haynes

JCP @ Raleigh, NC - Dorton Arena - November 28, 1984
Mike Davis & Tommy Lane defeated Gary Royal & Paul Kelly
Denny Brown defeated Sam Houston
The Assassin defeated Kareem Muhammad in a taped fist match
Buzz Tyler defeated Elijah Akeem
Manny Fernandez defeated Ivan Koloff via disqualification
Dick Slater defeated NWA TV Champion Tully Blanchard
NWA Tag Team Champion Dusty Rhodes & Ricky Steamboat defeated Ron Bass & Black Bart

FCW @ Miami, FL - Convention Hall - November 27, 1984
NWA World Champion Ric Flair defeated Billy Jack Haynes

Central States @ Kansas City, MO - November 29, 1984 (2,200)
NWA World Champion Ric Flair defeated Jerry Blackwell via count-out

JCP @ Lynchburg, VA - Armory - November 30, 1984
BattleStar 84 - prior to the show, Buzz Tyler, Brian Adidas, Johnny Weaver, and NWA Tag Team Champion Manny Fernandez took part in an autograph session; American flags were given away to the first 500 fans
Brian Adidas & Buzz Tyler vs. Mid-Atlantic Tag Team Champions Black Bart & Ron Bass
Mid-Atlantic TV Champion Tully Blanchard vs. Dick Slater
NWA Tag Team Champion Manny Fernandez vs. Ivan Koloff
Also included the Zambouie Express and Nikita Koloff

Central States @ Ft. Dodge, IA - November 30, 1984
NWA World Champion Ric Flair defeated Bob Brown

JCP @ Shelby, NC - Rec Center - November 1984

Worldwide - 12/1/84:
Sam Houston, Mike Davis, & Brian Adidas vs. Gary Royal, Joel Deaton, & Doug Vines
Buzz Tyler vs. Ben Alexander
NWA US Champion Wahoo McDaniel vs. Gene Ligon
The Assassin vs. an unknown
Ivan & Nikita Koloff vs. Ramsey & Diamond

JCP @ Morganton, NC - December 1, 1984
Barry Hart defeated Inferno
Tommy Lane defeated Doug Vines
The American Starships defeated JJ Dillon & Joel Deaton
Kareem Muhammad defeated Johnny Weaver
Black Bart & Ron Bass defeated Barry Hart & Brian Adidas
Dick Slater fought NWA TV Champion Tully Blanchard to a draw

Mid South @ Tulsa, OK - Fairgrounds Pavilion - December 2, 1984
Power Pro Wrestling: NWA World Champion Ric Flair pinned Magnum TA with a reversal into a backslide

JCP @ Sumter, SC - December 2, 1984
Denny Brown defeated Mike Davis
Kareem Muhammad defeated Sam Houston
Black Bart & Ron Bass defeated the Assassin & Brian Adidas
Dick Slater fought NWA TV Champion Tully Blanchard to a draw
Buzz Tyler defeated Elijah Akeem
Dusty Rhodes & Manny Fernandez defeated Ivan & Nikita Koloff

Springfield, MA - Civic Center - December 2, 1984
Rudy Diamond vs. Sgt. Muldoon
Tim & Shaun O'Reilly vs. Pete Mitchell & Mad Dog Richards
Bob Backlund vs. Superstar Billy Graham
NWA TV Champion Tully Blanchard vs. Carlos Colon

Mid South @ Oklahoma City, OK - December 3, 1984
NWA World Champion Ric Flair defeated Kerry Von Erich in a No DQ match

Continental @ Birmingham, AL - December 3, 1984
Bob Armstrong fought NWA World Champion Ric Flair to a 30-minute time-limit draw

GCW @ Baltimore, MD - Civic Center - December 4, 1984
Ron Slinker defeated Mr. Ito
Bob Roop fought Ron Ritchie to a draw
Rip Rogers & Ted Oates defeated Jerry Oates & Frank Lang (Frankie Lancaster)
Jimmy Valiant defeated the New York Assassin
Dusty Rhodes, Tommy Rich, & Ole Anderson defeated the Road Warriors & Paul Ellering
Ron Garvin fought NWA World Champion Ric Flair to a double count-out

JCP @ Columbia, SC - December 4, 1984
Denny Brown defeated Mike Davis
Elijah Akeem defeated Tommy Lane
The Assassin defeated Kareem Muhammad
Tully Blanchard defeated Brian Adidas

NWA US Champion Wahoo McDaniel defeated Randy Tyler
Manny Fernandez, Dick Slater, & Keith Larson defeated Black Bart, Ivan & Nikita Koloff
Ron Bass defeated Ricky Steamboat in a Texas Death Match

JCP @ Raleigh, NC - December 5, 1984
Denny Brown, Mike Davis, & Sam Houston defeated Gary Royal, Jeff Sword, & Doug Vines
Brian Adidas defeated Kareem Muhammad
The Assassin defeated Elijah Akeem in a taped fist match
Buzz Tyler defeated NWA US Champion Wahoo McDaniel via disqualification
NWA TV Champion Tully Blanchard defeated NWA World Champion Ric Flair via disqualification
Manny Fernandez & Keith Larson defeated Ivan & Nikita Koloff
Dick Slater & Ricky Steamboat defeated Black Bart & Ron Bass

JCP @ Norfolk, VA - December 6, 1984
Mike Davis & Sam Houston defeated Gary Royal & Jeff Sword
Denny Brown defeated Tommy Lane
The Zambuie Express defeated Brian Adidas in a handicap match
The Assassin defeated Rufus R. Jones
Buzz Tyler defeated Black Bart
Dusty Rhodes defeated NWA TV Champion Tully Blanchard via disqualification
Ron Bass, Ivan & Nikita Koloff defeated Dick Slater, Manny Fernandez, & Keith Larson
NWA World Champion Ric Flair defeated NWA US Champion Wahoo McDaniel

JCP @ Richmond, VA - Coliseum - December 7, 1984
Keith Larson defeated Gary Royal
Tommy Lane defeated Jeff Sword
Denny Brown fought Mike Davis to a draw
The Assassin & Brian Adidas defeated the Zambuie Express
Buzz Tyler fought Black Bart to a no contest
Ron Bass defeated Ricky Steamboat in a Texas Death Match
NWA TV Champion Tully Blanchard defeated Dick Slater via disqualification
Dusty Rhodes & Manny Fernandez defeated Ivan & Nikita Koloff

Worldwide - 12/8/84:
Buzz Tyler vs. Joel Deaton
NWA Tag Team Champion Manny Fernandez vs. Tommy Lane
Dick Slater, NWA Tag Team Champions Dusty Rhodes & Manny Fernandez vs. Joel Deaton, Jeff Sword, & Gary Royal
Black Bart vs. Lee Ramsey
Magnum TA vs. Inferno #1
NWA TV Champion Tully Blanchard vs. Mike Davis
Ivan & Nikita Koloff vs. Keith Larson & Sam Houston

JCP @ Greensboro, NC - Coliseum - December 8, 1984 (4,000)
Denny Brown defeated Sam Houston
American Starship defeated Gary Royal & Doug Vines
Kareem Muhammad defeated Brian Adidas
The Assassin defeated Gary Royal
Dusty Rhodes, Manny Fernandez, & Keith Larson defeated Krusher Kruschev, Ivan & Nikita Koloff
Black Bart & Ron Bass defeated Ricky Steamboat & Dick Slater via disqualification
NWA US Champion Wahoo McDaniel defeated Buzz Tyler
NWA World Champion Ric Flair defeated NWA TV Champion Tully Blanchard

JCP @ Charleston, SC - December 9, 1984
NWA World Champion Ric Flair defeated NWA TV Champion Tully Blanchard

JCP @ Charlotte, NC - December 9, 1984
Denny Brown defeated Sam Houston
Kareem Muhammad defeated Brian Adidas
The Assassin defeated Elijah Akeem in a taped fist match
Ricky Steamboat & Dick Slater defeated Black Bart & Ron Bass via disqualification
NWA US Champion Wahoo McDaniel defeated Buzz Tyler
NWA World Champion Ric Flair defeated NWA TV Champion Tully Blanchard
NWA Tag Team Champions Dusty Rhodes & Manny Fernandez defeated Ivan & Nikita Koloff in a steel cage match

JCP @ Greenville, SC - December 10, 1984 (2,000)
NWA World Champion Ric Flair defeated Wahoo McDaniel

JCP @ Spartanburg, SC - Memorial Auditorium - December 11, 1984
TV taping:
NWA World Champion Ric Flair vs. Mid-Atlantic Heavyweight Champion Ron Bass
Also included NWA Tag Team Champions Dusty Rhodes & Manny Fernandez, Ivan & Nikita Koloff, NWA TV Champion Tully Blanchard, and Magnum TA

JCP @ Charleston, SC - County Hall - December 14, 1984
Denny Brown defeated Mike Davis
Sam Houston defeated Gary Royal
Ivan & Nikita Koloff defeated Brian Adidas & Assassin #1
NWA TV Champion Tully Blanchard defeated Dick Slater via disqualification
NWA Tag Team Champions Dusty Rhodes & Manny Fernandez defeated the Zambouie Express
NWA World Champion Ric Flair defeated NWA US Champion Wahoo McDaniel

JCP @ Hampton, VA - December 15, 1984
The Assassin & the American Starships defeated Rufus R.

Jones, Jeff Sword, & the Masked Man
Denny Brown defeated Sam Houston
Brian Adidas defeated Inferno
Black Bart defeated Johnny Weaver
Dick Slater & Manny Fernandez defeated Ivan & Nikita Koloff
NWA World Champion Ric Flair defeated NWA TV Champion Tully Blanchard

Worldwide - 12/22/84:
The Road Warriors vs. Sam Houston & Dale Veasey
Ron Bass & Black Bart vs. Keith Larson & Barry Horowitz
NWA US Champion Wahoo McDaniel & NWA TV Champion Tully Blanchard vs. Randy Barber & Brinson

WCCW Christmas Star Wars - Dallas, TX - Reunion Arena - December 25, 1984 (17,000)
Kelly Kiniski defeated Buck Zumhofe
Jose Lothario defeated El Diablo Grande
Rip Oliver defeated Iceman King Parsons
Bobby Fulton & Tommy Rogers defeated Bobby Eaton & Dennis Condrey
Kevin Von Erich defeated Chris Adams in a lumberjack match
Terry Gordy, Buddy Roberts, & Chick Donovan defeated Mr. X (Mike York), Skandor Akbar, & the Missin Link in an elimination match; stipulations stated the loser of each fall would have to leave Texas; Gody was the sole survivor
Kerry Von Erich defeated NWA World Champion Ric Flair via disqualification at 18:30
Billy Jack Haynes & Mike Von Erich defeated Jake Roberts & Gino Hernandez

JCP @ Charlotte, NC - December 25, 1984
Television taping:
Steve Casey defeated Joel Deaton
American Starship defeated the Infernos
NWA Jr. Heavyweight Champion Denny Brown defeated Tommy Lane
Superstar Billy Graham (w/ Paul Jones) defeated Brian Adidas
Magnum TA defeated Super Destroyer (Magnum's debut)
Televised: Manny Fernandez fought Nikita Koloff to a draw
The Assassin defeated Kareem Muhammad (w/ Paul Jones)
Buzz Tyler defeated Inferno #1
The Barbarian (w/ Paul Jones) defeated Sam Houston
Magnum TA defeated Ben Alexander
Steve Casey defeated Gary Royal
Televised: Dusty Rhodes, Ricky Steamboat, & Dick Slater defeated Tully Blanchard, Black Bart, & Ron Bass in a bunkhouse match; JJ Dillon was tied to Magnum TA at ringside for the duration of the bout
Televised: Don Kernodle defeated Ivan Koloff in a flag match; Nikita Koloff and Keith Larson were barred from ringside for the match

Central States @ Topeka, KS - December 26, 1984
NWA World Champion Ric Flair defeated Marty Jannetty

JCP @ Norfolk, VA - December 27, 1984
Sam Houston & Keith Larson defeated Ben Alexander & Joel Deaton
Buzz Tyler defeated Inferno
Steve Casey defeated Jeff Sword
Superstar Billy Graham defeated Mike Davis
Magnum TA defeated Kareem Muhammad
Don Kernodle defeated Ivan Koloff
Dick Slater, NWA Tag Team Champions Dusty Rhodes & Manny Fernandez defeated NWA TV Champion Tully Blanchard, Black Bart, & Ron Bass

Central States @ Kansas City, MO - December 27, 1984 (2,700)
Bruiser Brody defeated NWA World Champion Ric Flair via disqualification

JCP @ Charleston, SC - County Hall - December 28, 1984
Steve Casey vs. Joel Deaton
Sam Houston vs. Doug Vines
Superstar Billy Graham vs. Johnny Weaver
Magnum TA vs. Mid-Atlantic Tag Team Champion Black Bart
Dick Slater vs. Nikita Koloff
Don Kernodle vs. Ivan Koloff (flag match)

149

Central States @ Wichita, KS - December 28, 1984
NWA World Champion Ric Flair defeated Rufus R. Jones

Worldwide - 12/29/84:
The Assassin vs. Kareem Muhammad
Buzz Tyler vs. Inferno #1
The Barbarian vs. Sam Houston
Magnum TA vs. Ben Alexander
Steve Casey vs. Gary Royal
NWA Tag Team Champion Dusty Rhodes, Ricky Steamboat, &
Dick Slater vs. NWA TV Champion Tully Blanchard, Black Bart,
& Ron Bass (bunkhouse match)

CWF @ Miami, FL - December 29, 1984 (5,000; sell out)
Scott McGhee pinned Jack Hart
Jesse Barr & B. Brian Blair defeated Mid Atlantic TV Champion
Tully Blanchard & Jim Neidhart
Jesse Barr pinned Billy Jack Hayes
NWA TV Champion Tully Blanchard fought Mike Graham to a
10-minute time-limit draw
Nicola Roberts defeated Stella Mae via disqualification
Dusty Rhodes, Mark & Chris Youngblood defeated the King
Cobra & PYTs
Michael Hayes & Dutch Mantell defeated Krusher Kruschev &
Jim Neidhart

JCP @ Greensboro, NC - Coliseum - December 29, 1984
Steve Casey defeated the Super Destroyer
Magnum TA defeated Doug Vines
Superstar Billy Graham defeated Mike Davis
Johnny Weaver & Tommy Lane defeated Inferno #2 & Joel
Deaton
Nikita Koloff defeated Manny Fernandez
Don Kernodle defeated Ivan Koloff in a flag match
Buzz Tyler defeated Zambouie Express #2
Dick Slater defeated NWA TV Champion Tully Blanchard in a
bunkhouse match
Ricky Steamboat defeated Mid-Atlantic Tag Team Champion
Ron Bass in a bunkhouse match
NWA Tag Team Champion Dusty Rhodes defeated Mid-
Atlantic Tag Team Champion Black Bart in a bunkhouse match

Central States @ St. Joseph, MO - December 30, 1984
NWA World Champion Ric Flair defeated Bob Brown

JCP @ Richmond, VA - Coliseum - December 30, 1984
Magnum TA vs. Kareem Muhammad
Don Kernodle & Buzz Tyler vs. Ivan & Nikita Kolof
Ricky Steamboat, NWA Tag Team Champion Dusty Rhodes, &
Dick Slater vs. NWA TV Champion Tully Blanchard, Mid-
Atlantic Tag Team Champions Black Bart & Ron Bass
(bunkhouse match; JJ Dillon handcuffed to Magnum TA at
ringside)

1985.

If 1984 was a year of transition for Jim Crockett Promotions, '85 was the breakthrough.

Despite losing longtime Crockett favorite Ricky Steamboat to the WWF, Crockett rebounded by strapping a rocket to the back of its new, young star.

Terry Allen, donning the moniker "Magnum TA" after Tom Selleck's "Magnum P.I.," made waves in Bill Watts' Mid-South Wrestling before joining Jim Crockett and Dusty Rhodes during the final weeks of 1984. It took only days for him to make an impact, as he won a $50,000 battle royal during the first Greensboro Coliseum show of the year. A feud with Wahoo McDaniel followed and Magnum would have Wahoo's US title belt by the spring.

The spring also saw Crockett buy the valuable WTBS Saturday 6:05 p.m. timeslot from the WWF, giving its own stars even more footing against the WWF machine. With the new timeslot came the inclusion of Georgia Championship Wrestling cities, venues and championships (the National Heavyweight and National Tag Team Titles) as well as talent.

Expanding on the Starrcade concept, JCP debuted the Great American Bash that summer which saw nearly 30,000 fans pack into the Memorial Stadium in Charlotte for an outdoor supercard. The event featured Ric Flair defending his heavyweight crown against Russian monster Nikita Koloff. Nikita's Russian cohorts and NWA tag team title holders Ivan Koloff & Krusher Kruschev faced the AWA's tag champions the Road Warriors in the undercard. Dusty Rhodes and Tully Blanchard ended the night in a steel cage, continuing their blood feud over the NWA TV Title.

1985 also saw the arrival of several new stars, chief among them the tag teams of the Rock 'n' Roll Express and Jim Cornette's Midnight Express. Meanwhile, Flair began surrounding himself with Blanchard, Blanchard's manager JJ Dillon, and Flair's "cousins" Ole & Arn Anderson in an attempt to keep a tighter hold on his championship against Rhodes.

By the end of the year, the stage was set for a series of ultimate showdowns. Leveraging Crockett's new hold in the Georgia market, Starrcade was held simultaneously in Greensboro and Atlanta and shared across the market via closed circuit. Top matches saw Magnum TA regain the US title from Blanchard in their famous I Quit steel cage match, the Rock 'n' Roll Express regain the tag team titles from the Koloffs, also in a cage, and Rhodes defeat Flair to win the NWA World Title. The belt was later returned to Flair due to interference from the Andersons.

With growing momentum, Crockett made its debut in St. Louis the very next night. Backed by regular appearances on network TV and a marketing machine, the WWF drew 4,300 that night to see Andre the Giant against King Kong Bundy. Crockett's show, featuring a Flair vs. Rhodes rematch, drew 3,600. A mere 700 fans separated the two shows that night.

The chase was on

1985

CWF @ Tampa, FL - Spartan Sports Center - January 1, 1985
Skip Young defeated King Cobra
Koko Ware & Norvell Austin fought Scott McGhee & Frankie Lane
Dutch Mantell defeated the Saint in a lumberjack match
Jesse Barr fought Florida Heavyweight Champion Brian Blair to a double disqualification
Jay & Mark Youngblood defeated US Tag Team Champions Jim Neidhart & Krusher Kruschev to win the titles
NWA World Champion Ric Flair defeated Pez Whatley

GCW @ Atlanta, GA - Omni - January 1, 1985
Tommy Rogers fought the Italian Stallion to a draw
Len Denton defeated Jerry Oates
Brian Adidas defeated Chick Donovan
Ron Ritchie defeated Ox Baker via disqualification
Ron Slinker defeated Bob Roop via disqualification
National Tag Team Champions Scott & Bill Irwin won a $50,000 tag team battle royal; other participants included NWA Tag Team Champions Dusty Rhodes & Manny Fernandez, Len Denton & Tony Anthony, Steve Keirn & Stan Lane, Tully Blanchard & Bob Roop, Ted Oates & Rip Rogers, and Tommy Rich & Michael Hayes
Ole Anderson & Thunderbolt Patterson defeated the Terminators
Tommy Rich & Abdullah the Butcher defeated Scott & Bill Irwin
National Heavyweight Champion Ron Garvin defeated Ox Baker (sub. for NWA US Champion Wahoo McDaniel)

JCP @ Raleigh, NC - Dorton Arena - January 2, 1985
TV taping:
The Barbarian defeated Sam Houston
Magnum TA defeated the Masked Inferno
Dick Slater defeated Superstar Billy Graham via count-out
Buzz Tyler defeated NWA TV Champion Tully Blanchard via disqualification
Don Kernodle defeated Ivan Koloff in a flag match
NWA Tag Team Champions Dusty Rhodes & Manny Fernandez defeated Mid-Atlantic Tag Team Champions Ron Bass & Black Bart
Worldwide - 1/5/85:
NWA TV Champion Tully Blanchard, Black Bart, & Ron Bass (w/ JJ Dillon) defeated Tommy Lane, Ramsey, & David Diamond when Blanchard pinned Ramsey with the slingshot suplex
The Barbarian (w/ Paul Jones) pinned Joel Deaton with the headbutt off the top
The Assassin defeated Curtis Harrison
Magnum TA pinned Doug Vines with the belly to belly suplex

CWF @ Miami Beach, FL - Convention Center - January 2, 1985 (3,240)
King Cobra defeated Mike Golden
Pez Whatley defeated Jim Neidhart
Michael Hayes defeated Krusher Kruschev
Mark & Jay Youngblood defeated Koko Ware & Norvell Austin
Dutch Mantell defeated the Saint in a lumberjack match
Jesse Barr defeated Brian Blair
Sweet Brown Sugar defeated NWA World Champion Ric Flair via disqualification

CWF @ Jacksonville, FL - January 3, 1985
Koko Ware & Norvell Austin defeated Mark & Jay Youngblood
Scott McGhee defeated Mike Golden
Michael Hayes & Sweet Brown Sugar defeated Jim Neidhart & Igor Latherjam
Dutch Mantell defeated the Saint in a lumberjack match
Brian Blair fought Jesse Barr to a draw
NWA World Champion Ric Flair defeated Pez Whatley

JCP @ Columbia, SC - Township Auditorium - January 3, 1985
Magnum TA defeated Kareem Muhammad
Buzz Tyler defeated Superstar Billy Graham
Manny Fernandez defeated Ivan Koloff via disqualification
Don Kernodle defeated Nikita Koloff in a flag match
Dusty Rhodes, Ricky Steamboat, & Dick Slater defeated NWA TV Champion Tully Blanchard, Ron Bass, & Black Bart in a bunkhouse match

JIM CROCKETT PROMOTIONS
presents

GOLDEN ANNIVERSARY

50 YEARS
1935
1985

JW CROCKETT
PROMOTIONS INC.

KICK-OFF '85
SPECTACULAR
SUNDAY, JAN. 6
7:30 PM

$50,000.00 TWENTY MAN BATTLE ROYAL
including

RICKY STEAMBOAT   OLE ANDERSON
NIKITA KOLOFF   BARBARIAN

N.W.A. WORLD TITLE MATCH
HARLEY RACE   VS   RIC FLAIR

LIGHTS OUT / CAGE MATCH
FLAG VS FLAG
DON KERNODLE   VS   IVAN KOLOFF

N.W.A. WORLD TAG TEAM TITLE MATCH
DUSTY RHODES
RAGIN' BULL   VS   ROAD WARRIORS

SPECIAL ATTRACTION
MAGNUM T.A.   VS   WAHOO McDANIEL

T.V. TITLE / $10,000.00
(TEXAS DEATH MATCH RULES)
TULLY BLANCHARD   VS   DICK SLATER

SIX MAN TAG MATCH
CHARLIE BROWN   SUPERSTAR BILLY GRAHAM
ASSASSIN #1   VS   RON BASS
BUZZ TYLER   J.J. DILLON

Tickets — $15 — $10 — $8
Children 10 and under ½ price in $10 & $8 sections.

On sale at Coliseum Box Office and all Ticketron Outlets.

Greensboro
Coliseum®

Central States @ St. Louis, MO - January 4, 1985
Dave Peterson, Marty Jannetty, & Mike Bond defeated Gary Royal, Sheik Abdullah, & TG Stone
Ken Timbs defeated Art Crews
Bob Brown & Rufus R. Jones defeated Mr. Pogo & Roger Kirby
Wahoo McDaniel defeated Terry Funk
Bob Backlund fought Harley Race to a draw
Kerry Von Erich defeated Buzz Sawyer
NWA World Champion Ric Flair fought Bruiser Brody to a double disqualification at the 23-minute mark

CWF @ Lakeland, FL - Civic Center - January 5, 1985
Scott McGhee defeated Jack Hart
Pez Whatley defeated Mike Golden
Mark & Jay Youngblood defeated Koko Ware & Norvell Austin
Brian Blair defeated Jesse Barr in an I Quit match
Michael Hayes, Sweet Brown Sugar, & the One Man Gang defeated Krusher Kruschev, Jim Neidhart, & the Saint
NWA World Champion Ric Flair defeated Dutch Mantell

JCP @ Richmond, VA - Coliseum - January 5, 1985
Tommy Lane defeated the Inferno
Johnny Weaver defeated Jeff Sword
American Starship defeated Mark Fleming & Doug Vines
Dick Slater defeated Kareem Muhammad
NWA US Champion Magnum TA fought Nikita Koloff to a double count-out
NWA TV Champion Tully Blanchard defeated Ricky Steamboat; Blanchard's $10,000 was also at stake
Don Kernodle defeated Ivan Koloff

JCP @ Greensboro, NC - Coliseum - January 6, 1985 (5,879)
Kickoff 85
Steve Casey defeated Black Bart
Cowboy Lang defeated Lord Littlebrook
Charlie Brown, Assassin #1, & Buzz Tyler defeated Superstar Billy Graham, Ron Bass, & JJ Dillon at the 13-minute mark when Tyler pinned Dillon with a powerslam
NWA TV Champion Tully Blanchard defeated Dick Slater in a $10,000 Texas Death Match with the slingshot suplex at the 8-minute mark
Magnum TA defeated NWA US Champion Wahoo McDaniel in a non-title match
NWA Tag Team Champion Dusty Rhodes & Manny Fernandez defeated the Road Warriors
Don Kernodle defeated Ivan Koloff in a lights out match
NWA World Champion Ric Flair defeated Harley Race at the 33-minute mark
Magnum TA won a 20-man $50,000 battle royal by last eliminating NWA US Champion Wahoo McDaniel; other participants included: Harley Race, Ole Anderson, Ricky Steamboat, the Barbarian, NWA Tag Team Champion Dusty Rhodes, and Nikita Koloff

JCP @ Charlotte, NC - Coliseum - January 6, 1985
NWA Tag Team Champions Dusty Rhodes & Manny Fernandez defeated the Road Warriors

JCP @ Fayetteville, NC - Cumberland County Civic Center - January 7, 1985
Cowboy Lang defeated Lord Littlebrook
NWA Tag Team Champion Dusty Rhodes defeated the Super Destroyer
The Barbarian defeated Mike Davis
The Assassin defeated Superstar Billy Graham via disqualification
NWA Tag Team Champion Manny Fernandez defeated Nikita Koloff
Don Kernodle defeated Ivan Koloff in a flag match

WCCW @ Ft. Worth, TX - January 7, 1985
Rip Oliver defeated Buck Zumhofe
The One Man Gang defeated Iceman King Parsons
Billy Jack Haynes defeated WCCW TV Champion Gino Hernandez to win the title
Bobby Fulton & Tommy Rogers defeated Kelly Kiniski & Buddy Landell
NWA World Champion Ric Flair fought Kerry Von Erich to a 60-minute time-limit draw; stipulations stated Von Erich could win the title on a disqualification

JCP @ Greenville, SC - Memorial Auditorium - January 7, 1985 (2,000)
Steve Casey defeated Kareem Muhammad
NWA Jr. Heavyweight Champion Denny Brown fought Keith Larson to a 20-minute time-limit draw
Charlie Brown defeated JJ Dillon
Black Bart & Ron Bass defeated Ricky Steamboat & Dick Slater in a No DQ match
Magnum TA defeated Harley Race via disqualification

WCCW @ Austin, TX - January 8, 1985
Terry Gordy defeated Rip Oliver via disqualification
Billy Jack Haynes defeated the Missing Link
Bobby Fulton & Tommy Rogers defeated Bobby Eaton & Dennis Condrey
The One Man Gang defeated Iceman King Parsons
NWA World Champion Ric Flair defeated Kerry Von Erich via disqualification at 27:48

JCP @ Raleigh, NC - Dorton Arena - January 9, 1985
Cowboy Lang defeated Little Littlebrook
Ricky Steamboat fought NWA TV Champion Tully Blanchard to a 20-minute time-limit draw
Magnum TA defeated Ron Bass
NWA Tag Team Champion Manny Fernandez defeated Black Bart
Superstar Billy Graham defeated Ricky Steamboat (sub. for Charlie Brown)

NWA Tag Team Champion Dusty Rhodes fought Harley Race to a double count-out; the bout was to determine the #1 contender for the NWA World Title
Dick Slater defeated NWA US Champion Wahoo McDaniel via disqualification

WCCW @ San Antonio, TX - January 10, 1985
The One Man Gang defeated Iceman King Parsons
Billy Jack Haynes defeated Gino Hernandez
Bobby Eaton & Dennis Condrey defeated Ricky Morton & Robert Gibson
Terry Gordy defeated Rip Oliver via disqualification
NWA World Champion Ric Flair fought Kerry Von Erich to a 60-minute time-limit draw in a No DQ match

JCP @ Charleston, SC - County Hall - January 10, 1985
Keith Larson vs. Denny Brown
Buzz Tyler defeated the Super Destroyer (sub. for NWA US Champion Wahoo McDaniel)
Magnum TA defeated Elijah Akeem (sub. for Doug Vines)
Cowboy Lang defeated Lord Littlebrook
Charlie Brown defeated Superstar Billy Graham
Don Kernodle & NWA Tag Team Champion Dusty Rhodes defeated Ivan & Nikita Koloff in a flag match

AWA @ Winnipeg, Manitoba - Arena - January 10, 1985 (5,628)
Greg Gagne & Jim Brunzell defeated Brian Jewel & Rob Rechsteiner
Jerry Blackwell, Greg Gagne, & Jim Brunzell defeated Paul Ellering & AWA Tag Team Champions the Road Warriors
Jimmy Garvin defeated John Nord via disqualification
Pro Wrestling USA - 1/26/85 - featured opening comments from Ken Resnick in which he promoted the Feb. 24 show at the Meadowlands, Star Wars 85, and announced there would be a $100,000 tag team challenge with the final two teams facing off in a one-fall match for the money and a trophy; Resnick & Blackjack Lanza provided commentary for the bout; included a backstage segment with Resnick promoting the Feb. 24 card, noting NWA World Champion Ric Flair would face Harley Race and Jimmy Garvin would challenge AWA World Champion Rick Martel; moments later, Resnick interviewed Garvin, who said he beat Martel in Las Vegas and would do it again at the Meadowlands; featured Resnick conducting a backstage interview with Martel regarding his upcoming title defense against Garvin:
Dino Bravo pinned Brian Jewel at 4:00 with a back suplex
AWA Tag Team Champions the Road Warriors (w/ Paul Ellering) defeated Brad Rheignans & Rick Phoebe at 2:57 when Road Warrior Hawk pinned Phoebe after Road Warrior Animal had Phoebe hoisted over his shoulder and Hawk came off the top behind the referee's back with a forearm to Phoebe; after the bout, Ken Resnick conducted an interview with the Road Warriors & Ellering regarding their upcoming participation in the Star Wars $100,000 tag team challenge, during which Hawk said there were two kinds of people in the world - weasels and weasel slappers, and they were weasel slappers
Curt Hennig pinned Rob Rechsteiner (Rick Steiner) at 4:18 with a dropkick from the middle turnbuckle
Jerry Blackwell & Baron Von Raschke defeated Rick Resnlow & Dave Wagner at 4:54 when Blackwell pinned Wagner with a powerslam, with Von Raschke then coming in the ring to prevent Renslow from making the save and putting the claw on Renslow; after the bout, Ken Resnick conducted an interview with Blackwell & Von Raschke regarding their participation in the upcoming $100,000 tag team battle royal at the Meadowlands
Sgt. Slaughter defeated Mr. Saito (w/ Sheik Adnan Al-Kaissie) via disqualification at 6:35 when, as Slaughter had an interfering Al-Kaissie in the Cobra Clutch, the Masked Superstar ran out and attacked Slaughter; moments later, Slaughter cleared the ring

WCCW @ Dallas, TX - Sportatorium - January 11, 1985
TV taping:
Kelly Kiniski defeated Buck Zumhofe
The One Man Gang pinned Sean Michael at 2:36 with a powerslam and splash (*Shawn Michaels: My Journey*)
Rip Oliver defeated Terry Daniels
Billy Haynes (w/ Sunshine) defeated Sean Michael via submission with the full nelson at 1:22 (*Shawn Michaels: Heartbreak & Triumph*)
NWA World Champion Ric Flair defeated Terry Gordy
American Heavyweight Champion Kerry Von Erich defeated Chris Adams (w/ Gary Hart)
Bobby Eaton & Dennis Condrey (w/ Jim Cornette) defeated American Tag Team Champions Bobby Fulton & Tommy Rogers to win the titles

Worldwide - 1/12/85:
Magnum TA & NWA Tag Team Champion Manny Fernandez defeated Joel Deaton & Jeff Sword when Magnum pinned Deaton with the belly to belly suplex
Steve Casey pinned Ben Alexander with an airplane spin into a backdrop
Ron Bass (w/ JJ Dillon) pinned Mike Davis with a powerslam
Buzz Tyler pinned Mike Fever with a powerslam
Nikita Koloff (w/ Ivan Koloff) defeated Tommy Lane via submission with the Cobra Clutch
Superstar Billy Graham & the Barbarian (w/ Paul Jones) defeated Mark Fleming & Sam Houston when Barbarian pinned Fleming with the headbutt off the top

WWC @ San Juan, Puerto Rico - ?, 1985
Dusty Rhodes fought NWA World Champion Ric Flair to a double disqualification at 15:24 after Flair kicked the referee and Rhodes threw the referee to the floor

JCP @ Bassett, VA - High School Gym - January 12, 1985
Included the Barbarian, Superstar Billy Graham, NWA Tag Team Champion Manny Fernandez, Jimmy Valiant, and American Starship

JCP @ Spartanburg, SC - Memorial Auditorium - January 12, 1985
Mike Davis defeated Gene Ligon
Sam Houston & Cowboy Lang defeated Jeff Sword & Ben Alexander
Tarzan Tyler defeated the Destroyer
NWA Tag Team Champion Dusty Rhodes defeated Nikita Koloff via count-out
Wahoo McDaniel defeated NWA World Champion Ric Flair via disqualification

SUNDAY, JAN. 13, 3:00 P.M.
DOUBLE MAIN EVENT
Asheville Civic Center

FLAG -vs- FLAG
USA
DON KERNODLE
-vs-
RUSSIAN BEAR
IVAN KOLOFF
TAG TEAM MATCH
AVALANCHE
BUZ TYLER
&
OLE ANDERSON
-vs-
U.S. CHAMP
WAHOO McDANIEL
&
T. V. Champ
TULLY BLANCHARD
SPECIAL CHALLENGE
(1/2 World's Tag Champs)
THE RAGIN' BULL
-vs-
THE GREAT
HARLEY RACE
CHARLIE BROWN
-vs-
(superstar)
BILLY GRAHAM
ASSASIN #1
-vs-
THE BARBARIAN
DENNY BROWN -vs- KEITH LARSON
MIDGETS
(Cow Boy Lang -vs- LORD LITTLEBROOK)
Ringside $7 Gen. Adm. $6 Children Under 10, $3
Box Office 255-5771 Mon.-Fri. 10-5:30, Sat. 11-4, Day of Match 1 PM
No Checks or Credit Cards Day of Match. Matches subject to change.
WIDE WORLD WRESTLING ON WLOS-TV 13 SUNDAY 12 NOON

JCP @ Asheville, NC - Civic Center - January 13, 1985 (matinee) (2,000)
Keith Larson fought NWA Jr. Heavyweight Champion Denny Brown to a draw
Cowboy Lang defeated Lord Littlebrook
Charlie Brown defeated Superstar Billy Graham
The Assassin defeated the Barbarian
Ole Anderson & Buzz Tyler defeated NWA US Champion Wahoo McDaniel & NWA TV Champion Tully Blanchard
NWA Tag Team Champion Manny Fernandez vs. Harley Race
Don Kernodle defeated Ivan Koloff in a flag match

JCP @ Charlotte, NC - Coliseum - January 13, 1985
Starship Eagle defeated Joel Deaton
Cowboy Lang defeated Lord Littlebrook
Superstar Billy Graham & the Barbarian defeated Charlie Brown & the Assassin
NWA Tag Team Champion Manny Fernandez defeated NWA TV Champion Tully Blanchard via disqualification
Harley Race fought Magnum TA to a draw
Ron Bass & Black Bart defeated Ricky Steamboat & Dick Slater via count-out
NWA US Champion Wahoo McDaniel defeated Buzz Tyler
Don Kernodle & NWA Tag Team Champion Dusty Rhodes defeated Ivan & Nikita Koloff

MID-ATLANTIC CHAMPIONSHIP WRESTLING

DORTON ARENA: TONIGHT!

N.C. STATE FAIRGROUNDS ... FREE PARKING
RINGSIDE $6.00 GEN. ADM. $5.00, CHILDREN (Under 12) $3.00 in Gen. Adm.
Box office at Dorton Arena Opens at Noon on day of matches...Call 733-2826

8:15 P.M.   8:15 P.M.

RETURN MATCH...2 REFEREES

FOR U.S. CHAMPIONSHIP
WAHOO McDANIEL
● VERSUS ●
DICK SLATER

DON KERNODLE & RICKY STEAMBOAT
● VERSUS ●
IVAN & NIKITA KOLOFF

FOR THE BRASS KNUCKS TITLE

BLACK BART   WITH JAMES J. DILLON   V S.   THE RAGIN' BULL

SUPERSTAR BILLY GRAHAM   AVALANCHE BUZZ TYLER

THE BARBARIAN   with PAUL JONES   THE ASSASSIAN #1

MAGNUM T.A.
● VERSUS ●
KAREEM MUHAMMAD

MIDGETS

LORD LITTLEBROOK   V S.   COWBOY LANG

158

JCP @ Greenville, SC - Memorial Auditorium - January 14, 1985 (2,000)
NWA Tag Team Champion Manny Fernandez defeated Superstar Billy Graham via disqualification
Magnum TA defeated Kareem Muhammad
NWA Tag Team Champion Dusty Rhodes defeated Super Destroyer
Dick Slater defeated Ron Bass via disqualification
Ricky Steamboat & Don Kernodle defeated Ivan & Nikita Koloff

CWF @ Tampa, FL - Spartan Sports Center - January 15, 1985
Jack Hart defeated King Cobra
Scott McGhee defeated Mike Golden
Sweet Brown Sugar defeated Jesse Barr
Koko Ware & Norvell Austin defeated Jay & Mark Youngblood via disqualification
Dutch Mantell, Michael Hayes, & Buddy Roberts defeated Jim Neidhart, Krusher Kruschev, & the Saint in an elimination match at the 20-minute mark; Krusher was eliminated; Mantell was eliminated; Neidhart pinned Roberts; Neidhart was eliminated; the Saint was disqualified when Neidhart & Kruschev interfered
NWA World Champion Ric Flair defeated Pez Whatley via disqualification at 22:30 when the challenger threw Flair over the top rope

JCP @ Raleigh, NC - Dorton Arena - January 16, 1985
Steve Casey fought NWA Jr. Heavyweight Champion Denny Brown to a draw
Magnum TA defeated Kareem Muhammad
The Assassin & Buzz Tyler defeated Superstar Billy Graham & the Barbarian
Black Bart defeated NWA Brass Knucks Champion Manny Fernandez to win the title
Don Kernodle & Ricky Steamboat defeated Ivan & Nikita Koloff
Dick Slater defeated NWA US Champion Wahoo McDaniel via disqualification; there were two referees for the bout

JCP @ Pittsburgh, PA - Civic Arena - January 17, 1985 (1,600)
Bob Backlund was scheduled to wrestle but instead came out to the ring in a suit and thanked the fans for coming out; he was booed
Magnum TA pinned Kareem Muhammad
Dick Slater pinned Ken Jugan
NWA Tag Team Champion Dusty Rhodes pinned Joel Deaton at the 27-second mark
Ron Garvin defeated Tully Blanchard via disqualification
Superstar Billy Graham defeated Mike Davis via submission with a full nelson
Don Kernodle & NWA Tag Team Champion Manny Fernandez defeated Ivan & Nikita Koloff via disqualification
NWA World Champion Ric Flair pinned Tommy Rich at the 45-minute mark; Flair was cheered and Rich booed in the match

CWF @ Tampa, FL - January 17, 1985
TV taping:
NWA World Champion Ric Flair vs. Jack Hart

GCW @ Pittsburgh, PA - January 17, 1985
NWA World Champion Ric Flair defeated Tommy Rich at the 45-minute mark

JCP @ Richmond, VA - Coliseum - January 18, 1985 (8,000)
Sam Houston defeated Jeff Sword
Johnny Weaver defeated Doug Vines
Nikita Koloff defeated Mike Davis
Magnum TA defeated Kareem Muhammad
Superstar Billy Graham & the Barbarian defeated Dick Slater & the Assassin
Mid-Atlantic TV Champion Tully Blanchard defeated NWA Tag Team Champion Dusty Rhodes via reverse decision; Rhodes originally won the match and title but the decision was reversed since Rhodes threw Blanchard over the top moments earlier
Ivan Koloff defeated Don Kernodle in a flag lumberjack match after Nikita Koloff interfered
NWA US Champion Wahoo McDaniel defeated NWA World Champion Ric Flair via disqualification when referee Tommy Young caught Flair with a steel chair, moments after McDaniel used it on Flair as Young was knocked down

JCP @ Charleston, SC - County Hall - January 18, 1985
Steve Casey vs. Inferno
Lord Littlebrook vs. Cowboy Lang
Denny Brown vs. Keith Larson
Manny Fernandez vs. Black Bart
Buzz Tyler vs. Mid-Atlantic Heavyweight Champion Ron Bass

Worldwide - 1/19/85 - featured an opening segment in which David Crockett conducted an interview with NWA Tag Team Champion Dusty Rhodes in which Rhodes showed his $10,000 in silver dollars, with Rhodes then challenging NWA TV Champion Tully Blanchard; included Tony Schiavone & Crockett on commentary; featured Crockett conducting an interview with Buzz Tyler, with the two then reviewing footage of Black Bart ripping up a sweatshirt that belonged to Tyler; Tyler then said he represented the fans there in South Carolina and he would come after Bart for what he did; included a vignette showing Mid-Atlantic TV Champion Tully Blanchard arriving to an airport in a limo; moments later, a private jet landed and a woman stepped out and joined Blanchard in the limo; the two kissed in the limo as it drove off; Motley Crue's "Looks that Kill" played throughout the segment (Baby Doll's debut); featured Crockett conducting an interview with Ivan & Nikita Koloff, with Nikita holding a giant trophy, regarding the addition of Krusher Kruschev to their family; during the segment, footage was shown of Ricky Steamboat coming through the crowd to confront Ivan only to be attacked from behind by Nikita and suffer the Russian Sickle; included

Crockett conducting an interview with NWA US Champion Wahoo McDaniel regarding his wanting a match with NWA World Champion Ric Flair, during which Wahoo noted National Heavyweight Champion Ron Garvin, Ole Anderson, Tyler, and "TA Magnum" were also wanting a shot with Flair but TA didn't deserve one; Wahoo then said he was going to be the longest reigning US champion; featured Crockett conducting an interview with Dillon & Funk in which Dillon said he didn't like Funk but knew he was the best, with Funk then saying he didn't wrestle for Dillon or Jim Crockett Promotions but for himself; Funk then said he wanted his money for taking out Slater and that he would go after "that steroid freak" Steamboat and "egg sucking dog" Rhodes:

NWA Tag Team Champion Manny Fernandez pinned Doug Vines with the flying forearm and a kneedrop off the top at 2:36

Inferno #1 defeated Dick Slater via disqualification at 3:59 when Slater threw his opponent over the top rope after noticing Terry Funk was ringside; during the bout, Funk & JJ Dillon joined the commentary team to discuss the bounty put on Slater; after the match, Slater fought off an interfering Ron Bass & Black Bart but was eventually triple teamed by Funk, Bass, & Bart and sustained a spike piledriver; moments later, several enhancement wrestlers ran out to try to make the save but were knocked to the floor; Funk then began choking Slater with his belt until Magnum TA, Buzz Tyler, NWA Tag Team Champions Dusty Rhodes & Manny Fernandez cleared the ring; Slater was helped out of the ring by several wrestlers while Funk screamed at him from the opposite side of the ring (Funk's surprise debut)

Assassin #1 & Steve Casey defeated Jeff Sword & Ben Alexander at 3:29 when Casey scored the pin following the airplane spin; during the bout, David Crockett said an event by the name of Lord of the Rings would take place later that year to celebrate 50 years of Jim Crockett Promotions; it was also noted Magnum TA had earned $50,000 by winning a battle royal in Greensboro earlier in the month to kick off the year of celebration

Superstar Billy Graham (w/ Paul Jones & the Barbarian) defeated Sharship Eagle in a full nelson challenge; stipulations stated Eagle had 30 seconds to break Graham's full nelson and would win $1,000 if he did

Mid-Atlantic Tag Team Champions - Mid-Atlantic Heavyweight Champion Ron Bass & Black Bart (w/ JJ Dillon) defeated NWA Jr. Heavyweight Champion Denny Brown & Tommy Lane at 1:27 when Bart pinned Lane with a running powerslam

NWA TV Champion Tully Blanchard (w/ Baby Doll) pinned Mike Davis with the slingshot suplex at 5:02; during the bout, Don Kernodle briefly joined the commentary team and spoke about his feud with Ivan & Nikita Koloff and said he would have a big surprise; after the bout, Crockett conducted an interview with Blanchard, alongside Baby Doll, in which Blanchard referenced the comments made by NWA Tag Team Champion Dusty Rhodes earlier in the show, noting he beat Ricky Steamboat under those same stipulations; moments later, Blanchard introduced Baby Doll, who said Tully had to go out to Texas to find a real woman because there weren't any nearby (Baby Doll's debut at ringside)

JCP @ Fredricksburg, VA - Stafford High School - January 19, 1985
Mike Davis (sub. for Joel Deaton) defeated Sam Houston
Johnny Weaver defeated Jeff Sword
Superstar Billy Graham defeated Mike Davis
Assassin #1 defeated the Barbarian via disqualification
NWA TV Champion Tully Blanchard fought Dick Slater to a draw; Slater would have won Blanchard's $10,000 by winning the title

JCP @ Lumberton, NC - Rec Center - January 19, 1985
Cowboy Lang vs. Lord Littlebrook
Denny Brown vs. Rocky Kernodle
Magnum TA vs. Black Bart
Buzz Tyler vs. Ron Bass
Don Kernodle & NWA Tag Team Champion Manny Fernandez vs. Ivan & Nikita Koloff

CWF @ Sarasota, FL - Robarts Arena - January 19, 1985
Scott McGhee defeated King Cobra
The Missing Link defeated Rocky King & Mike Golden in a handicap match
Sweet Brown Sugar, Mark & Jay Youngblood defeated Jack Hart, Koko Ware, & Norvell Austin
Pez Whatley fought Rick Rude to a draw
Brian Blair defeated Jesse Barr
NWA World Champion Ric Flair defeated Dutch Mantell via disqualification
Michael Hayes, Terry Gordy, & Buddy Roberts defeated the Saint, Boris Zhukov (sub. for Jim Neidhart), & Krusher Kruschev

Continental @ Pensacola, FL - January 20, 1985
NWA World Champion Ric Flair vs. Austin Idol

- 1/21/85: Florida Championship Wrestling promoter Eddie Graham committed suicide.

JCP @ Natural Bridge, VA - High School - January 21, 1985
Included Magnum TA, Ron Bass, Black Bart, Buzz Tyler, and NWA Tag Team Champion Manny Fernandez

JCP @ Spartanburg, SC - Memorial Auditorium - January 22, 1985
TV taping:
Buzz Tyler defeated Joe Young
NWA World Champion Ric Flair fought NWA US Champion Wahoo McDaniel to a no contest
Don Kernodle defeated Ben Alexander
Ricky Steamboat defeated Joel Deaton
Superstar Billy Graham & King Tonga defeated Lee Ramsey & Ron Rossi
NWA Tag Team Champion Manny Fernandez defeated NWA TV Champion Tully Blanchard via disqualification
Mid-Atlantic Championship Wrestling - 2/2/85:

Worldwide - 2/2/85:
Ricky Steamboat & Magnum TA defeated Frank Lang & Joe Young
Don Kernodle & Rocky Kernodle defeated Doug Vines & Ben Alexander via disqualification
Superstar Billy Graham defeated Ron Rossi
NWA Tag Team Champion Manny Fernandez defeated Joel Deaton
Dick Slater defeated the Inferno
Ivan & Nikita Koloff defeated Lee Ramsey & Gene Ligon

JCP @ Raleigh, NC - Dorton Arena - January 23, 1985
Black Bart defeated American Starship (sub. for Steve Casey)
Magnum TA defeated the Super Destroyer
Superstar Billy Graham & the Barbarian defeated Dick Slater & the Assassin
NWA TV Champion Tully Blanchard fought NWA Tag Team Champion Manny Fernandez to a draw
Buzz Tyler defeated NWA Mid Atlantic Heavyweight Champion Ron Bass via disqualification
Don Kernodle defeated Ivan Koloff in a death match

JCP @ Norfolk, VA - Scope - January 25, 1985
Denny Brown fought Keith Larson to a draw
Mike Davis defeated Joel Deaton
Magnum TA defeated Black Bart
Dick Slater defeated Terry Funk
NWA Tag Team Champion Dusty Rhodes fought NWA TV Champion Tully Blanchard to a draw
Ricky Steamboat & Don Kernodle defeated Ivan & Nikita Koloff in a double chain match

JCP @ Charleston, SC - County Hall - January 25, 1985
Frank Lang defeated Tommy Lane
Johnny Weaver defeated Ben Alexander (sub. for Joel Deaton)
Steve Casey defeated Inferno #1 (sub. for Ron Bass)
Superstar Billy Graham, the Barbarian, & Paul Jones defeated Buzz Tyler, the Assassin, & NWA Tag Team Champion Manny Fernandez

Central States @ St. Louis, MO - January 25, 1985
NWA World Champion Ric Flair defeated Kerry Von Erich at 38:04 in a No DQ match

Worldwide - 1/26/85:
Buzz Tyler pinned Doug Vines with a powerslam
Magnum TA pinned Mike Fever with the belly to belly suplex
Ron Bass & Black Bart (w/ JJ Dillon) defeated Denny Brown & Frank Lang when Bart pinned Lang with a powerslam
NWA US Champion Wahoo McDaniel pinned Sam Houston with a chop to the head
Superstar Billy Graham & the Barbarian (w/ Paul Jones) defeated American Starship when Barbarian pinned Starship Coyote with the headbutt off the top

161

Ivan Koloff (w/ Nikita Koloff) pinned Lee Ramsey with a clothesline off the top

JCP @ Greensboro, NC - Coliseum - January 26, 1985
Magnum TA defeated Ron Bass
NWA Mid Atlantic Heavyweight Champion Black Bart defeated Sam Houston
Superstar Billy Graham & the Barbarian defeated the Assassin & Steve Casey
The American Starship defeated the Masked Infernos
NWA TV Champion Tully Blanchard defeated NWA Tag Team Champion Dusty Rhodes
NWA US Champion Wahoo McDaniel defeated Buzz Tyler
Dick Slater defeated Terry Funk in a lights out bunkhouse bounty match

JCP @ Roanoke, VA - Civic Center - January 27, 1985 (matinee)
American Starship Eagle pinned Joel Deaton
Steve Casey pinned Doug Vines (sub. for Kareem Muhammad)
Buzz Tyler pinned the Barbarian
Superstar Billy Graham pinned Assassin #1
Dick Slater fought NWA TV Champion Tully Blanchard to a 20-minute time-limit draw; Blanchard's title and $10,000 were at stake
Magnum TA (sub. for NWA Tag Team Champions Dusty Rhodes) & NWA Tag Team Champion Manny Fernandez defeated Mid-Atlantic Tag Team Champions - Mid-Atlantic Heavyweight Champion Ron Bass & Black Bart
Don Kernodle defeated Nikita Koloff in a flag match; Ivan Koloff was banned from ringside for the bout
NWA US Champion Wahoo McDaniel defeated NWA World Chapion Ric Flair via disqualification

JCP @ Greenville, SC - Memorial Auditorium - January 28, 1985
Magnum TA vs. Ron Bass did not take place as advertised
Scott Casey defeated Joel Deaton
Johnny Weaver defeated Doug Vines
Superstar Billy Graham defeated American Starship Coyote
Buzz Tyler fought Black Bart to a no contest
Magnum TA (sub. for NWA Tag Team Champion Dusty Rhodes) fought NWA TV Champion Tully Blanchard to a draw
NWA World Champion Ric Flair defeated NWA US Champion Wahoo McDaniel

JCP @ Spartanburg, SC - Memorial Auditorium - January 29, 1985
TV taping:
Don Kernodle vs. Ivan Koloff
Also included NWA World Champion Ric Flair, NWA TV Champion Tully Blanchard, NWA US Champion Wahoo McDaniel, the Barbarian, and Buzz Tyler

JCP @ Mineral, VA - Louisa County High School Gym - January 31, 1985
Dick Slater & the Assassin vs. Superstar Billy Graham & the Barbarian
NWA World Champion Ric Flair vs. NWA TV Champion Tully Blanchard

JCP @ Sumter, SC - Exhibition Center - January 31, 1985
TV taping:
NWA Tag Team Champion Manny Fernandez defeated Joel Deaton
Magnum TA defeated the Golden Terror
Krusher Khruschev, Ivan & Nikita Koloff defeated Denny Brown, Mark Fleming, & Frank Lang
NWA TV Champion Tully Blanchard defeated Brian Adidas
Worldwide - 2/9/85:
Steve Casey defeated the Golden Terror
Dory Funk Jr. defeated Brian Adidas
Ricky Steamboat & Don Kernodle defeated Ivan & Nikita Koloff in a flag match
NWA Tag Team Champion Manny Fernandez defeated Frank Lang

JCP @ Charleston, SC - County Hall - February 1, 1985
Doug Vines vs. Mike Fever
Steve Casey vs. Joel Deaton
Superstar Billy Graham vs. Starship Eagle
Johnny Weaver vs. the Barbarian
Buzz Tyler vs. Black Bart (brass knuckles match)

JCP @ Norfolk, VA - Scope - February 1, 1985
Keith Larson defeated Mark Fleming
Don Kernodle defeated Frank Lang
Denny Brown defeated Sam Houston
Ron Bass defeated Dick Slater via disqualification
NWA Tag Team Champions Dusty Rhodes & Manny Fernandez defeated Ivan & Nikita Koloff
Magnum TA defeated NWA TV Champion Tully Blanchard via disqualification
NWA World Champion Ric Flair defeated NWA US Champion Wahoo McDaniel

MID-ATLANTIC CHAMPIONSHIP WRESTLING AT EAST SURRY HIGH SCHOOL
Pilot Mountain
SATURDAY, FEB. 2
8:15 P.M.

Featuring
IVAN KOLOFF
NIKITA KOLOFF
vs
BRONK BULL
DON KERNODLE

SUPERSTAR BILLY GRAHAM
vs
DICK SLATER

BARBARIAN
vs
STEVE CASEY

ZAMBOUIE / 2
vs
ASSASSIN / 1

JUNIOR HEAVYWEIGHT TITLE
DENNY BROWN   vs   KEITH LARSON

Sponsored By Pilot Mountain Jaycees
Proceeds Go To Cystic Fibrosis

JCP @ Pilot Mountain, NC - East Surry High School Gym - February 2, 1985
NWA Jr. Heavyweight Champion Denny Brown vs. Keith Larson
The Barbarian vs. Steve Casey
Zambouie Express #2 vs. Assassin #1
Dick Slater vs. Superstar Billy Graham
Don Kernodle & NWA Tag Team Champion Manny Fernandez vs. Ivan & Nikita Koloff

JCP @ Savannah, GA - Civic Center - February 3, 1985
Starship Coyote defeated Frank Lane
Denny Brown defeated Sam Houston
Magnum TA fought NWA TV Champion Tully Blanchard to a draw
NWA World Champion Ric Flair defeated NWA US Champion Wahoo McDaniel

JCP @ Charlotte, NC - Coliseum - February 3, 1985
Brian Adidas fought Doug Vines to a draw
Buzz Tyler defeated Black Bart
Magnum TA defeated Joel Deaton

Manny Fernandez defeated the Barbarian
Dick Slater defeated Ox Baker in a bounty match
Sheik Adnan defeated Doug Vines
NWA Tag Team Champion Dusty Rhodes fought NWA TV Champion Tully Blanchard to a draw
Ricky Steamboat & Don Kernodle defeated Ivan & Nikita Koloff in a flag match
NWA World Champion Ric Flair defeated NWA US Champion Wahoo McDaniel via disqualification

JCP @ Spartanburg, SC - Memorial Auditorium - February 4, 1985
TV taping:
Don Kernodle & Manny Fernandez vs. Nikita Koloff & Krusher Kruschev
Black Bart vs. Buzz Tyler
Steve Casey vs. the Golden Terror
Dory Funk Jr. vs. Brian Adidas
Ricky Steamboat & Don Kernodle vs. Ivan & Nikita Koloff (flag match)
Manny Fernandez vs. Frank Lane

JCP/AWA @ Philadelphia, PA - Convention Hall - February 5, 1985 (3,770)
Magnum TA pinned the Super Destroyer
Dick Slater pinned Joel Deaton (sub. for NWA National TV Champion Bob Roop)
Superstar Billy Graham defeated Brian Adidas
NWA National Tag Team Champions Ole Anderson & Thunderbolt Patterson defeated Rip Rogers & Ted Oates
NWA TV Champion Tully Blanchard pinned NWA Tag Team Champion Manny Fernandez
NWA World Champion Ric Flair defeated Ricky Steamboat at 44:12
NWA US Champion Wahoo McDaniel fought Ron Garvin to a no contest
Bob Backlund & NWA Tag Team Champion Dusty Rhodes defeated Mid-Atlantic Tag Team Champions Black Bart & Ron Bass

JCP @ Raleigh, NC - Dorton Arena - February 6, 1985
The Barbarian defeated Denny Brown
Black Bart fought Steve Casey to a draw
Krusher Khruschev, Ivan & Nikita Koloff defeated Ricky Steamboat, Don & Rocky Kernodle
Ron Bass defeated Dick Slater via disqualification
NWA TV Champion Tully Blanchard defeated NWA Tag Team Champion Manny Fernandez
Magnum TA defeated NWA US Champion Wahoo McDaniel via disqualification

JCP @ Raleigh, NC - Dorton Arena - February 6, 1985
The Barbarian fought Denny Brown to a draw
Black Bart fought Steve Casey to a draw
Krusher Kruschev, Ivan & Nikita Koloff defeated Ricky Steamboat, Don & Rocky Kernodle

WIDE WORLD WRESTLING

SUNDAY, FEB. 10th, 3:00 PM
TRIPLE MAIN EVENT
Asheville Civic Center

U.S. TITLE MATCH
(U.S. CHAMP)
WAHOO McDANIEL
—vs—
MAGNUM T.A.

TV TITLE MATCH
20 Min. $10,000
(T.V. CHAMP)
TULLY BLANCHARD
—vs—
DICK SLATER

SIX MAN TAG MATCH
DON KERNODLE
RICK STEAMBOAT
(½ World Tag Champs)
RAGIN' BULL
—vs—
IVAN KOLOFF
NIKITA KOLOFF
CRUSHER KRUSHCHEV

BUZ TYLER —vs— BLACK BART
STEVE CASEY —vs— SUPERSTAR
DENNY BROWN —vs— RON BASS

Ringside $7 Gen. Adm. $6 Children Under 10, $3
Box Office 255-5771 Mon.-Fri. 10-5:30, Sat. 11-4, Day of Match 1 PM
No Checks or Credit Cards Day of Match. Matches subject to change.

WIDE WORLD WRESTLING ON WLOS-TV 13 SUNDAY 12 NOON

Ron Bass defeated Dick Slater via disqualification
NWA TV Champion Tully Blanchard defeated NWA Tag Team Champion Manny Fernandez
Magnum TA defeated NWA US Champion Wahoo McDaniel via disqualification

JCP @ Columbia, SC - Township Auditorium - February 7, 1985

Sam Houston defeated Doug Vines
Denny Brown defeated Frank Lang
Sam Houston defeated Mike Fever
NWA Tag Team Champion Manny Fernandez defeated the Barbarian
NWA Tag Team Champion Dusty Rhodes fought NWA TV Champion Tully Blanchard to a draw
Magnum TA defeated NWA US Champion Wahoo McDaniel via disqualification

AAWA @ Singapore - Gay World Stadium - February 8, 1985

Royce Starr & the Sudanese Butcher vs. Bram Deve, Dhanraj, & Little Kevin (handicap match)
Lars Anderson vs. Ritchie Magnett
Kevin Sullivan vs. Mike George
NWA World Champion Ric Flair vs. Steve Rickard

JCP @ Richmond, VA - Coliseum - February 8, 1985

Krusher Kruschev, Ivan & Nikita Koloff defeated Johnny Weaver, Steve Casey, & Don Kernodle
Buzz Tyler defeated Black Bart
Dick Slater defeated Ron Bass
NWA TV Champion Tully Blanchard fought Magnum TA to a draw
NWA Tag Team Champions Dusty Rhodes & Manny Fernandez defeated Superstar Billy Graham & the Barbarian
Ricky Steamboat defeated NWA US Champion Wahoo McDaniel via disqualification

JCP @ Culpeper, VA - Junior High School - February 9, 1985

Black Bart defeated Keith Larson
Denny Brown defeated Doug Vines
Steve Casey defeated NWA Mid Atlantic Heavyweight Champion Ron Bass via disqualification
Buzz Tyler defeated Black Bart
NWA TV Champion Tully Blanchard fought Manny Fernandez to a draw

JCP @ Charlotte, NC - Coliseum - February 10, 1985

Magnum TA defeated NWA US Champion Wahoo McDaniel via count-out

JCP @ Asheville, NC - Civic Center - February 10, 1985

The Barbarian defeated Johnny Weaver
Buzz Tyler defeated Black Bart
Krusher Kruschev, Ivan & Nikita Koloff defeated Ricky Steamboat, Don Kernodle, & NWA Tag Team Champion Manny Fernandez
Dick Slater fought NWA TV Champion Tully Blanchard to a draw
Magnum TA defeated NWA US Champion Wahoo McDaniel via disqualification

JCP @ Greenville, SC - Memorial Auditorium - February 11, 1985

Steve Casey defeated Jeff Sword
Ron Bass & Black Bart defeated Dick Slater & Buzz Tyler
NWA Tag Team Champion Manny Fernandez defeated the Barbarian
NWA US Champion Wahoo McDaniel defeated ?
Krusher Khruschev, Ivan Koloff & Nikita Koloff defeated ?, ?, & ?

International @ Quebec City, Quebec - February 12, 1985

NWA World Champion Ric Flair defeated Dino Bravo
AWA World Champion Rick Martel defeated King Tonga

JCP @ Allentown, PA - February 12, 1985

Superstar Billy Graham defeated Johnny Weaver

JCP @ Spartanburg, SC - Memorial Auditorium - February 12, 1985

TV taping:
Buzz Tyler vs. Mid-Atlantic Heavyweight Champion Black Bart
Manny Fernandez & Don Kernodle vs. Nikita Koloff & Krusher Khruschev
Also included NWA US Champion Wahoo McDaniel, Ricky Steamboat, and Dick Slater
MACW - 2/16/85:
Worldwide - 2/16/85:
Nikita Koloff & Krusher Kruschev vs. Mark Fleming & Gene Ligon
Dory Funk Jr. vs. Denny Brown
Manny Fernandez vs. Joel Deaton
The Barbarian vs. Frank Lang
NWA TV Champion Tully Blanchard vs. Buzz Tyler

Polynesian Pacific @ Honolulu, HI - Blaisdell Arena - February 13, 1985

NWA World Champion Ric Flair fought Kerry Von Erich to a 60-minute time-limit draw; Von Erich was attempting to pin Flair by using the claw at the time of the bell

JCP / AWA @ Altoona, PA - Jaffa Mosque - February 13, 1985

Larry Zbyszko & Rocky Jones defeated Joel Deaton & Super Destroyer

Superstar Billy Graham defeated Steve Casey
Johnny Weaver defeated Doug Vines
JJ Dillon defeated Sam Houston
Bob Backlund defeated Ivan Koloff via disqualification
Sgt. Slaughter defeated Ron Bass

JCP @ Raleigh, NC - Dorton Arena - February 13, 1985
Denny Brown defeated Rocky Kernodle
NWA Tag Team Champion Manny Fernandez defeated the Barbarian
Buzz Tyler defeated Black Bart
Dick Slater & Don Kernodle defeated Nikita Koloff & Krusher Khruschev via disqualification
NWA TV Champion Tully Blanchard fought Magnum TA to a draw
NWA US Champion Wahoo McDaniel defeated Ricky Steamboat

JCP @ Columbia, SC - Township Auditorium - February 14, 1985
Denny Brown defeated Frank Lang
Sam Houston defeated the Inferno
Manny Fernandez defeated the Barbarian
NWA TV Champion Tully Blanchard fought Dusty Rhodes to a draw
Magnum TA defeated NWA US Champion Wahoo McDaniel via disqualification

Central States @ Kansas City, KS - February 14, 1985
Bruiser Brody defeated NWA World Champion Ric Flair via disqualification

JCP/AWA @ Trenton, NJ - CYO - February 14, 1985
JJ Dillon vs. Sam Houston
Brian Adidas vs. Doug Vines
Sika vs. Joel Deaton
Afa vs. the Super Destroyer
Superstar Billy Graham vs. Steve Casey
Sgt. Slaughter & Bob Backlund vs. Ivan Koloff & Ron Bass

JCP @ Sumter, SC - Exhibition Center - February 14, 1985
The Barbarian defeated Rocky Kernodle
Magnum TA defeated Frank Lang
Buzz Tyler defeated Black Bart
Dick Slater fought Tully Blanchard to a draw
Dusty Rhodes & Manny Fernandez defeated Krusher Khruschev & Nikita Koloff

JCP @ Hampton, VA - Coliseum - February 15, 1985
Brian Adidas defeated Scott Casey
Buzz Tyler defeated Black Bart
NWA Tag Team Champion Manny Fernandez defeated the Barbarian
Dick Slater defeated Ron Bass
NWA Tag Team Champion Dusty Rhodes fought NWA TV

Champion Tully Blanchard to a draw
Ivan & Nikita Koloff defeated Magnum TA & Don Kernodle
Jimmy Valiant defeated Superstar Billy Graham via disqualification

Central States @ St. Louis, MO - February 15, 1985
NWA World Champion Ric Flair fought Bruiser Brody to a 60-minute time-limit draw in a No DQ match

JCP/AWA @ Baltimore, MD - Civic Center - February 16, 1985
Denny Brown defeated Keith Larson
Bob Backlund & Jimmy Valiant defeated Superstar Billy Graham & the Barbarian via disqualification
Magnum TA defeated Doug Vines
Dick Slater defeated Dory Funk Jr.
NWA US Champion Wahoo McDaniel fought Ole Anderson to a no contest
NWA Tag Team Champions Dusty Rhodes & Manny Fernandez defeated Ivan & Nikita Koloff
NWA World Champion Ric Flair defeated Sgt. Slaughter via reverse decision; Slaughter originally won the title but another referee overruled the call

Continental @ Pensacola, FL - February 17, 1985
NWA World Champion Ric Flair vs. Austin Idol

JCP @ Greensboro, NC - Coliseum - February 17, 1985 (4,363)
The Barbarian defeated American Starship #1
Superstar Billy Graham defeated American Starship #2
Krusher Kruschev defeated Brian Adidas
Magnum TA defeated John Tatum
Dick Slater & Manny Fernandez defeated Dory Funk Jr. & Black Bart
Ivan Koloff defeated Don Kernodle in a Russian chain match
NWA Tag Team Champion Dusty Rhodes fought Mid Atlantic TV Champion Tully Blanchard to a draw
Worldwide - 2/23/85: NWA US Champion Wahoo McDaniel pinned Ricky Steamboat after hitting him in the face with the title belt, moments after Steamboat pushed referee Tommy Young out of his way

Continental @ Birmingham, AL - February 18, 1985
NWA World Champion Ric Flair defeated Bob Armstrong

JCP @ Fayetteville, NC - February 18, 1985
Superstar Billy Graham vs. Sam Houston

CWF @ St. Petersburg, FL - Bayfront Center - February 20, 1985
Buzz Tyler defeated Eric Embry
Von Erich defeated El Gran Apollo
Terry Funk & Dick Slater defeated Don Diamond & Jerry

Lawler
Bruiser Brody & Stan Hansen defeated Genichiro Tenryu & Jumbo Tsuruta
The Giant Baba defeated Iron Mike Sharpe
Dory Funk Jr. defeated Butch Reed via disqualification
Andre the Giant defeated the Iron Sheik
Andre the Giant won a 2-ring battle royal
NWA World Champion Ric Flair defeated Mike Graham via disqualification

JCP @ Pittsburgh, PA - Civic Arena - February 20, 1985
The Barbarian defeated Sean O'Reiley
Dick Slater defeated Leopard Man
JJ Dillon defeated Brian O'Reiley
Magnum TA defeated Davey G
Buzz Tyler fought Ron Bass to a draw
NWA Tag Team Champions Dusty Rhodes & Manny Fernandez defeated Ivan & Nikita Koloff
Bob Backlund defeated Black Bart
NWA US Champion Wahoo McDaniel defeated Ricky Steamboat

JCP @ Norfolk, VA - Scope - February 21, 1985
Sam Houston fought John Tatum to a draw
The Barbarian defeated Starship Coyote
Superstar Billy Graham defeated Starship Eagle
Dick Slater & Buzz Tyler defeated Ron Bass & Black Bart
Magnum TA fought NWA TV Champion Tully Blanchard to a draw
Don Kernodle, NWA Tag Team Champions Dusty Rhodes & Manny Fernandez defeated Krusher Kruschev, Ivan & Nikita Koloff via disqualification

CWF @ Jacksonville, FL - February 21, 1985
Jay Youngblood defeated Koko Ware
Mark Youngblood defeated Norvell Austin
Pez Whatley defeated Rick Rude
Jesse Barr defeated Brian Blair via disqualification
Dutch Mantell defeated Bill Irwin
Michael Hayes & Buddy Roberts defeated the Assassins
NWA World Champion Ric Flair defeated Terry Gordy via disqualification

CWF @ Miami, FL - February 22, 1985
NWA World Champion Ric Flair defeated Jesse Barr

JCP @ Richmond, VA - Coliseum - February 22, 1985
Black Bart fought Steve Casey to a draw
The Barbarian defeated Keith Larson
Buzz Tyler defeaed Ron Bass via disqualification
Dusty Rhodes, Jimmy Valiant, & Don Kernodle defeated NWA Six Man Tag Team Champions Ivan Koloff, Nikita Koloff, & Krusher Kruschev via disqualification
NWA TV Champion Tully Blanchard defeated Manny Fernandez; Blanchard's title and $10,000 were at stake
Magnum TA defeated NWA US Champion Wahoo McDaniel via disqualification
Dick Slater vs. Dory Funk Jr. (lights out bounty match)

167

Worldwide - 2/23/85 - included several minutes of the Ricky Steamboat vs. NWA US Champion Wahoo McDaniel match taped 2/17/85 at the Greensboro Coliseum:
Steve Casey vs. Doug Vines
John Tatum vs. Sam Houston
The Barbarian vs. Mark Fleming
Ivan Koloff & Krusher Kruschev vs. Lee Ramsey & Joel Deaton
NWA TV Champion Tully Blanchard vs. Keith Larson
Manny Fernandez & Buzz Tyler vs. Dory Funk Jr. & Black Bart

JCP/AWA @ Washington DC - Armory - February 24, 1985
Superstar Billy Graham defeated Walker
Dory Funk Jr. defeated Keith Larson
Manny Fernandez defeated Mark Fleming
Dick Slater fought NWA TV Champion Tully Blanchard to a draw
Dusty Rhodes & Jimmy Valiant defeated Ron Bass & Black Bart
Bob Backlund defeated Ivan Koloff via disqualification
Magnum TA defeated JJ Dillon
NWA US Champion Wahoo McDaniel defeated Ricky Steamboat

JCP @ Asheville, NC - Civic Center - February 24, 1985
Denny Brown vs. Sam Houston
Steve Casey vs. the Barbarian
Don Kernodle vs. Superstar Billy Graham
Mid-Atlantic Tag Team Champions Ron Bass & Black Bart vs. Dick Slater & Buzz Sawyer (elimination match)

Manny Fernandez vs. NWA TV Champion Tully Blanchard (Blanchard's $10,000 were also at stake)
Magnum TA vs. NWA US Champion Wahoo McDaniel (No DQ match)

JCP @ Charlotte, NC - Coliseum - February 24, 1985
Superstar Billy Graham defeated Starship Eagle
Magnum TA defeated John Tatum
NWA Six Man Tag Team Champions Ivan Koloff, Nikita Koloff, & Krusher Kruschev defeated Ricky Steamboat, Don & Rocky Kernodle
NWA World Champion Ric Flair defeated NWA US Champion Wahoo McDaniel
NWA TV Champion Tully Blanchard defeated NWA Tag Team Champion Dusty Rhodes via disqualification
Dick Slater & NWA Tag Team Champion Manny Fernandez defeated Ron Bass & Black Bart in an elimination match
Buzz Tyler defeated the Barbarian

JCP/AWA Star Wars - East Rutherford, NJ - Meadowlands - February 24, 1985 (18,600)
Jimmy Valiant, Jay & Mark Youngblood fought Larry Zbyszko, Nick Bockwinkel, & Dory Funk Jr. to a 15-minute time-limit draw
Kamala defeated Mark Pole & Lou Fabiano in a handicap match
Bob Backlund pinned Billy Robinson
Jim Brunzell & Greg Gagne fought Mr. Saito & the Masked Superstar to a double disqualification
Japan TV: Ivan & Nikita Koloff (w/ Krusher Kruschev) defeated Jimmy Valiant & Steve Keirn at around the 9:30 mark when Ivan pinned Valiant after Kruschev interfered behind the referee's back as Valiant had Ivan in the sleeper and Nikita fought with Keirn on the floor; after the match, several in the crowd chanted "Bullshit"
Japan TV: Jimmy Garvin (w/ Precious) defeated AWA World Champion Rick Martel via disqualification at 7:34 when Martel threw the challenger over the top rope; after the bout, Precious took the title belt from Martel, with she and Garvin then leaving ringside with it
Japan TV: AWA Tag Team Champions the Road Warriors (w/ Paul Ellering) defeated Jerry Lawler & Baron Von Raschke at 9:39 when Road Warrior Hawk pinned Von Raschke following a clothesline from Road Warrior Animal, the illegal man, on the apron behind the referee's back after Von Raschke ducked Hawk's clothesline
Japan TV: NWA World Champion Ric Flair pinned Harley Race at around the 20-minute mark when momentum of a crossbody off the top by Race put Flair on top for the win
Japan TV: Sgt. Slaughter won a $100,000 tag team battle royal by pinning Billy Robinson at around the 12-minute mark; following his entrance, Slaughter took the mic and said his scheduled tag team partner, Jerry Blackwell, was too injured to compete; other teams in the match included: AWA Tag Team Champions the Road Warriors (w/ Paul Ellering), Ivan & Nikita Koloff (w/ Krusher Kruschev), Greg Gagne & Jim Brunzell, Kamala (w/ Friday) & Billy Robinson, Jay & Mark Youngblood, Jerry Lawler & Baron Von Raschke, Bob Backlund & Jimmy

168

Valiant, Mr. Saito & the Masked Superstar, Nick Bockwinkel & Dory Funk Jr., Jimmy Garvin & Larry Zbyszko, and Jerry Oski & Steve Keim; stipulations stated the last two teams would face off in a one-fall contest; order of elimination: Ivan; Keirn; Bockwinkel; Backlund was eliminated following a knee to the back from Zbyszko; after the elimination, Backlund dragged Zbyszko out to the floor and attacked him; Valiant; Garvin; Gagne; Saito by Lawler; Superstar; Von Raschke by Road Warrior Hawk via a clothesline as Von Raschke had the claw applied on the ropes on Road Warrior Animal; both Road Warriors were eliminated when their own momentum sent them over the top rope as they tried to eliminate Slaughter; Kamala by Slaughter via a backdrop; Slaughter pinned Robinson with the Slaughter Cannon; after the bout, Kamala attacked Slaughter until Lawler, Von Raschke, and Gagne made the save; moments later, Slaughter was presented with a trophy

JCP @ Fayetteville, NC - February 25, 1985
Magnum TA & Manny Fernandez vs. Superstar Billy Graham & the Barbarian

★NWA★ WRESTLING

Mid-Atlantic
Championship Wrestling
Featuring...
U.S. Title Match
Wahoo McDaniel -vs- The Ragin' Bull
Others include
Ivan Koloff, Ric Flair, Ricky Steamboat,
Dusty Rhodes, Tully Blanchard & many more!
WEST ROWAN HIGH SCHOOL
Tuesday, February 26, 1985 - 7:30 p.m.
RINGSIDE TICKETS $6.00 | **T.V. TAPING!!** *Ticket Locations:* | GEN. ADMISSION TICKETS $5 ($3 under 10)
Both locations of Burger King; Dale's Sporting Goods, China Grove; Sports Unlimited, Mooresville, and at the school

JCP @ Steele, NC - West Rowan High School - February 26, 1985
TV taping:
NWA US Champion Wahoo McDaniel vs. Manny Fernandez
Also included Ivan Koloff, NWA World Champion Ric Flair, Ricky Steamboat, Dusty Rhodes, and NWA TV Champion Tully Blanchard

JCP/AWA @ Altoona, PA - February 26, 1985
Ron Garvin defeated Ron Starr
Superstar Billy Graham defeated Starship Eagle
Magnum TA defeated Bob Roop
Starship Eagle fought John Tatum to a draw
Bob Backlund defeated Ron Bass

CWF @ Tampa, FL - February 26, 1985
NWA World Champion Ric Flair defeated NWA US Champion Wahoo McDaniel

JCP/AWA @ Philadelphia, PA - Civic Center - Feburuary 28, 1985
Superstar Billy Graham defeated the Sharship Eagle
Magnum TA defeated Johnny Tatum
Manny Fernandez & Ricky Steamboat fought Ivan Koloff & Black Bart to a draw
Bob Backlund defeated Ron Bass
NWA US Champion Wahoo McDaniel defeated Dick Slater
NWA TV Champion Tully Blanchard defeated Dusty Rhodes via disqualification
NWA World Champion Ric Flair defeated Sgt. Slaughter via disqualification after the challenger accidentally hit the referee with the Slaughter Cannon; the bell didn't ring until Slaughter had Flair in the Cobra Clutch, leading the fans to believe he won the match

JCP @ Columbia, SC - Township Auditorium - March 1, 1985
The Barbarian defeated Gene Ligon
Denny Brown defeated Sam Houston
Superstar Billy Graham defeated Frankie Lane
Magnum TA, Manny Fernandez, & Don Kernodle defeated Krusher Kruschev, Ivan & Nikita Koloff via disqualification
NWA TV Champion Tully Blanchard defeated NWA Tag Team Champion Dusty Rhodes

Worldwide - 3/2/85:
Steve Casey vs. Joel Deaton
The Barbarian vs. David Cordinelli (Italian Stallion)
Nikita Koloff & Krusher Kruschev vs. two unknowns
Manny Fernandez vs. Chick Donovan
NWA World Champion Ric Flair vs. Doug Vines
NWA TV Champion Tully Blanchard vs. Denny Brown

GCW @ Atlanta, GA - WTBS Studios - March 2, 1985
TV taping:
NWA World Champion Ric Flair defeated Jackie Hines

JCP @ Greensboro, NC - Coliseum - March 2, 1985 (4,619)
Johnny Weaver fought John Tatum to a draw
Magnum TA defeated Joel Deaton
Nikita Koloff & Krusher Kruschev defeated Lee Ramsey & Gene Ligon
Tully Blanchard defeated Frank Lang & Mark Fleming in a

handicap match
Dick Slater defeated Dory Funk Jr.
Dusty Rhodes & Manny Fernandez defeated Superstar Billy Graham & the Barbarian
NWA World Champion Ric Flair defeated NWA US Champion Wahoo McDaniel

JCP @ Greenville, SC - Memorial Auditorium - March 2, 1985
Johnny Weaver fought John Tatum to a draw
Magnum TA defeated Joel Deaton
Nikita Koloff & Krusher Kruschev defeated Gene Ligon & Lee Ramsey
NWA TV Champion Tully Blanchard defeated Mark Fleming & Frank Lang in a handicap match
Dick Slater defeated Dory Funk Jr.
Dusty Rhodes & Manny Fernandez defeated Superstar Billy Graham & the Barbarian
NWA World Champion Ric Flair defeated NWA US Champion Wahoo McDaniel

Central States @ Des Moines, IA - March 3, 1985
NWA World Champion Ric Flair defeated Bob Brown

GCW @ Atlanta, GA - Omni - March 3, 1985
Devil Blue defeated Joe Polardy
The Italian Stallion defeated Vern Henderson
Rip Rogers defeated Paul Diamond
The Rock 'n' Roll RPMs defeated Chick Donovan & Doug Somers
Dick Slater fought Ron Starr to a no contest
Dusty Rhodes defeated Bob Roop in a bunkhouse match
Tommy Rich defeated Rip Rogers via disqualification
National Heavyweight Champion Ron Garvin defeated Ox Baker
Gene Anderson, National Tag Team Champions Thunderbolt Patterson & Ole Anderson defeated Ivan Koloff, Scott Irwin, & Kareem Muhammad

WCCW @ Ft. Worth, TX - March 4, 1985
Tommy Rogers defeated Gino Hernandez
Rip Oliver defeated Mike Von Erich
Brian Adias fought Dennis Condrey to a draw
Skip Young defeated El Diablo Grande
Rip Oliver defeated Jose Lothario
Chris Adams fought NWA World Champion Ric Flair to a draw

JCP @ Spartanburg, SC - Memorial Auditorium - March 5, 1985
Worldwide taping:
Manny Fernandez vs. the Barbarian
Black Bart & Ron Bass vs. Buzz Tyler & Jimmy Valiant
3/9/85:
Krusher Kruschev vs. Mark Fleming
Magnum TA, Dick Slater, & Buzz Tyler vs. Joel Deaton, Doug

Vines, & the Golden Terror
Arn Anderson vs. Sam Houston
Superstar Billy Graham vs. Frank Lane
The Great Kabuki vs. Mike Fever
Buddy Landell vs. Keith Larson
3/16/85:
Nikita Koloff & Krusher Kruschev vs. Joel Deaton & Frank Lane
Arn Anderson vs. Gene Ligon
The Great Kabuki & the Barbarian vs. Jimmy Valiant & Buzz Tyler
Manny Fernandez vs. Doug Vines
Magnum TA vs. the Golden Terror & Inferno (handicap match)
NWA TV Champion Tully Blanchard vs. Steve Casey

JCP @ Raleigh, NC - Dorton Arena - March 6, 1985
Buddy Landell defeated Denny Brown
Black Bart defeated Sam Houston
Steve Casey defeated Ron Bass via disqualification
Arn Anderson, Ivan Koloff, & Krusher Kruschev defeated Don Kernodle, Buzz Tyler, & Manny Fernandez
Tully Blanchard defeated Dusty Rhodes via disqualification
Magnum TA fought NWA US Champion Wahoo McDaniel to a no contest

JCP @ Charleston, SC - County Hall - March 8, 1985
Black Bart vs. Jim Cayce
John Tatum vs. Pez Whatley
Buzz Tyler vs. NWA Mid-Atlantic Heavyweight Champion Black Bart
Magnum TA & Jimmy Valiant vs. Superstar Billy Graham & the Barbarian

WCCW @ Dallas, TX - Sportatorium - March 8, 1985
TV taping:
Brian Adias defeated El Diablo Grande
Sweet Brown Sugar fought Johnny Mantell to a draw
Bobby Fulton & Tommy Rogers defeated Bobby Eaton & Dennis Condrey
NWA World Champion Ric Flair defeated Kevin Von Erich via count-out

JCP @ Richmond, VA - Coliseum - March 8, 1985
The Rock 'n' Roll RPMs vs. Steve Casey & Buzz Tyler
Ron Bass defeated Sam Houston
Magnum TA defeated John Tatum
Jimmy Valiant defeated Superstar Billy Graham
NWA TV Champion Tully Blanchard defeated Dusty Rhodes via disqualification; Blanchard's $10,000 were also at stake
Manny Fernandez & Dick Slater defeated Ron Bass & Black Bart

JCP @ Charlotte, NC - Coliseum - March 9, 1985
Buddy Landell defeated Sam Houston
Manny Fernandez defeated Black Bart
Steve Casey defeated Mike Davis

Dick Slater defeated Dory Funk Jr. in a bounty match
Jimmy Valiant defeated Superstar Billy Graham via disqualification
Ivan Koloff defeated Don Kernodle in a Russian chain match
NWA World Champion Ric Flair & Magnum TA won a tag team battle royal

JCP @ Sumter, SC - County Center - March 10, 1985
Buddy Landell defeated Sam Houston
Buzz Tyler & Steve Casey defeated the Rock 'n' Roll RPMs
Jimmy Valiant defeated Superstar Billy Graham via disqualification
Ivan Koloff defeated Don Kernodle in a Russian chain match
Magnum TA & Dick Slater defeated NWA US Champion Wahoo McDaniel & NWA TV Champion Tully Blanchard

JCP/AWA @ Mount Holly, NJ - March 11, 1985
Pete Sanchez fought Davey O'Hannon to a draw
Pez Whatley defeated JJ Dillon
Superstar Billy Graham defeated Manuel Soto
Larry Zbyszko defeated Rocky Jones
Bob Backlund defeated Ron Bass
Sgt. Slaughter defeated Ivan Koloff via count-out

Continental @ Birmingham, AL - March 11, 1985
NWA World Champion Ric Flair fought Bob Armstrong to a double disqualification in a steel cage match

JCP @ Greenville, SC - Memorial Auditorium - March 11, 1985
Johnny Weaver defeated Doug Vines
Denny Brown defeated Joel Deaton
Black Bart defeated Sam Houston
Magnum TA defeated John Tatum
Jimmy Valiant defeated the Barbarian
NWA US Champion Wahoo McDaniel & NWA TV Champion Tully Blanchard defeated Dusty Rhodes & Manny Fernandez via disqualification

JCP/AWA @ Allentown, PA - March 12, 1985
Manuel Soto fought Davey O'Hannon to a draw
Pez Whatley defeated JJ Dillon
Superstar Billy Graham defeated Steve King
Larry Zbyszko defeated Pete Sanchez
Sgt. Slaughter & Bob Backlund defeated Ivan Koloff & Ron Bass via disqualification

Central States @ Wichita, KS - March 12, 1985
NWA World Champion Ric Flair defeated Marty Jannetty

JCP @ Winchester, VA - Frederick County Middle School - March 12, 1985
The Golden Terror vs. Rocky King
Gene Ligon vs. Doug Vines
Johnny Weaver vs. Joel Deaton
Rocky Kernodle vs. Tommy Lane
Don Kernodle & Pez Whatley vs. Ivan & Nikita Koloff

N.W.A. Championship Wrestling

WEDNESDAY MARCH 13TH

8:00 P.M. — 8:00 P.M. — 8:00 P.M.

JAFFA MOSQUE
ALTOONA, PA.

SGT. **SLAUGHTER**
• VERSUS •
IVAN **KOLOFF**

COWBOY **RON BASS**
With His Mgr. James J. Dillon
• VERSUS •
PISTOL PEZ **WHATLEY**

SUPERSTAR BILLY **GRAHAM**
With His Mgr. Paul Jones
• Versus •
ROCKY JONES

BOB **BACKLAND**
• VERSUS •
LARRY **ZYBSZKO**

JAMES J. **DILLON**
• VERSUS •
MANNY **SOTO**

DAVEY O'HANNON V S PETE SANCHEZ

FOR TICKETS:
PHONE (814) 943-0838
THE BOOKSTORE in Park Hills Plaza, TOBACCO SHOP in the STATION MALL, LESLIE'S in Hollidaysburg, PA.

SILVER STAR '85

TONIGHT 8:15 PM

SGT. SLAUGHTER — WAHOO McDANIEL

WORLD HEAVYWEIGHT TITLE MATCH
INDIAN STRAP MATCH
Ric Flair vs Wahoo McDaniel

TV TITLE MATCH
1 fall, 20 minutes—no disqualification
$20,000 to winner
Tully Blanchard vs Dusty Rhodes
(Baby Doll will be inside a cage above the ring. If Tully wins, Dusty Rhodes leaves town.)

FLAG VS FLAG
6 MAN TAG MATCH
Sgt. Bob Slaughter
Magnum T.A.
Don Kernodle
VS
Ivan Koloff
Nikita Koloff
Krusher Khruschev

BOUNTY MATCH
Dick Slater vs The Barbarian

MID-ATLANTIC TITLE MATCH
Buzz Tyler vs Ron Bass

PLUS Jimmy Valiant vs Black Bart
and many others!

TICKETS—$20 $15 $10
Children 10 and under ½ price in $15 & $10 sections. On sale at Coliseum Box Office and all Ticketron Outlets.

172

JCP / AWA @ Altoona, PA - Jaffa Mosque - March 13, 1985
Pez Whatley fought Ron Bass to a 15-minute time-limit draw
Bob Backlund defeated Nikita Koloff via disqualification at the 29-minute mark Pez Whatley pinned JJ Dillon at the 24-second mark
Dominic DeNucci pinned Billy Berger at the 13-minute mark
Luis Martinez pinned Otto Von Mark at the 9-minute mark
Superstar Billy Graham pinned Ivan Koloff at the 15-minute mark

JCP/AWA @ Baltimore, MD - Civic Center - March 14, 1985
Manny Fernandez fought Superstar Billy Graham to a draw
Tom Zenk defeated Alaskan #1
The Freebirds defeated the Rock 'n' Roll RPMs
Rick Martel defeated Mr. Saito
Dusty Rhodes, Ole Anderson, & Sgt. Slaughter defeated Krusher Kruschev, Ivan & Nikita Koloff via disqualification
Tommy Rich fought Tully Blanchard to a draw
Bob Backlund defeated the Barbarian via disqualification

Central States @ Kansas City, KS - March 14, 1985
NWA World Champion Ric Flair defeated Rufus R. Jones

JCP @ Norfolk, VA - Scope - March 14, 1985
Arn Anderson defeated Scott Casey
Pez Whatley defeated John Tatum
Buddy Landell defeated Sam Houston
Jimmy Valiant defeated Black Bart
Ron Bass defeated Buzz Tyler
Dick Slater defeated Dory Funk Jr.
Magnum TA fought NWA US Champion Wahoo McDaniel to a no contest

JCP @ Elizabethtown, NC - East Bladen High School Gym - March 15, 1985
Johnny Weaver & Frank Lang vs. the Rock 'n Roll RPMs
Keith Larson vs. Krusher Khruschev
Sam Houston vs. Arn Anderson
Dick Slater & Don Kernodle vs. NWA Tag Team Champions Ivan & Nikita Koloff
NWA TV Champion Tully Blanchard vs. Manny Fernandez ($10,000 20-minute challenge)

Central States @ St. Joeseph, MO - March 15, 1985
NWA World Champion Ric Flair defeated Bob Brown

JCP @ Greensboro, NC - Coliseum - March 16, 1985 (9,947)
SilverStarr 85
TV taping:
Manny Fernandez fought Buddy Landell to a draw
Sam Houston defeated Arn Anderson

Jimmy Valiant defeated Black Bart
Dick Slater defeated the Barbarian in a bounty match
Magnum TA, Sgt. Slaughter, & Don Kernodle defeated Krusher Kruschev, Ivan & Nikita Koloff
Buzz Tyler defeated NWA Mid Atlantic Heavyweight Champion Ron Bass to win the title
Dusty Rhodes defeated NWA TV Champion Tully Blanchard (w/ Baby Doll) to win the title; stipulations stated Rhodes would have to leave JCP if he lost; each man put up $10,000 for the bout; Baby Doll was suspended over the ring in a cage during the contest
NWA World Champion Ric Flair defeated NWA US Champion Wahoo McDaniel in an Indian Strap match
Arn Anderson defeated Lee Ramsey via submission with an arm bar at around the 2:30 mark; after the bout, Manny Fernandez came out to check on Ramsey, with Anderson jumping him from behind; moments later, Anderson knocked down the referee, threw Fernandez to the floor, and dropped him across the ringside barrier; it was noted after the bout that Ramsey sustained a broken arm from the contest; Tony Schiavone & Ole Anderson provided commentary on the match after the fact
Arn Anderson pinned Gene Ligon with the gordbuster at 4:11; Tony Schiavone & Ole Anderson provided commentary for the bout after the fact; after the contest, Thunderbolt Patterson confronted Ole about Arn's tactics, with Ole saying he felt like a dummy for carrying Thunderbolt, Dusty Rhodes, and Tommy Rich and he was sick of it; moments later, Ole said it was a "free day" for Thunderbolt and he wouldn't touch him but the next time he saw him things would be different
Arn Anderson pinned Rocky King with the gordbuster; after the bout, Anderson condtinued to assault King until Manny Fernandez ran out and brawled with Anderson until several other wrestlers came out to break up the fight
NWA TV Champion Dusty Rhodes pinned an unknown; after the bout, Rhodes faced off with Baby Doll in the ring until he was jumped from behind by Tully Blanchard; moments later, Sam Houston ran out to make the save; Tony Schiavone then conducted an interview with Blanchard & Baby Doll in which Blanchard said he was taking back the TV title; Rhodes, with Houston, then confronted Blanchard, with Houston pulling Baby Doll away as Rhodes dragged Blanchard through the crowd and back into the ring; Rhodes then hit Blanchard with his own boot as the show came to an end

Worldwide - 3/23/85:
Pez Whatley vs. John Tatum
Arn Anderson vs. Steve Casey
Ivan Koloff & Krusher Khruschev vs. Sam Houston & Gene Ligon
Magnum TA & Manny Fernandez vs. Tommy Lane & Mike Davis
Jimmy Valiant vs. Superstar Billy Graham

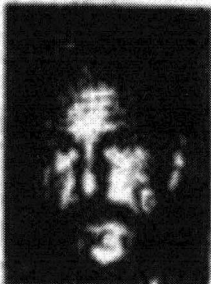

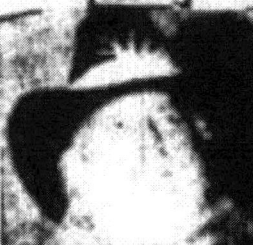

SUNDAY, MARCH 17 3:00 P.M.
TRIPLE MAIN EVENT
Asheville Civic Center

RETURN MAIN EVENT
U.S. TITLE MATCH
LUMBERJACK RULES
(U.S. CHAMP)
WAHOO McDANIEL
—vs—
MAGNUM T.A.
(GUARANTEED)
RETURN T.V. TITLE MATCH
(along with Baby Doll)
TULLY BLANCHARD
—vs—
(World Tag Champs)
**AMERICAN DREAM
DUSTY RHODES**
(BOOGIE WOOGIE MAN)
JIMMY VALIENT
—vs—
(Advised by Paul Jones)
**SUPERSTAR BILLY GRAHAM
JOHNNY WEAVER**
—vs—
(With Paul Jones)
THE BARBARIAN

TAG TEAM MATCH
(Jr. Champ)
**DENNY BROWN & MIKE SAM
HOUSTON**
—vs—
(R.P.M.'s)
DAVIS & LANE
Pedro Paz Whatley vs. Johnny Hollywood Tatum

WAHOO
TULLY
SUPERSTAR
MAGNUM
DUSTY
JIMMY

Ringside $7 Gen. Adm. $6 Children Under 10, $3
Box Office 255-5771 Mon.-Fri. 10-5:30, Sat. 11-4, Day of Match 1:00 P.M.
No Checks or Credit Cards Day of Match. Matches subject to change.

WIDE WORLD WRESTLING ON WLOS-TV 13 SUNDAY 12 NOON

WIDE WORLD WRESTLING

JCP @ Asheville, NC - Civic Center - March 17, 1985 (matinee)
Rock 'n' Roll RPMs vs. Denny Brown & Sam Houston
Johnny Weaver vs. the Barbarian
Jimmy Valiant vs. Superstar Billy Graham
Tully Blanchard vs. NWA TV Champion Dusty Rhodes
Magnum TA vs. NWA US Champion Wahoo McDaniel
(lumberjack match)

JCP @ Fayetteville, NC - March 18, 1985
Pez Whatley fought Buddy Landell to a draw
Arn Anderson defeated Sam Houston
Don Kernodle defeated Krusher Kruschev
Buzz Tyler defeated Tully Blanchard via disqualification
Magnum TA fought NWA US Champion Wahoo McDaniel to a no contest
Jimmy Valiant defeated the Great Kabuki
Ivan & Nikita Koloff defeated NWA Tag Team Champions - NWA Mid Atlantic TV Champion Dusty Rhodes & Manny Fernandez to win the titles after Krusher Kruschev interfered, hit Fernandez with a foreign object, and scored the pin himself

JCP @ Columbia, SC - Township Auditorium - March 19, 1985
The Barbarian defeated Gene Ligon
Denny Brown defeated Sam Houston
Superstar Billy Graham defeated Frankie Lane
Magnum TA, Manny Fernandez, & Don Kernodle defeated Krusher Krushchev, Ivan & Nikita Koloff via disqualification
NWA TV Champion Tully Blanchard defeated Dusty Rhodes via disqualification after Rhodes stole away a weapon thrown in the ring by Baby Doll; stipulations stated the winner would walk away with $10,000

JCP @ Raleigh, NC - Dorton Arena - March 20, 1985
Buddy Landell defeated Sam Houston
The Barbarian & Superstar Billy Graham defeated Denny Brown & Pez Whatley
Don Kernodle defeated Nikita Koloff
Arn Anderson defeated Manny Fernandez via disqualification
Jimmy Valiant defeated the Great Kabuki
Magnum TA defeated NWA US Champion Wahoo McDaniel via disqualification in a lumberjack match
NWA TV Champion Dusty Rhodes defeated Tully Blanchard

JCP @ Charlotte, NC - Coliseum - March 23, 1985
Buddy Landell defeated Denny Brown
Pez Whatley defeated the Barbarian via disqualification
Dick Slater & Don Kernodle defeated NWA Tag Team
Champions Ivan & Nikita Koloff via disqualification
Jimmy Valiant defeated the Great Kabuki
NWA TV Champion Dusty Rhodes fought Tully Blanchard to a
draw
Worldwide - 3/30/85: Superstar Billy Graham defeated Steve
Casey
Worldwide - 3/30/85: Arn Anderson defeated Manny
Fernandez via disqualification
Worldwide - 3/30/85: Magnum TA pinned NWA US Champion
Wahoo McDaniel to win the title in a steel cage match at 10:47
with the belly to belly suplex (*Crockett Cup 87*)

GCW @ Atlanta, GA - Omni - March 24, 1985
Brett Sawyer defeated Doug Somers
National Tag Team Champion Thunderbolt Patterson defeated
Kareem Muhammad
National Heavyweight Champion Ron Garvin defeated Ron
Starr via disqualification
NWA US Champion Magnum TA defeated Chic Donovan
Jimmy Valiant defeated Bob Roop via disqualification
Gene Anderson & National Tag Team Champion Ole Anderson
fought Ivan & Nikita Koloff to a no contest
Buzz Sawyer defeated Bill Irwin in a lights out match
Rip Rogers defeated Tommy Rich; stipulations stated the loser
would have his hair painted white

CWF @ Orlando, FL - March 24, 1985
Bill Irwin defeated Mike Golden
The Missing Link & Jesse Barr defeated Larry Hamilton & Mark
Ragin
Mike Graham defeated Buddy Roberts
Hector Guerrero defeated Rick Rude via disqualification
Bugsy McGraw & Brian Blair defeated Michael Hayes & Terry
Gordy
NWA World Champion Ric Flair defeated Wahoo McDaniel

JCP @ Steubenville, OH - March 25, 1985
Mike Davis defeated Jimmy Jackson
Sam Houston defeated John Tatum
Denny Brown & Pez Whatley defeated Tommy Lane & Mike
Davis
Jimmy Valiant defeated the Barbarian
Manny Fernandez defeated Ivan Koloff

CWF @ West Palm Beach, FL - March 25, 1985
NWA World Champion Ric Flair defeated Wahoo McDaniel

JCP @ Philadelphia, PA - Civic Center - March 26, 1985
Buzz Tyler defeated John Tatum
Buddy Landell defeated Sam Houston
Jimmy Valiant defeated the Barbarian

Pez Whatley & Denny Brown defeated the Rock 'n' Roll RPMs
Dusty Rhodes fought Tully Blanchard to a draw
Manny Fernandez defeated Arn Anderson via disqualification
NWA US Champion Magnum TA defeated Ivan Koloff

**CWF @ Tampa, FL - Spartan Sports Center - March 26,
1985 (4,000; sell out)**
Mike Golden defeated Jack Hart
Mark & Jay Youngblood defeated the Missing Link & the
Assassin
Jesse Barr defeated Hector Guerrero
Michael Hayes fought Bugsy McGraw to a double count-out
Terry Gordy defeated Mike Graham in a lumberjack match
NWA World Champion Ric Flair defeated Wahoo McDaniel

N.W.A. Championship Wrestling
TONIGHT
8:00 P.M.—4:00 P.M.—8:00 P.M.
JAFFA MOSQUE
ALTOONA, PA
The RAGIN' BULL
VERSUS
IVAN KOLOFF
ARNE ANDERSON VERSUS STEVE CASEY
THE PRM's VERSUS BUZZ TYLER & PEZ WHATLEY
KRUSHER KRUSCHEV VERSUS SAM HOUSTON
BUDDY LANDELL VS DENNY BROWN
FOR TICKETS PHONE (814) 943-0836

JCP @ Altoona, PA - Jaffa Mosque - March 27, 1985
Jimmy Jackson defeated the Super Assassin
Buddy Landell defeated Denny Brown
Sam Houston defeated John Tatum
Arn Anderson defeated Sam Houston (sub. for Steve Casey)
Byzz Tyler & Pez Whatley defeated Tommy Lane & Mike Davis
Manny Fernandez defeated Ivan Koloff via disqualification

**CWF @ Miami Beach, FL - Convention Center - March 27,
1985 (3,849)**
Jay Youngblood defeated the Missing Link via disqualification
Mark Youngblood fought Jesse Barr to a draw
Rick Rude defeated Hector Guerrero
Brian Blair defeated the Assassin
Mike Graham & Brian Blair won a $20,00 tag team battle royal
NWA World Champion Ric Flair defeated Wahoo McDaniel

**JCP @ Pittsburgh, PA - Convention Center - March 28,
1985**
Sam Houston & Denny Brown fought the Rock 'n Roll RPMs to
a 15-minute time-limit draw
Jimmy Jackson pinned the Super Assassin at 5:07

Manny Fernandez, NWA Mid-Atantic Heavyweight Champion Buzz Tyler, and Pez Whatley defeated Arn Anderson, Buddy Landell, and John Tatum at 23:30 when Fernandez pinned Tatum
Jimmy Valiant defeated the Barbarian via count-out at 8:25
NWA US Champion Magnum TA pinned Ivan Koloff at 19:25
Tully Blanchard defeated NWA TV Champion Dusty Rhodes via disqualification at 9:10

Central States @ St. Louis, MO - March 29, 1985
Kerry Von Erich defeated NWA World Champion Ric Flair via disqualification at the 29-minute mark

JCP @ Richmond, VA - Coliseum - March 29, 1985
Keith Larson & Denny Brown fought the Rock 'n' Roll RPMs to a draw
Pez Whatley defeated John Tatum
Buzz Tyler defeated Ivan Koloff via disqualification
NWA US Champion Magnum TA defeated Buddy Landell
Arn Anderson fought Manny Fernandez to a no contest
Jimmy Valiant defeated the Barbarian in a lumberjack match
NWA TV Champion Tully Blanchard defeated Dusty Rhodes via disqualification; there was a 20-minute time-limit for the bout and Rhodes put up $10,000; Baby Doll was locked in a cage for the duration of the contest

JCP @ Greensboro, NC - Coliseum - March 30, 1985
Sam Houston fought Rocky King to a draw
Pez Whatley & Rocky Kernodle defeated the Rock 'n' Roll RPMs
Arn Anderson fought Manny Fernandez to a no contest
The Barbarian defeated Jimmy Valiant
Buzz Tyler defeated Buddy Landell
NWA US Champion Magnum TA defeated Ivan Koloff
NWA World Champion Ric Flair & NWA TV Champion Dusty Rhodes defeated Wahoo McDaniel & Tully Blanchard

Continental @ Pensacola, FL - March 31, 1985
NWA World Champion Ric Flair vs. Austin Idol

JCP @ Sumter, SC - County Exhibition Center - March 31, 1985 (matinee)
Joel Deaton vs. Frank Lang
Johnny Weaver vs. the Golden Terror
John Tatum vs. Keith Larson
Manny Fernandez vs. Arn Anderson
Jimmy Valiant vs. the Barbarian

GCW @ Canton, OH - April 1, 1985
Brett Sawyer defeated Doug Somers
Paul Diamond defeated Randy Rose
Ron Garvin & the Italian Stallion defeated Ron Starr & Devil Blue
Thunderbolt Patterson defeated Bob Roop via disqualification
Buzz Sawyer, Gene & Ole Anderson defeated Kareem

Muhammad, Bill Irwin, & Rip Rogers
NWA World Champion Ric Flair defeated Tommy Rich

GCW @ Muskegon, MI - April 2, 1985
Brett Sawyer defeated Doug Somers
Paul Diamond defeated Randy Rose
Ron Garvin & the Italian Stallion defeated Ron Starr & Devil Blue
Thunderbolt Patterson defeated Bob Roop via disqualification
Buzz Sawyer, Gene & Ole Anderson defeated Kareem Muhammad, Bill Irwin, & Rip Rogers
NWA World Champion Ric Flair defeated Tommy Rich

JCP @ Spartanburg, SC - Memorial Auditorium - April 2, 1985
TV taping:
Buzz Tyler vs. Ivan Koloff
Manny Fernandez vs. Arn Anderson
Worldwide - 4/6/85:
Pez Whatley & Buzz Tyler vs. John Tatum & Joel Deaton
The Barbarian vs. Mark Fleming
NWA US Champion Magnum TA vs. Buddy Landell
Manny Fernandez vs. David Dillenger
Arn Anderson & Buddy Landell vs. Sam Houston & Denny Brown
NWA TV Champion Dusty Rhodes vs. Doug Vines

JCP @ Raleigh, NC - Dorton Arena - April 3, 1985
Arn Anderson defeated Manny Fernandez
Buzz Sawyer defeated Buddy Landell via disqualification
Jimmy Valiant defeated the Barbarian
Pez Whatley defeated Doug Vines
Sam Houston & Denny Brown defeated the Rock 'n' Roll RPMs
Dusty Rhodes defeated Tully Blanchard
NWA US Champion Magnum TA defeated Ivan Koloff

JCP @ Columbia, SC - Township Auditorium - April 5, 1985
Sam Houston defeated Doug Vines
Joel Deaton fought Rocky King to a draw
Buddy Landell defeated Sam Houston
Arn Anderson fought Manny Fernandez to a no contest
The Barbarian defeated Jimmy Valiant via disqualification
Dusty Rhodes defeated Tully Blanchard

GCW @ Lansing, MI - April 5, 1985
NWA World Champion Ric Flair defeated Tommy Rich

GCW @ Wheeling, WV - April 5, 1985
NWA World Champion Ric Flair defeated Tommy Rich

JCP @ Atlanta, GA - WTBS Studios - April 6, 1985
World Championship Wrestling - 4/6/85 - the first episode promoted by Jim Crockett Promotions - featured Tony Schiavone conducting an interview with NWA World Champion

JCP 1985

Ric Flair, alongside three women, in which Flair mentioned Dusty Rhodes, NWA US Champion Magnum TA, and Michael Hayes as his top contenders; included Schiavone conducting an interview with Tully Blanchard, alongside Baby Doll, regarding NWA TV Champion Dusty Rhodes and his quest to regain the belt; featured Schiavone conducting an interview with Ole & Arn Anderson regarding the altercation earlier in the show with Manny Fernandez and Thunderbolt Patterson, with Arn saying it was the rekindling of a dynasty; included Schiavone conducting an interview with the Andersons regarding Ole and Patterson being the NWA National Tag Team champions:
Ivan Koloff & Krusher Kruschev (w/ Nikita Koloff) vs. George South & Greg Stone
Jimmy Valiant vs. Mark Hill
Tully Blanchard (w/ Baby Doll) vs. Sam Houston
Superstar Billy Graham (w/ Paul Jones) vs. Rocky King
NWA World Champion Ric Flair vs. Gene Ligon
Manny Fernandez defeated Arn Anderson via disqualification at around the 7:15 mark when Ole Anderson helped Arn double team Fernandez on the floor; during the bout, Ole - who joined the commentary team for the bout - said he and Arn were brothers, though the story at the time was that they were cousins; after the contest, Thunderbolt Patterson came out to question Ole about his tactics, with Arn jumping Thunderbolt from behind; moments later, Thunderbolt gained the upper hand on Arn until Ole helped Arn double team him; Arn then held Thunderbolt down with Ole coming off the top; as Ole tried it a second time, Fernandez climbed back in the ring to take the blow
NWA US Champion Magnum TA vs. Paul Barnett
The Barbarian (w/ Paul Jones) vs. Joshua Stroud
Buddy Landell (w/ JJ Dillon) vs. David Dillinger
Black Bart (w/ JJ Dillon) vs. Ron Rossi

JCP @ Cincinnati, OH - April 6, 1985
Johnny Tatum defeated Rocky King
Black Bart defeated Denny Brown
Superstar Billy Graham defeated Pez Whatley
Arn Anderson defeated Rocky Kernodle
Jimmy Valiant defeated the Barbarian in a lumberjack match
Ron Garvin & the Italian Stallion defeated the Blue Devil & Ron Starr
NWA World Champion Ric Flair defeated Tommy Rich

Mid South @ Houston, TX - April 7, 1985 (sell out)
Brickhouse Brown defeated Jack Victory
Brad Armstrong defeated Kevin Kelly
Brickhouse Brown defeated Steve Williams via disqualification
Jake Roberts & Gino Hernandez defeated Bobby Fulton & Tommy Rogers
Jim Duggan defeated the One Man Gang in a bounty match
Nord the Barbarian defeated Butch Reed in a ghetto streetfight
Kevin Von Erich defeated Chris Adams via disqualification
Terry Taylor defeated Kamala via disqualification
Kerry Von Erich fought NWA World Champion Ric Flair to a 60-minute time-limit draw

JCP @ Troy, OH - April 1985
Tommy Rich defeated Rip Rogers
Buzz Sawyer, Ole & Gene Anderson defeated Kareem Muhammad, Scott Irwin, & Devil Blue
The Italian Stallion defeated Ron Starr
Brett Sawyer defeated Doug Somers
Ron Garvin fought NWA World Champion Ric Flair to a double count-out when both men began fighting on the floor

PNW @ Dallas, OR - April 8, 1985
NWA World Champion Ric Flair defeated Bobby Jaggers

JCP @ Pittsburgh, PA - April 1985
Buddy Landell defeated Denny Brown
Jimmy Valiant pinned the Barbarian with an elbowdrop
Buzz Tyler defeated Black Bart
NWA Tag Team Champions Ivan & Nikita Koloff defeated Manny Fernandez & Don Kernodle
NWA US Champion Magnum TA defeated Tully Blanchard

JCP @ Hampton, VA - April 1985
Buzz Tyler defeated John Tatum
Pez Whatley & Rocky Kernodle defeated the Rock 'n' Roll RPMs
Johnny Weaver defeated the Masked Inferno
Denny Brown defeated Mark Fleming
NWA US Champion Magnum TA pinned Ivan Koloff with a sunset flip

PNW @ Portland, OR - April 9, 1985
NWA World Champion Ric Flair defeated Curt Hennig

JCP @ Raleigh, NC - Dorton Arena - April 10, 1985
Arn Anderson defeated Manny Fernandez
Buzz Tyler defeated Buddy Landell via disqualification
Jimmy Valiant defeated the Barbarian
Pez Whatley defeated Doug Vines
Denny Brown & Sam Houston fought the Rock 'n' Roll RPMs to a draw
Dusty Rhodes defeated Tully Blanchard
NWA US Champion Magnum TA defeated Ivan Koloff

PNW @ Seattle, WA - April 10, 1985
NWA World Champion Ric Flair defeated Curt Hennig

JCP @ Pittsburgh, PA - April 10, 1985
LP defeated Jimmy Jackson
DJ defeated Brad Walsh
Arn Anderson defeated Sam Houston
Buddy Landell defeated Denny Brown
Buzz Tyler defeated Black Bart
NWA Tag Team Champions Ivan & Nikita Koloff defeated Manny Fernandez & Don Kernodle

Jimmy Valiant defeated the Barbarian
NWA US Champion Magnum TA defeated Tully Blanchard

PNW @ Salem, OR - April 11, 1985
NWA World Champion Ric Flair defeated Bobby Jaggers

JCP @ Fredricksburg, VA - Stafford Senior High School - April 11, 1985
Superstar Billy Graham pinned Mark Fleming
The Rock 'n' Roll RPMs fought Denny Brown & Sam Houston to a draw
Arn Anderson fought Manny Fernandez to a double count-out
Jimmy Valiant pinned the Barbarian
NWA US Champion Magnum TA pinned Buddy Landell

PNW @ Eugene, OR - April 12, 1985
NWA World Champion Ric Flair defeated Bobby Jaggers

JCP @ Norfolk, VA - Scope - April 12, 1985
Sam Houston fought LP to a draw
Buddy Landell defeated Denny Brown
Johnny Tatum pinned Mark Fleming
Buzz Tyler defeated Black Bart
Jimmy Valiant defeated Superstar Billy Graham in a lumberjack match
Manny Fernandez fought Arn Anderson to a no contest
NWA US Champion Magnum TA defeated Tully Blanchard

JCP @ Winchester, VA - Frederick County Middle School - April 12, 1985
Gene Ligon vs. Doug Vines
Rocky King vs. the Golden Terror
Keith Larson vs. a Rock 'n' Roll RPM
Johnny Weaver vs. Joel Deaton
NWA Tag Team Champions Ivan & Nikita Koloff vs. Don Kernodle & Pez Whatley

Worldwide - 4/13/85 - featured an opening segment in which roughly a dozen wrestlers had to come out to pull apart Arn Anderson and Manny Fernandez as they brawled in the ring; included Tony Schiavone & David Crockett on commentary; featured Crockett reviewing footage from a recent interview Schiavone conducted between NWA National Tag Team Champions Ole Anderson & Thunderbolt Patterson regarding Arn's actions, during which Ole complained that he was tired of carrying the likes of Patterson and Tommy Rich and told Patterson to watch out the next time he saw him; included Crockett conducting an interview with JJ Dillon & Buddy Landell in which they reviewed footage from the previous week of Landell attacking NWA US Champion Magnum TA and whipping him with the title belt; moments later, Magnum made a comeback with Landell sliding out to the floor; featured Crockett conducting an interview with Arn in which he said he wasn't living off the Anderson name and then commented on his feud with Fernandez and newfound partnership with Ole;

included Crockett conducting an interview with NWA Tag Team & NWA Six Man Tag Team Champions Nikita Koloff & Krusher Kruschev, with them in possession of the six man championship cup; moments later, Kruschev showed footage form the previous week of Rocky Kernodle cheating against Ivan Koloff; featured Crockett showing footage from WTBS Studios of Ole interfering in Fernandez' match with Arn, with the two then assaulting Patterson until Fernandez made the save:
Jimmy Valiant & Pez Whatley defeated Doug Vines & David Dillenger at 2:40 when Valiant scored the pin following a dropkick from Whatley and elbow drop from Valiant
NWA Mid Atlantic Tag Team Champion Black Bart (w/ JJ Dillon) pinned Gene Ligon with the legdrop off the top at 7:12
Manny Fernandez pinned Joel Deaton at 2:58 with a flying double thrust
Buddy Landell (w/ JJ Dillon) defeated Lee Ramsey via submission with the figure-4 at 2:48; after the bout, Landell kept the hold applied until Dillon and referee Tommy Young broke the hold
NWA Tag Team & NWA Six Man Tag Team Champion Nikita Koloff (w/ NWA Tag Team & NWA Six Man Tag Team Champion Krusher Kruschev) defeated Rocky King via submission with a cobra clutch at 1:22; after the bout, Koloff briefly kept the hold applied before then choking King
Arn Anderson defeated Ron Rossi via submission with an armbar at 2:25; after the match, Anderson refused to break the hold and then continued to assault Rossi until Fernandez made the save and cleared the ring; moments later, Anderson jumped Fernandez from behind, knocked him to the floor, rammed him into the ringpost, and continued to attack Rossi; Jimmy Valiant and Pez Whatley then ran out to make the save

JCP @ Atlanta, GA - WTBS Studios - April 13, 1985
World Championship Wrestling - 4/13/85 - featured Tony Schiavone conducting an interview with Ole & Arn Anderson regarding Manny Fernandez & Thunderbolt Patterson; included Schiavone conducting an interview with Tully Blanchard, alongside Baby Doll, regarding having lost the NWA TV title and $10,000 to Dusty Rhodes and his quest to be champion again; during which Blanchard made note of the fans heckling him and said they were illiterate:
Buddy Landell vs. Sam Houston
Michael Hayes vs. Joel Deaton
Thunderbolt Patterson & Manny Fernandez vs. Mike Jackson & Paul Garner
Tully Blanchard (w/ Baby Doll) vs. Paul Diamond
Ole & Arn Anderson vs. Gene Ligon & Rocky King
Ivan Koloff vs. Buzz Sawyer
Nikita Koloff vs. Josh Stroud
Superstar Billy Graham & the Barbarian (w/ Paul Jones) vs. Mack & Jim Jeffers
NWA US Champion Magnum TA defeated George South at the 13-second mark
Pez Whatley vs. Vernon Deaton
Krusher Kruschev vs. Mike Simone

MID ATLANTIC CHAMPIONSHIP WRESTLING

Mid-Atlantic and World-Wide Wrestling will return to Winchester, Va., on Friday, April 12, 1985 at 8:15 P.M. at the Frederick County Middle School, Linden Drive, Winchester.

** WORLD TAG TEAM TITLE **

IVAN KOLOFF NIKITA KOLOFF	VS	DON KERNODLE PISTOL PEZ WHATLEY

KEITH LARSON	VS	R.P.M. No. 1
JOHNNY WEAVER	VS	JOEL DEATON
GENE LIGON	VS	DOUG VINES
ROCKY KING	VS	GOLDEN TERROR

ADVANCE TICKET LOCATIONS:

PYRAMID SPORTS — APPLE BLOSSOM MALL, WINCHESTER, VA.
TONEY'S SUPERMARKET — STEPHENS CITY, VA.
TOWN OFFICE — MIDDLETOWN, VA.

Sponsored by
James Wood Concert Choir

RINGSIDE	GEN. ADM. ADULTS	GEN. ADM. CHILDREN UNDER 10
$6.00	$5.00	$3.00

Wide World
Wrestling

MID ATLANTIC CHAMPIONSHIP WRESTLING

PNW @ Portland, OR - April 13, 1985
NWA World Champion Ric Flair fought Karl Steiner to a draw

JCP @ Greensboro, NC - Coliseum - April 13, 1985 (3,467)
The Barbarian defeated Johnny Weaver
The Rock 'n' Roll RPMs defeated Sam Houston & Denny Brown
Jimmy Valiant defeated Superstar Billy Graham
Manny Fernandez defeated Arn Anderson
Buzz Tyler & Don Kernodle defeated NWA Tag Team Champions Ivan & Nikita Koloff
NWA US Champion Magnum TA defeated Buddy Landell
NWA TV Champion Dusty Rhodes defeated Tully Blanchard

JCP @ Richmond, VA - Coliseum - April 14, 1985 (matinee)
Buzz Tyler, Pez Whatley, & Don Kernodle vs. Krusher Kruschev, Ivan & Nikita Koloff
NWA TV Champion Dusty Rhodes vs. Tully Blanchard (barbed wire match)
NWA World Champion Ric Flair vs. Wahoo McDaniel (Indian strap match)

GCW @ Atlanta, GA - Omni - April 14, 1985
National Heavyweight Champion Ron Garvin defeated Bob Roop
Tully Blanchard defeated the Italian Stallion
NWA US Champion Magnum TA defeated Buddy Landel
Dusty Rhodes, Jimmy Valiant, & Buzz Sawyer defeated Krusher Kruschev, Ivan & Nikita Koloff
The Barbarian defeated Pez Whatley
Manny Fernandez & National Tag Team Champion Thunderbolt Patterson defeated Arn Anderson & National Tag Team Champion Ole Anderson via disqualification
NWA World Champion Ric Flair defeated Michael Hayes

JCP @ Asheville, NC - Civic Center - April 14, 1985 (matinee)
Gene Ligon vs. Joel Deaton
Rocky King vs. the Barbarian
Johnny Weaver vs. Dory Funk Jr.
Jimmy Valiant vs. Superstar Billy Graham
Manny Fernandez vs. Arn Anderson (No DQ)
NWA US Champion Magnum TA vs. Buddy Landell

JCP @ Altoona, PA - Jaffa Mosque - April 15, 1985
DJ defeated Red Walsh
Johnny Weaver defeated LP
DJ defeated Yukon Bob
Krusher Kruschev defeated Jimmy Jackson
Manny Fernandez fought Arn Anderson to a no contest

JCP @ Fayetteville, NC - Cumberland County Memorial Arena - April 15, 1985
Buzz Tyler vs. the Barbarian
Jimmy Valiant vs. Superstar Billy Graham (karate is legal)

NWA TV Champion Dusty Rhodes vs. Tully Blanchard (barbed wire match)

JCP @ Rock Hill, SC - Winthrop Coliseum - April 16, 1985 (3,300)
TV taping:
NWA Tag Team Champion Ivan & Nikita Koloff defeated Rocky King & Gene Ligon
Superstar Billy Graham defeated Lee Ramsey
Buddy Landell defeated David Dellinger via submission
Don Kernodle pinned Joel Deaton
NWA Mid-Atlantic Heavyweight Champion Buzz Tyler pinned Black Bart
NWA TV Champion Dusty Rhodes pinned Tully Blanchard in a steel cage match
Worldwide - 4/20/85:
NWA US Champion Magnum TA, Jimmy Valiant, & NWA Mid-Atlantic Heavyweight Champion Buzz Tyler defeated John Tatum, Doug Vines, & Joel Deaton
Nikita Koloff pinned Mark Fleming
Denny Brown pinned the Golden Terror
David Dellinger & Lee Ramsey defeated Superstar Billy Graham & the Barbarian via disqualification
Buddy Landell defeated Gene Ligon via submission
Sam Houston defeated Tully Blanchard via disqualification

JCP @ Allentown, PA - Agricultural Hall - April 16, 1985
Sam Houston vs. RPM #1
Pez Whatley vs. RPM #2
Tommy Rich vs. Krusher Kruschev
Manny Fernandez vs. Arn Anderson

PNW @ Portland, OR - April 16, 1985
Billy Jack Haynes defeated NWA World Champion Ric Flair via disqualification

JCP @ Talldega, AL - High School - April 16, 1985
The Italian Stallion defeated Doug Sommers
Ron Garvin defeated Ron Starr
Buzz & Bart Sawyer defeated Bob Roop & Scott Irwin
Thunderbolt Patterson defeated Kareem Muhammad
Pez Whatley defeated Rip Rogers

JCP @ Mareitta, OH - Ban Johnson Field - April 17, 1985

WIDE WORLD WRESTLING

Sunday, April 14, 3 P.M.
DOUBLE MAIN EVENT
Asheville Civic Center

US TITLE MAIN EVENT

(U.S. CHAMP)
MAGNUM T.A.
—VS—
Advised by J.J. Dillon
(NATURE BOY)
BUDDY LANDELL.

NO D.Q. MAIN EVENT
THE RAGIN' BULL
—VS—
Advised by J.J. Dillon
ARNE ANDERSON

(Boogie Woogie Man)
JIMMY VALIENT
—VS—
(Advised by Paul Jones)
SUPERSTAR BILLY GRAHAM

JOHNNY WEAVER
—VS—
DORY FUNK, JR.

ROCK KING —VS— THE BARBARIAN
GENE LIGON —VS— JOEN DEATON

Ringside $7 Gen. Adm. $6 Children Under 10, $3
Box Office 255-5771 Mon.-Fri. 10-5:30, Sat. 11-4, Day of Match 1:00 P.M.
No Checks or Credit Cards Day of Match. Matches subject to change.

WIDE WORLD WRESTLING ON WLOS-TV 13 SUNDAY 12 NOON

MAGNUM • SUPERSTAR • BULL • DORY • JIMMY • JOHNNY

MID-ATLANTIC CHAMPIONSHIP
WRESTLING

DORTON ARENA: TONIGHT

N.C. STATE FAIRGROUNDS. . .FREE PARKING
RINGSIDE $6.00 GEN. ADM. $5.00. CHILDREN (Under 12) $3.00 In Gen. Adm.
Box office at Dorton Arena Opens at Noon on day of matches...Call 733-3636

8:15 P.M.   8:15 P.M.

FOR U.S. CHAMPIONSHIP
BUDDY **LANDEL** v. s. **MAGNUM** T.A.
WITH JAMES J. DILLON

SPECIAL CHALLENGE MATCH
TULLY **BLANCHARD** & ARNE **ANDERSON**
WITH BABY DOLL THE • VERSUS • BUZZ
RAGIN' BULL & **TYLER**

KARATE WILL BE LEGAL
SUPERSTAR **BILLY GRAHAM** v. s. JIMMY **VALIANT**

FOR WORLD'S 6 MAN TAG TITLE
IVAN KOLOFF   V PEZ WAHTLEY
NIKITA KOLOFF   S. DON KERNODLE
KRUSHER KRUSCHEV   ROCKY KERNODLE

JOHNNY WEAVER V. THE BARBARIAN   BLACK BART V. SAM HOUSTON

183

JCP 1985

JCP @ Raleigh, NC - Dorton Arena - April 17, 1985
Superstar Billy Graham defeated Denny Brown
Black Bart defeated Sam Houston
Krusher Kruschev, NWA Tag Team Champions Ivan & Nikita Koloff defeated Don Kernodle & Johnny Weaver
Tully Blanchard & Arn Anderson defeated Manny Fernandez & Buzz Tyler
NWA US Champion Magnum TA defeated Buddy Landell via disqualification

JCP @ Columbia, SC - April 18, 1985
Sam Houston defeated LP
Denny Brown defeated Johnny Tatum
Black Bart defeated Johnny Weaver
Superstar Billy Graham defeated Denny Brown
Arn Anderson defeated Manny Fernandez
Buzz Tyler defeated Buddy Landell via disqualification
NWA US Champion Magnum TA defeated Tully Blanchard

JCP / AWA @ Washington DC - April 18, 1985
Larry Sharpe defeated Sean O'Reilly
Kamala defeated Tom Zenk & Steve O in a handicap match
The Samoans defeated Superstar Billy Graham & King Tonga
The Tonga Kid defeated Larry Zbyszko via disqualification
AWA Tag Team Champions the Road Warriors defeated NWA Tag Team Champions Ivan & Nikita Koloff via disqualification
AWA World Champion Rick Martel defeated Bob Backlund via count-out

JCP @ Lenoir, NC - April 19, 1985
Rocky King defeated Joel Deaton
Black Bart defeated Sam Houston
Rocky King defeated JJ Dillon
Buzz Tyler defeated the Barbarian via disqualification
NWA US Champion Magnum TA defeated Tully Blanchard

JCP @ Atlanta, GA - WTBS Studios - April 20, 1985
World Championship Wrestling - 4/20/85 - 90-minute edition; hosted by Tony Schiavone & David Crockett; included an opening interview with NWA Tag Team Champions Ivan & Nikita Koloff and Krusher Kruschev, who claimed he would capture the NWA TV Title from Dusty Rhodes later in the show, with Nikita sending a warning to NWA World Champion Ric Flair that he was coming for his title; featured Schiavone conducting an interview with Tully Blanchard, alongside Baby Doll, in which he challenged the winner of the match between Rhodes and Kruschev and said the title was coming back to him; included comments from Flair, who stated the fans deserved to see the best and he was just that, before stating he could have any woman he wanted and that Rhodes, NWA US Champion Magnum TA, Manny Fernandez, Buzz Sawyer, Jimmy Valiant, Harley Race, and Kerry Von Erich would always be second-best; included Schiavone interviewing Paul Jones, who showed off numerous scars on his hand and elbow that were a result of Valiant breaking his arm, with Jones promising his Army would take Valiant out; featured a confrontation between Rhodes and Ivan on the announce stage, with Rhodes requesting a shot at the NWA Six Man Tag Team Titles; included Schiavone interviewing Fernandez & National Tag Team Champion Thunderbolt Patterson, with Fernandez daring Arn & Ole Anderson to come and take Thunderbolt's half of the titles; featured a second interview with Patterson & Fernandez, who claimed they would settle the issue over the National Tag Team titles with the Andersons; included Schiavone interviewing Magnum TA who offered a US Title shot to anyone who wanted a piece of him; featured Schiavone conducting an interview with the Andersons, with Ole in possession of his half of the NWA National Tag Team Title belts; as the crowd chanted "We don't want to hear it," Ole said Thunderbolt's belt belonged to Arn:
Buddy Landell (w/ JJ Dillon) defeated Mack Jeffers via submission at 5:58 with the figure-4
NWA US Champion Magnum TA pinned Doug Vines at the 7-second mark in a non-title match with the belly to belly suplex; the announcers billed this as a world record for quickest match of all-time
NWA Tag Team Champion Ivan Koloff (w/ Nikita Koloff) defeated Josh Stroud via submission at 6:06 with the Cobra Clutch
Abdullah the Butcher (w/ Paul Jones) pinned Gene Ligon at 4:39 with an elbow drop
Tully Blanchard (w/ Baby Doll) pinned TJ Trippe at 5:12 with the slingshot suplex
NWA TV Champion Dusty Rhodes pinned Krusher Kruschev (w/ Ivan Koloff) with a roll up at 7:24 after the challenger missed a charge in the corner; after the bout, Kruschev, Koloff, and Nikita Koloff triple teamed Rhodes until NWA US Champion Magnum TA, Thunderbolt Patterson, and Manny Fernandez cleared the ring
Ole & Arn Anderson defeated Gerald Finley & George South at 3:02 when Arn forced South to submit to an armbar
Black Bart (w/ JJ Dillon) pinned Ron Rossi at 2:20 with a legdrop from the middle turnbuckle
Manny Fernandez & National Tag Team Champion Thunderbolt Patterson defeated Randy Barber & Jim Jeffers at 2:34 when Fernandez pinned Barber with the flying forearm

JCP @ Cleveland, OH - Convention Center - April 20, 1985
Bill Irwin defeated Ben Alexander
Joel Deaton defeated Paul Diamond
Thunderbolt Patterson defeated Kareem Muhammad in a lumberjack match
The Italian Stallion defeated Ron Starr
Ron Garvin defeated Bob Roop
Pez Whatley defeated Rip Rogers in a loser leaves town match
The Road Warriors defeated Brett & Buzz Sawyer

JCP @ Mansfield, OH - Local 711 Union Hall - April 21, 1985
Joel Deaton defeated Paul Diamond
The Italian Stallion defeated Ben Alexander
Thunderbolt Patterson defeated Kareem Muhammad
Brett & Buzz Sawyer defeated Bill Irwin & Bob Roop

Ron Garvin defeated Ron Starr
Pez Whatley defeated Rip Rogers in a loser leaves town match

JCP @ Sumter, SC - Exhibition Center - April 21, 1985
Doug Vines defeated Rocky King
Rocky Kernodle fought John Tatum to a draw
Buzz Tyler defeated Dory Funk Jr.
Arn Anderson defeated Denny Brown
Ivan & Nikita Koloff defeated Don Kernodle & Manny Fernandez
NWA US Champion Magnum TA defeated Tully Blanchard via disqualification

JCP @ Saginaw, MI - Civic Center - April 22, 1985
Included Rip Rogers, Thunderbolt Patterson, Buzz Sawyer, Kareem Muhammad, and Scott Irwin

AJPW @ Sagamihara, Japan - April 23, 1985
NWA World Champion Ric Flair fought Riki Choshu to a double count-out at 21:04

JCP @ Toledo, OH - April 23, 1985
Paul Diamond vs. Chic Donovan
Doug Somers vs. Italian Stallion
Thunderbolt Patterson vs. Kareem Muhammad
Bob Roop & Scott Irwin vs. Buzz & Brett Sawyer
NWA National Heavyweight Champion Ron Garvin vs. Ron Starr
Tommy Rich vs. Rip Rogers (loser leaves town)
Also included Pez Whatley

AJPW @ Yokohama, Japan - April 24, 1985
Jumbo Tsuruta fought NWA World Champion Ric Flair to a draw in a Best 2 out of 3 falls match at 26:01

AJPW @ Kisarazu, Japan - April 25, 1985
NWA World Champion Ric Flair & Dick Slater defeated Higo Hamaguchi & Masanobu Kurisu

JCP @ Norfolk, VA - Scope - April 25, 1985
Mark Fleming fought Doug Vines to a draw
Sam Houston defeated Joel Deaton
Pinky Larson defeated John Tatum
The Barbarian defeated Denny Brown
NWA US Champion Magnum TA & Don Kernodle defeated Ivan & Nikita Koloff
Jimmy Valiant defeated Superstar Billy Graham
NWA TV Champion Dusty Rhodes defeated Tully Blanchard in a bunkhouse match

AJPW @ Kisarasu, Japan - April 25, 1985
NWA World Champion Ric Flair & Dick Slater defeated Hiro Hamaguchi & Masanobu Kurisu

JCP @ Richmond, VA - Coliseum - April 26, 1985
John Tatum fought Denny Brown to a draw
Black Bart defeated Rocky Kernodle
Buddy Landell defeated Sam Houston
Don Kernodle defeated Krusher Krushev
Buzz Tyler defeated Ivan Koloff
Jimmy Valiant defeated Superstar Billy Graham via disqualification
NWA US Champion Magnum TA defeated Nikita Koloff
Tully Blanchard defeated NWA TV Champion Dusty Rhodes via disqualification

Worldwide - 4/27/85:
Manny Fernandez vs. Mike Davis
Superstar Billy Graham & the Barbarian vs. Rocky King & Gene Ligon
Nikita Koloff vs. George South
Arn Anderson vs. Mark Fleming
NWA US Champion Magnum TA vs. Black Bart

JCP @ Atlanta, GA - WTBS Studios - April 27, 1985
World Championship Wrestling - 4/27/85 - featured Tony Schiavone conducting an interview with NWA World Champion Ric Flair in which he said he never had to dress up as a cowboy like Dusty Rhodes to get girls in Texas and said Rhodes, NWA US Champion Magnum TA, Terry Taylor, Harley Race, Kevin Von Erich, Wahoo McDaniel, and Bob Armstrong could get a shot at his belt any time they wanted:
Ole & Arn Anderson vs. the Italian Stallion & Gerald Finlay
Manny Fernandez vs. Doug Vines
Bob Roop vs. the Golden Terror
Tully Blanchard (w/ Baby Doll) vs. Lee Ramsey
NWA National Heavyweight Champion Ron Garvin vs. George South
NWA US Champion Magnum TA vs. Hog Irwin
NWA Tag Team Champions Ivan & Nikita Koloff vs. Mike Jackson & Paul Garner
Thunderbolt Patterson defeated Randy Barber; after the bout, Ole & Arn Anderson - who provided guest commentary for the bout - attacked Patterson until Manny Fernandez came out and helped clear the ring
Pez Whatley vs. Vernon Deaton
Ron Bass (w/ JJ Dillon) vs. Rocky King
Superstar Billy Graham, the Barbarian, & Abdullah the Butcher vs. Gene Ligon, Ron Rossi, & Mike Simani

WCCW @ Tulsa, OK - April 27, 1985
NWA World Champion Ric Flair pinned Kerry Von Erich

JCP @ Columbus, GA - April 27, 1985
The Barbarian defeated Paul Diamond
Jimmy Valiant & Buzz Tyler defeated NWA Tag Team Champions Ivan & Nikita Koloff
The Italian Stallion fought Ron Starr to a draw
Pez Whatley defeated Scott Irwin

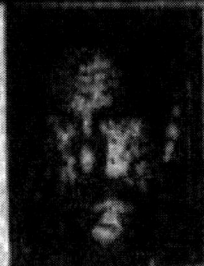

WIDE WORLD WRESTLING

SUNDAY, APRIL 28, 3PM
TRIPLE MAIN EVENT
Asheville Civic Center

RETURN LIGHTS OUT
TEXAS DEATH MATCH
(Boogie Woogie Man)
JIMMY VALIENT
—vs—
(Advised by Paul Jones)
SUPERSTAR BILLY GRAHAM

RETURN US TITLE MATCH
NO DQ
(US CHAMP)
MAGNUM TA
—vs—
(Advised by J.J. Dillon)
BUDDY LANDELL

TAG TEAM MATCH
THE RAGIN' BULL
&
THUNDERBOLT PATTERSON
—vs—
OLE ANDERSON
&
ARNE ANDERSON

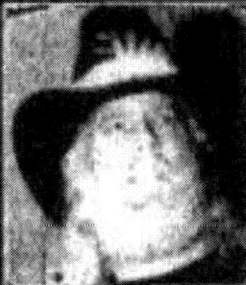

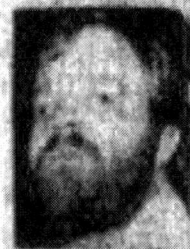

DON KERNODLE —vs— (½ World Tag Champs) NIKITA KOLOFF

PISTOL PEZ WHATLEY —vs— BLACK BART

BUZ TYLER —vs— R.P.M. DJ

DENNY BROWN —vs— R.P.M. LP

Ringside $7 Gen. Adm. $6 Children Under 10, $3
Box Office 255-5771 Mon.-Fri. 10-5:30, Sat. 11-4, Day of Match 1:00 P.M.
No Checks or Credit Cards Day of Match. Matches subject to change.

WIDE WORLD WRESTLING ON WLOS-TV 13 SUNDAY 12 NOON

186

Ron Garvin defeated Bob Roop
Thunderbolt Patterson fought Arn Anderson to a no contest

JCP @ Richmond, VA - Coliseum - April 27, 1985
Denny Brown fought John Tatum to a draw
NWA US Champion Magnum TA defeated Nikita Koloff
Jimmy Valiant defeated Superstar Billy Graham via
disqualification
Buzz Tyler defeated Ivan Koloff
Don Kernodle defeated Krusher Kruschev
Buddy Landell defeated Sam Houston
Black Bart defeated Rocky Kernodle
Tully Blanchard defeated NWA TV Champion Dusty Rhodes
via disqualification

**JCP @ Asheville, NC - Civic Center - April 28, 1985
(matinee)**
Denny Brown vs. LP
Buzz Tyler vs. DJ
Pez Whatley vs. Black Bart
Don Kernodle vs. NWA Tag Team Champion Nikita Koloff
Ole & Arn Anderson vs. Manny Fernandez & Thunderbolt
Patterson
NWA US Champion Magnum TA vs. Buddy Landell (No DQ)
Jimmy Valiant vs. Superstar Billy Graham (Texas Death
Match)

Mid South @ Oklahoma City, OK - April 28, 1985
NWA World Champion Ric Flair defeated Jake Roberts

**JCP @ Marietta, GA - Cobb County Civic Center - April 28,
1985**
The Italian Stallion defeated Kim Duk
The Barbarian defeated Johnny Weaver
Ron Starr defeated Rocky King
Pez Whatley fought Bob Roop to a draw
Ron Garvin defeated Scott Irwin
Buzz Tyler defeated Khrusher Khruschev

JCP @ Charlotte, NC - Coliseum - April 28, 1985
Jimmy Valiant defeated Superstar Billy Graham in a martial
arts match
Don Kernodle defeated Krusher Kruschev
Buzz Tyler fought Ron Bass to a draw
Ole & Arn Anderson defeated Thunderbolt Patterson & Manny
Fernandez; stipulations stated if Ole's team won then Arn
would win Thunderbolt's half of the National Tag Team
Champions and if Thunderbolt's team won then Fernandez
would win the belt
NWA US Champion Magnum TA & Dick Slater defeated NWA
Tag Team Champions Ivan & Nikita Koloff via disqualification
Tully Blanchard pinned NWA TV Champion Dusty Rhodes to
win the title after hitting him over the head with a foreign object,
thrown to him by Baby Doll, moments after referee Tommy

Young was knocked down; Rhodes feet were on the ropes
during the cover but the dazed Young didn't notice them

**JCP @ Fayetteville, NC - Cumberland County Memorial
Arena - April 29, 1985**
Ron Bass vs. Gene Ligon
Mark Fleming vs. Black Bart
Don & Rocky Kernodle vs. NWA Tag Team Champions Ivan &
Nikita Koloff
Jimmy Valiant vs. Superstar Billy Graham (Texas Death
Match)

**JCP @ Greenville, SC - Memorial Auditorium - April 29,
1985**
Stoney Burke defeated the Golden Terror
Ricky Reeves defeated Doug Vines
Buddy Landell defeated Sam Houston
NWA US Champion Magnum TA defeated Scott Irwin
Manny Fernandez & Thunderbolt Patterson defeated NWA
National Tag Team Champions Ole & Arn Anderson via
disqualification
Dusty Rhodes defeated NWA TV Champion Tully Blanchard in
a non-title match

JCP @ Vineland, NJ - High School - April 29, 1985
Included Ron Garvin, Bob Roop, Mid-Atlantic Heavyweight
Champion Buzz Tyler, Krusher Kruschev, the Rock 'n' Roll
RPMs, Pez Whatley, and Rocky Jones

JCP @ Philadelphia, PA - Civic Center - April 30, 1985
Denny Brown fought John Tatum to a draw
Buzz Tyler & Pez Whatley defeated the Rock 'n' Roll RPMs
Krusher Kruschev defeated Denny Brown
National Heavyweight Champion Ron Garvin defeated Bob
Roop
Manny Fernandez & Thunderbolt Patterson defeated National
Tag Team Champions Ole & Arn Anderson via disqualification
Dusty Rhodes defeated NWA TV Champion Tully Blanchard in
a non-title steel cage match

**JCP @ Spartanburg, SC - Memorial Auditorium - April 30,
1985**
TV taping:
NWA US Champion Magnum TA vs. Ivan Koloff
Also included Dusty Rhodes, NWA TV Champion Tully
Blanchard, Nikita Koloff, Superstar Billy Graham, Paul Jones,
Jimmy Valiant, JJ Dillon, and Thunderbolt Patterson

Mid South @ Shreveport, LA - April 30, 1985
NWA World Champion Ric Flair defeated Terry Taylor

JCP @ Trenton, NJ - CYO Building - May 1, 1985
Denny Brown defeated LP
Stoney Burke fought John Tatum to a draw

187

Buzz Tyler defeated Krusher Kruschev via disqualification
Pez Whatley defeated Bob Roop
Thunderbolt Patterson & Manny Fernandez defeated National Tag Team Champions Arn & Ole Anderson via disqualification
National Heavyweight Champion Ron Garvin defeated NWA TV Champion Tully Blanchard

JCP @ Marion, OH - County Fairgrounds Coliseum - May 1, 1985
Included Dusty Rhodes, Superstar Billy Graham, and Dick Slater

JCP @ Columbia, SC - May 2, 1985
Pat Tanaka fought Ron Starr to a draw
Sam Houston defeated Doug Vines
Black Bart defeated Johnny Weaver
Ron Bass defeated Rocky Kernodle
Nikita Koloff defeated Don Kernodle
NWA US Champion Magnum TA defeated Buddy Landell

JCP @ Pittsburgh, PA - May 2, 1985
Pez Whatley defeated LP
Denny Brown defeated John Tatum
Krusher Kruschev defeated Stoney Burke
Buzz Tyler fought Bob Roop to a draw
National Tag Team Champions Arn & Ole Anderson defeated Thunderbolt Patterson & Manny Fernandez
National Heavyweight Champion Ron Garvin defeated NWA TV Champion Tully Blanchard via disqualification

Mid South @ Houston, TX - May 3, 1985
NWA World Champion Ric Flair defeated Terry Taylor

JCP @ Columbus, OH - Fairgrounds - May 3, 1985
Included Dusty Rhodes, Ivan Koloff, Arn & Ole Anderson, and Manny Fernandez

JCP @ Bassett, VA - High School Gym - May 3, 1985

Worldwide - 5/4/85:
NWA US Champion Magnum TA vs. Doug Vines
The Barbarian vs. Gene Ligon
Ron Bass vs. Rocky King
Don Kernodle vs. Ben Alexander
Ivan & Nikita Koloff vs. Mark Fleming & Ron Rossi

Mid South @ Jackson, MS - May 4, 1985
Kerry Von Erich vs. NWA World Champion Ric Flair

JCP @ Atlanta, GA - WTBS Studios - May 1985
World Championship Wrestling - 5/4/85 - featured an opening segment with Tony Schiavone, David Crockett, NWA World Champion Ric Flair, and NWA US Champion Magnum TA in

which Flair made fun of Magnum's wardrobe and said he was the most recognizable sports personality in the world today; moments later, Magnum said he was the top contender and would soon face Flair in the ring; included Schiavone conducting an interview with the new NWA National Tag Team Champions Ole & Arn Anderson in which Ole said they would face anyone who wanted a shot; featured Schiavone conducting an interview with NWA TV Champion Tully Blanchard, with Baby Doll, regarding his title win over Dusty Rhodes:
Ron Bass vs. Gene Ligon
Jimmy Valiant vs. Randy Barber
Tully Blanchard vs. Dale Williams
Black Bart vs. Ken Glover
NWA US Champion Magnum TA vs. the Golden Terror
NWA World Champion Ric Flair defeated Rocky King; after the bout, Flair confronted NWA US Champion Magnum TA, said he was going to Florida next week to beat anyone they've got, and then challenged Magnum then and there; Magnum then took off his vest and slid in the ring; Flair soon followed but then walked off and said he didn't think Magnum was ready to be embarassed on national TV
Ole & Arn Anderson vs. Gerald Finley & Richard Dye
Pez Whatley vs. Jeff Sword
NWA Tag Team Champion Nikita Koloff vs. Alan Martin

JCP @ Greensboro, NC - Coliseum - May 4, 1985 (4,721)
Pat Tanaka defeated John Tatum
Buddy Landell defeated Ron Starr
Black Bart defeated Rocky Kernodle
Nikita Koloff defeated Don Kernodle
Buzz Tyler defeated Ron Bass
Dusty Rhodes defeated NWA TV Champion Tully Blanchard
NWA US Champion Magnum TA defeated Wahoo McDaniel

Mid South @ Jackson, MS - May 4, 1985
NWA World Champion Ric Flair vs. Kerry Von Erich

JCP @ Cincinnati, OH - May 4, 1985
Ricky Reeves defeated Kim Duk
Joel Deaton defeated Stoney Burke
Scott Irwin defeated the Italian Stallion
Buzz Tyler defeated Ivan Koloff
Manny Fernandez & Thunderbolt Patterson defeated National Tag Team Champions Arn & Ole Anderson

WCCW Parade of Champions II - Irving, TX - Texas Stadium - May 5, 1985 (26,153)
Kerry Von Erich (w/ Fritz Von Erich) defeated the One Man Gang (w/ Gary Hart) in a hair vs. hair match
Tommy Rogers & Bobby Fulton (w/ Little John) defeated Bobby Eaton & Dennis Condrey (w/ Jim Cornette) in a No DQ 2-ring match at 8:29; Cornette and John sat together at ringside for the match; Eaton & Condrey originally won the match and titles when Condrey pinned Fulton after Cornette hit Fulton with his tennis racquet but the second referee counted

Rogers covering Eaton with a roll up seconds later in the opposite ring; after some confusion, it was finally announced there were simultaneous pinfalls and the Fantastics were the winners; due to pre-match stipulations, Rogers & Fulton won the vacant American Tag Team Titles (*The Triumph & Tragedy of World Class Championship Wrestling*)
NWA World Champion Ric Flair fought Kevin Von Erich to a double count-out at 22:00
Kerry, Kevin, & Mike Von Erich, Michael Hayes, Terry Gordy, & Buddy Roberts defeated Chris Adams, Gino Hernandez, Rip Oliver, the One Man Gang, Kamala, & Steve Williams (w/ Skandar Akbar & Gary Hart); stipulations stated the winning team would split $100,000 and that the man to make the last elimination would win a new Lincoln Continental; Kevin pinned Williams to win the match; after the contest, Hernandez destroyed the car's windsheild with a chain

JCP @ Stuebenville, OH - May 5, 1985
Ricky Reeves defeated Kim Duk
The Italian Stallion fought Scott Irwin to a draw
Krusher Kruschev defeated Stoney Burke
Buzz Tyler defeated Ivan Koloff
Manny Fernandez & Thunderbolt Patterson defeated National Tag Team Champions Ole & Arn Anderson via disqualification

WCCW @ Dallas, TX - May 6, 1985
Kerry Von Erich defeated NWA World Champion Ric Flair via disqualification

CWF @ Ft. Myers, FL - May 6, 1985
Wahoo McDaniel vs. NWA World Champion Ric Flair

JCP @ Greenville, SC - May 6, 1985
Black Bart defeated Sam Houston
Ron Bass fought Buzz Tyler to a draw
Buddy Landell defeated Pez Whatley
Jimmy Valiant & Dick Slater defeated the Barbarian & Superstar Billy Graham
NWA TV Champion Tully Blanchard defeated Ron Garvin
NWA US Champion Magnum TA defeated Nikita Koloff via disqualification

JCP @ Spartanburg, SC - Memorial Auditorium - May 7, 1985
TV taping:
NWA US Champion Magnum TA vs. NWA Tag Team Champion Ivan Koloff

JCP @ Allentown, PA - Agricultural Hall - May 7, 1985
Scott Irwin vs. the Italian Stallion
Kareem Muhammad vs. Ron Starr
Buzz Sawyer vs. Krusher Kruschev
Manny Fernandez vs. National Tag Team Champion Arn Anderson (No DQ)

JCP @ Gainesville, GA - Georgia Mountains Center - May 7, 1985

CWF @ Tampa, FL - Sun Dome - May 7, 1985
Jay Youngblood defeated Jack Hart
Tiger Conway Jr. defeated Dale Veasey
Scott McGhee defeated Mike Golden
Brian Blair fought Rip Rogers to a time-limit draw
Southern Heavyweight Champion Hector Guerrero defeated Bill Irwin
Bugsy McGraw defeated the Missing Link
Wahoo McDaniel & Blackjack Mulligan defeated Jesse Barr & Bill Irwin (sub. for Rick Rude)
Kerry Von Erich defeated NWA World Champion Ric Flair via disqualification at 31:39 after Flair attacked an interfering Scott McGhee

JCP @ Raleigh, NC - Dorton Arena - May 8, 1985
NWA Tag Team Champions Ivan & Nikita Koloff defeated Dick Slater & Don Kernodle
Pat Tanaka fought Denny Brown to a draw
Pez Whatley defeated Black Bart
Buddy Landell defeated Sam Houston
Jimmy Valiant defeated Superstar Billy Graham in a Texas Death Match
Mid-Atlantic Heavyweight Champion Buzz Tyler defeated Ron Bass via disqualification
NWA US Champion Magnum TA fought NWA TV Champion Tully Blanchard to a no contest; only Blanchard's title was at stake in the match

CWF @ Miami Beach, FL - Convention Hall - May 8, 1985 (3,541)
Scott McGhee defeated Mike Golden
Tiger Conway Jr. defeated Jack Hart
The Missing Link defeated Bugsy McGraw
Hector Guerrero defeated Bill Irwin
Brian Blair fought Rip Rogers to a draw
Wahoo McDaniel & Blackjack Mulligan defeated Hercules Hernandez & Jesse Barr
Kerry Von Erich defeated NWA World Champion Ric Flair via disqualification when Flair hit the referee

JCP @ Norfolk, VA - May 9, 1985
Pez Whatley defeated Black Bart
Mark Fleming defeated DJ
Ron Bass defeated Buzz Tyler
NWA US Champion Magnum TA defeated Buddy Landell
Dick Slater & Jimmy Valiant defeated Superstar Billy Graham & the Barbarian
NWA Tag Team Champions Ivan & Nikita Koloff defeated Don & Rocky Kernodle

JCP @ Blackwood, NJ - Highland High School Gym - May 9, 1985
TV taping:
Superstar Billy Graham vs. Gene Ligon

JCP @ Richmond, VA - Coliseum - May 10, 1985
RPM defeated Stoney Burke
Buddy Landell defeated Don Kernodle
Dick Slater defeated the Barbarian
NWA TV Champion Tully Blanchard defeated NWA US Champion Magnum TA; only the TV title was at stake
Jimmy Valiant defeated Superstar Billy Graham in a steel cage match

CWF @ Orlando, FL - May 10, 1985
Tiger Conway Jr. fought Rip Rogers to a draw
Bill Irwin defeated Scott McGhee
Wahoo McDaniel & Blackjack Mulligan fought Abdullah the Butcher & the Missing Link to a draw
Hector Guerrero defeated Jesse Barr
Brian Blair defeated Rick Rude
NWA World Champion Ric Flair defeated Mike Graham

Worldwide - 5/11/85:
Dick Slater & Jimmy Valiant vs. Ron Rossi & the Golden Terror
Superstar Billy Graham vs. Gene Ligon
Buddy Landell vs. Mark Fleming
Nikita Koloff vs. Rocky King
NWA TV Champion Tully Blanchard vs. Don Kernodle
Manny Fernandez vs. Gene Ligon

JCP @ Atlanta, GA - WTBS Studios - May 1985
World Championship Wrestling - 5/11/85 - featured David

Crockett conducting an interview with NWA US Champion Magnum TA about NWA World Champion Ric Flair refusing to face him the previous week; moments later, Flair interrupted and said Magnum tried to embarass him without first paying his dues; Flair then told Magnum he would let him know when he was ready for a shot at the world title, with Magnum then reminding Flair he walked out last week after Magnum accepted his challenge; Flair then noted Magnum's belt was silver while Flair's was gold and he would get a title shot when Flair deemed him worthy; Magnum then said he would show Flair what he could do whenever they did face off in the ring; included Tony Schiavone conducting a closing interview with NWA National Tag Team Champions Ole & Arn Anderson regarding their controversial win earlier in the show, during which Ole said he was sick of being nice to Thunderbolt Patterson and he was at the top of their hit list
Ron Garvin vs. Larry Clark
Manny Fernandez vs. Paul Garner
NWA World Champion Ric Flair defeated Ron Rossi; after the bout, Tony Schiavone conducted an interview with Flair in which Flair said there was a misconception that pro wrestling was made up of clowns; Flair then mentioned Dusty Rhodes, NWA US Champion Magnum TA, Dick Slater, Manny Fernandez, Carlos Colon, Bob Armstrong, Harley Race, and the Von Erichs and said he was the best of the lot because he's got the belt
NWA US Champion Magnum TA vs. George South
Nikita Koloff vs. Kent Glover
Bob Roop, NWA National Tag Team Champions Ole & Arn Anderson defeated Buzz Sawyer, Pez Whatley, & the Italian Stallion
Thunderbolt Patterson vs. Randy Barber
Krusher Kruschev (w/ Ivan Koloff) vs. Alan Martin
Abdullah the Butcher (w/ Paul Jones) vs. Mack Jeffers
NWA TV Champion Tully Blanchard (w/ Baby Doll) vs. Jim Jeffers; prior to the bout, Schiavone conducted an interview with Blanchard, alongside Baby Doll, in which he said he would show just why he held a world title

JCP @ Charlotte, NC - Coliseum - May 11, 1985
The Barbarian defeated Sam Houston
Buddy Landell defeated Johnny Weaver
Dusty Rhodes defeated Scott Irwin
National Tag Team Champions Ole & Arn Anderson defeated Buzz Sawyer & Pez Whatley
NWA TV Champion Tully Blanchard defeated Manny Fernandez
Jimmy Valiant defeated Superstar Billy Graham in a New York streetfight
NWA US Champion Magnum TA & Dick Slater fought NWA Tag Team Champions Ivan & Nikita Koloff

CWF @ St. Petersburg, FL - Bayfront Center - May 11, 1985
Scott McGhee defeated Jack Hart
Tiger Conway Jr. defeated Rip Rogers
The Missing Link defeated Bugsy McGraw
Hector Guerrero fought Bill Irwin to a draw

Mike Graham & Brian Blair defeated Hercules Hernandez (sub. for Rick Rude) & Jesse Barr
Blackjack Mulligan fought Abdullah the Butcher to a double disqualification
NWA World Champion Ric Flair defeated Wahoo McDaniel

JCP @ Atlanta, GA - Omni - May 12, 1985
The Barbarian defeated Sam Houston
Superstar Billy Graham defeated the Italian Stallion
Buzz Sawyer fought Krusher Kruschev to a draw
NWA US Champion Magnum TA defeated John Tatum
Tully Blanchard defeated National Heavyweight Champion Ron Garvin
Jimmy Valiant fought Abdullah the Butcher (w/ Paul Jones) to a no contest
Thunderbolt Patterson & Manny Fernandez defeated National Tag Team Champions Ole & Arn Anderson
Dusty Rhodes & Dick Slater (mystery partner) defeated NWA Tag Team Champions Ivan & Nikita Koloff

JCP @ Sumter, SC - County Exhibition Center - May 12, 1985
Rocky King vs. Joel Deaton
Ricky Reeves vs. Pat Tanaka
Rocky Kernodle vs. Black Bart
Don Kernodle vs. Buddy Landell
Denny Brown & Stoney Burke vs. the Rock 'n Roll RPMs
Buzz Tyler vs. NWA Mid Atlantic Heavyweight Champion Ron Bass

Central States @ St. Louis, MO - May 12, 1985
NWA World Champion Ric Flair pinned Kevin Von Erich at 21:46

JCP @ Greenville, SC - May 13, 1985
Rocky King defeated the Golden Terror
Stoney Burke defeated Doug Vines
Krusher Kruschev defeated Ricky Reeves
Ivan Koloff defeated Joe Lightfoot
Dick Slater defeated the Barbarian
Jimmy Valiant defeated Superstar Billy Graham

Continental @ Birmingham, AL - May 13, 1985
NWA World Champion Ric Flair defeated Bob Armstrong

JCP @ Fayetteville, NC - Cumberland County Memorial Arena - May 13, 1985
Buddy Landel vs. Gene Ligon
Black Bart vs. Sam Houston
Ron Bass vs. Buzz Tyler
NWA US Champion Magnum TA vs. NWA Tag Team Champion Nikita Koloff
Dusty Rhodes vs. NWA TV Champion Tully Blanchard (60-minute time-limit)

Continental @ Florence, AL - May 14, 1985
NWA World Champion Ric Flair vs. Bob Armstrong

CWF @ Tampa, FL - May 14, 1985
Jay Youngblood defeated NWA World Champion Ric Flair

JCP @ Raleigh, NC - Dorton Arena - May 15, 1985
Buzz Tyler defeated Ron Bass
Buddy Landell defeated Gene Ligon
Krusher Kruschev defeated Sam Houston
Jimmy Valiant defeated Superstar Billy Graham
Dusty Rhodes defeated Tully Blanchard via disqualification
NWA Tag Team Champions Ivan & Nikita Koloff defeated NWA US Champion Magnum TA & Dick Slater

CWF @ Miami Beach, FL - Convention Hall - May 15, 1985 (3,051)
Dale Veasey defeated Jack Hart
Scott McGhee defeated Rip Rogers
Jesse Barr & Hercules Hernandez defeated Brian Blair & Tiger Conway Jr.
Bill Irwin defeated Hector Guerrero
Blackjack Mulligan & Bugsy McGraw defeated Abdullah the Butcher & the Missing Link
Wahoo McDaniel defeated NWA World Champion Ric Flair via disqualification

JCP @ Wheeling, WV - May 17, 1985
Scott Irwin defeated Joel Deaton
The Italian Stallion defeated Mike Davis via disqualification
Buzz Sawyer defeated Tommy Lane
Pez Whatley fought Bob Roop to a draw
Ron Garvin defeated John Tatum
Manny Fernandez & Thunderbolt Patterson defeated National Tag Team Champions Ole & Arn Anderson

Worldwide - 5/18/85:
Superstar Billy Graham & the Barbarian vs. Pat Tanaka & Mark Fleming
Ron Bass vs. Ron Rossi
Jimmy Valiant vs. Ben Alexander
Buzz Tyler vs. Doug Vines
Krusher Kruschev, Ivan & Nikita Koloff vs. Sam Houston, Ricky Reeves, & Stony Burks

World Championship Wrestling - 5/18/85 - featured Tony Schiavone conducting an opening interview with NWA US Champion Magnum TA, with NWA World Champion Ric Flair then interrupting and saying Magnum could watch him in action later in the show if he stuck around long enough; after Flair left, Magnum said the contract had been signed and Flair would have to prove himself against Magnum in the ring:
NWA Tag Team Champions Ivan & Nikita Koloff vs. two unknowns
Dick Slater vs. the Golden Terror

Black Bart vs. an unknown
Ron Bass vs. an unknown
NWA TV Champion Tully Blanchard vs. an unknown
NWA World Champion Ric Flair defeated Sam Houston via submission with the figure-4; after the bout, Flair shoved away referee Tommy Young and kept the hold applied; moments later, Flair took Houston's boot off and reapplied the hold until NWA US Champion Magnum TA - who provided guest commentary for the match - pulled Houston away and faced off with Flair both in and outside the ring; moments later, Jimmy Valiant appeared and said he wanted to see a match between Flair and Magnum
Abdullah the Butcher (w/ Paul Jones) vs. an unknown
NWA US Champion Magnum TA vs. an unknown
Buddy Landell vs. an unknown
Jimmy Valiant vs. an unknown

JCP @ Greensboro, NC - Coliseum - May 18, 1985 (3,758)
Ricky Reeves defeated Doug Vines
Pat Tanaka fought Denny Brown to a draw
Black Bart defeated Sam Houston
Ron Bass defeated Stoney Burke
NWA US Champion Magnum TA defeated Buddy Landell
Jimmy Valiant defeated Superstar Billy Graham
NWA TV Champion Tully Blanchard defeated Dusty Rhodes
NWA Tag Team Champions Ivan & Nikita Koloff defeated Dick Slater & Buzz Tyler

JCP @ Asheville, NC - Civic Center - May 19, 1985 (matinee)
Sam Houston defeated Black Bart
Krusher Kruschev defeated Ricky Reeves
Ivan Koloff defeated Rocky Kernodle
Buzz Tyler defeated Mid-Atlantic Heavyweight Champion Ron Bass via disqualification
The Barbarian defeated Sam Houston
Jimmy Valiant defeated Superstar Billy Graham in a streetfight

Central States @ Des Moines, IA - May 19, 1985
NWA World Champion Ric Flair defeated Rufus R. Jones

JCP @ Columbia, SC - Township Auditorium - May 19, 1985
Buddy Landell defeated Stoney Burke
Black Bart defeated Ricky Reeves
Buzz Tyler defeated Ron Bass
Dick Slater defeated Ivan Koloff
NWA TV Champion Tully Blanchard defeated NWA US Champion Magnum TA
Dusty Rhodes defeated Nikita Koloff
Jimmy Valiant defeated Superstar Billy Graham in a streetfight

JCP @ Roanoke, VA - Civic Center - May 19, 1985
Gene Ligon defeated Mark Fleming
The Golden Terror defeated Gene Ligon

Buddy Landell defeated Stoney Burke
Denny Brown fought Pat Tanaka to a draw
Dick Slater defeated Nikita Koloff via disqualification
NWA US Champion Magnum TA fought NWA TV Champion Tully Blanchard to a no contest

WCCW @ Dallas, TX - May 20, 1985
Chris Adams defeated NWA World Champion Ric Flair via disqualification

JCP @ Greenville, SC - May 20, 1985
Superstar Billy Graham vs. Dick Slater

PNW @ Portland, OR - Memorial Coliseum - May 21, 1985
Owen Promotions 60th Anniversary
Cowboy Lang defeated Little Tokyo
Mega Maharishi defeated Billy Two Eagles
Jerry Grey defeated Rocky Venturo
Karl Steiner defeated Steve Simpson
Bobby Jaggers & Ricky Vaughn defeated Timothy Flowers & Chris Colt
Sgt. Slaughter defeated Kendo Nagasaki
Roddy Piper defeated Buddy Rose
Larry & Curt Hennig defeated AWA Tag Team Champions the Road Warriors (w/ Paul Ellering) via disqualification when Curt was illegally double teamed in the ring; after the match, Billy Jack made the save and helped Curt clear the ring of the Road Warriors
NWA World Champion Ric Flair fought Billy Jack to a 45-minute time-limit draw; the challenger attempted to apply the full nelson when the time limit expired (Jack's first appearance using Diana Ross' "Muscles" as his theme song)
AWA World Champion Rick Martel pinned Pacific Northwest Heavyweight Champion Mike Miller with a cradle at 7:20 as the challenger attempted to apply the Boston Crab

JCP @ Raleigh, NC - Dorton Arena - May 22, 1985
Buzz Tyler defeated Ron Bass
National Tag Team Champion Arn Anderson defeated Pez Whatley
Jimmy Valiant defeated the Barbarian
Manny Fernandez defeated National Tag Team Champion Ole Anderson via disqualification
Dick Slater & Buzz Sawyer defeated Ivan Koloff & Krusher Kruschev
NWA US Champion Magnum TA defeated NWA TV Champion Tully Blanchard via disqualification

Mid South @ Shreveport, LA - May 23, 1985
TV taping:
NWA World Champion Ric Flair defeated Wendell Cooley

JCP @ Norfolk, VA - Scope - May 23, 1985
Sam Houston defeated John Tatum
The Barbarian defeated Mark Fleming

Jimmy Valiant defeated Superstar Billy Graham in a New York streetfight
Pat Tanaka fought Denny Brown to a draw
National Tag Team Champions Ole & Arn Anderson defeated Manny Fernandez & Sam Houston
NWA TV Champion Tully Blanchard defeated NWA US Champion Magnum TA via disqualification

Central States @ Kansas City, KS - May 23, 1985
Harley Race & Bob Brown defeated NWA World Champion Ric Flair & Mr. Pogo

JCP @ Richmond, VA - Coliseum - May 24, 1985
Denny Brown defeated John Tatum
Buddy Landell defeated Keith Larsen
National Tag Team Champions Ole & Arn Anderson defeated Manny Fernandez & Sam Houston
NWA US Champion Magnum TA defeated NWA TV Champion Tully Blanchard
Dusty Rhodes & Jimmy Valiant defeated Superstar Billy Graham & the Barbarian in a streetfight

Worldwide - 5/25/85:
Krusher Kruschev, Ivan & Nikita Koloff vs. Pat Tanaka, Stony Burks, & Gene Ligon
Manny Fernandez vs. Joel Deaton
Ole & Arn Anderson vs. Denny Brown & George South
Pez Whatley & Thunderbolt Patterson vs. Doug Vines & Ron Rossi
Buddy Landell vs. Ricky Reeves
NWA TV Champion Tully Blanchard vs. Buzz Sawyer

JCP @ Atlanta, GA - WTBS Studios - May 1985
World Championship Wrestling - 5/25/85 - featured Tony Schiavone conducting an interview with NWA World Champion Ric Flair in which he ran down Dusty Rhodes, NWA US Champion Magnum TA, Dick Slater, Billy Jack Haynes, Harley Race, and Thunderbolt Patterson and noted he would be in Huntington, WV, Pittsburg, PA, Philadelphia, PA, Greensboro, NC, and Columbia, SC over the next two weeks and invited all those who doubted him to see him in the ring; included Schiavone conducting an interview with NWA National Tag Team Champions Ole & Arn Anderson in which Ole noted Andre the Giant, Bruno Sammartino, Wahoo McDaniel, and Bill Watts had all been beaten by the Andersons and Thunderbolt Patterson would have the same fate; during the segment, Arn referred to them as the Anderson brothers:
Ivan Koloff & Krusher Kruschev (w/ Nikita Koloff) vs. Pat Dye & an unknown
The Italian Stallion vs. Terry Flynn
NWA TV Champion Tully Blanchard defeated Stoney Burke; after the bout, Blanchard & Baby Doll confronted Dusty Rhodes, who provided guest commentary for the match; after they walked off, Rhodes said he would slap Baby Doll and she wasn't a lady
Thunderbolt Patterson vs. Joel Deaton

Black Bart vs. Ricky Reeves
NWA National Heavyweight Champion Ron Garvin vs. Ron Bass (w/ JJ Dillon)
NWA National Tag Team Champions Ole & Arn Anderson vs. Vernon Deaton & Mike Simani
NWA US Champion Magnum TA vs. Paul Garner; after the bout, Magnum confronted NWA World Champion Ric Flair, with Flair telling Magnum he had a lot going for him but he needed to dress the part if he wanted to be a real man; moments later, Magnum grabbed Flair by the tie, with Flair then undressing to seemingly face Magnum in the ring but Flair backed off; moments later, Flair eventually got in the ring, jumped Magnum, and rubbed Magnum's face into the mat; Flair the continued to assault Magnum before leaving the ring
Buzz Sawyer vs. Randy Barber

Central States @ Ft. Scott, KS - May 25, 1985
NWA World Champion Ric Flair vs. Marty Jannetty

JCP @ Wilson, NC - Fleming Stadium - May 25, 1985
Ben Alexander defeated Doug Vines
Denny Brown fought Pat Tanaka to a draw
Rocky Kernodle & Mark Fleming defeated the Rock 'n' Roll RPMs
Pez Whatley defeated the Barbarian
Jimmy Valiant defeated Superstar Billy Graham in a streetfight

JCP @ Fayetteville, NC - Cumberland County Memorial Arena - May 26, 1985
Buddy Landel vs. Sam Houston
Denny Brown vs. Pat Tanaka
Don Kernodle & Dick Slater vs. NWA Tag Team Champions Ivan & Nikita Koloff
NWA World Champion Ric Flair & Jimmy Valiant vs. Superstar Billy Graham & the Barbarian
NWA US Champion Magnum TA vs. NWA TV Champion Tully Blanchard (only the TV title at stake)

JCP @ Greensboro, NC - Coliseum - May 26, 1985 (3,961)
Sam Houston defeated Joel Deaton
Buddy Landell defeated Denny Brown
NWA Tag Team Champions Ivan & Nikita Koloff defeated Rocky Kernodle & Pat Tanaka
NWA World Champion Ric Flair fought NWA US Champion Magnum TA to a 60-minute time-limit draw
NWA TV Champion Tully Blanchard defeated Dick Slater
Dusty Rhodes & Jimmy Valiant defeated Superstar Billy Graham & the Barbarian

JCP @ Fayetteville, NC - Cumberland County Memorial Arena - May 26, 1985
Buddy Landell vs. Sam Houston
Denny Brown vs. Pat Tanaka
Don Kernodle & Dick Slater vs. NWA Tag Team Champions Ivan & Nikita Koloff

NWA World Champion Ric Flair & Jimmy Valiant vs. Superstar Billy Graham & the Barbarian
NWA TV Champion Tully Blanchard vs. NWA US Champion Magnum TA (only the TV title at stake)

JCP @ Greenville, SC - May 27, 1985
Scott Irwin defeated Rocky King
Sam Houston defeated John Tatum
The Italian Stallion defeated Bob Roop
Buzz Sawyer defeated Khrusher Kruschev
Ron Garvin defeated Buddy Landell via disqualification
Pat Tanaka fought Denny Brown to a 20-minute time-limit draw
Buzz Tyler defeated Ron Bass

JCP @ Pittsburgh, PA - Three Rivers Stadium - May 27, 1985
The Barbarian pinned Ricky Reeves at 7:45
DJ pinned Stoney Burke at 10:25
NWA National Tag Team Champions Ole & Arn Anderson defeated Thunderbolt Patterson & Pez Whatley at 12:52 when Arn pinned Whatley
Manny Fernandez & Dick Slater defeated NWA Tag Team Champions Ivan & Nikita Koloff via disqualification at 17:22
Dusty Rhodes fought NWA TV Champion Tully Blanchard to a double count-out at 5:35
Jimmy Valian pinned Superstar Billy Graham at 6:10
NWA World Champion Ric Flair defeated NWA US Champion Magnum TA via disqualification at 56:00

JCP @ Altoona, PA - Jaffa Mosque - May 28, 1985
Jimmy Jackson defeated Yukon Eric
Scott Irwin defeated Mike Donatelli
Ricky Reeves defeated Tommy Lane
Mike Davis defeated Stoney Burke
Buzz Tyler defeated the Barbarian via disqualification
Jimmy Valiant defeated Superstar Billy Graham

JCP @ Marietta, GA - Cobb County Civic Center - May 28, 1985
Possibly canceled
Included Buzz Sawyer and Krusher Kruschev

JCP @ Lansing, MI - May 28, 1985
The Italian Stallion defeated John Tatum
Pez Whatley fought Bob Roop to a draw
Buzz Sawyer defeated Krusher Kruschev
Ron Garvin defeated Black Bart via disqualification
National Tag Team Champions Ole & Arn Anderson defeated Thunderbolt Patterson & Manny Fernandez

JCP @ Raleigh, NC - Dorton Arena - May 29, 1985
Sam Houston defeated Joel Deaton
Pat Tanaka fought Denny Brown to a draw
Buddy Landell defeated Rocky King
Ron Bass defeated Rocky Kernodle
NWA US Champion Magnum TA & Dick Slater defeated NWA Tag Team Champions Ivan & Nikita Koloff via disqualification
NWA World Champion Ric Flair defeated NWA TV Champion Tully Blanchard

Mid South @ Shreveport, LA - May 30, 1985
TV taping:
NWA World Champion Ric Flair vs. Terry Daniels

JCP @ Charleston, SC - County Hall - May 31, 1985
Rock 'n' Roll RPMs vs. Burke & Reeves
Denny Brown vs. Pat Tanaka
The Barbarian vs. ?
Buzz Tyler vs. Ron Bass
Jimmy Valiant vs. Superstar Billy Graham (streetfight)

Worldwide - 6/1/85:
Sam Houston vs. Ron Rossi
Ron Bass vs. David Diamond
Ivan & Nikita Koloff vs. Pat Tanaka & Rocky Kernodle
NWA US Champion Magnum TA vs. George South
Buddy Landell vs. Denny Brown
Buzz Sawyer vs. Doug Vines
Abdullah the Butcher vs. Gene Ligon

World Championship Wrestling - 6/1/85 - featured Tony Schiavone conducting an interview with NWA National Tag Team Champions Ole & Arn Anderson in which Arn said a lot

of men were saying they could beat the Andersons but it was all talk and Ole said Buzz Sawyer couldn't be a pimple on a hog's butt:
Buzz Sawyer & Ron Garvin vs. Mike Simani & Randy Barber
NWA US Champion Magnum TA vs. Larry Clark
NWA World Champion Ric Flair defeated George South; prior to the bout, Tony Schiavone conducted an interview with Flair in which Flair insulted Dick Slater, Harley Race, Dusty Rhodes, NWA US Champion Magnum TA, Kerry Von Erich, and Ron Garvin; moments later, Flair introduced a video clip that showcased his wins over Race at Starrcade 83, Kerry Von Erich in Japan, and Rhodes at Starrcade 84; Flair then said the greatest night in his life was laying out Magnum the previous week; Flair then pulled out a $1,500 suit he had personally made for Magnum to try to give him some class; after the contest, Magnum came in the ring with the suit and then tore it up in front of him; Flair then went to turn away but rushed Magnum and sustained the belly to belly suplex; Magnum then grabbed the world title belt, walked over to Tony Schiavone, and said he was leaving Flair's belt for him and the next time he saw the belt it would be his; Flair then yelled at Schiavone & Crockett and said no one touches his belt without earning it
Black Bart vs. Jim Jeffers
NWA TV Champion Tully Blanchard (w/ Baby Doll) vs. Paul Garner
NWA National Tag Team Champions Ole & Arn Anderson vs. Alan Martin & Mark Cooper; moments later, Buzz Sawyer came out to replace one of the Andersons' opponents; Sawyer was eventually double teamed until Dick Slater came out to make the save

JCP @ Atlanta, GA - WTBS Studios - June 1, 1985
World Championship Wrestling - 6/8/85 - featured Tony Schiavone conducting an interview with NWA World Champion Ric Flair in which Flair insulted Dusty Rhodes, Manny Fernandez, and NWA US Champion Magnum TA and said all the ladies asked "Rambo who?" when Flair walked through the airport and it took both Linda Carter and Bo Derek to make him flinch; he then noted he was heading to Wheeling, WV, Philadelphia, PA, and Greensboro, NC; Flair then took a parting shot at Buddy Landell; included Schiavone conducting an interview with NWA TV Champion Tully Blanchard, alongside Baby Doll and Abdullah the Butcher, in which Blanchard noted the injury Baby Doll gave Dusty Rhodes earlier in the show and how that wouldn't compare to what Abdullah would do to him; featured Schiavone conducting an interview with NWA National Tag Team Champion Arn Anderson in which he said NWA National Tag Team Champion Ole Anderson couldn't be there this week but Arn was sure Ole was proud of what he did to Brett Sawyer earlier in the show; included Schiavone conducting a closing interview with Flair in which Flair said pro wrestling wasn't rock 'n' roll and it wasn't Hollywood; Flair then said he would make Nikita Koloff his personal gardner if he didn't stop calling him out, he would take out Magnum, and told Landell in the ring that he would make himself available if Landell wanted a shot:
Manny Fernandez vs. George South
NWA US Champion Magnum TA vs. Mike Simani

NWA TV Champion Tully Blanchard (w/ Baby Doll) defeated Mark Hawk; after the bout, Dusty Rhodes came into the ring, with Baby Doll scratching Rhodes in the eye and allowing Blanchard to jump him
Buzz Sawyer vs. Joel Deaton
National Tag Team Champion Arn Anderson defeated Larry Clarke; after the bout, Anderson confronted Brett Sawyer, asking where Buzz Sawyer was; moments later, Arn took a cheap shot at Brett, with Brett then getting in the ring and challenging Arn to a fight; after a brawl, Anderson sent Sawyer falling out to the floor and followed with a gordbuster on the concrete and then a kick to the head; Dick Slater then came out to check on Sawyer, with Arn jumping him from behind and the two brawling in the ring until Anderson slid to the floor; Buzz then came out screaming at Arn while checking on Brett
Nikita Koloff vs. Rocky King
Black Bart pinned National Heavyweight Champion Ron Garvin to win the title in a loser leaves town match at 11:02 after hitting him with a loaded elbow pad
Dick Slater vs. Paul Garner
Thunderbolt Patterson, Pez Whatley, & the Italian Stallion vs. Randy Barber & the Rock 'n' Roll RPMs
Abdullah the Butcher vs. Mike Nichols
Ivan Koloff vs. the Green Shadow
Buddy Landell vs. Gerald Finley

JCP @ Cinncinati, OH - June 1, 1985
Buzz Sawyer vs. Nikita Koloff

JCP @ Charlotte, NC - Coliseum - June 1, 1985
Pat Tanaka defeated Doug Vines
Kendo Nagasaki defeated Ricky Reeves
Sam Houston defeated Joel Deaton
Buddy Landell defeated Gene Ligon
Buzz Tyler defeated Ron Bass
Jimmy Valiant & Dick Slater defeated Superstar Billy Graham & the Barbarian
NWA US Champion Magnum TA fought NWA TV Champion Tully Blanchard to a draw
Dusty Rhodes defeated Abdullah the Butcher

Mid South @ New Orleans, LA - Superdome - June 1, 1985 (11,000)
Dutch Mantell pinned Mark Ragin
The Nightmare (Randy Culley) pinned Frankie Lane
Wendell Cooley defeated Eddie Gilbert via disqualification
The Barbarian pinned Pat Rose
Bill Dundee pinned Tom Prichard
Michael Hayes & Buddy Roberts defeated Brad Armstrong & Brickhouse Brown
Mid South TV Champion the Snowman (w/ Muhammad Ali & Bundini Brown) pinned Jake Roberts (w/ Nord the Barbarian) with a powerslam at 10:37 after Ali repeatedly punched Roberts and Nord in the face from the ring apron; prior to the bout, Ernie Ladd helped escort Ali ringside (*Legends of Mid South Wrestling*)

WIDE WORLD WRESTLING

SUNDAY, JUNE 2, 1985
TRIPLE MAIN EVENT
Asheville Civic Center

RIC

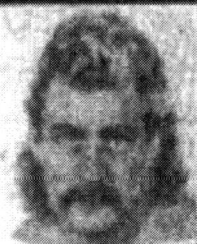
MAGNUM

NWA WORLD TITLE MATCH
(NATURE BOY)
RIC FLAIR
—VS—
MAGNUM T.A.

WORLD T.V. TITLE
(RETURN MATCH)

T.V. CHAMP
WITH BABY DOLL
TULLY BLANCHARD
—VS—
(AMERICAN DREAM)
DUSTY RHODES

TULLY

DUSTY

GRUDGE MATCH
JIMMY VALIANT
&
RAGIN' BULL—VS—
SUPERSTAR BILLY GRAHAM
&
(WITH PAUL JONES)
THE BARBARIAN

MID-ATL TITLE MATCH
BUZZ TYLER—VS—
RON BASS
ALSO
DENNY BROWN —VS—
KENDO NAGASAKI
SAM HOUSTON —VS—
THE ELIMINATOR

SUPERSTAR

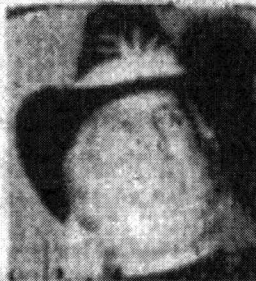
JIMMY

Ringside $7 Gen. Adm. $6 Children Under 10, $3
Box Office 255-5771 Mon.-Fri. 10-5:30, Sat. 11-4, Day of Match 1:00 P.M.
No Checks or Credit Cards Day of Match. Matches subject to change.

WIDE WORLD WRESTLING ON WLOS-TV 13 SUNDAY 12 NOON

NWA World Champion Ric Flair pinned Terry Taylor at 39:44 with a roll over and grabbing the tights for leverage; Boyd Pierce was the ring announcer for the match (*Legends of Mid South Wrestling*)

Sgt. Slaughter & Terry Daniels defeated the Dirty White Boys in a bootcamp match

Mid South Tag Team Champions Ted DiBiase & Steve Williams defeated Ricky Morton & Robert Gibson

Jim Duggan fought Kamala to a double disqualification

JCP @ Asheville, NC - Civic Center - June 2, 1985
Sam Houston vs. the Eliminator
Denny Brown vs. Kendo Nagasaki
Buzz Tyler vs. Mid Atlantic Heavyweight Champion Ron Bass
Jimmy Valiant & Manny Fernandez vs. Superstar Billy Graham & the Barbarian
Dusty Rhodes defeated NWA TV Champion Tully Blanchard via disqualification
NWA World Champion Ric Flair defeated NWA US Champion Magnum TA via disqualification

JCP @ Atlanta, GA - Omni - June 2, 1985
National Tag Team Champion Arn Anderson defeated the Italian Stallion
Bob Roop defeated Gerald Finley
Ron Garvin, Jimmy Valiant, & Buzz Sawyer defeated Superstar Billy Graham, Abdullah the Butcher, & the Barbarian
Tully Blanchard defeated Pez Whatley
Thunderbolt Patterson defeated National Tag Team Champion Ole Anderson via disqualification
Ivan Koloff & Krusher Kruschev defeated Dusty Rhodes & Dick Slater via disqualification
NWA World Champion Ric Flair fought NWA US Champion Magnum TA to a draw

JCP @ Fayetteville, NC - Cumberland County Memorial Arena - June 3, 1985
TV taping:
Jimmy Valiant vs. the Barbarian
Dusty Rhodes vs. Abdullah the Butcher (bounty match)
Also included NWA US Champion Magnum TA and NWA TV Champion Tully Blanchard

Continental @ Birmingham, AL - June 3, 1985
Lord Humongous defeated NWA World Champion Ric Flair via disqualification

JCP @ Spartanburg, SC - Memorial Auditorium - June 4, 1985
TV taping:
Kendo Nagasaki defeated Gene Ligon (sub. for Stoney Burke)
Nikita Koloff vs. Gene Ligon & Ricky Reeves (handicap match)
Abdullah the Butcher defeated Sam Houston
Rocky Kerndole vs. NWA Mid Atlantic Heavyweight Champion Ron Bass

NWA TV Champion Tully Blanchard defeated Buzz Tyler
Worldwide - 6/8/85:
Ron Bass vs. Ricky Reeves
Nikita Koloff & Krusher Kruschev vs. Sam Houston & Gene Ligon
NWA US Champion Magnum TA & Manny Fernandez vs. Joel Deaton & Ron Rossi
The Barbarian vs. Gerald Finley
Ivan Koloff vs. Stoney Burke
Abdullah the Butcher vs. Pat Tanaka
Dark match after the taping: Jimmy Valiant defeated Superstar Billy Graham in a lights out steel cage match

JCP @ Raleigh, NC - Dorton Arena - June 5, 1985
Kendo Nagasaki defeated Sam Houston
Denny Brown defeated Joel Deaton
Jimmy Valiant fought Abdullah the Butcher to a no contest
NWA TV Champion Tully Blanchard defeated Buzz Sawyer
Buzz Tyler defeated Ron Bass in a taped fist match
NWA Tag Team Champions Ivan Koloff & Kruscher Kruschev fought NWA US Champion Magnum TA & Manny Fernandez to a draw

JCP @ Norfolk, VA - Scope - June 6, 1985
Kendo Nagasaki defeated Mark Fleming
Superstar Billy Graham defeated Denny Brown
Ron Bass defeated Sam Houston
Jimmy Valiant defeated the Barbarian in a lumberjack match
Manny Fernandez & Buzz Tyler defeated NWA Tag Team Champions Ivan Koloff & Krusher Kruschev via disqualification
Dusty Rhodes & NWA US Champion Magnum TA fought NWA TV Champion Tully Blanchard & Abdullah the Butcher to a no contest

JCP @ Wilmington, NC - Legion Stadium - June 7, 1985 (2,100)
NWA World Champion Ric Flair vs. NWA US Champion Magnum TA did not take place as scheduled due to transportation problems; Ivan Koloff did not appear as advertised
Mark Fleming pinned Doug Vines
Ricky Reeves defeated Ron Bass via disqualification
Khrusher Khruschev pinned Mark Fleming
Buzz Tyler pinned Ron Bass; after the match, NWA TV Champion Tully Blanchard and Baby Doll came to the ring, and after Bass and Dillon left, Blanchard hit a bloody Tyler with the belt as Tyler tried to get to his feet
NWA TV Champion Tully Blanchard defeated Buzz Tyler via reverse decision; Tyler originally won the match and title but the desicion was changed for him throwing Blanchard over the top rope while the referee was knocked out

JCP @ Columbia, SC - Township Auditorium - June 7, 1985
Denny Brown vs. Pat Tanaka
Nikita Koloff vs. Burke & Reeves
Sam Houston vs. Superstar Billy Graham
National Tag Team Champions Ole & Arn Anderson vs. Dusty Rhodes & Manny Fernandez
Jimmy Valiant vs. the Barbarian (steel cage match)

Continental @ Dothan, AL - June 8, 1985
TV taping:
NWA World Champion Ric Flair vs. Josh Stroud

JCP @ Greensboro, NC - Coliseum - June 8, 1985
John Tatum defeated Sam Houston
Nikita Koloff defeated Denny Brown
Kendo Nagasaki defeated Ricky Reeves
National Tag Team Champion Arn Anderson defeated Pat Tanaka
Manny Fernandez defeated Ivan Koloff
Dusty Rhodes & NWA US Champion Magnum TA defeated NWA TV Champion Tully Blanchard & Abdullah the Butcher; after the bout, a fan ran into the ring and gave Blanchard something; Rhodes then tore a wig off the fan, revealing her to be Baby Doll, just before Blanchard shot a fireball into Rhodes' face; moments later, Magnum and several other wrestlers tended to Rhodes on the floor and helped him backstage
NWA World Champion Ric Flair defeated Buddy Landell

JCP @ Roanoke, VA - Civic Center - June 9, 1985
Denny Brown defeated Ron Rossie
Kendo Nagasaki defeated Mark Fleming
The Barbarian defeated George South
Buddy Landell defeated Pat Tanaka
Buzz Tyler defeated Ron Bass
Jimmy Valiant defeated Superstar Billy Graham

GCW @ Wheeling, WV - June 9, 1985
Dick Slater defeated NWA World Champion Ric Flair via disqualification

Continental @ Birmingham, AL - June 10, 1985
Bob Armstrong & Lord Humongous defeated NWA World Champion Ric Flair & Robert Fuller

JCP @ Greenville, SC - June 10, 1985
Ron Bass defeated Denny Brown
Nikita Koloff defeated Ricky Reeves & Stoney Burke via disqualification
Buddy Landell defeated Sam Houston
Buzz Tyler fought Ivan Koloff to a draw
NWA TV Champion Tully Blanchard defeated Manny Fernandez via disqualification
NWA US Champion Magnum TA, Dusty Rhodes, & Jimmy Valiant defeated Superstar Billy Graham, the Barbarian, & Paul Jones

Warwick, RI - June 11, 1985
NWA World Champion Ric Flair defeated David Schultz

JCP @ Philadelphia, PA - Civic Center - June 12, 1985
The Italian Stallion defeated Joel Deaton
Pez Whatley & Buzz Tyler defeated the Rock 'n' Roll RPMs
Black Bart defeated Brett Sawyer
Jimmy Valiant defeated the Eliminator
Thunderbolt Patterson defeated Ole Anderson
NWA World Champion Ric Flair fought NWA US Champion Magnum TA to a draw
NWA Tag Team Champions Ivan & Nikita Koloff defeated Manny Fernandez & Dick Slater via disqualification
Dusty Rhodes defeated NWA TV Champion Tully Blanchard in a non-title barbed wire match

JCP @ Salisbury, MD - June 14, 1985
Krusher Kruschev defeated Mark Fleming
Kendo Nagasaki defeated Denny Brown
Ron Bass defeated Stoney Burke
Krusher Kruschev defeated Sam Houston
NWA Tag Team Champions Ivan & Nikita Koloff defeated Manny Fernandez & Buzz Sawyer
NWA US Champion Magnum TA fought NWA TV Champion Tully Blanchard to a draw
NWA World Champion Ric Flair defeated Dusty Rhodes via disqualification

Worldwide - 6/15/85 - featured David Crockett conducting an interview with NWA Tag Team Champions Ivan & Nikita Koloff, during which Ivan said Nikita was the #1 contender to NWA World Champion Ric Flair and that Flair was avoiding the challenge; Crockett eventually told Ivan to shut up and brought up Flair's 1975 plane crash to show how tough Flair was; moments later, Crockett brought up the Koloffs attack people from behind, with Nikita then dropping Crockett with the Russian Sickle:
Sam Houston vs. George South
Krusher Kruschev vs. Denny Brown
The Barbarian (w/ Paul Jones) vs. Mike Lake
Ron Bass & Buddy Landell vs. Buzz Tyler & Manny Fernandez
Arn Anderson vs. Stoney Burke
Kendo Nagasaki vs. Ricky Reeves
Nikita Koloff vs. Mark Fleming

JCP @ Atlanta, GA - WTBS Studios - June 15, 1985
World Championship Wrestling - 6/15/85 - included opening footage of NWA TV Champion Tully Blanchard blinding Dusty Rhodes with a fireball during the 6/8/85 card in Greensboro; featured Tony Schiavone conducting an interview with Blanchard, alongside Baby Doll, regarding Rhodes' injury and noted that every time Rhodes insulted Blanchard or Baby Doll he ends up hurt and questioned what would happen next time:
Buzz Sawyer & Dick Slater vs. Ron Rossi & Hill
Manny Fernandez vs. Randy Barber
Kamala vs. Alan Martin

NWA National Tag Team Champions Ole & Arn Anderson vs. the Italian Stallion & Joe Lightfoot
The Barbarian vs. Jason Walker
NWA TV Champion Tully Blanchard vs. Gerald Finlay
NWA US Champion Magnum TA fought NWA World Champion Ric Flair to a 10-minute time-limit draw in a non-title match at 10:18; prior to the bout, Magnum interrupted an interview with Flair conducted by Tony Schiavone and put up $1,000 of his own money saying Flair couldn't beat him in whatever TV time was left; Flair accepted the challenge and faced Magnum instead of his scheduled opponent; early in the match, NWA National Tag Team Champions Ole & Arn Anderson joined Schiavone for guest commentary; the match ended as Magnum had Flair in the figure-4; after the contest, Flair attempted to jump Magnum from behind but Magnum fought him off only to be attacked by the Andersons; Dick Slater and Buzz Sawyer then cleared the ring after Magnum had been triple teamed (*The Rise and Fall of WCW*)

JCP @ Cleveland, OH - June 15, 1985
Jimmy Valiant defeated Superstar Billy Graham

JCP @ Richmond, VA - Coliseum - June 15, 1985
Kendo Nagasaki defeated Denny Brown
Ron Bass defeated Mark Fleming
Krusher Kruschev, NWA Tag Team Champions Ivan & Nikita Koloff defeated Sam Houston, Buzz Tyler, & Starship Eagle
Manny Fernandez fought the Barbarian to a no contest
NWA World Champion Ric Flair defeated Buddy Landell via disqualification
Dusty Rhodes & NWA US Champion Magnum TA defeated NWA TV Champion Tully Blanchard & Abdullah the Butcher in a steel cage match

SUNDAY, JUNE 16 3 PM
LIVE T.V. TAPING
Asheville Civic Center

WIDE WORLD WRESTLING

SUPER GRUDGE MATCH
"AMERICAN DREAM"
DUSTY RHODES
&
(U.S. CHAMP)
MAGNUM T.A.
—VS—
(462 lbs)
ABDULLAH THE BUTCHER
&
(WORLD T.V. CHAMP
WITH BABY DOLL)
TULLY BLANCHARD

GRUDGE MATCH
RAGIN' BULL
—VS—
(WITH PAUL JONES)
THE BARBARIAN

Other Matches With Such Stars As:
THE ROAD WARRIORS
IVAN & NIKITA KOLOFF
KRUSHER KRUSHCHEV
BUDDY LANDEL
KENDO NAGASAKI
SUPERSTAR BILLY GRAHAM
JIMMY VALIANT
BUZZ TAYLOR
RON BASS
SAM HOUSTON

DUSTY

MAGNUM

BULL

JIMMY

TULLY

BUZZ

Special T.V. Taping Prices '8 Ringside, Gen. Adm. '7, Children under 10, '3
Box Office 259-5771 Mon.-Fri. 10-5:30, Sat. 11-4, Day of Match 1:00 P.M.
No Checks or Credit Cards Day of Match. Matches subject to change.

WIDE WORLD WRESTLING ON WLOS-TV 13 SUNDAY 12 NOON

JCP @ Asheville, NC - Civic Center - June 16, 1985
(matinee)
TV taping:
Dusty Rhodes & NWA US Champion Magnum TA vs. Abdullah
the Butcher & NWA TV Champion Tully Blanchard

JCP @ Sumter, SC - County Exhibition Center - June 16,
1985
Pat Tanaka vs. Kendo Nagasaki
Denny Brown vs. Buddy Landell
Sam Houston vs. Krusher Khruschev
Buzz Tyler vs. Ron Bass
Manny Fernandez vs. the Barbarian (New York streetfight)
Jimmy Valiant vs. Superstar Billy Graham (New York
streetfight)

CWF @ Orlando, FL - June 16, 1985
Dale Veasey defeated Mike Golden
Bugsy McGraw defeated Rip Rogers
Kendall Windham defeated Jack Hart
Jesse Barr & Rick Rude defeated Tiger Conway Jr. & Scott
McGhee
Hercules Hernandez defeated Billy Jack Haynes via
disqualification
Wahoo McDaniel defeated NWA World Champion Ric Flair via
disqualification

JCP @ Greenville, SC - June 17, 1985
Krusher Kruschev defeated Starship Eagle
Kendo Nagasaki defeated Sam Houston
Jimmy Valiant & Manny Fernandez defeated Superstar Billy
Graham & the Barbarian
Buzz Tyler defeated Ron Bass in a bullrope match
NWA US Champion Magnum TA & Dusty Rhodes defeated
NWA TV Champion Tully Blanchard & Abdullah the Butcher in
a steel cage match

JCP @ Hickory, NC - June 18, 1985
Buddy Landell defeated Sam Houston
Superstar Billy Graham defeated Ricky Reeves
Jimmy Valiant defeated the Barbarian via disqualification
NWA US Champion Magnum TA defeated NWA TV Champion
Tully Blanchard

CWF @ Tampa, FL - June 18, 1985
Dale Veasey defeated Mike Golden
Tiger Conway Jr. defeated Jack Hart
Bugsy McGraw defeated Rip Rogers
Hercules Hernandez defeated Scott McGhee
Rick Rude & Jesse Barr defeated Billy Jack Haynes & Hector
Guerrero
Wahoo McDaniel defeated NWA World Champion Ric Flair via
disqualification

CWF @ Daytona Beach, FL - Spruce Creek High School -
June 19, 1985
US Tag Team Champions Rick Rude & Jesse Barr vs. Hector
Guerrero & Billy Jack Haynes
NWA World Champion Ric Flair vs. Wahoo McDaniel

Mid South @ Jackson, MS - June 20, 1985
NWA World Champion Ric Flair vs. Terry Taylor

WRESTLING
THURSDAY
JUNE 20
THE TOWNSHIP 8:15

MAGNUM T.A.   DUSTY RHODES
-vs-
TULLY BLANCHARD
WITH BABY DOLL
AND
ABDULLAH THE BUTCHER

RAGING BULL -vs- BARBARIAN

"BOOGIE WOOGIE" JIMMY VALIENT
- vs -
"NATURE BOY" BUDDY LANDELL

BUZZ TYLER -vs- RON BASS
HOUSTON -vs- KRUCHEV
DUPRE -vs- GRAHAM

RESERVED RINGSIDE $10
GENERAL ADMISSION $8
CHILD UNDER 8 YEARS $4
TICKETS NOW ON SALE
TAYLOR ST. PHARMACY

JCP @ Columbia, SC - Township Auditorium - June 20, 1985
Superstar Billy Graham defeated Stoney Burke
Krusher Kruschev defeated Sam Houston
Jimmy Valiant defeated Buddy Landell
Manny Fernandez defeated the Barbarian
Buzz Tyler defeated Ron Bass via TKO in a Texas Death Match
Dusty Rhodes & NWA US Champion Magnum TA defeated NWA TV Champion Tully Blanchard & Abdullah the Butcher

Central States @ St. Louis, MO - June 21, 1985
Dave Peterson fought Jim Waka to a draw
Marty Jannetty defeated Mike Vachon
Gustav the Giant defeated Monster Murdoch & Gil Guerrero in a handicap match
Larry & Curt Hennig defeated the Super Destroyer & Sheik Abdullah
Blackjack Lanza (sub. for Dick the Bruiser), Bob Brown, & Iceman King Parsons defeated Mr. Pogo, Starship Coyote, & Gary Royal
Harley Race defeated Bobby Duncum
Kerry Von Erich defeated NWA World Champion Ric Flair via disqualification

JCP @ Charleston, SC - County Hall - June 21, 1985
? vs. Doug Vines
Johnny Weaver vs. Joel Deaton
NWA Jr. Heavyweight Champion Denny Brown vs. Pat Tanaka (Best 2 out of 3 falls)
Ron Bass defeated Buzz Tyler in a bullrope match
Jimmy Valiant defeated The Barbarian in a steel cage match

JCP @ Hampton, VA - Coliseum - June 21, 1985
Buddy Landell defeated Stoney Burke
Krusher Kruschev defeated Sam Houston
Kendo Nagasaki defeated Ricky Reeves
Ivan Koloff defeated Starship Eagle
Manny Fernandez defeated Superstar Billy Graham
Dusty Rhodes & NWA US Champion Magnum TA defeated NWA TV Champion Tully Blanchard & Abdullah the Butcher

Worldwide - 6/22/85:
The Road Warriors vs. Ron Rossi & George South
NWA US Champion Magnum TA vs. Dave Dillenger
NWA TV Champion Tully Blanchard & Abdullah the Butcher vs. Pat Tanaka & Denny Brown
Buddy Landell vs. Joel Deaton
Starship Eagle vs. Lee Ramsey
Nikita Koloff vs. Sam Houston

World Championship Wrestling - 6/22/85 - featured Tony Schiavone conducting an interview with NWA TV Champion Tully Blanchard, with Baby Doll, regarding Dusty Rhodes' eye injury and Rhodes bringing in Wahoo McDaniel to help him:

Buzz & Brett Sawyer & Randy Barber & Larry Clark
Magnum TA vs. Paul Garner
Jimmy Valiant vs. Carl Styles
NWA TV Champion Tully Blanchard (w/ Baby Doll) defeated Terry Flynn; after the bout, Dusty Rhodes came out to the ring, confronted Baby Doll, pushed her and then fought with Blanchard before applying the figure-4; Baby Doll caused Rhodes to break the hold and distracted him long enough for Blanchard to hit Rhodes in the back of the head with a loaded elbow pad, knocking Rhodes to the floor
AWA Tag Team Champions the Road Warriors vs. Joel Deaton & David Dellenger
NWA Tag Team Champions Ivan & Nikita Koloff vs. Alan Martin & Mark Cooper
NWA World Champion Ric Flair, National Tag Team Champions Ole & Arn Anderson defeated the Italian Stallion, Pez Whatley, & Rocky King at around the 14-minute mark when Whatley submitted to Flair's figure-4 after sustaining Arn's gordbuster; late in the match, Magnum TA joined Tony Schiavone on commentary; after the bout, Flair & the Andersons confronted Magnum on the floor until Jimmy Valiant and ? appeared, scaring them off (*Ric Flair & the 4 Horsemen*)
Buddy Landell (w/ JJ Dillon) vs. Jason Walker
Thunderbolt Patterson vs. Tommy Lane
Kevin Sullivan vs. Gerald Finlay
Black Bart vs. Nick Busick

GCW @ Columbus, GA - June 22, 1985
NWA World Champion Ric Flair defeated Dick Slater via reverse decision

JCP @ Greensboro, NC - Coliseum - June 23, 1985
Kendo Nagasaki defeated Ricky Reeves
Nikita Koloff defeated Sam Houston
Buddy Landell defeated Pat Tanaka
NWA Tag Team Champions Ivan Koloff & Krusher Kruschev defeated Joe Lightfoot & Billy Thundercloud
Manny Fernandez defeated the Barbarian
Ron Bass fought Buzz Tyler to a double disqualification in a Texas Bullrope match
Dusty Rhodes & Wahoo McDaniel defeated NWA TV Champion Tully Blanchard & Abdullah the Butcher

JCP @ Atlanta, GA - Omni - June 23, 1985
Kevin Sullivan defeated Rocky King
Pez Whatley & the Italian Stallion defeated the Rock 'n' Roll RPMs
Thunderbolt Patterson defeated Bob Roop
Black Bart defeated Starship Eagle
Jimmy Valiant defeated Superstar Billy Graham
National Tag Team Champions Ole & Arn Anderson defeated Dick Slater & Buzz Sawyer
NWA US Champion Magnum TA defeated NWA World Champion Ric Flair via disqualification

JCP @ Greenville, SC - Memorial Auditorium - June 24, 1985
Joel Deaton defeated Lee Ramsey
Krusher Khrushchev defeated Ricky Reeves
Ivan Koloff defeated Stoney Burke
Nikita Koloff defeated Starship Eagle
NWA US Champion Magnum TA defeated NWA TV Champion Tully Blanchard
Dusty Rhodes defeated Buddy Landell via disqualification

Mid South @ New Orleans, LA - June 24, 1985
NWA World Champion Ric Flair defeated Butch Reed via reverse decision

JCP @ Lansing, MI - June 25, 1985
The Italian Stallion defeated Mike Davis
Joe Lightfoot fought Tommy Lane to a draw
Thunderbolt Patterson & Pez Whatley defeated Kevin Sullivan & Bob Roop
Black Bart defeated Brett Sawyer
Dick Slater & Buzz Sawyer fought Ole & Arn Anderson via disqualification

GCW @ Steubenville, OH - June 26, 1985
The Italian Stallion & Joe Lightfoot fought the Rock 'n' Roll RPMs to a draw
Thunderbolt Patterson defeated Bob Roop
Kevin Sullivan defeated Pez Whatley
Black Bart defeated Brett Sawyer
Dick Slater & Buzz Sawyer defeated Ole & Arn Anderson

JCP @ Raliegh, NC - Dorton Arena - June 26, 1985
Sam Houston defeated Mark Fleming
Ivan Koloff defeated Ricky Reeves
Krusher Kruschev defeated Starship Eagle
The Barbarian defeated Manny Fernandez
Kendo Nagasaki & Buddy Landell defeated Jimmy Valiant & Buzz Tyler via disqualification

JCP @ Norfolk, VA - Scope - June 27, 1985
Krusher Kruschev defeated Mark Fleming
Ivan Koloff defeated Sam Houston
Nikita Koloff defeated Starship Eagle
Ron Bass defeated Stoney Burke
Manny Fernandez defeated Kendo Nagasaki
NWA US Champion Magnum TA defeated Buddy Landell
NWA World Champion Ric Flair & Jimmy Valiant defeated Superstar Billy Graham & the Barbarian in a steel cage match
Dusty Rhodes defeated NWA TV Champion Tully Blanchard in a non-title steel cage match

JCP @ Richmond, VA - Coliseum - June 28, 1985
Buddy Landell defeated Ricky Reeves
The Barbarian defeated Manny Fernandez
Krusher Kruschev, Ivan & Nikita Koloff defeated Jimmy Valiant,
Buzz Tyler, & Starship Eagle
Kendo Nagasaki defeated Stoney Burke
Ron Bass defeated Sam Houston
Denny Brown defeated Mark Fleming
Dusty Rhodes defeated Tully Blanchard

Houston, TX - June 28, 1985
Magnum TA defeated NWA World Champion Ric Flair via reverse decision

Worldwide - 6/29/85:
Ron Bass vs. Mark Fleming
Ivan Koloff & Krusher Kruschev vs. Sam Houston & Paul Diamond
NWA US Champion Magnum TA & Manny Fernandez vs. Lee Ramsey & Joel Deaton
Jimmy Valiant vs. Ron Rossi
Superstar Billy Graham & the Barbarian vs. Ricky Reeves & Stoney Burke
NWA TV Champion Tully Blanchard vs. Gene Ligon

JCP @ Atlanta, GA - WTBS Studios - June 29, 1985 (matinee)
World Championship Wrestling - 6/29/85 - included Tony Schiavone conducting an interview with NWA World Champion Ric Flair in which he said he was heading to Los Angeles later in the day, NWA US Champion Magnum TA wasn't ready to challenge him, Nikita Koloff's recent attack on David Crockett, facing Koloff at the Great American Bash, and making Koloff his personal gardner; featured Schiavone conducting a closing interview with NWA TV Champion Tully Blanchard, with Baby Doll, about the attack he made on Sam Houston earlier in the show and said that was an example of what he was capable of; Blanchard wore Houston's hat and a Starrcade 84 t-shirt during the segment; Blanchard then noted he would face Rhodes in a ring surrounded by barbed wire and would continue to beat Rhodes:
NWA National Tag Team Champions Ole & Arn Anderson vs. Alan Martin & Joe Smith
Ivan Koloff (w/ Nikita Koloff) vs. Gerald Finlay
Buzz Sawyer vs. Jimmy Dill
Bobby Eaton & Dennis Condrey (w/ Jim Cornette) vs. Larry Clark & Joe Smith (debut of Eaton, Condrey, & Cornette)
Black Bart vs. the Italian Stallion
Sam Houston defeated an unknown; after the bout, NWA TV Champion Tully Blanchard ran into the ring, attacked Houston, and repeatedly whipped him with a belt until Dusty Rhodes came out

JCP @ Los Angeles, CA - Olympic Auditorium - June 29, 1985
Armando Guerrero & Jay York defeated Budda Khan & Pistol Pete via disqualification
Debbie the Killer Tomato defeated Charlie the Golden Cat to win the California Ladies Title
Jay Strongbow Jr. fought Jack Armstrong to a draw

Manny Fernandez defeated Krusher Kruschev
Dusty Rhodes defeated NWA TV Champion Tully blanchard
NWA World Champion Ric Flair defeated NWA US Champion
Magnum TA via disqualification

JCP @ Augusta, GA - June 29, 1985
Denny Brown defeated Stoney Burke
Starship Eagle defeated John Tatum
The Barbarian defeated Sam Houston
Ivan Koloff defeated the Italian Stallion
Dick Slater & Buzz Sawyer defeated NWA National Tag Team
Champions Ole & Arn Anderson via disqualification
Jimmy Valiant defeated Superstar Billy Graham

Mid South @ Tulsa, OK - June 30, 1985
NWA World Champion Ric Flair vs. Terry Taylor

- 6/30/85: Cody Rhodes (Runnels) was born.

JCP @ Greenville, SC - Memorial Auditorium - July 1, 1985
National Tag Team Champions Ole & Arn Anderson won a
$50,000, 10-team battle royal

JCP @ Columbia, SC - Township Auditorium - July 2, 1985
Buzz Tyler defeated John Tatum
Nikita Koloff defeated Sam Houston & Denny Brown in a
handicap match
The Barbarian defeated Manny Fernandez
Jimmy Valiant defeated Kendo Nagasaki
Buddy Landell defeated Ron Bass via disqualification;
stipulations stated Bass would face JJ Dillon if he won
NWA World Champion Ric Flair & Dusty Rhodes defeated
NWA Tag Team Champions Ivan Koloff & Krusher Kruschev
NWA US Champion Magnum TA defeated NWA TV Champion
Tully Blanchard in a lumberjack match

JCP @ Raleigh, NC - Dorton Arena - July 3, 1985
Buddy Landell defeated Sam Houston
Nikita Koloff defeated Starship Eagle
Manny Fernandez defeated the Barbarian via disqualification
NWA US Champion Magnum TA defeated Kendo Nagasaki
(sub. for Abdullah the Butcher)
NWA National Tag Team Champions Ole & Arn Anderson
fought Dick Slater & Buzz Sawyer to a draw
NWA Tag Team Champions Ivan Koloff & Krusher Kruschev
won a $50,000, 10-team battle royal; other participants
included: NWA US Champion Magnum TA & Manny
Fernandez, the Barbarian & Superstar Billy Graham, NWA
National Tag Team Champions Ole & Arn Anderson, Jimmy
Valiant & Starship Eagle, Buddy Landell & Kendo Nagasaki,
Dick Slater & Buzz Sawyer, Ron Bass & Buzz Tyler, Pat
Tanaka & Denny Brown, and Stoney Burke & Sam Houston

JCP @ Atlanta, GA - Omni - July 4, 1985 (13,000)
Bobby Eaton & Dennis Condrey defeated Brett Sawyer & the Italian Stallion (Eaton & Condrey's Omni debut)
Thunderbolt Patterson defeated Kevin Sullivan via disqualification
National Tag Team Champions Ole & Arn Anderson defeated Buzz & Brett Sawyer
Ron Garvin fought Black Bart to a no contest
Krusher Kruschev, NWA Tag Team Champions Ivan & Nikita Koloff defeated Dick Slater, Pez Whatley, & Bill Watts
NWA World Champion Ric Flair pinned NWA US Champion Magnum TA

JCP @ Norfolk, VA - July 4, 1985
Ricky Reeves fought Tommy Lane to a draw
Denny Brown defeated Mike Davis
Kendo Nagasaki defeated Stoney Burke
Superstar Billy Graham deeated Pat Tanaka
Buddy Landell defeated Ron Bass
Jimmy Valiant, Manny Fernandez, & Buzz Tyler defeated the Barbarian, Abdullah the Butcher, & Paul Jones

Worldwide - 7/6/85:
Jimmy Valiant vs. the Black Kat
Ole & Arn Anderson vs. Ricky Reeves & Stoney Burke
Buddy Landell vs. Sam Houston
Dick Slater vs. Tommy Lane
Krusher Kruschev, Ivan & Nikita Koloff vs. American Starship, Buzz Tyler, & Brett Sawyer
Manny Fernandez vs. John Tatum
NWA World Champion Ric Flair vs. Mike Davis

JCP @ Atlanta, GA - WTBS Studios - July 6, 1985 (matinee)
World Championship Wrestling - 7/6/85 - featured David Crockett on sole commentary; included Crockett conducting an interview with NWA TV Champion Tully Blanchard, with Baby Doll, in which he mentioned the arrival of Jim Cornette, Bobby Eaton & Dennis Condrey and noted his upcoming match later in the day against Dusty Rhodes as part of the Great American Bash; featured Crockett conducting an interview with NWA World Champion Ric Flair, during which it was noted one of Eaton & Condrey's opponents suffered a dislocated shoulder; Flair then mentioned his match against Nikita Koloff as part of the Great American Bash later in the day and soon facing Harley Race in Kansas City, MO as well as fending off challenges from Wahoo McDaniel, Dusty Rhodes, and NWA US Champion Magnum TA; included Crockett conducting an interview with NWA National Tag Team Champions Ole & Arn Anderson regarding Rhodes & Magnum, with Ole saying Rhodes knew the Andersons well enough to know he wanted no part of them; featured Crockett conducting an interview with Blanchard, with Baby Doll, in which he said he would still be champion after facing Rhodes at the Bash and would have the title as long as he wanted it:
Buzz & Brett Sawyer vs. Larry Clark & Vernon Deaton
Ron Garvin vs. Arthur Pritz

Bobby Eaton & Dennis Condrey vs. Alan Martin & Mark Cooper
Kevin Sullivan vs. Jason Walker
NWA US Champion Magnum TA vs. Ron Rossi
Krusher Kruschev, Ivan & Nikita Koloff vs. Mike Davis, Tommy Lane, & the Black Cat
NWA National Tag Team Champion Arn Anderson (w/ NWA National Tag Team Champion Ole Anderson) vs. Gene Ligon
Jimmy Valiant vs. Randy Barber
Sam Houston vs. Roy George
NWA Jr. Heavyweight Champion Denny Brown vs. Mike Simani
NWA National Heavyweight Champion Black Bart vs. Rocky King

JCP @ Columbus, GA - July 6, 1985
Bobby Eaton & Dennis Condrey defeated Brett Sawyer (sub. for Joe Lightfoot) & the Italian Stallion
Thunderbolt Patterson vs. Mike Davis
Brett Sawyer vs. Kendo Nagasaki
Pez Whatley vs. Kevin Sullivan
Ron Garvin vs. National Heavyweight Champion Black Bart (lights out match)
Also inclued a 12-man $20,000 battle royal

Great American Bash 85 - Charlotte, NC - Memorial Stadium - July 6, 1985 (27,000)
Featured an hour-long concert by David Allen Coe; during the concert, NWA World Champion Ric Flair, Dusty Rhodes, Jimmy Valiant, and NWA US Champion Magnum TA briefly joined Coe on stage, with Valiant helping out on vocals
Ron Bass fought Buddy Landell (w/ JJ Dillon) to a 20-minute time-limit draw; after the bout, Bass applied the claw to Dillon until Landell pulled him from the ring
NWA National Tag Team Champions Ole & Arn Anderson defeated Buzz Sawyer & Dick Slater when Ole pinned Sawyer with an elbow drop to the back of the head behind the referee's back as Sawyer had Arn covered following a flying forearm
Manny Fernandez, Sam Houston, & Buzz Tyler defeated Superstar Billy Graham, the Barbarian, & Abdullah the Butcher when Houston pinned Graham with a small package
Jimmy Valiant (w/ Buzz Tyler) pinned Paul Jones (w/ Abdullah the Butcher) in a dog collar chain match with the elbow drop after Jones accidentally hit an interfering Abdullah with the chain; after the bout, Abdullah attacked Valiant until Tyler cleared the ring with a chair
AWA Tag Team Champions the Road Warriors (w/ Paul Ellering) fought NWA Tag Team Champions Krusher Khruschev & Ivan Koloff to a double disqualification after Kruschev hit Road Warrior Animal with a steel chair as Animal attempted to powerslam Koloff off the top, with the Road Warriors then using the weapon on Kruschev & Koloff; after the bout, the two teams continued to brawl until the Road Warriors cleared the ring
NWA US Champion Magnum TA defeated Kamala (w/ Skandar Akbar) via disqualification at around the 6:45 mark when Akbar broke the cover after the champion hit a bodyslam

after Kamala missed a charge in the corner; after the bout, Kamala accidentally hit Akbar, with Magnum then dropping Kamala with the belly to belly suplex (*Crockett Cup 87*)

NWA World Champion Ric Flair pinned Nikita Koloff (w/ NWA Tag Team Champion Ivan Koloff) when Flair held onto the top rope as Nikita tried to slam him into the ring, with Flair landing on top for the win; David Crockett was the guest referee for the match; after the bout, Nikita and Ivan double teamed Flair as the ring announcer asked the fans to stay clear of the ring; moments later, Nikita hit a Russian Sickle off the middle turnbuckle as Ivan held Flair up in the air; Sam Houston and other wrestlers tried to make the save but were beaten down as well; Nikita then knocked a bloody Flair to the floor with another Russian Sickle

Dusty Rhodes pinned NWA TV Champion Tully Blanchard (w/ Baby Doll) in a non-sanctioned steel cage match to win the title at 11:30 with a piledriver; after the bout, Magnum TA, Manny Fernandez, and several other wrestlers came out to congratulate the new champion; due to pre-match stipulations, Rhodes won possession of Baby Doll for 30 days (*American Dream: The Dusty Rhodes Story*)

JCP @ Greenville, SC - Memorial Auditorium - July 7, 1985
Pat Tanaka & Denny Brown fought Gene Ligon & John Tatum to a draw
The Barbarian defeated Sam Houston
Nikita Koloff, NWA Tag Team Champions Ivan Koloff & Krusher Kruschev defeated Jimmy Valiant, Buzz Tyler, & Manny Fernandez
Buddy Landell defeated Ron Bass
NWA TV Champion Dusty Rhodes defeated Abdullah the Butcher via disqualification in a bullrope match
NWA World Champion Ric Flair defeated NWA US Champion Magnum TA via disqualification

JCP @ Marietta, GA - July 7, 1985
Thunderbolt Patterson & Rocky King defeated the Rock 'n' Roll RPMs
Bobby Eaton & Dennis Condrey defeated Brett Sawyer & the Italian Stallion
Kevin Sullivan defeated Pez Whatley
Ron Garvin defeated Black Bart via count-out
Buzz Sawyer defeated National Tag Team Champions Arn Anderson in a lights out match

JCP @ Swainsboro, GA - July 8, 1985
Bobby Eaton & Dennis Condrey defeated Rocky King & Pez Whatley

Mid South @ Oklahoma City, OK - July 8, 1985
NWA World Champion Ric Flair defeated NWA TV Champion Dusty Rhodes via disqualification

JCP @ Blackshear, GA - NFC Gym - July 9, 1985
Gerald Finley vs. the Eliminator

Rocky King vs. Rock 'n Roll RPM #2
Thunderbolt Patterson vs. Bob Roop
Bobby Eaton & Dennis Condrey defeated Pez Whatley & the Italian Stallion
Brett Sawyer vs. NWA National Heavyweight Champion Black Bart
Kevin Sullivan vs. National Tag Team Champion Arn Anderson
Buzz Sawyer vs. Dick Slater

WWC @ Puerto Rico - July 9, 1985
NWA World Champion Ric Flair & Dory Funk Jr. defeated Carlos Colon & Abdullah the Butcher

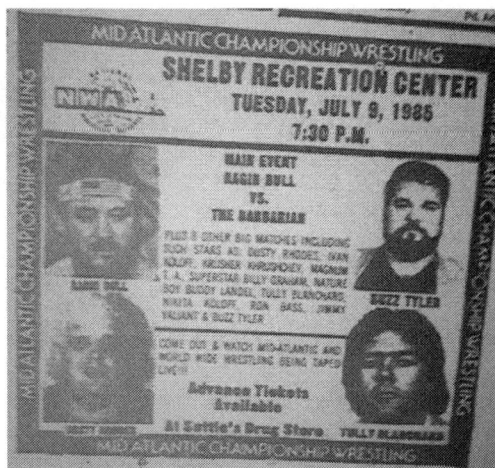

JCP @ Shelby, NC - Rec Center - July 9, 1985
Pro - 7/13/85:
Worldwide - 7/13/85
Ricky Morton & Robert Gibson defeated NWA Tag Team Champions Ivan Koloff & Krusher Kruschev to win the titles at around the 34-minute mark when Morton pinned Koloff with a victory roll; David Crockett, Magnum TA, and Tony Schiavone provided commentary for the match; after the contest, Jimmy Valiant, Manny Fernandez, Sam Houston, and several others came out to celebrate with the new champions (Morton & Gibson's debut) (*Allied Powers*)
Dark match: Manny Fernandez vs. the Barbarian

CWF @ Miami, FL - Dade County Youth Fair - July 10, 1985 (1,980)
Dale Veasey defeated the Masked Marauder
Tiger Conway Jr. defeated Tony Wonder
Kendall Windham defeated Jack Hart
Rip Oliver & the Grappler defeated Mike Graham & Cocoa Samoa
Billy Jack Haynes defeated Rick Rude
Wahoo McDaniel defeated Rip Rogers
NWA TV Champion Dusty Rhodes defeated NWA World Champion Ric Flair

JCP @ Raleigh, NC - Dorton Arena - July 10, 1985
Kendo Nagasaki defeated Gerald Findley
Superstar Billy Graham defeated Mark Fleming
Buddy Landell defeated Ron Bass
Ivan & Nikita Koloff defeated Sam Houston & Jimmy Valiant
NWA TV Champion Dusty Rhodes & NWA US Champion
Magnum TA fought Tully Blanchard & Abdullah the Butcher to
a double disqualification
Manny Fernandez defeated the Barbarian via disqualification

JCP @ Columbia, SC - July 11, 1985
Gene Ligon defeated George South
John Tatum defeated Lee Ramsey
Jimmy Valiant defeated the Barbarian
Jimmy Valiant defeated Paul Jones
Ron Bass defeated Kendo Nagasaki
NWA US Champion Magnum TA defeated Nikita Koloff
NWA TV Champion Dusty Rhodes defeated Buddy Landell

Central States @ Kansas City, KS - July 11, 1985
Harley Race defeated NWA World Champion Ric Flair in a
Best 2 out of 3 falls match; fall #3: Race won via
disqualification

JCP @ Dillwyn, VA - Bassett High School Gym - July 12, 1985
Superstar Billy Graham vs. Sam Houston
Buzz Tyler & American Starship vs. Ivan Koloff & Krusher Kruschev
Manny Fernandez vs. NWA TV Champion Tully Blanchard

Houston, TX - July 12, 1985
NWA World Champion Ric Flair defeated Wahoo McDaniel via disqualification

JCP @ Atlanta, GA - WTBS Studios - July 13, 1985 (matinee)
World Championship Wrestling - 7/13/85

JCP @ Greensboro, NC - Coliseum - July 13, 1985
Sam Houston defeated Joel Deaton
Rising Sun #2 defeated Stoney Burke
Ivan Koloff defeated Starship Eagle
Krusher Kruschev defeated Sam Houston
NWA TV Champion Dusty Rhodes defeated Nikita Koloff
NWA World Champion Ric Flair defeated Buddy Landell

JCP @ Cleveland, OH - July 13, 1985
Brett Sawyer defeated Mike Davis
Thunderbolt Patterson defeated Bob Roop
Dick Slater fought Kevin Sullivan to a no contest
Bobby Eaton & Dennis Condrey defeated Pez Whatley & the
Italian Stallion
Black Bart defeated Ron Garvin

Buzz Sawyer defeated Arn Anderson
Jimmy Valiant defeated the Barbarian via disqualification
Jimmy Valiant defeated Paul Jones via count-out

JCP @ Charlotte, NC - Coliseum - July 13, 1985
NWA World Champion Ric Flair defeated Buddy Landell

CWF @ Ft. Lauderdale, FL - July 13, 1985
Dale Veasey defeated Tony Wonder
The Grappler & Rip Oliver defeated Cocao Samoa & Tiger
Conway Jr.
Kendall Windham defeaetd Jack Hart
Wahoo McDaniel defeated Rick Rude
Rip Rogers defeated Bugsy McGraw
NWA World Champion Ric Flair defeated Billy Jack Haynes

JCP @ Asheville, NC - Civic Center - July 14, 1985 (matinee)
Gene Ligon defeated Lee Ramsey
Ricky Reeves defeated Tommy Lane
The Rising Suns defeated Starship Eagle & Sam Houston
Manny Fernandez defeated Ivan Koloff
NWA US Champion Magnum TA defeated Nikita Koloff
NWA TV Champion Dusty Rhodes defeated Buddy Landell

CWF @ Orlando, FL - July 14, 1985
Cocoa Samoa defeated Jack Hart
Kendall Windham defeated Tony Wonder
Bugsy McGraw defeated Rip Rogers
The Grappler & Rip Oliver defeated Mike Graham & Tiger
Conway Jr.
Rick Rude defeated Billy Jack Haynes via disqualification
NWA World Champion Ric Flair defeated Wahoo McDaniel

JCP @ Charleston, WV - July 14, 1985
Pez Whatley defeated Bob Roop
Thunderbolt Patterson defeated Mike Davis
Kevin Sullivan defeated the Italian Stallion
Bobby Eaton & Dennis Condrey defeated Dick Slater & Buzz
Sawyer
Brett Sawyer defeated Arn Anderson
Black Bart defeated Ron Garvin
Jimmy Valiant defeated the Barbarian
Jimmy Valiant defeated Paul Jones via disqualification

JCP @ Greenville, SC - Memorial Auditorium - July 15, 1985
Ron Bass defeated Joel Deaton
Ivan Koloff & Khrusher Khruschev defeated Sam Houston &
Starship Eagle
Manny Fernandez fought Abdullah The Butcher to a double
count-out
NWA Tag Team Champions Ricky Morton & Robert Gibson
defeated Superstar Billy Graham & Kendo Nagasaki
NWA TV Champion Dusty Rhodes fought Buddy Landell to a

draw
NWA US Champion Magnum TA defeated Nikita Koloff via disqualification

JCP @ Columbus, GA - July 15, 1985
Magnum TA defeated NWA World Champion Ric Flair via disqualification

JCP @ Canton, OH - July 15, 1985
Bobby Eaton & Dennis Condrey defeated Pez Whatley & the Italian Stallion

JCP @ Marion, OH - July 16, 1985
Bobby Eaton & Dennis Condrey defeated Dick Slater & Brett Sawyer

CWF @ Tampa, FL - July 16, 1985
Kendall Windham defeated Tony Wonder
Jack Hart defeated Dale Veasey
Rip Oliver & the Grappler defeated Tiger Conway Jr. & Cocoa Samoa
Rip Rogers defeated Bugsy McGraw
Rick Rude defeated Billy Jack Haynes via forfeit
NWA World Champion Ric Flair defeated Wahoo McDaniel

JCP @ Gaffney, SC - Timken Physical Education Center - July 16, 1985
Worldwide - 7/20/85 - featured Tony Schiavone & David Crockett on commentary; included Crockett introducing footage of NWA TV Champion Dusty Rhodes taking Baby Doll to Nelson Royal's ranch, with footage then airing of Baby Doll cleaning the horse stalls; moments later, Baby Doll found Rhodes and Royal outside and asked if she could ride one of the horses that she's been cleaning up after, with Rhodes agreeing; featured Crockett conducting an interview with Buddy Landell & JJ Dillon, with Dillon saying Landell should be the NWA World Champion then and there; moments later, footage aired of a recent bout between Flair and Landell in which Landell pinned Flair after hitting him with a foreign object; Rhodes then came out and told the referee what happened, with Landell assaulting Rhodes and then the referee; included Crockett conducting an interview with NWA Six-Man Tag Team Champions Krusher Kruschev, Ivan & Nikita Koloff regarding their NWA Tag Team Title loss to Ricky Morton & Robert Gibson and Nikita's loss to Flair at the Great American Bash in Charlotte, NC; the Russians then said they wouldn't stop until they reclaimed the tag team titles and Nikita took the world title; featured Crockett conducting an interview with Manny Fernandez regarding Paul Jones, with Jones then interrupting and distracting Fernandez until he was double teamed by the Barbarian & Superstar Billy Graham; included another segment of Baby Doll, Rhodes, and Royal in which Baby Doll rode Floyd the horse off the ranch; featured a closing segment in which Rhodes and Royal were shown at the ranch talking about Baby Doll's escape:

Jimmy Valiant pinned Joel Deaton with the elbow drop at the 28-second mark
The Barbarian (w/ Paul Jones) pinned NWA Jr. Heavyweight Champion Denny Brown in a non-title match at 3:49 with the headbutt off the top
NWA Tag Team Champions Ricky Morton & Robert Gibson defeated George South & Gene Ligon at 5:26 when Gibson pinned South following the double dropkick
Buddy Landell (w/ JJ Dillon) defeated Mark Fleming at 7:35 via submission with the figure-4
NWA US Champion Magnum TA pinned Kendo Nagasaki (w/ JJ Dillon) with the belly to belly suplex at the 58-second mark
NWA Six-Man Tag Team Champions Nikita Koloff & Krusher Kruschev (w/ NWA Six-Man Tag Team Champion Ivan Koloff) defeated Starship Eagle & Lee Ramsey at 3:16 when Nikita pinned Ramsey with the Russian Sickle as Kruschev held Ramsey in the air; prior to the bout, David Crockett conducted an interview with NWA Tag Team Champions Ricky Morton & Robert Gibson regarding their title win over the Russians; Morton & Gibson joined Crockett on commentary for the match; after the contest, Crockett spoke with Morton & Gibson regarding the challenge of the Road Warriors, NWA National Tag Team Champions Ole & Arn Anderson, NWA TV Champion Dusty Rhodes & NWA US Champion Magnum TA, and the Russians
Dark matches:
NWA TV Champion Dusty Rhodes vs. Buddy Landell
NWA US Champion Magnum TA vs. Ivan Koloff

JCP @ Cincinnati, OH - July 17, 1985
The Italian Stallion defeated Bob Roop
Thunderbolt Patterson defeated Mike Davis
NWA US Champion Magnum TA defeated Ivan Koloff
NWA TV Champion Dusty Rhodes defeated Tully Blanchard
Dick Slater defeated Abdullah the Butcher via disqualification
Bobby Eaton & Dennis Condrey defeated Pez Whatley & Brett Sawyer
Buzz Sawyer fought National Tag Team Champion Arn Anderson to a draw

CWF @ Ft. Lauderdale, FL - Stadium - July 17, 1985 (2,056)
Dale Veasey defeated Tony Wonder
Kendall Windham defeated Jack Hart
Rip Oliver & the Grappler defeated Tiger Conway Jr. & Cocoa Samoa
Rip Rogers defeated Bugsy McGraw
Wahoo McDaniel fought Rick Rude to a double disqualification
NWA World Champion Ric Flair defeated Billy Jack Haynes

JCP @ Columbia, SC - Township Auditorim - July 17, 1985
TV taping:
Mid-Atlantic Championship Wrestling - 7/20/85:
Manny Fernandez & Jimmy Valiant defeated Superstar Billy Graham & the Barbarian via disqualification at 5:27

JCP @ Columbus, OH - July 18, 1985
Brett Sawyer defeated Bob Roop
Thunderbolt Patterson defeated Mike Davis
Bobby Eaton & Dennis Condrey defeated Pez Whatley & the Italian Stallion
Dick Slater fought Kevin Sullivan to a no contest
NWA National Heavyweight Champion Black Bart defeated Ron Garvin
Buzz Sawyer defeated NWA National Tag Team Champion Arn Anderson in a Texas Death Match
Dusty Rhodes defeated Tully Blanchard
Magnum TA defeated NWA World Champion Ric Flair via disqualification

JCP @ Norfolk, VA - Scope - July 18, 1985
The Rising Suns defeated Sam Houston & Mark Fleming
Nikita Koloff defeated Ricky Reeves
Buddy Landell defeated Ron Bass
NWA Tag Team Champions Ricky Morton & Robert Gibson defeated the Barbarian & Superstar Billy Graham
Manny Fernandez defeated Abdullah the Butcher via disqualification
Jimmy Valiant defeated Paul Jones in a dog collar match

JCP @ Wheeling, WV - Civic Center - July 19, 1985
Brett Sawyer pinned Bob Roop at 7:43
Thunderbolt Patterson pinned DJ at 7:55
Bobby Eaton & Dennis Condrey defeated Pez Whatley & the Italian Stallion at 13:05 when Eaton pinned Whatley
Dick Slater defeated Kevin Sullivan via disqualification at 11:58
Buzz Sawyer defeated NWA National Tag Team Champion Arn Anderson in a Texas Death Match at 27:05
NWA National Heavyweight Champion Black Bart pinned Ron Garvin at 17:42

JCP @ Atlanta, GA - WTBS Studios - July 20, 1985 (matinee)
World Championship Wrestling - 7/20/85

JCP @ Philadelphia, PA - Civic Center - July 20, 1985
Sam Houston defeated JJ Dillon
Manny Fernandez defeated Superstar Billy Graham
Buddy Landell defeated Ron Bass
Dick Slater defeated the Barbarian
NWA US Champion Magnum TA defeated Nikita Koloff via count-out
NWA TV Champion Dusty Rhodes defeated Tully Blanchard in a bullrope match
Jimmy Valiant defeated Paul Jones in a dog collar match
NWA Tag Team Champions Ricky Morton & Robert Gibson defeated Ivan Koloff & Krusher Kruschev via disqualification

JCP @ Columbus, GA - Municipal Stadium - July 20, 1985
Joe Lightfoot vs. Bob Roop
Rocky King & Gerald Finlay vs. Mike Davis & Tommy Lane

NWA National Heavyweight Champion Black Bart vs. Pez Whatley (No DQ)
Bobby Eaton & Dennis Condrey defeated Pez Whatley (sub. for Bart Sawyer) & the Italian Stallion
Dick Slater vs. Kevin Sullivan
Buzz Sawyer vs. NWA National Tag Team Champion Arn Anderson (non-sanctioned steel cage match)

JCP @ Charlotte, NC - Coliseum - July 21, 1985
Thunderbolt Patterson defeated Joel Deaton
Krusher Kruschev defeated Starship Eagle
Ron Bass defeated Rising Sun #2
Jimmy Valiant defeated Rising Sun #1
Dusty Rhodes defeated Buddy Landell via disqualification
Tully Blanchard defeated NWA US Champion Magnum TA to win the title
Manny Fernandez defeated the Barbarian in a Mexican Death match
NWA Tag Team Champions Ricky Morton & Robert Gibson defeated Ivan & Nikita Koloff via disqualification

JCP @ Atlanta, GA - Omni - July 21, 1985
Prior to the show, National Tag Team Champions Ole & Arn Anderson attacked Magnum TA backstage as Magnum was cutting a promo for the Philadelphia market; during the assault, Magnum was repeatedly punched, kicked, and had his shirt torn
Terry Taylor defeated Bob Roop
Bobby Eaton & Dennis Condrey defeated Pez Whatley & the Italian Stallion
Jimmy Valiant defeated Paul Jones in a dog collar match
Tully Blanchard defeated Brett Sawyer
Dick Slater defeated Kevin Sullivan
Dusty Rhodes & Magnum TA fought National Tag Team Champions Ole & Arn Anderson to a no contest
Black Bart defeated Ron Garvin in a steel cage match

JCP @ Saginaw, MI - July 22, 1985
Bob Roop defeated Rocky King
Pez Whatley defeated Mike Davis
Thunderbolt Patterson defeated Tommy Lane
Black Bart defeated the Italian Stallion
Bobby Eaton & Dennis Condrey defeated Buzz & Brett Sawyer
Dick Slater defeated Kevin Sullivan via disqualification
Jimmy Valiant defeated the Barbarian
Jimmy Valiant fought Paul Jones to a draw

JCP @ Greenville, SC - Memorial Auditorium - July 22, 1985
Superstar Billy Graham defeated Denny Brown
Joel Deaton defeated Kareem Muhammad
Abdullah the Butcher defeated Sam Houston
Magnum TA fought NWA US Champion Tully Blanchard to a 30-minute time-limit draw
NWA TV Champion Dusty Rhodes defeated Nikita Koloff via disqualification

NWA World Champion Ric Flair pinned Buddy Landell at the 35-minute mark

JCP @ Lansing, MI - July 23, 1985
Tommy Lane defeated Rocky King
Thunderbolt Patterson defeated Mike Davis
Kevin Sullivan defeated the Italian Stallion
Pez Whatley defeated Bob Roop
Black Bart defeated Brett Sawyer
Bobby Eaton & Dennis Condrey defeated Dick Slater & Buzz Sawyer
Jimmy Valiant defeated the Barbarian
Jimmy Valiant defeated Paul Jones via disqualification

JCP @ Columbia, SC - July 23, 1985
Joel Deaton defeated Ricky Reeves
Superstar Billy Graham defeated Lee Ramsey
Jimmy Valiant defeated Abdullah the Butcher
Manny Fernandez defeated the Barbarian
NWA Tag Team Champions Ricky Morton & Robert Gibson defeated Ivan Koloff & Krusher Kruschev

JCP @ Newton, NC - July 24, 1985
Manny Fernandez defeated Superstar Billy Graham

CWF @ Miami Beach, FL - Convention Hall - July 24, 1985
Tiger Conway Jr. defeated Tony Wonder
Rip Rogers defeated Bugsy McGraw
The Grappler & Rip Oliver defeated Mike Graham & Cocoa Samoa
Jimmy Valiant defeated the Barbarian
Magnum TA fought Abdullah the Butcher to a double disqualification
Billy Jack Haynes defeated Rick Rude
Dusty Rhodes defeated NWA US Champion Tully Blanchard in a non-title barbed wire match
NWA World Champion Ric Flair defeated Wahoo McDaniel

Central States @ St. Louis, MO - July 24, 1985
NWA World Champion Ric Flair vs. Kevin Von Erich

JCP @ Athens, GA - July 25, 1985
Bobby Eaton & Dennis Condrey defeated Brett Sawyer & the Italian Stallion

JCP @ Albany, GA - Civic Center - July 26, 1985
Joe Lightfoot vs. Bob Roop
Rocky King vs. Mike Davis
NWA National Heavyweight Champion Black Bart vs. Pez Whatley
Bobby Eaton & Dennis Condrey defeated Brett Sawyer & the Italian Stallion
Dick Slater & Buzz Sawyer vs. Arn Anderson & Kevin Sullivan

(steel cage match)
Bobby Eaton & Dennis Condrey co-won a $10,000 battle royal

Houston, TX - July 26, 1985
NWA World Champion Ric Flair defeated Wahoo McDaniel in a No DQ match

JCP @ Hampton, VA - July 26, 1985
Denny Brown fought Pat Tanaka to a draw
The Rising Suns defeated Starship Eagle & Sam Houston
Ron Bass defeated Buddy Landell in a Texas Death Match
Magnum TA defeated Nikita Koloff via disqualification
NWA TV Champion Dusty Rhodes defeated NWA US Champion Tully Blanchard

JCP @ Atlanta, GA - WTBS Studios - July 27, 1985 (matinee)
World Championship Wrestling - 7/27/05

Worldwide - 7/27/85:
The Rising Suns vs. Denny Brown & Stony Burke
Buddy Landell vs. Joel Deaton
Bobby Eaton & Dennis Condrey vs. Dale Williams & Carry Clarke
NWA Tag Team Champions Ricky Morton & Robert Gibson vs. Mark Fleming & Lee Ramsey
NWA US Champion Tully Blanchard vs. Starship Eagle
Abdullah the Butcher vs. Ron Bass
Krusher Kruschev, Ivan & Nikita Koloff vs. Sam Houston, Burke, & Pat Tanaka

Mid South @ Tulsa, OK - July 27, 1985
NWA World Champion Ric Flair defeated Dusty Rhodes via disqualification

JCP @ Greensboro, NC - Coliseum - July 27, 1985
Ricky Reeves defeated Mark Fleming
Sam Houston defeated George South
Ron Bass defeated Joel Deaton
Jimmy Valiant defeated Paul Jones in a dog collar match
NWA Tag Team Champions Ricky Morton & Robert Gibson fought Ivan & Nikita Koloff to a draw
NWA TV Champion Dusty Rhodes defeated Buddy Landell
NWA World Champion Ric Flair defeated Nikita Koloff

JCP @ Asheville, NC - Civic Center - July 28, 1985 (matinee)
Denny Brown vs. Pat Tanaka
Sam Houston vs. Superstar Billy Graham
Manny Fernandez vs. the Barbarian
Jimmy Valiant vs. Paul Jones (dog collar match)
NWA US Champion Tully Blanchard vs. Magnum TA
NWA Tag Team Champions Ricky Morton & Robert Gibson vs. Ivan Koloff & Krusher Kruschev

JCP @ Augusta, GA - July 28, 1985
Bobby Eaton & Dennis Condrey defeated Brett Sawyer & the Italian Stallion

JCP @ Greenville, SC - Memorial Auditorium - July 29, 1985
Abdullah the Butcher defeated Ricky Reaves
Sam Houston pinned George South
Joel Deaton defeated Lee Ramsey
Ron Bass defeated Buddy Landell via disqualification
Jimmy Valiant pinned Paul Jones
NWA World Tag Team Champions Ricky Morton & Robert Gibson fought Ivan Koloff & Krusher Khruschev to 60-minute time-limit draw

JCP @ Jasper, GA - July 30, 1985
Bobby Eaton & Dennis Condrey defeated Brett Sawyer & the Italian Stallion

Mid South @ Jackson, MS - July 30, 1985
NWA World Champion Ric Flair vs. Dick Murdoch

JCP @ Raleigh, NC - Dorton Arena - July 31, 1985
Rising Sun #2 defeated Ricky Reeves
Rising Sun #1 defeated Sam Houston
Krusher Kruschev defeated Mark Fleming
NWA Tag Team Champions Ricky Morton & Robert Gibson defeated Ivan & Nikita Koloff via disqualification
Magnum TA fought NWA US Champion Tully Blanchard to a no contest
Terry Taylor defeated Black Bart
NWA World Champion Ric Flair vs. Buddy Landel

JCP @ Mount Holly, NJ - Burlington County Vo-Tech High School - August 1, 1985
Denny Brown fought Stoney Burke to a draw
Pat Tanaka defeated Gerald Finley
Ron Bass defeated the Barbarian via disqualification
Manny Fernandez defeated Superstar Billy Graham
NWA TV Champion Dusty Rhodes defeated Abdullah the Butcher via count-out

JCP @ Huntington, WV - August 1, 1985
Rising Sun #1 defeated Ricky Reeves
NWA National Tag Team Champions Arn & Ole Anderson defeated Johnny Weaver & Sam Houston
NWA US Champion Tully Blanchard defeated Starship Eagle
Jimmy Valiant defeated Paul Jones in a dog collar match
NWA Tag Team Champions Ricky Morton & Robert Gibson defeated Ivan & Nikita Koloff
NWA World Champion Ric Flair fought Magnum TA to a draw

JCP @ Charlotte, NC - Coliseum - August 2, 1985
Bobby Eaton & Dennis Condrey defeated Pat Tanaka & Denny Brown
National Tag Team Champion Arn Anderson defeated Starship Eagle
National Tag Team Champion Ole Anderson defeated Sam Houston
Ron Bass defeated Buddy Landell in a Texas Death Match
NWA Tag Team Champions Ricky Morton & Robert Gibson defeated Ivan Koloff & Krusher Kruschev via disqualification
NWA TV Champion Dusty Rhodes fought Nikita Koloff to a no contest
Magnum TA defeated NWA US Champion Tully Blanchard via count-out

JCP @ Charleston, SC - County Hall - August 2, 1985
Thunderbolt Patterson & Pez Whatley vs. the Rising Suns
Superstar Billy Graham vs. the Italian Stallion
Terry Taylor vs. NWA National Heavyweight Champion Black Bart
Dick Slater vs. Abdullah the Butcher
Manny Fernandez vs. the Barbarian (Mexican death match)
Jimmy Valiant vs. Paul Jones (dog collar match)

Central States @ St. Louis, MO - August 2, 1985
Missouri Heavyweight Champion Harley Race vs. NWA World Champion Ric Flair

JCP @ Atlanta, GA - WTBS Studios - August 3, 1985 (matinee)
World Championship Wrestling - 8/3/85

Polynesian Pacific @ Honolulu, HI - Aloha Stadium - August 3, 1985 (12,553; reported as 19,995)
WWF Jr. Heavyweight Champion the Cobra defeated Superfly Tui
Seiji Sakaguchi defeated Matt Borne
Kengo Kimura & Tatsumi Fujinami defeated Gary Fulton & Gary Lewis
Jimmy Snuka defeated Larry Sharpe
Manny Fernendez defeated Black Bart via disqualification
Mighty Milo fought AWA Light Heavyweight Champion Steve Regal to a draw
Debbie Combs defaeted Fallen Angel via disqualification
Farmer Boy Ipo & Leroy Brown defeated Joel & Verne Deaton
Mean Little Kevin defeated Pancho Boy
Richie Magnett defeated Gypsy Joe
Dusty Rhodes & Magnum TA defeated Nikita Koloff & Krusher Khruschev
Andre the Giant, Angelo Mosca, & Steve Collins defeated King Kong Bundy, Mark Lewin, & Kevin Sullivan
Lars Anderson defeated Polynesian Heavyweight Champion Bad News Allen to win the title
Polynesian Tag Team Champions Rocky & Ricky Johnson defeated the Dirty White Boys
NWA World Champion Ric Flair fought Sivi Afi to a no contest

Sunday, July 28th 3PM
TRIPLE MAIN EVENT
Asheville Civic Center

WORLD TAG TEAM TITLE
ROCK & ROLL EXPRESS
vs
IVAN KOLOFF &
KRUSHER KHRUSHCHEV

U.S. TITLE MATCH
U.S. Champion
MAGNUM T.A.
vs
TULLY BLANCHARD

DOG COLLAR MATCH
"Boogie Woogie Man"
JIMMY VALIANT
vs
"No. 1"
PAUL JONES

RAGIN' BULL
vs
BARBARIAN

SAM HOUSTON
vs
SUPERSTAR
BILLY GRAHAM

DENNY BROWN
vs
PATRICK TANAKA

PAUL

TULLY

JIMMY

MAGNUM

IVAN

KRALL

Ringside '7 Gen. Adm. '6 Children Under 10, '3
Box Office 259-5771 Mon.-Fri. 10-5:30, Sat. 11-4, Day of Match 1:00 P.M.
No Checks or Credit Cards Day of Match. Matches subject to change.

WIDE WORLD WRESTLING ON WLOS TV 13 SUNDAY 12 NOON

212

POLYNESIAN PACIFIC CHAMPIONSHIP
WRESTLING

Promoter Lia Maivia Goes To:

Aloha Stadium   7:30 pm   Saturday, August 3, 1985

'85 WORLD INVITATIONAL WRESTLING SPECTACULAR
(Hot Summer Night)

Champion

RIC FLAIR
U.S.A.

NWA WORLD CHAMPIONSHIP
— VS —

Challenger

SIVA AFI
Samoa

Polynesian Pacific Heavyweight

CHALLENGER
LARS ANDERSON

VS

CHAMPION
BAD NEWS ALLAN

Polynesian Pacific Tag Team
Winner take all.
No Disqualification

CHAMPION
"The Soul Patrol"
RICKY & RICKY JOHNSON
New York

VS

CHALLENGERS
THE DIRTY WHITE BOYS
Tennessee

WWF Jr. World Championship

CHAMPION
THE COBRA

VS

CHALLENGER
SUPER FLY TUI

NWA NATIONAL HEAVY-WEIGHT CHAMPIONSHIP

CHAMPION
BLACK BART

VS

CHALLENGER
MANNY FERNANDEZ

USA vs RUSSIA

Challengers
"The American Dream"
DUSTY RHODES & MAGNUM T.A.

VS

World Champions
NIKITA KOLOFF & KRUSHER KRUSCHEV

AWA LIGHTWEIGHT WORLD CHAMPIONSHIP

CHAMPION
STEVE REGAL

VS

CHALLENGER
MIGHTY MILO

Jimmy "Superfly" Snuka

VS

Larry Sharp

The Family vs Sullivans Army

$20,000 to any wrestler that can slam BUNDY
VS

"The Family"
Andre the Giant & Steve "The Kid" Collins
& "Big & Nasty" Angelo Mosca

"The Army"
King Kong Bundy & Kevin Sullivan & "Maniac" Mark Lewis

4 MAN TAG MATCH

KENGO KIMURA

VS

GENE LEWIS

4 MAN TAG MATCH

"The Samoan Connection"

VS

"Texas Outlaws"

MATCH OF THE CENTURY

ANTONIO INOKI
Japan

— VS —

BRUISER BRODIE
New Mexico
U.S.A.

TATSUMI FUJINAMI

VS

GARY FULTON

Seiji Sakaguchi

-VS-

Matt Borne

8 MAN TAG MATCH

Tonga Kid

Sam Anoai

All eight men in the ring at the same time
— VS —
$6,000 to winning team

Dick Murdoch

Adrian Adonis

Ritchie Magnet

VS

Super Joe

Women's Street Fight
"Answer to a Challenge"

DEBBIE COMBS

VS

THE FALLEN ANGEL

Afa & Sika

Royce Starr   Alexis Smirnoff

The Mighty Midgets

PANCHO BOY

VS

MEAN LITTLE KEVIN

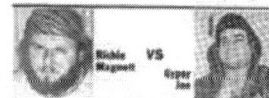

TICKET PRICES: 20.00   15.00 & 12.00 Reserved   9.00 Gen. Admission   6.00 Senior Citizen & Children 5 years to 12 years

TICKETS for SALE NOW at all FUNWAY OUTLETS 942-9696 and ALOHA STADIUM 488-7731

213

Worldwide - 8/3/85:
NWA US Champion Tully Blanchard & Abdullah the Butcher vs. Ricky Reeves & Stoney Burke
Buddy Landell vs. Pat Tanaka
Magnum TA vs. Gerald Finley
NWA TV Champion Dusty Rhodes (w/ Baby Doll) vs. Joel Deaton
Nikita Koloff vs. Sam Houston
Jimmy Valiant, Manny Fernandez, NWA Tag Team Champions Ricky Morton & Robert Gibson vs. Superstar Billy Graham, the Barbarian, & the Rising Suns

JCP @ Florence, SC - August 3, 1985
Rising Sun #1 defeated Stoney Burke
Rising Sun #2 defeated Denny Brown
Superstar Billy Graham defeated Sam Houston
Jimmy Valiant defeated Paul Jones in a dog collar match
Ron Bass defeated Buddy Landell in a Texas Death Match
NWA Tag Team Champions Ricky Morton & Robert Gibson defeated National Tag Team Champions Arn & Ole Anderson via disqualification

JCP @ Macon, GA - August 3, 1985
Bobby Eaton & Dennis Condrey defeated Buzz & Brett Sawyer

JCP @ Sumter, SC - County Exhibition Center - August 4, 1985
Gene Ligon vs. Lee Ramsey
Ricky Reeves vs. George South
Johnny Weaver vs. Superstar Billy Graham
NWA US Champion Tully Blanchard vs. Starship Eagle
NWA Tag Team Champions Ricky Morton & Robert Gibson vs. NWA National Tag Team Champions Ole & Arn Anderson

JCP @ Marietta, GA - August 4, 1985
Dick Slater, Buzz & Brett Sawyer defeated Bob Roop, Bobby Eaton & Dennis Condrey

JCP @ Greenville, SC - Memorial Auditorium - August 5, 1985
Rising Sun ? defeated Ricky Reeves
Denny Brown pinned Joe Lightfoot
Abdullah the Butcher defeated Starship Eagle
NWA US Champion Tully Blanchard defeated Manny Fernandez
NWA TV Champion Dusty Rhodes & Magnum TA defeated National Tag Team Champions Ole & Arn Anderson via disqualification
NWA World Champion Ric Flair fought Nikita Koloff to a double count-out

JCP @ Rock Hill, SC - Winthrop Coliseum - August 6, 1985 (5,123)
TV taping:
Worldwide - 8/10/85:

Jimmy Valiant & Manny Fernandez vs. Ron Rossi & the Golden Terror
Abdullah the Butcher & the Barbarian vs. Stoney Burke & Ricky Reeves
NWA Tag Team Champions Ricky Morton & Robert Gibson vs. Gerald Finley & Mark Fleming
Nikita Koloff & Krusher Kruschev vs. Denny Brown & George South
Buddy Landell vs. Lee Ramsey
NWA US Champion Tully Blanchard, Ole & Arn Anderson vs. American Starship, Ron Bass, & Sam Houston

JCP @ Gainesville, GA - August 6, 1985
Bobby Eaton & Dennis Condrey defeated Buzz & Brett Sawyer

JCP @ Wheeling, WV - Civic Center - August 7, 1985
The Italian Stallion pinned Bob Roop at 8:36
Dick Slater defeated Kevin Sullivan
Thunderbolt Patterson pinned Tommy Lane at 9:11
Pez Whatley pinned Mike Davis at 8:53
Bobby Eaton & Dennis Condrey defeated Buzz & Brett Sawyer at 19:47 when Eaton pinned Brett
Terry Taylor pinned National Heavyweight Champion Black Bart at 21:05 in a non-title match

JCP @ Raleigh, NC - Dorton Arena - August 7, 1985
Buddy Landel defeated Sam Houston
National Tag Team Champion Arn Anderson defeated Starship Eagle
Jimmy Valiant defeated the Barbarian
NWA TV Champion Tully Blanchard defeated Manny Fernandez via disqualification
National Tag Team Champion Ole Anderson defeated Magnum TA
NWA Tag Team Champions Ricky Morton & Robert Gibson vs. Ivan Koloff & Krusher Kruschev (No DQ)

JCP @ Canton, OH - August 8, 1985
Bobby Eaton & Dennis Condrey defeated Buzz & Brett Sawyer

JCP @ Norfolk, VA - August 8, 1985
Joel Deaton defeated Mark Fleming
Ron Bass fought Buddy Landell to a no contest
National Tag Team Champions Ole & Arn Anderson defeated Sam Houston & Starship Eagle
Jimmy Valiant defeated Superstar Billy Graham
Manny Fernandez defeated the Barbarian
Magnum TA defeated NWA US Champion Tully Blanchard via disqualification
NWA Tag Team Champions Ricky Morton & Robert Gibson fought Ivan Koloff & Krusher Kruschev to a draw

Central States @ Kansas City, KS - August 8, 1985
NWA World Champion Ric Flair defeated Missouri Heavyweight Champion Harley Race; Bob Brown was the

guest referee for the match

Mid South @ Baton Rouge, LA - August 9, 1985
NWA World Champion Ric Flair defeated Dick Murdoch via disqualification

JCP @ Charleston, WV - August 9, 1985
The Italian Stallion defeated Tommy Lane
Pez Whatley fought Bob Roop to a draw
Thunderbolt Patterson defeated Mike Davis
Black Bart defeated Terry Taylor via disqualification
Dick Slater defeated Kevin Sullivan in a No DQ match
Bobby Eaton & Dennis Condrey defeated Buzz & Brett Sawyer
Dusty Rhodes & Magnum TA defeated National Tag Team Champions Ole & Arn Anderson via disqualification

TV taping:
Jimmy Valiant defeated NWA US Champion Tully Blanchard via disqualification at around the 3:10 mark when Abdullah the Butcher attacked Valiant as Blanchard was caught in the sleeper; featured Bob Caudle & Johnny Weaver on commentary; after the bout, Magnum TA made the save, bodyslammed Abdullah, and ran Blanchard out of the ring

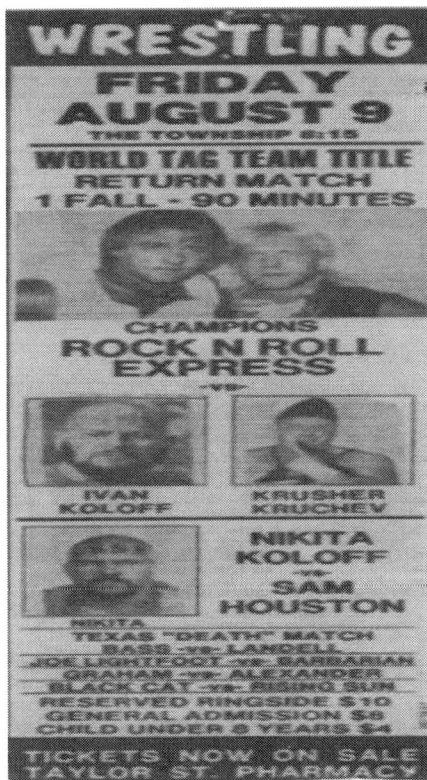

JCP @ Columbia, SC - Township Auditorium - August 9, 1985
Black Cat vs. Rising Sun
Superstar Billy Graham vs. Alexander
Joe Lightfoot vs. the Barbarian
Ron Bass vs. Buddy Landel (Texas Death Match)
Nikita Koloff vs. Sam Houston
NWA Tag Team Champions Ricky Morton & Robert Gibson vs. Ivan Koloff & Krusher Kruschev (90-minute time-limit)

JCP @ Atlanta, GA - WTBS Studios - August 10, 1985 (matinee)
World Championship Wrestling - 8/10/85 - 1 hour episode:
Ron Bass vs. Gerald Finley
NWA US Champion Tully Blanchard (w/ Baby Doll) fought Terry Taylor to a 20-minute time-limit draw; after the bout, Blanchard continued to attack Taylor
Harley Race vs. Jim Jeffers
Nikita Koloff vs. Brodie Chase
NWA Tag Team Champions Ricky Morton & Robert Gibson vs. Keith Erich & Alan Martin

JCP @ Columbus, GA - Municipal Auditorium - August 10, 1985
Kevin Sullivan defeated Adrian Bivens
Tommy Lane defeated Gerald Finley
Mike Davis defeated Rocky King
The Italian Stallion defeated Bob Roop
Black Bart defeated Terry Taylor via disqualification
Jimmy Valiant defeated Paul Jones in a dog collar match
Bobby Eaton & Dennis Condrey defeated Buzz & Brett Sawyer

JCP @ Greensboro, NC - Coliseum - August 10, 1985
Denny Brown defeated Joel Deaton
NWA National Tag Team Champion Arn Anderson defeated Sam Houston
NWA National Tag Team Champion Ole Anderson defeated Starship Eagle
Manny Fernandez defeated the Barbarian in a Mexican Death match
NWA TV Champion Dusty Rhodes, NWA Tag Team Champions Ricky Morton & Robert Gibson defeated Krusher Kruschev, Ivan & Nikita Koloff
Magnum TA fought NWA US Champion Tully Blanchard to a no contest

Mid South @ New Orleans, LA - Superdome - August 10, 1985 (15,800)
Bobby Fulton & Tommy Rogers defeated Bill Dundee & Dutch Mantell
Dick Murdoch defeated the Masked Champion
Mid South Tag Team Champions Ted DiBiase & Steve Williams defeated Nord the Barbarian & Jake Roberts in a steel cage match; Bob Sweetan was the guest referee for the bout
Kamala & Kareem Muhammad defeated Bill Watts & Jim

Duggan in a loser leaves town match when Watts was pinned
NWA World Champion Ric Flair defeated Butch Reed in a No DQ match

JCP @ Atlanta, GA - Omni - August 11, 1985
Bobby Eaton & Dennis Condrey defeated Buzz Sawyer & Manny Fernandez
Nikita Koloff fought NWA World Champion Ric Flair to a double count-out

JCP @ ? - August 11, 1985
George South vs. Stoney Burke
Joel Deaton vs. Sam Houston
Buddy Landel vs. Ron Bass
Jimmy Valiant vs. the Barbarian (dog collar match)
NWA Tag Team Champions Ricky Morton & Robert Gibson vs. Ivan Koloff & Krusher Kruschev
Magnum TA vs. NWA US Champion Tully Blanchard

JCP @ Greenville, SC - Memorial Auditorium - August 12, 1985
Bobby Eaton & Dennis Condrey defeated two unknowns
Bobby Eaton & Dennis Condrey defeated Jim Jeffers & Gerald Findlay
NWA Tag Team Champions Ricky Morton & Robert Gibson defeated Superstar Billy Graham & the Barbarian
Magnum TA defeated Buddy Landel via disqualification
Mid Atlantic Championship Wrestling:
Pro

CWF @ Tampa, FL - Spartan Sports Center - August 13, 1985
Scott McGhee defeated Tony Wonder
Kendall Windham defeated Rip Rogers
Cocoa Samoa fought Rip Oliver to a draw
Jack Hart defeated Tiger Conway Jr.
Mike Graham defeated Rick Rude via disqualification
Wahoo McDaniel & Billy Jack Haynes defeated NWA World Champion Ric Flair & the Grappler in a steel cage match

JCP @ Shelby, NC - Rec Center - August 13, 1985
Bobby Eaton & Dennis Condrey defeated Ron Rossi & an unknown
Bobby Eaton & Dennis Condrey defeated Denny Brown & Starship Eagle
Worldwide - 8/17/85 - featured an opening clip of Jimmy Valiant & Manny Fernandez vs. Joel Deaton & the Golden Terror; included Tony Schiavone & David Crockett on commentary; featured Jim Cornette joining David Crockett and cutting a promo saying he wasn't used to dealing with the lower tier of humanity and asked the fans to start showing he, Bobby Eaton & Dennis Condrey the respect they deserve; Cornette then cut a promo on the teams of Buzz & Brett Sawyer, NWA Tag Team Champions Ricky Morton & Robert Gibson, and NWA TV Champion Dusty Rhodes & Magnum TA;

included Crockett conducting an interview with Buddy Landell & JJ Dillon regarding the challenge of NWA World Champion Ric Flair; featured Crockett conducting an interview with Nikita Koloff regarding Morton & Gibson and that the Russians were still after the tag team titles, then adding he was also after Flair and was taking another piece of Flair each time they meet; included Crockett conducting an interview with Rhodes, Magnum, and Sam Houston regarding Houston's broken arm at the hands of NWA US Champion Tully Blanchard, National Tag Team Champions Ole & Arn Anderson; moments later, they reviewed footage of how Blanchard and the Andersons injured the arm weeks earlier in the ring; featured Crockett conducting an interview with Morton & Gibson regarding the challenge of the Russians; included Crockett conducting a closing interview with Blanchard & Baby Doll in which they made fun of Crockett's attire before bragging about their accomplishments and cutting a promo on Rhodes, Magnum, and Houston:
Jimmy Valiant & Manny Fernandez defeated Joel Deaton & the Golden Terror at 2:44 when Valiant pinned Terror with an elbow drop
Bobby Eaton & Dennis Condrey (w/ Jim Cornette) defeated Ricky Reeves & Jim Jeffers at 6:34 when Eaton pinned Jeffers following a bulldog double team; Cornette provided the ring introductions for his men
National Tag Team Champions Ole & Arn Anderson defeated Mike Starr & Ron Rossi at 4:58 when Ole forced a submission with a standing armbar after hitting a kneedrop off the top onto the opponent's shoulder; following the commercial break, David Crockett conducted an interview with the Andersons in which Ole talked about the recent attacks to Sam Houston and Magnum TA and said no one was in their caliber
Buddy Landell (w/ JJ Dillon) defeated Gerald Finley via submission with the figure-4 at 4:03; Landell kept the hold applied after the match, even grabbing Dillon for leverage, until referee Tommy Young broke it
NWA US Champion Tully Blanchard (w/ Baby Doll) pinned Vernon Deaton with the slingshot suplex at the 46-second mark
Abdullah the Butcher & the Barbarian (w/ Paul Jones) defeated Denny Brown & George South at 4:56 when Barbarian pinned South with a headbutt off the top
Dark match after the taping: NWA Tag Team Champions Ricky Morton & Robert Gibson defeated Bobby Eaton & Dennis Condrey via disqualification (the first Rock 'n' Roll Express vs. Midnight Express match in the Carolinas)

JCP @ Raleigh, NC - Dorton Arena - August 14, 1985
Buddy Landell defeated Denny Brown
Ron Bass fought Abdullah the Butcher to a no contest in a bounty match
NWA National Tag Team Champions Ole & Arn Anderson defeated Sam Houston & Starship Eagle
NWA US Champion Tully Blanchard defeated Manny Fernandez in a No DQ match
Jimmy Valiant, NWA Tag Team Champions Ricky Morton & Robert Gibson defeated Krusher Kruschev, Ivan & Nikita Koloff via disqualification

CWF @ Miami, FL - August 14, 1985
Kendall Windham defeated Tony Wonder
Rip Oliver & Rip Rogers defeated Cocoa Samoa & Tiger Conway Jr.
Jack Hart defeated Scott McGhee
Mike Graham defeated Rick Rude via disqualification
Wahoo McDaniel & Billy Jack Haynes defeated NWA World Champion Ric Flair & the Grappler

JCP @ Athens, GA - August 15, 1985
Bobby Eaton & Dennis Condrey defeated Pez Whatley & Brett Sawyer

CWF @ Orlando, FL - August 15, 1985
Dale Veasey defeated Tony Wonder
Frank Lang defeated Jack Hart
Rip Oliver defeated Tiger Conway Jr.
Cocoa Samoa defeated Rip Rogers
Rick Rude defeated Mike Graham
Wahoo McDaniel & Billy Jack Haynes defeated NWA World Champion Ric Flair & the Grappler

JCP @ Albany, GA - Civic Center - August 16, 1985
Pez Whatley vs. Mike Davis
Bob Roop vs. the Italian Stallion
Thunderbolt Patterson vs. Tommy Lane
Bobby Eaton & Dennis Condrey defeated Buzz & Brett Sawyer
Terry Taylor vs. NWA National Heavyweight Champion Black Bart
Dick Slater vs. Kevin Sullivan (Lights out match)

JCP/AWA Star Wars - East Rutherford, NJ - Meadowlands - August 16, 1985 (7,000)
Baron Von Raschke defeated Davey Gee
Brad Rheingans defeated Boris Zurcov via disqualification
AWA Light Heavyweight Champion Steve Regal pinned Buck Zumhoffe
Greg Gagne & Curt Hennig defeated Nick Bockwinkel & Ray Stevens at the 19-minute mark when Gagne pinned Bockwinkel
AWA World Champion Rick Martel pinned Larry Zbyszko at the 19-minute mark
Sgt. Slaughter defeated NWA World Champion Ric Flair via disqualification at the 34-minute mark when Boris Zhukov attacked Slaughter as Flair was caught in the Cobra Clutch; after the bout, Zhukov threw down the referee and continued to assault Slaughter; as Flair and Zhukov continued to double team Slaughter, Curt Hennig, Brad Rheingans, Buck Zumhoffe, and Tom Zenk made the save
The Road Warriors & Paul Ellering defeated Michael Hayes, Buddy Roberts, & Terry Gordy via disqualification

JCP @ Atlanta, GA - WTBS Studios - August 17, 1985 (matinee)
World Championship Wrestling - 8/17/85

JCP/AWA @ Landover, MD - Capital Centre - August 17, 1985
Bob Backlund defeated Larry Sharpe
Jimmy Valiant defeated Paul Jones
AWA World Champion Rick Martel defeated Larry Zbyszko
Dusty Rhodes fought NWA US Champion Tully Blanchard to a no contest
Magnum TA defeated NWA World Champion Ric Flair via disqualification

JCP @ Richmond, VA - Coliseum - August 1985
Krusher Khruschev defeated Sam Houston
National Tag Team Champion Arn Anderson defeated American Starship Eagle
Ron Bass defeated Buddy Landell via count-out in a Texas Death Match
NWA US Champion Tully Blanchard fought Magnum TA to a no contest when National Tag Team Champion Arn Anderson interfered
NWA Tag Team Champions Ricky Morton & Robert Gibson fought Ivan & Nikita Koloff to a 60-minute time-limit draw

JCP @ Columbus, GA - August 17, 1985
Bobby Eaton & Dennis Condrey defeated Buzz & Brett Sawyer

JCP @ Cleveland, OH - August 18, 1985
Bobby Eaton & Dennis Condrey defeated Buzz & Brett Sawyer

JCP @ Charlotte, NC - Coliseum - August 18, 1985
Sam Houston defeated Rising Sun #2
Denny Brown defeated Rising Sun #1
Starship Eagle defeated the Golden Terror
NWA Tag Team Champions Ricky Morton & Robert Gibson defeated Abdullah the Butcher & the Barbarian via disqualification
Ron Bass defeated Buddy Landell in a bunkhouse match
Wahoo McDaniel fought NWA US Champion Tully Blanchard to a no contest
NWA TV Champion Dusty Rhodes & Magnum TA defeated National Tag Team Champions Ole & Arn Anderson

AWA @ Chicago, IL - Rosemont Horizon - August 18, 1985 (6,000)
Scott Irwin defeated Rob Rechsteiner (Rick Steiner)
Curt Hennig fought Larry Zbyszko to a draw
Steve Regal defeated Buck Zumhoffe
Bill Irwin defeated Baron Von Raschke
Brad Rheingans defeated Boris Zhukov via disqualification
Michael Hayes, Terry Gordy, & Buddy Roberts defeated AWA World Champion Rick Martel, Jerry Blackwell, & Larry Hennig via disqualification
NWA World Champion Ric Flair defeated Billy Robinson
Sgt. Slaughter & Greg Gagne defeated Nick Bockwinkel & Ray Stevens

JCP @ Lovingston, VA - Nelson County High School Gym - August 22, 1985
Denny Brown & Rising Sun #1 vs. Stoney Burke & Ricky Reeves
Abdullah the Butcher vs. Starship Eagle
Manny Fernandez vs. the Barbarian (Mexican Death Match)
Jimmy Valiant vs. Paul Jones (dog collar match)

JCP @ Columbia, SC - Township Auditorium - August 22, 1985
National Tag Team Champion Arn Anderson defeated Sam Houston
Ron Bass defeated Buddy Landell in a bunkhouse match
NWA US Champion Tully Blanchard defeated Magnum TA
NWA TV Champion Dusty Rhodes defeated National Tag Team Champion Ole Anderson in a bullrope match
NWA Tag Team Champions Ricky Morton & Robert Gibson defeated Ivan Koloff & Krusher Kruschev
NWA World Champion Ric Flair defeated Nikita Koloff via disqualification

JCP @ Philadelphia, PA - Civic Center - August 23, 1985
Krusher Kruschev defeated Starship Eagle
National Tag Team Champions Ole & Arn Anderson defeated Jimmy Valiant & Pez Whatley
Ron Bass fought Buddy Landell to a draw
Magnum TA fought NWA US Champion Tully Blanchard to a draw
NWA World Champion Ric Flair defeated NWA TV Champion Dusty Rhodes via disqualification
Manny Fernandez defeated the Barbarian in a Mexican death match
NWA Tag Team Champions Ricky Morton & Robert Gibson defeated Ivan & Nikita Koloff via disqualification

JCP @ Atlanta, GA - WTBS Studios - August 24, 1985 (matinee)
World Championship Wrestling - 8/24/85:
Manny Fernandez vs. Jim Jeffers
The Barbarian vs. Lee Ramsey
Terry Taylor vs. Mike Davis
Ole & Arn Anderson vs. Brodie Chase & Jason Walker
Black Bart vs. Ron Rossi
Jimmy Valiant, Ron Bass, & Starship Eagle vs. NWA Six Man Tag Team Champions Krusher Kruschev, Ivan & Nikita Koloff
Buzz & Brett Sawyer vs. Randy Barber & George South
Buddy Landell vs. Gerald Finley
NWA Tag Team Champions Ricky Morton & Robert Gibson vs. Larry Clarke & Jim Jeffers

Worldwide - 8/24/85:
Ron Bass vs. Gerald Finley
Bobby Eaton & Dennis Condrey (w/ Jim Cornette) vs. Ron Rossi & Mark Fleming
NWA Tag Team Champions Ricky Morton & Robert Gibson vs. Joel Deaton & the Golden Terror

Buddy Landell vs. Jim Jeffers
Abdullah the Butcher & the Barbarian vs. George South & Mack Jeffers
NWA US Champion Tully Blanchard, Ole & Arn Anderson vs. Sam Houston, Starship Eagle, & Denny Brown

JCP @ Macon, GA - August 24, 1985
Terry Taylor, Buzz & Brett Sawyer defeated Jim Cornette, Bobby Eaton & Dennis Condrey

JCP @ Greensboro, NC - Coliseum - August 24, 1985
Stoney Burke defeated George South
National Tag Team Champion Arn Anderson defeated Starship Eagle
Sam Houston defeated Joel Deaton
Ivan Koloff & Krusher Kruschev defeated NWA Tag Team Champions Ricky Morton & Robert Gibson via disqualification
NWA TV Champion Dusty Rhodes defeated National Tag Team Champion Ole Anderson in a Texas bullrope match
Magnum TA defeated NWA US Champion Tully Blanchard
NWA World Champion Ric Flair defeated Nikita Koloff

JCP @ College Park, GA - August 25, 1985
Bobby Eaton & Dennis Condrey defeated Buzz & Brett Sawyer

JCP @ Greenville, SC - Memorial Auditorium - August 26, 1985 (4,100)
Starship Eagle fought the Rising Sun to a draw
Krusher Khruschev defeated Sam Houston
Little Coco pinned Cowboy Lane
Manny Fernandez fought Abdullah the Butcher to a double count-out
Ivan & Nikita Koloff defeated NWA Tag Team Champions Ricky Morton & Robert Gibson via disqualification
NWA TV Champion Dusty Rhodes, Magnum TA, & Ron Bass defeated NWA US Champion Tully Blanchard, NWA National Tag Team Champions Ole & Arn Anderson in a bunkhouse match

JCP @ Wildwood, NJ - August 26, 1985
Bobby Eaton & Dennis Condrey defeated Buzz & Brett Sawyer

JCP @ Allentown, PA - Fairgrounds - August 27, 1985
Bobby Eaton & Dennis Condrey defeated Buzz Sawyer & the Italian Stallion
Pez Whatley vs. the Barbarian
Black Bart vs. Terry Taylor
Jimmy Valiant vs. Superstar Billy Graham
Magnum TA vs. NWA US Champion Tully Blanchard

JCP @ Raleigh, NC - Dorton Arena - August 28, 1985
Manny Fernandez vs. Abdullah the Butcher
NWA Tag Team Champions Ricky Morton & Robert Gibson vs. Ivan & Nikita Koloff (No DQ match)

NWA US Champion Tully Blanchard vs. Jimmy Valiant
Dusty Rhodes & Magnum TA vs. NWA National Tag Team
Champions Ole & Arn Anderson

JCP @ Athens, GA - August 29, 1985
Jim Cornette, Bobby Eaton & Dennis Condrey defeated the
Italian Stallion, Buzz & Brett Sawyer

Worldwide - 8/31/85:
Ron Bass vs. Ron Rossi
Manny Fernandez vs. Tommy Lane
Ole & Arn Anderson vs. George South & Lee Ramsey
Buddy Landell vs. Joel Deaton
NWA Tag Team Champions Ricky Morton & Robert Gibson vs.
Jim & Mack Jeffers
Krusher Kruschev, Ivan & Nikita Koloff vs. Stoney Burke, Ricky
Reeves, & Denny Brown

JCP @ Charlotte, NC - Coliseum - August 31, 1985
Joel Deaton defeated Mark Fleming
Denny Brown defeated Pat Tanaka
Arn Anderson defeated Sam Houston
Krusher Kruschev, Ivan & Nikita Koloff defeated Jimmy Valiant,
NWA Tag Team Champions Ricky Morton & Robert Gibson
Dusty Rhodes defeated Ole Anderson
NWA US Champion Tully Blanchard defeated Magnum TA
NWA World Champion Ric Flair defeated Buddy Landell

JCP @ Columbus, GA - August 31, 1985
The Italian Stallion, Buzz & Brett Sawyer defeated Jim
Cornette, Bobby Eaton & Dennis Condrey via count-out

**JCP @ Atlanta, GA - WTBS Studios - September 1, 1985
(matinee)**
World Championship Wrestling - 9/1/85

JCP @ Raleigh, NC - Dorton Arena - September 1, 1985
Little Coco & Starship Eagle vs. Cowboy Lang & Joel Deaton
Buddy Landel vs. Ron Bass (bunkhouse match)
Manny Fernandez vs. Abdullah the Butcher (Texas Death
Match)
Jimmy Valiant, NWA Tag Team Champions Ricky Morton &
Robert Gibson vs. Ivan Koloff, Krusher Kruschev, & the
Barbarian
NWA US Champion Tully Blanchard vs. Magnum TA (No DQ)
NWA World Champion Ric Flair vs. Nikita Koloff

JCP @ Greensboro, NC - Coliseum - September 1, 1985
The Rising Suns defeated Stoney Burke & Pez Whatley
Joel Deaton defeated Ricky Reeves
Little Coco defeated Cowboy Lang
Manny Fernandez fought Abdullah the Butcher to a draw
NWA US Champion Tully Blanchard defeated Terry Taylor

NWA Tag Team Champions Ricky Morton & Robert Gibson
defeated Ivan Koloff & Krusher Kruschev

JCP @ Atlanta, GA - Omni - September 1, 1985
Superstar Billy Graham defeated Sam Houston
The Barbarian defeated Starship Eagle
Buddy Landell defeated the Italian Stallion
Ron Bass defeated Black Bart via disqualification
Jim Cornette, Bobby Eaton & Dennis Condrey defeated Jimmy
Valiant, Buzz & Brett Sawyer
Dusty Rhodes & Magnum TA defeated National Tag Team
Champions Ole & Arn Anderson
NWA World Champion Ric Flair defeated Nikita Koloff in a
lumberjack match

**JCP @ Fayetteville, NC - Cumberland County Memorial
Arena - September 2, 1985**
Rising Sun #1 vs. Denny Brown
Rising Sun #2 vs. Starship Eagle
NWA National Tag Team Champion Arn Anderson vs. Sam
Houston
Buddy Landel vs. Ron Bass (bunkhouse match)
Dusty Rhodes vs. NWA National Tag Team Champion Ole
Anderson
Magnum TA vs. NWA US Champion Tully Blanchard

**JCP @ Greenville, SC - Memorial Auditorium - September
2, 1985**
Terry Taylor fought Krusher Kruschev to a draw
Bobby Eaton & Dennis Condrey defeated Buzz & Brett Sawyer
Jimmy Valiant defeated Black Bart via disqualification
Manny Fernandez pinned Abdullah the Butcher
NWA Tag Team Champions Ricky Morton & Robert Gibson
defeated Ivan & Nikita Koloff

**CWF Battle of the Belts - Tampa, FL - Sun Dome -
September 2, 1985 (7,600)**
*Shown live in syndication - featured Gordon Solie & Mike
Graham on commentary:*
Hector & Chavo Guerrero defeated Rip Oliver & the Grappler
at 15:40 when Hector pinned the Grappler
Cocoa Samoa pinned Rip Rogers at the 11-minute mark
Kendall Windham pinned Jack Hart at the 12-minute mark
Southern Heavyweight Champion Rick Rude pinned Billy Jack
Hayes at the 14-minute mark
AWA Tag Team Champions the Road Warriors (w/ Paul
Ellering) fought Harley Race & Stan Hansen to a double count-
out at the 10-minute mark when all four men began brawling
on the floor
Nick Bockwinkel pinned Frankie Lane at the 4-minute mark
NWA World Champion Ric Flair defeated Wahoo McDaniel in a
Best 2 out of 3 falls match, 2-1; fall #1: McDaniel defeated Flair
via submission with a sleeper at the 24-minute mark; fall #2:
Flair pinned McDaniel at the 40-minute mark with a kneedrop
after twice ramming the challenger into the ringpost on the
floor; fall #3: Flair pinned McDaniel at 43:17 after kicking off the

ropes as Flair was caught in a sleeper, with Flair falling backwards for the win

JCP @ Gaffney, SC - September 3, 1985
TV taping:
Worldwide - 9/7/85:
Jimmy Valiant & Manny Fernandez vs. the Rising Sun & the Golden Terror
Superstar Billy Graham vs. George South
Magnum TA vs. Tommy Lane
Bobby Eaton & Dennis Condrey vs. Gerald Finley & Lee Ramsey
Sam Houston pinned NWA National Tag Team Champion Arn Anderson with a roll up at 4:48 after Anderson became distracted by Magnum TA on the apron; NWA National Tag Team Champion Ole Anderson provided guest commentary for the bout; Houston's arm was in a cast as a result of it being recently broken by the Andersons, NWA US Champion Tully Blanchard, and Baby Doll; mid-way through the bout, Magnum appeared ringside; after the bout, the Andersons double teamed Houston until NWA TV Champion Dusty Rhodes and Magnum cleared the ring
NWA US Champion Tully Blanchard vs. Rocky King
The Barbarian & Abdullah the Butcher vs. Starship Eagle & Mark Fleming

JCP @ Raleigh, NC - September 4, 1985
Nikita Koloff fought NWA World Champion Ric Flair to a double disqualification

Continental @ Lexington, KY - September 5, 1985 (9,000)
NWA Tag Team Champions Ricky Morton & Robert Gibson defeated Bobby Eaton & Dennis Condrey
NWA World Champion Ric Flair defeated Jerry Lawler via disqualification at 28:03; Lawler initially appeared to have won the match and title but the referee stopped the bout after noticing Lawler threw Flair over the top rope moments earlier

JCP @ Cincinnati, OH - September 6, 1985
Bobby Eaton & Dennis Condrey defeated Buzz & Brett Sawyer

JCP @ Hampton, VA - Coliseum - September 6, 1985
NWA World Champion Ric Flair defeated Buddy Landell

Central States @ St. Louis, MO - September 6, 1985
NWA World Champion Ric Flair defeated Sgt. Slaughter via disqualification

Mid Atlantic - featured Bob Caudle conducting an interview with NWA US Champion Tully Blanchard, with Baby Doll, in which Blanchard mentioned NWA TV Champion Dusty Rhodes and Magnum TA's comments earlier in the show and then showed off a new diamond watch Baby Doll bought him

JCP @ Richmond, VA - Coliseum - September 7, 1985
NWA Tag Team Champions Ricky Morton & Robert Gibson fought Bobby Eaton & Dennis Condrey to a 60-minute time-limit draw

JCP @ Philadelphia, PA - Civic Center - September 7, 1985
NWA World Champion Ric Flair defeated NWA TV Champion Dusty Rhodes; there were 2 referees for the match

JCP @ Asheville, NC - Civic Center - September 8, 1985 (matinee)
Little Coco vs. Cowboy Lang
Starship Eagle vs. Rising Sun
Sam Houston vs. Joel Deaton
Magnum TA, Ron Bass, & Manny Fernandez vs. NWA US Champion Tully Blanchard, NWA National Tag Team Champions Ole & Arn Anderson (bunkhouse match)
The Road Warriors vs. Ivan Koloff & Krusher Kruschev
NWA World Champion Ric Flair vs. Nikita Koloff

JCP @ Albany, GA - Civic Center - September 8, 1985 (matinee)
Jim Cornette, Bobby Eaton & Dennis Condrey defeated the Italian Stallion, Buzz & Brett Sawyer

JCP @ Marietta, GA - September 8, 1985
Terry Taylor, Buzz & Brett Sawyer defeated Jim Cornette, Bobby Eaton & Dennis Condrey

JCP @ Greenville, SC - Memorial Auditorium - September 9, 1985
The Barbarian defeated Starship Eagle
Terry Taylor defeated Joel Deaton
Sam Houston defeated Abdullah the Butcher via disqualification
NWA Tag Team Champions Ricky Morton & Robert Gibson fought Bobby Eaton & Dennis Condrey to a 45-minute time-limit draw
NWA TV Champion Dusty Rhodes & Magnum TA defeated NWA National Tag Team Champions Ole & Arn Anderson via disqualification
NWA World Champion Ric Flair defeated NWA US Champion Tully Blanchard

JCP @ Augusta, GA - Civic Center - September 9, 1985
Rocky King defeated Tommy Lane
Mike Davis defeated Stoney Burke
Buzz Sawyer defeated Superstar Billy Graham via disqualification
Ron Bass defeated Buddy Landell
Ivan Koloff & Krusher Kruschev defeated Manny Fernandez & Pez Whatley
Jimmy Valiant defeated Paul Jones in a dog collar match
NWA National Heavyweight Champion Ron Garvin defeated Black Bart

JCP @ Shelby, NC - Rec Center - September 10, 1985
Pro - 9/14/85:
Worldwide - 9/14/85 - included Tony Schiavone & David Crockett on commentary; featured opening footage of Superstar Billy Graham walking out to the ring; included Crockett conducting an interview with Jimmy Valiant, alongside Rocky King, regarding the recent attack King sustained from Bobby Eaton & Dennis Condrey; moments later, footage was shown of Eaton & Condrey attacking King and holding him so Jim Cornette could repeatedly slap King before Valiant made the save; featured Crockett conducting an interview with Manny Fernandez regarding Abdullah the Butcher and Paul Jones, with Fernandez saying he wanted to be the top contender fo the NWA World Title and would have to go through Abdullah to do that; included Crockett conducting an interview with Ivan Koloff in which he said Nikita Koloff & Krusher Kruschev were in the gym working to get bigger and stronger and said NWA TV Champion Dusty Rhodes and NWA World Champion Ric Flair were on their hit list; featured Crockett conducting an interview with Flair, wearing a Magnum TA hat, in which he agreed that Magnum TA was cool but he wasn't world champion; Flair then took the hat off, replied to Fernandez's comments earlier in the show, called Rhodes a fool, and said he NWA US Champion Tully Blanchard and NWA National Tag Team Champions Ole & Arn Anderson didn't have to take a back seat to anyone because they were champions like him; included Crockett conducting an interview with Graham, during which Graham issued a title challenge to Rhodes, Blanchard, and Flair; featured Crockett conducting an interview with Cornette regarding his actions against King, during which Cornette said NWA Tag Team Champions Ricky Morton & Robert Gibson would soon fall to Eaton & Condrey; Cornette then said King was a nobody and a bum, Valiant needed a blood test, and Valiant was now messing with the wrong people; Cornette then threatened to slap King and Valiant's faces:
Terry Taylor defeated Joel Deaton
Abdullah the Butcher (w/ Paul Jones) pinned Lee Ramsey with an elbow drop at 3:19; during the bout, the crowd chanted "Weasel" at Jones
Jimmy Valiant (w/ Rocky King) & Manny Fernandez defeated Jim Jeffers & Mark Fleming at 4:06 when Fernandez scored the pin following the flying forearm
NWA US Champion Tully Blanchard (w/ Baby Doll), NWA National Tag Team Champions Ole & Arn Anderson defeated Ron Rossi, Gerald Finley, & Vernon Deaton at 5:27 when Blanchard scored the pin following the slingshot suplex
NWA Tag Team Champions Ricky Morton & Robert Gibson defeated the Golden Terror & George South; during the bout, Ivan Koloff joined the commentary team and said he, Nikita

Koloff, & Krusher Kruschev would get the tag team titles back
Bobby Eaton & Dennis Condrey (w/ Jim Cornette) defeated Starship Eagle & Mack Jeffers at 2:19 when Condrey pinned Jeffers with a clothesline on his knees after Eaton pulled Jeffers up from the mat; prior to the match, David Crockett conducted an interview with NWA TV Champion Dusty Rhodes & Magnum TA, during which they spoke about Sam Houston's win over Arn Anderson the previous week and Magnum chasing Blanchard for the US title; Rhodes & Magnum joined Crockett on commentary for the match; after the match, Terry Taylor came out and told Rhodes & Magnum that something happened to Houston backstage; moments later, Crockett handed over his mic to Tony Schiavone and went backstage to investigate; Crockett was then shown outside the arena hovering over Houston as fans watched on; Rhodes, Taylor, Magnum, and another wrestler helped Houston to his feet and took him back inside the arena; after taking him inside, Houston was shown bleeding from the face; fans told Crockett that NWA US Champion Tully Blanchard, NWA National Tag Team Champions Ole & Arn Anderson were behind the assault; Houston was tended to by Rhodes, Taylor, Rocky King, Jimmy Valiant, and others as the show ended

JCP @ Kinston, NC - September 11, 1985
Bobby Eaton & Dennis Condrey defeated Starship Eagle & Brady Boone

CWF @ Miami Beach, FL - Convention Hall - September 11, 1985 (5,809)
Cocoa Samoa defeated Jack Hart
Hector Guerrero & Kendall Windham defeated the Grappler & Rip Oliver
Mike Graham fought Rick Rude to a draw
Buddy Rose defeated Frank Lang
Magnum TA fought NWA US Champion Tully Blanchard to a draw
Dusty Rhodes & Wahoo McDaniel defeated National Tag Team Champions Ole & Arn Anderson via disqualification
NWA World Champion Ric Flair defeated Billy Jack Haynes

JCP @ Wheeling, WV - Civic Center - September 12, 1985
The Italian Stallion & Pez Whatley vs. Mike Davis & Tommy Lane
Ron Garvin, Buzz & Brett Sawyer defeated Jim Cornette, Bobby Eaton & Dennis Condrey
Terry Taylor vs. National Heavyweight Champion Black Bart

221

WRESTLING

THURSDAY SEPTEMBER 12 The Township 8:15

6 MAN BUNKHOUSE MATCH

DUSTY RHODES, MANGUM TA, RAGING BULL
-vs.-
TULLY BLANCHARD, OLE AND ARN ANDERSON,
(WITH BABY DOLL)

Rock -n- Roll Express

WORLD'S TAG TEAM TITLE
CHAMPIONS
ROCK -N- ROLL EXPRESS
-vs.-
ABDULLAH AND THE BARBARIAN

"I QUIT" MATCH RON BASS -vs.- BUDDY LANDELL	HOUSTON -vs.- KRUSHER	GRAHAM -vs.- POLI	BURKE -vs.- KING

TICKETS NOW ON SALE TAYLOR ST. PHARMACY

RESERVED RINGSIDE $10
GENERAL ADMISSSION $8
CHILD UNDER 8 YEARS $4

222

JCP @ Columbia, SC - Township Auditorium - September 12, 1985
Stoney Burke vs. Rocky King
Superstar Billy Graham vs. Poli
Sam Houston vs. Krusher Kruschev
Ron Bass vs. Buddy Landel (I Quit match)
NWA Tag Team Champions Ricky Morton & Robert Gibson vs. Abdullah the Butcher & the Barbarian
Dusty Rhodes, Magnum TA, & Manny Fernandez vs. NWA US Champion Tully Blanchard, NWA National Tag Team Champions Ole & Arn Anderson

Continental @ Oxford, AL - September 13, 1985
NWA World Champion Ric Flair defeated Brad Armstrong

JCP @ Williamson, WV - Fieldhouse - September 13, 1985
Bobby Eaton & Dennis Condrey defeated Terry Taylor & the Italian Stallion
Also included Ron Garvin, Buzz Sawyer, and Bob Roop

JCP @ Columbus, GA - September 14, 1985
Bobby Eaton & Dennis Condrey defeated Buzz & Brett Sawyer in a steel cage loser leaves town match

JCP @ Atlanta, GA - WTBS Studios - September 15, 1985 (matinee)
World Championship Wrestling taping

JCP @ College Park, GA - Henderson's Arena - September 15, 1985
Pat Tanaka vs. Lee Ramsey
George South vs. the Italian Stallion
Starship Eagle vs. Tommy Lane
NWA Jr. Heavyweight Champion Denny Brown vs. Mike Davis
Buzz & Brett Sawyer vs. Superstar Billy Graham & Abdullah the Butcher
Ron Garvin vs. NWA National Heavyweight Champion Black Bart

JCP @ Norfolk, VA - September 15, 1985
Superstar Billy Graham defeated Mark Fleming
Starship Eagle & Tony Burke defeated Joe Deaton & the Golden Terror
Manny Fernandez defeated Abdullah the Butcher
Jimmy Valiant defeated Buddy Landell
The Road Warriors defeated Krusher Kruschev & Ivan Koloff
Ron Bass fought the Barbarian to a draw
Dusty Rhodes, Magnum TA, & Sam Houston defeated NWA US Champion Tully Blanchard, National Tag Team Champions Ole & Arn Anderson in a bunkhouse match

JCP @ Pensacola, FL - September 15, 1985 (2,000)
Buddy Landel pinned Sam Houston
Manny Fernandez pinned Krusher Kruschev

Brad & Steve Armstrong defeated National Tag Team Champions Ole & Arn Anderson via disqualification
Jimmy Valiant pinned the Barbarian
NWA Tag Team Champions Ricky Morton & Robert Gibson defeated Bobby Eaton & Dennis Condrey
Tommy Rich defeated Adrian Street via disqualification
Magnum TA fought NWA US Champion Tully Blanchard to a double count-out
The Road Warriors defeated Ivan & Nikita Koloff when Ivan was pinned
NWA World Champion Ric Flair defeated Dusty Rhodes via disqualification

JCP @ Fayetteville, NC - Cumberland County Memorial Arena - September 16, 1985
Gerald Finlay vs. Superstar Billy Graham
Buddy Landel vs. Jimmy Valiant
NWA Tag Team Champions Ricky Morton & Robert Gibson vs. Abdullah the Butcher & the Barbarian
Dusty Rhodes, Magnum TA, & Sam Houston vs. NWA US Champion Tully Blanchard, NWA National Tag Team Champions Ole & Arn Anderson (bunkhouse match)

JCP @ Unadilla, GA - September 16, 1985
Bobby Eaton defeated Buzz Sawyer

Continental @ Birmingham, AL - September 16, 1985
Tommy Rich defeated NWA World Champion Ric Flair via disqualification

JCP @ Chattanooga, TN - September 17, 1985
Bobby Eaton & Dennis Condrey defeated the Italian Stallion & Pez Whatley

CWF @ Tampa, FL - September 17, 1985
NWA World Champion Ric Flair defeated Billy Jack Haynes

JCP @ Raleigh, NC - Dorton Arena - September 18, 1985
Joe Deaton defeated Brady Boone
Superstar Billy Graham defeated Gerald Finley
The Barbarian defeated Rocky King
Bobby Eaton & Dennis Condrey defeated the Italian Stallion & Pat Tanaka
Jimmy Valiant defeated Black Bart via disqualification
NWA Tag Team Champions Ricky Morton & Robert Gibson fought National Tag Team Champions Ole & Arn Anderson to a draw
Manny Fernandez defeated Abdullah the Butcher in a steel cage match

JCP @ Madison Heights, VA - September 19, 1985
Bobby Eaton & Dennis Condrey defeated Starship Eagle & Denny Brown

JCP/AWA @ Baltimore, MD - Civic Center - September 19, 1985
Billy Robinson defeated Jerry Oski
Brad Rheingans defeated Kevin Kelly
Ron Garvin fought Black Bart to a no contest
Nick Bockwinkel & Larry Zbyszko defeated Sgt. Slaughter & Greg Gagne via disqualification
NWA TV Champion Dusty Rhodes fought Nikita Koloff to a draw
NWA Tag Team Champions Ricky Morton & Robert Gibson defeated Ivan Koloff & Krusher Kruschev via disqualification
NWA World Champion Ric Flair defeated Magnum TA

JCP @ Columbia, SC - Township Auditorium - September 20, 1985
Rising Sun vs. Pat Tanaka
Starship Eagle vs. George South
The Italian Stallion vs. Thunderfoot
Ron Garvin vs. Black Bart
Bobby Eaton & Dennis Condrey defeated Starship Eagle & Pat Tanaka (sub. for Buzz & Brett Sawyer)

JCP @ Richmond, VA - Coliseum - September 20, 1985
Mark Fleming defeated Stoney Burke
Tommy Lane defeated Brady Boone
Rocky King defeated Mike Davis
The Barbarian defeated Ricky Reeves
Terry Taylor defeated Arn Anderson
Ron Bass defeated Buddy Landell; stipulations stated Bass would get 5 minutes in the ring with JJ Dillon if he won
Nikita Koloff & Krusher Kruschev defeated NWA Tag Team Champions Ricky Morton & Robert Gibson in a non-title double chain match

JCP/AWA @ Ft. Wayne, IN - September 20, 1985 (5,000)
Brad Rheingans fought Steve Regal to a draw
Bill & Scott Irwin defeated Calypso Jim & Bobo Brazil
Superstar Billy Graham defeated Pez Whatley
Larry Zbyszko defeated Buck Zumhoffe
Sgt. Slaughter defeated Boris Zhukov via disqualification
Magnum TA fought NWA US Champion Tully Blanchard to a draw
NWA TV Champion Dusty Rhodes defeated Ivan Koloff

Central States @ St. Louis, MO - September 20, 1985
Art Crews vs. Sheik Abdullah
Bob Brown vs. Dave Peterson
Larry & Curt Hennig vs. Mr. Pogo & Boo Thomas
NWA Jr. Heavyweight Champion Denny Brown vs. Gary Royal
Jerry Blackwell vs. Kamala
AWA World Champion Rick Martel defeated Jimmy Garvin
Bruiser Brody vs. the One Man Gang
NWA World Champion Ric Flair defeated Missouri Heavyweight Champion Harley Race when the match was stopped due to blood

Worldwide - 9/21/85:
Magnum TA vs. Mack Jeffers
Jimmy Valiant & Rocky King vs. George South & Jim Jeffers
Ole & Arn Anderson vs. Brady Boone & Ricky Reeves
NWA US Champion Tully Blanchard vs. Ricky Reeves
Abdullah the Butcher & the Barbarian vs. Mark Fleming & Ben Alexander
Terry Taylor vs. Ron Rossi

JCP @ Charleston, SC - September 21, 1985
Bobby Eaton & Dennis Condrey defeated the Italian Stallion & Dan Spivey

WWC @ San Juan, Puerto Rico - September 21, 1985
NWA World Champion Ric Flair defeated Hercules Ayala

JCP/AWA @ Indianapolis, IN - September 21, 1985
NWA World Champion Ric Flair vs. Dusty Rhodes

JCP @ Greensboro, NC - Coliseum - September 21, 1985
Thunderfoot defeated Stoney Burke
Rocky King & Brady Boone defeated Mike Davis & Tommy Lane
The Barbarian defeated Pat Tanaka
Ron Garvin & Terry Taylor defeated NWA National Tag Team Champions Ole & Arn Anderson
Ron Bass defeated Buddy Landell in a bunkhouse match
Nikita Koloff & Krusher Kruschev defeated NWA Tag Team Champions Ricky Morton & Robert Gibson in a double chain match

JCP @ Asheville, NC - Civic Center - September 22, 1985 (matinee)
Bobby Eaton & Dennis Condrey defeated the Italian Stallion & Ricky Reeves
Sam Houston vs. NWA National Tag Team Champion Arn Anderson
Jimmy Valiant vs. the Barbarian
NWA Tag Team Champions Ricky Morton & Robert Gibson vs. Ivan & Nikita Koloff (double chain match)
Wahoo McDaniel vs. NWA US Champion Tully Blanchard

JCP @ Atlanta, GA - September 22, 1985
Terry Taylor pinned NWA National Heavyweight Champion Black Bart to win the title

JCP @ Charlotte, NC - Coliseum - September 22, 1985
Krusher Kruschev defeated Gene Ligon
Ron Bass defeated Superstar Billy Graham via disqualification
Nikita Koloff defeated Starship Eagle
Terry Taylor fought Buddy Landell to a draw
Jimmy Valiant defeated Black Bart
NWA Tag Team Champions Ricky Morton & Robert Gibson defeated Bobby Eaton & Dennis Condrey via disqualification in

a non-title match
Dusty Rhodes, Magnum TA, & Wahoo McDaniel defeated NWA US Chapion Tully Blanchard, NWA National Tag Team Champions Ole & Arn Anderson in a bunkhouse match

JCP @ Greenville, SC - September 23, 1985
Bobby Eaton & Dennis Condrey defeated Ron Garvin & Pez Whatley
Worldwide - 9/28/85 - included opening footage of the previous week's brawl between Jimmy Valiant & Rocky King and Bobby Eaton & Dennis Condrey; featured David Crockett conducting an interview with NWA US Champion Tully Blanchard & Baby Doll in which Blanchard said he was tired of only facing Magnum TA and would have a big surprise for Magnum that would bring an abrupt end to Magnum's title shots; included Crockett conducting an interview with NWA TV Champion Dusty Rhodes in which he said his goal was to regain the NWA World Title and responded to comments from NWA National Tag Team Champion Arn Anderson who claimed Rhodes wasn't defending his title on TV as much as he should; featured Crockett conducting an interview with Jimmy Valiant & Rocky King regarding their rivalry with Bobby Eaton, Dennis Condrey, & Jim Cornette; moments later, footage was shown of Rhodes showing up during an interview with Valiant & King and giving Valiant Big Mamma as his new valet; included Crockett conducting an interview with NWA National Heavyweight Champion Terry Taylor regarding his title win and defending against the likes of Buddy Landell and Black Bart; featured Crockett conducting a closing interview with Rhodes regarding Anderson:
Superstar Billy Graham defeated Mark Fleming via submission with the overhead backbreaker at 1:04
Bobby Eaton & Dennis Condrey (w/ Jim Cornette) defeated Ricky Reeves & Mack Jeffers at 5:16 when Condrey pinned Jeffers with one knee on his chest following a Hot Shot
Nikita Koloff pinned Stoney Burke at 5:18 with the Russian Sickle
NWA National Heavyweight Champion Terry Taylor vs. Jim Jeffers; during the bout, David Crockett conducted an interview with Jim Cornette regarding the comments made earlier in the show from Jimmy Valiant & Rocky King; after the contest, Cornette cut a promo on Big Mamma, with Big Mamma then showing up and scaring Cornette off
Ron Garvin vs. Gene Ligon
NWA US Champion Tully Blanchard (w/ Baby Doll), NWA National Tag Team Champion Arn Anderson, & Buddy Landell defeated Pez Whatley, the Italian Stallion, & Brady Boone at 3:54 when Anderson pinned Boone with the gordbuster; NWA TV Champion Dusty Rhodes provided guest commentary for the match alongside Crockett

PNW @ Seattle, WA - Coliseum - September 23, 1985 (4,975)
Billy Jack Haynes fought NWA World Champion Ric Flair to a draw

PNW @ Portland, OR - September 24, 1985 (8,000)
NWA World Champion Ric Flair fought Magnum TA to a draw

JCP @ Kenansville, NC - September 24, 1985
Bobby Eaton & Dennis Condrey defeated Starship Eagle & Pat Tanaka

JCP/AWA @ Queens, NY - Holy Cross High School Gym - September 25, 1985
Pez Whatley vs. Superstar Billy Graham
NWA National Heavyweight Champion Terry Taylor vs. Black Bart
Jimmy Valiant vs. Abdullah the Butcher
Also included Larry Zbyszko, Curt Hennig, Baron Von Rachke, and Tom Zenk

PNW @ Boise, ID - September 25, 1985
Included NWA World Champion Ric Flair

JCP @ Johnson City, TN - September 25, 1985
Bobby Eaton & Dennis Condrey defeated Starship Eagle & Pat Tanaka

JCP @ Harrisonburg, VA - High School - September 26, 1985
Mark Fleming vs. Thunderfoot
Johnny Weaver vs. Tommy Lane
Pat Tanaka vs. Buddy Landell
Bobby Eaton & Dennis Condrey defeated the Italian Stallion (sub. for Buzz Sawyer) & Starship Eagle
NWA US Champion Tully Blanchard vs. Magnum TA

JCP @ Norfolk, VA - Scope - September 27, 1985 (10,000+)
Bobby Eaton & Dennis Condrey defeated Ron Garvin & Starship Eagle
NWA US Champion Tully Blanchard defeated Dusty Rhodes via disqualification
Ivan & Nikita Koloff defeated NWA Tag Team Champions Ricky Morton & Robert Gibson in a non-title steel cage match
NWA World Champion Ric Flair fought Magnum TA to a 60-minute time-limit draw

Worldwide - 9/28/85 - included opening footage of the previous week's brawl between Jimmy Valiant & Rocky King and Bobby Eaton & Dennis Condrey; featured David Crockett conducting an interview with NWA US Champion Tully Blanchard & Baby Doll in which Blanchard said he was tired of only facing Magnum TA and would have a big surprise for Magnum that would bring an abrupt end to Magnum's title shots; included Crockett conducting an interview with NWA TV Champion Dusty Rhodes in which he said his goal was to regain the NWA World Title and responded to comments from NWA National Tag Team Champion Arn Anderson who claimed Rhodes wasn't defending his title on TV as much as he should;

Mid Atlantic Wrestling
Harrisonburg High School
Thursday, Sept. 26, 1985
8:15 P.M.

Main Event

Tully Blanchard & ''Baby Doll'' vs. Magnum TA
(For U.S. Heavyweight Championship)

Tag Team

Starship Eagle & ''Maddog' Buzz Sawyer
vs.
The Midnight Express managed by Jim Cornet

Also:

Pat Tanka vs. ''Nature Boy'' Buddy Landell
Mark Fleming vs. Thunder Foot
Johnny Weaver vs. Tommy Lane

Tickets on sale at Charles Mathias and Harrisonburg High School.
Ringside $6.00 and General Admission $5.00

WORLD T.V. TITLE MATCH
Saturday, September 28
8:15 p.m.

North Surry High School Gym--Mt. Airy, N.C.

*Featuring Many Top Stars Of
The National Wrestling Alliance:*

- Dusty Rhodes VS Tully Blanchard (with Baby Doll)
- ''Mad Dog'' Buzz Sawyer VS Superstar Billy Graham
- Starship Eagle VS J.J. Dillon
- Mark Fleming VS Lee Ramsey
- Ron Rossi VS Gene Ligon

BABY DOLL

SUBJECT TO CHANGE

Ticket Prices:

$10.00 Ringside
$8.00 General Admission
$3.00 General Admission-Children 10 yrs.
of age and under.

ADVANCE TICKET LOCATIONS:
Carpenter's Hardware (Surry Plaza Shopping Center)
Boyles Shoe Store (Main Street-Downstairs)
Zip Foods (Thruway Shopping Center)
Mt. Airy Tractor (Hwy. 89 West)

Event Sponsored By The Franklin Youth Foundation
Of Mt. Airy

JIM CROCKETT PROMOTIONS, INC.

featured Crockett conducting an interview with Jimmy Valiant & Rocky King regarding their rivalry with Bobby Eaton, Dennis Condrey, & Jim Cornette; moments later, footage was shown of Rhodes showing up during an interview with Valiant & King and giving Valiant Big Mamma as his new valet; included Crockett conducting an interview with NWA National Heavyweight Champion Terry Taylor regarding his title win and defending against the likes of Buddy Landell and Black Bart; featured Crockett conducting a closing interview with Rhodes regarding Anderson:

Superstar Billy Graham defeated Mark Fleming via submission with the overhead backbreaker at 1:04
Bobby Eaton & Dennis Condrey (w/ Jim Cornette) defeated Ricky Reeves & Mack Jeffers at 5:16 when Condrey pinned Jeffers with one knee on his chest following a Hot Shot
Nikita Koloff pinned Stoney Burke at 5:18 with the Russian Sickle
NWA National Heavyweight Champion Terry Taylor vs. Jim Jeffers; during the bout, David Crockett conducted an interview with Jim Cornette regarding the comments made earlier in the show from Jimmy Valiant & Rocky King; after the contest, Cornette cut a promo on Big Mamma, with Big Mamma then showing up and scaring Cornette off
Ron Garvin vs. Gene Ligon
NWA US Champion Tully Blanchard (w/ Baby Doll), NWA National Tag Team Champion Arn Anderson, & Buddy Landell defeated Pez Whatley, the Italian Stallion, & Brady Boone at 3:54 when Anderson pinned Boone with the gordbuster; NWA TV Champion Dusty Rhodes provided guest commentary for the match alongside Crockett

AWA SuperClash 85 - Chicago, IL - Comiskey Park - September 28, 1985 (21,000)
AWA Americas Champion Sgt. Slaughter defeated Boris Zhukov via disqualification at 9:34
IWA Champion Mil Mascaras pinned Buddy Roberts at 6:57
Jumbo Tsruta, the Giant Baba, & Genichiro Tenryu defeated Harley Race, Bill & Scott Irwin at 10:57 when Baba pinned Bill
Sherri Martell pinned Candi Devine at 11:24
WCCW Champion Kerry Von Erich pinned Jimmy Garvin at 6:47
AWA Tag Team Champions the Road Warriors (w/ Paul Ellering) defeated Michael Hayes & Terry Gordy (w/ Buddy Roberts) via reverse decision; the challengers originally won the match and titles at 9:59 when Gordy pinned Road Warrior Animal after Hayes came off the top with a double forearm behind the referee's back but the decision was changed after Verne Gagne had the replay shown on the big screen (The Life & Death of the Road Warriors)
NWA Midget Champion Little Tokyo pinned Little Mr. T at 6:54
Jerry Blackwell defeated Kamala in a bodyslam match at 9:50
AWA Jr. Heavyweight Champion Steve Regal pinned Brad Rheingans at 8:19
Greg Gagne, Scott Hall, & Curt Hennig defeated Ray Stevens, Nick Bockwinkel, & Larry Zbyszko at 12:20 when Hall pinned Stevens
NWA Six Man Tag Team Champions Krusher Kruschev, Ivan & Nikita Koloff defeated the Crusher, Dick the Bruiser, & Baron Von Raschke at 9:40 when Ivan pinned Raschke
NWA World Champion Ric Flair pinned Magnum TA with a roll over and grabbing the tights for leverage at 25:10; prior to the match, Larry Nelson conducted seperate interviews with Magnum and Flair about the match; after the bout, Nelson interviewed Flair at ringside in which Flair said Chicago wasn't used to seeing winners (The History of the World Heavyweight Championship)
AWA World Champion Rick Martel fought Stan Hansen to a double count-out at 2:30

JCP @ Mt. Airy, NC - North Surry High School Gym - September 28, 1985
Ron Rossi vs. Gene Ligon
Mark Fleming vs. Lee Ramsey
Starship Eagle vs. JJ Dillon
Buzz Sawyer vs. Superstar Billy Graham
NWA TV Champion Dusty Rhodes vs. Tully Blanchard

JCP @ Atlanta, GA - WTBS Studios - September 29, 1985 (matinee)
World Championship Wrestling taping

JCP @ Atlanta, GA - Omni - September 29, 1985 (12,000)
Buddy Landell defeated Denny Brown
Abdullah the Butcher defeated Sam Houston
Ron Bass defeated Black Bart via disqualification
Ron Garvin & Terry Taylor fought National Tag Team Champions Ole & Arn Anderson to a draw
NWA TV Champion Dusty Rhodes defeated the Barbarian
Ricky Morton & Robert Gibson defeated Ivan & Nikita Koloff via disqualification
Magnum TA fought NWA US Champion Tully Blanchard to a no contest
NWA World Champion Ric Flair defeated Nikita Koloff in a steel cage match; after the bout, Krusher Kruschev closed the cage door as Ivan & Nikita Koloff double teamed the champion; moments later, NWA TV Champion Dusty Rhodes came out to make the save and cleared the Russians from the ring; moments later, Ole & Arn Anderson came out and locked the cage behind them as they helped Flair triple team Rhodes, with Flair eventually hitting a kneedrop off the top to Rhodes' ankle as the Andersons held Rhodes' leg down; Flair then applied the figure-4 on Rhodes while Ricky Morton & Robert Gibson, Magnum TA, Sam Houston, and others came out to try to make the save; after the cage door was opened, Flair and the Andersons escaped while the other wrestlers tended to Rhodes

JCP @ Forest City, NC - September 30, 1985
Bobby Eaton & Dennis Condrey defeated ? & ?

JCP @ Charlotte, NC - Coliseum - September 30, 1985
Brady Boone defeated Tommy Lane
Pez Whatley defeated Mike Davis

227

Jimmy Valiant defeated Superstar Billy Graham
NWA Tag Team Champions Ricky Morton & Robert Gibson defeated Abdullah the Butcher & the Barbarian
Dusty Rhodes defeated Arn Anderson
NWA US Champion Tully Blanchard fought Magnum TA to a double count-out
NWA World Champion Ric Flair defeated Nikita Koloff

Memphis, TN - Mid-South Coliseum - September 30, 1985 (9,496)
Billy Travis, Tommy Wright, & Tojo Yamamoto defeated Buddy Wayne, Ron Sexton, & Mr. Class
Stan Lane & Steve Keirn defeated the Freebirds
Magnum TA fought NWA US Champion Tully Blanchard to a double disqualification
The Sheepherders fought Jimmy Valiant & Bill Dundee to a no contest
Pez Whatley (sub. for NWA TV Champion Dusty Rhodes) defeated Buddy Landell
Ron Bass defeated Terras Bulba
Mid-America Champion Koko Ware defeated Tom Prichard via disqualification
The Stomper defeated AWA International Heavyweight Champion Phil Hickerson to win the title
NWA Tag Team Champions Ricky Morton & Robert Gibson defeated Ivan & Nikita Koloff
NWA World Champion Ric Flair defeated Jerry Lawler via disqualification at 28:45; prior to the bout, Lawler was carried to the ring on a throne; Lawler initially appeared to have won the title but the referee stopped the match for seeing the challenger throw Flair over the top rope moments earlier

JCP @ Rock Hill, SC - Winthrop Coliseum - October 1, 1985
Worldwide - 10/5/85 - featured David Crockett conducting an interview with NWA US Champion Tully Blanchard, with Baby Doll, regarding Magnum TA in which he said he would take a 30 day vacation from facing Magnum and that Magnum would only get one more shot at the belt; included footage of NWA TV Champion Dusty Rhodes being tended to in the ring after being attacked by NWA World Champion Ric Flair, NWA National Tag Team Champions Arn & Ole Anderson at the Omni in Atlanta the previous week; during the segment, it was noted the injury was serious and his condition unknown; featured Crockett conducting an interview with Krusher Kruschev, Ivan & Nikita Koloff regarding the Road Warriors and their comments against the Soviet Union as well as their goal of taking back the NWA Tag Team Titles from Ricky Morton & Robert Gibson; included Crockett conducting an interview with Jimmy Valiant & Big Mamma regarding Bobby Eaton, Dennis Condrey, & Jim Cornette; featured Crockett conducting an interview with Don Kerndole regarding his return to the NWA, during which he said he was after NWA World Champion Ric Flair and Blanchard; included Crockett conducting an interview with Magnum regarding the comments made earlier in the show by Blanchard and the fact he would only get one more shot at the US title; featured Crockett

conducting an interview with Magnum regarding the injury to Rhodes and the hands of Flair, during which it was noted footage of the injury would be released the following week: Superstar Billy Graham defeated Mack Jeffers via submission with an overhead backbreaker at 1:11; during the bout, Paul Jones joined the commentary team and said Graham might have an attitude change but he was still under contract with him
Ron Garvin pinned Jim Jeffers following a right hand punch
Thunderfoot (w/ JJ Dillon) pinned Gene Ligon at 2:29 with a knee to the chest after sending Ligon to the ropes
NWA National Heavyweight Champion Terry Taylor vs. the Black Kat
Bobby Eaton & Dennis Condrey (w/ Jim Cornette) defeated Pez Whatley & Patrick Tanaka at 4:59 when Condrey pinned Tanaka following a brainbuster; NWA Tag Team Champions Ricky Morton & Robert Gibson joined David Crockett on commentary and spoke about Eaton & Condrey, Abdullah the Butcher & the Barbarian, and Ivan & Nikita Koloff being their top challengers
Ron Bass vs. Mike Lane
NWA US Champion Tully Blanchard (w/ Baby Doll) pinned Brady Boone with the slingshot suplex at 3:49; Magnum TA provided guest commentary for the match alongside David Crockett

JCP @ Mt. Vernon, NY - October 2, 1985
Bobby Eaton & Dennis Condrey defeated the Italian Stallion & Pat Tanaka

JCP @ Wheeling, WV - October 3, 1985
The Italian Stallion defeated Tommy Lane
Denny Brown fought Mike Davis to a draw
Thunderfoot defeated Brady Boone
Superstar Billy Graham defeated Starship Eagle
Ron Garvin defeated Black Bart
NWA Tag Team Champions Ricky Morton & Robert Gibson defeated Ivan Koloff & Krusher Kruschev

JCP @ Hampton, VA - Coliseum - October 4, 1985
Sam Houston defeated Mike Davis
The Italian Stallion defeated Mark Fleming
Superstar Billy Graham defeated Don Kernodle via disqualification
Buddy Landell defeated Pez Whatley
NWA Tag Team Champions Ricky Morton & Robert Gibson fought National Tag Team Champions Ole & Arn Anderson to a draw
NWA World Champion Ric Flair defeated Nikita Koloff

JCP @ Albany, GA - Civic Center - October 4, 1985
Brady Boone vs. Tommy Lane
Frank Dusek vs. Gerald Finley
NWA Jr. Heavyweight Champion Denny Brown vs. Thunderfoot
Brett Sawyer vs. the Barbarian

Bobby Eaton & Dennis Condrey defeated Ron Garvin & Rocky King
NWA National Heavyweight Champion Terry Taylor vs. Black Bart

JCP @ Greensboro, NC - Coliseum - October 5, 1985
Ricky Reeves fought Tommy Lane to a draw
Black Bart defeated Stoney Burke
Thunderfoot defeated Starship Eagle
Krusher Kruschev defeated Pez Whatley
Buddy Landell defeated Terry Taylor
Jimmy Valiant & Rocky King fought Bobby Eaton & Dennis Condrey to a double disqualification
NWA Tag Team Champions Ricky Morton & Robert Gibson defeated Ivan & Nikita Koloff

JCP @ Philadelphia, PA - Civic Center - October 5, 1985
Bulldog Brown fought the Italian Stallion to a draw
Sam Houston defeated Mike Davis
Superstar Billy Graham defeated Starship Eagle
Manny Fernandez defeated Arn Anderson
Magnum TA defeated NWA US Champion Tully Blanchard in a non-title steel cage match
Ron Bass defeated Abdullah the Butcher via disqualification
Ron Garvin defeated NWA World Champion Ric Flair via disqualification

JCP @ Atlanta, GA - WTBS Studios - October 6, 1985 (matinee)
World Championship Wrestling - 10/12/85 - featured Tony Schiavone conducting an interview with NWA US Champion Tully Blanchard, NWA National Tag Team Champion Arn Anderson, and Baby Doll regarding NWA TV Champion Dusty Rhodes, with Anderson claiming himself the new TV champion since Rhodes was too injured to compete and hadn't defended the title since 9/19/85 in Baltimore; included Schiavone conducting an interview with NWA World Champion Ric Flair regarding his attack on Rhodes, with David Crockett grilling Flair on his actions; Flair then said he and the Andersons were family and then brought in Arn; Crockett then told Flair to shut up before he and Schiavone introduced a clip of Crockett speaking with Rhodes' doctor, Dr. Joseph Estwanik, who said the recovery time was up in the air; as footage was shown of Terry Taylor, Magnum TA, and NWA Tag Team Champions Ricky Morton & Robert Gibson helping Rhodes backstage at the Omni, Estwanik said Rhodes suffered a third degree sprain; after the clip, Flair said he had been stabbed, hit by chairs, and beaten up by everyone and if you are a man, you don't cry about it; he then said no one was going to take his title unless it was in the ring and then sent a message to Rhodes; Crockett then said Rhodes should have left Flair to the Russians at the Omni

JCP @ Savannah, GA - Civic Center - October 6, 1985
Bobby Eaton & Dennis Condrey defeated Jimmy Valiant & Rocky King

JCP @ Cincinnati, OH - October 6, 1985
Starship Eagle defeated Mike Davis
Denny Brown defeated Pat Tanaka
Superstar Billy Graham defeated Sam Houston
National Heavyweight Champion Terry Taylor defeated Black Bart
NWA Tag Team Champions Ricky Morton & Robert Gibson defeated Abdullah the Butcher & Thunderfoot via disqualification
National Tag Team Champion Arn Anderson defeated Starship Eagle
NWA US Champion Tully Blanchard defeated Ron Garvin
Magnum TA fought NWA World Champion Ric Flair to a draw

JCP @ Canton, OH - October 7, 1985
Denny Brown fought Pat Tanaka to a draw
Black Bart defeated Starship Eagle
National Heavyweight Champion Terry Taylor defeated Mike Davis
National Tag Team Champion Arn Anderson defeated Sam Houston
NWA Tag Team Champions Ricky Morton & Robert Gibson defeated Abdullah the Butcher & Thunderfoot via disqualification
Superstar Billy Graham defeated Denny Brown
Magnum TA fought NWA US Champion Tully Blanchard to a no contest
NWA World Champion Ric Flair defeated Ron Garvin

JCP @ Greenville, SC - October 7, 1985
Buddy Landell defeated Brady Boone
Don Kernodle, Manny Fernandez, & Ron Bass defeated Krusher Kruschev, Ivan & Nikita Koloff via disqualification
Bobby Eaton & Dennis Condrey defeated Jimmy Valiant & Rocky King

JCP @ Shelby, NC - Rec Center - October 8, 1985
TV taping:
Pro - 10/12/85:
Worldwide - 10/12/85 - featured Tony Schiavone & David Crockett on commentary; included footage from the Omni of Ole & Arn Anderson attacking Dusty Rhodes after Rhodes saved NWA World Champion Ric Flair from an attack by the Russians; featured a backstage promo by Jimmy Valiant regarding Starrcade 85; included footage of Magnum TA, Terry Taylor, NWA Tag Team Champions Ricky Morton & Robert Gibson and others clearing Flair and the Andersons from the ring at the Omni and tending to Rhodes; featured Crockett speaking with Rhodes' doctor, Dr. Joseph Estwanik, who said the recovery time was up in the air; as footage was shown of Taylor, Magnum, Morton & Robert helping Rhodes backstage at the Omni, Estwanik said Rhodes suffered a third degree sprain; included Schiavone conducting an interview with NWA US Champion Tully Blanchard & Baby Doll regarding Starrcade 85; featured Crockett conducting an interview with Flair regarding the attack on Rhodes at the Omni; included

Crockett conducting an interview with Jimmy Valiant & Superstar Billy Graham regarding Graham recently saving Valiant from an attack by Bobby Eaton & Dennis Condrey:
Krusher Kruschev, Ivan & Nikita Koloff defeated Starship Eagle, Denny Brown, & ? when Nikita scored the pin following the Russian Sickle; during the bout, NWA Tag Team Champions Ricky Morton & Robert Gibson briefly joined the commentary team and said they would defend against the Russians any time they wanted a shot
Bobby Eaton & Dennis Condrey (w/ Jim Cornette) defeated George South & ? at 3:03 when Eaton pinned ? following a High-Low
? vs. ?
NWA National Tag Team Champion Arn Anderson pinned Gene Ligon with the gordbuster at the 57-second mark; prior to the bout, David Crockett conducted an interview with Anderson in which he proclaimed himself the new NWA TV Champion and said he was about to make his first title defense
NWA US Champion Tully Blanchard (w/ Baby Doll) pinned Sam Houston with the slingshot suplex at around the 8-minute mark; Magnum TA & Ron Garvin briefly joined the commentary team for the match; moments later, Magnum came ringside but was quickly ejected by the referee; after the match, Garvin made the save but was knocked out with a foreign object; Magnum then rushed into the ring, with Blanchard and Baby Doll then leaving ringside

JCP @ Raleigh, NC - Dorton Arena - October 9, 1985
NWA National Tag Team Champion Arn Anderson defeated Ron Bass
Superstar Billy Graham defeated Brady Boone
Bobby Eaton & Dennis Condrey defeated Jimmy Valiant & Rocky King
NWA US Champion Tully Blanchard defeated Terry Taylor
Don Kernodle, NWA Tag Team Champions Ricky Morton & Robert Gibson defeated Krusher Kruschev, Ivan & Nikita Koloff
Magnum TA defeated NWA World Champion Ric Flair via disqualification

JCP @ Norfolk, VA - Scope - October 10, 1985
Bobby Eaton & Dennis Condrey defeated Jimmy Valiant & Rocky King
Magnum TA defeated NWA World Champion Ric Flair via disqualification

JCP @ Wheeling, WV - Civic Center - October 10, 1985
The Italian Stallion pinned Tommy Lane at 13:06
NWA World Junior Heavyweight Champion Denny Brown fought Mike Davis to a 20-minute time-limit draw
Thunderfoot pinned Brady Boone at 11:47
Superstar Billy Graham pinned Starship Eagle at 5:00
Ron Garvin pinned Black Bart in a taped fist match at 15:38
NWA World Tag Team Champions Ricky Morton & Robert Gibson defeated Ivan Koloff & Krusher Khruschev at 17:18 when Gibson pinned Koloff

JCP @ Macon, GA - Coliseum - October 11, 1985
Bobby Eaton & Dennis Condrey defeated Jimmy Valiant & Rocky King

Mid South @ Houston, TX - October 11, 1985
NWA World Champion Ric Flair defeated Butch Reed via disqualification

Mid South @ Nashville, TN - October 12, 1985
NWA World Champion Ric Flair vs. Jim Duggan

Polynesian Pacivic @ Honolulu, HI - Blaisdel Arena - October 12, 1985 (announced at 7,000)
NWA World Champion Ric Flair fought Kerry Von Erich to a time-limit draw at around the 45-minute mark; prior to the bout, Lia Maivia presented leis to both men in the ring; Flair was caught in the claw for the last minute of the match

JCP/AWA @ Nashville, TN - October 12, 1985 (6,000)
Pat Rose, Bota the Witch Doctor, Tom Branch, & Taras Bulba defeated Tojo Yamamoto, Billy Travis, & the O'Reillys
Koko B. Ware defeated Tom Prichard via disqualification
The Masked Superstar defeated Phil Hickerson
Superstar Billy Graham defeated Starship Eagle
Rocky Johnson defeated Ron Sexton
Ron Garvin defeated Black Bart
Bill Dundee defeated the Mongolian Stomper
Jimmy Valiant & Manny Fernandez defeated Bobby Eaton & Dennis Condrey
Jackie Fargo defeated Buddy Wayne
Stan Lane & Steve Keirn defeated the Sheepherders in a hospital elimination match
NWA Tag Team Champions Ricky Morton & Robert Gibson defeated Ivan & Nikita Koloff
AWA World Champion Rick Martel defeated Jerry Lawler via disqualification

JCP @ Atlanta, GA - WTBS Studios - October 13, 1985 (matinee)
World Championship Wrestling taping

JCP @ Asheville, NC - Civic Center - October 13, 1985
Pat Tanaka vs. Stoney Burke
Sam Houston vs. Tommy Lane
Pez Whatley vs. Mike Davis
Don Kernodle, NWA Tag Team Champions Ricky Morton & Robert Gibson vs. Krusher Kruschev, Ivan & Nikita Koloff
NWA National Heavyweight Champion Terry Taylor vs. Buddy Landel
Ron Garvin vs. NWA US Champion Tully Blanchard
Magnum TA defeated NWA World Champion Ric Flair via disqualification

JCP @ Charlotte, NC - Coliseum - October 13, 1985
Jimmy Valiant & Don Kernodle defeated Bobby Eaton & Dennis Condrey via disqualification
Ivan & Nikita Koloff defeated NWA Tag Team Champions Ricky Morton & Robert Gibson to win the titles
Magnum TA defeated NWA World Champion Ric Flair via disqualification

JCP @ Fayetteville, NC - Cumberland County Memorial Arena - October 14, 1985
Bobby Eaton & Dennis Condrey defeated the Italian Stallion & Pat Tanaka
Don Kernodle vs. Krusher Kruschev
Manny Fernandez vs. NWA US Champion Tully Blanchard
NWA Tag Team Champions Ivan & Nikita Koloff vs. Ricky Morton & Robert Gibson (double chain match)

JCP @ Greenwood, SC - October 15, 1985
Television taping:

Dark match: Ricky Morton & Robert Gibson defeated Bobby Eaton & Dennis Condrey

JCP @ Lenoir, NC - October 16, 1985
Ricky Morton & Robert Gibson defeated Bobby Eaton & Dennis Condrey

JCP @ Columbia, SC - Township Auditorium - October 17, 1985
Ricky Morton & Robert Gibson defeated Bobby Eaton & Dennis Condrey

JCP @ Charleston, SC - County Hall - October 18, 1985
NWA Jr. Heavyweight Champion Denny Brown vs. Brady Boone
The Italian Stallion vs. Tommy Lane
Pat Tanaka vs. the Terror
Brett Sawyer vs. Thunderfoot
Bobby Eaton & Dennis Condrey defeated Jimmy Valiant & Rocky King
Ron Bass vs. Black Bart (taped fist match)

JCP @ Richmond, VA - Coliseum - October 18, 1985
Pez Whatley defeated Mike Davis
Superstar Billy Graham defeated Starship Eagle
National Tag Team Champion Arn Anderson defeated Manny Fernandez via count-out
Ron Garvin defeated Abdullah the Butcher via disqualification when Paul Jones interfered
National Heavyweight Champion Terry Taylor defeated Buddy Landell
Don Kernodle, NWA Tag Team Champions Ricky Morton & Robert Gibson defeated Krusher Kruschev, Ivan & Nikita Koloff when Kernodle pinned Ivan
Magnum TA defeated NWA US Champion Tully Blanchard via disqualification in a steel cage match when National Tag Team Champion Arn Anderson interfered; late in the bout, Dusty Rhodes entered the cage after the referee had been knocked down and counted Blanchard down for 3, with fans believing Magnum had won the title

- 10/19/85: Dusty Rhodes was stripped of the NWA TV Title due to the injury he sustained 9/28/85 at the Omni.

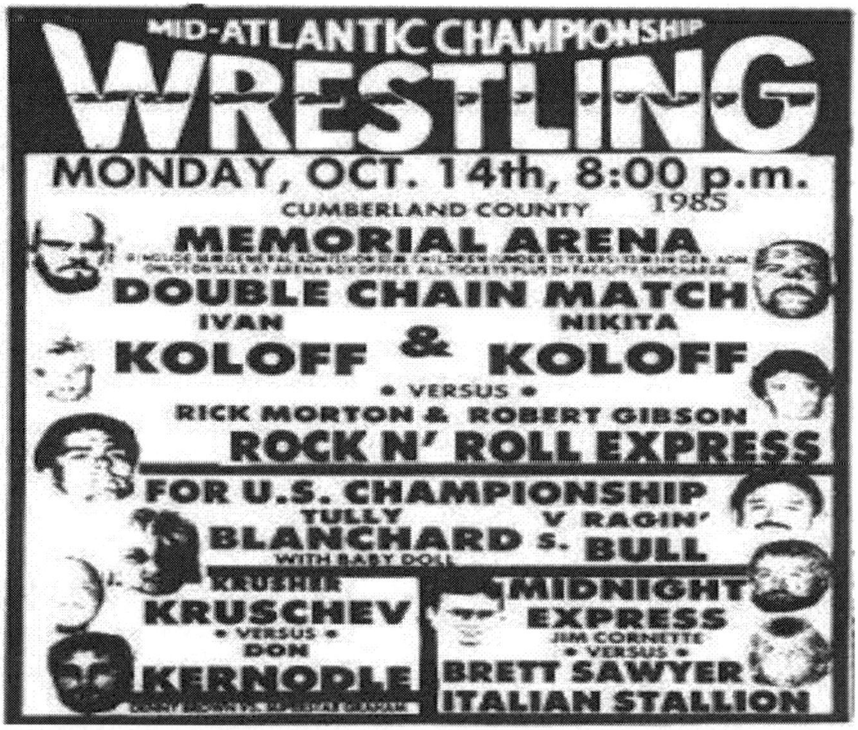
MID-ATLANTIC CHAMPIONSHIP
WRESTLING
MONDAY, OCT. 14th, 8:00 p.m.
1985
CUMBERLAND COUNTY
MEMORIAL ARENA
DOUBLE CHAIN MATCH
IVAN KOLOFF & NIKITA KOLOFF
• VERSUS •
RICK MORTON & ROBERT GIBSON
ROCK N' ROLL EXPRESS
FOR U.S. CHAMPIONSHIP
TULLY BLANCHARD
WITH BABY DOLL
VS.
RAGIN' BULL
KRUSHER KRUSCHEV
• VERSUS •
DON KERNODLE
MIDNIGHT EXPRESS
JIM CORNETTE
• VERSUS •
BRETT SAWYER
ITALIAN STALLION

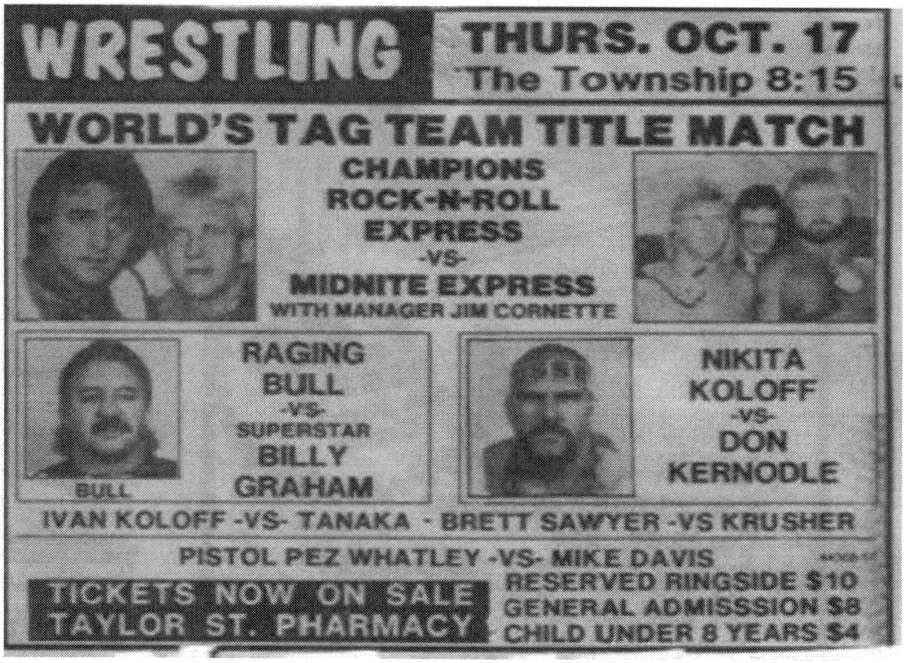
WRESTLING
THURS. OCT. 17
The Township 8:15
WORLD'S TAG TEAM TITLE MATCH
CHAMPIONS
ROCK-N-ROLL EXPRESS
-VS-
MIDNITE EXPRESS
WITH MANAGER JIM CORNETTE
RAGING BULL
-VS-
SUPERSTAR BILLY GRAHAM
BULL
NIKITA KOLOFF
-VS-
DON KERNODLE
IVAN KOLOFF -VS- TANAKA - BRETT SAWYER -VS KRUSHER
PISTOL PEZ WHATLEY -VS- MIKE DAVIS
TICKETS NOW ON SALE
TAYLOR ST. PHARMACY
RESERVED RINGSIDE $10
GENERAL ADMISSSION $8
CHILD UNDER 8 YEARS $4

JCP @ Greensboro, NC - Coliseum - October 19, 1985
Sam Houston defeated Thunderfoot
Ron Garvin defeated Buddy Landell
Don Kernodle defeated Krusher Kruschev
Superstar Billy Graham & Jimmy Valiant defeated Bobby Eaton
& Dennis Condrey via disqualification
NWA National Heavyweight Champion Terry Taylor defeated
Black Bart
NWA Tag Team Champions Ricky Morton & Robert Gibson
defeated Ole & Arn Anderson
NWA US Champion Tully Blanchard fought Magnum TA to a
double count-out

AJPW @ Tokyo, Japan - October 19, 1985
NWA World Champion Ric Flair fought Jumbo Tsuruta to a 15-
minute time-limit draw

JCP @ Atlanta, GA - WTBS Studios - October 20, 1985
(matinee)
World Championship Wrestling taping:
Superstar Billy Graham defeated Carl Styles via submission
with the backbreaker at 3:19

JCP @ Atlanta, GA - Omni - October 20, 1985
Superstar Billy Graham defeated Sam Houston
Thunderfoot defeated the Italian Stallion
Dennis Condrey defeated Rocky King
Jimmy Valiant defeated Bobby Eaton via disqualification
NWA National Heavyweight Champion Terry Taylor fought
Buddy Landell to a draw
NWA Tag Team Champions Ricky Morton & Robert Gibson
defeated Abdullah the Butcher & the Barbarian via
disqualification
Magnum TA, Ron Garvin, & Wahoo McDaniel defeated NWA
US Champion Tully Blanchard, National Tag Team Champions
Ole & Arn Anderson in a bunkhouse match

AJPW @ Shizuoka, Japan - October 20, 1985
NWA World Champion Ric Flair & AWA World Champion Rick
Martel fought Terry & Dory Funk Jr. to a double count-out

JCP @ Boiling Springs, NC - October 21, 1985
Jimmy Valiant & Manny Fernandez defeated Bobby Eaton &
Dennis Condrey

AJPW @ Tokyo, Japan - October 21, 1985
NWA World Champion Ric Flair fought AWA World Champion
Rick Martel to a double count-out at 34:00 after a crossbody by
Flair caused both men to fall over the top to the floor; prior to
the bout, the two men shook hands; AWA President Stanley
Blackburn gaven an in-ring announcement before the match
and presented Martel with the title belt after the contest; Giant
Baba provided guest commentary for the match

JCP @ Mooresville, NC - October 22, 1985
Television taping:
Dark match: Ricky Morton & Robert Gibson defeated Bobby
Eaton & Dennis Condrey

AJPW @ Kyoto, Japan - October 22, 1985
Genichiro Tenryu & Jumbo Tsuruta defeated NWA World
Champion Ric Flair & AWA World Champion Rick Martel via
count-out at 17:39 after all four men began brawling on the
floor; prior to the bout, the participants shook hands; Giant
Baba provided guest commentary for the match

AJPW @ Mito, Japan - October 23, 1985
NWA World Champion Ric Flair & AWA World Champion Rick
Martel fought Riki Choshu & the Great Yatsu to a double
disqualification at 16:13

Central States @ Kansas City, MO - October 24, 1985
(2,200)
NWA World Champion Ric Flair defeated Harley Race at the
22-minute mark when the match was stopped due to blood

JCP @ Roanoke, VA - Civic Center - October 25, 1985
Jimmy Valiant & Superstar Billy Graham defeated Bobby Eaton
& Dennis Condrey via disqualification

JCP @ Cleveland, OH - October 26, 1985
Magnum TA defeated NWA World Champion Ric Flair via
disqualification

JCP @ Atlanta, GA - WTBS Studios - October 27, 1985
Television taping:
Superstar Billy Graham vs. Mark Fleming

JCP @ Charlotte, NC - October 27, 1985
Jimmy Valiant & Superstar Billy Graham defeated Bobby Eaton
& Dennis Condrey via disqualification

WCCW @ Ft. Worth, TX - October 28, 1985
Scott Casey vs. John Tatum
Brian Adias defeated the Grappler via disqualification
Iceman King Parsons fought John Tatum to a draw
Gino Hernandez & Chris Adams defeated Kerry & Kevin Von
Erich
Rick Rude defeated Dave Peterson
NWA World Champion Ric Flair fought Lance Von Erich to a
no contest

TODAY, NOV. 3, 3 P.M.
WORLD TITLE MATCH NO DQ
ASHEVILLE CIVIC CENTER

WIDE WORLD WRESTLING

WORLD TITLE MATCH
NO DISQUALIFICATION
"Nature Boy"
RIC FLAIR
vs
Magnum T.A.

RIC

MAGNUM

SPECIAL GRUDGE MATCH
Jimmy "Boogie Woogie" Valient
& Superstar Billy Graham
vs
Midnight Express
(with Jim Cornette)

JIMMY

MIDNIGHT EXPRESS

RON BASS
vs
"Nature Boy" Buddy Landel
(with J.J. Dillon)

DON KERNODLE vs THUNDERFOOT

STARSHIP EAGLE vs TOMMY LANE

ROCKY KING vs ITALIAN STALLION

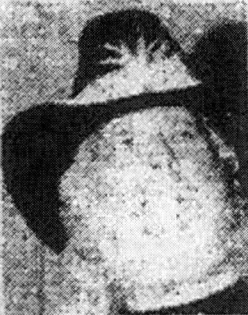

BUDDY

Ringside $10 Gen. Adm. $8 Children Under 10, $3
Box Office 259-5771 Mon.-Fri. 10-5:30 , Sat. 11-4, Day of Match 1:00 P.M.
No Checks or Credit Cards Day of Match. Matches subject to change.

WIDE WORLD WRESTLING ON WLOS-TV 13 SUNDAY 12 NOON

JCP @ Greenville, SC - Memorial Auditorium - October 28, 1985
TV taping:
Jimmy Valiant & Superstar Billy Graham defeated Bobby Eaton & Dennis Condrey via disqualification
Magnum TA defeated National Tag Team Champion Arn Anderson in a Texas Death Match

JCP @ Fayetteville, NC - Cumberland County Memorial Arena - October 28, 1985
Denny Brown vs. Mike Davis
Buddy Landel vs. Pez Whatley
Thunderfoot vs. Ron Bass
Don Kernodle, Ricky Morton & Robert Gibson vs. Krusher Kruschev, NWA Tag Team Champions Ivan & Nikita Koloff
Ron Garvin vs. NWA US Champion Tully Blanchard

JCP @ Richburg, SC - October 29, 1985
TV taping

JCP @ Atlanta, GA - WTBS Studios - November 2, 1985
TV taping

JCP @ Cincinnati, OH - November 2, 1985
Bobby Eaton & Dennis Condrey defeated Rocky King & Sam Houston

JCP @ Asheville, NC - Civic Center - November 3, 1985 (matinee) (2,500)
Starship Eagle was scheduled to face Tommy Lane and Don Kernodle was scheduled to face Thunderfoot but the matches were changed due to no shows from Eagle and Thunderfoot
Black Bart defeated Pat Tanaka
The Italian Stallion defeated Stoney Burke (sub. for Rocky King)
Don Kernodle defeated Tommy Lane
Ron Bass defeated Buddy Landell
Jimmy Valiant & Superstar Billy Graham defeated Bobby Eaton & Dennis Condrey
NWA World Champion Ric Flair defeated Magnum TA in a No DQ match

JCP @ Atlanta, GA - Omni - November 3, 1985
The Barbarian defeated Sam Houston
Dusty Rhodes defeated Mike Davis
Superstar Billy Graham defeated Abdullah the Butcher via disqualification
NWA National Heavyweight Champion Terry Taylor defeated Buddy Landell
Krusher Kruschev, NWA Tag Team Champions Ivan & Nikita Koloff defeated Jimmy Valiant, Ricky Morton & Robert Gibson via disqualification
NWA US Champion Tully Blanchard defeated Ron Garvin via disqualification
Dusty Rhodes, Magnum TA, & Billy Jack Haynes defeated

NWA World Champion Ric Flair, National Tag Team Champions Ole & Arn Anderson

JCP @ Greenville, SC - Memorial Auditorium - November 4, 1985
Rocky King defeated Jim Jeffers
Dusty Rhodes defeated Tommy Lane
Bobby Eaton & Dennis Condrey defeated Pez Whatley & Don Kernodle
Arn Anderson defeated Ron Bass
NWA US Champion Tully Blanchard defeated Ron Garvin
Jimmy Valiant & Superstar Billy Graham defeated Abdullah the Butcher & the Barbarian

JCP @ Charlotte, NC - Coliseum - November 4, 1985
Dusty Rhodes, Magnum TA, & Billy Jack Haynes defeated NWA World Champion Ric Flair, National Tag Team Champions Ole & Arn Anderson

JCP @ Sumter, SC - County Exhibition Center - November 5, 1985
Sam Houston vs. Tommy Lane
Ron Bass vs. the Barbarian
Dusty Rhodes vs. Mike Davis
Jimmy Valiant & Superstar Billy Graham defeated Bobby Eaton & Dennis Condrey via disqualification
Ron Garvin vs. NWA US Champion Tully Blanchard
Magnum TA vs. NWA National Tag Team Champion Arn Anderson

Baton Rouge, LA - November 5, 1985
Butch Reed defeated NWA World Champion Ric Flair via disqualification

Mid South @ Shreveport, LA - Irish McNeil's Boys Club - November 6, 1985
NWA World Champion Ric Flair vs. Al Perez
Butch Reed pinned NWA World Champion Ric Flair in a non-title match at 6:02
NWA World Champion Ric Flair defeated Ted DiBiase via count-out at 6:14 after Flair kicked DiBiase away during a figure-4 attempt, with a bloody DiBiase being flung over the top rope and into the ringside barricade; prior to the bout, Ross spoke with Flair, with Flair joking it was a shame Butch Reed couldn't be there and noted DiBiase would get a shot; moments later, Dick Murdoch interrupted and said he should be the one challenging Flair, not DiBiase; following the ring introductions, Murdoch came to the ring and told DiBiase to step aside and let him have the match instead, adding DiBiase didn't deserve it; after DiBiase said Murdoch was yesterday's news, Murdoch attacked DiBiase and rammed him head-first into the ringpost, busting his head open; moments later, Steve Williams and referees tended to DiBiase on the floor as Flair took the mic from Boyd Pierce and said he was going home; following the commercial break, Bill Watts gave a backstage

update on DiBiase in which he said DiBiase demanded the match go on and it would be allowed, but added DiBiase was wearing a pressure bandage that may lead to a bloody match; Ross & Joel Watts provided commentary for the match; after the bout, Murdoch returned ringside, attacked DiBiase, and hit the brainbuster on the floor before Williams tended to DiBiase (*Legends of Mid South Wrestling*)

JCP @ Raleigh, NC - Dorton Arena - November 6, 1985
Don Kernodle & Ron Bass vs. Thunderfoot & Buddy Landel
Dusty Rhodes vs. Mike Davis
NWA National Heavyweight Champion Terry Taylor vs. Black Bart
Jimmy Valiant & Manny Fernandez defeated Bobby Eaton & Dennis Condrey via disqualification
Ron Garvin vs. Tully Blanchard (taped fist match)
Magnum TA vs. NWA National Tag Team Champion Arn Anderson

JCP @ Norfolk, VA - Scope - November 7, 1985
Dusty Rhodes, Magnum TA, & Manny Fernandez defeated NWA World Champion Ric Flair, NWA National Tag Team Champions Ole & Arn Anderson

JCP @ Comfort, NC - November 7, 1985
Jimmy Valiant & Superstar Billy Graham defeated Bobby Eaton & Dennis Condrey via disqualification

JCP @ Richmond, VA - Coliseum - November 8, 1985
Tommy Lane vs. Pez Whatley
Mike Davis vs. Terry Taylor
Nikita Koloff vs. Superstar Billy Graham
Ricky Morton & Robert Gibson vs. NWA Tag Team Champions Ivan Koloff & Krusher Kruschev
Ron Garvin vs. NWA US Champion Tully Blanchard
Dusty Rhodes, Magnum TA, & Manny Fernandez defeated NWA World Champion Ric Flair, NWA National Tag Team Champions Ole & Arn Anderson

JCP @ Columbus, GA - November 8, 1985
Bobby Eaton & Dennis Condrey defeated Jimmy Valiant & Rocky King

JCP @ Atlanta, GA - WTBS Studios - November 10, 1985 (matinee)
World Championship Wrestling taping

JCP @ Charlotte, NC - November 10, 1985
Bobby Eaton & Dennis Condrey defeated Jimmy Valiant & Superstar Billy Graham via count-out

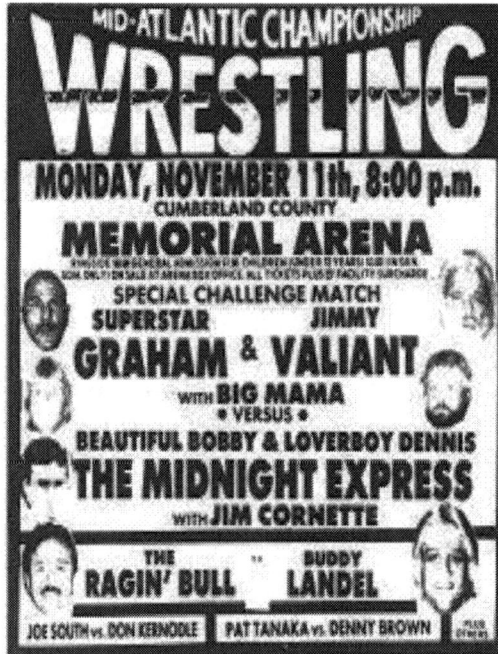

JCP @ Fayetteville, NC - Cumberland County Memorial Arena - November 11, 1985
George South vs. Don Kernodle
Pat Tanaka vs. Denny Brown
Manny Fernandez vs. Buddy Landel
Jimmy Valiant & Superstar Billy Graham defeated Bobby Eaton & Dennis Condrey

JCP @ Shelby, NC - Rec Center - November 12, 1985 (sell out)
Television taping:
Dark match: Jimmy Valiant & Superstar Billy Graham defeated Bobby Eaton & Dennis Condrey

JCP @ Monroe, NC - November 13, 1985 (sell out)
Jimmy Valiant & Superstar Billy Graham defeated Bobby Eaton & Dennis Condrey

JCP @ Harrisonburg, VA - High School - November 14, 1985
Stoney Burke vs. Mark Fleming
Ricky Reeves vs. Tommy Lane
The Italian Stallion vs. Mike Davis
Ron Bass vs. Black Bart (Texas Death match)
Manny Fernandez, Ricky Morton & Robert Gibson vs. Krusher Kruschev, NWA Tag Team Champions Ivan & Nikita Koloff

JCP @ Columbia, SC - Township Auditorium - November 14, 1985
Ron Garvin vs. the Barbarian
Starship Eagle vs. Jim Jeffers
Brown vs. Mack Jeffers
NWA National Heavyweight Champion Terry Taylor vs. Buddy Landell (if Taylor wins, he gets 5 minuts with JJ Dillon)
Bobby Eaton & Dennis Condrey defeated Jimmy Valiant & Superstar Billy Graham via count-out
Dusty Rhodes, Magnum TA, & Billy Jack Haynes vs. NWA US Champion Tully Blanchard, NWA National Tag Team Champions Ole & Arn Anderson

JCP @ Charleston, SC - St. Andrews High School Gym - November 15, 1985
Pat Tanaka vs. Jim Jeffers
Sam Houston vs. Mike Davis
Ron Bass vs. Buddy Landell
Ron Garvin vs. NWA US Champion Tully Blanchard (taped fist match)
Dusty Rhodes, Magnum TA, & Billy Jack Haynes vs. NWA World Champion Ric Flair, NWA National Tag Team Champions Ole & Arn Anderson

JCP @ Misenheimer, NC - November 15, 1985
Jimmy Valiant & Superstar Billy Graham defeated Bobby Eaton & Dennis Condrey

Worldwide - 11/16/85:
Bobby Eaton & Dennis Condrey vs. George South & Brady Boone
Billy Jack Haynes vs. the Golden Terror
Magnum TA vs. Gene Ligon
NWA US Champion Tully Blanchard vs. Pat Tanaka
Jimmy Valiant, Superstar Billy Graham, & Manny Fernandez vs. Vernon Deaton, Jim & Mack Jeffers
Ole & Arn Anderson vs. Rocky King & Tony Zane
NWA World Champion Ric Flair vs. Sam Houston

World Championship Wrestling - 11/16/85:
Jimmy Valiant vs. Tony Zane
Billy Jack Haynes vs. Gerald Finley
Krusher Kruschev vs. Larry Clark
Ron Bass vs. Paul Garner
The Barbarian vs. George South
NWA World Champion Ric Flair, NWA National Tag Team Champions Ole & Arn Anderson defeated Ron Garvin, Terry Taylor, & Pez Whatley when Arn pinned Whatley with an elbowdrop to the back of the head after Flair tripped Whatley from the floor and held the foot down during the cover
The Road Warriors vs. Jim & Mack Jeffers
NWA US Champion Tully Blanchard vs. Jimmy Backlund
Magnum TA vs. Joe Malcom
NWA Tag Team Champions Ivan & Nikita Koloff vs. Rocky King & Adrian Bivens

JCP @ Conway, SC - November 16, 1985
Jimmy Valiant & Superstar Billy Graham defeated Bobby Eaton & Dennis Condrey

JCP @ Cleveland, OH - November 16, 1985
Pez Whatley defeated Tommy Lane
Sam Houston defeated Mike Davis
Ron Bass fought Buddy Landell to a draw
Manny Fernandez fought Abdullah the Butcher to a no contest
NWA US Champion Tully Blanchard defeated Ron Garvin
Dusty Rhodes, Magnum TA, & Billy Jack Haynes defeated NWA World Champion Ric Flair, NWA National Tag Team Champions Ole & Gene Anderson

Central States @ Des Moines, IA - November 17, 1985
NWA World Champion Ric Flair vs. Harley Race

Lexington, KY - November 17, 1985
Stan Lane & Steve Keirn defeated Bobby Eaton & Dennis Condrey

Memphis, TN - Mid-South Coliseum - November 18, 1985 (7,500)
CWA International Champion Phil Hickerson defeated Dutch Mantell via count-out
Rip Morgan & Tarras Bulba defeated Tojo Yamamoto & Billy Joe Travis
Stan Lane & Steve Keirn defeated Tom Prichard & Pat Rose
Jimmy Valiant pinned Tony Falk
Stan Lane & Steve Keirn defeated Bobby Eaton & Dennis Condrey
Jerry Lawler, Dusty Rhodes, & Magnum TA defeated NWA US Champion Tully Blanchard (w/ Baby Doll), NWA National Tag Team Champions Ole & Arn Anderson in a bunkhouse match at 6:01 when Rhodes pinned Ole with an elbow drop off the top onto a standing Ole
NWA Tag Team Champions Ivan & Nikita Koloff defeated Ricky Morton & Robert Gibson in a steel cage match
NWA World Champion Ric Flair defeated Koko Ware (sub. for Bill Dundee)

JCP @ Greenville, SC - Memorial Auditorium - November 18, 1985
Pez Whatley defeated Jim Jeffers
Don Kernodle defeated Tommy Lane
Sam Houston defeated Mike Davis
Thunderfoot defeated Pez Whatley
Manny Fernandez defeated Krusher Kruschev
Billy Jack Haynes & Ron Bass defeated Black Bart, Buddy Landell, and JJ Dillon in a handicap match
The Barbarian defeated Superstar Billy Graham

Central States @ Lincoln, NE - November 19, 1985
NWA World Champion Ric Flair defeated Marty Jannetty

MID ATLANTIC WRESTLING
THURSDAY NOVEMBER 14
COLUMBIA TOWNSHIP AUDITORIUM 8:15
6 MAN TAG TEAM MATCH

DUSTY RHODES, MAGNUM T.A. & BILLY HAYNES
-VS.-
OLE & ARN ANDERSON & TULLY BLANCHARD
WITH BABY DOLL

BOOGIE WOOGIE

Jimmy Valiant and Super Star Billy Graham -vs.- Midnight Express

Terry Taylor -vs.- Buddy Landell
Note: If Taylor Beats Landell, Terry Gets a 5 Minute Match with J.J. Dillon

Garvin -vs.- Barbarian/Eagle -vs.- J. Jeffers/Brown -vs.- M. Jeffers

TICKETS NOW ON SALE TAYLOR ST. PHARMACY

RINGSIDE	$10.00
GEN. ADM.	8.00
CHILD UNDER 8	4.00

MID-ATLANTIC CHAMPIONSHIP WRESTLING
DORTON ARENA: TONIGHT

RHODES IS AFTER THE BELT

DUSTY RHODES v.s. ARN ANDERSON

MAGNUM T.A. v.s. OLE ANDERSON

JIMMY VALIANT
ROCKY KING
SUPERSTAR GRAHAM
• VERSUS •
JIM CORNETTE
The MIDNIGHT EXPRESS

| BLACK BART vs. ITALIAN STALLION | BILLY JACK vs. THUNDERFOOT | BARBARIAN vs. PEZ WHATLEY |

238

JCP @ Greenwood, SC - November 19, 1985
TV taping

JCP @ Canton, OH - November 20, 1985
Pat Tanaka fought Tommy Lane to a draw
Don Kernodle defeated Mike Davis
Krusher Kruschev defeated Sam Houston
Manny Fernandez defeated Buddy Landell
Ricky Morton & Robert Gibson defeated NWA Tag Team
Champions Ivan & Nikita Koloff
NWA National Heavyweight Champion Terry Taylor defeated
NWA US Champion Tully Blanchard via disqualification

Mid South @ Shreveport, LA - November 20, 1985
TV taping:
NWA World Champion Ric Flair & Butch Reed vs. Mark Hawk
& Bob Wayne

JCP @ Raleigh, NC - Dorton Arena - November 20, 1985
Denny Brown fought Brady Boone to a draw
Black Bart defeated the Italian Stallion
The Barbarian defeated Pez Whatley
Billy Jack Haynes defeated Thunderfoot
Jim Cornette, Bobby Eaton & Dennis Condrey defeated Jimmy
Valiant, Superstar Billy Graham, & Rocky King
Magnum TA defeated NWA National Tag Team Champion Ole
Anderson via disqualification
Dusty Rhodes defeated NWA National Tag Team Champion
Arn Anderson

JCP @ Wheeling, WV - Civic Center - November 21, 1985
Pat Tanaka fought Mike Davis to a draw
Don Kernodle defeated Tommy Lane
Buddy Landell defeated Sam Houston
Manny Fernandez fought Nikita Koloff to a no contest
NWA National Heavyweight Champion Terry Taylor defeated
NWA US Champion Tully Blanchard
NWA Tag Team Champions Ivan Koloff & Krusher Kruschev
defeated Ricky Morton & Robert Gibson in a double chain
match

**JCP @ Hendersonville, NC - East Henderson High School
Gym - November 22, 1985**
Rocky King vs. the Italian Stallion
NWA Jr. Heavyweight Champions Denny Brown vs. Brady
Boone
Pez Whatley vs. Black Bart
Ron Bass vs. Thunderfoot
Billy Jack Haynes vs. the Barbarian
Jimmy Valiant & Superstar Billy Graham defeated Bobby Eaton
& Dennis Condrey via disqualification

JCP @ Charleston, WV - November 22, 1985
Sam Houston defeated Tommy Lane
Mike Davis defeated Pat Tanaka

Don Kernodle fought Krusher Kruschev to a draw
Manny Fernandez defeated Buddy Landell
NWA US Champion Tully Blanchard defeated NWA National
Heavyweight Champion Terry Taylor
NWA Tag Team Champions Ivan Koloff & Krusher Kruschev
defeated Ricky Morton & Robert Gibson in a double chain
match
Dusty Rhodes & Magnum TA defeated NWA World Champion
Ric Flair & NWA National Tag Team Champion Arn Anderson

Worldwide - 11/23/85:
Ron Bass & Don Kernodle vs. Jim & Mack Jeffers
Superstar Billy Graham & Jimmy Valiant vs. Mike Davis &
Tommy Lane
Billy Jack Haynes vs. the Golden Terror
Manny Fernandez vs. Tony Zane
Buddy Landell vs. Pez Whatley
Ricky Morton & Robert Gibson vs. Gene Ligon & Mark Fleming
Tully Blanchard, Ole & Arn Anderson vs. Sam Houston, Denny
Brown, & Ricky Reeves

World Championship Wrestling - 11/23/85:
Terry Taylor vs. Black Kat
Don Kernodle vs. Don Turner
Superstar Billy Graham vs. Tony Zane
Buddy Landell vs. Manny Fernandez
Black Bart vs. Rocky King
Billy Jack Haynes vs. Jim Jeffers
Ron Bass, Pez Whatley, & the Italian Stallion vs. Carl Styles,
Kent Glover, & Larry Clarke
Sam Houston vs. the Golden Terror

CWF @ Lakeland, FL - Civic Center - November 23, 1985
Jimmy Valiant & Frankie Lane vs. Bobby Eaton & Dennis
Condrey
Magnum TA vs. NWA US Champion Tully Blanchard
Barry & Kendall Windham vs. Bob Roop & Kevin Sullivan (steel
cage match)
Southern Heavyweight Champion Wahoo McDaniel vs.
Abdullah the Butcher

**JCP @ Philadelphia, PA - Civic Center - November 23, 1985
(12,500; sell out)**
Sam Houston defeated Stan Lane
Pez Whatley defeated Mike Davis
Don Kernodle defeated the Barbarian via disqualification
NWA National Heavyweight Champion Terry Taylor fought
Buddy Landell to a 30-minute time-limit draw
NWA Tag Team Champions Ivan & Nikita Koloff defeated
Ricky Morton & Robert Gibson when Krusher Kruschev
interfered and pinned Morton
Superstar Billy Graham defeated Krusher Kruschev via
disqualification
Dusty Rhodes & the Road Warriors defeated NWA World
Champion Ric Flair, NWA National Tag Team Champions Ole
& Arn Anderson when Rhodes pinned Ole

? - November 24, 1985
NWA World Champion Ric Flair pinned Jake Roberts at 19:17 by reversing an inside cradle, though Roberts legs were touching the ropes during the cover; prior to the bout, Flair started a shoving match with the challenger, with Roberts then dropping the champion with the DDT; Roberts then told the referee to ring the bell but the referee refused for several minutes until Flair attempted to walk out of the match, with the referee then ringing the bell and begining a count on Flair; after the bout, Butch Reed, in a neckbrace, came out to dispute the call, with Flair and Reed briefly brawling until Reed cleared the champion from the ring

JCP @ Marietta, GA - November 24, 1985
Ricky Morton & Robert Gibson defeated Bobby Eaton & Dennis Condrey via disqualification

JCP/AWA @ Baltimore, MD - Civic Center - November 24, 1985
Mike Moore defeated Bill Irwin
Boris Zhukov defeated Larry Winters
AWA World Champion Rick Martel defeated Kamala via disqualification
Jimmy Valiant & Superstar Billy Graham fought the Barbarian & Abdullah the Butcher to a no contest
Magnum TA defeated Buddy Landell
Dusty Rhodes & the Road Warriors defeated NWA US Champion Tully Blanchard, NWA National Tag Team Champions Ole & Arn Anderson

JCP @ Fayetteville, NC - Cumberland County Memorial Arena - November 25, 1985
Television taping:
Magnum TA, Dusty Rhodes, & Billy Jack vs. NWA US Champion Tully Blanchard, NWA National Tag Team Champions Ole & Arn Anderson

JCP @ Easley, SC - November 25, 1985
Ricky Morton & Robert Gibson defeated Bobby Eaton & Dennis Condrey via disqualification

Mid South @ Jackson, MS - November 25, 1985
Butch Reed vs. NWA World Champion Ric Flair

JCP @ Lincolnton, NC - November 26, 1985
Ricky Morton & Robert Gibson defeated Bobby Eaton & Dennis Condrey via disqualification

JCP @ Raleigh, NC - Dorton Arena - November 27, 1985
Terry Taylor vs. Tully Blanchard did not take place as advertised
Sam Houston defeated Gene Ligon
The Italian Stallion defeated Tommy Lane
Pez Whatley defeated the Golden Terror

Manny Fernandez defeated Mike Davis
Ricky Morton & Robert Gibson defeated NWA US Champion Tully Blanchard (sub. for Thunderfoot) & the Barbarian via disqualification
Jimmy Valiant & Billy Jack defeated Bobby Eaton & Dennis Condrey

CWF @ Miami, FL - Convention Hall - November 27, 1985 (5,792)
Mike Fever defeated the Red Menace
Lex Luger defeated Frank Lang
Tyree Pride defeated the Cuban Assassin
Superstar Billy Graham defeated Abdullah the Butcher via disqualification
Barry Windham defeated Buddy Landell
Dusty Rhodes, Magnum TA, & Wahoo McDaniel defeated NWA World Champion Ric Flair, NWA National Tag Team Champions Ole & Arn Anderson

Mid South @ New Orleans, LA - Superdome - November 28, 1985
Featured a closed curcuit showing of Starrcade 85
Nick Patrick defeated Tommy Wright
Butch Reed & Nick Patrick defeated Dick Slater & Buzz Sawyer via disqualification
Jake Roberts defeated Lord Humongous via disqualification

Starrcade 85 - November 28, 1985 (sell out)
Greensboro, NC - Coliseum:
NWA Jr. Heavyweight Champion Denny Brown pinned Rocky King
Don Kernodle defeated Tommy Lane
Atlanta, GA - Omni (14,000; sell out):
Thunderfoot pinned the Italian Stallion
Pez Whatley defeated Mike Graham
Shown on closed circuit - featured Bob Caudle & Tony Schiavone on commentary:
Greensboro: *Mid-Atlantic Heavyweight Championship Tournament Finals*: Krusher Kruschev pinned Sam Houston with the Russian Sickle after Houston thought he had won the match following the bulldog, not realizing Kruschev's foot was on the bottom rope during the cover
Atlanta: Manny Fernandez defeated Abdullah the Butcher (w/ Paul Jones) in a Mexican Death Match after Abdullah missed a charge in the corner and hit his head on the ringpost, allowing Fernandez to climb up the pole and reach the sombraro
Greensboro: Ron Bass pinned Black Bart (w/ JJ Dillon) in a bullrope match after coming off the middle turnbuckle and hitting Bart with the cowbell; stipulations stated Bass would face Dillon for 5 minutes if he won
Greensboro: JJ Dillon pinned Ron Bass in a bullrope match after Black Bart interfered as the referee was knocked down and dropped Bass with a piledriver
Atlanta: Superstar Billy Graham defeated the Barbarian (w/ Paul Jones) in a $10,000 arm wrestling contest
Atlanta: Superstar Billy Graham defeated the Barbarian (w/

Paul Jones) via disqualification when Jones interfered with his cane as the Barbarian was caught in the bearhug; after the bout, Graham cornered Jones but was knocked to the floor by the Barbarian

Greensboro: Buddy Landell (w/ JJ Dillon) pinned National Heavyweight Champion Terry Taylor to win the title when Dillon grabbed Taylor's foot as the champion attempted a superplex, with Landell landing on top for the win; Dillon's head was heavily bandaged following his match earlier in the night

Atlanta: National Tag Team Champions Arn & Ole Anderson defeated NWA US Tag Team Champions Chief Wahoo McDaniel & Billy Jack Haynes when Arn pinned McDaniel at 8:59 after Ole tripped Wahoo and held the leg down during the cover; only the National titles were on the line (*Greatest Wrestling Stars of the 80s*)

Greensboro: Magnum TA defeated NWA US Champion Tully Blanchard (w/ Baby Doll) in an I Quit steel cage match to win the title at around the 15-minute mark when the challenger drove a broken piece of wood into the champion's forehead until Blanchard submitted (*Crockett Cup 87, The Best of Starrcade: 1983-1987, Bloodbath: Wrestling's Most Incredible Steel Cage Matches, Starrcade: The Essential Collection, The Top 25 WWE Rivalries*)

Atlanta: Jimmy Valiant (w/ Big Mama) & Ron Garvin (as Miss Atlanta Lively) defeated Bobby Eaton & Dennis Condrey (w/ Jim Cornette) in a streetfight at 6:36 when Garvin pinned Eaton with an uppercut as Eaton attempted the Alabama Jam on Valiant; after the bout, Cornette was stripped down to his boxers (*Falls Count Anywhere: The Greatest Street Fights and other Out of Control Matches*)

Greensboro: Ricky Morton & Robert Gibson (w/ Don Kernodle) defeated NWA Tag Team Champions Ivan & Nikita Koloff (w/ NWA Mid-Atlantic Heavyweight Champion Krusher Kruschev) in a no time limit, No DQ steel cage match to win the titles at 12:26 when Morton pinned Ivan with a roll up after Gibson made a blind tag; after the bout, the Koloffs and Kruschev attacked Morton, threw him over the top of the cage to the floor, attacked Kernodle, and then hit an elevated double clothesline off the top on Gibson; moments later, Gibson was whipped with a chain until other wrestlers came out to make the save (*The Best of Starrcade: 1983-1987, The Greatest Cage Matches of All Time*)

Atlanta: Dusty Rhodes pinned NWA World Champion Ric Flair with an inside cradle to win the title at 22:06, despite outside interference from Arn & Ole Anderson; after the match, Rhodes was congratulated in the ring by a number of wrestlers including Superstar Billy Graham; the title was later returned to Flair due to the controversial finish (*The Best of Starrcade: 1983-1987*)

JCP @ St. Louis, MO - November 29, 1985 (3,600)
Debut in the city; the WWF ran the city the same night
Tully Blanchard defeated Art Crews
NWA National Heavyweight Champion Buddy Landell fought Terry Taylor to a 20-minute time-limit draw
Jimmy Valiant & Superstar Billy Graham defeated Bobby Eaton & Dennis Condrey via disqualification
Jerry Blackwell defeated Tarzan Goto

NWA Six Man Tag Team Champions Ivan Koloff, Nikita Koloff, & NWA Mid-Atlantic Heavyweight Champion Krusher Kruschev defeated Billy Jack Haynes, NWA Tag Team Champions Ricky Morton & Robert Gibson
NWA US Champion Magnum TA pinned NWA TV Champion Arn Anderson to win the title; after the bout, Magnum vacated the belt and gave it to Jim Crockett
NWA World Champion Dusty Rhodes fought Ric Flair to a double disqualification

JCP @ Atlanta, GA - WTBS Studios - November 30, 1985
Television taping:
Superstar Billy Graham & Jimmy Valiant vs. the Golden Terror & Gene Ligon

JCP @ Macon, GA - November 30, 1985
Jimmy Valiant & Superstar Billy Graham defeated Bobby Eaton & Dennis Condrey

JCP @ Richmond, VA - Coliseum - November 30, 1985 (8,000)
Denny Brown defeated Brady Boone
Ivan Koloff defeated Sam Houston
Don Kernodle defeated Mike Davis
Billy Jack Haynes, NWA Tag Team Champions Ricky Morton & Robert Gibson defeated NWA National Heavyweight Champion Buddy Landell, JJ Dillon, & Black Bart
Arn Anderson defeated Ron Bass
The Road Warriors fought Nikita Koloff & NWA Mid-Atlantic Heavyweight Champion Krusher Kruschev to a double disqualification
NWA World Champion Dusty Rhodes & NWA US Champion Magnum TA defeated Ric Flair & Tully Blanchard in an elimination match; Flair and Magnum were both counted out; Rhodes pinned Blanchard

Jackson, TN - December 1, 1985
NWA World Champion Ric Flair defeated Koko Ware

JCP @ Columbia, SC - Township Auditorium - December 1, 1985
Reeves vs. Denton
Lee Ramsey vs. Gene Ligon
Pat Tanaka vs. Stoney Burke
Denny Brown vs. Rocky King
Ron Bass vs. JJ Dillon (bullrope match)
Manny Fernandez, Billy Jack, & Don Kernodle vs. NWA 6-man Tag Team Champions Krusher Kruschev, Ivan & Nikita Koloff

JCP @ Marietta, GA - December 1, 1985
Jimmy Valiant & Ron Garvin defeated Bobby Eaton & Dennis Condrey via disqualification

JCP @ Asheville, NC - Civic Center - December 1, 1985
George South defeated Gerald Finley
Denny Brown defeated the Golden Terror
Nelson Royal defeated Tony Zane
NWA Tag Team Champions Ricky Morton & Robert Gibson defeated Tully Blanchard & NWA National Heavyweight Champion Buddy Landell
NWA US Champion Magnum TA defeated Abdullah the Butcher via disqualification
Dusty Rhodes defeated NWA National Tag Team Champion Arn Anderson in a bullrope match

JCP @ Honea Path, SC - December 2, 1985
Bobby Eaton & Dennis Condrey defeated Jimmy Valiant & Sam Houston

JCP @ Spartanburg, SC - Memorial Auditorium - December 3, 1985
Pro - 12/7/85:
Worldwide - 12/7/85 - featured an opening segment showing the entrances of Dusty Rhodes and NWA World Champion Ric Flair at Starrcade 85; included Tony Schiavone & David Crockett conducting an interview with Terry Taylor regarding his quest to regain the NWA National Heavyweight Title; featured Schiavone conducting an interview with Tommy Young about the controversey regarding the Rhodes vs. Flair match at Starrcade and Rhodes pinning Flair but not being the champion; Young said he wanted to call for the disqualification earlier in the match but was knocked dizzy and helped backstage by Gene Ligon; included Crockett conducting an interview with Flair in which he said Rhodes would continue to be #2 because he was still #1; featured Crockett conducting an interview with NWA National Heavyweight Champion Buddy Landell & JJ Dillon regarding Landell's title win at Starrcade 85 and Landell's participation in the upcoming Bunkhouse Stampede matches; included Crockett conducting an interview with the Road Warriors & Paul Ellering regarding NWA Six-Man Tag Team Champions - NWA Mid Atlantic Heavyweight Champion Krusher Kruschev, Ivan & Nikita Koloff; featured Crockett conducting an interview with Krushev & the Koloffs regarding the Road Warriors and NWA Tag Team Champions Ricky Morton & Robert Gibson; included Crockett conducting an interview with NWA US Champion Magnum TA regarding his title win at Starrcade and taking part in the Bunkhouse Stampede; featured a video package of Starrcade highlights set to Frank Stallone's "Far From Over;" included Crockett conducting an interview with NWA National Tag Team Champions Ole & Arn Anderson regarding Rhodes, the Bunkhouse Stampedes, and defending the titles; Arn then discussed the upcoming tournament for the NWA TV Title and said he would walk out with the belt; featured Caudle conducting an interview with Rhodes regarding the outcome of Starrcade 85 in which Rhodes said he was a legend and Flair was just a man; footage was then shown of Rhodes pinning Flair at Starrcade:
The Road Warriors (w/ Paul Ellering) defeated Vernon Deaton & an unknown at the 38-second mark when Road Warrior

Hawk pinned Deaton following a modified Doomsday Device
Bobby Eaton & Dennis Condrey (w/ Jim Cornette) defeated Mack & Jim Jeffers at 1:45 when Eaton scored the pin following the High / Low
Tully Blanchard (w/ Baby Doll) pinned the Italian Stallion with the slingshot suplex at 1:41
Ron Bass pinned the Golden Terror with the claw at 1:06
NWA Tag Team Champions Ricky Morton & Robert Gibson defeated Black Bart & Thunderfoot at 6:35 when Gibson pinned Thunderfoot following the double dropkick
Sam Houston & Pez Whatley defeated NWA Mid Atlantic Heavyweight Champion & NWA Six Man Tag Team Champion Krusher Kruschev & NWA Six Man Tag Team Champion Nikita Koloff (w/ NWA Six Man Tag Team Champion Ivan Koloff) via disqualification at 1:00 when Kruschev threw Houston over the top rope; after the bout, the Russians double teamed Houston until the Road Warriors, with Paul Ellering, made the save; moments later, Ellering & the Road Warriors were assaulted with a chain and Kruschev hung Road Warrior Hawk over the top rope with the weapon
Billy Jack defeated Tommy Lane via submission with the full nelson at the 27-second mark; after the bout, Paul Jones appeared ringside, grabbed the mic, and challenged Jack to a test of strength against the Barbarian; moments later, the Barbarian attacked Billy Jack from behind and twice press slammed his head above his head as the show came to a close
Dark match after the taping: NWA Tag Team Champions Ricky Morton & Robert Gibson vs. NWA National Tag Team Champions Ole & Arn Anderson

JCP @ Raleigh, NC - Dorton Arena - December 4, 1985
Ron Garvin defeated Black Bart
Manny Fernandez defeated Thunderfoot
NWA Mid-Atlantic Heavyweight Champion Krusher Kruschev defeated Terry Taylor
NWA Tag Team Champions Ricky Morton & Robert Gibson fought Tully Blanchard & NWA National Heavyweight Champion Buddy Landell to a draw
NWA US Champion Magnum TA defeated Abdullah the Butcher via disqualification
Dusty Rhodes & the Road Warriors defeated NWA World Champion Ric Flair, NWA National Tag Team Champions Ole & Arn Anderson

JCP @ Amelia, VA - December 5, 1985
NWA Tag Team Champions Ricky Morton & Robert Gibson defeated Bobby Eaton & Dennis Condrey via disqualification

JCP @ Hampton, VA - Coliseum - December 6, 1985
Jimmy Valiant, Miss Atlanta Lively, & Ron Bass defeated Jim Cornette, Bobby Eaton & Dennis Condrey

World Championship Wrestling - 12/7/85:
NWA Tag Team Champions Ricky Morton & Robert Gibson vs. Jim & Mack Jeffers
Ron Garvin vs. Tommy Lane

Nikita Koloff vs. the Italian Stallion
The Road Warriors vs. Adrian Bivins & Paul Garner
NWA US Champion Magnum TA, Billy Jack Haynes, & Sam Houston vs. Tully Blanchard, NWA National Tag Team Champions Ole & Arn Anderson
Jimmy Valiant vs. Vernon Deaton
Terry Taylor vs. Brodie Chase
The Barbarian vs. George South
Buddy Landell vs. Jeff Smith
Ivan Koloff & Krusher Kruschev vs. Mark Cooper & Jim Backlund

JCP @ Cleveland, OH - December 7, 1985
Ron Garvin fought Ivan Koloff to a draw
NWA Tag Team Champions Ricky Morton & Robert Gibson defeated the Barbarian & Abdullah the Butcher
Jimmy Valiant defeated Black Bart
NWA US Champion Magnum TA defeated Ole Anderson
The Road Warriors defeated Nikita Koloff & NWA Mid-Atlantic Heavyweight Champion Krusher Kruschev
Dusty Rhodes defeated NWA National Tag Team Champion Arn Anderson in a Texas Death match
NWA US Champion Magnum TA won a 20-man Bunkhouse Stampede match

JCP @ Atlanta, GA - Omni - December 8, 1985
The Barbarian defeated Sam Houston
NWA Tag Team Champions Ricky Morton & Robert Gibson defeated Tully Blanchard & National Heavyweight Champion Buddy Landell via disqualification
Black Bart defeated the Italian Stallion
NWA US Champion Magnum TA defeated National Tag Team Champion Ole Anderson in a Texas Death Match
The Road Warriors defeated Ivan Koloff & Krusher Kruschev via disqualification
Dusty Rhodes defeated National Tag Team Champion Arn Anderson in a bullrope match
NWA US Champion Magnum TA won a 20-man Bunkhouse Stampede

JCP @ Rock Hill, SC - Winthrop Coliseum - December 11, 1985
TV taping:
Mid Atlantic Wrestling:
Ivan Koloff, Nikita Koloff, & Krusher Khruschev defeated Pat Tanaka, Ricky Reeves, & Stoney Burke
Bobby Eaton & Dennis Condrey defeated Mike Davis & Tommy Lane
Ricky Morton pinned Mark Fleming
Arn Anderson pinned Gene Ligon
NWA World Champion Ric Flair defeated Vernon Deaton via submission
The Barbarian pinned George South
Dusty Rhodes & NWA US Champion Magnum TA defeated Jim & Mack Jeffers
Worldwide:

Tully Blanchard pinned Mac Jeffers
NWA National Tag Team Champions Ole & Arn Anderson defeated Vernon Deaton & Mike Davis
Ricky Morton pinned Tommy Lane
Nikita Koloff & Krusher Khruschev defeated Jim Jeffers & George South
Dusty Rhodes & NWA US Champion Magnum TA defeated Mark Fleming & the Golden Terror
NWA World Champion Ric Flair defeated Rocky King via submission
Dark match after the taping: Dusty Rhodes & NWA US Champion Magnum TA defeated NWA World Champion Ric Flair & Tully Blanchard when Rhodes pinned Blanchard

JCP @ Richmond, VA - Coliseum - December 13, 1985 (4,000)
Tommy Lane vs. Don Kernodle
Abdullah th Butcher vs. Pez Whatley
Krusher Kruschev, Ivan & Nikita Koloff vs. Manny Fernandez, NWA Tag Team Champions Ricky Morton & Robert Gibson
Tully Blanchard vs. Billy Jack Haynes
Dusty Rhodes & NWA US Champion Magnum TA defeated NWA World Champion Ric Flair & NWA National Tag Team Champion Arn Anderson in a double bullrope match
Also included a 20-man $20,000 bunkhouse battle royal

JCP @ Fayetteville, NC - Cumberland County Memorial Arena - December 14, 1985
Krusher Kruschev vs. Manny Fernandez
Tommy Lane vs. Don Kernodle
NWA Tag Team Champions Ricky Morton & Robert Gibson vs. NWA National Tag Team Champions Ole & Arn Anderson
Billy Jack vs. Ivan Koloff
Dusty Rhodes, & NWA US Champion Magnum TA vs. NWA World Champion Ric Flair & Tully Blanchard
Also included a $20,000 20-man bunkhouse battle royal featuring NWA World Champion Ric Flair, NWA National Tag Team Champions Ole & Arn Anderson, Billy Jack, Dusty Rhodes, NWA US Champion Magnum TA, NWA Tag Team Champions Ricky Morton & Robert Gibson, Ivan & Nikita Koloff, Krusher Kruschev, Abdullah the Butcher, the Barbarian, Manny Fernandez, Don Kernodle, Pez Whatley, Tully Blanchard, Denny Brown, Tommy Lane, and the Golden Terror

JCP @ Conway, SC - December 14, 1985
Bobby Eaton & Dennis Condrey defeated Jimmy Valiant & Sam Houston

MID ATLANTIC WRESTLING

FRIDAY DECEMBER 27

COLUMBIA TOWNSHIP AUDITORIUM 8:15

ATLANTA STREET FIGHT!

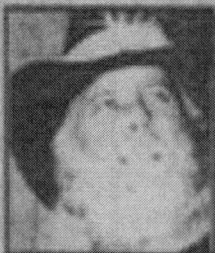

MS. ATLANTA LIVELY
AND
"BOOGIE WOOGIE" VALIENT
-VS-
THE MIDNITE EXPRESS

DON KERNODLE
AND
RON GARVIN
-VS-
IVAN KARLOFF
AND
KRUSHER KRUCHEV

PEZ WHATLEY -VS- GOLDEN TERROR

SUPERSTAR GRAHAM -VS- THE BARBARIAN

ITALIAN STALLION -VS- RICKY REEVES

STONEY BURKE -VS- TOMMY LANE

TICKETS NOW ON SALE
TAYLOR STREET PHARMACY

244

JCP @ Atlanta, GA - WTBS Studios - December 15, 1985 (matinee)
World Championship Wrestling - 12/21/85:
Ole Anderson vs. Bob Wayne
Nikita Koloff vs. Tony Zane
The Barbarian vs. Richard Dunn
Krusher Kruschev vs. Bill Mulkey
Tully Blanchard vs. Vernon Deaton
Sam Houston vs. Kent Glover
Ron Garvin & Manny Fernandez vs. Black Bart & Thunderfoot
NWA Tag Team Champions Ricky Morton & Robert Gibson vs. Larry Clarke & Randy Mulkey
NWA US Champion Magnum TA vs. George South
Arn Anderson vs. Josh Stroud
Ivan Koloff vs. Don Turner

JCP @ Greensboro, NC - Coliseum - December 15, 1985 (7,000+)
Ivan & Nikita Koloff defeated Ben Alexander & Gene Ligon
Dennis Condrey fought Don Kernodle to a 20-minute time-limit draw
Jimmy Valiant defeated Bobby Eaton via disqualification
NWA Mid-Atlantic Heavyweight Champion Krusher Kruschev defeated Pez Whatley
NWA Tag Team Champion Ricky Morton defeated the Barbarian
Ron Bass defeated JJ Dillon in a Texas Bullrope match
Dusty Rhodes, NWA US Champion Magnum TA, & Manny Fernandez defeated NWA World Champion Ric Flair, NWA National Tag Team Champions Ole & Arn Anderson
Dusty Rhodes won a 20-man Bunkhouse Stampede match

Worldwide - 12/21/85 - featured David Crockett conducting an interview with National Heavyweight Champion Buddy Landell & JJ Dillon in which Dillon argued Landell was the #1 contender to NWA World Champion Ric Flair:
Tully Blanchard vs. Mac Jeffers
Ole & Arn Anderson vs. Mike Davis & Vernon Deaton
NWA Tag Team Champion Ricky Morton vs. Tommy Lane
Nikita Koloff & Krusher Kruschev vs. George South & an unknown
Dusty Rhodes & NWA US Champion Magnum TA vs. Mark Fleming & the Golden Terror
NWA World Champion Ric Flair defeated Rocky King via submission with the figure-4 at 2:09 following a suplex; after the bout, Flair shook King's hand while King was still on the mat

JCP @ Charlotte, NC - Coliseum - December 25, 1985
Dusty Rhodes & NWA US Champion Magnum TA defeated NWA World Champion Ric Flair & Tully Blanchard

JCP @ Greenville, SC - December 25, 1985 (5,300; sell out)
Fan Appreciation Day - all seats were $3
Jimmy Valiant & Miss Atlanta Lively defeated Bobby Eaton & Dennis Condrey in a steel cage match

JCP @ Atlanta, GA - Omni - December 25, 1985
Manny Fernandez defeated Thunderfoot
Sam Houston fought Mid-Atlantic Heavyweight Champion Krusher Kruschev to a draw
Ron Garvin defeated JJ Dillon
Jimmy Valiant & Superstar Billy Graham defeated Black Bart & the Barbarian
NWA Tag Team Champions Ricky Morton & Robert Gibson defeated National Tag Team Champions Ole & Arn Anderson via disqualification
NWA US Champion Magnum TA defeated Tully Blanchard via disqualification
NWA World Champion Ric Flair defeated Dusty Rhodes

JCP @ Norfolk, VA - Scope - December 26, 1985
Pez Whatley defeated the Golden Terror (sub. for NWA National Champion Buddy Landell)
Black Bart defeated Mark Fleming
Don Kernodle defeated Thunderfoot
Denny Brown defeated Tommy Lane
Ron Bass defeated JJ Dillon in a bullrope match
Jimmy Valiant & Ron Garvin (as Miss Atlanta Lively) defeated Bobby Eaton & Dennis Condrey
NWA US Champion Magnum TA defeated Tully Blanchard

JCP @ Columbia, SC - Township Auditorium - December 27, 1985
Stoney Burke vs. Tommy Lane
The Italian Stallion vs. Ricky Reeves
Superstar Billy Graham vs. the Barbarian
Pez Whatley vs. the Golden Terror
Jimmy Valiant & Ms. Atlanta Lively defeated Bobby Eaton & Dennis Condrey in a streetfight
Don Kernodle & Ron Garvin vs. Ivan Koloff & Krusher Kruschev

JCP @ Richmond, VA - Coliseum - December 27, 1985
Ron Bass defeated Black Bart in a bullrope match
Abdullah the Butcher vs. Manny Fernandez (Mexican Death Match)
NWA Tag Team Champions Ricky Morton & Robert Gibson defeated National Tag Team Champions Ole & Arn Anderson via disqualification
Tully Blanchard defeated NWA US Champion Magnum TA
Billy Jack Haynes vs. Nikita Koloff
Dusty Rhodes fought NWA World Champion Ric Flair to a double count-out

Worldwide - 12/28/85:
NWA World Champion Ric Flair, National Tag Team Champions Arn & Ole Anderson defeated Dusty Rhodes, NWA US Champion Magnum TA, & Manny Fernandez at around the 14-minute mark when Ole pinned Fernandez after Arn grabbed a steel chair from the ringside area and hit Fernandez in the head with it behind the back of referee Tommy Young; at the time of the fall, Rhodes had Flair caught in the figure-4; after

245

the match, the Andersons attacked Rhodes, with Flair attempting to hit Rhodes with a chair until Magnum cleared him from the ring (*Nature Boy Ric Flair: The Definitive Collection*)

World Championship Wrestling - 12/28/85:
Sam Houston vs. Tony Zane
Bobby Eaton & Dennis Condrey vs. Josh Stroud & Mark Cooper
Arn Anderson vs. George South
Rocky King vs. Mack Jeffers
Black Bart vs. Jim Jeffers
NWA US Champion Magnum TA vs. Ole Anderson
NWA World Champion Ric Flair vs. Ron Garvin
The Italian Stallion vs. Pablo Crenshaw
Tully Blanchard vs. Kent Glover

JCP @ Greensboro, NC - Coliseum - December 28, 1985 (matinee)

Worldwide - 1/4/86 - hosted by Tony Schiavone & David Crockett, with the announcement NWA Tag Team Champion Dusty Rhodes defeated Buddy Landell in Albuquerque, NM to win the NWA National Heavyweight Title; moments later, they brought in NWA World Champion Ric Flair, with Flair saying he partied for two full days to celebrate the new year; Crockett then asked Flair about his antics with National Tag Team Champions Ole & Arn Anderson against the likes of Rhodes, NWA US Champion Magnum TA, and NWA Tag Team Champions Ricky Morton & Robert Gibson, with Flair simply saying he was out to make an example; featured footage of a recent fight between Rhodes & NWA Tag Team Champion Manny Fernandez against Flair and the Andersons, during which Arn hit Fernandez with a steel chair; included Crockett conducting an interview with Tully Blanchard, alongside Baby Doll, in which he said he was after Magnum and Rhodes' singles titles; Blanchard then asked Baby Doll where she had been, with Baby Doll saying JJ Dillon gave her tickets to Acapulco as a Christmas present; moments later, Dillon joined them on set, and told Baby Doll he thought the world of her but she was going to have to come up with a better story to cover her tracks; Blanchard then began yelling at Baby Doll, then knocked her down and dragged her by the hair as Dillon held Crockett away; Rhodes then intervened, punched Blanchard, and protected Baby Doll; Rhodes then took the mic, told Blanchard to never touch Baby Doll again because she now belonged to Rhodes; featured an ad promoting Starrcade 85 on VHS; included Crockett conducting an interview with Magnum about the events earlier in the show involving Blanchard, Baby Doll, and Rhdoes, with Magnum saying he didn't like Baby Doll but Blanchard had no right to put his hands on her as he did; featured Crockett conducting an interview with Dillon about the altercation earlier in the show, with Dillon saying he would not be held responsible for what happened, with Dillon saying he would send his men after Jimmy Valiant to help take the National Title from Rhodes; included Crockett conducting an interview with Mid-Atlantic Heavyweight Champion Krusher Kruschev & Ivan Koloff, with Kruschev discussing his feud with Sam Houston before adding

he wanted the Road Warriors in the ring; Ivan then said the Koloffs would be the team of 1986 as they were in 1985, adding he too wanted to show the Road Warriors how dominate they were:
Manny Fernandez pinned Thunderfoot with the flying forearm at the 26-second mark
NWA US Champion Magnum TA pinned Mike Davis with the belly to belly suplex at the 28-second mark
Black Bart pinned Pat Tanaka with a legdrop from the middle turnbuckle at 4:49
NWA Tag Team Champions Ricky Morton & Robert Gibson defeated George South & Gene Ligon at 2:59 when Gibson pinned South after the double dropkick; late in the match, Jim Cornette appeared ringside; after the match, Bobby Eaton & Dennis Condrey ran out and attacked the champions, eventually holding Morton against the ropes so Cornette could repeatedly hit Morton with his tennis racquet; moments later, Gibson ran back in to make the save
Ron Bass defeated Tommy Lane via TKO with the claw at 2:28
Tully Blanchard pinned NWA Jr. Heavyweight Champion Denny Brown in a non-title match with the slingshot suplex at 6:09; mid-way through the match, JJ Dillon appeared near the ring to watch the bout; after the contest, Dillon gave Blanchard a thumbs up; following the commercial break, Blanchard confronted David Crockett at the interview stage, saying Baby Doll was his and always would be his; Blanchard then stole the mic away and gave it to Dillon, with Dillon saying Baby Doll would eventually come crawling back on her hands and knees
NWA World Champion Ric Flair defeated Mack Jeffers via submission with the figure-4 at 1:34; after the match, Flair refused to break the hold, with NWA National Heavyweight Champion Dusty Rhodes then coming ringside; Tully Blanchard, alongside JJ Dillon, then attacked Rhodes from behind, with Flair then putting the figure-4 on Rhodes inside the ring as Blanchard pulled back on Rhodes' arms; after Rhodes was caught in the hold about 30 seconds, Baby Doll ran out to try to make the save, with Blanchard yanking her by the hair until NWA US Champion Magnum TA ran out; Magnum and a bloody Rhodes then began brawling with Flair and Blanchard on the floor; Flair and Blanchard eventually gained the upper hand in the fight as the show ended

JCP @ Philadelphia, PA - Civic Center - December 28, 1985 (10,000)

Don Kernodle fought Dennis Condrey to a 20-minute time-limit draw
Black Bart defeated Pez Whatley
Manny Fernandez defeated Thunderfoot
Ole & Arn Anderson defeated Ron Garvin & Sam Houston
Jimmy Valiant defeated the Barbarian via disqualification
Dusty Rhodes & NWA US Champion Magnum TA defeated NWA World Champion Ric Flair & Tully Blanchard
Dusty Rhodes won a Bunkhouse Stampede

JCP @ Asheville, NC - Civic Center - December 29, 1985 (matinee)

Jimmy Valiant & Miss Atlanta Lively defeated Bobby Eaton & Dennis Condrey in a steel cage match

JCP @ Savannah, GA - Civic Center - December 29, 1985
Jimmy Valiant & Miss Atlanta Lively defeated Bobby Eaton & Dennis Condrey in a streetfight

NWA/AWA Star Wars - East Rutherford, NJ - Meadowlands - December 29, 1985 (12,000)
Ron Bass defeted JJ Dillon
Little Tokyo defeated Cowboy Lang
Sherri Martel defeated Debbie Combs
Carlos Colon defeated Konga the Barbarian
Jake Roberts defeated Paul Ellering via disqualification
NWA Tag Team Champions Ricky Morton & Robert Gibson defeated Bill & Scott Irwin
Sgt. Slaughter defeated Chris Markoff & Boris Zhukov in a handicap match
NWA US Champion Magnum TA defeated Tully Blanchard
NWA World Champion Ric Flair defeated Dusty Rhodes via disqualification
The Road Warriors defeated Ivan Koloff & Krusher Kruschev
Stan Hansen defeated AWA World Champion Rick Martel via submission to win the title

JCP @ Baltimore, MD - Civic Center - December 30, 1985
NWA World Champion Ric Flair defeated Ron Garvin

JCP @ Fayetteville, NC - Cumberland County Memorial Arena - December 30, 1985
Sam Houston & Nelson Royal vs. Black Bart & Thunderfoot
Manny Fernandez vs. Ivan Koloff
Jimmy Valiant vs. Tully Blanchard
NWA Tag Team Champions Ricky Morton & Robert Gibson defeated Bobby Eaton & Dennis Condrey via disqualification in a non-title match

1986.

The year began with Harley Race again chasing Ric Flair across the Central States territory. Following Starrcade '83, Race remained one of the top names in the St. Louis promotion and even briefly regained the title from Flair during a tour of Asia in 1984.

But Race's glory days, and that of St. Louis, were done. Race, opting to end his in-ring career in the best financial way possible, joined the WWF in the spring of 1986. Within months, he won an untelevised King of the Ring tournament and was given the title and gimmick of "The King of Wrestling."

Race's departure spelled the end of the Central States territory under the ownership of Bob Geigel. Jim Crockett Promotions took control of the territory and its roster, and it was no coincidence that Flair regained the title from Dusty Rhodes around the same time in St. Louis.

JCP grew in '86 not only with the acquisition of the Central States territory and the official formation of the Four Horsemen but with the implementation of prime time TV specials and taking the Great American Bash concept on tour.

In February, Crockett fought back against the WWF's regular appearances on NBC by airing a "Superstars on the Superstation" prime time special on WTBS. The show featured highlights from the Omni event taped several days earlier, which saw the Midnight Express win the NWA Tag Team Titles from the Rock 'n' Roll Express, the Road Warriors facing the Koloffs, Dusty Rhodes against Tully Blanchard, and Flair against Ron Garvin. To counter the WWF's relationship with MTV and incorporation of celebrities into its broadcast, "Superstars on the Superstation" included an interview with Willie Nelson and music from both Nelson and Dire Straits.

In July, expanding on the successful Charlotte stadium show the previous summer, JCP took its top feuds, gave them stipulation rules, and sent them on tour in a loop that showcased its stars in front of new JCP cities (in the Central States, Georgia Championship Wrestling, and Championship Wrestling from Florida regions) as well as stepping into traditional WWF cities like Philadelphia and Washington DC. The tour culminated in front of a sold out Greensboro crowd which saw Rhodes pin Flair inside of a steel cage to win the title.

For all the steps forward, Crockett and the wrestling world took a step back when, on Oct. 14, Magnum TA was critically injured in a motorcycle wreck outside Charlotte. The wreck made regional headlines and spelled the end of Magnum's in-ring career. Magnum's departure led to a babyface turn for Nikita Koloff, who joined Rhodes in battling the Horsemen.

Six weeks later, a total of 30,000 fans packed into the Omni in Atlanta and Greensboro Coliseum - as they had done the previous year - for Starrcade. This year's event was headlined by the Road Warriors, now full-time members of the roster, against the Midnight Express in a scaffold match. Flair defended the world title against Nikita, Blanchard challenged Rhodes in a first blood match, and the Rock 'n' Roll Express faced the Andersons in a cage.

As the year ended, the promotion made even more strides with a tour that saw thousands of fans attend shows in the non-traditional JCP cities of Los Angeles, San Francisco, Minneapolis, and Philadelphia.

And as the promotion grew, so did its hold over the NWA World Title.

MID-ATLANTIC CHAMPIONSHIP • **FRI. JAN. 3rd**

WRESTLING
8:15 p.m. 8:15 p.m. 8:15 p.m.

STAFFORD SR. H.S. GYM
SPONSORED BY BOOSTER CLUB

SPECIAL CHALLENGE MATCH
RICK MORTON & ROBERT GIBSON

ROCK 'N ROLL EXPRESS
• VERSUS •

LOVERBOY DENNIS & BEAUTIFUL BOBBY

MIDNIGHT EXPRESS
with JIM CORNETTE

ARN	v	JIMMY
ANDERSON	s.	**VALIANT**

THE	v	RONNIE	P'n'd Por WHATLEY — vs — Mare FLEMING	Brady BOONE — vs — Denny BROWN	The Italian STALLION — vs — The Golden TERROR
BARBARIAN	s.	**GARVIN**			

Advance tickets are $7.00 for adults and $3.00 for children under 12. Tickets available at Athletic Attic in Spotsy Mall, Ross Music, Stafford High School (Jan. 2 & 3 only), Lafayette BP and Dennis Dodson Insurance at Stafford Courthouse.

250

1986

Central States @ St. Louis, MO - Kiel Auditorium - January 1, 1986
Brad & Bart Batten defeated Akio Sato & Sheik Abdullah
Tarzan Goto defeated Gary Jackson
Bob Brown defeated Marty Jannetty
Jimmy Valiant defeated Mr. Pogo
NWA US Champion Magnum TA defeated Tully Blanchard via disqualification
NWA National Heavyweight Champion Dusty Rhodes & the Road Warriors defeated Ivan Koloff, NWA National Tag Team Champions Ole & Arn Anderson
Harley Race fought NWA World Champion Ric Flair to a double disqualification

JCP @ Atlanta, GA - Omni - January 1, 1986 (14,000)
Fan Appreciation Day - all seats were $5
Sam Houston defeated Jim Jeffers
Manny Fernandez defeated Tony Zane
Ron Bass defeated Thunderfoot
Ron Garvin defeated Black Bart
Bobby Eaton & Dennis Condrey defeated NWA Tag Team Champions Ricky Morton & Robert Gibson in a non-title match
NWA US Champion Magnum TA defeated Tully Blanchard via disqualification
NWA National Heavyweight Champion Dusty Rhodes & the Road Warriors defeated NWA World Champion Ric Flair, National Tag Team Champions Ole & Arn Anderson via disqualification

Central States @ Kansas City, MO - January 2, 1986
Harley Race fought NWA World Champion Ric Flair to a draw

JCP @ Harrisonburg, VA - High School - January 2, 1986
Jimmy Valiant vs. the Barbarian
NWA Tag Team Champions Ricky Morton & Robert Gibson defeated Bobby Eaton & Dennis Condrey in a non-title match

JCP @ Fredricksburg, VA - Stafford High School Gym - January 3, 1986
Sponsored by the Booster Club
The Italian Stallion vs. the Golden Terror
NWA Jr. Heavyweight Champion Denny Brown vs. Brady Boone
Pez Whatley vs. Mark Fleming
Ron Garvin vs. the Barbarian
Jimmy Valiant vs. Arn Anderson
Bobby Eaton & Dennis Condrey defeated NWA Tag Team Champions Ricky Morton & Robert Gibson in a non-title match

JCP @ Atlanta, GA - WTBS Studios - January 4, 1986 (matinee)
World Championship Wrestling - 1/4/86:

NWA Tag Team Champions Ricky Morton & Robert Gibson vs. Jim Jeffers & Thunderfoot
Harley Race vs. Tony Zane
Ron Bass vs. Bill Tabb
Ron Garvin vs. Mack Jeffers
The Road Warriors vs. Gene Ligon & Josh Stroud
Manny Fernandez vs. Mark Hawk
Arn Anderson vs. Kent Glover
Jimmy Valiant vs. Diamond
Dennis Condrey vs. Rocky King
NWA US Champion Magnum TA defeated the Barbarian
Sam Houston & Nelson Royal vs. Pablo Crenshaw & Don Turner

JCP @ Greensboro, NC - Coliseum - January 4, 1986
NWA TV Championship Tournament Quarter-Finals: Tully Blanchard pinned Ron Bass by falling on top of him from the top rope as Bass had the claw applied
NWA TV Championship Tournament Quarter-Finals: NWA National Tag Team Champion Arn Anderson pinned Jimmy Valiant with a double leg pick up and putting his foot on the ropes for leverage
NWA TV Championship Tournament Quarter-Finals: Black Bart fought Road Warrior Animal to a double count-out
NWA TV Championship Tournament Quarter-Finals: Wahoo McDaniel pinned the Barbarian with a roll up after the Barbarian missed a charge into the corner
NWA TV Championship Tournament Semi-Finals: NWA National Tag Team Champion Arn Anderson pinned Ron Garvin by blocking a backdrop into a sunset flip and grabbing the ropes for leverage at around the 17-minute mark; after the bout, Garvin had a confrontation with Tully Blanchard, who was coming out for the next match
NWA TV Championship Tournament Semi-Finals: Wahoo McDaniel defeated Tully Blanchard via disqualification at around the 8-minute mark after referee Tommy Young spotted Blanchard hitting McDaniel with a foreign object; after the match, McDaniel cleared Blanchard from the ring
NWA Tag Team Champion Ricky Morton pinned Dennis Condrey after NWA Tag Team Champion Robert Gibson, who came ringside during the final moments to counter interference from Jim Cornette, tripped Condrey as he ran the ropes
Road Warrior Hawk defeated Ivan Koloff
Harley Race defeated NWA US Champion Magnum TA
NWA TV Championship Tournament Finals: NWA National Tag Team Champion Arn Anderson defeated Wahoo McDaniel
NWA National Heavyweight Champion Dusty Rhodes fought NWA World Champion Ric Flair to a no contest; after referee Tommy Young was knocked to the floor, Rhodes hit a clothesline on Flair, with NWA US Champion Magnum TA then running out and counting Flair down for 3; moments later, NWA TV Champion Arn Anderson attacked Magnum, with Anderson and Magnum fighting on the floor as Rhodes had the figure-4 applied on Flair in the ring; Young eventually came to his senses, with the match continuing until all four men began fighting on the floor

WIDE WORLD WRESTLING

TODAY 3 P.M.
CHALLENGE & TITLE MATCHES
ASHEVILLE CIVIC CENTER

WORLD TITLE
RAGIN' BULL
vs
RIC FLAIR
SPECIAL CHALLENGE MATCH
THE ROAD WARRIORS
(with Paul Ellering)
vs
BARBARIAN
IVAN KOLOFF
(with Paul Jones)
U.S. TITLE
MAGNUM T.A.
vs
ARN ANDERSON
ROCK & ROLL EXPRESS
vs
MIDNIGHT EXPRESS
JIMMY "BOOGIE WOOGIE"
VALIANT
vs
"NATURE BOY" BUDDY
LANDEL
(with J.J. Dillon)
RONNIE GAVIN
vs
THUNDERFOOT
DON KERNODLE
vs
MIKE DAVIS

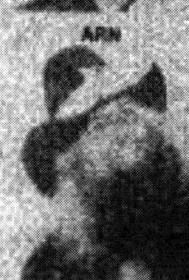

BULL · RIC · MAGNUM · ARN · ROCK N' ROLL EXPRESS · JIMMY

Ringside: $10, Balcony $8 Gen. Adm., & Children under 10 $3
Box Office 259-5771 Mon.-Fri. 10-5:30 , Sat. 11-4, Day of Match 1:00 P.M.
No Checks or Credit Cards Day of Match. Matches subject to change.

WIDE WORLD WRESTLING ON WLOS-TV 13 SUNDAY 12 NOON

252

JCP @ Asheville, NC - Civic Center - January 5, 1986 (2,500)
Don Kernodle defeated Pat Tanaka
Ron Garvin defeated Thunderfoot
Jimmy Valiant defeated Gene Ligon
Bobby Eaton & Dennis Condrey defeated NWA Tag Team Champions Ricky Morton & Robert Gibson in a non-title match
NWA US Champion Magnum TA defeated NWA TV Champion Arn Anderson via disqualification
The Road Warriors defeated Ivan Koloff & the Barbarian
NWA World Champion Ric Flair defeated Manny Fernandez

JCP @ Charlotte, NC - Coliseum - January 5, 1986 (10,200)
NWA TV Champion Arn Anderson defeated Don Kernodle
NWA Tag Team Champions Ricky Morton & Robert Gibson defeated the Barbarian & Black Bart
Road Warrior Hawk defeated Thunderfoot
Road Warrior Animal defeated Ivan Koloff
NWA US Champion Magnum TA defeated Tully Blanchard
NWA National Heavyweight Champion Dusty Rhodes fought NWA World Champion Ric Flair to a no contest

JCP @ Iva, SC - January 6, 1986
Jimmy Valiant & Miss Atlanta Lively defeated Bobby Eaton & Dennis Condrey

JCP @ Fayetteville, NC - Cumberland County Memorial Arena - January 6, 1986
Nelson Royal & Sam Houston vs. Tommy Lane & Mike Davis
Ron Bass vs. JJ Dillon
NWA Tag Team Champions Ricky Morton & Robert Gibson vs. Black Bart & the Barbarian
NWA US Champion Magnum TA vs. Tully Blanchard
NWA World Champion Ric Flair defeated NWA National Heavyweight Champion Dusty Rhodes

JCP @ Spartanburg, SC - Memorial Auditorium - January 7, 1986
TV taping:
Worldwide - 1/11/86:
Ron Bass & Don Kernodle defeated George South & Mark Fleming when Bass defeated Fleming with the claw
Ivan Koloff pinned Mack Jeffers with the Russian Sickle
The Barbarian pinned Stoney Burke with the headbutt off the top
Ron Garvin pinned Gene Ligon with a punch
Tully Blanchard pinned Rocky King with the slingshot suplex
NWA TV Champion Arn Anderson pinned Tony Zane with the gordbuster
NWA Tag Team Champions Ricky Morton & Robert Gibson defeated an unknown & Mike Jeffers; prior to the match, Bobby Eaton & Dennis Condrey attacked the champions

JCP @ Raleigh, NC - Dorton Arena - January 8, 1986
Sam Houston & Nelson Royal defeated Gene Ligon & Pat Tanaka
Ron Bass defeated Black Bart
Ron Garvin defeated Thunderfoot
Pez Whatley defeated the Golden Terror
NWA US Champion Magnum TA fought NWA TV Champion Arn Anderson to a no contest
NWA Tag Team Champions Ricky Morton & Robert Gibson defeated Bobby Eaton & Dennis Condrey via disqualification

JCP @ Canton, OH - January 9, 1986
Sam Houston defeated Jim Lancaster
Ron Bass defeated the Barbarian
NWA TV Champion Arn Anderson defeated Ron Garvin
NWA US Champion Magnum TA fought Tully Blanchard to a no contest
NWA Tag Team Champions Ricky Morton & Robert Gibson defeated Bobby Eaton & Dennis Condrey
NWA World Champion Ric Flair defeated NWA National Heavyweight Champion Dusty Rhodes via disqualification

Worldwide - 1986 - featured David Crockett conducting an interview with Tully Blanchard & JJ Dillon regarding Blanchard's recent attack on Jimmy Valiant, in which he dropped Valiant with a piledriver on the floor as a message to Dusty Rhodes; moments later, Blanchard said if Dusty Rhodes wanted a used up Baby Doll then he could have her

JCP @ Norfolk, VA - Scope - January 10, 1986
Denny Brown defeated Pat Tanaka
The Italian Stallion defeated Ron Rossi
NWA TV Champion Arn Anderson defeated Manny Fernandez
NWA Mid-Atlantic Heavyweight Champion Krusher Kruschev defeated Sam Houston
Jimmy Valiant & Miss Atlanta Lively (Ron Garvin) defeated Jim Cornette, Bobby Eaton & Dennis Condrey in a handicap match
NWA US Champion Magnum TA defeated Tully Blanchard
NWA World Champion Ric Flair defeated NWA National Heavyweight Champion Dusty Rhodes

JCP @ Cincinnati, OH - January 10, 1986
Jim Lancaster defeated Pat Tanaka
Black Bart defeated Larry Wilson
Don Kernodle defeated Thunderfoot
Pez Whatley defeated Al Snow
Ron Bass fought the Barbarian to a no contest
NWA Tag Team Champions Ricky Morton & Robert Gibson defeated Ivan & Nikita Koloff in a steel cage match

JCP @ Atlanta, GA - WTBS Studios - January 11, 1986 (matinee)
World Championship Wrestling - 1/11/86:
Ivan & Nikita Koloff vs. the Italian Stallion & Rocky King
Tully Blanchard vs. Mack Jeffers
The Barbarian vs. Art Pritts
NWA US Champion Magnum TA vs. Thunderfoot

Pez Whatley vs. George South
NWA Tag Team Champions Ricky Morton & Robert Gibson vs. Randy Mulkey & Vernon Deaton
Ron Garvin vs. Paul Garner
Bobby Eaton & Dennis Condrey vs. Bill Mulkey & Bill Tabb
Sam Houston defeated NWA Mid-Atlantic Heavyweight Champion Krusher Kruschev to win the title
NWA TV Champion Arn Anderson vs. Jim Jeffers

JCP @ Columbus, GA - January 11, 1986
NWA Tag Team Champions Ricky Morton & Robert Gibson defeated Bobby Eaton & Dennis Condrey via disqualification

JCP @ Cleveland, OH - January 12, 1986 (6,000)
Denny Brown defeated Pat Tanaka
NWA Tag Team Champion Robert Gibson defeated Black Bart
Manny Fernandez defeated the Barbarian
Bobby Eaton & Dennis Condrey defeated Jimmy Valiant & NWA Mid-Atlantic Heavyweight Champion Sam Houston
NWA World Champion Ric Flair defeated NWA National Heavyweight Champion Dusty Rhodes via disqualification
NWA US Champion Magnum TA defeated Tully Blanchard

JCP @ Greenwood, SC - January 13, 1986
TV taping:
Pez Whatley pinned Tony Zane with a superplex
NWA US Champion Magnum TA pinned Vernon Deaton with the belly to belly suplex
Manny Fernandez defeated the Golden Terror with a flying forearm from the middle turnbuckle
Jimmy Valiant pinned George South with an elbowdrop
Tully Blanchard pinned Mark Fleming with the slingshot suplex
Ron Bass & Don Kernodle defeated Gene Ligon & Stoney Burke when Kernodle pinned Ligon after a clothesline off the top tope
Bobby Eaton & Dennis Condrey defeated Pat Tanaka & Jim Jeffers when Condrey pinned Tanaka after a clothesline
Dark match after the taping: NWA Tag Team Champions Ricky Morton & Robert Gibson defeated Bobby Eaton & Dennis Condrey via disqualification

JCP @ Greenville, SC - Memorial Auditorium - January 14, 1986 (5,600)
Tully Blanchard defeated Pez Whatley
The Barbarian, Ivan & Nikita Koloff defeated Don Kernodle, Jimmy Valiant, & Ron Bass
NWA US Champion Magnum TA defeated Black Bart
Bobby Eaton & Dennis Condrey defeated NWA Tag Team Champions Ricky Morton & Robert Gibson via disqualification
NWA National Heavyweight Champion Dusty Rhodes fought NWA World Champion Ric Flair to a no contest

AWA @ Winnipeg, Manitoba - Arena - January 16, 1986 (6,800)
Candi Devine defeated AWA Women's Champion Sherri Martel

to win the title
Buddy Lane defeated Matt Jewell
Scott Hall defeated Earthquake Ferris
The Mongolian Stomper & Nord the Barbarian defeated the Alaskans
Jerry Blackwell defeated Boris Zhukov
AWA World Champion Stan Hansen defeated Rick Martel
The Road Warriors defeated AWA Tag Team Champions Steve Regal & Jimmy Garvin in a non-title match
NWA World Champion Ric Flair fought Nick Bockwinkel to a double count-out after both men tumbled over the top rope to the floor

JCP @ Richmond, VA - Coliseum - January 17, 1986 (8,500)
Ron Garvin fought the Barbarian to a draw
Ron Bass defeated Black Bart in a taped fist match
Ivan & Nikita Koloff defeated Manny Fernandez & Don Kernodle
NWA US Champion Magnum TA defeated NWA TV Champion Arn Anderson
Bobby Eaton & Dennis Condrey defeated NWA Tag Team Champions Ricky Morton & Robert Gibson via disqualification
Jimmy Valiant defeated Tully Blanchard via disqualification
NWA World Champion Ric Flair defeated NWA National Heavyweight Champion Dusty Rhodes

JCP @ Atlanta, GA - WTBS Studios - January 18, 1986 (matinee)
World Championship Wrestling - 1/18/86:
Ron Garvin vs. Pablo Crenshaw
Ivan Koloff vs. Benny Traylor
Jimmy Valiant vs. the Golden Terror
Baron Von Raschke vs. Tony Zane
NWA Mid-Atlantic Heavyweight Champion Sam Houston vs. Art Pritts
The Barbarian vs. Ray Taylor (Traylor)
NWA US Champion Magnum TA defeated Lee Peak
NWA Tag Team Champions Ricky Morton & Robert Gibson vs. Larry Clarke & Jerry Garmen
Bobby Eaton & Dennis Condrey vs. Larry Vickery & Bill Tabb
Tully Blanchard vs. Gene Ligon
Nikita Koloff vs. Mack Jeffers

JCP @ Philadelphia, PA - Civic Center - January 18, 1986 (8,500)
Don Kernodle defeated Mark Fleming
Jimmy Valiant defeated Ramblin Wreck
Bobby Eaton & Dennis Condrey defeated Ron Bass & Pez Whatley
Baron Von Raschke defeated the Italian Stallion
The Barbarian defeated NWA Mid-Atlantic Heavyweight Champion Sam Houston
NWA World Champion Ric Flair defeated NWA National Heavyweight Champion Dusty Rhodes in a Best 2 out of 3 falls match; fall #3: Flair won via disqualification

The Road Warriors defeated Ivan & Nikita Koloff in a Texas Tornado match
NWA US Champion Magnum TA defeated Tully Blanchard in an I Quit match

JCP @ York, SC - Comprehensive High School - January 18, 1986
Ricky Reeves vs. Jim Jeffers
Rocky King vs. Mack Jeffers
NWA Jr. Heavyweight Champion Denny Brown vs. Tommy Lane
Ron Garvin vs. Mike Davis
NWA Tag Team Champions Ricky Morton & Robert Gibson vs. Black Bart & Thunderfoot
Manny Fernandez vs. NWA TV Champion Arn Anderson

JCP @ Asheville, NC - Civic Center - January 19, 1986 (matinee)
Nelson Royal vs. Jim Jeffers
NWA Mid-Atlantic Heavyweight Champion Sam Houston vs. Krusher Kruschev
Pez Whatley & Ricky Reeves vs. Black Bart & Thunderfoot
Don Kernodle & Ron Bass vs. Ivan & Nikita Koloff
Manny Fernandez vs. NWA TV Champion Arn Anderson
Jimmy Valiant vs. Tully Blanchard

JCP @ Roanoke, VA - Civic Center - January 19, 1986 (matinee)
Mike Davis vs. NWA Jr. Heavyweight Champion Denny Brown
Superstar Billy Graham vs. the Barbarian (Texas Death match)
Bobby Eaton & Dennis Condrey defeated NWA Tag Team Champions Ricky Morton & Robert Gibson via disqualification

JCP @ Atlanta, GA - Omni - January 19, 1986 (10,000)
Baron Von Raschke defeated NWA Mid-Atlantic Heavyweight Champion Sam Houston
Manny Fernandez defeated Black Bart
Ron Bass fought the Barbarian to a draw
Bobby Eaton & Dennis Condrey defeated NWA Tag Team Champions Ricky Morton & Robert Gibson via disqualification
Tully Blanchard defeated Jimmy Valiant
NWA US Champion Magnum TA fought Nikita Koloff to a no contest
Ron Garvin fought NWA World Champion Ric Flair to a draw
NWA National Heavyweight Champion Dusty Rhodes defeated NWA TV Champion & National Tag Team Champion Arn Anderson in a non-title steel cage Texas Death match

JCP @ Greenville, SC - Memorial Auditorium - January 20, 1986 (700)
NWA Jr. Heavyweight Champion Denny Brown & Black Bart defeated Pez Whatley & Stoney Burke
Baron Von Raschke defeated Rocky King
Ron Garvin defeated the Barbarian via disqualification
Manny Fernandez defeated Thunderfoot

Tully Blanchard defeated Jimmy Valiant via disqualification
The Road Warriors defeated Ivan & Nikita Koloff via disqualification

JCP @ Fayetteville, NC - Cumberland County Memorial Arena - January 20, 1986
Don Kernodle vs. Jim Jeffers
Bobby Eaton & Dennis Condrey defeated NWA Tag Team Champions Ricky Morton & Robert Gibson via disqualification
NWA US Champion Magnum TA vs. NWA TV Champion Arn Anderson (title vs. title match)
NWA World Champion Ric Flair vs. NWA National Heavyweight Champion Dusty Rhodes (2 referees)

PNW @ Portland, OR - January 21, 1986
NWA US Champion Magnum TA & the Road Warriors defeated Timothy Flowers, Ivan & Nikita Koloff
NWA World Champion Ric Flair defeated NWA National Heavyweight Champion Dusty Rhodes via disqualification at 20:15

JCP @ Shelby, NC - Rec Center - January 21, 1986
TV taping:
Jimmy Valiant pinned Vernon Deaton with a elbowdrop
Baron Von Raschke defeated Pat Tanaka with the claw
Black Bart pinned George South with a legdrop from the middle turnbuckle
The Barbarian pinned The Italian Stallion with a headbutt off the top
Ron Garvin & Manny Fernandez defeated Mack & Jeff Jeffers
NWA Tag Team Champions Ricky Morton & Robert Gibson defeated Tony Zane & Thunderfoot when Zane was pinned after the double dropkick
Tully Blanchard & NWA TV Champion Arn Anderson defeated Pez Whatley & Rocky King

PNW @ Seattle, WA - January 22, 1986
NWA World Champion Ric Flair defeated NWA National Heavyweight Champion Dusty Rhodes via disqualification

JCP @ Raleigh, NC - Dorton Arena - January 22, 1986
Nelson Royal & NWA Mid-Atlantic Heavyweight Champion Sam Houston defeated Leo Burke & Pat Tanaka
Ron Garvin defeated the Barbarian
Tully Blanchard defeated Jimmy Valiant
The Italian Stallion defeated Thunderfoot
NWA TV Champion Arn Anderson fought Manny Fernandez to a draw
NWA Tag Team Champions Ricky Morton & Robert Gibson defeated Bobby Eaton & Dennis Condrey in a No DQ match

JCP @ Cheraw, SC - January 23, 1986 (sell out)
Bobby Eaton & Dennis Condrey defeated Pez Whatley & Ron Garvin

JCP @ Columbia, SC - Township Auditorium - January 23, 1986
Pez Whatley vs. Davis
Ron Bass vs. Thunderfoot
NWA Mid-Atlantic Heavyweight Champion Sam Houston vs. Lane
NWA Tag Team Champions Ricky Morton & Robert Gibson vs. Ivan Koloff & Krusher Kruschev
Jimmy Valiant vs. Tully Blanchard
NWA US Champion Magnum TA vs. Nikita Koloff
NWA World Champion Ric Flair vs. NWA National Heavyweight Champion Dusty Rhodes

JCP @ Johnson City, TN - January 24, 1986 (6,500; sell out)
NWA Tag Team Champions Ricky Morton & Robert Gibson defeated Bobby Eaton & Dennis Condrey

JCP @ Norfolk, VA - Scope - January 24, 1986
Nelson Royal defeated Mark Fleming
Black Bart defeated Gene Ligon
Don Kernodle & Ron Bass defeated Ivan Koloff & Baron Von Raschke via disqualification
NWA Mid-Atlantic Heavyweight Champion Sam Houston defeated Thunderfoot
NWA TV Champion Arn Anderson defeated Ron Garvin
NWA US Champion Magnum TA defeated Nikita Koloff via disqualification
Tully Blanchard defeated Jimmy Valiant

JCP @ Atlanta, GA - WTBS Studios - January 25, 1986 (matinee)
World Championship Wrestling - 1/25/86:
The Barbarian vs. George South
Ron Bass vs. Mike Simani
Ivan Koloff vs. Pat Tanaka
Manny Fernandez vs. Tony Zane
NWA Tag Team Champions Ricky Morton & Robert Gibson vs. Owens & Thunderfoot
Nikita Koloff vs. Bob Brown
Jimmy Valiant vs. Garner
Bobby Eaton vs. Wilkens
Ron Garvin vs. Mark Hawk
Black Bart vs. an unknown
Baron Von Raschke vs. an unknown
NWA TV Champion Arn Anderson & Tully Blanchard vs. Kernodle & the Italian Stallion

JCP @ Columbus, GA - January 25, 1986
NWA Tag Team Champions Ricky Morton & Robert Gibson defeated Bobby Eaton & Dennis Condrey

JCP @ Greensboro, NC - Coliseum - January 25, 1986 (6,222)
Nelson Royal defeated Jim Jeffers

Denny Brown defeated Mike Jeffers
NWA Mid-Atlantic Heavyweight Champion Sam Houston fought Black Bart to a draw
Don Kernodle & Ron Bass defeated Ivan & Nikita Koloff
Jimmy Valiant (w/ Baby Doll) defeated Tully Blanchard (w/ JJ Dillon) in a taped fist match after NWA National Heavyweight Champion Dusty Rhodes interfered
NWA US Champion Magnum TA defeated NWA TV Champion Arn Anderson
NWA World Champion Ric Flair defeated NWA National Heavyweight Champion Dusty Rhodes

JCP @ Marietta, GA - January 26, 1986
NWA Tag Team Champions Ricky Morton & Robert Gibson defeated Bobby Eaton & Dennis Condrey

JCP @ ? - 1986
Don Kernodle & Ron Bass defeated NWA Six Man Tag Team Champions Ivan & Nikita Koloff via disqualification when the referee saw Nikita hit Bass with his chain as Bass had a claw applied on Ivan; after the match, Bass cleared the ring with a steel chair
NWA US Champion Magnum TA pinned NWA TV Champion & NWA National Tag Team Champion Arn Anderson with a roll up at around the 20-minute mark as Anderson gloated over having kept his title; the TV title was only on the line for the first 20 minutes; the US title was on the line from that point on
Jimmy Valiant (w/ Baby Doll) defeated Tully Blanchard in a taped fist match when Blanchard couldn't answer the referee's standing 10-count after NWA National Heavyweight Champion Dusty Rhodes interfered behind the referee's back
NWA World Champion Ric Flair defeated NWA National Heavyweight Champion Dusty Rhodes via reverse decision; Rhodes originally won the match and title at around the 20-minute mark after hitting Flair with his cowboy boot but referee Tommy Young, who was at ringside, told referee Sonny Fargo what happened with Fargo then changing the call

JCP @ Greenville, SC - Memorial Auditorium - January 27, 1986 (2,000)
The Barbarian defeated NWA Mid-Atlantic Heavyweight Champion Sam Houston
Manny Fernandez fought NWA TV Champion Arn Anderson to a 20-minute time-limit draw
NWA US Champion Magnum TA defeated Baron Von Raschke via disqualification
The Road Warriors defeated Ivan & Nikita Koloff
NWA Tag Team Champions Ricky Morton & Robert Gibson defeated Bobby Eaton & Dennis Condrey
NWA World Champion Ric Flair defeated NWA National Heavyweight Champion Dusty Rhodes via disqualification

WRESTLING & TV TAPING
WINTHROP COLISEUM
TUES. JAN. 28, 1986 7:30 PM

ROAD WARRIORS
VS
NIKITA KOLOFF
&
KRUSHER KRUSHCHEV

DUSTY RHODES
The American Dream

MAGNUM T.A.

ALSO APPEARING:
- Dusty Rhodes
- Magnum T.A.
- Rock & Roll Express
- Barbarian
- Jimmy Valiant
- Ric Flair
- Midnight Express
- Tully Blanchard
- Ron Garvin
- Ivan Koloff

TULLY BLANCHARD **ADVANCE TICKET LOCATIONS**

JCP @ Rock Hill, SC - Winthrop Coliseum - January 28, 1986 (5,000)
TV taping:
NWA Tag Team Champions Ricky Morton & Robert Gibson defeated Mark & Jim Jeffers
Baron Von Raschke pinned Tony Zane
The Barbarian pinned Gene Ligon
The Road Warriors defeated Thunderfoot & the Golden Terror
Bobby Eaton & Dennis Condrey defeated Rocky King & Pez Whatley
The Road Warriors defeated George South & Mike Sumani
Ron Garvin pinned Tony Zane
Jimmy Valiant pinned Jim Jeffers
NWA TV Champion Arn Anderson pinned Rocky King
Baron Von Raschke, Ivan & Nikita Koloff defeated NWA Mid-Atlantic Heavyweight Champion Sam Houston, the Italian Stallion, & Pat Tanaka
Don Kernodle defeated the Barbarian via disqualification

NWA Tag Team Champions Ricky Morton & Robert Gibson defeated Black Bart & Thunderfoot via disqualification
NWA US Champion Magnum TA fought Ivan Koloff to a double disqualification
The Road Warriors defeated Ivan & Nikita Koloff

CWF @ Orlando, FL - January 29, 1986
Miss Linda defeated Despina Montagus
Cocoa Samoa & Hector Guerrero defeated the Cuban Assassin & Prince Iaukea
Kendall Windham defeated Bob Roop
Joe Savoldi & Mike Graham fought Kevin Sullivan & Purple Haze to a draw
Jesse Barr defeated Abdullah the Butcher
Wahoo McDaniel defeated NWA World Champion Ric Flair in a steel cage match

JCP @ Raleigh, NC - Dorton Arena - January 29, 1986
Ron Bass fought the Barbarian to a draw
Ron Garvin defeated Black Bart
Don Kernodle defeated Thunderfoot
Jimmy Valiant defeated Baron Von Raschke
NWA Tag Team Champions Ricky Morton & Robert Gibson defeated Bobby Eaton & Dennis Condrey in a No DQ, no time-limit match
The Road Warriors defeated Ivan & Nikita Koloff
NWA US Champion Magnum TA defeated Tully Blanchard in a No DQ match

JCP @ Washington, NC - January 30, 1986 (1,250)
Pez Whatley defeated Pat Tanaka
Don Kernodle defeated Gene Ligon
Ron Bass defeated Black Bart
NWA TV Chapion Arn Anderson fought Manny Fernandez to a draw
NWA Tag Team Champions Ricky Morton & Robert Gibson defeated Bobby Eaton & Dennis Condrey in a non-title match

JCP @ Beckley, WV - January 31, 1986 (2,500)
Rocky King defeated Mark Fleming
NWA Mid-Atlantic Heavyweight Champion Sam Houston defeated Thunderfoot
Ron Garvin defeated the Barbarian
Tully Blanchard defeated the Italian Stallion
NWA US Champion Magnum TA defeated Baron Von Raschke via disqualification
The Road Warriors defeated Ivan & Nikita Koloff

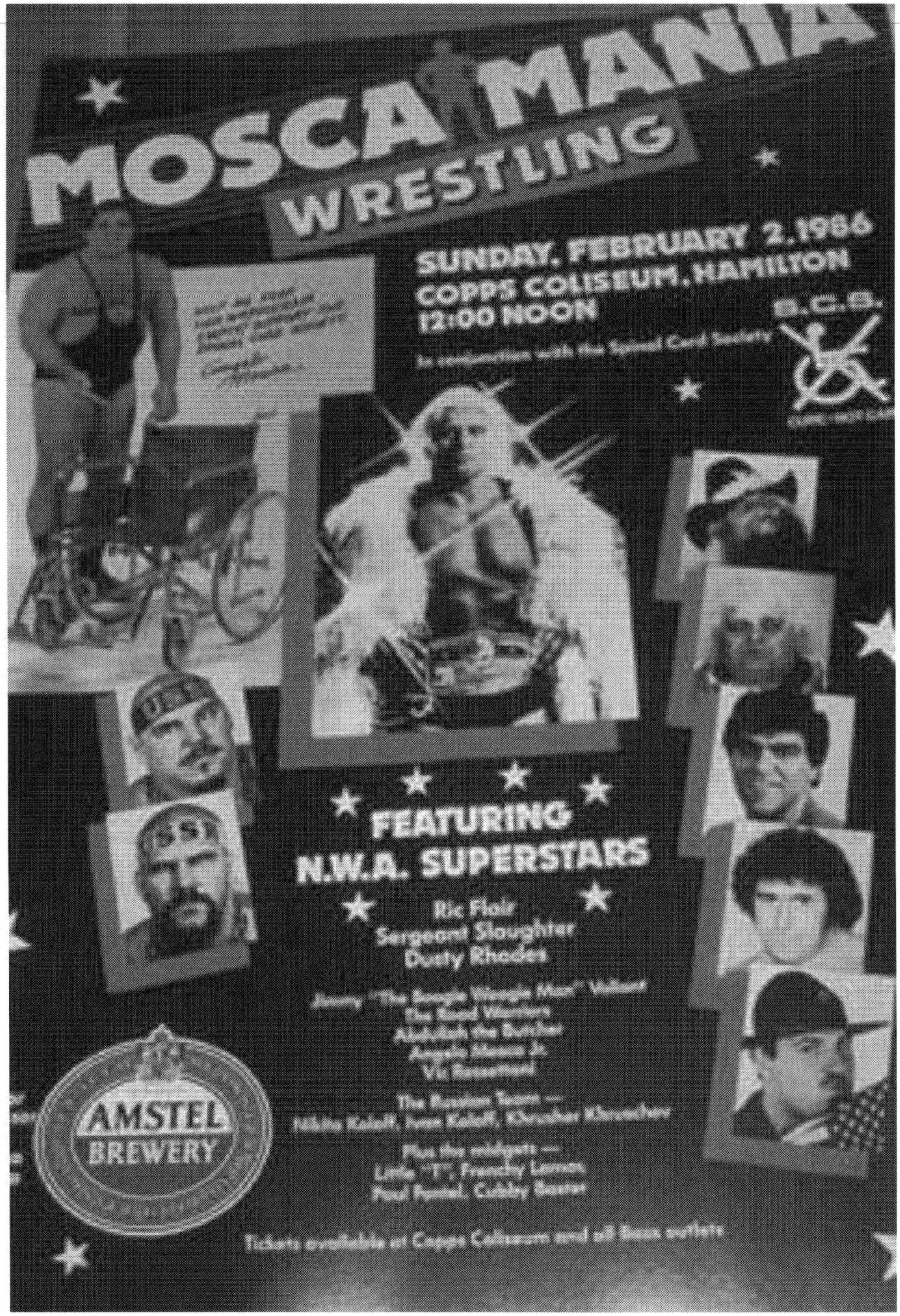
MOSCA MANIA
WRESTLING
SUNDAY, FEBRUARY 2, 1986
COPPS COLISEUM, HAMILTON
12:00 NOON
S.C.S.
FEATURING
N.W.A. SUPERSTARS
Ric Flair
Sergeant Slaughter
Dusty Rhodes
AMSTEL
BREWERY

JCP @ Columbia, SC - Township Auditorium - January 31, 1986
NWA Mid-Atlantic Heavyweight Champion Sam Houston & Gary Royal vs. Jim & Mack Jeffers
Ron Bass vs. the Barbarian
Ron Garvin vs. Zane
Pez Whatley vs. Wreck
NWA Tag Team Champions Ricky Morton & Robert Gibson defeated Bobby Eaton & Dennis Condrey
NWA National Heavyweight Champion Dusty Rhodes vs. NWA TV Champion Arn Anderson (title vs. title)

JCP @ Atlanta, GA - WTBS Studios - February 1, 1986 (matinee)
TV taping

JCP @ Philadelphia, PA - Civic Center - February 1, 1986 (6,500)
The Italian Stallion defeated Jim Jeffers
Ron Garvin defeated Thunderfoot
Baron Von Raschke defeated Pez Whatley
NWA National Heavyweight Champion Dusty Rhodes defeated Tully Blanchard
NWA Tag Team Champions Ricky Morton & Robert Gibson defeated Bobby Eaton & Dennis Condrey via disqualification at 13:59 when referee Earl Hebner caught Eaton hitting Gibson with Jim Cornette's tennis racquet as Gibson had Condrey in an abdominal stretch; after the bout, Morton & Gibson cleared the challengers from the ring (*Wrestling Rarities: The Midnight Express*)
NWA World Champion Ric Flair fought NWA US Champion Magnum TA to a 60-minute time-limit draw
The Road Warriors defeated Ivan & Nikita Koloff in a steel cage match

JCP @ Charlotte, NC - Coliseum - February 2, 1986 (matinee) (12,000; 10,200 paid; sell out)
Misty Blue defeated Linda Dallas
Ron Bass & Nelson Royal defeated Jim & Mack Jeffers
Don Kernodle defeated Thunderfoot
NWA Mid Atlantic Heavyweight Champion Sam Houston pinned Black Bart with a roll up
NWA US Champion Magnum TA pinned the Barbarian with a roll up after the challenger collided with Paul Jones on the apron
Ron Garvin fought Tully Blanchard to a 30-minute time-limit draw; Blanchard was caught in a Boston Crab for the last 15 seconds of the bout; after the contest, Garvin tried to get at JJ Dillon but Blanchard jumped him from behind and hit the slingshot suplex
NWA TV Champion Arn Anderson pinned Manny Fernandez by grabbing the tights for leverage after the momentum of a crossbody by Fernandez put Anderson on top
NWA Tag Team Champions Ricky Morton & Robert Gibson defeated Bobby Eaton & Dennis Condrey when Morton pinned Eaton with a sunset flip into the ring; Eaton & Condrey

originally won the match and titles moments earlier when Eaton pinned Gibson after hitting Gibson with Jim Cornette's tennis racquet behind the referee's back but referee Tommy Young ordered the match to continue

Mosca Mania - Hamilton, Ontario - Copps Coliseum - February 2, 1986 (matinee) (12,000)
Joey War Eagle defeated Jet Star via disqualification
Sgt. Slaughter defeated Danny Johnson
Little Farmer Pete pinned Frenchy Lamonte
Pat & Mike Kelly fought Angelo Mosca Jr. & Vic Rossitani to a no contest
Jimmy Valiant fought Abdullah the Butcher to a no contest
The Road Warriors (w/ Paul Ellering) defeated Nikita Koloff & Baron Von Raschke
NWA World Champion Ric Flair pinned NWA National Heavyweight Champion Dusty Rhodes (w/ Baby Doll) after hitting him in the back of the head as Rhodes was distracted by the referee

JCP @ Atlanta, GA - Omni - February 2, 1986 (10,000)
Ron Bass fought the Barbarian to a draw
Baron Von Raschke defeated the Italian Stallion
Jimmy Valiant defeated NWA TV Champion Arn Anderson via disqualification
Superstars on the Superstation - 2/7/86 - included an opening video package showing NWA US Champion Magnum TA arriving to the arena on his motorcycle, to the turne of Willie Nelson's "Georgia on a Fast Train;" hosted by Magnum & Linda Curry; featured Tony Schiavone & David Crockett on commentary; included Bob Caudle backstage with NWA Tag Team Champions Ricky Morton & Robert Gibson as they were getting dressed for their upcoming title defense; featured Caudle introducing footage of Morton & Gibson beating the Russians to win their first NWA Tag Team Titles; included an ad for the Starrcade 85 home video; included footage of the Russians assaulting Road Warrior Animal with a chain at WTBS Studios and hanging Road Warrior Hawk with the chain during a syndicated taping; featured Magnum speaking with racecar driver Benny Bartens; included a segment in which several of the fans onhand were asked who their favorite wrestlers were and why they watched wrestling; featured a look at the fans to the tune of Dire Straits' "Walk of Life;" included footage of Tony Schiavone conducting a sit-down interview with NWA National Heavyweight Champion Dusty Rhodes and Willie Nelson in Tucson, AZ, as Nelson was filming "Stagecoach;" featured Magnum speaking with Jim Crockett Jr. in which Crockett announced the first Jim Crockett Sr. Memorial Cup would take place later that year; footage then aired of Joel Watts speaking with Bob Johnson, executive vice president of the Superdome, regarding hosting the Crockett Cup; included Schiavone conducting a ringside interview with former MLB pitcher Gaylord Perry about the upcoming main event and the Atlanta Braves:
Bobby Eaton & Dennis Condrey (w/ Jim Cornette) defeated NWA Tag Team Champions Ricky Morton & Robert Gibson to win the titles at 16:27 when Eaton pinned Morton after Condrey

hit Morton with Cornette's tennis racquet as referee Randy Anderson was knocked down on the floor; following the commercial break, Bob Caudle conducted a backstage interview with Cornette, Eaton & Condrey regarding the title win

The Road Warriors (w/ Paul Ellering) defeated NWA Six Man Tag Team Champions Ivan & Nikita Koloff via disqualification at 6:55 when both Baron Von Raschke and Krusher Kruschev interfered; after the bout, the Koloffs & Von Raschke attempted to use the chain on Ellering until the Road Warriors made the save and used the chain on Ivan and Von Raschke

NWA National Heavyweight Champion Dusty Rhodes (w/ Baby Doll) fought Tully Blanchard (w/ JJ Dillon) to a 20-minute time-limit draw; Rhodes had Blanchard caught in a Boston Crab when the bell rang; after the bout, Rhodes confronted Dillon in the ring, with Blanchard jumping the champion from behind and dropping him with a piledriver; Blanchard and Dillon then left ringside in possession of the title belt

NWA World Champion Ric Flair pinned Ron Garvin at 14:33 with a knee to the back; Garvin's foot was on the rope during the cover but referee Tommy Young, who had been knocked down moments earlier, didn't notice it

Hamilton, Ontario - February 2, 1986
NWA World Champion Ric Flair defeated NWA National Heavyweight Champion Dusty Rhodes

GCW @ Saginaw, MI - February 3, 1986
NWA World Champion Ric Flair fought Ron Garvin to a draw

JPC @ Greenville, SC - February 3, 1986
Ricky Morton & Robert Gibson fought NWA Tag Team Champions Bobby Eaton & Dennis Condrey to a 60-minute time-limit draw in a Best 2 out of 3 falls match

GCW @ Lansing, MI - February 4, 1986
NWA World Champion Ric Flair vs. ?

JCP @ Spartanburg, SC - Memorial Auditorium - February 4, 1986
TV taping:
Ricky Morton & Robert Gibson vs. the Barbarian & Black Bart
Manny Fernandez vs. NWA TV Champion Arn Anderson Also included NWA National Heavyweight Champion Dusty Rhodes, NWA Tag Team Champions Bobby Eaton & Dennis Condrey, Superstar Billy Graham, Ron Bass, NWA Mid-Atlantic Heavyweight Champion Sam Houston, and Don Kernodle

GCW @ Grand Rapids, MI - February 5, 1986
NWA World Champion Ric Flair vs. ?

JCP @ Boone, NC - February 6, 1986
Ricky Morton & Robert Gibson defeated NWA Tag Team Champions Bobby Eaton & Dennis Condrey via disqualification

Central States @ Kansas City, MO - February 6, 1986
NWA World Champion Ric Flair fought Bruiser Brody to a double disqualification

JCP @ Canton, OH - February 6, 1986
Pez Whatley defeated Thunderfoot
Denny Brown defeated Pat Tanaka
Don Kernodle defeated Jim Lancaster
Misty Blue defeated Linda Dallas
Ron Garvin defeated Baron Von Raschke via disqualification
Tully Blanchard defeated Jimmy Valiant
The Road Warriors defeated Ivan & Nikita Koloff

Central States @ Des Moines, IA - February 7, 1986
NWA World Champion Ric Flair vs. Bruiser Brody

JCP @ Norfolk, VA - Scope - February 7, 1986
Ricky Morton & Robert Gibson fought NWA Tag Team Champions Bobby Eaton & Dennis Condrey to a 60-minute time-limit draw in a Best 2 out of 3 falls match

JCP @ Atlanta, GA - WTBS Studios - February 8, 1986 (matinee)
World Championship Wrestling taping

Central States @ St. Louis, MO - February 8, 1986 (3,200)
Rocky Johnson defeated Tim Flowers
Debbie Combs defeated Despina Montagus
Jerry Blackwell defeated Kareem Muhammad
Nick Bockwinkel defeated Larry Zbyszko via disqualification
Ricky Morton & Robert Gibson defeated NWA Tag Team Champions Bobby Eaton & Dennis Condrey via disqualification
Tully Blanchard defeated Jimmy Valiant
Harley Race defeated NWA World Champion Ric Flair in a non-title steel cage match at 22:46

JCP @ Asheville, NC - Civic Center - February 9, 1986
Teijo Khan vs. Mack Jeffers
Denny Brown vs. Jim Jeffers
Nelson Royal vs. Thunderfoot
NWA Mid-Atlantic Heavyweight Champion Sam Houston vs. the Barbarian
Jimmy Valiant vs. Tully Blanchard (taped fist match)
NWA World Champion Ric Flair vs. Ron Garvin

JCP @ Cleveland, OH - February 9, 1986 (7,000)
Black Bart defeated Jim Lancaster
Baron Von Raschke, Ivan & Nikita Koloff defeated Don Kernodle, Ron Bass, & Pez Whatley
Manny Fernandez defeated Ivan Koloff
Ricky Morton & Robert Gibson defeated NWA Tag Team Champions Bobby Eaton & Dennis Condrey in a non-title match

Tully Blanchard defeated Jimmy Valiant in a taped fist match
NWA World Champion Ric Flair defeated Ron Garvin

JCP @ Taylorsville, NC - February 10, 1986
Ricky Morton & Robert Gibson defeated NWA Tag Team
Champions Bobby Eaton & Dennis Condrey via disqualification

**CWF @ Ft. Pierce, FL - St. Lucie County Civic Center -
February 11, 1986**
Included NWA World Champion Ric Flair and the Road
Warriors

WRESTLING & TV TAPING WINTHROP COLISEUM
FEBRUARY 11, 1986 7:30 PM
FEATURING
MIDNIGHT EXPRESS (With Jim Cornette)
NIKITA KOLOFF
MAGNUM T.A.
KRUSHER KRUSHCHEV
DUSTY RHODES
ADVANCE TICKET LOCATIONS

**JCP @ Rock Hill, SC - Winthrop Coliseum - February 11,
1986**
TV taping:
Manny Fernandez defeated Mike Simani
Ricky Morton & Robert Gibson defeated Gene Ligon & Mark
Fleming
Black Bart defeated Ron Rossi
NWA Tag Team Champions Bobby Eaton & Dennis Condrey
defeated Ben Alexander & Rocky King
NWA Mid-Atlantic Heavyweight Champion Sam Houston &
Nelson Royal defeated Jim Jeffers & Tony Zane
Ron Bass defeated George South
NWA TV Champion Arn Anderson defeated the Italian Stallion
NWA Tag Team Champions Bobby Eaton & Dennis Condrey
defeated Pez Whatley & NWA Mid-Atlantic Heavyweight
Champion Sam Houston
Dark match after the taping: NWA National Heavyweight
Champion Dusty Rhodes & NWA US Champion Magnum TA
defeated NWA Tag Team Champions Bobby Eaton & Dennis
Condrey via disqualification

JCP @ Raleigh, NC - Dorton Arena - February 12, 1986
Don Kernodle defeated Teijo Khan
NWA Mid-Atlantic Heavyweight Champion Sam Houston
defeated the Barbarian
Baron Von Raschke defeated Ron Bass
NWA TV Champion Arn Anderson fought Ron Garvin to a draw
Jimmy Valiant defeated Tully Blanchard in a Texas Death
Match
NWA US Champion Magnum TA defeated Nikita Koloff
Ricky Morton & Robert Gibson defeated NWA Tag Team
Champions Bobby Eaton & Dennis Condrey via disqualification

**CWF @ Miami Beach, FL - Convention Center - February
12, 1986 (5,003)**
Joe Savoldi defeated Frank Lang
Kendall Windham defeated Prince Iaukea
Tyree Pride defeated Rick Rude via disqualification
Jesse Barr defeated Lex Luger via disqualification
Hector Guerrero defeated the Cuban Assassin in a pole match
The Road Warriors & Barry Windham defeated Kevin Sullivan,
Purple Haze, & Maya Singh
NWA World Champion Ric Flair defeated Wahoo McDaniel in a
steel cage match

**JCP @ Columbia, SC - Township Auditorium - February 13,
1986**
NWA Mid-Atlantic Heavyweight Champion Sam Houston &
Nelson Royal vs. Black Bart & Thunderfoot
NWA Jr. Heavyweight Champion Denny Brown vs. Mack
Jeffers
Manny Fernandez vs. Ivan Koloff
Baron Von Raschke vs. Pez Whatley
Ricky Morton & Robert Gibson defeated NWA Tag Team
Champions Bobby Eaton & Dennis Condrey via disqualification

AWA @ Winnipeg, Manitoba - February 14, 1986
NWA World Champion Ric Flair fought AWA World Champion
Nick Bockwinkel to a double disqualification

JCP @ Cincinnati, OH - February 14, 1986
Ricky Morton & Robert Gibson defeated NWA Tag Team
Champions Bobby Eaton & Dennis Condrey via disqualification

**CWF Battle of the Belts II - Orlando, FL - Eddie Graham
Sports Arena - February 14, 1986**
*Shown live in syndication - featured Gordon Solie & Mike
Graham on commentary; included Bobby Colt conducting a
backstage interview with Bahamas Champion Tyree Pride
regarding his win earlier in the show; featured Colt conducting
a backstage interview with Florida Heavyweight champion
Kendall Windham regarding his win earlier in the show;
included Colt conducting a backstage interview with the new
Southern Heavyweight Champion Lex Luger, with Hiro
Matsuda, regarding his title win; featured Colt conducting a
backstage interview with Paul Ellering, the Road Warriors, &
Blackjack Mulligan regarding their upcoming match and the
Road Warriors having stolen Kevin Sullivan's golden spike;
during the interview, a graphic on the screen said the Road
Warriors were the NWA Tag Team Champions; included Solie
conducting an interview in the crowd with Superstar Billy
Graham in which he said he had returned to Florida and would
team with Wahoo McDaniel to face Kevin Sullivan's group the
next night in Lakeland, FL; featured Colt conducting a
backstage interview with NWA World Champion Ric Flair
regarding his upcoming title defense against Barry Windham:*
Bahamas Champion Tyree Pride pinned Ron Slinker at 3:38
with a crossbody
Florida Heavyweight Champion Kendall Windham pinned
Rocky Iaukea with the bulldog at 8:39
NWA Jr. Heavyweight Champion Denny Brown defeated the
White Ninja (Keiji Mutoh) via disqualification at 12:39 when the
momentum of a crossbody by the champion caused Brown to
fall over the top rope while Ninja remained in the ring
Lex Luger (w/ Hiro Matsuda) pinned Southern Heavyweight
Champion Jesse Barr at 20:34 with a clothesline after holding
onto the ropes to avoid a roll up; Barr had his foot on the
bottom rope during the cover but Luger pushed it off
Bruiser Brody (w/ Gary Hart) fought Wahoo McDaniel to a
double count-out in a $20,000 bounty match at the 5-minute
mark after both men began brawling in the crowd and hitting
each other with steel chairs; after the bout, Brody & Hart left
ringside instead of continuing to fight McDaniel; moments later,
McDaniel ran up the aisle and brawled with Brody all the way
backstage
The Road Warriors (w/ Paul Ellering) & Blackjack Mulligan
fought Kevin Sullivan, Purple Haze (Mark Lewin), & Maya
Singh (Bob Roop) (w/ Luna Vachon) to a double count-out at
the 6-minute mark when, after the referee had been knocked
down, both teams battled their way backstage
NWA World Champion Ric Flair fought Barry Windham to a
double count-out at 41:44 when both men prevented the other
from getting back into the ring after a Flair crossbody sent both

men over the top to the floor; Flair used Phil Collins' "Easy
Lover" as his entrance music for the match (voted Match of the
Year by the Wrestling Observer Newsletter)

**JCP @ Atlanta, GA - WTBS Studios - February 15, 1986
(matinee)**
World Championship Wrestling taping:
NWA Tag Team Champions Bobby Eaton & Dennis Condrey
defeated Ron Bass & Don Kernodle

JCP @ Norfolk, VA - Scope - February 15, 1986
Don Kernodle defeated Thunderfoot
Ivan Koloff defeated NWA Mid-Atlantic Heavyweight Champion
Sam Houston
The Barbarian defeated Ron Rossi
Nelson Royal fought Denny Brown to a draw
Tully Blanchard defeated Jimmy Valiant
NWA US Champion Magnum TA defeated Nikita Koloff in a
lumberjack match

**JCP @ Greensboro, NC - Coliseum - February 15, 1986
(8,119)**
Rocky King defeated Tony Zane
Black Bart defeated Pat Tanaka
Pez Whatley defeated Teijo Khan
Manny Fernandez defeated Baron Von Raschke
Ricky Morton & Robert Gibson defeated NWA Tag Team
Champions Bobby Eaton & Dennis Condrey via disqualification
NWA National Heavyweight Champion Dusty Rhodes defeated
NWA TV Champion Arn Anderson
NWA World Champion Ric Flair fought Ron Garvin to a draw

CWF @ Miami, FL - February 16, 1986
NWA World Champion Ric Flair vs. Tyree Pride

JCP @ Charleston, SC - February 16, 1986
NWA Tag Team Champions Bobby Eaton & Dennis Condrey
defeated Ricky Morton & Robert Gibson after the 60-minute
mark; the bout was scheduled as a 60-minute time-limit draw
but reportedly the timekeeper forgot to ring the bell because he
expected the challengers to win; an impromptu finish was then
made

**JCP @ Fayetteville, NC - Cumberland County Memorial
Arena - February 17, 1986**
TV taping:
Ricky Morton & Robert Gibson defeated Dave Dillenger & Ben
Alexander Tully Blanchard defeated George South
Baron Von Raschke defeated Ron Rossi
The Barbarian & Tejho Khan defeated Rocky King & the Italian
Stallion
Ron Garvin, Manny Fernandez, & Ron Bass defeated Tony
Zane, Jim & Mack Jeffers
NWA Tag Team Champions Bobby Eaton & Dennis Condrey
defeated NWA Mid-Atlantic Heavyweight Champion Sam

Houston & Nelson Royal
NWA TV Champion Arn Anderson defeated Rocky Kernodle
NWA US Champion Magnum TA vs. NWA World Champion
Ric Flair

JCP @ Greenville, SC - Memorial Auditorium - February 18, 1986
NWA Mid-Atlantic Heavyweight Champion Sam Houston
defeated the Barbarian
Ivan Koloff & Baron Von Raschke deefated Ron Bass & the
Italian Stallion
Manny Fernandez defeated NWA TV Champion Arn Anderson
via disqualification
NWA US Champion Magnum TA defeated Nikita Koloff
Ricky Morton & Robert Gibson defeated NWA Tag Team
Champions Bobby Eaton & Dennis Condrey in a Best 2 out of
3 falls match; fall #3: Morton & Gibson won via disqualification;
there was a 90-minute time-limit for the match
NWA National Heavyweight Champion Dusty Rhodes pinned
Tully Blanchard
NWA World Champion Ric Flair fought Ron Garvin to a draw

JCP @ Rock Hill, SC - Winthrop Coliseum - February 18, 1986
Ron Garvin & NWA National Heavyweight Champion Dusty
Rhodes defeated NWA World Champion Ric Flair & NWA TV
Champion Arn Anderson

JCP @ King of Prussia, PA - Valley Forge Convention Center - February 19, 1986 (2,000)
Tully Blanchard defeated Pez Whatley
Ricky Morton & Robert Gibson defeated NWA Tag Team
Champions Bobby Eaton & Dennis Condrey in a non-title
match
Ron Bass fought Black Bart to a draw
Pez Whatley defeated Teijo Khan
Ivan Koloff, the Barbarian, & Baron Von Raschke defeated Ron
Garvin, NWA Mid-Atlantic Heavyweight Champion Sam
Houston, & Manny Fernandez
Jimmy Valiant defeated Tully Blanchard
NWA US Champion Magnum TA defeated Nikita Koloff via
disqualification

JCP/AWA @ Baltimore, MD - Civic Center - February 20, 1986 (13,000+; sell out)
Scott Hall defeated Boris Zhukov
Tully Blanchard defeated Jimmy Valiant
Nick Bockwinkel fought Larry Zbyszko to a no contest
NWA US Champion Magnum TA defeated Baron Von Raschke
NWA Tag Team Champions Bobby Eaton & Dennis Condrey
defeated Ricky Morton & Robert Gibson
Sgt. Slaughter defeated AWA World Champion Stan Hansen
via disqualification
NWA World Champion Ric Flair defeated NWA National
Heavyweight Champion Dusty Rhodes via disqualification

The Road Warriors defeated Ivan & Nikita Koloff in a steel
cage match

JCP @ Richmond, VA - Coliseum - February 21, 1986 (10,000)
Pez Whatley defeated Mark Fleming
Denny Brown defeated Mac Jeffers
Ron Garvin defeated Teijo Khan
Manny Fernandez defeated Baron Von Raschke
NWA US Champion Magnum TA defeated NWA TV Champion
Arn Anderson
NWA Tag Team Champions Bobby Eaton & Dennis Condrey
defeated Ricky Morton & Robert Gibson in a Best 2 out of 3
falls match
The Road Warriors fought Ivan & Nikita Koloff to a no contest
NWA World Champion Ric Flair defeated NWA National
Heavyweight Champion Dusty Rhodes via disqualification

JCP @ Atlanta, GA - WTBS Studios - February 22, 1986 (matinee)
*World Championship Wrestling - 2/22/86 - featured an
interview with NWA World Champion Ric Flair in which he
unveiled a new larger gold belt:*
The Road Warriors vs. Carl Styles & Bill Mulkey
Tully Blanchard vs. Mike Jackson
Baron Von Raschke vs. Rocky King
Teijo Khan vs. George South
Ron Garvin vs. Bob Owens
NWA TV Champion Arn Anderson vs. Denny Brown
The Barbarian vs. Kent Glover
Ivan Koloff vs. Brodie Chase
NWA Tag Team Champions Bobby Eaton & Dennis Condrey
vs. Mike Simani & Larry Clark
Ricky Morton & Robert Gibson vs. Black Bart & Thunderfoot
NWA US Champion Magnum TA vs. Bill Tabb

JCP @ Pilot Mountain, NC - East Surrey High School - February 22, 1986

JCP @ Roanoke, VA - Civic Center - February 22, 1986
Manny Fernandez & Ron Garvin defeated NWA Tag Team
Champions Bobby Eaton & Dennis Condrey via disqualification
at around the 20-minute mark when referee Tommy Young
caught Condrey hitting Garvin with Jim Cornette's tennis
racquet as Garvin had a sleeper applied on Eaton; after the
bout, the challengers were assaulted with the weapon until
Fernandez cleared the ring with a steel chair
NWA US Champion Magnum TA fought Nikita Koloff to a
double count-out at the 13-minute mark when both men began
brawling on the floor; after the match, it was announced NWA
National Heavyweight Champion Dusty Rhodes would
challenge NWA World Champion Ric Flair March 9

JCP @ Atlanta, GA - WTBS Studios - February 23, 1986 (matinee)
World Championship Wrestling taping

JCP @ Asheville, NC - Civic Center - February 23, 1986 (matinee)
The Italian Stallion vs. Thunderfoot
Pez Whatley vs. Black Bart
Ron Bass vs. Nikita Koloff
Jimmy Valiant vs. Ivan Koloff
Ricky Morton & Robert Gibson vs. Tully Blanchard & NWA TV Champion Arn Anderson
NWA US Champion Magnum TA vs. Baron Von Raschke
NWA World Champion Ric Flair vs. Ron Garvin

JCP @ Charlotte, NC - Coliseum - February 23, 1986 (12,000+; sell out)
Denny Brown fought Gary Royal to a draw
NWA Mid-Atlantic Heavyweight Champion Sam Houston defeated Teijo Khan
Don Kernodle defeated Baron Von Raschke
Tully Blanchard defeated Jimmy Valiant
Japanese TV: Ricky Morton & Robert Gibson defeated NWA Tag Team Champions Bobby Eaton & Dennis Condrey in a Best 2 out of 3 falls match; fall #1: Gibson pinned Eaton following the double dropkick at the 46-second mark; fall #2: Condrey pinned Gibson following a double clothesline behind the referee's back; fall #3: Morton & Gibson won via disqualification when Cornette threw powder into Morton's face after Morton stole away Cornette's tennis racquet from Eaton; after the bout, the champions assaulted both opponents with the racquet (*Wrestling Rarities: The Midnight Express*)
NWA World Champion Ric Flair defeated NWA US Champion Magnum TA
NWA National Heavyweight Champion Dusty Rhodes defeated NWA TV Champion Arn Anderson in a steel cage match

JCP @ Greenville, SC - Memorial Auditorium - February 24, 1986
Teijo Khan defeated the Italian Stallion
Pez Whatley defeated Thunderfoot
NWA Jr. Heavyweight Champion Denny Brown defeated Nelson Royal
NWA Mid-Atlantic Heavyweight Champion Sam Houston fought Black Bart to a no contest
The Barbarian defeated Ron Bass
Ron Garvin fought NWA TV Champion Arn Anderson to a draw

JCP/AWA Star Wars - East Rutherford, NJ - Meadowlands - February 24, 1986 (nearly 10,000)
Nord the Barbarian & the Mongolian Stomper defeated Buck Zumhoffe & Marty Jannetty
Jimmy Valiant defeated Tully Blanchard via disqualification
AWA Tag Team Champions Curt Hennig & Scott Hall defeated Scott & Bill Irwin
Larry Zbyszko defeated Nick Bockwinkel via disqualification

NWA National Heavyweight Champion Dusty Rhodes & the Road Warriors defeated Baron Von Raschke, Ivan & Nikita Koloff
NWA World Champion Ric Flair pinned NWA US Champion Magnum TA at 28:14
Ricky Morton & Robert Gibson defeated NWA Tag Team Champions Bobby Eaton & Dennis Condrey via disqualification in a non-title match
AWA World Champion Stan Hansen fought Sgt. Slaughter to a double count-out

JCP @ Greenwood, SC - February 25, 1986
TV taping:
Ricky Morton & Robert Gibson defeated Gene Ligon & Pat Tanaka; after the bout, Morton's hand was accidentally broken during an altercation with NWA Tag Team Champions Bobby Eaton & Dennis Condrey
NWA TV Champion Arn Anderson defeated Tony Zane
Jimmy Garvin defeated George South
Leo Burke defeated Mark Fleming
Thunderfoot defeated Mike Simani
Tully Blanchard defeated the Italian Stallion
NWA Tag Team Champions Bobby Eaton & Dennis Condrey defeated Pez Whatley & Rocky King

Columbus, MS - February 25, 1986
NWA World Champion Ric Flair defeated Tommy Rich

JCP @ North Wilkesboro, NC - February 26, 1986 (sell out)
Ricky Morton & Robert Gibson defeated NWA Tag Team Champions Bobby Eaton & Dennis Condrey via disqualification

Greenwood, MS - February 26, 1986
NWA World Champion Ric Flair defeated Tommy Rich via count-out

JCP @ Bennettsville, SC - February 27, 1986 (sell out)
Ricky Morton & Robert Gibson defeated NWA Tag Team Champions Bobby Eaton & Dennis Condrey in a non-title match

JCP @ Hampton, VA - Coliseum - February 28, 1986
Pat Tanaka defeated the Golden Terror
The Italian Stallion defeated Mark Fleming
Teijo Khan defeated Pez Whatley
NWA Mid-Atlantic Heavyweight Champion Sam Houston defeated Black Bart
The Barbarian defeated Ron Bass
Tully Blanchard defeated Jimmy Valiant
The Road Warriors fought Ivan & Nikita Koloff to a no contest

JCP @ Columbia, SC - Township Auditorium - February 28, 1986 (4,500+; sell out; the first sell out in Columbia since 1981)

Don Kernodle vs. Thunderfoot
Manny Fernandez vs. Baron Von Raschke
Denny Brown vs. Gary Royal
NwA World Champion Ric Flair vs. NWA US Champion
Magnum TA
NWA Tag Team Champions Bobby Eaton & Dennis Condrey
defeated Ricky Morton & Robert Gibson in a Best 2 out of 3
falls match
NWA National Heavyweight Champion Dusty Rhodes vs. NWA
TV Champion Arn Anderson (Texas Death steel cage match)

JCP @ Atlanta, GA - WTBS Studios - March 1, 1986 (matinee)
World Championship Wrestling - 3/1/86:
Jimmy Valiant pinned Bob Owens with an elbow drop
Baron Von Raschke pinned George South with the claw
Ivan Koloff pinned Rocky King with a clothesline off the top
The Barbarian pinned Tony Zane with the headbutt off the top
NWA US Champion Magnum TA pinned Randy Mulkey with
the belly to belly suplex
Tully Blanchard pinned Bill Tabb with the slingshot suplex
NWA Tag Team Champions Bobby Eaton & Dennis Condrey
defeated Paul Garner & Alan Martin
Ricky Morton & Robert Gibson defeated Bill Mulkey & Mike
Simani when Simani sustained the double dropkick
NWA TV Champion Arn Anderson fought Ron Garvin to a draw
NWA World Champion Ric Flair defeated Brodie Chase via
submission with the figure-4

JCP @ Greensboro, NC - Coliseum - March 1, 1986 (10,421)
Jimmy Garvin pinned NWA Mid-Atlantic Heavyweight
Champion Sam Houston in a non-title match with a knee to the
back and the brainbuster after Houston became distracted by
Precious on the floor
NWA National Heavyweight Champion Dusty Rhodes & the
Road Warriors defeated NWA Six-Man Tag Team Champions
Baron Von Raschke, Ivan & Nikita Koloff in a non-title match
when Road Warrior Animal press slammed Road Warrior
Hawk onto Ivan for the win; after the match, Von Raschke held
Hawk so the Koloffs could hit a clothesline on him while using
their chain; Hawk was then whipped with the chain until Animal
and Rhodes cleared the ring
NWA Tag Team Champions Bobby Eaton & Dennis Condrey
defeated Ricky Morton & Robert Gibson when Eaton pinned
Morton with a roll up after Jim Cornette threw powder into
Morton's face
NWA World Champion Ric Flair fought Ron Garvin to a double
count-out at around the 30-minute mark when, after Flair
repeatedly left the ring only to be chased back inside by
Garvin, Garvin began assaulting the champion on the floor;
after the bout, Garvin knocked Flair out with a punch in the
ring; after Flair struggled to his feet, Garvin knocked him out
with a second punch

JCP @ Charlotte, NC - Coliseum - March 2, 1986 (matinee) (8,000)

NWA Tag Team Champions Bobby Eaton & Dennis Condrey
defeated Ricky Morton & Robert Gibson in a No DQ Best 2 out
of 3 falls match

JCP @ St. Louis, MO - March 2, 1986
NWA Mid-Atlantic Heavyweight Champion Sam Houston
fought Don Kernodle to a draw
Baron Von Raschke defeated the Italian Stallion
Jimmy Garvin defeated NWA Mid-Atlantic Heavyweight
Champion Sam Houston
NWA US Champion Magnum TA defeated Nikita Koloff via
disqualification
Ricky Morton & Robert Gibson defeated NWA Tag Team
Champions Bobby Eaton & Dennis Condrey in a Best 2 out of
3 falls match; fall #3: Morton & Gibson won via disqualification
NWA National Heavyweight Champion Dusty Rhodes defeated
NWA TV Champion Arn Anderson in a non-title Texas Death
match
NWA World Champion Ric Flair defeated Ron Garvin

JCP @ Greenville, SC - March 3, 1986
NWA Tag Team Champions Bobby Eaton & Dennis Condrey
defeated Ricky Morton & Robert Gibson in a Best 2 out of 3
falls match

JCP @ Canton, OH - March 3, 1986
Teijo Khan defeated Jim Lancaster
Denny Brown fought Nelson Royal to a draw
The Barbarian & Black Bart defeated Ron Bass & Don
Kernodle
Manny Fernandez defeated Baron Von Raschke
The Road Warriors defeated Ivan & Nikita Koloff in a Russian
chain match

JCP @ Spartanburg, SC - Memorial Auditorium - March 4, 1986 (sell out)
TV taping:
NWA Tag Team Champions Bobby Eaton & Dennis Condrey
defeated Pez Whatley & Rocky King
NWA Tag Team Champions Bobby Eaton & Dennis Condrey
defeated Rocky Kernodle & the Italian Stallion
Tully Blanchard (w/ JJ Dillon) pinned NWA National
Heavyweight Champion Dusty Rhodes to win the title after
hitting him with a foreign object given to him by NWA World
Champion Ric Flair, who provided guest commentary for the
match
Also included Ricky Morton & Robert Gibson, NWA US
Champion Magnum TA, NWA TV Champion Arn Anderson,
Jimmy Garvin, Jimmy Valiant, and NWA Mid-Atlantic
Heavyweight Champion Sam Houston

JCP @ Wheeling, WV - March 4, 1986
Denny Brown fought Gary Royal to a draw
Black Bart & the Barbarian defeated Ron Bass & Don Kernodle
Ron Garvin defeated Teijo Khan

Manny Fernandez defeated Baron Von Raschke
The Road Warriors defeated Ivan & Nikita Koloff in a Russian chain match

JCP @ Raleigh, NC - Dorton Arena - March 5, 1986
Ben Alexander defeated George South
Thunderfoot defeated the Italian Stallion
Jimmy Garvin defeated NWA Mid-Atlantic Heavyweight Champion Sam Houston
NWA TV Champion Arn Anderson defeated Pez Whatley (sub. for NWA US Champion Magnum TA)
NWA National Heavyweight Champion Tully Blanchard defeated Jimmy Valiant in a lumberjack match
NWA Tag Team Champions Bobby Eaton & Dennis Condrey defeated Ricky Morton & Robert Gibson in a No DQ Best 2 out of 3 falls match

JCP @ Lenoir, NC - March 6, 1986
Rocky King defeated George South
Nelson Royal fought Denny Brown to a draw
The Barbarian defeated the Italian Stallion
Ivan & Nikita Koloff defeated Gary Royal & Rocky King
Dusty Rhodes defeated NWA National Heavyweight Champion Tully Blanchard

JCP @ Columbus, GA - March 6, 1986
NWA US Champion Magnum TA & Ron Garvin defeated NWA Tag Team Champions Bobby Eaton & Dennis Condrey via disqualification

JCP @ Norfolk, VA - Scope - March 7, 1986 (12,000; sell out; the first sell out in more than 6 years)
Teijo Khan defeated Rocky Kernodle
Black Bart defeated Pez Whatley
NWA Tag Team Champions Bobby Eaton & Dennis Condrey defeated Ricky Morton & Robert Gibson in a Best 2 out of 3 falls match
Jimmy Garvin defeated NWA Mid-Atlantic Heavyweight Champion Sam Houston
Ron Garvin fought NWA World Champion Ric Flair to a no contest
Dusty Rhodes defeated Ivan Koloff in a steel cage match
NWA US Champion Magnum TA defeated Nikita Koloff in a steel cage match

JCP @ Charleston, SC - St. Andrews High School Gym - March 7, 1986
Leo Burke vs. Italian Stallion
NWA Jr. Heavyweight Champion Denny Brown vs. Nelson Royal
Ron Bass vs. Black Bart
Manny Fernandez & Don Kernodle vs. Ivan Koloff & Baron Von Raschke
Jimmy Valiant vs. NWA National Heavyweight Champion Tully Blanchard (taped fist match)

JCP @ Atlanta, GA - WTBS Studios - March 8, 1986 (matinee)
World Championship Wrestling - 3/8/86:
Ron Garvin pinned Tony Zane with the punch to the face
The Barbarian pinned Bill Tabb with the headbutt off the top
Leo Burke pinned George South with a kneedrop
Pez Whatley pinned Art Pritts with a headbutt off the top
NWA Tag Team Champions Bobby Eaton & Dennis Condrey defeated Brodie Chase & Mike Simani
The Road Warriors defeated Carl Styles & Bill Mulkey
Ricky Morton & Robert Gibson defeated Bob Owens & Larry Clarke
Jimmy Garvin pinned Rocky King with the brainbuster
Black Bart pinned Dr. X with the legdrop off the top
Baron Von Raschke pinned Mike Jackson with the claw

JCP @ Cincinatti, OH - March 8, 1986 (10,700; sell out)
NWA World Champion Ric Flair vs. Dusty Rhodes
NWA Tag Team Champions Bobby Eaton & Dennis Condrey defeated Ricky Morton & Robert Gibson in a Best 2 out of 3 falls match

JCP @ Roanoke, VA - Civic Center - March 9, 1986 (matinee)
Mark Fleming defeated Gene Ligon
Baron Von Raschke defeated Pez Whatley
Ivan Koloff defeated NWA Mid-Atlantic Heavyweight Champion Sam Houston
NWA US Champion Magnum TA defeated Nikita Koloff (w/ Ivan Koloff) via disqualification at the 14-minute mark when Ivan interfered after the challenger sustained the belly to belly suplex; after the bout, the Koloffs double teamed Magnum and Nikita hit the Russian Sickle before Pez Whatley and NWA Mid-Atlantic Heavyweight Champion Sam Houston made the save
NWA Tag Team Champions Bobby Eaton & Stan Lane defeated Ricky Morton & Robert Gibson in a Best 2 out of 3 falls match; fall #1: Eaton pinned Morton at the 11-minute mark with a kneedrop off the top to Morton's broken hand; fall #2: Gibson pinned Eaton with a sunset flip out of the corner at the 10-minute mark; fall #3: Eaton pinned Gibson at the 51-second mark after hitting him with Jim Cornette's tennis racquet after the challengers knocked an interfering Cornette to the floor with the double dropkick
NWA World Champion Ric Flair defeated Dusty Rhodes (w/ Baby Doll) via disqualification at the 19-minute mark when referee Earl Hebner caught Rhodes assaulting Flair with his own leg brace, which Flair had torn off him moments earlier; a TV cameraman was ringside for the match; after the bout, Rhodes hit Hebner with the weapon as well

JCP @ ? - Spring 1986
Wahoo McDaniel defeated NWA National Heavyweight Champion Tully Blanchard via reverse decision at the 7:30 mark when - after McDaniel had been pinned following a knee to the back - the referee changed the call after realizing JJ

Dillon held McDaniel's foot down during the cover; after the match, Jimmy Garvin jumped McDaniel and repeatedly hit him over the back with a steel chair as Blanchard easily fought off two wrestlers that tried to make the save; moments later, NWA US Champion Magnum TA came out and cleared the ring
NWA World Champion Ric Flair defeated Dusty Rhodes via disqualification at around the 18-minute mark; both Tommy Young and Earl Hebner served as referees for the match; Rhodes and Baby Doll initially thought Rhodes had won the title following a clothesline and Young crawling over - making three slaps to the mat as he did so - but Young then said he saw Rhodes throw Flair over the top rope moments earlier
NWA US Champion Magnum TA defeated Nikita Koloff in a steel cage match at 8:51; both men were counted down by the referee after colliding into the cage, with the referee then telling the ring announcer that the first man to reach his feet would be declared the winner

JCP @ Atlanta, GA - Omni - March 9, 1986
Baron Von Raschke defeated Pez Whatley
Ivan Koloff defeated NWA Mid-Atlantic Heavyweight Champion Sam Houston
Nelson Royal fought Denny Brown to a draw
Rocky King defeated Tony Zane
NWA World Champion Ric Flair fought Ron Garvin to a no contest
Dusty Rhodes defeated NWA TV Champion Arn Anderson via disqualification
NWA US Champion Magnum TA defeated Nikita Koloff
Ricky Morton & Robert Gibson defeated NWA Tag Team Champions Bobby Eaton & Dennis Condrey via disqualification; Jim Cornette was held in a cage for the duration of the match

JCP @ Greenville, SC - Memorial Auditorium - March 10, 1986
TV taping:
NWA Tag Team Champions Bobby Eaton & Dennis Condrey defeated George South & Kernodle
Dark match after the taping: Dusty Rhodes & NWA US Champion Magnum TA defeated NWA Tag Team Champions Bobby Eaton & Dennis Condrey via disqualification

JCP @ Fayetteville, NC - Cumberland County Memorial Arena - March 10, 1986
Leo Burke defeated the Italian Stallion
Nelson Royal fought Denny Brown to a draw
NWA Mid-Atlantic Heavyweight Champion Sam Houston fought Black Bart to a no contest
Manny Fernandez defeated Teijo Khan
Ricky Morton & Robert Gibson defeated the Barbarian & Baron Von Raschke
NWA World Champion Ric Flair defeated Ron Garvin

CWF @ Miami Beach, FL - Convention Center - March 12, 1986 (4,257)
The White Ninja defeated Prince Iaukea
Jerry Grey defeated Ricky Santana
Stan Lane & Steve Keirn defeated Purple Haze & Maya Singh
Tyree Pride defeated Kevin Sullivan
Jesse Barr defeated Lex Luger via disqualification
Kendo Nagasaki defeated Wahoo McDaniel
NWA World Champion Ric Flair defeated Barry Windham

Greenwood, MS - March 12, 1986
NWA World Champion Ric Flair defeated Tommy Rich

CWF @ Tallahassee, FL - March 14, 1986
NWA World Champion Ric Flair vs. Wahoo McDaniel (steel cage match)

JCP @ Bassett, VA - March 14, 1986 (sell out)
Ricky Morton & Robert Gibson defeated NWA Tag Team Champions Bobby Eaton & Dennis Condrey in a non-title match

JCP @ Atlanta, GA - WTBS Studios - March 15, 1986 (matinee)
World Championship Wrestling - 3/15/86:
NWA National Heavyweight Champion Tully Blanchard vs. Don Turner
Jimmy Valiant vs. Bob Owens
Jimmy Garvin vs. Bill Mulkey
NWA Tag Team Champions Bobby Eaton & Dennis Condrey vs. Phil Brown & Lee Peak
NWA TV Champion Arn Anderson vs. Mike Jackson
Manny Fernandez vs. Tony Zane
Ron Garvin vs. Kent Glover
Black Bart vs. Carl Styles

JCP @ Charleston, WV - March 15, 1986
Rocky King defeated the Golden Terror
Leo Burke defeated the Italian Stallion
Black Bart defeated Don Kernodle
Ivan Koloff defeated Pez Whatley
Manny Fernandez defeated Nikita Koloff via disqualification
NWA Tag Team Champions Bobby Eaton & Dennis Condrey defeated Ricky Morton & Robert Gibson in a Best 2 out of 3 falls match

CWF @ Nassau, Bahamas - Stadium - March 15, 1986
Kendall Windham vs. Bob Roop
Tyree Pride vs. Jerry Grey
Barry Windham vs. Kendo Nagasaki
NWA World Champion Ric Flair vs. Wahoo McDaniel

JCP @ Asheville, NC - Civic Center - March 16, 1986 (matinee) (5,000; sell out; new record)
Rocky Kernodle vs. George South
NWA Jr. Heavyweight Champion Denny Brown vs. Nelson

Royal
Ron Bass vs. Thunderfoot
NWA US Champion Magnum TA vs. the Barbarian
Manny Fernandez vs. Black Bart
The Road Warriors vs. Nikita & Ivan Koloff (double chain match)
NWA Tag Team Champions Bobby Eaton & Dennis Condrey defeated Ricky Morton & Robert Gibson; Jim Cornette was held in a cage for the duration of the match

JCP @ Cleveland, OH - March 16, 1986 (10,000; sell out; new record)
NWA Mid-Atlantic Heavyweight Champion Sam Houston defeated Gene Ligon
Jimmy Valiant defeated the Golden Terror
NWA TV Champion Arn Anderson defeated Dusty Rhodes via disqualification
Leo Burke defeated Pez Whatley
Jimmy Garvin defeated Denny Brown
NWA US Champion Magnum TA defeated NWA National Heavyweight Champion Tully Blanchard
NWA Tag Team Champions Bobby Eaton & Dennis Condrey defeated Ricky Morton & Robert Gibson
Ron Garvin fought NWA World Champion Ric Flair to a no contest
The Road Warriors defeated Ivan & Nikita Koloff in a double Russian chain match

JCP @ Greenville, SC - Memorial Auditorium - March 17, 1986
Rocky Kernodle defeated George South
Jimmy Garvin defeated the Italian Stallion
NWA Mid-Atlantic Heavyweight Champion Sam Houston defeated Black Bart
Manny Fernandez defeated Thunderfoot
The Barbarian defeated Ron Bass
Ron Garvin defeated NWA National Champion Tully Blanchard via disqualification
Ricky Morton & Robert Gibson defeated NWA Tag Team Champions Bobby Eaton & Dennis Condrey in a non-title match; Jim Cornette was held in a cage for the duration of the match

JCP @ Mooresville, NC - March 18, 1986
TV taping:
NWA Tag Team Champions Bobby Eaton & Dennis Condrey defeated Don & Rocky Kernodle
Black Bart defeated NWA Mid-Atlantic Heavyweight Champion Sam Houston to win the title
Dark match after the taping: NWA Tag Team Champions Bobby Eaton & Dennis Condrey defeated Manny Fernandez & Ron Bass

JCP @ Raleigh, NC - Dorton Arena - March 19, 1986
Sam Houston fought NWA Mid-Atlantic Heavyweight Champion Black Bart to a draw

Jimmy Garvin defeated the Italian Stallion
Manny Fernandez defeated George South
The Barbarian defeated Ron Bass
Ron Garvin defeated NWA National Heavyweight Champion Tully Blanchard via disqualification
Ricky Morton & Robert Gibson defeated NWA Tag Team Champions Bobby Eaton & Dennis Condrey in a No DQ Best 2 out of 3 falls non-title match; Jim Cornette was held in a cage for the duration of the match

JCP @ Harrisonburg, VA - High School Gym - March 20, 1986
Rocky King vs. Pat Tanaka
NWA Jr. Heavyweight Champion Denny Brown vs. Leo Burke
Don Kernodle vs. George South
Ron Bass vs. Teijo Khan
Jimmy Valiant & Baron Von Raschke vs. ? & the Barbarian

Central States @ Kansas City, KS - March 20, 1986
Harley Race & Bruiser Brody defeated NWA World Champion Ric Flair & Bob Brown in a steel cage match; Pat O'Connor was the guest referee for the match

JCP @ Macon, GA - Coliseum - March 20, 1986
Ricky Morton & Robert Gibson defeated NWA Tag Team Champions Bobby Eaton & Dennis Condrey in a non-title match

JCP @ Huntington, WV - March 21, 1986 (6,000; sell out)
NWA Tag Team Champions Bobby Eaton & Dennis Condrey defeated Ricky Morton & Robert Gibson in a Best 2 out of 3 falls match; following the show, Jim Cornette was served with four warrants for his arrest for hitting fans with his tennis racquet while leaving the ring after the match; he later pleaded no contest and paid a $100 fine after police corroborated his story that he acted in self-defense
NWA World Champion Ric Flair vs. ?

JCP @ Atlanta, GA - WTBS Studios - March 22, 1986 (matinee)
World Championship Wrestling - 3/22/86:
Jimmy Valiant vs. Kent Glover
NWA Mid-Atlantic Champion Black Bart vs. Sam Houston
NWA Tag Team Champions Bobby Eaton & Dennis Condrey vs. Ray Traylor & Phil Brown
Leo Burke vs. Don Graves
Jimmy Garvin vs. Bill Mulkey
Wahoo McDaniel vs. Bob Owens
Baron Von Raschke & Teijo Khan vs. Tony Zane & the Italian Stallion
Ricky Morton & Robert Gibson vs. Larry Clarke & Paul Garner
NWA National Heavyweight Champion Tully Blanchard & NWA TV Champion Arn Anderson vs. Mike Simani & Ron Rossi
NWA US Champion Magnum TA vs. Dave Dellenger

Ivan Koloff vs. Rocky Kernodle
Ron Garvin vs. Brodie Chase

JCP @ Philadelphia, PA - Civic Center - March 22, 1986 (10,000+)
Pez Whatley fought Leo Burke to a draw
Jimmy Garvin defeated Sam Houston
NWA National Heavyweight Champion Tully Blanchard defeated Ron Bass
NWA Tag Team Champions Bobby Eaton & Dennis Condrey defeated Ricky Morton & Robert Gibson via disqualification at 10:32 after Morton hit Eaton with the tennis racquet; the decision was not announced until after Morton covered Eaton and referee Earl Hebner crawled into the ring, slapping his hand to the mat three times, thus the fans thought the titles had changed hands; after the bout, Morton was assaulted with the racquet until Gibson made the save with a steel chair (*Wrestling Rarities: The Midnight Express*)
NWA US Champion Magnum TA defeated Nikita Koloff via disqualification
Dusty Rhodes defeated NWA TV Champion Arn Anderson in a non-title steel cage Texas Death Match
NWA World Champion Ric Flair defeated Ron Garvin

JCP @ Greenville, SC - March 23, 1986 (matinee)
TV taping:
NWA Tag Team Champions Bobby Eaton & Dennis Condrey vs. two unknowns
NWA Tag Team Champions Bobby Eaton & Dennis Condrey vs. two unknowns
Japan TV: Ron Garvin defeated NWA National Heavyweight Champion Tully Blanchard (w/ JJ Dillon) when Dillon interfered
Japan TV: Wahoo McDaniel fought NWA TV Champion Arn Anderson to a double count-out
Japan TV: NWA World Champion Ric Flair pinned Robert Gibson with his feet on the ropes for leverage; during the bout, Flair had a brief brawl at ringside with Ricky Morton, whose face was bandaged
Japan TV: NWA US Champion Magnum TA defeated NWA Tag Team Champion Bobby Eaton

Central States @ Lincoln, NE - March 23, 1986
Bruiser Brody defeated NWA World Champion Ric Flair via disqualification

JCP @ Columbia, SC - Township Auditorium - March 23, 1986
Denny Brown vs. Gary Royal
The Italian Stallion vs. Ivan Koloff
Nikita Koloff vs. Ron Garvin
Jimmy Valiant vs. Sam Houston
NWA US Champion Magnum TA vs. NWA National Heavyweight Champion Tully Blanchard
NWA Tag Team Champions Bobby Eaton & Dennis Condrey defeated Ricky Morton & Robert Gibson via disqualification; Jim Cornette was handcuffed to Jimmy Valiant at ringside for the duration of the bout
Dusty Rhodes vs. NWA TV Champion Arn Anderson

Mid-South @ New Orleans, LA - March 24, 1986
NWA Tag Team Champions Bobby Eaton & Dennis Condrey defeated Ricky Morton & Robert Gibson

Central States @ Wichita, KS - March 24, 1986
Bruiser Brody defeated NWA World Champion Ric Flair via disqualification

JCP @ Fayetteville, NC - Cumberland County War Memorial Arena - March 24, 1986
Leo Burke defeated the Italian Stallion
Don Kernodle defeated Teijo Khan
The Barbarian defeated Rocky King
Ivan Koloff & Baron Von Raschke defeated Nelson Royal & Sam Houston
NWA TV Champion Arn Anderson defeated Jimmy Valiant
NWA US Champion Magnum TA fought Nikita Koloff to a no contest

PNW @ Portland, OR - March 25, 1986
NWA World Champion Ric Flair defeated Dusty Rhodes in a steel cage match

WRESTLING
WINTHROP COLISEUM
TUESDAY MARCH 25-7:30 PM

THE MIDNIGHT EXPRESS VS. THE ROCK & ROLL EXPRESS

MAGNUM T.A. VS. BARON VON RASCHKE

RAGIN' BULL VS. ARN ANDERSON

PLUS
RON GARVIN
TULLY BLANCHARD
NELSON ROYAL
SAM HOUSTON
BARBARIAN
TEIJHO KHAN
PISTOL PEZ WHATLEY
BLACK BART
ITALIAN SALLION
THUNDERFOOT

ADVANCE TICKET LOCATIONS

WINTHROP COLISEUM   GRANDMA'S HOME STYLE COOKIN' KIMBRELL'S FURNITURE
MR SPORT (ROCK HILL MALL) BLACK'S DRUG STORE (CHESTER) (TOWNCENTER MALL)
VIDEO CENTER (FORT MILL)   FRIENDLY GRILL
VIDEO CONNECTION (YORK)

JCP @ Rock Hill, SC - Winthrop Coliseum - March 25, 1986 (4,100)
Ron Garvin fought NWA National Heavyweight Champion Tully Blanchard to a double count-out
NWA TV Champion Arn Anderson pinned Jimmy Valiant (sub. for Manny Fernandez)
NWA US Champion Magnum TA pinned Baron Von Raschke
Ricky Morton & Robert Gibson defeated NWA Tag Team Champions Bobby Eaton & Dennis Condrey in a non-title match
Also included Nelson Royal, Sam Houston, the Barbarian, Teijho Khan, Pez Whatley, NWA Mid-Atlantic Heavyweight Champion Black Bart, the Italian Stallion, and Thunderfoot

JCP @ Raleigh, NC - Dorton Arena - March 26, 1986
Denny Brown fought Leo Burke to a draw
The Barbarian defeated Rocky King
Baron Von Raschke defeated Sam Houston
Jimmy Garvin defeated Rocky Kernodle
NWA TV Champion Arn Anderson defeated Don Kernodle
Ron Garvin fought NWA National Heavyweight Champion Tully Blanchard to a draw
NWA US Champion Magnum TA, Ricky Morton & Robert Gibson defeated Jim Cornette, NWA Tag Team Champions Bobby Eaton & Dennis Condrey in an elimination match

PNW @ Spokane, WA - March 27, 1986 (5,429)
Stoney Burke defeated Moondog Moretti
Bobby Jaggers defeated Jerry Sampson
Brady Boone & Scott Doring defeated Mike Miller & the Assassin
Sgt. Slaughter defeated Karl Steiner
NWA World Champion Ric Flair defeated Coco Samoa
The Road Warriors defeated Ivan & Nikita Koloff in a steel cage match

JCP @ Norfolk, VA - Scope - March 27, 1986
Denny Brown defeated George South
Leo Burke defeated the Italian Stallion
Jimmy Garvin defeated Rocky Kernodle
NWA TV Champion Arn Anderson defeated Pez Whatley
Ricky Morton & Robert Gibson defeated the Barbarian & Teijo Khan via disqualification
Ron Garvin defeated NWA National Heavyweight Champion Tully Blanchard via disqualification
NWA Tag Team Champions Bobby Eaton & Dennis Condrey defeated Dusty Rhodes & NWA US Champion Magnum TA via disqualification

JCP @ Richmond, VA - Coliseum - March 28, 1986 (10,000)
Don Kernodle fought NWA Mid-Atlantic Heavyweight Champion Black Bart to a 15-minute time-limit draw
Jimmy Garvin defeated Rocky Kernodle
Jimmy Valiant defeated Teijo Khan
Ricky Morton & Robert Gibson defeated NWA Tag Team Champions Bobby Eaton & Dennis Condrey in a non-title match; Jim Cornette was locked at ringside in a cage for the match
NWA US Champion Magnum TA defeated Baron Von Raschke
Dusty Rhodes & Wahoo McDaniel defeated NWA National Heavyweight Champion Tully Blanchard & NWA TV Champion Arn Anderson in a bullrope strap match when Dusty pinned Tully
The Road Warriors defeated Ivan & Nikita Koloff in a steel cage match when Road Warrior Animal pinned Ivan

CWF @ Daytona Beach, FL - March 28, 1986
Kendall Windham defeated Kevin Sullivan
Jesse Barr defeated Lex Luger in a taped fist match
NWA World Champion Ric Flair defeated Barry Windham

JCP @ Atlanta, GA - WTBS Studios - March 29, 1986 (matinee)
World Championship Wrestling - 3/29/86:
Wahoo McDaniel vs. Ron Rossi
NWA Tag Team Champions Bobby Eaton & Dennis Condrey vs. Phil Brown & Wee Willie Wilkens
Jimmy Garvin vs. Don Turner
Ivan Koloff vs. Ray Traylor
Ron Garvin vs. Tony Zane
NWA US Champion Magnum TA vs. Bob Owens
NWA National Heavyweight Champion Tully Blanchard vs. Bill Tabb
Ricky Morton & Robert Gibson vs. Art Pritts & Kent Glover
NWA TV Champion Arn Anderson vs. David Dillenger
The Road Warriors vs. Larry Clarke & Paul Garner

JCP @ Greensboro, NC - Coliseum - March 29, 1986 (12,339)
Nelson Royal defeated George South
Don Kernodle defeated Thunderfoot
Jimmy Garvin defeated the Italian Stallion
Ricky Morton & Robert Gibson defeated NWA Tag Team Champions Bobby Eaton & Dennis Condrey in a non-title match when Gibson pinned Condrey with a sunset flip after Morton prevented a double team; Jim Cornette was suspended above the ring in a cage for the duration of the match
NWA US Champion Magnum TA defeated Nikita Koloff (w/ Ivan Koloff) via disqualification when Ivan broke the cover after Magnum hit the belly to belly suplex; after the match, the champion was double teamed, with Nikita eventually hitting the Russian Sickle and then bringing out a Russian chain until the Italian Stallion, Don Kernodle, and another wrestler came out to make the save and helped Magnum backstage
Dusty Rhodes (w/ Baby Doll) & Wahoo McDaniel defeated NWA Natoinal Heavyweight Champion Tully Blanchard & NWA TV Champion Arn Anderson in a No DQ, no time-limit match leather strap / Texas bullrope match when McDaniel pinned Anderson at 6:36 following a standing elbow from Rhodes; after the match, JJ Dillon interfered which allowed McDaniel to be double teamed until Rhodes cleared the ring with the bullrope

NWA World Champion Ric Flair pinned Ron Garvin in a steel cage match at 25:24 when Garvin's leg went out as he attempted to catch Flair's crossbody; the match had a 90-minute time-limit

JCP @ Savannah, GA - Civic Center - March 30, 1986 (matinee)
NWA Tag Team Champions Bobby Eaton & Dennis Condrey defeated Ricky Morton & Robert Gibson

JCP @ Atlanta, GA - Omni - March 30, 1986 (5,300)
Hector Guerrero defeated Thunderfoot
Jimmy Garvin defeated Rocky Kernodle
Leo Burke defeated the Italian Stallion
Nighthawk, Ricky Morton & Robert Gibson defeated Jim Cornette, NWA Tag Team Champions Bobby Eaton & Dennis Condrey
NWA US Champion Magnum TA defeated Nikita Koloff in a lumberjack match
Dusty Rhodes & Wahoo McDaniel defeated NWA TV Champion Arn Anderson & NWA National Heavyweight Champion Tully Blanchard in a chain strap match
NWA World Champion Ric Flair defeated Ron Garvin in a steel cage match

JCP @ Baltimore, MD - Civic Center - March 31, 1986
Mike Kahlua defeated Tom Bradley
Jimmy Valiant defeated Jimmy Garvin via disqualification
NWA US Champion Magnum TA fought NWA National Heavyweight Champion Tully Blanchard to a draw
NWA Tag Team Champions Bobby Eaton & Dennis Condrey defeated Ricky Morton & Robert Gibson via disqualification; Jimmy Valiant was handcuffed to Jim Cornette for the duration of the bout
Road Warrior Animal & Paul Ellering defeated Ivan & Nikita Koloff via disqualification
NWA World Champion Ric Flair defeated Dusty Rhodes via disqualification

JCP @ ? - 1986
Dusty Rhodes & NWA US Champion Magnum TA defeated NWA World Champion Ric Flair & NWA National Heavyweight Champion Tully Blanchard in an elimination match; both Flair and Rhodes were counted out; Magnum pinned Blanchard moments later with a sunset flip into the ring

JCP @ Canton, OH - April 1, 1986
Don Kernodle fought Leo Burke to a draw
Thunderfoot defeated Rocky Kernodle
Don Kernodle defeated Teijo Khan
NWA Mid-Atlantic Heavyweight Champion Black Bart defeated Sam Houston
Jimmy Valiant defeated the Barbarian in a bunkhouse match
Ricky Morton & Robert Gibson defeated NWA Tag Team Champions Bobby Eaton & Dennis Condrey in a Best 2 out of 3 falls match; fall #3: Morton & Gibson won via disqualification

JCP @ California, PA - Hamer Hall - April 2, 1986
NWA Mid-Atlantic Heavyweight Champion Black Bart vs. Sam Houston
Ricky Morton & Robert Gibson defeated NWA Tag Team Champions Bobby Eaton & Dennis Condrey in a Best 2 out of 3 falls match; fall #3: Morton & Gibson won via disqualification

JCP @ St. Marys, PA - April 3, 1986
Ricky Morton & Robert Gibson defeated NWA Tag Team Champions Bobby Eaton & Dennis Condrey in a Best 2 out of 3 falls match; fall #3: Morton & Gibson won via disqualification

JCP @ Roanoke, VA - Civic Center - April 4, 1986
Denny Brown defeated Thunderfoot
Jimmy Garvin defeated the Italian Stallion
NWA Mid-Atlantic Heavyweight Champion Black Bart defeated Sam Houston
Wahoo McDaniel defeated NWA National Heavyweight Champion Tully Blanchard via disqualification
Ricky Morton & Robert Gibson defeated NWA Tag Team Champions Bobby Eaton & Dennis Condrey in a non-title match; Jim Cornette was held in a cage for the duration of the bout
NWA World Champion Ric Flair defeated Dusty Rhodes via disqualification

Worldwide - 4/5/86:
Jimmy Garvin vs. Ben Alexander
Ron Garvin vs. Ron Rossey
Hector Guerrero vs. Vernon Deaton
Wahoo McDaniel vs. Mr. Dillinger
Shaska Whatley vs. Rocky King (Pez Whatley's in-ring debut as Shaska)
NWA US Champion Magnum TA vs. Tony Zane

JCP @ Atlanta, GA - WTBS Studios - April 5, 1986 (matinee)
World Championship Wrestling - 4/5/86:
Wahoo McDaniel vs. Ray Traylor
Joe Coltrane vs. Tony Zane
Manny Fernandez vs. Bob Owens
Ivan Koloff vs. Gene Ligon
Hector Guerrero vs. Carl Styles
Baron Von Raschke, the Barbarian, & Shaska Whatley vs. Rocky Kernodle, Chase, & Tabb
Ricky Morton & Robert Gibson vs. Larry Clarke & Art Pritts
NWA US Champion Magnum TA vs. Randy Mulkey
NWA TV Champion Arn Anderson vs. Ron Garvin
NWA Tag Team Champions Bobby Eaton & Dennis Condrey vs. Mike Simani & Denny Brown

JCP @ Charleston, WV - April 5, 1986 (3,500)
Thunderfoot defeated the Italian Stallion
Pez Whatley defeated Nelson Royal
Sam Houston fought NWA Mid-Atlantic Heavyweight
Champion Black Bart to a no contest
Nighthawk defeated Teijo Khan
The Barbarian defeated Don Kernodle
Ricky Morton & Robert Gibson defeated NWA Tag Team
Champions Bobby Eaton & Dennis Condrey in a non-title
match; Jim Cornette was held in a cage for the duration of the
match

JCP @ Johnson City, TN - April 6, 1986 (matinee)
Ricky Morton & Robert Gibson defeated NWA Tag Team
Champions Bobby Eaton & Dennis Condrey in a non-title
match; Jim Cornette was held in a cage for the duration of the
match

JCP @ Savannah, GA - Civic Center - April 6, 1986
Ricky Morton & Robert Gibson defeated NWA Tag Team
Champions Bobby Eaton & Dennis Condrey in a non-title
match; Jim Cornette was held in a cage for the duration of the
match

JCP @ Gaffney, SC - April 7, 1986
Ricky Morton & Robert Gibson defeated NWA Tag Team
Champions Bobby Eaton & Dennis Condrey in a non-title
match

**JCP @ Fayetteville, NC - Cumberland County Memorial
Arena - April 7, 1986**
Nighthawk defeated Teijo Khan
Pez Whatley defeated the Italian Stallion
The Barbarian defeated Don Kernodle
Manny Fernandez fought NWA TV Champion Arn Anderson to
a draw
Wahoo McDaniel defeated Jimmy Garvin
NWA US Champion Magnum TA & the Road Warriors
defeated Baron Von Raschke, Ivan & Nikita Koloff

JCP @ Greenwood, SC - April 8, 1986
TV taping:
NWA Tag Team Champions Bobby Eaton & Dennis Condrey
defeated Rocky Kernodle & Denny Brown

JCP @ Raleigh, NC - Dorton Arena - April 9, 1986
Hector Guerrero defeated Thunderfoot
Pez Whatley defeated Sam Houston
Jimmy Garvin defeated Denny Brown
Misty Blue defeated Kat Leroux
Ricky Morton & Robert Gibson defeated the Barbarian & Baron
Von Raschke
Magnum TA & Manny Fernandez defeated NWA Tag Team
Champions Bobby Eaton & Dennis Condrey via disqualification

**JCP @ Hendersonville, NC - East Henderson High School
Gym - April 10, 1986**
Hector Guerrero vs. Thunderfoot
Misty Blue vs. Linda Dallas
Ron Garvin vs. Teijo Khan
Wahoo McDaniel vs. Jimmy Garvin
NWA US Champion Magnum TA vs. Baron Von Raschke
Dusty Rhodes vs. NWA TV Champion Arn Anderson (20
minute time-limit)

JCP @ Kershaw, SC - April 10, 1986
Ricky Morton & Robert Gibson defeated NWA Tag Team
Champions Bobby Eaton & Dennis Condrey in a non-title
match

JCP @ Hampton, VA - Coliseum - April 11, 1986
Misty Blue defeated Kat Leroux
NWA TV Champion Arn Anderson defeated Hector Guerrero
Wahoo McDaniel defeated NWA National Heavyweight
Champion Tully Blanchard via count-out
Ricky Morton & Robert Gibson defeated Ivan Koloff & Baron
Von Raschke
NWA US Champion Magnum TA defeated Nikita Koloff
NWA World Champion Ric Flair defeated Dusty Rhodes via
disqualification

**JCP @ Mt. Airy, NC - North Surry High School Gym - April
11, 1986**
Pez Whatley vs. the Italian Stallion
Don Kernodle vs. Leo Burke
NWA Jr. Heavyweight Champion Denny Brown vs. Nelson
Royal
Sam Houston vs. NWA Mid-Atlantic Heavyweight Champion
Black Bart
Manny Fernandez & Ron Garvin defeated NWA Tag Team
Champions Bobby Eaton & Dennis Condrey via disqualification

Worldwide - 4/12/86:
NWA Mid-Atlantic Heavyweight Champion Black Bart vs.
George South
The Road Warriors vs. Gene Ligon & Mark Fleming
Ricky Morton vs. Tony Zane

**JCP @ Atlanta, GA - WTBS Studios - April 12, 1986
(matinee)**
World Championship Wrestling - 4/12/86:
Manny Fernandez & Hector Guerrero vs. George South &
Tony Zane
NWA Mid-Atlantic Heavyweight Champion Black Bart vs. Gene
Ligon
NWA Six Man Tag Team Champions Baron Von Raschke,
Ivan & Nikita Koloff vs. the Italian Stallion, Nelson Royal, &
Denny Brown
Wahoo McDaniel vs. Ron Rossi
Jimmy Garvin vs. Rocky Kernodle

NWA TV Champion Arn Anderson vs. Sam Houston; NWA World Champion Ric Flair provided guest commentary for the match

The Barbarian & Shaska Whatley vs. Vernon Deaton & Randy Mulkey

Ricky Morton & Robert Gibson vs. Ray Traylor & Carl Styles

NWA Tag Team Champions Bobby Eaton & Dennis Condrey vs. Paul Garner & Bob Owens

JCP @ Charlotte, NC - Coliseum - April 12, 1986 (12,000; sell out)

Shown on closed-circuit at the Charlotte Park Center (600) and Spartanburg Memorial Auditorium; Tony Schiavone was the ring announcer for the show

Misty Blue vs. Linda Dallas

Jimmy Garvin vs. the Italian Stallion

Manny Fernandez vs. Teijo Khan

Japanese TV: Ricky Morton & Robert Gibson defeated NWA Tag Team Champions Bobby Eaton & Dennis Condrey in a non-title match at 10:41 when Morton pinned Condrey with a sunset flip as Gibson hit a dropkick on Eaton; Jim Cornette was held in a cage for the duration of the match (*Wrestling Rarities: The Midnight Express*)

Ron Garvin fought NWA TV Champion Arn Anderson to a 15-minute time-limit draw; Garvin punched Anderson with his injured right hand during the closing moments but wasn't able to make the cover before the time expired

NWA US Champion Magnum TA defeated Nikita Koloff via reverse decision; Koloff originally won the match and title around the 15-minute mark after hitting Magnum with a chain while the referee was down on the floor; after the decision was made, a second referee came out, told the initial referee what happened, and the call was changed; after the bout, Koloff assaulted Magnum until Magnum gained the upper hand and threw Koloff into the ringpost Dusty Rhodes & Wahoo McDaniel defeated NWA World Champion Ric Flair & NWA National Heavyweight Champion Tully Blanchard in a lights out bullrope / Indian strap match at 7:35 when McDaniel pinned Blanchard after hitting him with the strap as Blanchard came off the top; Rhodes had Flair in the figure-4 at the time of the fall; prior to the match, Jimmy Garvin attacked McDaniel from behind and then left ringside

JCP @ Atlanta, GA - WTBS Studios - April 13, 1986 (matinee)
TV taping

JCP @ Asheville, NC - Civic Center - April 13, 1986 (matinee)
Sam Houston vs. NWA Mid-Atlantic Heavyweight Champion Black Bart

Hector Guerrero vs. Thunderfoot

Wahoo McDaniel vs. Jimmy Garvin

The Road Warriors & NWA US Champion Magnum TA vs. Baron Von Raschke, Ivan & Nikita Koloff

Robert Gibson & Nighthawk vs. the Barbarian & Shaska Whatley

NWA World Champion Ric Flair vs. Ricky Morton

JCP @ Atlanta, GA - Omni - April 13, 1986 (5,300)
Nighthawk defeated Teijo Khan

Manny Fernandez fought NWA TV Champion Arn Anderson to a draw

Jimmy Garvin defeated Jimmy Valiant

Dusty Rhodes, NWA US Champion Magnum TA, & Manny Fernandez defeated Baron Von Raschke, Ivan & Nikita Koloff via disqualification

NWA National Heavyweight Champion Tully Blanchard defeated Ron Garvin

The Road Warriors defeated NWA Tag Team Champions Bobby Eaton & Dennis Condrey via disqualification

Ricky Morton fought NWA World Champion Ric Flair to a draw

GCW @ Saginaw, MI - April 14, 1986
Ricky Morton & Robert Gibson defeated NWA Tag Team Champions Bobby Eaton & Dennis Condrey via disqualification

GCW @ Lansing, MI - April 15, 1986
NWA Tag Team Champions Bobby Eaton & Dennis Condrey defeated Ricky Morton & Don Kernodle (sub. for Robert Gibson)

JCP @ Rock Hill, SC - Winthrop Coliseum - April 15, 1986
TV taping:
Manny Fernandez & Hector Guerrero defeated Vernon Deaton & Tony Zane
Baron Von Raschke defeated Gene Ligon via submission
Wahoo McDaniel pinned Thunderfoot
Shaska Whatley pinned George South
Jimmy Garvin defeated Mark Fleming
Leo Burke defeated Ron Rossi
Ivan Koloff pinned Rocky Kernodle
Manny Fernandez & Wahoo McDaniel defeated Ivan Koloff & Baron Von Raschke
Wahoo McDaniel (sub. for NWA US Champion Magnum TA, injured earlier in the show) fought Nikita Koloff to a double disqualification
Worldwide - 4/19/86:
Jimmy Garvin defeated Tony Zane
Ivan Koloff pinned Mark Fleming
Nighthawk pinned Ron Rossi
Wahoo McDaniel, Manny Fernandez, & Hector Guerrero defeated Thunderfoot, NWA Mid-Atlantic Heavyweight Champion Black Bart, & Leo Burke
Sam Houston & Nelson Royal defeated George South & Gene Ligon
Jimmy Valiant defeated Vernon Deaton
Baron Von Raschke & Shaska Whatley defeated Rocky Kerndole & Denny Brown

JCP @ Raliegh, NC - Dorton Arena - April 16, 1986
Ron Garvin defeated Leo Burke
Hector Guerrero defeated NWA Mid-Atlantic Heavyweight Champion Black Bart via disqualification
NWA Tag Team Champions Bobby Eaton & Dennis Condrey fought NWA US Champion Magnum TA & Manny Fernandez to a 60-minute time-limit draw
Jimmy Garvin defeated Wahoo McDaniel
Jimmy Valiant, Ricky Morton & Robert Gibson defeated Baron Von Raschke, Ivan & Nikita Koloff

CWF @ Miami Beach, FL - Convention Hall - April 16, 1986 (3,960)
Ricky Santana defeated Jerry Grey
Kendo Nagasaki defeated Jim Backlund
Kendall Windham defeated the White Ninja
Stan Lane & Steve Keirn defeated Kendo Nagasaki & the White Ninja
Jesse Barr defeated Bob Roop in a taped fist lumberjack match
Lex Luger defeated Barry Windham
NWA World Champion Ric Flair defeated Tyree Pride

JCP @ Bessemer City, NC - April 17, 1986
Ricky Morton & Robert Gibson defeated NWA Tag Team Champions Bobby Eaton & Dennis Condrey in a non-title match

JCP @ Norfolk, VA - Scope - April 17, 1986
Hector Guerrero defeated Mark Fleming
Shaska Whatley defeated the Italian Stallion
Manny Fernandez defeated NWA National Heavyweight Champion Tully Blanchard via disqualification
Jimmy Garvin defeated Wahoo McDaniel
Nikita Koloff defeated NWA US Champion Magnum TA in a non-title Russian chain match
NWA World Champion Ric Flair defeated Ron Garvin in a No DQ match

JCP @ Philadelphia, PA - Civic Center - April 18, 1986 (7,000)
NWA Tag Team Champions Bobby Eaton & Dennis Condrey defeated the Road Warriors via reverse decision; the challengers originally won the match and titles at 10:35 when Road Warrior Hawk pinned Eaton after hitting him with Jim Cornette's tennis racquet but Earl Hebner, the original referee, changed the call since Road Warrior Animal shoved him to the floor moments before the pinfall and he saw Hawk use the weapon to get the fall; after the match, the Road Warriors cleared the champions and Cornette from the ring (*Wrestling Rarities: The Midnight Express*)
NWA World Champion Ric Flair, NWA TV Champion Arn Anderson, & NWA National Heavyweight Champion Tully Blanchard defeated Dusty Rhodes, Ron Garvin, & Wahoo Mcdaniel

JCP @ Atlanta, GA - WTBS Studios - April 19, 1986
World Championship Wrestling - 4/19/86:
The Road Warriors vs. Bill Tabb & Ray Traylor
Nighthawk vs. Gene Ligon
NWA US Champion Magnum TA vs. Paul Garner
Jimmy Garvin vs. George South
Ivan Koloff vs. Tony Zane
NWA TV Champion Arn Anderson vs. Manny Fernandez
NWA Tag Team Champions Bobby Eaton & Dennis Condrey vs. Art Pritts & Bob Pearson

Crockett Cup 86 - New Orleans, LA - Superdome - April 19, 1986 (matinee)
Opening Round:
Wahoo McDaniel & Mark Youngblood defeated Bobby Jaggers & Mike Miller when McDaniel pinned Miller with a chop and elbow drop at 7:35
Nelson Royal & Sam Houston defeated the Batton Twins when Houston scored the pin following the bulldog at 8:17
Jimmy Valiant & Manny Fernandez defeated Baron Von Raschke & the Barbarian (w/ Paul Jones & Shaska Whatley) when Fernandez pinned Barbarian with a sunset flip into the ring
Terry Taylor & Steve Williams defeated Bill Dundee & Buddy Landel when Williams pinned Landel with the running powerslam
The Sheepherders (w/ Jack Victory) defeated Hector & Chavo Guerrero when Luke Williams pinned Hector following a double

clothesline behind the referee's back

UWF Tag Team Champions Bobby Fulton & Tommy Rogers defeated Stan Lane & Steve Keirn when Fulton pinned Keirn with a roll up

Buzz Sawyer & Rick Steiner defeated Koko B. Ware & the Italian Stallion when Sawyer pinned Stallion with a powerslam

NWA Mid-Atlantic Heavyweight Champion Black Bart & Jimmy Garvin (w/ Precious) defeated Brett Wayne & DJ Peterson when Garvin pinned Peterson following the brainbuster

Second Round:

NWA Tag Team Champions Bobby Eaton & Dennis Condrey (w/ Jim Cornette) defeated Sam Houston & Nelson Royal when Conrey pinned Royal after Eaton came off the top with an axe handle behind the referee's back as Royal had Condrey in an abdominal stretch

NWA US Champion Magnum TA & Ron Garvin defeated Buzz Sawyer & Rick Steiner when Magnum pinned Steiner with the belly to belly suplex after Garvin made the blind tag

The Road Warriors (w/ Paul Ellering) defeated Wahoo McDaniel & Mark Youngblood when Road Warrior Hawk pinned Youngblood with a clothesline from the middle turnbuckle

Ivan & Nikita Koloff defeated Jimmy Valiant & Manny Fernandez when Ivan pinned Valiant after Nikita hit the Russian Sickle from the apron behind the referee's back

Steve Williams & Terry Taylor defeated Rick Martel & Dino Bravo via forfeit; prior to the bout, ring announcer Bruce Prichard announced Dino Bravo was seriously injured and had been taken to the hospital; Martel appeared in a suit and shook Williams and Taylor's hands before leaving the ring

The Sheepherders (w/ Jack Victory) defeated Ricky Morton & Robert Gibson via disqualification when Morton attacked an interfering Victory with his own flagpole

UWF Tag Team Champions Bobby Fulton & Tommy Rogers defeated NWA TV Champion Arn Anderson & NWA National Heavyweight Champion Tully Blanchard (w/ JJ Dillon) when Rogers pinned Anderson after Fulton dropkicked Anderson behind the referee's back, with his partner falling on top for the win

The Giant Baba & Tiger Mask defeated Jimmy Garvin (w/ Precious) & NWA Mid-Atlantic Heavyweight Champion Black Bart when Baba pinned Bart with a boot to the chest

Non-tournament match: Mid South North American Champion Jim Duggan pinned Dick Slater with the running clothesline at 7:31 after the challenger shoved the referee; Jim Ross was the ring announcer for the bout

Crockett Cup 86 - New Orleans, LA - Superdome - April 19, 1986

Third Round:

Quarter finals: The Road Warriors (w/ Paul Ellering) defeated NWA Tag Team Champions Bobby Eaton & Dennis Condrey (w/ Jim Cornette) via disqualification when Cornette hit Road Warrior Animal with his tennis racquet; after the match, the Road Warriors cleared their opponents and Cornette from the ring

Quarter finals: Steve Williams & Terry Taylor fought Ivan & Nikita Koloff (w/ Krusher Kruschev & Eddie Gilbert) to a 20-minute time-limit draw; the bell rang just before Nikita hit the Russian Sickle on Taylor; after the match, the Russians further attacked their opponents

Quarter finals: UWF Tag Team Champions Bobby Fulton & Tommy Rogers fought the Sheepherders (w/ Jack Victory) to a no contest after the referee was knocked to the floor, all four men continued to brawl in and around the ring, Victory interfered, and the Fantastics used the flagpole as a weapon; the ensuing brawl saw all four men bleed from the face

Quarter finals: NWA US Champion Magnum TA & Ron Garvin defeated the Giant Baba & Tiger Mask when Magnum pinned Tiger by catching him coming off the top and hitting the belly to belly suplex

NWA World Champion Ric Flair defeated Dusty Rhodes (w/ Baby Doll) via disqualification at the 20-minute mark when Rhodes hit Flair with his own boot, moments after Flair did the same to him behind the back of referee Tommy Young; after the bout, Rhodes hit Young with the boot as well before then leaving ringside with Baby Doll and the title belt; Tony Schiavone announced the winner of the match

Finals: The Road Warriors (w/ Paul Ellering) defeated NWA US Champion Magnum TA & Ron Garvin when Road Warrior Animal pinned Garvin with a clothesline at 9:49 after Garvin landed a right hand punch on Hawk, further injuring his taped up hand; after the contest, Mrs. Jim Crockett Sr., Jim Crockett Jr., and Bill Watts awarded the Road Warriors with their $1 million check (*The Life & Death of the Road Warriors*)

JCP @ Savannah, GA - Civic Center - April 20, 1986

Manny Fernandez, Ricky Morton & Robert Gibson defeated Jim Cornette, NWA Tag Team Champions Bobby Eaton & Dennis Condrey

JCP @ Greensboro, NC - Coliseum - April 20, 1986

Hector Guerrero defeated the Italian Stallion

NWA Mid-Atlantic Heavyweight Champion Black Bart defeated Sam Houston

Ron Garvin defeated Ivan Koloff

Baron Von Raschke defeated Nighthawk

Jimmy Valiant defeated Pez Whatley

Dusty Rhodes, Ricky Morton & Robert Gibson defeated NWA World Champion Ric Flair, NWA National Heavyweight Champion Tully Blanchard, & NWA TV Champion Arn Anderson in an elimination match

Nikita Koloff defeated NWA US Champion Magnum TA in a non-title Russian chain match

JCP @ Greenville, SC - Memorial Auditorium - April 21, 1986

TV taping:

NWA World Champion Ric Flair pinned Robert Gibson

Worldwide - 4/26/86:

Hector Guerrero vs. George South

Ivan Koloff vs. Todd Champion

Jimmy Garvin vs. Rocky Kernodle

Ron Garvin vs. the Golden Terror

Robert Gibson vs. Ron Rossi
NWA Tag Team Champions Dennis Condrey & Bobby Eaton (w/ Jim Cornette) fought two unknowns to a no contest when Condrey & Eaton attacked their opponents before the match; moments later, Cornette called out Dusty Rhodes & Magnum TA, which led to a brawl between the two teams and Cornette hitting Baby Doll with his tennis racquet
Worldwide - 5/24/86:
Wahoo McDaniel fought NWA TV Champion Arn Anderson to a double count-out

JCP @ Fayetteville, NC - Cumberland County Memorial Arena - April 21, 1986
Rocky King defeated Gene Ligon
The Italian Stallion defeated Mark Fleming
Thunderfoot defeated Denny Brown
NWA Mid-Atlantic Heavyweight Champion Black Bart defeated Sam Houston
Manny Fernandez & Jimmy Valiant defeated Pez Whatley & Baron Von Raschke
Nikita Koloff defeated NWA US Champion Magnum TA in a non-title Russian chain match
Ricky Morton fought NWA World Champion Ric Flair to a no contest

Columbus, MS - April 22, 1986
NWA World Champion Ric Flair defeated the Bullet (Bob Armstrong)

JCP @ Columbia, SC - Township Auditorium - April 24, 1986
Sam Houston vs. Gene Ligon
Rocky Kernodle vs. Zale
Don Kernodle vs. Ivan Koloff
Manny Fernandez vs. Nikita Koloff
Jimmy Valiant & Nighthawk vs. Baron Von Raschke & Shaska Whatley
Ron Garvin, Ricky Morton & Robert Gibson defeated Jim Cornette, NWA Tag Team Champions Bobby Eaton & Dennis Condrey

JCP @ Richmond, VA - Coliseum - April 25, 1986
Hector Guerrero defeated NWA Mid-Atlantic Heavyweight Champion Black Bart
Jimmy Garvin fought Robert Gibson to a draw
Jimmy Valiant defeated Shaska Whatley via disqualification
Wahoo McDaniel defeated NWA TV Champion Arn Anderson
Dusty Rhodes defeated NWA National Heavyweight Champion Tully Blanchard in a non-title Texas Death Match
NWA Tag Team Champions Bobby Eaton & Dennis Condrey defeated the Road Warriors via disqualification
Nikita Koloff defeated NWA US Champion Magnum TA in a non-title Russian chain match
NWA World Champion Ric Flair fought Ricky Morton to a double count-out

JCP @ Atlanta, GA - WTBS Studios - April 26, 1986 (matinee)
World Championship Wrestling - 4/26/86:
Jimmy Valiant vs. Kent Glover
Manny Fernandez vs. an unknown
Ron Garvin vs. Paul Garner
The Road Warriors vs. Jeff Smith & Randy Mulkey
Baron Von Raschke & Shaska Whatley vs. Bill Tabb & Lee Peak
Wahoo McDaniel vs. Jim Dawson
Ricky Morton & Robert Gibson vs. Ron Rossi & Bob Owens
NWA Tag Team Champions Bobby Eaton & Dennis Condrey vs. Rocky King & George South
NWA National Heavyweight Champion Tully Blanchard vs. Mike Simani
NWA TV Champion Arn Anderson vs. Gene Ligon

JCP @ Baltimore, MD - Arena - April 26, 1986
NWA Tag Team Champions Bobby Eaton & Dennis Condrey defeated Manny Fernandez & Hector Guerrero

JCP @ Charlotte, NC - Coliseum - April 26, 1986

JCP @ Cleveland, OH - Convention Center - April 27, 1986
Teijo Khan defeated the Italian Stallion
Jimmy Valiant defeated Pez Whatley via disqualification
NWA Mid-Atlantic Heavyweight Champion Black Bart defeated Sam Houston
Magnum TA defeated Baron Von Raschke
Dusty Rhodes & Wahoo McDaniel defeated NWA National Heavyweight Champion Tully Blanchard & NWA TV Champion Arn Anderson in a bullrope Indian strap match
NWA Tag Team Champions Bobby Eaton & Dennis Condrey defeated the Road Warriors via disqualification
NWA World Champion Ric Flair defeated Ron Garvin in a No DQ, no count-out, no time limit match

Central States @ St. Louis, MO - April 27, 1986
NWA World Champion Ric Flair defeated Wahoo McDaniel

JCP @ Forest City, NC - April 28, 1986
Ricky Morton & Robert Gibson defeated NWA Tag Team Champions Bobby Eaton & Dennis Condrey in a non-title match

Continental @ Birmingham, AL - Boutwell Auditorium - April 28, 1986
Norvell Austin fought Frankie Lancaster to a draw
Tim Horner defeated Tom Prichard
Wendell Cooley defeated Adrian Street
Robert Fuller & Jimmy Golden defeated Tommy Rich & Steve Armstrong
Brad Armstrong fought Jerry Stubbs to a no contest
NWA World Champion Ric Flair defeated Bob Armstrong

JCP/AWA @ East Rutherford, NJ - Meadowlands - April 28, 1986 (5,000)
Col. DeBeers defeated Davey Gee
Mike Rotunda pinned Doug Somers
Bruiser Brody pinned Steve O
NWA US Champion Magnum TA defeated Baron Von Raschke
AWA Tag Team Champions Curt Hennig & Scott Hall defeated the Barbarian & Boris Zhukov when Hennig pinned Zhukov
Nick Bockwinkel defeated Larry Zbyszko in a Texas Death Match
NWA National Heavyweight Champion Tully Blanchard defeated Ron Garvin via disqualification
AWA World Champion Stan Hansen pinned Leon White
Dusty Rhodes pinned NWA TV Champion Arn Anderson in a non-title steel cage match
The Road Warriors defeated Ivan & Nikita Koloff in a steel cage match when Road Warrior Hawk pinned Ivan

JCP @ Macon, GA - Coliseum - April 29, 1986
Ricky Morton & Robert Gibson defeated NWA Tag Team Champions Bobby Eaton & Dennis Condrey in a non-title match

JCP @ Raleigh, NC - Dorton Arena - April 30, 1986
Baron Von Raschke defeated Sam Houston
NWA TV Champion Arn Anderson defeated Ron Garvin
Robert Gibson defeated NWA Tag Team Champion Bobby Eaton; stipulations stated Gibson would get 5 minutes in the ring with Jim Cornette if he won
Robert Gibson fought Jim Cornette to a 5-minute time-limit draw
Jim Valiant defeated Pez Whatley
Nikita Koloff defeated Magnum TA in a Russian chain match
Dusty Rhodes & Manny Fernandez defeated NWA National Heavyweight Champion Tully Blanchard & Jimmy Garvin
NWA World Champion Ric Flair defeated Ricky Morton

JCP @ Columbia, SC - Township Auditorium - May 1, 1986
Rocky Kernodle vs. Thunderfoot
Nikita Koloff vs. Nighthawk
Wahoo McDaniel vs. NWA TV Champion Arn Anderson
Robert Gibson vs. Jimmy Garvin
NWA Tag Team Champions Bobby Eaton & Dennis Condrey defeated Dusty Rhodes & NWA US Champion Magnum TA via disqualification
NWA World Champion Ric Flair vs. Ricky Morton

JCP @ Harrisonburg, VA - High School Gym - May 1, 1986
NWA Jr. Heavyweight Champion Denny Brown vs. Leo Burke
NWA Mid-Atlantic Heavyweight Champion Black Bart vs. Sam Houston
Don Kernodle vs. Teijo Khan
Hector Guerrero & Manny Fernandez vs. Baron Von Raschke & The Barbarian
Jimmy Valiant vs. Shaska Whatley

NWA National Heavyweight Champion Tully Blanchard vs. Ron Garvin

JCP @ Norfolk, VA - Scope - May 2, 1986
Don Kernodle defeated Mark Fleming
Leo Burke defeated Denny Brown
Dusty Rhodes & NWA US Champion Magnum TA defeated Ivan & Nikita Koloff
Robert Gibson defeated NWA National Heavyweight Champion Tully Blanchard via disqualification
NWA TV Champion Arn Anderson defeated Ron Garvin
Ricky Morton fought NWA World Champion Ric Flair to a draw

JCP @ ? - Return from April Charlotte card?
Jimmy Garvin defeated Wahoo McDaniel via count-out at 5:29 after throwing McDaniel head-first into the ringpost; after the bout, McDaniel attacked Garvin and cleared both he and Precious from ringside
Dusty Rhodes defeated NWA National Heavyweight Champion Tully Blanchard in a non-title no time limit Texas Death Match; fall #1: Rhodes pinned Blanchard with the Bionic Elbow at around the 25-second mark; fall #2: Rhodes pinned Blanchard at around the 1-minute mark following a series of standing elbows; fall #3: Rhodes pinned Blanchard with a clothesline; fall #4: Blanchard pinned Rhodes after hitting him with a taped fist; fall #5: Blanchard pinned Rhodes at the 30-second mark after hitting him with a taped fist after Rhodes became distracted by JJ Dillon on the apron; fall #6: Rhodes pinned Blanchard at the 2-minute mark with a tackle; fall #7: Blanchard pinned Rhodes with a figure-4 at at the 2-minute mark after taking off one of Rhodes' cowboy boots; fall #8: Rhodes pinned Blanchard at the 1-minute mark with an inside cradle as Blanchard attempted the figure-4; Rhodes was declared the winner after both men collided in the ring and referee Tommy Young began counting them both, with Rhodes reaching his feet first
NWA World Champion Ric Flair fought Ricky Morton to a 60-minute time-limit draw; prior to the bout, Robert Gibson escorted Morton to the ring; Flair kicked out of a hurricanrana just before the time limit expired

JCP @ Atlanta, GA - WTBS Studios - May 3, 1986 (matinee)
World Championship Wrestling - 5/3/86:
The Barbarian, Shaska Whatley, & Baron Von Raschke vs. Lee Peek, Rocky King, & Bill Mulkey
Frank & Jesse James (Dusty Rhodes & NWA US Champion Magnum TA under masks) defeated NWA Tag Team Champions Bobby Eaton & Dennis Condrey (w/ Jim Cornette) in a non-title match at 7:41 when Magnum pinned Eaton and Rhodes pinned Condrey following simultaneous belly to belly suplexes; after the bout, Baby Doll appeared and chased Cornette from ringside with a bullrope; after the bout, Tony Schiavone conducted an interview with the winners and Baby Doll
Ron Garvin vs. David Dillenger
NWA World Champion Ric Flair vs. Tony Zane

Wahoo McDaniel vs. Bob Owens
NWA TV Champion Arn Anderson vs. Randy Mulkey
Ivan & Nikita Koloff vs. Mike Samani & Brodie Chase

JCP @ Charleston, SC - May 3, 1986
Leo Burke defeated Rocky Kernodle
Teijo Khan defeated Denny Brown
Sam Houston defeated NWA Mid-Atlantic Heavyweight
Champion Black Bart in a Texas Death match
Jimmy Valiant defeated Pez Whatley via disqualification
The Barbarian & Baron Von Raschke defeated Manny
Fernandez & Hector Guerrero
Wahoo McDaniel fought Jimmy Garvin to a no contest

JCP @ Greensboro, NC - Coliseum - May 3, 1986 (7,549)
Nelson Royal defeated Thunderfoot
Ivan Koloff defeated Don Kernodle
Nikita Koloff defeated the Italian Stallion
NWA TV Champion Arn Anderson defeated Nighthawk
Robert Gibson fought NWA National Heavyweight Champion
Tully Blanchard to a draw
NWA Tag Team Champions Bobby Eaton & Dennis Condrey
defeated Dusty Rhodes & NWA US Champion Magnum TA
Ricky Morton fought NWA World Champion Ric Flair to a draw

Worldwide - 5/3/86:
Ron Garvin vs. NWA National Heavyweight Champion Tully
Blanchard

JCP @ Asheville, NC - Civic Center - May 4, 1986 (matinee)
Nighthawk vs. Teijo Khan
Denny Brown vs. the Barbarian
Manny Fernandez & Hector Guerrero vs. Ivan Koloff & Baron
Von Raschke
NWA Tag Team Champions Bobby Eaton & Dennis Condrey
defeated the Road Warriors via disqualification
NWA US Champion Magnum TA vs. Nikita Koloff (Russian
chain match)
NWA World Champion Ric Flair vs. Ricky Morton

JCP @ Philadelphia, PA - Civic Center - May 4, 1986
Robert Gibson defeated Thunderfoot
NWA Mid-Atlantic Heavyweight Champion Black Bart defeated
the Italian Stallion
Dusty Rhodes & NWA US Champion Magnum TA fought NWA
Tag Team Champions Bobby Eaton & Dennis Condrey to a no
contest
Baron Von Raschke, Ivan & Nikita Koloff defeated the Road
Warriors & Paul Ellering
Ricky Morton fought NWA World Champion Ric Flair to a no
contest
Wahoo McDaniel fought NWA TV Champion Arn Anderson to
a draw
Ron Garvin defeated NWA National Heavyweight Champion
Tully Blanchard via disqualification

JCP @ Fayetteville, NC - Cumberland County Memorial Arena - May 5, 1986
The Italian Stallion fought Thunderfoot to a draw
Barbarian & Teijo Khan defeated Nelson Royal & Sam
Houston
Jimmy Garvin defeated Hector Guerrero
Jimmy Valiant defeated Pez Whatley
NWA National Heavyweight Champion Tully Blanchard
defeated Ron Garvin
NWA Tag Team Champions Bobby Eaton & Dennis Condrey
defeated Dusty Rhodes & NWA US Champion Magnum TA

JCP @ Greenville, SC - Memorial Auditorium - May 5, 1986
Rocky Kernodle defeated George South
Denny Brown defeated Leo Burke
Don Kerndole defeated NWA Mid-Atlantic Heavyweight
Champion Black Bart via disqualification
Manny Fernandez defeated Baron Von Raschke
Wahoo McDaniel fought NWA TV Champion Arn Anderson to
a draw
The Road Warriors defeated Ivan & Nikita Koloff in a steel
cage match

JCP @ Spartanburg, SC - Memorial Auditorium - May 6, 1986 (sell out)
TV taping:
*Included the James Boys (Dusty Rhodes & NWA US
Champion Magnum TA under masks) kidnapping Jim Cornette
and trying to drive off with him until he was rescued by NWA
Tag Team Champions Bobby Eaton & Dennis Condrey*
NWA Tag Team Champions Bobby Eaton & Dennis Condrey
defeated Sam Houston & Gary Royal
NWA Tag Team Champions Bobby Eaton & Dennis Condrey
defeated the Road Warriors via disqualification
Also included Wahoo McDaniel, Ricky Morton & Robert
Gibson, NWA TV Champion Arn Anderson, NWA National
Heavyweight Champion Tully Blanchard, Ron Garvin, the
Barbarian, and NWA Mid-Atlantic Heavyweight Champion
Black Bart

JCP @ Rhonda, NC - May 7, 1986
Ricky Morton & Robert Gibson defeated NWA Tag Team
Champions Bobby Eaton & Dennis Condrey in a non-title
match

JCP @ Wheeling, WV - May 7, 1986
Nelson Royal defeated Jim Lancaster
Sam Houston defeated Al Snow
Manny Fernandez & Hector Guerrero defeated Baron Von
Raschke & Thunderfoot
Jimmy Valiant defeated Shaska Whatley via disqualification
Ron Garvin defeated NWA National Heavyweight Champion
Tully Blanchard vi adisqualification
Nikita Koloff defeated Magnum TA in a Russian chain match

JCP @ Whitmire, SC - May 8, 1986
NWA Tag Team Champions Bobby Eaton & Dennis Condrey defeated Rocky Kernodle & the Italian Stallion

JCP @ Concord, NC - Northwest Cabarrus High School - May 8, 1986
Ricky Morton & Robert Gibson vs. Ivan Koloff & NWA Mid-Atlantic Heavyweight Champion Black Bart
Dusty Rhodes vs. NWA TV Champion Arn Anderson

JCP @ Richmond, VA - Coliseum - May 9, 1986
NWA Mid-Atlantic Heavyweight Champion Black Bart defeated Todd Champion
Jimmy Garvin defeated Denny Brown
Manny Fernandez & Ron Garvin fought Ivan & Nikita Koloff to a draw
NWA TV Champion Arn Anderson defeated Wahoo McDaniel
Robert Gibson defeated NWA National Heavyweight Champion Tully Blanchard via disqualification
NWA Tag Team Champions Bobby Eaton & Dennis Condrey defeated Dusty Rhodes & Magnum TA via disqualification
Jimmy Valiant defeated Shaska Whatley via disqualification
NWA World Champion Ric Flair defeated Ricky Morton

JCP @ Atlanta, GA - WTBS Studios - May 10, 1986 (matinee)
World Championship Wrestling - 5/10/86:
Ron Garvin vs. Maurice Cooper
Robert Gibson vs. David Dellinger
Nikita Koloff vs. Tony Zane
NWA World Champion Ric Flair & NWA TV Champion Arn Anderson vs. Carl Styles & Bob Owens
Jimmy Valiant & Manny Fernandez vs. Larry Clark & Paul Garner
The Barbarian, Shaska Whatley, & Baron Von Raschke vs. Butch Brannigan, Art Pritts, & Kent Glover
Jimmy Garvin vs. Jim Dawson

JCP @ Charlotte, NC - Coliseum - May 10, 1986
NWA Tag Team Champions Bobby Eaton & Dennis Condrey defeated Dusty Rhodes & NWA US Champion Magnum TA via disqualification

JCP @ Atlanta, GA - Omni - May 11, 1986
Shaska Whatley defeated Sam Houston
Wahoo McDaniel defeated Jimmy Garvin via count-out
Robert Gibson fought NWA TV Champion Arn Anderson to a draw
Ron Garvin defeated NWA National Heavyweight Champion Tully Blanchard in a taped fist match
Baron Von Raschke, Ivan & Nikita Koloff defeated the Road Warriors & Paul Ellering
NWA Tag Team Champions Bobby Eaton & Dennis Condrey defeated Dusty Rhodes & Magnum TA via disqualification

Ricky Morton defeated NWA World Champion Ric Flair via disqualification

JCP @ Oakwood, VA - May 12, 1986
NWA Tag Team Champions Bobby Eaton & Dennis Condrey defeated Manny Fernandez & Hector Guerrero

JCP @ Greenville, SC - Memorial Auditorium - May 12, 1986
Thunderfoot defeated Rocky Kernodle
NWA Mid-Atlantic Heavyweight Champion Black Bart fought Don Kernodle to a draw
Ron Garvin defeated Ivan Koloff
Wahoo McDaniel defeated Jimmy Garvin via disqualification
NWA National Heavyweight Champion Tully Blanchard & NWA TV Champion Arn Anderson fought Ricky Morton & Robert Gibson to a no contest
Nikita Koloff defeated Magnum TA in a Russian chain match

JCP @ Richburg, SC - May 13, 1986
TV taping:
NWA Tag Team Champions Bobby Eaton & Dennis Condrey defeated Rocky Kernodle & Denny Brown
NWA Tag Team Champions Bobby Eaton & Dennis Condrey defeated Rocky King & Sam Houston

CWF @ Tampa, FL - May 13, 1986
Jim Backlund defeated Jerry Grey
Ron Bass defeated Ricky Santana
Stan Lane & Steve Keirn defeated Kendo Nagasaki & the White Ninja
Ron Bass defeated Lex Luger via disqualification
Lex Luger defeated Mike Rotundo via forfeit
NWA World Champion Ric Flair defeated Barry Windham

JCP @ Charleston, SC - Arthur Ravenel Stadium - May 14, 1986
Rocky Kernodle vs. the Golden Terror
Don Kernodle vs. Thunderfoot
Sam Houston vs. NWA Mid-Atlantic Heavyweight Champion Black Bart
Ron Garvin vs. Leo Burke
Ricky Morton & Robert Gibson vs. NWA TV Champion Arn Anderson & National Heavyweight Champion Tully Blanchard
NWA US Champion Magnum TA vs. Nikita Koloff (Russian chain match)

CWF @ Miami Beach, FL - Convention Hall - May 14, 1986 (4,287)
Jim Backlund defeated Jerry Grey
Ricky Santana defeated Steve Collins
Ron Bass defeated Mike Rotundo
Tyree Pride defeated Sir Oliver Humperdink in a strap match
Stan Lane & Steve Keirn defeated Kendo Nagasaki & the White Ninja

Barry Windham defeated Bob Roop in a taped fist match
Lex Luger defeated NWA World Champion Ric Flair via disqualification

JCP @ Raliegh, NC - Dorton Arena - May 14, 1986
Baron Von Raschke defeated the Italian Stallion
Teijo Khan defeated Denny Brown
The Barbarian defeated Todd Champion
Jimmy Garvin defeated Wahoo McDaniel in a Texas Death Match
Jimmy Valiant defeated Shaska Whatley in a lumberjack match
NWA Tag Team Champions Bobby Eaton & Dennis Condrey defeated Manny Fernandez & Hector Guerrero

JCP @ Lovingston, VA - May 15, 1986
NWA Tag Team Champions Bobby Eaton & Dennis Condrey defeated Manny Fernandez & Hector Guerrero in a non-title match

CWF @ Ocala, FL - Central Florida Community College - May 15, 1986
Kendall Windham defeated Jerry Grey
Ron Bass defeated Ricky Santana
Stan Lane & Steve Keirn defeated Kendo Nagasaki & the White Ninja
Tyree Pride defeated Sir Oliver Humperdink
Kendall Windham & Mike Rotundo defeated Lex Luger & Bob Roop in an elimination match
NWA World Champion Ric Flair defeated Barry Windham

JCP @ Atlanta, GA - WTBS Studios - May 17, 1986
World Championship Wrestling - 5/17/86:
Magnum TA vs. Art Pritts
Ron Garvin vs. Robert Burroughs
NWA Tag Team Champions Bobby Eaton & Dennis Condrey vs. Rocky Kernodle & Vernon Deaton
Jimmy Valiant & Manny Fernandez vs. Brodie Chase & Jerry Garmon
The Road Warriors vs. Ray Traylor & Carl Styles
Ivan & Nikita Koloff vs. Bob Peters & Jim Dawson
Ricky Morton & Robert Gibson vs. Gene Ligon & Randy Mulkey
The Barbarian & Shaska Whatley vs. Mike Simani & Bill Mulkey
Baron Von Raschke vs. Tony Zane

Central States @ St. Louis, MO - May 17, 1986
Canceled due to inclement weather
NWA World Champion Ric Flair vs. ?

JCP @ Baltimore, MD - Civic Center - May 17, 1986
Denny Brown fought Steve Regal to a draw
NWA Mid-Atlantic Heavyweight Champion Black Bart defeated Sam Houston
Manny Fernandez defeated Leo Burke

Ricky Morton & Robert Gibson defeated NWA Tag Team Champions Bobby Eaton & Dennis Condrey in a non-title match; Jim Cornette was held in a cage for the duration of the match
Ron Garvin defeated NWA TV Champion Arn Anderson
NWA US Champion Magnum TA fought NWA National Heavyweight Champion Tully Blanchard to a no contest
Dusty Rhodes & the Road Warriors defeated NWA Six Man Tag Team Champions Baron Von Raschke, Ivan & Nikita Koloff to win the titles

JCP @ Asheville, NC - Civic Center - May 18, 1986 (matinee)
Sam Houston & Nighthawk vs. the Barbarian & Teijo Khan
NWA Mid-Atlantic Heavyweight Champion Black Bart vs. Hector Guerrero
Don Kernodle vs. Baron Von Raschke
NWA TV Champion Arn Anderson vs. Manny Fernandez
Ricky Morton & Robert Gibson vs. Ivan & Nikita Koloff
Wahoo McDaniel vs. Jimmy Garvin (lumberjack match)

Continental @ Birmingham, AL - May 19, 1986
The Bullet defeated NWA World Champion Ric Flair via disqualification

JCP @ Fayetteville, NC - May 19, 1986
NWA Tag Team Champions Bobby Eaton & Dennis Condrey defeated Dusty Rhodes & NWA US Champion Magnum TA

JCP @ Greenville, SC - Memorial Auditorium - May 19, 1986
Hector Guerrero defeated Leo Burke
Denny Brown fought Steve Regal to a draw
Ivan Koloff defeated Sam Houston
Nikita Koloff defeated Ron Garvin
Ricky Morton & Robert Gibson defeated NWA TV Champion Arn Anderson & NWA National Heavyweight Champion Tully Blanchard in a Texas Tornado match
Jimmy Garvin defeated Wahoo McDaniel in a lumberjack match

PNW @ Portland, OR - May 20, 1986
NWA World Champion Ric Flair defeated Rip Oliver via disqualification

WRESTLING

WINTHROP COLISEUM
Rock Hill, S.C.
Tuesday, May 20, 7:30 PM

EIGHT BIG EVENTS

N.W.A. WORLD TAG TEAM TITLE MATCH
(2 out of 3 Falls)

Dusty Rhodes
(w/Baby Doll)
Magnum T.A.

VS

The Midnight
Express
(w/Jim Cornette)

N.W.A. National Title Match

Wahoo
McDaniel

VS

Tully
Blanchard

World Television Title Match
(1 fall 20 min Time Limit)

The
Ragin' Bull

VS

Arn
Anderson

Six Man Tag Team Match

The Rock N'
Roll Express
Sam
Houston

VS

Ivan Koloff
Nikita Koloff
Baron Von
Raschke

GRUDGE MATCH Jimmy Valient vs Shaska Whatley	Italian Stallion vs Jimmy Garvin (Precious)	Hector Guerrero Vs The Barbarian	Junior Heavy Wt. Denny Brown vs Steve Regal

Matches Subject to Change-No Returns
Ringside-$10.00 Gen. Ad. $8.00 Under 11 $4.00
For Coliseum Event Info-329-0440

ADVANCE TICKET LOCATIONS

KIMBRELL'S FURNITURE
(TOWNCENTER MALL)
GRANDMA'S HOME STYLE COOKIN
BLACK'S DRUG STORE (CHESTER)
FRIENDLY GRILL

WINTHROP COLISEUM
MR. SPORT (ROCK HILL MALL)
VIDEO CENTER (FORT MILL)
VIDEO CONNECTION (YORK)

JCP @ Rock Hill, SC - Winthrop Coliseum - May 20, 1986 (4,000)
NWA Jr. Heavyweight Champion Denny Brown defeated Leo Burke (sub. for Steve Regal)
The Barbarian defeated Hector Guerrero
Jimmy Garvin pinned the Italian Stallion
Jimmy Valiant defeated Shaska Whatley via disqualification
Baron Von Raschke, Ivan & Nikita Koloff defeated Sam Houston, Ricky Morton & Robert Gibson
NWA TV Champion Arn Anderson defeated Manny Fernandez
Wahoo McDaniel defeated NWA National Heavyweight Champion Tully Blanchard via disqualification
Dusty Rhodes & NWA US Champion Magnum TA defeated NWA Tag Team Champions Bobby Eaton & Dennis Condrey in a Best 2 out of 3 falls match via disqualification

PNW @ Seattle, WA - May 21, 1986
NWA World Champion Ric Flair defeated Ron Garvin

JCP @ Taylorsville, NC - May 21, 1986
Ricky Morton & Robert Gibson defeated NWA Tag Team Champions Bobby Eaton & Dennis Condrey in a non-title match

JCP @ San Antonio, TX - May 22, 1986
Ron Garvin defeated the Barbarian
Manny Fernandez defeated Baron Von Raschke
Wahoo McDaniel defeated Jimmy Garvin via disqualification
Jimmy Valiant defeated Pez Whatley in a taped fist match
NWA Tag Team Champions Bobby Eaton & Dennis Condrey defeated Ricky Morton & Robert Gibson
The Road Warriors defeated Ivan & Nikita Koloff in a double Russian chain match
NWA US Champion Magnum TA vs. NWA National Heavyweight Champion Tully Blanchard
Dusty Rhodes vs. NWA World Champion Ric Flair

JCP @ Columbia, SC - Township Auditorium - May 23, 1986
The Italian Stallion vs. Teijo Khan
Don Kernodle vs. Stoney Burke
NWA Tag Team Champion Dennis Condrey defeated Todd Champion (sub. for Bradford)
Manny Fernandez vs. the Barbarian
Robert Gibson defeated NWA Tag Team Champion Bobby Eaton; Jim Cornette was held in a cage for the duration of the match
Jimmy Valiant vs. Shaska Whatley (lumberjack match)
Wahoo McDaniel vs. Jimmy Garvin

JCP @ Norfolk, VA - Scope - May 23, 1986
Hector Guerrero defeated Mark Fleming
Denny Brown fought Steve Regal to a draw
NWA Mid-Atlantic Heavyweight Champion Black Bart defeated Sam Houston

Nelson Royal defeated Thunderfoot
Ron Garvin defeated Leo Burke (sub. for an injured NWA National Heavyweight Champion Tully Blanchard) (w/ Blanchard & JJ Dillon) following Tommy Young's standing 10-count; after the match, Blanchard jumped Garvin, revealing that his arm in a sling was a fake injury, and repeatedly punched Garvin in the face with a taped fist, bloodying his head; moments later, Blanchard dropped Garvin with a piledriver on a steel chair, with NWA US Champion Magnum TA and others then coming out to make the save
NWA US Champion Magnum TA & the Road Warriors defeated Baron Von Raschke, Ivan & Nikita Koloff
Ricky Morton fought NWA World Champion Ric Flair to a no contest

JCP @ Atlanta, GA - WTBS Studios - May 24, 1986 (matinee)
World Championship Wrestling - 5/24/86

JCP @ Cincinnati, OH - May 24, 1986
NWA Tag Team Champions Bobby Eaton & Dennis Condrey defeated the Road Warriors via disqualification
NWA World Champion Ric Flair vs. ?

JCP @ Cleveland, OH - Convention Center - May 25, 1986 (matinee) (4,000)
NWA Jr. Heavyweight Champion Denny Brown fought Steve Regal to a draw
Manny Fernandez defeated NWA Mid-Atlantic Heavyweight Champion Black Bart
Ricky Morton defeated Thunderfoot
NWA US Champion Magnum TA defeated Baron Von Raschke
Dusty Rhodes defeated NWA TV Champion Arn Anderson
NWA Tag Team Champions Bobby Eaton & Dennis Condrey fought the Road Warriors to a double count-out
NWA World Champion Ric Flair defeated Robert Gibson

JCP @ Greenville, SC - Memorial Auditorium - May 26, 1986
The Italian Stallion defeated Thunderfoot
Baron Von Raschke defeated Rocky Kernodle
Don Kernodle defeated NWA Mid-Atlantic Heavyweight Champion Black Bart via disqualification
NWA Tag Team Champions Bobby Eaton & Dennis Condrey defeated Manny Fernandez & Hector Guerrero
Wahoo McDaniel defeated Jimmy Garvin in a Texas Death Match
Dusty Rhodes, Ricky Morton & Robert Gibson defeated NWA World Champion Ric Flair, NWA National Heavyweight Champion Tully Blanchard, & NWA TV Champion Arn Anderson in an elimination match

Central States @ Joplin, MO - May 27, 1986
NWA World Champion Ric Flair vs. Bruiser Brody

JCP @ Greenwood, SC - May 27, 1986
TV taping:
Worldwide - 5/31/86 - featured the debut of Big Bubba
Shaska Whatley, the Barbarian, & Teijo Khan vs. the Italian Stallion, Gene Ligon, & Rocky Kernodle
Ivan & Nikita Koloff vs. George South & Mike Schiavone
Jimmy Valiant & Manny Fernandez vs. Vernon Deaton & Ron Rossi
Steve Regal vs. Rocky King
Hector Guerrero vs. NWA TV Champion Arn Anderson
The James Boys vs. Thunderfoot & Mulkey
Pro - 5/31/86:
Jimmy Garavin vs. Todd Champion
NWA Tag Team Champions Bobby Eaton & Dennis Condrey (w/ Jim Cornette & Big Bubba) vs. David Dillinger & Mike Simani
Wahoo McDaniel vs. Randy Mulkey
Robert Gibson (w/ Ricky Morton) vs. Gene Ligon
NWA National Heavyweight Champion Tully Blanchard & Steve Regal vs. Rocky Kernodle & George South
Nikita Koloff (w/ Ivan Koloff & Krusher Kruschev) vs. Tony Zane
Dark match after the taping: NWA Tag Team Champions Bobby Eaton & Dennis Condrey defeated Dusty Rhodes & NWA US Champion Magnum TA via disqualification

Central States @ Hutchinson, KS - Convention Hall - May 28, 1986
Rick McCord vs. Mr. Pogo
Broadway Joe & Debbie Combs vs. Athena & Tarzan Goto
Mike George vs. Akio Sato
Rufus R. Jones, Bart & Brad Batten vs. the Dream Team & Kevin the Magnificent
Butch Reed vs. Bob Brown
NWA World Champion Ric Flair vs. Bruiser Brody

JCP @ Raleigh, NC - Dorton Arena - May 28, 1986
Don Kernodle defeated Teijo Khan
NWA TV Champion Arn Anderson defeated the Italian Stallion
Ron Garvin defeated NWA National Heavyweight Champion Tully Blanchard in a non-title taped fist match
Jimmy Valiant & Manny Fernandez defeated the Barbarian & Shaska Whatley
Ricky Morton & Robert Gibson defeated Ivan & Nikita Koloff
Wahoo McDaniel defeated Jimmy Garvin in a combination death match
NWA Tag Team Champions Bobby Eaton & Dennis Condrey defeated Dusty Rhodes & NWA US Champion Magnum TA via disqualification

Central States @ Kansas City, KS - May 29, 1986
NWA World Champion Ric Flair fought Bruiser Brody to a double disqualification

JCP @ Amelia, VA - May 29, 1986
Ricky Morton & Robert Gibson defeated NWA Tag Team Champions Bobby Eaton & Dennis Condrey in a non-title match

JCP @ Hampton, VA - May 30, 1986
Teijo Khan defeated Mark Fleming
Wahoo McDaniel fought Jimmy Garvin to a no contest
Jimmy Valiant defeated Shaska Whatley
NWA Mid-Atlantic Heavyweight Champion Black Bart defeated Sam Houston
Nikita Koloff defeated NWA US Champion Magnum TA in a non-title Russian chain match
Ricky Morton & Robert Gibson defeated NWA Tag Team Champions Bobby Eaton & Dennis Condrey in a non-title match; Jim Cornette was held in a cage for the duration of the match

JCP @ Atlanta, GA - WTBS Studios - May 31, 1986 (matinee)
World Championship Wrestling - 5/31/86 - featured Tony Schiavone conducting an interview with NWA National Heavyweight Champion Tully Blanchard & JJ Dillon in which they showed footage from the 5/23/86 card in Norfolk, VA in which Leo Burke subbed for Blanchard against Ron Garvin; moments later, Blanchard bloodied Garvin and knocked him out with a piledriver on a steel chair:
Manny Fernandez & Hector Guerrero vs. Bob Owens & Thunderfoot
Wahoo McDaniel vs. Vernon Deaton
Shaska Whatley vs. Bill Mulkey
NWA Tag Team Champions Bobby Eaton & Dennis Condrey vs. Art Pritts & Brodie Chase
Ricky Morton & Robert Gibson vs. David Dellinger & Paul Garner
The Barbarian & Baron Von Raschke vs. the Italian Stallion & Rocky King
Ron Garvin vs. Kent Glover

JCP @ Florence, SC - May 31, 1986
NWA Tag Team Champions Bobby Eaton & Dennis Condrey defeated Manny Fernandez & Ron Garvin via disqualification

JCP @ Charleston, SC - June 1, 1986
Denny Brown fought Steve Regal to a draw
Ivan Koloff defeated Rocky Kernodle
Baron Von Raschke defeated the Italian Stallion
The Barbarian defeated Sam Houston
NWA Tag Team Champions Bobby Eaton & Dennis Condrey defeated Manny Fernandez & Ron Garvin via disqualification
Nikita Koloff defeated NWA US Champion Magnum TA in a non-title Russian chain match
Dusty Rhodes, Ricky Morton & Robert Gibson defeated NWA World Champion Ric Flair, NWA TV Champion Arn Anderson, & NWA National Heavyweight Champion Tully Blanchard in an elimination match

JCP @ Greensboro, NC - Coliseum - June 1, 1986
Ron Garvin defeated Thunderfoot
Jimmy Garvin defeated Hector Guerrero
Manny Fernandez defeated Teijo Khan
Nikita Koloff defeated Todd Champion
Jimmy Valiant defeated Shaska Whatley
Wahoo McDaniel defeated NWA TV Champion Arn Anderson
NWA World Champion Ric Flair & NWA National Heavyweight
Champion Tully Blanchard defeated Ricky Morton & Robert
Gibson
The James Boys (Dusty Rhodes & Magnum TA) defeated
NWA Tag Team Champions Bobby Eaton & Dennis Condrey in
a non-title lights out bunkhouse match

JCP @ Fayetteville, NC - June 2, 1986
Rocky King defeated George South
Steve Regal defeated Rocky Kernodle
Todd Champion defeated Thunderfoot
Ivan Koloff defeated the Italian Stallion
Dusty Rhodes & Wahoo McDaniel defeated NWA National
Heavyweight Champion Tully Blanchard & Jimmy Garvin
NWA World Champion Ric Flair & NWA TV Champion Arn
Anderson defeated Ricky Morton & Robert Gibson

**JCP @ Spartanburg, SC - Memorial Auditorium - June 3,
1986**
TV taping:
Ricky Morton & Robert Gibson vs. NWA World Champion Ric
Flair & NWA TV Champion Arn Anderson
Also included Dusty Rhodes, NWA US Champion Magnum TA,
NWA Tag Team Champions Bobby Eaton & Dennis Condrey,
Ivan & Nikita Koloff, Wahoo McDaniel, the Barbarian, Ron
Garvin, Jimmy Valiant, National Heavyweight Champion Tully
Blanchard, Manny Fernandez, and Jimmy Garvin

JCP @ Raleigh, NC - Dorton Arena - June 4, 1986
The Italian Stallion defeated Zane Grey
Denny Brown defeated Steve Regal
NWA Mid-Atlantic Heavyweight Champion Black Bart defeated
Todd Champion
Jimmy Garvin defeated Hector Guerrero
NWA Tag Team Champions Bobby Eaton & Dennis Condrey
defeated Wahoo McDaniel & Ron Garvin via disqualification
Dusty Rhodes, Ricky Morton & Robert Gibson defeated NWA
World Champion Ric Flair, NWA TV Champion Arn Anderson,
& NWA National Heavyweight Champion Tully Blanchard via
disqualification in an elimination match

**JCP @ Charleston, SC - Arthur Ravenel Stadium - June 4,
1986**
Rocky King vs. David Dillenger
Nelson Royal vs. Teijo Khan
Don Kernodle vs. the Golden Terror
Sam Houston vs. Ivan Koloff
Jimmy Valiant & Manny Fernandez vs. Shaska Whatley & the

Barbarian
NWA US Champion Magnum TA vs. Nikita Koloff

Central States @ Kansas City, KS - June 5, 1986
NWA World Champion Ric Flair defeated Sgt. Slaughter via
count-out

JCP @ Columbus, GA - June 5, 1986
NWA Tag Team Champions Bobby Eaton & Dennis Condrey
defeated Dusty Rhodes & Magnum TA via disqualification

JCP @ Norfolk, VA - Scope - June 6, 1986
Manny Fernandez defeated Teijo Khan
Jimmy Valiant defeated Shaska Whatley in a lumberjack match
Ivan Koloff defeated Hector Guerrero
Ron Garvin defeated the Barbarian
NWA National Heavyweight Champion Tully Blanchard
defeated Todd Champion
Wahoo McDaniel defeated Nikita Koloff via disqualification
NWA World Champion Ric Flair & NWA TV Champion Arn
Anderson defeated Ricky Morton & Robert Gibson
The James Boys defeated NWA Tag Team Champions Bobby
Eaton & Dennis Condrey in a non-title bunkhouse match

**JCP @ Atlanta, GA - WTBS Studios - June 7, 1986
(matinee)**
World Championship Wrestling - 6/7/86:
Ricky Morton & Robert Gibson vs. Kent Glover & Bob Owens
Manny Fernandez vs. Larry Clarke
NWA TV Champion Arn Anderson & NWA National
Heavyweight Champion Tully Blanchard vs. George South &
Randy Mulkey
Nikita Koloff vs. Todd Champion
The Barbarian & Shaska Whatley vs. the Italian Stallion & Jim
Dawson
Wahoo McDaniel vs. Lee Peak
NWA Tag Team Champions Bobby Eaton & Dennis Condrey
vs. Robert Burroughs & Vernon Deaton
Ron Garvin vs. Bill Tabb
World Championship Wrestling Sunday Edition - 6/8/86

JCP @ Roanoke, VA - Civic Center - June 7, 1986
NWA Tag Team Champions Bobby Eaton & Dennis Condrey
defeated Dusty Rhodes & Magnum TA via disqualification

**JCP @ Asheville, NC - Civic Center - June 8, 1986
(matinee)**
Denny Brown vs. Rocky King
The Italian Stallion vs. Steve Regal
Todd Champion vs. Ivan Koloff
NWA National Heavyweight Champion Tully Blanchard vs.
Wahoo McDaniel
NWA Tag Team Champions Bobby Eaton & Dennis Condrey
vs. Manny Fernandez & Hector Guerrero
NWA US Champion Magnum TA vs. Nikita Koloff

Ricky Morton & Robert Gibson vs. NWA World Champion Ric Flair & NWA TV Champion Arn Anderson (Texas Tornado match)

JCP @ Atlanta, GA - Omni - June 8, 1986 (5,000)
NWA Mid-Atlantic Heavyweight Champion Black Bart defeated Rocky Kernodle
The Barbarian defeated Hector Guerrero
Jimmy Garvin defeated Don Kernodle
Jimmy Valiant defeated Baron Von Raschke
Ron Garvin defeated Nikita Koloff via disqualification
Wahoo McDaniel defeated NWA TV Champion Arn Anderson via disqualification
NWA World Champion Ric Flair & NWA National Heavyweight Champion Tully Blanchard defeated Ricky Morton & Robert Gibson in a Texas Tornado Match
Dusty Rhodes & Magnum TA defeated NWA Tag Team Champions Bobby Eaton & Dennis Condrey in a non-title bunkhouse match

JCP @ Greenville, SC - Memorial Auditorium - June 9, 1986
Rocky Kernodle defeated Rocky King
Denny Brown defeated Steve Regal via disqualification
Jimmy Garvin defeated Todd Champion
Ricky Morton & Robert Gibson defeated Ivan Koloff & Baron Von Raschke
NWA National Heavyweight Champion Tully Blanchard defeated Wahoo McDaniel via disqualification
The James Boys defeated NWA Tag Team Champions Bobby Eaton & Dennis Condrey in a non-title bunkhouse match

CWF @ Orlando, FL - June 9, 1986
Ricky Santana defeated Jim Backlund
Sean Royal defeated the Marauder
Ricky Santana defeated Jerry Grey
Ed Gantner & Kendo Nagasaki defeated Stan Lane & Steve Keirn
Kendall Windham defeated Florida Heavyweight Champion the White Ninja to win the title in a steel cage match
Ron Bass defeated Barry Windham in a bullrope match
Steve Keirn won a battle royal
NWA World Champion Ric Flair defeated Lex Luger when the challenger was deemed unable to continue

JCP @ Salisbury, NC - June 10, 1986
TV taping

JCP @ Mission, TX - June 11, 1986 (sell out)
NWA Tag Team Champions Bobby Eaton & Dennis Condrey defeated Dusty Rhodes & Magnum TA via disqualification
NWA World Champion Ric Flair vs. Ron Garvin

JCP @ San Antonio, TX - June 12, 1986
NWA World Champion Ric Flair vs. Ricky Morton

The James Boys defeated NWA Tag Team Champions Bobby Eaton & Dennis Condrey in a non-title bunkhouse match

Continental @ Knoxville, TN - June 13, 1986
NWA World Champion Ric Flair defeated the Bullet

JCP @ Atlanta, GA - WTBS Studios - June 14, 1986 (matinee)
World Championship Wrestling - 6/14/86:
Ricky Morton & Robert Gibson vs. Ray Aaron & Mike Simani
Manny Fernandez & Jimmy Valiant vs. Pat Myers & Clement Fields
Ron Garvin vs. Vernon Deaton
Ole Anderson & NWA TV Champion Arn Anderson vs. Bill & Randy Mulkey
NWA World Champion Ric Flair vs. Tony Zane
World Championship Wrestling Sunday Edition - 6/15/86

JCP @ Baltimore, MD - Civic Center - June 14, 1986 (5,500)
Sam Houston pinned Teijo Khan
Jimmy Garvin pinned the Italian Stallion
The Barbarian (sub. for Ole Anderson) defeated Todd Champion
NWA Mid-Atlantic Heavyweight Champion Black Bart pinned Hector Guerrero
NWA TV Champion Arn Anderson fought Manny Fernandez to a time-limit draw after the 20-minute mark
NWA Tag Team Champions Bobby Eaton & Dennis Condrey defeated Wahoo McDaniel & Ron Garvin via disqualification when McDaniel hit Eaton with Jim Cornette's tennis racquet
Magnum TA pinned NWA National Heavyweight Champion Tully Blanchard in a non-title barbed wire match at 7:28

UWF @ New Orleans, LA - Superdome - June 14, 1986 (7,200)
The One Man Gang defeated Brett Sawyer
Robert Gibson defeated Baron Von Raschke
Koko B. Ware fought Jack Victory to a double disqualification
Terry Gordy & Buddy Roberts defeated the Blade Runners
The Missing Link defeated Kamala via disqualification
UWF TV Champion Terry Taylor defeated Buzz Sawyer
UWF Tag Team Champions Bobby Fulton & Tommy Rogers defeated the Sheepherders in a New Zealand Bootcamp match
Ted DiBiase defeated Michael Hayes via disqualification
NWA World Champion Ric Flair pinned Ricky Morton
Dusty Rhodes, Bill Watts, & Steve Williams defeated Kortsia Korchenko, Ivan & Nikita Koloff in a streetfight when Korchenko was pinned

JCP @ Wilmington, NC - Legion Stadium - June 15, 1986 (4,000)
Jimmy Valiant vs. Shaska Whatley (No DQ match)
NWA National Heavyweight Champion Tully Blanchard vs. Wahoo McDaniel
NWA Tag Team Champions Bobby Eaton & Dennis Condrey

defeated Ricky Morton & Robert Gibson in a non-title Best 2
out of 3 falls match
Also included Manny Fernandez

JCP @ Greenville, SC - June 16, 1986
Sam Houston & Denny Brown fought NWA Mid-Atlantic
Heavyweight Champion Black Bart & Steve Regal to a draw
The Warlord defeated the Italian Stallion
Baron Von Raschke defeated Hector Guerrero
Manny Fernandez defeated Jimmy Garvin via disqualification
Wahoo McDaniel defeated Ivan Koloff
Ricky Morton & Robert Gibson defeated NWA National
Heavyweight Champion Tully Blanchard & NWA TV Champion
Arn Anderson
Dusty Rhodes & Magnum TA defeated NWA Tag Team
Champions Bobby Eaton & Dennis Condrey in a lumberjack
match

JCP @ Greenwood, SC - June 17, 1986
TV taping:
*Featured a segment in which Big Bubba threw down Baby Doll,
with Dusty Rhodes then running out and smashing a wooden
chair over Bubba's head; Bubba didn't flinch from the blow;
moments later, Magnum TA came out with two shovels and
Jim Cornette had Bubba leave the ring*
Baron Von Raschke, Shaska Whatley, & Teijo Khan defeated
Mark Fleming, Bill & Randy Mulkey
The Warlord defeated Mike Simani
NWA Tag Team Champions Bobby Eaton & Dennis Condrey
defeated Todd Champion & Rocky Kernodle
Steve Regal defeated George South
Hector Guererro defeated the Golden Terror
Don Kernodle defeated Thnuderfoot
The Barbarian defeated Denny Brown
NWA TV Champion Arn Anderson & NWA National
Heavyweight Champion Tully Blanchard defeated Sam
Houston & Tony Zane

JCP @ Raleigh, NC - Dorton Arena - June 18, 1986
Don Kernodle defeated Teijo Khan
The Warlord defeated Rocky Kernodle
Magnum TA defeated Ivan Koloff in a Texas Death Match
Ricky Morton & Robert Gibson defeated NWA National
Heavyweight Champion Tully Blanchard & NWA TV Champion
Arn Anderson in a steel cage match
The Barbarian, Baron Von Raschke, & Pez Whatley defeated
Manny Fernandez, Jimmy Valiant, & Hector Guerrero
NWA Tag Team Champions Bobby Eaton & Dennis Condrey
defeated Ron Garvin & Wahoo McDaniel via disqualification

CWF @ Miami Beach, FL - Convention Hall - June 18, 1986
Jim Backlund defeated Steve Collins
Ricky Santana defeated the Maurauder
Sean Royal defeated Jerry Grey
The Shock Troops defeated Stan Lane & Steve Keim via
disqualification

Tyree Pride defeated Ron Bass via disqualification
Barry & Kendall Windham defeated Kendo Nagasaki & the
White Ninja in a bullrope match
Stan Lane won a battle royal
Southern Champion Lex Luger defeated NWA World
Champion Ric Flair; only Luger's title was at stake

JCP @ Columbia, SC - Township Auditorium - June 19, 1986
Rocky Kernodle vs. the Warlord
Don Kernodle vs. Thunderfoot
Denny Brown vs. Steve Regal
Wahoo McDaniel vs. Jimmy Garvin (lumberjack match)
Magnum TA vs. Ivan Koloff (Texas Death match)
Ricky Morton & Robert Gibson vs. NWA National Heavyweight
Champion Tully Blanchard & NWA TV Champion Arn
Anderson (steel cage match)

JCP @ Hillsville, VA - June 19, 1986 (600)
NWA Tag Team Champions Bobby Eaton & Dennis Condrey
defeated Manny Fernandez & Hector Guerrero
Jimmy Valiant defeated Shaska Whatley

CWF @ Ft. Pierce, FL - June 19, 1986
NWA World Champion Ric Flair vs. Southern Heavyweight
Champion Lex Luger

JCP @ Richmond, VA - Coliseum - June 20, 1986 (5,000)
NWA Mid-Atlantic Heavyweight Champion Black Bart pinned
Todd Champion
The Warlord pinned the Italian Stallion
Ole Anderson pinned Hector Guerrero
NWA TV Champion Arn Anderson defeated Ron Garvin in a
taped fist match after NWA National Heavyweight Champion
Tully Blanchard interfered
Magnum TA defeated Ivan Koloff in a Texas Death Match
NWA World Champion Ric Flair & NWA National Heavyweight
Champion Tully Blanchard defeated Ricky Morton & Robert
Gibson in a Texas Tornado match when Ole Anderson
interfered and helped gang up on Morton & Gibson
Dusty Rhodes & Magnum TA defeated NWA Tag Team
Champions Bobby Eaton & Dennis Condrey in a non-title
bunkhouse match

JCP @ Atlanta, GA - WTBS Studios - June 21, 1986 (matinee)
World Championship Wrestling - 6/21/86:
Ricky Morton & Robert Gibson vs. Ray Aaron & Mike Simani
Jimmy Valiant & Manny Fernandez vs. Clement Fields & Pat
Myers
NWA Tag Team Champions Bobby Eaton & Dennis Condrey
vs. Sam Houston & Rocky Kernodle
Ron Garvin vs. Vernon Deaton
Ole Anderson & NWA TV Champion Arn Anderson vs. Bill &
Randy Mulkey

MID-ATLANTIC CHAMPIONSHIP
WRESTLING

SCOPE COLISEUM
TONIGHT 8:15 PM

Ringside and Reserved seats $12.00. Gen. Adm. $10.00, Limited (800), Children under 12 $4.00 Gen. Adm. tax included at Box Office and all Ticket Outlets

LUMBERJACK MATCH FOR WORLD'S TAG TITLE
LUMBERJACK'S WILL BE ARMED WITH TENNIS RACKETS

MIDNIGHT EXPRESS
WITH JIM CORNETTE

• VERSUS •

MAGNUM T.A. DUSTY RHODES
WITH BABY DOLL

TEXAS DEATH MATCH
RIC **FLAIR** V S. RICKY **MORTON**

FOR WORLD'S TV TITLE
ARN **ANDERSON** V S. ROBERT **GIBSON**

FOR NATIONAL TITLE
TULLY **BLANCHARD** V S. WAHOO **McDANIEL**

GORGEOUS **JIMMY GARVIN** WITH PRECIOUS • VERSUS • **TODD CHAMPION**

STEVE **REGAL** V S. DENNY **BROWN**

THE **WAR LORDS** V S. ITALIAN **STALLION**

288

NWA World Champion Ric Flair vs. Tony Zane
World Championship Wrestling Sunday Edition - 6/22/86

JCP @ Norfolk, VA - Scope - June 21, 1986
The Warlord vs. the Italian Stallion
Jimmy Garvin vs. Todd Champion
NWA National Heavyweight Champion Tully Blanchard vs. Wahoo McDaniel
NWA TV Champion Arn Anderson vs. Robert Gibson
NWA World Champion Ric Flair vs. Ricky Morton (Texas Death Match)
NWA Tag Team Champions Bobby Eaton & Dennis Condrey defeated Dusty Rhodes & Magnum TA via disqualification

JCP @ Atlanta, GA - Omni - June 22, 1986 (matinee) (2,000)
Thunderfoot defeated Rocky King
The Warlord defeated the Italian Stallion
NWA National Heavyweight Champion Tully Blanchard defeated Todd Champion
Ivan Koloff defeated Hector Guerrero
Dusty Rhodes & Magnum TA defeated NWA Tag Team Champions Bobby Eaton & Dennis Condrey via disqualification in a lumberjack match
Arn & Ole Anderson defeated Ron Garvin & Robert Gibson
NWA World Champion Ric Flair defeated Ricky Morton in a steel cage match

JCP @ Asheville, NC - Civic Center - June 22, 1986 (matinee)
George South vs. Doug Dillenger
Rocky Kernodle vs. Steve Regal
Denny Brown vs. Teijho Khan
Sam Houston vs. NWA Mid-Atlantic Heavyweight Champion Black Bart (Texas Bullrope match)
Jimmy Valiant & Manny Fernandez vs. Shaska Whatley & Baron Von Raschke (elimination match)
Wahoo McDaniel vs. Jimmy Garvin (Texas Death Match)

JCP @ Greensboro, NC - Coliseum - June 22, 1986
Dusty Rhodes & Magnum TA defeated NWA Tag Team Champions Bobby Eaton & Dennis Condrey in a lumberjack match

JCP @ Fayetteville, NC - June 23, 1986
TV taping:
Ricky Morton & Robert Gibson defeated Mark Fleming & Ben Alexander
The Road Warriors defeated Bill & Randy Mulkey
NWA National Heavyweight Champion Tully Blanchard defeated Vernon Deaton
Magnum TA defeated Brodie Chase
The Warlord defeated Thunderfoot
Baron Von Raschke, Shasha Whatley, & the Barbarian defeated Mike Simani, George South, & Tony Zane
Ole & NWA TV Champion Arn Anderson defeated Sam

Houston & Denny Brown
Pro:
Worldwide

JCP @ Rock Hill, SC - Winthrop Coliseum - June 24, 1986
TV taping:
Ricky Morton & Robert Gibson defeated the Golden Terror & Thunderfoot
The Warlord pinned Mark Fleming
NWA TV Champion Arn Anderson & Ole Anderson defeated Don & Rocky Kernodle
The Road Warriors defeated Gene Ligon & Mike Sumani
NWA Tag Team Champions Bobby Eaton & Dennis Condrey defeated Nelson Royal & Todd Champion
Nikita Koloff pinned Tony Zane
The Barbarian & Baron Von Raschke defeated Bill & Randy Mulkey
Jimmy Valiant & Manny Fernandez defeated Baron Von Raschke & Shaska Whatley
NWA Tag Team Champions Bobby Eaton & Dennis Condrey defeated the Road Warriors via disqualification

Pro - 7/5/86:
Wahoo McDaniel & Ron Garvin defeated NWA Mid-Atlantic Heavyweight Champion Black Bart & Teijo Khan
The Road Warriors defeated Tony Zane & Vernon Deaton
The Warlord pinned Randy Mulkey
Jimmy Garvin pinned Gene Ligon
Krusher Kruschev, Ivan & Nikita Koloff defeated the Italian Stallion, Rocky King, & George South
Ole Anderson defeated Bill Mulkey via submission
Ricky Morton & Robert Gibson defeated Thunderfoot & Mark Fleming

CWF @ Miami Beach, FL - Convention Center - June 25, 1986 (3,022)
Ricky Santana defeated Jerry Grey
Sean Royal defeated the White Ninja
Kendall Windham defeated Kendo Nagasaki
Barry Windham defeated Ron Bass in a steel cage bunkhouse match
Stan Lane & Steve Keirn defeated the Shock Troops
Stan Lane defeated Sir Oliver Humperdink
NWA World Champion Ric Flair defeated Southern Champion Lex Luger via disqualification

JCP @ Laurinburg, NC - June 26, 1986
Ricky Morton & Robert Gibson defeated NWA Tag Team Champions Bobby Eaton & Dennis Condrey in a non-title match

Honolulu, HI - June 26, 1986
NWA World Champion Ric Flair defeated Sam Samoan via disqualification

JCP @ Harrisonburg, VA - High School - June 26, 1986
Denny Brown vs. Steve Regal
Rocky Kernodle vs. the Warlord
Don Kernodle vs. Thunderfoot
Jimmy Valiant, Manny Fernandez, & Hector Guerrero vs. the Barbarian, Shaska Whatley, & Baron Von Raschke
NWA National Heavyweight Champion Tully Blanchard vs. Ron Garvin
Wahoo McDaniel vs. Jimmy Garvin

JCP @ Columbia, SC - Township Auditorium - June 27, 1986
The Italian Stallion vs. Steve Regal
The Warlord vs. Terror
Todd Champion vs. NWA Mid-Atlantic Heavyweight Champion Black Bart
Wahoo McDaniel vs. NWA National Heavyweight Champion Tully Blanchard
Ricky Morton & Robert Gibson vs. Ole Anderson & NWA TV Champion Arn Anderson
The James Boys defeated NWA Tag Team Champions Bobby Eaton & Dennis Condrey in a non-title bunkhouse match

AWA @ Salt Lake City, UT - Salt Palace - June 27, 1986 (11,557)
Candi Devine defeated Sherri Martel
Col. DeBeers defeated Brad Rheingans
Greg Gagne & Jimmy Snuka defeated Boris Zhukov & Nord the Barbarian
Ali Kahn defeated Jerry Blackwell
Larry Zbyszko fought Scott LeDoux to a no contest
Shawn Michaels & Marty Jannetty defeated AWA Tag Team Champions Buddy Rose & Doug Somers via disqualification
NWA World Champion Ric Flair defeated Curt Hennig
AWA World Champion Stan Hansen defeated Nick Bockwinkel

JCP @ Atlanta, GA - WTBS Studios - June 28, 1986 (matinee)
World Championship Wrestling - 6/28/86:
NWA Tag Team Champions Bobby Eaton & Dennis Condrey defeated Sam Houston & George South
Krusher Kruschev, Ivan & Nikita Koloff defeated Vernon Deaton, Rocky King, & Gene Ligon
The Warlord defeated Mike Simani
Ole Anderson & NWA TV Champion Arn Anderson defeated Tony Zane & Rocky Kernodle
Ricky Morton & Robert Gibson defeated the Golden Terror & Thunderfoot
Baron Von Raschke & Shaska Whatley defeated Dave Spencer & Lee Peak
NWA National Heavyweight Champion Tully Blanchard defeated the Italian Stallion
Ron Garvin & Wahoo McDaniel defeated Paul Garner & Kent Glover

JCP @ Albuquerque, NM - June 28, 1986
Hillbilly Tooter defeated Jackson Brody
Tom Reynosa defeated Ted Heath
Dick Murdoch defeated Steve Regal
Wahoo McDaniel fought NWA National Heavyweight Champion Tully Blanchard to a no contest
The Road Warriors & Paul Ellering defeated Krusher Kruschev, Ivan & Nikita Koloff
NWA Tag Team Champions Bobby Eaton & Dennis Condrey defeated Dusty Rhodes & Magnum TA via disqualification
NWA World Champion Ric Flair defeated Ron Garvin

JCP @ Gainesville, GA - Georgia Mountains Center - June 29, 1986
TV taping:
Wahoo McDaniel & Ron Garvin defeated NWA Tag Team Champions Bobby Eaton & Dennis Condrey

JCP @ Marietta, GA - June 29, 1986
NWA Tag Team Champions Bobby Eaton & Dennis Condrey defeated Wahoo McDaniel & Ron Garvin

JCP @ Buckingham, VA - June 30, 1986
NWA Tag Team Champions Bobby Eaton & Dennis Condrey defeated Manny Fernandez & Hector Guerrero in a non-title match

JCP @ Greenville, SC - Memorial Auditorium - June 30, 1986
Steve Regal defeated Rocky King
The Warlord defeated George South
NWA Six-Man Tag Team Champions Ivan Koloff, Baron Von Raschke, & Krusher Krushchev defeated Wahoo McDaniel, Ron Garvin, & Sam Houston
NWA National Heavyweight Champion Tully Blanchard fought Robert Gisbon to a 30-minute time limit draw
Magnum TA defeated Nikita Koloff in a Texas Death match
NWA World Champion Ric Flair defeated Ricky Morton in a Texas death match

JCP @ Atlanta, GA - WTBS Studios - June 1986
World Championship Wrestling taping:
Robert Gibson (w/ Ricky Morton) fought NWA TV Champion Arn Anderson to a time-limit draw; immediately after the bell rang, Gibson had Anderson down with a backslide, with Morton then sliding in the ring and counting to 3

JCP @ Philadelphia, PA - Veterans Stadium - July 1, 1986 (10,900)
The Barbarian defeated Denny Brown
NWA Mid-Atlantic Heavyweight Champion Black Bart defeated Todd Champion
Manny Fernandez defeated Shaska Whatley in a bunkhouse match
Wahoo McDaniel defeated Jimmy Garvin in an Indian Death Match; the show was nearly shut down by Commissioner JJ Bins due to the blood loss during the match; there was speculation Bins had been paid off by the WWF to threaten to shut the show down; he reportedly said he attended the show with his kids and doesn't generally go to wrestling cards; however he appeared during the 6/28/86 Philadelphia Spectrum show, was part of the action, and - during the show - ordered the Junkyard Dog to face Don Muraco the following month in a dog collar match
Ron Garvin defeated NWA National Heavyweight Champion Tully Blanchard in a non-title taped fist match
Jimmy Valiant defeated Baron Von Raschke in a pole match
Baby Doll, Ricky Morton & Robert Gibson defeated Jim Cornette, Bobby Eaton & Dennis Condrey
NWA US Championship Best of 7 Series: Nikita Koloff defeated Magnum TA; Magnum: 0, Nikita: 1
NWA World Champion Ric Flair defeated Road Warrior Hawk (w/ Paul Ellering) via disqualification at 11:43 after Hawk accidentally knocked referee Tommy Young to the floor when the champion moved out of the way; the ball rang as Young crawled back in the ring as Hawk had Flair covered following a backbreaker, with fans thinking Young was counting to three as he crawled back in and that Hawk had won the title (*Great*

American Bash 86)
Dusty Rhodes & Road Warrior Animal defeated Ole & NWA TV Champion Arn Anderson in a steel cage match

JCP @ Washington DC - RFK Stadium - July 3, 1986 (6,300)
Baron Von Raschke defeated the Italian Stallion
Jimmy Garvin defeated Todd Champion
Don Kernodle defeated Thunderfoot
Ole Anderson defeated Hector Guerrero
Wahoo McDaniel defeated NWA TV Champion Arn Anderson in an Indian Strap Match
Manny Fernandez & Jimmy Valiant defeated the Barbarian & Shaska Whatley
NWA National Heavyweight Champion Tully Blanchard defeated Ron Garvin in a taped fist match
Ricky Morton & Robert Gibson defeated NWA Tag Team Champions Bobby Eaton & Dennis Condrey in a non-title steel cage match
Baby Doll defeated Jim Cornette at the 5-minute mark
NWA World Champion Ric Flair defeated Dusty Rhodes
The Road Warriors & Magnum TA defeated Krusher Kruschev, Ivan & Nikita Koloff in a steel cage match

JCP @ Memphis, TN - Liberty Bowl - July 4, 1986 (1,900)
NWA Mid-Atlantic Heavyweight Champion Black Bart defeated Todd Champion
Hector Guerrero defeated Thunderfoot
Wahoo McDaniel defeated Jimmy Garvin
Manny Fernandez defeated Shaska Whatley in a bunkhouse match
Jimmy Valiant defeated Baron Von Raschke
Ricky Morton & Robert Gibson fought Ole & NWA TV Champion Arn Anderson to a draw
NWA National Heavyweight Champion Tully Blanchard defeated Ron Garvin via disqualification in a taped fist match
The Road Warriors defeated Ivan Koloff & Krusher Kruschev in a double chain match
NWA World Champion Ric Flair defeated Nikita Koloff
Dusty Rhodes, Magnum TA, & Baby Doll defeated Jim Cornette, NWA Tag Team Champions Bobby Eaton & Dennis Condrey in a steel cage match

JCP @ Charlotte, NC - Memorial Stadium - July 5, 1986 (23,000)
NWA Jr. Heavyweight Champion Denny Brown fought Steve Regal to a 15-minute time-limit draw
Robert Gibson pinned NWA Mid-Atlantic Heavyweight Champion Black Bart with a crossbody off the top at the 8-minute mark
Ole & NWA TV Champion Arn Anderson defeated Sam Houston & Nelson Royal at the 12-minute mark when Ole pinned Houston
Manny Fernandez pinned Baron Von Raschke in a bunkhouse match at the 10-minute mark
Wahoo McDaniel defeated Jimmy Garvin in an Indian strap

match at the 9-minute mark after dragging Garvin to all four corners of the ring

Ron Garvin defeated NWA National Heavyweight Champion Tully Blanchard in a taped fist match via KO in the 5th round

The Road Warriors (w/ Paul Ellering) defeated Nikita & Ivan Koloff in a double Russian Chain Match at the 11-minute mark when Road Warrior Animal pinned Ivan after Ellering interfered and pushed Ivan off the top, causing him to crotch himself across the top rope; after the bout, the Warriors won a brawl over the Koloffs (*Great American Bash 86*, *The Life & Death of the Road Warriors*)

Jimmy Valiant pinned Shaska Whatley (w/ Paul Jones) at 8:53 after hitting him with Baron Von Raschke's loaded glove, moments after Von Raschke tried to interfere but was held back by Manny Fernandez; stipulations stated the loser of the match would have his head shaved; after the contest, Fernandez, Nelson Royal, NWA Jr. Heavyweight Champion Denny Brown, Ron Garvin, Sam Houston, and NWA Tag Team Champion Robert Gibson came out and held up Whatley while Valiant shaved him bald; moments later, Valiant grabbed the mic and said Jones was next (*Great American Bash 86*)

Dusty Rhodes, Magnum TA, & Boby Doll defeated Jim Cornette, NWA Tag Team Champions Bobby Eaton & Dennis Condrey (w/ Big Bubba) in a steel cage match when Baby Doll pinned Cornette with a right hand punch at 6:30; after the bout, Rhodes faced off with Bubba on the floor until he was jumped from behind by Eaton, with Eaton holding Dusty while Bubba landed a series of punches to the face; eventually, Magnum broke free of the cage to make the save (*Great American Bash 86*)

NWA World Champion Ric Flair pinned Ricky Morton in a steel cage match at 23:15 with his feet on the ropes for leverage after dropping Morton crotch-first across the top rope; Morton wore a protective mask over his face to shield his broken nose but Flair removed it mid-way through the contest; prior to the match, Flair arrived in a WSOC Channel 9 helicopter alongside sportscaster Harold Jackson, who was the guest ring announcer for the match (*Ric Flair & the 4 Horsemen*)

JCP @ Asheville, NC - Civic Center - July 6, 1986 (matinee)
NWA Jr. Heavyweight Champion Denny Brown vs. Hector Guerrero

Don Kernodle vs. the Barbarian

Robert Gibson vs. Steve Regal

Jimmy Valiant & Manny Fernandez vs. Shaska Whatley & Baron Von Raschke

Magnum TA vs. Ivan Koloff

The Road Warriors vs. NWA National Heavyweight Champion Tully Blanchard & NWA TV Champion Arn Anderson

Ricky Morton vs. NWA World Champion Ric Flair (Texas Death Match)

JCP @ Raleigh, NC - Dorton Arena - July 6, 1986 (8,500; sell out)
TV taping:

Magnum TA defeated Nikita Koloff in a Texas Death Match when Koloff couldn't answer the referee's standing 10 count

after 7 falls

World Championship Wrestling - 7/12/86:

The Warlord pinned Gene Ligon

Ivan Koloff pinned Rocky King

Ron Garvin pinned NWA Mid-Atlantic Heavyweight Champion Black Bart by using the ropes for leverage

Teijo Khan vs. Mark Fleming

Wahoo McDaniel defeated NWA National Heavyweight Champion Tully Blanchard via reverse decision; Blanchard originally won the match after hitting McDaniel with a foreign object but Ron Garvin came out, told referee Tommy Young what happened, and the decision was changed

Sam Houston vs. George South

The Road Warriors defeated NWA Tag Team Champions Bobby Eaton & Dennis Condrey via disqualification

Dusty Rhodes, Ricky Morton & Robert Gibson defeated NWA World Champion Ric Flair, Ole & NWA TV Champion Arn Anderson in a bunkhouse match when Morton pinned Flair; the first 3 minutes of the match aired on WTBS

JCP @ Greenville, SC - July 7, 1986
Baby Doll defeated Jim Cornette

JCP @ Rocky Mount, NC - July 7, 1986
Dusty Rhodes, Ricky Morton & Robert Gibson defeated NWA World Champion Ric Flair, Ole & NWA TV Champion Arn Anderson

JCP @ Spartanburg, SC - Memorial Auditorium - July 8, 1986 (sell out)
TV taping:

Dusty Rhodes, Magnum TA, Ricky Morton & Robert Gibson vs. NWA World Champion Ric Flair, NWA TV Champion Arn Anderson, Ole Anderson, & NWA National Heavyweight Champion Tully Blanchard

Pro - 7/12/86:

Ole & NWA TV Champion Arn Anderson defeated Mark Fleming & Gene Ligon

Manny Fernandez defeated Randy Mulkey

Don Kernodle defeated Golden Terror

Ron Garvin defeated Mike Simani

Jimmy Garvin defeated Bill Mulkey

Baron Von Raschke & Shaska Whatley defeated Rocky King & the Italian Stallion

NWA World Champion Ric Flair defeated NWA Jr. Heavyweight Champion Denny Brown

JCP @ Cincinnati, OH - Riverfront Stadium - July 9, 1986 (3,900 paid)
Featured a concert by George Jones

Hector Guerrero pinned NWA Mid-Atlantic Heavyweight Champion Black Bart

The Barbarian & Shaska Whatley defeated Sam Houston & Nelson Royal

Jimmy Valiant defeated Baron Von Raschke in a pole match

Jimmy Garvin defeated Todd Champion

Manny Fernandez & Ron Garvin fought Ivan Koloff & Krusher Kruschev to a 20-minute time-limit draw
NWA National Heavyweight Champion Tully Blanchard defeated Wahoo McDaniel via disqualification
Baby Doll, Ricky Morton & Robert Gibson defeated Jim Cornette, NWA Tag Team Champions Bobby Eaton & Dennis Condrey
Best of 7 Series for the NWA US Title: Nikita Koloff defeated Magnum TA; Koloff: 2, Magnum: 0
NWA World Champion Ric Flair defeated Road Warrior Animal via disqualification
Dusty Rhodes & Road Warrior Hawk defeated Ole & NWA TV Champion Arn Anderson in a steel cage match when Rhodes pinned Anderson

JCP @ Charleston, WV - Civic Center - July 10, 1986
Denny Brown defeated Thunderfoot
Hector Guerrero defeated Teijo Khan
Ole & NWA TV Champion Arn Anderson defeated Don Kernodle & Italian Stallion
Jimmy Valiant & Manny Fernandez defeated the Barbarian & Pez Whatley
Ron Garvin defeated NWA National Heavyweight Champion Tully Blanchard
Robert Gibson defeated NWA Tag Team Champion Dennis Condrey in a bunkhouse match
Magnum TA & Baby Doll defeated Jim Cornette & NWA Tag Team Champion Bobby Eaton
Wahoo McDaniel defeated Jimmy Garvin
Dusty Rhodes & the Road Warriors defeated Krusher Kruschev, Ivan & Nikita Koloff in a steel cage match
NWA World Champion Ric Flair defeated Ricky Morton

JCP @ Roanoke, VA - Civic Center - July 11, 1986
Arn & Ole Anderson defeated Hector Guerrero & Denny Brown
Robert Gibson defeated NWA Tag Team Champion Dennis Condrey
Jimmy Valiant & Manny Fernandez defeated Pez Whatley & the Barbarian
Wahoo McDaniel defeated Jimmy Garvin in an Indian Death Match
NWA National Heavyweight Champion Tully Blanchard defeated Ron Garvin via count-out
The Road Warriors & Paul Ellering defeated Krusher Kruschev, Ivan Koloff, & Baron Von Raschke
Nikita Koloff defeated Magnum TA
Dusty Rhodes & Baby Doll defeated Jim Cornette & NWA Tag Team Champion Bobby Eaton
NWA World Champion Ric Flair defeated Ricky Morton in a steel cage match

JCP @ Jacksonville, FL - Gator Bowl - July 12, 1986 (10,000)
Ron Garvin defeated NWA National Heavyweight Champion Tully Blanchard
Thunderfoot defeated Ricky Santana

Jimmy Garvin defeated the Italian Stallion
Ole Anderson defeated Hector Guerrero
Magnum TA defeated NWA TV Champion Arn Anderson
Ricky Morton & Robert Gibson defeated NWA Tag Team Champions Bobby Eaton & Dennis Condrey in a non-title match; Jim Cornette was placed in a cage for the duration of the bout
Baby Doll defeated Jim Cornette at the 5-minute mark
Dusty Rhodes defeated NWA World Champion Ric Flair via disqualification
The Road Warriors & Wahoo McDaniel defeated Krusher Kruschev, Ivan & Nikita Koloff in a steel cage match

JCP @ San Antonio, TX - July 13, 1986 (2,500)
Ken Fletcher defeated Ken Johnson
Mr. Ebony defeated Mike Williams
Hector Guerrero defeated Mr. X
Denny Brown fought Steve Regal to a draw
NWA National Heavyweight Champion Tully Blanchard defeated Manny Fernandez via disqualification
Wahoo McDaniel defeated Jimmy Garvin
The Road Warriors defeated NWA Tag Team Champions Bobby Eaton & Dennis Condrey via disqualification
NWA World Champion Ric Flair defeated Magnum TA

JCP @ Cleveland, OH - Stadium - July 13, 1986
Held during a Cleveland Indians game
The Barbarian defeated Todd Champion
Ron Garvin & Sam Houston fought NWA TV Champion Arn Anderson & Krusher Kruschev
Jimmy Valiant defeated Baron Von Raschke
Ricky Morton & Robert Gibson defeated Ivan & Nikita Koloff
Don Kernodle defeated NWA Mid-Atlantic Heavyweight Champion Black Bart

JCP @ Wilmington, NC - Legion Stadium - July 14, 1986 (5,000; sell out)
Dusty Rhodes & Magnum TA defeated NWA Tag Team Champions Bobby Eaton & Dennis Condrey in a non-title match
Ricky Morton vs. NWA World Champion Ric Flair

JCP @ Gaffney, SC - July 15, 1986 (sell out)
TV taping:
Dusty Rhodes & Magnum TA defeated NWA Tag Team Champions Bobby Eaton & Dennis Condrey in a non-title match
Pro - 7/19/86:
Don Kernodle defeated Mark Fleming
Ricky Morton & Robert Gibson vs. the Barbarian & Teijho Khan
Jimmy Garvin & Steve Regal defeated George South & Gene Ligon
Wahoo McDaniel defeated Bill Mulkey
Ole & NWA TV Champion Arn Anderson defeated Mike Simani & Randy Mulkey
NWA Tag Team Champions Bobby Eaton & Dennis Condrey

defeated Hector Guererro & Todd Champion
Krusher Khruschev defeated Rocky Kernodle

Central States @ Kansas City, KS - July 17, 1986
NWA World Champion Ric Flair defeated Cousin Junior

JCP @ Columbia, SC - Township Auditorium - July 17, 1986 (sell out)
TV taping:
Don Kernodle vs. Terror
The Warlord vs. Gene Ligon
Ivan Koloff vs. Todd Champion
NWA National Heavyweight Champion Tully Blanchard vs. Ron Garvin
MACW:
Worldwide:
Dark match: NWA Tag Team Champions Bobby Eaton & Dennis Condrey defeated Dusty Rhodes & Magnum TA via disqualification

JCP @ Richmond, VA - Coliseum - July 18, 1986
Steve Regal defeated the Italian Stallion
Teijo Khan & Pez Whatley defeated Sam Houston & Nelson Royal
Manny Fernandez defeated the Barbarian
Jimmy Garvin defeated Todd Champion
NWA National Heavyweight Champion Tully Blanchard defeated Ron Garvin via disqualification in a taped fist match
Ricky Morton & Robert Gibson fought NWA TV Champion Arn Anderson & Ole Anderson to a draw
Jimmy Valiant defeated Baron Von Raschke
The Road Warriors defeated Nikita Koloff & Krusher Kruschev
Dusty Rhodes, Magnum TA, & Baby Doll defeated Jim Cornette, NWA Tag Team Champions Bobby Eaton & Dennis Condrey
NWA World Champion Ric Flair defeated Wahoo McDaniel

JCP @ Baltimore, MD - Arena - July 19, 1986 (8,500)
Ivan Koloff & Krusher Kruschev defeated Hector Guerrero & Manny Fernandez
Magnum TA defeated Nikita Koloff
Steve Regal defeated Rocky King
The Road Warriors defeated NWA Tag Team Champions Bobby Eaton & Dennis Condrey via disqualification
Wahoo McDaniel defeated Jimmy Garvin
Ron Garvin defeated NWA National Heavyweight Champion Tully Blanchard
Dusty Rhodes, Ricky Morton & Robert Gibson defeated NWA World Champion Ric Flair, Ole & NWA TV Champion Arn Anderson in an elimination match

JCP @ Greenville, SC - Memorial Auditorium - July 20, 1986 (6,000; sell out)
Magnum TA & Baby Doll defeated Jim Cornette & NWA Tag Team Champion Bobby Eaton

Ricky Morton & Robert Gibson vs. NWA World Champion Ric Flair & Ole Anderson

JCP @ Fayetteville, NC - Cumberland County Memorial Arena - July 21, 1986 (sell out)
Hector Guerrero defeated Sam Houston
Ricky Morton defeated Baron Von Raschke in a pole match
Jimmy Valiant & Manny Fernandez defeated Shaska Whatley & the Barbarian
Wahoo McDaniel defeated Jimmy Garvin in a strap match
The Road Warriors defeated Ivan & Nikita Koloff in a steel cage match
Dusty Rhodes, Magnum TA, & Baby Doll defeated Jim Cornette, NWA Tag Team Champions Bobby Eaton & Dennis Condrey in a steel cage match
Ron Garvin defeated NWA National Heavyweight Champion Tully Blanchard in a non-title taped fist match
NWA World Champion Ric Flair defeated Robert Gibson

Quebec City, Quebec - Coliseum - July 22, 1986 (15,297)
Ron Ritchie & Gino Brito Jr. defeated Toshiaki & the Spoiler at 7:04
Dan Kraffat fought Sheik Ali to a draw
Alofa defeated Bob De La Serra at 12:20
Abdullah the Butcher defeated Kareem Muhammad at 15:25
Dino Bravo defeated the Great Samu at 11:45
NWA World Champion Ric Flair fought Rick Martel to a 45-minute time-limit draw
The Road Warriors & Tom Zenk defeated Steve Strong & the Long Riders via disqualification

JCP @ Greenwood, SC - July 22, 1986
TV taping:
Pro - 7/26/86:
Ricky Morton & Robert Gibson defeated Bill & Randy Mulkey
Nikita Koloff defeated Vernon Deaton
Ron Garvin defeated Gene Ligon
The Warlord defeated George South
Don Kernodle defeated Mike Simani
Baron Von Raschke & the Barbarian defeated Sam Houston & Rocky Kernodle
NWA National Heavyweight Champion Tully Blanchard, Arn & Ole Anderson defeated Hector Guerrero, Rocky King, & Denny Brown

JCP @ Johnson City, TN - Freedom Hall - July 23, 1986 (6,000+; sell out)
NWA World Champion Ric Flair defeated Ron Garvin
Dusty Rhodes, Magnum TA, & Baby Doll defeated Jim Cornette, NWA Tag Team Champions Bobby Eaton & Dennis Condrey in a steel cage match

JCP @ Norfolk, VA - Scope - July 25, 1986
Rocky Kernodle & Todd Champion defeated Thunderfoot & Teijo Khan

Ron Garvin & Manny Fernandez defeated Ivan & Nikita Koloff in a Texas Tornado Match

Jimmy Valiant defeated Baron Von Raschke in a pole match

NWA Mid-Atlantic Heavyweight Champion Black Bart defeated Sam Houston in a taped fist match

Denny Brown fought Steve Regal to a draw

Don Kernodle defeated the Barbarian via disqualification

Wahoo McDaniel defeated Jimmy Garvin in an Indian strap match

Baby Doll, Ricky Morton & Robert Gibson defeated Jim Cornette, NWA Tag Team Champions Bobby Eaton & Dennis Condrey

NWA World Champion Ric Flair defeated Magnum TA via disqualification

Dusty Rhodes & the Road Warriors defeated NWA National Heavyweight Champion Tully Blanchard, NWA TV Champion Arn Anderson, & Ole Anderson

JCP @ Greensboro, NC - Coliseum - July 26, 1986 (15,000; sell out)

Steve Regal pinned Sam Houston

NWA Mid-Atlantic Heavyweight Champion Black Bart & Konga the Barbarian defeated Denny Brown & the Italian Stallion when Konga pinned Stallion

Manny Fernandez pinned Baron Von Raschke in a loaded glove on a pole match

Wahoo McDaniel defeated Jimmy Garvin in an Indian strap match

NWA National Heavyweight Champion Tully Blanchard (w/ JJ Dillon) defeated Ron Garvin (w/ Wahoo McDaniel) in a taped fist match via KO in the 4th round after Blanchard hit Garvin with a foreign object, thrown to him moments before by Dillon (*Great American Bash 86*)

Ricky Morton & Robert Gibson defeated fought Ole Anderson & NWA TV Champion Arn Anderson to a 20-minute time-limit draw; Gibson had Arn in a sleeper when the bell rang; after the contest, Gibson made the save by clearing the ring with a steel chair; stipulations stated the winners would be the #1 contenders for the NWA Tag Team Titles (*Great American Bash 86*)

Paul Jones (w/ Baron Von Raschke) pinned Jimmy Valiant after Shaska Whatley hit Valiant with a chair, while the referee was distracted by Manny Fernandez fighting with Von Raschke in the ring, and put Jones on top for the win; stipulations stated the loser would have his head shaved; after the bout, the Italian Stallion, Sam Houston, and Fernandez protested the fall, with Sandy Scott then coming out to look into the controversial finish; after Valiant came to, he himself set up a chair in the ring and let Scott shave his head (*Great American Bash 86*)

Best of 7 Series for the NWA US Championship: Magnum TA pinned Nikita Koloff (w/ Ivan Koloff) at 7:28 with a sunset flip into the ring after referee Tommy Young prevented Koloff from grabbing the ropes for leverage; Magnum: 1, Koloff: 3 (*Great American Bash 86*)

The Road Warriors & Baby Doll defeated Jim Cornette, Bobby Eaton & Dennis Condrey in a steel cage match when Baby Doll pinned Cornette

Dusty Rhodes pinned NWA World Champion Ric Flair with an inside cradle to win the title in a steel cage match at 21:04; after the bout, Ricky Morton & Robert Gibson, Magnum TA, Baby Doll, Ron Garvin, and many others filled the ring to celebrate Rhodes' win (*Great American Bash 86, American Dream: The Dusty Rhodes Story*)

JCP @ Atlanta, GA - WTBS Studios - July 27, 1986 (matinee)
World Championship Wrestling taping

JCP @ Asheville, NC - Civic Center - July 27, 1986 (matinee)
Hector Guerrero vs. Steve Regal

The Italian Stallion vs. the Warlord

Nelson Royal vs. NWA Jr. Heavyweight Champion Denny Brown

Sam Houston vs. NWA Mid-Atlantic Heavyweight Champion Black Bart

Don Kernodle vs. NWA TV Champion Arn Anderson

Jimmy Valiant & Manny Fernandez vs. Shaska Whatley & the Barbarian (bunkhouse match)

Ron Garvin vs. NWA National Heavyweight Champion Tully Blanchard (taped fist match)

JCP @ Dallas, TX - Reunion Arena - July 27, 1986 (10,000)
Debut at the venue
Ricky Morton & Robert Gibson fought NWA Tag Team Champions Bobby Eaton & Dennis Condrey to a 20-minute time-limit draw

NWA World Champion Dusty Rhodes vs. Ric Flair

JCP @ Wilmington, NC - Legion Stadium - July 28, 1986 (2,000)
Thunderfoot vs. the Warlord

Don Kernodle vs. NWA Mid Atlantic Heavyweight Champion Black Bart

Todd Champion vs, Nikita Koloff

Ricky Morton & Robert Gibson vs. National Tag Team Champions Ole Anderson & NWA TV Champion Arn Anderson

NWA Tag Team Champions Bobby Eaton & Dennis Condrey defeated Dusty Rhodes & Magnum TA via disqualification

WRESTLING
WINTHROP COLISEUM
TUESDAY, JULY 29
7:30 PM-TV TAPING
FEATURING

Rock & Roll Express & DUSTY RHODES

VS
- **Ole Anderson**
- **Arne Anderson**
- **Tully Blanchard**

—PLUS—
- **Gorgeous Jimmy Garvin**
- **Wahoo McDaniel**
- **Ivan & Nikita Koloff**
- **Shaska Whatley**
- **Ron Garvin**
- **Magnum T.A.**
- **Midnight Express**
- **Baron Von Raschke**
- **Jimmy Vallant**
- **Barbarian**
- **Ragin' Bull**

Ticket Information 329-0440
ADVANCE TICKET LOCATIONS

JCP @ Rock Hill, SC - Winthrop Coliseum - July 29, 1986
TV taping:
Ron Garvin & Wahoo McDaniel defeated Randy & Bill Mulkey
Ricky Morton & Robert Gibson defeated George South & Ben Alexander
Nikita Koloff defeated Mark Fleming
Jimmy Garvin pinned Gene Ligon
Buddy Landell defeated Rocky King via submission
NWA National Heavyweight Champion Tully Blanchard pinned Vernon Deaton
NWA TV Champion Arn Anderson & Ole Anderson defeated Mike Simani & Rocky Kernodle
NWA Tag Team Champions Bobby Eaton & Dennis Condrey defeated the Italian Stallion & Rocky Kernodle
Ivan Koloff & Krusher Kruschev defeated Ron Rossi & Randy Mulkey
The Warlord pinned Mark Fleming
Buddy Landell defeated George South via submission
Todd Champion pinned Vernon Deaton

Magnum TA pinned Thunderfoot
Ricky Morton & Robert Gibson defeated NWA TV Champion Arn Anderson & Ole Anderson via disqualification
Dusty Rhodes, Ricky Morton & Robert Gibson defeated NWA National Heavyweight Champion Tully Blanchard, NWA TV Champion Arn Anderson, & Ole Anderson

JCP @ Raleigh, NC - Dorton Arena - July 30, 1986
Manny Fernandez fought Jimmy Garvin to a draw
Don Kernodle defeated NWA Mid-Atlantic Heavyweight Champion Black Bart via disqualification
Steve Regal defeated the Italian Stallion
The Warlord defeated Mark Fleming
Todd Champion defeated Thunderfoot
NWA National Heavyweight Champion Tully Blanchard, NWA TV Champion Arn Anderson, & Ole Anderson defeated Magnum TA, Ricky Morton & Robert Gibson
NWA Tag Team Champions Bobby Eaton & Dennis Condrey defeated Wahoo McDaniel & Ron Garvin

JCP @ Columbia, SC - Township Auditorium - July 31, 1986
Denny Brown vs. Rocky King
The Warlord vs. Teijo Khan
Ron Garvin fought NWA Tag Team Champion Dennis Condrey to a 30-minute time-limit draw
Wahoo McDaniel vs. Steve Regal (Indian strap match)
Magnum TA & Baby Doll defeated Jim Cornette & NWA Tag Team Champion Bobby Eaton

Central States @ Kansas City, KS - Memorial Hall - August 7, 1986
All Star Wrestling: NWA World Champion Dusty Rhodes defeated Ric Flair via disqualification at 15:57 when the referee, who was knocked to the floor moments earlier, saw Flair hit Rhodes with a steel chair; after the contest, Flair continued to assault Rhodes with the chair and rammed him into the ringside barrier; after the decision was announced, Flair took the mic and said he would continue to dog Rhodes until he got his belt back or Rhodes was six feet under; moments later, Flair was interviewed at ringside, with Flair saying he and Rhodes had only just begun

JCP @ San Antonio, TX - August 1, 1986
Baby Doll, Ricky Morton & Robert Gibson defeated Jim Cornette, NWA Tag Team Champions Bobby Eaton & Dennis Condrey

World Championship Wrestling - 8/2/86:
Krusher Kruschev, Ivan & Nikita Koloff vs. Randy Barber, Mike Simani, & Vernon Deaton
Bobby Eaton & Dennis Condrey vs. the Road Warriors
Ron Garvin vs. NWA Mid-Atlantic Heavyweight Champion Black Bart

Buddy Landell vs. George South
Dick Murdoch vs. Bill Mulkey

JCP @ Atlanta, GA - Fulton County Stadium - August 2, 1986 (12,000)
The end of the Great American Bash tour - all kids tickets were $5
Steve Regal defeated NWA Jr. Heavyweight Champion Denny Brown to win the title
Don Kernodle defeated the Barbarian
Baron Von Raschke, Ivan Koloff, & Krusher Kruschev defeated Manny Fernandez, Todd Champion, & Sam Houston
Jimmy Valiant defeated Shaska Whatley
Wahoo McDaniel defeated Jimmy Garvin
Magnum TA defeated Nikita Koloff
NWA National Heavyweight Champion Tully Blanchard defeated Ron Garvin in a brass knuckles match
Ricky Morton & Robert Gibson defeated Ole & NWA TV Champion Arn Anderson
The Road Warriors & Baby Doll defeated Jim Cornette, NWA Tag Team Champions Bobby Eaton & Dennis Condrey
NWA World Champion Dusty Rhodes defeated Ric Flair

JCP @ Greenville, SC - Memorial Auditorium - August 3, 1986
TV taping

Central States @ Kansas City, KS - August 7, 1986
Moondog Moretti defeated John Paul Demann
DJ Peterson defeated Mike George
Joe Lightfoot & Billy Two Eagles defeated the Masked Ape Man & Bob Owens
Sam Houston vs. Buddy Landell
Giant Baba & Hiroshi Wajima defeated JR Hogg & Earthquake Ferris
Rufus R. Jones defeated Butch Reed
NWA World Champion Dusty Rhodes defeated Ric Flair in a No DQ match at 18:52

JCP @ Richmond, VA - Coliseum - August 8, 1986
Bill Dundee defeated Denny Brown
NWA Tag Team Champion Dennis Condrey defeated Mark Fleming
Buddy Landell defeated the Italian Stallion
Dick Murdoch defeated Krusher Kruschev
Ron Garvin defeated Pez Whatley
Wahoo McDaniel defeated NWA Tag Team Champion Dennis Condrey
NWA Tag Team Champion Bobby Eaton defeated the Warlord
Magnum TA fought Nikita Koloff to a no contest

Central States @ St. Joseph, MO - Civic Arena - August 8, 1986
Joe Lightfoot & Billy Two Eagles defeated Moondog Moretti & Earthquake Ferris

DJ Peterson defeated Bob Brown
Rufus R. Jones defeated Butch Reed
NWA World Champion Dusty Rhodes defeated Ric Flair

JCP @ Atlanta, GA - WTBS Studios - August 9, 1986 (matinee)
World Championship Wrestling - 8/9/86:
Dutch Mantell & Bobby Jaggers vs. Bill Mulkey & Pat Myers
Jimmy Valiant vs. Tony Zane
The Warlord vs. George South
Nikita Koloff & Krusher Kruschev vs. Bill Bryant & Bill Tabb
Dick Murdoch vs. Vernon Deaton
Wahoo McDaniel & Sam Houston vs. Thunderfoot & NWA Mid-Atlantic Heavyweight Champion Black Bart
Rocky King vs. NWA Jr. Heavyweight Champion Steve Regal
NWA Tag Team Champions Bobby Eaton & Dennis Condrey vs. Darrin Evans & Tom Pittman
Ricky Morton & Robert Gibson vs. Pablo Crenshaw & Bob Burroughs
Buddy Landell vs. Randy Barber

JCP @ St. Louis, MO - Arena - August 9, 1986 (6,300)
Cousin Junior defeated Bob Owens
Rick McCord defeated Ron Powers
NWA National Heavyweight Champion Tully Blanchard defeated Sam Houston
Wahoo McDaniel defeated Jimmy Garvin in an Indian strap match
Ric Flair pinned NWA World Champion Dusty Rhodes (w/ Magnum TA) to win the title with a clip to the knee and applying the figure-4 for nearly 2 full minutes; after the bout, Magnum tended to Rhodes in the ring while NWA National Heavyweight Champion Tully Blanchard came ringside to congratulate Flair
Magnum TA, Dick Murdoch, & Baby Doll defeated Jim Cornette, NWA Tag Team Champions Bobby Eaton & Dennis Condrey in a steel cage match

JCP @ Asheville, NC - Civic Center - August 10, 1986
Included Ricky Morton & Robert Gibson in concert
Bill Dundee defeated the Italian Stallion
Buddy Landell defeated Rocky King
NWA Tag Team Champions Bobby Eaton & Dennis Condrey fought Dutch Mantell & Bobby Jaggers to a 20-minute time-limit draw
The Warlord defeated Big Bubba via disqualification
Jimmy Valiant defeated Paul Jones
Best of 7 Series: Magnum TA defeated Nikita Koloff
Dick Murdoch, Ricky Morton & Robert Gibson defeated NWA National Heavyweight Champion Tully Blanchard, NWA TV Champion Arn Anderson, & Ole Anderson
NWA World Champion Ric Flair defeated Dusty Rhodes via disqualification

JCP @ Camp Lejeune, NC - Goettge Fieldhouse - August 11, 1986 (3,500)

The Barbarian defeated the Italian Stallion
NWA Jr. Heavyweight Champion Denny Brown vs. Hector Guerrero
NWA Mid-Atlantic Heavyweight Champion Black Bart vs. Todd Champion
Dutch Mantell & Bobby Jaggers fought Ivan Koloff & Krusher Khruschev to a draw
Manny Fernandez vs. Baron Von Raschke
Ron Garvin defeated Nikita Koloff

JCP @ Greenville, SC - Memorial Auditorium - August 11, 1986
NWA Tag Team Champions Bobby Eaton & Dennis Condrey fought Ricky Morton & Robert Gibson to a 45-minute time-limit draw
NWA World Champion Ric Flair vs. Dusty Rhodes

JCP @ Spartanburg, SC - Memorial Auditorium - August 12, 1986
The Warlord vs. Teijo Khan
Sam Houston vs. NWA Mid-Atlantic Heavyweight Champion Black Bart
Dutch Mantell & Bobby Jaggers vs. Baron Von Raschke & the Barbarian
Jimmy Valiant vs. Paul Jones (lumberjack match)
Wahoo McDaniel & Dick Murdoch vs. Ivan Koloff & Krusher Kruschev
Magnum TA and Ricky Morton & Robert Gibson vs. NWA National Heavyweight Champion Tully Blanchard, NWA TV Champion Arn Anderson, and Ole Anderson (elimination match)

CWF @ Tampa, FL - August 12, 1986
Sean Royal defeated Chris Champion
The White Ninja defeated Mark Starr
Kendo Nagasaki defeated Tyree Pride
Kendall Windham defeated Ron Bass via disqualification
Stan Lane & Steve Keirn defeated Tatsumi Fujinami & Kendo Kimura
Southern Champion Lex Luger defeated Ed Ganter via disqualification
NWA World Champion Ric Flair defeated Barry Windham via disqualification

JCP @ Raleigh, NC - Dorton Arena - August 13, 1986 (8,000)
Bill Dundee defeated the Italian Stallion
Buddy Landell defeated Sam Houston
Jimmy Garvin defeated Todd Champion
Dick Murdoch & Don Kernodle defeated Ivan Koloff & Krusher Kruschev via disqualification
NWA National Heavyweight Champion Tully Blanchard defeated Wahoo McDaniel in a No DQ match
Magnum TA fought NWA TV Champion Arn Anderson to a draw
NWA Tag Team Champions Bobby Eaton & Dennis Condrey

defeated Ricky Morton & Robert Gibson
NWA World Champion Ric Flair defeated Dusty Rhodes via disqualification

CWF @ Ft. Lauderdale, FL - August 13, 1986
The Cuban Assassin defeated Steve Collins
Tyree Pride defeated Chris Champion via count-out
Sean Royal defeated the White Ninja
Kendall Windham defeated Ron Bass via disqualification
Barry Windham & Lex Luger defeated Kareem Muhammad & Ed Gantner in a steel cage match
Kendo Nagasaki defeated Stan Lane
NWA World Champion Ric Flair fought Steve Keirn to a double count-out

JCP @ Albany, GA - Civic Center - August 14, 1986
Denny Brown vs. Ricky Lee Jones
Todd Champion vs. NWA Mid-Atlantic Heavyweight Champion Black Bart
Hector Guerrero vs. Baron Von Raschke
Dutch Mantel & Bobby Jaggers vs. the Barbarian & Shaska Whatley
Jimmy Valiant vs. Paul Jones (lumberjack match)
NWA Tag Team Champions Bobby Eaton & Dennis Condrey defeated Ron Garvin & Manny Fernandez via disqualification

JCP @ Charleston, SC - Arthur Ravenel Stadium- August 15, 1986
Hector Guerrero vs. Tony Zane
Denny Brown vs. Thunderfoot
NWA Jr. Heavyweight Champion Steve Regal vs. Ricky Lee Jones
NWA Mid-Atlantic Heavyweight Champion Black Bart vs. the Warlord
Dutch Mantel & Bobby Jaggers vs. the Barbarian & Teijo Khan
Manny Fernandez vs. Shaska Whatley (Mexican death match)
Jimmy Valiant vs. Paul Jones

JCP @ Columbia, SC - Township Auditorium - August 15, 1986
Bill Dundee vs. the Italian Stallion
Sam Houston vs. Buddy Landell
Todd Champion vs. Baron Von Raschke
Dick Murdoch vs. Ivan Koloff
Wahoo McDaniel & Ron Garvin vs. Nikita Koloff & Krusher Kruschev
Dusty Rhodes, Magnum TA, Ricky Morton & Robert Gibson vs. NWA World Champion Ric Flair, NWA National Heavyweight Champion Tully Blanchard, NWA TV Champion Arn Anderson, & Ole Anderson

JCP @ Hays, NC - August 15, 1986
NWA Tag Team Champions Bobby Eaton & Dennis Condrey defeated Manny Fernandez & Hector Guerrero

JCP @ Atlanta, GA - WTBS Studios - August 16, 1986 (matinee)
World Championship Wrestling - 8/16/86:
Dutch Mantell & Bobby Jaggers defeated George South & Bill Mulkey
The Road Warriors defeated Pablo Crenshaw & Tom Pittman
Bill Dundee defeated Vernon Deaton
NWA National Heavyweight Champion Tully Blanchard, Ole & NWA TV Champion Arn Anderson defeated Sam Houston, Todd Champion, & the Italian Stallion
Dick Murdoch defeated Tony Zane
Krusher Kruschev, Ivan & Nikita Koloff defeated Randy Barber, Clement Fields, & Paul Garner
Ricky Morton & Robert Gibson defeated Bill Tabb & Art Pritts
World Championship Wrestling - 8/23/86:
Ricky Morton & Robert Gibson vs. Mike Rose & Phil Brown
NWA National Heavyweight Champion Tully Blanchard, Ole & NWA TV Champion Arn Anderson vs. Fields, Garner, & Bill Tabb
Magnum TA vs. Art Pritts
The Road Warriors vs. Lee Peek & Kent Glover
Bobby Eaton & Dennis Condrey vs. the Mulkeys
Wahoo McDaniel vs. Randy Barber

JCP @ Atlanta, GA - Omni - August 16, 1986 (2,800)
The Warlord defeated the Barbarian via disqualification
Manny Fernandez defeated Teijo Khan
Bill Dundee defeated Sam Houston
Buddy Landell defeated Todd Champion
Jimmy Valiant defeated Paul Jones
The Road Warriors & Paul Ellering defeated NWA National Heavyweight Champion Tully Blanchard, Ole & NWA TV Champion Arn Anderson in an elimination match
NWA World Champion Ric Flair defeated Dusty Rhodes via disqualification in a Best 2 out of 3 falls match

JCP @ Philadelphia, PA - Civic Center - August 16, 1986 (7,000)
Dick Murdoch defeated Steve Regal
Wahoo McDaniel pinned Baron Von Raschke
Ivan Koloff & Krusher Kruschev defeated Dutch Mantell & Bobby Jaggers
Ricky Morton & Robert Gibson defeated NWA Tag Team Champions Bobby Eaton & Dennis Condrey in a Best 2 out of 3 falls match to win the titles, 2-1; fall #1: Gibson pinned Eaton at 10:30 with an inside cradle as Eaton attempted a backdrop; fall #2: Condrey pinned Gibson at 1:29 following two backbreakers after Eaton pulled down the top rope behind the referee's back, causing Gibson to fall out to the floor; fall #3: Morton pinned Condrey at 6:13 by reversing a bodyslam into the ring into a cradle (*Wrestling Rarities: The Midnight Express*)
NWA US Championship Best of 7 Series - Match 7: Magnum TA fought Nikita Koloff to a no contest; Nikita: 3, Magnum: 3; Bob Geigel was the guest referee for the bout

JCP @ Huntington, WV - August 17, 1986 (matinee)
Dusty Rhodes, Magnum TA, & Baby Doll defeated Jim Cornette, Bobby Eaton & Dennis Condrey in a steel cage match

JCP @ Charlotte, NC - Coliseum - August 17, 1986 (11,000+; sell out)
TV taping:
Pro:
Worldwide - 8/23/86
NWA Tag Team Champions Ricky Morton & Robert Gibson defeated Bobby Eaton & Dennis Condrey via disqualification
NWA World Champion Ric Flair defeated Dusty Rhodes (w/ Baby Doll) via disqualification when, after Rhodes took a steel chair away from an interfering Baby Doll as referee Tommy Young was on the floor, Rhodes assaulted Flair with the chair; late in the bout, Baby Doll put Flair's foot on the bottom rope as Rhodes made the cover following a clothesline and later helped Flair grab the ropes after Rhodes reversed the figure-4; after the match, NWA National Heavyweight Champion Tully Blanchard assaulted Rhodes with the chair until Magnum TA, NWA Tag Team Champions Ricky Morton & Robert Gibson made the save, with Flair, Blanchard, and Baby Doll then leaving ringside together
NWA US Championship Best of 7 Series - Match 7: Nikita Koloff defeated Magnum TA to win the title; Nikita: 4, Magnum: 3

JCP @ Fayetteville, NC - Cumberland County Civic Center - August 18, 1986
NWA Tag Team Champions Ricky Morton & Robert Gibson defeated Bobby Eaton & Dennis Condrey via disqualification

JPC @ Norfolk, VA - Scope - August 18, 1986
Bill Dundee defeated the Italian Stallion
Buddy Landell defeated Sam Houston
The Warlord defeated Thunderfoot
Dick Murdoch & Don Kernodle defeated Ivan Koloff & Krusher Kruschev
NWA US Champion Nikita Koloff defeated Wahoo McDaniel
Dusty Rhodes, Magnum TA, NWA Tag Team Champions Ricky Morton & Robert Gibson defeated NWA World Champion Ric Flair, NWA National Heavyweight Champion Tully Blanchard, NWA TV Champion Arn Anderson, & Ole Anderson

JCP @ Indianapolis, IN - State Fair Coliseum - August 20, 1986
Sam Houston vs. the Barbarian
Todd Champion vs. Jimmy Garvin
Jimmy Valiant vs. Shaska Whatley
Manny Fernandez vs. NWA TV Champion Arn Anderson
Wahoo McDaniel vs. NWA National Heavyweight Champion Tully Blanchard
Magnum TA vs. NWA US Champion Nikita Koloff
NWA Tag Team Champions Ricky Morton & Robert Gibson

defeated Bobby Eaton & Dennis Condrey
NWA World Champion Ric Flair vs. Dusty Rhodes

JCP @ Cincinnati, OH - Riverfront Coliseum - August 21, 1986
Steve Regal defeated Denny Brown
Krusher Kruschev defeated the Italian Stallion
Ivan Koloff defeated the Warlord
Jimmy Garvin defeated Todd Champion
Ron Garvin defeated NWA US Champion Nikita Koloff
Ricky Morton & Robert Gibson fought NWA TV Champion Arn Anderson & Ole Anderson to a draw
NWA National Heavyweight Champion Tully Blanchard defeated Wahoo McDaniel
Bobby Eaton & Dennis Condrey defeated Dusty Rhodes & Magnum TA via disqualification

JCP @ Hampton, VA - Coliseum - August 22, 1986 (5,000)
Todd Champion fought the Italian Stallion to a draw
Bobby Jaggers & Dutch Mantell defeated the Barbarian & Teijo Khan
Ivan Koloff defeated the Warlord
Wahoo McDaniel & Manny Fernandez defeated Bobby Eaton & Dennis Condrey via disqualification
Jimmy Valiant defeated Shaska Whatley in a bunkhouse match
Magnum TA defeated NWA US Champion Nikita Koloff in a non-title Texas Death match
Dusty Rhodes defeated Big Bubba in a steel cage match

JCP @ Charleston, SC - County Hall - August 22, 1986
Buddy Landell defeated Rocky King
Steve Regal defeated Denny Brown
Krusher Kruschev defeated Rocky King
Jimmy Garvin defeated Don Kernodle
NWA National Heavyweight Champion Tully Blanchard defeated Ron Garvin
NWA TV Champion Arn Anderson & Ole Anderson defeated NWA Tag Team Champions Ricky Morton & Robert Gibson

JCP @ Cleveland, OH - Convocation Center - August 23, 1986
Buddy Landell defeated Denny Brown
Krusher Kruschev fought Ron Garvin to a no contest
Dick Murdoch defeated Ivan Koloff
Dutch Mantell & Bobby Jaggers defeated the Barbarian & Shaska Whatley
Jimmy Valiant defeated Paul Jones
Paul Ellering & the Road Warriors defeated Jim Cornette, Bobby Eaton & Dennis Condrey
Magnum TA defeated Nikita Koloff
Dusty Rhodes defeated Big Bubba in a steel cage match

JCP @ Asheville, NC - Civic Center - August 24, 1986 (matinee)
Bill Dundee defeated Rocky King

Buddy Landell defeated Todd Champion
Dennis Condrey defeated the Warlord
Wahoo McDaniel defeated Bobby Eaton
Ron Garvin defeated NWA US Champion Nikita Koloff
Magnum TA, Dick Murdoch, NWA Tag Team Chapions Ricky Morton & Robert Gibson defeated NWA National Heavyweight Champion Tully Blanchard, JJ Dillon, NWA TV Champion Arn Anderson, & Ole Anderson
Dusty Rhodes defeated Big Bubba in a steel cage match

JCP @ Roanoke, VA - Civic Center - August 24, 1986
Ricky Lee Jones vs. NWA Mid-Atlantic Heavyweight Champion Black Bart
Sam Houston vs. Steve Regal
Bobby Jaggers & Dutch Mantel vs. Ivan Koloff & Krusher Kruschev
Denny Brown vs. Jimmy Garvin
Bobby Eaton & Dennis Condrey defeated Manny Fernandez & Hector Guerrero
Wahoo McDaniel vs. NWA US Champion Nikita Koloff
Magnum TA, Dick Murdoch, NWA Tag Team Champions Ricky Morton & Robert Gibson vs. NWA National Heavyweight Champion Tully Blanchard, NWA TV Champion Arn Anderson, Ole Anderson, & JJ Dillon

JCP @ Greenville, SC - Memorial Auditorium - August 25, 1986
Steve Regal defeated George South
Hector Guerrero defeated Denny Brown
NWA Mid-Atlantic Champion Black Bart defeated Nelson Royal
Shaska Whatley defeated Sam Houston
Jimmy Garvin defeated Don Kernodle
Jimmy Valiant defeated Paul Jones in a lumberjack match
NWA Tag Team Champions Ricky Morton & Robert Gibson defeated Bobby Eaton & Dennis Condrey in a Best 2 out of 3 falls match; fall #3: Morton & Gibson won via disqualification

WRESTLING
WINTHROP COLISEUM
TUESDAY AUG. 26, 1986
TV TAPING

First Time For 8 Man Tag
TEAM IN THIS AREA

RIC FLAIR & **DUSTY RHODES**
ARN ANDERSON | **MAGNUM T.A.**
TULLY BLANCHARD | **Rock & Roll**
J.J. DILLON | **Express**

Other Big Matches Featuring:
Jimmy Valiant **Midnight Express**
Wahoo McDaniel **Ron Garvin**
Ivan Koloff **Nikita Koloff**
Krusher Krushchev
Kansas Jayhawks
Shaska Whatley
Barbarian

Join us for the live taping of N.W.A. Pro Wrestling & World Wide Wrestling

Ticket Information 329-0440
ADVANCE TICKET LOCATIONS

WINTHROP COLISEUM
MR. SPORT (ROCK HILL MALL)
VIDEO CENTER (FORT MILL)
VIDEO CONNECTION (YORK)
BLACK'S DRUG STORE (CHESTER)
FRIENDLY GRILL

JCP @ Rock Hill, SC - Winthrop Coliseum - August 26, 1986
TV taping:
Sam Houston pinned Vernon Deaton
George South & Rocky King defeated Randy & Bill Mulkey
The Italian Stallion defeated Tony Zane
Bobby Jaggers & Dutch Mantell defeated Thunderfoot & Mark Fleming
Ricky Morton & Robert Gibson defeated Bill Mulkey & Ron Rossi
Magnum TA pinned Jack Jackson
Manny Fernandez defeated Vernon Deaton
Baron Von Raschke defeated George South via submission
Wahoo McDaniel & Ron Garvin defeated Tony Zane & Colt Steele
NWA World Champion Ric Flair defeated Rocky Kernodle
The Warlord pinned Ron Rossi
Bobby Eaton & Dennis Condrey defeated Vernon Deaton & Bill Mulkey
Jimmy Garvin pinned Mitch Snow
Shaska Whatley pinned George South
NWA TV Champion Arn Anderson pinned Keith Patterson
NWA National Heavyweight Champion Tully Blanchard pinned Rocky Kernodle
Ivan Koloff & Krusher Kruschev defeated Jack Jackson & Todd Champion
Nikita Koloff defeated Sam Houston
Dusty Rhodes, Magnum TA, Ricky Morton & Robert Gibson defeated NWA World Champion Ric Flair, NWA TV Champion Arn Anderson, NWA National Heavyweight Champion Tully Blanchard, & JJ Dillon

JCP @ Inglewood, CA - Great Western Forum - August 28, 1986 (10,000)
Debut at the venue; Tony Schiavone was the ring announcer
Hector Guerrero pinned the Barbarian with a victory roll
Jimmy Valiant defeated Shaska Whatley in a streetfight
Wahoo McDaniel pinned NWA National Heavyweight Champion Tully Blanchard to win the title with a chop
Dick Murdoch fought NWA TV Champion Arn Anderson to a 20-minute time-limit draw; Murdoch drove Anderson to the mat with a knee to his back just before the bell rang
The Road Warriors defeated Ivan Koloff & Krusher Kruschev in a double Russian chain match when Road Warrior Animal pinned Koloff after Koloff became crotched on the top rope
Magnum TA fought NWA US Champion Nikita Koloff to a no contest
NWA Tag Team Champions Ricky Morton & Robert Gibson defeated Bobby Eaton & Dennis Condrey
NWA World Champion Ric Flair defeated Dusty Rhodes via disqualification

JCP @ Macon, GA - Coliseum - August 29, 1986
The Warlord fought Big Bubba to a double count-out in a streetfight

Continental @ Knoxville, TN - August 29, 1986
NWA World Champion Ric Flair vs. the Bullet

JCP @ Norfolk, VA - Scope - August 29, 1986
Denny Brown defeated Mark Fleming
Bill Dundee defeated the Italian Stallion
Buddy Landell defeated Hector Guerrero
Manny Fernandez defeated Baron Von Raschke in a Texas
Death Match
Jimmy Valiant defeated Paul Jones in a lumberjack match
Magnum TA fought NWA US Champion Nikita Koloff to a no
contest
NWA Tag Team Champions Ricky Morton & Robert Gibson
fought Bobby Eaton & Dennis Condrey to a no contest

**JCP @ Atlanta, GA - WTBS Studios - August 30, 1986
(matinee)**
World Championship Wrestling - 8/30/86:
Dick Murdoch vs. Mike Rose
Dutch Mantell & Bobby Jaggers vs. Randy Barber & Alan
Martin
NWA National Heavyweight Champion Wahoo McDaniel vs.
Tony Zane
Sam Houston vs. Jack Weathers
Ricky Morton & Robert Gibson vs. Phil Brown & Lee Peek
Bill Dundee & Buddy Landell vs. Rocky Johnson & Vernon
Deaton
Jimmy Garvin vs. Rocky Kernodle
Jimmy Valiant vs. Art Pritts
Ole & NWA TV Champion Arn Anderson vs. Henry Rutley &
the Italian Stallion
NWA World Champion Ric Flair vs. Mike Jackson
Nikita Koloff vs. Dave Spencer
Baron Von Raschke, Shaska Whatley, & Teijho Khan vs.
Johnnie Cook, Charles Freeman, & Mark Cooper
*World Championship Wrestling Sunday Edition - 8/31/86 -
debut episode*

JCP @ Greensboro, NC - Coliseum - August 30, 1986
Nelson Royal defeated Sam Houston
Bill Dundee defeated Mark Fleming
Don Kernodle defeated NWA Mid-Atlantic Heavyweight
Champion Black Bart
Buddy Landell defeated Hector Guerrero
Big Bubba defeated the Warlord via count-out in a streetfight
NWA National Heavyweight Champion Wahoo McDaniel &
Dick Murdoch defeated Bobby Eaton & Dennis Condrey via
disqualification
Dusty Rhodes, Magnum TA, NWA Tag Team Champions
Ricky Morton & Robert Gibson defeated NWA World
Champion Ric Flair, Tully Blanchard, NWA TV Champion Arn
Anderson, & Ole Anderson

**JCP @ Atlanta, GA - WTBS Studios - August 31, 1986
(matinee)**
World Championship Wrestling - 9/6/86:

Buddy Landell & Bill Dundee vs. Rocky King & Johnnie Cook
Ron Garvin & Dick Murdoch vs. Brodie Chase & Alan Martin
NWA National Heavyweight Champion Wahoo McDaniel vs.
Lee Peek
Ricky Morton & Robert Gibson vs. two unknowns
The Road Warriors vs. Art Pritts & Darrin Evans
Dutch Mantell & Bobby Jaggers defeated Ole Anderson &
NWA TV Champion Arn Anderson via disqualification
NWA US Champion Nikita Koloff vs. Randy Barber
Tully Blanchard & Jimmy Garvin vs. two unknowns
The Warlord vs. Jack Weathers
World Championship Wrestling Sunday Edition - 9/6/86:
NWA Tag Team Champions Ricky Morton & Robert Gibson
defeated Bobby Eaton & Dennis Condrey (w/ Jim Cornette &
Big Bubba) via reverse decision after the 20-minute mark;
Eaton & Condrey originally won the match and titles but the
decision was changed because Condrey hit Gibson with Jim
Cornette's tennis racquet; after the bout, Bubba attacked
Morton until Dusty Rhodes made the save

JCP @ Atlanta, GA - Omni - August 31, 1986 (matinee)
Dusty Rhodes defeated Big Bubba in a steel cage match

**JCP @ Charlotte, NC - Coliseum - August 31, 1986 (11,500;
sell out)**
NWA National Heavyweight Champion Wahoo McDaniel & the
Road Warriors vs. Tully Blanchard, Ole & NWA TV Champion
Arn Anderson
NWA Tag Team Champions Ricky Morton & Robert Gibson
defeated Bobby Eaton & Dennis Condrey via reverse decision
NWA US Champion Nikita Koloff vs. Ron Garvin
NWA World Champion Ric Flair vs. Dick Murdoch
Dusty Rhodes defeated Big Bubba in a Louisville streetfight
steel cage match

JCP @ Fayetteville, NC - September 1, 1986
NWA Mid-Atlantic Heavyweight Champion Black Bart defeated
Rocky Kernodle
Nelson Royal defeated Thunderfoot #1
The Warlord defeated Thunderfoot #2
NWA TV Champion Arn Anderson defeated Todd Champion
Bobby Eaton & Dennis Condrey defeated Bobby Jaggers &
Dutch Mantell
Magnum TA defeated Jimmy Garvin
Dusty Rhodes defeated Big Bubba in a streetfight

**JCP @ Greenville, SC - Memorial Auditorium - September
1, 1986**
Rocky King defeated George South
Misty Blue defeated Linda Dallas
Denny Brown defeated NWA Jr. Heavyweight Champion Steve
Regal to win the title
Buddy Landell defeated Don Kernodle
Ivan Koloff & Krusher Kruschev defeated Manny Fernandez &
Hector Guerrero
NWA US Champion Nikita Koloff defeated NWA National

Heavyweight Champion Wahoo McDaniel
Ron Garvin defeated Tully Blanchard in a lights out Texas barbedwire steel cage match)

CWF Battle of the Belts III - Daytona Beach, FL - Ocean Center - September 1, 1986 (8,000)
Jimmy Backlund pinned Bob Cook
Tyree Pride pinned the Cuban Assassin at 15:20
US Tag Team Champions Stan Lane & Steve Keirn defeated the Sheepherders at 7:45 when Lane pinned Butch Williams
The White Ninja pinned US Jr. Heavyweight Champion Tim Horner to win the title at the 11-minute mark; the belt was later returned to Horner due to outside interference
AWA World Champion Nick Bockwinkel defeated Kendo Nagasaki via disqualification at the 7-minute mark
The Road Warriors fought Ed Gantner & Kareem Muhammad to a double disqualification
Kendall Windham defeated Bahamas Champion Chris Champion via disqualification
NWA World Champion Ric Flair fought Lex Luger to a draw in a Best 2 out of 3 falls match; fall #1: Flair pinned Luger at 12:07; fall #2: Luger pinned Flair at 14:40; fall #3: the time limit expired at 34:40
Barry Windham pinned Florida Heavyweight Champion Ron Bass to win the title

JCP @ Spartanburg, SC - Memorial Auditorium - September 2, 1986
TV taping:
Featured Jimmy Garvin bloodying Magnum TA
Ron Garvin defeated NWA Mid-Atlantic Heavyweight Champion Black Bart to win the title
Magnum TA, NWA National Heavyweight Champion Wahoo McDaniel, & NWA Mid-Atlantic Heavyweight Champion Ron Garvin vs. NWA US Champion Nikita Koloff, Ivan Koloff, & Krusher Kruschev
Also included a women's match, NWA World Champion Ric Flair, NWA TV Champion Arn Anderson, Tully Blanchard, Dusty Rhodes, Bobby Eaton & Dennis Condrey, Jimmy Valiant, Manny Fernandez, Dutch Mantell & Bobby Jaggers, the Warlord, Buddy Landell, and Bill Dundee

JCP @ Raleigh, NC - Dorton Arena - September 3, 1986 (7,000)
Krusher Kruschev pinned the Warlord
Bobby Eaton & Dennis Condrey defeated Dutch Mantell & Bobby Jaggers
Buddy Landell pinned Hector Guerrero
Jimmy Valiant pinned Jimmy Garvin
Tully Blanchard pinned NWA Mid-Atlantic Heavyweight Champion Ron Garvin
NWA US Champion Nikita Koloff fought NWA National Heavyweight Champion Wahoo McDaniel to a double count-out
NWA World Champion Ric Flair pinned Magnum TA
Dusty Rhodes defeated Big Bubba in a steel cage match

JCP @ Cincinnati, OH - Cincinnati Gardens - September 4, 1986
Misty Blue vs. Linda Dallas
Black Bart vs. Todd Champion
Buddy Landell vs. Jimmy Valiant
Bobby Jaggers & Dutch Mantell vs. Ivan Koloff & Krusher Kruschev
Magnum TA vs. NWA US Champion Nikita Koloff
Dusty Rhodes & the Road Warriors vs. NWA World Champion Ric Flair, Tully Blanchard, & Ole Anderson

JCP @ Albany, GA - Civic Center - September 4, 1986
Hector Guerrero vs. Steve Regal
Denny Brown vs. Teijo Khan
The Barbarian vs. Don Kernodle
Sam Houston vs. Shaska Whatley
Big Bubba defeated the Warlord via count-out
Manny Fernandez vs. Jimmy Garvin
NWA National Heavyweight Champion Wahoo McDaniel & NWA Mid-Atlantic Heavyweight Champion Ron Garvin defeated Bobby Eaton & Dennis Condrey via disqualification

JCP @ Richmond, VA - Coliseum - September 5, 1986 (4,500)
Denny Brown defeated Mark Fleming
The Italian Stallion defeated George South
Misty Blue defeated Linda Dallas
Shaska Whatley defeated Todd Champion
Bobby Eaton & Dennis Condrey defeated Dutch Mantell & Bobby Jaggers
Buddy Landell pinned the Warlord
NWA National Heavyweight Champion Wahoo McDaniel & the Road Warriors defeated Tully Blanchard, Ole Anderson, & NWA TV Champion Arn Anderson when Wahoo pinned Ole at the 15-minute mark
NWA World Champion Ric Flair pinned NWA Mid-Atlantic Heavyweight Champion Ron Garvin
Dusty Rhodes defeated Big Bubba in a steel cage match

JCP @ Fayetteville, NC - Cumberland County Civic Center - September 6, 1986
Tim Horner fought Bill Dundee to a draw
Rick Rude defeated Allen West
NWA National Heavyewight Champion Wahoo McDaniel defeated Baron Von Raschke via disqualification
Bobby Jaggers & Dutch Mantell defeated Bobby Eaton & Dennis Condrey
Magnum TA defeated Jimmy Garvin
Dusty Rhodes defeated Tully Blanchard

JCP @ Baltimore, MD - Civic Center - September 6, 1986
Denny Brown defeated George South
Misty Blue defeated Linda Dallas
Jimmy Garvin defeated Sam Houston
The Warlord defeated Thunderfoot #1 & #2 in a handicap match

303

Baron Von Raschke defeated Todd Champion
Ole Anderson & NWA TV Champion Arn Anderson defeated NWA Tag Team Champions Ricky Morton & Robert Gibson
Tully Blanchard defeated NWA Mid-Atlantic Heavyweight Champion Ron Garvin
NWA World Champion Ric Flair defeated Dusty Rhodes

JCP @ Philadelphia, PA - Civic Center - September 6, 1986 (4,500)
Don Kernodle pinned Steve Regal
Buddy Landell defeated the Italian Stallion
Dutch Mantell pinned the Barbarian
Bobby Jaggers defeated Shaska Whatley via disqualification when Paul Jones tripped Jaggers
Ivan Koloff & Krusher Kruschev defeated Manny Fernandez & Hector Guerrero
Jimmy Valiant defeated Paul Jones in a lumberjack match
NWA National Heavyweight Champion Wahoo McDaniel & Dick Murdoch defeated Bobby Eaton & Dennis Condrey via disqualification when Condrey used Jim Cornette's tennis racquet as a weapon; after the bout, McDaniel & Murdoch assaulted Eaton & Condrey with the weapon
NWA US Champion Nikita Koloff defeated Magnum TA in a steel cage match

JCP @ Atlanta, GA - WTBS Studios - September 7, 1986 (matinee)
World Championship Wrestling - 9/13/86:
World Championship Wrestling Sunday Edition - 9/14/86:
Tully Blanchard & NWA TV Champion Arn Anderson vs. Vernon Deaton & Tony Zane

JCP @ Asheville, NC - Civic Center - September 7, 1986 (matinee)
Nelson Royal vs. George South
Rocky Kernodle vs. Black Bart
Jimmy Valiant, Manny Fernandez, & Hector Guerrero vs. Shaska Whatley, the Barbarian, & Teijo Khan
Don Kernodle vs. Baron Von Raschke
Dick Murdoch & NWA National Heavyweight Champion Wahoo McDaniel vs. Ivan Koloff & Krusher Kruschev
NWA US Champion Nikita Koloff vs. Magnum TA (Best 2 out of 3 falls)

JCP @ Marietta, GA - Cobb County Civic Center - September 8, 1986 (sell out)
NWA Tag Team Champions Ricky Morton & Robert Gibson defeated Bobby Eaton & Dennis Condrey
Dusty Rhodes defeated Big Bubba via count-out in a streetfight

JCP @ Wallace, SC - September 9, 1986
NWA Tag Team Champions Ricky Morton & Robert Gibson defeated Bobby Eaton & Dennis Condrey in a non-title match

JCP @ Columbia, SC - Township Auditorium - September 9, 1986
TV taping:
Bobby Eaton & Dennis Condrey defeated Bobby Jaggers & Dutch Mantel
NWA National Heavyweight Champion Wahoo McDaniel, Ricky Morton & Robert Gibson vs. Krusher Kruschev, NWA US Champion Nikita Koloff, & Ivan Koloff
Pro - 9/13/86:
Dick Murdoch vs. Thunderfoot
Manny Fernandez vs. Teijo Khan
Jimmy Valiant vs. Vernon Deaton
Dusty Rhodes pinned NWA TV Champion Arn Anderson to win the title with a DDT onto a steel chair, moments after referee Earl Hebner was knocked to the floor and Anderson attempted to use the chair as a weapon
Dark match: NWA World Champion Ric Flair vs. Magnum TA

JCP @ Norfolk, VA - Scope - September 11, 1986
Buddy Landell defeated Hector Guerrero
The Italian Stallion defeated Mark Fleming
Misty Blue defeated Linda Dallas
Arn Anderson defeated the Warlord
NWA National Heavyweight Champion Wahoo McDaniel defeated Ivan Koloff
NWA US Champion Nikita Koloff defeated Magnum TA via disqualification
NWA Tag Team Champions Ricky Morton & Robert Gibson defeated Bobby Eaton & Dennis Condrey in a Best 2 out of 3 falls match
NWA TV Champion Dusty Rhodes defeated Big Bubba via count-out in a streetfight
NWA World Champion Ric Flair defeated Dick Murdoch via disqualification

JCP @ Charleston, SC - County Hall - September 12, 1986
Dutch Mantell defeated Thunderfoot #2
Misty Blue defeated Linda Dallas
Bobby Jaggers defeated Thunderfoot #1
Jimmy Garvin defeated Sam Houston
Dick Murdoch, NWA Tag Team Champions Ricky Morton & Robert Gibson defeated Big Bubba, Bobby Eaton & Dennis Condrey
NWA National Heavyweight Champion Wahoo McDaniel defeated Tully Blanchard
Magnum TA defeated NWA US Champion Nikita Koloff

JCP @ Charlotte, NC - Coliseum - September 13, 1986
NWA TV Champion Dusty Rhodes, NWA Tag Team Champions Ricky Morton & Robert Gibson defeated Big Bubba, Bobby Eaton & Dennis Condrey
NWA World Champion Ric Flair defeated Dick Murdoch

- 9/86: Jim Crockett Promotions purchased the Central States territory.

JCP @ Atlanta, GA - WTBS Studios - September 14, 1986 (matinee)
World Championship Wrestling - 9/20/86:
Baron Von Raschke vs. Tom Barrett
Ricky Morton & Robert Gibson vs. Gene Ligon & Mike Simani
Arn Anderson vs. Jack Jackson
The Road Warriors vs. Vernon Deaton & Mike Simani
Dutch Mantell & Bobby Jaggers vs. Pablo Crenshaw & Tony Zane
Dick Murdoch & NWA Mid-Atlantic Heavyweight Champion Ron Garvin vs. the Mulkeys
World Championship Wrestling Sunday Edition - 9/21/86:
NWA Tag Team Champions Ricky Morton & Robert Gibson vs. the Golden Terror & Randy Barber
Jimmy Garvin vs. Bill Mulkey
Manny Fernandez vs. Randy Mulkey
Dick Murdoch vs. Brodie Chase
Baron Von Raschke, the Barbarian, & Shaska Whatley vs. Lee Peak, Art Pritts, & Paul Garner
Bobby Eaton & Dennis Condrey vs. Ken Glover & Alan Martin

JCP @ Cleveland, OH - Convocation Center - September 14, 1986
Bill Dundee defeated Sam Houston
NWA Mid-Atlantic Heavyweight Champion Ron Garvin fought Buddy Landell to a draw
Misty Blue defeated Linda Dallas
Dick Murdoch defeated Arn Anderson
NWA National Heavyweight Champion Wahoo McDaniel defeated Tully Blanchard via disqualification
The Road warriors & Paul Ellering defeated Baron Von Raschke, Ivan Koloff, & Krusher Kruschev
NWA Tag Team Champions Ricky Morton & Robert Gibson defeated Bobby Eaton & Dennis Condrey
NWA US Champion Nikita Koloff defeated Magnum TA in a steel cage match

JCP @ Green Bay, WI - Brown County Veterans Memorial Arena - September 18, 1986
NWA Mid-Atlantic Heavyweight Champion Ron Garvin pinned Ole Anderson
Arn Anderson defeated Baron Von Raschke via disqualification when Von Raschke refused to break the claw after Anderson reached the ropes
Jimmy Valiant pinned Shaska Whatley
Paul Ellering pinned JJ Dillon with his feet on the ropes for leverage
Dick Murdoch defeated Tully Blanchard via disqualification
NWA National Heavyweight Champion Wahoo McDaniel defeated Jimmy Garvin in an Indian strap match
NWA Tag Team Champions Ricky Morton & Robert Gibson defeated Bobby Eaton & Dennis Condrey
NWA US Champion Nikita Koloff fought Magnum TA to a double count-out
The Road Warriors defeated Ivan Koloff & Krusher Kruschev
NWA World Champion Ric Flair pinned NWA TV Champion Dusty Rhodes

JCP @ Minneapolis, MN - Met Center - September 19, 1986
NWA Mid-Atlantic Heavyweight Champion Ron Garvin defeated JJ Dillon
Baron Von Raschke defeated Jimmy Garvin via disqualification
Arn Anderson defeated Jimmy Valiant
Dick Murdoch defeated Shaska Whatley
Tully Blanchard defeated Magnum TA via disqualification
NWA Tag Team Champions Ricky Morton & Robert Gibson defeated Bobby Eaton & Dennis Condrey
NWA World Champion Ric Flair defeated NWA TV Champion Dusty Rhodes via disqualification
The Road Warriors & Paul Ellering defeated NWA US Champion Nikita Koloff, Ivan Koloff, & Krusher Kruschev

JCP @ Greensboro, NC - Coliseum - September 20, 1986 (8,223)
Dutch Mantell & Bobby Jaggers defeated Bill Dundee & Buddy Landell
Mitch Snow defeated Bill Mulkey
Krusher Kruschev defeated Nelson Royal
Don Kernodle defeated Baron Von Raschke
Dick Murdoch defeated Jimmy Garvin
NWA TV Champion Dusty Rhodes defeated Big Bubba via count-out in a streetfight
Ole & Arn Anderson defeated NWA Tag Team Champions Ricky Morton & Robert Gibson via disqualification
NWA US Champion Nikita Koloff defeated Magnum TA

WWC @ Mayaguez, Puerto Rico - September 20, 1986
NWA World Champion Ric Flair defeated Miguel Perez Jr.

JCP @ Atlanta, GA - WTBS Studios - September 21, 1986 (matinee)
World Championshp Wrestling - 9/27/86:
Jimmy Garvin vs. Vernon Deaton
Shaska Whatley & the Barbarian vs. the Mulkeys
Hector Guerrero & Manny Fernandez vs. the Golden Terror & Tony Zane
NWA US Champion Nikita Koloff vs. Bill Tabb
Jimmy Valiant vs. Brodie Chase
Bobby Eaton & Dennis Condrey vs. Art Pritts & Paul Garner
World Championshp Wrestling Sunday Edition - 9/28/86:
Dutch Mantell & Bobby Jaggers vs. Vernon Deaton & Charles Freeman
Jimmy Valiant vs. an unknown
Tully Blanchard vs. Rocky Kernodle
Dick Murdoch vs. Mike Simani
Buddy Landell & Bill Dundee vs. Bill & Randy Mulkey
Bobby Eaton & Dennis Condrey vs. Lee Peak & Bill Tabb
Manny Fernandez vs. Randy Barber

JCP @ Asheville, NC - Civic Center - September 21, 1986 (matinee) (1,500)
Tim Horner defeated Mike Simani
Bill Dundee defeated Joe Jackson
NWA Mid-Atlantic Heavyweight Champion Ron Garvin

defeated Buddy Landell via disqualification
Dutch Mantell & Bobby Jaggers fought Ivan Koloff & Krusher Kruschev to a draw
NWA National Heavyweight Champion Wahoo McDaniel defeated Tully Blanchard
Ole & Arn Anderson defeated NWA Tag Team Champions Ricky Morton & Robert Gibson via disqualification

WWC @ San Juan, Puerto Rico - September 21, 1986
Invader #1 defeated NWA World Champion Ric Flair via disqualification

JCP @ Charlotte, NC - Coliseum - September 21, 1986
Bobby Eaton & Dennis Condrey defeated Bobby Jaggers & Dutch Mantel
NWA Tag Team Champions Ricky Morton & Robert Gibson fought Ole & Arn Anderson to a draw

JCP @ Greenville, SC - Memorial Auditorium - September 22, 1986
Nelson Royal defeated the Golden Terror
Manny Fernandez defeated Tony Zane
Bill Dundee defeated Rocky Kernodle
NWA Mid-Atlantic Heavyweight Champion Ron Garvin fought Buddy Landell to a 20-minute time-limit draw
Magnum TA fought Jimmy Garvin to a double disqualification
NWA National Heavyweight Champion Wahoo McDaniel fought NWA US Champion Nikita Koloff to a double count-out
Tully Blanchard defeated NWA TV Champion Dusty Rhodes via disqualification

Continental @ Birmingham, AL - September 22, 1986
NWA World Champion Ric Flair defeated Wendell Cooley

JCP @ Saginaw, MI - Civic Center - September 22, 1986
NWA Tag Team Champions Ricky Morton & Robert Gibson defeated Bobby Eaton & Dennis Condrey

JCP @ Lansing, MI - September 23, 1986
NWA Tag Team Champions Ricky Morton & Robert Gibson defeated Bobby Eaton & Dennis Condrey in a Best 2 out of 3 falls match

JCP @ Cincinnati, OH - Cincinnati Gardens - September 23, 1986 (1,600)
Don Kernodle defeated the Barbarian
Manny Fernandez & Jimmy Valiant defeated Baron Von Raschke & Shaska Whatley
NWA National Heavyweight Champion Wahoo McDaniel vs. Jimmy Garvin
NWA World Champion Ric Flair vs. NWA Mid-Atlantic Heavyweight Champion Ron Garvin
NWA TV Champion Dusty Rhodes vs. Arn Anderson (steel cage match)

Magnum TA vs. NWA US Champion Nikita Koloff (steel cage match)

JCP @ Grand Rapids, MI - September 24, 1986
Bobby Eaton & Dennis Condrey defeated Bobby Jaggers & Dutch Mantell
NWA World Champion Ric Flair fought NWA TV Champion Dusty Rhodes to a double count-out

JCP @ Columbia, SC - Township Auditorium - September 25, 1986
Bobby Eaton & Dennis Condrey defeated Bobby Jaggers & Dutch Mantel
Magnum TA vs. Jimmy Garvin
NWA National Heavyweight Champion Wahoo McDaniel vs. Tully Blanchard
NWA TV Champion Dusty Rhodes vs. Arn Anderson
Also included 2 other bouts

JCP @ Norfolk, VA - Scope - September 26, 1986
Bobby Eaton & Dennis Condrey defeated Bobby Jaggers & Dutch Mantell

Central States @ Kansas City, MO - Memorial Hall - September 26, 1986 (1,100)
Sam Houston (sub. for Mitch Snow) defeated Mark Fleming
Jimmy Garvin defeated Mitch Snow
The Italian Stallion defeated Colt Steele
The MOD Squad & Colt Steele defeated George South, Rufus R. Jones, & Mitch Snow
The Italian Stallion defeated Mark Fleming
Bill Dundee defeated Rocky King
Denny Brown defeated Teijo Khan
The Thunderfoots defeated Todd Champion & DJ Peterson
Sam Houston fought Buddy Landell to a draw
NWA Tag Team Champions Ricky Morton & Robert Gibson defeated Big Bubba & the Warlord via disqualification
Tully Blanchard defeated NWA TV Champion Dusty Rhodes via disqualification

JCP @ Macon, GA - Coliseum - September 27, 1986
TV taping

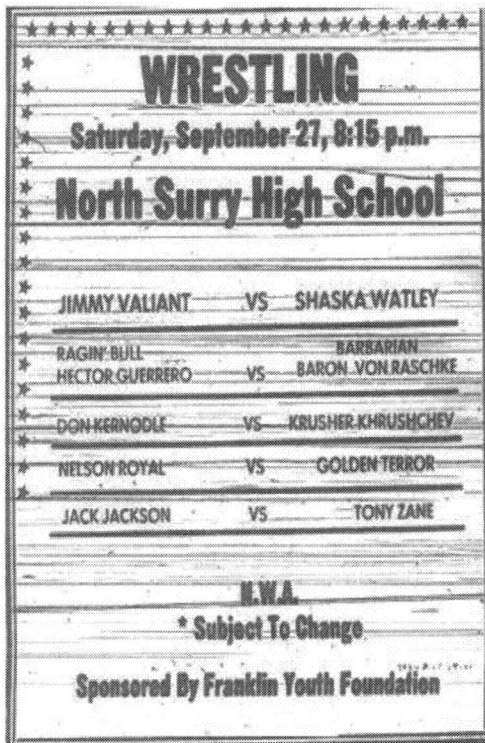

WRESTLING
Saturday, September 27, 8:15 p.m.
North Surry High School

JIMMY VALIANT   VS   SHASKA WATLEY

RAGIN' BULL   BARBARIAN
HECTOR GUERRERO   VS   BARON VON RASCHKE

DON KERNODLE   VS   KRUSHER KHRUSHCHEV

NELSON ROYAL   VS   GOLDEN TERROR

JACK JACKSON   VS   TONY ZANE

N.W.A.
* Subject To Change

Sponsored By Franklin Youth Foundation

JCP @ Mt. Airy, NC - North Surry High School - September 27, 1986
Jack Jackson vs. Tony Zane
Nelson Royal vs. the Golden Terror
Don Kernodle vs. Krusher Kruschev
Manny Fernandez & Hector Guerrero vs. the Barbarian & Baron Von Raschke
Jimmy Valiant vs. Shaska Whatley

JCP @ Atlanta, GA - WTBS Studios - September 28, 1986 (matinee)
World Championship Wrestling - 10/4/86:
Magnum TA vs. Vernon Deaton
Manny Fernandez vs. Mike Siamni
Tim Horner vs. Randy Mulkey
Tully Blanchard, Ole & Arn Anderson vs. Rocky Kernodle, Bill Tabb, & Charles Freeman
Baron Von Raschke & Shaska Whatley vs. Bill Mulkey & Lee Peek
Bobby Eaton & Dennis Condrey vs. Randy Barber & Pablo Crenshaw
NWA Mid-Atlantic Heavyweight Champion Ron Garvin vs. Gary Royal

JCP @ Atlanta, GA - Omni - September 28, 1986 (3,000)
NWA US Tag Team Championship Tournament Quarter

Finals: Ivan Koloff & Krusher Kruschev defeated Tim Horner & Nelson Royal
NWA US Tag Team Championship Tournament Quarter Finals: Tully Blanchard & Jimmy Garvin defeated Jimmy Valiant & Manny Fernandez
NWA US Tag Team Championship Tournament Quarter Finals: Dick Murdoch & NWA Mid-Atlantic Heavyweight Champion Ron Garvin fought Bobby Eaton & Dennis Condrey to a 20-minute time-limit draw
NWA US Tag Team Championship Tournament Quarter Finals: NWA TV Champion Dusty Rhodes & Magnum TA defeated Baron Von Raschke & Shaska Whatley
NWA US Tag Team Championship Tournament Quarter Finals: Dutch Mantell & Bobby Jaggers defeated Bill Dundee & Buddy Landell
NWA US Tag Team Championship Tournament Semi Finals: Ivan Koloff & Krusher Kruschev defeated NWA TV Champion Dusty Rhodes & Magnum TA via disqualification
NWA US Tag Team Championship Tournament Semi Finals: Dutch Mantell & Bobby Jaggers defeated Tully Blanchard & Jimmy Garvin
NWA US Tag Team Championship Tournament Finals: Ivan Koloff & Krusher Kruschev defeated Dutch Mantell & Bobby Jaggers to win the titles
Ole & Arn Anderson defeated NWA Tag Team Champions Ricky Morton & Robert Gibson via disqualification
All Star Wrestling (Central States): NWA US Champion Nikita Koloff (w/ NWA US Tag Team Champion Ivan Koloff) pinned NWA National Heavyweight Champion Wahoo McDaniel to win the title in a unification match after more than 11 minutes with a knee to the back as McDaniel attempted to help referee Tommy Young back into the ring; McDaniel's foot was on the bottom rope during the cover until Nikita knocked it off

Central States @ Wichita, KS - September 29, 1986 (2,600)
Rufus R. Jones defeated Mark Fleming
The MOD Squad defeated Rocky King & George South
Denny Brown defeated Thunderfoot #1
Thunderfoot #2 defeated the Italian Stallion
Magnum TA fought Buddy Landell to a draw
Todd Champion & DJ Peterson defeated Big Bubba & the Warlord via disqualification
Sam Houston defeated Teijo Khan
NWA Tag Team Champions Ricky Morton & Robert Gibson defeated Bobby Eaton & Dennis Condrey
NWA World Champion Ric Flair defeated NWA TV Champion Dusty Rhodes via disqualification

WRESTLING

WINTHROP COLISEUM

Rock Hill, S.C.

Tuesday, Sept. 30 7:30 PM

NWA WORLD HEAVYWEIGHT TITLE

DUSTY RHODES   RIC FLAIR

MAGNUM T.A.
VS.
GORGEOUS JIMMY GARVIN
(WITH PRECIOUS)
KANSAS JAYHAWKS
VS
MIDNIGHT EXPRESS
(WITH JIM CORNETTE)
RON GARVIN
VS
IVAN KOLOFF
HECTOR GUERRERO
MIDNIGHT EXPRESS
(WITH JIM CORNETTE)
RON GARVIN
VS
IVAN KOLOFF
HECTOR GUERRERO
VS
TIM HORNER
EDDIE ROBERTS
VS
DANNY DAVIS
NELSON ROYAL
VS
GARY ROYAL
ALLEN WEST
VS
KEN WAYNE

Matches Subject to Change-No Returns
Ringside-$10.00 Gen. Ad. $8.00 Under 11 $4.00
For Coliseum Event Info-329-6448

ADVANCE TICKET LOCATIONS

•Central Newsstand (TownCenter Mall)
•Video Center (Ft. Mill)
•Black s Drug Store (Chester)
•Friendly Grill
•Mr. Sport
•Video Connection (York)

JCP @ Rock Hill, SC - Winthrop Coliseum - September 30, 1986
TV taping:
Ken Wayne vs. Allen West
Nelson Royal vs. Gary Royal
Eddie Roberts vs. Danny Davis
Hector Guerrero vs. Tim Horner
NWA Mid-Atlantic Heavyweight Champion Ron Garvin vs. Ivan Koloff
Bobby Eaton & Dennis Condrey defeated Bobby Jaggers & Dutch Mantell
Magnum TA vs. Jimmy Garvin
NWA World Champion Ric Flair vs. NWA TV Champion Dusty Rhodes

JCP @ Raleigh, NC - Dorton Arena - October 1, 1986 (4,800)
Dutch Mantell & Bobby Jaggers defeated the Barbarian & Gary Royal
Manny Fernandez defeated Baron Von Raschke
Wahoo McDaniel defeated the Barbarian
Brad Armstrong defeated NWA US Tag Team Champion Ivan Koloff
Magnum TA defeated Jimmy Garvin via disqualification
NWA Tag Team Champions Ricky Morton & Robert Gibson defeated Ole & Arn Anderson
NWA World Champion Ric Flair defeated Dick Murdoch

Central States @ Des Moines, IA - October 2, 1986
The Italian Stallion defeated Teijo Khan
The MOD Squad defeated Rocky King & George South
Jimmy Valiant defeated Shaska Whatley
Todd Champion & DJ Peterson fought the Thunderfoots to a draw
Sam Houston defeated the Warlord via disqualification
NWA Tag Team Champions Ricky Morton & Robert Gibson defeated Ole & Arn Anderson
NWA World Champion Ric Flair defeated NWA TV Champion Dusty Rhodes

JCP @ Hampton, VA - Coliseum - October 3, 1986
Bobby Eaton & Dennis Condrey fought Bobby Jaggers & Dutch Mantell to a 20-minute time-limit draw

Central States @ Kansas City, MO - Kemper Arena - October 3, 1986 (1,200)
The MOD Squad defeated Rocky King & Mitch Snow
The Italian Stallion defeated Teijo Khan
Denny Brown pinned Mark Fleming
Dave Peterson & Todd Champion fought Thunderfoot #1 & #2 to a draw
Sam Houston defeated the Warlord via disqualification
Jimmy Valiant defeated Pez Whatley
NWA Tag Team Champions Ricky Morton & Robert Gibson defeated Ole & Arn Anderson
NWA World Champion Ric Flair pinned NWA Mid-Atlantic

Heavyweight Champion Ron Garvin after the Warlord interfered and attacked the challenger while Big Bubba distracted the referee

JCP @ Albany, GA - Civic Center - October 4, 1986
Danny Davis vs. Keith Patterson
Eddie Roberts vs. Gary Royal
Ken Wayne vs. Alan West
Ivan Koloff vs. Jimmy Valiant
Bobby Jaggers & Dutch Mantell defeated Bobby Eaton & Dennis Condrey via disqualification

JCP @ Charlotte, NC - Coliseum - October 4, 1986
Tim Horner defeated the Grim Reaper
Rick Rude defeated Allen West
Brad Armstrong defeated the Barbarian
Shaska Whatley & Baron Von Raschke defeated Manny Fernandez & Jimmy Valiant
Tully Blanchard defeated Dick Murdoch
NWA Tag Team Champions Ricky Morton & Robert Gibson defeated Ole & Arn Anderson
NWA World Champion Ric Flair defeated NWA TV Champion Dusty Rhodes

JCP @ Atlanta, GA - WTBS Studios - October 5, 1986 (matinee)
World Championship Wrestling - 10/11/86:
Bobby Eaton & Dennis Condrey vs. Paul Garner & Art Pritts
Brad Armstrong vs. Randy Barber
Tim Horner vs. Bill Tabb
Rick Rude vs. Lee Peek
Tully Blanchard vs. Tony Zane
Manny Fernandez vs. Randy Glover

JCP @ Asheville, NC - Civic Center - October 5, 1986 (matinee)
Tony Zane vs. Allen West
Gary Royal vs. Don Kernodle
Bobby Jaggers & Dutch Mantel vs. Danny Davis & Ken Wayne
Wahoo McDaniel vs. Baron Von Raschke
Magnum TA vs. Jimmy Garvin
NWA Tag Team Champions Ricky Morton & Robert Gibson vs. Ole & Arn Anderson
NWA World Champion Ric Flair vs. Dick Murdoch

JCP @ Roanoke, VA - Civic Center - October 5, 1986
Brad Armstrong (sub. for injured NWA Tag Team Champion Robert Gibson) & NWA Tag Team Champion Ricky Morton defeated Bobby Eaton & Dennis Condrey via disqualification
NWA World Champion Ric Flair vs. ?

JCP @ Fayetteville, NC - Cumberland County Civic Center - October 6, 1986
Bobby Jaggers & Dutch Mantell defeated Bobby Eaton & Dennis Condrey

JCP @ Greenville, SC - Memorial Auditorium - October 6, 1986
Shaska Whatley defeated Eddie Roberts
Brad Armstrong defeated Tony Zane
Hector Guerrero defeated Gary Royal
Manny Fernandez defeated the Grim Reaper
NWA Mid-Atlantic Heavyweight Champion Ron Garvin defeated Ivan Koloff
NWA Tag Team Champions Ricky Morton & Robert Gibson defeated Ole & Arn Anderson in a No DQ match
NWA World Champion Ric Flair defeated Dick Murdoch

JCP @ Spartanburg, SC - Memorial Auditorium - October 7, 1986
TV taping:
Worldwide - 10/11/86:
Bobby Eaton & Dennis Condrey vs. Tony Zanek & Gary Royal
Brad Armstrong vs. Eddie Roberts
Jimmy Garvin vs. Ben Alexander
Rick Rude, Manny Fernandez, & Baron Von Raschke vs. Rocky Kernodle, Keith Patterson, & a Mulkey
Tully Blanchard & Arn Anderson vs. Nelson Royal & Tim Horner
Ricky Morton vs. Ole Anderson
Championship Wrestling - 10/18/86:
World Championship Wrestling - 10/18/86:
Dark match: Magnum TA vs. Jimmy Garvin
Dark match: NWA TV Champion Dusty Rhodes vs. NWA World Champion Ric Flair
Also included Jimmy Valiant, Dick Murdoch, Buddy Landell, Bill Dundee, Dutch Mantell & Bobby Jaggers, and Ivan Koloff

JCP @ Lenoir, NC - October 8, 1986 (sell out)
Magnum TA defeated Jimmy Garvin
Brad Armstrong (sub. for injured NWA Tag Team Champion Robert Gibson) & NWA Tag Team Champion Ricky Morton defeated Bobby Eaton & Dennis Condrey via disqualification

CWF @ Tampa, FL - October 8, 1986
NWA World Champion Ric Flair fought Lex Luger to a draw in a Best 2 out of 3 falls match

JCP @ Raleigh, NC - Dorton Arena - October 9, 1986
Don Kernodle & Hector Guerrero defeated Bill & Randy Mulkey
Rick Rude defeated Allen West
Gary Royal defeated Eddie Roberts
Wahoo McDaniel defeated Bill Dundee
Bobby Jaggers & Dutch Mantell defeated Bobby Eaton & Dennis Condrey in a bunkhouse match
Magnum TA defeated Jimmy Garvin

JCP @ Baltimore, MD - Civic Center - October 9, 1986
NWA Mid-Atlantic Heavyweight Champion Ron Garvin defeated NWA US Tag Team Champion Ivan Koloff
Jimmy Valiant defeated Baron Von Raschke
Brad Armstrong defeated the Grim Reaper
Tim Horner fought Shaska Whatley to a draw
NWA TV Champion Dusty Rhodes defeated Tully Blanchard
NWA Mid-Atlantic Heavyweight Champion Ron Garvin (sub. for injured NWA Tag Team Champion Robert Gibson) & NWA Tag Team Champion Ricky Morton defeated Ole & Arn Anderson via disqualification
NWA World Champion Ric Flair defeated Dick Murdoch

JCP @ Norfolk, VA - Scope - October 10, 1986
Wahoo McDaniel defeated Bobby Eaton via disqualification

JCP @ Charleston, SC - St. Andrews High School Gym - October 11, 1986
Eddie Roberts vs. Keith Patterson
Allen West vs. Gary Royal
Nelson Royal vs. the Grim Reaper
Hector Guerrero vs. Bill Dundee
Jimmy Valiant vs. Buddy Landell
Wahoo McDaniel & NWA Mid-Atlantic Heavyweight Champion Ron Garvin vs. Ole & Arn Anderson

JCP @ Greensboro, NC - Coliseum - October 11, 1986
Rick Rude defeated Tim Horner
Brad Armstrong defeated NWA US Tag Team Champion Ivan Koloff
Don Kernodle defeated Baron Von Raschke
Magnum TA defeated Jimmy Garvin
Brad Armstrong (sub. for injured NWA Tag Team Champion Robert Gibson) & NWA Tag Team Champion Ricky Morton defeated Bobby Eaton & Dennis Condrey via disqualification
NWA World Champion Ric Flair defeated Dick Murdoch
Tully Blanchard defeated NWA TV Champion Dusty Rhodes via disqualification when Rhodes assaulted Blanchard's knee with a chair

JCP @ Atlanta, GA - WTBS Studios - October 12, 1986 (matinee)
World Championship Wrestling - 10/18/86:
Ole & Arn Anderson vs. Keith Patterson & Vernon Deaton
NWA Mid-Atlantic Heavyweight Champion Ron Garvin vs. the Grimm Reaper
Ivan Koloff vs. Mike Simani
Shaska Whatley, Rick Rude, & Baron Von Raschke vs. Brad Armstrong, Dutch Mantell & Bobby Jaggers
Bobby Eaton & Dennis Condrey vs. Alan West & Eddie Robberts

Central States @ St. Louis, MO - Arena - October 12, 1986 (2,500)
Sam Houston defeated the Warlord via disqualification
Bill Dundee defeated the Italian Stallion
Denny Brown defeated Colt Steele
Thunderfoot #1 & #2 defeated Mark Fleming & Mitch Snow
Todd Champion & DJ Peterson fought the MOD Squad to a draw
NWA Tag Team Champion Ricky Morton defeated Arn Anderson
NWA TV Champion Dusty Rhodes defeated Teijo Khan
NWA World Champion Ric Flair defeated Dick Murdoch

JCP @ Cincinnati, OH - October 12, 1986
Bobby Jaggers & Dutch Mantell defeated Bobby Eaton & Dennis Condrey

JCP @ Greenville, SC - Memorial Auditorium - October 13, 1986

Eddie Roberts defeated Randy Mulkey
Manny Fernandez defeated Hector Guerrero
Allen West defeated Tony Zane
Shaska Whatley defeated Bill Mulkey
Dick Murdoch defeated Rick Rude
Bobby Jaggers & Dutch Mantell defeated Bobby Eaton & Dennis Condrey in a bunkhouse match
Magnum TA defeated Jimmy Garvin in a lumberjack match (Magnum's last match)

- 10/14/86: Magnum TA was hospitalized after the car he was driving crashed into a telephone poll. Magnum sustained a broken neck, was paralyzed from the chest down, and was initially put on life support. He was returning to his home in Matthews, NC from a bar in Charlotte but had not been drinking and was driving 55 mph on a 45 mph zone. The roads were wet due to rain.

JCP @ Columbia, SC - Township Auditorium - October 14, 1986
TV taping:
Pro - 10/18/86:
Brad Armstrong defeated Mike Simani
Rick Rude & Manny Fernandez defeated Bill & Randy Mulkey
Hector Guerrero defeated John Savage
Bobby Eaton & Dennis Condrey defeated Alan West & Vernon Deaton
Jimmy Garvin defeated Eddie Roberts
Worldwide - 10/18/86:
Bobby Eaton & Dennis Condrey defeated John Savage & Rocky Kernodle
Rick Rude, Manny Fernandez, & Shaska Whatley defeated Eddie Roberts, Alan West, & Bill Mulkey
Brad Armstrong defeated Vernon Deaton
Jimmy Garvin defeated Randy Mulkey
Dick Murdoch defeated Mike Simani
Dark match: Bobby Jaggers & Dutch Mantell defeated Bobby Eaton & Dennis Condrey
Dark match: NWA TV Champion Dusty Rhodes & Magnum TA vs. NWA World Champion Ric Flair & Jimmy Garvin

JCP @ Grand Rapids, MI - October 15, 1986 (1,500)
Keith Patterson defeated the Grim Reaper
Nelson Royal fought Bill Dundee to a draw
Tim Horner defeated Gary Royal
NWA US Tag Team Champion Ivan Koloff defeated Keith Patterson
Mid-Atlantic Heavyweight Champion Ron Garvin defeated Baron Von Raschke
Wahoo McDaniel (sub. for injured NWA Tag Team Champion Robert Gibson) & NWA Tag Team Champion Ricky Morton defeated Ole & Arn Anderson

JCP @ Cambridge, MD - October 16, 1986
Brad Armstrong (sub. for injured NWA Tag Team Champion Robert Gibson) & NWA Tag Team Champion Ricky Morton defeated Bobby Eaton & Dennis Condrey

JCP @ Richmond, VA - Coliseum - October 17, 1986 (4,000)
Tim Horner pinned the Grim Reaper
Ivan Koloff pinned Eddie Roberts
Jimmy Valiant & Nelson Royal defeated Baron Von Raschke & Pez Whatley when Valiant pinned Von Raschke with a roll up after Von Raschke accidentally put the claw on Whatley; after the bout, Von Raschke and Whatley argued but then shook hands
Wahoo McDaniel defeated Rick Rude via disqualification
Jimmy Garvin pinned Hector Guerrero (sub. for Magnum TA)
Bobby Eaton & Dennis Condrey defeated Bobby Jaggers & Dutch Mantel when Jim Cornette interfered with the tennis racquet
Dick Murdoch defeated JJ Dillon at the 90-second mark
Brad Armstrong (sub. for injured NWA Tag Team Champion Robert Gibson) & NWA Tag Team Champion Ricky Morton defeated Ole & Arn Anderson when Morton pinned Arn

Central States @ Kansas City, MO - Memorial Hall - October 17, 1986 (600)
Rocky King defeated Colt Steele
Mitch Snow defeated Mark Fleming
Denny Brown & the Italian Stallion fought the MOD Squad to a draw
Bill Dundee defeated Rufus R. Jones
Sam Houston defeated Teijo Khan
Todd Champion & DJ Peterson defeated Thunderfoot #1 & #2 via disqualification
NWA Mid-Atlantic Heavyweight Champion Ron Garvin defeated the Warlord via disqualification

JCP @ Philadelphia, PA - Civic Center - October 18, 1986 (7,000)
Bobby Eaton & Dennis Condrey defeated Tim Horner & Don Kernodle
NWA US Champion Nikita Koloff, Ivan Koloff, & Krusher Kruschev defeated Jimmy Valiant, Dick Murdoch, & Wahoo McDaniel when Valiant was pinned
Brad Armstrong defeated Jimmy Garvin via disqualification
Manny Fernandez pinned Hector Guerrero
NWA Tag Team Champions Ricky Morton & Robert Gibson defeated Ole & Arn Anderson via disqualification
NWA TV Champion Dusty Rhodes pinned JJ Dillon (sub. for Tully Blanchard) at the 30-second mark; after the bout, Rhodes grabbed the mic and said "Tell Hulk Hogan that Dusty's in town," noting the WWF was running a show across town at the Spectrum

JCP @ Atlanta, GA - WTBS Studios - October 19, 1986 (matinee)
World Championship Wrestling - 10/25/86:
Brad Armstrong & Tim Horner vs. Bill Tabb & Brodie Chase

Jimmy Garvin (w/ Precious) vs. John Savage
Ole & Arn Anderson vs. Randy Barber & Clement Fields
Rick Rude & Manny Fernandez (w/ Paul Jones) vs. Kent Glover & Alan Martin

JCP @ Charlotte, NC - Coliseum - October 19, 1986
Bobby Jaggers & Dutch Mantell defeated Bobby Eaton & Dennis Condrey in a lumberjack match
NWA TV Champion Dusty Rhodes & NWA US Champion Nikita Koloff defeated Ole Anderson & JJ Dillon (sub. for Tully Blanchard) in a steel cage match

JCP @ Greenville, SC - Memorial Auditorium - October 20, 1986
Gary Royal defeated Allen West
Brad Armstrong defeated Randy Mulkey
Tim Horner defeated Tony Zane (sub. for Bill Dundee)
NWA Mid-Atlantic Heavyweight Champion Ron Garvin defeated the Grim Reaper (sub. for Krusher Kruschev); Reaper was to have fought Nelson Royal as well
NWA Tag Team Champions Ricky Morton & Robert Gibson defeated Ivan Koloff & Krusher Kruschev (sub. for Tully Blanchard & Jimmy Garvin)
NWA TV Champion Dusty Rhodes & NWA US Champion Nikita Koloff (sub. for Brad Armstrong) defeated Ole & Arn Anderson in a steel cage match

JCP @ Fayetteville, NC - Cumberland County Civic Center - October 20, 1986
Rocky Kernodle defeated Eddie Roberts
Don Kernodle defeated Keith Patterson
Rick Rude defeated Hector Guerrero
Wahoo McDaniel defeated Manny Fernandez
Jimmy Valiant defeated Dick Murdoch
Bobby Jaggers & Dutch Mantell defeated Bobby Eaton & Dennis Condrey

JCP @ Greenwood, SC - October 21, 1986
TV taping:
Ivan Koloff & Krusher Kruschev defeated Rocky Kernodle & an unknown
Worldwide - 10/25/86:
Brad Armstrong defeated Gary Royal
Jimmy Garvin defeated Keith Patterson
NWA Tag Team Champions Ricky Morton & Robert Gibson defeated the Grim Reaper & Gary Royal
Tully Blanchard, Ole & Arn Anderson defeated John Savage, Tony Zane, & Mike Simani
Bobby Eaton & Dennis Condrey defeated Bill & Randy Mulkey
Pro - 10/25/86:
Ole & Arn Anderson defeated Nelson Royal & Tim Horner
Ricky Morton & Robert Gibson vs. the Grim Reaper & Gary Royal
Rick Rude & Manny Fernandez defeated Eddie Roberts & Alan West

Brad Armstrong defeated Vernon Deaton
Wahoo McDaniel defeated Tony Zane

Central States @ Concordia, KS - Bryant Gymnasium - October 23, 1986
Mitch Snow vs. Colt Steele
Denny Brown vs. Thunderfoot #2
Italian Stallion vs. Thunderfoot #1
Rufus R. Jones, Rocky King and George South vs. the MOD Squad & Teijo Khan
Todd Champion & Dave Peterson vs. Ivan Koloff & Baron Von Raschke
Sam Houston vs. the Warlord
Jimmy Valiant vs. Shaska Whatley

JCP @ Sumter, SC - Exhibition Center - October 23, 1986
Bobby Eaton & Dennis Condrey defeated Bobby Jaggers & Dutch Mantell

JCP @ Pittsburgh, PA - Civic Arena - October 24, 1986 (10,000)
Rick Rude defeated Tim Horner
Jimmy Garvin defeated Hector Guerrero (sub. for Brad Armstrong)
NWA US Champion Nikita Koloff defeated Brad Armstrong (sub. for Magnum TA)
Wahoo McDaniel defeated Tully Blanchard via disqualification
NWA Mid-Atlantic Heavyweight Champion Ron Garvin & Dick Murdoch fought Bobby Eaton & Dennis Condrey to a 20-minute time-limit draw
NWA Tag Team Champions Ricky Morton & Robert Gibson defeated Ole & Arn Anderson
NWA World Champion Ric Flair defeated NWA TV Champion Dusty Rhodes via disqualification

Central States @ Kansas City, KS - October 24, 1986
Teijo Khan defeated Rufus R. Jones & Rocky King
The MOD Squad defeated Denny Brown & Mitch Snow
George South defeated Colt Steele
The Italian Stallion defeated Baron Von Raschke
Rufus R. Jones defeated the Assassin
Thunderfoot #1 & #2 defeated Todd Champion & DJ Peterson in a Texas Tornado match
Sam Houston defeated Bill Dundee via disqualification
Jimmy Valiant defeated Shaska Whatley

JCP @ Greensboro, NC - Coliseum - October 25, 1986
Jimmy Valiant defeated Gary Royal
Rick Rude defeated Hector Guerrero
Tully Blanchard defeated Tim Horner
Wahoo McDaniel defeated Manny Fernandez
NWA TV Champion Dusty Rhodes & NWA US Champion Nikita Koloff defeated Arn & Ole Anderson in a steel cage match
NWA Tag Team Champions Ricky Morton & Robert Gibson

defeated Bobby Eaton & Dennis Condrey in a steel cage match

JCP @ Asheville, NC - Civic Center - October 26, 1986 (matinee)
Bill Mulkey vs. Allen West
Eddie Roberts vs. Randy Mulkey
Manny Fernandez vs. Hector Guerrero
Wahoo McDaniel vs. Tully Blanchard
Brad Armstrong vs. Jimmy Garvin
NWA US Tag Team Champions Ivan Koloff & Krusher Kruschev vs. Bobby Jaggers & Dutch Mantel
NWA World Champion Ric Flair vs. Dick Murdoch (steel cage match)

JCP @ Atlanta, GA - Omni - October 26, 1986
Rick Rude defeated Nelson Royal
Tully Blanchard defeated Rocky Kernodle
NWA Mid-Atlantic Heavyweight Champion Ron Garvin defeated Shaska Whatley
Manny Fernandez defeated Hector Guerrero
Brad Armstrong & Tim Horner defeated NWA US Tag Team Champions Ivan Koloff & Krusher Kruschev
Wahoo McDaniel, NWA Tag Team Champions Ricky Morton & Robert Gibson defeated Big Bubba, Bobby Eaton & Dennis Condrey via disqualification
NWA TV Champion Dusty Rhodes & NWA US Champion Nikita Koloff defeated Ole & Arn Anderson
NWA World Champion Ric Flair defeated Dick Murdoch

JCP @ Misenheimer, NC - October 27, 1986
Bobby Eaton & Dennis Condrey defeated Bobby Jaggers & Dutch Mantell

JCP @ Greenville, SC - Memorial Auditorium - October 27, 1986
Brad Armstrong defeated Bill Dundee
Baron Von Raschke defeated the Grim Reaper
Wahoo McDaniel defeated Shaska Whatley
NWA Tag Team Champions Ricky Morton & Robert Gibson defeated Manny Fernandez & Rick Rude
Ole Anderson defeated Dick Murdoch
NWA TV Champion Dusty Rhodes & NWA US Champion Nikita Koloff defeated Tully Blanchard & Arn Anderson in a double bullrope match

WRESTLING
WINTHROP COLISEUM
TUESDAY, OCTOBER 28, 1986
TV TAPING
7:30 P.M.

GRUDGE MATCH-FENCE MATCH

DUSTY RHODES
ROCK 'N ROLL
EXPRESS
&
RIC FLAIR
OLE ANDERSON
ARN ANDERSON

Plus Other Big Matches Featuring Such Stars As:
GORGEOUS JIMMY GARVIN   MIDNIGHT EXPRESS
PRECIOUS   DICK MURDOCH
IVAN KOLOFF   RAGIN' BULL
TULLY BLANCHARD   RONNI GARVIN
NIKITA KOLOFF   WAHOO McDANIEL
JAYHAWKS

Plus Others

Join us for the live taping of N.W.A. Pro Wrestling & World Wide Wrestling
Matches Subject To Change

**Ticket Inforation 329-0440
ADVANCE TICKET LOCATIONS**

WINTHROP COLISEUM
VIDEO CENTER (FORT MILL)
VIDEO CONNECTION (YORK)
BLACK'S DRUG STORE (CHESTER)
FRIENDLY GRILL
CENTRAL NEWSSTAND

JCP @ Rock Hill, SC - Winthrop Coliseum - October 28, 1986
TV taping:
Tully Blanchard pinned Rocky Kernodle
Bobby Eaton, Dennis Condrey, & Big Bubba defeated Gary Royal, Keith Patterson, & Mike Simani
Brad Armstrong pinned John Savage
Bobby Jaggers & Dutch Mantell defeated Allen West & Eddie Roberts
Jimmy Garvin pinned Brodie Chase
Ricky Lee Jones pinned Tony Zane
Rick Rude & Manny Fernandez defeated Bill & Randy Mulkey
Bobby Eaton & Dennis Condrey defeated Allen West & Eddie Roberts
Rick Rude & Manny Fernandez defeated Gary Royal & Tony

313

Zane
Arn & Ole Anderson defeated Bill Mulkey & John Savage
Big Bubba defeated Vernon Deaton & Mike Siamani in a handicap match
Ivan Koloff & Krusher Khruschev defeated Rocky Kerndole & Keith Patterson
Brad Armstrong pinned the Grim Reaper
Japan TV: NWA TV Champion Dusty Rhodes, NWA World Tag Team Champions Ricky Morton & Robert Gibson defeated NWA World Champion Ric Flair, Arn & Ole Anderson in a steel cage match at around the 15-minute mark when Rhodes pinned Ole after Ole missed an elbow drop off the top; Gibson's ribs were heavily taped for the match

JCP @ Boone, NC - October 29, 1986
Bobby Jaggers & Dutch Mantell defeated Bobby Eaton & Dennis Condrey via disqualification

JCP @ Charleston, SC - October 30, 1986
Nelson Royal defeated Alan West
Rocky Kernodle defeated Gary Royal
Don Kernodle fought Shaska Whatley to a draw
Wahoo McDaniel defeated Tully Blanchard via disqualification
Jimmy Garvin defeated Hector Guerrero
NWA Tag Team Champions Ricky Morton & Robert Gibson defeated Ole & Arn Anderson in a double bullrope match
NWA World Champion Ric Flair defeated NWA TV Champion Dusty Rhodes via disqualification

JCP @ Philadelphia, PA - Civic Center - November 1, 1986
Baron Von Raschke fought Shaska Whatley to a draw
Jimmy Garvin defeated Tim Horner
NWA US Tag Team Champions Ivan Koloff & Krusher Kruschev defeated Hector Guerrero & Don Kernodle
Brad Armstrong defeated Rick Rude via disqualification
Manny Fernandez defeated Wahoo McDaniel
NWA TV Champion Dusty Rhodes & NWA US Champion Nikita Koloff defeated NWA World Champion Ric Flair & Tully Blanchard
NWA Tag Team Champions Ricky Morton & Robert Gibson defeated Ole & Arn Anderson
Big Bubba, Bobby Eaton & Dennis Condrey defeated NWA Mid-Atlantic Heavyweight Champion Ron Garvin, Bobby Jaggers & Dutch Mantell

JCP @ Atlanta, GA - WTBS Studios - November 2, 1986 (matinee)
World Championship Wrestling - 11/8/86:
Big Bubba, Bobby Eaton & Dennis Condrey vs. Tony Zane, Vernon Deaton, & Brodie Chase
NWA US Tag Team Champions Ivan Koloff & Krusher Kruschev vs. Mike Simani & John Savage
Arn Anderson vs. Eddie Roberts
Jimmy Garvin (w/ Precious) vs. Pablo Crenshaw
Brad Armstrong vs. the Grim Reaper

JCP @ Omaha, NE - Civic Auditorium - November 2, 1986
Mitch Snow defeated Mark Fleming
Bill Dundee & the MOD Squad defeated Rocky King, George South, & the Italian Stallion
Teijo Khan defeated Denny Brown
Sam Houston defeated the Warlord in a Texas Death Match
Thunderfoot #1 & #2 defeated Todd Champion & DJ Peterson
NWA Tag Team Champions Ricky Morton & Robert Gibson defeated Bobby Eaton & Dennis Condrey
NWA World Champion Ric Flair defeated NWA TV Champion Dusty Rhodes

JCP @ Greenville, SC - Memorial Auditorium - November 3, 1986
Allen West defeated Tony Zane
Tim Horner defeated Randy Mulkey
Nelson Royal defeated Bill Mulkey
Jimmy Garvin defeated Don Kernodle
NWA US Tag Team Champions Ivan Koloff & Krusher Kruschev fought Bobby Jaggers & Dutch Mantell to a double disqualification
Brad Armstrong, NWA Tag Team Champions Ricky Morton & Robert Gibson defeated Big Bubba, Bobby Eaton & Dennis Condrey

JCP @ Fayetteville, NC - Cumberland County Memorial Arena - November 3, 1986
Gary Royal defeated Eddie Roberts
Rocky Kernodle defeated the Grim Reaper
Hector Guerrero fought Shaska Whatley to a draw
Baron Von Raschke defeated Rick Rude via disqualification
Manny Fernandez defeated Wahoo McDaniel
NWA Mid-Atlantic Heavyweight Champion Ron Garvin fought Arn Anderson to a no contest
NWA TV Champion Dusty Rhodes & NWA US Champion Nikita Koloff defeated NWA World Champion Ric Flair & Tully Blanchard

JCP @ Spartanburg, SC - Memorial Auditorium - November 4, 1986
TV taping:
Jumbo Tsuruta & Genichiro Tenryu defeated Brodie Chase & Tony Zane
Hiroshi Wajima defeated Randy Mulkey
Tully Blanchard & Arn Anderson defeated John Savage & Ron Rossi
Big Bubba, Bobby Eaton & Dennis Condrey defeated Alan West, Ed Roberts, & Tony Zane
Dark match: NWA TV Champion Dusty Rhodes, NWA Tag Team Champions Ricky Morton & Robert Gibson defeated Big Bubba, Bobby Eaton & Dennis Condrey via disqualification

JCP @ Wheeling, WV - Civic Center - November 4, 1986
Tim Horner pinned The Grim Reaper at 8:31
Jimmy Valiant pinned Bill Dundee at 9:00
Baron Von Raschke pinned Shaska Whatley

314

Manny Fernandez fought Wahoo McDaniel to a double count-out at 9:52
Dutch Mantell & Bobby Jaggers defeated NWA US Tag Team Champions Ivan Koloff & Krusher Khruschev in a non-title Texas Tornado match at 8:22 when Jaggers pinned Koloff
NWA World Champion Ric Flair pinned Brad Armstrong at 31:40

JCP @ Canton, OH - November 5, 1986
NWA Tag Team Champions Ricky Morton & Robert Gibson defeated Bobby Eaton & Dennis Condrey in a non-title match

JCP @ Raleigh, NC - Dorton Arena - November 6, 1986
Ricky Lee Jones defeated Gary Royal
Brad Armstrong defeated Rick Rude
Baron Von Raschke defeated Shaska Whatley
Manny Fernandez defeated Hector Guerrero
Arn Anderson defeated Wahoo McDaniel
Big Bubba, Bobby Eaton & Dennis Condrey defeated NWA Mid-Atlantic Heavyweight Champion Ron Garvin, NWA Tag Team Champions Ricky Morton & Robert Gibson
NWA TV Champion Dusty Rhodes & NWA US Champion Nikita Koloff defeated NWA World Champion Ric Flair & Tully Blanchard

JCP @ Roanoke, VA - Civic Center - November 7, 1986
Rocky Kernodle defeated Eddie Roberts
Don Kernodle defeated the Grip Reaper
Tim Horner defeated Tony Zane
Brad Armstrong defeated Jimmy Garvin via disqualification
NWA Mid-Atlantic Heavyweight Champion Ron Garvin defeated Shaska Whatley
Jimmy Valiant, NWA Tag Team Champions Ricky Morton & Robert Gibson defeated Big Bubba, Bobby Eaton & Dennis Condrey

JCP @ Kansas City, KS - November 7, 1986 (300)
Denny Brown pinned Colt Steele
MOD Squad Basher defeated Rocky King
MOD Squad Spike defeated George South
Sam Houston & Rufus R. Jones fought Bill Dundee & the Barbarian to a double disqualification
DJ Peterson & Todd Champion defeated Central States Tag Team Champions Thunderfoot #1 & #2 to win the titles

JCP @ Charlotte, NC - Coliseum - November 8, 1986
Don Kernodle defeated Tony Zane
Tim Horner defeated Bill Dundee
Rick Rude defeated Hector Guerrero
Big Bubba, Bobby Eaton & Dennis Condrey defeated Brad Armstrong, NWA Tag Team Champions Ricky Morton & Robert Gibson
Manny Fernandez defeated Wahoo McDaniel
Road Warrior Animal defeated Arn Anderson
Jumbo Tsuruta & Genichiro Tenryu defeated the Grim Reaper

& Art Pritts
The Giant Baba & Wajima defeated Gary Royal & American Eagle
NWA TV Champion Dusty Rhodes & NWA US Champion Nikita Koloff defeated NWA World Champion Ric Flair & Tully Blanchard

JCP @ Atlanta, GA - WTBS Studios - November 9, 1986 (matinee)
World Championship Wrestling - 11/15/86:
Big Bubba, Bobby Eaton & Dennis Condrey (w/ Jim Cornette) vs. Lee Peek, Alan West, & Vernon Deaton
Tim Horner & Ricky Lee Jones vs. Randy & Bill Mulkey
Tully Blanchard (w/ JJ Dillon) vs. Keith Patterson
Brad Armstrong vs. Tony Zane
Rick Rude (w/ Paul Jones) vs. Paul Garner

JCP @ Asheville, NC - Civic Center - November 9, 1986 (matinee)
Rocky Kernodle vs. Vernon Deaton
Bobby Jaggers & Dutch Mantel vs. Gary Royal & the Grim Reaper
Jimmy Valiant vs. Jimmy Garvin
Wahoo McDaniel vs. Manny Fernandez
The Road Warriors vs. NWA US Tag Team Champions Ivan Koloff & Krusher Kruschev
NWA Tag Team Champions Ricky Morton & Robert Gibson vs. Ole & Arn Anderson

JCP @ Cincinnati, OH - Cincinnati Gardens - November 9, 1986 (6,500)
Rick Rude pinned Hector Guerrero
Manny Fernandez pinned Wahoo McDaniel after Rick Rude interfered
Brad Armstrong, NWA Tag Team Champions Ricky Morton & Robert Gibson defeated Big Bubba, Dennis Condrey & Bobby Eaton via disqualification
Road Warrior Animal pinned Ole Anderson in a steel cage match; the bout was to have been a tag team match but Road Warrior Hawk was said to have car trouble
NWA TV Champion Dusty Rhodes & NWA US Champion Nikita Koloff defeated NWA World Champion Ric Flair & Arn Anderson in a steel cage match

JCP @ Greenville, SC - Memorial Auditorium - November 10, 1986
Baron Von Raschke defeated Gary Royal
Ivan Koloff defeated Dutch Mantell
Bobby Jaggers defeated Krusher Kruschev
Bobby Eaton & Dennis Condrey defeated Brad Armstrong & Tim Horner; stipulations stated the winners would be the #1 contenders to the NWA Tag Team Titles
NWA Tag Team Champion Robert Gibson defeated Rick Rude
Manny Fernandez defeated Rick Rude
Big Bubba defeated NWA Tag Team Champion Ricky Morton in a streetfight

NWA CHAMPIONSHIP WRESTLING

FRIDAY, NOV 14, 8PM

DC ARMORY STARPLEX

DUSTY RHODES + NIKITA KOLOFF
VS.
RIC FLAIR + TULLY BLANCHARD

The Road Warriors & Paul Ellering
VS.
The Midnight Express & Big Bubba

World Tag Team Title
The Rock & Roll Express
VS.
Ole & Arn Anderson

Plus Much More

Tickets At RFK Box Office
Hecht Co., All Ticket Center Outlets

Watch NWA Wrestling Every
Sat & Sun At 10:00 AM On

WFTY 50
WASHINGTON•DC

Central States @ Wichita, KS - November 10, 1986
NWA TV Champion Dusty Rhodes & NWA US Champion Nikita Koloff defeated NWA World Champion Ric Flair & Tully Blanchard

JCP @ Columbia, SC - Township Auditorium - November 11, 1986
TV taping:
Brad Armstrong, NWA Tag Team Champions Ricky Morton & Robert Gibson defeated Big Bubba, Bobby Eaton & Dennis Condrey via disqualification
The Road Warriors defeated NWA US Tag Team Champions Ivan Koloff & Krusher Kruschev

Worldwide - 11/15/86:
Bill Dundee defeated Randy Mulkey
Tully Blanchard defeated Eddie Roberts
Ole & Arn Anderson defeated Gary Royal & an unknown
Bobby Eaton & Dennis Condrey defeated John Savage & Keith Petterson
Road Warrior Animal defeated Tony Zane & Vernon Deaton in a handicap match
Pro - 11/15/86:
Rick Rude & Manny Fernandez defeated Jack Johnson & John Savage
Big Bubba, Bobby Eaton & Dennis Condrey vs. Hector Guerrero, Ricky Lee Jones, & Tim Horner
Road Warrior Animal defeated Bill & Randy Mulkey in a handicap match
Ole & Arn Anderson defeated Brodie Chase & Vernon Deaton
Dutch Mantell & Bobby Jaggers defeated Eddie Roberts & Alan West
Wahoo McDaniel & Brad Armstrong vs. Tony Zane & Keith Petterson

JCP @ Norfolk, VA - Scope - November 13, 1986
Brad Armstrong, NWA Tag Team Champions Ricky Morton & Robert Gibson defeated Big Bubba, Bobby Eaton & Dennis Condrey via disqualification

JCP @ Washington DC - Armory - November 14, 1986 (4,000)
The Barbarian pinned Nelson Royal
Rick Rude pinned Hector Guerrero
NWA US Tag Team Champions Ivan Koloff & Krusher Kruschev fought Tim Horner & Brad Armstrong to a 15-minute time-limit draw
Manny Fernandez pinned Wahoo McDaniel after Rick Rude interfered
Road Warrior Animal & Paul Ellering defeated Dennis Condrey & Bobby Eaton via disqualification when Condrey hit Animal with Jim Cornette's tennis racquet at around the 11-minute mark; the match was originally scheduled as a six man tag team match also involving Road Warrior Hawk and Big Bubba but Hawk couldn't compete
NWA Tag Team Champions Ricky Morton & Robert Gibson

defeated Ole & Arn Anderson at 14:30 when Morton pinned Ole
NWA TV Champion Dusty Rhodes & NWA US Champion Nikita Koloff defeated NWA World Champion Ric Flair & Tully Blanchard via disqualification at the 13-minute mark

JCP @ Huntington, WV - November 15, 1986
Road Warrior Animal & Paul Ellering defeated Dennis Condrey & Bobby Eaton via disqualification

JCP @ Atlanta, GA - WTBS Studios - November 16, 1986 (matinee)
World Championship Wrestling - 11/22/86 - featured Tony Schiavone conductin gan interview with Brad Armstrong, NWA Tag Team Champions Ricky Morton & Robert Gibson; featured Schiavone conducting an interview with Jim Cornette, Big Bubba, Bobby Eaton & Dennis Condrey; featured Schiavone conducting an interview with NWA US Champion Nikita Koloff & NWA TV Champion Dusty Rhodes; included Schiavone conducting an interview with Paul Ellering; featured a Starrcade 86 Control Center; included Schiavone conducting an interview with Paul Jones; featured Schiavone conducting an interview with JJ Dillon, Tully Blanchard, Ole & Arn Anderson; included Schiavone conducting an interview with Wahoo McDaniel, Baron Von Raschke, Bobby Jaggers & Dutch Mantell; featured Schiavone conducting an interview with NWA World Champion Ric Flair; included Schiavone conducting an interview with Flair, Ole & Arn, Blanchard, and Dillon:
Tully Blanchard (w/ JJ Dillon) pinned Allen West with the slingshot suplex at the 41-second mark
Brad Armstrong pinned Bill Mulkey at 2:06 with the side Russian legsweep
NWA US Tag Team Champion Krusher Kruschev pinned Keith Patterson at the 29-second mark with the Russian Sickle
Rick Rude & Manny Fernandez (w/ Paul Jones) defeated Bill Tabb & Brodie Chase at 2:00 when Fernandez pinned Chase following the flying forearm
Bobby Eaton & Dennis Condrey (w/ Jim Cornette & Big Bubba) defeated Art Pritts & Vernon Deaton at 1:42 when Deaton submitted to Condrey's Boston Crab following a kneedrop off the top by Eaton
Arn Anderson pinned Tony Zane with the gordbuster at the 30-second mark

JCP @ Johnson City, TN - November 16, 1986
Road Warrior Animal & Paul Ellering defeated Dennis Condrey & Bobby Eaton via disqualification

Central States @ St. Louis, MO - November 16, 1986 (1,500 - 1,800)
Denny Brown & the Italian Stallion defeated Thunderfoot #1 & #2
Mitch Snow pinned Mark Fleming
The MOD Squad & Colt Steele defeated Rufus R. Jones, Rocky King, & George South

Arn Anderson pinned Dave Patterson
Rick Rude fought Brad Armstrong to a draw
NWA TV Champion Dusty Rhodes pinned the Warlord; midway through the bout, Bob Brown interfered on behalf of Warlord but Rhodes beat him up
Tully Blanchard pinned Sam Houston
Teijo Khan pinned an unknown
Bill Dundee defeated Sam Houston
NWA World Champion Ric Flair pinned NWA Tag Team Champion Ricky Morton

JCP @ Greenville, SC - Memorial Auditorium - November 17, 1986
Neslon Royal defeated Eddie Roberts
Ricky Lee Jones defeated Allen West
Hector Guerrero defeated Gary Royal
Jimmy Garvin defeated Tim Horner
Dutch Mantell & Bobby Jaggers defeated NWA US Tag Team Champions Ivan Koloff & Krusher Khruschev in a non-title Texas Tornado match
Baron Von Raschke defeated Shaska Whatley
NWA TV Champion Dusty Rhodes, NWA US Champion Nikita Koloff, Road Warrior Animal, & Paul Ellering defeated NWA World Champion Ric Flair, Tully Blanchard, Ole & Arn Anderson via disqualification

JCP @ Fayetteville, NC - Cumberland County Memorial Arena - November 17, 1986
Don Kernodle defeated John Savage
Bill Dundee defeated Tony Zane
The Barbarian defeated Keith Patterson
Jimmy Valiant defeated Rick Rude via disqualification
Manny Fernandez defeated Wahoo McDaniel in a Texas Death Match
Brad Armstrong, NWA Tag Team Champions Ricky Morton & Robert Gibson defeated Big Bubba, Bobby Eaton & Dennis Condrey via disqualification

JCP @ Spartanburg, SC - Memorial Auditorium - November 18, 1986
Bill Dundee & Jimmy Garvin vs. Don Kernodle & Jimmy Valiant
Hector Guerrero vs. Rick Rude
Manny Fernandez vs. Wahoo McDaniel
Brad Armstrong, NWA Tag Team Champions Ricky Morton & Robert Gibson vs. Big Bubba, Bobby Eaton & Dennis Condrey
NWA TV Champion Dusty Rhodes & NWA US Champion Nikita Koloff vs. NWA World Champion Ric Flair & Tully Blanchard

JCP @ Lansing, MI - November 18, 1986
Road Warrior Animal & Paul Ellering defeated Dennis Condrey & Bobby Eaton via disqualification

JCP @ Green Bay, WI - Brown County Arena - November 19, 1986

Tim Horner fought Shaska Whatley to a draw
The Barbarian defeated Alan West
Jimmy Garvin defeated Hector Guerrero
NWA US Tag Team Champions Ivan Koloff & Krusher Kruschev defeated Dutch Mantell & Bobby Jaggers
Brad Armstrong, NWA Tag Team Champions Ricky Morton & Robert Gibson defeated Big Bubba, Bobby Eaton & Dennis Condrey via disqualification
Wahoo McDaniel fought Arn Anderson to a no contest
NWA TV Champion Dusty Rhodes & NWA US Champion Nikita Koloff defeated NWA World Champion Ric Flair & Tully Blanchard

JCP @ Grand Rapids, MI - November 20, 1986
Road Warrior Animal & Paul Ellering defeated Big Bubba (sub. for an injured Dennis Condrey) & Bobby Eaton

Central States @ Omaha, NE - November 20, 1986
NWA World Champion Ric Flair defeated NWA TV Champion Dusty Rhodes via disqualification

JCP @ Saginaw, MI - Civic Center - November 21, 1986
Brad Armstrong defeated Big Bubba via disqualification
Road Warrior Animal defeated Bobby Eaton

JCP @ Cleveland, OH - Convocation Center - November 22, 1986
Nelson Royal defeated Eddie Roberts
Shaska Whatley defeated Allan West
Don Kernodle defeated Bill Dundee via disqualification
NWA US Tag Team Champions Ivan Koloff & Krusher Kruschev defeated Brad Armstrong & Tim Horner
Wahoo McDaniel defeated the Barbarian in an Indian strap match
NWA Tag Team Champions Ricky Morton & Robert Gibson defeated Rick Rude & Manny Fernandez

JCP @ Baltimore, MD - Arena - November 22, 1986 (14,000; sell out)
Larry Winters defeated Ron Shaw
Ricky Lee Jones Gibson defeated Rocky Kernodle
Hector Guerrero defeated Tony Zane
Jimmy Valiant pinned Gary Royal
Ole & Arn Anderson defeated Dutch Mantell & Bobby Jaggers in a Texas Tornado match when Arn pinned Mantell
Road Warrior Animal & Paul Ellering defeated Bobby Eaton & Dennis Condrey via disqualification when Condrey hit Animal with Jim Cornette's tennis racquet
NWA TV Champion Dusty Rhodes & NWA US Champion Nikita Koloff defeated NWA World Champion Ric Flair & Tully Blanchard in a steel cage match at around the 20-minute mark when Rhodes pinned Blanchard after Koloff hit Blanchard with the Russian Sickle

JCP @ Atlanta, GA - WTBS Studios - November 23, 1986 (matinee)

World Championship Wrestling - 11/29/86 - featured Tony Schiavone conducting an interview with Jimmy Garvin & Precious; included Schiavone conducting an interview with Jim Cornette, Big Bubba, Bobby Eaton & Dennis Condrey; featured Schiavone conducting an interview with Brad & Bob Armstrong; included Schiavone conducting an interview with the Barbarian & Shaska Whatley; featured Schiavone conducting an interview with Dutch Mantell & Bobby Jaggers; included Schiavone conducting an interview with NWA Tag Team Champions Ricky Morton & Robert Gibson; featured Schiavone conducting an interview with Cornette:

Bill Dundee pinned Alan Martin at 2:19 with a sit-down splash off the top

Dennis Condrey & Bobby Eaton (w/ Jim Cornette & Big Bubba) defeated Bill & Randy Mulkey at 3:23 when Eaton pinned Randy

The Barbarian (w/ Shaska Whatley) pinned Paul Garner at 2:45 with a headbutt off the top

Tim Horner pinned Art Pritts at 2:54 with a roll up into a bridge

Don Kernodle pinned Randy Barber at 2:52 with a clothesline off the top

Dutch Mantell & Bobby Jaggers defeated Bill Tabb & Phil Brown at 4:04 when Mantell pinned Brown following a double clothesline

Bill Dundee & Jimmy Garvin (w/ Precious) fought Bob & Brad Armstrong to a double disqualification at 12:57 when all four men began brawling in the ring

JCP @ Kitchener, Ontario - Memorial Auditorium - November 23, 1986 (1,500)

Promoted by Angelo Mosca

Angelo Mosca Jr. defeated Sweet Daddy Siki via disqualification

Gino Brito & Tony Parisi defeated the Destroyer & Gilles Poisson

David Schultz defeated Danny Johnson

Jimmy Valiant defeated the Hangman

NWA US Tag Team Champions Ivan Koloff & Krusher Kruschev defeated Road Warrior Animal & Paul Ellering (sub. for Road Warrior Hawk)

NWA US Champion Nikita Koloff pinned Wahoo McDaniel

JCP @ Asheville, NC - Civic Center - November 23, 1986

Gary Royal fought Rocky Kernodle to a draw

The Barbarian defeated Nelson Royal

Ricky Lee Jones defeated Shaska Whatley

Manny Fernandez defeated Tim Horner

Big Bubba, Bobby Eaton & Dennis Condrey defeated Don Kernodle, Dutch Mantell & Bobby Jaggers

Brad Armstrong defeated Rick Rude via disqualification

NWA Tag Team Champions Ricky Morton & Robert Gibson defeated NWA World Champion Ric Flair & Arn Anderson

JCP @ Greenville, SC - Memorial Auditorium - November 24, 1986

TV taping:

The Road Warriors defeated NWA US Tag Team Champions Ivan Koloff & Krusher Khruschev

NWA Tag Team Champions Ricky Morton & Robert Gibson defeated Rick Rude & Manny Fernandez via disqualification

Also included Tim Horner, Jimmy Garvin, Wahoo McDaniel, Big Bubba, Bobby Jaggers & Dutch Mantell, Bobby Eaton & Dennis Condrey, Brad Armstrong, Tully Blanchard, Arn Anderson, Jimmy Valiant, NWA World Champion Ric Flair, and NWA TV Champion Dusty Rhodes

JCP @ Spartanburg, SC - Memorial Auditorium - November 25, 1986

Jimmy Valiant & Don Kernodle vs. Jimmy Garvin & Bill Dundee

Hector Guerrero vs. Rick Rude

Wahoo McDaniel vs. Manny Fernandez

Brad Armstrong, NWA Tag Team Champions Ricky Morton & Robert Gibson defeated Big Bubba, Bobby Eaton & Dennis Condrey

NWA TV Champion Dusty Rhodes & NWA US Champion Nikita Koloff vs. NWA World Champion Ric Flair & Tully Blanchard

Central States @ Kansas City, MO - November 27, 1986 (3,700)

George South defeated Colt Steele

The Italian Stallion defeated Thunderfoot #2

Thunderfoot #1 defeated Mitch Snow

The MOD Squad defeated Rufus R. Jones & Rocky King

The Warlord defeated Denny Brown

Todd Champion & DJ Peterson defeated Bulldog Brown & Teijo Khan via disqualification

Starrcade 86 - November 27, 1986
Greensboro, NC - Coliseum (16,000; sell out)
Atlanta, GA - Omni (14,000)

Closed-circuit locations included Columbia, SC (which sold out), Charleston, WV, Kansas City, MO, Jacksonville, FL, Cincinnati, OH, Norfolk, VA, Charlotte, NC, and Albany, GA Shown on closed circuit - featured Bob Caudle & Johnny Weaver on commentary in Greensboro and Tony Schiavone & Rick Stewart on commentary in Atlanta; included a music video tribute to Magnum TA:

Greensboro: Tim Horner & Nelson Royal defeated Don & Rocky Kernolde at 7:30 when Horner pinned Rocky with a rolling reverse cradle

Atlanta: Brad Armstrong fought Jimmy Garvin (w/ Precious) to a 15-minute time-limit draw at 15:08; the time limit ended just as Garvin missed a dive off the top; after the match, Armstrong cleared Garvin from the ring, with Precious then confronting Armstrong; Garvin tried to sneak up behind Armstrong but Armstrong again cleared him from the ring

Greensboro: Hector Guerrero & Baron Von Raschke defeated Shaska Whatley & the Barbarian at 7:30 when Von Raschke pinned Whatley with an elbow drop after Whatley missed a charge in the corner; during the bout, Weaver left ringside to go backstage for an interview with NWA TV Champion Dusty Rhodes; after the bout, the Barbarian kicked Von Raschke in the face and then hit a headbutt off the top as Whatley held Von Raschke down; moments later, Guerrero made the save

Atlanta: NWA US Tag Team Champions Krusher Khruschev & Ivan Koloff defeated Bobby Jaggers & Dutch Mantel in a No DQ match at 7:51 when Koloff pinned Jaggers after Kruschev hit Jaggers in the back with a chain as the challenger ran the ropes

Greensboro: Wahoo McDaniel defeated Rick Rude (w/ Paul Jones) in an Indian strap match at 9:05 after dragging Rude to all four corners; after the match, Jones attacked McDaniel until Hector Guerrero and Baron Von Raschke made the save

Atlanta: Central States Heavyweight Champion Sam Houston defeated Bill Dundee via disqualification at 10:21 when, after referee Scrappy McGowan was knocked down, Dundee hit Houston with his own boot; McGowan came to just after the assault and then helped Houston from the ring

Greensboro: Jimmy Valiant (w/ Big Mama) pinned Paul Jones at 4:00 after hitting him with Jones' own foreign object; stipulations stated Jones would be shaved bald if he lost and Big Mama would be shaved bald if Valiant lost; after the bout, Rick Rude and Manny Fernandez attacked Valiant, eventually dropping him with a double DDT onto a steel chair

Atlanta: Big Bubba (w/ Jim Cornette) defeated NWA Mid-Atlantic Heavyweight Champion Ron Garvin in a non-title streetfight at 11:50; after the referee counted both men down for 10, it was ruled that the first man to reach his feet would be the winner; when Garvin got up behind the referee's back, Cornette hit him with his tennis racquet, giving Bubba the win

Greensboro: Tully Blanchard (w/ JJ Dillon) defeated NWA TV Champion Dusty Rhodes in a first blood match to win the title at 8:41 after hitting him with a roll of coins; prior to the match, Rhodes busted open Dillon with an elbow to the head; Rhodes made Blanchard bleed first, at the 11-minute mark, but referee Earl Hebner was knocked out, allowing Dillon to wipe away the blood, rub Vasoline on the wound, and hand the challenger the roll of coins; after the bout, Rhodes threw Hebner to the floor (*Ric Flair & the 4 Horsemen*)

Atlanta: The Road Warriors (w/ Paul Ellering) defeated Bobby Eaton & Dennis Condrey (w/ Jim Cornette & Big Bubba) in a scaffold match at 7:07 after Condrey and Eaton were kicked off the scaffold; after the bout, Ellering chased Cornette up the scaffold, where Cornette eventually fell off and blew out both knees (*The Best of Starrcade: 1983-1987*, *The Life & Death of the Road Warriors*, *Starrcade: The Essential Collection*)

Greensboro: NWA Tag Team Champions Ricky Morton & Robert Gibson defeated Arn & Ole Anderson in a steel cage match at 19:03 when Gibson dropkicked Morton onto Ole for the pin (*The Best of Starrcade: 1983-1987*, *Bloodbath: Wrestling's Most Incredible Steel Cage Matches*)

Atlanta: NWA World Champion Ric Flair fought NWA US Champion Nikita Koloff to a double disqualification at 19:12 after the challenger repeatedly shoved referee Tommy Young to the mat as Young tried to get Koloff and Flair out of the corner; earlier in the match, both Young and referee Scrappy

McGowan were knocked down; after the bout, Jimmy Garvin, Bill Dundee, and Big Bubba came out and helped Flair gang up on Koloff until Bobby Jaggers, NWA Mid-Atlantic Heavyweight Champion Ron Garvin, Dutch Mantel, Sam Houston, and Brad Armstrong made the save; the two men were then held apart

JCP @ Richmond, VA - Coliseum - November 28, 1986 (9,000)
Hector Guerrero fought Bill Dundee to a draw
Bobby Jaggers & Dutch Mantel defeated NWA US Tag Team Champions Ivan Koloff & Krusher Kruschev
Brad Armstrong defeated Jimmy Garvin via disqualification
Wahoo McDaniel defeated Manny Fernandez in an Indian strap match
Ole & Arn Anderson defeated NWA Tag Team Champions Ricky Morton & Robert Gibson in a non-title Texas Tornado match
Road Warrior Animal & Paul Ellering defeated Bobby Eaton & Dennis Condrey via disqualification; the bout was advertised as Big Bubba, Eaton & Condrey vs. Ellering & the Road Warriors
Dusty Rhodes & NWA US Champion Nikita Koloff defeated NWA World Champion Ric Flair & NWA TV Champion Tully Blanchard in a steel cage match

JCP @ Minneapolis, MN - Met Center - November 29, 1986
Tim Horner vs. Big Bubba
The Road Warriors vs. Bobby Eaton & Dennis Condrey
NWA World Champion Ric Flair vs. Dusty Rhodes

JCP @ Philadelphia, PA - Civic Center - November 29, 1986
Hector Guerrero defeated Alan West
Don Kernodle defeated Gary Royal
Jimmy Valiant defeated Tony Zane
NWA Mid-Atlantic Heavyweight Champion Ron Garvin defeated Bill Dundee via count-out
NWA US Tag Team Champions Ivan Koloff & Krusher Kruschev defeated Dutch Mantell & Bobby Jaggers
NWA US Champion Nikita Koloff defeated NWA TV Champion Tully Blanchard
NWA Tag Team Champions Ricky Morton & Robert Gibson defeated Rick Rude & Manny Fernandez via disqualification

JCP @ Peoria, IL - November 30, 1986
Big Bubba, Bobby Eaton & Dennis Condrey vs. Paul Ellering & the Road Warriors

JCP @ Fayetteville, NC - Cumberland County Memorial Arena - December 1, 1986
Tim Horner defeated Bill Dundee
Brad Armstrong fought Ivan Koloff to a draw
Krusher Kruschev defeated Bobby Jaggers
NWA Mid-Atlantic Heavyweight Champion Ron Garvin defeated Bobby Eaton (sub. for Big Bubba)
Dusty Rhodes & NWA US Champion Nikita Koloff defeated

NWA World Champion Ric Flair & NWA TV Champion Tully Blanchard in a chain & bullrope match
Road Warrior Animal won a $25,000 25-man Bunkhouse Stampede match; other participants included Barry Windham, Road Warrior Hawk, NWA Tag Team Champions Ricky Morton & Robert Gibson, Rick Rude, Bobby Eaton & Dennis Condrey, Wahoo McDaniel, Brad Armstrong, Dick Murdoch, Big Bubba, Arn Anderson, Manny Fernandez, Krusher Kruschev, Ivan Koloff, NWA Mid-Atlantic Heavyweight Champion Ron Garvin, Baron Von Raschke, Jimmy Valiant, Jimmy Garvin, Bobby Jaggers & Dutch Mantel

JCP @ Rock Hill, SC - Winthrop Coliseum - December 2, 1986
TV taping:
Rick Rude & Manny Fernandez defeated Allen West & Eddie Roberts
Barry Windham pinned Mike Simani
Brad Armstrong defeated Ron Rossi
NWA TV Champion Tully Blanchard pinned John Savage
Wahoo McDaniel & Baron Von Raschke defeated Tony Zane & Vernon Deaton
Arn Anderson pinned Keith Patterson
Jimmy Garvin defeated Randy Mulkey
Bobby Eaton & Dennis Condrey defeated Nelson Royal & Tim Horner
NWA Mid-Atlantic Heavyweight Champion Ron Garvin defeated John Savage
Rick Rude & Manny Fernandez defeated Ron Rossi & Vernon Deaton
Barry Windham defeated Bill Mulkey
NWA TV Champion Tully Blanchard & Arn Anderson defeated Randy Mulkey & Keith Patterson
Bobby Jaggers & Dutch Mantell defeated Allen West & Eddie Roberts
NWA US Champion Nikita Koloff pinned Mike Simani
Big Bubba defeated NWA Mid-Atlantic Heavyweight Champion Ron Garvin via count-out in a Louisville streetfight
NWA Tag Team Champions Ricky Morton & Robert Gibson defeated Rick Rude & Manny Fernandez via disqualification

JCP @ Raleigh, NC - Dorton Arena - December 3, 1986
Denny Brown defeated Hector Guerrero
Tim Horner defeated Bill Dundee
Nelson Royal defeated Shaska Whatley
Brad Armstrong defeated the Barbarian
Dutch Mantell fought Ivan Koloff to a no contest
Dusty Rhodes & NWA US Champion Nikita Koloff defeated NWA World Champion Ric Flair & NWA TV Champion Tully Blanchard in a chain and bullrope match
Big Bubba won a Bunkhouse Stampede match

JCP @ Columbus, GA - December 4, 1986
NWA Mid-Atlantic Heavyweight Champion Ron Garvin, NWA Tag Team Champions Ricky Morton & Robert Gibson vs. Big Bubba, Bobby Eaton & Dennis Condrey

JCP @ Hampton, VA - Coliseum - December 5, 1986
NWA Mid-Atlantic Heavyweight Champion Ron Garvin vs. Big Bubba (streetfight)
Included a Bunkhouse Stampede match

Central States @ Kansas City, KS - Memorial Hall - December 5, 1986
Bulldog Brown defeated Russell Sapp
Brad & Bart Batten defeated Thunderfoot #1 & #2
Rufus R. Jones defeated Bill Dundee via disqualification
Sam Houston defeated Colt Steele

321

ALLSTAR CHAMPIONSHIP WRESTLING

SUNDAY DECEMBER 7
VETERANS AUDITORIUM
DES MOINES, IA

NWA NATIONAL WRESTLING ALLIANCE

RUSSIAN CHAIN & TEXAS BULLROPE

"AMERICAN DREAM"   "NATURE BOY"

DUSTY RHODES   vs   RIC FLAIR
NIKITA KOLOFF   TULLY BLANCHARD

$25,000 BUNKHOUSE BATTLE ROYAL!

ROAD WARRIORS - ROBERT GIBSON - RICK MORTON
PAUL ELLERING - BARRY WINDHAM - BIG BUBBA
JIMMY GARVIN - RAGING BULL - MIDNITE EXPRESS
SAM HOUSTON - DAVE PETERSON - RUFUS JONES
BARBARIAN - MOD SQUAD - ARN ANDERSON
STALLION - TODD CHAMPION - PAUL JONES -
DICK MURDOCH
COLT STEEL - BRAD ARMSTRONG WARLORD - DENNY BROWN

CENTRAL STATES HWT. TITLE!   **SAM HOUSTON vs ARN ANDERSON**
(CHAMPION)   (CHALLENGER)

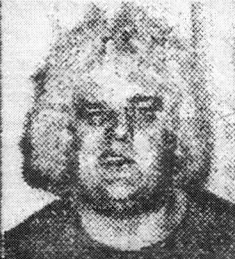

ADVANCE TICKETS AT:
VETS AUDITORIUM
AMES HILTON - CONV. CENTER

RINGSIDE	GEN. ADM ADULTS	GEN. ADM CHILDREN
$15.00	$10.00	$5.00

WATCH TV WRESTLING
SUN 11 AM CH. 17

TAG TITLE
PETERSON
CHAMPION
vs
MOD SQUAD

RUFUS vs D. BROWN
SNOW vs STEEL

ALLSTAR CHAMPIONSHIP WRESTLING

322

The Warlord won a Bunkhouse Stampede match
Bulldog Brown defeated Mitch Snow
Todd Champion & DJ Peterson defeated the Warlord & the Barbarian
The Italian Stallion defeated Thunderfoot #2
Sam Houston defeated Jimmy Garvin via disqualification
Wahoo McDaniel fought Manny Fernandez to a no contest

JCP @ Atlanta, GA - WTBS Studios - December 6, 1986 (matinee)
World Championship Wrestling - 12/6/86 - featured Tony Schiavone conducting an interview with NWA World Champion Ric Flair in which he compared himself to Barry Windham, Wahoo McDaniel, NWA Mid-Atlantic Heavyweight Champion Ron Garvin, the Road Warriors, and NWA US Champion Nikita Koloff and then complained about having to be put in bullrope chain matches, which weren't his speciality; Flair then told David Crockett that he wouldn't work for him if he didn't put him in actual wrestling matches; Arn Anderson, NWA TV Champion Tully Blanchard, and JJ Dillon then came out, with Flair then saying the Horsemen would tear down Baltimore, Chicago, and Philadelphia:
NWA TV Champion Tully Blanchard (w/ JJ Dillon) pinned Mike Jackson
Brad Armstrong pinned Vernon Deaton
Arn Anderson pinned Alan Martin
Bobby Eaton & Dennis Condrey (w/ Baby Doll & Big Bubba) defeated Art Pritts & Dave Spearman when Eaton pinned Pritts
Barry Windham pinned Randy Barber
Rick Rude & Manny Fernandez (w/ Paul Jones) defeated NWA Tag Team Champions Ricky Morton & Robert Gibson to win the titles at 26:58 when Fernandez pinned Gibson with a roll over and grabbing the tights for leverage after Rude hit a clothesline on Gibson behind the referee's back as Gibson had Fernandez covered with a roll up

Central States @ St. Louis, MO - December 6, 1986
NWA US Champion Nikita Koloff defeated NWA World Champion Ric Flair via disqualification

JCP @ Cleveland, OH - Convocation Center - December 6, 1986
Tim Horner defeated Buddy Roberts
Jimmy Valiant & Baron Von Raschke defeated Shaska Whatley & Gary Royal
Ricky Lee Jones defeated the Super Destroyer
Denny Brown fought Hector Guerrero to a draw
NWA TV Champion Tully Blanchard defeated Brad Armstrong via count-out
Bobby Jaggers & Dutch Mantell defeated Ivan Koloff & Krusher Kruschev in a Texas Tornado match
Big Bubba defeated NWA Mid-Atlantic Heavyweight Champion Ron Garvin via count-out in a streetfight

Central States @ Des Moines, IA - December 7, 1986
Dusty Rhodes & NWA US Champion Nikita Koloff defeated

NWA World Champion Ric Flair & NWA TV Champion Tully Blanchard
Also included a Bunkhouse Stampede match featuring Bobby Eaton & Dennis Condrey

Central States @ Kansas City, MO - December 7, 1986
Dusty Rhodes & NWA US Champion Nikita Koloff defeated NWA World Champion Ric Flair & NWA TV Champion Tully Blanchard in a bullrope chain match

JCP @ Saginaw, MI - December 8, 1986
NWA Mid-Atlantic Heavyweight Champion Ron Garvin vs. Big Bubba (streetfight)
Bobby Eaton & Dennis Condrey vs. Brad Armstrong & Tim Horner

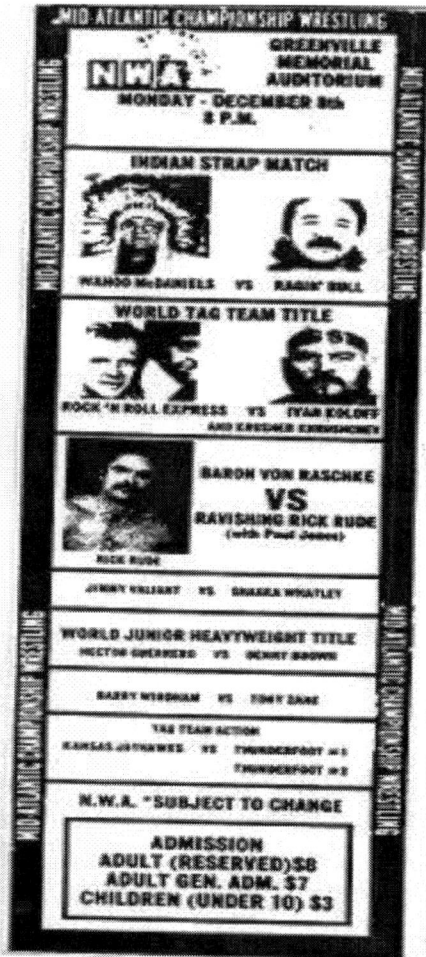

JCP @ Greenville, SC - Memorial Auditorium - December 8, 1986
Bobby Jaggers & Dutch Mantell vs. Thunderfoot #1 & #2
Barry Windham vs. Tony Zane
Hector Guerrero vs. NWA Jr. Heavyweight Champion Denny Brown
Jimmy Valiant vs. Shaska Whatley
Baron Von Raschke vs. NWA Tag Team Champion Rick Rude
Ricky Morton & Robert Gibson vs. Ivan Koloff & Krusher Kruschev
Wahoo McDaniel vs. NWA Tag Team Champion Manny Fernandez (Indian strap match)

JCP @ Spartanburg, SC - Memorial Auditorium - December 9, 1986
TV taping:
Ricky Morton & Robert Gibson vs. NWA Tag Team Champions Rick Rude & Manny Fernandez
NWA Mid-Atlantic Heavyweight Champion Ron Garvin & Barry Windham defeated NWA US Tag Team Champions Ivan Koloff & Krusher Kruschev to win the titles

JCP @ Asheville, NC - Civic Center - December 10, 1986
Don Kernodle vs. Thunderfoot #2
NWA Jr. Heavyweight Champion Denny Brown vs. Nelson Royal
Wahoo McDaniel vs. Ivan Koloff
Ricky Morton & Robert Gibson vs. NWA Tag Team Champions Rick Rude & Manny Fernandez
Dusty Rhodes & NWA US Champion Nikita Koloff vs. NWA World Champion Ric Flair & NWA TV Champion Tully Blanchard
Also included a $25,000 25-man Bunkhouse Stampede featuring Ricky Morton & Robert Gibson, Barry Windham, Wahoo McDaniel, Jimmy Valiant, Don Kernodle, Thunderfoot #1, Thunderfoot #2, Arn Anderson, the Road Warriors, Bobby Eaton & Dennis Condrey, Big Bubba, Dick Murdoch, NWA Tag Team Champions Rick Rude & Manny Fernandez, Shaska Whatley, Baron Von Raschke, Bobby Jaggers, Dutch Mantel, Nelson Royal, Krusher Kruschev, and Ivan Koloff

JCP @ Norfolk, VA - Scope - December 11, 1986
Big Bubba vs. NWA Mid-Atlantic Heavyweight Champion Ron Garvin (streetfight)
Included a Bunkhouse Stampede match featuring Bobby Eaton & Dennis Condrey

JCP @ Charlotte, NC - Coliseum - December 12, 1986 (9,000 paid)
TV taping:
Ivan Koloff defeated Rocky King
Denny Brown fought Hector Guerrero to a draw
The Road Warriors defeated Randy & Bill Mulkey
Barry Windham defeated Art Pritts
Big Bubba defeated NWA Mid-Atlantic Heavyweight Champion Ron Garvin in a streetfight

Bobby Eaton & Dennis Condrey defeated George South & Rocky King
NWA US Tag Team Champions Barry Windham & NWA Mid-Atlantic Heavyweight Champion Ron Garvin defeated Mike Simani & Vernon Deaton
Jimmy Valiant defeated Tony Zane
Ricky Morton & Robert Gibson defeated NWA Tag Team Champions Rick Rude & Manny Fernandez
Worldwide - 12/86:
Dusty Rhodes & NWA US Champion Nikita Koloff defeated NWA World Champion Ric Flair & Arn Anderson (w/ JJ Dillon) in a bullrope chain match; only the first 2 minutes of the match were shown before the broadcast ended

JCP @ Atlanta, GA - WTBS Studios - December 13, 1986 (matinee)
World Championship Wrestling - 12/13/86 - featured Tony Schiavone conducting a closing interview with NWA World Champion Ric Flair, NWA TV Champion Tully Blanchard, Ole & Arn Anderson, and JJ Dillon in which Arn said he felt naked standing beside so many champions and not having a belt for himself; Blanchard, Flair, Ole, and Dillon then discussed the prestige of the Horsemen, with Ole finishing by saying he had his eye on the National Tag Team Titles

JCP @ Baltimore, MD - Arena - December 13, 1986 (just under 10,000) (matinee)
Brad Armstrong defeated Shaska Whatley
Bobby Jaggers & Dutch Mantell defeated Ivan Koloff & Krusher Kruschev
Big Bubba defeated NWA Mid-Atlantic Heavyweight Champion & NWA US Tag Team Champion Ron Garvin in a streetfight
The Road Warriors defeated Bobby Eaton & Dennis Condrey
Dusty Rhodes won a Bunkhouse Stampede match
NWA World Champion Ric Flair defeated NWA US Champion Nikita Koloff

JCP @ Philadelphia, PA - Civic Center - December 13, 1986 (10,000)
Denny Brown defeated Hector Guerrero
Jimmy Valiant defeated Shaska Whatley
Brad Armstrong & Tim Horner defeated Ivan Koloff & Krusher Kruschev
Barry Windham defeated the Barbarian
Dusty Rhodes & the Road Warriors defeated Big Bubba, Bobby Eaton, & Dennis Condrey
NWA US Champion Nikita Koloff defeated NWA World Champion Ric Flair via disqualification
Dusty Rhodes won a Bunkhouse Stampede match

JCP @ Atlanta, GA - WTBS Studios - December 14, 1986 (matinee)
World Championship Wrestling - 12/20/86 - featured Tony Schiavone conducting an interview with NWA TV Champion Tully Blanchard & JJ Dillon in which they discussed Dusty Rhodes recently winning back to back Bunkhouse Stampedes

in Philadelphia and Baltimore, with Blanchard saying Rhodes would have to regroup after the punishment he sustained if he hoped to win back the TV title; included Schiavone conducting an interview with NWA World Champion Ric Flair in which he spoke about his recent matches in Philadelphia and Baltimore against NWA US Champion Nikita Koloff and said Koloff was out of breath at the 20-minute mark; Flair then brought up the fact Dusty Rhodes was friends with Bruce Springsteen, David Allen Coe, and Willie Nelson but he was waking up next to a beautiful woman every morning; Flair then spoke about going to Minneapolis and Los Angeles, said Rhodes was a Boston Celtics fan, and wanted Jack Nicholson in the front row to see him wipe the mat with Rhodes:

Bobby Eaton & Dennis Condrey defeated David Isley & Zane Smith when Condrey pinned Isley
NWA Mid-Atlantic Heavyweight Champion & NWA US Tag Team Champion Ron Garvin pinned Vernon Deaton
Brad Armstrong pinned Brodie Chase
Ole & Arn Anderson defeated Rocky King & George South when South submitted to Ole
NWA US Champion Nikita Koloff pinned Art Pritts; prior to the bout, Tony Schiavone conducted an interview with Ole & Arn Anderson in which Ole said the Andersons needed titles and said Dusty Rhodes was hiding from them; Arn then said he had come from relative obscurity over the past 2 years to become a Horseman and repeated title holder; Arn then pointed to Koloff in the ring and said he wanted a title and didn't care which it was
NWA US Tag Team Champion Barry Windham pinned Tony Zane
The Road Warriors defeated Larry Stevens & Butch Cooper
Ivan Koloff & Krusher Kruschev defeated Bill Tabb & Al Garrett when Koloff pinned Garrett
NWA Tag Team Champions Rick Rude & Manny Fernandez defeated Bill & Randy Mulkey when Rude pinned Randy
NWA TV Champion Tully Blanchard pinned Randy Barber
Wahoo McDaniel pinned Paul Garner

Central States @ Maysville, KS - December 14, 1986
Brad & Bart Batten defeated Pork Chop Cash & Colt Steele
Pat Rose defeated Mitch Snow
Todd Champion & DJ Peterson defeated Teijo Khan & the Warlord
The Italian Stallion & Rufus R. Jones defeated the MOD Squad
Sam Houston fought Bulldog Brown to a no contest

JCP @ Chicago, IL - Rosemont Horizon - December 14, 1986 (12,500)
Debut at the venue
Tim Horner defeated Shaska Whatley
Brad Armstrong fought Jimmy Garvin to a draw
Wahoo McDaniel defeated NWA Tag Team Champion Rick Rude
Ricky Morton & Robert Gibson defeated Ivan Koloff & Krusher Kruschev
The Road Warriors defeated Bobby Eaton & Dennis Condrey
The Road Warriors co-won a $50,000 Bunkhouse Stampede;

other participants included: Bobby Eaton & Dennis Condrey, Big Bubba, Bob Armstrong, Wahoo McDaniel, Ole Anderson, Arn Anderson, Ivan Koloff, Krusher Kruschev, Shaska Whatley, Dick Murdoch, Ricky Morton & Robert Gibson, Dutch Mantell & Bobby Jaggers, Jimmy Valiant, Tim Horner, Barry Windham, NWA Tag Team Champions Rick Rude & Manny Fernandez, Jimmy Garvin, the Barbarian, and Baron Von Raschke
Dusty Rhodes & NWA US Champion Nikita Koloff defeated NWA World Champion Ric Flair & NWA TV Champion Tully Blanchard

JCP @ Greenville, SC - Memorial Auditorium - December 15, 1986
TV taping:
Pro - 1/3/87:
Hector Guerrero vs. Eddie Roberts
Barry Windham vs. Gary Royal
The Barbarian vs. Baron Von Raschke
NWA Tag Team Champion Rick Rude vs. Robert Gibson
Dark match after the taping: Big Bubba won a $25,000 20-man Bunkhouse Stampede match
Dark match after the taping: Dusty Rhodes & NWA US Champion Nikita Koloff defeated NWA World Champion Ric Flair & Arn Anderson in a steel cage match

JCP @ Greenville, SC - Memorial Auditorium - December 25, 1986 (3,566) (matinee)
$4 fan appreciation night
Big Bubba did not appear due to injury
Thunderfoot #1 & #2 defeated George South & Rocky King
Rocky Kernodle defeated Allen West
Don Kernodle defeated Ricky Lee Jones
NWA Jr. Heavyweight Champion Denny Brown fought Nelson Royal to a draw
Bobby Jaggers & Dutch Mantell defeated Ivan Koloff & Krusher Kruschev
Brad Armstrong defeated Jimmy Garvin
Ivan Koloff (sub. for Big Bubba), Bobby Eaton & Dennis Condrey defeated Dutch Mantell & Bobby Jaggers (sub. for Wahoo McDaniel & Dick Murdoch), NWA Mid-Atlantic Heavyweight Champion & NWA Us Tag Team Champion Ron Garvin

JCP @ Charlotte, NC - December 25, 1986 (matinee) (10,200)
Hector Guerrero defeated Eddie Roberts
Barry Windham defeated Gary Royal
Barry Windham defeated Shaska Whatley
Jimmy Valiant defeated Bill Dundee
Ricky Morton defeated NWA Tag Team Champion Manny Fernandez
Robert Gibson fought NWA Tag Team Champion Rick Rude to a draw
Dusty Rhodes, NWA US Champion Nikita Koloff, & the Road Warriors defeated NWA World Champion Ric Flair, NWA TV Champion Tully Blanchard, Arn & Ole Anderson

MID-ATLANTIC CHAMPIONSHIP WRESTLING

NWA
GREENVILLE MEMORIAL AUDITORIUM
Monday, December 15th
7:30 PM
TV Taping

10 FOOT STEEL CAGE MATCH

DUSTY RHODES VS "RIC FLAIR"

NIKITA KOLOFF VS ARN ANDERSON

BUNKHOUSE STAMPEDE
$25,000 — 20 MAN BUNKHOUSE STAMPEDE
OVER THE TOP BATTLE ROYAL

PLUS LIVE T.V.
TAPING OF N.W.A. PRO WRESTLING
AND
WORLD WIDE WRESTLING
FEATURING THESE ABOVE STARS

N.W.A. * SUBJECT TO CHANGE

ADMISSION
ADULT (RESERVED)-$15
ADULT GEN. ADM. $10
CHILDREN (UNDER 10) $5

MID-ATLANTIC CHAMPIONSHIP WRESTLING

NWA
GREENVILLE MEMORIAL AUDITORIUM
Christmas Day
December 25th
2:00 P.M.

FAN APPRECIATION DAY
ALL SEATS $4

SIX MAN TAG TEAM ELIMINATION

WAHOO McDANIEL, RONNIE GARVIN VS MIDNIGHT EXPRESS, BIG BUBBA (With Jim Cornette)

DICK MURDOCH

BIG GRUDGE MATCH

BRAD ARMSTRONG VS GORGEOUS JIMMY GARVIN

TAG TEAM MATCH
IVAN KOLOFF, KRUSHER KHRUSHCHEV VS KANSAS JAYHAWKS

WORLD JUNIOR HEAVYWEIGHT TITLE
DENNY BROWN VS NELSON ROYAL
DON KERNODLE VS RICKY LEE JONES
ALLEN WEST VS ROCKY KERNODLE
ROCKY KING VS THUNDERFOOT #1
GEORGE SOUTH VS THUNDERFOOT #2

TICKET PRICES : $4 — ALL SEATS
*NWA SUBJECT TO CHANGE

ADMISSION
ALL SEATS
$4
FAN APPRECIATION DAY

MID-ATLANTIC CHAMPIONSHIP WRESTLING

The Toughest Of All
NWA PRO WRESTLING
featuring
"Bunkhouse Stampede" PLUS! WORLD HEAVYWEIGHT TITLE MATCH

"Nature Boy" Ric Flair
vs
Nikita Koloff

SAT. DEC. 27, 8:00 PM
MET CENTER
Tickets at Met Center & Dayton's
CALL: 853-9300

Watch NWA every Sat
noon on KTMA-TV23 on
KXLI-TV41 Fridays and
Sundays at 10 30 p m

326

JCP @ Atlanta, GA - Omni - December 25, 1986 (18,000)
All tickets were $5
Denny Brown fought Nelson Royal to a draw
Dick Murdoch defeated Bobby Eaton
NWA US Tag Team Champions Barry Windham & NWA Mid-Atlantic Heavyweight Champion Ron Garvin defeated Ivan Koloff & Krusher Kruschev
Robert Gibson defeated NWA Tag Team Champion Rick Rude via disqualification
Ricky Morton fought NWA Tag Team Champion Manny Fernandez to a no contest
Bobby Eaton & Dennis Condrey defeated Brad Armstrong & Tim Horner
Dusty Rhodes, NWA US Champion Nikita Koloff, & the Road Warriors defeated NWA World Champion Ric Flair, NWA TV Champion Tully Blanchard, Arn & Ole Anderson

JCP @ Charleston, SC - December 26, 1986 (3,750)
Thunderfoot #1 & #2 defeated Alan West & Eddie Roberts
Tim Horner & Don Kernodle defeated Ivan Koloff & Krusher Kruschev
NWA Tag Team Champion Manny Fernandez defeated Hector Guerrero
Denny Brown fought Nelson Royal to a draw
Jimmy Garvin fought Brad Armstrong to a draw
Ricky Lee Jones defeated Alan West
NWA US Champion Nikita Koloff defeated NWA World Champion Ric Flair via disqualification

JCP @ Richmond, VA - Coliseum - December 26, 1986
Bill Dundee defeated Mark Fleming
Baron Von Raschke defeated Shaska Whatley
Ricky Morton defeated NWA Tag Team Champion Rick Rude via disqualification
Robert Gibson defeated Arn Anderson
Dick Murdoch fought NWA TV Champion Tully Blanchard to a draw
The Road Warriors defeated Bobby Eaton & Dennis Condrey
Dusty Rhodes won a Bunkhouse Stampede match

JCP @ Atlanta, GA - WTBS Studios - December 27, 1986 (matinee)
World Championship Wrestling - 12/27/86 - featured Tony Schiavone conducting an interview with NWA Mid-Atlantic Heavyweight Champion & NWA US Tag Team Champion Ron Garvin in which Garvin vacated the title and handed it over to Jim Crockett Jr.:
Dick Murdoch pinned Brodie Chase
NWA US Tag Team Champions Ron Garvin & Barry Windham fought Bobby Eaton & Dennis Condrey (w/ Jim Cornette & Big Bubba) to a time-limit draw
The Road Warriors (w/ Paul Ellering) defeated Randy & Bill Mulkey with simultaneous pinfalls
NWA Tag Team Champions Rick Rude & Manny Fernandez (w/ Paul Jones) defeated Pablo Crenshaw & Dave Spencer when Rude pinned Spencer

NWA TV Champion Tully Blanchard (w/ JJ Dillon) pinned Pat O'Brian
Bill Dundee pinned Clement Fields
Ole & Arn Anderson (w/ JJ Dillon) defeated Bill Tabb & Randy Barber when Arn pinned Barber
Brad Armstrong pinned Mike Jackson
Jimmy Garvin (w/ Precious) pinned Alan Martin
World Championship Wrestling Sunday Edition - 12/28/86

Worldwide - 12/27/86:
NWA Tag Team Champions Rick Rude & Manny Fernandez vs. Allen West & Eddie Roberts
Big Bubba, Dennis Condrey, & Bobby Eaton vs. Rocky King, George South, & Ricky Lee Jones
Ole & Arn Anderson vs. Nelson Royal & Mike Simani
Barry Windham vs. Ron Rossi
Ivan Koloff & Krusher Kruschev vs. Bill & Randy Mulkey
NWA TV Champion Tully Blanchard vs. Gary Royal
Jimmy Garvin vs. Tony Zane

JCP @ Minneapolis, MN - Met Center - December 27, 1986
Big Bubba did not appear as scheduled due to a high fever
Dusty Rhodes & the Road Warriors defeated Jimmy Garvin (sub. for Big Bubba), Bobby Eaton, & Dennis Condrey
NWA World Champion Ric Flair vs. NWA US Champion Nikita Koloff
Also included a Bunkhouse Stampede match

JCP @ Greensboro, NC - December 28, 1986 (matinee) (8,121)
Tim Horner defeated Shaska Whatley
Denny Brown fought Hector Guerrero to a draw
Robert Gibson defeated NWA Tag Team Champion Rick Rude
Ricky Morton defeated NWA Tag Team Champion Manny Fernandez
Barry Windham & Brad Armstrong defeated Ivan Koloff & Krusher Kruschev
Dusty Rhodes & NWA US Champion Nikita Koloff defeated NWA World Champion Ric Flair & Arn Anderson
Big Bubba won a Bunkhouse Stampede match

JCP @ Albuquerque, NM - December 28, 1986 (5,251; 5,002 paid)
Big Bubba did not appear as scheduled due to a high fever
Teijo Khan fought the Italian Stallion to a draw
Todd Champion pinned Rose
Sam Houston pinned the Warlord
NWA US Champion Nikita Koloff pinned MOD Squad Basher (sub. for Big Bubba) at the 29-second mark
NWA World Champion Ric Flair defeated Dusty Rhodes via disqualification
The Road Warriors defeated Bobby Eaton & Dennis Condrey at 5:46
NWA US Champion Nikita Koloff won a Bunkhouse Stampede

JCP @ Fayetteville, NC - Cumberland County Memorial Arena - December 29, 1986 (4,500)
Wahoo McDaniel vs. NWA Tag Team Champion Rick Rude in an Indian strap match did not take place as advertised
Baron Von Raschke defeated Shaska Whatley (sub. for the Barbarian) in a Texas Death Match
NWA Tag Team Champion Rick Rude (sub. for Shaska Whatley) pinned Jimmy Valiant in under a minute
Ron Garvin defeated Bill Dundee
Brad Armstrong defeated Jimmy Garvin via disqualification
Dutch Mantell & Bobby Jaggers defeated NWA US Tag Team Champions Ivan Koloff & Krusher Kruschev in a steel cage match

JCP @ Inglewood, CA - Great Western Forum - December 29, 1986 (7,000)
Several of the matches were taped by Nippon television and aired in Japan over the weekend; Big Bubba did not appear as scheduled due to a high fever; Mr. T was in attendance; Tony Schiavone was the ring announcer
Sam Houston pinned Teijo Khan
Todd Champion defeated Ken Timbs
Dick Murdoch pinned the Warlord with a roll up
Ricky Morton & Robert Gibson defeated Ole & Arn Anderson when Morton pinned Ole with a sunset flip into the ring
The Giant Baba & Hiroshi Wajima defeated the MOD Squad
Televised on Japan TV: NWA Six-Man Tag Team Champions the Road Warriors (w/ Paul Ellering) defeated Bobby Eaton & Dennis Condrey (w/ Jim Cornette) via disqualification
Dusty Rhodes & NWA US Champion Nikita Koloff defeated NWA World Champion Ric Flair & NWA TV Champion Tully Blanchard at the 20-minute mark
Televised on Japan TV: Road Warrior Hawk (w/ Paul Ellering) won a Bunkhouse Stampede at 7:30 by winning a coin flip between he and Road Warrior Animal after both men eliminated Bobby Eaton & Dennis Condrey; other participants included: Ricky Morton & Robert Gibson, NWA Tag Team Champions Manny Fernandez & Rick Rude, Ole & Arn Anderson, Teijo Khan, Ken Timbs, the Italian Stallion, the Warlord, Sam Houston, Pat Rose, the MOD Squad, Dick Murdoch, and Barry Windham; order of elimination: Houston, Basher, Stallion, Rose, Khan, Champion, Arn, Fernandez, Morton, Murdoch, Windham, Ole, Warlord, Gibson, Condrey, and Eaton

JCP @ San Francisco, CA - Civic Auditorium - December 30, 1986 (8,500; sell out)
Big Bubba did not appear as scheduled due to a high fever
Todd Champion pinned Pat Rose at around the 8-minute mark with an elbow drop
Sam Houston pinned Teijo Khan at around the 8-minute mark with a small package
Dick Murdoch pinned the Warlord at around the 7-minute mark
The Road Warriors defeated Bobby Eaton & Dennis Condrey via disqualification when Eaton & Condrey used Jim Cornette's tennis racquet as a weapon
NWA World Champion Ric Flair defeated Dusty Rhodes via reverse decision; Rhodes originally won the match and title but the decision was overruled because Rhodes had knocked down the referee moments earlier
NWA US Champion Nikita Koloff pinned NWA TV Champion Tully Blanchard at the 16-minute mark after hitting the Russian Sickle on both the challenger and JJ Dillon, moments after Blanchard thought he had won the match and title with the slingshot suplex, not realizing Koloff's foot was on the ropes
Road Warrior Animal won a Bunkhouse Stampede; other participants included: Dave Peterson, Todd Champion, Pat Rose, Sam Houston, Teijo Khan, Dick Murdoch, the Warlord, Bobby Eaton & Dennis Condrey, Road Warrior Hawk, the Italian Stallion, the MOD Squad, Ken Timbs, Barry Windham, and Manny Fernandez; the Road Warriors eliminated Eaton & Condrey and then flipped a coin to determine which of them would win the match

1987.

As the year began, Jim Crockett Promotions was arguably positioned as the second top wrestling promotion in the US, behind the World Wrestling Federation.

Pro Wrestling USA was no more, a failed experiment that did more to highlight mistrust among the top promoters than it did to put a dent in the WWF's success. But as the WWF made its national expansion - even breaking into international TV markets - Crockett made its own westward movement.

The ownership of the Central States territory was short-lived but strength in the Georgia and Florida territories grew and, within months, Bill Watts' Universal Wrestling Federation also became part of the JCP family.

An influx of new talent like Steve Williams, Eddie Gilbert, Lex Luger, Rick Steiner, Sting, and the Sheepherders paired with returning names like Barry Windham, the Fabulous Freebirds, Mike Rotunda, Kevin Sullivan, and Dory Funk Jr. kept the roster fresh.

The company hosted a two-day Crockett Cup tag team tournament in Baltimore, traditionally a WWF city, and used stacked line ups to sell a bigger and better Great American Bash tour headlined by the debut of the Wargames concept.

JCP sold out arenas from Pittsburgh to Chicago during '87. And it was that national mindset that sold them on moving Starrcade, traditionally a Greensboro and Atlanta event, to the UIC Pavilion in Chicago on Thanksgiving Day. It would be the first ever JCP event made available through pay-per-view.

Leveraging the first meeting of Hulk Hogan and Andre the Giant following WrestleMania III, the WWF premiered the inaugural Survivor Series on the same day as Starrcade and forced cable companies to choose between them and Starrcade, using the following year's WrestleMania IV as a bargaining chip.

Some argue that it was Starrcade '87 that set the stage for the demise of Jim Crockett Promotions. Many point to the Road Warriors not leaving the event, in their "hometown," with the tag team title belts. But maybe more importantly it was the overall concept of the supercard more so than the result of a single match that ultimately turned fans away.

Starrcade '83-86 were bigger than life events featuring roughly a dozen matches. The latter years were so big in fact that they necessitated two cities hosting them simultaneously.

Despite an expanded roster of top domestic and international stars, JCP's pay-per-view debut saw a scaled down 3-hour show of only seven matches, with Dusty Rhodes and Ric Flair emerging victorious in the two top bouts. Closed circuit showings in New Orleans and Greensboro featured additional talent in live matches, but the pay-per-view audience only saw the Chicago card.

Starrcade '83 set the stage for Flair vs. Rhodes. Starrcade '84 and '85 were headlined by Flair vs. Rhodes. At Starrcade '86, transitioning their feud somewhat, Flair and Rhodes were in the top two singles matches.

By the end of Starrcade '87, the stage was again set for Flair vs. Rhodes, whether the fans wanted to see it or not.

Change was in the air as 1988 approached. Luger, who spent much of the year on the side of the Horsemen, was now chasing his former partners. A charismatic man with a surfer persona by the name of Sting was looking to make waves. And Watts' mouthpiece in the UWF, Jim Ross, was now the weekly host of World Championship Wrestling.

But would it be enough to keep Crockett in the fight against the WWF?

1987

JCP @ Atlanta, GA - Omni - January 1, 1987 (3,000)
Tim Horner pinned Bill Dundee
Baron Von Raschke defeated Tony Zane
Barry Windham pinned Pez Whatley
Manny Fernandez pinned Denny Brown
The Road Warriors & Paul Ellering defeated Big Bubba, Bobby Eaton & Dennis Condrey when Condrey was pinned
Dusty Rhodes & NWA US Champion Nikita Koloff defeated NWA World Champion Ric Flair & Tully Blanchard in a bullrope chain match
Big Bubba won a Bunkhouse Stampede match

JCP @ Johnson City, TN - January 2, 1987
Included a Bunkhouse Stampede match

JCP @ Atlanta, GA - WTBS Studios - January 3, 1987 (matinee)
World Championship Wrestling - 1/3/87 - featured opening footage from the previous week of Bobby Eaton & Dennis Condrey attacking NWA US Tag Team Champions Ron Garvin & Barry Windham; included Tony Schiavone & David Crockett conducting an interview with Ricky Morton & Robert Gibson regarding NWA Tag Team Champions Rick Rude & Manny Fernandez, with Morton & Gibson challenging them to a title rematch; included Schiavone conducting an interview with Jim Cornette, alongside Big Bubba, with Cornette stating Bubba was winning Bunkhouse Stampedes around the country and Eaton & Condrey would get revenge against the Road Warriors in their upcoming Scaffold match; Cornette then said he would take great pleasure in putting Paul Ellering in the hospital; Cornette then cut a promo on Garvin & Windham, saying they would end Garvin's career to take the US tag team titles before the Crockett Cup in April; featured Schiavone conducting an interview with NWA US Tag Team Champions Ron Garvin & Barry Windham, during which Garvin issued a challenge to NWA Tag Team Champions Rick Rude & Manny Fernandez and responded to Cornette's attack on him the previous week; Windham then said Cornette had sent him letters asking him to join Cornette's men but he was talking to the wrong man; Garvin then said Big Bubba might have won their match at Starrcade but he beat Bubba from one end of the ring to the other; included Schiavone conducting an interview with NWA TV Champion Tully Blanchard & JJ Dillon, with Dillon saying Dusty Rhodes wasn't in the building and Blanchard has proven his win over Rhodes at Starrcade wasn't a fluke because he still has the belt; moments later, Dillon pulled out $10,000 in cash and said the money would be on the line as well as the belt for Blanchard's match later in the show against Tim Horner; Blanchard then said putting up the money would just prove no one could beat him and he would expand the 20-minute time-limit to 25 minutes, then adding he makes the rules because he's the champion; featured Schiavone conducting an interview with Dick Murdoch, who spoke about the show later that night in Amarillo and then said the NWA

has the biggest shows in wrestling and he was proud to be part of it; included an ad for the Rock 'n' Roll Express Fan Club; featured Schiavone conducting an interview with NWA World Champion Ric Flair, during which he picked Eaton & Condrey to beat the Road Warriors in the scaffold matches; Flair also said Ivan Koloff's new man would get rid of NWA US Champion Nikita Koloff, which would leave Flair with only Windham and Dusty Rhodes; included Schiavone conducting an interview with Ole & Arn Anderson, with Ole saying his time was running out but he would take a list of men down with him, including a fat cowboy in Oklahoma; Arn then cut a promo on Nikita and Rhodes, saying he would take the US title and end Rhodes' career; featured Schiavone conducting an interview with Nikita regarding Petrov, during which Nikita also discussed the challenge of Arn Anderson as Anderson stood feet away; including a complete replay of Petrov's debut to close the program:
Brad Armstrong pinned Kent Glover with a reversal into the side Russian legsweep at 3:57
Ricky Morton & Robert Gibson defeated Alan Martin & Zane Smith at 2:20 when Morton pinned Smith following the double dropkick
NWA US Tag Team Champion Ron Garvin pinned the White Knight at 2:01 by sitting on him after the right hand punch
NWA US Tag Team Champion Barry Windham pinned Randy Barber with the lariat at 1:46
Bobby Eaton & Dennis Condrey (w/ Jim Cornette & Big Bubba) defeated George South & Mike Jackson when Condrey pinned South at 5:00 following a flapjack after Eaton hit a kneedrop off the top; prior to the bout, Cornette and Bubba approached Tony Schiavone, with Cornette then cutting a promo on Eaton & Condrey facing the Road Warriors in upcoming scaffold matches; Cornette joined the commentary team for the bout, during which he said his team should be in the Crockett Cup
NWA TV Champion Tully Blanchard (w/ JJ Dillon) pinned Tim Horner at around the 16-minute mark by grabbing the tights for leverage after the momentum of a crossbody off the top by the challenger put Blanchard on top for the win; stipulations stated an extra 5 minutes were added to the time limit, making it a 25-minute time-limit, and Horner would win $10,000 in addition to the title if he won; Barry Windham provided guest commentary for the contest; mid-way through the bout, Dillon approached the commentary table to object to Windham getting the spotlight and making excuses for Dusty Rhodes not being in the building, with Windham saying Rhodes was out spending all the money he won from Dillon's men; after the contest, Windham argued the decision and brawled with Blanchard until NWA World Champion Ric Flair, Ole & Arn Anderson ran out, jumped Horner, threw the referee to the floor, and then ganged up on Windham; Blanchard then hit the slingshot suplex on Windham, with Flair then slapping Windham before the Horsemen left the ring; Tony Schiavone then conducted an interview with the Horsemen, with Blanchard telling Windham to stay out of his matches and Flair noting that when you jump on one Horsemen, you jump on them all; Arn then noted that the same was in store for NWA US Champion Nikita Koloff
NWA Tag Team Champions Rick Rude & Manny Fernandez (w/ Paul Jones) defeated Allan West & Eddie Roberts when

Rude pinned Roberts at the 49-second mark with the Rude Awakening DDT; after the bout, Schiavone conducted an interview with Jones, Rude & Fernandez regarding the challenges of the Road Warriors, Dusty Rhodes & NWA US Champion Nikita Koloff, NWA US Tag Team Champions Ron Garvin & Barry Windham, and Ricky Morton & Robert Gibson
Vladimir Petrov (w/ Ivan Koloff) defeated Bill Tabb, Bill & Randy Mulkey in a handicap match when Petrov pinned Tabb at the 33-second mark following a clothesline and choke; prior to the bout, Schiavone conducted an interview with Ivan regarding Petrov and his mission to end Nikita Koloff; after the bout, Ivan got in the ring and instructed Petrov to throw the Mulkeys to the floor; moments later, Schiavone conducted an interview with Ivan & Petrov (Petrov's debut)
Dick Murdoch pinned Henry Rutley with the brainbuster at 4:18
Ole & Arn Anderson defeated Larry Stephens & David Isley when Arn pinned Stephens with the spinebuster at 3:24
NWA US Champion Nikita Koloff pinned Chance Mcquade with the Russian Sickle at the 44-second mark
NWA Six-Man Tag Team Champions the Road Warriors (w/ Paul Ellering) defeated Dave Spearman & Clement Fields when Road Warrior Hawk pinned Fields at the 48-second mark with the clothesline off the top after an atomic drop from Road Warrior Animal; prior to the bout, Tony Schiavone conducted an interview with the Road Warriors & Ellering, holding the six-man title trophy, in which they responded with Road Warrior Hawk saying Jim Cornette is a little man with a big mouth, Big Bubba is a big man with a little brain, and Bobby Eaton & Dennis Condrey are little men with no brains and big mouths; Hawk then cut a promo on NWA Tag Team Champions Rick Rude & Manny Fernandez, noting Fernandez was a burrito that gave him gas, and NWA World Champion Ric Flair

JCP @ Amarillo, TX - Civic Center - January 3, 1987
The Road Warriors defeated Bobby Eaton & Dennis Condrey
Also included Dusty Rhodes, Dick Murdoch, and NWA TV Champion Tully Blanchard

Central States @ Topeka, KS - January 3, 1987
Bill Dundee defeated Central States Heavyweight Champion Sam Houston to win the title

JCP @ Charlotte, NC - Coliseum - January 3, 1987
Ricky Morton defeated NWA Tag Team Champion Manny Fernandez via disqualification
Barry Windham defeated Shaska Whatley
Jimmy Valiant defeated Bill Dundee
Dusty Rhodes, NWA US Champion Nikita Koloff, & the Road Warriors defeated NWA World Champion Ric Flair, Ole & Arn Anderson, & NWA TV Champion Tully Blanchard

JCP @ Huntington, WV - January 4, 1987 (matinee)
The Road Warriors defeated Bobby Eaton & Dennis Condrey in a scaffold match

JCP @ St. Joseph, MO - January 4, 1987

JCP @ Cincinnati, OH - Cincinnati Gardens - January 4, 1987 (7,000)
Vladimir Petrov pinned Jim Lancaster within seconds (Petrov's house show debut)
Big Bubba defeated Ron Garvin in a streetfight
Bobby Eaton pinned Baron Von Raschke
NWA US Champion Nikita Koloff defeated NWA World Champion Ric Flair via disqualification
Rick Rude & Manny Fernandez defeated Dick Murdoch & Tim Horner
Dusty Rhodes won a Bunkhouse Stampede

JCP @ Baltimore, MD - Arena - January 5, 1987 (6,000)
Jimmy Valiant defeated Mark Fleming
Hector Guerrero defeated Eddie Roberts
Bill Dundee defeated Alan West
Jimmy Garvin defeated Hector Guerrero
Big Bubba defeated Ricky Lee Jones
Bobby Eaton & Dennis Condrey defeated Dick Murdoch & NWA US Tag Team Champion Ron Garvin
Ricky Morton & Robert Gibson defeated NWA Tag Team Champions Rick Rude & Manny Fernandez
NWA US Tag Team Champion Barry Windham fought NWA TV Champion Tully Blanchard to a draw

JCP @ Spartanburg, SC - Memorial Auditorium - January 5, 1987
TV taping:
Worldwide - 1/10/87:
Jimmy Valiant vs. Brodie Chase
Bobby Eaton & Dennis Condrey vs. Vernon Deaton & Gary Royal
Brad Armstrong vs. Larry Stevens
Vladimir Pietrov vs. Tony Zane
NWA US Champion Nikita Koloff vs. David Isley
Barry Windham & Ron Garvin vs. the Thunderfoots
Bill & Randy Mulkey vs. NWA Tag Team Champions Rick Rude & Manny Fernandez
Pro - 1/10/87:
NWA Tag Team Champions Rick Rude & Manny Fernandez vs. Keith Patterson & Mike Simani
Barry Windham vs. Thunderfoot #1
Ricky Morton & Robert Gibson vs. Gary Royal & Larry Stevens
Dick Murdoch vs. Thunderfoot #2
Big Bubba, Bobby Eaton & Dennis Condrey vs. Rocky King, Ricky Lee Jones, & Tim Horner
Vladimir Pietrov vs. Eddie Roberts, Alan West, & George South (handicap match)
Brad Armstrong vs. Brodie Chase
Dark match: NWA US Champion Nikita Koloff vs. NWA TV Champion Tully Blanchard

JCP @ Greenville, SC - Memorial Auditorium - January 5, 1987

Nelson Royal vs. Denny Brown
Rocky King vs. Tony Zane
Bobby Jaggers & Dutch Mantell vs. Thunderfoot #1 & #2
Tim Horner vs. Shaska Whatley
Baron Von Raschke vs. Arn Anderson
Dusty Rhodes & NWA US Champion Nikita Koloff vs. Ivan Koloff & Krusher Kruschev
NWA World Champion Ric Flair vs. Brad Armstrong

JCP @ Raleigh, NC - Dorton Arena - January 8, 1987 (5,900)

Brad Armstrong defeated Bill Dundee
Jimmy Garvin defeated Bobby Jaggers
Ivan Koloff defeated Dutch Mantell
Vladimir Petrov defeated Gary Royal
Bobby Eaton & Dennis Condrey defeated Ron Garvin & Dick Murdoch
Ricky Morton & Robert Gibson defeated Rick Rude & Manny Fernandez via disqualification
Barry Windham fought NWA TV Champion Tully Blanchard to a draw
NWA US Champion Nikita Koloff defeated NWA World Champion Ric Flair via disqualification

Kansas City, MO - January 9, 1987 (200)

The Battens defeated Porkchop Cash & Pat Rose
The MOD Squad defeated Todd Champion & Dave Peterson
Sam Houston defeated Bob Brown in a bullrope match

JCP @ Norfolk, VA - Scope - January 9, 1987

Barry Windham, Ricky Morton & Robert Gibson defeated Big Bubba, Bobby Eaton & Dennis Condrey via disqualification

JCP @ Atlanta, GA - WTBS Studios - January 10, 1987 (matinee)

World Championship Wrestling - 1/10/87 - included the announcement that the Sunday Edition program would begin at 5:30 p.m. the following day; included a replay of Tony Schiavone conducting an interview with Jim Cornette, alongside Big Bubba, from NWA Pro in which Cornette said Bubba should have won the Bunkhouse Stampede finals because Bubba won the $100,000 match; however, Cornette said, Jim Crockett Jr. told Cornette Bubba wasn't the winner because he and Dusty Rhodes won the same number of battle royals and so Bubba would face Rhodes Feb. 25 in the finals during a steel cage match in Pittsburgh, Pa.:
Jimmy Garvin (w/ Precious) pinned Keith Vincent
Brad Armstrong pinned Tommy Angel
Central States Champion Bill Dundee pinned Randy Barber
NWA US Champion Nikita Koloff pinned Larry Stevens
NWA TV Champion Tully Blanchard pinned Alan Martin
Ricky Morton & Robert Gibson defeated Allan West & Eddie Roberts when Morton pinned Roberts
The Road Warriors (w/ Paul Ellering) defeated David Isley & Ray Allen when Road Warrior Animal pinned Isley
NWA US Tag Team Champions Barry Windham & Ron Garvin defeated Bill & Randy Mulkey when Windham pinned Bill
Vladimir Petrov (w/ Ivan Koloff) defeated Vernon Deaton & George South in a handicap match by pinning Deaton
Ivan Koloff (w/ Vladimir Petrov) pinned Zane Smith
Dick Murdoch pinned Brodie Chase

JCP @ Philadelphia, PA - Civic Center - January 10, 1987 (11,000; sell out)

Vladimir Petrov defeated Tim Horner

NWA US Tag Team Champion Ron Garvin defeated Ivan Koloff

Jimmy Garvin defeated Brad Armstrong in a Texas Death Match

Dick Murdoch, Ricky Morton & Robert Gibson defeated Shaska Whatley, Rick Rude & Manny Fernandez

NWA TV Champion Tully Blanchard defeated Dusty Rhodes via disqualification

Super Towns on the Superstation - 2/7/87: NWA US Tag Team Champion Barry Windham pinned Arn Anderson with a sunset flip into the ring at 15:05; after the bout, Anderson dropped Windham with the gordbuster

NWA US Champion Nikita Koloff fought NWA World Champion Ric Flair to a double count-out

The Road Warriors defeated Bobby Eaton & Dennis Condrey in a scaffold match

JCP @ Charlotte, NC - Coliseum - January 11, 1987 (matinee) (sell out)
Denny Brown fought Ricky Lee Jones to a draw
Brad Armstrong defeated Bill Dundee
Barry Windham defeated Arn Anderson
Ron Garvin, Ricky Morton & Robert Gibson defeated Big Bubba, Bobby Eaton & Dennis Condrey
Ivan Koloff & Vladimir Petrov defeated Eddie Roberts & Hector Guerrero
The Road Warriors defeated NWA Tag Team Champions Rick Rude & Manny Fernandez via disqualification
NWA TV Champion Tully Blanchard defeated Dusty Rhodes
NWA World Champion Ric Flair defeated NWA US Champion Nikita Koloff

JCP @ Atlanta, GA - Omni - January 11, 1987
Brad Armstrong defeated Jimmy Garvin
Ricky Morton & Robert Gibson defeated Arn & Ole Anderson
NWA Tag Team Champions Rick Rude & Manny Fernandez defeated Dick Murdoch & Baron Von Raschke
Dusty Rhodes & the Road Warriors defeated Big Bubba, Bobby Eaton & Dennis Condrey
NWA US Champion Nikita Koloff fought NWA World Champion Ric Flair to a draw
Also included NWA TV Champion Tully Blanchard

JCP @ Wichita, KS - January 12, 1987
Included NWA World Champion Ric Flair

JCP @ Greenville, SC - Memorial Auditorium - January 12, 1987
Ricky Lee Jones defeated Allen West
Tim Horner defeated Thunderfoot #1
Ron Garvin fought Arn Anderson to a draw
The Road Warriors & Barry Windham defeated Big Bubba, Bobby Eaton, and Dennis Condrey
NWA Tag Team Champions Rick Rude & Manny Fernandez defeated Ricky Morton & Robert Gibson
NWA TV Champion Tully Blanchard defeated Dusty Rhodes
NWA US Champion Nikita Koloff defeated NWA World Champion Ric Flair via disqualification

JCP @ Columbia, SC - Township Auditorium - January 13, 1987
TV taping:
Worldwide - 1/17/87:
Barry Windham vs. Allen West
Dutch Mantell & Bobby Jaggers vs. the Thunderfoots
Ricky Morton & Robert Gibson vs. Gary Royal & George South
NWA Tag Team Champions Rick Rude & Manny Fernandez vs. David Isley & Eddie Roberts
Big Bubba vs. Vernon Deaton
Ron Garvin vs. Larry Stevens
NWA World Champion Ric Flair, NWA TV Champion Tully Blanchard, & Arn Anderson vs. Tim Horner, Denny Brown, & Hector Guerrero
NWA World Champion Ric Flair vs. Barry Windham (lumberjack match)
Pro - 1/17/87:
Ricky Morton & Robert Gibson vs. Mark Fleming & Brodie Chase
NWA Tag Team Champions Rick Rude & Manny Fernandez vs. Gary Royal & Randy Mulkey
Vladimir Pietrov vs. Rocky King
Ole Anderson vs. Bill Mulkey

JCP @ Salina, KS - January 13, 1987 (800)
The MOD Squad defeated Rufus R. Jones & the Italian Stallion
Ivan Koloff & Vladimir Pietrov defeated Dick Murdoch & Baron Von Raschke
Bob Brown defeated Sam Houston
Brad Armstrong & Jimmy Valiant defeated Bill Dundee & Jimmy Garvin
The Battens defeated Pat Rose & Ken Timbs

JCP @ Grand Rapids, MI - January 14, 1987 (2,500)
NWA US Tag Team Champion Barry Windham pinned Ivan Koloff
Big Bubba, Bobby Eaton & Dennis Condrey defeated Baron Von Raschke & the Road Warriors when Eaton pinned Von Raschke after Jim Cornette interfered with his tennis racquet
Ricky Morton & Robert Gibson defeated Ole & Arn Anderson
NWA US Champion Nikita Koloff defeated NWA World Champion Ric Flair via disqualification

JCP @ Marquette, MI - Lakeview Arena - January 15, 1987
Big Bubba, Bobby Eaton & Dennis Condrey defeated the Road Warriors & Baron Von Raschke
Also included NWA World Champion Ric Flair, NWA US Champion Nikita Koloff, Ricky Morton & Robert Gibson

JCP @ Hollywood, FL - Sportatorium - January 16, 1987
Super Towns on the Superstation - 2/7/87: Ricky Morton & Robert Gibson defeated Ivan Koloff & Vladimir Pietrov via disqualification at 8:57 when Petrov hit Morton with a chain as Morton had Koloff in a sleeper; after the bout, Koloff & Petrov assaulted Morton with the chain until Gibson stole it away and cleared the ring

NWA World Champion Ric Flair defeated Dusty Rhodes via disqualification
The Road Warriors defeated Bobby Eaton & Dennis Condrey in a scaffold match

JCP @ Atlanta, GA - WTBS Studios - January 17, 1987 (matinee)
World Championship Wrestling - 1/17/87 - featured Tony Schiavone conducting an interview with Dusty Rhodes in which he said he and Magnum TA were responsible for NWA US Champion Nikita Koloff choosing freedom and then challenged Ivan Koloff; included Schiavone & David Crockett introducing Lex Luger, with Luger saying he can do it all and would one day become a member of the Four Horsemen:
NWA Tag Team Champions Rick Rude & Manny Fernandez (w/ Paul Jones) defeated Rocky King & William Tabb when Rude pinned Tabb
Dutch Mantell & Bobby Jaggers defeated Allen West & Eddie Roberts when Jaggers pinned West
Barry Windham pinned Thunderfoot #2
Dick Murdoch & Baron Von Raschke defeated Randy Barber & Gary Royal when Murdoch pinned Barber
Big Bubba, Bobby Eaton & Dennis Condrey (w/ Jim Cornette) defeated Larry Stevens, David Isley, & Ronnie Angle when Eaton pinned Stevens
Vladimir Petrov (w/ Ivan Koloff) pinned Zane Smith
Lex Luger defeated George South via submission with the Torture Rack (Luger's debut)
Tim Horner pinned Thunderfoot #1
Jimmy Garvin (w/ Precious) pinned Bill Mulkey
Brad Armstrong pinned Vernon Deaton
NWA TV Champion Tully Blanchard (w/ JJ Dillon) pinned Randy Mulkey

JCP @ Charlotte, NC - Coliseum - January 17, 1987
NWA US Tag Team Champion Barry Windham defeated Alan West
Bobby Jaggers & Dutch Mantell defeated Thunderfoot #1 & #2
Ricky Morton & Robert Gibson defeated George South & Gary Royal
NWA Tag Team Champions Rick Rude & Manny Fernandez defeated David Isley & Brodie Chase
Big Bubba defeated Vernon Deaton
NWA US Tag Team Champion Ron Garvin defeated Larry Stephens
NWA World Champion Ric Flair, NWA TV Champion Tully Blanchard, & Arn Anderson defeated Tim Horner, Hector Guerrero, & Denny Brown
NWA US Tag Team Champion Barry Windham Barry Windham defeated NWA World Champion Ric Flair in a lumberjack match

JCP @ Greensboro, NC - Coliseum - January 17, 1987
Hector Guerrero defeated Denny Brown
Arn Anderson defeated Tim Horner
Brad Armstrong defeated Jimmy Garvin

Ivan Koloff & Vladimir Petrov defeated Dick Murdoch & Baron Von Raschke
NWA TV Champion Tully Blanchard defeated Barry Windham
Ricky Morton & Robert Gibson defeated NWA Tag Team Champions Rick Rude & Manny Fernandez
Dusty Rhodes & the Road Warriors defeated Big Bubba, Bobby Eaton & Dennis Condrey
NWA World Champion Ric Flair defeated NWA US Champion Nikita Koloff via disqualification

JCP @ Asheville, NC - Civic Center - January 18, 1987 (matinee)
Eddie Roberts & Allen West vs. Ricky Lee Jones & Tim Horner
Jimmy Valiant vs. Bill Dundee
Barry Windham vs. Shaska Whatley
Wahoo McDaniel vs. Arn Anderson
Dick Murdoch vs. NWA TV Champion Tully Blanchard
Ricky Morton & Robert Gibson vs. NWA Tag Team Champions Rick Rude & Manny Fernandez
NWA US Champion Nikita Koloff vs. NWA World Champion Ric Flair

JCP @ - January 1987
Super Towns on the Superstation - 2/7/87: NWA World Champion Ric Flair fought NWA US Champion Nikita Koloff to a double count-out in a No DQ match at around the 15-minute mark when an interfering NWA TV Champion Tully Blanchard attacked Koloff on the floor as Flair was on the floor injured; moments later, Dusty Rhodes helped make the save, with Koloff eventually leaving the ring with Flair's title belt

JCP @ Chesterfield, SC - January 19, 1987
Dick Murdoch fought Big Bubba to a double count-out
Bobby Eaton & Dennis Condrey defeated Ron Garvin & Baron Von Raschke

JCP @ Fayetteville, NC - Cumberland County Crown Coliseum - January 20, 1987
TV taping:
Ole Anderson defeated Bill Mulkey
Vladimir Petrov defeated Rocky King
NWA Tag Team Champions Rick Rude & Manny Fernandez defeated Gary Royal & Randy Mulkey
Ricky Morton & Robert Gibson defeated Mark Fleming & Brodie Chase
Worldwide - 1/24/87:
NWA World Champion Ric Flair fought Barry Windham to a time-limit draw (*The Ultimate Ric Flair Collection*)
Pro - 1/24/87

JCP @ Jacksonville, FL - Memorial Coliseum - January 21, 1987 (8,000; sell out)
Dutch Mantell & Bobby Jaggers defeated Jimmy Garvin & Bill Dundee via disqualification
NWA Tag Team Champions Rick Rude & Manny Fernandez

defeated Dick Murdoch & Baron Von Raschke
Denny Brown fought Hector Guerrero to a draw
NWA TV Champion Tully Blanchard defeated Barry Windham via disqualification
Dusty Rhodes & the Road Warriors defeated Big Bubba, Bobby Eaton & Dennis Condrey
NWA US Champion Nikita Koloff defeated NWA World Champion Ric Flair via disqualification

JCP @ Washington DC - Armory - January 22, 1987
Cancelled due to inclement weather; rescheduled for 1/24/87

JCP @ Raleigh, NC - Dorton Arena - January 22, 1987 (3,100)
The show took place during a blizzard
Jimmy Garvin defeated Eddie Roberts
Bill Dundee defeated Gary Royal
Ricky Lee Jones defeated Thunderfoot #1
NWA TV Champion Tully Blanchard defeated Dusty Rhodes via disqualification
NWA Tag Team Champions Rick Rude & Manny Fernandez defeated Ricky Morton & Robert Gibson in a Best 2 out of 3 falls match
NWA US Champion Nikita Koloff fought NWA World Champion Ric Flair to a double count-out

JCP @ Norfolk, VA - Scope - January 23, 1987
Dusty Rhodes & the Road Warriors defeated Big Bubba, Bobby Eaton & Dennis Condrey

JCP @ Atlanta, GA - WTBS Studios - January 24, 1987 (matinee)
World Championship Wrestling - 1/24/87 - Tony Schiavone provided sole commentary and all interviews for the show; featured an opening clip showing the ring introductions for the NWA US Tag Team Champion Barry Windham vs. NWA World Champion Ric Flair match from the 1/24/87 Worldwide; included Tony Schiavone conducting an interview with Ivan Koloff, with Vladimir Petrov, regarding their wanting revenge on NWA US Champion Nikita Koloff & Dusty Rhodes; Koloff then said another surprise, the Big Red Machine, was on his way to go after Nikita as well; featured Schiavone conducting an interview with Tim Horner regarding the Four Horsemen, with Horner saying he, Brad Armstrong, & Windham would put a stop to them; moments later, Jimmy Valiant interrupted, after his match, and said it was National Grandpa Day and wished his own grandpa a happy day; included Schiavone conducting an interview with Armstrong regarding the recent attack he sustained from the Horsemen and said he wanted to take them on in the ring one-on-one; footage was then shown from a recent episode of Pro in which NWA World Champion Ric Flair interrupted Armstrong's interview time and told him to get off the set, with Armstrong then calling Flair out until NWA TV Champion Tully Blanchard, Arn & Ole Anderson, with JJ Dillon, jumped Armstrong from behind, with Arn dropping Brad with a gordbuster onto a steel chair; moments later, NWA US Tag

Team Champions Windham & Ron Garvin as well as Ricky Morton & Robert Gibson made the save; featured an ad promoting the Rock 'n' Roll Express Fan Club; included Schiavone reviewing several minutes of footage from the Flair vs. Windham match from Worldwide; moments later, Schiavone showed footage of Bob Caudle conducting a backstage interview with Flair, and the Horsemen, after the title defense, in which he said Windham was the loser because he still had the title; Schiavone, in the studio, then conducted an interview with Windham regarding the recent match in which Windham said he would soon pin Flair; featured Schiavone conducting an interview with the Road Warriors, with Paul Ellering, in which they said no one had answered their open challenge to face them, or a combo of them, Dusty Rhodes, & Nikita Koloff; they then hyped their scaffold match that night in Washington DC against Bobby Eaton & Dennis Condrey; Schiavone then presented Ellering with a copy of Starrcade 86, which was now available on home video; included Schiavone conducting an interview with Morton & Gibson regarding their feud with Paul Jones, NWA Tag Team Champions Rick Rude & Manny Fernandez and wanting the belts back, with Morton & Gibson then bringing out David Allan Coe who said the Rock 'n' Roll Express would win the belts back and Magnum TA took his first step four days earlier and was on his way after Flair; Coe then noted he and his band were performing that night at Center Stage Theatre; featured Schiavone conducting an interview with Rhodes & Nikita regarding the Horsemen, with Nikita finishing by saying he would see Flair that night in Richmond, VA; included Schiavone conducting an interview with Central States Heavyweight Champion Bill Dundee, Jimmy Garvin, with Precious, in which Dundee said the Barbarian was on his way back to the territory and that many other names were on their way in; Garvin then said he would be going to Richmond and DC and would, unfortunately, miss the Coe concert that night at Center Stage; featured an ad promoting the Starrcade 86 home video:

Jimmy Valiant pinned Randy Barber at the 10-second mark with an elbow drop; Valiant worked the match without taking off his leather jacket, shirt, and stocking cap

Dick Murdoch & Baron Von Raschke defeated Brody Chase & Larry Stevens at 2:40 when Murdoch pinned Stevens with the brainbuster; after the bout, Tony Schiavone conducted an interview with Murdoch & Von Raschke in which they talked about wanting to be part of the Crockett Cup in April

NWA TV Champion Tully Blanchard (w/ JJ Dillon) pinned Zane Smith with the slingshot suplex at 1:23; both the title and Blanchard's $10,000 were at stake in the match

Lex Luger defeated Randy Mulkey via submission with the Torture Rack at 1:39; prior to the bout, Tony Schiavone conducted an interview with JJ Dillon, alongside NWA TV Champion Tully Blanchard & Arn Anderson in which Dillon said there were no plans to expand the Horsemen, despite Luger's recent comments, and that each member of the current Horsemen group was integral to their overall success; Dillon remained ringside to watch Luger in action; after the bout, Dillon whispered something into Luger's ear and shook his hand; moments later, Schiavone conducted an interview with Luger in which he said his phone had been ringing off the hook

since his national debut and he wanted to be a Horseman; moments later, NWA US Tag Team Champion Barry Windham came out and said he was looking out for Luger and that Luger did not want to be a member of the Horsemen, with Luger taking exception to Windham taking his interview time; after Windham left, Luger said Windham needed to grow up and there was more to life than blue jeans and car payments

Brad Armstrong pinned Gary Royal with the side Russian legsweep at around the 6-minute mark

Ricky Morton & Robert Gibson defeated Eddie Roberts & David Isley at 4:06 when Gibson pinned Isley after the double dropkick

NWA Tag Team Champions Rick Rude & Manny Fernandez (w/ Paul Jones) defeated Tommy Angel & Chance McQuaid at 4:14 when Rude pinned Angel with one finger after hitting the Rude Awakening DDT; after the bout, Schiavone conducted an interview with Jones and the champions in which Jones said they didn't have a fan club but were still the champions, with Rude then cutting a promo on facing the Road Warriors Feb. 1 at the Omni and Fernandez talking about facing Ricky Morton & Robert Gibson

Vladimir Petrov (w/ Ivan Koloff) pinned Alan Martin at the 49-second mark with a clothesline off the top; after the bout, Schiavone conducted an interview with Koloff, alongside Petrov, regarding NWA US Champion Nikita Koloff & Dusty Rhodes

Big Bubba, Bobby Eaton & Dennis Condrey (w/ Jim Cornette) defeated NWA Jr. Heavyweight Champion Denny Brown, Bill Mulkey, & George South at 5:18 when Bubba pinned Mulkey with a sit-down powerbomb after Eaton & Condrey lifted Mulkey into the air and put him into position; prior to the bout, Cornette yelled at Tony Schiavone for hyping the Starrcade home video and called all the fans sick for wanting to watch him hurt himself as bad as he did that night; Cornette joined Schiavone on commentary for the bout and talked about Bubba facing Dusty Rhodes Feb. 27 in a cage in Pittsburgh, PA to determine the winner of the Bunkhouse Stampede; after the bout, Schiavone conducted an interview with Cornette, Bubba, Eaton, & Condrey in which Cornette said Eaton & Condrey were the NWA US Tag Team Champions but just didn't have the belts; as Cornette was talking, Mulkey was taken out of the ring by other wrestlers

Arn Anderson pinned Bill Tabb with the spinebuster at 1:37; after the bout, Tony Schiavone conducted an interview with Lex Luger, well dressed, in which he talked about how he wanted to be a member of the Horsemen

World Championship Wrestling Sunday Edition - 1/25/87

JCP @ Richmond, VA - Coliseum - January 24, 1987 (8,500)

Tim Horner pinned Bill Dundee in under 2 minutes

Arn Anderson pinned Jimmy Valiant

Dusty Rhodes fought NWA TV Champion Tully Blanchard to a time-limit draw after the 25-minute mark

Barry Windham, Ricky Morton & Robert Gibson defeated Big Bubba, Bobby Eaton & Dennis Condrey in an elimination match in under 5 minutes

Ivan Koloff & Vladimir Peitrov defeated Dick Murdoch & Baron

Von Raschke
Brad Armstrong defeated Jimmy Garvin in a Death Match
The Road Warriors defeated NWA Tag Team Champions Rick
Rude & Manny Fernandez via disqualification when Paul Jones
interfered
NWA US Champion Nikita Koloff defeated NWA World
Champion Ric Flair via disqualification at the 35-minute mark
when Flair threw the challenger over the top rope

JCP @ Washington DC - Armory - January 24, 1987 (5,000)
*Bobby Eaton, Dennis Condrey, Jim Cornette, and Dusty
Rhodes were flown in immediately after their matches in
Richmond; the preliminary matches were told to go long to buy
them time and intermission lasted an hour; as a result, the
main event went on at 11:50 p.m.*
Gary Michael Cappetta was the ring announcer
Super Towns on the Superstation - 2/7/87: Brad Armstrong
defeated Jimmy Garvin (w/ Precious) via disqualification at
8:19 when Garvin threw Armstrong over the top rope; after the
bout, Armstrong cleared Garvin and Precious from the ring
The Road Warriors defeated Bobby Eaton & Dennis Condrey
in a scaffold match
Also included Dusty Rhodes

**JCP @ Greenville, SC - Memorial Auditorium - January 26,
1987**
Ricky Lee Jones (sub. for Tim Horner) defeated Shaska
Whatley
Ivan Koloff defeated Jimmy Valiant
Bobby Eaton & Dennis Condrey defeated Brad Armstrong &
Tim Horner (sub. for Wahoo McDaniel)
Jimmy Garvin defeated Baron Von Raschke
Arn Anderson defeated Dick Murdoch
NWA Tag Team Champion Rick Rude & Manny Fernandez
defeated Ricky Morton & Robert Gibson via disqualification
Barry Windham fought NWA TV Champion Tully Blanchard to
a time-limit draw; the title and Blanchard's $10,000 were at
stake in the match
NWA World Champion Ric Flair fought NWA US Champion
Nikita Koloff to a double count-out

**JCP @ Rock Hill, SC - Winthrop Coliseum - January 27,
1987**
TV taping:
Japan TV: Dick Murdoch, Ricky Morton & Robert Gibson
defeated Big Bubba, Bobby Eaton & Dennis Condrey (w/ Jim
Cornette) in an elimination match at around 9:30; Eaton pinned
Gibson with his feet on the ropes for leverage at around the 6-
minute mark; Morton pinned Eaton with a roll up at around
6:30; Bubba and Murdoch fought to a double count-out when
both men began brawling at ringside at around 7:40; Murdoch
and Bubba remained ringside after the elimination; Morton
pinned Condrey with a sunset flip into the ring after referee
Tommy Young prevented Cornette from grabbing Condrey for
leverage (*Wrestling Rarities: The Midnight Express*)
Worldwide - 1/31/87:
NWA Tag Team Champions Rick Rude & Manny Fernandez
vs. Vernon Deaton & Gary Royal
Dick Murdoch vs. Keith Patterson
Barry Windham vs. Larry Stevens
NWA TV Champion Tully Blanchard vs. Rocky King
NWA US Champion Nikita Koloff vs. Thunderfoot
Pro - 1/31/87

**JCP @ Odessa, TX - Ector County Coliseum - January 28,
1987**
Ricky Romero defeated Ted Heath
Ron Garvin fought Arn Anderson to a draw
NWA Tag Team Champions Rick Rude & Manny Fernandez
fought Barry Windham & Baron Von Raschke to a draw
NWA TV Champion Tully Blanchard defeated Dick Murdoch
via disqualification
Dusty Rhodes & the Road Warriors defeated Big Bubba,
Bobby Eaton & Dennis Condrey
NWA US Champion Nikita Koloff defeated NWA World
Champion Ric Flair via disqualification

**JCP @ Inglewood, CA - Great Western Forum - January 29,
1987 (4,750)**

338

Todd Champion defeated Teijo Khan
Big Bubba defeated Ron Garvin in a Louisville streetfight
Super Towns on the Superstation - 2/7/87: Dusty Rhodes
defeated NWA TV Champion Tully Blanchard (w/ JJ Dillon) via
disqualification at around the 9-minute mark after NWA US Tag
Team Champion Barry Windham came out to counter the
interference of Arn Anderson, with all four men then brawling in
the ring and Windham counting a pinfall for Rhodes; after the
match, Rhodes was bloodied with a shoe until Windham made
the save
Barry Windham fought Arn Anderson to a no contest
NWA Tag Team Champions Rick Rude & Manny Fernandez
defeated Dick Murdoch & Baron Von Raschke
NWA US Champion Nikita Koloff defeated NWA World
Champion Ric Flair via disqualification
Super Towns on the Superstation - 2/7/87: The Road Warriors
(w/ Paul Ellering) defeated Bobby Eaton & Dennis Condrey (w/
Jim Cornette & Big Bubba) in a scaffold match at around the 7-
minute mark

JCP @ St. Louis, MO - Arena - January 30, 1987 (1,900)
Porkchop Cash defeated Dave Peterson
Super Towns on the Superstation - 2/7/87: Central States Tag
Team Champions the MOD Squad defeated Brad & Bart
Batton when Basher pinned Brad at around the 12-minute
mark when the other MOD Squad grabbed Brad's leg from the
floor and tripped him, with Basher falling on top for the win
Bill Dundee defeated Brady Boone
Big Bubba, Bobby Eaton & Dennis Condrey defeated Ron
Garvin, the Italian Stallion, & Todd Champion
NWA Tag Team Champions Rick Rude & Manny Fernandez
defeated Dick Murdoch & Baron Von Raschke
Dusty Rhodes defeated NWA TV Champion Tully Blanchard in
a non-title first blood match
NWA US Champion Nikita Koloff defeated Arn Anderson
NWA World Champion Ric Flair defeated Barry Windham via
disqualification at the 55-minute mark

JCP @ Atlanta, GA - WTBS Studios - January 31, 1987 (matinee)
World Championship Wrestling - 1/31/87:
Jimmy Garvin (w/ Precious) vs. George South
Ron Garvin vs. Gary Royal
NWA TV Champion Tully Blanchard vs. Brad Armstrong
Lex Luger (w/ JJ Dillon) vs. Tommy Angel
NWA World Champion Ric Flair & Ole Anderson vs. Tim
Horner & Eddie Roberts
Vladimir Pietrov vs. Mike Simani
NWA Tag Team Champions Rick Rude & Manny Fernandez
vs. Rocky King & Kent Glover
Bobby Eaton & Dennis Condrey vs. Vernon Deaton & Larry
Stevens
Arn Anderson vs. Tim Horner
World Championship Wrestling Sunday Edition - 2/1/87:
NWA US Champion Nikita Koloff vs. Dave Spencer
NWA US Tag Team Champions Ron Garvin & Barry Windham
vs. Alan Martin & Bill Tabb

Tim Horner vs. Tommy Angel
NWA TV Champion Tully Blanchard & Lex Luger vs. George
South & Rocky King
Vladimir Petrov vs. Eddie Roberts
Arn Anderson vs. Chance McQuade
Jimmy Garvin vs. Randy Barber

JCP @ Kansas City, MO - January 31, 1987
The Batten Twins defeated Bobby Eaton & Dennis Condrey via
disqualification
Dick Murdoch defeated Big Bubba in a barbed wire match

JCP @ Charleston, WV - January 31, 1987
Bobby Jaggers & Dutch Mantell defeated Thunderfoot #1 & #2
Baron Von Raschke defeated Shaska Whatley
Ivan Koloff & Vladimir Petrov defeated Ron Garvin & Tim
Horner
NWA TV Champion Tully Blanchard defeated Barry Windham
via disqualification
Ricky Morton & Robert Gibson fought NWA Tag Team
Champions Rick Rude & Manny Fernandez to a draw
NWA World Champion Ric Flair fought NWA US Champion
Nikita Koloff to a draw

JCP @ Atlanta, GA - Omni - February 1, 1987 (4,500)
Bill Dundee defeated Dutch Mantell
Bob Armstrong defeated Jimmy Garvin
Arn Anderson (w/ JJ Dillon & Lex Luger) pinned Brad
Armstrong after Luger tripped Armstrong as he attempted a
suplex, with Arn falling on top
NWA TV Champion Tully Blanchard (w/ JJ Dillon & Lex Luger)
pinned Wahoo McDaniel after Luger hit McDaniel in the head
with the title belt
Robert Gibson & Ron Garvin (sub. for Ricky Morton) defeated
Bobby Eaton & Dennis Condrey (w/ Jim Cornette & Big Bubba)
in an elimination match; Eaton pinned Gibson after Cornette hit
Gibson with the tennis racquet; Garvin pinned Eaton with a roll
up moments later; Garvin pinned Condrey after ramming him
into Bubba's boot; after the match, Garvin was assaulted by
the racquet until Gibson made the save
Dusty Rhodes & NWA US Champion Nikita Koloff defeated
Ivan Koloff & Vladimir Petrov via disqualification when Petrov
assaulted Koloff with the Russian chain and threw the referee
to the floor; Rhodes & Koloff cleared the ring moments later
The Road Warriors (w/ Paul Ellering) defeated NWA Tag Team
Champions Rick Rude & Manny Fernandez (w/ Paul Jones) via
disqualification when Jones broke the cover as Road Warrior
Animal had Fernandez covered following a powerslam
Barry Windham fought NWA World Champion Ric Flair to a 60-
minute time-limit draw

JCP @ Bassett, VA - February 2, 1987
Ron Garvin fought Big Bubba to a double count-out
Ricky Morton & Robert Gibson defeated Bobby Eaton &
Dennis Condrey

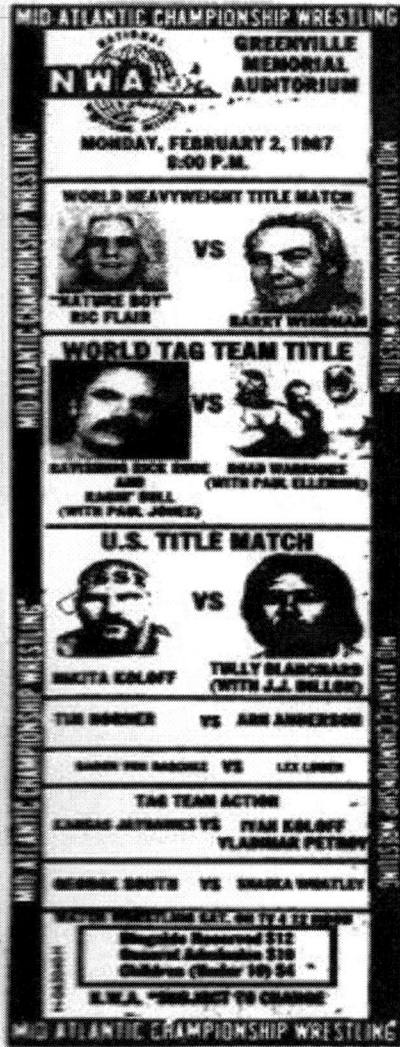

JCP @ Greenville, SC - Memorial Auditorium - February 2, 1987
Shaska Whatley defeated George South
Ivan Koloff & Vladimir Petrov defeated Dutch Mantell & Bobby Jaggers
Lex Luger defeated Baron Von Raschke
Arn Anderson defeated Wahoo McDaniel (sub. for Tim Horner)
NWA US Champion Nikita Koloff defeated NWA TV Champion Tully Blanchard via disqualification; only the US title was at stake
The Road Warriors defeated NWA Tag Team Champions Rick Rude & Manny Fernandez via disqualification
NWA World Champion Ric Flair fought Barry Windham to a 60-minute time-limit draw

JCP @ Spartanburg, SC - Memorial Auditorium - February 3, 1987
TV taping:
Worldwide - 2/7/87:
Barry Windham & Ron Garvin vs. Rocky King & George South
Ricky Morton & Robert Gibson vs. two unknowns
Bob Armstrong vs. Thunderfoot
Lex Luger vs. Eddie Roberts
Vladimir Pietrov vs. Mike Simani
Arn Anderson vs. Tommy Angel
NWA Tag Team Champions Rick Rude & Manny Fernandez vs. Tim Horner & Ricky Lee Jones
Pro - 2/7/87:
Jimmy Garvin vs. Rocky King
Dutch Mantell & Bobby Jaggers vs. John Savage & Randy Mulkey
Vladimir Pietrov vs. David Isley
Bob Armstrong vs. Vernon Deaton
Bobby Eaton & Dennis Condrey vs. Eddie Roberts & Tommy Angel
Lex Luger vs. George South
Barry Windham vs. Thunderfoot
Dark matches after the taping:
Ricky Morton & Robert Gibson vs. NWA Tag Team Champions Rick Rude & Manny Fernandez
Barry Windham vs. NWA TV Champion Tully Blanchard

JCP @ Kenansville, NC - February 4, 1987
Ron Garvin & Tim Horner defeated Big Bubba & Dennis Condrey

JCP @ Harrisonburg, VA - High School Gym - February 5, 1987 (1,600; sell out)
Denny Brown fought Hector Guerrero to a draw
Lex Luger defeated Tim Horner
Brad Armstrong defeated Arn Anderson
Bob Armstrong defeated Jimmy Garvin
NWA US Tag Team Champion Ron Garvin & Bob Armstrong (sub. for NWA US Tag Team Champion Barry Windham) defeated Bobby Eaton & Dennis Condrey

JCP @ Richmond, VA - Coliseum - February 6, 1987 (5,500)
Ivan Koloff defeated Gary Royal
Lex Luger defeated Tim Horner
The Road Warriors defeated NWA Tag Team Champions Rick Rude & Manny Fernandez via disqualification
Bob Armstrong defeated Jimmy Garvin
NWA US Champion Nikita Koloff fought NWA World Champion Ric Flair to a no contest in a No DQ match
Dusty Rhodes defeated Vladimir Petrov via disqualification
NWA TV Champion Tully Blanchard defeated Jimmy Valiant
Ron Garvin & Bob Armstrong defeated Arn & Ole Anderson

JCP @ Baltimore, MD - Arena - February 6, 1987 (11,000)
Dutch Mantell defeated Ricky Lee Jones
Baron Von Raschke defeated Thunderfoot

Hector Guerrero fought Denny Brown to a draw
Bobby Jaggers defeated Shaska Whatley
Ricky Morton & Robert Gibson defeated NWA Tag Team Champions Rick Rude & Manny Fernandez via disqualification
Lex Luger defeated Wahoo McDaniel
NWA US Champion Nikita Koloff fought NWA World Champion Ric Flair to a double count-out at the 20-minute mark
Dusty Rhodes & the Road Warriors defeated Big Bubba, Bobby Eaton & Dennis Condrey in a steel cage match

Super Towns on the Superstation - 2/7/87 - included an opening graphic which read wrestling was struck a major blow Oct. 14, 1986 when Magnum TA suffered his injury but Magnum was now back; featured Tony Schiavone & David Crockett on commentary from the studio; featured the Barry Windham vs. Arn Anderson match taped 1/10/87 in Philadelphia; included the Brad Armstrong vs. Jimmy Garvin match taped 1/24/87 in Washington DC; featured the MOD Squad vs. Brad & Bart Batten match 1/30/87 in St. Louis; included a promo by Paul Jones, NWA Tag Team Champions Rick Rude & Manny Fernandez regarding the Crockett Cup, during which Jones argued his team should be the #1 seed in the tournament; featured the Ricky Morton & Robert Gibson vs. Ivan Koloff & Vladimir Pietrov match taped 1/16/87 in Hollywood, FL; included Schiavone conducting an interview in the Baltimore Arena with Gary Juster and Charles Neustadt regarding the upcoming Crockett Cup in April, the crowd expected for the two-day event, and the rennovations to the facility; featured the Dusty Rhodes vs. Tully Blanchard match from 1/29/87 in Inglewood, CA; included Schiavone conducting a sit-down interview with Magnum TA regarding his injury, road to recovery, and what's been going on in wrestling since Magnum's injury; featured the Ric Flair vs. Nikita Koloff match taped ? in Charlotte, NC; included the Road Warriors vs. Bobby Eaton & Dennis Condrey scaffold match taped 1/29/87 in Inglewood, CA

JCP @ Greensboro, NC - Coliseum - February 7, 1987 (13,000)
Tim Horner defeated Shaska Whatley
Jimmy Valiant defeated Thunderfoot
Bob Armstrong defeated Jimmy Garvin
Arn Anderson & Lex Luger defeated Wahoo McDaniel & Baron Von Raschke
NWA US Tag Team Champions Ron Garvin & Barry Windham defeated Bobby Eaton & Dennis Condrey
NWA TV Champion Tully Blanchard defeated Dusty Rhodes via disqualification
NWA World Champion Ric Flair fought NWA US Champion Nikita Koloff to a no contest
NWA Tag Team Champions Rick Rude & Manny Fernandez defeated Ricky Morton & Robert Gibson in a steel cage match

JCP @ Cincinnati, OH - Cincinnati Gardens - February 8, 1987
Bobby Jaggers & Dutch Mantell defeated Thunderfoot #1 & #2

Lex Luger defeated Ricky Lee Jones
Bob Armstrong defeated Jimmy Garvin
Dick Murdoch, Wahoo McDaniel, & NWA US Tag Team Champion Ron Garvin defeated Jim Cornette, Bobby Eaton, & Dennis Condrey
Tully Blanchard defeated Barry Windham via disqualification
NWA Tag Team Champions Rick Rude & Manny Fernandez defeated Ricky Morton & Robert Gibson in a steel cage match
NWA World Champion Ric Flair fought NWA US Champion Nikita Koloff to a draw

341

JCP @ Greenville, SC - Memorial Auditorium - February 9, 1987
Bill Dundee defeated Randy Mulkey (sub. for Bob Armstrong)
Dick Murdoch (sub. for Jimmy Valiant) defeated Thunderfoot #1
Bobby Eaton & Dennis Condrey defeated Dutch Mantell & Bobby Jaggers; stipulations stated the winners would be the #1 contenders to the NWA US Tag Team Titles
Arn Anderson & Lex Luger defeated Bob Armstrong & Jimmy Valiant (sub. for Brad Armstrong & Tim Horner)
Big Bubba defeated NWA US Tag Team Champion Ron Garvin in a lumberjack match
Ricky Morton & Robert Gibson defeated NWA Tag Team Champions Rick Rude & Manny Fernandez
NWA US Champion Nikita Koloff defeated NWA TV Champion Tully Blanchard; only the US title was at stake
NWA World Champion Ric Flair defeated NWA US Tag Team Champion Barry Windham

JCP @ Columbia, SC - Township Auditorium - February 10, 1987
TV taping:
Worldwide - 2/14/87:
Ole & Arn Anderson vs. Larry Stevens & Johnny Ace
Barry Windham vs. Thunderfoot #2
Lex Luger vs. Vernon Deaton
NWA TV Champion Tully Blanchard vs. Gary Royal
Pro - 2/14/87

JCP @ Marion, NC - February 11, 1987
NWA US Tag Team Champions Ron Garvin & Barry Windham defeated Bobby Eaton & Dennis Condrey

JCP @ Raleigh, NC - Dorton Arena - February 12, 1987 (5,200)
Ivan Koloff & Vladimir Petrov defeated Brad Armstrong & Tim Horner
Wahoo McDaniel defeated Shaska Whatley
Ricky Lee Jones defeated Denny Brown
NWA US Champion Nikita Koloff defeated Arn Anderson
Bob Armstrong defeated Gary Royal
Lex Luger & NWA TV Champion Tully Blanchard defeated Dutch Mantel & Bobby Jaggers
NWA World Champion Ric Flair defeated NWA US Tag Team Champion Barry Windham
Ricky Morton & Robert Gibson defeated NWA Tag Team Champions Rick Rude & Manny Fernandez in a steel cage match

JCP @ Columbus, GA - February 13, 1987
NWA US Tag Team Champions Ron Garvin & Barry Windham defeated Bobby Eaton & Dennis Condrey

JCP @ Atlanta, GA - WTBS Studios - February 14, 1987 (matinee)

World Championship Wrestling - 2/14/87:
Jimmy Valiant pinned Tommy Angel at 1:48
Barry Windham & Ron Garvin defeated Randy Barber & Jack Jackson at 6:29
Lex Luger defeated Kent Glover via submission with the Torture Rack at 4:06
Arn Anderson pinned Zane Smith with the gordbuster at 4:25
Jimmy Garvin vs. David Isley
Bobby Eaton & Dennis Condrey vs. Ricky Sullivan & Larry Stevens
Dick Murdoch, Ivan Koloff & Krusher Kruschev vs. Alan Martin, Randy Mulkey, & Chance McQuade
Big Bubba vs. George South
Dutch Mantell & Bobby Jaggers vs. Keith Vincent & Vernon Deaton
Bob Armstrong vs. the Demon
World Championship Wrestling Sunday Edition - 2/15/87:
NWA TV Champion Tully Blanchard & Lex Luger vs. Zane Smith & Tommy Angel
Bobby Jaggers & Dutch Mantel vs. Randy Barber & Jack Jackson
Bob Armstrong vs. Keith Vincent
Tim Horner vs. Randy Barber
Dick Murdoch vs. Zane Smith

JCP @ Charlotte, NC - Coliseum - February 14, 1987 (8,000)
TV taping:
Lex Luger defeated Randy Mulkey
Tim Horner defeated David Isley
Jimmy Garvin defeated George South
NWA TV Champion Tully Blanchard defeated Ricky Lee Jones
NWA World Champion Ric Flair defeated NWA US Champion Nikita Koloff
Pro - 2/21/87:
NWA US Tag Team Champions Ron Garvin & Barry Windham defeated Bobby Eaton & Dennis Condrey (w/ Jim Cornette) via disqualification when Cornette threw a fireball into Garvin's face; after the bout, Jimmy Garvin ran out to make the save
Worldwide - 2/21/87:
Bob Armstrong vs. Thunderfoot
Ivan Koloff & Dick Murdoch vs. Keith Patterson & Tommy Angel
NWA Tag Team Champions Rick Rude & Manny Fernandez vs. Ricky Morton & Robert Gibson
Dusty Rhodes vs. Vladimir Petrov

Mosca Mania II - Hamilton, Ontario - Copps Coliseum - February 15, 1987 (matinee) (3,000)
Angelo Mosca Jr. defeated Shaska Whatley
Joey War Eagle defeated Danny Johnson
Lex Luger defeated Ricky Lee Jones
Bobby Eaton & Dennis Condrey defeated Barry Windham & Hector Guerrero (sub. for Ron Garvin)
Arn Anderson defeated Tim Horner (sub. for Baron Von Raschke)
NWA Tag Team Champions Rick Rude & Manny Fernandez

defeated Ricky Morton & Bob Armstrong (sub. for Robert Gibson)
NWA TV Champion Tully Blanchard defeated Dusty Rhodes via disqualification
NWA US Champion Nikita Koloff defeated NWA World Champion Ric Flair via disqualification

JCP @ Toronto, Ontario - February 15, 1987
Angelo Mosca Jr. defeated Shaska Whatley
Joey War Eagle defeated Dan Johnson
Lex Luger defeated Ricky Lee Jones
Bobby Eaton & Dennis Condrey defeated Barry Windham & Hector Guerrero
Arn Anderson defeated Tim Horner
NWA Tag Team Champions Rick Rude & Manny Fernandez defeated Ricky Morton & Bob Armstrong
NWA TV Champion Tully Blanchard defeated Dusty Rhodes via disqualification
NWA US Champion Nikita Koloff defeated NWA World Champion Ric Flair via disqualification

JCP @ Brantford, Ontario - February 16, 1987
Television taping:
Big Bubba defeated Frank Marconi
NWA TV Champion Tully Blanchard defeated Ricky Lee Jones
NWA US Champion Nikita Koloff defeated Eric the Red
Barry Windham defeated Shaska Whatley
Bobby Eaton & Dennis Condrey defeated Troy Little Bear & Mad Dog Vachon
NWA Tag Team Champions Rick Rude & Manny Fernandez defeated Terry Morgan & Bob Armstrong
Lex Luger defeated Ron Hutchinson
Arn Anderson defeated Hector Guerrero
Tim Horner defeated Sildent Boyd
NWA US Champion Nikita Koloff defeated NWA TV Champion Tully Blanchard
Ricky Morton & Barry Windham defeated Bobby Eaton & Dennis Condrey

JCP @ Peterborough, Ontario - February 17, 1987
Ricky Lee Jones defeated Lex Luger via disqualification
Big Bubba defeated Chico Fernandez
Arn Anderson defeated Hector Guerrero
NWA Tag Team Champions Rick Rude & Manny Fernandez defeated Ricky Lee Jones & Bob Armstrong
NWA TV Champion Tully Blanchard fought Barry Windham to a no contest
Ricky Morton & Tim Horner defeated Bobby Eaton & Dennis Condrey

JCP @ Jacksonville, FL - Memorial Coliseum - February 20, 1987 (8,000)
NWA TV Champion Tully Blanchard fought Barry Windham to a no contest
Ricky Morton & Robert Gibson defeated NWA Tag Team Champions Rick Rude & Manny Fernandez via disqualification

NWA World Champion Ric Flair fought NWA US Champion Nikita Koloff to a no contest
Dusty Rhodes defeated Big Bubba
Also included the Road Warriors

World Championship Wrestling - 2/21/87:
Jimmy Valiant pinned Thunderfoot #2 with an elbow drop at 4:24; after the bout, Tony Schiavone conducted an interview with Valiant, during which Valiant said the fans wanted to see him give some sugar to Schiavone; he then said he was going to Gainesville, GA and would then hibernate for 3 or 4 days and would then work out hard and find a partner to compete in the Crockett Cup; Valiant then said, if his team won, he would give all his winnings to those in need
Brad Armstrong vs. Larry Stevens
Dick Murdoch, Ivan Koloff, & Vladimir Petrov vs. Rick Sullivan, David Isley, & Tommy Angel
NWA Tag Team Champions Rick Rude & Manny Fernandez vs. Rick Nelson & Alan Martin
Tim Horner vs. Randy Barber
Big Bubba vs. Kent Glover
Bobby Eaton & Dennis Condrey vs. Randy Mulkey & Zane Smith
Denny Brown vs. Rocky King
Baron Von Raschke vs. Brodie Chase
NWA TV Champion Tully Blanchard, Lex Luger, Ole & Arn Anderson vs. Bob Armstrong, Dutch Mantell, Eddie Roberts, & Ricky Lee Jones
World Championship Wrestling Sunday Edition - 2/22/87:
Jimmy Valiant vs. Brodie Chase
Ole & Arn Anderson vs. David Isley & Tommy Angel
Ivan Koloff & Dick Murdoch vs. George South & Rocky King
Baron Von Raschke vs. Thunderfoot #2
Bob & Brad Armstrong vs. Randy Mulkey & Thunderfoot #1
Big Bubba, Dennis Condrey & Bobby Eaton vs. Bill Tabb, Eric Long, & Jack Jackson

JCP @ Philadelphia, PA - Civic Center - February 21, 1987 (7,216)
Bob Armstrong defeated Gary Royal
Arn Anderson defeated Ricky Lee Jones
Lex Luger defeated Eddie Roberts
NWA TV Champion Tully Blanchard defeated Tim Horner
Wahoo McDaniel & Jimmy Garvin defeated Bobby Eaton & Dennis Condrey
Dusty Rhodes & NWA US Champion Nikita Koloff defeated Ivan Koloff & Vladimir Pietrov
NWA Tag Team Champions Rick Rude & Manny Fernandez defeated Ricky Morton & Robert Gibson
NWA World Champion Ric Flair defeated Barry Windham at the 20-minute mark

JCP @ Asheville, NC - Civic Center - February 22, 1987 (matinee)
The Barbarian defeated Hector Guerrero
Jimmy Valiant defeated Bill Dundee

Vladimir Pietrov defeated Dutch Mantell
NWA Tag Team Champions Rick Rude & Manny Fernandez fought Ricky Morton & Robert Gibson to a draw in a Best 2 out of 3 falls match
Lex Luger & Arn Anderson defeated Denny Brown & Ricky Lee Jones
Dick Murdoch & Ivan Koloff defeated Bob & Brad Armstrong
NWA TV Champion Tully Blanchard defeated Barry Windham

World Championship Wrestling Sunday Edition - 2/22/87:
Jimmy Valiant vs. Brodie Chase
Ole & Arn Anderson vs. David Isley & Tommy Angel
Ivan Koloff & Dick Murdoch vs. George South & Rocky King
Baron Von Raschke vs. Thunderfoot #2
Bob & Brad Armstrong vs. Randy Mulkey & Thunderfoot #1
Big Bubba, Bobby Eaton & Dennis Condrey vs. Bill Tabb, Eric Long, & Jack Jackson

JCP @ Greenville, SC - Memorial Auditorium - February 23, 1987
George South & Rocky King defeated Randy & Bill Mulkey
Hector Guerrero defeated Gary Royal
Jimmy Valiant defeated Brody Chase (sub. for the Barbarian)
Wahoo McDaniel & Baron Von Raschke fought Bobby Eaton & Dennis Condrey to a 20-minute time-limit draw
Bob & Brad Armstrong defeated the Barbarian (sub. for Jimmy Garvin) & Bill Dundee
Robert Gibson defeated NWA Tag Team Champion Rick Rude in a Texas Death Match
NWA Tag Team Champion Manny Fernandez defeated Ricky Morton in a Mexican Death Match

JCP @ Fayetteville, NC - February 23, 1987
Nelson Royal defeated Thunderfoot #1
Shaska Whatley defeated Mark Fleming
Misty Blue defeated Linda Dallas
Ivan Koloff & Dick Murdoch defeated Dutch Mantell & Denny Brown
Lex Luger defeated Ricky Lee Jones
NWA TV Champion Tully Blanchard defeated Tim Horner
Jimmy Garvin defeated Arn Anderson
NWA World Champion Ric Flair defeated Barry Windham via disqualification

JCP @ Rock Hill, SC - Winthrop Coliseum - February 24, 1987
Television taping:
Lex Luger defeated Vernon Deaton via submission
Barry Windham pinned Thunderfoot #2
Arn & Ole Anderson defeated Tommy Angel & Johnny Ace
NWA TV Champion Tully Blanchard pinned Gary Royal
Bob Armstrong pinned Brodie Chase
Ivan Kolov, Vladimir Petrov, & Dick Murdoch defeated Rocky King, Johnny Ace, & George South
Brad Armstrong pinned Bill Mulkey
Arn Anderson, NWA TV Champion Tully Blanchard, & Lex Luger defeated Denny Brown, Ricky Lee Jones, & Eddie Roberts
Barry Windham pinned Brodie Chase
Ricky Morton & Robert Gibson defeated Randy Mulkey & David Isley
NWA Tag Team Champions Rick Rude & Manny Fernandez defeated Rocky King & Tommy Angel
Jimmy Valiant pinned Randy Mulkey
Ivan Koloff & Vladimir Petrov defeated George South & Gary Royal
Ricky Morton & Robert Gibson defeated NWA World Tag Team Champions Rick Rude & Manny Fernandez in a steel cage match

JCP @ Hammond, IN - Civic Center - February 25, 1987 (500)
Debut in the city
Dick Murdoch (sub. for Ivan Koloff) defeated Ricky Lee Jones
Misty Blue defeated Linda Dallas

Lex Luger defeated Baron Von Raschke
Ron Garvin defeated Arn Anderson via disqualification; the bout was advertised as Garvin & Wahoo McDaniel vs. Arn & Ole Anderson
NWA TV Champion Tully Blanchard defeated Tim Horner
Ricky Morton & Robert Gibson defeated NWA Tag Team Champions Rick Rude & Manny Fernandez via disqualification
NWA World Champion Ric Flair defeated Barry Windham via disqualification

JCP @ Minneapolis, MN - Met Center - February 26, 1987 (1,100)
Dick Murdoch defeated Ricky Lee Jones
Lex Luger, Arn & Ole Anderson defeated Wahoo McDaniel, Tim Horner, & Baron Von Raschke
Misty Blue defeated Linda Dallas
Jimmy Garvin defeated Big Bubba in a streetfight
Ricky Morton & Robert Gibson defeated NWA Tag Team Champions Rick Rude & Manny Fernandez via disqualification
NWA US Champion Nikita Koloff defeated NWA TV Champion Tully Blanchard; only the US title was on the line
NWA World Champion Ric Flair defeated Barry Windham

JCP @ Albany, GA - Civic Center - February 27, 1987 (3,000)
Rocky King & George South defeated Randy Mulkey & John Savage
Misty Blue defeated Linda Dallas
NWA Jr. Heavyweight Champion Denny Brown defeated Thunderfoot #2
Bob Armstrong defeated Thunderfoot #1
Arn Anderson pinned Brad Armstrong
Barry Windham & Jimmy Garvin defeated Bobby Eaton & Arn Anderson (sub. for Dennis Condrey) when Windham pinned Anderson

JCP @ Pittsburgh, PA - Civic Arena - February 27, 1987 (either 17,521 or 16,600; sell out)
Hector Guerrero fought Shaska Whatley to a draw
Vladimir Petrov pinned Jim Lancaster
Ivan Koloff & Dick Murdoch defeated Wahoo McDaniel & Dutch Mantell
Lex Luger pinned Ricky Lee Jones
NWA TV Champion Tully Blanchard pinned Tim Horner
NWA World Tag Team Champions Rick Rude & Manny Fernandez defeathed Ricky Morton & Robert Gibson when Rude pinned Gibson
NWA US Champion Nikita Koloff defeated NWA World Champion Ric Flair via disqualification
Bunkhouse Stampede Finals: Dusty Rhodes defeated Big Bubba in a steel cage match; stipulations stated the winner would win the $100,000 Bunkhouse Stampede cash prize

Worldwide - 2/28/87:
NWA TV Champion Tully Blanchard & Arn Anderson vs. Mitch Snow & Larry Stevens

Baron Von Raschke vs. Bill Mulkey
NWA Tag Team Champions Rick Rude & Manny Fernandez vs. Chance McQuade & Randy Mulkey

Pro - 2/28/87:
Ivan Koloff & Dick Murdoch vs. George South & Gary Royal
Jimmy Valiant vs. Bill Mulkey
NWA Tag Team Champions Rick Rude & Manny Fernandez vs. Rocky King & Johnny Ace
NWA TV Champion Tully Blanchard, Arn Anderson, & Lex Luger vs. Denny Brown, Chance McQuade, & Eddie Roberts
Barry Windham vs. Brodie Chase
Ricky MOrton & Robert Gibson vs. Randy Mulkey & David Isley

JCP @ Atlanta, GA - WTBS Studios - February 28, 1987 (matinee)
World Championship Wrestling - 2/28/87 - featured Tony Schiavone conducting an interview with JJ Dillon, NWA TV Champion Tully Blanchard, and Lex Luger in which Dillon noted the record crowd the night before at the Philadelphia Civic Center; moments later, Blanchard said they were getting ready for Baltimore and Luger said more security was being hired to keep the women in their seats when he walks out:
NWA TV Champion Tully Blanchard & Lex Luger vs. Ricky Sullivan & Chance McQuade
Barry Windham vs. Thunderfoot #2
Brad Armstrong vs. Keith Vincent
NWA Tag Team Champions Rick Rude & Manny Fernandez vs. Zane Smith & Jack Evans
Tim Horner vs. Kent Glover
Jimmy Garvin vs. Thunderfoot #1
Bobby Eaton vs. Larry Stevens
Ron Garvin vs. Tommy Angel
Big Bubba vs. George South
Ole & Arn Anderson defeated Alan Martin & Randy Mulkey via submission when Ole applied an arm bar; after the bout, Ole confronted Blanchard at the commentary area, with Ole punching Blanchard in the face when Blanchard told him he should have been paying attention to business instead of his snot nosed kid
Misty Blue vs. Linda Dallas

JCP @ Taylorsville, NC - Alexander Central High School Gym - February 28, 1987
Tim Horner vs. Gary Royal
Shaska Whatley vs. Ricky Lee Jones
NWA Jr. Heavyweight Champion Denny Brown vs. Hector Guerrero
Bob Armstrong vs. Arn Anderson
Also included NWA Tag Team Champions Manny Fernandez & Rick Rude

JCP @ Kingsport, TN - February 28, 1987
Ricky Morton & Robert Gibson defeated Bobby Eaton & Dennis Condrey

NWA US Champion Nikita Koloff defeated NWA World Champion Ric Flair via disqualification

JCP @ Richmond, VA - Coliseum - March 1, 1987 (matinee) (9,000)
Dutch Mantell & Bobby Jaggers defeated Ricky Lee Jones & Shaska Whatley
Bobby Eaton fought Jimmy Valiant to a 15-minute time-limit draw
Lazertron defeated Mark Fleming
Lex Luger defeated Baron Von Raschke
NWA TV Champion Tully Blanchard defeated Brad Armstrong
NWA Tag Team Champions Rick Rude & Manny Fernandez fought Ricky Morton & Robert Gibson to a no contest
Jimmy Garvin defeated Big Bubba via count-out
Dusty Rhodes & NWA US Champion Nikita Koloff defeated Ivan Koloff & Dick Murdoch via disqualification
NWA World Champion Ric Flair defeated Barry Windham

JCP @ Atlanta, GA - Omni - March 1, 1987 (4,500)
The Barbarian defeated the Italian Stallion
Bob Armstrong defeated Thunderfoot #1
Mike Rotundo defeated Thunderfoot #2
Arn Anderson & Lex Luger defeated Bob Armstrong & Tim Horner
NWA Tag Team Champions Rick Rude & Manny Fernandez fought Ricky Morton & Robert Gibson to a no contest
Brad Armstrong defeated NWA TV Champion Tully Blanchard via disqualification
Jimmy Garvin defeated Bobby Eaton
Dusty Rhodes & NWA US Champion Nikita Koloff defeated Ivan Koloff & Dick Murdoch
NWA World Champion Ric Flair defeated Barry Windham at the 30-minute mark

JCP @ Greenville, SC - Memorial Auditorium - March 2, 1987
Ricky Lee Jones vs. Bill Dundee
Mike Rotunda defeated Dennis Condrey via disqualification
Bob Armstrong & Tim Horner vs. Lex Luger & Arn Anderson
Brad Armstrong, Ricky Morton & Robert Gibson vs. Paul Jones, NWA Tag Team Champions Rick Rude & Manny Fernande
NWA TV Champion Tully Blanchard vs. Baron Von Raschke
Jimmy Garvin defeated Bobby Eaton
NWA US Champion Nikita Koloff vs. Dick Murdoch
Dusty Rhodes vs. Ivan Koloff
NWA World Champion Ric Flair vs. Barry Windham (Best 2 out of 3 falls)

JCP @ Sapartanburg, SC - Memorial Auditorium - March 3, 1987
TV taping:
Pro - 3/7/87:
Barry Windham vs. Colt Steele
Ron & Jimmy Garvin vs. Vernon Deaton & an unknown
Ricky Morton & Robert Gibson vs. Randy Mulkey & Gary Royal
Lazortron vs. Bill Mulkey
Lex Luger & NWA TV Champion Tully Blanchard vs. Chance McQuade & Eddie Roberts
Arn Anderson vs. Tommy Angel
Dick Murdoch, Ivan Koloff & Vladimir Pietrov vs. George South, Mitch Snow, & the Italian Stallion
Worldwide - 3/7/87:
Lazortron vs. Keith Vincent
Dick Murdoch, Ivan Koloff, & Vladimir Pietrov vs. Randy Mulkey & two unknowns
Bob & Brad Armstrong vs. George South & Mark Fleming
Lex Luger vs. Gary Royal
NWA TV Champion Tully Blanchard & Arn Anderson vs. Brady Boone & Eddie Roberts
Dark match after the taping: Ricky Morton & Robert Gibson vs. NWA TV Champion Tully Blanchard & Lex Luger

JCP @ Wytheville, VA - March 4, 1987
Dutch Mantell & Bobby Jaggers defeated the MOD Squad
Baron Von Raschke pinned Shaska Whatley
Lazertron defeated Teijo Khan
Ivan Koloff & Vladimir Pietrov defeated Tim Horner & the Italian Stallion
Wahoo McDaniel defeated Dick Murdoch via disqualification

JCP @ Birmingham, AL - BJCC - March 4, 1987 (750)
Jimmy Valiant pinned the Barbarian
Bob Armstrong, Ron & Jimmy Garvin defeated Bobby Eaton, Dennis Condrey, & Big Bubba at 9:22 when Armstrong pinned Eaton
Brad Armstrong pinned Bill Dundee at 7:15
Barry Windham defeated Lex Luger via disqualification at 7:04 when JJ Dillon tripped Windham
NWA TV Champion Tully Blanchard defeated Dusty Rhodes via reverse decision at 7:15; Rhodes originally won the match and title after hitting Blanchard with the champion's own foreign object but JJ Dillon showed the referee the weapon and the referee changed his call
NWA US Champion Nikita Koloff pinned Arn Anderson at 11:29 with the Russian Sickle
NWA Tag Team Champions Rick Rude & Manny Fernandez defeated Ricky Morton & Robert Gibson at 11:46 when Rude pinned Gibson after using a foreign object

JCP @ Memphis, TN - Mid-South Coliseum - March 5, 1987
The Barbarian fought Bob Armstrong to a draw
Brad Armstrong defeated Big Bubba
Jimmy Valiant defeated Arn Anderson
Ron & Jimmy Garvin defeated Bobby Eaton & Dennis Condrey

Barry Windham defeated Lex Luger via disqualification
NWA US Champion Nikita Koloff defeated NWA TV Champion Tully Blanchard
NWA Tag Team Champions Rick Rude & Manny Fernandez defeated Ricky Morton & Robert Gibson
Bill Dundee defeated Dusty Rhodes in a King of Tennessee match

JCP @ Morganton, NC - March 6, 1987 (sell out)
Ron & Jimmy Garvin defeated Bobby Eaton & Dennis Condrey

AJPW @ Mizusawa, Japan - March 6, 1987
NWA World Champion Ric Flair & Art Crews defeated Teranishi & Yoshiaki Yatsu

JCP @ Atlanta, GA - WTBS Studios - March 7, 1987 (matinee)
World Championship Wrestling - 3/7/87 - featured the debut of a new theme song and entrance video:
Lex Luger vs. Rocky King
The MOD Squad vs. Mitch Snow & George South
Mike Rotunda vs. Thunderfoot
Arn Anderson vs. Mike Anderson
Lazortron defeated NWA Jr. Heavyweight Champion Denny Brown to win the title
Jimmy Valiant vs. Tommy Angel
The Barbarian vs. Randy Mulkey
Wahoo McDaniel & Baron Von Raschke vs. Rick Sullivan & Randy Barber
Dick Murdoch, Ivan Koloff, & Vladimir Pietrov vs. Alan Martin, Zane Smith, & Cougar Jay
Barry Windham vs. Chance McQuade
Ron & Jimmy Garvin vs. Larry Stevens & Darrell Dalton
World Championship Wrestling Sunday Edition - 3/8/87

AJPW @ Akita, Japan - March 7, 1987
Yoshiaki Yatsu fought NWA World Champion Ric Flair to a double count-out at 17:08

JCP @ Norfolk, VA - Scope - March 7, 1987
Bobby Eaton fought Tim Horner to a 20-minute time-limit draw
Jimmy Garvin defeated Bobby Eaton

JCP @ Beckley, WV - Armory - March 8, 1987 (5,000; sell out)
Bob & Brad Armstrong defeated Thunderfoot #1 & #2
Nelson Royal defeated Johnny Ace
Baron Von Raschke defeated Pez Whatley
Bobby Jaggers defeated Gary Royal
Mark Fleming defeated Teijo Khan
Wahoo McDaniel pinned Arn Anderson
Ricky Morton & Brad Armstrong (sub. for Robert Gibson) defeated NWA Tag Team Champions Rick Rude & Manny Fernandez in a non-title match

MID-ATLANTIC CHAMPIONSHIP WRESTLING

NATIONAL NWA WRESTLING ALLIANCE

GREENVILLE MEMORIAL AUDITORIUM
SUNDAY - MARCH 8, 1987
2:00 P.M.

U.S. HEAVYWEIGHT TITLE MATCH
NIKITA KOLOFF
VS
LEX LUGER
(WITH J.J. DILLON)
NIKITA KOLOFF

GRUDGE MATCH
DUSTY RHODES VS DICK MURDOCH

6 MAN TAG ACTION
BARRY WINDHAM, RON GARVIN, GORGEOUS JIMMY VS MIDNIGHT EXPRESS AND BIG BUBBA
(WITH PRECIOUS) (WITH JIM CORNETTE)

WORLD T.V. TITLE 25 MINUTES
TULLY BLANCHARD (J.J. DILLON) VS DUTCH MANTEL

TAG ACTION
JIMMY VALIANT BRADY BOONE VS THE BARBARIAN SUPERSTAR BILL DUNDEE

DENNY BROWN VS VLADIMAR PIETROV

ROCKY KING GEORGE SOUTH VS THE MOD SQUAD

NWA TICKET PRICES: $12, $10, & $4 *SUBJECT TO CHANGE

MID-ATLANTIC CHAMPIONSHIP WRESTLING

JCP @ Greenville, SC - Memorial Auditorium - March 8, 1987
The MOD Squad defeated Rocky King & George South
Vladimir Pietrov defeated Denny Brown
The Barbarian & Bill Dundee defeated Jimmy Valiant & Brady Boone
NWA TV Champion Tully Blanchard defeated Dutch Mantell
Barry Windham, Ron & Jimmy Garvin defeated Big Bubba, Bobby Eaton & Dennis Condrey
Dick Murdoch defeated Dusty Rhodes
NWA US Champion Nikita Koloff defeated Lex Luger

AJPW @ Togane, Japan - March 8, 1987
Genichiro Tenryu, Ishikawa, & the Great Wajima defeated NWA World Champion Ric Flair, Art Crews, & El Olympico

JCP @ Fayetteville, NC - March 9, 1987
Pro - 3/14/87:
NWA TV Champion Tully Blanchard, Arn Anderson, & Lex Luger vs. Keith Anderson, Colt Steele, & the Italian Stallion
Wahoo McDaniel & Baron Von Raschke vs. Thunderfoot #1 & #2
Ricky Morton & Robert Gibson vs. Larry Stevens & Tommy Angel
NWA Tag Team Champions Rick Rude & Manny Fernandez vs. Bill & Randy Mulkey
Ron & Jimmy Garvin vs. Gary Royal & Johnny Ace
Bobby Eaton & Stan Lane vs. Brodie Chase & Mitch Snow
Worldwide - 3/14/87

AJPW @ Takasaki, Japan - March 9, 1987
NWA World Champion Ric Flair defeated Tiger Mask II

JCP @ Greenwood, SC - March 10, 1987
Ron & Jimmy Garvin defeated Bobby Eaton & Dennis Condrey

AJPW @ Koriyama, Japan - March 10, 1987 (4,100)
NWA World Champion Ric Flair defeated Jumbo Tsuruta via disqualification at 17:29

JCP @ Thomasville, NC - March 11, 1987
Ron Garvin defeated Bobby Eaton
Brad Armstrong defeated Dennis Condrey

AJPW @ Shizuoka, Japan - March 11, 1987 (2,900)
Genichiro Tenryu, Tiger Mask, & the Great Wajima defeated NWA World Champion Ric Flair, Art Crews, & Mike George

JCP @ Sunrise, FL - Musical Theatre - March 12, 1987 (4,700)
Jimmy Valiant pinned the Barbarian
Barry Windham fought Lex Luger to a 20-minute time-limit draw
NWA Tag Team Champions Rick Rude & Manny Fernandez

defeated Ricky Morton & Robert Gibson at the 20-minute mark
NWA US Champion Nikita Koloff pinned Arn Anderson
NWA TV Champion Tully Blanchard defeated Dusty Rhodes
via disqualification

JCP @ Raleigh, NC - Dorton Arena - March 12, 1987
Bob Armstrong & Denny Brown defeated the MOD Squad
Eddie Roberts & Brady Boone defeated Thunderfoot #1 & #2
Big Bubba defeated Brad Armstrong via count-out in a
Louisville streetfight
Ivan Koloff & Dick Murdoch defeated Baron Von Raschke &
Wahoo McDaniel
The Italian Stallion defeated Colt Steele
Vladimir Petrov defeated Tim Horner
Ron & Jimmy Garvin defeated Bobby Eaton & Dennis Condrey

AJPW @ Tokyo, Japan - Budokan Hall - March 12, 1987 (12,900)
NWA World Champion Ric Flair defeated the Great Wajima at
18:29

JCP @ Albany, GA - Civic Center - March 13, 1987
Denny Brown defeated Brady Boone
Thunderfoot #1 defeated Rocky King
The Barbarian defeated the Italian Stallion
Vladimir Petrov defeated Baron Von Raschke
Bob & Brad Armstrong defeated Arn Anderson & Lex Luger
NWA TV Champion Tully Blanchard defeated NWA US Tag
Team Champion Barry Windham via disqualification
Dusty Rhodes & NWA US Champion Nikita Koloff defeated
Ivan Koloff & Dick Murdoch via disqualification

JCP @ Washington DC - Armory - March 13, 1987
Mark Fleming defeated Tiejo Khan
Tim Horner defeated Johnny Ace
Lazertron defeated Shaska Whatley
Dutch Mantell & Bobby Jaggers defeated the MOD Squad
Wahoo McDaniel defeated Big Bubba via disqualification
Ron Garvin defeated Bobby Eaton
Jimmy Garvin defeated Dennis Condrey via disqualification
NWA Tag Team Champions Rick Rude & Manny Fernandez
defeated Ricky Morton & Robert Gibson in a steel cage match

JCP @ Atlanta, GA - WTBS Studios - March 14, 1987 (matinee)
*World Championship Wrestling - 3/14/87 - featured Tony
Schiavone & David Crockett conducting an interview with NWA
US Tag Team Champions Ron Garvin & Barry Windham
regarding their title defense later in the show against Ivan
Koloff & Dick Murdoch; included Schiavone conducting an
interview with Dusty Rhodes & NWA US Champion Nikita
Koloff, the #2 seed in the Crockett Cup, regarding their
participation in the tournament; Rhodes finished the interview
by noting he would soon be facing Big Bubba at the Boston
Garden; featured footage of Jim Cornette recently sending Big*

*Bubba out to fight with Ole Anderson; included an ad
promoting the Starrcade 86 home video; featured a video
package hosted by Francis Crockett regarding Baltimore
hosting the Crockett Cup and the historic sights in the city:*
Jimmy Garvin (w/ Precious) pinned Randy Barber with the
brainbuster at 3:45; during the bout, it was noted the
Gladiators, Steve Keirn & Stan Lane, Mike Graham & Nelson
Royal would be part of the Crockett Cup in April
The Barbarian (w/ Bill Dundee) pinned Zane Smith with a
tombstone and headbutt off the top; during the bout, it was
announced Big Bubba would face Ole Anderson that night in
Greensboro, NC; Dundee joined the commentary team during
the match to advertise that he, Kevin Sullivan, and the MOD
Squad would be in Daytona Beach, FL the next night for Night
of the Thunderdome
Ivan Koloff & Dick Murdoch (w/ Vladimir Pietrov) defeated
NWA US Tag Team Champions Ron Garvin & Barry Windham
to win the titles at 22:52 when Koloff pinned Garvin after Jim
Cornette and Bobby Eaton appeared ringside, with Eaton
hitting Garvin with Cornette's tennis racquet behind the
referee's back
Brad Armstrong vs. El Lobo
NWA TV Champion Tully Blanchard, Arn Anderson, & Lex
Luger vs. Alan Martin, Larry Stevens, & Bill Mulkey
Lazortron vs. Tommy Angel
Bobby Eaton & Stan Lane vs. Dexter Wescott & Mike Jackson
Ricky Morton & Robert Gibson vs. Darrel Dalton & Randy
Mulkey

JCP @ Greensboro, NC - Coliseum - March 14, 1987 (15,000+; sell out)
Dutch Mantell & Bobby Jaggers defeated the MOD Squad
Tim Horner defeated Lex Luger via disqualification
Dennis Condrey (w/ Jim Cornette) defeated Baron Von
Raschke
NWA Super Bouts - 5/16/87: Jimmy Garvin (w/ Precious)
pinned Bobby Eaton (w/ Jim Cornette & Big Bubba) at 6:30
with an inside cradle as Eaton attempted a backdrop; after the
bout, Dennis Condrey ran out and helped in ganging up on
Garvin, with Garvin being hit in the head repeatedly with
Cornette's tennis racquet until Ron Garvin came out to clear
the ring
NWA Super Bouts - 5/9/87: NWA TV Champion Tully
Blanchard (w/ JJ Dillon) pinned Brad Armstrong at 12:53 when
Blanchard blocked a sunset flip into the ring, then held onto
Dillon from the floor for added leverage; both the title and
Blanchard's $10,000 were at stake in the match
NWA Super Bouts - 5/16/87: Wahoo McDaniel, Ricky Morton &
Robert Gibson defeated Paul Jones, NWA Tag Team
Champions Rick Rude & Manny Fernandez at around the 7-
minute mark when McDaniel pinned Jones after Morton &
Gibson hit Jones with the double dropkick; Jones covered his
face with a mask for the match
NWA US Tag Team Champions Ivan Koloff & Dick Murdoch
defeated Dusty Rhodes & NWA US Champion Nikita Koloff
NWA Super Bouts - 5/9/87: Ole Anderson defeated Big Bubba
via disqualification
NWA World Champion Ric Flair defeated Barry Windham

JCP @ Atlanta, GA - WTBS Studios - March 15, 1987 (matinee)
TV taping:
World Championship Wrestling - 3/21/87:
Arn Anderson & Lex Luger vs. Tommy Angel & Larry Stevens
Brad Armstrong vs. Paul Garner
Tim Horner vs. El Lobo
Wahoo McDaniel vs. Randy Barber
Ron Garvin vs. Dexter Wescott
Bobby Eaton vs. Alan Fox
Ricky Morton & Robert Gibson vs. Darel Dalton & Zane Smith
Barry Windham vs. Bill Tabb
World Championship Wrestling Sunday Edition - 3/22/87

JCP @ Daytona Beach, FL - Ocean Center - March 15, 1987
The Night of the Thunderdome
Included the MOD Squad, Bill Dundee, and Kevin Sullivan

JCP @ Minneapolis, MN - Met Center - March 15, 1987 (2,500)
Bobby Jaggers & Dutch Mantell defeated Thunderfoot #1 & #2
Jimmy Garvin defeated Bobby Eaton
Lex Luger defeated Baron Von Raschke
NWA US Champion Nikita Koloff defeated Vladimir Petrov
The Road Warriors defeated NWA Tag Team Champions Rick Rude & Manny Fernandez
NWA World Champion Ric Flair defeated Barry Windham
Dusty Rhodes defeated Big Bubba in a steel cage match

JCP @ Lenoir, NC - March 16, 1987
Ron & Jimmy Garvin defeated Bobby Eaton & Dennis Condrey

JCP @ Greenville, SC - Memorial Auditorium - March 16, 1987
Bobby Jaggers & Dutch Mantell vs. the MOD Squad did not take place as advertised
Tim Horner defeated the Italian Stallion
Bob Armstrong fought Vladimir Petrov to a draw
Brad Armstrong defeated Ivan Koloff
Tim Horner & Bobby Jaggers defeated Gary Royal & the Barbarian
NWA US Champion Nikita Koloff fought Lex Luger to a double count-out in a No DQ match
Ricky Morton defeated NWA Tag Team Champion Rick Rude in a steel cage match; the match was scheduled for Morton & Robert Gibson vs. Rude & Manny Fernandez
NWA World Champion Ric Flair defeated Barry Windham in a Best 2 out of 3 falls, 90-minute time limit match

MID-ATLANTIC CHAMPIONSHIP WRESTLING

GREENVILLE MEMORIAL AUDITORIUM

NWA NATIONAL WRESTLING ALLIANCE

MONDAY, MARCH 16, 1987

NWA WORLD HEAVYWEIGHT TITLE
2 OUT OF 3 FALLS - 90 MINUTE TIME LIMIT
"NATURE BOY" RIC FLAIR VS. BARRY WINDHAM

WORLD TAG TEAM TITLE IN A 10 FOOT STEEL CAGE
ROCK 'N ROLL EXPRESS VS. RAGING BULL RAVISHING RICK RUDE (WITH #1 PAUL JONES)

U.S. HEAVYWEIGHT TITLE NO DISQUALIFICATION
NIKITA KOLOFF VS. LEX LUGER (WITH J.J. DILLON)

TAG ACTION VS.
KANSAS JAYHAWKS   MOD SQUAD #1 & 2

BRAD ARMSTRONG VS. IVAN KOLOFF

"BULLET" BOB ARMSTRONG VS. VALDIMIR PETROV

NWA *SUBJECT TO CHANGE
TIM HORNER VS. SHASKA WHATLEY

TICKET PRICES:
Ring Side (Res.) $12
Adults Gen. Adm. $10
Children (under 10) $4

MID-ATLANTIC CHAMPIONSHIP WRESTLING

JCP @ Daytona Beach, FL - Ocean Center - March 15, 1987
The Night of the Thunderdome
Included the MOD Squad, Bill Dundee, and Kevin Sullivan

JCP @ Minneapolis, MN - Met Center - March 15, 1987 (2,500)
Bobby Jaggers & Dutch Mantell defeated Thunderfoot #1 & #2
Jimmy Garvin defeated Bobby Eaton
Lex Luger defeated Baron Von Raschke
NWA US Champion Nikita Koloff defeated Vladimir Petrov
The Road Warriors defeated NWA Tag Team Champions Rick Rude & Manny Fernandez
NWA World Champion Ric Flair defeated Barry Windham
Dusty Rhodes defeated Big Bubba in a steel cage match

JCP @ Lenoir, NC - March 16, 1987
Ron & Jimmy Garvin defeated Bobby Eaton & Dennis Condrey

JCP @ China Grove, NC - South Rowan Senior High School Gym - March 17, 1987
TV taping:
Barry Windham defeated John Savage
Wahoo McDaniel & Baron Von Raschke defeated Gary Royal & Tommy Angel
NWA Tag Team Champions Manny Fernandez & Rick Rude vs. Ricky Morton & Robert Gibson
Worldwide - 3/21/87:
Tim Horner defeated Vernon Deaton
Barry Windham, Ron & Jimmy Garvin defeated John Savage, Thunderfoot #1 & Thunderfoot #2
Lazortron defeated Rocky King
Pro - 3/21/87:
Jimmy Garvin defeated Mark Fleming

JCP @ Las Cruces, NM - Pan American Center - March 18, 1987 (5,000)
Bobby Jaggers defeated Thunderfoot #2
Dutch Mantell pinned the Barbarian
Barry Windham pinned Arn Anderson
Wahoo McDaniel, Ron & Jimmy Garvin defeated Big Bubba, Bobby Eaton & Dennis Condrey when Ron pinned Eaton
Dusty Rhodes & Barry Windham defeated Lex Luger & NWA TV Champion Tully Blanchard when Rhodes pinned Blanchard
Ricky Morton & Robert Gibson defeated NWA Tag Team Champions Rick Rude & Manny Fernandez via disqualification
NWA US Champion Nikita Koloff defeated NWA World Champion Ric Flair via disqualification

JCP @ Inglewood, CA - Great Western Forum - March 19, 1987 (3,000)
Bobby Jaggers defeated Thunderfoot #2
Dutch Mantell defeated the Barbarian
Ricky Morton & Robert Gibson fought Arn Anderson & Lex Luger to a draw
Ron & Jimmy Garvin defeated Bobby Eaton & Dennis Condrey

in a bunkhouse match
NWA TV Champion Tully Blanchard defeated Wahoo McDaniel via disqualification
NWA Tag Team Champions Rick Rude & Manny Fernandez defeated Dusty Rhodes & NWA US Champion Nikita Koloff via disqualification
NWA World Champion Ric Flair defeated Barry Windham at 23:29
Road Warrior Animal defeated Big Bubba via count-out in a Louisville streetfight

JCP @ Albuquerque, NM - Tingley Coliseum - March 20, 1987 (3,632)
Bobby Jaggers defeated Thunderfoot #2
Dutch Mantell defeated the Barbarian
Ron & Jimmy Garvin defeated Bobby Eaton & Dennis Condrey
Wahoo McDaniel defeated Lex Luger via disqualification
NWA US Champion Nikita Koloff & Road Warrior Animal defeated NWA TV Champion Tully Blanchard & Arn Anderson
NWA World Champion Ric Flair defeated Barry Windham at 21:14
NWA Tag Team Champions Rick Rude & Manny Fernandez defeated Ricky Morton & Robert Gibson
Dusty Rhodes defeated Big Bubba in a chain match

JCP @ Cincinnati, OH - Cincinnati Gardens - March 21, 1987 (3,500)
Dutch Mantell pinned the Italian Stallion
NWA Jr. Heavyweight Champion Lazertron pinned Denny Brown
Bob & Brad Armstrong defeated Thunderfoot #1 & Gary Royal
Wahoo McDaniel defeated Vladimir Petrov via count-out
Barry Windham defeated Lex Luger via disqualification
Ron & Jimmy Garvin defeated Bobby Eaton & Dennis Condrey in a steel cage match
Ole Anderson defeated Big Bubba in a steel cage match

JCP @ Chicago, IL - UIC Pavilion - March 21, 1987
Tim Horner defeated Ricky Lee Jones
Bobby Jaggers defeated Thunderfoot #1
Arn Anderson defeated Baron Von Raschke
Ricky Morton & Robert Gibson defeated Ivan Koloff & Vladimir Petrov
NWA TV Champion Tully Blanchard defeated Dusty Rhodes via disqualification
The Road Warriors defeated NWA Tag Team Champions Rick Rude & Manny Fernandez via disqualification
NWA World Champion Ric Flair fought NWA US Champion Nikita Koloff to a no contest at 35:00

JCP @ Waco, TX - Heart O'Texas Coliseum - March 22, 1987 (matinee) (1,100)
NWA TV Champion Tully Blanchard defeated Dusty Rhodes via disqualification
The Road Warriors defeated Bobby Eaton & Dennis Condrey

NWA US Champion Nikita Koloff defeated NWA World Champion Ric Flair via disqualification

JCP @ Houston, TX - Summit - March 22, 1987
Ron & Jimmy Garvin defeated Bobby Eaton & Dennis Condrey in a bunkhouse match
Also included NWA World Champion Ric Flair, Dusty Rhodes, Ricky Morton & Robert Gibson, and the Road Warriors

JCP @ Fayetteville, NC - March 23, 1987
Nelson Royal defeated Gary Royal
Baron Von Raschke defeated Mark Fleming
Lazertron defeated Denny Brown
Ivan Koloff & Vladimir Petrov defeated Bob Armstrong & Tim Horner
Brad Anderson defeated Dennis Condrey via disqualification
Jimmy Garvin defeated Big Bubba in a streetfight
Ron Garvin defeated Bobby Eaton in a steel cage match

JCP @ Greenville, SC - Memorial Auditorium - March 23, 1987
TV taping:
Ricky Morton & Robert Gibson fought Lex Luger & NWA TV Champion Tully Blanchard to a 20-minute time-limit draw
The Road Warriors defeated NWA Tag Team Champions Rick Rude & Manny Fernandez via disqualification
Also included Dusty Rhodes, Barry Windham, Wahoo McDaniel, Arn Anderson, the Barbarian, NWA US Champion Nikita Koloff, Jimmy Valiant, NWA World Champion Ric Flair, Bill Dundee, and the MOD Squad

JCP @ Lincolnton, NC - March 24, 1987
TV taping:
Bobby Jaggers & Dutch Mantell defeated Tommy Angel & Ricky Nelson
Lex Luger & NWA TV Champion Tully Blanchard defeated Tim Horner & the Italian Stallion
NWA Tag Team Champions Rick Rude & Manny Fernandez defeated Mike Simani & Vernon Deaton
Arn Anderson defeated John Savage
Lex Luger, NWA TV Champion Tully Blanchard, & Arn Anderson defeated Ricky Lee Jones, the Italian Stallion, & Johnny Ace
Ron & Jimmy Garvin defeated Bobby Eaton & Dennis Condrey (Condrey's last appearance for 18 months)
Worldwide - 3/28/87:
NWA Tag Team Champions Rick Rude & Manny Fernandez defeated George South & Rocky King
NWA TV Champion Tully Blanchard, Arn Anderson, & Lex Luger (w/ JJ Dillon) defeated Ricky Lee Jones, the Italian Stallion, & Johnny Ace; during the bout, NWA World Champion Ric Flair joined Bob Caudle on commentary until Ole Anderson appeared and ripped up Flair's clothing until the other Horsemen came after him; moments later, Flair cut a promo saying Ole just made the mistake of a lifetime

JCP @ San Francisco, CA - Civic Auditorium - March 25, 1987 (2,733)
Tim Horner defeated Frank Dusek
Robert Gibson fought NWA Tag Team Champion Rick Rude to a draw
NWA Tag Team Champion Manny Fernandez defeated Tim Horner
Barry Windham defeated Big Bubba via count-out
Jimmy Garvin defeated Bobby Eaton
Dusty Rhodes & the Road Warriors defeated Arn Anderson, NWA TV Champion Tully Blanchard, & Lex Luger
NWA US Champion Nikita Koloff defeated NWA World Champion Ric Flair via disqualification at 19:39

JCP @ Amarillo, TX - Civic Center - March 26, 1987
Ricky Morton & Robert Gibson defeated Bobby Eaton & Big Bubba (sub. for Dennis Condrey)
Also included Dick Murdoch, Ivan Koloff, NWA US Champion Nikita Koloff, and Vladimir Pietrov

WIDE WORLD WRESTLING

**SUNDAY, MARCH 29 AT 2 PM
IN THE ASHEVILLE CIVIC CENTER
Featuring a "LOUISVILLE STREETFIGHT"**

JIMMY

BUBBA

BEAUTIFUL BOBBY WITH JIM

LOUISVILLE STREET FIGHT
OLE ANDERSON
VS
BIG BUBBA

GEORGEOUS JIMMY GARVIN
(WITH PRECIOUS)
VS
BEAUTIFUL BOBBY
(WITH JIM CORNETTE)

WORLD HEAVYWEIGHT TITLE
"NATURE BOY" RIC FLAIR
VS
BRAD ARMSTRONG

SIX MAN TAG ACTION
NIKITA KOLOFF
BARRY WINDHAM
WAHOO MCDANIEL
VS
TULLY BLANCHARD
LEX LUGER
ARN ANDERSON
(WITH J.J. DILLON)

RONNIE GARVIN
VS
LOVERBOY DENNIS

TAG ACTION
KANSAS JAYHAWKS
VS
MOD SQUAD

JIMMY VALIANT
VS
COLT STEELE

RICKY LEE JONES
VS
BRADY BOONE

LOVERBOY

RIC

BARRY

**Ringside: $10, Balcony $8, $4 for Children under 10
Box Office 259-5771 Mon.-Fri. 10-5:30, Sat. 11-4, Day of Match 12 Noon
No Checks or Credit Cards Day of Match. Matches subject to change.**

WIDE WORLD WRESTLING ON WLOS-TV 13 SUNDAY 12 NOON

JCP @ Norfolk, VA - Scope - March 27, 1987
Jimmy Garvin defeated Bobby Eaton

JCP @ Atlanta, GA - Omni - March 27, 1987 (4,500)
Bobby Jaggers & Dutch Mantell defeated Thunderfoot #1 & #2
Denny Brown defeated George South
Tim Horner defeated Gary Royal
The Barbarian defeated Todd Champion
NWA TV Champion Tully Blanchard, Arn Anderson, & Lex Luger defeated Barry Windham, Bob Armstrong, & Baron Von Raschke
NWA World Champion Ric Flair defeated Brad Armstrong at the 24-minute mark
Ole Anderson defeated Big Bubba in a steel cage match
Dusty Rhodes & NWA US Champion Nikita Koloff defeated Ivan Koloff & Dick Murdoch in a steel cage match

JCP @ Atlanta, GA - WTBS Studios - March 28, 1987 (matinee)
World Championship Wrestling - 3/28/87:
Ricky Morton & Robert Gibson vs. Chance McQuade & Bill Tabb
Bobby Eaton vs. Vernon Deaton
Ole Anderson vs. Kent Glover
Wahoo McDaniel & Baron Von Raschke vs. Larry Clarke & Rick Sullivan
Big Bubba vs. Cougar Jay
Lex Luger & NWA TV Champion Tully Blanchard vs. Todd Champion & Denny Brown
Arn Anderson vs. Tim Horner
Barry Windham vs. Dave Spearman
NWA Tag Team Champion Rick Rude vs. Larry Stephens
Bill & Randy Mulkey defeated the Gladiators

Pro - 3/28/87:
Bobby Eaton & Stan Lane vs. George South & Rocky King
Lex Luger, NWA TV Champion Tully Blanchard, & Arn Anderson vs. the Italian Stallion, Dexter Westcott, & Tim Horner
Ivan Koloff & Vladimir Pietrov vs. Mike Simani & Mark Fleming

JCP @ Philadelphia, PA - Civic Center - March 28, 1987 (3,916)
Lazertron defeated Denny Brown
Baron Von Raschke defeated Gary Royal
Lex Luger defeated Tim Horner
Dusty Rhodes, Wahoo McDaniel, & NWA US Champion Nikita Koloff defeated Ivan Koloff, Dick Murdoch, & Vladimir Petrov in a bunkhouse match
Ole Anderson defeated NWA TV Champion Tully Blanchard via disqualification
NWA World Champion Ric Flair defeated Brad Armstrong
NWA Tag Team Champions Rick Rude & Manny Fernandez fought Ricky Morton & Robert Gibson to a no contest
Ron Garvin defeated Bobby Eaton in a steel cage match

JCP @ Asheville, NC - Civic Center - March 29, 1987 (matinee)
Bob Armstrong defeated Gary Royal
Ron Garvin defeated the Italian Stallion (sub. for Dennis Condrey)
Bobby Jaggers & Dutch Mantell defeated Thunderfoot #1 & #2 (sub. for the MOD Squad)
NWA US Champion Nikita Koloff, Barry Windham, & Wahoo McDaniel defeated NWA TV Champion Tully Blanchard, Arn Anderson, & Lex Luger
NWA World Champion Ric Flair defeated Brad Armstrong
Jimmy Garvin defeated Bobby Eaton
Ole Anderson defeated Big Bubba in a Louisville streetfight

JCP @ Charlotte, NC - Coliseum - March 29, 1987
Tim Horner defeated George South
Jimmy Garvin defeated Ricky Nelson
Lex Luger & Arn Anderson defeated Wahoo McDaniel & Brad Armstrong
Ole Anderson defeated NWA TV Champion Tully Blanchard via disqualification
Ron Garvin defeated Bobby Eaton in a lights out match
Dusty Rhodes & NWA US Champion Nikita Koloff Ivan Koloff & Dick Murdoch via disqualification
NWA World Champion Ric Flair defeated Barry Windham
NWA Tag Team Champions Rick Rude & Manny Fernandez defeated Ricky Morton & Robert Gibson

MID-ATLANTIC CHAMPIONSHIP WRESTLING

NWA
NATIONAL WRESTLING ALLIANCE

GREENVILLE
MEMORIAL
AUDITORIUM
MONDAY, MARCH 30
8:00 P.M.

LOUISVILLE STREET FIGHT

OLE ANDERSON
VS
BIG BUBBA
(WITH JIM CORNETTE)

BUNKHOUSE MATCH

RON GARVIN
VS
MIDNIGHT EXPRESS
(WITH JIM CORNETTE)

GORGEOUS JIMMY GARVIN
(WITH PRECIOUS)

WORLD T.V. TITLE
1 FALL - 25 MINUTES

TULLY BLANCHARD (WITH J.J. DILLON)	VS	RICKY MORTON
ROBERT GIBSON	VS	LEX LUGER
TIM HORNER	VS	ARN ANDERSON
LAZOR-TRON	VS	DENNY BROWN
ITALIAN STALLION	VS	BRODY CHASE

Ringside Reserved $12
General Admission $10
Children (Under 10) $4

N017610

MID-ATLANTIC CHAMPIONSHIP WRESTLING

JCP @ Greenville, SC - Memorial Auditorium - March 30, 1987
The Italian Stallion defeated Brodie Chase
Lazortron defeated Denny Brown
Tim Horner defeated Arn Anderson via disqualification
Lex Luger defeated Robert Gibson
Ricky Morton fought NWA TV Champion Tully Blanchard to a double count-out
Ron Garvin defeated Bobby Eaton; the match was scheduled for Ron & Jimmy Garvin vs. Eaton & Dennis Condrey
Ole Anderson defeated Big Bubba in a streetfight

JCP @ Gastonia, NC - March 31, 1987
Worldwide - 4/4/87 - featured the announcement that NWA US Tag Team Champion Dick Murdoch had been suspended 30 days and the US Tag Team Titles had been stripped due to Murdoch dropping NWA US Champion Nikita Koloff with a brainbuster on the floor.
Jimmy Garvin vs. Tommy Angel
Bobby Jaggers vs. George South
Lazortron vs. Larry Stevens
NWA Tag Team Champions Rick Rude & Manny Fernandez vs. Johnny Ace & Mike Force
NWA TV Champion Tully Blanchard & Lex Luger vs. Denny Brown & Nelson Royal
Ricky Morton & Robert Gibson vs. Vernon Deaton & Brodie Chase
Bobby Eaton & Big Bubba vs. the Italian Stallion & Ricky Lee Jones

JCP @ Laurinburg, NC - April 1, 1987
Big Bubba defeated Brad Armstrong
Ron Garvin defeated Bobby Eaton

CWF @ Sunrise, FL - April 1, 1987
The Tahitian Prince defeated Eddie Roberts
Teijo Khan defeated Mitch Snow
Ron Simmons defeated Shaska Whatley via disqualification
Wahoo McDaniel defeated Ed Gantner
Scott Hall, Tracy Smothers, & Steve Armstrong defeated Bill Dundee & the MOD Squad
Mike Rotundo defeated the Barbarian via disqualification
Ole Anderson defeated Arn Anderson via disqualification
Dusty Rhodes & NWA US Champion Nikita Koloff defeated NWA TV Champion Tully Blanchard & Lex Luger

JCP @ Columbia, SC - April 2, 1987
Ron Garvin defeated Bobby Eaton

JCP @ Albany, GA - Civic Center - April 3, 1987
Ron Garvin defeated Bobby Eaton
Big Bubba defeated Bob Armstrong via count-out

JCP @ Greensboro, NC - Coliseum - April 3, 1987
Bill & Randy Mulkey defeated Chris Champion & Sean Royal

Lazertron defeated Denny Brown
Baron Von Raschke defeated John Savage
Chris Champion & Sean Royal defeated Bobby Jaggers & Tim Horner
NWA Super Bouts - 5/23/87: Ole Anderson defeated Arn Anderson (w/ JJ Dillon) via disqualification at around the 4-minute mark when Dillon interfered as Ole had Arn in a standing armbar; after the bout, Ole cleared the two from the ring; after the contest, a bloody Arn returned to the ring but lost the ensuing brawl with Ole
NWA Super Bouts - 5/23/87: NWA US Champion Nikita Koloff defeated Vladimir Petrov (w/ Ivan Koloff) at around the 6:20 mark by pinning an interfering Ivan with the Russian Sickle; the champion wore a neckbrace for the match; late in the bout, referee Tommy Young was knocked to the floor, with Ivan then interfering and hitting Nikita with the Russian chain; moments later, Ivan put Young back into the ring but turned around and sustained the Russian Sickle, with the dazed referee counting the pinfall not realizing it wasn't Petrov
NWA Super Bouts - 5/30/87: Ricky Morton & Robert Gibson fought NWA TV Champion Tully Blanchard & Lex Luger (w/ JJ Dillon) to a 15-minute time-limit draw; the time limit expired as Morton had Blanchard covered with a crossbody off the top; after the match, Morton & Gibson cleared their opponents from ringside
NWA Super Bouts - 5/23/87: Dusty Rhodes defeated NWA World Champion Ric Flair via disqualification; only the first two minutes of the match aired

JCP @ Atlanta, GA - WTBS Studios - April 4, 1987 (matinee)

World Championship Wrestling - 4/4/87 - featured Tony Schiavone & David Crockett on commentary; included Schiavone conducting an interview with Jim Crockett Jr. in which he announced Ivan Koloff would team with Vladimir Petrov at the Crockett Cup instead of Dick Murdoch because Murdoch had been suspended for 30 days, due to dropping NWA US Champion Nikita Koloff with a brainbuster on the floor the previous week, and he and Koloff had been stripped of the NWA US Tag Team Titles; Crockett said a tournament would determine the next champions and he is considering further actions against Murdoch; moments later, Schiavone conducted an interview with Koloff & Petrov regarding Murdoch's suspension, during which Koloff said they would target Dusty Rhodes & Nikita; featured Schiavone conducting an interview with Ricky Morton & Robert Gibson regarding their being the #4 seed in the Crockett Cup the following week; included a pretaped promo by Murdoch replying to his suspension from Crockett, during which he said his lawyer had contacted Crockett and he would be back at work in two weeks, Crockett couldn't ban the brainbuster, and that he would take out Rhodes just like he took out Nikita; featured a pretaped promo by NWA Florida Heavyweight Champion Mike Rotundo regarding his participation at the Crockett Cup with Tim Horner; featured Schiavone conducting an interview with JJ Dillon & NWA TV Champion Tully Blanchard regarding the Crockett Cup, during which it was noted Blanchard would face Ole Anderson the next night at the Omni; included Schiavone

conducting an interview with Nikita, in a neckbrace, regarding his recovery from Murdoch's brainbuster the previous week and being part of the Crockett Cup with Rhodes; featured Schiavone conducting an interview with Baron Von Raschke regarding his teaming with Wahoo McDaniel in the Crockett Cup; included a pretaped promo by NWA Florida Tag Team Champions the MOD Squad regarding their participation in the Crockett Cup; featured an ad promoting the Starrcade 86 home video; included a video segment focusing on the history of Baltimore and tourist sites in the city; featured Schiavone conducting an interview with Flair regarding his defense against Barry Windham during the Crockett Cup, during which Flair again said Precious wanted Flair and that she should go ahead and jump onboard before any blood is spilled between he and Jimmy Garvin; moments later, Flair asked for Precious to come out, with Precious then doing so and Flair praising her until she slapped him across the face and walked off; moments later, Flair said he would be back out next week with two of the best Space Mountainettes and would again ask Precious to come out, then stating the next time Precious slapped him it would be behind closed doors; included Schiavone conducting an interview with Windham regarding his challenging Flair in Baltimore; featured Schiavone conducting an interview with Ron Garvin regarding Jim Cornette & the New Midnight Express, with Garvin implying Dennis Condrey quit because he was the only one that had any sense; included Schiavone conducting an interview with Cornette, Bubba, Eaton & Lane regarding Lane now being a member of the Midnight Express and responding to Ron Garvin's comments earlier in the show; moments later, Lane said he was on Clearwater Beach, FL 24 years earlier when Cornette called him and said he could win $1 million and get to beat up Ron Garvin; featured a pretaped promo by Kevin Sullivan regarding his teaming with Arn Anderson as part of the Crockett Cup; included Schiavone conducting a closing interview with Jimmy Garvin & Precious regarding the altercation between Precious and Flair earlier in the show, with Garvin taking exception to Flair hitting on Precious:

Jimmy Garvin (w/ Precious) & Ron Garvin defeated Larry Clarke & Mike Force at 5:55 when Jimmy scored the pin following the brainbuster; during the match, NWA World Champion Ric Flair joined the commentary team to scout Jimmy, during which he said Precious wanted to be with him; Flair called out to Precious several times during the contest
NWA Tag Team Champions Rick Rude & Manny Fernandez (w/ Paul Jones) defeated Cougar Jay & Dexter Wescott at the 15-second mark when both men scored simulteanous pinfalls following Rude's DDT and Fernandez' flying forearm; after the bout, Schiavone conducted an interview with Rude, Fernandez, & Jones regarding their being the #1 seed in the Crockett Cup, during which they targetted Dusty Rhodes & NWA US Champion Nikita Koloff, Lex Luger & NWA TV Champion Tully Blanchard, the Road Warriors, and Ricky Morton & Robert Gibson
International Tag Team Champions the Road Warriors (w/ Paul Ellering) defeated Bill Tabb & Tommy Angel at 1:04 when Road Warrior Hawk pinned Angel following the Doomsday Device; after the bout, David Crockett conducted a ringside

interview with the Road Warriors & Ellering regarding their having won the International tag team titles in Japan, their return to the US, and being part of the Crockett Cup; during the segment, it was noted they would face Bobby Eaton & Stan Lane that night in Boston and griped that they were the #3 seed in the tournament instead of #1; Hawk noting they would face "the new Midnight Express" was made before the announcement later in the show that the team had changed

Big Bubba (w/ Jim Cornette) pinned Gary Royal at 4:00 with the sidewalk slam; during the bout, Cornette joined Schiavone on commentary and spoke about Bubba's upcoming steel cage matches that night in Boston against Dusty Rhodes and the following Friday against Ole Anderson in Baltimore; after the match, Cornette said he met with his mother in Louisville and she ordered later in the show that a change had to be made to get rid of the weak link in the Midnight Express; Cornette said the weak link had been made strong and then introduced the New Midnight Express - Bobby Eaton & Stan Lane; Cornette then predicted they would win the Crockett Cup, world and US tag team titles (Lane's surprise debut with the Midnight Express)

Lex Luger (w/ JJ Dillon) defeated the Italian Stallion via submission with the Torture Rack at 6:16; during the bout, Dillon briefly joined the commentary team to talk about Luger & NWA TV Champion Tully Blanchard being part of the Crockett Cup

Ole Anderson (w/ Tim Horner) defeated Brodie Chase via submission with an armbar at 1:57; Horner, baseball bat in hand, briefly joined the commentary team for the match; after the bout, Schiavone conducted an interview with Horner & Anderson regarding Ole's upcoming matches with NWA TV Champion Tully Blanchard at the Omni and Big Bubba in Baltimore

Ivan Koloff & Vladimir Petrov defeated Johnny Ace & Ricky Lee Jones at 3:20 when Koloff pinned Ace with the Russian Sickle; after the bout, Schiavone conducted an interview with Koloff & Petrov regarding their participation in the Crockett Cup and facing the Road Warriors the following day at the Omni

NWA TV Champion Tully Blanchard (w/ JJ Dillon) pinned Larry Stephens with the slingshot suplex at 2:33; Blanchard's $10,000 and the title were at stake in the match

Arn Anderson pinned Alan Martin with the gordbuster at 1:55; after the bout, Schiavone conducted an interview with JJ Dillon & Anderson regarding Anderson teaming with Kevin Sullivan as part of the Crockett Cup, with Arn then discussed Ole Anderson & Tim Horner, saying they were in a war they can't win

Brad & Bob Armstrong defeated Cougar Jay & Mike Jackson at 5:20 when Brad pinned Jay with the Russian legsweep; during the bout, it was noted Steve Armstrong & Tracy Smothers were teaming in Florida as the Southern Boys

Barry Windham pinned Chance McQuade with the lariat at the 43-second mark

Tim Horner pinned Thunderfoot #1 at 2:17 with a roll up into a bridge

JCP @ St. Petersburg, FL - April 4, 1987
Included NWA Tag Team Champions Rick Rude & Manny Fernandez

JCP @ Boston, MA - Boston Garden - April 4, 1987 (11,000)
Debut at the venue
Misty Blue defeated Linda Dallas
Jimmy & Ron Garvin defeated Thunderfoot #1 & #2
Lex Luger defeated Baron Von Raschke
Ole Anderson defeated Arn Anderson via disqualification
Ricky Morton & Robert Gibson defeated Ivan Koloff & Vladimir Pietrov
The Road Warriors defeated Bobby Eaton & Stan Lane
NWA US Champion Nikita Koloff defeated NWA TV Champion Tully Blanchard
NWA World Champion Ric Flair defeated Barry Windham at the 23-minute mark
Dusty Rhodes defeated Big Bubba in a steel cage match

JCP @ Atlanta, GA - WTBS Studios - April 5, 1987
World Championship Wrestling - 4/11/87:
Ole Anderson vs. Ray Aaron
Bobby Eaton & Stan Lane vs. Larry Stevens & Tommy Angel
Arn Anderson vs. Zane Smith
The Road Warriors vs. Randy Barber & Thunderfoot #2
Baron Von Raschke vs. Brodie Chase
Ivan Koloff vs. Dexter Wescott
Jimmy Garvin vs. Thunderfoot #1
The New Breed vs. Cougar Jay & Chance McQuade
NWA TV Champion Tully Blanchard vs. Alan Martin
Ron Garvin vs. Bill Tabb
Lex Luger vs. Larry Clarke
Tim Horner vs. Mike Force
World Championship Wrestling Sunday Edition - 4/12/87

CWF @ Orlando, FL - April 5, 1987
Bob Armstrong, Tracy Smothers, & Steve Armstrong defeated Bill Dundee & the MOD Squad
Teijo Khan & the Tahitian Prince defeated Brady Boone & Mitch Snow
Scott Hall defeated Ed Gantner
Mike Rotundo defeated the Barbarian
NWA Tag Team Champions Rick Rude & Manny Fernandez defeated Brad Armstrong & Wahoo McDaniel
Bill & Randy Mulkey fought Colt Steele & Snake Brown to a draw
Kevin Sullivan defeated Jimmy Valiant in a Texas Death Match

JCP @ Atlanta, GA - Omni - April 5, 1987 (4,000)
Tim Horner defeated Sean Royal
Lazertron defeated Chris Champion
Baron Von Raschke defeated Ricky Lee Jones
Bobby Eaton & Stan Lane defeated Barry Windham & Ron Garvin
The Road Warriors fought Ivan Koloff & Vladimir Pietrov to a no contest
Ole Anderson defeated NWA TV Champion Tully Blanchard
Dusty Rhodes defeated Arn Anderson
Lex Luger defeated NWA US Champion Nikita Koloff via disqualification

NWA World Champion Ric Flair defeated Jimmy Garvin via disqualification at the 12-minute mark

JCP @ Toccoa, GA - April 6, 1987 (sell out)
Ron & Jimmy Garvin, Ricky Morton & Robert Gibson defeated Jim Cornette, Big Bubba, Bobby Eaton & Stan Lane

JCP @ Spartanburg, SC - Memorial Auditorium - April 7, 1987
Worldwide - 4/11/87:
Chris Champion & Sean Royal vs. George South & Rocky King
Jimmy Garvin vs. John Savage
Lex Luger vs. Todd Champion
Bobby Eaton & Stan Lane vs. Vernon Deaton & Gary Royal
The Road Warriors vs. Tommy Angel & Ricky Nelson
Pro - 4/11/87:
Dark match after the taping: The Road Warriors vs. NWA Tag Team Champions Rick Rude & Manny Fernandez
Also included NWA World Champion Ric Flair, Dusty Rhodes, NWA US Champion Nikita Koloff, NWA TV Champion Tully Blanchard, Ole Anderson, Ricky Morton & Robert Gibson, Barry Windham, Ivan Koloff, Big Bubba, and Dick Murdoch

JCP @ Spokane, WA - April 1987
Ricky Morton & Robert Gibson defeated NWA Tag Team Champions Rick Rude & Manny Fernandez (w/ Paul Jones) in a non-title match when Morton pinned Fernandez with a sunset flip into the ring; footage of the match was later aired in June to explain Morton & Gibson's title win after Rude left for the WWF

CWF @ Miami, FL - April 8, 1987
NWA World Champion Ric Flair defeated Wahoo McDaniel

JCP @ Raleigh, NC - Dorton Arena - April 9, 1987
Baron Von Raschke defeated Thunderfoot #1
The Italian Stallion defeated Thunderfoot #2
Lazortron defeated John Savage
Johnny Ace defeated Mark Fleming
Wahoo McDaniel & Brad Armstrong defeated NWA Tag Team Champions Rick Rude & Manny Fernandez via disqualification
Chris Champion & Sean Royal defeated Bobby Jaggers & Todd Champion
Ron & Jimmy Garvin, Ricky Morton & Robert Gibson defeated Jim Cornette, Big Bubba, Bobby Eaton & Stan Lane

JCP @ Johnstown, PA - April 9, 1987
Michael Hayes & Buddy Roberts defeated Bill Irwin & the Angel of Death

Crockett Cup 87 Day 1 - Baltimore, MD - Arena - April 10, 1987 (9,300)
Crockett Cup Opening Round: Thunderfoot #1 & #2 defeated Rocky King & Bobby Jaggers at 5:54 when #1 pinned King following a kick to the chest as King attempted a backdrop

Crockett Cup Opening Round: Bill Dundee & the Barbarian defeated Tim Horner & Florida Heavyweight Champion Mike Rotundo at 8:37 when Barbarian pinned Horner after Dundee hit Horner with a foreign object behind the referee's back as Horner was on the Barbarian's back applying a sleeper
Crockett Cup Opening Round: Shaska Whatley & Teijo Khan defeated Jimmy Valiant & NWA Jr. Heavyweight Champion Lazertron via disqualification at 4:35 when Lazertron sent Whatley over the top rope with a backdrop
Crockett Cup Opening Round: Ron & Jimmy Garvin (w/ Precious) defeated Ricky Lee Jones & the Italian Stallion at 2:13 when Jimmy pinned Stallion with a sunset flip
Crockett Cup Opening Round: Denny Brown & Todd Champion defeated Bill & Randy Mulkey at 3:58 when Brown pinned Randy with an Oklahoma roll
Crockett Cup Opening Round: Steve Keirn & George South fought Mike Graham & Nelson Royal to a 20-minute time-limit draw at 20:04
Crockett Cup Opening Round: Bob & Brad Armstrong defeated Ivan Koloff & Vladimir Petrov via disqualification at 4:14 when referee Randy Anderson caught Petrov hitting Brad with the Russian chain as Brad had Ivan in a sleeper
Crockett Cup Opening Round: Florida Tag Team Champions the MOD Squad (w/ Bill Dundee) defeated Wahoo McDaniel & Baron Von Raschke at 4:48 when Spike pinned Von Raschke after Basher hit Von Raschke with a foreign object as Von Raschke had the claw applied to Spike
Crockett Cup Second Round: Bob & Brad Armstrong defeated Arn Anderson & Kevin Sullivan
Crockett Cup Second Round: NWA TV Champion Tully Blanchard & Lex Luger defeated Florida Tag Team Champions the MOD Squad
Crockett Cup Second Round: The Giant Baba & Isao Takagi defeated Denny Brown & Todd Champion
Crockett Cup Second Round: The Road Warriors defeated Shaska Whatley & Teijo Khan
Crockett Cup Second Round: Bobby Eaton & Stan Lane (w/ Jim Cornette) defeated Ron & Jimmy Garvin (w/ Precious) via count out after Cornette hit Ron in the back with his tennis racquet as Garvin attempted a piledriver on Eaton outside the ring; after the bout, the Garvins cleared their opponents from ringside; moments later, Ron punched out referee Earl Hebner until Jimmy pulled him away
Crockett Cup Second Round: NWA Tag Team Champions Rick Rude & Manny Fernandez defeated Thunderfoot #1 & #2
Crockett Cup Second Round: Dusty Rhodes & NWA US Champion Nikita Koloff defeated Bill Dundee & the Barbarian Ole Anderson pinned Big Bubba (w/ Jim Cornette) in a last man standing steel cage match when Bubba failed to reach his feet by referee Tommy Young's standing 10 count after missing a kneedrop off the top and then sustaining a piledriver

JCP @ New Orleans, LA - April 11, 1987

Crockett Cup 87 Day 2- Baltimore, MD - Arena - April 11, 1987 (13,000)
Crockett Cup Quarter Finals: NWA TV Champion Tully

Blanchard & Lex Luger (w/ JJ Dillon) defeated Bob & Brad Armstrong at 17:46 when Blanchard pinned Bob after Blanchard and Dillon hit a double clothesline behind the referee's back while Dillon was on the apron
Crockett Cup Quarter Finals: The Giant Baba & Isao Takagi defeated Ricky Morton & Robert Gibson via forfeit when it was announced Morton sustained an eye injury two days before and could not compete
Crockett Cup Quarter Finals: Bobby Eaton & Stan Lane (w/ Jim Cornette & Big Bubba) defeated NWA International Tag Team Champions the Road Warriors (w/ Paul Ellering) via disqualification in a non-title match at 12:17 when Ellering interfered, moments after Cornette interfered while the referee was down and shot a fireball into Road Warrior Animal's face, and hit both Cornette and Lane with Cornette's tennis racquet; after the bout, Road Warrior Animal knocked Bubba to the floor and into the retaining barrier before the Road Warriors dropped Eaton with a modified Doomsday Device; upon the announcement of the decision, the crowd chanted "bullshit;" after the ring cleared, Road Warrior Hawk too the mic and said the Midnight Express were "dead meat"
Crockett Cup Quarter Finals: Dusty Rhodes & NWA US Champion Nikita Koloff defeated NWA Tag Team Champions Rick Rude & Manny Fernandez (w/ Paul Jones) in a non-title match at 9:39 when Rhodes pinned Fernandez after the momentum of a crossbody off the top by Fernandez put Rhodes on top for the win
Crockett Cup Semi Finals: NWA TV Champion Tully Blanchard & Lex Luger (w/ JJ Dillon) defeated the Giant Baba & Isao Takagi at 8:38 when Luger pinned Takagi with an elbow drop after failing to lift him up for the Torture Rack
Crockett Cup Semi Finals: Dusty Rhodes & NWA US Champion Nikita Koloff defeated Bobby Eaton & Stan Lane (w/ Jim Cornette & Big Bubba) at 11:10 when Koloff pinned Eaton with the Russian Sickle after Eaton accidentally knocked Lane to the floor with a kneelift
NWA World Champion Ric Flair pinned Barry Windham at 25:52 with a roll over and grabbing the tights for leverage after Windham attempted an O'Connor roll
Crockett Cup Finals: Dusty Rhodes & NWA US Champion Nikita Koloff defeated NWA TV Champion Blanchard & Lex Luger (w/ JJ Dillon) when Rhodes pinned Blanchard at 17:29 with a crossbody off the top as Blanchard attempted a piledriver on Koloff; prior to the bout, Magnum TA was introduced to the crowd and hugged Rhodes & Koloff at ringside; Koloff wore a neckbrace for the match but it was removed by the Horsemen mid-way through the bout; after the bout, Mrs. Jim Crockett Sr. and Jim Crockett Jr. presented Rhodes & Koloff with the Crockett Cup trophy and a check for $1 million (Magnum's first arena appearance following his wreck 6 months earlier) (*Allied Powers*)

JCP @ Charlotte, NC - Coliseum - April 12, 1987
The Road Warriors & Ron Garvin defeated Big Bubba, Bobby Eaton & Stan Lane

JCP @ Charleston, SC - April 12, 1987 (3,500)
Todd Champion defeated Mark Fleming
Ivan Koloff defeated Bobby Jaggers
Lazertron defeated Gary Royal
The Road Warriors & NWA US Champion Nikita Koloff defeated NWA World Champion Ric Flair, Lex Luger, & Arn Anderson
Ron Garvin defeated NWA Tag Team Champion Rick Rude
Ole Anderson defeated NWA TV Champion Tully Blanchard via disqualification

JCP @ Marietta, GA - April 12, 1987
Bobby Jaggers defeated Thunderfoot #1
Vladimir Pietrov defeated Baron Von Raschke
Brad Armstrong defeated NWA Tag Team Champion Rick Rude

JCP @ Marion, VA - April 13, 1987 (sell out)
Jimmy Valiant defeated Big Bubba via disqualification
Ron & Jimmy Garvin defeated Bobby Eaton & Stan Lane

MID-ATLANTIC CHAMPIONSHIP WRESTLING
NWA
GREENVILLE MEMORIAL AUDITORIUM
Monday, April 13
8:00 pm

Lights Out, 10ft. Steel Cage
Ole Anderson vs Tully Blanchard w/ J.J. Dillon

World Heavyweight Title Match
Ric Flair vs Dusty Rhodes

U.S. Heavyweight Title Match
Nikita Koloff vs Vladimar Petrov

Tag Action
Tim Horace / Baron Von Rasche vs Lex Luger & Arn Anderson
Nelson Royal / Todd Champion vs Ivan Koloff / Bobby Jaggers
Bob Armstrong / Brad Armstrong vs New Breed 1 & 2

Opening Match
Italian Stallion vs George South

Ringside Reserved $15
General Admission $10
Children (Under 10) $5

MID-ATLANTIC CHAMPIONSHIP WRESTLING

MID ATLANTIC CHAMPIONSHIP WRESTLING
NWA
WORLD HEAVYWEIGHT
CHAMPIONSHIP!!!
NATURE BOY RIC FLAIR vs DUSTY RHODES
THURSDAY NIGHT
APRIL 16th
8:00pm
LIVE
UGA COLISEUM
JIM CROCKETT PROMOTIONS
VARIETY DIVISION
STUDENTS $8
RINGSIDE $12
GEN ADM ADULTS $10
GEN ADM CHILDREN $4
TICKET LOCATIONS
ATHLETIC ATTIC
GEORGIA SQUARE
RUTHLESS RECORDS
COLLEGE SQUARE
University Union
STUDENT TICKETS
TATE CENTER
CASHIER
TICKETS ON SALE
AT THE DOOR
MID ATLANTIC CHAMPIONSHIP WRESTLING

JCP @ Greenville, SC - Memorial Auditorium - April 13, 1987
The Italian Stallion defeated George South
Bob & Brad Armstrong fought Chris Champion & Sean Royal to a draw
Bobby Jaggers defeated Todd Champion
Ivan Koloff defeated Nelson Royal
Arn Anderson & Lex Luger defeated Baron Von Raschke & Tim Horner
NWA US Champion Nikita Koloff defeated Vladimir Petrov
Dusty Rhodes defeated NWA World Champion Ric Flair via disqualification
Ole Anderson defeated NWA TV Champion Tully Blanchard in a non-title steel cage match

JCP @ Salisbury, NC - April 14, 1987
Worldwide - 4/18/87:
Jimmy Garvin vs. Tommy Angel
Barry Windham vs. Denny Brown
NWA US Champion Nikita Koloff vs. John Savage
The New Breed vs. Bobby Jaggers & Todd Champion
Bobby Eaton & Stan Lane vs. the Italian Stallion & Nelson Royal
Bob & Brad Armstrong vs. Gary Royal & Vernon Deaton
Lex Luger (w/ JJ Dillon) vs. Rocky King
Pro - 4/18/87

JCP @ Charleston, SC - April 15, 1987
Big Bubba defeated Tim Horner
Ron & Jimmy Garvin defeated Bobby Eaton & Stan Lane

JCP @ Harrisonburg, VA - High School Gym - April 16, 1987 (450)
The Italian Stallion defeated Gary Royal
Bruce Bonner defeated John Savage
Ricky Lee Jones defeated Thunderfoot #2
Lazertron defeated George South
Todd Champion defeated Thunderfoot #1
The New Breed defeated Bobby Jaggers & Nelson Royal
Jimmy Valiant defeated the Barbarian

JCP @ Athens, GA - Coliseum - April 16, 1987
Ron Garvin, Wahoo McDaniel, Jimmy Garvin, & Barry Windham defeated Big Bubba, Jim Cornette, Bobby Eaton & Stan Lane
Bob Armstrong vs. Ivan Koloff
Baron Von Raschke vs. NWA Tag Team Champion Rick Rude
Brad Armstrong vs. Arn Anderson
Ole Anderson vs. NWA TV Champion Tully Blanchard
Dusty Rhodes vs. NWA World Champion Ric Flair

JCP @ Richmond, VA - Coliseum - April 17, 1987 (5,000)
Johnny Ace defeated Mark Fleming
The Barbarian defeated the Italian Stallion
Lazertron defeated Thunderfoot #1

Ivan Koloff defeated Baron Von Raschke
NWA US Champion Nikita Koloff defeated NWA Tag Team Champion Rick Rude
Wahoo McDaniel defeated Vladimir Pietrov via disqualification
Ole Anderson defeated NWA TV Champion Tully Blanchard via disqualification
Dusty Rhodes & the Road Warriors defeated NWA World Champion Ric Flair, Arn Anderson, & Lex Luger

JCP @ Macon, GA - Coliseum - April 17, 1987
Ron & Jimmy Garvin defeated Bobby Eaton & Stan Lane

JCP @ Atlanta, GA - WTBS Studios - April 18, 1987 (matinee)
World Championship Wrestling - 4/18/87 - featured an opening clip from the Crockett Cup of Magnum TA's introduction to the crowd, with Magnum then hugging Dusty Rhodes & NWA US Champion Nikita Koloff just prior to their victory in the finals of the tournament; included Tony Schiavone & David Crockett on commentary; featured the announcement that the NWA US Tag Team Championship tournament would kick off the following week; included Schiavone conducting an interview with Tim Horner and Ole Anderson regarding NWA World Champion Ric Flair, Arn Anderson, NWA TV Champion Tully Blanchard, & Lex Luger, with Horner noting he had a baseball bat and was ready and willing to use it if the Horsemen wanted to gang up on him; featured Schiavone conducting an interview with Ivan Koloff & Vladimir Petrov regarding the challenge of Rhodes & Nikita and the impending return of Dick Murdoch from suspension, with Ivan then saying he would get the NWA US Tag Team Titles back that were stripped from he and Murdoch; moments later, Ivan challenged Nikita to a Russian chain match, then adding he has won more than 250 of them and was undefeated; included Schiavone conducting an interview with Nikita regarding his Crockett Cup victory, during which Nikita called out Ivan and noted challenges of Dick Murdoch and Lex Luger; featured Schiavone conducting an interview with NWA World Champion Ric Flair in which Flair discussed the challenge of Jimmy Garvin before noting he was defending against Brad Armstrong in Los Angeles; Flair then discussed the comments earlier in the show from the Road Warriors and the Horsemen facing them in Daytona Beach, FL; included a video package recapping highlights from the previous weekend's Crockett Cup in Baltimore; featured Schiavone conducting an interview with Blanchard and Dillon regarding Blanchard's $10,000 and the title that are on the line each time he gets in the ring and the challenges of Horner, Barry Windham, and Ricky Morton; included Schiavone conducting a closing interview with Jim Cornette, alongside Big Bubba, Bobby Eaton & Stan Lane regarding Bubba's services being rented out and Eaton & Lane helping him against the challenge of Ron Garvin:
Bobby Eaton & Stan Lane (w/ Jim Cornette & Big Bubba) defeated Dave Diamond & Alan Martin at 5:18 when Eaton scored the pin with one foot on his opponent's chest following the Rocket Launcher; Cornette joined the commentary team for the match, during which he bragged about the Midnight

Express eliminating the Road Warriors from the Crockett Cup and blamed their loss to Dusty Rhodes & NWA US Champion Nikita Koloff on a biased referee; Cornette also discussed facing Ron Garvin in a steel cage match during the month of May; after the bout, David Crockett conducted a ringside interview with Cornette and his men, during which Cornette said an old friend of his offered a big sum of money for Bubba's services in the near future; Cornette then addressed Garvin, saying Garvin was trying to assassinate him but he would get Eaton & Lane to take Garvin out

Ivan Koloff & Vladimir Petrov defeated Mike Force & Russ Taylor at 4:15 when Ivan pinned Taylor after a modified Doomsday Device

Brad Armstrong pinned Randy Barber with the side Russian legsweep at 3:47; after the bout, Schiavone conducted an interview with Brad and Bob Armstrong regarding their performance in the Crockett Cup and potentially challenging for the NWA US Tag Team Titles

Ron Garvin pinned Tony Beason with one hand on his chest after hitting the right hand punch at around the 5-minute mark

The Road Warriors (w/ Paul Ellering) defeated Dexter Wescott & Rick Sullivan at 1:51 when Road Warrior Hawk scored the pin following the Doomsday Device; after the bout, Schiavone conducted an interview with the Road Warriors & Ellering, during which they noted they would team with Dusty Rhodes & NWA US Tag Team Champion Nikita Koloff to face the Horsemen in Daytona, FL and were also after the NWA Tag Team Titles; Ellering then noted the LOD were also coming to Phoenix

Lex Luger (w/ JJ Dillon) defeated Larry Clarke at 3:08 via submission with the Torture Rack; after the bout, Tony Schiavone conducted an interview with Dillon and Luger, during which Dillon discussed the Horsemen's recent loss at the Crockett Cup and said that $1 million paycheck would continue to make NWA US Champion Nikita Koloff soft; Luger then said he was after the US title

Sean Royal & Chris Champion defeated Chance McQuade & Larry Stevens at 1:54 when Champion scored the pin following a suplex / crossbody off the top double team; after the bout, Tony Schiavone conducted an interview with Royal & Champion in which Champion mocked Road Warrior Hawk before referring to Jimmy Valiant as "Father Time" and Royal said they would end him and Lazortron as well as Ricky Morton & Robert Gibson

Ole Anderson & Tim Horner defeated Bill Tabb & Vernon Deaton at 2:56 when Horner forced the submission with a standing armbar

Arn Anderson pinned the Italian Stallion with the gordbuster at 2:18; after the bout, David Crockett conducted a ringside interview with Anderson in which Anderson cut a promo on Barry Windham, saying he was the #1 contender and had beaten people up north, down south, and out west but was in JCP because he wanted to face the best; Anderson then took exception to people thinking Windham was better than him

NWA World Champion Ric Flair defeated Brodie Chase via submission with the figure-4 at 4:08; throughout the bout, Flair called for Precious

NWA Jr. Heavyweight Champion Lazortron pinned Darrell

Dalton at 1:26; during the bout, Jimmy Valiant appeared ringside to cheer on Lazortron; after the bout, Schiavone conducted an interview with the two regarding comments earlier in the show from Chris Champion & Sean Royal

Jimmy Garvin (w/ Precious) pinned Billy Moore with the brainbuster at the 13-second mark; after the bout, Schiavone conducted an interview with Garvin, with Precious, in which he discussed challenging Flair

The Barbarian pinned Clement Fields with a tombstone piledriver and headbutt off the top at 1:07

World Championship Wrestling Sunday Edition - 4/19/87

JCP @ Roanoke, VA - Civic Center - April 18, 1987
Ron & Jimmy Garvin defeated Bobby Eaton & Stan Lane

CWF @ Orlando, FL - April 19, 1987
Brady Boone defeated Mitch Snow
Scott Hall & Denny Brown defeated Colt Steele & Teijo Khan
Ron Simmons defeated Pez Whatley
Tracy Smothers, Steve Armstrong, & Kendall Windham defeated Bill Dundee & the MOD Squad
Jimmy Valiant defeated Vladimir Petrov
Baron Von Raschke defeated Ivan Koloff
Dusty Rhodes & Barry Windham defeated Kevin Sullivan & the Tahitian Prince
NWA World Champion Ric Flair defeated Mike Rotunda

JCP @ Huntington, WV - April 19, 1987
Brad Armstrong defeated Stan Lane via disqualification
Ron Garvin defeated Bobby Eaton in a bunkhouse match

JCP @ Fayetteville, NC - April 20, 1987 (2,300)
Lazertron defeated Gary Royal
Ivan Koloff defeated Tim Horner
Vladimir Pietrov defeated Baron Von Raschke
Ole Anderson defeated JJ Dillon
Barry Windham defeated Lex Luger via disqualification
NWA US Champion Nikita Koloff defeated NWA Tag Team Champion Rick Rude
Dusty Rhodes defeated NWA World Champion Ric Flair via disqualification

MID-ATLANTIC CHAMPIONSHIP WRESTLING

GREENVILLE MEMORIAL AUDITORIUM

NWA

April 20
8:00 pm

Lites Out Bunkhouse Match

Ronnie Garvin

Midnight Express (with Jim Cornette)

Jimmy Garvin (with Precious)

VS

Special Challenge Match

Rock n Roll Express

VS

New Breed

"Bullet" Bob Armstrong

VS

Big Bubba

JIMMY VALIANT VS THUNDERFOOT #2

TODD CHAMPION VS THUNDERFOOT #1

DENNIS BROWN VS JOHNNY ACE

ITALIAN STALLION VS JOHN SAVAGE

Ringside Reserved $10
General Admission $8
Children (Under 10) $4

MID-ATLANTIC CHAMPIONSHIP WRESTLING

PRO WRESTLING

JCP @ Greenville, SC - Memorial Auditorium - April 20, 1987
The Italian Stallion defeated John Savage
Neslon Royal defeated Johnny Ace
Todd Champion defeated Thunderfoot #1
Jimmy Valiant defeated Thunderfoot #2
Bob Armstrong defeated Big Bubba via disqualification
Ricky Morton & Robert Gibson fought Chris Champion & Sean Royal to a 30-minute time-limit draw
Ron & Jimmy Garvin defeated Bobby Eaton & Stan Lane in a bunkhouse match

JCP @ Columbia, SC - Township Auditorium - April 21, 1987
TV taping:
Ricky Morton & Robert Gibson vs. Mike Force & Rocky King
Pro - 4/25/87:
Barry Windham & Brad Armstrong fought NWA World Champion Ric Flair & Lex Luger to a draw
Ivan Koloff & Vladimir Pietrov defeated George South & Tommy Angel
NWA TV Champion Tully Blanchard (w/ JJ Dillon) pinned Bob Armstrong after hitting him behind the referee's back with the briefcase full of $10,000 after Armstrong chased Dillon around and into the ring
Worldwide - 4/25/87 - featured an opening clip of Lex Luger attacking Barry Windham and putting him in the Torture Rack; included Tony Schiavone & David Crockett on commentary; featured Crockett conducting a ringside interview with NWA World Champion Ric Flair, Lex Luger, and JJ Dillon in which Flair said there were 2,000 people in the arena so 1,800 potential Space Mountainettes; Luger then took off his shirt to flex while Flair said Precious would soon be his; included Bob Caudle conducting an interview with Dillon & NWA TV Champion Tully Blanchard in which Blanchard pulled out a briefcase full of $10,000 that would be on the line whenever the TV title is at stake; featured Caudle conducting an interview with Bob Armstrong regarding him recently challenging Blanchard and having him beaten until Dillon interfered, allowing Blanchard to hit Armstrong with his briefcase; included Caudle conducting an interview with Ricky Morton & Robert Gibson regarding the injury that took them out of the Crockett Cup, with Morton then saying they've studied footage of Dusty Rhodes & NWA US Champion Nikita Koloff's win over NWA Tag Team Champions Rick Rude & Manny Fernandez in Baltimore and now knew Rude & Fernandez's weaknesses; featured Caudle conducting an interview with Ivan Koloff & Vladimir Petrov in which Ivan said he would soon teach Nikita that he was the master of the Russain chain match and that he and Petrov would win the vacant NWA US Tag Team Titles; included Caudle conducting an interview with Jim Cornette, Bobby Eaton & Stan Lane in which Cornette said his mother was giving him a hard time until they got titles; Cornette then said he would have to face Ron Garvin in steel cage matches during the month of May but Eaton & Lane would make sure Garvin would be in no shape to make the matches; featured Caudle conducting an interview with Nikita regarding Dick Murdoch recently attacking him, facing the challenge of Luger,

and responding to the comments made earlier in the show by Ivan:
Chris Champion & Sean Royal defeated Brodie Chase & Tommy Angel at 4:01 when Champion scored the pin following a suplex / crossbody off the top double team; after the bout, David Crockett conducted a ringside interview in which Champion & Royal cut a promo on Jimmy Valiant & Lazortron and Ricky Morton & Robert Gibson
Ricky Morton & Robert Gibson defeated Johnny Ace & Vernon Deaton at 1:05 when Gibson pinned Deaton following the double dropkick
Jimmy Garvin (w/ Precious) pinned Mike Force with the brainbuster at 1:36
Brad Armstrong pinned George South at 2:03 with the side Russian legsweep after South missed a charge in the corner
Lex Luger (w/ JJ Dillon) defeated Ricky Nelson via submission with the Torture Rack at 2:27
Jimmy Valiant & NWA Jr. Heavyweight Champion Lazortron defeated Thunderfoot #1 & Dexter Wescott at 2:15 when Lazortron pinned Wescott with a crossbody off the top
Bobby Eaton & Stan Lane (w/ Jim Cornette) defeated Todd Champion & Gary Royal at 3:19 when Eaton pinned Royal following the Rocket Launcher; Cornette joined the commentary team for the duration of the bout; after the match, Crockett conducted a ringside interview with Cornette, Eaton & Lane regarding Cornette's upcoming steel cage matches against Ron Garvin, with Cornette telling the fans to sign letters and petitions to get him out of it

JCP @ Miami, FL - Miami Beach Convention Center - April 22, 1987

JCP @ Inglewood, CA - Great Western Forum - April 22, 1987
Baron Von Raschke defeated the Barbarian
Bob Armstrong fought Ivan Koloff to a draw
Jimmy Garvin defeated Bobby Eaton via disqualification
Ron Garvin defeated Stan Lane in a taped fist match
NWA US Champion Nikita Koloff & the Road Warriors defeated Paul Jones, NWA Tag Team Champions Rick Rude & Manny Fernandez
NWA World Champion Ric Flair defeated Brad Armstrong
Ole Anderson defeated NWA TV Champion Tully Blanchard via disqualification

JCP @ San Francisco, CA - Civic Auditorium - April 23, 1987 (between 1,500 and 1,700)
Baron Von Raschke defeated the Barbarian via count-out at 9:53
Bob Armstrong fought Ivan Koloff to a 15-minute time-limit draw
Ron & Jimmy Garvin defeated Bobby Eaton & Stan Lane via disqualification at 16:01
Ole Anderson defeated NWA TV Champion Tully Blanchard via disqualification at 7:35
The Road Warriors & Brad Armstrong defeated Paul Jones,

NWA Tag Team Champions Rick Rude & Manny Fernandez
NWA World Champion Ric Flair fought NWA US Champion Nikita Koloff to a no contest

JCP @ Raleigh, NC - Dorton Arena - April 23, 1987
Lazertron defeated Nelson Royal
John Savage defeated Gary Royal
Tim Horner defeated Thunderfoot #2
Todd Champion defeated Thunderfoot #1
Chris Champion & Sean Royal defeated the Italian Stallion & Bobby Jaggers
Ricky Morton defeated Lex Luger via disqualification

JCP @ Columbus, GA - April 24, 1987
Jimmy Garvin defeated Stan Lane

JCP @ Chicago, IL - UIC Pavilion - April 24, 1987
NWA TV Champion Tully Blanchard defeated Tim Horner
Brad Armstrong defeated the Barbarian
Ivan Koloff defeated Baron Von Raschke
Ole Anderson defeated JJ Dillon in a bunkhouse match
NWA Tag Team Champions Rick Rude & Manny Fernandez defeated Ricky Morton & Robert Gibson
NWA US Champion Nikita Koloff & the Road Warriors defeated NWA TV Champion Tully Blanchard, Lex Luger, & Arn Anderson
NWA World Champion Ric Flair defeated Dusty Rhodes via disqualification

JCP @ Atlanta, GA - WTBS Studios - April 25, 1987 (matinee)
World Championship Wrestling - 4/25/87:
Ron Garvin & Barry Windham defeated Ivan Koloff & Vladimir Petrov via disqualification
World Championship Wrestling Sunday Edition - 4/26/87

JCP @ Philadelphia, PA - Civic Center - April 25, 1987 (2,500)
Ricky Lee Jones defeated Mark Fleming
Todd Champion defeated John Savage
Bobby Jaggers & the Italian Stallion defeated Thunderfoot #1 & #2
NWA TV Champion Tully Blanchard pinned Tim Horner at the 15-minute mark; Blanchard put $10,000 of his own money at stake in the match
Ole Anderson pinned Arn Anderson at the 6-minute mark after a low blow
The Road Warriors defeated NWA Tag Team Champions Rick Rude & Manny Fernandez via disqualification when Paul Jones interfered

JCP @ Greensboro, NC - Coliseum - April 25, 1987 (7,829)
Nelson Royal defeated Johnny Ace
Lazertron defeated Gary Royal
Ricky Morton & Robert Gibson defeated Chris Champion &

Sean Royal
Ron Garvin, Barry Windham, & Bob Armstrong defeated Big
Bubba, Bobby Eaton, & Stan Lane
Brad Armstrong defeated the Barbarian
Lex Luger defeated NWA US Champion Nikita Koloff via
disqualification
Dusty Rhodes defeated Ivan Koloff
NWA World Champion Ric Flair defeated Jimmy Garvin via
disqualification

JCP @ Rock Hill, SC - Winthrop Coliseum - April 26, 1987
Television taping:
Ron Garvin pinned Thunderfoot #2
Jimmy Garvin pinned George South
Ole Anderson defeated NWA TV Champion Tully Blanchard by
disqualification
NWA US Champion Nikita Koloff & The Road Warriors
defeated NWA World Champion Ric Flair, NWA TV Champion,
& Lex Luger
Pro - 5/2/87:
The Road Warriors defeated Tommy Angel & Brodie Chase
NWA Jr. Heavyweight Champion Lazertron pinned Rocky King
Bobby Eaton & Stan Lane defeated Ricky Nelson & Todd
Champion
NWA US Champion Nikita Koloff pinned Gary Royal
NWA World Champion Ric Flair, NWA TV Champion Tully
Blanchard, & Lex Luger defeated Tim Horner, Bob & Brad
Armstrong
Worldwide - 5/2/87:
Lex Luger defeated Brodie Chase via submission
NWA Tag Team Champions Rick Rude & Manny Fernandez
defeated Ricky Nelson & Tommy Angel
Ivan Koloff & Vladimir Petrov defeated Johnny Ace & the Italian
Stallion
Ron Garvin pinned George South
Jimmy Garvin pinned Rocky King
Bobby Eaton & Stan Lane defeated Gary Royal & Dexter
Wescott
NWA TV Champion Tully Blanchard defeated Nelson Royal

CWF @ Daytona Beach, FL - April 26, 1987
Dusty Rhodes, NWA US Champion Nikita Koloff, & the Road
Warriors defeated NWA World Champion Ric Flair, Lex Luger,
Arn Anderson, & NWA TV Champion Tully Blanchard

JCP @ Phoenix, AZ - Veterans Memorial Coliseum - April 27, 1987
Ricky Morton & Robert Gibson defeated Bobby Eaton & Stan
Lane
Also included the Road Warriors, NWA Tag Team Champions
Rick Rude & Manny Fernandez, and Jimmy Garvin

JCP @ El Paso, TX - County Coliseum - April 28, 1987
Ricky Morton & Robert Gibson defeated Bobby Eaton & Stan
Lane

Also included NWA TV Champion Tully Blanchard and Arn
Anderson

JCP @ Marion, NC - April 29, 1987
Ron Garvin defeated Stan Lane
Jimmy Garvin defeated Bobby Eaton via disqualification

JCP @ Pembroke, NC - April 30, 1987
Ron & Jimmy Garvin defeated Bobby Eaton & Stan Lane

JCP @ Birmingham, AL - BJCC - April 30, 1987
Brad Armstrong defeated the Barbarian
Ole Anderson & Tim Horner defeated Lex Luger & Arn
Anderson
Bob Armstrong, Ricky Morton & Robert Gibson defeated Paul
Jones, NWA Tag Team Champions Rick Rude & Manny
Fernandez
NWA US Champion Nikita Koloff defeated NWA TV Champion
Tully Blanchard
Dusty Rhodes defeated NWA World Champion Ric Flair via
disqualification

JCP @ Atlanta, GA - Omni - May 1, 1987 (3,200)
Chris Champion & Sean Royal defeated Jeff Sampson & Jeff
Belk
Baron Von Raschke defeated Thunderfoot #1
Vladimir Pietrov defeated Jimmy Valiant
Bobby Eaton & Stan Lane defeated Bob & Brad Armstrong
Barry Windham defeated Lex Luger via disqualification
Arn Anderson & NWA TV Champion Tully Blanchard defeated
Ole Anderson & Tim Horner
NWA US Champion Nikita Koloff defeated Ivan Koloff in a
Russian chain match
NWA World Champion Ric Flair defeated Jimmy Garvin in a
lumberjack match at the 17-minute mark

JCP @ Atlanta, GA - WTBS Studios - May 2, 1987 (matinee)
World Championship Wrestling - 5/2/87:
Jimmy Valiant & Lazortron vs. Randy Barber & Alan Martin
Lex Luger vs. Jeff Belk
*NWA US Tag Team Championship Tournament Quarter
Finals:* Bob & Brad Armstrong fought Sean Royal & Chris
Champion to a draw
Ivan Koloff & Vladimir Pietrov vs. Cougar Jay & Jeff Sampson
Bobby Eaton & Stan Lane vs. Bill Tabb & Larry Clark
The Road Warriors vs. David Isley & Mike Force
Ron Garvin vs. Larry Stevens
Jimmy Garvin vs. Paul Garner

JCP @ Chattanooga, TN - UTC Arena - May 2, 1987
Bob & Brad Armstrong defeated Bobby Eaton & Stan Lane via
disqualification

JCP @ Charleston, WV - May 3, 1987 (matinee) (2,200)
Chris Champion & Sean Royal defeated Rocky King & the Italian Stallion
Jimmy Valiant defeated Thunderfoot #1
Lazertron pinned Nelson Royal
Bobby Eaton & Stan Lane defeated Bob & Brad Armstrong
Ole Anderson defeated Arn Anderson via disqualification
Lex Luger & NWA TV Champion Tully Blanchard fought the Road Warriors to a double count-out
NWA World Champion Ric Flair defeated Jimmy Garvin via disqualification when Garvin hit the referee; earlier in the match, Lex Luger interfered on behalf of the champion while the referee was knocked down

JCP @ Cincinnati, OH - May 3, 1987
Baron Von Raschke defeated Jim Lancaster
Ivan Koloff defeated Tim Horner
Lazertron defeated Denny Brown
Bobby Eaton & Stan Lane defeated Bob & Brad Armstrong
Ole Anderson fought Arn Anderson to a no contest
The Road Warriors fought Lex Luger & NWA TV Champion Tully Blanchard to a no contest
NWA World Champion Ric Flair defeated Jimmy Garvin via disqualification

JCP @ Fayetteville, NC - May 4, 1987
Todd Champion defeated the Italian StallioN
Rocky King defeated Tommy Angel
Bob & Brad Armstrong defeated Ivan Koloff & Vladimir Petrov
The Road Warriors defeated Chris Champion & Sean Royal
Lex Luger fought Barry Windham to a no contest
Dusty Rhodes defeated Dick Murdoch

JCP @ Greenville, SC - Memorial Auditorium - May 4, 1987
Thunderfoot #1 defeated George South (sub. for the Italian Stallion)
Gary Royal (sub. for Bobby Jaggers) defeated Johnny Ace
The Barbarian defeated Denny Brown
NWA Jr. Heavyweight Champion Lazertron defeated Nelson Royal via disqualification
Jimmy Valiant defeated John Savage
Arn Anderson & NWA TV Champion Tully Blanchard defeated Ole Anderson & Tim Horner
Ricky Morton & Robert Gibson fought Bobby Eaton & Stan Lane to a double count-out; stipulations stated the winners would be the #1 contenders to the NWA US Tag Team Titles
NWA World Champion Ric Flair defeated Jimmy Garvin

MID-ATLANTIC CHAMPIONSHIP WRESTLING

NWA

GREENVILLE MEMORIAL AUDITORIUM
MONDAY, MAY 4, 1987
8:00 P.M.

WORLD HEAVYWEIGHT TITLE MATCH

Ric Flair VS Jimmy Garvin (With Precious)

MATCH TO DETERMINE #1 CONTENDER FOR U.S. TAG TEAM TITLE

Rock 'N Roll Express VS Midnight Express (With Jim Cornette)

Special Challenge Match

Ole Anderson Tim Horner VS Arn Anderson Tully Blanchard (With J.J. Dillon)

Jimmy Valiant vs John Savage

World Junior Heavyweight Title
Lazer-Tron vs Nelson Royal

Denny Brown vs Barbarian

Bobby Jaggers vs Johnny Ace

Italian Stallion vs Thunderfoot #1

NWA
* Subject to Change

Ringside Reserved $12
General Admission $10
Children (Under 10) $8
* Subject to Change

MID-ATLANTIC CHAMPIONSHIP WRESTLING

JCP @ Spartanburg, SC - Memorial Auditorium - May 5, 1987
TV taping:
Chris Champion & Sean Royal defeated Rocky King & Brody Chase
Jimmy Garvin defeated Thunderfoot #2
Bobby Eaton & Stan Lane defeated Rocky King & Larry Stevens
Worldwide - 5/9/87 - featured Tony Schiavone conducting a ringside interview with JJ Dillon & NWA TV Champion Tully Blanchard regarding Dusty Rhodes; included Bob Caudle conducting an interview with NWA World Champion Ric Flair in which he challenged NWA Six Man Tag Team Champions Rhodes & the Road Warriors to face the Horsemen and then commented on Magnum TA's recent comments; featured Caudle conducting an interview with Dillon & Lex Luger in which Luger targetted NWA Us Champion Nikita Koloff:
Chris Champion & Sean Royal defeated Mike Force & Ricky Nelson
Ron Garvin defeated Tommy Angel
Barry Windham defeated Thunderfoot #2
Ricky Morton & Robert Gibson defeated the Gladiators
NWA TV Champion Tully Blanchard defeated Chance McQuade
Lex Luger defeated Mike Simani
Pro - 5/9/87 - featured Dusty Rhodes escorting Magnum TA, his arm in a sling, to ringside to speak with Bob Caudle & Johnny Weaver; Magnum then commented on comments recently made by the Four Horsemen and NWA TV Champion Tully Blanchard before Rhodes grabbed a paper bag and showed off the cash inside; Rhodes then told Blanchard and NWA World Champion Ric Flair to stop BSing the people and then said he had $50,000 to match JJ Dillon's $50,000 if Dillon would only accept his challenge (Magnum's return to TV); included Caudle conducting a ringside interview with Dillon and Blanchard regarding Magnum's appearance earlier in the show and Rhodes' comments, with Blanchard saying it wasn't his fault he and the Horsemen were the best wrestlers in the world; featured Caudle conducting an interview with Flair in which he said Magnum's comments put him on the Horsemen's hit list; Flair then said Precious was his and he would take Jimmy Garvin out any time he wanted:
The Road Warriors defeated Dexter Wescott & Mike Force
Barry Windham defeated Tommy Angel
Lex Luger defeated David Isley
Arn Anderson vs. Larry Stevens
Ricky Morton & Robert Gibson defeated Mike Simani & Vernon Deaton

CWF @ Miami, FL - May 6, 1987
Tracy Smothers & Steve Armstrong defeated Bill & Randy Mulkey
Jerry Gray defeated Jim Backlund
Ed Gantner defeated Sam Bass
Jimmy Valiant defeated Colt Steele
Ron Simmons defeated Shaska Whtley
Ricky Morton & Robert Gibson defeated the MOD Squad via disqualification

Dusty Rhodes & Mike Rotundo defeated Kevin Sullivan & Teijo Khan
NWA World Champion Ric Flair defeated Jimmy Garvin via disqualification

JCP @ Raleigh, NC - Dorton Arena - May 7, 1987
Thunderfoot #1 & #2 defeated Ricky Lee Jones & Mark Fleming
The Italian Stallion defeated John Savage
Denny Brown defeated John Savage
Lazertron defeated Nelson Royal via disqualification
Jimmy Valiant defeated Gladiator #2
Ricky Morton & Robert Gibson defeated Bobby Eaton & Stan Lane
NWA TV Champion Tully Blanchard defeated Ole Anderson in a steel cage match

JCP @ Waldorf, MD - May 7, 1987
NWA World Champion Ric Flair defeated Brad Armstrong

JCP @ Baltimore, MD - Arena - May 8, 1987 (10,000)
Bob & Brad Armstrong fought Chris Champion & Sean Royal to a draw
Arn Anderson defeated Tim Horner
Vladimir Peitrov defeated Baron Von Raschke
Lex Luger defeated Ron Garvin via disqualification
The Road Warriors defeated NWA Tag Team Champions Rick Rude & Manny Fernandez via disqualification
Dick Murdoch defeated Dusty Rhodes in a Texas Death Match
NWA US Champion Nikita Koloff defeated Ivan Koloff in a Russian chain match
NWA World Champion Ric Flair defeated Jimmy Garvin via disqualification at the 15-minute mark

JCP @ Atlanta, GA - WTBS Studios - May 9, 1987 (matinee)
World Championship Wrestling - 5/9/87:
Jimmy Garvin vs. Larry Clark
The New Breed vs. Alan Martin & Clement Fields
NWA US Tag Team Championship Tournament Semi-Finals:
Bobby Eaton & Stan Lane (w/ Jim Cornette) defeated Ricky Morton & Robert Gibson via disqualification
Dick Murdoch vs. Cougar Jay
Ron Garvin vs. Mike Force
Bob Armstrong vs. Randy Barber
Jimmy Valiant vs. Terry Jones
Barry Windham vs. Rick Sullivan
NWA US Champion Nikita Koloff vs. Chance McQuade
NWA TV Champion Tully Blanchard, Arn Anderson, & Lex Luger vs. Rocky King, Howell Moore, & Larry Stephens
The Road Warriors vs. Bill Tabb & the Shadow
World Championship Wrestling Sunday Edition - 5/10/87 - featured Tony Schiavone conducting an interview with JJ Dillon & Lex Luger in which Dillon said NWA TV Champion Tully Blanchard's match earlier in the show against Barry Windham showed just why the Horsemen are champions; Luger then discussed his hunt for Nikita Koloff and the NWA US Title:

N.W.A.

PRO WRESTLING
EDDIE GRAHAM MEMORIAL
BAYFRONT CENTER
ST. PETERSBURG

FLAIR · SATURDAY, MAY 9, 8:30 PM · RHODES

WORLD TITLE
RIC FLAIR —VS— DUSTY RHODES

WORLD TAG TITLES
THE RAGING BULL AND RAVISHING RICK RUDE
VERSUS THE ROAD WARRIORS

FLORIDA TITLE
MIKE ROTUNDA —VS— KEVIN SULLIVAN

MIKE GRAHAM —VS— DORY FUNK, JR.

PLUS FIVE MORE MATCHES
INCLUDING . . . BRAD & BOB ARMSTRONG, JIMMY
GARVIN AND MANY, MANY MORE!

TICKETS AT BAYFRONT, ALL
SELECT-A-SEATS AND SPORTATORIUM
TELEPHONE 893-7251 OR 253-0841

PORTIONS OF
PROCEEDS TO
FLA. SHERIFFS'
YOUTH
RANCHES

Barry Windham fought NWA TV Champion Tully Blanchard (w/ JJ Dillon) to a time-limit draw at around the 15-minute mark; both men were brawling on the floor at the time the bell rang; after the contest, the two continued to brawl around ringside
Chris Champion & Sean Royal vs. Chance McQuade & Rick Sullivan

NWA Super Bouts - 5/9/87 - debut episode; featured Tony Schiavone & JJ Dillon providing commentary for the match from the studio; included the NWA TV Champion Tully Blanchard vs. Brad Armstrong and Ole Anderson vs. Big Bubba matches taped 3/14/87 at the Greensboro Coliseum

CWF Eddie Graham Memorial - St. Petersburg, FL - Bayfront Center - May 9, 1987
Jimmy Valiant defeated Colt Steele
Bob & Brad Armstrong defeated the MOD Squad
Mike Graham defeated Dory Funk Jr.
Florida Heavyweight Champion Mike Rotundo defeated Kevin Sullivan
Jimmy Garvin defeated Teijo Khan
NWA Florida Tag Team Champions Steve Kiern & Stan Lane defeated the MOD Squad
Barry Windham & Ed Gantner defeated Dory Funk Jr. & the Tahitian Prince
The Road Warriors (w/ Paul Ellering) fought NWA Tag Team Champions Rick Rude & Manny Fernandez (w/ Paul Jones) to a double disqualification at 5:07 when both Ellering and Jones interfered as Road Warrior Animal had Fernandez covered following a powerslam off the top
Dusty Rhodes defeated NWA World Champion Ric Flair via disqualification

JCP @ Charlotte, NC - Coliseum - May 9, 1987 (9,000+)
Ivan Koloff defeated Todd Champion
Chris Champion & Sean Royal defeated Rocky King & the Italian Stallion
Baron Von Raschke defeated Thunderfoot
Lazertron pinned Nelson Royal
NWA TV Champion Tully Blanchard defeated Ole Anderson
NWA US Champion Nikita Koloff defeated Lex Luger via disqualification
Ricky Morton & Robert Gibson defeated Vladimir Pietrov & Dick Murdoch
Ron Garvin defeated Jim Cornette in a steel cage match after both Ricky Morton & Robert Gibson and Bobby Eaton & Stan Lane interfered

CWF @ Orlando, FL - May 10, 1987
Mike Rotunda vs. NWA World Champion Ric Flair

JCP @ Newton, NC - May 11, 1987
Ron & Jimmy Garvin defeated Bobby Eaton & Stan Lane

MID-ATLANTIC CHAMPIONSHIP WRESTLING
NWA
GREENVILLE MEMORIAL AUDITORIUM
MAY 11, 1987
8:00 P.M.

LITE OUT - RUSSIAN CHAIN MATCH
NIKITA KOLOFF VS IVAN KOLOFF

SPECIAL CHALLENGE MATCH
OLE ANDERSON TIM HORNER VS RIC FLAIR ARN ANDERSON

SPECIAL EVENT
BRAD ARMSTRONG VS LEX LUGER

WORLD JUNIOR TITLE MATCH NO DISQUALIFICATION
LAZOR-TRON VS NELSON ROYAL

ITALIAN STALLION VS NEW BREED #1
"BULLET" BOB ARMSTRONG VS NEW BREED #2
JEFF SAMPSON VS DENNY BROWN
JEFF BELK VS GEORGE SOUTH

NWA
TICKET PRICES: $12, $10, & $4
SUBJECT TO CHANGE
Ringside Reserved $12
General Admission $10
Children (Under 10) $4

JCP @ Greenville, SC - Memorial Auditorium - May 11, 1987
Jeff Belk vs. George South did not take place as advertised
Denny Brown defeated Jeff Sampson
Bob Armstrong fought New Breed #2 to a 20-minute time-limit draw
New Breed #1 defeated the Italian Stallion
NWA Jr. Heavyweight Champion Lazortron defeated Nelson Royal in a No DQ match
Lex Luger defeated Brad Armstrong
NWA World Champion Ric Flair & Arn Anderson defeated Ole Anderson & Tim Horner
NWA US Champion Nikita Koloff defeated Ivan Koloff in a Russian chain match

JCP @ Columbia, SC - May 12, 1987
TV taping:
Jimmy Garvin defeated Johnny Ace
Jimmy Valiant defeated Jeff Sampson
Ron Garvin & Barry Windham defeated Vernon Deaton & Brodie Chase
NWA Tag Team Champions Rick Rude & Manny Fernandez defeated the Italian Stallion & Tim Horner
Sean Royal defeated George South
NWA TV Champion Tully Blanchard, Lex Luger, & Arn Anderson defeated Todd Champion, Tommy Angel, & David Isley
Pro - 5/16/87 - featured Tony Schiavone conducting an interview with NWA World Champion Ric Flair regarding his attack earlier on the show on Ricky Morton; Flair then noted Dusty Rhodes recently told him to cut the BS, with Flair then saying the BS was Rhodes claiming he and others like him could take his title; Flair then cut a promo on Jimmy Garvin and Precious having walked off with his $15,000 coat:
Arn Anderson defeated Jeff Sampson; after the bout, Bob Caudle conducted a ringside interview with Anderson in which he said NWA US Champion Nikita Koloff was so preoccupied by NWA World Champion Ric Flair and Lex Luger that he had forgotten about Anderson
NWA TV Champion Tully Blanchard (w/ JJ Dillon) defeated Robert Gibson (w/ Ricky Morton) via disqualification at around the 17-minute mark when - after the referee was knocked to the floor and Morton and Dillon interfered - Gibson backdropped Blanchard over the top rope; after the bout, NWA World Champion Ric Flair came out, attacked Morton in and out of the ring, and helped triple team him before Gibson made the save
Bobby Eaton & Stan Lane defeated David Isley & Tommy Angel
NWA World Champion Ric Flair & Lex Luger (w/ JJ Dillon) defeated Todd Champion & the Italian Stallion; after the bout, Dillon commented on Dusty Rhodes' remarks the previous week and told Rhodes he had a meeting scheduled with the Horsemen's attorney
Worldwide - 5/16/87:
Dark match: Ricky Morton & Robert Gibson fought Bobby Eaton & Stan Lane to a 20-minute time-limit draw

JCP @ Westminster, SC - May 13, 1987
Ricky Morton & Robert Gibson defeated Bobby Eaton & Stan Lane

CWF @ Ft. Lauderdale, FL - May 13, 1987
Ron Simmons defeated Shaska Whatley
Mike Rotundo defeated Dory Funk Jr.
Kendall Windham & Ed Gantner defeated Kevin Sullivan & the Tahitian Prince
NWA World Champion Ric Flair defeated Jimmy Garvin

JCP @ Hartwell, GA - May 14, 1987
Jimmy Garvin defeated Stan Lane via disqualification
Ron Garvin defeated Bobby Eaton

JCP @ Johnson City, TN - Freedom Hall Convention Center - May 15, 1987

JCP @ Albany, GA - Civic Center - May 15, 1987
Bobby Eaton & Stan Lane defeated Bob & Brad Armstrong

JCP @ Atlanta, GA - WTBS Studios - May 16, 1987 (matinee)
World Championship Wrestling - 5/16/87 - featured a music video hyping the Fabulous Freebirds' return to the Omni to the tune of Michael Hayes' "The Boys Are Back in Town;" included Tony Schiavone & David Crockett on commentary; featured Schiavone conducting an interview with JJ Dillon regarding the Horsemen facing the Freebirds June 7 at the Omni, during which Dillon said the Horsemen in any combination could beat any other combination in wrestling; included a music video on Dusty Rhodes to the tune of Bo Diddley's "You Can't Judge a Book by the Cover;" featured an ad promoting the 1987 Crockett Cup on home video; included a vignette of NWA World Champion Ric Flair to the tune of his entrance music; featured Schiavone & Crockett conducting an interview with NWA US Tag Team Champions Bobby Eaton & Stan Lane regarding their title win, with Lane saying they were now going after the NWA Tag Team titles; moments later, Crockett interrupted to review the finish of the match; moments later, Jim Cornette came out, still recovering from the sleeper Ron Garvin gave him, and bragged about the title win:
NWA US Tag Team Championship Tournament Finals: Bobby Eaton & Stan Lane (w/ Jim Cornette) defeated Barry Windham & Ron Garvin at 26:54 when Eaton pinned Garvin when, as Windham had Cornette in a sleeper on the floor and referee Teddy Long had been knocked to the floor moments earlier, Lane hit Garvin with a chair; moments after the finish, Windham hit a clothesline on Lane and made the cover, not realizing the match was over
World Championship Wrestling Sunday Edition - 5/17/87:
Dick Murdoch vs. Randy Barber
Barry Windham vs. Alan Martin
Ron Garvin vs. Larry Clarke
Brad Armstrong vs. Brodie Chase

Arn Anderson vs. David Isley
NWA US Tag Team Champions Bobby Eaton & Stan Lane vs.
Bill Tabb & Art Pritts

JCP @ Chesterfield, SC - May 16, 1987
NWA US Tag Team Champions Bobby Eaton & Stan Lane
defeated Bob Armstrong & Ron Garvin

*NWA Super Bouts - 5/16/87 - included Jimmy Garvin vs.
Bobby Eaton and Wahoo McDaniel, Ricky Morton, & Robert
Gibson vs. Paul Jones, NWA Tag Team Champions Rick Rude
& Manny Fernandez taped 3/14/87 at the Greensboro
Coliseum*

**JCP @ Asheville, NC - Civic Center - May 17, 1987
(matinee)**
NWA US Tag Team Champion Stan Lane defeated Todd
Champion
Ron Garvin defeated NWA US Tag Team Champion Bobby
Eaton

JCP @ Daytona Beach, FL - Ocean Center - May 17, 1987
Ricky Morton & Robert Gibson defeated NWA US Tag Team
Champions Bobby Eaton & Stan Lane in a non-title match
NWA World Champion Ric Flair defeated Jimmy Garvin

JCP @ Fayetteville, NC - May 18, 1987
Ron & Jimmy Garvin defeated NWA US Tag Team Champions
Bobby Eaton & Stan Lane in a non-title match

**JCP @ Greenville, SC - Memorial Auditorium - May 18,
1987**
The Italian Stallion defeated Gary Royal
Thunderfoot #1 defeated John Savage (sub. for Bobby
Jaggers)
Baron Von Raschke defeated Thunderfoot #2
NWA Tag Team Champion Rick Rude defeated Johnny Ace
(sub. for Tim Horner)
Jimmy Valiant & Lazertron defeated Chris Champion & Sean
Royal via disqualification
NWA TV Champion Tully Blanchard defeated Bob Armstrong
Ricky Morton & Robert Gibson defeated NWA World
Champion Ric Flair & Lex Luger

MID-ATLANTIC CHAMPIONSHIP WRESTLING

NWA

GREENVILLE
MEMORIAL
AUDITORIUM
MONDAY
MAY 18, 1987
8:00 P.M.

SPECIAL CHALLENGE MATCH

ROCK'N ROLL EXPRESS
VS
"NATURE BOY" RIC FLAIR
LEX LUGER
(WITH J.J. DILLON)

**WORLD T.V. TITLE
1 FALL 25 MINUTES**

"BULLET"
BOB ARMSTRONG
VS
TULLY BLANCHARD
(WITH J.J. DILLON)

SPECIAL CHALLENGE MATCH

JIMMY VALIENT
LAZOR-TRON
VS
NEW BREED

SPECIAL ATTRACTION

TIM HORNER
VS
RAVISHING RICK RUDE
(WITH PAUL JONES)

BARON VON RASCHKE
VS
THUNDER-FOOT #2

BOBBY JAGGERS
VS
THUNDER-FOOT #1

ITALIAN STALLION
VS
GARY ROYAL

NWA
*SUBJECT TO CHANGE

Ringside Reserved $12
General Admission $10
Children (Under 10) $4

N077017 H

MID-ATLANTIC CHAMPIONSHIP WRESTLING

JCP @ Raleigh, NC - Dorton Arena - May 19, 1987
TV taping:
Worldwide - 5/23/87:
The New Breed vs. Rocky King & John Savage
Barry Windham vs. Gladiator #1
NWA US Tag Team Champions Bobby Eaton & Stan Lane vs.
Dexter Wescott & an unknown
Bob Armstrong vs. Mark Fleming
Vladimir Pietrov vs. the Italian Stallion
Arn Anderson vs. Tommy Angel
Ricky Morton & Robert Gibson vs. Ricky Nelson & Gary Young
*Pro - 5/23/87 - featured Tony Schiavone conducting an
interview with JJ Dillon and NWA TV Champion Tully
Blanchard in which Dillon introduced Dark Journey as
Blanchard's new secretary and then discussed the $100,000
match with Dusty Rhodes on June 6 in Greensboro; Blanchard
then brought up his history with Rhodes, bragging over beating
Rhodes at Starrcade 86 to win the TV title:*
Ricky Morton & Robert Gibson vs. Gene Ligon & John Savage
Jimmy Garvin vs. Gladiator #1
Ron Garvin vs. Gladiator #2
Ivan Koloff & Vladimir Pietrov vs. Dexter Wescott & Ricky
Nelson
Dusty Rhodes & NWA US Champion Nikita Koloff defeated
NWA World Champion Ric Flair & Lex Luger (w/ JJ Dillon) via
disqualification at 5:26 when NWA TV Champion Tully
Blanchard and Arn Anderson interfered as Flair was caught in
Rhodes' figure-4 and Blanchard repeatedly hit Rhodes in the
leg with a steel briefcase; after the bout, the Horsemen ganged
up on Rhodes, with Blanchard hitting a kneedrop off the top;
moments later, NWA Tag Team Champions Ricky Morton &
Robert Gibson cleared the ring and tended to Rhodes

JCP @ Hillsville, VA - May 20, 1987 (850)
Mark Fleming defeated David Diamond
Denny Brown defeated John Savage
Gary Royal defeated Mark Fleming
Nelson Royal defeated Rocky King
The Italian Stallion defeated Larry Stephens
Vladimir Petrov defeated Todd Champion
Jimmy Valiant & the Italian Stallion defeated Chris Champion &
Sean Royal via disqualification

JCP @ Savannah, GA - Civic Center - May 20, 1987
Ron Garvin & Barry Windham defeated NWA US Tag Team
Champions Bobby Eaton & Stan Lane in a non-title match
NWA World Champion Ric Flair vs. ?

JCP @ Salisbury, MD - May 21, 1987
Baron Von Raschke defeated Mark Fleming
Vladimir Petrov defeated Brad Armstrong
Ivan Koloff defeated Tim Horner
Ron Garvin & Barry Windham defeated NWA US Tag Team
Champions Bobby Eaton & Stan Lane in a non-title match
NWA US Champion Nikita Koloff defeated NWA TV Champion
Tully Blanchard

NWA Tag Team Champions Rick Rude & Manny Fernandez
defeated Ricky Morton & Robert Gibson

CWF @ Tallahassee, FL - May 21, 1987
Big Bubba fought Ed Gantner to a double count-out
Michael Hayes & Terry Gordy defeated Sting & Rick Steiner
Kendall Windham fought Lex Luger to a double disqualification
Dusty Rhodes defeated NWA World Champion Ric Flair via
disqualification

CWF @ Jacksonville, FL - May 22, 1987
The Freebirds defeated Sting & Rick Steiner
Dusty Rhodes defeated Big Bubba via disqualification
NWA World Champion Ric Flair defeated Florida Heavyweight
Champion Mike Rotunda

JCP @ Richmond, VA - Coliseum - May 22, 1987
Todd Champion & Denny Brown defeated Thunderfoot #1 &
Thunderfoot #2
Tim Horner defeated Mark Fleming
Vladimir Petrov defeated Baron Von Raschke
Lazertron defeated Chris Champion
Jimmy Valiant defeated Sean Royal via disqualification
NWA Tag Team Champions Rick Rude & Manny Fernandez
defeated Brad & Bob Armstrong
NWA US Champion Nikita Koloff defeated Ivan Koloff in a
Russian chain match
Ricky Morton & Robert Gibson defeated Jim Cornette, NWA
US Tag Team Champions Bobby Eaton & Stan Lane in a
handicap match

**JCP @ Atlanta, GA - WTBS Studios - May 23, 1987
(matinee)**
*World Championship Wrestling - 5/23/87 - featured Tony
Schiavone conducting an interview with NWA World Champion
Ric Flair regarding the Road Warriors and the return of the
Fabulous Freebirds; Flair then discussed Jimmy Garvin &
Precious and said he would eventually have Precious; included
Schiavone conducting an interview with JJ Dillon and NWA TV
Champion Tully Blanchard, with Dark Journey, regarding the
upcoming $100,000 match with Dusty Rhodes; featured
Schiavone conducting an interview with Lex Luger in which he
said there was nothing common about the Four Horsemen,
referring to Rhodes, and then said NWA US Champion Nikita
Koloff had become soft and was a shell of his former self;
included Schiavone conducting an interview with Flair,
Blanchard, Journey, Luger, and Dillon in which Flair made fun
of the Road Warriors and repeatedly had Luger flex; Flair then
referred to the Freebirds as the "fruit birds":*
World Championship Wrestling Sunday Edition - 5/24/87

*NWA Super Bouts - 5/23/87 - featured the Arn Anderson vs.
Ole Anderson, NWA US Champion Nikita Koloff vs. Vladimir
Petrov, and Dusty Rhodes vs. NWA World Champion Ric Flair
matches taped 4/3/87 at the Greensboro Coliseum*

JCP @ Columbus, GA - May 23, 1987
Ron & Jimmy Garvin defeated NWA US Tag Team Champions
Bobby Eaton & Stan Lane in a non-title bunkhouse match

JCP @ Roanoke, VA - Civic Center - May 24, 1987
Chris Champion & Sean Royal defeated Jimmy Valiant &
Lazortron
NWA TV Champion Tully Blanchard defeated Bob Armstrong
NWA US Champion Nikita Koloff defeated Ivan Koloff in a
Russian chain match
The Road Warriors defeated NWA World Champion Ric Flair &
Lex Luger via disqualification

**JCP @ Chicago, IL - UIC Pavilion - May 24, 1987 (9,000;
sell out)**
Debut at the venue
Tim Horner fought Eddie Gilbert to a draw
Terry Gordy & Buddy Roberts defeated Sting & Rick Steiner
Terry Taylor fought Chris Adams to a no contest
Ricky Morton & Robert Gibson defeated NWA US Tag Team
Champions Bobby Eaton & Stan Lane in a non-title Best 2 out
of 3 falls match
Michael Hayes defeated Big Bubba via disqualification
Manny Fernandez & Vladimir Petrov defeated Barry Windham
& Brad Armstrong
NWA US Champion Nikita Koloff defeated Ivan Koloff in a
chain match
Dusty Rhodes & the Road Warriors defeated NWA World
Champion Ric Flair, NWA TV Champion Tully Blanchard, &
Lex Luger

**JCP @ Greenville, SC - Memorial Auditorium - May 25,
1987**
*Ricky Lee Jones vs. Johnny Ace did not take place as
advertised*
The Italian Stallion defeated Brodie Chase (sub. for Jeff Belk)
Nelson Royal defeated John Savage (sub. for Bobby Jaggers)
Jimmy Valiant & Lazortron defeated Thunderfoot #1 & #2
NWA Tag Team Champion Manny Fernandez defeated Baron
Von Raschke
Ron Garvin defeated Ivan Koloff (sub. for NWA Tag Team
Champion Rick Rude)
NWA US Tag Team Champions Bobby Eaton & Stan Lane
defeated Barry Windham & Brad Armstrong
NWA US Champion Nikita Koloff defeated Vladimir Petrov

★★ UWF-NWA ★★
"SCHOOLS OUT"
WRESTLING SPECTACULAR
TONIGHT - 7:30 PM
THE MYRIAD

★★★★★★★★★★★★★★★★★★★★★★★★★

WORLD HEAVYWEIGHT TITLE

"NATURE BOY"
RIC FLAIR **VS.** **JIMMY GARVIN** "GORGEOUS"
WITH PRECIOUS

WORLD TAG TEAM TITLE

1st TIME EVER IN OKC!
THE ROAD WARRIORS **VS.** **RICK RUDE RAGIN' BULL** "RAVISHING"
WITH PAUL ELLERING WITH PAUL JONES

UWF WORLD HEAVYWEIGHT TITLE
BARRY WINDHAM VS. **BIG BUBBA RODGERS**

"GENTLEMAN" CHRIS ADAMS VS. TERRY TAYLOR

U.S. TITLE MATCH
NIKITA KOLOFF VS. **LEX LUGER**

ALL THIS ACTION PLUS: ROCK N' ROLL EXPRESS - STEVE COX - SAVANNAH JACK - STING - RICK STEINER - EDDIE GILBERT - CHAVO GUERRERO - BLACK BART.

TICKETS ON SALE NOW AT ALL "OK TICKET" LOCATIONS

DON'T MISS THIS AWESOME EVENT!

JCP @ Greenwood, SC - May 26, 1987
TV taping:
Pro - 5/30/87 - - featured Johnny Weaver & Bob Caudle on commentary; included Weaver & Caudle conducting an opening ringside interview with Ricky Morton & Robert Gibson regarding their quest for the NWA Tag Team Championship and Paul Jones replacing Rick Rude with Ivan Koloff on the championship team; featured Tony Schiavone conducting an interview with Chris Champion & Sean Royal regarding Jimmy Valiant & NWA Jr. Heavyweight Champion Lazortron, during which they made fun of Dusty Rhodes; included Schiavone conducting an interview with NWA TV Champion Tully Blanchard, alongside Dark Journey, regarding his $100,000 match against Rhodes June 6 at the Greensboro Coliseum; featured Schiavone conducting an interview with Lex Luger & JJ Dillon regarding NWA US Champion Nikita Koloff, during which Luger said Koloff had become soft and was a shadow of his former self; included a Dusty Rhodes music video to the tune of Bo Diddley's "You Can't Judge a Book by It's Cover;" featured Schiavone conducting an interview with Valiant & Lazotron regarding the comments made earlier in the show by Champion & Royal:
NWA US Champion Nikita Koloff pinned Gladiator #2 with the Russian Sickle at the 41-second mark; following the bout, Bob Caudle conducted a ringside interview with Koloff regarding the challenge of Lex Luger
NWA US Tag Team Champions Bobby Eaton & Stan Lane (w/ Jim Cornette) defeated Randy & Bill Mulkey; Cornette joined the commentary team for the match
Barry Windham vs. Brodie Chase
NWA TV Champion Tully Blanchard vs. George South
NWA Tag Team Champions Manny Fernandez & Ivan Koloff vs. Larry Stevens & Ricky Nelson
Lex Luger (w/ JJ Dillon) defeated Dexter Wescott; after the bout, Luger grabbed the mic and called out NWA US Champion Nikita Koloff, with Koloff then coming out and brawling with Luger in and out of the ring and down the aisle until other wrestlers came out to break up the fight Barry Windham pinned Brodie Chase with the lariat at 3:09
NWA TV Champion Tully Blanchard (w/ Dark Journey) pinned George South with the slingshot suplex at around the 4-minute mark; Blanchard's $10,000 was on the line in the match; during the bout, Tony Schiavone conducted an interview with JJ Dillon regarding the June 6 match in Greensboro between Blanchard and Dusty Rhodes
NWA Tag Team Champions Manny Fernandez & Ivan Koloff (w/ Paul Jones & Vladimir Petrov) defeated Larry Stephens & Ricky Nelson at 3:02 when Koloff pinned Nelson following Fernandez' Flying Burrito; Jones briefly joined the commentary team during the bout and said any combination of Fernandez, Koloff, and Petrov could defend the titles
Lex Luger (w/ JJ Dillon) defeated Dexter Wescott via submission with the Torture Rack at 1:01; after the bout, Luger cut an in-ring promo in which he challenged NWA US Champion Nikita Koloff to fight him immediately; moments later, Koloff came out to the ring, shoved Dillon to the mat, and brawled with Luger in and around the ring until Ricky Nelson, Gladiator #2, other wrestlers, and referees came out to try to

break up the fight; they two were held apart by the exit doors just as the show ended
Worldwide - 5/30/87 - featured an opening announcement by Paul Jones that NWA Tag Team Champion Rick Rude was injured and would be replaced by Ivan Koloff; included Bob Caudle conducting an interview with NWA World Champion Ric Flair regarding Jimmy Garvin & Precious, with Flair saying Precious would be his; Flair then spoke about the Road Warriors and said they never beat the Horsemen and the Horsemen would beat them in the upcoming steel cage match in Chicago; featured Caudle conducting an interview with JJ Dillon, NWA TV Tully Blanchard, and Dark Journey regarding the upcoming $100,000 match with Dusty Rhodes on June 6; included Caudle conducting an interview with Flair, Lex Luger, Blanchard, Dillon, Arn Anderson, and Dark Journey regarding the attack the previous week on Rhodes; during the segment, Flair repeatedly praised Tully for acquiring Dark Journey:
Lex Luger defeated David Isley
NWA US Tag Team Champions Bobby Eaton & Stan Lane defeated George South & Vernon Deaton
Barry Windham, Ron & Jimmy Garvin vs. three unknowns
Vladimir Pietrov defeated Ricky Nelson
The New Breed defeated the Italian Stallion & Bill Mulkey
NWA TV Champion Tully Blanchard defeated Randy Mulkey
Ricky Morton & Robert Gibson defeated the Gladiators

CWF @ Miami, FL - May 27, 1987
Bob & Brad Armstrong defeated the MOD Squad
Tracy Smothers & Steve Armstrong defeated Krusher Knopf & Ron Bass
Jimmy Garvin defeated Teijo Khan
Mike Graham defeated Dory Funk Jr. via disqualification
Barry Windham & Ed Gantner defeated the Tahitian Prince & Teijo Khan
Barry Windham & Ed Gantner defeated Dory Funk Jr. & the Tahitian Prince
The Road Warriors defeated NWA Tag Team Champions Rick Rude & Manny Fernandez via disqualification

JCP / UWF @ Oklahoma City, OK - Myriad - May 27, 1987
Chris Adams vs. Terry Taylor
NWA US Champion Nikita Koloff vs. Lex Luger
Barry Windham vs. Big Bubba
The Road Warriors vs. NWA Tag Team Champions Rick Rude & Manny Fernandez
NWA World Champion Ric Flair vs. Jimmy Garvin
Also included: Ricky Morton & Robert Gibson, Steve Cox, Savannah Jack, Sting, Rick Steiner, Eddie Gilbert, Chavo Guerrero, and Black Bart

JCP @ Silver City, NC - May 28, 1987
NWA US Tag Team Champions Bobby Eaton & Stan Lane defeated the Italian Stallion & Todd Champion

CWF @ Gainesville, FL - O'Connell Center - May 29, 1987
Tracy Smothers & Steve Armstrong and ? vs. Colt Steel and

Randy & Bill Mulkey
Steve Keirn vs. Jerry Gray
Ron Simmons vs. Shaska Whatley
Kendall Windham vs. Teijo Khan
Mike Rotunda vs. Manny Fernandez
The Road Warriors & Ed Gantner vs. Dory Funk Jr., Kevin Sullivan, & the Tahitan Prince
NWA US Champion Nikita Koloff vs. Rick Rude
Dusty Rhodes vs. NWA World Champion Ric Flair

JCP @ Beckley, WV - May 29, 1987 (3,000)
Ricky Morton & Robert Gibson defeated NWA US Tag Team Champions Bobby Eaton & Stan Lane in a non-title match; during the bout, a fan by the name of Roy Massey threw an object into the ring and struck Eaton & Lane; moments later, Massey sustained fractured bones in his face from a punch from Lane; he was later arrested and charged with two counts of battery

JCP @ Joplin, MO - Memorial Hall - May 29, 1987

JCP @ Atlanta, GA - WTBS Studios - May 30, 1987 (matinee)
World Championship Wrestling - 5/30/87 - 60-minute episode; featured Tony Schiavone & David Crockett conducting an opening interview with Magnum TA regarding his being in Dusty Rhodes' corner for the June 6 match at the Greensboro Coliseum between Dusty Rhodes and NWA TV Champion Tully Blanchard; moments later, NWA US Champion Nikita Koloff came out to welcome Magnum before going to the ring for the opening match; included Schiavone conducting an interview with Lex Luger & JJ Dillon regarding Luger's quest for Koloff's US title; featured a closing announcement that the following day's Sunday Edition would air at 5:30 EST:
NWA US Champion Nikita Koloff pinned Art Pritts with the Russian Sickle at the 52-second mark; after the bout, Tony Schiavone conducted an interview with Koloff regarding the challenge of Lex Luger, during which they reviewed footage of Koloff and Luger brawling at the end of the 5/30/87 Pro
Jimmy Garvin (w/ Precious) pinned Tim Davis with the brainbuster at the 50-second mark
International Tag Team Champions the Road Warriors (w/ Paul Ellering) defeated Mike Force & Rick Sullivan at 1:08 when Road Warrior Hawk scored the pin following the Doomsday Device; after the bout, Schiavone conducted an interview with the Road Warriors & Ellering regarding the Four Horsemen
Ron Garvin pinned Barry Phelps at 1:16 with a right hand punch

NWA Super Bouts - 5/30/87 - featured the Ricky Morton & Robert Gibson vs. NWA TV Champion Tully Blanchard & Lex Luger match taped 4/3/87 at the Greensboro Coliseum

JCP @ Sarasota, FL - May 30, 1987

JCP @ Florence, SC - May 30, 1987
The show was to have seen Ricky Morton & Robert Gibson defeat NWA Tag Team Champions Rick Rude & Manny Fernandez to regain the titles but Rude left the promotion

JCP @ Philadelphia, PA - Civic Center - May 30, 1987 (5,500)
Denny Brown defeated Thunderfoot #2
Baron Von Raschke defeated Mark Fleming
Todd Champion defeated Thunderfoot #1
NWA US Tag Team Champions Bobby Eaton & Stan Lane fought Barry Windham & Ron Garvin to a 30-minute time-limit draw
NWA TV Champion Tully Blanchard, Arn Anderson, & Lex Luger defeated Dusty Rhodes & the Road Warriors via disqualification
NWA US Champion Nikita Koloff defeated Ivan Koloff in a chain match
NWA World Champion Ric Flair defeated Jimmy Garvin via disqualification

JCP @ Little Rock, AR - Barton Coliseum - May 31, 1987

NWA Super Bouts - 6/87 - hosted by Tony Schiavone & JJ Dillon; included footage of the NWA World Champion Ric Flair & Lex Luger vs. Dusty Rhodes & NWA US Champion Nikita Koloff match taped at a NWA Pro taping, with NWA TV Champion Tully Blanchard attacking Rhodes with a steel briefcase to end the match and targetting Rhodes' leg:
NWA TV Champion Tully Blanchard (w/ Dark Journey & JJ Dillon) defeated NWA Tag Team Champion Ricky Morton via disqualification at around the 10-minute mark when Morton threw the champion over the top rope; after the bout, Morton cleared Blanchard from the ring (held at NWA Pro taping site)

CWF @ West Palm Beach, FL - June 1, 1987
Mike Rotunda vs. NWA World Champion Ric Flair

JCP @ Spartanburg, SC - Memorial Auditorium - June 2, 1987
TV taping:
Pro - 6/6/87 - featured the announcement that Ricky Morton & Robert Gibson had won the NWA Tag Team Titles; included an announcement by Jim Crockett Jr. that 'the Match Beyond' would debut as part of the Atlanta Omni stop of the Great American Bash tour the following month:
Lex Luger vs. Gene Ligon
The New Breed vs. Mike Force & Cougar Jay
NWA US Tag Team Champions Bobby Eaton & Stan Lane vs. John Savage & Ricky Nelson
Ivan Koloff & Vladimir Pietrov vs. Tommy Angel & Rocky King
NWA TV Champion Tully Blanchard (w/ Dark Journey) pinned Todd Champion at 6:53 with the slingshot suplex after the challenger failed an elbow drop; both Blanchard's title and $10,000 were on the line in the bout; during the match, Tony

Schiavone conducted an insert interview with JJ Dillon in which he said Blanchard and the Horsemen would dominate the Great American Bash

Worldwide - 6/6/87:
Arn Anderson & NWA TV Champion Tully Blanchard vs. Rick Nelson & Tommy Angel
Jimmy Valiant & Lazertron vs. two unknowns
Ivan Koloff & Vladimir Pietrov vs. the Italian Stallion & Todd Champion
Nikita Koloff vs. Cougar Jay
Ron & Jimmy Garvin vs. Mike Force & John Savage
Kendall Windham vs. Thunderfoot #1 (Kendall's debut)
NWA US Tag Team Champions Bobby Eaton & Stan Lane vs. George South & Gary Royal
Dark match: Barry Windham & Ron Garvin defeated NWA US Tag Team Champions Bobby Eaton & Stan Lane

JCP @ Raleigh, NC - Dorton Arena - June 4, 1987
NWA US Tag Team Champions Bobby Eaton & Stan Lane defeated the Italian Stallion & Todd Champion
NWA Tag Team Champion Robert Gibson defeated Arn Anderson
NWA Tag Team Champion Ricky Morton fought NWA TV Champion Tully Blanchard to a draw
NWA US Champion Nikita Koloff defeated Lex Luger via disqualification

JCP @ Richmond, VA - Coliseum - June 5, 1987 (4,500)
Chris Champion & Sean Royal defeated Denny Brown & Baron Von Raschke
Vladimir Petrov pinned the Italian Stallion
Arn Anderson defeated Todd Champion
NWA US Tag Team Champions Bobby Eaton & Stan Lane defeated Jimmy Valiant & Lazortron
NWA TV Champion Tully Blanchard pinned Kendall Windham with the slingshot suplex
Ivan Koloff & Vladimir Petrov (sub. for Rick Rude & Manny Fernandez) defeated Ricky Morton & Robert Gibson via disqualification in a No DQ match when Morton & Gibson were caught using the Russian chain
NWA World Champion Ric Flair & Lex Luger defeated Dusty Rhodes & NWA US Champion Nikita Koloff when Flair pinned Rhodes after NWA TV Champion Tully Blanchard interfered
Ron Garvin defeated Jim Cornette in a steel cage match at the 2-minute mark following a punch

NWA Super Bouts - 6/6/87 - featured the closing moments of the Ricky Morton & Robert Gibson vs. NWA Tag Team Champoins Rick Rude & Manny Fernandez match explaining Morton & Gibson's title victory; the footage was actually from a non-title match earlier in the year; during the segment, the commentary team never referred to Rude by name, only as "Fernandez's partner"

JCP @ Atlanta, GA - WTBS Studios - June 6, 1987 (matinee)

World Championship Wrestling - 6/6/87 - 60-minute episode - featured an opening announcement that Ricky Morton & Robert Gibson won the NWA Tag Team Titles from Rick Rude & Manny Fernandez and that the Freebirds would be at the Omni the following night to face the Horsemen; included footage of how Morton & Gibson won the titles; featured Schiavone announcing that the Great American Bash would kick off July 1 at in Lakeland, FL and would hit Landover, MD, Baltimore, Philadelphia, Dallas, San Francisco, Los Angeles and the Freebirds would be part of the event; Schiavone then spoke with Jim Crockett Jr. about the July 4 show at the Omni in which Crockett announced the Match Beyond would take place at the show; included a Dusty Rhodes music video to the tune of Bo Diddley's "You Can't Judge a Book by It's Cover;" featured Schiavone conducting an interview with NWA TV Champion Tully Blanchard, Dark Journey, & JJ Dillon regarding Blanchard's $100,000 match later that night against Dusty Rhodes in Greensboro; included a vignette of NWA World Champion Ric Flair; featured Schiavone conducting an interview with Barry Windham regarding his challenge of Big Bubba and being part of a tournament in Houston to determine the Western States Heritage champion, during which it was noted Windham would face Bubba the following night at the Omni; included footage of Schiavone conducting an interview with Rhodes regarding his match June 6 against Blanchard; featured Schiavone conducting an interview with Jimmy Garvin, with Precious, regarding the Bash and challenging Flair; included Schiavone conducting an interview with Flair regarding facing the Freebirds the next night at the Omni, moments later, Flair pulled a crew member aside and asked if he wanted to spend a night with Dark Journey, with the man saying yes; Flair replied by saying he can't because she's Blanchard's; featured Schiavone conducting an interview with NWA US Champion Nikita Koloff regarding the challenge of Lex Luger and facing Dick Murdoch the next night at the Omni; included footage from the UWF of Dick Murdoch assaulting Steve Williams after Williams beat Eddie Gilbert and breaking Williams' arm; Jim Ross & Ted DiBiase provided commentary on the footage; featured Schiavone conducting an interview with JJ Dillon & Luger regarding the Bash and challenging Koloff:
Chris Champion & Sean Royal defeated Alan Martin & Mike Force at 3:58 when Champion scored the pin following a suplex / missile dropkick double team
NWA Tag Team Champions Ricky Morton & Robert Gibson defeated Randy Barber & Cougar Jay at 2:56 when both men scored the pin following the double dropkick; following the commercial break, Tony Schiavone conducted an interview with Morton & Gibson regarding their recent title win and facing NWA World Champion Ric Flair & Lex Luger the following night in Greensboro
Jimmy Garvin (w/ Precious) pinned Terry Jones with the brainbuster at the 55-second mark
NWA US Tag Team Champions Bobby Eaton & Stan Lane (w/ Jim Cornette) defeated Trent Knight & Larry Stephens when Lane pinned Knight at 4:05 following the flapjack; Cornette joined the commentary team for the bout, during which the champions brought one of the opponents over to the broadcast

booth for Cornette to talk to him; after the contest, Schiavone conducted an interview with Cornette, Eaton & Lane in which they challenged NWA Tag Team Champions Ricky Morton & Robert Gibson to a title match during the Great American Bash
Arn Anderson pinned Chance McQuade with the gordbuster at 2:23; MLB Hall of Famer Lou Brock was shown on camera during the bout
Michael Hayes, Terry Gordy, & Buddy Roberts defeated Gladiator #1, Thunderfoot #1 & #2 at around the 3-minute mark when Hayes pinned the Gladiator following an elbow off the top as Gordy had the Gladiator in a fireman's carry; after the match, Schiavone conducted an interview with the Freebirds regarding their match the next night at the Omni against the Horsemen (the Freebirds' return)
Vladimir Petrov (w/ Paul Jones) pinned Gary Phelps at the 23-second mark with the Russian Sickle
Barry Windham pinned Gladiator #2 with the lariat at around the 15-second mark
Ron Garvin pinned Rick Sullivan at the 39-second mark by sitting on him after two right hand punches; after the bout, Schiavone conducted a ringside interview with Garvin and Barry Windham regarding their challenge of NWA US Tag Team Champions Bobby Eaton & Stan Lane, during which they said they would take Jim Cornette out of the picture before the match even begins NWA World Champion Ric Flair & Lex Luger (w/ JJ Dillon) defeated Ricky Nelson & John Savage at 1:32 when Nelson submitted to Flair's figure-4; following the bout, Schiavone conducted a ringside interview with Flair, Luger, Dillon, NWA TV Champion Tully Blanchard, Arn Anderson, and Dark Journey regarding the challenge of the Freebirds, during which Flair referred to them as the "Fruitbirds" and implied Dark Journey tried Michael Hayes and he didn't meet her standards

JCP @ Greensboro, NC - Coliseum - June 6, 1987 (12,837)
TV taping:
Eddie Gilbert pinned Kendall Windham
Ivan Koloff & Vladimir Petrov defeated Ron Garvin & Baron Von Raschke
Terry Taylor fought Chris Adams to a double count-out
NWA Super Bouts - 7/87: Michael Hayes & Terry Gordy (w/ Buddy Roberts) defeated Sting & Rick Steiner (w/ Eddie Gilbert) at around the 9-minute mark when Gordy pinned Sting after Gilbert accidentally hit Sting with a clothesline off the top, behind the referee's back when Gordy moved out of the way; prior to the bout, Hayes took the mic and told the crowd that if they were ready to rock 'n' roll they the Freebirds were "ready to kick ass;" after the contest, Sting argued with Gilbert
NWA Super Bouts - 7/87: Barry Windham defeated UWF Heavyweight Champion Big Bubba (w/ Skandar Akbar) via disqualification at around the 10-minute mark when Akbar tripped the challenger as Windham attempted the lariat; after the match, Windham cleared Bubba from the ring
NWA US Champion Nikita Koloff pinned Dick Murdoch
NWA Super Bouts - 8/87: NWA World Champion Ric Flair & Lex Luger defeated NWA Tag Team Champions Ricky Morton & Robert Gibson in a non-title match at around the 19-minute mark when Flair pinned Morton with his feet on the ropes for

leverage after Luger hit a clothesline to the back of the head, behind the referee's back, as Morton had Flair covered with a roll up; Morton & Gibson came out with the title belts as their phantom title victory was announced the same day on television
Worldwide - 6/13/87: NWA TV Champion Tully Blanchard defeated Dusty Rhodes via count-out when Rhodes went after JJ Dillon outside the ring after Dillon stole a bag containing $100,000 from Magnum TA; stipulations stated the winner would walk away with the $100,000

CWF @ St. Petersburg, FL - June 6, 1987
Television taping:
NWA US Tag Team Champions Bobby Eaton & Stan Lane (w/ Jim Cornette) defeated Tracy Smothers & Steve Armstrong; Cornette joined Sir Oliver Humperdink on commentary for the bout

JCP @ Atlanta, GA - Omni - June 7, 1987 (7,000)
Chris Champion & Sean Royal defeated Jimmy Valiant & Lazertron at 10:31 when Champion pinned Valiant
UWF TV Champion Eddie Gilbert pinned Kendall Windham at 9:40
Rick Steiner & Sting defeated Todd Champion & Baron Von Raschke at 9:35 when Steiner pinned Von Raschke following a double team move; after the bout, Steiner and Sting argued with Sting then walking out
Terry Taylor fought Chris Adams to a double count-out
NWA Tag Team Champions Ricky Morton & Robert Gibson defeated Ivan Koloff & Vladimir Petrov at 9:08 when Morton pinned Koloff after a leap off the top
Barry Windham defeated UWF Heavyweight Champion Big Bubba via disqualification at 7:30 after Skandar Akbar tripped Windham from the floor
NWA World Champion Ric Flair, Lex Luger, & Tully Blanchard defeated Michael Hayes, Terry Gordy, & Buddy Roberts at 17:25 when Flair pinned Roberts after JJ Dillon hit Roberts with his shoe
NWA US Champion Nikita Koloff defeated Dick Murdoch in a steel cage match at 6:37 after the challenger missed the splash

CWF @ Orlando, FL - June 7, 1987
NWA US Tag Team Champions Bobby Eaton & Stan Lane defeated Ron Simmons & Ed Gantner

MID-ATLANTIC CHAMPIONSHIP WRESTLING

NWA

GREENVILLE MEMORIAL AUDITORIUM
June 8, 1987
8:00 p.m.

WORLD T.V. TITLE
1 FALL - 25 MINUTES
AND $10,000

Tully Blanchard (with Dark Journey)
VS
1/2 Rock 'N Roll Express Ricky Morton

U.S. Tag Team Championship

Midnight Express (with Jim Cornette)
VS
Barry Windham Ron Garvin

U.S. Heavyweight Title

Nikita Koloff
VS
Ragin' Bull (with Paul Jones)

Special Grudge Match
"Bullet" Bob Armstrong "Gorgeous" Jimmy Garvin (with Precious)
VS
Lex Luger Arn Anderson

Italian Stallion	VS	"Ravishing" Rick Rude
Todd Champion	VS	Vladimir Petrov

Tag Team Action

Lazer-Tron Jimmy Valiant	VS	New Breed
Kendall Windham	VS	Denny Brown

NWA   Subject To Change

Ticket Prices:
$12, $10, & $4

N077776-H

MID-ATLANTIC CHAMPIONSHIP WRESTLING

JCP @ Greenville, SC - Memorial Auditorium - June 8, 1987
Denny Brown defeated Gary Royal (sub. for Kendall Windham)
Chris Champion & Sean Royal defeated Jimmy Valiant & Lazertron
Vladimir Petrov defeated Todd Champion
The Italian Stallion defeated Thunderfoot #1 (sub. for NWA Tag Team Champion Rick Rude)
Arn Anderson & Lex Luger defeated Jimmy Garvin & Kendall Windham (sub. for Bob Armstrong)
NWA US Champion Nikita Koloff defeated NWA Tag Team Champion Manny Fernandez
Barry Windham & Ron Garvin defeated NWA US Tag Team Champions Bobby Eaton & Stan Lane via disqualification
Ricky Morton fought NWA TV Champion Tully Blanchard to a double count-out; Blanchard's title and his $10,000 were at stake in the match

JCP @ Columbia, SC - June 9, 1987
Worldwide - 6/13/87 - featured the Dusty Rhodes vs. NWA TV Champion Tully Blanchard match taped 6/6/87 in Greensboro:
NWA Tag Team Champions Ricky Morton & Robert Gibson vs. Gene Ligon & Tommy Angel
NWA US Tag Team Champions Bobby Eaton & Stan Lane vs. Vernon Deaton & an unknown
NWA TV Champion Tully Blanchard, Arn Anderson, & Lex Luger vs. Ricky Nelson & two unknowns
Pro - 6/13/87:
NWA US Tag Team Champions Bobby Eaton & Stan Lane vs. John Savage & Ricky Nelson
Barry Windham vs. Brodie Chase

JCP @ Cincinnati, OH - Cincinnati Gardens - June 11, 1987 (1,500)
Thunderfoot #1 pinned Jim Lancaster
Rocky King defeated Thunderfoot #2
NWA US Tag Team Champions Bobby Eaton & Stan Lane defeated Kendall Windham & the Italian Stallion
NWA TV Champion Tully Blanchard pinned Todd Champion
NWA US Champion Nikita Koloff defeated Arn Anderson via disqualification at the 18-minute mark when JJ Dillon interfered
Ron Garvin defeated Jim Cornette in a steel cage match at the 3-minute mark after stripping Cornette down to his underwear
NWA World Champion Ric Flair pinned Jimmy Garvin in a steel cage match at the 15-minute mark

- 6/11/87: Terry Taylor was injured in a car wreck. Six inches of his small intestine, four inches of his large intestine and his appendix were removed following a subsequent operation.

JCP @ Norfolk, VA - Scope - June 12, 1987 (6,000)
NWA US Tag Team Champions Bobby Eaton & Stan Lane defeated Kendall Windham & Todd Champion
Arn Anderson & Lex Luger defeated Dusty Rhodes & NWA US Champion Nikita Koloff
Ron Garvin defeated Jim Cornette in a steel cage match

NWA World Champion Ric Flair defeated Jimmy Garvin in a steel cage match

JCP @ Charleston, WV - June 12, 1987
Chris Champion & Sean Royal defeated Jimmy Valiant & Lazertron in a Texas Tornado match
Manny Fernandez pinned Robert Gibson in a lumberjack match
NWA TV Champion Tully Blanchard fought Ricky Morton to a time-limit draw

JCP @ Lake Charles, LA - Civic Center - June 12, 1987

JCP @ Atlanta, GA - WTBS Studios - June 13, 1987 (matinee)
World Championship Wrestling - 6/13/87 - featured the Dusty Rhodes vs. NWA TV Champion Tully Blanchard bout taped 6/6/87 at the Greensboro Coliseum; included Tony Schiavone conducting an interview with NWA World Champion Ric Flair in which he said Precious was playing hard to get after walking off with his $15,000 fur coat; Flair then shook the hands of NWA TV Champion Tully Blanchard, Arn Anderson, Lex Luger, and JJ Dillon in the ring :
Kendall Windham vs. Art Pritts
Jimmy Garvin vs. Rick Sullivan
Arn Anderson, NWA TV Champion Tully Blanchard, & Lex Luger (w/ JJ Dillon) vs. Mike Force, Cougar Jay, & Chance McQuade
World Championship Wrestling Sunday Edition - 6/14/87

NWA Super Bouts - 6/13/87 - included Tony Schiavone as the sole host, without JJ Dillon; featured an ad promoting the 1987 Crockett Cup on VHS; included the NWA TV Champion Tully Blanchard vs. Todd Champion bout from the 6/6/87 Pro; featured the announcement that the 7/18/87 show in Charlotte, NC would be part of the Great American Bash tour NWA US Champion Nikita Koloff defeated Ivan Koloff in a Russian chain match at 9:07 when, after Nikita touched three corners, Ivan knocked him into the fourth; David Crockett was the guest ring announcer for the bout and explained the rules of the match, with referee Tommy Young having to clarify to him that the winner would have to drag his opponent to the four corners consecutively

- 6/13/87: Chris Champion & Sean Royal were injured in a car wreck driving from the TV studio in Atlanta to Florence, SC. The car hydroplaned in rain, with both men being thrown through the windshield before the car exploded. Royal suffered major burns while Champion's arm was broken in two places.

JCP @ Florence, SC - June 13, 1987

JCP @ Baltimore, MD - Arena - June 13, 1987 (5,200)
NWA Tag Team Champion Ricky Morton defeated Mark Fleming
Arn Anderson defeated Kendall Windham
Manny Fernandez defeated Brickhouse Brown
NWA US Tag Team Champions Bobby Eaton & Stan Lane defeated Tracy Smothers & Steve Armstrong
NWA TV Champion Tully Blanchard defeated Ron Garvin
NWA US Champion Nikita Koloff defeated Lex Luger via disqualification
NWA World Champion Ric Flair defeated Jimmy Garvin

JCP @ New Orleans, LA - Superdome - June 13, 1987

JCP @ Charlotte, NC - Coliseum - June 14, 1987 (7,500)
The MOD Squad fought Tracy Smothers & Steve Armstrong to a draw
Jimmy Valiant & Lazertron defeated Gladiator #1 & #2
Arn Anderson defeated Kendall Windham
Manny Fernandez & Vladimir Petrov defeated Ron Garvin & Todd Champion
NWA Tag Team Champions Ricky Morton & Robert Gibson defeated NWA US Tag Team Champions Bobby Eaton & Stan Lane
Lex Luger fought NWA US Champion Nikita Koloff to a no contest
Dusty Rhodes defeated NWA TV Champion Tully Blanchard in a non-title Texas Death Match
NWA World Champion Ric Flair defeated Jimmy Garvin

JCP @ Tulsa, OK - Civic Center - June 14, 1987

JCP @ Greenville, SC - Memorial Auditorium - June 15, 1987
The MOD Squad defeated Tracy Smothers & Steve Armstrong
Lazertron defeated Gladiator #2 (sub. for New Breed #2)
Kendall Windham defeated Gladiator #1 (sub. for New Breed #1)
Vladimir Petrov defeated Denny Brown (sub. for Todd Champion)
Manny Fernandez defeated Todd Champion (sub. for Denny Brown)
NWA TV Champion Tully Blanchard defeated Barry Windham; Blanchard's title and $10,000 were at stake in the match
NWA US Tag Team Champions Bobby Eaton & Stan Lane fought Ron & Jimmy Garvin to a double count-out in a No DQ match
NWA Tag Team Champions Ricky Morton & Robert Gibson defeated Lex Luger & Arn Anderson

JCP @ Fayetteville, NC - Cumberland County Memorial Arena - June 16, 1987
TV taping:

Pro - 6/20/87:
Ron & Jimmy Garvin vs. John Savage & David Isley
Tracy Smothers & Steve Armstrong vs. Cougar Jay & Tommy Angel
Barry Windham vs. Thunderfoot #2
Manny Fernandez, Ivan Koloff, & Vladimir Pietrov vs. the Italian Stallion, Rocky King, & Todd Champion
NWA US Champion Nikita Koloff vs. Gladiator #1
NWA TV Champion Tully Blanchard vs. Ricky Nelson
NWA US Tag Team Champions Bobby Eaton & Stan Lane vs. Nelson Royal & Mike Force
Worldwide - 6/20/87:
Arn Anderson defeated an unknown; after the bout, Bob Caudle conducted a ringside interview with Anderson in which he said NWA US Champion Nikita Koloff was so preoccupied by NWA World Champion Ric Flair and Lex Luger that he had forgotten about Anderson

JCP @ Baton Rouge, LA - Centroplex - June 16, 1987

JCP @ Atlanta, GA - WTBS Studios - June 17, 1987
World Championship Wrestling - 6/20/87:
Barry Windham vs. Brodie Chase
Jimmy Valiant & Lazortron vs. Thunderfoot #1 & #2
NWA US Champion Nikita Koloff vs. Hal Moore
The MOD Squad vs. Mike Jackson & Alan Martin
Manny Fernandez & Ivan Koloff vs. Todd Champion & Denny Brown
Ron Garvin vs. John Hardy
Jimmy Garvin vs. Terry Jones
Kendall Windham vs. Tim Hardy
Lex Luger vs. Dexter Wescott
The Italian Stallion vs. Tommy Angel
NWA US Tag Team Champions Bobby Eaton & Stan Lane vs. Mike Force & Larry Stephens

NWA TV Champion Tully Blanchard & Arn Anderson vs. Dalton & Sullivan
World Championship Wrestling Sunday Edition - 6/21/87

JCP @ Alexandria, LA - Rapides Parish Coliseum - June 18, 1987

JCP @ Atlanta, GA - WTBS Studios - June 18, 1987
World Championship Wrestling - 6/27/87:
The MOD Squad vs. Martin & El Negro
Arn Anderson vs. Dexter Wescott
NWA World Champion Ric Flair & Lex Luger fought Ron & Jimmy Garvin to a double disqualification
NWA Tag Team Champion Ricky Morton vs. Freddy Smith
NWA US Champion Nikita Koloff vs. Brodie Chase
UWF Western States Heritage Champion Barry Windham vs. Gary Phelps
NWA TV Champion Tully Blanchard vs. Hal Moore
NWA US Tag Team Champions Bobby Eaton & Stan Lane vs. Mike Force & Larry Stevens

Thunderfoot #2 vs. Darrel Dalton
World Championship Wrestling Sunday Edition - 6/28/87

CWF @ Tallahassee, FL - Leon County Civic Center - June 19, 1987
NWA US Tag Team Champions Bobby Eaton & Stan Lane defeated Ron & Jimmy Garvin

JCP @ Lafayette, LA - Cajundome - June 19, 1987

UWF / JCP @ Houston, TX - Summit - June 20, 1987
Steve Cox won a $10,000 pole battle royal; other participants included: Shane Douglas, Gary Young, Bob Bradley, Ken Massey, Mike Boyette, Jeff Raitz, and David Haskins
UWF Western States Heritage Championship Tournament Quarter Finals: Shaska Whatley pinned Buddy Roberts at 5:23
UWF Western States Heritage Championship Tournament Quarter Finals: Black Bart pinned Sting at 7:00
UWF Western States Heritage Championship Tournament Quarter Finals: Rick Steiner fought Terry Gordy to a double disqualification at 6:35
UWF Western States Heritage Championship Tournament Quarter Finals: Barry Windham pinned Chris Adams at 8:13
UWF Tag Team Champions Tim Horner & Brad Armstrong defeated the Enforcer & the Terminator at 5:25
NWA Tag Team Champions Ricky Morton & Robert Gibson defeated the Angel of Death & Big Bubba at 9:45
NWA World Champion Ric Flair pinned Michael Hayes at 20:12
UWF Western States Heritage Championship Tournament Semi Finals: Barry Windham pinned Shaska Whatley at 7:32
Dusty Rhodes & Steve Williams defeated Eddie Gilbert & Dick Murdoch in a bunkhouse tornado match at 11:00
UWF Western States Heritage Championship Tournament Finals: Barry Windham pinned Black Bart at 9:00 to win the title

CWF @ Lakeland, FL - June 20, 1987
NWA US Tag Team Champions Bobby Eaton & Stan Lane defeated Ron & Jimmy Garvin

JCP @ Amarillo, TX - Civic Center - June 21, 1987

JCP @ Greensboro, NC - Coliseum - June 21, 1987 (4,500)
Kendall Windham pinned Denny Brown
Jimmy Valiant & Lazortron fought the MOD Squad to a time-limit draw after the 15-minute mark
Manny Fernandez pinned the Italian Stallion
Ivan Koloff pinned Todd Champion
NWA US Tag Team Champions Bobby Eaton & Stan Lane defeated Ron & Jimmy Garvin via disqualification
NWA US Champion Nikita Koloff pinned Arn Anderson
Dusty Rhodes defeated NWA TV Champion Tully Blanchard via count-out in a Texas Death Match after hitting him with Magnum TA's cane, knocking Blanchard to the floor
NWA Tag Team Champions Ricky Morton & Robert Gibson

MID-ATLANTIC CHAMPIONSHIP WRESTLING

NWA NATIONAL WRESTLING ALLIANCE

GREENVILLE MEMORIAL AUDITORIUM
MONDAY - JUNE 15, 1987
8:00 P.M.

WORLD TAG TEAM TITLE

ROCK 'N ROLL EXPRESS VS. **LEX LUGER ARN ANDERSON (WITH J.J. DILLON)**

WORLD T.V. TITLE
1 FALL - 25 MINUTES AND $10,000

TULLY BLANCHARD (WITH DARK JOURNEY) VS. **Barry Windham**

U.S. TAG TEAM TITLE
NO DISQUALIFICATION

MIDNIGHT EXPRESS (WITH JIM CORNETTE) VS. **GORGEOUS JIMMY GARVIN (WITH PRECIOUS)**

DENNY BROWN VS. RAGIN' BULL (WITH PAUL JONES)

TODD CHAMPION vs. VLADIMIR PETROV

KENDALL WINDHAM vs. NEW BREED #1

LAZOR-TRON vs. NEW BREED #2

SOUTHERN BOYS vs. MOD SQUAD

Ringside Reserved $12
General Admission $10
Children (Under 10) $4

*Subject to Change

NO77821 H

MID-ATLANTIC CHAMPIONSHIP WRESTLING

MID-ATLANTIC CHAMPIONSHIP WRESTLING

NWA NATIONAL WRESTLING ALLIANCE

GREENVILLE MEMORIAL AUDITORIUM
MONDAY JUNE 22, 1987
7:30 P.M.

SIX MAN TAG ACTION

ROCK 'N ROLL EXPRESS AND BARRY WINDHAM VS. **LEX LUGER plus ARN ANDERSON TULLY BLANCHARD (WITH J.J. DILLON) (DARK JOURNEY)**

SPECIAL CHALLENGER MATCH

GORGEOUS JIMMY GARVIN RON GARVIN (WITH PRECIOUS) **MIDNIGHT EXPRESS**

JIMMY VALIANT VS. ½ NEW BREED SEAN ROYAL

JOIN US FOR LIVE T.V. TAPING OF NWA PRO WRESTLING
AND
WORLD WIDE WRESTLING WITH SUCH STARS AS:

NIKITA KOLOFF   RAGIN' BULL

DUSTY RHODES   IVAN KOLOFF

LAZOR-TRON   VLADIMIR PETROV

Ringside Reserved $10
General Admission $8
Children (Under 10) $4

NO7785S-H

MID-ATLANTIC CHAMPIONSHIP WRESTLING

382

defeated NWA World Champion Ric Flair & Lex Luger via disqualification when NWA TV Champion Tully Blanchard interfered

JCP @ Greenville, SC - Memorial Auditorium - June 22, 1987
TV taping:
Worldwide - 6/27/87
Pro - 6/27/87:
NWA Tag Team Champions Ricky Morton & Robert Gibson defeated Gladiator #2 & Thunderfoot #2
UWF Western States Heritage Champion Barry Windham vs. Larry Stevens
Arn Anderson & NWA TV Champion Tully Blanchard vs. Tommy Angel & Ricky Nelson
Bobby Eaton & Stan Lane vs. Rocky King & David Isley
Manny Fernandez vs. the Italian Stallion
Jimmy & Ron Garvin vs. Cougar Jay & Thunderfoot #1 *Dark match*: NWA US Tag Team Champions Bobby Eaton & Stan Lane fought Ron & Jimmy Garvin to a double count-out
Dark match: Barry Windham & NWA Tag Team Champion Ricky Morton & Robert Gibson defeated NWA TV Champion Tully Blanchard, Arn Anderson, & Lex Luger
Also included Lazortron, NWA US Champion Nikita Koloff, Dusty Rhodes, Ivan Koloff, and Vladimir Petrov

JCP @ Albuquerque, NM - Tingley Coliseum - June 22, 1987
NWA World Champion Ric Flair vs. Barry Windham

CWF @ Tampa, FL - June 23, 1987
The Sheepherders defeated Mike Graham & Steve Keirn
Ed Gantner fought Kevin Sullivan to a no contest
Steve Williams defeated the Tahitian Prince
NWA Tag Team Champions Ricky Morton & Robert Gibson defeated Arn Anderson & Lex Luger via disqualification

JCP @ Beaumont, TX - Civic Center - June 24, 1987

JCP @ Macon, GA - Coliseum - June 25, 1987
NWA Tag Team Champions Ricky Morton & Robert Gibson defeated NWA US Tag Team Champions Bobby Eaton & Stan Lane

JCP @ Greenville, NC - June 26, 1987
Ron & Jimmy Garvin defeated NWA US Tag Team Champions Bobby Eaton & Stan Lane via disqualification

JCP @ Philadelphia, PA - Civic Center - June 27, 1987 (5,500)
Todd Champion pinned Thunderfoot #2
The Italian Stallion defeated Thunderfoot #1

Kendall Windham defeated Mark Fleming
Barry Windham pinned Ivan Koloff
NWA Tag Team Champions Ricky Morton & Robert Gibson defeated NWA US Tag Team Champions Bobby Eaton & Stan Lane in a Best 2 out of 3 falls match; fall #3: Morton & Gibson won via disqualification when Jim Cornette interfered with his tennis racquet; Jim Cornette sustained a knee injury which required arthroscopic surgery the following week
NWA US Champion Nikita Koloff fought Lex Luger to a double count-out
Dusty Rhodes defeated NWA TV Champion Tully Blanchard after using Magnum TA's cane as a weapon
NWA World Champion Ric Flair pinned Jimmy Garvin

JCP @ Fayetteville, NC - June 27, 1987 (6,300)
The Italian Stallion defeated Thunderfoot #1
The Barbarian defeated Todd Champion
Paul Ellering defeated Paul Jones
Lazertron defeated MOD Squad Basher
Jimmy Valiant defeated MOD Squad Spike
Bobby Eaton & Stan Lane defeated NWA Western States Heritage Champion Barry Windham & Kendall Windham
NWA Tag Team Champions Ricky Morton & Robert Gibson defeated Arn Anderson & NWA TV Champion Tully Blanchard
The Road Warriors defeated Ivan Koloff & Manny Fernandez in a double chain match
Ron Garvin defeated NWA World Champion Ric Flair via disqualification
NWA US Champion Nikita Koloff defeated Lex Luger via disqualification

JCP @ Rock Hill, SC - Winthrop Coliseum - June 28, 1987 (matinee) (600)
TV taping:
Jimmy Garvin defeated Thunderfoot #2
Barry Windham defeated Larry Stephens
NWA Tag Team Champions Ricky Morton & Robert Gibson defeated Gladiator #2 & Rick Sullivan
Ivan Koloff defeated Tommy Angel
NWA US Champion Nikita Koloff defeated Chance McQuade
Lex Luger defeated John Savage
Arn Anderson & NWA TV Champion Tully Blanchard defeated Ricky Nelson & Dexter Wescott
Lex Luger defeated Larry Stephens
Ivan Koloff defeated Ricky Nelson
Jimmy Garvin defeated Gladiator #2
NWA US Champion Nikita Koloff defeated Dexter Wescott
NWA US Champion Nikita Koloff fought Lex Luger to a draw
Pro - 7/11/87:
NWA Tag Team Champions Ricky Morton & Robert Gibson defeated NWA US Tag Team Champions Bobby Eaton & Stan Lane via disqualification when referee Teddy Long was knocked to the floor; after the bout, Lane hit the Alabama Jam on Gibson before Eaton & Lane left ringside with both title belts

JCP @ Wilmington, NC - June 28, 1987
NWA Tag Team Champions Ricky Morton & Robert Gibson vs. NWA US Tag Team Champions Bobby Eaton & Stan Lane

MID-ATLANTIC CHAMPIONSHIP WRESTLING

GREENVILLE MEMORIAL AUDITORIUM June 29, 1987 8:00 p.m.

WORLD TAG TEAM TITLE

Rock 'N Roll Express VS Tully Blanchard Arn Anderson (with J.J. Dillon) (with Dark Journey)

Barry Windham VS Lex Luger

U.S. Tag Team Title

Midnight Express (with Jim Cornette) VS Jimmy Valiant Lazer-Tron

Italian Stallion	VS	Barbarian
Nelson Royal	VS	Gladiator #1
Ric Nelson	VS	Gladiator #2
Denny Brown	VS	John Savage

NWA
*SUBJECT TO CHANGE

Ringside Reserved $12
General Admission $10
Children (Under 10) $4

Subject to change

MID-ATLANTIC CHAMPIONSHIP WRESTLING

JCP @ Greenville, SC - Memorial Auditorium - June 29, 1987
Denny Brown defeated David Diamond
Gladiator #2 defeated Ricky Nelson
Nelson Royal defeated Gladiator #1
The Italian Stallion defeated Brodie Chase
NWA US Tag Team Champions Bobby Eaton & Stan Lane defeated Jimmy Valiant & Lazertron
UWF Western States Heritage Champion Barry Windham defeated Lex Luger via disqualification
NWA Tag Team Champion Ricky Morton & Robert Gibson fought NWA TV Champion Tully Blanchard & Arn Anderson to a 60-minute time-limit draw

JCP @ Columbia, SC - June 30, 1987
NWA US Tag Team Champions Bobby Eaton & Stan Lane vs. Ron & Jimmy Garvin

JCP @ Lakeland, FL - Civic Center - July 1, 1987 (5,000+)
The start of the Great American Bash tour
The Cuban Connection defeated Bill & Randy Mulkey
Ron Simmons defeated the Tahitian Prince
Terry Gordy & Buddy Roberts defeated the MOD Squad
Florida Tag Team Champions Mike Graham & Steve Keirn defeated the Sheepherders via disqualification
NWA Southern Professional Wrestling - 7/12/87: Jimmy Garvin (w/ Precious) fought Arn Anderson to a 10-minute time-limit draw
NWA Southern Professional Wrestling - 7/12/87: NWA Tag Team Champions Ricky Morton & Robert Gibson defeated NWA US Tag Team Champions Bobby Eaton & Stan Lane via disqualification when the referee caught Lane coming off the top with a double axe handle to Morton as Eaton was covered; in commentary, Jim Cornette's absence was explained in that he sustained an injury in a prior altercation with Morton & Gibson
NWA US Champion Nikita Koloff defeated Lex Luger
Blackjack Mulligan, Bugsy McGraw, & Ed Gantner defeated Dory Funk Jr., Sir Oliver Humperdink, & the Black Assassin in a bunkhouse match
Florida Heavyweight Champion Mike Rotunda defeated the Barbarian
NWA Southern Professional Wrestling - 7/12/87: NWA TV Champion Tully Blanchard (w/ Dark Journey) fought UWF Western States Heritage Champion Barry Windham to a draw; only Blanchard's title was at stake in the match
Dusty Rhodes defeated NWA World Champion Ric Flair in a Best 2 out of 3 falls match; fall #1: Rhodes pinned Flair at 17:07; fall #2: Flair pinned Rhodes at the 10-minute mark; fall #3: Rhodes won via disqualification when NWA TV Champion Tully Blanchard interfered

JCP @ Landover, MD - Capital Centre - July 2, 1987 (15,000)

Debut at the venue - Gary Michael Cappetta was the ring announcer

Pro - 7/11/87 - featured Tony Schiavone conducting a ringside interview with Dick Murdoch & UWF TV Champion Eddie Gilbert regarding Murdoch's match later in the show against Steve Williams, during which Murdoch also cut a promo on Dusty Rhodes and Terry Gordy and said he would become the next UWF World Champion; included Schiavone conducting a ringside interview with Lex Luger & JJ Dillon regarding the July 25 card at the Philadelphia Civic Center in which Luger would be part of an in-ring segment of The Dating Game with three members of the audience, during which both said Luger would leave Philadelphia with the NWA US Title

Kendall Windham pinned Thunderfoot #1 at 3:28

Pro - 7/11/87: Rocky King pinned Thunderfoot #2 at 6:30 with a sunset flip

Pro - 7/11/87: Terry Gordy & Buddy Roberts (w/ Michael Hayes) defeated Paul Jones & Ivan Koloff at 9:14 when Gordy pinned Jones with an elbow drop

Pro - 7/11/87: Dick Murdoch (w/ UWF TV Champion Eddie Gilbert) defeated Steve Williams in a Texas Death Match at 10:51; both men were counted down by referee Dick Whorle followed by the announcement the first man to reach his feet would be the winner; Williams reached his feet first but Gilbert tripped him behind the referee's back; after the match, Williams cornered Gilbert before Murdoch pulled Gilbert from the ring

UWF World Champion Big Bubba defeated Barry Windham via count-out in a Louisville Streetfight at 7:15

Worldwide - 7/11/87: UWF TV Champion Eddie Gilbert pinned Mark Fleming at 3:27

NWA Tag Team Champions Ricky Morton & Robert Gibson defeated NWA US Tag Team Champions Bobby Eaton & Stan Lane via reverse decision; Eaton & Lane originally won the match and titles after Big Bubba interfered and hit a sidewalk slam on Morton but another referee came in and told the official what happened, with the call then being changed

Worldwide - 7/11/87: Dusty Rhodes, NWA US Champion Nikita Koloff, & the Road Warriors defeated NWA World Champion Ric Flair, Arn Anderson, Tully Blanchard, & Lex Luger in a steel cage match at the 18-minute mark when Rhodes pinned Anderson

JCP @ Richmond, VA - Coliseum - July 3, 1987 (8,500)

Misty Blue pinned Kat Laroux

The Italian Stallion pinned Mark Fleming

The Barbarian pinned Todd Champion; the Barbarian was cheered in the match

UWF TV Champion Eddie Gilbert pinned Kendall Windham by grabbing the tights for leverage

Michael Hayes, Terry Gordy, & Buddy Roberts defeated Ivan Koloff, Manny Fernandez, & Vladimir Pietrov when Gordy pinned Pietrov

Steve Williams pinned Dick Murdoch after hitting him with his arm cast; after the bout, UWF TV Champion Eddie Gilbert and Murdoch double teamed Williams until Terry Gordy made the save

Barry Windham defeated Big Bubba via count-out in a Louisville Streetfight

NWA Tag Team Champions Ricky Morton & Robert Gibson defeated NWA US Tag Team Champions Bobby Eaton & Stan Lane in a Best 2 out of 3 falls match; fall #1: Morton & Gibson won at the 30-second mark; fall #2: Eaton & Lane won after Big Bubba interfered; fall #3: Morton & Gibson won via disqualification after Bubba dropped Morton with the sidewalk slam

NWA US Champion Nikita Koloff pinned Arn Anderson

The Road Warriors defeated NWA World Champion Ric Flair & Lex Luger via disqualification when Flair hit Road Warrior Hawk with JJ Dillon's shoe

Dusty Rhodes defeated NWA TV Champion Tully Blanchard in a non-title I Quit steel cage match after taking JJ Dillon's shoe and grinding it into Blanchard's face

JCP @ Nassau, Bahamas - Stadium - July 3, 1987

Randy & Bill Mulkey vs. the Sheepherders

Bugsy McGraw vs. Johnny Ace

Mike Rotundo vs. the Tahitian Prince

Blackjack Mulligan & Kevin Sullivan vs. Dory Funk Jr. & Sir Oliver Humperdink

Worldwide - 7/4/87

Pro - 7/4/87

JCP @ Atlanta, GA - WTBS Studios - July 4, 1987 (matinee)

World Championship Wrestling - 7/4/87 - featured Tony Schiavone & David Crockett on commentary; included

Schiavone conducting an interview with Dusty Rhodes regarding his team facing the Four Horsemen later that night at the Omni in Wargames and facing NWA TV Champion Tully Blanchard at Charlotte Memorial Stadium for $100,000; featured Schiavone conducting an interview with Blanchard, with Dark Journey, regarding that night's Wargames; included comments from University of Oklahoma football coach Barry Switzer in which he told the fans not to miss the Great American Bash on tour; featured ads promoting Wargames at the Omni; included Schiavone conducting an interview with UWF Western States Heritage Champion Barry Windham regarding his title win and being in Rhodes corner for the upcoming show in Charlotte, during which Windham said Arn Anderson wanted a shot at his belt; featured an ad promoting the Crockett Cup 87 home video; included Schiavone conducting an interview with Paul Ellering regarding that night's Wargames; featured Schiavone conducting an interview with NWA World Champion Ric Flair regarding Ellering's comments and that night's Wargames; footage then aired of a recent match between Jimmy & Ron Garvin and Flair & Luger in which Precious was helped to safety backstage and Garvin knocked Flair out with the brainbuster; Flair then commented on his upcoming match against Jimmy in Greensboro with both his belt and a date with Precious on the line, during which Flair said he can be beat but noted he's only been beat three times in five years; included footage of Steve Williams in training at the University of Oklahoma for his match against UWF World Champion Big Bubba July 11 in Oklahoma City; Switzer was shown working with Williams during the segment and the segment ended with comments from Jim Ross on the college campus; featured Schiavone conducting an interview with Ron Simmons regarding his football history with Williams and said he would give Williams all the help he could; included a music video of the Fabulous Freebirds to the tune of "The Boys are Back in Town;" featured Schiavone conducting an interview with Lex Luger & JJ Dillon regarding them hosting "The Dating Game" July 25 in Philadelphia with the winner getting a date with Luger and Luger's challenge of NWA US Champion Nikita Koloff:

Ron Simmons pinned Larry Stephens at around the 2-minute mark with a shoulderblock; Tony Schiavone provided sole commentary for the match

Lex Luger (w/ JJ Dillon) defeated David Isley via submission with the Torture Rack at 5:24; during the bout, David Crockett joined Schiavone on commentary and said he just came from the Omni as final preparations were being made for that night's Great American Bash card

NWA Tag Team Champions Ricky Morton & Robert Gibson defeated David Diamond & Terry Jones at 1:59 when both men scored the pin following the double dropkick; during the bout, it was noted Jim Cornette was sidelined with an injury

Arn Anderson pinned David Wescott with the gordbuster at 4:25

UWF Western States Heritage Champion Barry Windham pinned El Negro with the lariat at 2:38

NWA Florida Heavyweight Champion Mike Rotundo fought Dory Funk Jr. to a time-limit draw at 14:10; the match ended as Rotundo had Funk in the airplane spin; after the contest, the

Black Assassin attacked the champion and double teamed him with Funk until several enhancement workers cleared the ring

JJ Dillon (w/ NWA World Champion Ric Flair, Arn Anderson, NWA TV Champion Tully Blanchard, Arn Anderson, Lex Luger, & Dark Journey) pinned Alan Martin at 3:58 with the figure-4 after hitting the slingshot suplex, gordbuster, and briefly applying the Torture Rack; prior to the bout, Crockett conducted a ringside interview with Dark Journey regarding the match in which she said it was a warm up for Wargames later that night; after the contest, Schiavone conducted an interview with Anderson regarding Wargames and his challenging UWF Western States Heritage Champion Barry Windham

Paul Ellering (w/ Dusty Rhodes) pinned Cougar Jay with a clothesline at the 39-second mark

Ivan Koloff (w/ Paul Jones) pinned Hal Moore at 1:27 with a clothesline off the top; prior to the bout, Schiavone conducted an interview with Jones in which he said he would regroup and his men Manny Fernandez, the Barbarian, Koloff, and Vladimir Petrov would win at the Great American Bash; moments later, Koloff appeared and said he was looking forward to doing battle at the Bash

The Black Assassin (w/ Dory Funk Jr.) pinned Darrel Dalton at 2:19 with a flying clothesline; after the bout, Schiavone conducted an interview with Funk regarding his match earlier in the show and the Black Assassin's interference afterwards, during which he said he would be facing Blackjack Mulligan and Kevin Sullivan during the Great American Bash and aimed to take the Florida title

NWA TV Champion Tully Blanchard vs. Trent Knight

JCP @ Atlanta, GA - Omni - July 4, 1987 (13,500)
Opened with a Michael Hayes concert; featured a David Allen Coe concert

Kendall Windham pinned Gladiator #1 (Gary Royal) with a bulldog at 4:59

Sting pinned Thunderfoot #1 (Joel Deaton) with a flying fist drop at 5:40

Jimmy Valiant pinned Basher of the MOD Squad with a roll up at 5:10

UWF Western States Heritage Champion Barry Windham pinned Rick Steiner in a non-title match at 5:00 with a cradle as Steiner attempted a powerslam from the apron into the ring (Great American Bash 87)

Jimmy & Ron Garvin defeated Vladimir Petrov & Konga the Barbarian at 6:00 when Ron pinned the Barbarian

UWF Tag Team Champions Brad Armstrong & Tim Horner defeated UWF World Champion Big Bubba & the Angel of Death at 6:00 when Horner pinned Angel

Chris Adams defeated Black Bart via reverse decision at 4:35; Bart originally won via pinfall after using his branding iron but Sting came out and told the referee what happened

Michael Hayes, Terry Gordy, & Buddy Roberts defeated Paul Jones, Ivan Koloff, & Manny Fernandez at 3:58 when Gordy pinned Jones with an elbow drop (Great American Bash 87)

NWA Tag Team Champions Ricky Morton & Robert Gibson defeated NWA US Tag Team Champions Bobby Eaton & Stan Lane (w/ Jim Cornette & Big Bubba) via disqualification in a title vs. title match after referee Tommy Young found Bubba's hat and sunglasses in the ring after Bubba interfered behind his back and dropped Morton with a sidewalk slam (*Great American Bash 87*)

Steve Williams (w/ Magnum TA) defeated Dick Murdoch (w/ Eddie Gilbert) in a Texas Death Match at 8:00 when Murdoch failed to get to his feet after Williams hit Murdoch with the cast on his left arm as Murdoch came off the top rope; after the bout, Williams hit Gilbert with the cast but was assaulted from behind by Murdoch wielding a steel chair; Magnum then gave Williams his cane, with Williams hitting Murdoch with the weapon and clearing him from the ring (*Great American Bash 87*)

Dusty Rhodes, NWA US Champion Nikita Koloff, the Road Warriors, & Paul Ellering defeated NWA World Champion Ric Flair, Arn Anderson, Tully Blanchard, Lex Luger, & JJ Dillon in Wargames at 21:20 when Dillon submitted as Road Warrior Hawk stood on his throat (the first Wargames match) (*Great American Bash 87*, *WarGames: WCW's Most Notorious Matches*)

MID-ATLANTIC CHAMPIONSHIP WRESTLING

NWA

GREENVILLE MEMORIAL AUDITORIUM
Sunday, July 5, 1987
2:00 p.m.

"BIG INDEPENDENCE WEEK-END SPECIAL"

SPECIAL CHALLENGE MATCH

ROAD WARRIORS (WITH PAUL ELLERING) VS TULLY BLANCHARD ARN ANDERSON (WITH DARK JOURNEY)

WORLD TAG TEAM TITLE

ROCK 'N ROLL EXPRESS VS IVAN KOLOFF (WITH PAUL JONES) RAGIN' BULL

U.S. HEAVYWEIGHT TITLE
2 OUT OF 3 FALLS
Nikita Koloff VS LEX LUGER (WITH J.J. DILLON)

JIMMY VALIANT VS MOD SQUAD #1

LASOR-TRON VS MOD SQUAD #2

NELSON ROYAL VS GLADIATOR #1

ROCKY KING VS JOHN SAVAGE

NWA

Ringside Reserved $15
General Admission $12
Children (Under 10) $5

*Subject to change

MID-ATLANTIC CHAMPIONSHIP WRESTLING

JCP @ Greenville, SC - Memorial Auditorium - July 5, 1987 (matinee)
Rocky King defeated John Savage
Nelson Royal defeated Clark (sub. for Gladiator #1)
Lazortron defeated MOD Squad #2
Jimmy Valiant defeated MOD Squad #1
NWA US Champion Nikita Koloff defeated Lex Luger in a Best 2 out of 3 falls match
NWA Tag Team Champions Ricky Morton & Robert Gibson defeated Manny Fernandez & Ivan Koloff
The Road Warriors defeated Arn Anderson & NWA TV Champion Tully Blanchard

JCP @ Charleston, WV - July 5, 1987
The Italian Stallion defeated Gladiator #2
Kendall Windham defeated Thunderfoot #1
Misty Blue defeated Kat Leroux
The Barbarian defeated Todd Champion
Mike Rotundo fought Dory Funk Jr. to a draw
Jimmy Garvin defeated Ivan Koloff
Ron Garvin defeated Manny Fernandez via disqualification
Barry Windham defeated Vladimir Petrov
The Road Warriors defeated NWA US Tag Team Champions Bobby Eaton & Stan Lane
NWA World Champion Ric Flair defeated Dusty Rhodes via disqualification
NWA US Champion Nikita Koloff, NWA Tag Team Champions Ricky Morton & Robert Gibson defeated NWA TV Champion Tully Blanchard, Arn Anderson, & Lex Luger in a steel cage match

JCP @ Inglewood, CA - Great Western Forum - July 6, 1987
Misty Blue defeated Kat Leroux
Mike Rotunda fought Dory Funk Jr. to a draw
Chris Adams defeated Black Bart via disqualification
Barry Windham defeated UWF Heavyweight Champion Big Bubba (w/ Skandar Akbar) in a streetfight
Jimmy & Ron Garvin defeated Ivan Koloff & Manny Fernandez
NWA Tag Team Champions Ricky Morton & Robert Gibson defeated NWA US Tag Team Champions Bobby Eaton & Stan Lane via disqualification when UWF Heavyweight Champion Big Bubba hit the sidewalk slam on Morton
Steve Williams defeated Dick Murdoch
Dusty Rhodes pinned NWA TV Champion Tully Blanchard in a non-title steel cage match with an elbow off the top to a standing Blanchard; after the match, NWA World Champion Ric Flair, Lex Luger, & Arn Anderson ran out and attacked Rhodes in the cage, with NWA US Champion Nikita Koloff & the Road Warriors then making the save
NWA US Champion Nikita Koloff & the Road Warriors defeated NWA World Champion Ric Flair, Lex Luger, & Arn Anderson in a steel cage match when Road Warrior Animal pinned Anderson with a clothesline as Anderson came off the middle turnbuckle; the cage was too small for wrestlers to stand on the apron, so they stood in the corner within the ring while waiting for the tag

JCP @ San Francisco, CA - Civic Auditorium - July 7, 1987
Misty Blue defeated Kat Leroux
Big Bubba defeated Chris Adams
Barry Windham defeated Black Bart
Mike Rotunda fought Dory Funk Jr.
Jimmy & Ron Garvin defeated Ivan Koloff & Manny Fernandez
Dick Murdoch defeated Steve Williams
NWA US Champion Nikita Koloff defeated Arn Anderson
The Road Warriors defeated NWA US Tag Team Champions Bobby Eaton & Stan Lane
NWA Tag Team Champions Ricky Morton & Robert Gibson defeated NWA World Champion Ric Flair & Lex Luger
Dusty Rhodes defeated NWA TV Champion Tully Blanchard in a non-title steel cage match

JCP @ Atlanta, GA - WTBS Studios - July 8, 1987
TV taping

JCP @ Cincinnati, OH - Cincinnati Gardnes - July 9, 1987
Lazortron & Kendall Windham defeated Ivan Koloff & Paul Jones
Misty Blue defeated Kat Leroux
Jimmy Valiant defeated MOD Squad Basher
Ron Garvin defeated MOD Squad Spike
Michael Hayes & Buddy Roberts defeated Big Bubba & the Angel of Death
Jimmy Garvin defeated Manny Fernandez via disqualification
NWA Tag Team Champions Ricky Morton & Robert Gibson defeated NWA US Tag Team Champions Bobby Eaton & Stan Lane via disqualification
UWF Western States Heritage Champion Barry Windham defeated the Barbarian
Steve Williams & Terry Gordy defeated Dick Murdoch & Eddie Gilbert
Dusty Rhodes, NWA US Champion Nikita Koloff, & the Road Warriors defeated NWA World Champion Ric Flair, NWA TV Champion Tully Blanchard, Arn Anderson, & Lex Luger in a steel cage match

JCP @ Pittsburgh, PA - Civic Arena - July 10, 1987
Misty Blue defeated Kat Leroux
Sting & Chris Adams defeated the Barbarian & Thunderfoot #1
Black Bart defeated the Italian Stallion
Buddy Roberts defeated Jerry Jackson
Brad Armstrong & Tim Horner defeated Rick Steiner & Eddie Gilbert
Jimmy Garvin defeated Big Bubba via disqualification
Michael Hayes & Terry Gordy defeated the MOD Squad
Steve Williams defeated Dick Murdoch
Barry Windham & Ron Garvin defeated NWA US Tag Team Champions Bobby Eaton & Stan Lane via disqualification
Dusty Rhodes, NWA US Champion Nikita Koloff, & the Road Warriors defeated NWA World Champion Ric Flair, NWA TV Champion Tully Blanchard, Arn Anderson, & Lex Luger

Worldwide - 7/11/87 - featured the Eddie Gilbert vs. Mark Fleming, NWA Tag Team Champions Ricky Morton & Robert Gibson vs. NWA US Tag Team Champions Bobby Eaton & Stan Lane, and Dusty Rhodes, NWA US Champion Nikita Koloff, & the Road Warriors vs. NWA World Champion Ric Flair, Lex Luger, NWA TV Champion Tully Blanchard, & Arn Anderson matches taped 7/2/87 at the Capital Centre

Pro - 7/11/87 - included Tony Schiavone & Bob Caudle on commentary; featured Schiavone conducting a ringside interview with Dick Murdoch & UWF TV Champion Eddie Gilbert regarding Murdoch's match later in the show against Steve Williams, during which Murdoch also cut a promo on Dusty Rhodes and Terry Gordy and said he would become the next UWF World Champion; included Schiavone conducting a ringside interview with Lex Luger & JJ Dillon regarding the July 25 card at the Philadelphia Civic Center in which Luger would be part of an in-ring segment of The Dating Game with three members of the audience, during which both said Luger would leave Philadelphia with the NWA US Title; featured comments from University of Oklahoma football coach Barry Switzer in which he told fans not to miss the Great American Bash on tour; included footage from the 6/28/87 match in Rock Hill, SC between NWA Tag Team Champions Ricky Morton & Robert Gibson vs. NWA US Tag Team Champions Bobby Eaton & Stan Lane; featured the Rocky King vs. Thunderfoot #2, Gordy & Buddy Roberts vs. Paul Jones & Ivan Koloff, and Murdoch vs. Williams matches taped 7/2/87 at the Capital Centre

World Championship Wrestling - 7/11/87 - featured an opening segment showing the team introductions from Wargames, held 7/4/87 at the Atlanta Omni, after which it was noted both JJ Dillon and NWA US Champion Nikita Koloff both suffered injuries in the match; moments later, Tony Schiavone & David Crockett spoke with Jim Crockett Jr., with Jim saying Wargames II would be held July 31 at the Orange Bowl and that Dillon would have a personal substitute for the bout; included Schiavone conducting an interview with Dillon, his arm in a sling, alongside NWA World Champion Ric Flair, NWA TV Champion Tully Blanchard, with Dark Journey, Lex Luger, and Arn Anderson in which they discussed Wargames and the pending rematch, during which Dillon showed footage of the Road Warriors hitting a modified Doomsday Device on him during Wargames; moments later, Dillon introduced footage of him alongside a masked man, described at 6'9 and 440lbs. and named the War Machine who would replace him in Wargames II; after the footage was shown, Flair cut a promo saying he would have Precious later that night in Greensboro, Blanchard would beat Dusty Rhodes in Charlotte, and Flair and Luger soon facing the Road Warriors in singles matches; featured Schiavone conducting an interview with Jimmy Garvin, Precious, & Ron Garvin regarding Jimmy's match that night against Flair in Greensboro, with a night with Precious on the line against Flair's title; included Schiavone conducting an interview with Bugsy McGraw, during which he discussed his upcoming tour stops; featured Schiavone conducting an interview with Rhodes regarding facing the Horsemen during

the Bash tour and the injury to Nikita, during which he showed footage of Nikita sustaining a spike piledriver from Flair & Blanchard in Wargames; moments later, Rhodes brought out Nikita, with Nikita throwing off his T-shirt, discussing his neckbrace, and cutting a promo on the Horsemen:
NWA Tag Team Champions Ricky Morton & Robert Gibson defeated Gary Phelps & Eric Long at 3:28 when Morton scored the pin with a backslide; after the bout, David Crockett conducted a ringside interview with Morton & Gibson, during which they spoke about their rivalry with Jim Cornette, NWA US Tag Team Champions Bobby Eaton & Stan Lane and their reaction to the debut of Wargames
Steve Williams pinned Alan Martin with the Oklahoma Stampede at 2:33; during the bout, it was noted Williams would challenge UWF Heavyweight Champion Big Bubba that night in Oklahoma City, OK and that Williams would have the cast on his left hand removed for the match; following the commercial break, Tony Schiavone conducted an interview with Williams regarding his upcoming title shot; moments later, Ron Simmons appeared and wished Williams the best going into his match with Bubba
Bugsy McGraw pinned Dexter Wescott with a splash at 2:58
UWF Western States Heritage Champion Barry Windham pinned Clement Fields with the lariat at 1:34
Michael Hayes, Buddy Roberts, & Terry Gordy defeated David Isley, Cougar Jay, & Larry Stephens at 4:47 when Roberts pinned Jay with a crossbody off the top; after the bout, Tony Schiavone conducted an interview with the Fabulous Freebirds, during which they discussed the Great American Bash tour and Hayes said he wanted the NWA World Title
Ron Simmons pinned Tommy Angel with a tackle at 4:00
NWA US Tag Team Champions Bobby Eaton & Stan Lane (w/ Jim Cornette) defeated Mike Jackson & Terry Jones at 4:22 when Jones submitted to a Scorpion Deathlock from Lane; prior to the bout, Cornette came out on crutches, introduced his team, and then joined the commentary team; following the commercial break, Tony Schiavone conducted an interview with Cornette, Eaton & Lane, with Cornette saying he would get payback on NWA Tag Team Champions Ricky Morton & Robert Gibson for forcing him to use crutches
NWA US Women's Champion Misty Blue Simmes vs. Kat Leroux; the match went 4 minutes before the broadcast ended without a winner

UWF @ Oklahoma City, OK - Myriad - July 11, 1987
Brad Armstrong & Tim Horner defeated Gary Young & the Terminator
Dave Haskins & Shane Douglas defeated the Enforcer & Bob Bradley
Steve Cox won a pole battle royal
Terry Gordy defeated Black Bart in a taped fist match
The Road Warriors defeated NWA US Tag Team Champions Bobby Eaton & Stan Lane in a non-title match
Dusty Rhodes, Sting, & Chris Adams defeated Eddie Gilbert, Rick Steiner, & the Angel of Death in a bunkhouse match
UWF TV - 7/11/87: UWF Western States Heritage Champion Barry Windham fought Dick Murdoch (w/ Eddie Gilbert) to a time-limit draw at around the 29:41 mark; Jim Ross & Terry

Taylor provided commentary for the match; the bout ended just after Murdoch dropped Windham with the brainbuster Steve Williams pinned UWF Heavyweight Champion Big Bubba to win the title

NWA Southern Professional Wrestling - 7/12/87 - hosted by Sir Oliver Humperdink & JJ Dillon; included comments from Blackjack Mulligan & Kevin Sullivan on facing Dory Funk Jr. & Humperdink the following day in Orlando, with Mulligan warning Sullivan not to double cross him and Sullivan stating they could be teammates without being friends; moments later, UWF Western States Heritage Champion Barry Windham stormed in and objected to his father teaming with Sullivan; featured two live event promos for the Great American Bash tour, featuring NWA World Champion Ric Flair and Dusty Rhodes, respectively; included comments from Bugsy McGraw, who urged fans to celebrate their freedom at the Bash tour events; featured the Jimmy Garvin vs. Arn Anderson, NWA Tag Team Champions Ricky Morton & Robert Gibson vs. NWA US Tag Team Champions Stan Lane & Bobby Eaton, and NWA TV Champion Tully Blanchard vs. Windham matches taped 7/1/87 in Lakeland, FL

NWA Super Bouts - 7/87 - featured the Barry Windham vs. UWF Heavyweight Champion Big Bubba and Michael Hayes & Terry Gordy vs. Sting & Eddie Gilbert matches taped 6/6/87 at the Greensboro Coliseum

JCP @ Greensboro, NC - Coliseum - July 11, 1987
Kendall Windham defeated Thunderfoot #1
Nelson Royal defeated Thunderfoot #2
The MOD Squad defeated Jimmy Valiant & Lazertron in a bunkhouse match at 6:16 when Basher pinned Lazertron after Spike hit Lazertron with brass knuckles behind the referee's back as Basher was caught in an abdominal stretch
Worldwide - 7/18/87: Michael Hayes & Buddy Roberts fought Manny Fernandez & Ivan Koloff (w/ Paul Jones) to a time-limit draw at around the 13-minute mark; Fernandez kicked out of a sunset flip from Hayes just before the bell rang
Ole Anderson defeated the Barbarian
Arn Anderson & NWA TV Champion Tully Blanchard defeated NWA Tag Team Champions Ricky Morton & Robert Gibson via disqualification
Worldwide - 7/18/87; NWA Super Bouts - 12/87: NWA World Champion Ric Flair pinned Jimmy Garvin (w/ Precious) in a steel cage match with the figure-4 and holding the ring ropes for added leverage at around the 14-minute mark; stipulations stated Flair would win a date with Precious if he won; mid-way through the bout, Ron Garvin appeared ringside to offer moral support to the challenger; after the match, Precious climbed in the ring to tend to Jimmy but was grabbed by Flair, with Ron then assaulting Flair until he left the cage (Great American Bash 87)
Worldwide - 7/18/87: Lex Luger (w/ JJ Dillon) defeated NWA US Champion Nikita Koloff in a steel cage match via KO with the Torture Rack after hitting him in the back with a steel chair

thrown in the ring by Dillon while referee Earl Hebner was knocked out; Koloff came into the ring wearing a neckbrace but Luger took it off mid-way through the match; after the bout, NWA TV Champion Tully Blanchard & Arn Anderson celebrated in the ring with Luger and Dillon (*Great American Bash 87*)

CWF @ Orlando, FL - July 12, 1987 (4,000)
Lazertron defeated Jerry Gray
The Sheepherders defeated Mike Graham & Steve Keirn
NWA Tag Team Champions Ricky Morton & Robert Gibson defeated the Cuban Connection
Kevin Sullivan defeated the Tahitian Prince
Florida Heavyweight Champion Mike Rotundo defeated Ivan Koloff
Blackjack Mulligan & Kevin Sullivan defeated Dory Funk Jr. & Sir Oliver Humperdink

JCP @ Asheville, NC - Civic Center - July 12, 1987

JCP @ Baltimore, MD - Arena - July 12, 1987 (13,500)
Misty Blue defeated Kat Leroux
Terry Gordy defeated Thunderfoot #1
Rick Steiner defeated Sting
Jimmy Garvin defeated Manny Fernandez via disqualification
NWA US Tag Team Champions Bobby Eaton & Stan Lane defeated Michael Hayes & Buddy Roberts
Barry Windham defeated Big Bubba
Ron Garvin defeated NWA US Tag Team Champion Bobby Eaton (sub. for an injured Jim Cornette); Cornette came out to the ring on crutches before the bout
Steve Williams defeated Dick Murdoch
Nikita Koloff & the Road Warriors defeated NWA World Champion Ric Flair, NWA US Champion Lex Luger, & Arn Anderson in an elimination match
Dusty Rhodes defeated NWA TV Champion Tully Blanchard in a non-title barbed wire match

JCP @ Salisbury, MD - July 13, 1987
Misty Blue defeated Kat Leroux
Terry Gordy defeated Thunderfoot #2
Eddie Gilbert defeated Mark Fleming
Michael Hayes & Buddy Roberts defeated the MOD Squad
Sting defeated Rick Steiner
UWF Western States Heritage Champion Barry Windham defeated Big Bubba
UWF World Champion Steve Williams defeated Dick Murdoch

JCP @ West Palm Beach, FL - Auditorium - July 13, 1987
Jimmy Valiant defeated Ricky Santana
David Sierra defeated Bill Mulkey
Ron Simmons & Scott Hall defeated Bill Tabb & Incubus
The Sheepherders defeated Ed Gantner & Steve Keirn
Florida Heavyweight Champion Mike Rotunda defeated Ivan Koloff

Ron & Jimmy Garvin defeated NWA TV Champion Tully Blanchard & Arn Anderson
NWA US Champion Lex Luger fought Nikita Koloff to a double disqualification
NWA World Champion Ric Flair defeated Dusty Rhodes via disqualification
Blackjack Mulligan & Bugsy McGraw defeated Dory Funk Jr. & Sir Oliver Humperdink

JCP @ Baton Rouge, LA - Centroplex - July 14, 1987
Dave Haskins & Shane Douglas fought the Enforcer (Doug Gilbert) & Gary Young to a draw
Angel of Death defeated Buddy Roberts
Shaska Whatley defeated Steve Cox
Michael Hayes defeated the Terminator
Brad Armstrong & Tim Horner defeated Ivan Koloff & Paul Jones
Chris Adams & Sting defeated Rick Steiner & Black Bart
UWF Western States Heritage Champion Barry Windham defeated Big Bubba via disqualification
Brad Armstrong (sub. for NWA Tag Team Champion Ricky Morton) & NWA Tag Team Champion Robert Gibson defeated NWA US Tag Team Champions Bobby Eaton & Stan Lane via disqualification
Steve Williams & Terry Gordy defeated UWF TV Champion Eddie Gilbert & Dick Murdoch in a bunkhouse match

JCP @ Gaffney, SC - Timken Gym - July 14, 1987
George South defeated Gladiator #1
The Italian Stallion defeated Thunderfoot #2
Rocky King defeated Thunderfoot #1
NWA Jr. Heavyweight Champion Lazertron fought Nelson Royal to a draw
The MOD Squad defeated Kendall Windham & Todd Champion
Jimmy Valiant defeated Arn Anderson via disqualification
Ron & Jimmy Garvin defeated Manny Fernandez & the Barbarian

JCP @ Key West, FL - July 14, 1987

JCP @ Little Rock, AR - Barton Coliseum - July 15, 1987
UWF Western States Heritage Champion Barry Windham (sub. for NWA Tag Team Champion Ricky Morton) & NWA Tag Team Champion Robert Gibson defeated NWA US Tag Team Champions Bobby Eaton & Stan Lane via disqualification

JCP @ Johnson City, TN - Freedom Hall - July 16, 1987
Ron & Jimmy Garvin defeated NWA US Tag Team Champions Bobby Eaton & Stan Lane via disqualification

JCP @ Tallahassee, FL - July 17, 1987

JCP @ Norfolk, VA - Scope - July 17, 1987
Mark Fleming defeated Gladiator #1
Nelson Royal defeated Thunderfoot #2
Lazertron defeated Thunderfoot #1
The MOD Squad defeated the Italian Stallion & Todd Champion
Manny Fernandez defeated Rocky King
The Barbarian defeated Kendall Windham
Paul Ellering defeated Paul Jones in a bunkhouse match
Robert Gibson defeated Sean Royal
Ron & Jimmy Garvin defeated NWA US Tag Team Champions Bobby Eaton & Stan Lane via disqualification
Dusty Rhodes, Nikita Koloff, & the Road Warriors defeated NWA World Champion Ric Flair, NWA US Champion Lex Luger, NWA TV Champion Tully Blanchard, & Arn Anderson in a steel cage match

Worldwide - 7/18/87 - featured the Michael Hayes & Buddy Roberts vs. Ivan Koloff & Manny Fernandez, NWA US Champion Nikita Koloff vs. Lex Luger, and NWA World Champion Ric Flair vs. Jimmy Garvin matches taped 7/11/87 in Greensboro

Pro - 7/18/87:
Sean Royal vs. Todd Champion
Nelson Royal vs. Colt Steele
Barry Windham vs. NWA TV Champion Tully Blanchard

World Championship Wrestling - 7/18/85 - featured the announcement that Steve Williams had beaten Big Bubba for the UWF Heavyweight Title and Lex Luger had defeated Nikita Koloff for the NWA US Title:
Ron Simmons vs. Gladiator #1
The MOD Squad vs. Martin & Long
Jimmy Valiant vs. Gladiator #2
Kendall Windham vs. Thunderfoot #2
Todd Champion & the Italian Stallion vs. Force & David Isley
NWA US Champion Lex Luger vs. Rocky King
Ron Garvin vs. El Negro

JCP @ Sarasota, FL - July 18, 1987

JCP @ Charlotte, NC - Memorial Stadium - July 18, 1987 (25,000)
Pro - 7/25/87: Vladimir Petrov (w/ Paul Jones) pinned Todd Champion with the Russian Sickle at 2:11
Pro - 7/25/87: Jimmy Valiant, Kendall Windham, & Lazertron defeated Sean Royal, Gladiators #1 & #2 when Windham pinned a Gladiator with a crossbody
Chris Adams defeated Black Bart
Pro - 7/25/87: UWF Western States Heritage Champion Barry Windham pinned Big Bubba (w/ Skandar Akbar) with a crossbody off the top at around the 6-minute mark; after the bout, Bob Caudle conducted a ringside interview with Windham regarding his recent title win and defending against

the likes of Bubba, Dick Murdoch, and the Four Horsemen
Worldwide - 7/25/87: UWF World Champion Steve Williams & Terry Gordy defeated UWF TV Champion Eddie Gilbert & Dick Murdoch in a bunkhouse match
Pro - 7/25/87: NWA US Tag Team Champions Bobby Eaton & Stan Lane (w/ Jim Cornette) defeated Michael Hayes & Buddy Roberts when Lane pinned Roberts after hitting him with Cornette's tennis racquet behind the referee's back; Cornette briefly joined the commentary team for the match; after the contest, Terry Gordy came out to dispute the call and then cleared the champions and Cornette from ringside; the commentary team of Bob Caudle & Johnny Weaver said the decision was overturned after Gordy told the referee what happened but the ring announcer did not indicate that; moments later, Caudle & Weaver conducted a ringside interview with Hayes regarding the match
Worldwide - 7/25/87: NWA Tag Team Champions Ricky Morton & Robert Gibson defeated the MOD Squad
Road Warrior Animal defeated Arn Anderson
NWA US Champion Lex Luger defeated Nikita Koloff
Worldwide - 7/25/87: NWA World Champion Ric Flair defeated Road Warrior Hawk via disqualification
Dusty Rhodes (w/ UWF Western States Heritage Champion Barry Windham) defeated NWA TV Champion Tully Blanchard (w/ JJ Dillon & Dark Journey) in a non-title $100,000 barbed wire ladder match at 7:14 after hitting Blanchard with his own loaded glove as Windham prevented Dillon from interfering (*Great American Bash 87*)

JCP @ Roanoke, VA - Civic Center - July 19, 1987 (matinee)
The Italian Stallion defeated Gene Ligon
The Barbarian defeated Kendall Windham
Jimmy Valiant & Lazortron defeated Sean Royal & Thunderfoot #2
Jimmy Garvin defeated Manny Fernandez via disqualification
Ron Garvin defeated Ivan Koloff in a chain match
NWA Tag Team Champions Ricky Morton & Robert Gibson defeated NWA US Tag Team Champions Bobby Eaton & Stan Lane via disqualification
Sean Royal defeated Rocky King
The Barbarian defeated the Italian Stallion
UWF Western States Heritage Champion Barry Windham defeated Thunderfoot #2
Mike Rotunda fought Dory Funk Jr. to a draw
Dusty Rhodes, Nikita Koloff, & the Road Warriors defeated NWA World Champion Ric Flair, NWA US Champion Lex Luger, NWA TV Champion Tully Blanchard, & Arn Anderson in a steel cage match

JCP @ Chicago, IL - UIC Pavilion - July 19, 1987 (10,000; sell out)
Ivan Koloff defeated Todd Champion
Sting defeated Rick Steiner
Michael Hayes & Buddy Roberts defeated the MOD Squad
Black Bart defeated Chris Adams
Brad Armstrong & Tim Horner defeated Big Bubba & the Angel

of Death
Steve Williams & Terry Gordy defeated Dick Murdoch & Eddie Gilbert
NWA US Champion Lex Luger fought Road Warrior Hawk to a no contest
Nikita Koloff defeated Arn Anderson
NWA Tag Team Champions Ricky Morton & Robert Gibson defeated NWA US Tag Team Champions Bobby Eaton & Stan Lane via disqualification

JCP @ Greenville, SC - Memorial Auditorium - July 20, 1987
Sean Royal defeated Rocky King
The Barbarian defeated Kendall Windham
Ivan Koloff defeated Todd Champion
Ron & Jimmy Garvin defeated Thunderfoot #1 & #2
Jimmy Valiant & Lazertron defeated the MOD Squad
UWF Western States Heritage Champion Barry Windham defeated Manny Fernandez
NWA Tag Team Champions Ricky Morton & Robert Gibson defeated NWA US Tag Team Champions Bobby Eaton & Stan Lane via disqualification
Paul Ellering defeated Paul Jones in a bunkhouse match
Dusty Rhodes (w/ Magnum TA) defeated NWA TV Champion Tully Blanchard
Nikita Koloff & the Road Warriors defeated NWA World Champion Ric Flair, NWA US Champion Lex Luger, & Arn Anderson in a steel cage match

JCP @ Atlanta, GA - WTBS Studios - July 22, 1987 (matinee)
TV taping

JCP @ Columbus, GA - July 22, 1987
NWA Tag Team Champions Ricky Morton & Robert Gibson defeated NWA US Tag Team Champions Bobby Eaton & Stan Lane via disqualification

JCP @ Dallas, TX - Reunion Arena - July 23, 1987
UWF Tag Team Champions Brad Armstrong & Tim Horner defeated NWA US Tag Team Champions Bobby Eaton & Stan Lane via disqualification

JCP @ Harrisonburg, VA - High School Gym - July 23, 1987
Denny Brown vs. Gladiator #2
The Italian Stallion vs. Gladiator #1
Todd Champion vs. the Barbarian
Kendall Windham vs. Vladimir Petrov
Jimmy Valiant & Lazer Tron vs. Thunderfoot #1 & #2
Ron Garvin vs. Ivan Koloff
NWA Tag Team Champions Ricky Morton & Robert Gibson vs. Chris Champion & Sean Royal

UWF @ Houston, TX - Summit - July 24, 1987
Shane Douglas vs. the Enforcer
Buddy Roberts vs. the Terminator
Steve Cox vs. the Angel of Death
Sting vs. Rick Steiner
UWF Tag Team Champions Brad Armstrong & Tim Horner vs. NWA US Champion Lex Luger & Arn Anderson
UWF Western States Heritage Champion Barry Windham vs. NWA TV Champion Tully Blanchard (only the UWF title was at stake)
Chris Adams vs. UWF TV Champion Eddie Gilbert

NWA Tag Team Champions Ricky Morton & Robert Gibson, Michael Hayes & Terry Gordy fought NWA US Tag Team Champions Bobby Eaton & Stan Lane, Big Bubba, & Black Bart to a double count-out; both Jim Cornette & Skandar Akbar were suspended in a cage above the ring for the bout
NWA World Champion Ric Flair vs. Dusty Rhodes
Steve Williams vs. Dick Murdoch (barbed wire match)

JCP @ St. Petersburg, FL - July 24, 1987

Worldwide - 7/25/87

Pro - 7/25/87 - included Johnny Weaver & Bob Caudle on commentary; featured Caudle conducting a backstage interview with Nikita Koloff regarding the recovery of his neck injury and loss of the NWA US Title; Caudle and Koloff then reviewed footage from the cage match loss to Lex Luger on 7/11/87 in Greensboro; included Dusty Rhodes cutting a backstage promo on Luger regarding his title win, during which Rhodes challenged Luger to a title match; featured the Jimmy Valiant, Kendall Windham, & Lazortron vs. Sean Royal, Gladiator #1, & Gladiator #2, Vladimir Petrov vs. Todd Champion, UWF Western States Heritage Champion Barry Windham vs. Big Bubba, and NWA US Tag Team Champions Bobby Eaton & Stan Lane vs. Michael Hayes & Buddy Roberts matches taped 7/18/87 in Charlotte

World Championship Wrestling - 7/25/87 - featured footage of Ron Garvin interrupting Precious' date with NWA World Champion Ric Flair:
Arn Anderson & NWA TV Champion Tully Blanchard vs. Tommy Angel & Stevens
Barry Windham vs. Alan Martin
NWA US Tag Team Champions Bobby Eaton & Stan Lane vs. Mike Jackson & Jay
NWA Tag Team Champions Ricky Morton & Robert Gibson vs. Keith Steinborn & Jones
Ron Garvin vs. Art Pritts

NWA Super Bouts - ?/87 - hosted by Tony Schiavone & JJ Dillon:
UWF Western States Heritage Champion Barry Windham fought NWA TV Champion Tully Blanchard (w/ JJ Dillon) to a time-limit draw at around the 15-minute mark; the bell rang just as Windham had Blanchard covered following a dropkick off the top

JCP @ Philadelphia, PA - Civic Center - July 25, 1987
Future ECW referee Jim Molineaux was in attendance for the show
Kendall Windham & Todd Champion defeated the MOD Squad
NWA Jr. Heavyweight Champion Lazortron defeated Nelson Royal
Sean Royal defeated the Italian Stallion
Florida Heavyweight Champion Mike Rotundo fought Dory

Funk Jr. to a 20-minute time-limit draw
The Barbarian defeated Jimmy Valiant
Michael Hayes, Terry Gordy, & Buddy Roberts defeated Ivan Koloff, Vladimir Petrov, & Manny Fernandez
UWF Western States Heritage Champion Barry Windham defeated Arn Anderson
NWA Tag Team Champions Ricky Morton & Robert Gibson defeated NWA US Tag Team Champions Bobby Eaton & Stan Lane in a non-title lumberjacks with tennis racquets match
UWF World Champion Steve Williams defeated Dick Murdoch in a bunkhouse match
Jimmy Garvin & Precious defeated Paul Jones (sub. for JJ Dillon) & Dark Journey
Dusty Rhodes & Ron Garvin defeated NWA World Champion Ric Flair & NWA TV Champion Tully Blanchard in a double bullrope match when Rhodes pinned Blanchard
Nikita Koloff defeated NWA US Champion Lex Luger via disqualification in a steel cage match

JCP @ Daytona Beach, FL - Ocean Center - July 26, 1987

JCP @ Cleveland, OH - Municipal Stadium - July 26, 1987
Non-Great American Bash show held after a Cleveland Indians game
Ron Garvin defeated the Barbarian
Jimmy Valiant defeated Ivan Koloff
NWA TV Champion Tully Blanchard fought Jimmy Garvin to a draw
NWA Tag Team Champions Ricky Morton & Robert Gibson defeated NWA US Tag Team Champions Bobby Eaton & Stan Lane

JCP @ Fayetteville, NC - Cumberland County Memorial Arena - July 27, 1987
The Italian Stallion defeated Thunderfoot #1
The Barbarian defeated Todd Champion
Paul Ellering defeated Paul Jones
NWA Jr. Heavyweight Champion Lazertron defeated MOD Squad Basher
NWA US Tag Team Champions Bobby Eaton & Stan Lane defeated UWF Western States Heritage Champion Barry Windham & Kendall Windham
NWA Tag Team Champions Ricky Morton & Robert Gibson defeated NWA TV Champion Tully Blanchard & Arn Anderson
The Road Warriors defeated Manny Fernandez & Ivan Koloff
Ron Garvin defeated NWA World Champion Ric Flair
Nikita Koloff defeated NWA US Champion Lex Luger

JCP @ Rock Hill, SC - Winthrop Coliseum - July 28, 1987
Manny Fernandez defeated Kendall Windham
The Barbarian defeated Lazortron
Jimmy Valiant defeated Ivan Koloff via disqualification
Todd Champion & The Italian Stallion defeated Thunderfoot #1 & #2
Ron & Jimmy Garvin fought NWA US Tag Team Champions Bobby Eaton & Stan Lane to a 30-minute time-limit draw

NWA US Champion Lex Luger defeated Barry Windham
NWA Tag Team Champions Ricky Morton & Robert Gibson defeated Arn Anderson & NWA TV Champion Tully Blanchard

JCP @ Atlanta, GA - WTBS Studios - July 29, 1987
TV taping

JCP @ Jacksonville, FL - Coliseum - July 30, 1987
NWA Tag Team Champions Ricky Morton & Robert Gibson defeated NWA US Tag Team Champions Bobby Eaton & Stan Lane via disqualification

JCP @ Miami, FL - Orange Bowl - July 31, 1987 (16,000)
The last show of the Great American Bash tour
Scott Hall defeated Bob Cook
Jimmy Valiant & Bugsy McGraw defeated Ricky Santana & the Cuban Assassin
Manny Fernandez (w/ Paul Jones) defeated Randy & Bill Mulkey in a handicap match following a flying forearm
UWF Western States Heritage Champion Barry Windham pinned Incubus with a clothesline off the top
NWA Florida Tag Team Champions the Sheepherders fought Ron & Jimmy Garvin to a double disqualification
NWA Florida Heavyweight Champion Mike Rotundo pinned Ivan Koloff (w/ Paul Jones) with an inside cradle and fast count from referee Earl Hebner, moments after the challenger shoved Hebner
Kevin Sullivan defeated Dory Funk Jr. in a Texas Death Match
NWA Tag Team Champions Ricky Morton & Robert Gibson defeated NWA US Tag Team Champions Bobby Eaton & Stan Lane (w/ Jim Cornette) via disqualification at 10:15 when Lane accidentally hit Eaton with Cornette's tennis racquet; after the bout, Cornette hit Morton with the racquet before Eaton & Lane dropped Morton with a spike piledriver
Dusty Rhodes, Nikita Koloff, the Road Warriors, & Paul Ellering defeated NWA World Champion Ric Flair, Arn Anderson, NWA TV Champion Tully Blanchard, NWA US Champion Lex Luger, & the War Machine (Ray Traylor) (sub. for JJ Dillon) at 19:38 when War Machine submitted as Road Warrior Animal repeatedly rammed a spike elbowpad into War Machine's eye (*Great American Bash 87, WarGames: WCW's Most Notorious Matches*)

Worldwide - 8/1/87:
Sean Royal vs. Rocky King
The Barbarian vs. the Italian Stallion
Barry Windham vs. Thunderfoot #2

Pro - 8/1/87:
The Italian Stallion vs. Gene Ligon
Kendall Windham vs. the Barbarian
Jimmy Valiant & Lazortron vs. Sean Royal & Thunderfoot #1
Jimmy Garvin vs. Manny Fernandez

World Championship Wrestling - 8/1/87:
NWA US Tag Team Champions Bobby Eaton & Stan Lane vs. George South & Cougar Jay
Jimmy Garvin vs. Thunderfoot #2
Nikita Koloff vs. David Isley
Barry Windham vs. Dave Spearman
Arn Anderson & NWA TV Champion Tully Blanchard vs. Wescott & Patterson
Sean Royal vs. Ricky Nelson
Ron Garvin vs. Thunderfoot #1
NWA US Champion Lex Luger vs. Alan Martin
Ivan Koloff vs. Dale Laperouse
NWA Tag Team Champion Ricky Morton vs. NWA TV Champion Tully Blanchard

JCP @ Richmond, VA - Coliseum - August 1, 1987 (7,500)
Thunderfoot #1 & Sean Royal defeated the Italian Stallion & Nelson Royal
Ivan Koloff defeated Todd Champion
The Barbarian defeated Kendall Windham
Jimmy Valiant & Bugsy McGraw defeated the MOD Squad
Jimmy Garvin defeated Manny Fernandez
Nikita Koloff defeated NWA US Champion Lex Luger via disqualification
NWA Tag Team Champions Ricky Morton & Robert Gibson defeated NWA TV Champion Tully Blanchard & Arn Anderson
Ron Garvin defeated NWA World Champion Ric Flair via disqualification

UWF @ New Orleans, LA - Superdome - August 1, 1987 (5,000)
Shane Doglas pinned Gary Young
Davey Haskins pinned Mike Boyette
Terry Gordy pinned the Angel of Death
Terry Taylor pinned Steve Cox
UWF Western States Heritage Champion Barry Windham pinned Shaska Whatley
Rick Steiner defeated Chris Adams in a taped fist match in the 5th round
Sting pinned the Enforcer
UWF Tag Team Champions Brad Armstrong & Tim Horner defeated NWA US Tag Team Champions Bobby Eaton & Stan Lane via reverse decision
Dusty Rhodes & UWF World Champion Steve Williams defeated Eddie Gilbert & Dick Murdoch in a double bullrope match when Williams pinned Gilbert
Michael Hayes, Terry Gordy, & Buddy Roberts defeated Big Bubba, Black Bart, & the Terminator in a steel cage first blood elimination match; Roberts was eliminated; Terminator was eliminated; Hayes and Bart were eliminated; Rogers was eliminated

JCP @ Huntington, WV - August 2, 1987 (matinee)
NWA Tag Team Champions Ricky Morton & Robert Gibson defeated NWA US Tag Team Champions Bobby Eaton & Stan Lane in a non-title match

JCP @ Charlotte, NC - Coliseum - August 2, 1987
NWA Tag Team Champions Ricky Morton & Robert Gibson defeated NWA US Tag Team Champions Bobby Eaton & Stan Lane in a bunkhouse match

JCP @ Greenville, SC - Memorial Auditorium - August 3, 1987
Lazortron defeated Gladiator #1
Sean Royal defeated the Italian Stallion
Jimmy Valiant & Bugsy McGraw defeated the MOD Squad
NWA Tag Team Champions Ricky Morton & Robert Gibson defeated Ivan Koloff & the Barbarian (sub. for Vladimir Petrov)
Jimmy Garvin defeated Manny Fernandez
NWA TV Champion Tully Blanchard defeated Nikita Koloff; Blanchard's title and his $10,000 were at stake
NWA US Champion Lex Luger defeated UWF Western States Heritage Champion Barry Windham; only the US title was at stake
NWA World Champion Ric Flair defeated Ron Garvin

JCP @ Spartanburg, SC - Memorial Auditorium - August 4, 1987
TV taping:
Worldwide - 8/8/87:
Nikita Koloff vs. Arn Anderson
Nelson Royal vs. Keith Patterson
NWA US Champion Lex Luger vs. Dusty Rhodes
Pro - 8/8/87:
NWA US Tag Team Champions Bobby Eaton & Stan Lane vs. Ricky Nelson & David Isley
Jimmy Garvin & Barry Windham vs. Thunderfoot #1 & #2
Ron Garvin vs. Gladiator #1
Arn Anderson & NWA TV Champion Tully Blanchard vs. John Savage & Mike Force
Bugsy McGraw vs. Tommy Angel
Nikita Koloff vs. Gary Royal
NWA World Champion Ric Flair vs. Rocky King
Dark match: NWA Tag Team Champions Ricky Morton & Robert Gibson vs. Arn Anderson & NWA TV Champion Tully Blanchard

JCP @ Atlanta, GA - WTBS Studios - August 5, 1987
World Championship Wrestling - 8/8/87:
Sean Royal vs. George South
NWA TV Champion Tully Blanchard & Arn Anderson vs. Larry Stephens & Rocky King
NWA Tag Team Champions Ricky Morton & Robert Gibson vs. Phelps & Franks
NWA US Tag Team Champions Bobby Eaton & Stan Lane vs. Ricky Nelson & David Isley
Mike Jackson vs. David Isley
Michael Hayes & Buddy Roberts vs. Dexter Wescott & Art Pritts
Eddie Gilbert vs. Alan Martin
UWF Western States Heritage Champion Barry Windham & Nikita Koloff vs. Thunderfoot #2 & Savage
UWF World Champion Steve Williams vs. John Force
Ivan Koloff & the Barbarian vs. Max McGyver & Patterson

JCP @ St. Louis, MO - August 7, 1987 (7,000)
Sting fought Rick Steiner to a draw

Ron Simmons defeated Ivan Koloff
Terry Gordy defeated Black Bart
NWA US Tag Team Champions Bobby Eaton & Stan Lane defeated Ron & Jimmy Garvin via disqualification
NWA US Champion Lex Luger defeated Nikita Koloff via count-out
Barry Windham defeated Big Bubba
Dusty Rhodes & Steve Williams defeated Dick Murdoch & Eddie Gilbert in a bunkhouse match
NWA World Champion Ric Flair defeated Michael Hayes

JCP @ Pittsburgh, PA - August 8, 1987
Denny Brown defeated Jimmy Jackson
The Italian Stallion & Nelson Royal defeated Thunderfoot #2 & Gladiator #1
Sean Royal defeated Kendall Windham
Jimmy Valiant & NWA Jr. Heavyweight Champion Lazertron defeated the MOD Squad
Ron Garvin defeated Thundertoot #1
Jimmy Garvin defeated Manny Fernandez
NWA Tag Team Champions Ricky Morton & Robert Gibson defeated NWA TV Champion Tully Blanchard & Arn Anderson
Nikita Koloff defeated NWA US Champion Lex Luger via disqualification

JCP @ Kansas City, MO - August 8, 1987
NWA US Tag Team Champions Bobby Eaton & Stan Lane defeated the Freebirds via disqualification

JCP @ Asheville, NC - Civic Center - August 9, 1987 (matinee)
Rocky King defeated John Savage
Sean Royal defeated NWA Jr. Heavyweight Champion Lazertron
Manny Fernandez defeated Colt Steele
The MOD Squad defeated Kendall Windham & the Italian Stallion
UWF Western States Heritage Champion Barry Windham defeated Arn Anderson
NWA TV Champion Tully Blanchard defeated Nikita Koloff
NWA Tag Team Champions Ricky Morton & Robert Gibson defeated NWA US Tag Team Champions Bobby Eaton & Stan Lane in a non-title Best 2 out of 3 falls match

JCP @ Atlanta, GA - Omni - August 9, 1987 (14,100)
Denny Brown defeated George South
Ron Simmons defeated Teijo Khan
Barry Windham defeated Dick Murdoch
NWA US Tag Team Champions Bobby Eaton & Stan Lane fought Terry Gordy & Buddy Roberts to a 20-minute time-limit draw
Steve Williams defeated Big Bubba
Nikita Koloff fought Ivan Koloff to a draw
Dusty Rhodes defeated NWA US Champion Lex Luger via disqualification
NWA Tag Team Champions Ricky Morton & Robert Gibson

defeated Arn Anderson & Tully Blanchard
NWA World Champion Ric Flair defeated Ron Garvin via disqualification

JCP @ Buckingham, VA - August 10, 1987
Ron & Jimmy Garvin defeated NWA US Tag Team Champions Bobby Eaton & Stan Lane in a non-title match

JCP @ Stockton, CA - August 10, 1987 (1,500)
Ron Simmons pinned Shaska Whatley at 4:49 with a shoulderblock off the top
Michael Hayes pinned the Terminator at 12:39 with a crossbody
Terry Taylor defeated Chris Adams via disqualification at 9:00; Adams originally won the match and title with a powerslam but the referee caught him moments later with a foreign object that Taylor had tried to use moments earlier and then stuffed into the challenger's tights, with the referee thinking the weapon was Adams'
UWF Tag Team Champions Brad Armstrong & Tim Horner defeated Big Bubba & Black Bart at 15:40 when Armstrong pinned Bart with a cradle after switching places in the ring with Horner
NWA Tag Team Champion Robert Gibson & Sting (sub. for NWA Tag Team Champion Ricky Morton) defeated NWA TV Champion Tully Blanchard & Arn Anderson at 16:00 when Gibson pinned Anderson with a roll up
Nikita Koloff defeated NWA US Champion Lex Luger via disqualification at 16:00
Steve Williams & Terry Gordy defeated Eddie Gilbert & Dick Murdoch in a bunkhouse match when Williams pinned Gilbert after hitting him with his own cowboy boot at 11:00

JCP @ Columbia, SC - Township Auditorium - August 11, 1987
TV taping:
Worldwide - 8/22/87:
Jimmy Valiant vs. John Savage
Dusty Rhodes (w/ Johnny Weaver) vs. Colt Steele
The Italian Stallion vs. MOD Squad Basher
Ivan Koloff & the Barbarian vs. George South & Rocky King
Sean Royal vs. Ricky Nelson
Kendall Windham vs. Denny Brown
Barry Windham & Jimmy Garvin vs. Teijo Khan & Cougar Jay
Pro - 8/22/87 - featured Bob Caudle & Johnny Weaver on commentary:
Dusty Rhodes defeated Gladiator #1 via submission with the sleeper at the 40-second mark; after the bout, Johnny Weaver left the commentary table to have Rhodes wake his opponent up
The MOD Squad vs. George South & Rocky King
Manny Fernandez, the Barbarian, & Ivan Koloff vs. Denny Brown, Ricky Nelson, & Larry Stevens
NWA US Tag Team Champions Bobby Eaton & Stan Lane (w/ Jim Cornette) defeated Ron & Jimmy Garvin via disqualification

JCP @ San Jose, CA - August 11, 1987 (1,800)
Buddy Roberts defeated Steve Pardee
Sting & Ron Simmons defeated Pez Whatley & Rick Steiner
Michael Hayes defeated the Terminator
Brad Armstrong & Tim Horner defeated Big Bubba & Black Bart via disqualification
Chris Adams defeated Terry Taylor via disqualification
Nikita Koloff defeated Eddie Gilbert
Terry Gordy fought Dick Murdoch to a no contest
UWF Heavyweight Champion Steve Williams, NWA Tag Team Champions Ricky Morton & Robert Gibson defeated NWA US Champion Lex Luger, NWA TV Champion Tully Blanchard, & Arn Anderson

JCP @ Atlanta, GA - WTBS Studios - August 12, 1987
World Championship Wrestling - 8/15/87:
Jimmy Garvin vs. Cougar Jay
Kendall Windham vs. Gladiator #1
Jimmy Valiant vs. Terry Jones
Sean Royal vs. Larry Stephens
Ron Garvin vs. Dexter Wescott
Manny Fernandez & the Barbarian vs. George South & Rocky King
Teijo Khan vs. Keith Steinborn
NWA US Tag Team Champions Bobby Eaton & Stan Lane vs. Ricky Nelson & Diamond
The MOD Squad vs. the Italian Stallion & Denny Brown
UWF Western States Heritage Champion Barry Windham vs. Ed Franks
Ivan Koloff vs. Colt Steele

JCP @ Los Angeles, CA - August 12, 1987
Chris Adams defeated Terry Taylor
Buddy Roberts defeated Tau Lugo
Ron Simmons defeated Rodney Anoia
NWA Tag Team Champions Ricky Morton & Robert Gibson defeated Big Bubba & Black Bart via disqualification
Michael Hayes fought NWA TV Champion Tully Blanchard to a draw
Shaska Whatley defeated Tim Patterson
Terry Taylor & Eddie Gilbert defeated Harry Hell & Billy Anderson
Arn Anderson defeated Brad Armstrong
Tim Horner defeated the Terminator
Eddie Gilbert & Dick Murdoch defeated UWF Heavyweight Champion Steve Williams & Terry Gordy,BR> Nikita Koloff defeated NWA US Champion Lex Luger via disqualification

JCP @ Raleigh, NC - Dorton Arena - August 13, 1987
Nelson Royal defeated MOD Squad Basher
MOD Squad Spike defeated Rocky King
The Italian Stallian defeated Colt Steele
Denny Brown defeated Thunderfoot #1
Jimmy Valiant & Lazertron defeated the Barbarian & Ivan Koloff
UWF Western States Heritage Champion Barry Windham &

Jimmy Garvin defeated NWA US Tag Team Champions Bobby Eaton & Stan Lane in a Best 2 out of 3 falls match; fall #3: Windham & Garvin won via disqualification
NWA World Champion Ric Flair fought Ron Garvin to a double count-out

JCP @ Norfolk, VA - Scope - August 14, 1987
The MOD Squad fought the Italian Stallion & Lazertron
Sean Royal defeated Colt Steele
Jimmy Garvin defeated Manny Fernandez
Ivan Koloff defeated Kendall Windham
Dusty Rhodes defeated NWA US Champion Lex Luger via disqualification
Nikita Koloff & UWF Western States Heritage Champion Barry Windham defeated NWA US Tag Team Champions Bobby Eaton & Stan Lane via disqualification
NWA Tag Team Champions Ricky Morton & Robert Gibson defeated NWA TV Champion Tully Blanchard & Arn Anderson
NWA World Champion Ric Flair defeated Ron Garvin via disqualification

JCP @ Charlotte, NC - Coliseum - August 15, 1987
UWF Western States Heritage Champion Barry Windham & Jimmy Garvin fought NWA US Tag Team Champions Bobby Eaton & Stan Lane to a draw

Worldwide - 8/15/87:
Jimmy Valiant & Bugsy McGraw vs. Thunderfoot #1 & Thunderfoot #2
NWA Tag Team Champions Ricky Morton & Robert Gibson vs. Ricky Nelson & Gary Royal
Barry Windham vs. Mike Force
Ivan Koloff & the Barbarian vs. David Isley & Tommy Angel
NWA TV Champion Tully Blanchard vs. Colt Steele
Arn Anderson vs. Brodie Chase
NWA US Tag Team Champions Bobby Eaton & Stan Lane vs. George South & Larry Stevens

JCP @ Baltimore, MD - Arena - August 15, 1987
Steve Cox defeated Thunderfoot #1
Lazertron fought Nelson Royal to a draw
Jimmy Valiant defeated Angel of Death
Sting defeated Eddie Gilbert via disqualification
Michael Hayes & Terry Gordy defeated Manny Fernandez & Shaska Whatley
The Road Warriors defeated Ivan Koloff & the Barbarian
NWA World Champion Ric Flair fought Ron Garvin to a draw at the 50-minute mark

JCP @ Kingsport, TN - Dobyns-Bennett High School Gym - August 16, 1987 (matinee)
Todd Champion vs. Ed Gantner
The Italian Stallion vs. Teijo Khan
Denny Brown & Rocky King vs. Thunderfoot #1 & #2
Jimmy Valiant & Lazertron vs. the MOD Squad

Kendall Windham vs. Manny Fernandez
NWA Tag Team Champions Ricky Morton & Robert Gibson defeated NWA US Tag Team Champions Bobby Eaton & Stan Lane
Nikita Koloff vs. NWA US Champion Lex Luger
Ron Garvin vs. NWA World Champion Ric Flair

JCP @ Chicago, IL - UIC Pavilion - August 16, 1987 (8,700; sell out)
UWF Heavyweight Champion Steve Williams defeated Eddie Gilbert
NWA Tag Team Champions Ricky Morton & Robert Gibson defeated NWA US Tag Team Champions Bobby Eaton & Stan Lane
UWF Western States Heritage Champion Barry Windham defeated Rick Steiner
Ron Simmons defeated Sean Royal
Sting defeated Black Bart
Ivan Koloff defeated the Italian Stallion
Ron Garvin, Dusty Rhodes, Nikita Koloff, & the Road Warriors defeated NWA World Champion Ric Flair, Lex Luger, NWA TV Champion Tully Blanchard, Arn Anderson, & JJ Dillon in a Wargames match

JCP @ Denver, CO - August 17, 1987
Ron Simmons defeated Rick Steiner
Sting defeated Black Bart
UWF Western States Heritage Champion Barry Windham defeated Big Bubba
NWA Tag Team Champions Ricky Morton & Robert Gibson defeated NWA US Tag Team Champions Bobby Eaton & Stan Lane in a non-title match
UWF Heavyweight Champion Steve Williams defeated Dick Murdoch
The Road Warriors & Nikita Koloff defeated NWA US Champion Lex Luger, NWA TV Champion Tully Blanchard, & Arn Anderson
NWA World Champion Ric Flair defeated Dusty Rhodes via disqualification

JCP @ Fayetteville, NC - Cumberland County Civic Center - August 19, 1987
TV taping:
Pro - 8/29/87 - included opening clips from the MOD Squad vs. Denny Brown & Italian Stallion match; featured Bob Caudle & Johnny Weaver on commentary; included Tony Schiavone conducting an interview with NWA World Champion Ric Flair in which Flair spoke of the challenges of Dusty Rhodes, Nikita Koloff, the Road Warriors, Ron Garvin, NWA Tag Team Champions Ricky Morton & Robert Gibson, then adding Garvin would never pin him or make him give up to win the title; featured Schiavone discussing the Horsemen's challenge of Morton & Gibson for the tag team titles; included Schiavone conducting an interview with Garvin regarding his challenging Flair; featured Schiavone conducting an interview with NWA US Champion Lex Luger in which he discussed the challenge

of Dusty Rhodes and Rhodes using Johnny Weaver's sleeper:
The MOD Squad defeated Denny Brown & the Italian Stallion when Stallion was pinned following a double clothesline behind the referee's back (the match was joined in progress)
Ivan Koloff (w/ Paul Jones) pinned Kendall Windham with the Russian Sickle at around the 3:30 mark after Windham became distracted by Jones on the apron; after the bout, UWF Western States Heritage Champion Barry Windham ran out and cleared Koloff and Jones from the ring; moments later, Bob Caudle conducted a ringside interview with the Windhams in which Barry said Kendall would do well for himself but he wouldn't stand for someone taking advantage of him; Barry then spoke of the challenge of Arn Anderson, saying they could settle it anytime in the ring
NWA Super Bouts: Nikita Koloff pinned NWA TV Champion Tully Blanchard (w/ JJ Dillon) to win the title after more than 16 minutes after hitting the Russian Sickle on an interfering Dillon and hitting Blanchard with his own foreign object behind the back of referee Earl Hebner; late in the bout, Arn Anderson appeared ringside, at which time Blanchard hit Koloff with the weapon; moments later, UWF Western States Heritage Champion Barry Windham came out, stopped the referee from making the count, and tried to tell him what happened before then brawling with Blanchard in the ring in plain view of the referee; after the bout, Windham, NWA Tag Team Champions Ricky Morton & Robert Gibson, Kendall Windham, Lazortron, the Italian Stallion, Ron Garvin, and others filled the ring to celebrate the win; moments later, Bob Caudle conducted a ringside interview with Koloff regarding the win
NWA Super Bouts - 9/87: NWA US Tag Team Champions Bobby Eaton & Stan Lane (w/ Jim Cornette) defeated UWF Western States Heritage Champion Barry Windham & Jimmy Garvin (w/ Precious) at around the 15-minute mark when Lane pinned Garvin after Eaton hit Garvin over the back with Cornette's tennis racquet behind the referee's back as Garvin attempted to drop Lane with a suplex

JCP @ Forest City, NC - August 19, 1987
Ron Garvin & UWF Western States Heritage Champion Barry Windham defeated NWA US Tag Team Champions Bobby Eaton & Stan Lane via disqualification

JCP @ Pennington Gap, VA - August 20, 1987
NWA US Tag Team Champions Bobby Eaton & Stan Lane defeated Jimmy Valiant & Lazortron

JCP @ Cincinnati, OH - Cincinnati Gardens - August 20, 1987 (2,500)
Kendall Windham pinned Jim Lancaster
Rocky King pinned Teijo Khan
Denny Brown pinned Gladiator #1
Sean Royal pinned the Italian Stallion
Jimmy Garvin pinned Colt Steele
UWF Western States Heritage Champion Barry Windham pinned Ivan Koloff
NWA TV Champion Nikita Koloff fought NWA US Champion

Lex Luger to a double-disqualification
NWA Tag Team Champions Ricky Morton & Robert Gibson defeated Arn Anderson & Tully Blanchard when Morton pinned Blanchard
NWA World Champion Ric Flair defeated Ron Garvin via disqualification at the 25-minute mark

JCP @ Charleston, WV - August 21, 1987 (3,500)
Mark Fleming pinned Cougar Jay
Teijo Khan defeated Keith Patterson
Colt Steele defeated Ricky Nelson
Sean Royal defeated Denny Brown
UWF Western States Heritage Champion Barry Windham pinned Ivan Koloff
NWA TV Champion Nikita Koloff defeated the Barbarian
Dusty Rhodes defeated NWA US Champion Lex Luger via disqualification
NWA Tag Team Champions Ricky Morton & Robert Gibson defeated Arn Anderson & Tully Blanchard

JCP @ Macon, GA - Coliseum - August 21, 1987
Jimmy Valiant & Jimmy Garvin defeated NWA US Tag Team Champions Bobby Eaton & Stan Lane in a Best 2 out of 3 falls match; fall #3: Valiant & Garvin won via disqualification

World Championship Wrestling - 8/22/87 - included the Dusty Rhodes vs. Gladiator #1 match from the 8/22/87 Pro; featured Tony Schiavone & David Crockett on commentary; included Schiavone conducting an interview with Dory Funk Jr., wearing a suit, in which he showed the NWA Florida Heavyweight Title that he had stolen from NWA Florida Heavyweight Champion Mike Rotundo, with Funk then saying - for the fans that didn't live in Florida - he pinned Rotundo to win the belt; Funk then said he was coming after Kevin Sullivan, Blackjack Mulligan, and Bugsy McGraw to defend his title; featured vignettes of Rhodes to the tune of Bo Diddley's "You Can't Judge a Book by It's Cover;" included an ad promoting the Great American Bash 87 home video; featured a vignette of NWA World Champion Ric Flair; included Schiavone conducting an interview with Sullivan in which he said he needed Rhodes to come to Florida with him to get rid of the Sheepherders and, in turn, he would help Rhodes against the Four Horsemen:
NWA Florida Heavyweight Champion Mike Rotundo pinned Alan Martin with the airplane spin at 2:33; after the bout, Tony Schiavone conducted an interview with Rotundo regarding Dory Funk Jr. and Terry Funk jumping him during a TV match in Tampa, FL and stealing his title belt
Jimmy Valiant pinned El Negro with an elbow drop at 1:41
Kendall Windham & NWA Jr. Heavyweight Champion Lazortron defeated Dexter Wescott & Dale Laperouse at 5:21 when Windham pinned Laperouse with the bulldog
UWF Tag Team Champions Brad Armstrong & Tim Horner defeated Tommy Angel & Cougar Jay at 4:13 when Armstrong pinned Jay after Armstrong lifted Horner in the air so he could hit a legdrop; following the commercial break, Schiavone conducted an interview with Armstrong & Horner regarding

their return to WTBS and winning the titles, during which they mentioned Skandar Akbar, Big Bubba & Black Bart, Eddie Gilbert & Terry Taylor as their top competition
Terry Taylor pinned the Italian Stallion with a reverse roll up and grabbing the tights for leverage at 5:03; following the commercial break, Schiavone conducted an interview with Terry regarding his return to WTBS, his rivalry with Chris Adams, and responded to comments earlier in the night made by UWF Tag Team Champions Brad Armstrong & Tim Horner
Ivan Koloff & Manny Fernandez defeated George South & Rocky King at 3:35 when Koloff pinned South following a Russian Sickle off the top as Fernandez held South in the air for a back suplex
Chris Adams pinned Colt Steele with the superkick at 5:12; after the match, Terry Taylor ran in the ring and jumped Adams from behind but Adams eventually cleared him from the ring; moments later, Schiavone conducted an interview with Adams regarding Taylor
Ron Garvin pinned Keith Steinborn at 2:09 after the right hand punch; after the match, Schiavone conducted an interview with Garvin regarding his quest for Ric Flair's NWA World Title
Kevin Sullivan pinned Larry Stevens at 1:47 with a gutwrench suplex and several punches to the face
Bugsy McGraw pinned Terry Jones with a splash at 1:27; after the match, Schiavone conducted an interview with McGraw regarding the comments earlier in the show by Dory Funk Jr.; moments later, Jimmy Valiant appeared and said he and McGraw would be coming to all the towns together
Michael Hayes & Terry Gordy defeated Thunderfoot #1 & #2 at 2:12 when Gordy scored the pin following a backdrop / powerbomb combo; after the bout, Schiavone conducted an interview with Hayes regarding Jim Cornette

JCP @ Philadelphia, PA - Civic Center - August 22, 1987 (4,500)
The MOD Squad defeated Denny Brown & Mark Fleming
Lazertron defeated Gladiator #2
Jimmy Valiant defeated Sean Royal via disqualification
Jimmy Garvin pinned Manny Fernandez by using the ropes for leverage
UWF World Champion Steve Williams pinned Big Bubba with the Oklahoma Stampede
NWA TV Champion Nikita Koloff & UWF Western States Heritage Champion Barry Windham defeated NWA Tag Team Champions Bobby Eaton & Stan Lane via disqualification when Koloff was caught using Jim Cornette's tennis racket as a weapon
The Road Warriors defeated Ivan Koloff & the Barbarian when Animal pinned the Barbarian after Barbarian missed a headbutt off the top

JCP @ Minneapolis, MN - Met Center - August 23, 1987 (2,500)
UWF Western States Heritage Champion Barry Windham pinned Eddie Gilbert
Ron Garvin pinned Sean Royal
Ivan Koloff pinned Jimmy Garvin

Chris Adams defeated Terry Taylor via disqualification

UWF World Champion Steve Williams pinned Big Bubba at the 10-minute mark

NWA Tag Team Champions Ricky Morton & Robert Gibson defeated the Barbarian (sub. for NWA US Tag Team Champion Stan Lane) & NWA US Tag Team Champion Bobby Eaton when Gibson pinned Eaton; Barbarian had Morton pinned at the same time as the fall

Dusty Rhodes, the Road Warriors, & NWA TV Champion Nikita Koloff defeated NWA World Champion Ric Flair, Arn Anderson, Tully Blanchard, & NWA US Champion Lex Luger when Road Warrior Animal pinned Anderson

JCP @ Greenville, SC - Memorial Auditorium - August 24, 1987

Lazortron vs. MOD Squad #2 and Todd Champion vs. Ed Von Ganter did not take place as advertised

MOD Squad Spike defeated Larry Stephens (sub. for Denny Brown)

The Italian Stallion defeated Colt Steele (sub. for the Barbarian)

Ivan Koloff & Manny Fernandez defeated Kendall Windham & Jimmy Valiant

The Barbarian defeated Rocky King

Arn Anderson & NWA TV Champion Tully Blanchard defeated Barry Windham & Jimmy Garvin; stipulations stated the winners would be the #1 contenders for the NWA Tag Team Titles

Dusty Rhodes defeated NWA US Champion Lex Luger via disqualification

NWA World Champion Ric Flair defeated Ron Garvin in a No DQ match

JCP @ Weslaco, TX - August 24, 1987

NWA Tag Team Champions Ricky Morton & Robert Gibson defeated NWA US Tag Team Champions Bobby Eaton & Stan Lane in a non-title match

JCP @ Corpus Christi, TX - Memorial Coliseum - August 25, 1987

NWA Tag Team Champions Ricky Morton & Robert Gibson defeated NWA US Tag Team Champions Bobby Eaton & Stan Lane in a non-title match

JCP @ Rock Hill, SC - Winthrop Coliseum - August 25, 1987

Television taping:

Ivan Koloff, Manny Fernandez, & the Barbarian defeated George South, Rocky King, & Ricky Nelson

Sean Royal defeated Cougar Jay

Ron Garvin defeated Vernon Deaton

The Road Warriors defeated Brodie Chase & Larry Stevens

NWA US Champion Lex Luger defeated John Savage

Jimmy Valiant defeated Brodie Chase

The MOD Squad defeated David Isley & Ricky Nelson

Ivan Koloff defeated Rocky King

Arn Anderson & Tully Blanchard defeated The Italian Stallion & Denny Brown

The Road Warriors defeated Cougar Jay & the Gladiator

NWA Western States Heritage Champion Barry Windham defeated Vernon Deaton

Teijo Khan defeated John Savage

Jimmy & Ron Garvin defeated Manny Fernandez & the Barbarian

NWA Western States Heritage Champion Barry Windham defeated Ivan Koloff

NWA US Champion Lex Luger & Tully Blanchard defeated the Road Warriors

NWA Western States Heritage Champion Barry Windham defeated Arn Anderson

JCP @ Galveston, TX - August 26, 1987
NWA Tag Team Champions Ricky Morton & Robert Gibson defeated NWA US Tag Team Champions Bobby Eaton & Stan Lane in a non-title match

JCP @ Miami, FL - Miami Beach Convention Center - August 26, 1987
Johnny Ace defeated Luis Astea
Ricky Santana defeated Robbie Idol
Jimmy Backlund defeated Rick Rider
The Samurai Warriors defeated Rex King & Bill Mulkey
Mike Graham & Steve Keirn defeated the Sheepherders
Mike Rotunda defeated the Black Assassin
Barry Windham defeated Ivan Koloff
Kevin Sullivan & Bugsy McGraw defeated the Mighty Yankees via disqualification
Blackjack Mulligan defeated Dory Funk Jr.
The Road Warriors defeated Arn Anderson & Tully Blanchard
NWA World Champion Ric Flair fought Ron Garvin to a double count-out

JCP @ Amarillo, TX - August 27, 1987
Brad Armstrong & Tim Horner defeated NWA US Tag Team Champions Bobby Eaton & Stan Lane in a non-title match

JCP @ Tallahassee, FL - Leon County Civic Center - August 27, 1987

JCP @ Hampton, VA - Coliseum - August 28, 1987
NWA Tag Team Champions Ricky Morton & Robert Gibson defeated NWA US Tag Team Champions Bobby Eaton & Stan Lane

JCP @ Daytona Beach, FL - Ocean Center - August 28, 1987

Worldwide - 8/29/87:
Arn Anderson vs. George South
Lazortron vs. Gladiator #2
NWA US Tag Team Champions Bobby Eaton & Stan Lane vs. Greg Stevens & David Isley
NWA Tag Team Champions Ricky Morton & Robert Gibson vs. Dexter Wescott & an unknown
NWA US Champion Lex Luger vs. Mike Force

JCP @ Atlanta, GA - WTBS Studios - August 29, 1987
World Championship Wrestling - 8/29/87 - featured an opening clip from the Nikita Koloff vs. NWA TV Champion Tully Blanchard match that aired that same day as part of NWA Pro; included Tony Schiavone on commentary for the program; featured a vignette of Rhodes to the tune of Bo Diddley's "You

Can't Judge a Book by It's Cover;" included Koloff's title win over Blanchard taped 8/19/87, nearly shown in full, as well as the post-match celebration; featured Schiavone conducting an interview with Rhodes regarding Koloff's title win, with Rhodes then saying he didn't have to beat Luger but Luger had to beat him to become a bigger star; moments later, Rhodes led Schiavone to the ring, then laid across the apron before yelling that he would be the next US champion; included a pre-taped segment in which David Crockett conducted a ringside interview with NWA World Champion Ric Flair, alongside Luger, Dillon, Arn Anderson, and Blanchard, in which he bragged about the Horsemen; featured a vignette on Flair set to his theme music; included footage from NWA Worldwide of Bob Caudle conducting an interview with Ron Garvin regarding his challenge of Flair, during which he said he had his sights set on the world title:
NWA US Champion Lex Luger (w/ JJ Dillon) defeated Cougar Jay via submission with the Torture Rack at 5:10; after the bout, Tony Schiavone conducted an interview with Luger & Dillon regarding the challenge of Dusty Rhodes and Rhodes' use of Johnny Weaver's sleeper, during which Dillon argued the hold was an illegal choke
Jimmy Garvin (w/ Precious) pinned John Savage with the brainbuster at 3:38; after the bout, Schiavone conducted a ringside interview with Garvin, alongside Precious, in which he said Ron Garvin would beat NWA World Champion Ric Flair and Dusty Rhodes would beat NWA US Champion Lex Luger
The MOD Squad fought Kendall Windham & the Italian Stallion to a 10-minute time-limit draw at 9:30; after the bout, the MOD Squad double teamed Stallion in the ring, with Stallion sustaining an elbow drop off the top before Windham made the save; moments later, Tony Schiavone held up a copy of the soon to be released 'Great American Bash 87: Wargames' VHS tape and said Starrcade 87 would be even bigger; the MOD Squad then walked in and said what just happened was a sign of things to come, that they weren't getting the title shots they said they deserved, and were after NWA Tag Team Champions Ricky Morton & Robert Gibson
Jimmy Valiant pinned Tim Hardy with the elbow drop at 2:44
The Barbarian (w/ Paul Jones) pinned Rocky King with a powerslam and headbutt off the top at 5:52
Denny Brown pinned Mike Jackson at 6:44 by lifting his shoulder as Jackson had him down with a bridged suplex; Jackson was billed by Schiavone as the Alabama Jr. Heavyweight Champion in the match but he did not appear with a belt; Brown played the heel in the match; referee Teddy Long hesitated before making the third count

NWA Super Bouts - 9/87 - hosted by Tony Schiavone & JJ Dillon:
Ron Garvin defeated Arn Anderson (w/ JJ Dillon) via disqualification at around the 16-minute mark when, as Garvin had Anderson in the figure-4, Anderson poked referee Tommy Young in the eye; Bob Caudle & Dusty Rhodes provided commentary for the bout; moments later, Rhodes attacked Dillon, with NWA World Champion Ric Flair, Tully Blanchard, and NWA US Champion Lex Luger then coming out, with Flair attacking Garvin as Luger put Rhodes in the Torture Rack;

Barry Windham, Ricky Morton & Robert Gibson, NWA TV Champion Nikita Koloff and others then ran out to make the save (held at NWA Pro taping site)

JCP @ St. Petersburg, FL - Bayfront Center - August 29, 1987
The Road Warriors defeated NWA US Tag Team Champions Bobby Eaton & Stan Lane in a non-title match

JCP @ Houston, TX - Summit - August 29, 1987 (1,800)
Night of Champions
Misty Blue pinned Comrade Orca at the 5-minute mark; the match was billed as for the NWA World Women's title
UWF TV Champion Shane Douglas pinned Pez Whatley at 6:48 with an inside cradle
Ron Simmons pinned the Enforcer at 3:30 after a second rope flying tackle
Steve Cox pinned Gary Young at 10:00
UWF Tag Team Champions Brad Armstrong & Tim Horner defeated Black Bart & the Terminator at 10:12 when Horner pinned Terminator after Armstrong hit a missile dropkick
Terry Taylor pinned Chris Adams at 10:05 after Taylor used a foreign object
UWF World Champion Steve Williams pinned Big Bubba at 7:28 after the Oklahoma Stampede
Sting pinned Eddie Gilbert at the 12-minute mark in a Texas death match
Dusty Rhodes defeated NWA US Champion Lex Luger via disqualification at the 14-minute mark when JJ Dillon interfered when Rhodes had Luger in the sleeper; Rhodes then put Dillon in the sleeper, with Arn Anderson & Tully Blanchard coming out; moments later, NWA Tag Team Champions Ricky Morton & Robert Gibson came out to make the save
NWA Tag Team Champions Ricky Morton & Robert Gibson defeated Arn Anderson & Tully Blanchard at 14:33 when Morton pinned Blanchard; Anderson hit Morton with a tag title belt after the match
NWA World Champion Ric Flair pinned UWF Western States Heritage Champion Barry Windham at 26:45 when Flair fell on top of Windham after a collision

JCP @ Charlotte, NC - Coliseum - August 30, 1987 (matinee) (10,200)
Kendall Windham pinned Gladiator #1
Denny Brown pinned Colt Steele
Robert Gibson fought Arn Anderson to a draw
NWA US Tag Team Champions Bobby Eaton & Stan Lane fought NWA TV Champion Nikita Koloff & UWF Western States Heritage Champion Barry Windham to a double count-out
Tully Blanchard defeated NWA Tag Team Champion Ricky Morton
The Road Warriors defeated Ivan Koloff & the Barbarian
Dusty Rhodes defeated NWA US Champion Lex Luger via disqualification after JJ Dillon interfered

NWA World Champion Ric Flair pinned Ron Garvin when Flair held on to JJ Dillon as Garvin attempted a sunset flip

JCP @ Atlanta, GA - Omni - August 30, 1987 (9,000)
Back to school special - upper balcony tickets were $5
MOD Squad Basher fought the Italian Stallion to a draw
Teijo Khan pinned Denny Brown
UWF Western States Heritage Champion Barry Windham pinned Manny Fernandez after the 11-minute mark
NWA TV Champion Nikita Koloff pinned Sean Royal after the 9-minute mark
NWA US Tag Team Champions Bobby Eaton & Stan Lane fought UWF Western States Heritage Champion Barry Windham & Michael Hayes to a double count-out after the 16-minute mark
Jimmy Garvin pinned Ivan Koloff
NWA Six-Man Tag Team Champions Dusty Rhodes & the Road Warriors defeated NWA US Champion Lex Luger, Arn Anderson, and Tully Blanchard after the 11-minute mark
NWA World Champion Ric Flair pinned Ron Garvin after the 22-minute mark when Flair held on to JJ Dillon for leverage as Garvin attempted a sunset flip

JCP @ Savannah, GA - Civic Center - August 31, 1987
Jimmy Garvin & Jimmy Valiant defeated NWA US Tag Team Champions Bobby Eaton & Stan Lane via disqualification

JCP @ Biloxi, MS - September 3, 1987
Included Dusty Rhodes and NWA World Champion Ric Flair

JCP @ Anderson, SC - September 3, 1987
NWA US Tag Team Champions Bobby Eaton & Stan Lane defeated the Mulkey Brothers

JCP @ Richmond, VA - Coliseum - September 4, 1987 (7,000)
Denny Brown defeated David Isley
Sean Royal defeated Kendall Windham
The Road Warriors defeated Ivan Koloff & Gladiator #1
NWA Tag Team Champions Ricky Morton & Roberts Gibson defeated Arn Anderson & Tully Blanchard when Morton pinned Blanchard
NWA US Champion Lex Luger pinned Jimmy Garvin; after the match, Precious slapped the referee
NWA World Champion Ric Flair defeated Ron Garvin in a Best 2 out of 3 falls match, 2-1; fall #1: Flair pinned Garvin with feet on the ropes; fall #2: Garvin pinned Flair after the right hand punch; fall #3: Flair pinned Garvin at the 40-minute mark by holding on to JJ Dillon for leverage as Garvin attempted a sunset flip

JCP @ Columbus, OH - Ohio Center - September 4, 1987
Brad Armstrong & Tim Horner defeated NWA US Tag Team Champions Bobby Eaton & Stan Lane via disqualification

Worldwide - 9/5/87:
Jimmy Valiant vs. Brodie Chase
The MOD Squad vs. Ricky Nelson & David Isley
Ivan Koloff vs. Rocky King
Arn Anderson & Tully Blanchard vs. the Italian Stallion & Denny Brown
The Road Warriors vs. Gladiator #1 & Cougar Jay
UWF Western States Heritage Champion Barry Windham vs. Vernon Deaton
Teijo Khan vs. John Savage

World Championship Wrestling - 9/5/87:
NWA TV Champion Nikita Koloff vs. Alan Martin
NWA US Champion Lex Luger vs. Keith Steinborn
Tully Blanchard vs. Ed Franks
Arn Anderson vs. Mike Jackson
Ron Garvin vs. Terry Jones
NWA US Tag Team Champions Bobby Eaton & Stan Lane vs. Barry & Kendall Windham

JCP @ Philadelphia, PA - Civic Center - September 5, 1987 (3,200)
Lazertron pinned Mark Fleming
Denny Brown defeated MOD Squad Basher
MOD Squad Spike defeated the Italian Stallion
Lazertron (sub. for Todd Champion) defeated Gladiator #1
NWA World Champion Ric Flair pinned Ron Garvin after the 20-minute mark when Flair held on to JJ Dillon for leverage as Garvin attempted a sunset flip
Jimmy Valiant & Kendall Windham defeated Sean Royal & Teijo Khan (sub. for Chris Champion)
NWA Tag Team Champions Ricky Morton & Robert Gibson defeated Arn Anderson & Tully Blanchard when Morton pinned Blanchard
Jimmy Garvin pinned Manny Fernandez after the 5-minute mark

JCP @ Baltimore, MD - Civic Center - September 5, 1987 (9,000)
The preliminary matches were drawn out to allow time for NWA World Champion Ric Flair, Arn Anderson, Tully Blanchard, and JJ Dillon to arrive from Philadelphia; the main event didn't start until after 11:30 p.m.
Ron Simmons defeated the Barbarian
NWA US Tag Team Champions Bobby Eaton & Stan Lane defeated UWF Tag Team Champions Brad Armstrong & Tim Horner (sub. for the Freebirds) after Jim Cornette hit Armstrong with his tennis racket
Sting & Chris Adams defeated UWF TV Champion Terry Taylor & Rick Steiner when Sting pinned Steiner
UWF Western States Heritage Champion Barry Windham pinned Eddie Gilbert
UWF World Champion Steve Williams defeated Ivan Koloff via disqualification after Paul Jones interfered
NWA TV Champion Nikita Koloff fought NWA US Champion Lex Luger to a draw in a Best 2 out of 3 falls match after the

42-minute mark
Dusty Rhodes & the Road Warriors defeated NWA World Champion Ric Flair, Arn Anderson, & Tully Blanchard in a steel cage match when Road Warrior Animal pinned Blanchard

JCP @ Asheville, NC - Civic Center - September 6, 1987 (matinee)
TV taping

JCP @ Greenville, SC - Memorial Auditorium - September 7, 1987
Rocky King vs. Vernon Deaton did not take place as advertised
John Savage defeated Brody Chase
Colt Steele defeated David Isley
Denny Brown defeated Gladiator #2
Kendall Windham defeated Teijo Khan
UWF Western States Heritage Champion Barry Windham fought Arn Anderson to a double count-out
NWA US Champion Lex Luger defeated NWA TV Champion Nikita Koloff in a Russian chain match
NWA World Champion Ric Flair defeated Ron Garvin in a No DQ match; no managers were allowed ringside for the bout

403

NWA WRESTLING UWF
UNIVERSAL WRESTLING FEDERATION

Saturday, Sept. 12 8:00 pm

St. Louis ARENA

WORLD HEAVYWEIGHT TITLE
Nature Boy Ric Flair
vs.
Ronnie Garvin

WORLD SIX MAN TAG TEAM TITLE
Dusty Rhodes &
The Road Warriors
vs.
The Midnight Express &
Big Bubba

U.W.F. HEAVYWEIGHT TITLE
Steve "Dr. Death" William vs. Dory Funk, Jr.

Special Grudge Tag Team Match
Chris Adams & Sting vs. Terry Taylor & Eddie Gilbert

Plus the Fabulous Freebirds and much more!

Tickets $10, 9, 8; 7 on sale now at the Arena
Box Office and Famous Barr Tickets Now locations

Watch the UWF Every Sat. and Sun., at 10:00 a.m. and NWA
every Sat. at 10:00 pm and Sun. at 11:00 am on KDNL-TV

JCP @ Wilmington, NC - September 7, 1987
Outdoor show was canceled due to rain

JCP @ Amherst, VA - September 8, 1987
Ron & Jimmy Garvin defeated NWA US Tag Team Champions Bobby Eaton & Stan Lane via disqualification

JCP @ Miami, FL - Miami Beach Convention Center - September 9, 1987

JCP @ Atlanta, GA - WTBS Studios - September 9, 1987
World Championship Wrestling taping

JCP @ Jackson, MS - September 10, 1987
NWA US Tag Team Champions Bobby Eaton & Stan Lane defeated Michael Hayes & Shane Douglas when Eaton pinned Douglas after Jim Cornette hit Douglas with his tennis racquet

JCP @ Memphis, TN - Mid-South Coliseum - September 11, 1987
UWF World Champion Steve Williams & the Road Warriors defeated Big Bubba, NWA US Tag Team Champions Bobby Eaton & Stan Lane

JCP @ Charleston, WV - September 11, 1987 (3,000)
George South pinned Mark Fleming
Lazertron pinned Denny Brown
The MOD Squad defeated Italian Stallion & Keith Patterson
Arn Anderson defeated NWA Tag Team Champion Robert Gibson in a No DQ match after Tully Blanchard intefered
NWA Tag Team Champion Ricky Morton defeated Tully Blanchard in a Texas Death match
NWA US Champion Lex Luger defeated NWA TV Champion Nikita Koloff via disqualification
NWA World Champion Ric Flair pinned Ron Garvin

Worldwide - 9/12/87:
Sean Royal vs. Larry Stevens
Ivan Koloff vs. George South
UWF Western States Heritage Champion Barry Windham vs. Vernon Deaton
NWA US Tag Team Champions Bobby Eaton & Stan Lane vs. Dexter Wescott & Ricky Nelson
NWA TV Champion Nikita Koloff vs. Colt Steele
The MOD Squad vs. Rocky King & John Savage

World Championship Wrestling - 9/12/87 - featured Sting vs. Ron Ellis from UWF TV:
Sean Royal vs. Alan Martin
NWA TV Champion Nikita Koloff vs. NWA US Tag Team Champion Bobby Eaton
UWF Western States Heritage Champion Barry Windham vs. Arn Anderson
NWA US Tag Team Champion Stan Lane vs. Mike Jackson

JCP @ St. Louis, MO - Arena - September 12, 1987
Michael Hayes & Sting defeated Eddie Gilbert & Terry Taylor
Black Bart & the Terminator defeated Steve Cox & Shane Douglas
Tim Horner fought Tiger Conway Jr. to a draw
Dusty Rhodes & Road Warrior Hawk defeated NWA US Tag Team Champions Bobby Eaton & Stan Lane in a non-title match
Steve Williams defeated Dory Funk Jr.
Ron Garvin fought NWA World Champion Ric Flair to a draw

JCP @ Greensboro, NC - Coliseum - September 12, 1987 (3,725)
Denny Brown defeated Gladiator #1
The Barbarian pinned George South
The Italian Stallion pinned Teijo Khan
Sean Royal & the MOD Squad defeated Jimmy Valiant, Kendall Windham, & Lazertron
UWF Western States Heritage Champion Barry Windham defeated Ivan Koloff
Jimmy Garvin pinned Manny Fernandez
NWA US Champion Lex Luger defeated NWA TV Champion Nikita Koloff via disqualification; both titles were at stake in the match
NWA Tag Team Champions Ricky Morton & Robert Gibson fought Arn Anderson & Tully Blanchard to a 60-minute time-limit draw

JCP @ Cincinnati, OH - September 13, 1987
NWA US Tag Team Champions Bobby Eaton & Stan Lane defeated Jimmy Valiant & Kendall Windham

JCP @ Dallas, TX - Reunion Arena - September 13, 1987
Gary Young defeated Steve Cox
Ron Simmons defeated Rick Steiner via count-out
Michael Hayes, Shane Douglas, Tim Horner, & Brad Armstrong defeated Shaska Whatley, Tiger Conway Jr., the Terminator, & the Enforcer
Ron Simmons defeated the Enforcer
Sting defeated Terry Taylor via disqualification
Ron Simmons defeated Big Bubba via count-out
Barry Windham defeated Eddie Gilbert
Dusty Rhodes defeated NWA US Champion Lex Luger via disqualification
Steve Williams defeated Black Bart
NWA World Champion Ric Flair fought Ron Garvin to a no contest

JCP @ Kansas City, MO - Kemper Arena - September 18, 1987

JCP @ Pittsburgh, PA - Civic Arena - September 18, 1987
Sean Royal defeated Jimmy Jackson
Denny Brown defeated Colt Steele
The Barbarian defeated Rocky King

Ivan Koloff defeated Kendall Windham
NWA US Tag Team Champions Bobby Eaton & Stan Lane fought UWF Western States Heritage Champion Barry Windham & Jimmy Garvin to a 30-minute time-limit draw
NWA US Champion Lex Luger defeated NWA TV Champion Nikita Koloff via disqualification
NWA Tag Team Champions Ricky Morton & Robert Gibson defeated Arn Anderson & Tully Blanchard
NWA World Champion Ric Flair defeated Ron Garvin

Worldwide - 9/19/87:
NWA Tag Team Champion Ricky Morton vs. Tully Blanchard (death match)
Sting vs. Ron Ellis
UWF Western States Heritage Champion Barry Windham vs. Larry Stevens
NWA US Tag Team Champions Bobby Eaton & Stan Lane vs. Ricky Nelson & George South
Jimmy Valiant vs. John Savage
Dusty Rhodes & Road Warrior Animal vs. NWA US Champion Lex Luger & Arn Anderson (double bullrope match)

JCP @ Charlotte, NC - Coliseum - September 19, 1987
TV taping:
NWA US Tag Team Champions Bobby Eaton & Stan Lane defeated NWA TV Champion Nikita Koloff & UWF Western States Heritage Champion Barry Windham via disqualification
Dusty Rhodes & Road Warrior Animal defeated NWA US Champion Lex Luger & Arn Anderson
NWA Tag Team Champion Ricky Morton defeated Tully Blanchard in a Texas Death Match
NWA World Champion Ric Flair defeated Ron Garvin

JCP @ Raleigh, NC - Dorton Arena - September 1987
TV taping:
World Championship Wrestling - 9/19/87 - hosted by Tony Schiavone; included an ad for the 1987 Great American Bash home video; featured a Ron Garvin training vignette, which showed Garvin running, swimming, and lifting weights in preparation to challenge NWA World Champion Ric Flair; included a feature on the Garvin vs. Flair feud set to Frank Sinatra's "My Way;" featured Schiavone conducting a ringside interview with Dusty Rhodes who claimed NWA US Champion Lex Luger needed to beat him and not the other way around, with Rhodes vowing to put Luger to sleep; moments later, Luger came ringside, with Arn Anderson holding him back; included Schiavone interviewing Sean Royal, who claimed he had been physically upgraded and Chris Champion was currently in the year 2002 undergoing the same process; featured Schiavone conducting a ringside interview with Flair, who claimed Ron Garvin had a date with destiny and that Garvin lacked class and style:
The Barbarian (w/ Paul Jones) pinned Colt Steele at 4:58 with the diving headbutt; the match was joined in progress
UWF Western States Heritage Champion Barry Windham defeated NWA US Champion Lex Luger (w/ JJ Dillon) via

disqualification at 11:58 when, as Luger had Windham covered, referee Earl Hebner interrupted referee Tommy Young's three count and alerted him that Arn Anderson had tripped Windham; only Luger's title was on the line; after the match, Luger and Anderson double teamed Windham, with Luger applying the Torture Rack until NWA Tag Team Champions Ricky Morton & Robert Gibson made the save; after the commercial break, Tony Schiavone conducted a ringside interview with Luger & Dillon, with Luger claiming he would take the US Title to new heights
Ivan Koloff (w/ Paul Jones) pinned George South at 3:07 with the Russian Sickle from the middle turnbuckle
Jimmy Valiant pinned Tommy Angel at the 41-second mark with the elbow drop; the match was joined in progress
Jimmy Garvin (w/ Precious) pinned John Savage at the 59-second mark with the brainbuster
NWA TV Champion Nikita Koloff pinned David Isley at 1:52 with the Russian Sickle; after the match, Schiavone conducted a ringside interview with Koloff about the challenge made by Eddie Gilbert & UWF TV Champion Terry Taylor, with Koloff stating Taylor had a big mouth and he would face him to determine the true TV Champion
NWA Tag Team Champions Ricky Morton & Robert Gibson fought Arn Anderson & Tully Blanchard (w/ JJ Dillon) to a double count-out in a No DQ match at 24:03 (shown) when the two teams began brawling on the floor and fought to the back; moments earlier, Blanchard had pinned Morton after hitting him in the head with Dillon's shoe, but referee Earl Hebner entered the ring and informed referee Tommy Young of what happened, with Young then restarting the match; after the bout, Schiavone conducted a ringside interview with the champions, who claimed they would hold onto their titles no matter what

Pro - 9/19/87:
NWA US Tag Team Champions Bobby Eaton & Stan Lane vs. NWA TV Champion Nikita Koloff & UWF Western States Heritage Champion Barry Windham
The Warlord vs. George South
NWA US Champion Lex Luger vs. Larry Stevens
Jimmy Garvin vs. Teijo Khan
Manny Fernandez vs. Colt Steele (Fernandez' last appearance)
Sean Royal vs. Ricky Nelson

JCP @ Roanoke, VA - Civic Center - September 20, 1987

JCP @ Atlanta, GA - Omni - September 20, 1987 (2,300)
Teijo Khan pinned Larry Clarke
Todd Champion pinned Gladiator #2
The MOD Squad defeated Denny Brown & Rocky King
The Italian Stallion pinned Gladiator #1
Manny Fernandez pinned Kendall Windham
NWA TV Champion Nikita Koloff pinned Big Bubba after the Russian Sickle
Michael Hayes & Jimmy Garvin defeated NWA US Tag Team

Champions Bobby Eaton & Stan Lane via disqualification when Lane hit Hayes with Jim Cornette's tennis racket; Cornette and Precious got into an altercation during the match
NWA Tag Team Champions Ricky Morton & Robert Gibson defeated Arn Anderson & Tully Blanchard in a steel cage match after the 14-minute mark when Morton pinned Anderson after Morton leaped off of the top of the cage

JCP @ Chicago, IL - UIC Pavilion - September 20, 1987
Rick Steiner fought Ron Simmons to a draw
Jimmy Valiant defeated Sean Royal
UWF Western States Heritage Champion Barry Windham defeated Black Bart
Brad Armstrong & Tim Horner defeated Shaska Whatley & Tiger Conway Jr.
Terry Taylor defeated Shane Douglas
Eddie Gilbert defeated Sting
UWF World Champion Steve Williams defeated Ivan Koloff
NWA US Champion Lex Luger defeated Dusty Rhodes via disqualification
NWA World Champion Ric Flair fought Ron Garvin to a no contest

JCP @ Winnsboro, SC - Fairfield Central High School Gym - September 21, 1987
Gladiator #2 vs. Larry Stephens
Gladiator #1 vs. the Italian Stallion
Cougar Jay vs. Rick Nelson
Lazertron & Todd Champion vs. the MOD Squad
Jimmy Garvin vs. Manny Fernandez
UWF Western States Heritage Champion Barry Windham vs. Ivan Koloff

JCP @ Greenville, SC - Memorial Auditorium - September 21, 1987
Denny Brown defeated John Savage (sub. for Teijo Khan)
Colt Steele defeated Rocky King
Jimmy Valiant & Kendall Windham defeated Sean Royal & Teijo Khan (sub. for Chris Champion)
NWA Tag Team Champion Robert Gibson defeated the Barbarian
NWA Tag Team Champion Ricky Morton defeated Tully Blanchard in a Texas Death Match
NWA US Champion Lex Luger & Arn Anderson defeated Dusty Rhodes & NWA TV Champion Nikita Koloff in a Texas Tornado Match
NWA World Champion Ric Flair defeated Ron Garvin in a steel cage match

JCP @ Tampa, FL - Sundome - September 22, 1987
Pro taping:
NWA Super Bouts - 10/87: Dusty Rhodes defeated NWA US Champion Lex Luger (w/ JJ Dillon) via disqualification in a non-title match at around the 12-minute mark when Dillon interfered as Rhodes had Luger in a sleeper; after the bout, Rhodes and Luger continued to brawl, with Luger shoving down referee Bill Alphonso as Luger and Dillon double teamed Rhodes; moments later, Johnny Weaver left the broadcast table and applied the sleeper on Dillon while Rhodes cleared Luger from the ring and prevented him from reentering; Luger eventually pulled Dillon to the floor and helped him backstage

JCP @ Inglewood, CA - Great Western Forum - September 23, 1987
Steve Cox defeated Gary Young
Shane Douglas, Brad Armstrong, & Tim Horner defeated the Enforcer, Shaska Whatley, & Tiger Conway Jr.
Michael Hayes & Ron Simmons defeated Big Bubba & the Terminator
UWF Western States Heritage Champion Barry Windham defeated Rick Steiner
Terry Taylor & Eddie Gilbert defeated Sting & Shane Douglas
UWF World Champion Steve Williams defeated Black Bart
NWA US Champion Lex Luger defeated NWA TV Champion Nikita Koloff
NWA World Champion Ric Flair fought Ron Garvin to a no contest

JCP @ Las Vegas, NV - September 24, 1987
Steve Cox defeated Gary Young
Michael Hayes & Ron Simmons defeated Big Bubba & the Terminator
UWF Western States Heritage Champion Barry Windham defeated Rick Steiner
NWA US Champion Lex Luger defeated NWA TV Champion Nikita Koloff via disqualification
Brad Armstrong & Tim Horner defeated Shaska Whatley & Tiger Conway Jr.
Sting defeated Eddie Gilbert
UWF TV Champion Terry Taylor defeated Shane Douglas
UWF World Champion Steve Williams defeated Black Bart
NWA World Champion Ric Flair defeated Ron Garvin

JCP @ Harrisonburg, VA - High School - September 24, 1987
Rikki Nelson vs. Teijo Khan
Colt Steele vs. John Savage
Rocky King vs. Chris Champion
The Italian Stallion vs. Sean Royal
Todd Champion vs. Manny Fernandez
NWA US Tag Team Champions Bobby Eaton & Stan Lane vs. Ron & Jimmy Garvin

JCP @ Detroit, MI - Joe Louis Arena - September 25, 1987 (8,000)

Debut at the venue
The Barbarian defeated Shane Douglas
Tiger Conway Jr. defeated Gary Young
Sting defeated Eddie Gilbert
Tim Horner defeated Shaska Whatley
NWA Western States Heritage Champion Barry Windham defeated Rick Steiner
Nikita Koloff defeated Ivan Koloff
NWA Super Bouts - 10/87: NWA Tag Team Champions Ricky Morton & Robert Gibson defeated NWA US Tag Team Champions Bobby Eaton & Stan Lane (w/ Jim Cornette) via disqualification at around the 16-minute mark when Eaton hit Gibson in the face with Cornette's tennis racquet; after the bout, Morton stole the racquet away and cleared the ring
Michael Hayes defeated the Terminator
UWF TV Champion Terry Taylor defeated Brad Armstrong
UWF Heavyweight Champion Steve Williams defeated Big Bubba
Dusty Rhodes & the Road Warriors defeated NWA US Champion Lex Luger, Arn Anderson, & Tully Blanchard in a steel cage match
Worldwide - 9/26/87: Ron Garvin pinned NWA World Champion Ric Flair in a steel cage match to win the title with a sunset flip off the top

Pro - 9/26/87:
Mike Rotundo vs. Bobbie Idol
Steve Keirn & Mike Graham vs. the Masked Yankees
NWA US Champion Lex Luger vs. Jim Backlund
NWA TV Champion Nikita Koloff vs. the Black Assassin
UWF Western States Heritage Champion Barry Windham vs. the Masked Villian
Bugsy McGraw vs. Rick Ryder
Kevin Sullivan vs. Rex King
The Sheepherders vs. Bill Mulkey & Rick McCord

World Championship Wrestling - 9/26/87 - featured footage of Ron Garvin winning the NWA World Title from Ric Flair in a steel cage match in Detroit held 9/25/87:
NWA Tag Team Champions Ricky Morton & Robert Gibson vs. Tommy Angel & Mike Force
Kevin Sullivan vs. Larry Stevens
Arn Anderson vs. Art Pritts
Tully Blanchard vs. the Menace
Mike Rotundo vs. Dave Spearman

JCP @ Norfolk, VA - Scope - September 26, 1987
Dusty Rhodes & NWA TV Champion Nikita Koloff defeated NWA US Tag Team Champions Bobby Eaton & Stan Lane via disqualification

World Championship Wrestling Sunday Edition - 9/27/87:
Arn Anderson & Tully Blanchard vs. Mike Force & Mike Jackson
Mike Rotundo vs. Tommy Angel

JCP @ Oklahoma City, OK - Grandstands State Fair - September 27, 1987 (matinee)

JCP @ Greensboro, NC - Coliseum - September 27, 1987
Kendall Windham & Lazortron defeated the MOD Squad
Jimmy Garvin defeated Manny Fernandez
Sting defeated Eddie Gilbert
UWF World Champion Steve Williams defeated Black Bart
NWA Tag Team Champion Ricky Morton defeated NWA US Tag Team Champion Bobby Eaton
NWA Tag Team Champion Robert Gibson defeated NWA US Tag Team Champion Stan Lane via disqualification
NWA World Champion Ron Garvin defeated Big Bubba
Dusty Rhodes, NWA TV Champion Nikita Koloff, & the Road Warriors defeated Ric Flair, NWA US Champion Lex Luger, Arn Anderson, & Tully Blanchard in a steel cage match

JCP @ Greenville, SC - Memorial Auditorium - September 28, 1987
Thunderfoot #1 defeated Rocky King
Teijo Khan defeated Larry Stephens (sub. for Denny Brown)
Denny Brown defeated Gladiator #1
The Italian Stallion & Todd Champion fought the MOD Squad to a draw
NWA US Tag Team Champion Stan Lane defeated Denny Brown
NWA Tag Team Champion Ricky Morton defeated NWA US Tag Team Champion Bobby Eaton
Dusty Rhodes & NWA Tag Team Champion Robert Gibson (sub. for NWA TV Champion Nikita Koloff) defeated Ric Flair & NWA US Champion Lex Luger; the match was initially NWA World Champion Ron Garvin, Rhodes, & Koloff vs. Flair, Luger, & Arn Anderson in an elimination match
NWA World Champion Ron Garvin defeated Arn Anderson

JCP @ Misenheimer, NC - September 29, 1987
TV taping:
Pro - 10/3/87:
NWA World Champion Ron Garvin vs. Tommy Angel
The Warlord vs. David Isley
Arn Anderson & Tully Blanchard (w/ JJ Dillon) defeated NWA Tag Team Champions Ricky Morton & Robert Gibson to win the titles when Gibson told the referee to stop the match as Blanchard had Morton in an arm bar; prior to the bout, NWA US Tag Team Champions Bobby Eaton & Stan Lane, with Jim Cornette, ambushed the champions from behind as they made their way out to the ring; Gibson eventually worked the match alone, with Morton returning late in the bout heavily bandaged and with his left arm in a sling; moments later, Dusty Rhodes, NWA World Champion Ron Garvin, Barry Windham, and others surrounded the ring in support of the champions
Sean Royal vs. Gary Royal

JCP @ Charleston, SC - September 30, 1987
UWF Western States Heritage Champion Barry Windham & Jimmy Garvin defeated NWA US Tag Team Champions Bobby Eaton & Stan Lane via disqualification

JCP @ Raleigh, NC - Dorton Arena - October 1, 1987
NWA Tag Team Champion Arn Anderson defeated Jimmy Garvin in a steel cage match

JCP @ Richmond, VA - Coliseum - October 2, 1987 (3,000)
Rick Steiner pinned Lazertron
Ricky Santana fought MOD Squad Spike to a draw
Denny Brown pinned Colt Steele
Sting pinned John Savage (sub. for the Barbarian, who was in Japan) after the 1-minute mark
Michael Hayes & Jimmy Garvin defeated UWF TV Champion Terry Taylor & Eddie Gilbert when Hayes pinned Gilbert
Florida Heavyweight Champion Mike Rotundo fought Dick Murdoch to a double count-out
The Road Warriors defeated NWA US Tag Team Champions

Bobby Eaton & Stan Lane via disqualification after Lane used Jim Cornette's tennis racket
NWA Tag Team Champions Arn Anderson & Tully Blanchard defeated Ricky Morton & Robert Gibson in a steel cage match when Morton was pinned
The Road Warriors defeated NWA US Tag Team Champions Bobby Eaton & Stan Lane via disqualification

Worldwide - 10/3/87:
UWF Western States Heritage Champion Barry Windham vs. Gary Royal
The Warlord vs. Tommy Angel
Kevin Sullivan vs. Ricky Nelson
Sean Royal vs. John Savage
NWA World Champion Ron Garvin & NWA TV Champion Nikita Koloff vs. NWA US Champion Lex Luger & NWA Tag Team Champion Arn Anderson

World Championship Wrestling - 10/3/87:
The Road Warriors vs. Fields & Franks
UWF TV Champion Terry Taylor vs. Terry Jones
NWA Tag Team Champions Arn Anderson & Tully Blanchard vs. Force & Tommy Angel
NWA US Champion Lex Luger vs. Max McGyver
Ivan Koloff & the Warlord vs. Keith Steinborn & Rusty Riddle
NWA TV Champion Nikita Koloff vs. El Negro

JCP @ Pittsburgh, PA - Civic Arena - October 3, 1987
The Road Warriors defeated NWA US Tag Team Champions Bobby Eaton & Stan Lane via disqualification

JCP @ Charlotte, NC - Coliseum - October 3, 1987
NWA Tag Team Champions Arn Anderson & Tully Blanchard defeated Ricky Morton & Robert Gibson in a steel cage match

JCP @ Asheville, NC - Civic Center - October 4, 1987 (matinee)
Robert Gibson defeated NWA US Tag Team Champion Bobby Eaton

JCP @ Macon, GA - Coliseum - October 4, 1987
Robert Gibson & Jimmy Valiant (sub. for Ricky Morton, selling the injury sustained in Misenheimer) defeated NWA US Tag Team Champions Bobby Eaton & Stan Lane in a non-title match

GREENVILLE, SOUTH CAROLINA
GREENVILLE MEMORIAL AUDITORIUM
MONDAY-OCTOBER 5, 1987
8:00 P.M.

U.S. TITLE MATCH
LEX LUGER (WITH J.J. DILLON) VS BARRY WINDHAM

RONNIE GARVIN VS TULLY BLANCHARD
RONNIE GARVIN

WORLD TAG TEAM TITLE
2 OUT OF 3 FALLS NO DISQUALIFICATIONS
ROCK N ROLL EXPRESS VS MIDNIGHT EXPRESS

TAG ACTION
KENDALL WINDHAM & ITALIAN STALLION VS BILL MULKEY & RANDY MULKEY
BUGSY McGRAW VS THUNDERFOOT #
KEVIN SULLIVAN VS WARLORD
CUBAN CONNECTION VS COLT STEELE & TEIJHO KHAN

NWA
*SUBJECT TO CHANGE
Ringside Reserved $12
General Admission $10
Children (Under 10) $4

410

JCP @ Greenville, SC - Memorial Auditorium - October 5, 1987
Ricky Santana defeated Colt Steele
Kevin Sullivan defeated Teijo Khan
Bugsy McGraw defeated the Warlord
Kendall Windham & Lazortron defeated Gladiator #1 & Thunderfoot #1
Ricky Morton & Robert Gibson defeated NWA US Tag Team Champions Bobby Eaton & Stan Lane in a non-title Best 2 out of 3 falls match
NWA World Champion Ron Garvin defeated NWA Tag Team Champion Tully Blanchard
NWA US Champion Lex Luger defeated UWF Western States Heritage Champion Barry Windham

JCP @ Spartanburg, SC - October 6, 1987
TV taping:
NWA World Champion Ron Garvin vs. NWA Tag Team Champion Tully Blanchard
Dusty Rhodes, Ricky Morton & Robert Gibson vs. NWA Tag Team Champion Arn Anderson, NWA US Champion Lex Luger, and JJ Dillon

JCP @ Cleveland, OH - October 7, 1987
TV taping:
Ric Flair, NWA US Champion Lex Luger, NWA Tag Team Champions Arn Anderson & Tully Blanchard defeated UWF Western States Heritage Champion Barry Windham, Florida Heavyweight Champion Mike Rotunda, Brad Armstrong, & Tim Horer
NWA Super Bouts - 10/87; Power Pro Wrestling - 10/87: UWF Western States Heritage Champion Barry Windham defeated Eddie Gilbert (w/ UWF TV Champion Terry Taylor) via disqualification at around the 20-minute mark when, as Windham had Gilbert covered with a roll up, Taylor entered the ring, hit the champion with his shoe and helped Gilbert double team Windham; Jim Ross provided sole commentary for the bout
Worldwide - 10/87:
NWA World Champion Ron Garvin defeated NWA Tag Team Champion Tully Blanchard (w/ JJ Dillon) via disqualification at around the 6-minute mark when Ric Flair and NWA US Champion Lex Luger interfered after Garvin knocked out both Blanchard and Dillon with punches; after the bout, Luger rammed Garvin's head into a ringside table, busting his head open, and helped gang up on him until the Road Warriors & Paul Ellering made the save and cleared the ring
Dark match after the taping: Dusty Rhodes & the Road Warriors defeated Ric Flair, NWA US Champion Lex Luger, & NWA Tag Team Champion Arn Anderson in a steel cage match

JCP @ Hammond, IN - October 8, 1987
The Road Warriors defeated NWA US Champion Lex Luger & NWA Tag Team Champion Tully Blanchard
NWA World Champion Ron Garvin defeated Ric Flair

JCP @ Albany, GA - Civic Center - October 9, 1987
Big Bubba defeated George South
NWA US Tag Team Champion Bobby Eaton defeated Chris Champion

JCP @ Charleston, WV - October 9, 1987
Robert Gibson defeated NWA Tag Team Champion Arn Anderson

JCP @ ? - October 1987
TV taping:
Pro - 10/87 - featured Bob Caudle & Johnny Weaver on commentary; included footage of JJ Dillon hosting a demonstration by Hiro Matsuda of his version of the sleeper on referee Tommy Young, which almost immediately put Young to sleep; moments later, Johnny Weaver ran in the ring to tend to Young and then slapped Dillon before Matsuda also put him out with the sleeper; NWA World Champion Ron Garvin, Windham, and Dusty Rhodes then ran in the ring to protect Weaver as Dillon announced Rhodes would face Matsuda Oct. 25 at the Greensboro Coliseum:
The Mighty Wilbur (w/ Paul Jones) pinned Ricky Nelson with a splash at 1:15; prior to the bout, Jones yelled at Wilbur for being friendly with the fans; after the match, Johnny Weaver came ringside to interview the two, with Wilbur calling Jones "puddin head" and Jones yelling at him some more

World Championship Wrestling - 10/10/87:
NWA US Champion Lex Luger vs. Ricky Nelson
NWA Tag Team Champions Arn Anderson & Tully Blanchard vs. Martin & Rusty Riddle
The Road Warriors vs. Stevens & David Isley
Eddie Gilbert vs. the Menace
Ivan Koloff vs. Mike Jackson
The Kodiaks vs. Rocky King & Jones
Kevin Sullivan vs. George South
Ron Garvin vs. Mike Force
The Sheepherders vs. Keith Steinborn & Franks
The Warlord vs. Max McGyver
UWF TV Champion Terry Taylor vs. Tommy Angel

JCP @ Denver, CO - October 10, 1987
The Road Warriors defeated Big Bubba & NWA US Tag Team Champion Stan Lane

JCP @ Greensboro, NC - Coliseum - October 10, 1987
Teijo Khan defeated Rocky King
Mike Rotundo defeated Mighty Wilbur
Chris Champion & Sean Royal defeated Teijo Khan & the Warlord
Kevin Sullivan defeated MOD Squad #1
NWA US Champion Lex Luger defeated Sting
Robert Gibson defeated NWA Tag Team Champion Arn Anderson
NWA Tag Team Champion Tully Blanchard defeated Ricky

Morton in a lumberjack match
NWA World Champion Ron Garvin defeated Ric Flair

JCP @ Columbus, OH - October 11, 1987 (2,437)
Barry Windham defeated Dick Murdoch via disqualification
Black Bart defeated Jimmy Valiant
The Kodiaks defeated the Italian Stallion & Kendall Windham
Bobby Eaton & Stan Lane fought Michael Hayes & Jimmy Garvin to a draw
Terry Taylor defetaed Ron Simmons
Tim Horner & Brad Armstrong defetaed the Sheepherders
NWA World Champion Ron Garvin defeated Ric Flair

JCP @ Greenville, SC - Memorial Auditorium - October 12, 1987
The Warlord defeated Todd Champion
Mighty Wilbur defeated the Italian Stallion
Lazortron defeated Teijo Khan
Mike Rotundo defeated Colt Steele
The Road Warriors defeated NWA Tag Team Champions Tully Blanchard & Arn Anderson in a non-title bunkhouse match
Ric Flair & NWA US Champion Lex Luger defeated NWA World Champion Ron Garvin & Robert Gibson

JCP @ Philadelphia, PA - Civic Center - October 14, 1987
Bugsy McGraw defeated Teijo Khan
Mike Rotundo defeated Rick Steiner
Jimmy Valiant defeated the Warlord via disqualification
Michael Hayes & Jimmy Garvin fought Luke Williams & Johnny Ace (sub. for Butch Miller) to a draw
Mighty Wilbur defeated Ivan Koloff
Sting defeated Eddie Gilbert
NWA US Tag Team Champions Bobby Eaton & Stan Lane defeated Chris Champion & Sean Royal
Ric Flair defeated NWA TV Champion Nikita Koloff via disqualification

JCP @ Norfolk, VA - Scope - October 16, 1987
Sean Royal fought MOD Squad Basher to a draw
Bugy McGraw defeated MOD Squad Spike
Kendall Windham defeated Samurai Warrior #1
Mike Rotundo defeated Samurai Warrior #2
Kevin Sullivan fought the Warlord to a draw
Chris Champion & Sean Royal defeated NWA US Tag Team Champions Bobby Eaton & Stan Lane via disqualification
NWA US Champion Lex Luger defeated NWA Western States Heritage Champion Barry Windham
NWA Tag Team Champions Arn Anderson & Tully Blanchard defeated Ricky Morton & Robert Gibson in a steel cage match

JCP @ Atlanta, GA - WTBS Studios - October 17, 1987 (matinee)
World Championship Wrestling - 10/17/87 - featured Tony Schiavone & David Crockett on commentary; included a vignette of Ric Flair with clips from various Starrcades; featured Schiavone conducting an interview with UWF Western States Heritage Champion Barry Windham regarding his upcoming match at Starrcade against UWF World Champion Steve Williams; featured the announcement that Wargames IV would be held Nov. 25 at Long Island's Nassau Coliseum, the night before Starrcade; included footage from Pro of JJ Dillon hosting a demonstration by Hiro Matsuda of his version of the sleeper on referee Tommy Young, which almost immediately put Young to sleep; moments later, Johnny Weaver ran in the ring to tend to Young and then slapped Dillon before Matsuda also put him out with the sleeper; NWA World Champion Ron Garvin, Windham, and Dusty Rhodes then ran in the ring to protect Weaver as Dillon announced Rhodes would face Matsuda Oct. 25 at the Greensboro Coliseum; featured

Schiavone conducting an interview with NWA US Champion Lex Luger & Dillon in which Luger said he would agree to face Rhodes at Starrcade but only with Luger's stipulations; included the Mighty Wilbur vs. Ricky Nelson match from Pro, during which Paul Jones repeatedly yelled at Wilbur not to be friendly with the fans and to be more aggressive against Nelson; moments later, Schiavone conducted an interview at WTBS Studios with Jones regarding Wilbur's behavior, with Jones saying the fans would see a changed man later in the show; featured Schiavone conducting an interview with Rhodes regarding his upcoming match against Matsuda in Greensboro; included a vignette of Rhodes with clips from various Starrcades; featured Schiavone conducting an interview with Dillon, NWA Tag Team Champions Arn Anderson & Tully Blanchard in which they said they didn't care who they would defend against at Starrcade - the Road Warriors, Ricky Morton & Robert Gibson, or the Sheepherders - and noted they too were hurt when they took the titles from Morton & Gibson yet they stuck it out in the match and came out with the belts; Blanchard then responded to comments made earlier in the show by Eddie Gilbert and said he should go sell out some buildings before he starts making fun of the NWA; included Schiavone conducting an interview with Ric Flair in which he discussed the Road Warriors perhaps facing Anderson & Blanchard at Starrcade, responded to Gilbert & Terry Taylor's comments earlier in the show, challenging Garvin at Starrcade, and said the women in New York were starved for a real man like himself:

Sting pinned Gladiator #1 at 2:29 following a Stinger Splash in the corner; after the bout, Tony Schiavone conducted an interview with Sting regarding his WTBS debut and being part of Starrcade (Sting's WTBS debut)

The Sheepherders (w/ Johnny Ace) defeated David Isley & John Savage at 3:57 when Luke Williams pinned Savage following the double gutbuster; after the bout, David Crockett conducted a ringside interview with the Sheepherders & Ace, who said they wanted Brad Armstrong & Tim Horner at Starrcade 87

NWA Tag Team Champions Arn Anderson & Tully Blanchard (w/ JJ Dillon) defeated Rocky King & George South at 3:12 when Blanchard pinned South with the slingshot suplex; after the bout, Anderson dropped King with the gordbuster

UWF TV Champion Terry Taylor (w/ Eddie Gilbert) defeated Larry Stephens via submission with the figure-4 at 1:43; after the bout, Schiavone conducted an interview with Taylor & Gilbert regarding Taylor being in possession of both the NWA and UWF TV titles and Taylor facing NWA TV Champion Nikita Koloff in a title vs. title match at Starrcade

Kevin Sullivan defeated Tony Suber at 1:15 via submission with a modified Cobra Clutch; after the contest, Schiavone conducted an interview with Sullivan in which he guessed the Road Warriors might want NWA Tag Team Champions Arn Anderson & Tully Blanchard at Starrcade in Chicago and that Ricky Morton & Robert Gibson would get their hands on Jim Cornette; Sullivan then discussed the NWA World Champion Ron Garvin vs. Ric Flair and Dusty Rhodes vs. NWA US Champion Lex Luger matches, then said Rhodes would be in big trouble with Hiro Matsuda

Jimmy Valiant & Bugsy McGraw defeated Rex King & Alan Martin at the 45-second mark when McGraw scored the pin with a splash; after the bout, Schiavone conducted an interview with Valiant & McGraw in which they said they would team up at the Atlanta Omni and Nassau Coliseum

Ricky Morton & Robert Gibson defeated Robbie Idol & Eric Long at 1:39 when both men scored the pin following a double DDT; Morton's shoulder was heavily taped for the match

Michael Hayes & Jimmy Garvin (w/ Precious) defeated Thunderfoot #1 & #2 at 1:18 when Hayes scored the pin following the bulldog; after the match, Crockett conducted a ringside interview with Hayes, Garvin, & Precious about being part of Starrcade and Garvin's brother, NWA World Champion Ron Garvin, facing Ric Flair in a cage in Chicago

NWA World Champion Ron Garvin pinned Tommy Angel at 1:18 after two right hand punches; after the match, Schiavone conducted an interview with Garvin regarding his upcoming steel cage match with Ric Flair at Starrcade, during which he said Flair was now nothing more than an ex champion

The Mighty Wilbur (w/ Paul Jones) pinned the Italian Stallion with the splash at 1:23; after the match, Wilbur wouldn't continue to attack Stallion, with the Warlord and Ivan Koloff then coming out and doing it for him; moments later, Crockett attempted to conduct an interview with Wilbur at ringside until Jones repeatedly cut him off and wouldn't let him answer, with Wilbur calling him "puddin head" and Jones then ordering Wilbur backstage

NWA US Tag Team Champions Bobby Eaton & Stan Lane (w/ Jim Cornette & Big Bubba) defeated Rick Ryder & Mike Jackson at 2:01 when Eaton pinned Ryder following the Gravedigger; Cornette provided guest commentary for the match alongside Schiavone; after the bout, Schiavone conducted an interview with Cornette, Bubba, Eaton & Lane regarding Ricky Morton & Robert Gibson

JCP @ Baltimore, MD - Arena - October 17, 1987 (8,000)
The Italian Stallion fought Samurai Warrior #2 to a draw
Kendall Windham defeated Samurai Warrior #1
Mike Rotundo defeated Black Bart
Sting defeated the Terminator
NWA US Tag Team Champions Bobby Eaton & Stan Lane defeated Brad Armstrong & Tim Horner
NWA Tag Team Champions Arn Anderson & Tully Blanchard defeated Ricky Morton & Robert Gibson
NWA World Champion Ron Garvin defeated Ric Flair

JCP @ Atlanta, GA - Omni - October 18, 1987 (about 2,000)
David Sierra, Kendall Windham, & Nelson Royal defeated the Black Assassin & the Samurai Warriors
Kevin Sullivan defeated Teijo Khan
Jimmy Valiant & Bugsy McGraw defeated the MOD Squad
Sting defeated UWF TV Champion Terry Taylor via disqualification
NWA US Tag Team Champions Bobby Eaton & Stan Lane defeated Chris Champion & Sean Royal
NWA TV Champion Nikita Koloff defeated Eddie Gilbert

NWA Tag Team Champion Tully Blanchard defeated Ricky Morton in a lumberjack strap match

JCP @ Roanoke, VA - Civic Center - October 18, 1987 (3,500)
Gary Royal & Colt Steele defeated Larry Stephens & John Savage
Mighty Wilbur defeated Thunderfoot #1
Kendall Windham defeated George South
Robert Gibson defeated Thunderfoot #2
NWA TV Champion Nikita Koloff defeated Big Bubba
Chris Champion & Sean Royal defeated NWA US Tag Team Champions Bobby Eaton & Stan Lane
Ricky Morton defeated NWA Tag Team Champion Tully Blanchard via disqualification

JCP @ Detroit, MI - Joe Louis Arena - October 18, 1987 (1,000)
Shaska Whatley defeated the Italian Stallion
Tim Horner defeated Tiger Conway Jr.
Brad Armstrong fought Rick Steiner to a draw
Florida Heavyweight Champion Mike Rotundo defeated Dory Funk Jr. via disqualification
Michael Hayes & Jimmy Garvin defeated Ivan Koloff & the Warlord
NWA Western States Heritage Champion Barry Windham fought NWA Tag Team Champion Arn Anderson to a no contest
Ric Flair & NWA US Champion Lex Luger defeated NWA World Champion Ron Garvin & Dusty Rhodes

JCP @ New Orleans, LA - Lakefront Arena - October 19, 1987

JCP @ Greenville, SC - Memorial Auditorium - October 19, 1987
Kendall Windham & the Italian Stallion fought the Cuban Connection to a draw
Mighty Wilbur defeated Teijo Khan
Nelson Royal (sub. for Lazortron) defeated Denny Brown
Jimmy Valiant & Bugsy McGraw defeated the MOD Squad
NWA Tag Team Champion Arn Anderson defeated Robert Gibson in a taped fist match
NWA US Tag Team Champions Bobby Eaton & Stan Lane defeated Chris Champion & Sean Royal
Ricky Morton defeated NWA Tag Team Champion Tully Blanchard in a bunkhouse match

JCP @ Baton Rouge, LA - Centroplex - October 20, 1987

JCP @ Monroe, LA - Civic Center - October 21, 1987

JCP @ West Palm Beach, FL - October 22, 1987
Mike Graham defeated Ivan Koloff
Chris Champion & Sean Royal defeated NWA US Tag Team Champions Bobby Eaton & Stan Lane
Robert Gibson defeated Dory Funk Jr. via disqualification
Ricky Morton defeated NWA Tag Team Champion Tully Blanchard in a Texas Death Match
Dusty Rhodes, NWA TV Champion Nikita Koloff, & Kevin Sullivan defeated Ric Flair, NWA US Champion Lex Luger, & NWA Tag Team Champion Arn Anderson

JCP @ Biloxi, MS - Mississippi Coast Coliseum - October 22, 1987

JCP @ Charlotte, NC - Coliseum - October 23, 1987

JCP @ ? - October 1987
Pro taping:
NWA Super Bouts - 10/87: Robert Gibson defeated NWA Tag Team Champion Arn Anderson via count-out in a death match at around the 17-minute mark when, as both men were fighting on the floor, Gibson crawled back in and punched Anderson in the face, preventing him from answering referee Teddy Long's 10-count; Gibson's victory drew audible boos from the crowd; Tony Schiavone & JJ Dillon provided ringside commentary for the match; after the match, it was announced UWF Western States Heritage Champion Barry Windham would face Eddie Gilbert the following week

Pro - 10/24/87:
Jimmy Valiant & Bugsy McGraw vs. George South & John Savage
Mike Rotunda vs. Gladiator #1
Kevin Sullivan vs. Rocky King
UWF Western States Heritage Champion Barry Windham vs. Samurai Warrior #1
Ivan Koloff, the Warlord, & Mighty Wilbur vs. Ricky Santana, David Sierra, & Ricky NelsoN
NWA Tag Team Champions Arn Anderson & Tully Blanchard vs. Kendall Windham & the Italian Stallion
NWA US Tag Team Champions Bobby Eaton & Stan Lane vs. the New Breed

Worldwide - 10/24/87:
NWA Tag Team Champions Arn Anderson & Tully Blanchard vs. John Savage & Rocky King
UWF Western States Heritage Champion Barry Windham vs. George South
Ricky Morton & Robert Gibson vs. Thunderfoot #1 & #2
NWA US Tag Team Champions Bobby Eaton & Stan Lane vs.

Ricky Nelson & David Isley
NWA US Champion Lex Luger vs. Kendall Windham
Mighty Wilbur vs. Tommy Angel

World Championship Wrestling - 10/24/87:
Jimmy Valiant & Bugsy McGraw vs. two unknowns
Barry Windham vs. John Savage
The Mighty Wilbur vs. David Isley
The New Breed vs. Bob Riddle & Gladiator #1
Ivan Koloff & the Warlord vs. Rick Ryder & Rex King
Michael Hayes & Jimmy Garvin vs. Rick Idol & Thunderfoot #1
Kevin Sullivan vs. Terry Jones
NWA Tag Team Champions Arn Anderson & Tully Blanchard vs. Keith Steinborn & Ricky Nelson
Mike Rotundo vs. Alan Martin
Ricky Morton & Robert Gibson vs. Larry Stevens & Tony Suber
NWA US Tag Team Champions Bobby Eaton & Stan Lane vs. George South & the Italian Stallion
Ricky Santana vs. Thunderfoot #2

JCP @ Philadelphia, PA - Civic Center - October 24, 1987
Bugsy McGraw defeated Teijo Khan
Florida Heavyweight Champion Mike Rotundo defeated Rick Steiner
Jimmy Valiant defeated the Warlord via disqualification
Luke Williams & Johnny Ace (sub. for Butch Miller) fought Michael Hayes & Jimmy Garvin to a draw
Mighty Wilbur defeated Ivan Koloff via count-out
Sting defeated Eddie Gilbert
NWA US Tag Team Champions Bobby Eaton & Stan Lane fought Chris Champion & Sean Royal to a draw
Ric Flair defeated NWA TV Champion Nikita Koloff via disqualification

JCP @ Jonesboro, AR - October 25, 1987 (250)
David Haskins fought the Terminator to a draw
Steve Cox pinned Gary Young
The Kodiaks defeated Ken Massey & the Enforcer (Doug Gilbert)
Tim Horner pinned Black Bart
David Haskins pinned Terry Taylor at the 20-minute mark
Brad Armstrong & Tim Horner defeated the Jive Tones

JCP @ Greensboro, NC - Coliseum - October 25, 1987 (3,500)
Ricky Santana defeated MOD Squad Basher
Kendall Windham defeated MOD Squad Spike
Mighty Wilbur defeated Thunderfoot #1
Ivan Koloff fought Kevin Sullivan to a no contest
Dusty Rhodes defeated Hiro Matsuda
NWA US Tag Team Champions Bobby Eaton & Stan Lane defeated Chris Champion & Sean Royal
NWA Western States Heritage Champion Barry Windham defeated NWA Tag Team Champion Arn Anderson
Ric Flair, NWA US Champion Lex Luger, & NWA Tag Team

Champion Tully Blanchard defeated NWA TV Champion Nikita Koloff, Ricky Morton & Robert Gibson

JCP @ Greenville, SC - Memorial Auditorium - October 26, 1987

Cuban Connection #1 vs. Nelson Royal did not take place as advertised

John Savage defeated David Sierra

Kendall Windham & the Italian Stallion defeated the MOD Squad

Mike Rotundo fought Ivan Koloff to a draw

NWA US Tag Team Champions Bobby Eaton & Stan Lane defeated Chris Champion & Sean Royal

UWF Western States Heritage Champion Barry Windham defeated Arn Anderson

NWA TV Champion Nikita Koloff vs. NWA Tag Team Champion Tully Blanchard

Ricky Morton & Robert Gibson defeated Ric Flair & NWA US Champion Lex Luger

JCP @ Harrisonburg, VA - High School Gym - October 29, 1987

The scheduled bouts of Denny Brown vs. Teijo Khan, Cuban Assassin #2 vs. the Warlord, and Jimmy Valiant vs. Samurai #2 did not take place as advertised

Denny Brown defeated David Sierra

The Italian Stallion defeated Thunderfoot #1

Jimmy Valiant defeated Teijo Khan

Mighty Wilbur defeated Ivan Koloff via disqualification

Ricky Morton & Robert Gibson defeated NWA Tag Team Champions Arn Anderson & Tully Blanchard via disqualification

416

JCP @ Norfolk, VA - Scope - October 30, 1987

Pro - 10/31/87:
Ivan Koloff & the Warlord vs. David Isley & Larry Stevens
NWA World Champion Ron Garvin vs. George South
NWA Tag Team Champions Arn Anderson & Tully Blanchard
vs. Ricky Santana & Cougar Jay
Mighty Wilbur vs. Thunderfoot #2
NWA TV Champion Nikita Koloff vs. Gladiator #2
Jimmy Valiant & Bugsy McGraw vs. Chance McQuade &
Tommy Angel
NWA US Tag Team Champions Bobby Eaton & Stan Lane vs.
the Texas Cowboys (Ricky Morton & Robert Gibson under
masks)

World Championship Wrestling - 10/31/87:
Michael Hayes & Jimmy Garvin vs. Gladiator #1 & #2
Ricky Santana vs. Larry Stephens
Dick Murdoch vs. Tommy Angel
Ivan Koloff & the Warlord vs. Rocky King & David Isley
The Mighty Wilbur vs. Cougar Jay
NWA Florida Heavyweight Champion Mike Rotundo vs.
Thunderfoot #2
NWA US Tag Team Champions Bobby Eaton & Stan Lane vs.
Ed Franks & Alan Martin
Sean Royal & Chris Champion vs. Rick Ryder & Robbie Idol
Ricky Morton vs. Joe Lynn
Eddie Gilbert vs. Tony Suber
NWA Tag Team Champions Arn Anderson & Tully Blanchard
vs. Keith Steinborn & Rex King
UWF TV Champion Terry Taylor vs. an unknown

- 10/31/87: Eddie Gilbert and Missy Hyatt were married.

**JCP @ Asheville, NC - Civic Center - November 1, 1987
(matinee)**
Ricky Morton & Robert Gibson defeated NWA US Tag Team
Champions Bobby Eaton & Stan Lane in a non-title bunkhouse
match

JCP @ Orlando, FL - November 1, 1987
Ricky Morton & Robert Gibson defeated NWA US Tag Team
Champions Bobby Eaton & Stan Lane in a non-title bunkhouse
match
Kevin Sullivan defeated Big Bubba via count-out

**JCP @ Salisbury, MD - Wicomico Youth & Civic Center -
November 1, 1987**
TV taping

MID-ATLANTIC CHAMPIONSHIP WRESTLING

GREENVILLE MEMORIAL AUDITORIUM
Monday, Nov. 2
8:00 p.m.

LITES OUT - BUNKHOUSE MATCH
Rock n' Roll Express VS Midnight Express (with Jim Cornette) (and Big Bubba)

SPECIAL CHALLENGE MATCH
Ron Garvin VS Warlord

TEXAS DEATH MATCH
Barry Windham VS Arn Anderson

SPECIAL ATTRACTION
Bugsy McGraw Jimmy Valiant VS Ivan Koloff Barbarian
Ron Simmons VS Hiro Matsuda
"New Breed" Sean Royal VS Mod Squad #1
Todd Champion VS Larry Zbyszko
"New Breed" Chris Champion VS Mod Squad #2

NWA
Ticket Prices: $10, $8, & $4
*subject to change
Ringside Reserved $10
General Admission $8
Children (Under 10) $4

NO49531

MID-ATLANTIC CHAMPIONSHIP WRESTLING

JCP @ Greenville, SC - Memorial Auditorium - November 2, 1987
TV taping:
Chris Champion vs. MOD Squad #2
Todd Champion vs. Larry Zbsyzko
Ron Simmons vs. Hiro Matsuda
Jimmy Valiant & Bugsy McGraw vs. Ivan Koloff & the Barbarian
NWA World Champion Ron Garvin defeated the Warlord
NWA Western States Heritage Champion Barry Windham defeated NWA Tag Team Champion Arn Anderson in a Texas Death Match
Dark match after the taping: Ricky Morton & Robert Gibson defeated NWA US Tag Team Champions Bobby Eaton & Stan Lane in a non-title bunkhouse match

JCP @ Rock Hill, SC - Winthrop Coliseum - November 3, 1987
TV taping:
Johnny Weaver vs. JJ Dillon
Barry Windham vs. NWA Tag Team Champion Arn Anderson (Texas Death match)
NWA World Champion Ron Garvin & NWA TV Champion Nikita Koloff vs. Ric Flair & NWA US Champion Lex Luger
Also featured Michael Hayes, Sting, Kevin Sullivan, Rick Steiner, UWF TV Champion Terry Taylor, Ron Simmons, Larry Zbyszko, Eddie Gilbert, the Sheepherders, Mighty Wilbur, Brad Armstrong & Tim Horner, the Terminator, the Kodiaks, and Black Bart

JCP @ Winston-Salem, NC - Memorial Coliseum - November 3, 1987
Ricky Morton & Robert Gibson defeated NWA US Tag Team Champions Bobby Eaton & Stan Lane in a non-title bunkhouse match

JCP @ Monroe, NC - November 4, 1987
NWA US Tag Team Champions Bobby Eaton & Stan Lane defeated Sean Royal & Chris Champion in a non-title match

JCP @ Portsmouth, OH - Grant Middle School Gym - November 4, 1987
Ron Simmons vs. Larry Zbyszko
Brad Armstrong & Tim Horner vs. the Sheepherders
Sting vs. UWF TV Champion Terry Taylor
Michael Hayes vs. Tully Blanchard
NWA World Champion Ron Garvin & NWA TV Champion Nikita Koloff vs. Ric Flair & NWA US Champion Lex Luger

JCP @ Raleigh, NC - Dorton Arena - November 5, 1987
Rick Steiner defeated Denny Brown
The Italian Stallion & John Savage defeated the Kodiaks
Jimmy Valiant defeated the Terminator
Bugsy McGraw defeated the Barbarian
Mighty Wilbur defeated UWF TV Champion Terry Taylor via

disqualification
Florida Heavyweight Champion Mike Rotundo, Michael Hayes & Jimmy Garvin defeated NWA US Champion Lex Luger, NWA Tag Team Champion Tully Blanchard, & JJ Dillon
NWA TV Champion Nikita Koloff defeated Eddie Gilbert
Ricky Morton & Robert Gibson defeated NWA US Tag Team Champions Bobby Eaton & Stan Lane in a non-title bunkhouse match

JCP @ Marion, NC - November 6, 1987
NWA US Tag Team Champions Bobby Eaton & Stan Lane defeated Sean Royal & Chris Champion in a non-title match

JCP @ Pensacola, FL - Civic Center - November 6, 1987

JCP @ Atlanta, GA - WTBS Studios - November 1987
World Championship Wrestling - 11/7/87 - featured Tony Schiavone & David Crockott on commentary; included Schiavone conducting an interview with Ricky Santana in which he said Dusty Rhodes would beat NWA US Champion Lex Luger and NWA World Champion Ron Garvin would beat Ric Flair at Starrcade; featured Schiavone conducting an interview with Flair regarding his upcoming steel cage match against Garvin at Starrcade, during which he responded to the comments earlier in the show from Santana, made fun of Sean Royal & Chris Champion who were leaving the ring following their match, and said the Four Horsemen would win all their matches at the show; Flair then said the Horsemen and Jim Crockett Promotions would take over New York on Nov. 25; included a Dusty Rhodes vignette showing clips from past Starrcades; featured a Starrcade control center hosted by Schiavone in which it was announced Sting, Michael Hayes, & Jimmy Garvin would face Larry Zbyszko, Rick Steiner, & Eddie Gilbert; Schiavone then said he would speak next week about someone important to the show and the upcoming Bunkhouse Stampede; during the segment, it was noted there would be more than 100 closed circuit locations around the country that would air the event:
Sean Royal & Chris Champion defeated Rex King & Robbie Idol at 5:16 when Champion pinned King with a crossbody off the top as Royal held King up for a suplex
Kevin Sullivan pinned David Isley at 3:05 with the double stomp
Sting pinned Tommy Angel at 3:29 after a Stinger Splash in the corner
NWA US Tag Team Champions Bobby Eaton & Stan Lane (w/ Jim Cornette & Big Bubba) defeated Joe Lynn & Bob Emory at 4:27 when Eaton scored the pin following the Rocket Launcher; Cornette provided guest commentary for the match; during the bout, Cornette said Eaton & Lane along with NWA Tag Team Champions Arn Anderson & Tully Blanchard would face Ricky Morton, Robert Gibson, Chris Champion, & Sean Royal the following night at the Omni; moments later, Eaton brought one of the opponents over to where Cornette was
NWA World Champion Ron Garvin vs. Alan Martin
Hiro Matsuda (w/ JJ Dillon) defeated Rocky King via

submission with the sleeper at 1:56
Ricky Santana vs. Rick Ryder
NWA TV Champion Nikita Koloff vs. Gladiator #1
Kendall Windham vs. Thunderfoot #2
Michael Hayes & Jimmy Garvin vs. Thompson & Tony Suber
Dick Murdoch vs. Bob Cook
Luke Williams & Johnny Ace vs. Phelps & Long

Worldwide - 11/7/87:
NWA TV Champion Nikita Koloff vs. David Isley
NWA Tag Team Champions Arn Anderson & Tully Blanchard vs. Cougar Jay & Gary Royal
Mike Rotunda vs. Thunderfoot #1
Ricky Santana vs. Rick Nelson
NWA US Champion Lex Luger & Hiro Matsuda vs. the Italian Stallion & Larry Stevens
Kevin Sullivan vs. George South
Dusty Rhodes vs. Hiro Matsuda
Mighty Wilbur, Ricky Morton & Robert Gibson vs. Thunderfoot #2, Ivan Koloff, & the Warlord

Pro - 11/7/87:
The New Breed vs. Thunderfoot #1 & #2
NWA US Champion Lex Luger vs. Larry Stevens
Hiro Matsuda vs. Rocky King
NWA US Tag Team Champions Bobby Eaton & Stan Lane vs. George South & Gary Royal
UWF Western States Heritage Champion Barry Windham & Ricky Santana vs. Ivan Koloff & the Warlord

JCP @ Akron, OH - James Rhodes Arena - November 7, 1987 (1,800)
Kendall Windham pinned Thunderfoot #1
Bugsy McGraw & Jimmy Valiant defeated the Kodiaks
Florida Heavyweight Champion Mike Rotunda defeated Big Bubba via disqualification
Jimmy Garvin & Mighty Wilbur defeated the Barbarian & the Warlord when Garvin pinned the Barbarian
Michael Hayes pinned Ivan Koloff
Ricky Morton & Robert Gibson defeated NWA US Tag Team Champions Bobby Eaton & Stan Lane in a non-title bunkhouse match when Gibson pinned Lane after kicking Lane's powder into his own face
Dusty Rhodes defeated NWA US Champion Lex Luger via disqualification when JJ Dillon interfered

JCP @ Anaheim, CA - Convention Center - November 8, 1987 (matinee)
Ron Simmons defeated Black Bart
UWF World Champion Steve Williams defeated Dory Funk Jr. via disqualification
Brad Armstrong & Tim Horner defeated the Canadian Kodiaks (w/ Skandar Akbar)
Shaska Whatley defeated Samoan Tau
The Terminator defeated the Golden Bear
NWA Western States Heritage Champion Barry Windham

fought Larry Zbyszko to a draw
The Road Warriors defeated Luke Williams & Johnny Ace when Road Warrior Animal pinned Ace with a powerslam off the top

JCP @ Atlanta, GA - Omni - November 8, 1987 (3,800)
Rick Steiner fought Kevin Sullivan to a draw
Michael Hayes defeated the Warlord
Mighty Wilbur defeated the Barbarian via disqualification
Ivan Koloff defeated Florida Heavyweight Champion Mike Rotundo
NWA World Champion Ron Garvin defeated Gladiator #1 & #2 in a handicap match
Ric Flair defeated Kendall Windham & the Italian Stallion in a handicap match
Hiro Matsuda defeated Johnny Weaver
NWA US Champion Lex Luger defeated Jimmy Garvin
Dusty Rhodes & NWA TV Champion Nikita Koloff defeated UWF TV Champion Terry Taylor & Eddie Gilbert
Ricky Morton, Robert Gibson, Chris Champion, & Sean Royal fought NWA Tag Team Champions Arn Anderson & Tully Blanchard, NWA US Tag Team Champions Bobby Eaton & Stan Lane to a double disqualification

JCP @ San Francisco, CA - Civic Auditorium - November 9, 1987
Shaska Whatley defeated George Wells
Ron Simmons defeated Black Bart
Brad Armstrong & Tim Horner defeated the Kodiaks
NWA TV Champion Nikita Koloff defeated Eddie Gilbert
UWF Western States Heritage Champion Barry Windham fought Larry Zbyszko to a no contest
The Road Warriors defeated Luke Williams & Johnny Ace
UWF World Champion Steve Williams defeated Dory Funk Jr. via disqualification
NWA World Champion Ron Garvin & Jimmy Garvin defeated Ric Flair & NWA US Champion Lex Luger

JCP @ Toccoa, GA - November 9, 1987
Ricky Morton & Robert Gibson defeated NWA US Tag Team Champions Bobby Eaton & Stan Lane via disqualification

JCP @ Jacksonville, FL - November 10, 1987
NWA US Tag Team Champions Bobby Eaton & Stan Lane defeated Chris Champion & Sean Royal

JCP @ Atlanta, GA - WTBS Studios - November 11, 1987
TV taping

JCP @ Atlanta, GA - WTBS Studios - November 12, 1987
TV taping

JCP @ West Palm Beach, FL - South Florida Fairgrounds - November 13, 1987

Admission was free with a paid ticket to the Florida Heritage Festival
Louis Astia vs. Rick Ryder
Jimmy Valiant & Busgy McGraw vs. the Mighty Yankees
Misty Blue vs. Linda Dallas
Kevin Sullivan, Mike Graham, & Rex King defeated Big Bubba, NWA US Tag Team Champions Bobby Eaton & Stan Lane
UWF Western States Heritage Champion Barry Windham vs. Dory Funk Jr.

JCP @ Hampton, VA - Coliseum - November 13, 1987
Rick Steiner fought Ricky Santana to a draw
Mike Rotundo defeated Thunderfoot #1 (Joel Deaton)
Robert Gibson defeated the Barbarian via disqualification
Ricky Morton defeated NWA Tag Team Champion Arn Anderson in a lumberjack match
UWF TV Champion Terry Taylor defeated Mark Fleming
Dusty Rhodes & Johnny Weaver defeated NWA US Champion Lex Luger & Hiro Matsuda
The Road Warriors defeated Ivan Koloff & the Warlord
NWA World Champion Ron Garvin & NWA TV Champion Nikita Koloff defeated Ric Flair & NWA Tag Team Champion Tully Blanchard when Garvin pinned Flair

Pro - 11/14/87:
Sting vs. Tommy Angel
Larry Zbyszko vs. Curtis Thompson
UWF TV Champion Terry Taylor & Eddie Gilbert vs. Rocky King & Rick Nelson
UWF Western States Heritage Champion Barry Windham vs. Rick Steiner

World Championship Wrestling - 11/14/87:
UWF World Champion Steve Williams vs. Rex King
Michael Hayes & Jimmy Garvin vs. Long & Phelps
Ricky Santana vs. Bob Emory
NWA Tag Team Champions Arn Anderson & Tully Blanchard vs. Washington & El Negro
Ivan Koloff & the Warlord vs. Thompson & Max McGyver
NWA US Champion Lex Luger vs. Tony Suber
Larry Zbyszko vs. Ricky Nelson
UWF TV Champion Terry Taylor & Eddie Gilbert vs. Knight & Fox
UWF Western States Heritage Champion Barry Windham vs. Cougar Jay
Luke Williams & Johnny Ace vs. David Isley & Tommy Angel
Shaska Whatley & Tiger Conway Jr. vs. Martin & the Menace

JCP @ Sarasota, FL - Robarts Arena - November 14, 1987
NWA US Tag Team Champions Bobby Eaton & Stan Lane defeated Mike Graham & Rex King
NWA Super Bouts - 11/87: UWF Western States Heritage Champion Barry Windham fought Dory Funk Jr. to a 20-minute time-limit draw; after the bout, Funk attacked the champion but Windham hit him with a dropkick and left the ring with the title belt

JCP @ Oklahoma City, OK - November 15, 1987 (500) (matinee)
Big Bubba defeated an unknown
NWA US Tag Team Champion Bobby Eaton defeated an unknown
Kevin Sullivan defeated NWA US Tag Team Champion Stan Lane

JCP @ Tulsa, OK - Convention Center - November 15, 1987 (3,000)
TV taping:
NWA Super Bouts - 11/21/87: NWA Western States Heritage Champion Barry Windham defeated Larry Zbyszko (w/ Baby Doll) via reverse deicison; Zbyszko initially won the match and title at around the 15-minute mark after hitting Windham with a foreign object but Tim Horner came out, told the referee what happened, and the referee changed the decision after the weapon fell out of the challenger's tights; after the match, Zbyszko assaulted both Windham and Horner with the title belt before shoving the referee
Dusty Rhodes & NWA TV Champion Nikita Koloff defeated UWF TV Champion Terry Taylor & Eddie Gilbert

JCP @ Inglewood, CA - Great Western Forum - November 16, 1987 (1,500)
Shaska Whatley & Tiger Conway Jr. defeated Billy Anderson & Tim Patterson
Ron Simmons pinned the Terminator
Sting pinned Black Bart by using the ropes for leverage
Brad Armstrong & Tim Horner defeated Luke Williams & Johnny Ace at around the 16-minute mark when Horner pinned Luke after Brad tripped Luke from the floor
Michael Hayes defeated UWF TV Champion Terry Taylor via disqualification when Eddie Gilbert interfered
NWA Western States Heritage Champion Barry Windham fought Larry Zbyszko to a double count-out at 22:17
NWA TV Champion Nikita Koloff pinned Eddie Gilbert at 5:38
Ric Flair & NWA US Champion Lex Luger defeated NWA World Champion Ron Garvin & UWF Heavyweight Champion Steve Williams at 22:13 in an elimination match; Flair pinned Garvin after hitting him with his shoe; following the pinfall, it was announced Luger and Williams, who had been fighting on the floor during the pinfall, had been counted-out

MID-ATLANTIC CHAMPIONSHIP WRESTLING

NWA

GREENVILLE MEMORIAL AUDITORIUM

MONDAY, NOVEMBER 16, 1987
8:00 P.M.

U.S. TAG TITLE

NEW BREED VS **MIDNIGHT EXPRESS (WITH JIM CORNETTE) (AND BIG BUBBA)**

SIX MAIN TAG ACTION

ROCK 'N ROLL EXPRESS MIGHTY WILBUR VS **IVAN KOLOFF WARLORD BARBARIAN**

KEVIN SULLIVAN VS HIRO MATSUDA

JOHN SAVAGE VS RICK STEINER

ROCKY KING DENNY BROWN VS CANADIAN KODIAKS (WITH AKBAR)

LARRY STEPHENS VS TEIJO KANN

RIC NELSON VS BILL MULKEY

*NWA

Ticket Prices
Ringside Reserved $10
General Admission $8
Children (Under 16) $4
*subject to change

MID-ATLANTIC CHAMPIONSHIP WRESTLING

JCP @ Greenville, SC - Memorial Auditorium - November 16, 1987
Rocky King & Denny Brown vs. the Canadian Kodiaks (w/ Skandar Akbar), Larry Stephens vs. Teijo Khan, and Ricky Nelson vs. Bill Mulkey did not take place as advertised
Ricky Nelson fought Larry Stephens to a draw
John Savage defeated Thunderfoot #1 (sub. for Rick Steiner)
Denny Brown defeated Rocky King
Kevin Sullivan & the Barbarian defeated Hiro Matsuda & Rick Steiner
Mighty Wilbur, Ricky Morton & Robert Gibson defeated Ivan Koloff, the Warlord, & Barbarian
NWA US Tag Team Champions Bobby Eaton & Stan Lane defeated Chris Champion & Sean Royal

JCP @ El Paso, TX - Civic Center - November 17, 1987

JCP @ Columbia, SC - Township Auditorium - November 17, 1987
Worldwide - 11/28/87:
NWA Florida Heavyweight Champion Mike Rotundo pinned David Isley at 2:02
Mighty Wilbur pinned Gene Ligon at the 49-second mark
Ricky Santana pinned Thunderfoot #1 at 3:55
Nelson Royal pinned Denny Brown; stipulations stated the winner would become the new NWA Jr. Heavyweight Champion
Rick Steiner pinned George South at 2:28
Ivan Koloff, the Barbarian, & the Warlord defeated Curtis Thompson, Max McGyver, & Chance McQuade when Barbarian pinned McQuade at 3:33
Pro - 11/28/87:
Bugsy McGraw & Jimmy Valiant defeated Thunderfoot #1 & George South at 2:44 when McGraw pinned Thunderfoot
Ricky Santana pinned Gary Royal
Rick Steiner pinned Tommy Angel at 3:20
NWA US Tag Team Champions Bobby Eaton & Stan Lane defeated Ricky Morton & Robert Gibson via disqualification

JCP @ Lincolnton, NC - November 18, 1987
NWA US Tag Team Champions Bobby Eaton & Stan Lane defeated Chris Champion & Sean Royal

JCP @ Troy, OH - Hobart Arena - November 19, 1987
NWA US Tag Team Champions Bobby Eaton & Stan Lane vs. Ricky Morton & Robert Gibson

NWA WRESTLING PRESENTS

WRESTLING

Brushfork Armory Civic Center
Bluefield, W.Va.

Friday Nov. 20th, 8:00 P.M.
Sponsored by: **Spanishburg Athletic Dept.**
Advance Tickets: **Brushfork Armory, Bluefield**
Douglas Sporting Goods, Princeton, Deli-Mart, Athens
* * * * * * * * * * * * * * * *

RONNIE GARVIN & JIMMY GARVIN vs TULLY BLANCHARD & ARN ANDERSON	MIGHTY WILBUR vs IVAN KOLOFF
	NEW BREED vs BARBARIAN & WARLORD
KENDALL WINDHAM vs RICK STEINER	CUBAN CONNECTION vs SAMURAI WARRIOR 2
DENNY BROWN vs JOHN SAVAGE	RICKY SANTANA vs SAMURAI WARRIOR 1

JCP @ Bluefield, WV - Brushfork Armory Civic Center - November 20, 1987
Ricky Santana vs. Samurai Warrior #1
Denny Brown vs. John Savage
Cuban Connection vs. Samurai Warrior #2
Chris Champion & Sean Royal vs. the Powers of Pain
Mighty Wilbur vs. Ivan Koloff
Rick Steiner vs. Kendall Windham
Ron & Jimmy Garvin vs. NWA Tag Team Champions Arn Anderson & Tully Blanchard

JCP @ Williamson, WV - Fieldhouse - November 20, 1987
Michael Hayes vs. Larry Zbyszko
Barry Windham vs. NWA US Champion Lex Luger
Ricky Morton & Robert Gibson vs. NWA US Tag Team Champions Bobby Eaton & Stan Lane (bunkhouse match)
Nikita Koloff vs. Ric Flair (#1 contenders match)
Also included Sting, UWF TV Champion Terry Taylor, Brad Armstrong, and Black Bart

World Championship Wrestling - 11/21/87:
Chris Champion & Sean Royal vs. David Isley & Jones
NWA Florida Heavyweight Champion Mike Rotundo vs. Tommy Angel
Sting vs. Cougar Jay

Kevin Sullivan vs. Alan Martin
UWF World Champion Steve Williams vs. Thunderfoot #2
Rick Steiner vs. Ricky Nelson
NWA US Tag Team Champions Bobby Eaton & Stan Lane vs. King & Max McGyver
The Road Warriors vs. Laperouse & Thompson
Larry Zbyszko vs. Larry Stephens
Shaska Whatley & Tiger Conway Jr. vs. Washington & El Negro
Eddie Gilbert vs. George Fox
UWF TV Champion Terry Taylor vs. Bob Emory

JCP @ Washington DC - Armory - November 21, 1987
Kevin Sullivan fought the Barbarian to a draw
Sting defeated Larry Zbyszko via disqualification
UWF Heavyweight Champion Steve Williams defeated Rick Steiner
Michael Hayes & Jimmy Garvin defeated Eddie Gilbert & UWF TV Champion Terry Taylor
NWA World Champion Ron Garvin defeated NWA Tag Team Champion Arn Anderson
Ricky Morton & Robert Gibson defeated NWA US Tag Team Champions Bobby Eaton & Stan Lane in a non-title bunkhouse match
The Road Warriors defeated Ric Flair & NWA Tag Team Champion Tully Blanchard via disqualification
Dusty Rhodes defeated NWA US Champion Lex Luger in a non-title bullrope match

Pro - 11/21/87:
Larry Zbyszko vs. David Isley
NWA Tag Team Champions Arn Anderson & Tully Blanchard vs. Mike Rotunda & Ricky Santana
Ricky Morton & Robert Gibson vs. Tony Suber & Max McGyver
NWA TV Champion Nikita Koloff vs. Eddie Gilbert

JCP @ Johnstown, PA - War Memorial Arena - November 22, 1987 (2,000) (matinee)
Eddie Gilbert pinned Jimmy Jackson
Big Bubba pinned John Gavin
Kevin Sullivan fought Rick Steiner to a draw
Paul Ellering pinned JJ Dillon
NWA Tag Team Champion Arn Anderson pinned Robert Gibson at 10:30 by using the ropes for leverage
Ricky Morton pinned NWA Tag Team Champion Tully Blanchard at 9:30 by using the ropes for leverage
The Road Warriors defeated NWA US Tag Team Champions Bobby Eaton & Stan Lane in a non-title match after Road Warrior Hawk hit Lane with Jim Cornette's tennis racquet

JCP @ Boone, NC - November 22, 1987
Ricky Morton & Robert Gibson defeated NWA US Tag Team Champions Bobby Eaton & Stan Lane in a non-title match

MID-ATLANTIC CHAMPIONSHIP WRESTLING

NWA
GREENVILLE MEMORIAL AUDITORIUM

MONDAY, NOVEMBER 23, 1987
8:00 P.M.

SIX-MAN TAG MATCH

ROAD WARRIORS
AND
PAUL ELLERING

VS.

"NATURE BOY" RIC FLAIR

TULLY BLANCHARD
J.J. DILLON

SPECIAL EVENT
JOHNNY WEAVER **VS.** HIRO MATSUDA

NIKITA KOLOFF **VS.** EDDIE GILBERT

BARRY WINDHAM **VS.** RICK STEINER

NEW BREED **VS.** BLACK BART BARBARIAN

KEVIN SULLIVAN **VS.** GLADIATOR #1

JOHN SAVAGE **VS.** NELSON ROYAL

*NWA

Ticket Prices
Ringside Reserved '10
General Admission '8
Children (Under 10) '4

*subject to change

MID-ATLANTIC CHAMPIONSHIP WRESTLING

JCP @ Greenville, SC - Memorial Auditorium - November 23, 1987
John Savage vs. Nelson Royal
Kevin Sullivan vs. Gladiator #1
Chris Champion & Sean Royal vs. Black Bart & the Barbarian
Barry Windham vs. Rick Steiner
NWA TV Champion Nikita Koloff vs. Eddie Gilbert
Johnny Weaver vs. Hiro Matsuda
The Road Warriors & Paul Ellering vs. Ric Flair, NWA Tag Team Champion Tully Blanchard, & JJ Dillon

JCP @ Bennettsville, SC - November 23, 1987
Ricky Morton & Robert Gibson defeated NWA US Tag Team Champions Bobby Eaton & Stan Lane in a non-title match

JCP @ Hillsville, VA - November 24, 1987 (800)
John Savage pinned Gladiator #1 (Gary Royal)
Ricky Santana defeated Rocky King
NWA Florida Heavyweight Champion Mike Rotundo defeated Thunderfoot #1
Kevin Sullivan pinned Eddie Gilbert by using the ropes for leverage
Rick Steiner pinned Kendall Windham by using the tights for leverage
Jimmy Valiant, Bugsy McGraw, & Mighty Wilbur defeated Ivan Koloff, the Warlord, & the Barbarian via disqualification
NWA Western States Heritage Champion Barry Windham pinned NWA Tag Team Champion Arn Anderson at the 15-minute mark

JCP @ Long Island, NY - Nassau Coliseum - November 25, 1987 (11,500)
Debut at the venue
Sting & Ron Simmons fought UWF TV Champion Terry Taylor & the Barbarian to a draw
Larry Zbyszko defeated Kevin Sullivan
Jimmy Valiant, Bugsy McGraw, & Mighty Wilbur defeated Black Bart, the Warlord, & Ivan Koloff
Michael Hayes & Jimmy Garvin defeated the Jive Tones
UWF Heavyweight Champion Steve Williams defeated Rick Steiner
The Sheepherders defeated Brad Armstrong & Tim Horner
NWA TV Champion Nikita Koloff defeated Eddie Gilbert
The Road Warrior defeated Ric Flair & NWA US Champion Lex Luger via disqualification
NWA World Champion Ron Garvin, Dusty Rhodes, NWA Western States Heritage Champion Barry Windham, Ricky Morton & Robert Gibson defeated Big Bubba, NWA Tag Team Champions Arn Anderson & Tully Blanchard, NWA US Tag Team Champions Bobby Eaton & Stan Lane when Eaton submitted to Rhodes' figure-4

MID-ATLANTIC CHAMPIONSHIP WRESTLING

STARRCADE '87
ON THE WIDE SCREEN
IN COLOR VIA CLOSED CIRCUIT TV

Sumter, S.C.
Exhibition Center 8 PM
THANKSGIVING NITE - NOV. 26

NWA WORLD'S HEAVYWEIGHT TITLE BOUT

Champion
RON GARVIN
-vs-
RIC FLAIR

Cage Match
*No Time Limit
*No D.Q.

GARVIN

FLAIR

DUSTY RHODES -vs- **LEX LUGER**

ROCK 'N ROLL EXPRESS -vs- **MIDNITE EXPRESS**

ROAD WARRIORS
with Paul Ellering
-vs-
ARN ANDERSON
and
TULLY BLANCHARD

N.W.A. TV Title
NIKITA KOLOFF -vs- **TERRY TAYLOR**

"DR. DEATH" WILLIAMS
-vs-
BARRY WINDHAM
8 Man Tag Team Match
"FREEBIRD" MICHAEL HAYES
"STING"
JIMMY GARVIN with PRECIOUS
-vs-
GILBERT, ZBYSZKO, STEINER

GENERAL ADMISSION
$10.00

Tickets On Sale Sumter-SEACO Music and Weynick's Pharmacy, Alice Drive

Tickets on Sale at The Exhibition Center Thursday, Nov. 26th - Box Office Opens at 12 Noon

424

JCP @ New Orleans, LA - Lakefront Arena - November 26, 1987 (1,610)
Starrcade 87 was shown in closed circuit following the live matches
Jimmy Valiant & Bugsy McGraw defeated Tiger Conway Jr. & Shaska Whatley at 7:32 when Valiant pinned Conway
Ron Simmons pinned Johnny Ace at 4:00 with a flying shoulderblock
Sean Royal pinned Killer Khalifa at 4:11 with a kneedrop off the top
UWF Tag Team Champions the Sheepherders (w/ Johnny Ace) defeated Brad Armstrong & Tim Horner via disqualification when Horner grabbed the flagpole from Ace and used it as a weapon; the match was advertised as Chris Champion & Sean Royal vs. the Sheepherders in a steel cage match but both Champion and the cage did not appear

JCP @ Greensboro, NC - Coliseum - November 26, 1987 (6,000)
Starrcade 87 was shown in closed circuit following the live matches
The Warlord defeated Ricky Santana
Florida Heavyweight Champion Mike Rotunda defeated Black Bart
Misty Blue won a $15,000 7-woman battle royal; other participants included Kat Leroux, Linda Dallas, Jamie West, Venus, Mad Dog Debbie, and Whitney Hansen
Kevin Sullivan defeated Hiro Matsuda
Mighty Wilbur defeated Ivan Koloff

Starrcade 87 - Chicago, IL - UIC Pavilion - November 26, 1987 (8,000; sell out)
Pay-per-view bouts - featured Jim Ross & Tony Schiavone on commentary:
Michael Hayes, Jimmy Garvin, & Sting fought Eddie Gilbert, Rick Steiner, & Larry Zbyszko to a 15-minute time-limit draw
UWF Heavyweight Champion Steve Williams pinned NWA Western States Heritage Champion Barry Windham
Ricky Morton & Robert Gibson defeated NWA US Tag Team Champions Bobby Eaton & Stan Lane (w/ Jim Cornette & Big Bubba) in a scaffold match at around the 9-minute mark; prior to the bout, Bubba dropped Morton with the sidewalk slam inside the ring; order of elimination: Morton knocked Lane off the scaffold (8-minute mark); Lane appeared to injure his knee in the fall; Eaton by Morton & Gibson after being repeatedly hit with Cornette's tennis racquet; after the match, Bubba climbed the scaffold to face Morton but Morton landed a low blow before climbing back down and putting on Bubba's hat and jacket (*Starrcade: The Essential Collection*)
NWA TV Champion Nikita Koloff pinned UWF TV Champion Terry Taylor in a unification match
NWA Tag Team Champions Arn Anderson & Tully Blanchard (w/ JJ Dillon) defeated the Road Warriors (w/ Paul Ellering) via reverse decision; the challengers originally won the match and titles at 13:24 when Road Warrior Animal pinned Anderson following the Doomsday Device but referee Tommy Young overruled Earl Hebner's decision since he saw Animal throw Anderson over the top moments before the pinfall; after the bout, the Road Warriors left ringside with the title belts (*The Life & Death of the Road Warriors, Starrcade: The Essential Collection*)
Dusty Rhodes pinned NWA US Champion Lex Luger (w/ JJ Dillon) in a steel cage match to win the title at 16:24 with a DDT onto a steel chair thrown over the top and into the cage by Dillon; pre-match stipulations stated if Rhodes lost he couldn't wrestle for 90 days; Johnny Weaver was in possession of the cage key until late in the match when he was knocked down by Dillon outside the ring (*The Best of Starrcade: 1983-1987, American Dream: The Dusty Rhodes Story*)
Ric Flair (w/ JJ Dillon) pinned NWA World Champion Ron Garvin to win the title in a steel cage match at 17:38 after catching Garvin running off the ropes and ramming his head into the cage (*The Best of Starrcade: 1983-1987*)

JCP @ Atlanta, GA - WTBS Studios - November 28, 1987 (matinee)
World Championship Wrestling - 11/28/87:
Ricky Morton & Robert Gibson vs. Larry Stephens & Trent Knight
Michael Hayes & Jimmy Garvin vs. Gladiator #1 & #2
Larry Zbyszko vs. Bob Riddle
Sting vs. David Isley
NWA US Tag Team Champions Bobby Eaton & Stan Lane vs. Thunderfoot #1 & #2
UWF World Champion Steve Williams vs. Tommy Angel
Rick Steiner vs. Ron Simmons
NWA Tag Team Champions Arn Anderson & Tully Blanchard vs. King & Chance McQuade
UWF Western States Heritage Champion Barry Windham, Mighty Wilbur, & Ricky Santana vs. Ivan Koloff, the Warlord, & the Barbarian
World Championship Wrestling Sunday Edition - 11/29/87

JCP @ St. Petersburg, FL - Bayfront Center - November 28, 1987
Mighty Yankee #2 defeated Rick Ryder
Bugsy McGraw defeated Mighty Yankee #1
Sting, Michael Hayes, & Jimmy Garvin defeated Ivan Koloff, the Warlord, & the Barbarian
NWA TV Champion Nikita Koloff defeated Eddie Gilbert
NWA Western States Heritage Champion Barry Windham fought Larry Zbyszko to a draw
Ricky Morton & Robert Gibson defeated NWA US Tag Team Champions Bobby Eaton & Stan Lane in a non-title bunkhouse match
NWA US Champion Dusty Rhodes & the Road Warriors defeated Lex Luger, NWA Tag Team Champions Tully Blanchard & Arn Anderson via disqualification
NWA World Champion Ric Flair defeated Ron Garvin

JCP @ Little Rock, AR - Barton Coliseum - November 29, 1987

JCP @ Monroe, LA - December 1, 1987
TV taping:
Included NWA US Tag Team Champions Bobby Eaton & Stan Lane and a Bunkhouse Stampede match
Pro - 12/5/87 - included Jim Ross & Bob Caudle on commentary; featured Tony Schiavone conducting an interview with NWA Tag Team Champions Arn Anderson & Tully Blanchard, alongside JJ Dillon, regarding Michael Hayes & Jimmy Garvin, during which Anderson called out Lex Luger for being the sole member of the Horsemen to not win their respective match at Starrcade; included Schiavone conducting an interview with Jim Crockett Jr., with Crockett saying Hayes & Garvin heard Anderson & Blanchard's comments and wanted a match against them, with Crockett saying they would face the Horsemen in the last match on the show:
Steve Williams vs. Tug Taylor
Michael Hayes vs. an unknown
Larry Zbyszko vs. Ron Ellis
The Road Warriors vs. Terry Hays & Chan Torrez
Ricky Morton & Robert Gibson vs. Jerry Newton & Craig Wintford
Michael Hayes & Jimmy Garvin defeated NWA Tag Team Champions Arn Anderson & Tully Blanchard (w/ JJ Dillon) via disqualification in a non-title match at around the 7-minute mark when Blanchard hit Hayes with Dillon's shoe as Hayes had Anderson covered after hitting a bulldog; after the contest, Hayes & Garvin cleared the champions from the ring (the match began during the commercial break)

JCP @ Miami, FL - Knight Center - December 2, 1987 (2,000)
TV taping:
NWA US Tag Team Champion Bobby Eatong defeated Rex King
NWA US Tag Team Champion Stan Lane defeated Kendall Windham
NWA Western States Heritage Champion Barry Windham fought Larry Zbyszko to a time-limit draw after the 20-minute mark
NWA World Champion Ric Flair pinned Michael Hayes at the 25-minute mark
Lex Luger won a Bunkhouse Stampede by last eliminating JJ Dillon; eliminations late in the match: Ricky Santana by Luger; NWA Tag Team Champion Tully Blanchard eliminated himself; NWA Tag Team Champion Arn Anderson eliminated himself; after the eliminations, Anderson climbed on the apron to tell Luger to take a dive like the rest of them so Dillon could win; after the match, Luger press slammed Blanchard and dropped Anderson with a powerslam before putting him in the Torture Rack; moments later, Blanchard hit Luger in the back of the knee with a steel chair before he, Anderson, and Dillon ganged up on Luger's leg; Mike Rotundo and others then came out to make the save

JCP @ Atlanta, GA - WTBS Studios - December 3, 1987

World Championship Wrestling - 12/5/87 - Jim Ross' debut as host:
NWA Western States Heritage Champion Barry Windham vs. Larry Zbyszko
The Powers of Pain vs. Towers & Idol
Steve Williams vs. Jerry Grey
Sting vs. Bob Cook
NWA US Tag Team Champion Stan Lane vs. Kendall Windham
NWA Tag Team Champions Arn Anderson & Tully Blanchard vs. Gary Royal & the Italian Stallion
NWA TV Champion Nikita Koloff vs. Mark Starr
Kevin Sullivan vs. Rick Ryder
NWA US Tag Team Champion Bobby Eaton vs. Rex King
Mike Rotundo vs. Thunderfoot #1
NWA World Champion Ric Flair vs. Michael Hayes
World Championship Wrestling Sunday Edition - 12/6/87

JCP @ Hampton, VA - Coliseum - December 4, 1987
TV taping:
Also included a Bunkhouse Stampede match
Pro - 12/12/87:
Michael Hayes & Jimmy Garvin vs. Cougar Jay & David Isley
The Powers of Pain vs. Tommy Angel & an unknown
NWA TV Champion Nikita Koloff vs. John Savage
Mighty Wilbur vs. an unknown
NWA US Tag Team Champions Bobby Eaton & Stan Lane defeated NWA Florida Heavyweight Champion Mike Rotundo & Ricky Santana when Rotunda left ringside with Kevin Sullivan

JCP @ Lakeland, FL - December 5, 1987
Included a 25-man Bunkhouse Stampede match involving NWA US Tag Team Champions Bobby Eaton & Stan Lane

JCP @ Charlotte, NC - Coliseum - December 6, 1987 (matinee)
Mighty Wilbur defeated NWA Tag Team Champion Arn Anderson
The Road Warriors & Paul Ellering defeated JJ Dillon, NWA Tag Team Champions Arn Anderson & Tully Blanchard
NWA World Champion Ric Flair pinned Sting
Worldwide - 12/19/87:
NWA TV Champion Nikita Koloff vs. Thunderfoot #2
Ivan Koloff & the Warlord vs. Rocky King & Jessie McClain
Mike Rotunda vs. John Savage
Steve Williams vs. Gladiator #1
Larry Zbyszko vs. the Italian Stallion
Michael Hayes & Jimmy Garvin defeated NWA US Tag Team Champions Bobby Eaton & Stan Lane via disqualification

JCP @ Atlanta, GA - Omni - December 6, 1987 (8,800)
Balcony seats were $5 for adults and $1 for children
Bugsy McGraw fought the Barbarian to a time-limit draw
Larry Zbyszko pinned Ricky Santana (sub. for NWA Western States Heritage Champion Barry Windham) at the 11-minute

mark by using the ropes for leverage
UWF Tag Team Champions the Sheepherders fought Brad Armstrong & Tim Horner to a 15-minute time-limit draw
Sting pinned Terry Taylor with a sunset flip
UWF Heavyweight Champion Steve Williams & Ron Simmons defeated Kevin Sullivan & the Black Assassin (Bill Tabb) when Williams pinned Assassin with the Oklahoma Stampede
NWA TV Champion Nikita Koloff defeated Eddie Gilbert in a chain match by dragging Gilbert to all four corners
The Road Warriors defeated NWA World Champion Ric Flair & NWA Tag Team Champion Arn Anderson (sub. for Lex Luger) via disqualification when NWA Tag Team Champion Tully Blanchard interfered
NWA Tag Team Champions Arn Anderson & Tully Blanchard, NWA US Tag Team Champions Bobby Eaton & Stan Lane defeated Ricky Morton & Robert Gibson, Chris Champion & Sean Royal in a steel cage match at 10:30 when Anderson pinned Gibson; after the bout, Morton & Gibson and Champion & Royal argued

JCP @ Lafayette, LA - December 7, 1987
Included a 26-man Bunkhouse Stampede match involving NWA US Tag Team Champions Bobby Eaton & Stan Lane

JCP @ Greenville, SC - Memorial Auditorium - December 7, 1987
Kids under 10 were admitted for $1
Denny Brown defeated Ricky Nelson
Nelson Royal defeated the Italian Stallion
Rocky King defeated John Savage
Jimmy Valiant defeated Thunderfoot #1
The Barbarian defeated Bugsy McGraw
Ivan Koloff & the Warlord defeated Chris Champion & Sean Royal; stipulations stated the winners would be the #1 contenders for the NWA US Tag Team Titles

JCP @ Baton Rouge, LA - December 8, 1987
NWA TV Champion Nikita Koloff pinned NWA Florida Heavyweight Champion Mike Rotundo; after the bout, Rotundo & Kevin Sullivan attacked Koloff
Big Bubba won a 28-man Bunkhouse Stampede match

JCP @ Atlanta, GA - WTBS Studios - December 9, 1987
World Championship Wrestling - 12/12/87:
Brad Armstrong & Tim Horner vs. Gary Royal & Cougar Jay
UWF Western States Heritage Champion Barry Windham vs. Trent Knight
Michael Hayes & Jimmy Garvin vs. David Isley & Savage
UWF World Champion Steve Williams vs. Gladiator #2
Ron Garvin vs. Larry Stephens
Mighty Wilbur & Ricky Santana vs. Brown & Lynn
Sting vs. Tommy Angel
Larry Zbyszko vs. Rocky King
NWA TV Champion Nikita Koloff vs. Thunderfoot #1
NWA US Tag Team Champions Bobby Eaton & Stan Lane vs. George South & the Italian Stallion
World Championship Wrestling - 12/19/87:
NWA TV Champion Nikita Koloff vs. David Isley
NWA US Tag Team Champions Bobby Eaton & Stan Lane vs. King & Cougar Jay
UWF World Champion Steve Williams vs. Trent Knight
The Barbarian vs. Larry Stephens
NWA Florida Heavyweight Champion Mike Rotundo vs. the Italian Stallion
Larry Zbyszko vs. Tony Suber
Michael Hayes & Jimmy Garvin vs. Gladiator #1 & #2
Sting & Ricky Morton vs. Thompson & Savage
The Road Warriors vs. Thunderfoot #1 & #2
NWA Tag Team Champions Arn Anderson & Tully Blanchard vs. Kendall Windham & Denny Brown

JCP @ Raleigh, NC - Dorton Arena - December 10, 1987 (4,000)
NWA World Champion Ric Flair fought Jimmy Garvin to a no contest
World Championship Wrestling - 12/26/87 - featured Tony Schiavone & Jim Ross on commentary; included David Crockett conducting an interview in the arena with Lex Luger in which he responded to comments made by NWA Tag Team Champions Arn Anderson & Tully Blanchard in which they said they were just trying to spank Luger when they jumped him in Miami, FL; Luger said they tried to cripple him, they crossed a line, and he would start his payback with Anderson; featured Schiavone & Ross announcing that 5 men would take part in a Wildcard Bunkhouse Stampede Jan. 1 at the Omni to determine the final name entered into the Jan. 24 Bunkhouse Stampede Finals in Long Island and the participants would be NWA TV Champion Nikita Koloff, NWA US Tag Team Champion Bobby Eaton, Dick Murdoch, Black Bart, and NWA US Champion Dusty Rhodes; it was also announced that Big Bubba, Anderson & Blanchard, the Warlord, the Barbarian, Ivan Koloff, Luger, Mighty Wilbur, UWF World Champion Steve Williams, and Road Warrior Animal had already qualified for

the Bunkhouse Stampede Finals; included Crockett conducting an interview with Rhodes & Nikita regarding their match later in the show against NWA US Tag Team Champions Eaton & Stan Lane, during which Rhodes said he would give title shots to the likes of Eaton, Larry Zbyszko, Blanchard, and Anderson, the possibility of facing Koloff one-on-one at the Omni as part of the Bunkhouse Stampede, and teaming with Koloff before it was cool for America and Russia to work together; Koloff then cut a promo on Mike Rotundo and Kevin Sullivan and the match later in the show; featured an ad promoting "The Danger Zone" home video; included Crockett conducting an interview with UWF Western States Heritage Champion Barry Windham in the arena in which he spoke about his match at Starrcade against Williams and said he wouldn't make the same mistake again; featured Crockett conducting an interview in the arena with Ricky Morton regarding the Sheepherders; included Crockett conducting an interview in the arena with International Tag Team Champions the Road Warriors & Paul Ellering regarding Road Warrior Animal being in the Bunkhouse Stampede Finals; featured footage of Ole Anderson coming to Luger's aid Christmas Day at the Omni against Anderson, Blanchard, and JJ Dillon and Ross conducting an in-ring interview with Luger & Ole moments later, setting up Luger & Ole vs. Anderson & Blanchard Jan. 1 at the Omni; included Crockett conducting an interview in the arena with NWA World Champion Ric Flair, Anderson, & Blanchard regarding the challenge of Luger, during which Flair cut a promo on Michael Hayes as well:
Ron Garvin & Mighty Wilbur defeated Chance McQuade & Tommy Angel at 5:00 when Wilbur pinned McQuade with a splash after Garvin hit McQuade with the right hand punch; during the bout, a graphic appeared on the screen noting the show was being taped at the "Dorn Arena" instead of the Dorton Arena; after the contest, Tony Schiavone conducted a ringside interview with Garvin & Wilbur in which Garvin said Wilbur had his respect and was the top contender to NWA World Champion Ric Flair; Wilbur then said he was very excited about teaming with Garvin and called all his friends to let them know
International Tag Team Champions the Road Warriors (w/ Paul Ellering) defeated Bob Emory & Trent Knight at the 54-second mark when Road Warrior Hawk pinned Knight following the Doomsday Device
Larry Zbyszko (w/ Baby Doll) pinned Ricky Nelson at 5:03 with a swinging neckbreaker; during the bout, a graphic appeared on the screen noting the show was being taped at the "Dorn Arena" instead of the Dorton Arena
Sting defeated Mark Fleming via submission with the Scorpion Deathlock at 5:39
UWF World Champion Steve Williams pinned Curtis Thompson with the Oklahoma Stampede at 3:10
Eddie Gilbert pinned George South with the Hot Shot at 4:34
Michael Hayes pinned Larry Stephens at the 48-second mark
NWA US Champion Dusty Rhodes & NWA TV Champion Nikita Koloff defeated NWA US Tag Team Champions Bobby Eaton & Stan Lane (w/ Jim Cornette & Big Bubba) via disqualification at around the 22-minute mark when Cornette climbed in the ring and tried to hit Rhodes with the tennis

racquet as Rhodes had Eaton in the figure-4; after the bout, Rhodes put Cornette out with a sleeper before Eaton, Lane, & Bubba assaulted Rhodes & Koloff; eventually, Bubba carried Cornette backstage as Eaton & Lane double teamed Koloff in the ring, with Rhodes then covering Koloff's body to cushion the blow of the Rocket Launcher

NWA Florida Heavyweight Champion Mike Rotundo (w/ Kevin Sullivan) pinned David Isley with the butterfly suplex at 4:37; Sullivan provided guest commentary for the match, during which he responded to comments made earlier in the show by NWA TV Champion Nikita Koloff and said Koloff's true enemy was NWA US Champion Dusty Rhodes because Rhodes took the US title shot that Koloff deserved and made Koloff soft

Michael Hayes won a Bunkhouse Stampede; other participants included: NWA Tag Team Champion Arn Anderson, Mighty Wilbur, the Road Warriors, Kendall Windham, NWA US Tag Team Champions Bobby Eaton & Stan Lane, Ron Garvin, Paul Ellering, Sting, Kevin Sullivan, Big Bubba, Ricky Morton, NWA Florida Heavyweight Champion Mike Rotundo, Eddie Gilbert, UWF World Champion Steve Williams, and Gladiator; eliminations: Rotundo by Gilbert via a backdrop; only 2 minutes of the match was shown (the match was joined in progress; the finish was not shown)

JCP @ Baltimore, MD - Arena - December 12, 1987 (4,000) (matinee)
Larry Zbyszko defeated Mighty Wilbur
Sting fought the Barbarian to a draw
Eddie Gilbert defeated NWA TV Champion Nikita Koloff via disqualification
UWF Heavyweight Champion Steve Williams pinned Terry Taylor
Michael Hayes defeated NWA World Champion Ric Flair via disqualification
Road Warrior Hawk won a 25-man Bunkhouse Stampede match by last eliminating Big Bubba; NWA US Tag Team Champions Bobby Eaton & Stan Lane were also in the match

JCP @ Greensboro, NC - Coliseum - December 12, 1987 (6,000)
TV taping:
Lex Luger won a 25-man Bunkhouse Stampede; NWA US Tag Team Champions Bobby Eaton & Stan Lane were also in the match
Pro - 1/2/88:
NWA US Tag Team Champions Bobby Eaton & Stan Lane defeated Mike Force & Cougar Jay
Kevin Sullivan defeated Rocky King
UWF Heavyweight Champion Steve Williams defeated Tommy Salvage
NWA Tag Team Champions Tully Blanchard & Arn Anderson defeated Gary Royal & John Salvage
The Road Warriors defeated Chance McQuade & Larry Stevens
The Warlord defeated George South
NWA World Champion Ric Flair pinned Sting
Worldwide - 1/2/88 - featured Bob Caudle conducting an

opening ringside interview with Lex Luger in which he took off his T-shirt and challenged NWA Tag Team Champion Arn Anderson to come out and show him what he's got; Anderson then rushed down as the opening credits began; included Tony Schiavone & David Crockett on commentary, with Crockett then interviewing Larry Zbyszko & Baby Doll in which they said they were after Barry Windham's NWA Western States Heritage Title and Dusty Rhodes' NWA US Title; featured an ad promoting the Bunkhouse Stampede Finals on Jan. 24 on pay-per-view; included Schiavone running down the 11 participants entered into the Bunkhouse Stampede Finals - Rhodes, Anderson, NWA Tag Team Champion Tully Blanchard, Steve Williams, Mighty Wilbur, Road Warrior Animal, Warlord, Barbarian, Big Bubba, Ivan Koloff, and Luger - and clarifying the rules of the $500,000 match; Schiavone brought in Jim Crockett Jr. who said NWA World Champion Ric Flair would face Road Warrior Hawk as part of the event, with Schiavone then conducting an interview with Rhodes about his participation in the match, his match later in the night with NWA TV Champion Nikita Koloff against Anderson & Blanchard, and replied to the comments made earlier in the show from Zbyszko & Baby Doll; featured Schiavone conducting an interview with Luger about his recent brawl with Anderson, with Luger saying it was all on the line for both of their careers, said Anderson drew first blood, and there wasn't a building where Anderson was safe; included Schiavone conducting an interview with Flair in which he discussed the challenges of Michael Hayes, Sting, and Road Warrior Hawk; featured Schiavone conducting an interview with Paul Ellering & the Road Warriors about the upcoming weightlifting challenge against the Powers of Pain, Animal being in the Bunkhouse Stampede Finals, and Hawk facing Flair; included Schiavone conducting an interview with Paul Jones, Koloff, & the Warlord about the upcoming benchpress challenge against the Road Warriors:

Ricky Morton pinned Mike Force at the 47-second mark with a backslide; moments later, David Crockett conducted a ringside interview with Morton in which he discussed the Sheepherders putting down America and said he wouldn't stand for it
Ron Garvin pinned Thunderfoot #1 at the 42-second mark after the Garvin Stomp
Sting defeated Thunderfoot #2 via submission with the Scorpion Deathlock at the 31-second mark
Eddie Gilbert pinned George South with the Hot Shot at 1:25; on his way to the ring, Gilbert smacked away an NWA calender a fan had open to Sting's month; Gilbert used what would later be Sting's theme music for the bout
NWA US Champion Dusty Rhodes & NWA TV Champion Nikita Koloff defeated NWA Tag Team Champions Arn Anderson & Tully Blanchard via disqualification in a non-title match at 9:44 when Anderson threw Koloff over the top rope; after the match, NWA World Champion Ric Flair ran out and attacked Koloff on the floor, with Lex Luger then running out and chasing Anderson backstage
Big Bubba, NWA US Tag Team Champions Bobby Eaton & Stan Lane (w/ Jim Cornette) defeated Kendall Windham, the Italian Stallion, & Mighty Wilbur at 3:41 when Lane pinned

Stallion after the Flapjack; Cornette joined the commentary team for the bout

JCP @ Albany, GA - December 13, 1987 (matinee) (4,000)
Television taping:
Ivan Koloff (w/ Paul Jones) pinned Chris Champion after Jones interfered
NWA US Tag Team Champions Bobby Eaton & Stan Lane defeated Denny Brown & George South
NWA US Champion Dusty Rhodes & NWA TV Champion Nikita Koloff defeated NWA Tag Team Champions Arn Anderson & Tully Blanchard via disqualification
NWA World Champion Ric Flair pinned Ron Garvin
NWA Tag Team Champion Tully Blanchard won a 25-man Bunkhouse Stampede by last eliminating Mighty Wilbur

JCP @ Cincinatti, OH - December 13, 1987
UWF World Champion Steve Williams defeated Jim Lancaster
Ivan Koloff defeated Mike Rotunda
Larry Zbyzsko defeated the Mighty Wilbur via count-out
NWA Tag Team Champions Tully Blanchard & Arn Anderson fought NWA US Champion Dusty Rhodes & NWA TV Champion Nikita Koloff to a draw
NWA World Champion Ric Flair defeated Sting
Mighty Wilbur won a 25-man Bunkhouse Stampede match

Pro - 12/19/87:
The Sheepherders vs. Ricky Morton & Robert Gibson
Sting vs. Gene Miller
Steve Williams vs. Keith Steinborn
Larry Zbyszko vs. Ed Franks
NWA TV Champion Nikita Koloff vs. NWA Florida Heavyweight Champion Mike Rotundo (w/ Kevin Sullivan)

JCP @ Greenville, SC - Memorial Auditorium - December 25, 1987 (matinee)
The Sheepherders vs. Chris Champion & Sean Royal, Bugsy McGraw vs. Black Bart, and Ron Simmons & Mike Rotundo vs. Shaska Whatley & Tiger Conway Jr. did not take place as advertised
Nelson Royal (sub. for Johnny Ace) fought Kendall Windham to a draw
Ricky Santana defeated Thunderfoot #1
Mike Rotunda defeated the Italian Stallion
Shaska Whatley defeated Rocky King
Brad Armstrong & Tim Horner defeated the Barbarian & John Savage
The Barbarian won a $20,000 25-man Bunkhouse Stampede; other participants included: Eddie Gilbert, Terry Taylor, Ricky Santana, Bugsy McGraw, the Sheepherders, Brad Armstrong, Jimmy Valiant, Chris Champion & Sean Royal, Johnny Ace, Shaska Whatley, Tiger Conway Jr., Ron Simmons, Black Bart, Tim Horner, Rocky King, John Savage, Kendall Windham, Mike Rotundo, Denny Brown, Italian Stallion, Thunderfoot #1, and Nelson Royal

MID-ATLANTIC CHAMPIONSHIP WRESTLING

NWA

GREENVILLE MEMORIAL AUDITORIUM
Friday, Dec. 25, 1987
2:00 p.m.

BUNKHOUSE STAMPEDE
$20,000 - 25 MAN OVER TOP ROPE

Jimmy Valiant

New Breed

Brad Armstrong

Tim Horner

EDDIE GILBERT
TERRY TAYLOR
RICKY SANTANA
BUGSY McGRAW
SHEEPHERDERS
BRAD ARMSTRONG
JIMMY VALIANT
NEW BREED
JOHNNY ACE
SHASKA WHATLEY
TIGER CONWAY
RON SIMMONS
BARBARIAN
BLACK BART
TIM HORNER
ROCKY KING
JOHN SAVAGE
KENDALL WINDHAM
MIKE ROTUNDA
DENNY BROWN
ITALLION STALLION
THUNDERFOOT #1
NELSON ROYAL

UWF TAG TEAM TITLE

THE SHEEPHERDERS (WITH ACE) VS THE NEW BREED

TAG ACTION

RON SIMMONS
MIKE ROTUNDA VS JIVE TONES
SHASKA WHATLEY & TIGER CONWAY

RICKY SANTANA VS THUNDERFOOT #1

BUGSY McGRAW VS BLACK BART (WITH ARBAR)

KENDALL WINDHAM VS JOHNNY ACE

*NWA SUBJECT TO CHANGE

ALL SEATS $4.00
FAN APPRECIATION DAY
2:00 P.M.
CHRISTMAS DAY

MID-ATLANTIC CHAMPIONSHIP WRESTLING

JCP @ Charlotte, NC - Coliseum - December 25, 1987 (matinee)
Included a 27-man Bunkhouse Stampede match involving NWA US Tag Team Champions Bobby Eaton & Stan Lane

JCP @ Atlanta, GA - Omni - December 25, 1987
Lex Luger won a 26-man Bunkhouse Stampede by last eliminating NWA Tag Team Champion Tully Blanchard after NWA Tag Team Champion Arn Anderson interfered and attacked Luger, with the momentum knocking Blanchard over the top; other participants included: NWA US Tag Team Champions Bobby Eaton & Stan Lane, Michael Hayes, and others; eliminations late in the bout: Hayes by Blanchard; Anderson by Luger; after the bout, Luger was triple teamed by Anderson, Blanchard, and JJ Dillon until Ole Anderson made the save and helped clear the ring; Luger and Ole then brawled with Blanchard & Anderson all the way backstage; moments later, Jim Ross conducted an in-ring interview with Luger & Ole in which they challenged Anderson & Blanchard to a title match on Jan. 1

Worldwide - 12/26/87:
Michael Hayes & Jimmy Garvin vs. Dave Spencer & an unknown
NWA US Tag Team Champion Bobby Eaton vs. Randy Mulkey
Larry Zbyszko vs. Tim Horner
Ron Garvin vs. Alan Martin
Sting vs. Steve Atkinson
The Road Warriors vs. the Menace & an unknown

JCP @ Richmond, VA - Coliseum - December 26, 1987 (matinee)
Television taping:
Included NWA US Tag Team Champions Bobby Eaton & Stan Lane and a 28-man Bunkhouse Stampede match

JCP @ Detroit, MI - December 26, 1987
Black Bart fought Tim Horner to a draw
Mike Rotunda defeated the Italian Stallion
Jimmy Garvin defeated Ivan Koloff
NWA TV Champion Nikita Koloff fought Dick Murdoch to a draw
Road Warrior Hawk won a Bunkhouse Stampede match

JCP @ Philadelphia, PA - Civic Center - December 26, 1987
NWA US Tag Team Champion Bobby Eaton fought UWF Western States Heritage Champion Barry Windham to a 20-minute time-limit draw
NWA World Champion Ric Flair defeated Sting
Also included a 20-man Bunkhouse Stampede match

JCP @ Charleston, WV - Civic Center - December 27, 1987 (matinee)
NWA US Tag Team Champion Bobby Eaton defeated Chris Champion

Also included a 24-man Bunkhouse Stampede match
World Championship Wrestling - Sunday Edition - 1/3/88 - included Tony Schiavone on commentary; featured Schiavone conducting an opening ringside interview with NWA World Champion Ric Flair regarding Sting, Lex Luger, and the Horsemen still running the NWA into 1988; included Schiavone conducting a ringside interview with Luger regarding the Horsemen in which he said he couldn't take all the Horsemen on himself but he could take them one by one and wanted to start with Anderson; featured Schiavone conducting a ringside interview with the Road Warriors & Paul Ellering regarding their $50,000 benchpress contest against the Powers of Pain Jan. 30 in Greensboro and Road Warrior Hawk's upcoming match against Flair Jan. 24 at the Nassau Coliseum; included an ad for The Danger Zone home video:
NWA Tag Team Champions Arn Anderson & Tully Blanchard (w/ JJ Dillon) defeated Kendall Windham & Larry Stephens at 3:39 when Anderson pinned Stephens following the spinebuster and gordbuster; following the bout, Tony Schiavone conducted a ringside interview with Dillon, Anderson & Blanchard in which they bragged about having the gold while all the other teams were just contenders
Black Bart (w/ Skandar Akbar) pinned George South with a legdrop off the middle turnbuckle at 3:15
Shaska Whatley & Tiger Conway Jr. defeated Mike Force & Gene Ligon at 4:26 when Whatley pinned Force following a double Russian legsweep; after the match, Schiavone conducted a ringside interview with Whatley & Conway in which they said they would dominate 1988
Florida Heavyweight Champion Mike Rotunda (w/ Kevin Sullivan) pinned Chance McQuade with a butterfly suplex at 1:53; after the bout, Schiavone conducted a ringside interview with Sullivan & Rotunda in which Rotunda said he was the first member of the Varsity Club and wanted the belts of either NWA US Champion Dusty Rhodes or NWA TV Champion Nikita Koloff
NWA US Tag Team Champion Bobby Eaton (w/ Jim Cornette) pinned Mark Fleming with a kneedrop off the top at 3:41; during the bout, Cornette joined Schiavone on commentary to say Eaton would be the next NWA US Champion; after the contest, NWA US Tag Team Champion Stan Lane joined Cornette and Eaton for a ringside interview with Schiavone, during which Cornette said Lane would be the next NWA TV Champion and that he and the Midnight Express would retire Rhodes
The Sheepherders (w/ Johnny Ace) defeated Tommy Angel & David Isley at 4:18 when Luke Williams pinned Isley following the double gutbuster; Ace briefly joined Schiavone on commentary during the match; after the contest, Schiavone conducted a ringside interview with the Sheepherders & Ace in which they said they would begin crippling people in the NWA and said they started with Ricky Morton & Robert Gibson

JCP @ Norfolk, VA - Scope - December 27, 1987
NWA US Tag Team Champion Bobby Eaton fought UWF Western States Heritage Champion Barry Windham to a 20-minute time-limit draw

JCP @ St. Louis, MO - Arena - December 28, 1987 (matinee)
TV taping:
Ron Garvin defeated NWA Tag Team Champion Arn Anderson via disqualification
NWA US Champion Dusty Rhodes & the Road Warriors defeated Ivan Koloff & the Powers of Pain
Michael Hayes & Jimmy Garvin defeated NWA Tag Team Champions Arn Anderson & Tully Blanchard via disqualification
Steve Williams won a bunkhouse battle royal
NWA World Champion Ric Flair defeated Sting

JCP @ Savannah, GA - Civic Center - December 29, 1987
Included a 20-man Bunkhouse Stampede match

JCP @ Albuquerque, NM - Tingley Coliseum - December 29, 1987

JCP @ Johnson City, TN - Freedom Hall - December 30, 1987

JCP @ Chicago, IL - UIC Pavilion - December 30, 1987
Jimmy Garvin defeated Eddie Gilbert
Ron Simmons defeated Johnny Ace
NWA Western States Heritage Champion Barry Windham defeated Larry Zbyszko via disqualification
NWA TV Champion Nikita Koloff fought Dick Murdoch to a draw
NWA World Champion Ric Flair defeated Sting
Road Warrior Animal won a Bunkhouse Stampede

JCP @ Atlanta, GA - WTBS Studios - December 31, 1987 (matinee)
World Championship Wrestling taping:
1/2/88:
Michael Hayes & Jimmy Garvin vs. Bradley & Martin
Lex Luger vs. Keith Steinborn
Dick Murdoch vs. Jason Walker
Eddie Gilbert vs. Steve Atkinson
NWA US Tag Team Champions Bobby Eaton & Stan Lane vs. Mike Jackson & Mark Starr
Larry Zbyszko vs. Lee Peak
NWA TV Champion Nikita Koloff vs. the Menace
NWA Tag Team Champion Arn Anderson vs. Ron Garvin
NWA US Champion Dusty Rhodes & the Road Warriors vs. Ivan Koloff, the Warlord & the Barbarian

1988.

Jim Crockett Promotions was still chasing the WWF. But only because there wasn't much else competition left.

Ric Flair was no longer touring Toronto, Seattle, Dallas, and St. Louis, working for different promoters each night against varied challengers. The NWA World Champion worked for JCP. There was still limo driving and jet flying, but it was on Jim Crockett Jr.'s tab.

Crockett and Vince McMahon alone hosted live pro wrestling on cable TV and pay-per-view. It would be December '88 before the AWA could share in that, and then it was only one event.

Flair and the Horsemen, now featuring Barry Windham, were running strong, chased from town to town by the likes of Lex Luger, Sting, Dusty Rhodes, Nikita Koloff, and Steve Williams. The Varsity Club and Powers of Pain became prominent players. And Crockett leveraged gimmick matches - the Triple Cage of Doom, barbed wire matches, scaffold matches, the Prince of Darkness match, and others - in an attempt to give the audience as much spectacle as that of the WWF.

Fans could argue that Crockett had the more athletic wrestling, but when it came to marketing and production value there was no contest. The WWF still wasn't winning over fans in all of its new markets (Hulk Hogan vs. Andre the Giant in '88 failed to sell out the Omni and Greensboro Coliseum), but had already solidified its foothold internationally through TV deals and European tours. And the company went so far as to book the Omni to host a closed-circuit showing of WrestleMania IV.

JCP was reeling from the disaster of Starrcade '87. Their first pay-per-view attempt of '88 was a live airing of the Bunkhouse Stampede finals, from Long Island's Nassau Coliseum. Six thousand fans packed inside the arena, a far cry from the 15,000-seat sell outs when Hulk Hogan came to town. To make matters worse, the WWF aired its own live TV special on the USA Network that night, the inaugural Royal Rumble which also served to hype Hogan vs. Andre as part of a live primetime NBC special. Two months later, Crockett fired back by airing the first Clash of the Champions primetime special on WTBS, opposite the WWF's pay-per-view offering of WrestleMania IV. And while the Clash is regarded as the stronger show of the night, its ability to sway fans away from the WWF product was negligible.

Perhaps the most noticeable change in '88 was the fans' growing frustration with Rhodes positioned as a top babyface. Rhodes, JCP's longtime booker, began the year not only as the US title holder but also by three-peating as the winner of the Bunkhouse Stampede finals. Akin to a modern reaction to John Cena, Dusty began hearing more and more boos during his segments. The reaction was heightened when, for several weeks, he wrestled as the masked Midnight Rider while "on suspension." Windham's heel turn to join the Horsemen, feuding with Rhodes in the process, did more to sway fans to the side of the Horsemen than it did to create sympathy for Dusty.

Rhodes' problems weren't confined to his on-screen appearances. The impressive stadium crowds of the Great American Bash tour were no more. The crowd at the Charlotte Memorial Stadium was less than half the size of '85 and '86. Greensboro shows started the year with 12,000-plus fans in attendance but fell to little more than 2,000. Even the Crockett Cup tag team tournament, held in the heart of the JCP territory, could only fill up roughly half of the Coliseum.

And as the crowds dissipated, so did the talent. As the year progressed, more and more talent became frustrated with their position in the company and the falling size of their paychecks. Robert Gibson left, splitting up the Rock 'n' Roll Express. Ron Garvin left for the AWA and then WWF. Tully Blanchard & Arn Anderson, cornerstones of the Horsemen and two of the territory's top workhorses, jumped ship to the WWF along with the Sheepherders and Powers of Pain. Nikita Koloff took time off to be with his ailing wife and wouldn't return on a full-time basis until 1991.

By the fall, the writing was on the wall. JCP was bleeding money at the expense of fans and wrestlers.

Enter Ted Turner.

The Georgia-based media mogul had long been a fan of professional wrestling. His WTBS had aired pro wrestling dating back to Georgia Championship Wrestling in 1972.

For months, the two sides aimed to work out a buyout that would keep the product on TV, the wrestlers employed and the live events profitable. The deal was signed on Nov. 2, 1988.

And while it ensured the continuation of the NWA, improved production quality and a spot within the Turner media family, it spelled the end of Jim Crockett Promotions.

1988

JCP @ Atlanta, GA - Omni - January 1, 1988 (12,700)
Jimmy Garvin, Sting, & Ricky Santana defeated Terry Taylor, Mike Rotundo, & Kevin Sullivan at 10:14 when Sting pinned Taylor
Ron Garvin pinned Eddie Gilbert at 12:14
The Sheepherders defeated Ricky Santana & Robert Gibson at 10:15 when Luke Williams pinned Santana after Butch Miller hit him with the flagpole
NWA Western States Heritage Champion Barry Windham fought Larry Zybzsko to a 20-minute time-limit draw
Road Warrior Animal defeated the Warlord via disqualification at 8:00 when the Barbarian interfered; after the bout, Sting made the save; the match was scheduled for the Road Warriors vs. the Powers of Pain but Road Warrior Hawk didn't appear as scheduled
Lex Luger & Ole Anderson defeated NWA Tag Team Champions Arn Anderson & Tully Blanchard after 19 minutes in a non-title match when Luger pinned Anderson after Anderson ran into a steel chair held up by Blanchard
NWA World Champion Ric Flair pinned Michael Hayes at 15:46 by using the ropes for leverage
NWA US Champion Dusty Rhodes defeated NWA TV Champion Nikita Koloff, Dick Murdoch, Black Bart, and NWA US Tag Team Champion Bobby Eaton in a Bunkhouse Stampede match at the 7-minute mark by last eliminating Eaton; stipulations stated the winner would earn the final spot in the 3rd annual Bunkhouse Stampede

JCP @ Asheville, NC - Civic Center - January 2, 1988
NWA US Tag Team Champion Stan Lane defeated Chris Champion
NWA TV Champion Nikita Koloff defeated NWA US Tag Team Champion Bobby Eaton

JCP @ Greensboro, NC - Coliseum - January 2, 1988 (12,457)
Dick Murdoch pinned the Italian Stallion
Brad Armstrong & Tim Horner defeated the Gladiators (sub. for Sean Royal & Chris Champion)
The Sheepherders defeated Ricky Santana & Robert Gibson
NWA Tag Team Champion Tully Blanchard defeated Jimmy Garvin in a Texas Death Match
The Road Warriors defeated Ivan Koloff & the Warlord
NWA US Champion Dusty Rhodes defeated Larry Zbyzsko via disqualification
Lex Luger pinned NWA Tag Team Champion Arn Anderson
NWA World Champion Ric Flair defeated Michael Hayes via disqualification at the 23-minute mark

JCP @ Roanoke, VA - Civic Center - January 3, 1988 (matinee)

JCP @ Greenville, SC - Memorial Auditorium - January 3, 1988 (matinee)
Shaska Whatley fought Jimmy Valiant to a draw
Steve Williams defeated Dick Murdoch
Brad Armstrong & Tim Horner defeated the Italian Stallion & Chris Champion
Ricky Santana defeated Terry Taylor
Sting defeated Eddie Gilbert
NWA Tag Team Champion Tully Blanchard defeated Jimmy Garvin
NWA World Champion Ric Flair defeated Michael Hayes
Lex Luger defeated NWA Tag Team Champion Arn Anderson

JCP @ Baltimore, MD - Arena - January 3, 1988
TV taping:
NWA World Champion Ric Flair vs. Michael Hayes
Worldwide - 1/9/88:
Michael Hayes & Jimmy Garvin vs. two unknowns
Kevin Sullivan vs. George South
Dick Murdoch vs. an unknown
NWA Western States Heritage Champion Barry Windham vs. an unknown
Eddie Gilbert vs. an unknown
NWA TV Champion Nikita Koloff vs. Tommy Angel
NWA World Champion Ric Flair, NWA Tag Team Champions Arn Anderson & Tully Blanchard vs. three unknowns
Pro - 1/9/88:
Sting vs. the Warlord
Pro - 1/16/88:
Dick Murdoch (w/ Jim Cornette) fought NWA TV Champion Nikita Koloff to a 20-minute time-limit draw

JCP @ Macon, GA - Coliseum - January 4, 1988

JCP @ Spartanburg, SC - Memorial Auditroium - January 5, 1988
Brad Armstrong vs. Chris Champion
Tim Horner vs. Sean Royal
The Italian Stallion vs. Larry Zbyszko
Mighty Wilbur vs. Dick Murdoch
NWA US Tag Team Champions Bobby Eaton & Stan Lane defeated Sting & Ron Simmons
Ricky Morton & Robert Gibson vs. the Sheepherders

JCP @ Albany, GA - Gray Civic Center - January 5, 1988
The first 500 kids 12 and under were admitted for $1 if the ticket was purchased the day of the show
Ron Garvin vs. Terry Taylor
Lex Luger vs. Black Bart
The Road Warriors vs. Ivan Koloff & the Warlord
Michael Hayes & Jimmy Garvin vs. NWA Tag Team Champions Arn Anderson & Tully Blanchard
NWA World Champion Ric Flair vs. NWA TV Champion Nikita Koloff
Also included 3 other matches

JCP @ Atlanta, GA - WTBS Studios - January 6, 1988
World Championship Wrestling - 1/9/88:
Sting & NWA Western States Heritage Champion Barry Windham vs. Martin & Tommy Angel
Bobby Eaton & Stan Lane vs. McGyver & Peek
NWA TV Champion Nikita Koloff vs. Jeff Crews
The Barbarian vs. Steve Atkins
Ron Simmons vs. David Isley
Larry Zbyzsko vs. Cougar Jay
Brad Armstrong & Tim Horner vs. Bob Riddle & Trent Knight
The Warlord vs. Larry Stevens
Lex Luger vs. Curtis Thompson
Dick Murdoch vs. Ricky Nelson

The Road Warriors defeated Bolin & Laperouse
The Sheepherders vs. the Italian Stallion & Jackson
World Championship Wrestling Sunday Edition - 1/10/88 - featured Tony Schiavone & Magnum TA on commentary; included a pretaped promo by NWA World Champion Ric Flair in which he said Lex Luger didn't have what it takes to be a Horseman and Michael Hayes was just another contender; included Schiavone conducting an interview with the Sheepherders, with Johnny Ace, regarding their recent attack on Ricky Morton & Robert Gibson; featured Magnum conducting an interview with Morton & Gibson regarding the Sheepherders, during which they said they were on their way back to get revenge and become 5-time NWA Tag Team Champions; included an ad for the Starrcade 87 home video; featured Schiavone conducting an interview with the Road Warriors & Paul Ellering regarding the challenge of the Powers of Pain, participating in the Bunkhouse Stampede Jan. 24, and the benchpress contest against the Powers of Pain Jan. 30 in Greensboro:
Black Bart (w/ Skandar Akbar) pinned Ricky Nelson with the legdrop from the middle turnbuckle at 3:42
Eddie Gilbert & Terry Taylor defeated the Italian Stallion & Tommy Angel at 4:24 when Gilbert pinned Angelo following a Hot Shot double team
Dick Murdoch (w/ NWA US Tag Team Champion Bobby Eaton) pinned David Isley with the brainbuster at 4:22; after the bout, Jim Cornette came out and gave a ringside interview with Schiavone; Cornette then said he had arranged for Murdoch to meet his mom and would soon be collecting a lot of money for putting NWA US Champion Dusty Rhodes out of the business; Murdoch then referred to Dusty as Virgil Runnels and said the whole world was ready to see him face Rhodes; Cornette then said Murdoch would collect on the bounty after facing Rhodes Jan. 23 in Lakeland, FL
The Warlord & the Barbarian (w/ Paul Jones) defeated Larry Stephens & Trent Knight at 4:48 when Barbarian pinned Knight following a modified Decapitation in which he came off the top with a headbutt; during the bout, Jones briefly joined the commentary team regarding his team being part of the Bunkhouse Stampede finals Jan. 24 in Long Island, NY
Sting defeated Lee Peak via submission with the Scorpion Deathlock at the 27-second mark; following the bout, Schiavone conducted an interview with Sting regarding his team with Barry Windham and going after NWA World Champion Ric Flair, NWA Tag Team Champions Arn Anderson & Tully Blanchard
NWA US Tag Team Champions Bobby Eaton & Stan Lane (w/ Jim Cornette) defeated Mike Jackson & Alan Martin at 1:28 when Lane pinned Martin following the flapjack; after the bout, Schiavone conducted an interview with Cornette, Dick Murdoch, Eaton & Lane in which he showed off Eaton & Lane's Pro Wrestling Illustrated Tag Team of the Year award and their spread in the magazine; Cornette then said Eaton & Lane would be the next NWA TV and NWA US champions and would retire Rhodes

JCP @ Jacksonville, FL - Veterans Memorial Coliseum - January 7, 1988

436

JCP @ Newton, NC - January 8, 1988
Canceled due to snow

JCP @ Huntington, WV - Civic Center - January 9, 1988
NWA US Champion Dusty Rhodes & NWA TV Champion Nikita Koloff defeated NWA US Tag Team Champions Bobby Eaton & Stan Lane in a non-title steel cage match

JCP @ Greenville, SC - Memorial Auditorium - January 10, 1988 (matinee)
Chris Champion defeated John Savage
Kendall Windham defeated Johnny Ace
Jimmy Valiant defeated Black Bart
Ron Simmons defeated Kevin Sullivan
The Warlord defeated the Italian Stallion
Mike Rotundo defeated Ricky Santana
Robert Gibson defeated Luke Williams
Ron Garvin & Sting defeated NWA US Tag Team Champions Bobby Eaton & Stan Lane via disqualification
NWA TV Champion Nikita Koloff defeated NWA Tag Team Champion Tully Blanchard

JCP @ Charlotte, NC - Coliseum - January 10, 1988
Dick Murdoch, NWA US Tag Team Champions Bobby Eaton & Stan Lane defeated the Italian Stallion, Brad Armstrong, & Tim Horner
NWA US Tag Team Champions Bobby Eaton & Stan Lane fought NWA US Champion Dusty Rhodes & NWA TV Champion Nikita Koloff to a no contest in a steel cage match

JCP @ Columbus, OH - January 10, 1988 (2,300)
Brad Armstrong pinned Jim Lancaster
Jimmy Garvin defeated Al Snow at the 12-second mark
Road Warrior Hawk pinned Ivan Koloff; after the bout, Road Warrior Animal and the Barbarian took part in a brawl
NWA Western States Heritage Champion Barry Windham fought the Barbarian to a double count-out
Lex Luger pinned NWA Tag Team Champion Arn Anderson
NWA World Champion Ric Flair pinned Michael Hayes at 14:29

JCP @ Fayetteville, NC - Cumberland County Memorial Arena - January 11, 1988
Ron Simmons defeated Black Bart
NWA US Tag Team Champion Stan Lane defeated Jimmy Valiant
Sting, Ron & Jimmy Garvin defeated Kevin Sullivan, Dick Murdoch, & Mike Rotundo
NWA Tag Team Champion Tully Blanchard fought NWA TV Champion Nikita Koloff to a draw
Ricky Morton & Robert Gibson defeated the Sheepherders
Lex Luger defeated NWA Tag Team Champion Arn Anderson

JCP @ North Wilkesboro, NC - January 12, 1988
Ron Garvin & Sting defeated NWA US Tag Team Champions Bobby Eaton & Stan Lane in a non-title match

JCP @ Sumter, SC - Exhibition Center - January 12, 1988
Nelson Royal vs. Denny Brown
The Italian Stallion vs. John Savage
Jimmy Valiant vs. Black Bart
Chris Champion vs. the Gladiator
Brad Armstrong & Tim Horner vs. Shaska Whatley & Tiger

Conway Jr.
Ivan Koloff vs. Ron Simmons
NWA Western States Heritage Champion Barry Windham vs. Larry Zbyszko
Ricky Morton & Robert Gibson vs. the Powers of Pain

JCP @ Atlanta, GA - WTBS Studios - January 13, 1988
World Championship Wrestling - 1/16/88 - included the match from NWA Pro between NWA TV Champion Nikita Koloff and Dick Murdoch:
Michael Hayes & Jimmy Garvin defeated Tony Suber & George South when Hayes pinned Suber
The Warlord & the Barbarian defeated Clement Fields & Keith Steinborn when Barbarian pinned Fields
Ron Simmons pinned Cody Starr with a shoulderblock from the middle turnbuckle
Ricky Morton & Robert Gibson defeated Steve Atkinson & Alan Martin when Gibson pinned Atkinson
NWA Tag Team Champions Arn Anderson & Tully Blanchard defeated Ed Franks & Lee Peek when Blanchard pinned Franks with the slingshot suplex
Mike Rotundo pinned Larry Wayne
Dick Murdoch pinned Dave Spencer
Ivan Koloff defeated Mike Jackson

JCP @ Fisherville, VA - January 14, 1988 (1,200)
TV taping:
Chris Champion defeated Rocky King
Rick Steiner defeated the Italian Stallion
Ricky Santana defeated John Savage
Eddie Gilbert defeated Ron Simmons
Brad Armstrong & Tim Horner defeated Jive Tones
Ivan Koloff defeated Jimmy Valiant

JCP @ Norfolk, VA - Scope - January 14, 1988 (4,000)
TV taping:
World Championship Wrestling Sunday Edition - 1/24/88 - included an opening in-ring segment in which Sting challenged NWA World Champion Ric Flair to come out and face him while being interviewed by Jim Ross; featured Ross & Tony Schiavone on commentary; included Schiavone conducting an opening ringside interview with Larry Zbyzsko, with Baby Doll, regarding him facing NWA Western States Heritage Champion Barry Windham in Long Island, NY later that night; featured Schiavone conducting a ringside interview with Dick Murdoch regarding his association with Jim Cornette, feud with NWA US Champion Dusty Rhodes, and upcoming Texas barbed wire bunkhouse match against NWA TV Champion Nikita Koloff Feb. 6 in Charlotte; included Schiavone conducting a ringside interview with Flair & JJ Dillon regarding Flair facing Road Warrior Hawk later that night in Long Island, during which Flair said he would beat Hawk and NWA Tag Team Champions Arn Anderson & Tully Blanchard would split the $50,000 after co-winning the Bunkhouse Stampede finals; featured an ad for the Starrcade 87 home video; included Schiavone conducting a ringside interview with Lex Luger regarding the Bunkhouse

Stampede finals later that night and facing Blanchard & Anderson as part of the match; featured Schiavone conducting a ringside interview with the Road Warriors & Paul Ellering regarding Hawk facing Flair later that night and Road Warrior Animal being part of the Bunkhouse Stampede finals:
NWA Tag Team Champions Arn Anderson & Tully Blanchard (w/ JJ Dillon) defeated Tommy Angel & Cougar Jay at 3:15 when Blanchard pinned Jay with the slingshot suplex; following the commercial break, Schiavone conducted a ringside interview with Anderson, Blanchard, & Dillon regarding the Bunkhouse Stampede finals later that night on pay-per-view
The Warlord & the Barbarian (w/ Paul Jones) defeated Larry Stephens & Trent Knight at 3:01 when Barbarian pinned Knight following a modified Decapitation where Barbarian came off the top with a headbutt; following the bout, Schiavone conducted a ringside interview with Jones, Warlord, & Barbarian regarding their participation in the $50,000 Bunkhouse Stampede finals and the $50,000 benchpress challenge against the Road Warriors Jan. 30 in Greensboro
Black Bart (w/ Skandar Akbar) pinned Mark Cruz with a legdrop at 3:20; during the bout, Akbar briefly joined the commentary team
Ricky Morton & Robert Gibson defeated George South & Gene Ligon at 2:32 when Morton pinned Ligon following the double dropkick
Sting defeated Mark Fleming via submission with the Scorpion Deathlock at 2:56
Florida Heavyweight Champion Mike Rotunda (w/ Kevin Sullivan) pinned Bob Riddle with the butterfly suplex at 1:06; after the bout, Schiavone conducted a ringside interview with Rotunda & Sullivan regarding NWA TV Champion Nikita Koloff and the show later that night in Long Island
Dark matches:
NWA Western States Heritage Champion Barry Windham pinned Larry Zbyzsko
The Road Warriors fought the Powers of Pain to a double disqualification
NWA TV Champion Nikita Koloff defeated Mike Rotundo via disqualification
Lex Luger pinned NWA Tag Team Champion Arn Anderson
NWA World Champion Ric Flair defeated NWA US Champion Dusty Rhodes in a steel cage match

JCP @ Richmond, VA - Coliseum - January 15, 1988 (6,000)
TV taping:
The Road Warriors defeated Ivan Koloff & the Warlord
Lex Luger pinned NWA Tag Team Champion Arn Anderson
NWA Western States Heritage Champion Barry Windham fought NWA Tag Team Champion Tully Blanchard to a double disqualification at the 27-minute mark when NWA Tag Team Champion Arn Anderson and NWA World Champion Ric Flair attacked Windham, with Lex Luger then coming out to make the save; after clearing the ring of the Horsemen, Luger and Windham shook hands
Dick Murdoch (sub. for an injured NWA US Tag Team Champion Bobby Eaton) & NWA US Tag Team Champion Stan Lane defeated two unknowns

NWA World Champion Ric Flair pinned Michael Hayes by blocking a sunset flip into the ring and grabbing the ropes for leverage
NWA US Champion Dusty Rhodes & NWA TV Champion Nikita Koloff defeated Dick Murdoch & Stan Lane (w/ Jim Cornette) in a steel cage match when Rhodes pinned Lane after hitting him with Cornette's tennis racquet
Worldwide - 1/16/88:
Steve Williams vs. Mark Fleming
The Road Warriors vs. two unknowns
Ivan Koloff & the Powers of Pain vs. three unknowns
Mike Rotunda vs. Bob Riddle
Sting & NWA Western States Heritage Champion Barry Windham vs. NWA Tag Team Champions Arn Anderson & Tully Blanchard

JCP @ Philadelphia, PA - Arena - January 16, 1988 (7,500)
Dick Murdoch, Eddie Gilbert, & Kevin Sullivan defeated Sting, Ron Simmons, & Kendall Windham at the 8-minute mark when Murdoch pinned Windham with the brainbuster
Jimmy Garvin pinned Black Bart with a roll up at 3:30
NWA Tag Team Champion Tully Blanchard fought Ron Garvin to a 20-minute time-limit draw
NWA TV Champion Nikita Koloff defeated Mike Rotunda via disqualification when Kevin Sullivan interfered
The Road Warriors fought the Powers of Pain to a double count-out at the 7-minute mark
NWA US Champion Dusty Rhodes pinned NWA US Tag Team Champion Stan Lane at 8:43
Lex Luger pinned NWA Tag Team Champion Arn Anderson at 9:11 by reversing a small package
NWA World Champion Ric Flair pinned Michael Hayes at the 13-minute mark; the match was shorter than usual because it was approaching 11 p.m. and local workers would have had to be paid overtime if the show went late

JCP @ Charleston, WV - Civic Center - January 17, 1988 (matinee)
TV taping:
Ricky Morton & Robert Gibson vs. Tommy Angel & Cougar Jay
Sting vs. Gladiator #1
Ivan Koloff & the Warlord vs. Mark Fleming & Bob Riddle
The Sheepherders vs. Larry Stephens & Trent Knight
Dick Murdoch & NWA US Tag Team Champion Stan Lane vs. Andrew Bellamy & Jeff Crews
NWA Tag Team Champion Arn Anderson vs. George South
Ron Garvin vs. Gene Ligon
NWA Western States Heritage Champion Barry Windham vs. NWA Tag Team Champion Tully Blanchard

JCP @ St. Louis, MO - Arena - January 17, 1988 (5,900)
The show started an hour late
NWA TV Champion Nikita Koloff fought NWA Tag Team Champion Tully Blanchard to a draw
Mike Rotunda pinned Kendall Windham
Sting defeated Larry Zbyzsko

Ricky Morton & Robert Gibson defeated Gary Royal & Max Mcgyver (sub. for NWA US Tag Team Champions Bobby Eaton & Stan Lane, who were double booked)
NWA US Champion Dusty Rhodes defeated Dick Murdoch via disqualification
Lex Luger pinned NWA Tag Team Champion Arn Anderson
NWA World Champion Ric Flair pinned Michael Hayes in a steel cage match at around the 14-minute mark after Flair crotched the challenger on the ropes

JCP @ Columbia, SC - Township Auditorium - January 18, 1988
Sting defeated Dick Murdoch via disqualification

JCP @ Georgetown, SC - High School - January 20, 1988
Ron Garvin & Jimmy Valiant defeated NWA US Tag Team Champions Bobby Eaton & Stan Lane via disqualification in a non-title match
Also included Ivan Koloff, NWA TV Champion Mike Rotundo, Ricky Morton & Robert Gibson

JCP @ Honolulu, HI - Blaisdell Arena - January 20, 1988 (7,200; near sell out)
Super Fly Tui defeated Mighty Milo
Farmer Boy Ipo defeated Kinipopo
NWA Western States Heritage Champion Barry Windham, Ricky Morton & Robert Gibson defeated Larry Zbyzsko, NWA US Tag Team Champions Bobby Eaton & Stan Lane
The Road Warriors defeated the Powers of Pain
Lex Luger defeated NWA Tag Team Champion Arn Anderson
NWA US Champion Dusty Rhodes defeated NWA Tag Team Champion Tully Blanchard
NWA World Champion Ric Flair pinned NWA TV Champion Nikita Koloff with his feet on the ropes for leverage
NWA Western States Heritage Champion Barry Windham defeated Larry Zbyzsko
Michael Hayes defeated Kevin Sullivan via disqualification

JCP @ Inglewood, CA - Great Western Forum - January 21, 1988 (3,000)
Kevin Sullivan defeated the Hurricane Kid
NWA Western States Heritage Champion Barry Windham defeated Samoan Tau
NWA TV Champion Nikita Koloff fought NWA Tag Team Champion Tully Blanchard to a draw
The Road Warriors fought the Powers of Pain to a no contest
Lex Luger defeated NWA Tag Team Champion Arn Anderson
NWA US Champion Dusty Rhodes defeated Larry Zbyzsko via disqualification
NWA World Champion Ric Flair defeated Michael Hayes

JCP @ Chesterfield, SC - January 21, 1988
Ron & Jimmy Garvin defeated NWA US Tag Team Champions Bobby Eaton & Stan Lane via disqualification in a non-title match

WRESTLING
Sunday, Jan. 17
7:30 pm

SAINT LOUIS
ARENA

ALL UPPER BALCONY
SEATS $3

STEEL CAGE MATCH —
WORLD TITLE

Nature Boy
RIC FLAIR vs. Freebird **MICHAEL HAYES**

SPECIAL GRUDGE MATCH
Lex Luger vs. Arn Anderson
U.S. HEAVYWEIGHT TITLE
Dusty Rhodes vs. Dick Murdoch
WORLD T.V. TITLE
Nikita Koloff vs. Tully Blanchard
The Road Warriors vs. The Barbarian & the Warlord and more!

Tickets $10, 9, 3 on sale at Arena Box Office
and all Famous-Barr Tickets Now locations
Watch the NWA every Sat and Sun on KDNL Ch 30

440

JCP @ Elberton, GA - January 22, 1988
NWA Western States Heritage Champion Barry Windham (sub. for Ricky Morton) & Robert Gibson defeated NWA US Tag Team Champions Bobby Eaton & Stan Lane via disqualification in a non-title match

JCP @ Atlanta, GA - WTBS Studios - January 1988
World Championship Wrestling - 1/23/88:
Ricky Morton & Robert Gibson defeated Tommy Angel & Cougar Jay when Gibson pinned Jay
Sting defeated Gladiator #1 via submission with the Scorpion Deathlock
Ivan Koloff & the Warlord defeated Mark Fleming & Bob Riddle when Koloff pinned Riddle
The Sheepherders defeated Larry Stephens & Trent Knight when Luke pinned Knight
Stan Lane & Dick Murdoch defeated Andrew Bellamy & Stan Crews when Murdoch pinned Bellamy
NWA Tag Team Champion Arn Anderson pinned George South
Ron Garvin pinned Gene Ligon
NWA Western States Heritage Champion Barry Windham fought NWA Tag Team Champion Tully Blanchard to a no contest

JCP @ Lakeland, FL - January 23, 1988
NWA Western States Heritage Champion Barry Windham & Ron Garvin defeated NWA US Tag Team Champions Bobby Eaton & Stan Lane via disqualification in a non-title match

JCP @ Cincinnati, OH - Cincinnati Gardens - January 23, 1988
Jimmy Valiant defeated Jim Lancaster
NWA Tag Team Champion Tully Blanchard defeated Jimmy Garvin via count-out
Ivan Koloff & the Warlord defeated Ricky Morton & Robert Gibson
NWA TV Champion Nikita Koloff fought Larry Zbyszko to a draw
Lex Luger defeated NWA Tag Team Champion Arn Anderson
Sting defeated NWA World Champion Ric Flair via disqualification

Bunkhouse Stampede 88 - Long Island, NY - Nassau Coliseum - January 24, 1988 (6,000)
Sting & Jimmy Garvin (sub. for Ricky Morton & Robert Gibson) defeated the Sheepherders via disqualification
Pay-per-view bouts - featured Jim Ross & Bob Caudle on commentary; included Tony Schiavone as the ring announcer:
NWA TV Champion Nikita Koloff fought NWA US Tag Team Champion Bobby Eaton (w/ Jim Cornette) to a 20-minute time-limit draw; Koloff hit the Russian Sickle just as the time limit expired; after the bout, Koloff attempted to go after an interfering Cornette until NWA US Tag Team Champion Stan Lane appeared, with Eaton & Lane double teaming Koloff with Cornette's tennis racquet and knocking him to the floor

Larry Zbyzsko (w/ Baby Doll) pinned Western States Heritage Champion Barry Windham to win the title at 19:16 after hitting Windham with Baby Doll's high heel after referee Dick Kroll had been knocked down
Road Warrior Hawk (w/ Paul Ellering) defeated NWA World Champion Ric Flair via disqualification at 22:40 when Flair hit the challenger with a steel chair; moments later, Hawk sent the bloody Flair to the floor
NWA US Champion Dusty Rhodes won a $500,000 8-man Bunkhouse Stampede by last eliminating the Barbarian at 26:20; other participants included: NWA Tag Team Champions Arn Anderson & Tully Blanchard (w/ JJ Dillon), Road Warrior Animal (w/ Paul Ellering), Lex Luger, Ivan Koloff, the Warlord, and the Barbarian (w/ Paul Jones); eliminations: Koloff by Animal via over the cage (16:39); Warlord by Animal via out the door (18:07); Animal by Barbarian via a boot to the head from behind, through the door (18:09); Luger, Anderson, and Blanchard were eliminated via out the door as Anderson & Blanchard attempted to eliminate Luger (22:37); Barbarian by Rhodes via two elbows to the head, over the cage; after the bout, Rhodes was presented with the oversized Bunkhouse Stampede boot for his win (*3rd Annual Jim Crockett Sr. Memorial Cup*)

JCP @ Orlando, FL - Orange County Convention Center - January 24, 1988
Tiger Conway Jr. defeated Rex King
Pez Whatley defeated Robbie Idol
Ricky Santana defeated Black Bart
Ron Simmons defeated Mighty Yankee #2 (Bob Cook)
Bugsy McGraw defeated Mighty Yankee #1 (Jerry Grey)
Brad Armstrong & Ricky Santana defeated Eddie Gilbert & the Terminator
Ron Garvin defeated Dick Murdoch in a steel cage match

MID-ATLANTIC CHAMPIONSHIP WRESTLING

NWA NATIONAL WRESTLING ALLIANCE

GREENVILLE MEMORIAL AUDITORIUM
MONDAY
JAN. 25, 1988
8:00 P.M.

**WORLD HEAVYWEIGHT TITLE
NO. D.Q. - 10 FOOT STEEL CAGE**

"NATURE BOY" RIC FLAIR VS. "FREEBIRD" MICHAEL HAYES

NIKITA KOLOFF VS. MIKE ROTUNDO (WITH KEVIN SULLIVAN)

MATCH TO DETERMINE #1 CONTENDER FOR WORLD TAG TITLE

ROCK 'N ROLL EXPRESS VS. DICK MURDOCH BLACK BART

STING VS. BARBARIAN (WITH PAUL JONES)

RON SIMMONS VS. WARLORD

JIMMY VALIANT VS. IVAN KOLOFF

ITALIAN STALLION VS. KEVIN SULLIVAN

RICKY SANTANA VS. GLADIATOR #1

*NWA - SUBJECT TO CHANGE

TICKET PRICES:
$12 Ringside
$10 Gen. Adm.
$4 Children (under 10)

JCP @ Greenville, SC - Memorial Auditorium - January 25, 1988
Butch Miller defeated George South
Luke Williams defeated Larry Stephens
Ivan Koloff defeated Jimmy Valiant
Ron Simmons defeated the Warlord to a double count-out
Sting defeated the Barbarian
Dick Murdoch & Black Bart defeated Ricky Santana & the Italian Stallion (sub. for Ricky Morton & Robert Gibson); stipulations for the bout stated the winners would be the #1 contenders for the NWA Tag Team Titles
NWA TV Champion Nikita Koloff fought Mike Rotundo to a draw
NWA World Champion Ric Flair defeated Barry Windham (sub. for Michael Hayes) in a steel cage match

JCP @ Fayetteville, NC - Cumberland County Civic Center - January 25, 1988
Nelson Royal defeated John Savage
Tiger Conway Jr. defeated Rocky King
Pez Whatley defeated Chris Champion
Larry Zbyszko defeated Gary Royal
NWA Tag Team Champion Arn Anderson defeated Kendall Windham
Ron & Jimmy Garvin defeated NWA US Tag Team Champions Bobby Eaton & Stan Lane via disqualification in a non-title match
Lex Luger defeated NWA Tag Team Champion Tully Blanchard

JCP @ Raleigh, NC - Dorton Arena - January 26, 1988
TV taping:
Also featured Ricky Morton & Robert Gibson (Morton's last appearance for several months) (Gibson's last appearance for 2 years)
Pro - 2/6/88:
Mike Rotundo (w/ Kevin Sullivan) pinned NWA TV Champion Nikita Koloff to win the title at around the 13-minute mark after Sullivan hit the champion in the throat with a foreign object as Rick Steiner who appeared ringside late in the bout, distracted referee Earl Hebner from the floor Dick Murdoch, NWA US Tag Team Champions Bobby Eaton & Stan Lane defeated Kendall Windham, the Italian Stallion, & Tommy Angel
Ricky Santana defeated Bob Emory
The Powers of Pain defeated George South & Rocky King
Butch Miller defeated David Isley
Worldwide - 2/6/88 - featured a segment in which NWA World Champion Ric Flair was driven into the arena in a white limo, with Flair, NWA Tag Team Champions Arn Anderson & Tully Blanchard, JJ Dillon, and several women stepping out of the limo for Flair to receive the 1987 Wrestler of the Year award from the NWA Pro Wrestling Digest; moments later, Jim Ross conducted an interview with Flair in which Flair said Raleigh was the place where he won the Mid-Atlantic TV Title and he and the Horsemen would party later that night; Flair then cut a promo on Lex Luger; following the commercial break, Tony Schiavone conducted an in-ring interview with Sting, who was

in the ring during the presentation, who cut a promo on Flair and challenged Flair to come to the ring and face him; Dillon then came out to the ring in Flair's place and said Sting was showing no class by interrupting Flair's big day; after Sting talked back to Dillon, Dillon threw champagne in his face, with Sting then attacking Dillon and hitting the Stinger Splash on him before locking him in the Scorpion Deathlock; moments later, Flair, Anderson, and Blanchard rushed the ring, with Sting escaping unharmed; Flair then called for Sting to come back out and then accepted Sting's challenge to a match, saying he wouldn't appear on the program again until he had a match set with Sting:

Barry Windham defeated David Isley
NWA US Tag Team Champion Bobby Eaton defeated NWA US Champion Dusty Rhodes via disqualification
Sting defeated Bob Emory
NWA Western States Heritage Champion Larry Zbyszko defeated George South

JCP @ Atlanta, GA - WTBS Studios - January 27, 1988
World Championship Wrestling taping:
1/30/88 - featured the NWA TV Champion Nikita Koloff vs. Mike Rotundo match from NWA Pro:
NWA US Tag Team Champions Bobby Eaton & Stan Lane defeated Dave La Parouse & El Negro when Eaton pinned Negro
NWA Western States Heritage Champion Larry Zbyzsko pinned Alan Martin
Shaska Whatley & Tiger Conway Jr. defeated Kendall Windham & the Italian Stallion when Conway pinned Stallion
Ron & Jimmy Garvin defeated Charles Ryan & Tony Suber when Ron pinned Ryan
Sting & Barry Windham defeated Mike Jackson & Gary Royal via submission with the Scorpion Deathlock
The Barbarian & Warlord defeated Max McGyver & Ed Franks when Barbarian pinned McGyver

JCP @ Hammond, IN - Civic Center - January 28, 1988
Nikita Koloff defeated NWA Western States Heritage Champion Larry Zbyszko
The Road Warriors & Paul Ellering defeated Ivan Koloff, the Warlord, & Paul Jones
Lex Luger defeated NWA Tag Team Champion Arn Anderson
NWA US Champion Dusty Rhodes defeated NWA Tag Team Champion Tully Blanchard
NWA World Champion Ric Flair defeated Jimmy Garvin

JCP @ Harrisonburg, VA - High School - January 28, 1988
Matches originally advertised were Barry Windham vs. Steve Williams, the Mighty Wilbur vs. Pez Whatley, and Tiger Conway Jr. vs. Kendall Windham
Rick Steiner defeated John Savage
Kendall Windham defeated Pez Whatley
Black Bart defeated the Italian Stallion
Eddie Gilbert defeated Mark Fleming (sub. for Ron Garvin)
Brad Armstrong & Tim Horner defeated NWA US Tag Team

Champions Bobby Eaton & Stan Lane
Barry Windham & Ron Garvin (sub. for Ricky Morton & Robert Gibson) defeated the Sheepherders in a Texas Tornado match

JCP @ Pittsburgh, PA - Civic Arena - January 29, 1988
NWA US Tag Team Champion Stan Lane defeated Ricky Santana
The Warlord defeated Jimmy Jackson
NWA Tag Team Champion Tully Blanchard defeated Jimmy Garvin
Nikita Koloff defeated NWA TV Champion Mike Rotundo via disqualification
Road Warrior Hawk & Paul Ellering defeated Ivan Koloff & the Barbarian
Lex Luger pinned NWA Tag Team Champion Arn Anderson
NWA US Champion Dusty Rhodes defeated NWA US Tag Team Champion Bobby Eaton
Sting defeated NWA World Champion Ric Flair via disqualification when Flair knocked Sting over the top rope with a backdrop

JCP @ Greensboro, NC - Coliseum - January 30, 1988
TV taping:
NWA US Champion Dusty Rhodes & Nikita Koloff defeated NWA US Tag Team Champions Bobby Eaton & Stan Lane in a double bullrope match
NWA Tag Team Champion Arn Anderson beat Kendall Windham
Lex Luger & Barry Windham defeated Tommy Angel & Trent Knight
Black Bart defeated Curtis Thompson
Dick Murdoch defeated Joe Cruz
Jimmy & Ron Garvin defeated Bob Emory & Bob Riddle
Brad Armstrong & Tim Horner defeated Bob Emory & Trent Knight
NWA Tag Team Champions Arn Anderson & Tully Blanchard defeated Tommy Angel & Gary Royal
NWA TV Champion Mike Rotundo & Florida Heavyweight Champion Rick Steiner beat Bob Riddle & Larry Stevens
Kevin Sullivan beat Joe Cruz
NWA World Champion Ric Flair defeated Barry Windham
Worldwide - featured a benchpress contest between the Road Warriors and the Powers of Pain:
NWA US Champion Dusty Rhodes defeated NWA US Tag Team Champion Bobby Eaton (w/ Jim Cornette) in a No DQ match by pinning an interfering Cornette
NWA TV Champion Mike Rotundo & Florida Heavyweight Champion Rick Steiner (w/ Kevin Sullivan) defeated Gary Royal & George South
Lex Luger & Barry Windham defeated Cougar Jay & an unknown
Pro:

JCP @ Atlanta, GA - Omni - January 31, 1988 (16,002)
NWA TV Champion Mike Rotundo pinned Nikita Koloff
Road Warrior Hawk & Paul Ellering defeated the Powers of

Pain in a $50,000 ladder match

NWA US Champion Dusty Rhodes defeated NWA Western States Heritage Champion Larry Zbyzsko via disqualification when Kevin Sullivan attacked Rhodes with a hanger given to him by Baby Doll; after the bout, NWA TV Champion Mike Rotundo joined in attacking Rhodes until Barry Windham made the save; only the US title was at stake

Lex Luger & Ole Anderson defeated NWA Tag Team Champions Arn Anderson & Tully Blanchard via disqualification

NWA World Champion Ric Flair pinned Sting

JCP @ Newton, NC - February 1, 1988

Sting & Barry Windham defeated NWA US Tag Team Champions Bobby Eaton & Stan Lane via disqualification in a non-title match

JCP @ Spartanburg, SC - Memorial Auditorium - February 2, 1988

Ricky Santana vs. the Terminator

Kendall Windham vs. Black Bart

The Italian Stallion vs. Tiger Conway Jr.

Ron Simmons vs. Shaska Whatley

Jimmy Valiant vs. Chris Champion

Steve Williams vs. NWA Tag Team Champion Arn Anderson

Sting, Brad Armstrong, & Tim Horner defeated Dick Murdoch, NWA US Tag Team Champions Bobby Eaton & Stan Lane

JCP @ Miami, FL - Knight Center - February 2, 1988

Debut at the venue

Bugsy McGraw defeated Mighty Yankee #1

Ricky Santana defeated Kevin Sullivan via disqualification

Barry Windham fought NWA Western States Heritage Champion Larry Zbyzsko to a draw

Nikita Koloff defeated NWA TV Champion Mike Rotundo via disqualification

Road Warrior Hawk & Paul Ellering defeated Ivan Koloff & the Warlord

NWA US Champion Dusty Rhodes & Lex Luger defeated NWA World Champion Ric Flair & NWA Tag Team Champion Tully Blanchard

JCP @ Atlanta, GA - WTBS Studios - February 3, 1988

TV taping:

World Championship Wrestling - 2/6/88:

NWA Western States Heritage Champion Larry Zbyszko pinned Larry Stephens

Sting defeated David Isley via submission with the Scorpion Deathlock

Tim Horner pinned Gladiator #1

Dick Murdoch pinned Bob Emory

NWA Tag Team Champions Arn Anderson & Tully Blanchard defeated Max McGyver & John Savage when Anderson pinned McGyver

The Italian Stallion pinned Gene Ligon with a powerslam

Lex Luger & Barry Windham defeated Tony Suber & Bob Riddle when Windham pinned Riddle

NWA TV Champion Mike Rotundo & Rick Steiner defeated Andrew Bellamy & Dave Spearman

Ryan Wagner defeated Kevin Sullivan via disqualification when NWA TV Champion Mike Rotundo and Rick Steiner attacked Wagner

NWA US Tag Team Champions Bobby Eaton & Stan Lane defeated Alan Martin & Mike Jackson when Eaton pinned Martin

World Championship Wrestling Sunday Edition - 2/7/88 - featured Tony Schiavone on commentary; included opening comments from Magnum TA in which he said he would be in Norfolk on Feb. 20 and Charlotte Feb. 21 with a surprise for the Horsemen; featured Schiavone conducting a ringside interview with NWA Western States Heritage Champion Larry Zbyzsko, with Baby Doll, in which Zbyzsko said he didn't care to defend the title because he wanted to move up higher in the rankings by taking the NWA US Title from Dusty Rhodes and then the NWA World Title; included footage from the previous night's World Championship Wrestling of David Crockett conducting an interview with Road Warrior Hawk & Paul Ellering regarding the injury sustained from Road Warrior Animal at the hands of the Warlord & the Barbarian Jan. 30 in Greensboro, during which Ellering said they would still defend the NWA Six Man Tag Team Titles Feb. 13 in Philadelphia against Paul Jones' men; featured an ad for the Starrcade 87 home video; included Schiavone conducting an interview with Sting:

NWA TV Champion Mike Rotunda (w/ Florida Heavyweight Champion Rick Steiner & Kevin Sullivan) pinned Ryan Wagner with the butterfly suplex at 2:42; following the bout, Tony Schiavone conducting an interview with the Varsity Club in which Sullivan said the TV title was the second most prestigious title in the world and then responded to recent comments made by Jimmy Garvin

Tim Horner pinned John Savage with a roll up into a bridge at 2:55

Joe Cruze defeated Kevin Sullivan (w/ NWA TV Champion Mike Rotunda & Florida Heavyweight Champion Rick Steiner) via disqualification at 1:51 when Steiner and Rotunda helped in triple teaming Cruze and Sullivan shoved referee Teddy Long

Lex Luger & Barry Windham defeated David Isley & Tommy Angel at 2:38 when Angel submitted to Luger's Torture Rack; after the bout, Schiavone conducted an interview with Luger & Windham regarding the Horsemen and Varsity Club

The Warlord & the Barbarian (w/ Paul Jones & Ivan Koloff) defeated Dave Spearman & Bob Riddle at 3:38 when Warlord pinned Spearman following a catapult / clothesline double team; during the bout, it was noted Jones has taken the $50,000 that was up for grabs in the benchpress challenge against the Road Warriors and put it aside for a future ladder match between the two teams; after the bout, Schiavone conducted an interview with Jones and his men about the injury to Road Warrior Animal, the ladder match for the money, and their NWA Six Man Tag Team Title shot Feb. 13 in Philadelphia (Warlord & Barbarian's first appearance with theme music)

NWA Tag Team Champions Arn Anderson & Tully Blanchard (w/ JJ Dillon) defeated Alan Martin & Larry Stephens at 1:42

when Blanchard pinned Martin following the slingshot suplex; after the bout, Schiavone conducted an interview regarding comments recently made by Ole Anderson and facing Ole at the Omni

JCP @ Jacksonville, FL - Memorial Coliseum - February 3, 1988

JCP @ Chattanooga, TN - UTC Arena - February 4, 1988
NWA US Tag Team Champions Bobby Eaton & Stan Lane defeated Jimmy Garvin & Mike Jackson (sub. for Ron Garvin)
Nikita Koloff defeated Dick Murdoch

JCP @ Charlotte, NC - Coliseum - February 6, 1988
Nikita Koloff defeated Dick Murdoch in a Texas barbed wire bunkhouse match

JCP @ Fayetteville, NC - Cumberland County Memorial Arena - February 7, 1988

JCP @ Columbia, SC - February 7, 1988
Sting & Jimmy Garvin defeated NWA US Tag Team Champions Bobby Eaton & Stan Lane via disqualification

JCP @ Macon, GA - Coliseum - February 8, 1988
Barry Windham, Brad Armstrong, & Tim Horner defeated Jim Cornette, NWA US Tag Team Champions Bobby Eaton & Stan Lane

JCP @ Greenville, SC - Memorial Auditorium - February 8, 1988
Nelson Royal defeated Gladiator #1
Shaska Whatley defeated Rocky King
Tiger Conway Jr. defeated Larry Stephens
Ivan Koloff, Warlord & Barbarian defeated Kendall Windham, Italian Stallion, & Jimmy Valiant
Ricky Santana & Sting defeated Rick Steiner & Kevin Sullivan
NWA TV Champion Mike Rotundo defeated Nikita Koloff
Lex Luger & Ole Anderson defeated NWA World Champion Ric Flair & NWA Tag Team Champion Arn Anderson

MID-ATLANTIC CHAMPIONSHIP WRESTLING

NWA

GREENVILLE MEMORIAL AUDITORIUM

MONDAY FEB. 8, 1988 8:00 P.M.

SPECIAL CHALLENGE MATCH

LEX LUGER AND OLE ANDERSON

VS

"NATURE BOY" RIC FLAIR
ARN ANDERSON (WITH J.J. DILLON)

WORLD T.V. TITLE - 1 FALL - 45 MINUTES

NIKITA KOLOFF VS. MIKE ROTUNDA WITH KEVIN SULLIVAN

STING "DR. DEATH" STEVE WILLIAMS VS KEVIN SULLIVAN RIC STEINER

SIX MAN TAG ACTION
RICKY SANTANA ITALIAN STALLION KENDALL WINDHAM VS IVAN KOLOFF WARLORD BARBARIAN (WITH PAUL JONES)

JIMMY VALIANT VS TIGER CONWAY

TIM HORNER VS SHASKA WHATLEY

NELSON ROYAL VS GLADIATOR #1

*NWA - SUBJECT TO CHANGE

TICKET PRICES:
$12 Reserved Ringside
$10 General Adm.
$4 Children (Under 10)

N-049862-G

MID-ATLANTIC CHAMPIONSHIP WRESTLING

JCP @ Albany, GA - Civic Center - February 9, 1988
Jimmy Valiant defeated Tiger Conway Jr.
Pez Whatley defeated Rocky King
Eddie Gilbert defeated Ron Garvin
Barry Windham & Sting defeated NWA US Tag Team Champions Bobby Eaton & Stan Lane via disqualification
Jimmy Garvin defeated Black Bart
Brad Armstrong & Tim Horner defeated the Sheepherders

JCP @ Johnson City, TN - February 10, 1988
Sting defeated NWA World Champion Ric Flair via disqualification

JCP @ Columbus, GA - Municipal Auditorium - February 11, 1988

JCP @ Raliegh, NC - February 11, 1988
Chris Champion defeated Black Bart
Rick Steiner defeated Rocky King
Jimmy Valiant defeated the Terminator
NWA Tag Team Champion Arn Anderson defeated the Italian Stallion
NWA TV Champion Mike Rotundo defeated Ricky Santana
Road Warrior Hawk & Nikita Koloff fought the Powers of Pain to a no contest
Lex Luger & Barry Windham defeated NWA World Champion Ric Flair & NWA Tag Team Champion Tully Blanchard via disqualification

JCP @ Baltimore, MD - Arena - February 12, 1988 (about 10,000)
The show took place during a snowstorm
Ron Simmons defeated the Terminator
NWA Tag Team Champion Arn Anderson defeated Kendall Windham
Jimmy Garvin fought NWA TV Champion Mike Rotundo to a draw
Road Warrior Hawk & Paul Ellering fought the Powers of Pain to a no contest
Lex Luger & Ron Garvin defeated NWA World Champion Ric Flair & NWA Tag Team Champion Tully Blanchard via disqualification
NWA US Champion Dusty Rhodes, Nikita Koloff, Barry Windham, & Misty Blue defeated Dick Murdoch, Jim Cornette, NWA US Tag Team Champions Bobby Eaton & Stan Lane

JCP @ Atlanta, GA - WTBS Studios - February 10, 1988 (matinee)
World Championship Wrestling taping:
2/13/88:
NWA Tag Team Champion Arn Anderson defeated John Savage
Eddie Gilbert defeated David Isley
Road Warrior Hawk defeated Keith Steinborn & Ryan Wagner in a handicap match

Shaska Whatley & Tiger Conway Jr. defeated Mike Jackson & Gary Royal
Lex Luger defeated Alan Martin
Ricky Santana defeated Tommy Angel
Brad Armstrong & Tim Horner defeated Max McGyver & Curtis Thompson
NWA TV Champion Mike Rotundo defeated Rocky King
Sting defeated Bob Riddle
Ivan Koloff & the Powers of Pain defeated Steve Atkinson, Randy Hogan & Gene Miller
Jimmy & Ron Garvin defeated Joe Cruz & the Red Raider
Shane Douglas defeated George South
World Championship Wrestling Sunday Edition - 2/14/88 - featured Tony Schiavone on commentary with opening comments from Magnum TA on his upcoming return to the Norfolk Scope; included Schiavone conducting an interview with JJ Dillon & NWA Tag Team Champion Arn Anderson regarding the non-title steel cage match that night at the Omni between Anderson & Tully Blanchard and Lex Luger & Ole Anderson; featured Schiavone conducting an interview with Jimmy & Ron Garvin, with Precious, in which Jimmy targetted the Varsity Club; included Schiavone conducting an interview with NWA World Champion Ric Flair, Anderson, & Dillon in which Flair said Anderson might break Luger's bones that night at the Omni and then cut a promo on facing Sting later that night; featured an ad for the Starrcade 87 home video; included Schiavone conducting an interview with Shaska Whatley & Tiger Conway Jr. in which they challenged such teams as NWA US Champion Dusty Rhodes & Nikita Koloff and Brad Armstrong & Tim Horner; featured Schiavone conducting an interview with Armstrong & Horner regarding the attack they sustained the night before from the Sheepherders, during which Armstrong said the US never bombed any sheep in New Zealand so he didn't know what problem they had with America; Armstrong then noted his brother Brian was stationed at Camp Lejeune:
NWA TV Champion Mike Rotundo & Florida Heavyweight Champion Rick Steiner (w/ Kevin Sullivan) defeated John Savage & David Isley at 3:04 when Savage passed out while in a modified full nelson from Steiner; after the bout, Tony Schiavone conducted an interview with Sullivan, Rotundo, & Steiner regarding Jimmy Garvin's comments the previous night in which he told Sullivan to never mention Precious' name again; moments later, all three began chanting "Precious"
Eddie Gilbert pinned Joe Cruz with the Hot Shot at 2:57; Gilbert briefly left the ring to give his own commentary for the match
Sting, Lex Luger, & Barry Windham defeated George South, Gary Royal, & Tommy Angel at 3:22 when South submitted to Sting's Scorpion Deathlock; following the bout, Schiavone conducted a ringside interview with Sting, Luger, & Windham regarding the Horsemen and the show later that night at the Omni
Black Bart (w/ Skandar Akbar) pinned Randy Hogan at 1:22 with a bodyslam and legdrop; following the match, Schiavone conducted an interview with Akbar & Bart in which they complained they weren't getting the competition they wanted and Bart said he kicked NWA US Champion Dusty Rhodes out

of Florida and would do the same in the Carolinas
NWA US Tag Team Champions Bobby Eaton & Stan Lane (w/ Jim Cornette) defeated Bob Riddle & Curtis Thompson at 1:44 when Lane pinned Riddle following the Flapjack; Cornette provided guest commentary for the match; after the match, Schiavone conducted an interview with Cornette, Eaton & Lane in which Cornette argued Eaton should be the NWA US Champion and not Rhodes; Cornette then said the Powers of Pain had his respect for taking out the Road Warriors and said Eaton & Lane didn't have worthy opponents; he then said Dick Murdoch would be back the next week; Schiavone said the Rhodes vs. Eaton match would air the following Saturday morning Shane Douglas defeated Alan Martin via submission with the sleeper at the 57-second mark

JCP @ Johnson City, TN - Freedom Hall - February 10, 1988
Sting defeated NWA World Champion Ric Flair via disqualification

JCP @ Columbus, GA - Municipal Auditorium - February 11, 1988
Ron & Jimmy Garvin defeated NWA US Tag Team Champions Bobby Eaton & Stan Lane via disqualification

JCP @ Raleigh, NC - Dorton Arena - February 11, 1988
Florida Heavyweight Champion Rick Steiner defeated Rocky King
Chris Champion defeated Black Bart
Jimmy Valiant defeated the Terminator
NWA Tag Team Champion Arn Anderson defeated the Italian Stallion
NWA TV Champion Mike Rotundo defeated Ricky Santana
Nikita Koloff (sub. for Road Warrior Animal) & Road Warrior Hawk fought the Powers of Pain to a no contest
Lex Luger & Barry Windham defeated NWA World Champion Ric Flair & NWA Tag Team Champion Tully Blanchard via disqualification

JCP @ Baltimore, MD - Arena - February 12, 1988 (about 10,000)
The show took place during a snowstorm
Ron Simmons defeated the Terminator
NWA Tag Team Champion Arn Anderson defeated Kendall Windham
NWA TV Champion Mike Rotundo fought Jimmy Garvin to a draw
The Powers of Pain fought Road Warrior Hawk & Paul Ellering (sub. for Road Warrior Animal) to a no contest
Lex Luger & Ron Garvin defeated NWA World Champion Ric Flair & NWA Tag Team Champion Tully Blanchard via disqualification
NWA US Champion Dusty Rhodes, Nikita Koloff, Barry Windham, & Misty Blue defeated Dick Murdoch, Jim Cornette, NWA US Tag Team Champions Stan Lane & Bobby Eaton

JCP @ Philadelphia, PA - Arena - February 13, 1988 (6,000)
TV taping:
shane Douglas defeaetd Curtis Thompson
NWA Tag Team Champions Arn Anderson & Tully Blanchard defeated Tom Marker & Bob Emory
Sting defeated Tony Suber
Barry Windham defeated Steve Sampson
NWA TV Champion Mike Rotundo defeated Joe Cruz
Jimmy & Ron Garvin defeated NWA US Tag Team Champions Stan Lane & Bobby Eaton via disqualification
Nikita Koloff defeated Dick Murdoch
Lex Luger & Barry Windham defeated Ric Flair & NWA Tag Team Champion Tully Blanchard via disqualification
The Powers of Pain defeated Tony Suber & Tom Marker
NWA World Champion Ric Flair, NWA Tag Team Champions Arn Anderson & Tully Blanchard defeated Curtis Thompson, Steve Sampson, & Joe Cruz
Shane Douglas defeated Jimmy Miller
NWA US Champion Dusty Rhodes defeated NWA US Tag Team Champion Bobby Eaton
Ivan Koloff & the Powers of Pain defeated NWA 6 Man Tag Team Champions - NWA US Champion Dusty Rhodes, Road Warrior Hawk, & Paul Ellering to win the titles

JCP @ Chicago, IL - UIC Pavilion - February 14, 1988 (matinee)
JT the Spider defeated Catfish Charlie
Barry Windham, Jimmy & Ron Garvin fought Dick Murdoch, NWA US Tag Team Champions Bobby Eaton & Stan Lane to a draw
NWA Tag Team Champion Tully Blanchard defeated Ricky Santana
NWA TV Champion Mike Rotundo defeated Nikita Koloff
NWA US Champion Dusty Rhodes defeated NWA Western States Heritage Champion Larry Zbyszko via disqualification
Road Warrior Hawk & Paul Ellering (sub. for Road Warrior Animal) defeated the Powers of Pain in a $50,000 ladder match
Lex Luger defeated NWA Tag Team Champion Arn Anderson in a steel cage match
Sting defeated NWA World Champion Ric Flair via disqualification

CHAMPIONSHIP WRESTLING

GREENVILLE MEMORIAL AUDITORIIUM

NWA

**FEB. 14th
2 P.M. SUNDAY
SPECIAL KIDS
VALENTINE'S DAY**

MATCH TO DETERMINE #1 CONTENDER
FOR U.S. TAG TEAM TITLE OR WORLD TAG TEAM TITLE

**LIGHTIN EXPRESS
BRAD ARMSTRONG** VS **THE SHEEPHERDERS
(WITH JOHNNY ACE)**

TIM HORNER

JIMMY VALIANT

VS

**"HOT STUFF"
EDDIE GILBERT**

**"NEW BREED"
CHRIS CHAMPION** VS **BLACK BART
(WITH SCANDOR AKBAR)**

**KENDALL WINDHAM
STALLION** VS **JIVE TONES**

GIRLS - GIRLS

LINDA DALLAS VS **MISTY BLUE**

ROCKY KING VS **RIC STEINER**

GEORGE SOUTH VS **TERMINATOR**

*NWA - SUBJECT TO CHANGE
N-065640-G

**TICKETS: $10 Reserved Ringside
$8 General Adm.
$1 Children (UNDER 10)**

CHAMPIONSHIP WRESTLING

JCP @ Greenville, SC - Memorial Auditorium - February 14, 1988 (matinee)
Chris Champion vs. Black Bart did not take place as advertised
The Terminator defeated George South
Shane Douglas fought Rick Steiner to a draw
Misty Blue defeated Kat Laroux
Shaska Whatley & Tiger Conway Jr. defeated Kendall Windham & the Italian Stallion
Rocky King defeated the Gladiator
Jimmy Valiant defeated Eddie Gilbert
Ron Simmons defeated Ivan Koloff
Brad Armstrong & Tim Horner defeated the Sheepherders; stipulations stated the winners would become the #1 contenders for either the NWA World Tag Team Titles or NWA US Tag Team Titles

JCP @ Atlanta, GA - Omni - February 14, 1988
Ivan Koloff defeated Ron Simmons
NWA TV Champion Mike Rotundo defeated Nikita Koloff
Barry Windham, Ron & Jimmy Garvin defeated Dick Murdoch, NWA US Tag Team Champions Bobby Eaton & Stan Lane
Road Warrior Hawk & Paul Ellering (sub. for Road Warrior Animal) defeated the Powers of Pain in a ladder match
NWA World Champion Ric Flair defeated Sting
NWA Tag Team Champions Tully Blanchard & Arn Anderson defeated Lex Luger & Ole Anderson in a non-title steel cage match

JCP @ Atlanta, GA - WTBS Studios - February 15, 1988
World Championship Wrestling - 2/20/88:
NWA TV Champion Mike Rotundo & Florida Heavyweight Champion Rick Steiner vs. Curtis Thompson & Max McGyver
Shane Douglas vs. Thunderfoot #2
Ron Simmons vs. David Isley
Eddie Gilbert vs. George South
NWA Western States Heritage Champion Larry Zbyzsko vs. Trent Knight
NWA 6 Man Tag Team Champions the Powers of Pain & Ivan Koloff vs. Mike Jackson, the Raider, & Steve Atkinson
NWA Tag Team Champions Arn Anderson & Tully Blanchard vs. Larry Stephens & Tony Suber
Lex Luger & Barry Windham vs. Bear Collie & Cougar Jay
Ricky Santana vs. Keith Steinborn
Shaska Whatley & Tiger Conway Jr. vs. Martin & Bob Riddle
World Championship Wrestling Sunday Edition - 2/21/88 - featured Tony Schiavone on commentary; included Schiavone conducting an opening interview with Paul Jones, NWA Six Man Tag Team Champions Ivan Koloff & the Powers of Pain regarding their win over NWA US Champion Dusty Rhodes & the Road Warriors and facing them the following week in Greensboro; featured a video promoting the Starrcade 87 home video; included Schiavone conducting an interview with NWA World Champion Ric Flair & JJ Dillon regarding the six man tag team match the following week at the Omni; featured Schiavone conducting an interview with Sting regarding Flair;
Shane Douglas & Ricky Santana defeated Mike Jackson & Alan Martin at 3:57 when Douglas pinned Martin with the belly

to belly suplex; during the bout, it was noted NWA US Champion Dusty Rhodes, Ole Anderson, & Lex Luger would face NWA World Champion Ric Flair, NWA Tag Team Champions Arn Anderson & Tully Blanchard the following week at the Omni and Magnum TA would be in the corner of Rhodes' team while JJ Dillon would be in the corner of the Horsemen; following the bout, Jim Ross conducted an interview with Douglas & Santana regarding the youth movement, the upcoming Crockett Cup, and Douglas working with Magnum

Lex Luger & Barry Windham defeated David Isley & Larry Stephens at 3:16 when Windham pinned Isley with a lariat; during the match, it was noted Windham would challenge NWA Western States Heritage Champion Larry Zbyszko later that night at the Nassau Coliseum; it was also announced that the site of the 1988 Crockett Cup would be announced the following Saturday; after the contest, Schiavone conducted a ringside interview with Luger & Windham regarding NWA Tag Team Champions Arn Anderson & Tully Blanchard and Luger teaming with Rhodes the following week at the Omni against the Horsemen

NWA Tag Team Champions Arn Anderson & Tully Blanchard (w/ JJ Dillon) defeated Curtis Thompson & George South at 5:23 when Anderson pinned South following the gordbuster; following the commercial break, Schiavone conducted an interview with Dillon, Anderson & Blanchard regarding next week's show at the Omni

Kevin Sullivan & NWA Florida Heavyweight Champion Rick Steiner (w/ NWA TV Champion Mike Rotunda) defeated Tony Suber & Ryan Wagner at 2:10 when Sullivan scored the pin following the double stomp; following the match, Schiavone conducted an interview with the Varsity Club regarding NWA US Champion Dusty Rhodes

NWA TV Champion Mike Rotunda (w/ Kevin Sullivan & NWA Florida Heavyweight Champion Rick Steiner) pinned Steve Adkinson with the butterfly suplex at 1:09

NWA Western States Heritage Champion Larry Zbyszko (w/ Baby Doll) pinned Barry Collie with a neckbreaker at the 41-second mark; following the match, Schiavone conducted an interview with Zbyszko & Baby Doll regarding the NWA US Champion Dusty Rhodes

JCP @ Albuquerque, NM - Tingley Coiseum - February 16, 1988
NWA Western States Heritage Champion Larry Zbyzsko defeated Tim Chappa
Ricky Santana defeated Kevin Sullivan
Dick Murdoch defeated Hillbilly Tooter
NWA US Tag Team Champions Bobby Eaton & Stan Lane fought Sting & Jimmy Garvin to a 30-minute time-limit draw
Road Warrior Hawk & Paul Ellering fought Sting & Jimmy Garvin to a draw
Road Warrior Hawk & Paul Ellering defeated the Powers of Pain
NWA US Champion Dusty Rhodes, Lex Luger, & Barry Windham defeated NWA World Champion Ric Flair, NWA Tag Team Champions Arn Anderson & Tully Blanchard

JCP @ Inglewood, CA - Great Western Forum - February 17, 1988
Ricky Santana defeated the Hurricane Kid
Dick Murdoch defeated Billy Anderson
NWA Tag Team Champion Arn Anderson defeated Tim Patterson
NWA US Tag Team Champions Bobby Eaton & Stan Lane fought Sting & Jimmy Garvin to a 30-minute time-limit draw
Road Warrior Hawk & Paul Ellering defeated the Powers of Pain in a ladder match
NWA US Champion Dusty Rhodes defeated NWA Western States Heritage Champion Larry Zbyzsko
Lex Luger & Barry Windham defeated NWA World Champion Ric Flair & NWA Tag Team Champion Tully Blanchard via disqualification

JCP @ Sioux City, IA - Municipal Auditorium - February 18, 1988 (2,750; sell out)
Dick Murdoch defeated JT the Spider
Larry Zbyzsko defeated Richard Starling
NWA US Tag Team Champions Bobby Eaton & Stan Lane fought Jimmy Garvin & Ricky Santana to a 20-minute draw in a non-title match
Barry Windham pinned NWA Tag Team Champion Tully Blanchard
Sting, Road Warrior Hawk, & Paul Ellering defeated Paul Jones & the Powers of Pain at 17:13 when Ellering pinned Jones
Lex Luger pinned NWA Tag Team Champion Arn Anderson at 22:18
NWA World Champion Ric Flair defeated NWA US Champion Dusty Rhodes via disqualification at 33:55; Rhodes initially won the match and title with a clothesline but the decision was changed because Rhodes hit the referee earlier in the match

JCP @ Richmond, VA - Coliseum - February 19, 1988
TV taping:
NWA US Tag Team Champions Bobby Eaton & Stan Lane defeated Barry Windham & Ron Garvin
Jimmy Garvin defeated Kevin Sullivan
Sting, Road Warrior Hawk, & Paul Ellering (sub. for Road Warrior Animal) defeated NWA 6 Man Tag Team Champions Ivan Koloff & the Powers of Pain
NWA US Champion Dusty Rhodes defeated NWA Western States Heritage Champion Larry Zbyszko via disqualification
Lex Luger & Ole Anderson defeated NWA Tag Team Champions Arn Anderson & Tully Blanchard in a non-title steel cage match

JCP @ Hillsville, VA - February 19, 1988 (900)
The Italian Stallion defeated John Savage
Chris Champion defeated Gladiator #1
Ron Simmons defeated the Terminator (Marc Laurinidas)
Jimmy Valiant pinned Black Bart at the 4-minute mark
Ron Garvin pinned Dick Murdoch
Brad Armstrong & Tim Horner defeated the Sheepherders via

disqualification when the Sheepherders used their flag as a weapon

JPC @ Charleston, WV - Civic Center - February 20, 1988

JCP @ Norfolk, VA - Scope - February 20, 1988 (8,000)
Tiger Conway pinned Mark Fleming
Misty Blue defeated Linda Dallas
Shane Douglas pinned Pez Whatley
Rick Steiner defeated Kendall Windham
Larry Zbyzsko pinned Sting after Baby Doll hit Sting with her high heel shoe
NWA US Tag Team Champions Bobby Eaton & Stan Lane defeated Barry Windham & Jimmy Garvin after Kevin Sullivan interfered
NWA US Champion Dusty Rhodes, Lex Luger, & Ole Anderson (w/ Magnum TA) defeated NWA World Champion Ric Flair, NWA Tag Team Champions Arn Anderson & Tully Blanchard when Luger pinned Anderson after hitting him with Magnum TA's baseball bat

JCP @ Charlotte, NC - Coliseum - February 21, 1988 (matinee)

JCP @ Long Island, NY - Nassau Coliseum - February 21, 1988
NWA US Tag Team Champion Stan Lane fought Ron Simmons to a 20-minute time-limit draw
Misty Blue pinned Linda Dallas
NWA US Tag Team Champion Bobby Eaton pinned Ricky Santana
Sting fought NWA TV Champion Mike Rotundo to a draw
Ron Garvin defeated Kevin Sullivan
Barry Windham defeated NWA Western States Heritage Champion Larry Zbyzsko via count-out
Road Warrior Hawk & Paul Ellering defeated the Powers of Pain in a $50,000 ladder match after an injured Road Warrior Animal interfered
NWA US Champion Dusty Rhodes & Lex Luger defeated NWA World Champion Ric Flair & NWA Tag Team Champion Tully Blanchard via disqualification after JJ Dillon hit Luger with his shoe

JCP @ Poughkeepsie, NY - Mid-Hudson Civic Center - February 22, 1988
Florida Heavyweight Champion Rick Steiner defeated Steve Flemming
NWA US Tag Team Champions Bobby Eaton & Stan Lane defeated Ron Garvin & Ron Simmons

JCP @ Savannah, GA - Civic Center - February 23, 1988

JCP @ Asbury Park, NJ - Convention Hall - February 23, 1988

JCP @ Elizabeth, NJ - February 23, 1988
The show was cancelled due to almost no advance sales
Barry Windham vs. NWA Western States Heritage Champion Larry Zbyzsko
Was to also feature NWA US Tag Team Champions Bobby Eaton & Stan Lane

JCP @ Atlanta, GA - WTBS Studios - February 24, 1988
World Championship Wrestling - 2/27/88:
Sting vs. John Savage
Shane Douglas & Ricky Santana vs. Cruel Connection
The Sheepherders vs. Brad Armstrong & Tim Horner
NWA US Tag Team Champions Bobby Eaton & Stan Lane defeated Curtis Thompson & Cody Starr
Lex Luger & Barry Windham defeated Gene Ligon & Rick Orasi
Ron & Jimmy Garvin defeated David Isley & Paul Lee
NWA 6-Man Tag Team Champions the Powers of Pain & Ivan Koloff defeated Joe Cruz, Mike Jackson, & Allen Martin
Ron Simmons pinned Ryan Wagner
NWA TV Champion Mike Rotundo & Rick Steiner defeated Trent Knight & Gary Phelps
NWA Tag Team Champions Arn Anderson & Tully Blanchard defeated Barry Collie & Tony Suber
Larry Zbyzsko vs. Max McGyver
World Championship Wrestling Sunday Edition - 2/28/88:
Tim Horner & Brad Armstrong defeated Curtis Thompson & Bob Emory
NWA Tag Team Champions Arn Anderson & Tully Blanchard defeated Trent Knight & Gary Phelps
Lex Luger defeated Cruel Connection #1 via submission with the Torture Rack
Pez Whatley & Tiger Conway Jr. defeated Tony Suber & David Isley
Barry Windham pinned Cruel Connection #2
Black Bart pinned Gene Legion

JCP @ Akron, OH - James Rhodes Arena - February 25, 1988
Brad Armstrong & Tim Horner defeated the Sheepherders
Ron Simmons defeated Florida Heavyweight Champion Rick Steiner via disqualification
Jimmy Valiant defeated Ivan Koloff
Sting defeated NWA TV Champion Mike Rotundo by pinning an interfering Kevin Sullivan
Barry Windham fought NWA Western States Heritage Champion Larry Zbyzsko to a double count-out
The Powers of Pain defeated the Road Warriors in a streetfight

JCP @ Columbia, SC - Township Auditorium - February 25, 1988
Ron & Jimmy Garvin defeated NWA US Tag Team Champions Bobby Eaton & Stan Lane via disqualification

- 2/26/88: NWA World Champion Ric Flair's son Reid was born.

JCP @ Lynchburg, VA - Armory - February 26, 1988
Jimmy & Ron Garvin defeated NWA US Tag Team Champions Bobby Eaton & Stan Lane

JCP @ Cincinnati, OH - Cincinnati Gardens - February 26, 1988 (3,500)
TV taping - 3/12:
Sting defeated the Terminator at the 15-second mark
Barry Windham defeated NWA TV Champion Mike Rotundo via disqualification when Rick Steiner and Kevin Sullivan interfered; after the bout, Lex Luger made the save
Shane Douglas defeated an unknown
The Powers of Pain defeated Max McGyver & an unknown
NWA Tag Team Champions Arn Anderson & Tully Blanchard defeated two unknowns
Lex Luger defeated an unknown
Lex Luger & Ole Anderson defeated NWA Tag Team Champions Arn Anderson & Tully Blanchard (w/ JJ Dillon) via disqualification when Dillon interfered
Lex Luger & Barry Windham defeated Tony Super & the Terminator
NWA TV Champion Mike Rotundo & Florida Heavyweight Champion Rick Steiner defeated Max MacGyver & an unknown
Ron Simmons defeated David Isley
NWA Western States Heritage Champion Larry Zbyszko defeated George Cox
Shane Douglas defeated an unknown
Sting defeated Bob Emory
NWA Tag Team Champions Tully Blanchard & Arn Anderson defeated Joe Cruz & an unknown
The Warlord & The Barbarian defeated Trent Knight & Curtis Thompson
NWA World Champion Ric Flair (w/ JJ Dillon) pinned Sting at 17:00 after Dillon hit the challenger with his shoe

JCP @ Greensboro, NC - Coliseum - February 27, 1988 (10,000)
Upper deck seats were $5
Ricky Santana pinned Black Bart
Jimmy Valiant pinned John Savage
Brad Armstrong & Tim Horner defeated the Sheepherders when Armstrong pinned Luke Williams
Jimmy Garvin pinned Kevin Sullivan at the 5-minute mark
Ron Garvin pinned Ivan Koloff
Sting defeated Larry Zybzsko via disqualification when Baby Doll interfered
Barry Windham defeated NWA TV Champion Mike Rotundo via disqualification when Rick Steiner and Kevin Sullivan interfered; after the bout, Jimmy Garvin made the save
Road Warrior Hawk & Paul Ellering defeated the Powers of Pain in a ladder match at the 4-minute mark after both Ivan Koloff and Road Warrior Animal, wearing a protective face mask, interfered
NWA US Champion Dusty Rhodes, Lex Luger, & Ole Anderson defeated NWA World Champion Ric Flair, NWA Tag Team Champions Arn Anderson & Tully Blanchard at the 12-minute mark

JCP @ Atlanta, GA - Omni - February 28, 1988 (7,300)
Upper deck seats were $5
Ricky Santana pinned Black Bart at 3:17
Rick Steiner pinned the Italian Stallion at 6:44
The Jive Tones defeated Ron Simmons & Kendall Windham at 10:33 when Pez Whatley pinned Simmons
NWA US Tag Team Champions Bobby Eaton & Stan Lane defeated Jimmy & Ron Garvin at 9:40 after Kevin Sullivan interfered and hit Jimmy in the back of the head with a spike
Sting defeated Larry Zbyzsko via disqualification at 7:19 when Baby Doll interfered; prior to the bout, Sting grabbed the mic and called Zbyzsko an "asshole," with the crowd then chanting that throughout the match
Barry Windham defeated NWA TV Champion Mike Rotunda via disqualification at 12:50 when Rick Steiner interfered; after the bout, Jimmy Garvin made the save against Rotunda, Steiner, and Kevin Sullivan
Road Warrior Hawk & Paul Ellering fought the Powers of Pain to a double disqualification at 14:35 after both Ivan Koloff and Road Warrior Animal, wearing a protective mask, interfered
NWA US Champion Dusty Rhodes, Lex Luger, & Ole Anderson defeated NWA World Champion Ric Flair, NWA Tag Team Champions Arn Anderson & Tully Blanchard at 17:58 after Luger hit Anderson with a baseball bat given to him by Magnum TA

JCP @ Washington DC - Armory - February 29, 1988
Jimmy & Ron Garvin defeated NWA US Tag Team Champions Bobby Eaton & Stan Lane via disqualification

CHAMPIONSHIP WRESTLING

NWA

GREENVILLE MEMORIAL AUDITORIUM
Monday, Feb. 29
8:00 p.m.

10-FOOT STEEL CAGE MATCH

Barry Windham and **Lex Luger**

VS

Tully Blanchard and **Arn Anderson** (with J.J. Dillon)

World Title T.V. Match
One Fall - 20 Minutes

MIKE ROTUNDO (WITH KEVIN SULLIVAN) **VS** **STING**

Tag Action

Lightnin' Express
Brad Armstrong & Tim Horner **VS** The Sheepherders (with Johnny Ace)

JOHN SAVAGE VS. RIC STEINER

RON SIMMONS VS. GLADIATOR #1

ROCKY KING VS. THE TERMINATOR

* NWA - SUBJECT TO CHANGE

Ringside Reserved $12
General Admission $10
Children (Under 10) $4

CHAMPIONSHIP WRESTLING

JCP @ Greenville, SC - Memorial Auditorium - February 29, 1988
Shane Douglas defeated the Terminator
Ron Simmons defeated Gladiator #1
Rick Steiner defeated John Savage
Brad Armstrong & Tim Horner defeated Johnny Ace (sub. for Butch Miller) & Luke Williams
Sting defeated NWA TV Champion Mike Rotundo via disqualification
Lex Luger & Barry Windham defeated NWA Tag Team Champions Arn Anderson & Tully Blanchard in a non-title steel cage match

JCP @ Gainesville, GA - Georgia Mountains Center - March 1, 1988
Jimmy & Ron Garvin defeated NWA US Tag Team Champions Bobby Eaton & Stan Lane

JCP @ Atlanta, GA - WTBS Studios - March 2, 1988
World Championship Wrestling - 3/5/88:
Shane Douglas pinned Gene Ligon
NWA TV Champion Mike Rotundo pinned Ricky Santana
Barry Windham pinned Gary Phelps
NWA Western States Heritage Champion Larry Zbyszko pinned Randy Hogan
Shaska Whatley & Tiger Conway Jr. defeated Keith Steinborn & Ryan Wagner
Kevin Sullivan & Rick Steiner defeated Allen Martin & Steve Atkinson
The Road Warriors defeated Rick Orasi & Bob Riddle
Tony Suber pinned the Super Destroyer
NWA World Champion Ric Flair, NWA Tag Team Champions Arn Anderson & Tully Blanchard defeated Mike Jackson, Trent Knight, & Rocky King
World Championship Wrestling Sunday Edition - 3/6/88:
Lex Luger & Barry Windham defeated Alan Martin & Randy Hogan
Shaska Whatley & Tiger Conway Jr. defeated Rocky King & Bob Riddle
NWA Tag Team Champions Arn Anderson & Tully Blanchard defeated Tony Suber & Gene Legion
Rick Steiner pinned an unknown
Ricky Santana pinned Curtis Thompson
NWA Western States Heritage Champion Larry Zbyszko pinned Cody Starr

JCP @ Harrisonburg, VA - High School - March 3, 1988
George South vs. the Terminator
Ron Simmons vs. John Savage
Shane Douglas vs. Black Bart
Jimmy Valiant vs. the Big Green Machine
Ron Garvin vs. Ivan Koloff
Barry Windham vs. NWA Western States Heritage Champion Larry Zbyszko

JCP @ Pittsburgh, PA - Civic Arena - March 4, 1988 (3,000)
The Green Machine defeated the Italian Stallion
Jimmy Valiant defeated Jerry Jackson
Chris Champion defeated Pez Whatley
Ricky Santana fought Ivan Koloff to a draw
The Lightning Express defeated the Sheepherders
Lex Luger & Ole Anderson defeated NWA Tag Team
Champions Arn Anderson & Tully Blanchard via disqualification
The Road Warriors defeated the Powers of Pain in a streetfight

JCP @ Houston, TX - Sam Houston Coliseum - March 4, 1988 (3,000)
Linda Dallas won a women's battle royal
Kendall Windham fought Black Bart to a draw
Shane Douglas defeated Tiger Conway
Ron Simmons defeated Rick Steiner
Barry Windham defeated NWA TV Champion Mike Rotundo via disqualification
NWA US Champion Dusty Rhodes defeated Larry Zybzsko via disqualification
NWA US Tag Team Champions Bobby Eaton & Stan Lane defeated Jimmy & Ron Garvin
NWA World Champion Ric Flair defeated Sting

Worldwide - 3/5/88:
NWA TV Champion Mike Rotundo pinned an unknown
Sting defeated an unknown via submission with the Scorpion Deathlock
NWA 6-Man Tag Team Champions Ivan Koloff & the Powers of Pain defeated George South & two unknowns
Shaska Whatley & Tiger Conway Jr. defeated two unknowns
NWA Western States Heritage Champion Larry Zbyszko pinned an unknown
Lex Luger & Ole Anderson defeated NWA World Champion Ric Flair & NWA Tag Team Champion Tully Blanchard in a steel cage match when Luger pinned Blanchard with a roll up; after the bout, JJ Dillon and NWA Tag Team Champion Arn Anderson attacked Luger & Ole until Dusty Rhodes made the save

JCP @ Louisville, KY - Convention Center - March 5, 1988
TV taping:
Worldwide - 3/12/88:
Lex Luger & Barry Windham defeated the Terminator & Tony Suber
NWA TV Champion Mike Rotundo & Rick Steiner defeated Barry Collie & Max McGyver
Ron Simmons pinned an unknown
NWA Western States Heritage Champion Larry Zbyszko pinned an unknown
Shane Douglas pinned Rick Orasi
Sting defeated an unknown via submission with the Scorpion Deathlock
NWA Tag Team Champions Arn Anderson & Tully Blanchard defeated two unknowns
The Powers of Pain defeated Curtis Thompson & an unknown

JCP @ Raleigh, NC - Dorton Arena - March 6, 1988
Chris Champion defeated Pez Whatley
Ivan Koloff defeated Tommy Angel
Black Bart defeated the Italian Stallion
The Green Machine defeated Jimmy Valiant
Ron Simmons defeated Tiger Conway Jr.
Jimmy & Ron Garvin defeated NWA US Tag Team Champions Bobby Eaton & Stan Lane via disqualification
The Road Warriors defeated the Powers of Pain in a streetfight

JCP @ St. Louis, MO - Arena - March 6, 1988
Kendall Windham pinned Johnny Ace
Shane Douglas defeated Mr. Missouri
Ricky Santana fought Florida Heavyweight Champion Rick Steiner to a 20-minute time-limit draw
Brad Armstrong & Tim Horner defeated the Sheepherders
NWA US Champion Dusty Rhdoes defeated NWA TV Champion Mike Rotundo via disqualification
Lex Luger & Barry Windham defeated NWA Tag Team Champions Arn Anderson & Tully Blanchard via disqualification
NWA World Champion Ric Flair defeated Sting

CHAMPIONSHIP WRESTLING

NWA

GREENVILLE MEMORIAL AUDITORIUM
MONDAY - MAR. 7
8:00 P.M.

MID-ATLANTIC CHAMPIONSHIP WRESTLING

N.W.A. WORLD TITLE

"NATURE BOY" RIC FLAIR VS **STING**

WORLD TAG TITLE

ARN ANDERSON WITH J.J. DILLON TULLY BLANCHARD VS **BARRY WINDHAM LEX LUGER**

WORLD T.V. TITLE
ONE FALL - 30 MINUTES

MIKE ROTUNDO (WITH KEVIN SULLIVAN) VS **GORGEOUS JIMMY GARVIN (WITH PRECIOUS)**

JIMMY VALIANT VS THE GREEN MACHINE

SHANE DOUGLAS VS GARY ROYAL

RON SIMMONS VS BLACK BART (WITH SKANDOR AKBAR)

JOHN SAVAGE VS RIC STEINER

ROCKY KING VS THE TERMINATOR

* NWA - SUBJECT TO CHANGE

Ringside Reserved '15
General Admission '10
Children (Under 10) '5

CHAMPIONSHIP WRESTLING

JCP @ Greenville, SC - Memorial Auditorium - March 7, 1988
Rocky King vs. the Terminator did not take place as advertised
Kendall Windham (sub. for Rick Steiner) defeated John Savage
Rick Steiner defeated Rocky King
Ron Simmons defeated Black Bart
Shane Douglas defeated Gary Royal
Green Machine defeated Jimmy Valiant
Jimmy Garvin defeated NWA TV Champion Mike Rotundo via disqualification; the match had a 30-minute time limit
Lex Luger & Barry Windham defeated JJ Dillon (sub. for NWA Tag Team Champion Arn Anderson) & NWA Tag Team Champion Tully Blanchard
Sting defeated NWA World Champion Ric Flair via disqualification

JCP @ Macon, GA - Coliseum - March 7, 1988
Shaska Whatley & Tiger Conway Jr. vs. Chris Champion & the Italian Stallion
Nelson Royal fought George South to a double count-out
Ron Garvin vs. Ivan Koloff
Brad Armstrong & Tim Horner vs. the Sheepherders
The Road Warriors vs. the Powers of Pain
Also included a 7-woman battle royal including Misty Blue, Kat Laroux, Linda Dallas, Venus, Comrade Olga, Wendy Witney Hensen, and Mad Dog Debbie

JCP @ Spartanburg, SC - Memorial Auditorium - March 8, 1988
Shane Douglas vs. Eddie Gilbert
The Italian Stallion & Ricky Santana vs. the Sheepherders
Kendall Windham vs. Florida Heavyweight Champion Rick Steiner
Jimmy Valiant vs. the Green Machine
Jimmy Garvin vs. NWA TV Champion Mike Rotundo
Brad Armstrong & Tim Horner vs. NWA US Tag Team Champions Bobby Eaton & Stan Lane

JCP @ Atlanta, GA - WTBS Studios - March 9, 1988 (matinee)
World Championship Wrestling - 3/12/88:
The Road Warriors vs. Keith Steinborn & Phelps
Shaska Whatley & Tiger Conway Jr. vs. Gene Ligon & King
NWA US Tag Team Champions Bobby Eaton & Stan Lane vs. Thompson & Knight
Ricky Stanana vs. Bob Riddle
Lex Luger vs. Dal Laperouse
The Powers of Pain vs. Orasi & Randy Hogan
NWA TV Champion Mike Rotundo vs. Jimmy Garvin
NWA Tag Team Champions Arn Anderson & Tully Blanchard vs. Atkinson & Spearman
Florida Heavyweight Champion Rick Steiner vs. Gary Royal
World Championship Wrestling Sunday Edition - 3/13/88 - featured Tony Schiavone on commentary; included Schiavone

conducting an interview with Jimmy Garvin, with Precious, regarding the attack he recently sustained at the hands of Kevin Sullivan, NWA TV Champion Mike Rotunda, & Rick Steiner, called out the Varsity Club, and said someone was going to get hurt; featured a graphic advertising the Clash of the Champions; included an ad promoting the Starrcade 87 home video; featured Schiavone conducting an interview with Paul Jones & NWA Six-Man Tag Team Champions the Powers of Pain regarding their & Ivan Koloff's barbed wire match against NWA US Champion Dusty Rhodes & the Road Warriors as part of the Clash of the Champions, with Jones saying he didn't have proper time to train his men against barbed wire but that the Powers of Pain had taken more from the Road Warriors than any other team; included Schiavone conducting an interview with Paul Ellering & the Road Warriors, Animal's face covered in a mask, regarding the upcoming barbed wire match; featured a vignette promoting the debut of the Fantastics; included an ad promoting the Clash of the Champions hotline; included an ad promoting the Clash of the Champions, focusing around the Rhodes & Road Warriors vs. Koloff & Powers of Pain match; featured Schiavone conducting an interview with NWA World Champion Ric Flair regarding his match with Sting as part of the Clash, during which Flair noted Lex Luger & Barry Windham would face NWA Tag Team Champions Arn Anderson & Tully Blanchard:

Shaska Whatley & Tiger Conway Jr. defeated Tony Suber & Ryan Wagner at 3:02 when Whatley pinned Wagner following a double Russian legsweep; during the bout, it was noted the Top 10 seeds for the Crockett Cup would be announced during the upcoming Clash of the Champions NWA TV Champion Mike Rotunda & Florida Heavyweight Champion Rick Steiner (w/ Kevin Sullivan) defeated Gary Phelps & Rocky King at 2:28 when Rotunda pinned Phelps following the butterfly suplex; moments later, Tony Schiavone conducted a ringside interview with the Varsity Club regarding Jimmy Garvin & Precious and dominating the NWA
Lex Luger defeated Alan Martin at 2:10 via submission with the Torture Rack
Ricky Santana pinned Gary Royal at 3:59 with a splash off the top after Royal missed a reverse crossbody off the top
NWA Tag Team Champions Arn Anderson & Tully Blanchard (w/ JJ Dillon) defeated Trent Knight & Gene Ligon at 3:19 when Anderson pinned Knight following the gordbuster; during the bout, Schiavone said Baby Doll would soon reveal the photos regarding NWA US Champion Dusty Rhodes that she has thus far kept to herself; Dillon was wired with a mic for the match so the fans could hear his encouragement and comments directed at the champions; after the match, Schiavone conducted a ringside interview with Dillon, Anderson, & Blanchard regarding their title defense at the Clash against Luger & Windham and the upcoming Crockett Cup
NWA US Tag Team Champions Bobby Eaton & Stan Lane (w/ Jim Cornette) defeated Randy Hogan & Steve Atkinson at 3:17 when Lane pinned Hogan following the flapjack; Cornette was wired with a mic for the match, giving the fans a chance to hear his comments at ringside; Cornette also briefly joined

Schiavone on commentary for the bout; after the contest, Schiavone conducted an interview with Cornette, Eaton & Lane in which Cornette said no one wanted them as the #1 seed in the Crockett Cup because all the other teams were scared of them for their 10-month reign as US tag team champions

JCP @ Wadesboro, NC - March 9, 1988
Brad Armstrong & Tim Horner defeated NWA US Tag Team Champions Bobby Eaton & Stan Lane via disqualification

JCP @ Marion, VA - March 10, 1988
Brad Armstrong & Tim Horner defeated NWA US Tag Team Champions Bobby Eaton & Stan Lane

JCP @ Baltimore, MD - Arena - March 10, 1988
Shane Douglas defeated Black Bart
Rick Steiner defeated Kendall Windham
Ricky Santana defeated Gary Royal
Jimmy Garvin defeated NWA TV Champion Mike Rotundo via disqualification
Lex Luger & Barry Windham defeated NWA Tag Team Champions Arn Anderson & Tully Blanchard via disqualification
The Road Warriors defeated the Powers of Pain in a ladder match
NWA World Champion Ric Flair defeated Sting

JCP @ Lenoir, NC - March 11, 1988
Brad Armstrong & Tim Horner defeated NWA US Tag Team Champions Bobby Eaton & Stan Lane

JCP @ Norfolk, VA - Scope - March 12, 1988
TV taping:
NWA Tag Team Champions Arn Anderson & Tully Blanchard defeated Lex Luger & Barry Windham
NWA US Champion Dusty Rhodes defeated Larry Zbyzsko
Pro: Sting defeated NWA World Champion Ric Flair (w/ JJ Dillon) via disqualification at around the 12-minute mark when Dillon threw referee Gene Ligon into the ringpost as Flair was caught in the Scorpion Deathlock, with NWA Tag Team Champion Arn Anderson coming out to attack Sting until Lex Luger & Barry Windham appeared; moments later, the ring filled with wrestlers as Anderson helped Flair to the floor; after the commercial break, Flair was helped backstage
Pro - 3/26/88 - featured Jim Ross & Bob Caudle on commentary; included Tony Schiavone as the ring announcer:
Bobby Fulton & Tommy Rogers defeated NWA US Tag Team Champions Bobby Eaton & Stan Lane (w/ Jim Cornette) in a non-title match at around the 27-minute mark when Fulton pinned Eaton with the Rocket Launcher after Eaton failed to hit the move himself (Fulton & Rogers' debut)

JCP @ Columbus, OH - Fairgrounds Coliseum - March 13, 1988 (matinee)
Mickey Doyle defeated Ben Patrick
Jim Lancaster defeated Al Snow

Shane Douglas & Ricky Santana defeated NWA US Tag Team Champions Bobby Eaton & Stan Lane via disqualification

NWA Western States Heritage Champion Larry Zbyszko fought Ron Garvin to a double count-out

The Road Warriors & Paul Ellering defeated Paul Jones & the Powers of Pain at 6:06 in a streetfight

Sting defeated NWA World Champion Ric Flair via disqualification

JCP @ Atlanta, GA - Omni - March 13, 1988

Gary Royal defeated Florida Heavyweight Champion Rick Steiner

Ron Garvin defeated NWA Western States Heritage Champion Larry Zbyszko via disqualification

NWA US Tag Team Champions Bobby Eaton & Stan Lane defeated Brad Armstrong & Tim Horner

NWA TV Champion Mike Rotundo defeated Jimmy Garvin

NWA Tag Team Champions Arn Anderson & Tully Blanchard defeated Lex Luger & Barry Windham

The Powers of Pain defeated NWA US Champion Dusty Rhodes & Road Warrior Hawk

Sting defeated NWA World Champion Ric Flair via disqualification

JCP @ Atlanta, GA - WTBS Studios - March 14, 1988

World Championship Wrestling - 3/19/88:
NWA TV Champion Mike Rotundo & Florida Heavyweight Champion Rick Steiner vs. Keith Stienborn & Wagner
Shane Douglas vs. Barry Collie
Sting vs. Joe Cruz
The Powers of Pain vs. Bob Riddle & Max McGyver
Ron Simmons vs. Trent Knight
The Road Warriors vs. Atkinson & El Negro
Lex Luger vs. Andrew Bellamy
Al Perez vs. Tony Suber
NWA US Tag Team Champions Bobby Eaton & Stan Lane vs. Mike Jackson & Gary Martin

World Championship Wrestling: Sunday Edition - 3/20/88 - the last episode; featured Tony Schiavone on commentary; included Schiavone conducting an interview with Sting regarding his upcoming match with NWA World Champion Ric Flair the following week during the Clash of the Champions, with JJ Dillon suspended above the ring in a cage; featured an ad for Starrcade 87 on home video; included an ad promoting the Clash; featured Schiavone conducting an interview with Kevin Sullivan, NWA TV Champion Mike Rotunda, & Florida Heavyweight Champion Rick Steiner in which Sullivan discussed Dusty Rhodes, Barry Windham, Jimmy Garvin, and Lex Luger:
The Road Warriors (w/ Paul Ellering) defeated Keith Stienborn & Gene Miller at the 17-second mark when Road Warrior Animal pinned Miller following a clothesline; Animal wore a protective face mask for the match; after the bout, Tony Schiavone conducted an interview with Ellering & the Road Warriors regarding their barbed wire match with NWA US Champion Dusty Rhodes against Ivan Koloff & the Powers of Pain as part of the Clash of the Champions

Tommy Rogers & Bobby Fulton defeated Max McGyver & Alan Martin at 5:28 when Rogers scored the pin following the Rocket Launcher; after the commercial break, Schiavone conducted a ringside interview with Rogers & Fulton regarding the attack they sustained the previous day at the hands of NWA US Tag Team Champions Bobby Eaton & Stan Lane and facing them as part of the Clash of the Champions

NWA Six-Man Tag Team Champions Ivan Koloff & the Powers of Pain (w/ Paul Jones) defeated Joe Cruz, Trent Knight, & David Isley at 6:42 when Koloff pinned Isley after coming off the top with a blow to Isley's throat as Warlord held Isley above his head; following the commercial break, Schiavone conducted an interview with Jones, alongside his men, in which Jones said the Powers of Pain should be seeded #1 in the Crockett Cup and that the Road Warriors might not even make it to the tournament after the upcoming barbed wire match at the Clash of the Champions

Lex Luger & Barry Windham defeated Bob Riddle & Big Bear Collie at 3:19 when Windham pinned Riddle following the lariat; after the bout, Schiavone conducted a ringside interview with Luger & Windham regarding their upcoming match at the Clash against NWA Tag Team Champions Arn Anderson & Tully Blanchard and being part of the Crockett Cup; during the segment, Luger responded to Kevin Sullivan's comments made earlier in the show and said he also wanted a piece of NWA World Champion Ric Flair

NWA US Tag Team Champions Bobby Eaton & Stan Lane (w/ Jim Cornette) defeated Ryan Wagner & Steve Atkinson at 3:12 when Eaton scored the pin following the Rocket Launcher; Cornette was wired with a mic for the match, giving fans the opportunity to listen to his comments from ringside; Cornette joined Schiavone on commentary for the majority of the bout; after the match, Schiavone conducted an interview with Cornette, alongside Eaton & Lane, regarding the challenge of Tommy Rogers & Bobby Fulton

Al Perez (w/ Gary Hart) defeated Andrew Bellamy via submission with the spinning toe hold at 2:35; after the bout, Schiavone conducted a ringside interview with Hart & Perez regarding Perez's arrival to the NWA, during which Hart said he wanted Perez to have a title shot against NWA US Champion Dusty Rhodes and that Perez would team with Larry Zbyszko as part of the Crockett Cup

JCP @ Reno, NV - Lawlor Events Center - March 15, 1988

NWA World Champion Ric Flair defeated Sting

JCP @ Columbia, SC - Township Auditorium - March 15, 1988

NWA US Tag Team Champion Stan Lane defeated Shane Douglas

NWA US Champion Dusty Rhodes defeated NWA US Tag Team Champion Bobby Eaton

JCP @ San Francisco, CA - Civic Auditorium - March 16, 1988 (4,500)

George Wells fought Earthquake Ferris to a no contest

456

Rick Steiner defeated Rex Farmer
Larry Zbyzsko defeated Jimmy Garvin
Lex Luger & Barry Windham defeated NWA Tag Team Champions Arn Anderson & Tully Blanchard via disqualification
The Road Warriors defeated the Powers of Pain
NWA World Champion Ric Flair defeated Sting

JCP @ Inglewood, CA - Great Western Forum - March 17, 1988
Mando Guerrero fought Tony Rocco to a 10-minute time-limit draw
Rick Steiner pinned Pistol Pete
Larry Zbyzsko pinned Ron Garvin
NWA TV Champion Mike Rotundo fought Jimmy Garvin to a 30-minute time-limit draw
Lex Luger & Barry Windham defeated NWA Tag Team Champions Arn Anderson & Tully Blanchard via disqualification
The Road Warriors defeated the Powers of Pain in a lumberjack match
NWA World Champion Ric Flair defeated Sting

JCP @ Cincinnati, OH - Cincinnati Gardens - March 18, 1988
TV taping:
NWA Tag Team Champions Arn Anderson & Tully Blanchard defeated Lex Luger & Barry Windham via disqualification when Magnum TA interfered with a baseball bat
Ron & Jimmy Garvin defeated NWA TV Champion Mike Rotundo & Rick Steiner via disqualification
The Road Warriors defeated the Powers of Pain in a lumberjack match
Sting fought NWA World Champion Ric Flair to a no contest

JCP @ Chicago, IL - UIC Pavilion - March 19, 1988
Ivan Koloff pinned Shane Douglas
Rick Steiner pinned Kendall Windham
NWA Tag Team Champion Arn Anderson fought Barry Windham to a double disqualification
NWA US Tag Team Champions Bobby Eaton & Stan Lane defeated Jimmy & Ron Garvin when Eaton pinned Jim
Lex Luger defeated NWA Tag Team Champion Tully Blanchard
NWA US Champion Dusty Rhodes defeated NWA TV Champion Mike Rotundo (w/ Kevin Sullivan) via disqualification in a title vs. title match
NWA World Champion Ric Flair pinned Sting
The Road Warriors defeated the Powers of Pain in a lumberjack streetfight

JCP @ St. Louis, MO - March 1988
Kendall Windham pinned Johnny Ace
Shane Douglas defeated Mr. Missouri
Ricky Santana fought Rick Steiner to a 20-minute time-limit draw
Brad Armstrong & Tim Horner defeated the Sheepherders
NWA US Champion Dusty Rhodes defeated NWA TV

Champion Mike Rotundo via disqualification when Kevin Sullivan interfered
Lex Luger & Barry Windham defeated NWA Tag Team Champions Arn Anderson & Tully Blanchard via disqualification
NWA World Champion Ric Flair defeated Sting after JJ Dillon interfered

JCP @ Charleston, WV - Civic Center Coliseum - March 20, 1988 (matinee) (3,000)
Florida Heavyweight Champion Rick Steiner pinned Kendall Windham
NWA US Tag Team Champion Stan Lane fought Shane Douglas to a draw
Pez Whatley, Tiger Conway, & the Green Machine defeated Jimmy Valiant, Chris Champion, & the Italian Stallion
Lex Luger & Barry Windham defeated JJ Dillon (sub. for NWA Tag Team Champion Arn Anderson) & NWA Tag Team Champion Tully Blanchard
NWA TV Champion Mike Rotundo pinned Jimmy Garvin after Kevin Sullivan interfered
Dusty Rhodes pinned NWA US Tag Team Champion Bobby Eaton

JCP @ Peoria, IL - Civic Center - March 20, 1988 (matinee)
Larry Cameron defeated Johnny Love
Steve Regal defeated Spike Huber
Ron Garvin defeated Ivan Koloff
The Road Warriors defeated the Powers of Pain via disqualification
NWA World Champion Ric Flair defeated Sting

JCP @ Charlotte, NC - Coliseum - March 20, 1988
TV taping:
NWA US Tag Team Champions Bobby Eaton & Stan Lane defeated Shane Douglas & Ricky Santana

JCP @ Sumter, SC - Exhibition Center - March 22, 1988
John Savage vs. Rick Snyder
Ricky Santana vs. the Terminatior
Ron Simmons & Kendall Windham vs. the Sheepherders
Kevin Sullivan vs. the Italian Stallion
Brad Armstrong, Tim Horner, & Shane Douglas vs. NWA Six-Man Tag Team Champions Ivan Koloff & the Powers of Pain
Dusty Rhodes vs. NWA TV Champion Mike Rotunda
Sting vs. NWA World Champion Ric Flair

JCP @ Athens, GA - March 22, 1988
Ron & Jimmy Garvin defeated NWA US Tag Team Champions Bobby Eaton & Stan Lane via disqualification

JCP @ Atlanta, GA - WTBS Studios - March 23, 1988
World Championship Wrestling - 3/26/88 - featured David Crockett conducting an interview with Magnum TA, with a baseball bat, in which he spoke about his I Quit win over Tully Blanchard at Starrcade 85; moments later, Blanchard

appeared, with Barry Windham then following to protect Magnum; in the ensuing melee, NWA US Champion Dusty Rhodes appeared after Magnum was bloodied, hit Blanchard with the bat, and struck Jim Crockett; moments later, Jim Ross, Paul Boesch, Tony Schiavone came to Crockett's aid while Sting, Bobby Fulton & Tommy Rogers appeared and pulled Rhodes off Blanchard; the incident later saw Rhodes stripped of the title and suspended for 120 days:
The Sheepherders vs. Bowman & Wagner
Bobby Fulton & Tommy Rogers vs. Gene Ligon & Atkinson
NWA TV Champion Mike Rotundo & Rick Steiner vs. Tommy Angel & the Italian Stallion
Ron Simmons vs. David Diamond
Sting vs. Max McGyver
NWA US Tag Team Champions Bobby Eaton & Stan Lane vs. Kendall Windham & Collie
The Big Green Machine vs. El Negro
Jimmy Garvin & Shane Douglas vs. Mike Jackson & Pritts

JCP @ Gastonia, NC - March 23, 1988
NWA US Tag Team Champion Stan Lane defeated Shane Douglas
Ron Garvin defeated NWA US Tag Team Champion Bobby Eaton

JCP @ Columbia, SC - Township Auditorium - March 24, 1988
Shane Douglas pinned Doug Savage
Chris Champion fought the Terminator to a draw
Ricky Santana defeated Johnny Ace
Black Bart defeated the Italian Stallion
NWA Tag Team Champion Arn Anderson pinned Kendall Windham
Ron & Jimmy Garvin defeated NWA US Tag Team Champions Bobby Eaton & Stan Lane via disqualification
Lex Luger pinned NWA Tag Team Champion Tully Blanchard

JCP @ Raleigh, NC - Dorton Arena - March 25, 1988
TV taping

JCP @ Biscoe, NC - March 25, 1988
Ron & Jimmy Garvin defeated NWA US Tag Team Champions Bobby Eaton & Stan Lane via disqualification

JCP @ Richmond, VA - Coliseum - March 26, 1988 (2,000)
Tiger Conway pinned Kendall Windham
Ricky Santana pinned Shaska Whatley
Steve Williams & Ron Garvin defeated Kevin Sullivan & Rick Steiner when Williams pinned Steiner
NWA TV Champion Mike Rotundo fought Nikita Koloff to a draw
Bobby Fulton & Tommy Rogers defeated NWA US Tag Team Champions Bobby Eaton & Stan Lane via disqualification
NWA US Champion Dusty Rhodes pinned Larry Zbyszko
NWA World Champion Ric Flair pinned Sting

- 3/27/88: The WWF booked the Omni in Atlanta for a closed-circuit airing of WrestleMania IV.

Clash of the Champions - Greensboro, NC - Coliseum - March 27, 1988 (6,000)
Shown live on TBS - included opening comments from Tony Schiavone & Bob Caudle, with the announcement that the board of directors would be meeting to discuss the incident the previous day involving NWA US Champion Dusty Rhodes, Magnum TA, and David Crockett; featured Jim Ross & Schiavone on commentary:
NWA TV Champion Mike Rotunda (w/ Kevin Sullivan) pinned Jimmy Garvin (w/ Precious) in an amateur wrestling match; the match was scheduled for 3 5-minute rounds in which a one count would be sufficient for a pinfall; Rotunda pinned Garvin at the 55-second mark of the second round with a roll up after Garvin went after Sullivan on the apron, after setting Rotunda up for the brainbuster, after Sullivan grabbed Precious; after the match, Garvin hit the brainbuster on the champion until he was attacked by Rick Steiner, with Precious then hitting Steiner with a 2x4 and choking Sullivan with a coat hanger
NWA US Tag Team Champions Bobby Eaton & Stan Lane (w/ Jim Cornette) defeated Bobby Fulton & Tommy Rogers via reverse decision at 10:19; during the bout, Jim Ross announced that stand-by matches scheduled for later in the show included Shane Douglas vs. NWA Western States Heritage Champion Larry Zbyzsko and Ricky Santana vs. Rick Steiner; the challengers originally won the match and titles when Fulton pinned Eaton with a Rocket Launcher, with replacement referee Tommy Young counting the pinfall, but the initial referee Randy Anderson changed the call because he had been thrown over the top by Fulton earlier in the match; after the contest, the champions whipped Fulton with a leater strap and Cornette hit Young with his tennis racquet
NWA US Champion Dusty Rhodes & the Road Warriors defeated Ivan Koloff & the Powers of Pain (w/ Paul Jones) in a non-sanctioned barbed wire match when Road Warrior Animal pinned the Warlord at around the 4-minute mark after hitting a powerslam and the Barbarian accidentally hitting his partner with a diving headbutt when Animal moved out of the way; Animal wore a protective mask for the match to protect an eye injury sustained at the hands of the Powers of Pain but the POP removed the mask after the match and assaulted him until Rhodes made the save; the ring ropes were wrapped in barbed wire for the match (*American Dream: The Dusty Rhodes Story*)
Lex Luger & Barry Windham defeated NWA Tag Team Champions Arn Anderson & Tully Blanchard (w/ JJ Dillon) to win the titles at 9:33 when Luger pinned Anderson after throwing him into the corner, with Anderson hitting a steel chair held in the corner by Dillon (*Ric Flair & the 4 Horsemen, Legends of Wrestling, The Best of Clash of the Champions*)
Sting fought NWA World Champion Ric Flair (w/ JJ Dillon) to a 45-minute time-limit draw at 39:14; during the bout, Dillon was suspended above the ring in a shark cage; Sandy Scott, Gary Juster, and 1988 Penthouse Pet of the Year Patty Mullen served as judges for the match, with Scott ruling it a draw, Juster voting for Sting, and Mullen voting for Flair; Jason

Hervey, of "The Wonder Years," and Ken Osmond, Eddie Haskel of "The New Leave it to Beaver," sat ringside with the judges (voted Match of the Year by the Wrestling Observer Newsletter) (*Nature Boy Ric Flair: The Definitive Collection*, *The Best of Clash of the Champions*)

MID-ATLANTIC CHAMPIONSHIP WRESTLING

NWA

GREENVILLE MEMORIAL AUDITORIUM

MONDAY, MAR. 28 8 P.M.

WORLD TITLE MATCH
NO DISQUALIFICATIONS

"NATURE BOY" RIC FLAIR **VS** STING

GRUDGE TAG MATCH

DUSTY RHODES OLE ANDERSON **VS** TULLY BLANCHARD ARN ANDERSON (WITH J.J. DILLON)

U.S. TAG TITLE

MIDNIGHT EXPRESS **VS** THE FANTASTICS

Midnight Express with Jim Cornette

WESTERN STATES HERITAGE TITLE

LARRY ZBYSZKO (WITH BABY DOLL) **VS** SHANE DOUGLAS

RON SIMMONS **VS** SHASKA WHATLEY

KENDALL WINDHAM **VS** TIGER CONWAY

ITALIAN STALLION **VS** TERMINATOR

*NWA - SUBJECT TO CHANGE

Ringside Reserved $15
General Admission $10
Children (Under 10) $5

N014947-G

MID-ATLANTIC CHAMPIONSHIP WRESTLING

JCP @ Greenville, SC - Memorial Auditorium - March 28, 1988
The Italian Stallion vs. the Terminator did not take place as advertised
Arn Anderson & Tully Blanchard defeated Rocky King & John Savage (sub. for NWA US Champion Dusty Rhodes & Ole Anderson)
Nelson Royal defeated George South
Kendall Windham defeated Tiger Conway Jr.
Ron Simmons defeated Shaska Whatley
NWA Western States Heritage Champion Larry Zbyszko defeated Shane Douglas
Bobby Fulton & Tommy Rogers defeated NWA US Champion Bobby Eaton & Stan Lane
NWA World Champion Ric Flair defeated Sting in a No DQ match

JCP @ North Wilkesboro, NC - March 29, 1988
Ron & Jimmy Garvin defeated NWA US Tag Team Champions Bobby Eaton & Stan Lane

JCP @ Columbia, SC - Township Auditorium - March 29, 1988
Shane Douglas pinned Doug Savage
Chris Champion fought the Terminator to a draw
Ricky Santana defeated Johnny Ace
Black Bart defeated the Italian Stallion
Arn Anderson pinned Kendall Windham
Ron & Jimmy Garvin defeated NWA US Tag Team Champions Bobby Eaton & Stan Lane via disqualification
NWA Tag Team Champion Lex Luger pinned Tully Blanchard, despite interference from JJ Dillon

JCP @ Atlanta, GA - WTBS Studios - March 30, 1988
World Championship Wrestling - 4/2/88:
Bobby Fulton & Tommy Rogers vs. Keith Steinborn & Martin
Sting vs. Barry Collie
The Sheepherders vs. Stevens & King
NWA Tag Team Champion Arn Anderson vs. Art Pritts
The Road Warriors vs. Joe Cruz & El Negro
Ron & Jimmy Garvin vs. Atkinson & Wagner
Al Perez vs. Mike Jackson
NWA US Tag Team Champions Bobby Eaton & Stan Lane vs. Trent Knight & Tony Suber
Kevin Sullivan, NWA TV Champion Mike Rotundo, & Florida Heavyweight Champion Rick Steiner vs. Riddle, Davis, & George South
Ivan Koloff vs. Curtis Thompson

JCP @ Spartanburg, SC - Memorial Auditorium - March 31, 1988
The Main Event taping:
4/3/88 - debut episode - included Jim Ross as the guest ring announcer; featured Tony Schiavone on commentary; included a backstage promo by NWA World Champion Ric Flair, Arn Anderson, Tully Blanchard, & JJ Dillon regarding their

scheduled match later in the show against Sting, NWA Tag Team Champions Lex Luger & Barry Windham; featured a closing announcement that Windham would face Blanchard, Anderson would face Steve Williams, and the Warlord & the Barbarian would face Brad Armstrong & Tim Horner:
The Road Warriors (w/ Paul Ellering) defeated NWA Western States Heritage Champion Larry Zbyzsko (w/ Baby Doll) & the Super Destroyer at 3:23 when Road Warrior Hawk pinned Destroyer following the Doomsday Device
NWA US Champion Dusty Rhodes pinned Ivan Koloff (w/ Paul Jones) with a crossbody off the top at 6:38 after punching Jones on the floor; Kevin Sullivan cut an insert promo during the match regarding Rhodes (American Dream: The Dusty Rhodes Story)
NWA World Champion Ric Flair, Arn Anderson, & Tully Blanchard (w/ JJ Dillon) defeated Sting, NWA Tag Team Champions Lex Luger & Barry Windham at around the 13-minute mark when Blanchard pinned Windham after repeatedly punching Windham in the face with a foreign object thrown in the ring by Dillon; during the match, Dillon cut an insert promo on the match and the suspension of Dusty Rhodes; Jim Ross joined Tony Schiavone on commentary for the match (The Rise and Fall of WCW)
4/10/88 - featured Tony Schiavone on commentary; included Jim Ross as the ring announcer; featured a split screen backstage segment in which NWA Tag Team Champion Barry Windham and Tully Blanchard discussed their upcoming match later in the show; included a closing announcement that Windham & Steve Williams would face Blanchard & Arn Anderson, Nikita Koloff would face Tiger Conway Jr., and the Sheepherders would be in action the following week:
The Warlord & the Barbarian (w/ Paul Jones) defeated Tim Horner & the Italian Stallion (sub. for Brad Armstrong) at around the 5-minute mark when Barbarian pinned Stallion following a headbutt off the top
Steve Williams fought Arn Anderson to a double count-out at 9:46 when both men began brawling on the floor and Anderson left ringside; NWA World Champion Ric Flair provided guest commentary for the match; after the contest, Flair and Williams had words, with Williams then challenging Flair to get in the ring and face him
NWA Tag Team Champion Barry Windham pinned Tully Blanchard (w/ JJ Dillon) with a sunset flip into the ring at 15:34 after Arn Anderson and Steve Williams appeared ringside and brawled with each other; Jim Ross joined Tony Schiavone on commentary for the bout; during the match, Sting cut an insert promo in which he said he was targetting NWA World Champion Ric Flair; after the match, NWA US Champion Dusty Rhodes came out to congratulate Windham on the win

JCP @ Norfolk, VA - Scope - April 1, 1988
Tim Horner defeated Tiger Conway Jr.
Pez Whatley defeated Mark Fleming
Steve Williams defeated Rick Steiner
NWA US Tag Team Champions Bobby Eaton & Stan Lane fought Tommy Rogers & Bobby Fulton to a draw
Dusty Rhodes defeated NWA TV Champion Mike Rotundo via disqualification

Arn Anderson & Tully Blanchard defeated NWA Tag Team Champions Lex Luger & Barry Windham via disqualification
NWA World Champion Ric Flair defeated Sting in a steel cage match after hitting him with a steel chair thrown in the ring by Arn Anderson, who appeared ringside early in the match with Tully Blanchard; after the bout, the Horsemen ganged up on Sting until Dusty Rhodes, Steve Williams, NWA Tag Team Champions Lex Luger & Barry Windham made the save

-4/88: Baby Doll was released.

JCP @ Charlotte, NC - Coliseum - April 2, 1988
TV taping

JCP @ Bluefield, WV - Armory - April 2, 1988
Bobby Fulton & Tommy Rogers defeated NWA US Tag Team Champions Stan Lane & Bobby Eaton via disqualification

JCP @ Atlanta, GA - Omni - April 3, 1988
Florida Heavyweight Champion Rick Steiner defeated Ricky Santana
Tim Horner defeated Shaska Whatley
Tiger Conway Jr. defeated Brad Armstrong
NWA Tag Team Champion Arn Anderson defeated the Italian Stallion
Bobby Fulton & Tommy Rogers defeated the Sheepherders
NWA US Tag Team Champions Bobby Eaton & Stan Lane defeated Steve Williams & Nikita Koloff via disqualification
Barry Windham defeated NWA Tag Team Champion Tully Blanchard
Lex Luger defeated NWA TV Champion Mike Rotundo via disqualification
The Road Warriors defeated the Powers of Pain
NWA World Champion Ric Flair defeated Sting

JCP @ Hartwell, GA - April 4, 1988
Bobby Fulton & Tommy Rogers defeated NWA US Tag Team Champions Bobby Eaton & Stan Lane via disqualification

JCP @ Gaffney, SC - April 5, 1988
TV taping:
The Sheepherders defeated the Italian Stallion & Nelson Royal
Cruel Connection #1 defeated Rock Riddle
Green Machine defeated Jimmy Valiant
Nikita Koloff defeated the Warlord
Bobby Fulton & Tommy Rogers defeated NWA US Tag Team Champions Bobby Eaton & Stan Lane via disqualification

JCP @ Macon, GA - Coliseum - April 5, 1988

JCP @ Atlanta, GA - WTBS Studios - April 6, 1988
World Championship Wrestling - 4/9/88 - featured an opening clip highlighting the finish and aftermath of the Bobby Fulton & Tommy Rogers vs. NWA US Tag Team Champions Bobby

Eaton & Stan Lane during the Clash of the Champions; included Jim Ross & Tony Schiavone on commentary; featured the announcement NWA US Champion Dusty Rhodes had been suspended for 120 days; included Schiavone conducting an interview with Road Warrior Animal & Paul Ellering, in which Animal responded to the ruling regarding Dusty Rhodes and said the Road Warriors were always available to help Rhodes; moments later, Ellering discussed the Road Warriors being part of the Crockett Cup; featured Schiavone conducting an interview with NWA Tag Team Champions Lex Luger & Barry Windham, during which Luger apologized for hogging last week's interview and put the spotlight on Windham; Windham then commented on Rhodes' suspension and being part of the Crockett Cup; moments later, it was noted Luger & Windham were seeded #6 in the tournament; included a vignette promoting the debut of the Midnight Rider, alongside Magnum TA; featured Schiavone conducting an interview with NWA World Champion Ric Flair, during which Flair said Rhodes would soon be gone from the NWA; included Ross conducting an interview with Jim Crockett Jr. regarding the suspension of Rhodes, which takes affect April 16 after his match the night before at the Boston Garden; moments later, Jim Cornette, Eaton & Lane interrupted, with Cornette saying Ray Charles could see the Midnight Rider was Rhodes and that Eaton & Lane would be facing Fulton & Rogers in Boston; Cornette then said he'd like to whip Rogers' mom and the fans but he didn't have the time to do that so he would instead whip Rogers & Fulton at every chance he gets:
Bobby Fulton & Tommy Rogers defeated Bear Collie & Art Pritts at 5:07 when Rogers pinned Pritts following the Rocket Launcher; during the bout, it was noted Fulton & Rogers were the #7 seed in the Jim Crockett Sr. Memorial Cup; following the commercial break, Jim Ross conducted an interview with Fulton & Rogers regarding the attack they sustained from Jim Cornette at the Clash of the Champions and being part of the Crockett Cup, during which Rogers wished his dad a fast recovery
NWA Western States Heritage Champion Larry Zbyszko & Al Perez (w/ Gary Hart) defeated Ricky Santana & Tommy Angel at 4:39 when Angel submitted to Perez's spinning toe hold; during the match, it was noted Santana would team with Shane Douglas during the Crockett Cup; following the commercial break, Tony Schiavone conducted an interview with Hart, Zbyszko, & Perez in which Hart said he had gone to the Board of Directors to reinstate Zbyszko's piledriver and then cut a promo on his team potentially facing Dusty Rhodes & Nikita Koloff during the Cup (Zbyszko & Perez's first match as a team)
Steve Williams pinned Alan Martin with the Oklahoma Stampede at 2:29; during the match, it was noted Williams would team with Ron Simmons during the Crockett Cup
Nikita Koloff pinned Ryan Wagner with the Russian Sickle at 1:54; after the match, Ross conducted a ringside interview with Koloff regarding the suspension of NWA US Champion Dusty Rhodes and their team no longer being part of the Crockett Cup; moments later, Koloff responded to Gary Hart's comments earlier in the show (Koloff's return match after a several week absence; his first appearance with hair)

Arn Anderson & Tully Blanchard (w/ JJ Dillon) defeated Kendall Windham & Mike Jackson at around the 1:45 mark when Anderson pinned Jackson with the DDT; after the match, Ross conducted an interview with Anderson, Blanchard, & Dillon regarding their participation in the Crockett Cup, during which Dillon argued about the coming debut of the Midnight Rider when he said he knew and everyone else knew it was Dusty Rhodes
Sting defeated the Destroyer via submission with the Scorpion Deathlock at 1:11; during the match, it was noted Sting would team with Ron Garvin during the Crockett Cup and would have Magnum TA at ringside; after the match, Ross conducted an interview with Sting regarding the Cup and facing NWA World Champion Ric Flair; moments later, after being questioned about Rhodes' suspension, Sting said he would have done the same thing Rhodes did
Ron Garvin pinned Bob Emory with the right hand punch at the 35-second mark
NWA TV Champion Mike Rotundo & Kevin Sullivan (w/ Forida Heavyweight Champion Rick Steiner) defeated Tony Bowman & El Negro when Sullivan pinned Bowman with the double stop after Rotundo hit the butterfly suplex; during the match, it was noted Sullivan would face Jimmy Garvin in a Prince of Darkness match during the Crockett Cup; following the commercial break, Schiavone conducted an interview with Sullivan, Rotundo, & Steiner, during which Sullivan said he remembered the first time Dusty Rhodes became the Midnight Rider, and mentioned what happened to the likes of Angelo Mosca, Purple Haze, and Malachai the last time the Rider showed up; Sullivan then said he didn't like the Horsemen or Jim Cornette's group but they would have to work together to eliminate the Rider
Dick Murdoch, NWA Six-Man Tag Team Champions the Powers of Pain (w/ Paul Jones) defeated the Italian Stallion, Tony Suber, & Larry Davis at 2:07 when Murdoch pinned Davis with the brainbuster; during the match, it was noted The Main Event would air the following Saturday morning due to Atlanta Braves baseball; after the match, Ross conducted an interview with Jones' men, during which Jones said he would have two teams in the Crockett Cup - Murdoch & Ivan Koloff as the #10 seed and the Powers of Pain as the #3 seed; Murdoch then said everyone - including Jim Crockett Sr. and Jim Barnett - knew the Midnight Rider was Dusty Rhodes

JCP @ Kings Mountain, NC - April 7, 1988
Bobby Fulton & Tommy Rogers defeated NWA US Tag Team Champions Bobby Eaton & Stan Lane

JCP @ Long Island, NY - Nassau Coliseum - April 8, 1988 (4,500)
Mighty Wilbur pinned the Terminator; during the bout, Wilbur reinjured his knee
Ron Simmons pinned Johnny Ace
Jimmy Valiant pinned the Green Machine (Bugsy McGraw)
Brad Armstrong & Tim Horner defeated the Sheepherders after Johnny Ace accidentally hit Butch Miller with the flagpole
Dick Murdoch pinned Shane Douglas

NWA Tag Team Champions Lex Luger & Barry Windham defeated Arn Anderson & Tully Blanchard via disqualification
The Road Warriors defeated the Powers of Pain

JCP @ Richmond, VA - Coliseum - April 8, 1988
Tiger Conway Jr. pinned Kendall Windham
Ricky Santana pinned Shaska Whatley
Steve Williams & Ron Garvin defeated Kevin Sullivan & Florida Heavyweight Champion Rick Steiner
NWA TV Champion Mike Rotundo fought Nikita Koloff to a draw
Bobby Fulton & Tommy Rogers defeated NWA US Tag Team Champions Bobby Eaton & Stan Lane via disqualification
NWA US Champion Dusty Rhodes pinned NWA Western States Heritage Champion Larry Zbyszko in a non-title match
NWA World Champion Ric Flair pinned Sting

JCP @ Houston, TX - Sam Houston Coliseum - April 8, 1988
Ricky Santana & Kendall Windham defeated the Sheepherders via disqualification
Nikita Koloff defeated Tiger Conway Jr.
Barry Windham & Steve Williams fought NWA Tag Team Champions Arn Anderson & Tully Blanchard to a draw

JCP @ Philadelphia, PA - Civic Center - April 9, 1988 (matinee) (4,000)
Ron Simmons pinned the Terminator
Jimmy Valiant fought the Green Machine to a draw
The Road Warriors defeated the Powers of Pain when Road Warrior Animal pinned Barbarian after Paul Ellering tripped Barbarian as he was on the top rope
Sting defeated Ric Flair via disqualification
Ron Garvin fought Dick Murdoch to a double count-out
Brad Armstrong & Tim Horner defeated the Sheepherders when Johnny Ace's interference backfired
Steve Williams pinned Larry Zbyszko at the 5-minute mark
NWA Tag Team Champions Lex Luger & Barry Windham defeated Arn Anderson & Tully Blanchard when Windham pinned Anderson

JCP @ Baltimore, MD - Arena - April 9, 1988 (9,000)
Tiger Conway Jr. fought Chris Champion to a draw
Shaska Whatley pinned the Italian Stallion
Kevin Sullivan & Rick Steiner defeated Ricky Santana & Kendall Windham
NWA TV Champion Mike Rotundo fought Nikita Koloff to a time-limit draw
Bobby Fulton & Tommy Rogers defeated NWA US Tag Team Champions Bobby Eaton & Stan Lane via disqualification at the 42-minute mark
The Powers of Pain & Ivan Koloff defeated Dusty Rhodes & the Road Warriors via disqualification
NWA World Champion Ric Flair pinned Sting

JCP @ Roanoke, VA - Civic Center - April 10, 1988 (matinee)
TV taping:
Worldwide - 4/23/88 - featured an opening clip showing Nikita Koloff having a ringside altercation with Al Perez, alongside Gary Hart, and Koloff then challenging Perez to face him in the ring; hosted by Tony Schiavone, with Schiavone saying David Crockett was on assignment and Jim Ross would join him later in the show; Schiavone then brought in Nikita, who discussed his championship past, said he was close with the Midnight Rider, and would close Hart's big mouth; included Ross conducting an interview with Kevin Sullivan & NWA TV Champion Mike Rotundo in which Sullivan offered his support to JJ Dillon against the Midnight Rider and his group, then saying he would welcome Gary Hart to their group as well; Sullivan said the Rider was the evil side of Dusty Rhodes; featured Ross conducting an interview with Steve Williams regarding his chase of Ric Flair's NWA World Title; included Ross conducting an interview with Hart & Perez regarding the vacant NWA US Title tournament upcoming, the Midnight Rider, and Perez saying he would wrestle Koloff for free to prove he was worthy of being #1 contender and not Koloff; featured a local promo by Rotundo & Rick Steiner regarding Rotundo's upcoming title defense against Jimmy Garvin in Fayetteville, NC, during which Rotundo referred to Steiner as "Rob;" included Ross conducting an interview with Flair regarding the Midnight Rider; featured Ross conducting an interview with JJ Dillon regarding the Rider, with Dillon saying Rhodes should be under suspension and the NWA was turning a blind eye, then adding if the Rider was unmasked as Rhodes then Rhodes would be suspended for a year:
The Road Warriors (w/ Paul Ellering) defeated Steve Riddle & Larry Stephens at the 42-second mark with a simultaneous pinfall after Road Warrior Hawk hit a double clothesline off the top; following the commercial break, Tony Schiavone conducted a ringside interview with the Road Warriors & Ellering in which they offered their support to the Midnight Rider and said they were after the Crockett Cup
Dick Murdoch & NWA Six-Man Tag Team Champions the Powers of Pain (w/ Paul Jones) defeated Mark Fleming, Rocky King, & an unknown at 3:27 when Murdoch pinned the unknown with the brainbuster
The Midnight Rider (w/ Magnum TA) pinned Bear Collie with a DDT onto a steel chair at the 28-second mark; Rider came into the arena riding on a horse and used Willie Nelson's "Midnight Rider" as his entrance song; after the match, Rider hit the move a second time onto the chair; moments later, Jim Ross conducted a ringside interview with Magnum as other wrestlers ran in the ring to tend to Collie; Rider then cleared the ring and motioned that he would take off his mask, with Ross then entering the ring and Rider telling him he was going to raise some hell in Roanoke; the Rider then cut a promo on the Four Horsemen and said he would bring them violence
Al Perez (w/ Gary Hart) defeated David Diamond via submission with the spinning toe hold at 1:29; after the match, Perez briefly reapplied the hold
NWA Tag Team Champions Lex Luger & Barry Windham defeated Trent Knight & Joe Cruz at 2:08 when Knight

submitted to Luger's Torture Rack; after the bout, Tony Schiavone conducted a ringside interview with Luger & Windham in which they discussed the challenge of the Varsity Club, Sheepherders, and Powers of Pain

Sting defeated Thunderfoot #2 via submission with the Scorpion Deathlock at the 42-second mark after a Stinger Splash in the corner

The Sheepherders defeated Max McGyver & Curtis Thompson at 2:11 when Butch pinned McGyver after a double gutbuster

Steve Williams pinned Tony Suber with the Oklahoma Stampede at 1:43

JCP @ Salisbury, MD - April 10, 1988
Bobby Fulton & Tommy Rogers defeated NWA US Tag Team Champions Bobby Eaton & Stan Lane via disqualification

JCP @ Fayetteville, NC - Cumberland County Civic Center - April 11, 1988
Bobby Fulton & Tommy Rogers defeated NWA US Tag Team Champions Bobby Eaton & Stan Lane via disqualification

JCP @ Las Cruces, NM - Pan American Center - April 11, 1988

JCP @ Kingstree, SC - April 12, 1988
Bobby Fulton & Tommy Rogers defeated NWA US Tag Team Champions Bobby Eaton & Stan Lane via disqualification

JCP @ Albuquerque, NM - Tingley Coliseum - April 12, 1988

JCP @ Atlanta, GA - WTBS Studios - April 13, 1988
World Championship Wrestling - 4/16/88:
NWA US Champion Bobby Eaton & Stan Lane vs. George South & Trent Knight
Dick Murdoch vs. Larry Stevens
NWA Tag Team Champion Lex Luger vs. Art Pritts
The Powers of Pain vs. Atkinson & Bob Riddle
NWA TV Champion Mike Rotundo & Florida Heavyweight Champion Rick Steiner vs. Spearman & Starr
Arn Anderson & Tully Blanchard vs. Bowman & Paradise
Nikita Koloff vs. El Negro
Jimmy Garvin vs. Larry Davis
Bobby Fulton & Tommy Rogers vs. Keith Steinborn & Martin
Al Perez vs. Ryan Wagner

JCP @ Greenwood, SC - April 14, 1988
The Main Event taping:
4/17/88 - featured Tony Schiavone & Peter Birkholz on commentary; included an opening announcement that Houston, TX would host the upcoming NWA US Title tournament; featured Jim Ross as the ring announcer; included footage of David Crockett conducting an interview with Dusty Rhodes in an empty arena regarding his 120-day suspension,

during which Rhodes said he felt he did what he had to do and would be going home and training until he returned to action Aug. 14; Rhodes finished the interview by saying he was not the Midnight Rider but there was a little Midnight Rider in everyone; featured the announcement the Sheepherders would face Ricky Santana & Kendall Windham in a rematch the following week; included the announcement that Sting would be in action the following week and Nikita Koloff would face Al Perez:
Ricky Santana & Kendall Windham defeated the Sheepherders (w/ Johnny Ace) via disqualification at 9:04 when Ace accidentally struck Luke Williams with the flag pole while trying to break a cover after Santana hit a crossbody off the top; after the bout, Butch Williams yelled at Ace for the mistake
Nikita Koloff pinned Tiger Conway Jr. with the Russian Sickle immediately after Conway threw Koloff into the corner; during the bout, it was mentioned Dusty Rhodes would be in Houston, TX for the NWA US Title tournament, despite his suspension
Arn Anderson & Tully Blanchard (w/ JJ Dillon) fought Steve Williams & NWA Tag Team Champion Barry Windham to a time-limit draw at 14:23; both teams were fighting in and out of the ring when the match ended; after the bout, Williams & Windham fought off their opponents and cleared them from the ring
4/24/88 - featured Tony Schiavone & Peter Birkholz on commentary; included Jim Ross as the ring announcer; featured a backstage promo by JJ Dillon regarding the Midnight Rider in which he said he had been working behind the scenes with Jim Cornette, Gary Hart, and Kevin Sullivan to help rid the NWA of the Rider; Dillon then said if his men or the men of the other managers was to unmask the Rider as Dusty Rhodes then Rhodes' 120-day suspension would be extended to a year; included a closing segment in which Johnny Ace came ringside and told Schiavone he had a challenge for he, Ricky Santana, & Kendall Windham to face the Sheepherders & Rip Morgan the following week; it was also announced NWA Tag Team Champion Lex Luger & Sting would face NWA World Champion Ric Flair & Arn Anderson the next week:
Sting pinned Shaska Whatley at 5:51 with a sunset flip into the ring
Ricky Santana & Kendall Windham defeated the Sheepherders (w/ Johnny Ace) at 9:21 when Santana pinned Butch with a roll up after Butch and Ace fought over possession of the New Zealand flag; after the bout, Ace fought the Sheepherders until another man came out and helped triple team Ace; Santana & Windham eventually cleared the ring and tended to Ace; following the commercial break, the man's identity was revealed to be Rip Morgan, the Sheepherders' nephew (the surprise debut of Rip Morgan)
Nikita Koloff defeated Al Perez (w/ Gary Hart) via disqualification at 14:08 when Hart assaulted Koloff with a foreign object after Koloff hit the Russian Sickle; after the bout, Perez repeatedly applied the spinning toe hold until Sting slid in the ring; moments later, Hart held Perez back as the referee tended to Koloff

JCP @ Columbia, SC - Township Auditorium - April 14, 1988

Bobby Fulton & Tommy Rogers defeated NWA US Tag Team Champions Bobby Eaton & Stan Lane via disqualification

- 4/15/88: Dusty Rhodes was stripped of the NWA US Title and suspended for 120 days after attacking Jim Crockett.

JCP @ Boston, MA - Boston Garden - April 15, 1988
Al Perez defeated Ricky Santana (sub. for Shane Douglas)
Kevin Sullivan & Florida Heavyweight Champion Rick Steiner defeated Kendall Windham & the Italian Stallion (sub. for Brad Armstrong & Tim Horner)
Nikita Koloff defeated Western States Heritage Champion Larry Zbyszko
Bobby Fulton & Tommy Rogers defeated NWA US Tag Team Champions Bobby Eaton & Stan Lane via disqualification
Steve Williams fought NWA TV Champion Mike Rotunda to a draw
The Road Warriors defeated the Powers of Pain
Dusty Rhodes, Sting, NWA Tag Team Champions Lex Luger & Barry Windham defeated NWA World Champion Ric Flair, Ivan Koloff, Arn Anderson, & Tully Blanchard in a steel cage match

JCP @ Chicago, IL - UIC Pavilion - April 16, 1988 (3,500)
Shaska Whatley & Tiger Conway Jr. defeated the Rebel & Mike Tolos
Ron Simmons defeated the Terminator
The Sheepherders defeated Brad Armstrong & Tim Horner
Dick Murdoch defeated Ricky Santana
NWA Tag Team Champions Lex Luger & Barry Windham defeated Arn Anderson & Tully Blanchard via disqualification
The Road Warriors & Steve Williams defeated Paul Jones & the Powers of Pain
Sting vs. NWA World Champion Ric Flair

JCP @ Rock Hill, SC - Winthrop Coliseum - April 16, 1988
The Sheepherders & Rip Morgan vs. Johnny Ace, Ricky Santana, & Kendall Windham

JCP @ Cincinnati, OH - Cincinnati Gardens - April 16, 1988
Bobby Fulton & Tommy Rogers defeated NWA US Tag Team Champions Bobby Eaton & Stan Lane via disqualification

JCP @ Asheville, NC - Civic Center - April 17, 1988 (matinee)
TV taping:
World Championship Wrestling - 4/23/88 - featured the NWA Tag Team Champions Lex Luger & Barry Windham vs. Arn Anderson & Tully Blanchard match taped 4/20/88 in Jacksonville, FL:
Sting defeated David Isley via submission with the Scorpion Deathlock
Bobby Fulton & Tommy Rogers defeated Carey Stevens & Snake Watson when Rogers pinned Stevens
Steve Williams pinned Bob Riddle with the Oklahoma Stampede

Bobby Eaton & Stan Lane (w/ Jim Cornette) defeated Tommy Angel & Rocky King when Eaton pinned Angel
NWA 6 Man tag Team Champions Ivan Koloff, the Warlord & Barbarian (w/ Paul Jones) defeated Max McGyver, Bob Emory, & Curtis Thompson
Al Perez (w/ Gary Hart) pinned Larry Stephens
Nikita Koloff pinned Krusher Knault with the Russian Sickle
NWA TV Champion Mike Rotunda (w/ Kevin Sullivan) pinned Sam Bass

JCP @ Charlotte, NC - Coliseum - April 17, 1988
Bobby Fulton & Tommy Rogers defeated NWA US Tag Team Champions Bobby Eaton & Stan Lane via disqualification
The Road Warriors vs. Tiger Conway Jr. & Pez Whatley
The Midnight Rider vs. NWA Tag Team Champion Tully Blanchard
Lex Luger & NWA Tag Team Champion Barry Windham vs. NWA world Champion Ric Flair & Arn Anderson

JCP @ West Palm Beach, FL - Auditorium - April 18, 1988 (2,000)
Rick Steiner pinned Kendall Windham
Kevin Sullivan fought Jimmy Garvin to a no contest
Bobby Fulton & Tommy Rogers defeated NWA US Tag Team Champions Bobby Eaton & Stan Lane via disqualification
NWA Tag Team Champion Barry Windham fought NWA TV Champion Mike Rotundo to a draw
The Midnight Rider, Sting, & NWA Tag Team Champion Lex Luger defeated NWA World Champion Ric Flair, Arn Anderson, & Tully Blanchard at the 14-minute mark when the Rider pinned Blanchard

JCP @ Miami, FL - Knight Center - April 19, 1988 (4,000)
Ricky Santana pinned Rocky King
Bugsy McGraw pinned Crusher Balboa
Rick Steiner pinned Kendall Windham
Bobby Fulton & Tommy Rogers defeated NWA US Tag Team Champions Bobby Eaton & Stan Lane via disqualification at the 18-minute mark
Kevin Sullivan pinned Jimmy Garvin after Sullivan hit him with a weapon, handed to him by NWA TV Champion Mike Rotunda
Lex Luger defeated Arn Anderson via count-out
The Midnight Rider defeated Tully Blanchard via disqualification
Sting defeated NWA World Champion Ric Flair via disqualification at the 17-minute mark when Flair threw the challenger over the top rope

JCP @ Jacksonville, FL - Memorial Coliseum - April 20, 1988
TV taping:
World Championship Wrestling - 4/23/88:
Sting defeated David Isley via submission with the Scorpion Deathlock
Bobby Fulton & Tommy Rogers defeated Carey Stevens &

Snake Watson when Rogers pinned Stevens
Steve Williams pinned Bob Riddle with the Oklahoma
Stampede
Bobby Eaton & Stan Lane (w/ Jim Cornette) defeated Tommy
Angel & Rocky King when Eaton pinned Angel
NWA Six Man tag Team Champions Ivan Koloff, the Warlord &
Barbarian (w/ Paul Jones) defeated Max McGyver, Bob Emory,
& Curtis Thompson
Al Perez (w/ Gary Hart) pinned Larry Stephens
Nikita Koloff pinned Krusher Knault with the Russian Sickle
NWA TV Champion Mike Rotunda (w/ Kevin Sullivan) pinned
Sam Bass
Arn Anderson & Tully Blanchard (w/ JJ Dillon) defeated NWA
Tag Team Champions Lex Luger & Barry Windham to win the
titles when Anderson pinned Luger after Windham tagged an
injured Luger into the match, powerslammed him into the ring,
and then hit the lariat on his partner; after the bout, Windham
left ringside with Dillon, Anderson & Blanchard; after the bout,
the Midnight Rider, Steve Williams, Nikita Koloff, and Ron
Garvin tended to a bleeding Luger inside the ring; after Luger
was helped to the back, the Rider confronted Windham in the
heel locker room, with the Horsemen and others beating the
Rider down until Sting and others covered his body and pulled
him from safety

JCP @ Harrisonburg, VA - High School - April 21, 1988
Chris Champion vs. Cruel Connection #2
Johnny Ace vs. Cruel Connection #1
Brad Armstrong & Tim Horner vs. the Sheepherders
Jimmy Valiant vs. the Big Green Machine
Barry Windham & Ron Garvin vs. Rick Steiner & Al Perez
Jimmy Garvin vs. NWA TV Champion Mike Rotunda

JCP @ Sumter, SC - Exhibition Center - April 21, 1988
Bobby Fulton & Tommy Rogers defeated NWA US Tag Team
Champions Bobby Eaton & Stan Lane via disqualification

**3rd Annual Jim Crockett Sr. Memorial Cup - Greenville, SC
- Memorial Auditorium - April 22, 1988 (4,440)**
*Featured an opening announcement by Tony Schiavone that
Barry Windham would not be part of the tournament; included
Tony Schiavone conducting an interview with NWA World
Champion Ric Flair regarding his match the following night
against Nikita Koloff*
Opening Round: Kendall Windham & the Italian Stallion
defeated the Terminator & the Green Machine via forfeit when
Machine did not appear
Opening Round: Dick Murdoch & Ivan Koloff (w/ Paul Jones)
defeated Jimmy Valiant & Mighty Igor at 6:14 when Koloff
pinned Valiant with the Russian Sickle after Murdoch landed a
knee to the back as Valiant ran the ropes
Opening Round: Tiger Conway & Shaska Whatley defeated
Rocky King & Nelson Royal at 6:05 when King was pinned
following a double Russian leg sweep
Opening Round: Chris Champion & Mark Starr defeated the
Twin Devils (Curtis Thompson & Gene Ligon in red outfits) at

7:46 when Champion pinned Ligon with a slingshot splash
Opening Round: Brad Armstrong & Tim Horner defeated
Johnny Ace & John Savage (sub. for a Japanese team) at 6:43
when Armstrong pinned Savage following the double team
legdrop
Opening Round: The Sheepherders (w/ Rip Morgan) defeated
the Cruel Connection (Gary Royal & George South) at 7:20
when South was pinned following a double gutbuster
Opening Round: Larry Zbyzsko & Al Perez defeated Ricky
Santana & Joe Cruz (sub. for Shane Douglas, who quit earlier
in the week) at 4:57 when Cruz submitted to Perez' spinning
toe hold
Opening Round: NWA TV Champion Mike Rotundo & Rick
Steiner (w/ Kevin Sullivan) defeated Steve Williams & Ron
Simmons via count-out at 9:20 after Sullivan hit Simmons with
a foreign object on the floor; the bell rang just as Williams
dropped Rotundo with the Oklahoma Stampede
Non-tournament match: Jimmy Garvin (w/ Precious) pinned
Kevin Sullivan (w/ Rick Steiner) in a blindfold match with an
inside cradle at 7:20; after the match, Steiner unmasked
Sullivan and attacked Garvin from behind; moments later, Ron
Garvin came out to make the save, with NWA TV Champion
Mike Rotundo appearing as well; during the brawl, Sullivan hit
Garvin in the chest with his golden spike; moments later,
Kendall Windham, Ricky Santana, and Johnny Ace came out
to tend to the Garvins; as a result of Ron Garvin's injury, Sting
was left without a tag team partner for the tournament; it was
later announced that Sting would team with Lex Luger, who
also was without a partner
Second Round: NWA Tag Team Champions Arn Anderson &
Tully Blanchard defeated Kendall Windham & the Italian
Stallion in a non-title match when Anderson pinned the Stallion
at 6:24 with the DDT as Stallion attempted a backdrop
Second Round: Lex Luger & Sting (w/ Magnum TA) defeated
Dick Murdoch & Ivan Koloff (w/ Paul Jones) at 9:41 when Sting
pinned Murdoch by reversing a bodyslam from the apron into
the ring into a cradle
Second Round: The Road Warriors (w/ Paul Ellering) defeated
Pez Whatley & Tiger Conway at 5:26 when Road Warrior
Hawk pinned Whatley with the clothesline off the top after
avoiding a flying clothesline from Whatley
Second Round: The Powers of Pain defeated Chris Champion
& Mark Starr at 8:04 when Barbarian pinned Starr following a
powerslam off the middle turnbuckle
Second Round: The Sheepherders (w/ Rip Morgan) defeated
Brad Armstrong & Tim Horner at 9:32 when Luke pinned
Armstrong after hitting him with the flagpole as Armstrong had
a sleeper applied on an interfering Morgan
Second Round: Bobby Fulton & Tommy Rogers defeated NWA
Western States Heritage Champion Larry Zbyzsko & Al Perez
(w/ Gary Hart) at 5:03 when Fulton pinned Zybzsko with an
inside cradle as Zbyzsko & Perez attempted a double team,
with Rogers then knocking Perez to the floor with a dropkick
Second Round: NWA US Tag Team Champions Bobby Eaton
& Stan Lane (w/ Jim Cornette) defeated the Sheepherders (w/
Rip Morgan) at 4:44 when Lane pinned Butch after Eaton hit
Butch from behind with Cornette's tennis racquet; the
champions were heavily cheered in the contest

465

3rd Annual Jim Crockett Sr. Memorial Cup - Greensboro, NC - Coliseum - April 23, 1988 (6,200 paid)

Featured an opening announcement of Ron Garvin's injury and Barry Windham's joining the Horsemen, thus forming the Sting & Lex Luger team

Quarter-Finals: Tommy Rogers & Bobby Fulton defeated NWA TV Champion Mike Rotunda & Rick Steiner (w/ Kevin Sullivan) at 27:20 when Rogers pinned Steiner with a sunset flip into the ring

Quarter-Finals: Sting & Lex Luger defeated Bobby Eaton & Stan Lane (w/ Jim Cornette) at 13:40 when Sting pinned Lane with a Thesz Press

Quarter-Finals: The Powers of Pain (w/ Paul Jones & Ivan Koloff) defeated the Road Warriors (w/ Paul Ellering) via reverse decision at 9:10; Road Warrior Animal originally pinned the Barbarian following a double clothesline after the Barbarian missed a diving headbutt, with replacement referee Teddy Long counting the pinfall; however, the initial referee Randy Anderson disqualified the Road Warriors for Animal accidentally hitting a clothesline on him

Non-tournament match: The Midnight Rider (Dusty Rhodes under a mask) pinned JJ Dillon in a Texas Bullrope match at 4:10 after coming off the middle turnbuckle and hitting Dillon with the cowbell; stipulations stated that if Dillon were to unmask the Rider and reveal him as Rhodes then Rhodes would be suspended for a year; after the bout, another masked man appeared as Rhodes choked Dillon, with the second man attacking Rhodes until Steve Williams attempted to make the save; as Dillon choked the Rider, the second masked man assaulted Williams with the cowbell until Rider eventually cleared the ring

Semi-Finals: Sting & Lex Luger (w/ Magnum TA) defeated the Powers of Pain (w/ Paul Jones & Ivan Koloff) at 6:50 when Luger pinned the Warlord after Sting hit a dropkick on Warlord as he had Luger up for a slam, with Luger falling on top for the win

Semi-Finals: NWA Tag Team Champions Arn Anderson & Tully Blanchard defeated Bobby Fulton & Tommy Rogers in a non-title match at 14:35 when Anderson pinned Rogers after hitting him with the shoe of JJ Dillon, who appeared ringside during the contest

Non-tournament match: Nikita Koloff defeated NWA World Champion Ric Flair via disqualification at 30:08 when Flair backdropped Koloff over the top rope to the floor; prior to the bout, Flair was escorted to the ring by Barry Windham, with Flair then cutting an in-ring promo regarding Windham joining the Four Horsemen; moments later, as Windham left ringside, he was greeted in the aisle by JJ Dillon, NWA Tag Team Champions Arn Anderson & Tully Blanchard; late in the match, Koloff hit the Russian Sickle but Flair kicked out at 2

Finals: Sting & Lex Luger (w/ Magnum TA) defeated NWA Tag Team Champions Arn Anderson & Tully Blanchard (w/ JJ Dillon) in a non-title match at 16:05 when Luger pinned Anderson with a roll up as Anderson grabbed at Magnum on the floor, moments after Magnum interfered; after the bout, Elizabeth Crockett, the widow of Jim Crockett Sr., and Jim Crockett Jr. presented Sting & Luger with the Crockett Cup and

the $1 million prize; moments later, Luger cut an in-ring promo thanking the fans for their support

JCP @ Charleston, SC - Civic Center - April 24, 1988 (matinee) (2,500)

TV taping:

Jimmy Garvin defeated NWA TV Champion Mike Rotundo via disqualification

Dark match: Bobby Fulton & Tommy Rogers fought NWA US Tag Team Champions Bobby Eaton & Stan Lane to a double disqualification

Sting & Lex Luger defeated NWA Tag Team Champions Arn Anderson & Tully Blanchard in a non-title steel cage match

JCP @ Atlanta, GA - Omni - April 24, 1988 (1,400)

Brad Armstrong & Tim Horner fought NWA TV Champion Mike Rotunda & Florida Heavyweight Champion Rick Steiner to a draw after the 15-minute mark; after the bout, Rotunda & Steiner argued

Ivan Koloff pinned Jimmy Valiant at 5:34

Ron Garvin pinned the Terminator at 3:02

Bobby Fulton & Tommy Rogers fought NWA US Tag Team Champions Bobby Eaton & Stan Lane to a double count-out at 14:40

NWA Tag Team Champion Arn Anderson defeated the Midnight Rider via disqualification at the 49-second mark after hitting Anderson with a chair and punching the referee

Jimmy Garvin pinned Dick Murdoch at 7:45 with a cradle after Murdoch went to grab at Precious; Kevin Sullivan appeared ringside late in the match; after the bout, Murdoch challenged Sullivan to a match

NWA World Champion Ric Flair & NWA Tag Team Champion Tully Blanchard defeated Sting & Lex Luger at 19:20 when Sting was pinned after Barry Windham interfered and dropped Sting with a lariat behind the referee's back as Sting had Blanchard in the Scorpion Deathlock

The Road Warriors & Paul Ellering defeated the Powers of Pain & Paul Jones in a steel cage match at 4:50 when Road Warrior Hawk was the last man of his team to escape the cage, leaving the Barbarian alone in the ring

JCP @ Fayetteville, NC - Cumberland County Memorial Arena - April 25, 1988

Kendall Windham vs. the Terminator

Jimmy Valiant vs. Al Perez

The Italian Stallion vs. the Warlord

Ricky Santana & Shane Douglas vs. Kevin Sullivan & Rick Steiner

Ron Garvin vs. the Barbarian

Nikita Koloff vs. NWA Western States Heritage Champion Larry Zbyszko

Jimmy Garvin vs. NWA TV Champion Mike Rotunda

JCP @ Nashville, TN - Municipal Auditorium - April 25, 1988 (2,500)

NWA World Champion Ric Flair did not appear as scheduled;

refunds were offered as a result
Bobby Fulton & Tommy Rogers fought NWA US Tag Team
Champions Bobby Eaton & Stan Lane to a double count-out
Road Warrior Hawk vs. ? (sub. for NWA World Champion Ric
Flair)

JCP @ Chattanooga, TN - UTC Arena - April 26, 1988 (2,500)

NWA World Champion Ric Flair did not appear as scheduled; refunds were offered as a result
TV taping:
Sting defeated John Savage
Ivan Koloff defeated Joe Cruz
The Sheepherders defeated Brad Armstrong & Tim Horner
NWA Tag Team Champions Arn Anderson & Tully Blanchard
defeated Tommy Angel & Trent Knight
Bobby Fulton & Tommy Rogers defeated Andrew Bellamy &
Bob Riddle
Shaska Whatley defeated Larry Stephens
Pro - 5/14/88:
NWA US Champion Barry Windham (w/ JJ Dillon) pinned
George South with one knee after hitting the lariat; after the
match, Dillon gave Windham a black glove to put on on, with
Windham then applying the claw on South; moments later,
other enhancement wrestlers tried to pull Windham away
without success; eventually, Windham releaesd the hold under
his own will as South was shown bleeding from the head
*Worldwide - 5/14/88 - featured Tony Schiavone conducting an
interview with the Midnight Rider regarding Barry Windham
coming after him to take off the mask, with the Rider saying
Dusty Rhodes had a heavy heart and he would be there all
summer until Rhodes returned to the ring; the Rider then talked
about Rhodes raising Windham in Florida and Texas, then
telling Windham not to follow the Four Horsemen and don't
push him into hurting him; included footage of Windham
beating George South, then putting on a black glove to apply
the claw on South; moments later, other enhancement
wrestlers tried to pull Windham away without success;
eventually, Windham releaesd the hold under his own will as
South was shown bleeding from the head; David Crockett then
conducted a ringside interview with Windham, alongside JJ
Dillon, NWA Tag Team Champions Arn Anderson & Tully
Blanchard, in which Windham discussed Lex Luger; Anderson
then said Windham was following his own American dream
and Rhodes should be smart enough to leave him be:*
Bobby Fulton & Tommy Rogers defeated NWA US Tag Team
Champions Bobby Eaton & Stan Lane (w/ Jim Cornette) to win
the titles at around the 30-minute mark when Fulton pinned
Eaton with a roll up following a missile dropkick from Rogers;
late in the match, referee Randy Anderson went to stop the
match as a result of Fulton bleeding from the head until Rogers
convinced him to do otherwise; Jim Ross was the ring
announcer for the bout; Tony Schiavone & David Crockett
provided commentary for the match
Shaska Whatley & Tiger Conway Jr. defeated Tommy Angel &
John Savage; only the first 2 minutes of the match were shown
before the announcers broke away to recap the final several

minutes of the NWA US Tag Team Title change earlier in the
show

JCP @ Atlanta, GA - WTBS Studios - April 27, 1988

*NWA World Champion Ric Flair did not appear as scheduled
World Championship Wrestling - 4/30/88 - featured an opening
pretaped promo by JJ Dillon in which he announced Barry
Windham was now part of the Four Horsemen and Arn
Anderson & Tully Blanchard had regained the NWA Tag Team
Titles; Dillon then said the only void was the vacant NWA US
Title, which he said Windham would win; included the
announcement Tommy Rogers & Bobby Fulton had won the
NWA US Tag Team Titles from Bobby Eaton & Dennis
Condrey; featured Tony Schiavone & Jim Ross on
commentary; included an ad promoting the Four Horsemen
Top Performance System diet supplements; featured several
minutes of footage from the Wimdham & Lex Luger vs.
Anderson & Blanchard match taped 4/20/88 in Jacksonville, FL
in which Anderson & Blanchard won the tag team titles;
included Schiavone conducting an interview with Dillon
regarding Windham joining the Horsemen, during which Dillon
said Windham knew he had to break away from Dusty Rhodes
and Luger and that the personal appearances, endorsements,
and movie roles should go to Windham; following the
commercial break, Windham came out to join Schiavone and
Dillon, as the fans chanted "Barry sucks;" Windham then said
Luger would spend the rest of his career flat on his back as he
was in Jacksonville; the two then discussed the Midnight Rider,
with Windham then showing the Rider's mask; footage then
aired from Jacksonville of the Rider in the ring going backstage
as Nikita Koloff, Steve Williams, and Sting helped Luger
backstage; moments later, the Rider going into the heel's
dressing room, yelling at Windham, and then being jumped by
the Horsemen until Sting, Koloff, and Williams covered his
body and pulled him to safety; moments later, Schiavone
spoke with Windham, Dillon, Anderson, & Blanchard in which
Blanchard said the last part of Rhodes' mystique as the Rider's
mask, and the Horsemen had taken that too; Anderson then
said Windham had achieved the American Dream and that
Rhodes shouldn't blame him for doing so; included Ross
holding the Jim Crockett Sr. Memorial Cup home video, with
footage then showing highlights from the 2-day event; featured
a pretaped interview between Schiavone and Luger regarding
Windham turning on him in Jacksonville; included Crockett
conducting an interview with Jim Cornette regarding Rogers &
Fulton winning the NWA US Tag Team Titles, during which
footage from Chattanooga, TN was shown; moments later,
Cornette said his mother took the video tape to Jim Crockett
and Crockett would have a decision for him the following week,
noting that the following week would have marked Bobby
Eaton & Stan Lane's one-year anniversary of being
champions; included Crockett conducting an interview with the
Midnight Rider, to a mixed reaction, in which he told Windham
not to force him or Dusty Rhodes to come after him:*
Al Perez (w/ Gary Hart) defeated George South via submission
with the spinning toe hold at 3:17; after the bout, David
Crockett conducted a ringside interview with Perez & Hart
regarding Perez' involvement in the NWA US Title tournament

in Houston, TX on May 13, during which Hart said all the Latin fans would turn out to see Perez in action; moments later, Hart objected to Dusty Rhodes taking part in the tournament as the Midnight Rider

NWA Six-Man Tag Team Champion Ivan Koloff (w/ Paul Jones) pinned Larry Davis with a clothesline from the middle turnbuckle at 3:49; during the bout, it was noted Koloff would be part of the NWA US Title tournament; it was also noted Jim Cornette could be lashed by NWA US Tag Team Champions Bobby Fulton & Tommy Rogers at the Omni on May 22 and that Sting & Lex Luger would face NWA World Champion Ric Flair & NWA Tag Team Champion Arn Anderson the following night on The Main Event

The Sheepherders (w/ Rip Morgan) defeated Tommy Angel & Larry Stevens when Butch pinned Stevens following the double gutbuster at 2:55; during the bout, it was noted the Sheepherders & Morgan would face Ricky Santana, Johnny Ace, & Kendall Windham and that Steve Williams would wrestle the Terminator the following night on The Main Event

Jimmy Garvin (w/ Precious) pinned Alan Martin with the brainbuster at 2:52; during the match, it was noted Paul Boesch had invited Dusty Rhodes to be his special guest May 13 in Houston, TX; after the bout, David Crockett conducted a ringside interview with Garvin & Precious in which Garvin discussed the situation between Barry Windham and Lex Luger, Kevin Sullivan's attack on Ron Garvin, and his claims about Precious; footage was then shown of Garvin beating Sullivan in the Prince of Darkness match and Sullivan hitting Ron with the golden spike

NWA TV Champion Mike Rotunda & Florida Heavyweight Champion Rick Steiner (w/ Kevin Sullivan) defeated Andrew Bellamy & Joe Cruz at 2:03 when Rotunda pinned Bellamy with the butterfly suplex after Steiner hit a belly to belly suplex; after the commercial break, David Crockett conducted an interview with Sullivan, Rotunda, & Steiner regarding the Midnight Rider, during which Sullivan implied he had been speaking to Precious behind Jimmy Garvin's back

Sting defeated Steve Atkinson via submission with the Scorpion Deathlock at 1:00; following the bout, Crockett conducted a ringside interview with Sting regarding Barry Windham joining the Horsemen and held his four fingers upside down to show what he thought of the Horsemen

Nikita Koloff pinned Trent Knight with the Russian Sickle at 1:05; after the bout, Crockett conducted an interview with Koloff, alongside the Midnight Rider, in which he discussed his match against NWA World Champion Ric Flair during the Crockett Cup and said Flair took the coward's way out by throwing Koloff over the top rope; Koloff then cut a promo on Windham

NWA Six-Man Tag Team Champions the Powers of Pain (w/ Paul Jones & NWA Six-Man Tag Team Champion Ivan Koloff) defeated Keith Steinborn & Jerry Price at 3:58 when Warlord pinned Price following the Hart Attack

Rip Morgan (w/ the Sheepherders) pinned Ryan Wagner with a splash off the middle turnbuckle at 1:52; prior to the bout, Crockett conducted an interview with the Sheepherders & Morgan, in which they said Johnny Ace was a traitor and that

they would take the NWA Six-Man Tag Team Titles, NWA Tag Team Titles, and unmask the Midnight Rider

JCP @ Rock Hill, SC - Winthrop Coliseum - April 28, 1988
NWA World Champion Ric Flair did not appear as scheduled; refunds were offered as a result
TV taping:
The Main Event - 5/1/88 - featured Tony Schiavone on commentary and as ring announcer; included an opening announcement that the previously announced Lex Luger & Sting vs. NWA World Champion Ric Flair & Arn Anderson match would now simply be Luger vs. Anderson because Luger wanted to go on his own to gain revenge on the Horsemen; featured pretaped footage of an interview with JJ Dillon & Barry Windham regarding Windham being the newest member of the Four Horsemen and turning on Luger; included the announcement of the following matches for the next week's program: Sting & Steve Williams vs. NWA TV Champion Mike Rotunda & Rick Steiner, Kevin Sullivan vs. Ricky Stanana, and Lex Luger vs. Bobby Eaton:
Steve Williams pinned the Terminator with the Oklahoma Stampede at 4:51
The Sheepherders & Rip Morgan defeated Ricky Santana, Kendall Windham, & Johnny Ace at 9:38 when Morgan pinned Ace with a running stomp to the head (Morgan's in-ring debut)
Lex Luger defeated NWA Tag Team Champion Arn Anderson (w/ JJ Dillon) via disqualification at around the 10-minute mark when Barry Windham, who appeared ringside late in the match, began brawling with Luger on the floor; moments later, Anderson continued to attack Luger in the ring while Windham cut a promo at ringside; Sting and Steve Williams then ran out to make the save
The Main Event - 5/8/88 - featured Tony Schiavone on commentary; included pretaped footage of a ringside interview with Lex Luger in which Luger spoke about Barry Windham recently turning on Luger to join the Four Horsemen and said he would hand Windham his own head when they meet in the ring:
Sting & Steve Williams fought NWA TV Champion Mike Rotunda & Rick Steiner (w/ Kevin Sullivan) to a 15-minute time-limit draw; the bell rang as Sting had Steiner in the Scorpion Deathlock
Kevin Sullivan pinned Ricky Santana with the double stomp to the chest at 1:16
Lex Luger pinned Bobby Eaton (w/ Jim Cornette) with a roll up at around the 9:30 mark after Eaton missed an elbow drop off the top; Magnum TA provided guest commentary for the match (the bout began during the commercial break)

JCP @ Washington DC - Armory - April 29, 1988
Jimmy Valiant defeated Mark Fleming
Ron Simmons defeated the Terminator
Al Perez defeated Chris Champion
The Sheepherders defeated Brad Armstrong & Tim Horner
Nikita Koloff defeated Ivan Koloff
Bobby Eaton & Stan Lane fought NWA US Tag Team Champions Bobby Fulton & Tommy Rogers to a double count-

out
The Road Warriors defeated the Powers of Pain in a steel cage match

JCP @ Norfolk, VA - April 29, 1988
Ron & Jimmy Garvin defeated Kevin Sullivan & Rick Steiner
NWA TV Champion Mike Rotundo & Kevin Sullivan defeated Ricky Santana & the Challenger
The Green Machine (Bugsy McGraw) defeated Gene Ligon
Pez Whatley & Tiger Conway Jr. defeated Kendall Windham & the Italian Stallion
Steve Williams defeated NWA Western States Heritage Champion Larry Zbyzsko
The Midnight Rider defeated Tully Blanchard in a barbed wire match
NWA World Champion Ric Flair & Arn Anderson defeated Sting & Lex Luger after Barry Windham interfered and caused Sting to be pinned

JCP @ Miami, FL - Knight Center - April 29, 1988
Ricky Santana defeated Rocky King
Bugsy McGraw defeated Crusher Balboa
Florida Heavyweight Champion Rick Steiner defeated Kendall Windham
NWA US Tag Team Champions Bobby Fulton & Tommy Rogers defeated Bobby Eaton & Stan Lane via disqualification
Kevin Sullivan defeated Jimmy Garvin
Barry Windham fought NWA TV Champion Mike Rotundo to a draw
Lex Luger defeated NWA Tag Team Champion Arn Anderson via count-out
The Midnight Rider defeated NWA Tag Team Champion Tully Blanchard via disqualification
Sting defeated NWA World Champion Ric Flair via disqualification

Worldwide - 4/30/88 - hosted by Tony Schiavone & David Crockett, with the two interviewing NWA World Champion Ric Flair at ringside to open the show with Flair saying the mask of the Midnight Rider would come off and Dusty Rhodes would be suspended for a year; Flair went on to comment on the challenges for the Horsemen against the likes of Sting, Steve Williams, Magnum TA, and NWA Tag Team Champions Lex Luger & Barry Windham; featured Crockett conducting an empty arena interview with Rhodes regarding his 120-day suspension, with Rhodes noting there were fans that loved him and hated him and he needed all the help and support he could get; Rhodes then said he would be back in the ring on Sunday, Aug. 14; Rhodes then said he was not the Midnight Rider, then saying there was a Midnight Rider in each and every one of us; included Schiavone conducting an interview with the Road Warriors & Paul Ellering in which they said it didn't matter who they get in the ring with; featured Schiavone conducting an interview with Blanchard, alongside JJ Dillon and Arn Anderson, regarding the attack he sustained the previous week from the Rider, adding he would face the Rider

anywhere and any time; included Schiavone conducting an interview with Ron & Jimmy Garvin, alongside Precious, in which they reviewed footage of the Varsity Club attacking Jimmy before then trying to kidnap Precious from ringside before Ron made the save; included footage of Jim Ross in Jacksonville, FL in which he said Anderson & Blanchard had just won the NWA Tag Team Titles, then showing extended highlights of the Anderson & Blanchard vs. Luger & Windham title change and Windham joining the Four Horsemen:
NWA US Tag Team Champions Bobby Eaton & Stan Lane (w/ Jim Cornette) defeated John Savage & an unknown at 2:47 when Eaton pinned Savage with the Rocket Launcher; Cornette briefly joined the commentary team during the match to cut a promo on Tommy Rogers & Bobby Fulton and his team facing them in upcoming lash matches
The Midnight Rider (w/ Magnum TA) pinned Bob Riddle with the Bionic elbow at the 26-second mark; the Rider used Willie Nelson's "Midnight Rider" as his theme song for the match; after the match, the Rider hung Riddle with his bullrope until other enhancement wrestlers ran out to pull Riddle away; Rider then attacked one of the enhancement wrestlers, then helped the man to his feet and told him to leave the ring; after the match, Jim Ross - who provided commentary for the match with Bob Caudle - conducted a ringside interview with Magnum in which he said they would get vengeance; Ross then climbed onto the apron to conduct an interview with the Rider, in which he called out Tully Blanchard and said he was going to serve up violence
Al Perez (w/ Gary Hart) defeated Gene Ligon via submission with the spinning toe hold at 1:35; during the bout, Nikita Koloff cut an insert promo saying he was after Perez and the vacant NWA US Title in Houston, TX
Sting defeated Cruel Connection via submission with the Scorpion Deathlock at 1:31
Dick Murdoch pinned George South with an elbow drop at the 49-second mark; Murdoch assaulted South with a steel chair at ringside during the bout, in plain view of referee Tommy Young
Steve Williams pinned an unknown with the Oklahoma Stampede at the 46-second mark; during the bout, it was announced a man by the name of the Texan was coming in to unmask the Midnight Rider; after the bout, David Crockett conducted a ringside interview with Williams regarding him chasing NWA World Champion Ric Flair and the title
Bobby Fulton & Tommy Rogers defeated two unknowns at 2:03 when Fulton scored the pin with the Rocket Launcher; after the bout, Crockett conducted a ringside interview with Fulton & Rogers in which they commented about their upcoming lash matches against NWA US Tag Team Champions Bobby Eaton & Stan Lane, with Jim Cornette getting lashed as well if his team lost

JCP @ Detroit, MI - Cobo Arena - April 30, 1988 (4,000)
Ivan Koloff pinned Jimmy Valiant at the 5-minute mark
The Sheepherders defeated Brad Armstrong & Tim Horner at 15:24 when Armstrong was pinned after being hit with the flagpole
NWA Western States Heritage Champion Larry Zbyzsko pinned Ron Simmons at 6:15 by using the ropes for leverage

Kevin Sullivan & Rick Steiner fought Ron & Jimmy Garvin to a double count-out at 10:50
NWA TV Champion Mike Rotundo fought Steve Williams to a 20-minute time-limit draw
Sting defeated NWA World Champion Ric Flair via disqualification at 19:29 when Flair threw the challenger over the top rope
The Road Warriors defeated the Powers of Pain at 7:07 when Road Warrior Hawk pinned Warlord after the Barbarian accidentally struck his partner with a chain

JCP @ Laurinburg, NC - Pate Stadium - April 30, 1988 (620)
Chris Champion fought the Terminator to a draw
Pez Whatley pinned Kendall Windham
Ricky Santana pinned the Green Machine
Barry Windham pinned Rocky King with the claw
Nikita Koloff defeated Al Perez via disqualification
NWA US Tag Team Champions Bobby Fulton & Tommy Rogers defeated Bobby Eaton & Stan Lane
The Midnight Rider & Lex Luger defeated JJ Dillon, NWA Tag Team Champions Arn Anderson & Tully Blanchard in a handicap match when Luger pinned Dillon (Rhodes' last appearance as the Rider)

JCP @ Indianapolis, IN - Convention Center - May 1, 1988
Jimmy Garvin defeated Kevin Sullivan
Brad Armstrong & Tim Horner defeated Bobby Eaton & Stan Lane
Steve Williams defeated NWA Tag Team Champion Arn Anderson
The Road Warriors defeated the Powers of Pain
Lex Luger & Nikita Koloff defeated the Sheepherders
Dusty Rhodes fought NWA Tag Team Champion Tully Blanchard to a double count-out when both men began fighting on the floor
NWA World Champion Ric Flair pinned Sting

JCP @ Greenville, SC - Municipal Auditorium - May 2, 1988
Tiger Conway Jr. defeated John Savage
Shaska Whatley defeated Johnny Ace
Barry Windham defeated the Italian Stallion
Mighty Wilbur defeated the Terminator
Nikita Koloff fought Dick Murdoch to a double count-out
Lex Luger & Sting defeated the Sheepherders
Dusty Rhodes & Steve Williams defeated NWA Tag Team Champions Tully Blanchard & Arn Anderson in a lights out match; Rhodes was initially advertised as the Midnight Rider for the match

MID-ATLANTIC CHAMPIONSHIP WRESTLING

GREENVILLE MEMORIAL AUDITORIUM

NWA

MONDAY, MAY 2, 1988
8:00 P.M.

LIGHTS OUT - GRUDGE MATCH

MIDNIGHT RIDER DR. DEATH

VS

TULLY BLANCHARD ARN ANDERSON (WITH J.J. DILLON)

SPECIAL CHALLENGE MATCH

LEX LUGER   STING

VS

THE SHEEPHERDERS (WITH RIP MORGAN)

NIKITA KOLOFF
vs.
DICK MURDOCH

MIGHTY WILBUR
vs.
TERMINATOR

ITALIAN STALLION
vs.
BARRY WINDHAM

JOHNNY ACE
vs.
SHASKA WHATLEY

JOHN SAVAGE
vs.
TIGER CONWAY

*NWA - SUBJECT TO CHANGE

Ringside Reserved	$12
General Admission	$10
Children (Under 10)	$4

N-105681-G

JCP @ Bishopville, SC - May 2, 1988
NWA US Tag Team Champions Bobby Fulton & Tommy Rogers defeated Bobby Eaton & Stan Lane in a non-title match

JCP @ Schallote, NC - West Brunswick High School - May 3, 1988

JCP @ Atlanta, GA - WTBS Studios - May 4, 1988 (matinee)
World Championship Wrestling - 5/7/88:
Bobby Eaton & Stan Lane vs. Price & Starr
Sting vs. Bob Emory
Al Perez vs. Gary Royal
The Powers of Pain vs. Thompson & Paradise
Steve Williams vs. Keith Stienborn
Kevin Sullivan vs. Robbie Aumen
Barry Windham vs. Larry Davis
NWA US Tag Team Champions Bobby Fulton & Tommy Rogers vs. Strickland & Bowman
Ivan Koloff vs. David Isley

JCP @ Raleigh, NC - Dorton Arena - May 5, 1988 (1,900)
TV taping:
Dusty Rhodes, Lex Luger, & Nikita Koloff vs. NWA World Champion Ric Flair, Barry Windham, & NWA Tag Team Champion Tully Blanchard; after the bout, Steve Williams appeared and fought with Flair
Pro - 5/21/88:
Barry Windham (w/ JJ Dillon) pinned the Italian Stallion with the claw; after the match, Jim Ross conducted an in-ring interview with Windham, alongside Dillon, with Windham saying Dusty Rhodes means nothing to him and he was done living in his shadow; moments later, Rhodes came into the ring and asked whether Windham was man enough to look him in the eye; moments later, Rhodes struck Dillon, with NWA Tag Team Champions Arn Anderson & Tully Blanchard attacking Rhodes and allowing Windham to lock Rhodes in the claw; Lex Luger then ran out to make the save but was then attacked by NWA World Champion Ric Flair; moments later, Nikita Koloff and Steve Williams then ran out to clear the Horsemen from the ring
Worldwide - 5/21/88 - included an opening backstage segment in which Tony Schiavone conducted an interview with Paul Boesch in which he said the punishment against Dusty Rhodes was too harsh and he didn't vote for it; moments later, Schiavone & David Crockett announced Rhodes had been reinstated; featured Jim Ross conducting an interview with NWA Tag Team Champion Tully Blanchard regarding Rhodes' suspension being lifted, with Blanchard saying the NWA dropped the ball in not carrying out its own punishment against Rhodes; Blanchard then said Barry Windham now knows what it means to be part of an elite group and Rhodes' son left him for something bigger and better; included footage from NWA Pro of Windham defeating the Italian Stallion with the claw; moments later, Ross conducted an in-ring interview with Windham, alongside JJ Dillon, with Windham saying Rhodes

means nothing to him and he was done living in his shadow; moments later, Rhodes came into the ring and asked whether Windham was man enough to look him in the eye; moments later, Rhodes struck Dillon, with NWA Tag Team Champions Arn Anderson & Tully Blanchard attacking Rhodes and allowing Windham to lock Rhodes in the claw; Lex Luger then ran out to make the save but was then attacked by NWA World Champion Ric Flair; moments later, Nikita Koloff and Steve Williams then ran out to clear the Horsemen from the ring; featured Crockett conducting an interview with Windham, alongside Dillon, Anderson & Blanchard, about Rhodes and Luger; included Crockett conducting an interview with Gov. Jim Martin in the crowd about the show, with Martin saying a lot of the wrestlers were from North Carolina as are a lot of the stock car racers; featured Ross conducting an interview with Rhodes regarding his official return to the NWA and the threat of the Horsemen; Rhodes then said he was obsessed with two men - Terry Funk, who was now retired, and Blanchard, who he said he would never stop hunting; included Ross conducting an interview with Flair in which Flair said the Horsemen and Windham would rule the summer over the likes of Rhodes, Sting, and Steve Williams:
Kevin Sullivan & Rick Steiner defeated two unknowns at 1:05 when Sullivan scored the pin with his knee after hitting the double stomp; Steiner came to the ring in possession of the Florida Heavyweight Title; North Carolina Gov. Jim Martin was shown in the crowd during the match
Nikita Koloff & Steve Williams defeated Cruel Connection at 2:38 when Koloff scored the pin with the Russian Sickle; moments later, David Crockett conducted a ringside interview with Koloff & Williams, with Koloff commenting about Al Perez & Gary Hart before the two turned their attention to the Four Horsemen, adding they would both like to be NWA World Champion or NWA Tag Team Champions; Williams then said everyone in the world thought he was going to jump the fence but it ended up being Barry Windham, then targetted Flair
NWA Tag Team Champion Arn Anderson pinned Chris Champion with the DDT at 1:23
Bobby Eaton & Stan Lane (w/ Jim Cornette) defeated Tony Suber & an unknown at 2:31 when Lane pinned the unknown after the Flap Jack; during the match, Cornette joined the commentary team and complained about Paul Boesch's call of reinstating Dusty Rhodes while Eaton & Lane were cheated out of the NWA US Tag Team Titles; after the bout, Crockett conducted a ringside interview with Cornette, Eaton & Lane in which they reviewed footage of how Bobby Fulton & Tommy Rogers won the US tag team titles, despite Fulton being too bloody to continue
Al Perez (w/ Gary Hart) defeated an unknown via submission with the spinning toe hold at 2:16
NWA US Tag Team Champions Bobby Fulton & Tommy Rogers defeated two unknowns at 1:10 when Rogers scored the pin following the Rocket Launcher; the champions came to the ring with a leather strap as a message to Jim Cornette
Lex Luger defeated Gene Ligon via submission with the Torture Rack at 1:09; after the match, Crockett conducted a ringside interview with Luger regarding Barry Windham, with Luger saying Windham was scum as well as the rest of the

Horsemen and that the time for talking was over *Dark match*: NWA US Tag Team Champions Bobby Fulton & Tommy Rogers defeated Bobby Eaton & Stan Lane via disqualification in a non-title match

JCP @ Johnstown, PA - War Memorial Arena - May 5, 1988 (680)
Sy Youngblood defeated Johnny Rotten
Rip Morgan defeated Jimmy Jackson
Butch Miller fought Johnny Ace to a draw
The Mighty Wilbur defeated Luke Williams via disqualification
NWA US Tag Team Champions Bobby Fulton & Tommy Rogers defeated Bobby Eaton & Stan Lane via disqualification
Sting defeated NWA Western States Heritage Champion Larry Zbyzsko
The Road Warriors defeated the Powers of Pain

JCP @ Pittsburgh, PA - Civic Arena - May 6, 1988 (3,800)
The Sheepherders defeated Johnny Ace & Mighty Wilbur
Sting pinned Dick Murdoch
Barry Windham & NWA Tag Team Champion Arn Anderson defeated Brad Armstrong & Tim Horner
NWA US Tag Team Champions Bobby Fulton & Tommy Rogers defeated Bobby Eaton & Stan Lane
Nikita Koloff fought Al Perez to a double count-out
Dusty Rhodes defeated NWA Tag Team Champion Tully Blanchard in a bullrope match
Steve Williams defeated NWA World Champion Ric Flair via disqualification at the 15-minute mark when JJ Dillon interfered as Williams had Flair up for the Oklahoma Stampede; Flair was heavily cheered in the match and Williams booed
The Road Warriors defeated the Powers of Pain in a steel cage match

Worldwide - 5/7/88 - featured opening comments from JJ Dillon regarding Barry Windham now being part of the Four Horsemen; included Jim Ross backstage saying he would have interviews later in the show pertaining to Windham joining the Horsemen; featured Tony Schiavone & David Crockett on commentary; included Ross conducting an interview with Dillon regarding Windham, with Dillon reminding Ross that NWA World Champion Ric Flair went on national TV in late 1987 and said his pick to join the Horsemen was Windham and that planted the seeds; Dillon then said if Windham never broke away from Dusty Rhodes, he would never make a career for himself, and that all the Hollywood buzz surrounded Lex Luger and not Windham; extended highlights then aired of the Luger & Windham match against Arn Anderson & Tully Blanchard taped 4/20/88 in Jacksonville, FL; Dillon then said Windham had his sights on the vacant NWA US Title tournament in Houston, TX, adding he would like to address the Midnight Rider situation after the commercial break; following the break, Dillon said Windham told him he would be the man to unmask the Midnight Rider, then showed footage of the Rider busting into the Horsemen's locker room in Jacksonville and being jumped by them, Rick Steiner, Kevin Sullivan, NWA TV

Champion Mike Rotundo, and NWA US Tag Team Champions Bobby Eaton & Stan Lane; after the Rider was unmasked - but his face not shown on TV - Nikita Koloff, Sting, and Steve Williams helped him out into the hallway; featured Ross showing footage from Richmond, VA on 12/26/87 in which Flair said he would like Windham to be part of the group, with Ross then conducting an interview with Flair about how Windham was lured to the Horsemen; included Schiavone conducting an interview with Luger in which he watched footage of Windham turning on him in Jacksonville and commented on losing the titles and Windham joining the Horsemen; Luger then said Windham would pay for his actions and the Horsemen weren't really his friends; featured Ross conducting an interview with Sullivan, Rotundo, & Steiner in which Sullivan commented on Windham joining the Horsemen, saying he never thought "he would see the day when the son would leave the father;" Sullivan then said he was on the phone with Precious earlier in the week, in a message to Jimmy Garvin; included Ross conducting a closing interview with Windham and Dillon, with Windham responding to Luger's comments before he was joined by Flair, NWA Tag Team Champions Tully Blanchard & Arn Anderson:
The Sheepherders (w/ Rip Morgan) defeated Tony Suber & Trent Knight at 1:49 when Luke pinned Knight after the double gutbuster
Sting & Nikita Koloff defeated Cruel Connection at 1:24 when Sting scored the submission with the Scorpion Deathlock following a Stinger Splash in the corner; after the bout, David Crockett conducted a ringside interview with Sting & Koloff regarding the Four Horsemen and Barry Windham now being part of the group, with both men saying they couldn't believe what Windham did; Koloff then said Sting, Dusty Rhodes, himself, and the Road Warriors would show Windham he made a mistake
Jimmy Garvin (w/ Precious) pinned an unknown with the brainbuster at the 40-second mark
Stve Williams pinned an unknown with the Oklahoma Stampede at the 54-second mark; moments later, Crockett conducted a ringside interview with Williams regarding chasing NWA World Champion Ric Flair and Windham joining the Horsemen
Al Perez (w/ Gary Hart) defeated an unknown via submission with the spinning toe hold at 1:04
Tommy Rogers & Bobby Fulton defeated two unknowns at the 58-second mark when Rogers scored the pin with the Rocket Launcher

JCP @ Baltimore, MD - Arena - May 7, 1988 (5,500)
Larry Zbyzsko pinned Johnny Ace
Dick Murdoch pinned Mighty Wilbur
Barry Windham pinned Tim Horner
NWA US Tag Team Champions Bobby Fulton & Tommy Rogers defeated Bobby Eaton & Stan Lane
Al Perez fought Nikita Koloff to a double count-out
The Road Warriors defeated the Sheepherders
Dusty Rhodes & Steve Williams defeated NWA Tag Team Champions Arn Anderson & Tully Blanchard via disqualification; Anderson & Blanchard were heavily cheered in

the match
NWA World Champion Ric Flair pinned Sting after Barry Windham interfered

JCP @ Roanoke, VA - Civic Center - May 8, 1988 (matinee) (3,000)
The Sheepherders defeated Johnny Ace & Bugsy McGraw
Jimmy Garvin pinned Rick Steiner
Ron Garvin defeated Larry Zbyzsko via disqualification
Al Perez pinned Ricky Santana
Barry Windham defeated the Italian Stallion
NWA US Tag Team Champions Bobby Fulton & Tommy Rogers defeated Bobby Eaton & Stan Lane via disqualification
Steve Williams defeated Kevin Sullivan at the 3-minute mark
NWA Six-Man Tag Team Champions the Powers of Pain & Ivan Koloff defeated Nikita Koloff & the Road Warriors via disqualification at the 13-minute mark when Road Warrior Hawk hit the referee
NWA World Champion Ric Flair pinned Sting in a steel cage match at the 13-minute mark after Sting hit the cage when Flair avoided a Stinger Splash

JCP @ Fayetteville, NC - May 9, 1988
The Main Event - 5/15/88 - featured Tony Schiavone on commentary; included Schiavone conducting a ringside interview with NWA US Champion Barry Windham & JJ Dillon, with Windham claiming he was the reason Lex Luger finally obtained a title and he easily took it away from him:
NWA Six Man Tag Team Champion the Warlord (w/ Paul Jones & NWA Six Man Tag Team Champion Ivan Koloff) pinned Tim Horner at 6:29 with an elbow drop after Warlord avoided a monkey flip with an assist from Koloff
The Sheepherders (w/ Rip Morgan) defeated the Mighty Wilbur & Johnny Ace at 4:40 when Luke Williams pinned Ace after Morgan hit Ace with the New Zealand flag as he had Williams in a sleeper
Ron Garvin defeated NWA Tag Team Champion Arn Anderson (w/ JJ Dillon) via disqualification at 16:00 after NWA Tag Team Champion Tully Blanchard interfered as Garvin had Anderson covered following a punch; after the bout, Anderson, Blanchard, & NWA US Champion Barry Windham triple teamed Garvin, with Windham applying the claw until Sting and Dusty Rhodes made the save
The Main Event - 5/22/88 - featured Tony Schiavone & Jim Cornette on commentary; included Schiavone conducting a ringside interview with NWA US Champion Barry Windham, along with NWA Tag Team Champions Arn Anderson & Tully Blanchard and JJ Dillon, with Windham stating no one would take his title away and that Ron Garvin learned a lesson the previous week:
Tim Horner fought Rip Morgan to a time-limit draw at 8:45 as Horner had a sleeper applied
Kevin Sullivan pinned the Italian Stallion at 4:03 with the double stomp; after the commercial break, Tony Schiavone conducted a ringside interview with Sullivan, who claimed claimed he was constructing a Tower of Doom for the summer, where two sides would enter and only one would leave
NWA US Tag Team Champions Bobby Fulton & Tommy

Rogers defeated NWA Six Man Tag Team Champions Ivan Koloff & the Warlord (w/ Paul Jones) via disqualification at 12:32 after referee Tommy Young, who had been pulled to the floor by Warlord, saw commentator Jim Cornette enter the ring and count Koloff's pinfall on Fulton; Fulton & Rogers then dropkicked Cornette, with Bobby Eaton & Stan Lane pulling him out of the ring
Dark match after the taping: NWA US Tag Team Champions Bobby Fulton & Tommy Rogers defeated Bobby Eaton & Stan Lane in a non-title match

JCP @ Greenville, SC - Municipal Auditorium - May 9, 1988
Jimmy Valiant vs. the Barbarian did not take place as advertised
Ricky Santana fought Kendall Windham (sub. for Larry Zbyszko) to a draw
Brad Armstrong defeated Chris Champion (sub. for Ron Simmons)
Bugsy McGraw defeated the Terminator
Ron Simmons defeated Cruel Connection #1
The Road Warriors & Jimmy Garvin defeated Larry Zbyszko (sub. for one of the Varsity Club) & the Varsity Club

Nikita Koloff defeated Al Perez via disqualification
Steve Williams defeated NWA World Champion Ric Flair via disqualification

NWA @ Miami, FL - Knight Center - May 10, 1988 (2,943)
Al Perez defeated Bobby Brooks
NWA Tag Team Champion Arn Anderson defeated Ricky Santana
NWA TV Champion Mike Rotunda & Rick Steiner defeated Ron & Jimmy Garvin
The Road Warriors defeated the Powers of Pain
Dusty Rhodes & Sting fought NWA Tag Team Champion Tully Blanchard & Barry Windham to a double count-out
Steve Williams defeated NWA World Champion Ric Flair via disqualification after JJ Dillon interfered

JCP @ Cherryville, NC - May 10, 1988
NWA US Tag Team Champions Bobby Fulton & Tommy Rogers defeated Bobby Eaton & Stan Lane in a non-title match

JCP @ Tallahassee, FL - Leon County Civic Center - May 11, 1988

World Championship Wrestling - 5/14/88:
NWA US Tag Team Champions Bobby Fulton & Tommy Rogers defeated Aumen & Price
Steve Williams pinned Gary Phelps
NWA TV Champion Mike Rotundo & Rick Steiner fought Ron & Jimmy Garvin (w/ Precious) to a no contest when Kevin Sullivan carried Precious over his shoulder backstage; after the commercial break, the Garvins found Precious screaming hysterically in the locker room
Al Perez defeated Russ Mosley via submission
Sting vs. Larry Davis
Ricky Santana pinned Mike Jackson
NWA Tag Team Champion Arn Anderson pinned Ryan Wagner
Barry Windham pinned Keith Steinborn
The Road Warriors defeated the Powers of Pain via disqualification when NWA Tag Team Champions Arn Anderson & Tully Blanchard interfered; after the bout, Road Warrior Hawk was beaten down and eventually taken backstage on a stretcher; the stretcher footage did not air on TV
Dusty Rhodes vs. NWA Tag Team Champion Tully Blanchard (bullrope match)

JCP @ Walterboro, SC - May 12, 1988
NWA US Tag Team Champions Bobby Fulton & Tommy Rogers defeated Bobby Eaton & Stan Lane in a non-title match

JCP @ Weslaco, TX - High School Stadium - May 12, 1988

JCP @ Hammond, IN - May 13, 1988
NWA US Tag Team Champions Bobby Fulton & Tommy Rogers defeated Bobby Eaton & Stan Lane in a non-title match

JCP @ Houston, TX - Sam Houston Coliseum - May 13, 1988 (4,800)
Larry Zybzsko defeated Rudy Gonzalez at 3:29
NWA US Championship Tournament Quarter Finals: Barry Windham pinned the Midnight Rider (Italian Stallion); after the bout, Dusty Rhodes made the save
NWA US Championship Tournament Quarter Finals: Lex Luger fought Al Perez to a double count-out at 15:05
NWA US Championship Tournament Quarter Finals: Nikita Koloff pinned Ivan Koloff at 8:17
Steve Williams pinned NWA Tag Team Champion Arn Anderson at 8:32 with a small package
Pro: The Road Warriors defeated the Powers of Pain at 10:33 when Road Warrior Hawk pinned the Barbarian
NWA US Championship Tournament Semi Finals: Nikita Koloff pinned NWA Tag Team Champion Tully Blanchard at 9:33 with a roll up after Blanchard became distracted by Dusty Rhodes at ringside; Blanchard received a bye into the semi finals
Pro: *NWA US Championship Tournament Finals*: Barry Windham (w/ JJ Dillon) pinned Nikita Koloff to win the title at the 15-minute mark by using the ropes for leverage after Dillon tripped Koloff from the floor
NWA World Chammpion Ric Flair pinned Sting in a steel cage match at the 15-minute mark with his feet on the ropes for leverage

JCP @ Chicago, IL - UIC Pavilion - May 14, 1988
NWA TV Champion Mike Rotundo defeated Jimmy Garvin
Al Perez fought Nikita Koloff to a no contest
The Road Warriors defeated Bobby Eaton & Stan Lane
Sting defeated NWA World Champion Ric Flair via disqualification

JCP @ Wilmington, NC - Legion Stadium - May 15, 1988 (matinee)
Nikita Koloff vs. NWA TV Champion Mike Rotundo
NWA US Tag Team Champions Bobby Fulton & Tommy Rogers defeated Bobby Eaton & Stan Lane in a non-title match
The Road Warriors vs. the Powers of Pain
Lex Luger & Dusty Rhodes vs. NWA US Champion Barry Windham & NWA Tag Team Champion Tully Blanchard
Sting vs. NWA World Champion Ric Flair (No DQ)

The Main Event - 5/15/88:
The Warlord vs. Tim Horner
The Sheepherders vs. Mighty Wilbur & Johnny Ace
Ron Garvin vs. NWA Tag Team Champion Arn Anderson

JCP @ Asheville, NC - Civic Center - May 15, 1988 (500)

The Main Event - 5/29/88 - featured Tony Schiavone & JJ Dillon on commentary; included Schiavone conducting a ringside interview with Lex Luger regarding the Four Horsemen in which Luger noted Sting, Dusty Rhodes, the Road Warriors, Nikita Koloff, and Steve Williams were all standing beside him; featured the announcement Kevin Sullivan would face Big Bear Collie, Rick Steiner would face Kendall Windham, and Ron Garvin & Mighty Wilbur would face NWA Tag Team Champions Arn Anderson & Tully Blanchard the following week:

NWA Western States Heritage Champion Larry Zbyszko & Al Perez (w/ Gary Hart) defeated the Italian Stallion & Tommy Angel when Angel submitted to Perez' spinning toe hold / claw combo

NWA US Champion Barry Windham (w/ JJ Dillon) defeated Mighty Wilbur via count-out in a non-title match at 9:22 after applying the claw on the floor after Dillon distracted Wilbur from ringside; after the bout, Windham kept the hold applied until Ron Garvin came out to clear the ring

Ron Garvin defeated NWA TV Champion Mike Rotundo (w/ Kevin Sullivan & Rick Steiner) via disqualification at around the 12:30 mark when both Sullivan & Steiner interfered after Garvin hit Rotundo with the right hand punch; after the contest, Garvin fought off all three men until he was eventually triple teamed

Dark match after the taping: NWA US Tag Team Champions Bobby Fulton & Tommy Rogers defeated Bobby Eaton & Stan Lane

Dark match after the taping: Sting & the Road Warriors vs. NWA World Champion Ric Flair, NWA Tag Team Champions Arn Anderson & Tully Blanchard

JCP @ Greenville, SC - Municipal Auditorium - May 16, 1988
Bugsy McGraw fought Tiger Conway Jr. to a draw
Ron Simmons defeated Shaska Whatley
NWA Tag Team Champion Arn Anderson defeated the Italian Stallion
NWA US Tag Team Champions Bobby Fulton & Tommy Rogers defeated the Sheepherders
The Road Warriors defeated Bobby Eaton & Stan Lane
NWA TV Champion Mike Rotundo defeated Jimmy Garvin
Lex Luger, Ron Garvin, & Sting defeated NWA World Champion Ric Flair, NWA US Champion Barry Windham, & NWA Tag Team Champion Tully Blanchard via disqualification

MID-ATLANTIC CHAMPIONSHIP WRESTLING

NWA

GREENVILLE MEMORIAL AUDITORIUM

MONDAY - MAY 16, 1988
8:00 P.M.

SIX MAN TAG ACTION

STING
DUSTY RHODES
LEX LUGER

"NATURE BOY" RIC FLAIR

VS

BARRY WINDHAM
TULLY BLANCHARD
(WITH J.J. DILLON)

GRUDGE MATCH

GORGEOUS JIMMY GARVIN
RON GARVIN

VS

MIKE ROTUNDO
KEVIN SULLIVAN

TAG ACTION

VS

ROAD WARRIORS
(WITH PAUL ELLERING)

MIDNIGHT EXPRESS
(WITH JIM CORNETTE)

TAG ACTION

THE FANTASTICS	VS	THE SHEEPHERDERS (WITH MR MORGAN)
ITALIAN STALLION	VS	ARN ANDERSON
JIMMY VALIANT	VS	SHASKA WHATLEY
BUGSY McGRAW	VS	TIGER CONWAY

NWA - SUBJECT TO CHANGE

Ringside Reserved	$12
General Admission	$10
Children (Under 10)	$4

NI05027-G

MID-ATLANTIC CHAMPIONSHIP WRESTLING

JCP @ West Jefferson, NC - May 17, 1988
NWA US Tag Team Champions Bobby Fulton & Tommy
Rogers defeated Bobby Eaton & Stan Lane in a non-title match

JCP @ Fisherville, VA - May 19, 1988 (3,500)
*Nikita Koloff, Kevin Sullivan, Brad Armstrong, Ricky Santana,
and NWA Tag Team Champion Arn Anderson did not appear
as scheduled, causing the line up to be changed*
Ron Simmons pinned Chris Champion
Jimmy Valiant & Bugsy McGraw defeated the Cruel
Connection (Gary Royal & George South)
Mighty Wilbur pinned Tommy Angel
Rick Steiner defeated Mark Fleming
The Powers of Pain defeated Kendall Windham & the Italian
Stallion
NWA TV Champion Mike Rotundo fought Jimmy Garvin to a
draw
Lex Luger pinned NWA Tag Team Champion Tully Blanchard

JCP @ Norfolk, VA - Scope - May 20, 1988 (4,000)
Television taping - 6/4
Worldwide: Bugsy McGraw & Ron Simmons defeated Kevin
Sullivan & Rick Steiner via disqualification
Worldwide: Nikita Koloff defeated NWA Western States
Heritage Champion Larry Zybzsko via disqualification when
Gary Hart and Al Perez interfered
Dark match: NWA TV Champion Mike Rotundo pinned Jimmy
Garvin after hitting him with Kevin Sullivan's spike
Dark match: Dusty Rhodes, Lex Luger, Sting, & Nikita Koloff
defeated NWA World Champion Ric Flair, NWA US Champion
Barry Windham, NWA Tag Team Champions Arn Anderson &
Tully Blanchard via disqualification

JCP @ Atlanta, GA - WTBS Studios - May 21, 1988
World Championship Wrestling - 5/21/88:
NWA Tag Team Champion Arn Anderson (w/ J.J. Dillon)
pinned David Isley with the gordbuster
NWA TV Champion Mike Rotundo (w/ Kevin Sullivan & Rick
Steiner) pinned Trent Knight
Sting defeated Max McGyver via submission with the Scorpion
Deathlock
NWA US Champion Barry Windham (w/ J.J. Dillon) pinned
Ryan Wagner with the lariat
Al Perez (w/ Gary Hart) defeated Keith Steinborn via
submission with the spinning toe hold
NWA Tag Team Champion Tully Blanchard (w/ J.J. Dillon)
pinned Dave Spearman with a slingshot suplex
Kevin Sullivan & Rick Steiner (w/ Mike Rotundo) defeated Rick
Allen & Rick Paradise when Sullivan pinned Allen
Nikita Koloff pinned Bob Riddle with the Russian Sickle
NWA Western States Heritage Champion Larry Zbyszko
pinned Dark Star with a neckbreaker

JCP @ Richmond, VA - Coliseum - May 21, 1988 (7,000)
The show took place during a hailstorm
Bugsy McGraw & Ron Simmons defeated the Cruel

Connection
Al Perez pinned Chris Champion with the spinning toe hold
Jimmy Garvin pinned Rick Steiner
The Sheepherders defeated Mighty Wilbur & Gary Royal
NWA TV Champion Mike Rotundo defeated Steve Williams via
disqualification when Williams threw the champion over the top
rope
Dusty Rhodes, Lex Luger, & Nikita Koloff fought NWA US
Champion Barry Windham, NWA Tag Team Champions Arn
Anderson & Tully Blanchard to a no contest
NWA World Champion Ric Flair pinned Sting at the 25-minute
mark after NWA US Champion Barry Windham interfered and
hit the challenger with a lariat; there were three judges
advertised for the match, should it go to a time-limit draw, but
no judges were used
The Road Warriors defeated the Powers of Pain in a steel
cage match

The Main Event - 5/22/88:
Tim Horner vs. Rip Morgan
Kevin Sullivan vs. the Italian Stallion
NWA US Tag Team Champions Bobby Fulton & Tommy
Rogers vs. Ivan Koloff & the Warlord

JCP @ Atlanta, GA - Omni - May 22, 1988 (7,300)
Rick Steiner pinned Kendall Windham
NWA Western States Heritage Champion Larry Zbyzsko fought
Brad Armstrong to a 10-minute time-limit draw
The Powers of Pain & Ivan Koloff defeated Tim Horner, the
Italian Stallion, & Bugsy McGraw when Warlord pinned Stallion
Ron & Jimmy Garvin defeated Kevin Sullivan & NWA TV
Champion Mike Rotundo in an elimination match; Rotundo and
Ron were counted-out; Jimmy pinned Sullivan after Precious
tripped Sullivan
Nikita Koloff defeated Al Perez via disqualification at 17:01
when Perez threw Koloff over the top rope
The Road Warriors defeated the Sheepherders at 8:05 after
Rip Morgan accidentally hit Butch Miller with the flagpole
NWA US Tag Team Champions Tommy Rogers & Bobby
Fulton defeated Bobby Eaton & Stan Lane at 16:10;
stipulations for the bout stated the winners would get to whip
the losers; after the contest, the champions whipped Eaton &
Lane and Jim Cornette before they were jumped from behind
by the challengers, who then whipped Rogers & Fulton
Dusty Rhodes, Lex Luger, & Sting (w/ Magnum TA) fought
NWA US Champion Barry Windham, NWA Tag Team
Champions Arn Anderson & Tully Blanchard to a double count-
out at 17:42 when Windham and Luger fought their way
backstage
Steve Williams defeated NWA World Champion Ric Flair via
disqualification at the 20-minute mark when JJ Dillon interfered

JCP @ Hartsville, SC - May 23, 1988
NWA US Tag Team Champions Bobby Fulton & Tommy
Rogers defeated Bobby Eaton & Stan Lane in a non-title match

JCP @ Fayetteville, NC - Cumberland County Memorial Arena - May 23, 1988
Included Dusty Rhodes, the Road Warriors, and Lex Luger

JCP @ Elberton, GA - May 24, 1988
NWA US Tag Team Champions Bobby Fulton & Tommy Rogers defeated Bobby Eaton & Stan Lane in a non-title match

JCP @ Hillsville, VA - May 24, 1988 (800)
Kendall Windham pinned Tony Suber
Rip Morgan defeated Rocky King
The Sheepherders defeated George South & Gary Royal
Al Perez pinned Chris Champion
Lex Luger & Nikita Koloff defeated NWA Tag Team Champions Arn Anderson & Tully Blanchard in a non-title match
Jimmy Garvin defeated NWA TV Champion Mike Rotundo via disqualification

JCP @ Louisville, KY - Commonwealth Convention Center - May 26, 1988
Bobby Eaton & Stan Lane fought NWA US Tag Team Champions Bobby Fulton & Tommy Rogers to a double count-out

JCP @ St. Louis, MO - Arena - May 27, 1988 (3,100)
The Sheepherders defeated Bugsy McGraw & Gary Royal
Sting defeated NWA TV Champion Mike Rotundo
Nikita Koloff defeated Al Perez via disqualification
NWA US Tag Team Champions Tommy Rogers & Bobby Fulton defeated Bobby Eaton & Stan Lane via reverse decision
The Road Warriors defeated the Powers of Pain in a steel cage match
Dusty Rhodes & Lex Luger fought NWA US Champion Barry Windham & NWA Tag Team Champion Tully Blanchard to a no contest
Steve Williams defeated NWA World Champion Ric Flair via disqualification

JCP @ Atlanta, GA - WTBS Studios - May 28, 1988 (matinee)
World Championship Wrestling - 5/28/88:
NWA US Tag Team Champions Bobby Fulton & Tommy Rogers vs. Stevens & Knight
Sting, Nikita Koloff, & Steve Williams vs. Wagner, Laperouse, & Phelps
Al Perez vs. Bob Riddle
NWA Tag Team Champion Arn Anderson vs. Keith Steinborn
Ron Garvin & Mighty Wilbur vs. Aumen & Grundy

JCP @ Charleston, WV - May 28, 1988 (2,500)
Ron Simmons defeated Tiger Conway
NWA Tag Team Champion Arn Anderson defeated the Italian Stallion
Ivan Koloff defeated Kendall Windham
NWA Western States Heritage Champion Larry Zbyszko

defeated Ron Garvin via count-out
NWA US Tag Team Champions Tommy Rogers & Bobby Fulton defeated Bobby Eaton & Stan Lane via reverse decision
Dusty Rhodes defeated NWA Tag Team Champion Tully Blanchard in a bullrope match
Lex Luger fought NWA US Champion Barry Windham to a no contest
Steve Williams defeated NWA World Champion Ric Flair via disqualification

JCP @ Greensboro, NC - Coliseum - May 29, 1988 (4,000)
The Sheepherders fought Ron Simmons & Mighty Wilbur to a draw
NWA Tag Team Champion Arn Anderson defeated the Italian Stallion
NWA TV Champion Mike Rotundo & Rick Steiner defeated Kendall Windham & Bugsy McGraw
The Powers of Pain defeated Sting & the Road Warriors via disqualification
Nikita Koloff defeated Al Perez via disqualification
NWA US Tag Team Champions Bobby Fulton & Tommy Rogers defeated Bobby Eaton & Stan Lane in a non-title match
Dusty Rhodes & Lex Luger defeated NWA US Champion Barry Windham & NWA Tag Team Champion Tully Blanchard when Rhodes pinned Blanchard
Steve Williams defeated NWA World Champion Ric Flair via disqualification when JJ Dillon interfered

JCP @ Union, SC - May 30, 1988
NWA US Tag Team Champions Bobby Fulton & Tommy Rogers defeated Bobby Eaton & Stan Lane in a non-title match

JCP @ Savannah, GA - Civic Center - May 30, 1988
Television taping:
Sting defeated Tommy Angel
NWA Tag Team Champions Arn Anderson & Tully Blanchard vs. David Isley & Larry Stephens
NWA US Champion Barry Windham defeated Tommy Angel
Steve Williams defeated an unknown
Kevin Sullivan defeated Curtis Thompson
Nikita Koloff defeated Bob Riddle
Al Perez defeated Joe Cruz
Pro - 6/88 - featured Bob Caudle conducting a ringside interview with NWA US Champion Barry Windham, alongside JJ Dillon, in which Windham said Dusty Rhodes was the reason he became a member of the Four Horsemen; moments later, Rhodes confronted Windham with the two brawling; NWA Tag Team Champions Arn Anderson & Tully Blanchard then ran out but were held off in the ring by Rhodes, Sting, Steve Williams, and Nikita Koloff:
Dark match after the taping: Dusty Rhodes vs. NWA US Champion Barry Windham

JCP @ Sumter, SC - Exhibition Center Arena - May 31, 1988
The Main Event taping:

6/12/88 - featured Tony Schiavone conducting an opening ringside interview with Steve Williams regarding his participation in Wargames against the Four Horsemen during the Great American Bash tour; included Schiavone on commentary and as the ring announcer; featured Schiavone conducting a ringside interview with Kevin Sullivan regarding the Bash kicking off in Orlando, during which Sullivan said his men were creating a five story Tower of Doom so that Sullivan could destroy Jimmy Garvin and take back Precious:
Bobby Eaton (w/ Jim Cornette & Stan Lane) pinned NWA US Tag Team Champion Tommy Rogers (w/ NWA US Tag Team Champion Bobby Fulton) at 5:51 when Cornette hit Rogers with his tennis racquet behind the referee's back as Lane and Fulton fought on the floor; the match was not shown in full; just before the fall, it was noted that 3 minutes remained in the 15-minute time-limit
Sting pinned Stan Lane (w/ Jim Cornette) at 8:47 when Sting fell on Lane as Lane attempted to suplex Sting into the ring
Lex Luger defeated NWA Tag Team Champion Arn Anderson (w/ JJ Dillon) via disqualification at 8:07 when NWA US Champion Barry Windham attacked Luger, as Luger had an interfering Dillon in a full nelson, and applied the claw; moments later, Sting, Steve Williams, and Nikita Koloff ran out to make the save
6/19/88 - featured Tony Schiavone & JJ Dillon on commentary; included Schiavone as the ring announcer; featured Dillon conducting a ringside interview with Kevin Sullivan regarding the Great American Bash and Sullivan's Tower of Doom and the fact that Precious would be at the bottom:
NWA US Tag Team Champion Bobby Fulton defeated Al Perez (w/ Gary Hart) via disqualification at the 5:30 mark when Perez threw Fulton over the top rope; the match was not shown in full; Perez originally won the match when the momentum of a crossbody off the top by Fulton put Perez on top for the win but referee Teddy Long had the match continue after noticing Fulton's foot was on the ropes during the pin; after the contest, Perez assaulted Fulton on the floor, applied the spinning toe hold on him inside the ring, and shoved Long to the mat
NWA US Champion Barry Windham & NWA Tag Team Champion Tully Blanchard (w/ JJ Dillon) defeated Ron Garvin & Mighty Wilbur at 10:11 when Windham pinned Wilbur with the claw; during the bout, Dillon spoke highly of Garvin while on commentary
Nikita Koloff & Steve Williams fought Bobby Eaton & Stan Lane (w/ Jim Cornette) to a double count-out at 10:24 when both teams began brawling on the floor; after the bout, Williams attempted to gorilla press slam Cornette until Eaton hit him with Cornette's tennis racquet
6/26/88 - featured Tony Schiavone on commentary; included Schiavone as the ring announcer; featured Schiavone conducting a closing ringside interview with Kevin Sullivan in which he said Al Perez would be joining his team in the Tower of Doom match against Jimmy Garvin's team in Baltimore for the Great American Bash:
NWA Tag Team Champion Arn Anderson (w/ JJ Dillon) pinned Tommy Angel with the gordbuster at around the 2-minute mark; the match was not shown in full; following the

commercial break, Tony Schiavone conducted a ringside interview with Anderson & Dillon in which they discussed the Wargames and scaffold matches scheduled for the Great American Bash tour; Anderson then said the Horsemen had momentum on their side after several wins on The Main Event
Bobby Eaton & Stan Lane (w/ Jim Cornette) defeated Kendall Windham & the Italian Stallion at around the 5-minute mark when Eaton pinned Stallion following the Rocket Launcher; the match was not shown in full; Jim Cornette joined Schiavone on commentary
NWA US Tag Team Champions Tommy Rogers & Bobby Fulton defeated NWA Western States Heritage Champion Larry Zbyzsko & Al Perez (w/ Gary Hart) at 16:58 when Fulton pinned Zbyzsko after Zbyzsko tripped over Rogers while attempting a bodyslam
7/17/88 - featured Jim Ross & Tony Schiavone as hosts from the studio; included Schiavone as the ring announcer; featured a replay of the NWA US Champion Barry Windham vs. Mighty Wilbur match from the 5/29/88 episode and the Al Perez vs Bobby Fulton and Bobby Eaton & Stan Lane vs. Steve Williams & Nikita Koloff matches from the 6/19/88 episode

JCP @ Bluefield, WV - Brushfork Armory - June 2, 1988
Ron Simmons defeated Cruel Connection #2
NWA Western States Heritage Champion Larry Zbyzsko defeated the Italian Stallion
Rip Morgan defeated Rocky King
Brad Armstrong & Tim Horner fought the Sheepherders to a draw
Ron Garvin defeated Al Perez via disqualification
Sting defeated NWA TV Champion Mike Rotundo via disqualification
NWA US Tag Team Champions Tommy Rogers & Bobby Fulton defeated Bobby Eaton & Stan Lane

JCP @ Richmond, VA - Coliseum - June 3, 1988
Ron Simmons defeated Tiger Conway
Mighty Wilbur defeated Cruel Connection
NWA Western States Heritage Champion Larry Zbyzsko defeated Chris Champion
Ivan Koloff defeated Kendall Windham
The Powers of Pain defeated Brad Armstrong & Tim Horner
Al Perez defeated Mark Fleming
NWA TV Champion Mike Rotundo defeated Steve Williams via count-out
Sting & Nikita Koloff defeated NWA Tag Team Champions Arn Anderson & Tully Blanchard via disqualification
Lex Luger fought NWA US Champion Barry Windham to a no contest

JCP @ Atlanta, GA - WTBS Studios - June 4, 1988 (matinee)
World Championship Wrestling - 6/4/88:
Ron Garvin vs. Russ Tyler
NWA US Tag Team Champions Bobby Fulton & Tommy Rogers vs. Keith Steinborn & Spearman

NWA TV Champion Mike Rotundo vs. Trent Knight
NWA US Champion Barry Windham vs. Curtis Thompson
Nikita Koloff & Steve Williams vs. Bob Riddle & Bob Emory
The Powers of Pain & Ivan Koloff vs. Tony Suber, Paradise, &
Starr
Kevin Sullivan & Rick Steiner vs. Price & Grundy
Jimmy Garvin vs. Bobby Rose
Larry Zbyszko & Al Perez vs. Phelps & Laperouse
Sting vs. Tommy Royal
NWA Tag Team Champions Arn Anderson & Tully Blanchard
vs. Allen & Aumen

JCP @ Charlotte, NC - Coliseum - June 4, 1988
Bobby Eaton & Stan Lane defeated Brad Armstrong & Tim
Horner

JCP @ Roanoke, VA - Civic Center - June 5, 1988 (matinee)
TV taping

JCP @ Columbus, OH - June 5, 1988
NWA US Tag Team Champions Bobby Fulton & Tommy
Rogers defeated Bobby Eaton & Stan Lane

JCP @ Gainesville, FL - June 6, 1988
Jimmy & Ron Garvin vs. Rick Steiner & Kevin Sullivan
NWA Tag Team Champions Arn Anderson & Tully Blanchard
vs. Sting & Nikita Koloff
NWA TV Champion Mike Rotundo vs. Steve Williams
Dusty Rhodes & Lex Luger vs. NWA World Champion Ric Flair
& NWA US Champion Barry Windham

JCP @ Greenville, SC - Municipal Auditorium - June 6,
1988
*The Italian Stallion vs. Terminator match did not take place as
advertised*
Cruel Connection #1 defeated Tony Suber
Jimmy Valiant & the Italian Stallion (sub. for Bugsy McGraw)
defeated Tiger Conway Jr. & John Savage (sub. for Shaska
Whatley)
Larry Zbyszko defeated Trent Knight (sub. for Brad Armstrong)
Ivan Koloff & the Powers of Pain defeated Mighty Wilbur, Ron
& Jimmy Garvin
NWA US Tag Team Champion Bobby Fulton defeated Bobby
Eaton; the match was scheduled as Fulton & Tommy Rogers
vs. Eaton & Stan Lane in a No DQ match
Lex Luger fought NWA US Champion Barry Windham to a
double count-out

MID-ATLANTIC CHAMPIONSHIP WRESTLING

NWA

GREENVILLE MEMORIAL AUDITORIUM
MONDAY - JUNE 6, 1988
8:00 P.M.

SPECIAL CHALLENGE MATCH
LEX LUGER VS. BARRY WINDHAM

U.S. TAG TEAM TITLE
NO DISQUALIFICATIONS
THE FANTASTICS VS THE MIDNIGHT EXPRESS
(WITH JIM CORNETTE)

WORLD SIX MAN TAG TITLE MATCH
MIGHTY WILBUR
RONNIE GARVIN
GORGEOUS
JIMMY GARVIN
VS
BARBARIAN
WARLORD
IVAN KOLOFF
(WITH PAUL JONES)

BRAD ARMSTRONG VS LARRY ZBYSZKO

TAG ACTION
JIMMY VALIANT
BUGSY McGRAW
VS
"THE JIVE TONES"
SHASKA WHATLEY
TIGER CONWAY

ITALIAN STALLION VS TERMINATOR

TONY SUBER VS CRUEL CONNECTION #1

NWA *SUBJECT TO CHANGE

Ringside Reserved	$12
General Admission	$10
Children (Under 10)	$4

N04177-G

MID-ATLANTIC CHAMPIONSHIP WRESTLING

JCP @ Columbia, SC - June 7, 1988
Bobby Eaton defeated Tim Horner

JCP @ Gainesville, FL - O'Connell Center - June 7, 1988
Al Perez vs. Ricky Santana
Kendall Windham vs. Larry Zbyszko
Steve Williams vs. NWA TV Champion Mike Rotundo
Ron & Jimmy Garvin vs. Kevin Sullivan & Rick Steiner
Sting & Nikita Koloff vs. NWA Tag Team Champions Arn
Anderson & Tully Blanchard
Dusty Rhodes & Lex Luger vs. NWA World Champion Ric Flair
& NWA US Champion Barry Windham

Clash of the Champions II "Miami Mayhem" - Miami, FL -
Knight Center - June 8, 1988
Shown live on TBS - featured Tony Schiavone & Bob Caudle
on commentary:
NWA US Champion Barry Windham (w/ JJ Dillon) pinned Brad
Armstrong at 13:56 with the claw after rolling through the
challenger's crossbody off the top
NWA US Tag Team Champions Tommy Rogers & Bobby
Fulton defeated the Sheepherders (w/ Rip Morgan) at around
the 19-minute mark when Fulton pinned Luke Williams with a
roll up; the match began as Jim Ross attempted to interview
Lex Luger outside the arena, who arrived in a limo; just after
Luger exited the car, he was attacked by NWA World
Champion Ric Flair, Windham, and NWA Tag Team
Champions Arn Anderson & Tully Blanchard while JJ Dillon
looked on; after the bout, the challengers attacked the
champions
Ron & Jimmy Garvin (w/ Precious) defeated NWA TV
Champion Mike Rotundo & Rick Steiner (w/ Kevin Sullivan) at
13:14 when Jimmy pinned Steiner with a roll up; Steve
Williams provided guest commentary for the bout, subbing for
Bob Caudle; after the bout, Williams came to Precious' aid
after Sullivan freed himself from a shark cage at ringside;
moments later, Precious shoved away both Jimmy and
Williams and left ringside
Nikita Koloff defeated Al Perez (w/ Gary Hart) via
disqualification at 11:50 when NWA Western States Heritage
Champion Larry Zbyszko interfered while Hart had Koloff
distracted from the apron; after the bout, Perez, Zbyszko, and
Hart triple teamed Koloff in the corner with a chain
Sting & Dusty Rhodes fought NWA Tag Team Champions Arn
Anderson & Tully Blanchard (w/ JJ Dillon) to a double
disqualification at 11:01 after both challengers shoved referee
Teddy Long, with NWA US Champion Barry Windham then
running out, attacking Rhodes, and applying the claw hold
outside the ring; after the bell rang, NWA World Champion Ric
Flair came out as well and with the champions triple teamed
Sting inside the ring (American Dream: The Dusty Rhodes
Story, The Best of Clash of the Champions)

JCP @ Tallahassee, FL - Leon County Civic Center - June
9, 1988

JCP @ Dunn, NC - Tritan High School - June 9, 1988
Chris Champion defeated Cruel Connection #2
Cruel Connection #1 defeated Larry Stephens
Rip Morgan defeated Gene Ligon
Bugsy McGraw & Rocky King defeated Tiger Conway Jr. &
Tony Suber
Rick Steiner defeated Jimmy Valiant
Jimmy Garvin defeated NWA TV Champion Mike Rotundo via
disqualification
Brad Armstrong & Tim Horner defeated the Sheepherders via
disqualification

JCP @ Houston, TX - Sam Houston Coliseum - June 10,
1988
Kevin Sullivan defeated an unknown
Rick Steiner defeated Randy Hogan
NWA Western States Heritage Champion Larry Zbyzsko
defeated Chris Champion
The Powers of Pain & Ivan Koloff defeated Ron Garvin, Mighty
Wilbur, & Kendall Windham
NWA US Tag Team Champions Bobby Fulton & Tommy
Rogers defeated Bobby Eaton & Stan Lane in a Best 2 out of 3
falls match
Al Perez defeated Jimmy Garvin
Sting defeated NWA TV Champion Mike Rotundo via
disqualification
Lex Luger, Nikita Koloff, & Steve Williams fought NWA World
Champion Ric Flair, NWA Tag Team Champion Arn Anderson,
& NWA US Champion Barry Windham to a no contest
Dusty Rhodes defeated NWA Tag Team Champion Tully
Blanchard in a barbed wire match

AJPW @ Tokyo, Japan - Budokan Hall - June 10, 1988
(11,800)
Mitsuo Momota pinned Tsuyoshi Kikuchi at 6:42
Masa Fuchi pinned Tatsumi Kitamura at 6:23
Motoshi Okuma & Haruka Eigen defeated Takagi & Kenta
Kobashi at 9:24
Shunji Takano defeated Boone via submission at 5:13
Rusher Kimura & Goro Tsurumi defeated Mighty Inoue &
Isamu Teranishi at 10:05
John Tenta defeated Havanna the Terror via submission at
6:03
The Great Kabuki defeated Rip Rogers via submission at 6:44
Ashura Hara, Toshiaki Kawada, & Samson Fuyuki defeated
Tiger Mask (Misawa), Shinichi Nakano, & Takashi Ishikawa at
19:18
Giant Baba & Hiroshi Wajima defeated Tiger Jeet Singh &
Jimmy Jack Funk at 14:33
United National Champion Genichiro Tenryu pinned Danny
Spivey at 13:30
PWF Tag Team Champions Jumbo Tsuruta & Yoshiaki Yatsu
defeated NWA International Tag Team Champions the Road
Warriors via count-out at 13:48 to win the titles; the combined
championships were renamed the All Japan World Tag Team
Title

JCP @ Atlanta, GA - WTBS Studios - June 11, 1988 (matinee)

World Championship Wrestling - 6/11/88 - featured an opening clip showing the entrance of Dusty Rhodes & Sting at Clash of the Champions II earlier in the week; included Jim Ross & Tony Schiavone on commentary; featured the announcement Rhodes would challenge NWA US Champion Barry Windham at the Great American Bash in Baltimore the following month; featured footage of Rhodes and Windham brawling during a recent episode of Pro taped in Savannah, Ga.; included footage of the Four Horsemen attacking Lex Luger at the Clash; featured Schiavone conducting an interview with NWA World Champion Ric Flair & JJ Dillon regarding the attack on Luger and facing Luger the following month in Baltimore; Flair then said Luger got 30 stitches for the attack and Sting would be next, along with Williams, Rhodes, and the Road Warriors; toward the end of his promo, some of Flair's words were muted; he might have said something to the effect of "The shit's on;" included Ross conducting an interview with Luger, his head bandaged, regarding the attack from the Horsemen and facing Flair in Baltimore, during which Luger said he didn't want Jim Crockett Jr. to fine or suspend Flair or do anything that would stop him from getting his title shot; some of Luger's comments were muted when he used the word "ass;" featured the announcement that Wargames and scaffold matches would take place during the Great American Bash tour and that the Tower of Doom would include a three-story cage with trap doors; it was also noted the Road Warriors would soon return to face the Powers of Pain in scaffold matches, followed by footage recapping the feud between the two teams; included several minutes of footage from the Nikita Koloff vs. Al Perez match at the Clash:

Sting defeated Rick Allen via submission with the Scorpion Deathlock at 3:24; Butch Patrick, Eddie Munster from "The Munsters," was shown in attendance during the match; following the bout, David Crockett conducted a ringside interview with Sting and Steve Williams regarding facing the Four Horsemen during the Great American Bash tour

NWA US Champion Barry Windham (w/ JJ Dillon) pinned Curtis Thompson with a lariat at 3:11; after the bout, David Crockett conducted an interview with Windham & Dillon regarding the challenge of Dusty Rhodes in Baltimore and Lex Luger going after Ric Flair's NWA World Title

Steve Williams pinned Trent Knight with the Oklahoma Stampede at 4:09; during the bout, it was noted Williams would soon be facing NWA TV Champion Mike Rotundo and would team with Sting on July 4 in Dallas, TX

NWA Tag Team Champion Tully Blanchard (w/ JJ Dillon) pinned Dave Spearman with the slingshot suplex at 3:59; prior to the bout, David Crockett conducted an interview with Dillon, Blanchard, & NWA Tag Team Champion Arn Anderson regarding the attack on Lex Luger at the Clash and the comments made earlier in the show by Sting; during the bout, Dillon briefly joined the commentary team

Kevin Sullivan pinned Bob Riddle with a clothesline at 3:33; during the bout, Sullivan attacked Riddle with the commentary team's podium and a steel chair but referee Teddy Long didn't stop the match; after the contest, Crockett conducted an

interview with Sullivan in which he claimed Jimmy Garvin stole Precious from him years before and said he would get his revenge in the Tower of Doom; during the segment, Sullivan accidentally called it the Temple of Doom

NWA Tag Team Champion Arn Anderson (w/ JJ Dillon) pinned Tommy Angel with the gordbuster at 4:35; during Anderson's entrance, he stopped by Jim Ross and said Luger was a scared man

Bobby Eaton & Stan Lane (w/ Jim Cornette) defeated Lee Wagner & Bob Emory at 7:02 when Eaton scored the win following the Rocket Launcher; during the bout, Cornette joined the commentary team, during which it was noted Cornette would be put in a straightjacket and suspended above the ring during the Great American Bash tour when Eaton & Lane face NWA US Tag Team Champions Bobby Fulton & Tommy Rogers; after the match, it was noted Ricky Morton & Robert Gibson would return to the NWA as part of the Bash tour; moments later, Crockett conducted an interview with Cornette, Eaton, & Lane regarding Fulton & Rogers

NWA US Tag Team Champions Bobby Fulton & Tommy Rogers defeated the Grappler & Joe Cruz at 2:18 when Rogers pinned Cruz with the Rocket Launcher; during the bout, Tony Schiavone wished a speedy recovery to Granny Louise Billon, a front row regular at the Omni, who was recovering in the hospital; after the match, Jim Ross conducted an interview with Fulton & Rogers regarding the attack they sustained the previous week from Cornette, Eaton, & Lane and facing them as part of the Bash tour

JCP @ Baltimore, MD - Arena - June 11, 1988 (5,500)
Brad Armstrong defeated the Bounty Hunter
Ivan Koloff defeated Larry Winters
Al Perez defeated Mark Fleming
The Powers of Pain defeated Ron Garvin & Mighty Wilbur
NWA TV Champion Mike Rotundo fought Steve Williams to a draw
Sting & Nikita Koloff defeated NWA Tag Team Champions Arn Anderson & Tully Blanchard via disqualification
Dusty Rhodes & Lex Luger fought NWA World Champion Ric Flair & NWA US Champion Barry Windham to a no contest

JCP @ Florence, SC - Civic Center - June 11, 1988
NWA US Tag Team Champions Bobby Fulton & Tommy Rogers defeated Bobby Eaton & Stan Lane in a steel cage match

JCP @ Asheville, NC - Civic Center - June 12, 1988 (matinee)
NWA US Tag Team Champions Bobby Fulton & Tommy Rogers defeated Bobby Eaton & Stan Lane

JCP @ Albany, GA - Civic Center - June 12, 1988
TV taping:
Sting & Steve Williams fought Bobby Eaton & Stan Lane to a 20-minute time-limit draw
NWA US Tag Team Champions Bobby Fulton & Tommy

Rogers defeated Bob Riddle & Tommy Angel
Lex Luger fought NWA US Champion Barry Windham to a no contest
Sting & Nikita Koloff defeated NWA World Champion Ric Flair & NWA Tag Team Champion Tully Blanchard via disqualification
Dark match after the taping: NWA US Tag Team Champions Bobby Fulton & Tommy Rogers defeated Bobby Eaton & Stan Lane

JCP @ Columbus, GA - June 13, 1988
NWA US Tag Team Champions Bobby Fulton & Tommy Rogers defeated Bobby Eaton & Stan Lane

JCP @ Spartanburg, SC - Memorial Auditorium - June 14, 1988
Rick Steiner defeated Kendall Windham
Rip Morgan defeated the Italian Stallion
Ron Simmons defeated Tiger Conway Jr.
Larry Zbyszko (sub. for Shaska Whatley) defeated Bugsy McGraw
Bobby Eaton & Stan Lane defeated Brad Armstrong & Tim Horner
Ivan Koloff defeated Mighty Wilbur (sub. for Ron Garvin)
NWA US Tag Team Champions Bobby Fulton & Tommy Rogers defeated the Sheepherders

JCP @ Harrisonburg, VA - High School Gym - June 16, 1988
The Italian Stallion defeated Cruel Connection #2
Kendall Windham defeated Cruel Connection #1
Ivan Koloff defeated Mark Fleming
Jimmy Garvin defeated Kevin Sullivan
Ron Garvin & Mighty Wilbur defeated Ivan Koloff & Larry Zbyzsko
The Road Warriors defeated NWA TV Champion Mike Rotundo & Rick Steiner

JCP @ Charleston, WV - Civic Center - June 17, 1988
Bugsy McGraw defeated Chris Champion
Ron Garvin defeated Gary Royal
Ivan Koloff defeated Mark Fleming
Jimmy Garvin defeated Cruel Connection #1
Al Perez defeated Mighty Wilbur
Sting & Steve Williams defeated Larry Zbyzsko & Cruel Connection #2
NWA US Tag Team Champions Bobby Fulton & Tommy Rogers defeated Bobby Eaton & Stan Lane
The Road Warriors defeated NWA TV Champion Mike Rotundo & Rick Steiner

JCP @ Atlanta, GA - WTBS Studios - June 18, 1988 (matinee)
World Championship Wrestling - 6/18/88:
NWA US Tag Team Champions Bobby Fulton & Tommy

Rogers defeated Curtis Thompson & Agent Steel when Rogers pinned Thompson with the Rocket Launcher
Nikita Koloff & Steve Williams defeated Bob Riddle & Max McGyver when Williams pinned McGyver
The Road Warriors (w/ Paul Ellering) defeated Robbie Aumen & JC Wilde when Road Warrior Animal pinned Wilde
Al Perez (w/ Gary Hart) defeated Dark Star via submission
The Russian Assassin (w/ Paul Jones & Ivan Koloff) pinned the Italian Stallion with a backbreaker
Ron Garvin pinned Jerry Price
NWA Tag Team Champions Arn Anderson & Tully Blanchard (w/ JJ Dillon) defeated Tommy Angel & Don Grundy when Anderson pinned Grundy
Kevin Sullivan pinned Ryan Wagner
The Sheepherders, Bobby Eaton & Stan Lane (w/ Jim Cornette) vs. Jimmy Garvin, Mighty Wilbur, Brad Armstrong & Tim Horner; the show ended with the match still in progress

JCP @ Philadelphia, PA - Civic Center - June 18, 1988 (5,900)
Al Perez defeated Kendall Windham
Bobby Eaton & Stan Lane defeated Brad Armstrong & Tim Horner
NWA TV Champion Mike Rotundo defeated Jimmy Garvin
Steve Williams defeated Larry Zbyzsko
The Road Warriors defeated Kevin Sullivan & Rick Steiner
Paul Ellering defeated Paul Jones via count-out
Sting & Nikita Koloff defeated NWA Tag Team Champions Arn Anderson & Tully Blanchard via disqualification
Dusty Rhodes & Lex Luger fought NWA World Champion Ric Flair & NWA US Champion Barry Windham to a no contest

JCP @ Johnson City, TN - Freedom Hall - June 19, 1988 (matinee)
Television taping Al Perez pinned Max McGyver
Sting, Nikita Koloff, & Steve Williams defeated Joe Cruz, Doug Savage, & Mark Starr
The Road Warriors defeated NWA Tag Team Champions Arn Anderson & Tully Blanchard via disqualification
Lex Luger fought NWA US Champion Barry Windham (w/ JJ Dillon) to a double count-out

JCP @ Montgomery, AL - Garrett Coliseum - June 20, 1988
The Italian Stallion defeated Ron Simmons
Rick Steiner defeated Kendall Windham
NWA TV Champion Mike Rotundo fought Brad Armstrong to a draw
Ivan Koloff defeated Tim Horner
The Road Warriors defeated the Sheepherders
Sting, Steve Williams, & Brad Armstrong defeated NWA World Champion Ric Flair, NWA Tag Team Champions Arn Anderson & Tully Blanchard
Lex Luger fought NWA US Champion Barry Windham to a no contest

JCP @ Birmingham, AL - Civic Center - June 21, 1988

JCP @ Atlanta, GA - WTBS Studios - June 22, 1988
World Championship Wrestling - 6/25/88:
Sting defeated Jerry Price via submission with the Scorpion Deathlock
Ivan Koloff & the Russian Assassin (w/ Paul Jones) defeated Keith Steinborn & Robbie Aumen
Brad Armstrong, Tim Horner, & Kendall Windham defeated Max McGyver & Cruel Connection when Windham pinned McGyver with the bulldog
Scott Putski pinned David Isley
The Road Warriors defeated Gary Royal & JC Wilde when Road Warrior Animal pinned Royal
Nikita Koloff pinned Ryan Wagner with the Russian Sickle
The Sheepherders defeated the Italian Stallion & Rick Allen when Butch pinned Allen
NWA Tag Team Champions Arn Anderson & Tully Blanchard (w/ JJ Dillon) defeated Tony Bowen & Joe Cruz when Blanchard pinned Cruz with the slingshot suplex
Steve Williams pinned Bear Collie
NWA US Champion Barry Windham pinned Bobby Rose

NWA @ Nashville, TN - Municipal Auditorium - June 23, 1988
Jimmy Garvin vs. Kevin Sullivan
Steve Williams vs. NWA TV Champion Mike Rotunda
NWA US Tag Team Champions Bobby Fulton & Tommy Rogers defeated Bobby Eaton & Stan Lane
Sting & Nikita Koloff vs. NWA Tag Team Champions Arn Anderson & Tully Blanchard
Lex Luger vs. NWA US Champion Barry Windham
Also included 2 other matches

JCP @ Charlottesville, VA - University Hall - June 24, 1988
Bobby Eaton & Stan Lane defeated Brad Armstrong & Tim Horner
Sting & Nikita Koloff vs. NWA Tag Team Champions Arn Anderson & Tully Blanchard

JCP @ Orlando, FL - Orange County Convention Center - June 26, 1988 (6,000)
The start of the Great American Bash tour
Larry Zbyzsko pinned Bugsy McGraw
Ivan Koloff & the Russian Assassin defeated Jimmy & Ron Garvin when the Assassin pinned Jimmy after Kevin Sullivan interfered and the Assassin hit Jimmy with Sullivan's spike
Ricky Morton & Robert Gibson defeated the Sheepherders
NWA US Tag Team Champions Bobby Fulton & Tommy Rogers defeated Bobby Eaton & Stan Lane; stipulations stated the losing team would be lashed 10 times
Steve Williams defeated Kevin Sullivan via disqualification when Sullivan used a chair
Sting defeated NWA TV Champion Mike Rotunda via disqualification when Rick Steiner interfered
Al Perez defeated Nikita Koloff in a Texas Death Match after Gary Hart interfered
Dusty Rhodes, Lex Luger, the Road Warriors, & Paul Ellering

defeated NWA World Champion Ric Flair, NWA US Champion Barry Windham, JJ Dillon, NWA Tag Team Champions Arn Anderson & Tully Blanchard in Wargames when Dillon submitted to Rhodes' figure-4

JCP @ Greenville, SC - Memorial Auditorium - June 27, 1988 (4,700; a few hundred short of a sell out)
TV taping:
Included a David Allen Coe concert which began an hour before the show
Chris Champion vs. Shaska Whatley
Mighty Wilbur defeated Ivan Koloff via disqualification when Koloff used a chain
Larry Zbyzsko & Al Perez defeated Kendall Windham & the Italian Stallion
Kevin Sullivan & Rick Steiner defeated Jimmy Garvin & Chris Champion (sub. for Ron Garvin)
Bobby Eaton & Stan Lane defeated Brad Armstrong & Tim Horner via count-out
NWA US Tag Team Champions Bobby Fulton & Tommy Rogers defeated the Sheepherders (sub. for Brad Armstrong & Tim Horner)
Steve Williams fought NWA TV Champion Mike Rotunda to a 20-minute time-limit draw
The Road Warriors defeated Ivan Koloff & the Russian Assassin in a scaffold match
Dusty Rhodes, Lex Luger, Nikita Koloff, & Sting fought NWA World Champion Ric Flair, NWA US Champion Barry Windham, NWA Tag Team Champions Arn Anderson & Tully Blanchard to a double count-out

JCP @ Columbia, SC - Township Auditorium - June 28, 1988 (sell out)
Television taping
NWA US Tag Team Champions Bobby Fulton & Tommy Rogers defeated Jim Cornette, Bobby Eaton & Stan Lane in a handicap bunkhouse match

JCP @ Atlanta, GA - WTBS Studios - June 29, 1988
World Championship Wrestling - 7/2/88:
Ron Garvin vs. Larry Stevens
Sting vs. Gary Phelps
Al Perez vs. George South
Jimmy Garvin vs. Agent Steele
NWA TV Champion Mike Rotundo vs. Tony Suber
NWA US Tag Team Champions Bobby Fulton & Tommy Rogers vs. Thompson & Mike Jackson
Ricky Morton & Robert Gibson vs. Bob Riddle & Joe Cruz
Ivan Koloff & the Russian Assassin vs. Keith Steinborn & Davis
Steve Williams vs. Ryan Wagner
The Sheepherders vs. Wilde & Little

JCP @ Norfolk, VA - Scope - July 1, 1988
Bugsy McGraw & the Italian Stallion defeated Tiger Conway Jr. & Rip Morgan
Ron Garvin defeated Larry Zbyszko
Ivan Koloff, Rick Steiner, & the Russian Assassins defeated the Mighty Wilbur, Brad Armstrong, & Tim Horner
Ricky Morton & Robert Gibson defeated the Sheepherders
Jimmy Garvin defeated Kevin Sullivan in a Prince of Darkness match
NWA TV Champion Mike Rotundo defeated Steve Williams via disqualification
Nikita Koloff defeated Al Perez in a Russian chain match
NWA US Tag Team Champions Bobby Fulton & Tommy Rogers defeated Jim Cornette, Bobby Eaton & Stan Lane in a handicap bunkhouse match
Dusty Rhodes defeated NWA Tag Team Champion Tully Blanchard in an I Quit match
Sting, Lex Luger, & the Road Warriors defeated NWA World Champion Ric Flair, NWA US Champion Barry Windham, NWA Tag Team Champion Arn Anderson, & JJ Dillon in a steel cage match

JCP @ Charlotte, NC - Memorial Stadium - July 2, 1988 (about 10,000)
Included a performance by David Allen Coe
The Main Event - 8/14/88: Brad Armstrong, Tim Horner, (sub. for Ron Simmons & Jimmy Valiant) & Bugsy McGraw defeated Tiger Conway Jr., Chris Champion, & Cruel Connection #1 (Gary Royal) at 7:49 when Horner pinned Conway following a double elbow to the face by Horner & Armstrong
The Main Event - 8/14/88: NWA Western States Heritage Champion Larry Zbyzsko pinned Kendall Windham at 5:32 when the momentum of a crossbody by Windham put Zbyzsko on top
Al Perez pinned Mighty Wilbur at the 4-minute mark
Ron Garvin pinned Rick Steiner in a taped fist match after Kevin Sullivan's interference backfired and Garvin knocked out Steiner with Sullivan's foreign object
The Main Event - 8/21/88: Ricky Morton & Robert Gibson defeated the Sheepherders (w/ Rip Morgan) at 13:10 when Morton pinned Luke Williams with a crossbody off the top
The Main Event - 8/28/88: Jimmy Garvin pinned Kevin Sullivan in a blindfold match
The Main Event - 9/4/88: NWA US Tag Team Champions Bobby Fulton & Tommy Rogers defeated Jim Cornette, Bobby Eaton & Stan Lane in a handicap bunkhouse match
The Main Event - 9/18/88: Steve Williams defeated NWA TV Champion Mike Rotunda via disqualification; Williams originally won the match and title following the Oklahoma Stampede but the decision was changed because Rotunda knocked down the referee moments earlier
The Road Warriors defeated Ivan Koloff & the Russian Assassin in a scaffold match in under 5 minutes
Dusty Rhodes, Lex Luger, Sting, Nikita Koloff, & Paul Ellering defeated NWA World Champion Ric Flair, NWA US Champion Barry Windham, JJ Dillon, NWA Tag Team Champions Arn Anderson & Tully Blanchard in Wargames when Dillon submitted to Luger's Torture Rack

JCP @ Amarillo, TX - Civic Center - July 3, 1988 (6,000; near sell out)
Brad Armstrong & Tim Horner fought the Sheepherders to a draw
Larry Zbyszko defeated Bugsy McGraw
Ricky Morton & Robert Gibson defeated Rick Steiner & Kevin

Sullivan
Ron Garvin fought Dick Murdoch to a double count-out
NWA TV Champion Mike Rotundo defeated Jimmy Garvin
NWA US Tag Team Champions Bobby Fulton & Tommy Rogers defeated Jim Cornette, Bobby Eaton & Stan Lane in a handicap streetfight
Nikita Koloff defeated Al Perez in a Russian chain match
Sting & Steve Williams defeated NWA Tag Team Champions Arn Anderson & Tully Blanchard via disqualification
Dusty Rhdoes & Lex Luger defeated NWA World Champion Ric Flair & NWA US Champion Barry Windham in a bullrope match
The Road Warriors defeated Ivan Koloff & the Russian Assassin in a scaffold match

JCP @ Dallas, TX - Reunion Arena - July 4, 1988 (5,000)
Nikita Koloff vs. Al Perez (Russian Chain match)
Sting & Steve Williams vs. NWA Tag Team Champions Tully Blanchard & Arn Anderson
NWA US Tag Team Champions Bobby Fulton & Tommy Rogers defeated Jim Cornette, Bobby Eaton & Stan Lane in a handicap bunkhouse match
The Road Warriors defeated Ivan Koloff & the Russian Assassin in a scaffold match
Lex Luger & Dusty Rhodes defeated NWA World Champion Ric Flair & NWA US Champion Barry Windham in a steel cage match

JCP @ Miami, FL - Knight Center - July 5, 1988

JCP @ Tampa, FL - Stadium - July 6, 1988
Al Perez defeated Kendall Windham
Bugsy McGraw defeated Tiger Conway Jr.
Sting, Ron Garvin, & Ron Simmons defeated Ivan Koloff, Larry Zbyszko, & the Russian Assassin
Ricky Morton & Robert Gibson defeated the Sheepherders
NWA US Tag Team Champions Bobby Fulton & Tommy Rogers defeated Jim Cornette, Bobby Eaton & Stan Lane in a handicap match
Jimmy Garvin fought Dick Murdoch to a draw
NWA TV Champion Mike Rotundo defeated Steve Williams via disqualification
Dusty Rhodes, Nikita Koloff, Lex Luger, & the Road Warriors defeated NWA World Champion Ric Flair, NWA US Champion Barry windham, Kevin Sullivan, NWA Tag Team Champions Arn Anderson & Tully Blanchard in Wargames

JCP @ Raleigh, NC - Dorton Arena - July 7, 1988
Kendall Windham fought Rick Steiner to a draw
Brad Armstrong defeated Cruel Connection #1
Ron Garvin & Mighty Wilbur defeated Larry Zbyszko & Al Perez
Jimmy Garvin defeated Dick Murdoch
Ricky Morton & Robert Gibson defeated the Sheepherders
NWA TV Champion Mike Rotunda defeated Steve Williams via disqualification

NWA US Tag Team Champions Bobby Fulton & Tommy Rogers defeated Jim Cornette, Bobby Eaton & Stan Lane in a handicap match
The Road Warriors defeated Ivan Koloff & the Russian Assassin
Dusty Rhodes, Lex Luger, Sting, & Nikita Koloff defeated NWA World Champion Ric Flair, NWA US Champion Barry Windham, NWA Tag Team Champions Arn Anderson & Tully Blanchard

JCP @ Pittsburgh, PA - Civic Arena - July 8, 1988
Chris Champion fought Kendall Windham to a draw
Rip Morgan fought Bugsy McGraw to a no contest
Al Perez & Larry Zbyszko defeated Brad Armstrong & Tim Horner
Ron Garvin defeated Rick Steiner
Ricky Morton & Robert Gibson defeated the Sheepherders
NWA TV Champion Mike Rotunda defeated Jimmy Garvin
Sting, Nikita Koloff, & Steve Williams defeated Dick Murdoch, Ivan Koloff, & the Russian Assassin
The Road Warriors defeated NWA Tag Team Champions Arn Anderson & Tully Blanchard via disqualification
NWA US Tag Team Champions Bobby Fulton & Tommy Rogers defeated Bobby Eaton & Stan Lane in a scaffold match
Lex Luger & Dusty Rhodes defeated NWA World Champion Ric Flair & NWA US Champion Barry Windham

World Championship Wrestling - 7/9/88:
Brad Armstrong vs. Mike Jackson
Ricky Morton & Robert Gibson vs. Gary Royal & Mike Phelps
Sting vs. Larry Stevens
Bobby Eaton & Stan Lane vs. Wagner & Little
Steve Williams vs. Joe Cruz
The Varsity Club vs. George South & Allen
NWA Tag Team Champions Arn Anderson & Tully Blanchard vs. Tony Suber & Wilde
NWA US Champion Barry Windham vs. Max McGyver
The Sheepherders vs. Keith Steinborn & Tommy Angel
Al Perez vs. Agent Steele

JCP @ Chicago, IL - UIC Pavilion - July 9, 1988 (6,500)
Steve Williams pinned Al Perez
Ron Garvin fought NWA TV Champion Mike Rotunda to a no contest
Jimmy Garvin pinned Kevin Sullivan in a blindfold match with a small package; after the bout, Sullivan attacked Garvin and chased after Precious
The Russian Assassin (Angel of Death) pinned Kendall Windham
Rick Steiner fought Tim Horner to a draw
Ricky Morton & Robert Gibson defeated the Sheepherders
Sting & Nikita Koloff defeated Ivan Koloff & Dick Murdoch
NWA US Tag Team Champions Bobby Fulton & Tommy Rogers defeated Jim Cornette, Bobby Eaton & Stan Lane in a handicap bunkhouse match
Lex Luger defeated NWA US Champion Barry Windham via

count-out in a Texas Death Match

Dusty Rhodes & the Road Warriors defeated NWA World Champion Ric Flair, NWA Tag Team Champions Arn Anderson & Tully Blanchard in a steel cage match; pre-match stipulations stated the victors would win the vacant NWA Six-Man Tag Team Championship

The Main Event - 7/10/88 - hosted by Jim Ross & Tony Schiavone - hype show for the Great American Bash pay-per-view later that night

Great American Bash 88 - Baltimore, MD - Arena - July 10, 1988 (13,000)

The Main Event - 7/24/88: Florida Heavyweight Champion Rick Steiner & Dick Murdoch defeated Tim Horner & Kendall Windham at around the 7-minute mark when Murdoch pinned Windham with an elbow to the face and elbow drop

Pay-per-view bouts - featured Jim Ross & Tony Schiavone on commentary:

Nikita Koloff & Sting fought NWA Tag Team Champions Arn Anderson & Tully Blanchard (w/ JJ Dillon) to a 20-minute time-limit draw at 20:07; the bell rang as Sting had Blanchard caught in the Scorpion Deathlock, making some fans believe there was a title change; after the bout, Sting & Koloff left ringside with the belts (*Ric Flair & the 4 Horsemen, Allied Powers*)

Bobby Eaton & Stan Lane (w/ Jim Cornette) defeated NWA US Tag Team Champions Bobby Fulton & Tommy Rogers to win the titles at 16:23 when Eaton pinned Fulton after hitting him in the face with a chain after referee Tommy Young was knocked down; pre-match stipulations stated the champions would get to whip Cornette 10 times if they won; Cornette was hung above the ring in a shark cage and wearing a straight jacket for the duration of the bout; after the match, Fulton assaulted Eaton with the chain before he and Rogers chased Cornette into the ring and lashed him 10 times (*Allied Powers*)

Jimmy & Ron Garvin, the Road Warriors (w/ Paul Ellering), & Steve Williams defeated Kevin Sullivan, NWA TV Champion Mike Rotunda, Al Perez (w/ Gary Hart), the Russian Assassin, & Ivan Koloff (w/ Paul Jones) in a Tower of Doom match when Sullivan knocked Jimmy out of the cage after Precious gave Jimmy the key to unlock it; stipulations for the bout stated a wrestler from each team would enter at 2-minute intervals and would battle down the three cages; the team to get to the bottom first would have to go through Precious, who had the only key to the lock; after the bout, Sullivan locked himself in the cage with Precious, with Jimmy then climbing back to the top of the cage and going through each level to get back to Sullivan, with Road Warrior Hawk making the save as Garvin freed Precious (*WarGames: WCW's Most Notorious Matches*)

NWA US Champion Barry Windham (w/ JJ Dillon) pinned Dusty Rhodes with the claw after Ron Garvin interfered and knocked Rhodes out with a punch after referee Tommy Young was knocked down; after the bout, Steve Williams tended to Rhodes in the ring; moments later, footage backstage showed Garvin celebrating with Gary Hart and Dillon (*The Rise and Fall of WCW*)

NWA World Champion Ric Flair (w/ JJ Dillon) defeated Lex Luger when referee Tommy Young, under orders of the athletic commissioner at ringside, stopped the bout due to Luger bleeding above the eye as Luger had Flair caught in the Torture Rack; after the bout, Sting, Steve Williams, and Nikita Koloff came out to celebrate Luger's victory until the official decision was announced

JCP @ Salisbury, MD - July 11, 1988
Television taping:
Rick Steiner fought Kendall Windham to a draw
Bobby Fulton & Tommy Rogers defeated Jim Cornette, NWA US Tag Team Champions Bobby Eaton & Stan Lane in a handicap match
Steve Williams & Nikita Koloff defeated NWA Tag Team Champions Arn Anderson & Tully Blanchard via disqualification
NWA World Champion Ric Flair & NWA US Champion Barry Windham fought Lex Luger & Sting to a no contest
The Road Warriors defeated Ivan Koloff & the Russian Assassin in a scaffold match

JCP @ Huntsville, AL - Von Braun Civic Center - July 12, 1988 (3,000)
Larry Zbyzsko pinned Bugsy McGraw
Al Perez pinned Kendall Windham
Ron Garvin pinned the Italian Stallion
Brad Armstrong & Tim Horner defeated Tiger Conway Jr. & Rip Morgan
Dick Murdoch, Ivan Koloff, & the Russian Assassin defeated Chris Champion, Ron Simmons, & Mighty Wilbur when Murdoch pinned Simmons
Ricky Morton & Robert Gibson defeated the Sheepherders
NWA TV Champion Mike Rotunda defeated Steve Williams via disqualification
Bobby Fulton & Tommy Rogers defeated Jim Cornette, NWA US Tag Team Champions Bobby Eaton & Stan Lane in a handicap match
Lex Luger, Sting, the Road Warriors, & Nikita Koloff defeated NWA World Champion Ric Flair, NWA US Champion Barry Windham, JJ Dillon, NWA Tag Team Champions Arn Anderson & Tully Blanchard in Wargames

JCP @ Louisville, KY - July 13, 1988
Bobby Fulton & Tommy Rogers defeated Jim Cornette, NWA US Tag Team Champions Bobby Eaton & Stan Lane in a handicap bunkhouse match

JCP @ Chattanooga, TN - UTC Arena - July 14, 1988
Bugsy McGraw defeated Tiger Conway Jr.
Tim Horner defeated Larry Zbyzsko
Ron Garvin defeated the Italian Stallion
Dick Murdoch, Ivan Koloff, & the Russian Assassin defeated Chris Champion, Kendall Windham, & Mighty Wilbur
Ricky Morton & Robert Gibson defeated the Sheepherders
NWA TV Champion Mike Rotunda defeated Brad Armstrong
Nikita Koloff defeated Al Perez in a chain match

Bobby Fulton & Tommy Rogers defeated NWA US Tag Team Champions Bobby Eaton & Stan Lane in a non-title scaffold match
Lex Luger, Sting, the Road Warriors, & Steve Williams defeated NWA World Champion Ric Flair, NWA US Champion Barry Windham, JJ Dillon, NWA Tag Team Champions Arn Anderson & Tully Blanchard in Wargames

JCP @ Richmond, VA - Coliseum - July 15, 1988
Kevin Sullivan & Rick Steiner defeated the Italian Stallion & Kendall Windham
Bugsy McGraw defeated Rip Morgan
Larry Zbyszko defeated Tim Horner
Al Perez defeated Brad Armstrong
Dick Murdoch, Ivan Koloff, & the Russian Assassin defeated Ron Simmons, Jimmy Garvin, & Mighty Wilbur
Ricky Morton & Robert Gibson defeated the Sheepherders
Ron Garvin defeated Chris Champion
Steve Williams defeated NWA TV Champion Mike Rotunda via disqualification
Bobby Fulton & Tommy Rogers defeated NWA US Tag Team Champions Bobby Eaton & Stan Lane in a non-title scaffold match
Lex Luger, Sting, the Road Warriors, & Nikita Koloff defeated NWA World Champion Ric Flair, NWA US Champion Barry Windham, JJ Dillon, NWA Tag Team Champions Arn Anderson & Tully Blanchard in Wargames

JCP @ Atlanta, GA - WTBS Studios - July 16, 1988 (matinee)
World Championship Wrestling - 7/16/88:
Sting & Steve Williams vs. Green Hornet & Laperouse
Brad Armstrong vs. Larry Stevens
Dick Murdoch vs. Curtis Thompson
NWA Tag Team Champions Arn Anderson & Tully Blanchard vs. Tommy Angel & Trent Knight
Al Perez vs. Agent Steele
The Road Warriors vs. Phelps & Allen
NWA US Tag Team Champions Bobby Eaton & Stan Lane vs. Spearman & Wilde
Nikita Koloff vs. Tommy Royal

Worldwide - 7/16/88 - featured an opening interview by David Crockett of the Road Warriors, alongside Paul Ellering and a young fan, in which Road Warrior Animal said they were the #1 contenders and were coming after NWA Tag Team Champions Arn Anderson & Tully Blanchard; Road Warrior Hawk then said Anderson & Blanchard could forget about the Great American Bash and everything else, save hospital insurance; included Crockett conducting an interview with Sting regarding Anderson & Blanchard and the Bash tour; featured Tony Schiavone & Crockett on commentary; included a segment with Jim Ross in which he announced Dusty Rhodes & the Road Warriors are once again the NWA Six-Man Tag Team Champions and Bobby Eaton & Stan Lane had regained the NWA US Tag Team Titles; featured Ross conducting an interview with Steve Williams and his chasing NWA TV Champion Mike Rotundo, during which he had the cameraman zoom in on his swollen eye, then said he would have the TV title by the end of the summer; Williams then offered his help to Dusty Rhodes after the recent attack he sustained from the Horsemen; included Bob Caudle conducting a backstage interview in Baltimore with Dusty Rhodes regarding Ron Garvin turning on him and costing him his match against NWA US Champion Barry Windham; Rhodes then said he knew Gary Hart was also involved in Garvin being paid off for $50,000, then saying Garvin, Hart, and JJ Dillon now had to deal with him; featured Caudle conducting a backstage interview in Baltimore with NWA World Champion Ric Flair regarding keeping the belt after facing Lex Luger, with Flair saying the sports commission stopped the match before he sent Luger to the hospital; included Caudle conducting a backstage interview with Luger in Baltimore regarding his match with Flair, with Luger's forehead bandaged; Luger then said he wasn't disappointed because he knew he would get his rematch because he, the NWA, and the fans would call for it and that he now knew what it takes to beat Flair and be champion:
Jimmy Garvin (w/ Precious) pinned Cruel Connection #1 at 1:34 with the brainbuster
NWA Tag Team Champions Arn Anderson & Tully Blanchard (w/ JJ Dillon) defeated Joe Cruz & an unknown at 4:43 when Anderson pinned Cruz with the DDT
Brad Armstrong pinned Cruel Connection #2 with the side Russian legsweep at 2:16 after Cruel Connection missed a charge in the corner
Kevin Sullivan, NWA TV Champion Mike Rotundo, & Rick Steiner defeated the Italian Stallion, Kendall Windham, & Tim Horner at 4:35 when Sullivan pinned Stallion with the double stomp after Rotundo dropped Stallion with the butterfly suplex; Steiner came to the ring in possession of the Florida Heavyweight Title
Al Perez (w/ Gary Hart) defeated Trent Knight via submission with the spinning toe hold at 2:00; after the bout, Perez briefly reapplied the hold
Ricky Morton & Robert Gibson defeated Bob Riddle & an unknown at 1:48 when Morton pinned Riddle with the double dropkick
The Russian Assassin (w/ Ivan Koloff & Paul Jones) defeated Tommy Angel & Larry Stephens in a handicap match at 1:35 when Stephens submitted to the Russian Guillotine (Cobra Clutch); after the match, David Crockett conducted a ringside interview with Jones and his men, during which the team of Koloff & the Assassin were referred to as the Powers of Pain and they discussed their upcoming scaffold matches against the Road Warriors during the Great American Bash tour

JCP @ Greensboro, NC - War Memorial Stadium - July 16, 1988
Tony Schiavone was the ring announcer for the show
Bugsy McGraw & Tim Horner defeated Rip Morgan & Larry Zbyzsko
Ron Garvin defeated the Italian Stallion
Dick Murdoch defeated Gary Royal
Jimmy Garvin defeated Rick Steiner

Ricky Morton & Robert Gibson defeated the Sheepherders
Al Perez (w/ Gary Hart) pinned Brad Armstrong after Hart grabbed Armstrong's foot as Armstrong attempted to suplex Perez into the ring, with Perez falling on top and and Hart holding the foot down during the cover
Bobby Fulton & Tommy Rogers defeated Jim Cornette, NWA US Tag Team Champions Bobby Eaton & Stan Lane in a handicap match
The Road Warriors defeated Ivan Koloff & the Russian Assassin in a scaffold match
Sting defeated NWA TV Champion Mike Rotunda (w/ Kevin Sullivan & Rick Steiner) via disqualification at 8:20 when Steiner interfered as Sting applied the Scorpion Deathlock (*Great American Bash 88*)
Lex Luger, Steve Williams, Nikita Koloff, Dusty Rhodes, & Paul Ellering defeated NWA World Champion Ric Flair, NWA US Champion Barry Windham, JJ Dillon, NWA Tag Team Champions Arn Anderson & Tully Blanchard in Wargames at 21:07 when Dillon submitted to Rhodes' figure 4, with Rhodes grabbing the bottom rope for added leverage; order of entry: Rhodes, Anderson, Windham, Williams, Flair, Luger, Blanchard, Nikita, Dillon, Ellering (*Ric Flair & the 4 Horsemen, WarGames: WCW's Most Notorious Matches*)

JCP @ Charleston, WV - Civic Center - July 17, 1988 (6,500)

Tim Horner pinned Larry Zybzsko
NWA TV Champion Mike Rotundo pinned Bugsy McGraw
Ricky Morton & Robert Gibson defeated the Sheepherders
Al Perez pinned Brad Armstrong after Gary Hart distracted Armstrong from the floor
Bobby Fulton & Tommy Rogers defeated NWA US Tag Team Champions Bobby Eaton & Stan Lane in a bunkhouse match; Jim Cornette was to have been involved in the match, making it a handicap match, but he missed his plane connection
Ron Garvin pinned Mighty Wilbur at the 23-second mark
Jimmy Garvin pinned Kevin Sullivan in a blindfold match
The Road Warriors defeated Ivan Koloff & the Russian Assassin in a scaffold match
Lex Luger, Sting, Nikita Koloff, & Steve Williams defeated NWA World Champion Ric Flair, NWA US Champion Barry Windham, NWA Tag Team Champions Arn Anderson & Tully Blanchard in a steel cage match when Luger pinned Anderson

JCP @ Columbus, GA - Municipal Auditorium - July 18, 1988 (4,200)

The largest crowd at the venue in 3 years; featured a David Allen Coe concert
TV taping:
Sting defeated NWA TV Champion Mike Rotunda via disqualification
Bobby Fulton & Tommy Rogers defeated Jim Cornette, NWA US Tag Team Champions Bobby Eaton & Stan Lane in a handicap match
Dusty Rhodes, Nikita Koloff, & Steve Williams fought NWA World Champion Ric Flair, NWA US Champion Barry Windham, & NWA Tag Team Champion Tully Blanchard to a

no contest
The Road Warriors defeated Ivan Koloff & the Russian Assassin in a scaffold match

JCP @ Atlanta, GA - WTBS Studios - July 19, 1988

World Championship Wrestling - 7/23/88 - included an opening shot of the Tower of Doom from the Great American Bash, followed by the announcement another Tower of Doom match would take place at the upcoming Capital Centre card; featured Jim Ross & Tony Schiavone on commentary; included an ad promoting the Great American Bash 88 home video; featured David Crockett conducting an interview with Jim Cornette, NWA US Tag Team Champions Bobby Eaton & Stan Lane in which Cornette said he wanted the NWA Tag Team Titles and complained that they were the #1 contenders to the titles but had been ignored; Cornette said he and JJ Dillon had been business associates and Eaton and Arn Anderson were best friends, then added that Eaton & Lane were better than Anderson & Tully Blanchard; moments later, Cornette said they would still be Dillon, Anderson & Blanchard's friends after they beat them for the belts; included a promo by Dusty Rhodes regarding Gary Hart & Ron Garvin costing him the NWA US Title at the Great American Bash in Baltimore:
The Russian Assassin (w/ Paul Jones & Ivan Koloff) defeated Trent Knight via submission with the Cobra Clutch at 4:04; after the bout, David Crockett conducted a ringside interview with Jones, Koloff, & the Russian Assassin regarding their scaffold matches with the Road Warriors; during the segment, Jones threatened Koloff to get the job done and get rid of the Road Warriors or he would get rid of Koloff & the Assassin
Bobby Fulton & Tommy Rogers defeated Chris Champion & Gary Royal at 3:51 when Rogers pinned Royal with a roll up
Ron Garvin (w/ Gary Hart) pinned Tommy Angel with the punch at 4:38; after the bout, Garvin executed the Garvin Stomp to Angel; moments later, Crockett conducted an interview with Hart, Garvin, & Al Perez in which Hart said Garvin cost Dusty Rhodes the NWA US Title and said the next goal was to put Rhodes out of wrestling; Hart then called out Steve Williams if Williams wanted a chance to get in the ring with Garvin
Al Perez (w/ Gary Hart) defeated David Isley via submission with the spinning toe hold at 4:20; after the bout, Perez briefly continued to assault his opponent
Ricky Morton & Robert Gibson defeated Agent Steele & George South at 4:46 when Morton pinned Steele following the double dropkick; following the commercial break, Crockett conducted an interview with Morton & Gibson in which they said they were back in the NWA for their fifth NWA Tag Team Titles
NWA Six-Man Tag Team Champions the Road Warriors (w/ Paul Ellering) defeated Ric Allen & JC Wilde at 1:23 when Road Warrior Animal scored the pin following a powerslam from the middle turnbuckle; after the bout, Crockett conducted a ringside interview with the Road Warriors & Ellering in which they protested Jim Cornette's claim that NWA US Tag Team Champions Bobby Eaton & Stan Lane were the #1 contenders to the NWA Tag Team Titles, citing they were ranked #1 contenders by all the wrestling magazines; moments later,

Road Warrior Hawk cut a promo on Ron Garvin
NWA TV Champion Mike Rotunda (w/ Kevin Sullivan & Florida Heavyweight Champion Rick Steiner) pinned Gary Phelps with the butterfly suplex at 3:59; during the bout, Steiner briefly climbed in the ring and assaulted Phelps before referee Teddy Long sent him out of the ring; after the match, Crockett conducted an interview with Rotunda, Sullivan, & Steiner in which Rotunda replied to a challenge from Steve Williams; moments later, Sullivan spoke about his upcoming cage match in Detroit with Dick Murdoch against Dusty Rhodes & the Sheik and said Rhodes would have to face Sullivan in Daytona Beach, FL before he gets to Detroit
NWA Tag Team Champion Tully Blanchard (w/ JJ Dillon) pinned Ryan Wagner with the slingshot suplex at 3:00; following the commercial break, Crockett conducted an interview with Blanchard, Arn Anderson, & Dillon regarding the the challenge of Jim Cornette, NWA US Tag Team Champions Bobby Eaton & Stan Lane, during which Anderson told Eaton to be happy where he was and not worry about he and Blanchard
NWA US Champion Barry Windham (w/ JJ Dillon) pinned Dale Laperyouse at 2:08 with the claw after hitting the superplex and lariat; following the bout, Crockett conducted a ringside interview with Windham & Dillon regarding the win over Dusty Rhodes in Baltimore, during which Dillon said Ron Garvin was nothing more than a little insurance that they didn't need
Lex Luger defeated Keith Steinborn via submission with the Torture Rack at 1:51; following the bout, Crockett conducted an interview with Luger regarding the outcome of his match with NWA World Champion Ric Flair in Baltimore
Sting, Nikita Koloff, & Steve Williams defeated the Green Hornet, Larry Stephens, & Cruel Connection #2 at 7:43 when Williams pinned Stephens following the Oklahoma Stampede
NWA World Champion Ric Flair defeated Curtis Thompson via submission with the figure-4 at 4:30; after the bout, Crockett conducted a ringside interview with Flair & Dillon in which Dillon said the ratings would pay off for Flair wrestling on the show and Flair cut a promo on Lex Luger

JCP @ Macon, GA - Coliseum - July 19, 1988
TV taping:
Bobby Fulton & Tommy Rogers defeated Jim Cornette, NWA US Tag Team Champions Stan Lane & Bobby Eaton in a handicap bunkhouse match

JCP @ Cincinnati, OH - Cincinnati Gardens - July 21, 1988 (4,000)
Bugsy McGraw pinned Rip Morgan
Rick Steiner pinned Ron Simmons at 1:29
Al Perez pinned Tim Horner after Gary Hart hit Horner with a foreign object
Ron Garvin pinned Chris Champion at 1:03
Ricky Morton & Robert Gibson defeated the Sheepherders at the 17-minute mark
Jimmy Garvin & Mighty Wilbur defeated Ivan Koloff & the Russian Assassin when Garvin pinned Ivan
Bobby Fulton & Tommy Rogers defeated Jim Cornette, NWA

US Tag Team Champions Bobby Eaton & Stan Lane in a bunkhouse handicap match
NWA TV Champion Mike Rotunda fought Steve Williams to a double count-out
Lex Luger, Sting, Nikita Koloff, & Dusty Rhodes defeated NWA World Champion Ric Flair, NWA US Champion Barry Windham, JJ Dillon, NWA Tag Team Champions Arn Anderson & Tully Blanchard in Wargames when Dillon submitted to Sting's Scorpion Deathlock

JCP @ St. Louis, MO - Arena - July 22, 1988 (6,000)
Ron Garvin pinned Mighty Wilbur
Ricky Morton & Robert Gibson defeated the Sheepherders
NWA Western States Heritage Champion Larry Zbyzsko & Al Perez defeated Jimmy Garvin & Kendall Windham
Bugsy McGraw pinned Rip Morgan
Sting fought NWA TV Champion Mike Rotundo to a draw
Bobby Fulton & Tommy Rogers defeated Jim Cornette, NWA US Tag Team Champions Bobby Eaton & Stan Lane in a handicap bunkhouse match
The Road Warriors defeated Ivan Koloff & the Russian Assassin in a scaffold match
Dusty Rhodes, Lex Luger, Nikita Koloff, & Steve Williams defeated NWA World Champion Ric Flair, NWA US Champion Barry Windham, NWA Tag Team Champions Arn Anderson & Tully Blanchard when Luger pinned Blanchard

Pro - 7/88:
NWA US Tag Team Champions Bobby Eaton & Stan Lane (w/ Jim Cornette) defeated Larry Stephens & an unknown at 4:25 when Eaton pinned Stephens with one hand on his chest following the Rocket Launcher; after the bout, Bob Caudle conducted a ringside interview with Cornette, Eaton & Lane in which they talked about wanting a shot against NWA Tag Team Champions Arn Anderson & Tully Blanchard; moments later, JJ Dillon, Blanchard & Anderson came out with all six men arguing

JCP @ Philadelphia, PA - Civic Center - July 23, 1988 (7,520)
Ron Garvin pinned the Italian Stallion
NWA Western States Heritage Champion Larry Zbyzsko pinned Bugsy McGraw
Rick Steiner pinned Kendall Windham
Ricky Morton & Robert Gibson defeated the Sheepherders
Al Perez pinned Mighty Wilbur
Steve Williams & Jimmy Garvin defeated Ivan Koloff & the Russian Assassin
Bobby Fulton & Tommy Rogers defeated Jim Cornette, NWA US Tag Team Champions Bobby Eaton & Stan Lane in a handicap bunkhouse match
Sting defeated NWA TV Champion Mike Rotundo via disqualification when Kevin Sullivan interfered
Dusty Rhodes, Lex Luger, Nikita Koloff, & the Road Warriors defeated NWA World Champion Ric Flair, NWA US Champion

Barry Windham, JJ Dillon, NWA Tag Team Champions Arn Anderson & Tully Blanchard in Wargames

JCP @ Roanoke, VA - Civic Center - July 24, 1988 (matinee)
Bobby Fulton & Tommy Rogers defeated Jim Cornette, NWA US Tag Team Champions Stan Lane & Bobby Eaton in a handicap bunkhouse match

JCP @ Johnson City, TN - Freedom Hall - July 24, 1988
The Italian Stallion vs. Cruel Connection #2
Bugsy McGraw vs. Cruel Connection #1
Ricky Morton & Robert Gibson vs. Al Perez & Larry Zbyzsko
Bobby Fulton & Tommy Rogers vs. Jim Cornette, Bobby Eaton & Stan Lane (handicap match)
Steve Williams vs. NWA TV Champion Mike Rotunda
Lex Luger, Sting, Nikita Koloff, & the Road Warriors vs. NWA World Champion Ric Flair, NWA US Champion Barry Windham, NWA Tag Team Champions Arn Anderson & Tully Blanchard, & JJ Dillon (Wargames)

JCP @ Atlanta, GA - WTBS Studios - July 25, 1988
World Championship Wrestling - 7/30/88 - included an ad for the Great American Bash 88 home video; featured the NWA US Tag Team Champions Bobby Eaton & Stan Lane vs. Larry Stephens & ? match from NWA Pro, followed by the post-match altercation between Jim Cornette, Eaton, Lane, JJ Dillon, NWA Tag Team Champions Arn Anderson & Tully Blanchard; included David Crockett conducting an interview with Lex Luger regarding his rematch with NWA World Champion Ric Flair, in which he talked about everything Flair wanted backstage in order to agree to the rematch, how many limos he wanted, and how he wanted a private jet to fly him to the show, and said he himself would wrestle Flair for free and he could take a cab to the show:
NWA US Champion Barry Windham (w/ JJ Dillon) & Ron Garvin defeated Tommy Angel & Dale Lapeyrouse at 5:05 when Garvin pinned Lapeyrouse after twice hitting the right hand punch and then sitting on his chest; after the bout, Garvin used the Garvin Stomp on Lapeyrouse while Windham assaulted Angel; Dillon briefly joined the commentary team during the contest; following the commercial break, David Crockett conducted an interview with Dillon, Windham, & Garvin in which Dillon forced Crockett off the set before the three cut a promo on Dusty Rhodes and Sting; moments later, Gary Hart & Al Perez came out, with Hart discussing Rhodes; Dillon then showed footage from Hart recently being interviewed at ringside by Jim Ross & Bob Caudle; Rhodes then attacked Hart from behind, laid him out, and took the mic saying he was looking for Garvin; after reviewing the footage, Hart said not even Mike Tyson was safe from Garvin's punch
NWA Tag Team Champions Arn Anderson & Tully Blanchard (w/ JJ Dillon) defeated JC Wilde & Trent Knight at 3:15 when Blanchard scored the pin following the slingshot suplex; prior to the bout, David Crockett conducted an interview with NWA World Champion Ric Flair regarding his rematch with Lex

Luger, with Flair saying it could be Luger's last shot; moments later, Flair spoke about upcoming tours of Los Angeles, Milwaukee, Detroit, Los Vegas, Seattle, and San Francisco as Dillon, Anderson & Blanchard joined him on the set; moments later, Dillon & Anderson cut a promo on Jim Cornette, NWA US Tag Team Champions Bobby Eaton & Stan Lane
Sting defeated Rick Allen via submission with the Scorpion Deathlock at 1:56 following the Stinger Splash; after the bout, David Crockett conducted an interview with Sting from the ring apron, with Sting doing a Blackjack Mulligan impression before saying he was after the NWA US Title and Barry Windham
Bobby Fulton & Tommy Rogers defeated Mike Jackson & Larry Stephens at 4:53 when Fulton pinned Stephens after being slammed onto his opponent by Rogers; after the bout, David Crockett conducted an interview with Fulton & Rogers in which they said they and Ricky Morton & Robert Gibson could take out the Horsemen and the Midnight Express and gave a shout out to Dusty Hill of ZZ Top

JCP @ Fayetteville, NC - Cumberland County Memorial Arena - July 25, 1988
Bobby Fulton & Tommy Rogers defeated Jim Cornette, NWA US Tag Team Champions Stan Lane & Bobby Eaton in a handicap bunkhouse match

JCP @ Savannah, GA - Civic Center - July 26, 1988
TV taping:
Bobby Fulton & Tommy Rogers defeated NWA US Tag Team Champions Bobby Eaton & Stan Lane in a non-title scaffold match
Worldwide - 8/13/88 - featured an opening segment in which Jim Ross conducted an interview in the arena with Sting, who he said could be the next NWA US Champion, with Sting saying he was after Barry Windham and would do to Windham what he did months earlier with NWA World Champion Ric Flair; included Tony Schiavone & David Crockett on commentary, with the two saying the NWA TV Title match would have an extra stipulation that Steve Williams would win $10,000 if he was able to win the belt; featured Ross conducting an interview with Lex Luger regarding his chasing Flair for the title, with Luger saying the Four Horsemen was a sinking ship because of he, Sting, Dusty Rhodes & Dick Murdoch; included Ross conducting an interview with Flair about the challenge of Luger:
Steve Williams fought NWA TV Champion Mike Rotundo (w/ Kevin Sullivan) to a 20-minute time-limit draw at 15:38, moments after Williams hit the Oklahoma Stampede while referee Tommy Young was knocked down on the floor; moments later, as Young climbed back into the ring, Williams rolled up Rotundo and pinned him at 15:44, with Young then awarding the title to Williams, not realizing the time limit had expired; referee Teddy Long then came out to the ring and, with Sullivan, told Young about the time limit, thus implying the title would remain with Rotundo; Tony Schiavone was the ring announcer for the bout; stipulations stated Williams would win $10,000 from Rotundo if he could win the title
NWA US Tag Team Champions Bobby Eaton & Stan Lane (w/

Jim Cornette) defeated Kendall Windham & George South at 1:36 when Lane pinned South after the Flapjack; during the bout, the announce team clarified that Mike Rotundo was still the NWA TV Champion following the opening bout; Cornette joined the commentary team for the contest and cut a promo on NWA Tag Team Champions Arn Anderson & Tully Blanchard; after the match, David Crockett conducted a ringside interview with Cornette, Eaton & Lane regarding them chasing the Horsemen for the tag team titles

Kevin Sullivan, Ron Garvin, & Al Perez (w/ Gary Hart) defeated Brad Armstrong, Tim Horner, & Joe Cruz at 3:15 when Garvin pinned Cruz by sitting on him after a right hand punch; during the bout, Bobby Fulton & Tommy Rogers cut an insert promo in which they challenged NWA US Tag Team Champions Bobby Eaton & Stan Lane to a title rematch; Hart briefly joined the commentary team to remind them Garvin was a former NWA World Champion; after the contest, Crockett conducted a ringside interview with Hart, Garvin, Sullivan, & Perez in which Hart gave Garvin an envelope of cash and then cut a promo on Dusty Rhodes & Dick Murdoch as a tag team

Nikita Koloff pinned an unknown with the Russian Sickle at the 59-second mark; Koloff wore his red Soviet outfit for the bout; after the contest, Crockett conducted a ringside interview with Dusty Rhodes, Dick Murdoch, & Koloff about Gary Hart and Ron Garvin; Murdoch then said he didn't like Koloff but respected him, then extending his hand to Koloff before saying he would take out Hart; Koloff then said he would stand by Murdoch as long as Murdoch stood by Rhodes

The Road Warriors (w/ Paul Ellering) defeated two unknowns at the 22-second mark when Road Warrior Hawk scored the pin after the Doomsday Device; after the bout, Crockett conducted a ringside interview with the Road Warriors & Ellering in which they ranted about Ron Garvin sucker punching Dusty Rhodes before saying they would face the winners of whomever came out with the NWA Tag Team Titles between Bobby Eaton & Stan Lane and Arn Anderson & Tully Blanchard

JCP @ Jacksonville, FL - Memorial Coliseum - July 27, 1988

TV taping:

Worldwide - 8/20/88 - featured an opening clip of NWA Tag Team Champions Arn Anderson & Tully Blanchard vs. Sting & Nikita Koloff; included Tony Schiavone & David Crockett on commentary; featured Jim Ross conducting an interview with the Road Warriors, alongside Paul Ellering, in which they said they were after the NWA Tag Team Titles and didn't care who had them; they then noted NWA US Champion Barry Windham recently jumped Sting and that they would always be in Sting's corner; Road Warrior Hawk then said it was convenient that the NWA US Tag Team Champions Bobby Eaton & Stan Lane were busy facing Anderson & Blanchard so neither team would have to face them; featured Ross conducting an interview with Steve Williams regarding his chasing NWA TV Champion Mike Rotundo and the $10,000 that have been put up; Williams then said he wanted to go 60 minutes with Rotundo and not have to deal with Kevin Sullivan and Rick Steiner interfering; included Ross showing footage of Sting & Koloff against Anderson &

Blanchard, with NWA US Champion Barry Windham then interfering and applying the claw on Sting outside the ring; moments later, Koloff ran Windham off with a steel chair and tended to the bloody Sting; Ross then conducted an interview with Sting, his head bandaged, alongside Koloff about the attack by Windham; featured Ross conducting an interview with JJ Dillon, Anderson & Blanchard regarding the challenge of Jim Cornette, NWA US Tag Team Champions Bobby Eaton & Stan Lane, during which Anderson said he was man enough to say he once loved Eaton as a brother but he can't give up the titles for any friendship:

Ricky Morton pinned Cruel Connection with a crossbody off the top at 1:20

Rick Steiner (w/ Kevin Sullivan), Ron Garvin, & Al Perez (w/ Gary Hart) defeated Curtis Thompson, Larry Stephens, & an unknown at 3:58 when Garvin pinned Stephens after landing several punches in the corner; during the bout, Hart briefly joined the commentary team to remind them that Garvin was a former NWA World Champion; after the contest, David Crockett conducted a ringside interview with Garvin, Sullivan, Hart, Perez, & Steiner in which Crockett said Dusty Rhodes had accepted Hart's challenge to face Garvin in a dog collar match; moments later, Hart gave Garvin an envelope of cash before then cutting a promo on what Garvin would do to Rhodes in the match

NWA US Tag Team Champions Bobby Eaton & Stan Lane (w/ Jim Cornette) defeated George South & an unknown at 2:37 when Eaton pinned South after hitting the Double Goozle; during the bout, JJ Dillon cut an insert promo in which he said Cornette's mother obviously wore the pants in the family and he would put Cornette over his knee and teach him the manners his father never did

Ivan Koloff & the Russian Assassin (w/ Paul Jones) defeated Trent Knight & Bob Emory at 3:58 when Emory submitted to the Assassin's Cobra Clutch; after the bout, Koloff pulled the Assassin off Emory and shoved him; moments later, Crockett conducted a ringside interview with Jones, Koloff, & the Assassin in which Jones said he wanted victims, not necessarily victories; Jones then said he had a rocky summer but he would have Koloff & Assassin bring him victims

Dick Murdoch pinned Agent Steel with the brainbuster at 2:31

Lex Luger & Dusty Rhodes (w/ Magnum TA) vs. NWA World Champion Ric Flair & NWA US Champion Barry Windham (w/ JJ Dillon); Rhodes came to the ring wearing a Road Warriors T-shirt; Jim Ross was the ring announcer for the match; less than a minute of the match aired before the broadcast ended

JCP @ Daytona Beach, FL - Ocean Center - July 28, 1988 (5,500)

Bugsy McGraw pinned NWA Western Stages Heritage Champion Larry Zbyszko

Rick Steiner pinned the Italian Stallion

Ron Garvin pinned Will Clifford following a right hand punch

Al Perez pinned Kendall Windham

Ricky Morton, Brad Armstrong, & Tim Horner defeated Ivan Koloff, Dick Murdoch, & the Russian Assassin when Morton pinned Assassin; after the bout, Murdoch argued with Paul Jones over the loss

491

Bobby Fulton & Tommy Rogers defeated Jim Cornette, NWA US Tag Team Champions Stan Lane & Bobby Eaton in a handicap bunkhouse match
NWA TV Champion Mike Rotundo fought Steve Williams to a double count-out
NWA US Champion Barry Windham pinned Lex Luger in a Texas Death Match; Luger was accidentally announced as the winner after the match
Sting, Dusty Rhodes, Nikita Koloff, & the Road Warriors defeated NWA World Champion Ric Flair, Kevin Sullivan, JJ Dillon, NWA Tag Team Champions Arn Anderson & Tully Blanchard in Wargames when Dillon submitted to Sting's Scorpion Deathlock

JCP @ Houston, TX - Sam Houston Coliseum - July 29, 1988
Bobby Fulton & Tommy Rogers defeated Jim Cornette, NWA US Tag Team Champions Bobby Eaton & Stan Lane in a handicap bunkhouse match

- 7/88: Robert Gibson quit the NWA after being paid $1,100 for a week's worth of Great American Bash house shows.

JCP @ Landover, MD - Capital Centre - July 30, 1988
Tim Horner defeated Rick Steiner
Bugsy McGraw fought Larry Zbyszko to a draw
Dick Murdoch defeated Rip Morgan
The Russian Assassin defeated Mighty Wilbur
Brad Armstrong (sub. for Robert Gibson) & Ricky Morton defeated the Sheepherders
Bobby Fulton & Tommy Rogers defeated Jim Cornette, NWA US Tag Team Champions Bobby Eaton & Stan Lane in a handicap bunkhouse match
NWA TV Champion Mike Rotundo fought Steve Williams to a double count-out
Dusty Rhodes, Lex Luger, the Road Warriors, Sting, & Paul Ellering defeated NWA World Champion Ric Flair, NWA US Champion Barry Windham, Kevin Sullivan, JJ Dillon, NWA Tag Team Champions Arn Anderson & Tully Blanchard in a Tower of Doom match

JCP @ Detroit, MI - Cobo Arena - July 31, 1988 (7,000)
Larry Zbyszko fought Bugsy McGraw to a draw after the 10-minute mark
Jimmy Garvin pinned Ivan Koloff at 5:45; after the bout, Paul Jones argued with Koloff over the loss
Ron Garvin pinned Tim Horner at the 50-second mark with the right hand punch
Ricky Morton & Brad Armstrong defeated the Sheepherders at 12:00
Rick Steiner pinned Kendall Windham
Nikita Koloff defeated Al Perez in a Russian Chain Match
Sting, Lex Luger, & the Road Warriors defeated NWA World Champion Ric Flair, NWA US Champion Barry Windham, NWA Tag Team Champions Arn Anderson & Tully Blanchard when Luger pinned Blanchard at the 21-minute mark; the bout was advertised as a steel cage match
Bobby Fulton & Tommy Rogers defeated NWA US Tag Team Champions Bobby Eaton & Stan Lane in a scaffold match
Dusty Rhodes & the Sheik defeated Kevin Sullivan & Dick Murdoch in a steel cage match at 3:55 when Rhodes pinned Sullivan; after the bout, the Sheik attacked Rhodes until Murdoch made the save

JCP @ Milwaukee, WI - Mecca - August 1, 1988
Dick Murdoch defeated the Russian Assassin
Jimmy Garvin defeated Rick Steiner
Al Perez defeated Kendall Windham
Larry Zbyszko defeated Tim Horner
Bugsy McGraw defeated Rip Morgan
Ricky Morton & Brad Armstrong defeated the Sheepherders
Bobby Fulton & Tommy Rogers defeated NWA US Tag Team Champions Bobby Eaton & Stan Lane in a non-title bunkhouse match
NWA TV Champion Mike Rotundo defeated Nikita Koloff
Dusty Rhodes, Lex Luger, Sting, & the Road Warriors defeated NWA World Champion Ric Flair, NWA US Champion Barry Windham, NWA Tag Team Champions Arn Anderson & Tully Blanchard, and JJ Dillion in Wargames

JCP @ Columbus, GA - Municipal Auditorium - August 1988
Nikita Koloff defeated Al Perez via disqualification
Bobby Fulton & Tommy Rogers defeated Kevin Sullivan & NWA TV Champion Mike Rotundo
The Italian Stallion defeated Kendall Windham
Ron Simmons pinned Rip Morgan
Steve Williams pinned Rick Steiner
NWA US Tag Team Champions Bobby Eaton & Stan Lane fought NWA Tag Team Champions Arn Anderson & Tully Blanchard to a double disqualification
Lex Luger & Sting defeated NWA World Champion Ric Flair & NWA US Champion Barry Windham via disqualification

JCP @ Sioux City, IA - Municipal Auditorium - August 2, 1988
Larry Zbyszko defeated Ed Tossel
NWA TV Champion Mike Rotundo defeated Kendall Windham
Ron Garvin fought Dick Murdoch to a draw
Al Perez defeated Jimmy Garvin
The Road Warriors defeated Ivan Koloff & the Russian Assassin
Bobby Fulton & Tommy Rogers defeated Jim Cornette, NWA US Tag Team Champions Bobby Eaton & Stan Lane in a handicap match
Lex Luger defeated NWA US Champion Barry Windham
Sting, Steve Williams, & Nikita Koloff defeated NWA World Champion Ric Flair, NWA Tag Team Champions Arn Anderson & Tully Blanchard

JCP & Don Owen Promotions @ Seattle, WA - Arena - August 3, 1988

492

Avalanche (Paul Neu) defeated Billy Two Eagles
Mike Golden defeated the Grappler via disqualification
Steve Doll & Scott Peterson defeated Buddy Rose & Col. DeBeers
Larry Zbyszko defeated Kendall Windham
Bobby Fulton & Tommy Rogers defeaeted Jim Cornette, NWA US Tag Team Champions Bobby Eaton & Stan Lane in a non-title handicap bunkhouse match
Al Perez defeated the Mighty Wilbur via forfeit
Sting & Dick Murdoch defeated Ivan Koloff & Ron Garvin
Jimmy Garvin defeated Kevin Sullivan in a taped fist match
Steve Williams fought NWA TV Champion Mike Rotundo to a double count-out
Lex Luger, Nikita Koloff, & the Road Warriors defeated NWA World Champion Ric Flair, NWA US Champion Barry Windham, NWA Tag Team Champions Arn Anderson & Tully Blanchard in a steel cage match

JCP @ Las Vegas, NV - Thomas & Mack Center - August 4, 1988 (3,200)
Debut at the venue
Jimmy Garvin pinned NWA Western States Heritage Champion Larry Zbyzsko at 5:07 in a non-title match
Al Perez defeated Kendall Windham at 5:37 via submission with the spinning toe hold
Ron Garvin fought Dick Murdoch to a 15-minute time-limit draw
Bobby Fulton & Tommy Rogers defeated Jim Cornette, NWA US Tag Team Champions Bobby Eaton & Stan Lane in a handicap bunkhouse match at the 18-minute mark when Cornette was pinned following a double clothesline
NWA TV Champion Mike Rotundo vs. Kendall Windham (sub. for Steve Williams) (6:06); after the bout, Kevin Sullivan attacked Windham until Williams, in street clothes, came out to make the save
The Road Warriors defeated Ivan Koloff & the Russian Assassin in a scaffold match at 5:31
Sting & Nikita Koloff defeated NWA Tag Team Champions Arn Anderson & Tully Blanchard via disqualification at 19:15 when Anderson threw Koloff over the top
Dusty Rhodes & Lex Luger defeated NWA World Champion Ric Flair & NWA US Champion Barry Windham at 14:44 when Luger pinned Windham with an inside cradle

JCP @ Atlanta, GA - WTBS Studios - August 1988
World Championship Wrestling - 8/6/88 - featured the Dick Murdoch vs. Trent Knight match from NWA Pro:
NWA TV Champion Mike Rotundo & Rick Steiner (w/ Kevin Sullivan) defeated Brad Holiday & Bob Emory when Steiner pinned Holiday with the belly to belly suplex
The Sheepherders (w/ Rip Morgan) defeated Tony Suber & Bret Holiday when Luke pinned Holiday
Brad Armstrong pinned Joe Cruz with a Russian legsweep
Kevin Sullivan pinned JC Wilde by putting a foot on Wilde's chest during the cover
Mike Jackson & Curtis Thompson defeated Tommy Angel & Bob Riddle when Thompson pinned Riddle
Chris Champion pinned Don Valentine with the crane kick

NWA US Tag Team Champion Bobby Eaton (w/ Jim Cornette) pinned Gary Phelps with a kneedrop off the top
Al Perez (w/ Gary Hart) pinned Rick Allen via submission with the spinning toe hold
Rip Morgan (w/ the Sheepherders) pinned Bear Collie

JCP @ Inglewood, CA - Great Western Forum - August 5, 1988
Sting defeated NWA TV Champion Mike Rotundo via disqualification
Steve Williams defeated Rick Steiner
Jimmy Garvin pinned Kevin Sullivan
Larry Zbyszko fought Dick Murdoch to a double count-out
Nikita Koloff pinned Al Perez; the bout was billed as a Russian Chain Match
Bobby Fulton & Tommy Rogers defeated Jim Cornette, NWA US Tag Team Champions Bobby Eaton & Stan Lane in a bunkhouse match
Rick Steiner pinned Jose Rossand
Dusty Rhodes, Lex Luger, Paul Ellering, & the Road Warriors defeated NWA World Champion Ric Flair, NWA US Champion Barry Windham, JJ Dillon, NWA Tag Team Champions Arn Anderson & Tully Blanchard in Wargames when Rhodes forced Dillon to submit to the figure-4

JCP @ Oakland, CA - Kaiser Convention Center - August 6, 1988 (6,000)
Ivan Koloff pinned Kendall Windham at 10:02 by using the tights for leverage when the momentum of a crossbody by Kendall put Koloff on top
Jimmy Garvin pinned Kevin Sullivan at 5:05 with a cradle, despite interference by Rick Steiner
Nikita Koloff defeated Al Perez in a Russian Chain match at 16:00
Dick Murdoch fought Ron Garvin to a 20-minute time-limit draw
Sting pinned NWA Western Stages Heritage Champion Larry Zbyzsko in a non-title match at 6:12 with a sunset flip
NWA TV Champion Mike Rotundo fought Steve Williams to a double count-out at 16:00; after the bout, Williams cleared both Rotundo and Rick Steiner from the ring
Bobby Fulton & Tommy Rogers defeated NWA US Tag Team Champions Bobby Eaton & Stan Lane via disqualification at 12:00 when Jim Cornette interfered
Dusty Rhodes, Lex Luger, the Road Warriors & Paul Ellering defeated NWA World Champion Ric Flair, NWA US Champion Barry Windham, NWA Tag Team Champions Arn Anderson & Tully Blanchard, & JJ Dillon in Wargames at 24:00 when Dillon submitted to Luger's Torture Rack

The Main Event - 8/7/88 - featured Jim Ross & Tony Schiavone on commentary; included a replay of the Lex Luger vs. NWA Tag Team Champion Arn Anderson match that aired on the 5/1/88 episode; included an ad for the Great American Bash 88 home video:
Florida Heavyweight Champion Rick Steiner (w/ Kevin Sullivan) pinned Kendall Windham with an elbow drop at

around the 5:30 mark after blocking a monkey flip out of the corner

Ricky Morton & Robert Gibson, Tommy Rogers & Bobby Fulton defeated NWA TV Champion Mike Rotunda & Florida Heavyweight Champion Rick Steiner, Ivan Koloff & the Russian Assassin (w/ Paul Jones) when Morton pinned Koloff after Fulton came off the top with a double axe handle, knocking Koloff into the Assassin, who had Morton in a Cobra Clutch; after the bout, Jones yelled at Koloff for the loss

JCP @ Kansas City, MO - Kemper Arena - August 7, 1988 (6,800)
The end of the Great American Bash tour
Rick Steiner fought Larry Zbyszko to a draw after the 10-minute mark; Steiner played the babyface for the bout
Al Perez defeated JR Hogg at 1:03
Jimmy Garvin pinned Kevin Sullivan at 4:37
Ron Garvin defeated Kendall Windham at 5:01 via KO
Bobby Fulton & Tommy Rogers defeated NWA US Tag Team Champions Bobby Eaton & Stan Lane via disqualification at 14:08 when Jim Cornette interfered
Sting defeated NWA TV Champion Mike Rotunda via disqualification at 12:18 when Rick Steiner and Kevin Sullivan interfered
Steve Williams defeated NWA Tag Team Champion Arn Anderson via count-out
The Road Warriors defeated Ivan Koloff & the Russian Assassin in a scaffold match
Dusty Rhodes, Lex Luger, & Dick Murdoch defeated NWA World Champion Ric Flair, NWA US Champion Barry Windham, & NWA Tag Team Champion Arn Anderson in a steel cage match at 15:09 when Luger pinned Blanchard

JCP @ Atlanta, GA - Center Stage Theatre - August 10, 1988
World Championship Wrestling - 8/13/88 - featured opening footage of Al Perez attacking Brad Armstrong as Kevin Sullivan held Armstrong's foot from the floor; included a segment in which Jim Cornette, NWA US Tag Team Champions Bobby Eaton & Stan Lane interrupted Jim Ross, Tony Schiavone, & David Crockett in which Cornette said the Four Horsemen vitamins were nothing more than Flintstone's vitamins and then cut a promo on Gary Hart for Hart's recent comments directed toward him; featured an ad promoting the Great American Bash 88 home video; included Crockett conducting an interview with Lex Luger regarding his rematch with NWA World Champion Ric Flair; Luger received a mixed reaction during the segment; featured Crockett conducting an interview with Paul Jones, alongside the Russian Assassin, in which he said he would take out the Road Warriors & Paul Ellering but they were still around; Jones said there was something wrong in his camp and it was Ivan Koloff; Jones said he spoke with Koloff and Koloff said he would give him 110% from now on, and that's all Jones needed to eliminate the Road Warriors; included Crockett conducting an interview with Flair, NWA Tag Team Champions Arn Anderson & Tully Blanchard, NWA US Champion Barry Windham, and JJ Dillon regarding their challengers:

Ricky Morton pinned Lee Ramsey with a crossbody off the top at 2:06; after the bout, David Crockett conducted a ringside interview with Morton regarding his new team with Nikita Koloff; moments later, Koloff appeared and said he and Morton were after the NWA Tag Team, NWA US Tag Team, and NWA World Title belts
Kevin Sullivan, NWA TV Champion Mike Rotundo, & Rick Steiner (w/ Gary Hart) defeated Don Valentine, Rick Allen, & Gary Phelps at 4:05 when Steiner scored the pin with a belly to belly suplex after Rotundo hit the butterfly suplex, and Sullivan hit the double stomp four times
Brad Armstrong pinned Dave Spearman at 3:01 with the side Russian leg sweep
Al Perez (w/ Gary Hart) defeated Max McGyver via submission with the spinning toe hold at 1:34; after the bout, Crockett conducted a ringside interview with Hart, alongside Perez, regarding Dusty Rhodes and said his combination of Perez & Ron Garvin or Perez & Kevin Sullivan could take out Rhodes & Dick Murdoch
NWA US Champion Barry Windham (w/ JJ Dillon) defeated Curtis Thompson via submission with the claw at 2:53; during the bout, NWA Tag Team Champions Arn Anderson & Tully Blanchard cut an insert promo on NWA US Tag Team Champions Bobby Eaton & Stan Lane, during which Anderson compared Eaton & Lane to women; after the match, Crockett conducted an interview with Dillon and Windham regarding the challenge of Sting and Dusty Rhodes
Bobby Fulton & Tommy Rogers defeated Brad & Brett Holiday at 1:07 when Fulton scored the pin after Rogers slammed him onto one of the opponents; prior to the bout, it was noted the Boys Club of Florence, SC was on hand for the show

JCP @ Norfolk, VA - Scope - August 12, 1988 (9,500)
TV taping:
The Masked Maniac defeated Trent Knight
NWA TV Champion Mike Rotundo defeated Kendall Windham
Brad Armstrong defeated Al Perez via disqualification
NWA US Champion Barry Windham defeated Nikita Koloff
NWA US Tag Team Champions Bobby Eaton & Stan Lane fought NWA Tag Team Champions Arn Anderson & Tully Blanchard to a double disqualification
Lex Luger defeated NWA World Champion Ric Flair via disqualification

Worldwide - 8/13/88:
Steve Williams vs. NWA TV Champion Mike Rotundo
NWA US Tag Team Champions Bobby Eaton & Stan Lane vs. Kendall Windham & George South
Kevin Sullivan, Ron Garvin, & Al Perez vs. Brad Armstrong, Tim Horner, & Joe Cruz
Nikita Koloff vs. an unknown
The Road Warriors vs. two unknowns

JCP @ Macon, GA - Coliseum - August 13, 1988
NWA US Tag Team Champions Bobby Eaton & Stan Lane

fought NWA Tag Team Champions Arn Anderson & Tully Blanchard to a double disqualification

JCP @ Atlanta, GA - Center Stage Theatre - August 17, 1988
World Championship Wrestling - 8/20/88:
Al Perez vs. Jerry Price
Bobby Fulton & Tommy Rogers vs. the Menace & Boss
The Russian Assassin vs. Robbie Alumen
Kendall Windham & the Italian Stallion vs. Keith Steinborn & Valentine
Rick Steiner vs. Tony Suber
Brad Armstrong vs. Max McGyver
NWA US Tag Team Champions Bobby Eaton & Stan Lane vs. Collie & Shadow
NWA TV Champion Mike Rotundo vs. Rick Allen
Nikita Koloff vs. Russ Tyler
The Sheepherders vs. Brad & Brett Holiday
NWA US Champion Barry Windham vs. Lee Ramsey

JCP @ Raleigh, NC - Dorton Arena - August 18, 1988
The Russian Assassin defeated the Italian Stallion
Brad Armstrong defeated Ivan Koloff
Bobby Fulton & Tommy Rogers defeated the Sheepherders
Sting defeated Al Perez
Ricky Morton defeated NWA US Champion Barry Windham via disqualification
The Road Warriors defeated Rick Steiner & NWA TV Champion Mike Rotundo
NWA US Tag Team Champion Stan Lane fought NWA Tag Team Champion Arn Anderson to a double disqualification
Lex Luger defeated NWA World Champion Ric Flair via disqualification

JCP @ Richmond, VA - Coliseum - August 19, 1988 (13,000; near sell out)
Ron Simmons fought Larry Zbyszko to a draw
Ricky Morton, Nikita Koloff, & Brad Armstrong defeated Rip Morgan & the Sheepherders
Sting defeated Al Perez
The Road Warriors defeated Rick Steiner & NWA TV Champion Mike Rotundo
NWA US Champion Barry Windham defeated Steve Williams via count-out
Dusty Rhodes defeated the Russian Assassin
NWA US Tag Team Champions Bobby Eaton & Stan Lane fought NWA Tag Team Champions Arn Anderson & Tully Blanchard to a double disqualification
Lex Luger defeated NWA World Champion Ric Flair via disqualification

Worldwide - 8/20/88:
Ricky Morton vs. Cruel Connection
Ron Garvin, Rick Steiner, & Al Perez vs. Curtis Thompson & two unknowns
NWA US Tag Team Champions Bobby Eaton & Stan Lane vs. two unknowns
Ivan Koloff & the Russian Assassin vs. two unknowns
Dick Murdoch vs. Agent Steel
Lex Luger & Dusty Rhodes vs. NWA World Champion Ric Flair & NWA US Champion Barry Windham

JCP @ Philadelphia, PA - Civic Center - August 20, 1988
Ron Simmons & Brad Armstrong fought Rick Steiner & NWA TV Champion Mike Rotundo to a draw
Bobby Fulton & Tommy Rogers defeated the Sheepherders
Sting, Steve Williams, Ricky Morton, & Brad Armstrong defeated Al Perez, Larry Zbyszko, NWA Tag Team Champions Arn Anderson & Tully Blanchard
NWA US Champion Barry Windham defeated Nikita Koloff via count-out
Dusty Rhodes defeated the Russian Assassin
The Road Warriors defeated NWA US Tag Team Champions Bobby Eaton & Stan Lane via disqualification

JCP @ Cincinnatti, OH - Cincinnati Gardens - August 21, 1988
Bobby Fulton & Tommy Rogers defeated NWA TV Champion Mike Rotundo & Rick Steiner
Sting pinned Al Perez
Steve Williams pinned the Russian Assassin
NWA US Tag Team Champions Bobby Eaton & Stan Lane defeated Ricky Morton & Brad Armstrong (sub. for Robert Gibson)
NWA US Champion Barry Windham defeated Nikita Koloff via count-out
The Road Warriors defeated NWA Tag Team Champions Arn Anderson & Tully Blanchard via disqualification
Lex Luger defeated NWA World Champion Ric Flair via disqualification; Luger originally won the match and title with a sunset flip but the decision was changed by the original referee who saw Flair throw Luger over the top rope moments earlier

JCP @ Sumter, SC - Fairgrounds Exhibition Center - August 23, 1988 (sell out)
TV taping:
NWA US Tag Team Champions Bobby Eaton & Stan Lane fought NWA Tag Team Champions Arn Anderson & Tully Blanchard to a double disqualification

JCP @ Atlanta, GA - WTBS Studios - August 24, 1988
World Championship Wrestling - 8/27/88 - featured the NWA US Tag Team Champion Stan Lane vs. Curtis Thompson match from NWA Worldwide:
Nikita Koloff & Ricky Morton vs. Price & McGyver
The Russian Assassin vs. Bret Holiday
Rick Steiner vs. Keith Steinborn
Al Perez vs. Gary Royal
NWA Tag Team Champions Arn Anderson & Tully Blanchard vs. Bret Holiday & Ramsey
Brad Armstrong vs. Gary Phelps
Sting vs. Cruel Connection #1

Steve Williams vs. the Menace
Jimmy Garvin vs. Agent Steele
NWA TV Champion Mike Rotundo vs. Eddie Sweat

JCP @ Columbus, GA - Municipal Auditorium - August 25, 1988
Nikita Koloff defeated Al Perez via disqualification
Bobby Fulton & Tommy Rogers defeated Kevin Sullivan & NWA TV Champion Mike Rotundo
The Italian Stallion defeated Kendall Windham
Ron Simmons pinned Rip Morgan
Steve Williams pinned Rick Steiner
NWA US Tag Team Champions Bobby Eaton & Stan Lane fought NWA Tag Team Champions Arn Anderson & Tully Blanchard to a double disqualification
Lex Luger & Sting defeated NWA World Champion Ric Flair & NWA US Champion Barry Windham via disqualification

JCP @ Atlanta, GA - Omni - August 26, 1988 (13,700)
Ron Simmons (sub. for Tim Horner) defeated Rip Morgan
The Italian Stallion defeated Kendall Windham (sub. for Al Perez)
Bobby Fulton & Tommy Rogers defeated the Sheepherders
Sting fought NWA US Champion Barry Windham to a draw
Dusty Rhodes defeated the Russian Assassin (sub. for Ron Garvin)
The Road Warriors defeated NWA Tag Team Champions Arn Anderson & Tully Blanchard via disqualification
Lex Luger defeated NWA World Champion Ric Flair via disqualification
Jimmy Garvin, Steve Williams, Nikita Koloff, Brad Armstrong, & Ricky Morton defeated Kevin Sullivan, NWA TV Champion Mike Rotundo, Rick Steiner, Ivan Koloff, & Al Perez (sub. for the Russian Assassin) in a Tower of Doom match

Worldwide - 8/27/88:
Bobby Fulton & Tommy Rogers vs. Larry Stevens & Trent Knight
Rick Steiner, NWA US Tag Team Champions Bobby Eaton & Stan Lane vs. George South & two unknowns
Al Perez vs. an unknown
NWA Tag Team Champions Arn Anderson & Tully Blanchard vs. two unknowns
Nikita Koloff & Ricky Morton vs. Agent Steel & an unknown
NWA US Champion Barry Windham vs. Bob Riddle

JCP @ Charlotte, NC - Coliseum - August 27, 1988 (13,500)
Debut at the new coliseum
Rip Morgan & the Sheepherders defeated Kendall Windham, Ron Simmons, & the Italian Stallion
Ricky Morton defeated Cruel Connection #1
Nikita Koloff defeated Al Perez in a chain match
Dusty Rhodes & Sting defeated NWA US Champion Barry Windham & Larry Zbyzsko
NWA US Tag Team Champions Bobby Eaton & Stan Lane fought NWA Tag Team Champions Arn Anderson & Tully

Blanchard to a no contest
The Road Warriors, Jimmy Garvin, Brad Armstrong, & Steve Williams defeated Kevin Sullivan, Rick Steiner, NWA TV Champion Mike Rotundo, Ivan Koloff, & the Russian Assassin in a Tower of Doom match
Lex Luger defeated NWA World Champion Ric Flair via disqualification

JCP @ Greensboro, NC - Coliseum - August 28, 1988 (6,000)
TV taping:
Sting (sub. for Dusty Rhodes) & the Road Warriors defeated Kevin Sullivan, NWA TV Champion Mike Rotundo, & Florida Heavyweight Champion Rick Steiner via disqualification
NWA US Champion Barry Windham defeated Steve Williams via count-out
NWA US Tag Team Champions Bobby Eaton & Stan Lane fought NWA Tag Team Champions Arn Anderson & Tully Blanchard to a no contest
Lex Luger & Dusty Rhodes defeated NWA World Champion Ric Flair & Al Perez

JCP @ Daytona Beach, FL - Ocean Center - August 28, 1988
Bugsy McGraw vs. Krusher Knoff
Tim Horner vs. Larry Zbyszko
Brad Armstrong vs. Rick Steiner
Kendall Windham vs. Al Perez
Jimmy Garvin, Ricky Morton & Robert Gibson vs. Ivan Koloff, Dick Murdoch, & the Russian Assassin
NWA US Tag Team Champions Bobby Eaton & Stan Lane vs. Bobby Fulton & Tommy Rogers
Steve Williams vs. NWA TV Champion Mike Rotundo
Lex Luger vs. NWA US Champion Barry Windham
Dusty Rhodes, Paul Ellering, Nikita Koloff, & the Road Warriors vs. NWA World Champion Ric Flair, JJ Dillon, Kevin Sullivan, NWA Tag Team Champions Arn Anderson & Tully Blanchard

MID-ATLANTIC CHAMPIONSHIP WRESTLING

NWA

GREENVILLE MEMORIAL AUDITORIUM
MONDAY, AUGUST 29, 1988
8:00 P.M.

WORLD TAG TEAM TITLE VS. U.S. TAG TEAM TITLE

TULLY BLANCHARD

VS.

ARN ANDERSON WITH JJ DILLON

MIDNIGHT EXPRESS WITH JIM CORNETTE

BIG 8 MAN TAG MATCH

VS.

ROCK & ROLL EXPRESS, RICKY MARTON
THE FANTASTICS
STING

THE RUSSIAN ASSASSIN
IVAN KOLOFF
THE SHEEPHERDERS
WITH RIP MORGAN

TAG ACTION

ROAD WARRIORS	VS	MIKE ROTUNDI RIC STEINER
RON SIMMONS	VS	AL PEREZ
KENDALL WINDHAM	VS	KEVIN SULLIVAN
LARRY ZBYSZKO	VS	ITALIAN STALLION

* NWA - SUBJECT TO CHANGE

TICKET PRICES:
$12 Reserved Ringside
$10 General Adm.
$5 Children (Under 10)

N-40074-G

MID-ATLANTIC CHAMPIONSHIP WRESTLING

JCP @ Greenville, SC - Municipal Auditorium - August 29, 1988
Kendall Windham vs. Kevin Sullivan did not take place as advertised
Kevin Sullivan (sub. for Larry Zbyszko) defeated the Italian Stallion
Al Perez defeated Chris Champion (sub. for Ron Simmons)
NWA TV Champion Mike Rotundo & Rick Steiner defeated Brad Armstrong & Ron Simmons (sub. for the Road Warriors)
Sting, Ricky Morton, Bobby Fulton & Tommy Rogers defeated Ivan Koloff, Russian Assassin, Luke Williams, & Rip Morgan
NWA US Tag Team Champions Bobby Eaton & Stan Lane fought NWA Tag Team Champions Arn Anderson & Tully Blanchard to a double disqualification

JCP @ Savannah, GA - Civic Center - August 30, 1988
TV taping:
Dark match after the taping: NWA US Tag Team Champions Bobby Eaton & Stan Lane fought NWA Tag Team Champions Arn Anderson & Tully Blanchard to a double disqualification

JCP @ Atlanta, GA - WTBS Studios - August 31, 1988
World Championship Wrestling - 9/3/88 - featured opening footage of Dusty Rhodes & Brad Armstrong vs. Kevin Sullivan & Al Perez; included Tony Schiavone & Jim Ross on commentary; featured David Crockett conducting an interview with Dusty Rhodes regarding Kevin Sullivan and Gary Hart; moments later, Rhodes called out a woman in the crowd who had cat called him and said he had turned down uglier women than her; included an ad for Clash of the Champions III which announced NWA US Tag Team Champions Bobby Eaton & Stan Lane would be on the card, which didn't happen; featured Crockett conducting an interview with Sting regarding his wanting Barry Windham's NWA US Title; included a pretaped promo by NWA World Champion Ric Flair bragged about being the champion and said Herschel Walker, the Atlanta Braves' Dale Murphy, Lex Luger, Dusty Rhodes, Ricky Morton, and Steve Williams all had to look up to him; featured an ad for the Great American Bash 88 home video:
Bobby Fulton & Tommy Rogers defeated George South & Keith Steinborn at 3:24 when Rogers pinned Steinborn following the Rocket Launcher
Mike Jackson & Gary Royal defeated NWA US Tag Team Champions Bobby Eaton & Stan Lane (w/ Jim Cornette) via disqualification at 3:33 when Cornette hit Jackson with the tennis racquet; after the match, Eaton & Lane continued to assault their opponents; moments later, David Crockett conducted an interview with Cornette, Eaton & Lane regarding JJ Dillon, NWA Tag Team Champions Arn Anderson & Tully Blanchard and the attack Eaton recently sustained from Anderson & Blanchard backstage; during the segment, Cornette noted the injuries his men had given Ron Garvin and Bobby Fulton and the fact Anderson & Blanchard won the belts only after Eaton & Lane attacked Ricky Morton & Robert Gibson earlier that night
NWA TV Champion Mike Rotundo (w/ Kevin Sullivan) pinned Bob Emory (sub. for Jimmy Garvin) with the butterfly suplex at

497

1:30; Garvin was the scheduled challenger for the title; following his entrance, Sullivan grabbed Precious on the floor, with Garvin and Sullivan then brawling until Rotundo jumped Garvin from behind; Sullivan then shoved Precious to the floor and hit referee Teddy Long; moments later, Rotundo held Garvin as Sullivan threw a cinder block onto Garvin's leg; Garvin screamed "My god, my leg is broken" as Sting, Mike Jackson, Dusty Rhodes, Steve Williams, Ricky Morton, Brad Armstrong, Bobby Fulton & Tommy Rogers, and Precious tended to Garvin; moments later, Garvin was taken backstage on a backboard; following the commercial break, Jim Ross conducted an interview with Rotundo in which he and Sullivan demanded that they wanted the #1 contender to come out and get a title shot; moments later, Emory, an enhancement wrestler, came out instead; after the match, Williams ran out and knocked Rotundo to the floor; following the commercial break, David Crockett said Garvin's injury was very severe and that he had been taken to the hospital

NWA US Champion Barry Windham (w/ JJ Dillon) pinned the Italian Stallion with the lariat at 2:35; during the bout, it was noted Dusty Rhodes and Dick Murdoch would team up the following week in Houston, TX; following the commercial break, Crockett conducted an interview with Windham & Dillon regarding the challenge of Sting, during which Windham said Sting wouldn't win the US title just like he couldn't take the NWA World Title from Ric Flair

Ron Simmons pinned Joe Cruze with a spinebuster at 1:49; after the match, Ross & Crockett conducted an interview with Simmons, who returned from the locker room, in which he said he was worthy of title shots and then told the kids that his success came without the use of drugs and that it wasn't worth it to get involved with drugs

Ricky Morton & Steve Williams vs. the Menace & Jerry Price
Ivan Koloff & the Russian Assassin vs. Jones & Wilde
NWA Tag Team Champions Arn Anderson & Tully Blanchard vs. Tommy Angel & Trent Knight
Al Perez vs. Rick Allen

JCP @ Raleigh, NC - Dorton Arena - September 1, 1988
The Italian Stallion defeated Gary Royal
Ivan Koloff defeated George South
The Russian Assassin (Dave Shelton) defeated Chris Champion
Brad Armstrong & Ricky Morton, Bobby Fulton & Tommy Rogers defeated NWA TV Champion Mike Rotundo, Rick Steiner, & the Sheepherders
Dick Murdoch defeated Larry Zbyzsko
Kevin Sullivan & Al Perez defeated Sting & Nikita Koloff
NWA US Champion Barry Windham defeated Steve Williams via count-out
NWA US Tag Team Champions Bobby Eaton & Stan Lane fought NWA Tag Team Champions Arn Anderson & Tully Blanchard to a no contest

JCP @ Norfolk, VA - Scope - September 2, 1988
Worldwide taping:
Featured the debut of Magnum TA's Straight Talk segment,
with guest Kendall Windham
Ron Simmons defeated Cruel Connection #1
Larry Zbyzsko pinned Mark Fleming
Bobby Fulton & Tommy Rogers defeated the Sheepherders
Steve Williams, Dick Murdoch, & Nikita Koloff defeated NWA TV Champion Mike Rotundo, Al Perez, & Kevin Sullivan
Ricky Morton defeated the Russian Assassin when Ivan Koloff's interference backfired
Sting defeated NWA US Champion Barry Windham via disqualification
NWA Tag Team Champions Arn Anderson & Tully Blanchard defeated NWA US Tag Team Champions Bobby Eaton & Stan Lane in a No DQ match after NWA US Champion Barry Windham interfered
Lex Luger defeated NWA World Champion Ric Flair via count-out in a No DQ match

Worldwide - 9/3/88:
NWA US Tag Team Champion Stan Lane vs. Curtis Thompson
NWA TV Champion Mike Rotundo pinned the Italian Stallion
Nikita Koloff, Steve Williams, & Jimmy Garvin vs. Rick Steiner, Lee Ramsey, & Cruel Connection
The Sheepherders vs. Kendall Windham & an unknown
The Russian Assassin vs. an unknown
Sting vs. Agent Steel
Al Perez vs. an unknown

JCP @ Baltimore, MD - Arena - September 3, 1988 (11,000)
Ricky Morton, Ron Simmons, & Brad Armstrong defeated the Sheepherders & Larry Zbyzsko
Bobby Fulton & Tommy Rogers defeated Ivan Koloff & Russian Assassin #1
Nikita Koloff pinned Rip Morgan
NWA TV Champion Mike Rotunda defeated Steve Williams via disqualification
Dick Murdoch defeated Kevin Sullivan via disqualification
Dusty Rhodes & Sting defeated NWA US Champion Barry Windham & Al Perez
NWA US Tag Team Champions Bobby Eaton & Stan Lane fought NWA Tag Team Champions Arn Anderson & Tully Blanchard to a double disqualification
Lex Luger defeated NWA World Champion Ric Flair via disqualification

JCP @ Detroit, MI - Cobo Hall - September 4, 1988 (7,500)
Ron Simmons defeated Rip Morgan
Rick Steiner defeated the Italian Stallion
Brad Armstrong, Bobby Fulton & Tommy Rogers defeated NWA TV Champion Mike Rotundo & the Sheepherders
Steve Williams defeated Ivan Koloff
NWA US Champion Barry Windham defeated Sting via disqualification
Dusty Rhodes & Dick Murdoch defeated Kevin Sullivan & Larry Zbyzsko
NWA US Tag Team Champions Bobby Eaton & Stan Lane fought NWA Tag Team Champions Arn Anderson & Tully Blanchard to a no contest

498

Lex Luger defeated NWA World Champion Ric Flair via disqualification

JCP @ Covington, GA - September 5, 1988 (5,500)
George South defeated Rip Morgan
Ron Simmons & the Italian Stallion defeated the Sheepherders in a Best 2 out of 3 falls match
Brad Armstrong pinned Ivan Koloff

JCP @ Seattle, WA - Sports Arena - September 1988
The Avalanche defeated Billy Two Eagles
The Southern Rockers fought Col. DeBeers & Buddy Rose to a draw
Mike Golden defeated the Grappler via disqualification
Larry Zbyszko pinned Kendall Windham
Al Perez defeated Mighty Wilbur via forfeit
Sting & Dick Murdoch defeated Ron Garvin & Ivan Koloff
Jimmy Garvin defeated Kevin Sullivan in a taped fist match
Bobby Fulton & Tommy Rogers defeated Jim Cornette, NWA US Tag Team Champions Bobby Eaton & Stan Lane in a bunkhouse match
Steve Williams fought NWA TV Champion Mike Rotundo to a double count-out
Lex Luger, Nikita Koloff, & the Road Warriors defeated NWA World Champion Ric Flair, NWA US Champion Barry Windham, NWA Tag Team Champions Arn Anderson & Tully Blanchard in a steel cage match

JCP @ Atlanta, GA - WTBS Studios - September 7, 1988
World Championship Wrestling taping:
9/10/88:
Sting vs. Tommy Angel
Ron Simmons vs. Bob Riddle
Bobby Fulton & Tommy Rogers vs. Price & Scott
The Russian Assassin vs. Keith Steinborn
Ricky Morton & Brad Armstrong vs. Steele & Menace
The Varsity Club vs. Stevens & David Isley
Steve Williams vs. Don Valentine
Larry Zbyszko vs. Tony Suber
Al Perez vs. Mike Justice

Clash of the Champions III "Fall Brawl" - Albany, GA - Civic Center - September 7, 1988 (3,700)
Shown live on TBS - featured Jim Ross & Bob Caudle on commentary; included Tony Schiavone conducting a closing interview with NWA World Champion Ric Flair regarding the altercation earlier in the show by John Ayres and defending his title against Lex Luger:
Brad Armstrong fought NWA TV Champion Mike Rotunda (w/ Kevin Sullivan) to a 20-minute time-limit draw; late in the bout, Steve Williams appeared ringside to cheer on Armstrong; Armstrong repeatedly kicked out of the champion's pin attempts as the time limit expired; after the bout, Williams celebrated with Armstrong in the ring before helping him from ringside
Nikita Koloff & Steve Williams defeated the Sheepherders (w/

Rip Morgan) when Koloff pinned Luke Williams with the Russian Sickle
Dusty Rhodes defeated Kevin Sullivan (w/ Gary Hart) at 7:00 by pinning an interfering Hart with an inside cradle; late in the bout, Al Perez appeared and helped in double teaming Rhodes with a dog collar and chain but referee Tommy Young allowed the match to continue; after the bout, Rhodes briefly took a seat at ringside before eventually going backstage
Ricky Morton defeated Ivan Koloff (w/ Paul Jones) in a Russian chain match, despite interference by Jones; after the bout, the Russian Assassin appeared and threw Morton to the floor; moments later, Jones began blaming Koloff for the loss - even though it was his own fault - with Koloff eventually knocking Jones down; the Assassin then attacked Koloff, with another masked Russian appearing; the Russians and Jones then assaulted Koloff with the chain before hanging him over the top rope with it (debut of the second Russian Assassin) (*The Best of Clash of the Champions*)
Sting defeated NWA US Champion Barry Windham (w/ JJ Dillon) via disqualification after the Atlanta Falcons' John Ayres climbed in the ring as Windham had Sting covered and told referee Tommy Young that Windham hit Sting with a steel chair; after the bout, Sting and Ayres cleared Windham and Dillon from the ring; Ayres sat ringside for the bout because he was scheduled to referee an upcoming NWA World Title match

JCP @ Houston, TX - Sam Houston Coliseum - September 9, 1988 (3,000)
Brad Armstrong pinned Rick Steiner
Bobby Fulton & Tommy Rogers defeated Tug Taylor & Rip Morgan (sub. for the Sheepherders, who were in Puerto Rico)
Nikita Koloff pinned Russian Assassin #1
NWA US Champion Barry Windham defeated Sting via count-out
Ricky Morton pinned Rip Morgan (sub. for NWA TV Champion Mike Rotunda)
Dusty Rhodes & Steve Williams (sub. for Dick Murdoch) defeated Kevin Sullivan & Al Perez when Williams pinned Perez
NWA US Tag Team Champions Bobby Eaton & Stan Lane fought NWA Tag Team Champions Arn Anderson & Tully Blanchard to a double disqualification
Lex Luger defeated NWA World Champion Ric Flair via disqualification

Worldwide - 9/10/88:
The Road Warriors defeated two unknowns
Brad Armstrong vs. Trent Knight
Kevin Sullivan & Al Perez vs. George South & an unknown
The Russian Assassin vs. Agent Steel
The Sheepherders defeated two unknowns
Steve Williams vs. NWA US Champion Barry Windham

JCP @ Philadelphia, PA - Civic Center - September 10, 1988 (6,532)
Children's tickets were sold for $1

Steve Corino and Stevie Richards were in attendance for the show

Ron Simmons defeated Agent Steel

Ricky Morton pinned Curtis Thompson

Brad Armstrong, Bobby Fulton & Tommy Rogers defeated Rick Steiner, Larry Zbyzsko, & Al Perez at the 10-minute mark

Dusty Rhodes defeated Kevin Sullivan in a dog collar match when Brad Armstrong (sub. for Dick Murdoch), who was handcuffed to Al Perez at ringside for the duration of the bout, hit Sullivan with the timekeeper's bell

Sting defeated NWA US Champion Barry Windham via disqualification when the champion refused to break the claw after Sting reached the ring ropes

The Road Warriors defeated Rip Morgan & Russian Assassin #1 when Road Warrior Hawk pinned Morgan; after the bout, Ivan Koloff attacked Paul Jones until Koloff was attacked by the Russian Assassins; the Road Warriors eventually made the save

NWA TV Champion Mike Rotundo defeated Nikita Koloff via disqualification at the 20-minute mark

NWA US Tag Team Champions Bobby Eaton & Stan Lane defeated NWA Tag Team Champions Arn Anderson & Tully Blanchard to win the titles at 14:50 when Eaton pinned Anderson with the Alabama Jam at the same time Blanchard pinned Lane with the slingshot suplex; because Eaton and Anderson were the legal men, the challengers won the titles; prior to the bout, Jim Cornette, JJ Dillon, and Anderson exchanged words on the mic; the match was advertised as a Best 2 out of 3 falls match (Anderson's last appearance for a year; Blanchard's last appearance for 6 years) (*Wrestling Rarities: The Midnight Express*)

Lex Luger defeated NWA World Champion Ric Flair via disqualification after JJ Dillon hit Luger with his shoe and NWA US Champion Barry Windham interfered; former NFL player John Ayres was the guest referee for the bout

JCP @ Fayetteville, NC - Cumberland County Memorial Arena - September 11, 1988 (matinee)

TV taping:

Worldwide - 9/24/88 - featured an opening clip showing how John Ayers took part in the Clash of the Champions and gave Sting a disqualification victory over NWA US Champion Barry Windham; included David Crockett conducting a ringside interview with JJ Dillon in which he said Lex Luger has become the toughest challenger ever for NWA World Champion Ric Flair and Sting was becoming a threat to NWA US Champion Barry Windham, then saying Jim Cornette's team recently proved they were the better team that night in Philadelphia but then questioned whether they would stand the test of time; featured a backstage promo by Dusty Rhodes in which he noted Stan Lane & Bobby Eaton were the new NWA Tag Team Champions before turning his attention to Kevin Sullivan wanting a dog collar match with him; Rhodes then discussed Al Perez and Gary Hart were talking about his family, with Rhodes saying America was his family and he's got the support of Lugor, Ron Simmons, Steve Williams, Sting, and Nikita Koloff; included Jim Ross conducting an interview with Williams about his chasing NWA TV Champion Mike Rotundo,

with Williams saying he was happy about it being football season, then challenging Rotundo to put the title on the line in a 60-minute time-limit match; featured Magnum TA hosting a segment of Straight Talk with the Boss with Ivan Koloff as his guest, with Koloff saying he's always respected Magnum as a person and wrestler and responded to Paul Jones's comments about him; Koloff said Jones was greedy and took advantage of everyone whereas he himself has principles; Ivan then said he would fight his own fight and come after Jones and his men; included Ross conducting an interview with Flair about the challenge of Luger; featured Ross conducting a closing interview with Luger in which he said all the promoters around the country were after him and he was in the NWA because he wanted to be there and he woudl take the title from Flair.

NWA TV Champion Mike Rotundo & Rick Steiner (w/ Kevin Sullivan) defeated two unknowns at 1:26 when Rotundo scored the pin with the butterfly suplex; Steiner came to the ring in possession of the Florida Heavyweight Title; Steiner had the match won until Sullivan ordered him to tag out to Rotundo for the pinfall, with Steiner then looking dejected after the bout; moments later, David Crockett conducted a ringside interview with the Varsity Club in which Sullivan noted Stan Lane & Bobby Eaton were the new NWA Tag Team Champions, ranted on Dusty Rhodes, and said he wasn't the only one coming for Rhodes; Sullivan then said there was a movement growing against Rhodes and he would do to him what Ron Garvin couldn't, then saying he knew it was Rhodes' last run; during the segment, Sullivan physically abused Steiner

The Russian Assassins (w/ Paul Jones) defeated Curtis Thompson & an unknown at 1:08 when Thompson was pinned after sustaining a loaded headbutt; during the bout, Ricky Morton & Nikita Koloff came out to cut an insert promo on the Russian Assassins; after the match, Crockett conducted a ringside interview with Jones and his men in which Jones cut a promo on Ivan Koloff before reviewing footage of Jones & the Assassins triple teaming Koloff with his own Russian chain before Nikita made the save

Ron Simmons pinned an unknown with a shoulderblock from the middle turnbuckle at 1:30; after the match, Crockett conducted a ringside interview with Simmons in which Simmons said he had been speaking to the kids about the dangers of drugs and noted he spent 15 years of his life living in the projects

Sting & Ricky Morton vs. Agent Steel & an unknown at 2:03 when Steel submitted to Sting's Scorpion Deathlock

NWA Tag Team Champions & NWA US Tag Team Champions Bobby Eaton & Stan Lane (w/ Jim Cornette) defeated George South & John Savage at the 58-second mark when Eaton pinned South after the Double Goozle and Lane pinned Savage after a kick; Eaton & Lane came out with both sets of titles; during the contest, Tony Schiavone named past tag team championship duos and said "Ole and ... Gene Anderson" so as not to mention Arn Anderson; after the contest, Crockett conducted a ringside interview with Cornette, Eaton & Lane in which they said Horsemen vitamins, alcohol, and painted ladies don't make tag team champions; Cornette then said Tully Blanchard was an Eddie Munster look-a-like and Arn looked like Dom Delouise

Chris Champion pinned David Isley with the crane kick at 1:08 after a springboard clothesline into the ring (Champion's debut with the Karate Kid gimmick)

JCP @ Greensboro, NC - Coliseum - September 11, 1988 (2,500)
NWA TV Champion Mike Rotundo & Rick Steiner defeated Brad Armstrong & the Italian Stallion
Steve Williams pinned Rip Morgan
The Road Warriors defeated the Sheepherders
The Russian Assassins defeated Ricky Morton & Nikita Koloff via disqualification when Ivan Koloff interfered
Dusty Rhodes defeated Al Perez in a dog collar match; after the bout, Kevin Sullivan interfered and helped double team Rhodes
Sting defeated NWA US Champion Barry Windham via disqualification when the champion began choking Sting on the ropes
NWA World & US Tag Team Champions Bobby Eaton & Stan Lane defeated Bobby Fulton & Tommy Rogers when Eaton pinned Rogers
Lex Luger defeated NWA World Champion Ric Flair via disqualification when Flair threw the challenger over the top rope; former NFL player John Ayres was scheduled as the guest referee but did not appear; Luger originally won the match and title when replacement referee Teddy Long made the pinfall but initial referee Tommy Young overruled it due to Flair throwing Luger over the top earlier in the match

JCP @ Greenville, SC - Memorial Auditorium - September 12, 1988
Brad Armstrong defeated Luke Williams; the match was scheduled as Armstrong & Kendall Windham vs. the Sheepherders
Russian Assassin #1 defeated the Italian Stallion; the match was scheduled as the Russian Assassins vs. Bobby Fulton & Tommy Rogers
Ricky Morton defeated Al Perez
Nikita Koloff defeated Rip Morgan (sub. for Larry Zbyszko)
The Road Warriors & Steve Williams defeated NWA TV Champion Mike Rotundo, Rick Steiner, & Kevin Sullivan
NWA Tag Team Champions Bobby Eaton & Stan Lane defeated Bobby Fulton & Tommy Rogers (sub. for Arn Anderson & Tully Blanchard); the initial match was scheduled as No DQ
Sting defeated NWA US Champion Barry Windham via disqualification

MID-ATLANTIC CHAMPIONSHIP WRESTLING
NWA
GREENVILLE MEMORIAL AUDITORIUM
MONDAY, SEPT. 12, 1988
8:00 P.M.

U.S. TITLE MATCH
BARRY WINDHAM VS. STING

WORLD TAG TITLE
NO DISQUALIFICATION
TULLY BLANCHARD
ARN ANDERSON
VS.
THE MIDNIGHT EXPRESS WITH JIM CORNETTE

6 MAN TAG MATCH
"DR. DEATH"/ STEVE WILLIAMS
THE ROAD WARRIORS
WITH PAUL ELLERING
MIKE ROTUNDA
RIC STEINER
KEVIN SULLIVAN

GRUDGE MATCH
NIKITA KOLOFF VS. LARRY ZBYSZKO

SPECIAL EVENT
RICKY MORTON (ROCK & ROLL EXPRESS) VS. AL PEREZ WITH GARY HART

TAG ACTION
THE FANTASTICS VS. RUSSIAN ASSASINS WITH PAUL JONES

TAG ACTION
BRAD ARMSTRONG
KENDALL WINDHAM VS. THE SHEEPHERDERS WITH RIP MORGAN

NWA Subject To Change
WATCH WYFF TV 4
NWA Wrestling Sat. 11 AM-Noon
TICKET PRICES:
$12 Reserved Ringside
$10 General Adm.
$4 Children (Under 10)
N-4079-G

MID-ATLANTIC CHAMPIONSHIP WRESTLING

JCP @ Columbia, SC - Township Auditorium - September 13, 1988
TV taping:
NWA Tag Team Champions Bobby Eaton & Stan Lane defeated Bobby Fulton & Tommy Rogers

JCP @ Atlanta, GA - WTBS Studios - September 14, 1988
TV taping

JCP @ Atlanta, GA - WTBS Studios - September 15, 1988
TV taping

Worldwide - 9/17/88:
Ron Simmons & Brad Armstrong vs. Agent Steel & an unknown
The Russian Assassin vs. George South
Bobby Fulton & Tommy Rogers vs. two unknowns
NWA US Champion Barry Windham vs. an unknown
Steve Williams vs. an unknown
The Sheepherders vs. two unknowns

JCP @ Richmond, VA - Coliseum - September 16, 1988
Ivan Koloff defeated Rip Morgan
The Sheepherders defeated Chris Champion & Mark Fleming
The Russian Assassins defeated Nikita Koloff & the Italian Stallion
The Road Warriors & Steve Williams defeated NWA TV Champion Mike Rotundo, Rick Steiner, & Larry Zbyszko
NWA Tag Team Champions Bobby Eaton & Stan Lane defeated Bobby Fulton & Tommy Rogers
Dusty Rhodes defeated Kevin Sullivan in a dog collar match
Sting defeated NWA US Champion Barry Windham via disqualification
NWA World Champion Ric Flair fought Lex Luger to a no contest

JCP @ Charleston, SC - Johnson-Hagwood Stadium - September 17, 1988
The Road Warriors defeated NWA US Tag Team Champions Bobby Eaton & Stan Lane

JCP @ Roanoke, VA - Civic Center - September 18, 1988 (3,200)
Larry Zbyszko pinned Curtis Thompson
The Sheepherders defeated Chris Champion & Mark Fleming
The Russian Assassins defeated Nikita Koloff & the Italian Stallion when the Stallion was pinned
The Road Warriors defeated NWA TV Champion Mike Rotunda & Rick Steiner; after the bout, Steiner and Rotunda argued over the loss
Sting defeated NWA US Champion Barry Windham via disqualification
Lex Luger defeated NWA World Champion Ric Flair via disqualification

NWA US Tag Team Champions Bobby Eaton & Stan Lane defeated Bobby Fulton & Tommy Rogers

- 9/20/88: Nikita Koloff and Mandy Smithson were married.

JCP @ Atlanta, GA - WTBS Studios - September 21, 1988
World Championship Wrestling - 9/24/88:
The Road Warriors defeated the Menace #1 & #2
NWA US Champion Barry Windham defeated Agent Steele
Sting defeated Jerry Price
NWA Tag Team Champions Bobby Eaton & Stan Lane defeated Curtis Thompson & Cruel Connection #1
Bobby Fulton & Tommy Rogers defeated Mike Justice & Griffin
Nikita Koloff defeated Eddie Sweat
Steve Williams & Brad Armstrong defeated Keith Steinborn & Jones
Kevin Sullivan, NWA TV Champion Mike Rotunda, & Rick Steiner defeated Bill Mulkey, Gary Royal, & Hallis
Al Perez defeated Max Mcgyver
Russian Assassin #1 & #2 defeated the Italian Stallion & Miles

N.W.A. WRESTLING
"The Major League of Professional Wrestling"
FRIDAY, SEPT. 23   8:00 p.m. (Doors Open at 7:00)
FREDERICK COMMUNITY COLLEGE FIELDHOUSE

SPECIAL TAG TEAM CHALLENGE
STING & LEX LUGER
VS
RICK FLAIR & BARRY WINDHAM
"WORLD TAG TEAM TITLE MATCH"
TULLY BLANCHARD & ARN ANDERSON
With J.J. Dillon
VS
THE MIDNIGHT EXPRESS
With Jim Cornette
"WORLD TV TITLE MATCH"
MIKE ROTUNDO w/Kevin Sullivan
VS.
STEVE "DR. DEALTH" WILLIAMS
PLUS FOUR OTHER EXCITING MATCHES
SHEEPHERDERS   VS.   THE FANTASTICS
NIKITA KOLOFF   VS RUSSIAN ASSASSIN I
RICKY MORTON   VS.   AL PEREZ W/GARY HART
BRAD ARMSTON   VS RUSSIAN ASSASSIN II
TICKET INFORMATION
Ringside $15   General Information $9
AVAILABLE IN FREDERICK
Varsity Shop Sporting Goods - FSK Mall   662-6632
B&B Video - Amber Meadows   662-6627
B&B Video - West Pointe Rt 40   695-7747
Note: Tickets are not available thru the Community College so don't call.

JCP @ Frederick, MD - Community College Fieldhouse - September 23, 1988
Brad Armstrong vs. Russian Assassin #2
Ricky Morton vs. Al Perez
Nikita Koloff vs. Russian Assassin #1
The Sheepherders vs. Bobby Fulton & Tommy Rogers
Steve Williams vs. NWA TV Champion Mike Rotundo
NWA US Tag Team Champions Bobby Eaton & Stan Lane vs.

NWA Tag Team Champions Arn Anderson & Tully Blanchard
Sting & Lex Luger vs. NWA World Champion Ric Flair & NWA
US Champion Barry Windham

JCP @ Washington DC - Armory - September 24, 1988
Al Perez defeated the Italian Stallion
The Russian Assassins defeated the Sheepherders
NWA TV Champion Mike Rotundo fought Steve Williams to a
draw
Sting fought NWA US Champion Barry Windham to a double
count-out
Dusty Rhodes defeated Kevin Sullivan
NWA Tag Team Champions Bobby Eaton & Stan Lane
defeated Tommy Rogers & Bobby Fulton
Lex Luger defeated NWA World Champion Ric Flair via
disqualification

JCP @ Atlanta, GA - Omni - September 25, 1988 (6,700)
Luke Williams (w/ Butch Miller & Rip Morgan) pinned Curtis
Thompson
Dick Murdoch pinned Larry Zbyszko at the 12-minute mark
Mike Rotunda, Rick Steiner, & Al Perez defeated Steve
Williams, Nikita Koloff, & the Italian Stallion at 15:29 when
Steiner pinned Stallion
Russian Assassin #2 (Jack Victory) pinned Ivan Koloff at 8:50
when the other Russian Assassin switched places and
headbutted Koloff with a loaded mask; after the bout, Nikita
Koloff made the save for Ivan
The Midnight Express defeated the Fantastics when Stan Lane
pinned Tommy Rogers
Dusty Rhodes pinned Kevin Sullivan at 8:15 in a collar match
after ramming his head into a chair
Sting defeated NWA US Champion Barry Windham via
disqualification at 10:30
Lex Luger defeated NWA World Champion Ric Flair via
disqualification at the 19-minute mark when JJ Dillon interfered

JCP @ Greenville, SC - Municipal Auditorium - September
26, 1988
Gary Royal defeated Agent Steele
Russian Assassin #2 defeated Curtis Thompson
Russian Assassin #1 defeated George South
Bobby Fulton & Tommy Rogers defeated Rick Steiner & Larry
Zbyszko
The Italian Stallion (sub. for Brad Armstrong) defeated NWA
TV Champion Mike Rotundo
Al Perez defeated Ron Simmons
Steve Williams & Dick Murdoch defeated NWA Tag Team
Champions Bobby Eaton & Stan Lane
NWA US Champion Barry Windham defeated Sting

MID-ATLANTIC CHAMPIONSHIP WRESTLING

GREENVILLE MEMORIAL AUDITORIUM
Monday September 26, 1988
8:00 P.M.

U.S. TITLE 1 FALL/1 HOUR TIME LIMIT
BARRY WINDHAM VS STING

WORLD TITLE TAG MATCH
DICK MURDOCH "DR. DEATH"/ STEVE WILLIAMS VS. MIDNIGHT EXPRESS WITH JIM CORNETTE

SPECIAL GRUDGE MATCH
RON SIMMONS VS AL PEREZ WITH GARY HART

WORLD T.V. TITLE - 1 FALL 30 MINUTES
MIKE ROTUNDA WITH KEVIN SULLIVAN VS BRAD ARMSTRONG

TAG ACTION
THE FANTASTICS VS LARRY ZBYSZKO RIC STEINER
ITALION STALLION VS RUSSIAN ASSASSIAN #1 WITH PAUL JONES
VS
CURTIS THOMPSON VS RUSSIAN ASSASSIAN #2
AGENT STEELE VS GARY ROYAL

TICKET PRICES:
$12 Reserved Ringside
$10 General Adm.
$4 Children (Under 10)

MID-ATLANTIC CHAMPIONSHIP WRESTLING

JCP @ Columbus, GA - Municipal Auditorium - September 27, 1988
TV taping:
NWA Tag Team Champions Bobby Eaton & Dennis Condrey defeated Bobby Fulton & Tommy Rogers

JCP @ Atlanta, GA - WTBS Studios - September 28, 1988
World Championship Wrestling - 10/1/88:
Ron Simmons vs. Eddie Sweat
Ivan Koloff vs. Agent Steele
Rick Steiner vs. the Italian Stallion
Bam Bam Bigelow vs. Trent Knight
Bobby Fulton & Tommy Rogers vs. the Menace & Nightmare
NWA US Champion Barry Windham vs. George South
Steve Williams vs. Joe Cruz
Sting vs. Terry Jones
NWA Tag Team Champions Bobby Eaton & Stan Lane vs. Gary Royal & Price
Dick Murdoch vs. JC Wilde
Larry Zbyzsko & Al Perez vs. Mike Jackson & Keith Steinborn

JCP @ Hammond, IN - Civic Center - September 29, 1988

JCP @ Winnipeg, Manitoba - Arena - September 30, 1988 (4,000)
Rip Morgan defeated the Masked Invader
Bobby Fulton & Tommy Rogers defeated Rick Steiner & Larry Zbyzsko
Nikita & Ivan Koloff defeated the Russian Assasins via disqualification
NWA TV Champion Mike Rotundo defeated the Italian Stallion
Sting fought NWA US Champion Barry Windham to a no contest
Bobby Eaton & Stan Lane defeated the Sheepherders
Lex Luger defeated NWA World Champion Ric Flair via disqualification

Worldwide - 10/1/88:
NWA Tag Team Champions Bobby Eaton & Stan Lane vs. Agent Steel & KC Wild
Sting vs. an unknown
Steve Williams & Brad Armstrong vs. two unknowns
The Road Warriors vs. two unknowns
The Sheepherders vs. two unknowns
Al Perez, NWA TV Champion Mike Rotundo, & Rick Steiner vs. the Italian Stallion, Randy Mulkey, & an unknown
The Russian Assassin vs. an unknown

JCP @ Brandon, Manitoba - October 1, 1988 (1,000)
Rick Steiner pinned Larry Zbyzsko
The Sheepherders defeated Ron Ritchie & Bill Cody
NWA TV Champion Mike Rotunda defeated the Italian Stallion
Ivan Koloff pinned Russian Assassin #2
Nikita Koloff defeated Russian Assassin #1 via disqualification
Bobby Eaton & Stan Lane defeated the Fantastics

Sting & Lex Luger defeated NWA World Champion Ric Flair & NWA US Champion Barry Windham via disqualification

JCP @ Chicago, IL - UIC Pavilion - October 2, 1988
Ron Simmons defeated Rip Morgan
NWA TV Champion Mike Rotunda defeated the Italian Stallion
Bobby Eaton & Stan Lane fought Dick Murdoch & Dusty Rhodes to a draw
Bobby Fulton & Tommy Rogers defeated the Sheepherders
The Russian Assassins defeated Ivan & Nikita Koloff via disqualification
Sting defeated NWA US Champion Barry Windham via disqualification
NWA World Champion Ric Flair fought Lex Luger to a draw

JCP @ Atlanta, GA - WTBS Studios - October 1988
World Championship Wrestling - 10/8/88 - featured the Bam Bam Bigelow vs. David Isley match from NWA Worldwide:
The Road Warriors vs. Allen & Jones
Ron Simmons vs. the Menace
Bobby Fulton & Tommy Rogers vs. Keith Steinborn & Price
Dick Murdoch vs. Cruel Connection #1
Russian Assassin #1 vs. Brett Holiday
The Sheepherders vs. Justice & Wilde
Rick Steiner vs. Curtis Thompson
NWA Tag Team Champions Bobby Eaton & Stan Lane vs. Agent Steele & Mike Jackson
NWA US Champion Barry Windham vs. Gary Royal
Nikita Koloff vs. the Blue Demon
Larry Zbyzsko vs. Eddie Sweat

JCP @ Macon, GA - Coliseum - October 4, 1988 (2,900)
TV taping:
NWA US Champion Barry Windham pinned Dick Murdoch at 15:40
Lex Luger defeated NWA World Champion Ric Flair via disqualification at 15:02

JCP @ Raleigh, NC - October 6, 1988 (700)
The Italian Stallion defeated Rip Morgan
Bobby Fulton pinned Luke Williams; the bout was to have been the Fantastics vs. the Sheepherders but Tommy Rogers no-showed; after the bout, Fulton did a stretcher job for the Sheepherders
NWA TV Champion Mike Rotunda pinned Ron Simmons
The Road Warriors defeated Al Perez & Larry Zbyzsko
Bobby Eaton & Stan Lane defeated Kevin Sullivan & Rick Steiner when Sullivan was pinned
Nikita Koloff fought Russian Assassin #1 to a double disqualification
Lex Luger & Sting defeated NWA World Champion Ric Flair & NWA US Champion Barry Windham in a lumberjack match when Sting pinned Flair

JCP @ Richmond, VA - Coliseum - October 7, 1988
TV taping:
NWA Pro: NWA Six-Man Tag Team Champions Sting (sub. for Dusty Rhodes) & the Road Warriors (w/ Paul Ellering) defeated Kevin Sullivan, NWA TV Champion Mike Rotundo, & Rick Steiner via disqualification when, as Sting set Rotunda up for the Scorpion Deathlock, the Road Warriors attacked their partner, double teamed him, and hit the Doomsday Device; moments later, Lex Luger came out and was also double teamed; several wrestlers, including Nikita Koloff, then tended to Sting and Luger as the Road Warriors left ringside; Steiner then helped in bringing a stretcher into the ring for Sting; after the bout, Tony Schiavone conducted a backstage interview with Ellering & the Road Warriors in which they said they were threw carrying guys like Sting and Rhodes and that all they needed was each other; Ellering then blamed Rhodes for not appearing as scheduled, instead appearing at a charity, and Sting's injury came as a result of that
Larry Zbyzsko defeated the Italian Stallion
The Russian Assassins defeated Ivan & Nikita Koloff via disqualification
NWA World Champion Ric Flair & NWA US Champion Barry Windham defeated Lex Luger & Ron Simmons (sub. for an injured Sting) when Flair pinned Simmons with the figure-4

Worldwide - 10/8/88 - included Tony Schiavone & David Crockett on commentary; featured NWA US Champion Barry Windham, with JJ Dillon, as a guest of Straight Shooting with the Boss in which Magnum TA noted Sting was the #1 contender to Windham's title but then questioned why Dusty Rhodes had only received one shot at the title; Magnum then said the only reason Windham beat Rhodes at the Great American Bash was because of the interference of a man who isn't in the NWA anymore; Windham then proposed Sting wrestle Rhodes to determine whether or not Rhodes could get a title shot; Windham then said he would never put the title up again against Rhodes; included Ross conducting an interview with NWA World Champion Ric Flair in which Flair complained about Sting interfering in his matches, then noting Sting already had his title shot; Flair said Sting siding with Lex Luger has made him a target and added all the big stars were in the NWA because they were all after his belt; Flair continued by saying he always got along with Sir Oliver Humperdink but Humperdink bringing Bam Bam Bigelow in made him a target, then noted Ron Simmons and Steve Williams as other potential challengers:
Bobby Fulton & Tommy Rogers fought the Sheepherders (w/ Rip Morgan) to a double disqualification after both teams shoved referee Tommy Young to the mat, Rogers used the Sheepherders' flag pole as a weapon, and Morgan interfered; during the bout, an insert promo aired from Jim Cornette, NWA Tag Team Champions Bobby Eaton & Stan Lane in which Cornette said the Sheepherders and Fantastics were battling to see who would challenge them, then adding it didn't matter whether it was the Road Warriors or Varsity Club, they would take on any team; after the match, both teams fought into the crowd before Rogers and a bloody Fulton returned to the ring
Steve Williams & Ron Simmons defeated Agent Steel & Larry

Stephens at 2:35 when Simmons pinned Stephens with a shoulderblock off the middle turnbuckle; during the bout, Kevin Sullivan & NWA TV Champion Mike Rotunda appeared ringside to watch the match; after the contest, David Crockett conducted a ringside interview with Williams & Simmons in which they told kids not to do drugs
Rick Steiner (w/ Kevin Sullivan & NWA TV Champion Mike Rotunda) pinned Bob Riddle with the belly to belly suplex at the 40-second mark; after the match, Crockett conducted a ringside interview with the Varsity Club in which Steiner gave Sullivan a Michigan sweater, with Sullivan then taking a Syracuse sweater from Rotunda, praising him as the greatest TV champion of all time, and then walking off, leaving Steiner behind
Bam Bam Bigelow (w/ Sir Oliver Humperdink) pinned David Isley with the face-first suplex at 3:04; after the bout, Crockett conducted a ringside interview with Humperdink & Bigelow in which Humperdink said he was happy to be back where he started in the NWA and said Bigelow was after anyone who has a belt, including NWA World Champion Ric Flair and NWA US Champion Barry Windham; Humperdink then said he had a partner for Bigelow and when he revealed who it was, Jim Cornette would be without the NWA Tag Team Titles
Ivan & Nikita Koloff defeated two unknowns at 2:33 when Ivan scored the pin with a clothesline from the middle turnbuckle; during the bout, an insert promo aired from Paul Jones & the Russian Assassins in which Jones commented about the Koloffs and said he would end them both; moments later, the commentary team alluded to a legend coming to the NWA and JJ Dillon perhaps making the Four Horsemen whole again soon

JCP @ Charlotte, NC - Coliseum - October 8, 1988

The Main Event - 10/9/88:
Kevin Sullivan vs. Big Bear Colley
Sting & Steve Williams vs. NWA TV Champion Mike Rotunda & Rick Steiner
Nikita Koloff vs. Al Perez

JCP @ Greensboro, NC - Coliseum - October 9, 1988 (4,000)
The Sheepherders defeated Chris Champion & the Italian Stallion
Rip Morgan pinned Curtis Thompson
The Fantastics defeated Rick Steiner & Kevin Sullivan
The Road Warriors defeated Al Perez & Larry Zbyzsko at the 5-minute mark
NWA TV Champion Mike Rotunda pinned Ron Simmons
Sting fought NWA US Champion Barry Windham to a double count-out at the 5-minute mark
The Russian Assassins defeated Ivan & Nikita Koloff when Jack Victory pinned Nikita after hitting him with a loaded mask headbutt
Lex Luger defeated NWA World Champion Ric Flair via

disqualification at the 20-minute mark when Barry Windham and JJ Dillon interfered

JCP @ Greenville, SC - Municipal Auditorium - October 10, 1988
Ron Simmons defeated Rip Morgan
The Sheepherders defeated Gary Royal & Chris Champion
Rick Steiner defeated Agent Steele
Dick Murdoch defeated Kevin Sullivan
Bobby Fulton & Tommy Rogers defeated Al Perez & Larry Zbyszko
NWA TV Champion Mike Rotundo defeated the Italian Stallion
The Russian Assassins defeated Ivan & Nikita Koloff
NWA Tag Team Champions Bobby Eaton & Stan Lane defeated the Road Warriors via disqualification

JCP @ Fayetteville, NC - October 11, 1988 (300)
The Road Warriors vs. NWA Tag Team Champions Bobby Eaton & Stan Lane

JCP @ Sumter, SC - Exhibition Center - October 13, 1988
TV taping:
NWA Tag Team Champions Bobby Eaton & Stan Lane defeated the Road Warriors via disqualification

JCP @ Norfolk, VA - Scope - October 14, 1988
NWA Tag Team Champions Bobby Eaton & Stan Lane defeated the Road Warriors via disqualification

JCP @ Charleston, SC - October 1988
The Sheepherders defeated the Italian Stallion & Curtis Thompson
Steve Williams pinned Rip Morgan
Nikita Koloff pinned Russian Assassin #1 with the Russian Sickle; after the bout, Russian Assassin #2 helped double team Koloff until Ivan Koloff made the save
Bobby Fulton & Tommy Rogers defeated the Varsity Club
The Road Warriors defeated Bobby Eaton & Stan Lane
Lex Luger & Sting defeated NWA World Champion Ric Flair & NWA US Champion Barry Windham via disqualification

JCP @ Philadelphia, PA - Civic Center - October 15, 1988 (4,418)
Lex Luger had the night off and Ric Flair was attending his 20 year high school reunion in Minnesota
Larry Zbyszko pinned the Italian Stallion at the 8-minute mark
Al Perez fought Ron Simmons to a 15-minute draw
The Road Warriors defeated Rick Steiner & Mike Rotunda via count-out when Steiner and Rotunda began arguing with one another
Kevin Sullivan pinned Eddie Gilbert after hitting him with a foreign object
Russian Assassin #1 & #2 defeated Ivan & Nikita Koloff when Nikita was pinned after sustaining a loaded mask headbutt
NWA US Champion Barry Windham defeated Sting via count-out after dropping the challenger throat-first across the guard rail; Sting wore a neckbrace for the duration of the bout
NWA Tag Team Champions Bobby Eaton & Stan Lane

defeated Tommy Rogers & Bobby Fulton
JJ Dillon pinned Jim Cornette in a steel cage match at 9:08 with a kick to the groin and forearm to the face, with an exhausted and bloody Dillon then collapsing ontop of Cornette; prior to the bout, the two exchanged words on the mic (*Wrestling Rarities: The Midnight Express*)

Worldwide - 10/15/88 - featured an opening clip of the Sheepherders vs. Bobby Fulton & Tommy Rogers; included Tony Schiavone & David Crockett on commentary; featured Jim Ross conducting an interview with Sir Oliver Humperdink regarding his bringing Bam Bam Bigelow into the NWA, then introducing the pretaped Bigelow vs. South match; after the match aired, Humperdink said his goal was to have gold for Bigelow and his mystery partner, specifically noting NWA World Champion Ric Flair and NWA US Champion Barry Windham; included Ross conducting an interview with NWA Six-Man Tag Team Champions Dusty Rhodes & the Road Warriors, alongside Paul Ellering, during which Road Warrior Animal said he and Road Warrior Hawk were the #1 contenders for the NWA Tag Team Titles and would soon have all the belts; featured a segment of Straight Talk with the Boss hosted by Magnum TA in which he discussed the recent attack Jimmy Garvin sustained at the hands of the Varsity Club; Magnum then said Garvin was on the mend and was on his way back, then introducing Al Perez and NWA Western States Heritage Champion Larry Zbyszko who discussed the NWA US Tag Team Title Tournament, also naming such teams as the Road Warriors, Sheepherders, Fulton & Rogers, Rhodes & Dick Murdoch, and NWA Tag Team Champions Bobby Eaton & Stan Lane; Magnum then said he would have Lex Luger as his guest the following week; included Ross conducting an interview with Luger about his chasing NWA World Champion Ric Flair, during which Flair and NWA US Champion Barry Windham had yet to cleanly beat he or Sting:
Bobby Fulton & Tommy Rogers defeated Mike Jackson & Keith Steinborn at 3:48 when Fulton pinned Steinborn with a splash; after the contest, David Crockett conducted a ringside interview with Fulton & Rogers regarding their participation in the upcoming NWA US Tag Team Title tournament and their feud with the Sheepherders, then showing footage of how the two teams recently brawled, using the Sheepherders' flagpole as a weapon, and fought to a double disqualification
Bam Bam Bigelow (w/ Sir Oliver Humperdink) pinned George South at 2:13 with the front suplex; Jim Ross was the ring announcer for the bout; Ross & Bob Caudle provided commentary for the match
The Sheepherders (w/ Rip Morgan) defeated two unknowns at 2:42 when Luke scored the pin after the double gutbuster
Ron Simmons pinned Bob Riddle with a spinebuster at the 59-second mark
NWA World Champion Ric Flair & NWA US Champion Barry Windham (w/ JJ Dillon) defeated Agent Steel & an unknown at 3:44 when Windham pinned Steel with a lariat; during the bout, Jim Cornette, NWA Tag Team Champions Bobby Eaton & Stan Lane cut an insert promo in which Cornette ranted about Flair & Windham and said the Road Warriors would never hold the belts, then noting the guys they beat to win the belts "would

rather switch than fight;" after the match, Crockett conducted a ringside interview with Dillon, Flair, & Windham about the comments of Cornette, Sting challenging Windham, Bam Bam Bigelow & Sir Oliver Humperdink; Flair then said he needed a "fat boy" to clean up the backyard at his new 12,000 sq. foot house, referring to Bigelow, before cutting a promo on Lex Luger; moments later, Flair pulled a young woman out of the crowd and carried her around while laughing and celebrating
The Russian Assassins defeated Tony Suber & Bob Emory at 2:20 when one Assassin pinned Emory after the other landed a loaded headbutt; after the match, Suber was thrown to the floor before the Assassins cut an in-ring promo challenging Nikita & Ivan Koloff; moments later, the Koloffs ran out and brawled with the Assassins as the show ended

JCP @ Atlanta, GA - WTBS Studios - October 1988
World Championship Wrestling - 10/15/88:
Larry Zbyszko & Al Perez vs. David Isley & Mike Justice
Bam Bam Bigelow vs. George South
Nikita Koloff vs. Russian Assassin #2
Ron Simmons vs. John Savage
Eddie Gilbert vs. Trent Knight
The Sheepherders vs. Thompson & Tommy Angel
The Varsity Club vs. Gene Ligon & Joe Cruz
Kevin Sullivan vs. Bob Emory
Dick Murdoch vs. Agent Steele
NWA Tag Team Champions Bobby Eaton & Stan Lane vs. George South & Gary Royal

JCP @ Baltimore, MD - Arena - October 16, 1988 (6,000)
Larry Zbyszko fought Eddie Gilbert to a draw
The Fantastics defeated Kevin Sullivan & Rick Steiner via reverse decision when Sullivan scored the pin after using a foreign object but Steiner told the referee what happened
Bobby Eaton & Stan Lane defeated the Road Warriors via disqualification
NWA US Champion Barry Windham defeated Sting via count-out
The Russian Assassins defeated Ivan & Nikita Koloff
Al Perez pinned Ron Simmons
NWA TV Champion Mike Rotunda pinned the Italian Stallion
Rick Steiner (sub. for Lex Luger who had conjunctivitis) defeated NWA World Champion Ric Flair via disqualification when NWA US Champion Barry Windham interfered

Worldwide - 10/22/88:
Sting & the Road Warriors vs. NWA TV Champion Mike Rotundo, Kevin Sullivan, & Rick Steiner
The Russian Assassins vs. two unknowns
Larry Zbyszko & Al Perez vs. Agent Steel & David Isley
Eddie Gilbert vs. an unknown
Ron Simmons vs. an unknown
NWA Tag Team Champions Bobby Eaton & Stan Lane vs. two unknowns
NWA TV Champion Mike Rotundo & Kevin Sullivan vs. two unknowns

JCP @ Atlanta, GA - WTBS Studios - October 1988
World Championship Wrestling - 10/22/88 - featured footage from NWA Pro of Sting & the Road Warriors vs. the Varsity Club in which the Road Warriors attacked Sting:
Ron Simmons vs. Keith Steinborn
Russian Assassin #1 & #2 vs. Price & Allen
NWA Tag Team Champions Bobby Eaton & Stan Lane vs. Jackson & Jones
Dick Murdoch vs. Larry Stevens
Ivan & Nikita Koloff vs. Menace #1 & #2
Larry Zbyzsko vs. Tony Suber
Eddie Gilbert vs. Gary Royal
NWA TV Champion Mike Rotundo vs. Eddie Sweat

JCP @ Lansing, MI - October 19, 1988
The Main Event - 11/6/88 - featured Jim Ross & Tony Schiavone on commentary; included Schiavone as the ring announcer:
Road Warrior Animal & Paul Ellering (sub. for Road Warrior Hawk) defeated NWA Tag Team Champions Bobby Eaton & Stan Lane (w/ Jim Cornette) via disqualification at 3:39 after Lane accidentally hit Eaton with Cornette's tennis racquet after Animal moved out of the way
Brad Armstrong defeated Al Perez (w/ Gary Hart) via disqualification at 10:47 when Kevin Sullivan came ringside, with Sullivan and Perez then double teaming Armstrong

JCP @ Saginaw, MI - October 20, 1988
TV taping:
Sting (sub. for Lex Luger who had conjunctivitis) defeated NWA World Champion Ric Flair via disqualification
Worldwide - 11/5/88:
Bobby Eaton & Stan Lane vs. Mike Jackson & Bruce
NWA US Tag Team Championship Tournament Quarter-Finals: Eddie Gilbert & Ron Simmons defeated Larry Zbyzsko & Al Perez after Zbyzsko accidentally hit Perez with nunchucks
The Sheepherders vs. two unknowns
Ivan Koloff vs. an unknown
Worldwide - 11/12/88:
The Sheepherders vs. two unknowns
NWA US Tag Team Championship Tournament Quarter-Finals: The Russian Assassins fought Ivan & Nikita Koloff to a double disqualification
Eddie Gilbert vs. an unknown
Larry Zbyzsko vs. an unknown
Kevin Sullivan & Rick Steiner vs. Randy Hogan & an unknown

JCP @ Detroit, MI - Coboa Arena - October 21, 1988 (1,300)
The Sheepherders defeated Ron Simmons & Tony Zon at 9:45
Bobby Fulton & Tommy Rogers defeated Larry Zbyzsko & Rip Morgan
NWA TV Champion Mike Rotunda pinned the Italian Stallion with a butterfly suplex
Eddie Gilbert defeated Kevin Sullivan via reverse decision; Sullivan orginally won the match at 3:32 after hitting Gilbert with a weapon but Rick Steiner came out and showed the

referee the foreign object, with the referee then changing the call
NWA Tag Team Champions Bobby Eaton & Stan Lane defeated the Road Warriors via disqualification at 6:30 after Paul Ellering interfered using Jim Cornette's tennis racquet
Ivan & Nikita Koloff defeated the Russian Assassins when Ivan pinned Jack Victory
Sting (sub. for Lex Luger who had conjunctivitis) defeated NWA World Champion Ric Flair via disqualification at 21:05 when JJ Dillon hit referee Tommy Young to prevent Flair from losing the title

JCP @ Cincinnati, OH - October 22, 1988 (1,800)
NWA Tag Team Champions Bobby Eaton & Stan Lane defeated the Road Warriors via disqualification
NWA World Champion Ric Flair & NWA US Champion Barry Windham defeated Sting & Ron Simmons (sub. for Lex Luger who had conjunctivitis)

JCP @ Charleston, WV - Civic Center - October 23, 1988
NWA Tag Team Champions Bobby Eaton & Stan Lane defeated the Road Warriors via disqualification

JCP @ Little Rock, AR - October 24, 1988
NWA Tag Team Champions Bobby Eaton & Stan Lane defeated the Road Warriors via disqualification

JCP @ Jackson, TN - October 25, 1988
NWA Tag Team Champions Bobby Eaton & Stan Lane defeated the Road Warriors via disqualification

JCP @ Greenwood, MS - October 26, 1988
NWA Tag Team Champions Bobby Eaton & Stan Lane defeated the Road Warriors via disqualification

JCP @ Atlanta, GA - WTBS Studios - October 1988
World Championship Wrestling - 10/29/88:
NWA Tag Team Champions Bobby Eaton & Stan Lane vs. Mike Justice & David Isley
Eddie Gilbert vs. Tommy Angel
NWA US Champion Barry Windham vs. Bob Riddle
Bobby Fulton & Tommy Rogers vs. Price & Jackson
Varsity Club vs. Brad & Brett Holiday
Larry Zbyzsko & Al Perez vs. Sweat & Allen
Ivan Koloff vs. the Executioner
The Itallian Stallion vs. Gary Royal
Russian Assassin #1 & #2 vs. Bob Emory & Keith Steinborn
The Sheepherders vs. Hollis & Jones
Ron Simmons vs. George South

JCP @ Jackson, MS - October 27, 1988
Eddie Gilbert pinned Larry Zbyzsko with the Hot Shot
Ron Simmons, Bobby Fulton & Tommy Rogers defeated Rip Morgan & the Sheepherders

NWA TV Champion Mike Rotunda pinned the Italian Stallion
Ivan Koloff defaeted Russian Assassin #2 via disqualification
Dick Murdoch defeated NWA US Champion Barry Windham
via disqualification
Dusty Rhodes pinned Kevin Sullivan
Lex Luger & Nikita Koloff defeated NWA World Champion Ric
Flair & Al Perez
NWA Tag Team Champions Bobby Eaton & Stan Lane
defeated the Road Warriors via disqualification

JCP @ Baton Rouge, LA - October 28, 1988
NWA Tag Team Champions Bobby Eaton & Stan Lane
defeated the Road Warriors via disqualification

Worldwide - 10/29/88:
The Russian Assassins vs. Agent Steel & an unknown
Larry Zbyszko & Al Perez vs. two unknowns
Eddie Gilbert vs. an unknown
Ron Simmons vs. Bob Riddle
NWA Tag Team Champions Bobby Eaton & Stan Lane vs.
Curtis Thompson & an unknown
NWA TV Champion Mike Rotundo & Kevin Sullivan vs. an
unknown

JCP @ New Orleans, LA - Municipal Auditorium - October 29, 1988
Kevin Sullivan defeated Dusty Rhodes via disqualification
Steve Williams defeated Larry Zbyszko
Worldwide - 11/19/88: The Road Warriors (w/ Paul Ellering)
defeated NWA Tag Team Champions Bobby Eaton & Stan
Lane (w/ Jim Cornette) to win the titles at around the 4:30 mark
when Road Warrior Animal pinned Bobby Eaton with a
clothesline, immediately after Animal was sent into the corner;
prior to the bout, Ellering attacked Cornette on the floor while
Eaton was double teamed and had his head busted open on
the outside of the ring (*The Life & Death of the Road Warriors*)
Lex Luger defeated NWA World Champion Ric Flair via
disqualification

JCP @ Alexandria, LA - October 30, 1988 (2,792)
Ron Simmons, Bobby Fulton & Tommy Rogers defeated Rip
Morgan & the Sheepherders
Ivan Koloff defeated Russian Assassin #2
NWA TV Champion Mike Rotunda defeated the Italian Stallion
Eddie Gilbert defeated Russian Assassin #1 via disqualification
Sting fought NWA US Champion Barry Windham to a no
contest
Lex Luger & Nikita Koloff defeated NWA World Champion Ric
Flair & Al Perez
NWA Tag Team Champions the Road Warriors defeated
Bobby Eaton & Stan Lane

JCP @ Savannah, GA - Civic Center - November 1, 1988
TV taping:
The Sheepherders defeated Eddie Gilbert & Ron Simmons

Dark match after the taping: NWA Tag Team Champions the
Road Warriors defeated Bobby Eaton & Stan Lane

**- 11/2/88: Jim Crockett Promotions was officially sold to
Ted Turner.**

NWA @ Atlanta, GA - WTBS Studios - November 2, 1988
*World Championship Wrestling - 11/5/88 - included Jim Ross &
Tony Schiavone on commentary; featured the Road Warriors
vs. NWA Tag Team Champions Bobby Eaton & Stan Lane
match taped 10/29/88 in New Orleans; included David Crockett
conducting a ringside interview with NWA Tag Team
Champions the Road Warriors & Paul Ellering regarding their
title win, during which they said they were tired of carrying the
likes of Dusty Rhodes, Lex Luger, and Sting and Ellering said
they were never friends with those men, they just used them to
make money; featured an ad promoting "The Best of
Starrcade: 1983-1987" home video; included a graphic stating
Clash of the Champions IV would take place Dec. 7; featured
Crockett conducting an interview with NWA World Champion
Ric Flair & JJ Dillon in which Flair made reference to several
Turner employees in the audience, responded to the
comments made earlier in the show by Bam Bam Bigelow &
Sir Oliver Humperdink*:
Ron Simmons pinned Rip Morgan with a spinebuster at 11:27;
after the bout, the Sheepherders came out and helped triple
team Simmons, throwing down referee Teddy Long in the
melee; moments later, Eddie Gilbert came out and helped
Simmons clear the ring; David Crockett then conducted a
ringside interview with Simmons & Gilbert regarding the attack;
it was noted during the segment that both Simmons & Gilbert
and the Sheepherders would be part of the upcoming NWA US
Tag Team Title tournament
Russian Assassin #1 & #2 (w/ Paul Jones) defeated Brett
Holiday & Terry Jones at 4:42 when Holiday was pinned after
sustaining a loaded headbutt; during the match, it was noted
the Assassins along with Nikita & Ivan Koloff would be part of
the upcoming NWA US Tag Team Title tournament
Bam Bam Bigelow (w/ Sir Oliver Humperdink) pinned Trent
Knight with a gordbuster at 3:54; after the bout, David Crockett
conducted an interview with Bigelow & Humperdink in which
they targetted NWA World Champion Ric Flair and NWA US
Champion Barry Windham; moments later, Humperdink said
Bigelow would be soon teaming with Dusty Rhodes
Bobby Fulton & Tommy Rogers defeated George South &
Gary Royal at 3:00 when Fulton pinned South following a
double team move off the top; prior to the bout, Fulton &
Rogers came out with the American flag; after the bout,
Crockett conducted a ringside interview with Fulton & Rogers
regarding their feud with the Sheepherders and being part of
the NWA US Tag Team Title tournament
Lex Luger defeated Agent Steele via submission with the
Torture Rack at 1:56; after the bout, Crockett conducted a
ringside interview with Luger regarding he and Sting soon
facing NWA Tag Team Champions the Road Warriors
Stan Lane (w/ Jim Cornette & Bobby Eaton) fought Menace #2
to a no contest at around the 2:30 mark; prior to the match,

Crockett conducted an interview with Cornette, Eaton, & Lane regarding their loss of the tag team titles, during which Cornette said it was their fault they loss because they trusted the Road Warriors a little too much and said his men had more guts than the Road Warriors put together; Cornette then challenged them to a rematch and said Lane would be in singles action because Eaton was still recovering from the injury he sustained in New Orleans; Cornette joined the commentary team for the match until Tony Schiavone was told that an important phone call came in for Cornette; Cornette then took the call and challenged whomever was on the other line to show up with his "two geeks" whenever he wanted; moments later, Dennis Condrey & Randy Rose jumped Eaton & Lane, with Cornette then sliding in the ring to make the save but he was jumped by Paul E. Dangerously and hit in the head with his phone; Lane was triple teamed in the ring before a bloody Cornette was dragged into the ring and slapped by Dangerously (Dangerously's surprise debut; Rose's surprise debut; Condrey's surprise return after an 18-month absence)
Eddie Gilbert pinned Mike Jackson with the Hot Shot at 4:21; during the match, it was noted Jim Cornette was receiving medical treatment backstage and that NWA World Champion Ric Flair would be in action the following week
Abdullah the Butcher (w/ Gary Hart) pinned David Isley at 2:26 with an elbow drop; after the bout, David Crockett conducted a ringside interview with Hart, as Abdullah chewed on the bottom rope behind them (Abdullah's debut)
NWA TV Champion Mike Rotundo vs. Bob Emory
The Sheepherders vs. Price & Allen

NWA @ Atlanta, GA - WTBS Studios - November 3, 1988

NWA @ Louisville, KY - November 4, 1988
Stan Lane fought Tommy Rogers to a 20-minute time-limit draw

NWA @ Dayton, OH - UD Arena - November 5, 1988
Bobby Fulton defeated Stan Lane

NWA @ Roanoke, VA - Civic Center - November 6, 1988 (matinee)
Rick Steiner pinned Larry Zbyszko
Bobby Fulton & Tommy Rogers defeated the Sheepherders
Russian Assassin #1 & #2 defeated Ivan & Nikita Koloff
Bam Bam Bigelow defeated NWA US Champion Barry Windham via disqualification when Windham refused to break the claw after the challenger reached the ring ropes
NWA World Champion Ric Flair fought Lex Luger to a double count-out

NWA @ Johnson City, TN - Freedom Hall - November 6, 1988

NWA @ Greenwood, SC - Civic Center - November 9, 1988
Television taping:

Dark match after the taping: NWA Tag Team Champions the Road Warriors defeated Bobby Eaton & Stan Lane

NWA @ Johnstown, PA - Cambria County War Memorial Arena - November 10, 1988 (1,549)
Dennis Condrey & Randy Rose defeated Dante DeNucci & the Italian Stallion at 12:10 when Rose pinned DeNucci
Steve Williams pinned Ron Simmons at 9:41
Kevin Sullivan pinned Eddie Gilbert at 9:42
NWA TV Champion Mike Rotunda fought Bam Bam Bigelow to a double count-out at 11:05
NWA Tag Team Champion The Road Warriors defeated Bobby Eaton & Stan Lane at 7:49 when Road Warrior Animal pinned Lane
Lex Luger & Sting defeated NWA World Champion Ric Flair & NWA US Champion Barry Windham via disqualfication at 18:25

NWA @ Pittsburgh, PA - Civic Arena - November 11, 1988
Dennis Condrey & Randy Rose defeated Dante DeNucci & Jumping Jack Flash at 4:52 when Condrey pinned DeNucci
Steve Williams pinned Eddie Gilbert at 10:52
NWA TV Champion Mike Rotunda fought Nikita Koloff to a draw
NWA Tag Team Champions The Road Warriors defeated Ron Simmons & the Italian Stallion at 5:34 when Stallion was pinned
Sting defeated NWA US Champion Barry Windham via disqualification
Dusty Rhodes & Bam Bam Bigelow defeated Bobby Eaton & Stan Lane at 12:35 when Rhodes pinned Eaton
Lex Luger fought NWA World Champion Ric Flair to a double count-out at 22:15

NWA @ Atlanta, GA - WTBS Studios - November 1988
World Championship Wrestling taping:
11/12/88 - featured Jim Ross & Tony Schiavone on commentary; included a graphic advertising the Clash of the Champions Dec. 7; featured a contest in which NWA fans could win tickets to see "They Live" starring Roddy Piper; included David Crockett conducting an interview with the Sheepherders, alongside Rip Morgan, in which they showed off a diagram demonstrating their goal of winning the NWA US Tag Team Titles; featured Schiavone conducting an interview with Cornette, alongside Eaton & Lane, in which he brought out the stained white suit he wore the previous week when he was beaten bloody by Paul E. Dangerously, Dennis Condrey, & Randy Rose; after reviewing footage from the attack, Cornette held up the bloodstained suit, ran down the injuries he's taken in wrestling, and he wouldn't let a punk like Dangerously put him out of the industry and that he, Eaton, & Lane would take the suit into three pieces and ram it up their opponents; included an ad promoting "The Best of Starrcade: 1983-1987" home video; featured Crockett conducting an interview with Paul Ellering & NWA Tag Team Champions the Road Warriors regarding the comments made earlier in the show by Lex

Luger and their rivalry with Luger & Sting:
Dennis Condrey & Randy Rose (w/ Paul E. Dangerously) defeated Jerry Price & Rick Allen at 5:56 when Condrey pinned Price following a side Russian legsweep and kneeling on him for the cover; prior to the match, Dangerously introduced his team from the commentary table; after the contest, David Crockett conducted a ringside interview with Dangerously, Condrey, & Rose regarding their attack the previous week on Jim Cornette, Bobby Eaton, & Stan Lane, during which Dangerously said Condrey carried Cornette and Eaton for 5 years
NWA US Champion Barry Windham (w/ JJ Dillon) pinned Curtis Thompson with the superplex and a lariat at 10:47; during the bout, Dillon briefly joined the commentary team to comment on Bam Bam Bigelow, during which Dillon said the Four Horsemen were far from being a thing of the past and were about to reclaim their dominance; when questioned about adding to the Horsemen, Dillon said the Horsemen already had the best in Flair and Windham and weren't immediately looking to add to their ranks; following the bout, Crockett conducted an interview with Windham & Dillon regarding challenges made by Bigelow & Sir Oliver Humperdink; moments later, Bigelow & Humperdink interrupted Dillon, with Bigelow then assaulting Windham around ringside; a brawl then ensued in the ring with Windham eventually knocking Bigelow to the floor and ramming him into the ringpost; Windham soon attempted the claw but Bigelow hit a gorilla press slam and went up for the headbutt but Dillon pulled Windham from the ring; Dusty Rhodes then appeared and cut a promo at ringside, saying Bigelow had what it takes to take out Windham and NWA World Champion Ric Flair and he was proud to be his partner
NWA TV Champion Mike Rotundo (w/ Kevin Sullivan & Rick Steiner) pinned David Isley with the butterfly suplex at 5:07; prior to the bout, the crowd chanted "Retardo" at the champion and "Steiner's number one;" during the contest, it was announced Steve Williams would appear the following week to officially join the Varsity Club following his tour of Japan; Steiner briefly sat in the crowd and chanted with the crowd until Sullivan brought him back to ringside; following the match, the crowd continued their chants against Rotundo before Crockett conducted a ringside interview with Sullivan regarding the Varsity Club's quest to win the vacant NWA US Tag Team Titles; during the segment, Sullivan took off his University of Michigan jacket to put on Rotundo's University of Syracuse jacket, prompting Steiner to yell that he could beat Rotundo, Sullivan, Steve Williams, and Ric Flair; Steiner then stormed off as the crowd cheered
Bam Bam Bigelow (w/ Sir Oliver Humperdink) pinned Bill Holiday with a splash off the top at 3:10
Lex Luger defeated Trent Knight via submission with the Torture Rack at 1:36; during the bout, the commentary team advertised they would be back for a TV taping Thanksgiving afternoon, hours before that night's show at the Omni; after the contest, Crockett conducted an interview with Luger in which he commented on he and Sting's feud with NWA Tag Team Champions the Road Warriors, during which he said he and Road Warrior Animal used to be friends but he had no use for Road Warrior Hawk and that Sting was the finest athlete in

wrestling today
NWA World Champion Ric Flair (w/ JJ Dillon) defeated George South via submission with the figure-4 at 11:28; after the bout, Crockett conducted a ringside interview with Flair, alongside Dillon, regarding the comments made earlier in the show from Rhodes & Bigelow; moments later, a dazed Windham came out as Flair said he and Windham would beat up Rhodes & Bigelow around the country
Abdullah the Butcher (w/ Gary Hart) pinned Randy Hogan with an elbow drop at 2:25; after the match, Abdullah continued to attack his opponent until Hart covered Abdullah's face with a hood; moments later, Crockett conducted an interview with Hart, alongside Abdullah who began chewing away at the interview podium
Ron Simmons & Eddie Gilbert defeated Brett Holiday & Gary Royal at 2:45 when Simmons pinned Holiday following a shoulderblock off the top
Bobby Fulton & Tommy Rogers defeated Agent Steel & Terry Jones at 2:05 when Rogers pinned Steel following a somersault splash off the top double team; following the match, Crockett conducted an interview with Fulton & Rogers regarding their participation in the NWA US Tag Team Title tournament and rivalry with the Sheepherders

NWA @ Johnstown, PA - War Memorial Arena - November 10, 1988 (1,549)
Dennis Condrey & Randy Rose defeated Dante DeNucci & the Italian Stallion
Steve Williams defeated Ron Simmons
Kevin Sullivan defeated Eddie Gilbert
NWA TV Champion Mike Rotunda fought Bam Bam Bigelow to a no contest
NWA Tag Team Champions the Road Warriors defeated Bobby Eaton & Stan Lane
Lex Luger & Sting defeated NWA World Champion Ric Flair & NWA US Champion Barry Windham via disqualification

NWA @ Pittsburgh, PA - Civic Arena - November 11, 1988 (3,400)
Dennis Condrey & Randy Rose defeated Dante DeNucci & Jumping Jack Flash
NWA Tag Team Champions the Road Warriors defeated the Italian Stallion & Ron Simmons
Steve Williams defeated Eddie Gilbert
NWA TV Champion Mike Rotunda fought Nikita Koloff to a draw
Sting defeated NWA US Champion Barry Windham via disqualification
Dusty Rhodes & Bam Bam Bigelow defeated Bobby Eaton & Stan Lane via disqualification
Lex Luger fought NWA World Champion Ric Flair to a no contest

NWA @ Columbus, OH - Fairgrounds Coliseum - November 12, 1988 (2,500-3,000)
Dennis Condrey & Randy Rose defeated two unknowns

Steve Williams pinned Eddie Gilbert
NWA TV Champion Mike Rotunda fought Nikita Koloff to a draw
NWA Tag Team Champions the Road Warriors defeated the Italian Stallion & Ron Simmons
Sting defeated NWA US Champion Barry Windham via disqualification
Lex Luger & Bam Bam Bigelow defeated Bobby Eaton & Stan Lane
NWA World Champion Ric Flair pinned Dusty Rhodes

NWA @ Huntington, WV - Civic Center - November 13, 1988 (matinee) (5,000)
Curtis Thompson defeated Gary Royal
Dennis Condrey & Randy Rose defeated the Italian Stallion & Ron Simmons
Steve Williams defeated Eddie Gilbert
NWA TV Champion Mike Rotunda fought Nikita Koloff to a draw
NWA Tag Team Champions the Road Warriors defeated Bobby Eaton & Stan Lane
Bam Bam Bigelow fought NWA US Champion Barry Windham to a no contest
Sting defeated NWA World Champion Ric Flair via disqualification

NWA @ Atlanta, GA - WTBS Studios - November 14, 1988
World Championship Wrestling taping:
11/19/88 - featured Tony Schiavone & Jim Ross on commentary; included a graphic advertising the Clash of the Champions Dec. 7; featured an ad promoting "The Best of Starrcade: 1983-1987" home video; included David Crockett conducting an interview with Jim Cornette, Bobby Eaton & Stan Lane in which Cornette said Dennis Condrey left the Midnight Express because he let his personal problems get in the way of business and he was dragging the team down with him; Cornette then said Lane far exceeded what Condrey brought to the team; Cornette then cut a promo on Condrey, Randy Rose, & Paul E. Dangerously and held up a white sheet that had blood on it from when he and his team were jumped by Dangerously and his team and said it was a reminder and he would shove it down their throats; included the Lex Luger & Sting vs. David Isley & Trent Knight match from NWA Pro; featured the Bobby Fulton & Tommy Rogers vs. Steve Williams & NWA TV Champion Mike Rotunda match from Worldwide: Bam Bam Bigelow (w/ Sir Oliver Humperdink) pinned Trent Knight with a gordbuster at 3:12; following the match, David Crockett conducted a ringside interview with Bigelow & Humperdink regarding Bigelow's partnership with Dusty Rhodes against NWA World Champion Ric Flair & NWA US Champion Barry Windham; during the segment, Humperdink said Rhodes & Bigelow could also challenge Bobby Eaton & Stan Lane for the tag team titles, even though Eaton & Lane had lost the belts weeks earlier
Tommy Rogers & Bobby Fulton defeated Mike Jackson & Joe Cruz at 4:27 when Fulton pinned Cruz with a modified splash; Rogers & Fulton brought the American flag out with them prior to the match
Eddie Gilbert pinned David Isley with the Hot Shot at 5:36
Ron Simmons vs. Terry Jones
Steve Williams & NWA TV Champion Mike Rotundo vs. the Italian Stallion & Randy Hogan
Dennis Condrey & Randy Rose vs. Brad & Brett Holiday
Russian Assassin #1 & #2 vs. Thompson & Justice
NWA US Champion Barry Windham
Abdullah the Butcher vs. Eddie Sweat

NWA @ Albany, GA - Civic Center - November 15, 1988
NWA Tag Team Champions the Road Warriors defeated Bobby Eaton & Stan Lane

NWA @ Raleigh, NC - Dorton Arena - November 16, 1988
Dennis Condrey & Randy Rose defeated Mike Justice & Curtis Thompson
Eddie Gilbert defeated the Italian Stallion
Bobby Fulton defeated Cruel Connection #1
Steve Williams defeated Ron Simmons
Ivan & Nikita Koloff defeated the Russian Assassins
NWA Tag Team Champions the Road Warriors defeated Bobby Eaton & Stan Lane in a steel cage match

NWA @ Norfolk, VA - Scope - November 17, 1988

NWA @ Washington DC - Armory - November 18, 1988
Dennis Condrey & Randy Rose defeated Bobby Fulton & Tommy Rogers
Bam Bam Bigelow pinned Russian Assassin #2
Nikita Koloff pinned Russian Assassin #1
NWA TV Champion Mike Rotundo pinned Stan Lane after hitting him with a foreign object, given to the champion by Kevin Sullivan
Rick Steiner defeated NWa US Champion Barry Windham via disqualification
Lex Luger & Sting defeated NWA World Champion Ric Flair & NWA Tag Team Champion Road Warrior Animal

Worldwide - 11/19/88 - featured the Road Warriors vs. NWA Tag Team Champions Bobby Eaton & Stan Lane match taped 10/29/88 in New Orleans, LA
The Russian Assassins vs. two unknowns
Bam Bam Bigelow vs. an unknown
The Sheepherders vs. Ron Simmons & Eddie Gilbert
Dennis Condrey & Randy Rose vs. two unknowns

NWA @ Philadelphia, PA - Civic Center - November 19, 1988 (5,000)
Stan Lane defeated the Italian Stallion
Dennis Condrey & Randy Rose defeated Bobby Fulton & Tommy Rogers
Ivan Koloff defeated Russian Assassin #2
NWA TV Champion Mike Rotunda & Steve Williams defeated Bam Bam Bigelow & Ron Simmons

Rick Steiner defeated NWA US Champion Barry Windham via disqualification
Lex Luger & Sting fought NWA Tag Team Champions the Road Warriors to a no contest

NWA @ ? - November 1988
The Main Event - 11/20/88:
NWA TV Champion Mike Rotunda vs. Kendall Windham
Rick Steiner, Bobby Eaton & Stan Lane vs. George South, Gary Royal, & Brett Holiday
Bobby Fulton & Tommy Rogers vs. NWA TV Champion Mike Rotunda & Steve Williams

NWA @ Chicago, IL - UIC Pavilion - November 20, 1988
Randy Rose & Dennis Condrey defeated Jonnie Stewart & the Mighty Thor
Ron Simmons defeated Steve Williams via disqualification
NWA TV Champion Mike Rotunda defeated the Italian Stallion
Ivan & Nikita Koloff defeated the Russian Assassins
Rick Steiner defeated NWA US Champion Barry Windham via disqualification
Sting & Lex Luger fought NWA World Tag Team Champions Hawk & Animal to a double count-out

NWA @ Sumter, SC - November 22, 1988
Television taping:
The Main Event - 12/18/88: NWA US Champion Barry Windham (w/ JJ Dillon) defeated NWA US Tag Team Champion Bobby Fulton (w/ NWA US Tag Team Champion Tommy Rogers) via disqualification in a non-title match at 13:40 when Bam Bam Bigelow attacked the champion as Windham had the claw applied; moments earlier, Dillon attacked Fulton behind the referee's back, leading to Rogers attacking Dillon on the floor; after the contest, Bigelow hit a splash off the top onto Windham before he, Sir Oliver Humperdink, and Rogers checked on Fulton; Tony Schiavone was the ring announcer for the match; Fulton & Rogers did not come out with the title belts nor were they introduced as champions because they had yet to win the titles at the time the match was taped

NWA @ Baltimore, MD - Arena - November 23, 1988 (9,000)
Steve Williams, Ron Simmons, Eddie Gilbert, the Sheepherders, Al Perez, and Abdullah the Butcher were all scheduled to appear but did not; Abdullah was touring Japan
Dennis Condrey & Randy Rose defeated the Italian Stallion & Joey Maggs
Tommy Rogers pinned Rip Morgan
Bobby Eaton & Stan Lane defeated Ted Tyson & Tony Stetson
Bobby Fulton defeated NWA TV Champion Mike Rotunda via disqualification at the 17-minute mark
Ivan & Nikita Koloff defeated the Russian Assassins in a chain match when Nikita pinned Assassin #2
Dusty Rhodes (w/ Bam Bam Bigelow) defeated NWA US Champion Barry Windham to win the title via submission with a sleeper; after intermission, it was announced Windham was still the champion since he knocked out the first referee with a foreign object as he was caught in the sleeper and Rhodes was awarded the match via disqualification
Sting & Lex Luger fought NWA Tag Team Champions the Road Warriors to a double count-out at the 13-minute mark
NWA World Champion Ric Flair pinned Rick Steiner at the 15-minute mark with a suplex and putting his feet on the ropes for leverage

NWA @ Atlanta, GA - WTBS Studios - November 24, 1988 (matinee)
Thanksgiving Day
World Championship Wrestling - 11/26/88 - included the Dusty Rhodes / Road Warriors segment in which the Warriors assaulted Dusty with their shoulder spikes, causing a bloody gash to Rhodes' face; the segment, devised by Rhodes, was the final straw in him being replaced on the booking committee and resulted in over 300 angry phone calls from TBS viewers:
Eddie Gilbert & Ron Simmons vs. Trent Knight & Bob Emory
Nikita Koloff vs. Terry Jones
Sting & Lex Luger vs. Adams & Price
The Commandos vs. Mulkey & Sweat
Bam Bam Bigelow vs. Keith Steinborn
Dennis Condrey & Randy Rose vs. Brad & Brett Holiday
NWA TV Champion Mike Rotundo & Steve Williams vs. Anderson & Jackson
Rick Steiner vs. Joe Cruz
Bobby Eaton & Stan Lane vs. Morgan & Miles
Bobby Fulton & Tommy Rogers vs. Cruel Connection

Worldwide - 11/26/88:
Dennis Condrey & Randy Rose vs. two unknowns
NWA World Champion Ric Flair & NWA US Champion Barry Windham vs. the Italian Stallion & George South
Bobby Fulton & Tommy Rogers vs. NWA TV Champion Mike Rotundo & Steve Williams

NWA @ Atlanta, GA - WTBS Studios - November 1988
World Championship Wrestling taping:
12/3/88:
Dennis Condrey & Randy Rose vs. Isley & Knight
Sting vs. Joe Cruz
Bobby Eaton & Stan Lane vs. Bob Emory & El Negro
The Commandos vs. Wilde & Keith Steinborn
NWA World Champion Ric Flair vs. Jerry Price
NWA US Champion Barry Windham vs. Tony Suber
Rick Steiner vs. Randy Hogan
Steve Williams & NWA TV Champion Mike Rotundo vs. Mulkey & Mr. Pain
Lex Luger vs. Terry Jones
Bam Bam Bigelow vs. Max Miles

NWA @ Atlanta, GA - Omni - November 24, 1988 (8,000)
Thanksgiving Day
Tommy Rogers pinned Rip Morgan
NWA TV Champion Mike Rotunda & Steve Williams defeated

NWA
WRESTLING
MAIN EVENT
GRUDGE MATCH
VS
SPECIAL CHALLENGE
TAG TEAM MATCH
VS
DUSTY RHODES
SPECIAL EVENT
VS STEVE WILLIAMS
KEVIN SULLIVAN
WORLD T.V. TITLE
VS
TAG TEAM
THE ORIGINAL
MIDNIGHT EXPRESS
MIDNIGHT EXPRESS
VS
PAUL E. DANGEROUSLY
AND

Rick Steiner & Ron Simmons
Dennis Condrey & Randy Rose defeated Eddie Gilbert & the Italian Stallion
Ivan & Nikita Koloff defeated the Russian Assassins in a chain match
Dusty Rhodes & Bam Bam Bigelow defeated NWA World Champion Ric Flair & NWA US Champion Barry Windham via disqualification
Sting & Lex Luger fought NWA Tag Team Champions the Road Warriors to a double count-out

NWA @ Charlotte, NC - Coliseum - November 25, 1988 (5,000)
The Main Event - 12/25/88: Rick Steiner pinned Mike Samani with a belly to belly suplex at 2:36
The Main Event - 12/25/88: Al Perez, Rip Morgan, Dennis Condrey & Randy Rose (w/ Paul E. Dangerously) defeated Eddie Gilbert, the Italian Stallion, NWA US Tag Team Champions Bobby Fulton & Tommy Rogers at around the 17-minute mark when Condrey pinned Stallion following a double DDT behind the referee's back; the match was not shown in full
The Main Event - 12/18/88: Bobby Eaton & Stan Lane (w/ Jim Cornette) defeated the Cruel Connection when Eaton scored the pin following the Veg-O-Matic at around the 5-minute mark; the match was not shown in full
The Main Event - 12/18/88: Russian Assassin #2 (w/ Paul Jones) defeated Ivan Koloff in a death match at 10:44 when, as referee Teddy Long was giving both men the standing 10-count, Jones knocked Koloff to the mat behind the referee's back, allowing the Assassin to reach his feet
NWA US Champion Barry Windham vs. Dusty Rhodes (JJ Dillon suspended in a cage above the ring)
NWA World Champion Ric Flair vs. Bam Bam Bigelow
The Main Event - 12/25/88: NWA Tag Team Champions the Road Warriors (w/ Paul Ellering) fought Lex Luger & Sting to a double disqualification at 13:26 when Road Warrior Hawk threw Luger over the top rope and Luger then knocked Hawk off the top with a steel chair

NWA @ Greensboro, NC - Coliseum - November 26, 1988 (7,500)
Tommy Rogers & Bobby Fulton defeated Rip Morgan & Larry Zbyzsko
Dennis Condrey & Randy Rose defeated Curtis Thompson & Mike Justice
Al Perez defeated the Italian Stallion
Bobby Eaton & Stan Lane defeated the Cruel Connection
NWA TV Champion Mike Rotunda pinned Ron Simmons when Steve Williams tripped Simmons as he attempted a suplex and Rotunda fell on top for the win
Rick Steiner fought Steve Williams to a double disqualification
Ivan & Nikita Koloff defeated the Russian Assassins when Nikita pinned Assassin #2 (Nikita's last appearance for 5 months)
Dusty Rhodes & Bam Bam Bigelow defeated NWA World Champion Ric Flair & NWA US Champion Barry Windham via disqualification when JJ Dillon interfered as Rhodes had

Windham in a sleeper
NWA Tag Team Champions the Road Warriors defeated Sting & Lex Luger via disqualification when Luger hit Road Warrior Animal with a chair

- 11/27/88: Nikita Koloff quit.

NWA @ Atlanta, GA - WTBS Studios - November 27, 1988
World Championship Wrestling - 12/3/88:
Dennis Condrey & Randy Rose vs. Isley & Knight
Sting vs. Joe Cruz
Bobby Eaton & Stan Lane vs. Bob Emory & El Negro
The Commandos vs. Wilde & Keith Steinborn
NWA World Champion Ric Flair vs. Jerry Price
NWA US Champion Barry Windham vs. Tony Suber
Rick Steiner vs. Randy Hogan
Steve Williams & NWA TV Champion Mike Rotundo vs. Mulkey & Mr. Pain
Lex Luger vs. Terry Jones
Bam Bam Bigelow vs. Max Miles

NWA @ Richmond, VA - Coliseum - November 27, 1988 (3,500)
Nikita Koloff, Dusty Rhodes, NWA US Champion Barry Windham, NWA TV Champion Mike Rotunda, the Sheepherders, and Kevin Sullivan were all scheduled to appear but did not
Dennis Condrey & Randy Rose defeated Curtis Thompson & Mike Justice
Bobby Eaton & Stan Lane defeated the Cruel Connection
Tommy Rogers & Bobby Fulton defeated Thunderfoot & the Italian Stallion
Ron Simmons pinned Rip Morgan
Ivan Koloff pinned Russian Assassin #2 in a chain match; after the bout, both Russian Assassins bloodied Ivan
Rick Steiner & Bam Bam Bigelow defeated NWA World Champion Ric Flair & Steve Williams (sub. for NWA US Champion Barry Windham) via disqualification when JJ Dillon interfered
Sting & Lex Luger fought NWA Tag Team Champions the Road Warriors to a double count-out

NWA @ Macon, GA - Coliseum - November 28, 1988
Television taping

NWA @ Las Vegas, NV - Showboat - November 29, 1988 (2,500)
Ron Simmons pinned the Italian Stallion (sub. for Larry Zbyszko) at 6:35 with a flying shoulder tackle
Bobby Eaton & Stan Lane fought Dennis Condrey & Randy Rose to a 20-minute time-limit draw; after the bout, Condrey & Rose attacked their opponents
NWA TV Champion Mike Rotunda pinned Ron Simmons (sub. for Nikita Koloff) at 8:39 by using the ropes for leverage
Rick Steiner defeated Steve Williams via disqualification at

9:57 when Mike Rotunda interfered; Steiner cleared both from the ring afterwards
NWA World Champion Ric Flair & NWA US Champion Barry Windham defeated Eddie Gilbert (sub. for Dusty Rhodes) & Bam Bam Bigelow at 18:27 when Flair pinned Gilbert after Windham hit a lariat as Gilbert had Flair covered
NWA Tag Team Champions the Road Warriors defeated Sting & Lex Luger via disqualification at 11:50 when Luger hit Hawk with a chair

- 11/30/88: Dusty Rhodes resigned as head booker of the NWA in a move forced by TBS executives. His position was filled by Jim Crockett.

NWA @ San Francisco, CA - Civic Auditorium - November 30, 1988 (2,700)
Ron Simmons pinned the Italian Stallion at 5:53 with a flying shoulder block
Bobby Eaton & Stan Lane fought Dennis Condrey & Randy Rose to a 20-minute time limit draw
NWA World Champion Ric Flair & NWA US Champion Barry Windham defeated Eddie Gilbert (sub. for Dusty Rhodes) & Bam Bam Bigelow at 14:36 when Flair pinned Gilbert
NWA TV Champion Mike Rotunda pinned Ron Simmons (sub. for Nikita Koloff) at 16:06 when Steve Williams swept the challenger's leg out as he attempted a suplex into the ring
Rick Steiner defeated Steve Williams via disqualification at 2:51 when Mike Rotunda interfered; after the bout, Ron Simmons helped make the save
NWA Tag Team Champions the Road Warriors fought Sting & Lex Luger to a double count-out at 12:41

NWA @ Albuquerque, NM - Tingley Coliseum - December 1, 1988 (4,700)
Ron Simmons defeated the HalfBreed (Tim Chappa) at 1:15
Dennis Condrey & Randy Rose defeated Bobby Eaton & Stan Lane via disqualification at 13:15 when Jim Cornette and Paul E. Dangerously interfered; the match was scheduled for a 20-minute time-limit draw but Cornette changed the finish; Cornette, Eaton, & Lane were suspended by JJ Dillon until Cornette spoke to Jim Crockett Jr. the following day
Bam Bam Bigelow & Eddie Gilbert defeated NWA US Champion Barry Windham & JJ Dillon (sub. for NWA World Champion Ric Flair who had to fly home) when Gilbert pinned Dillon at 12:39
NWA TV Champion Mike Rotunda pinned the Italian Stallion
Rick Steiner defeated Steve Williams via disqualification when Mike Rotunda interfered
NWA Tag Team Champions the Road Warriors fought Sting & Lex Luger to a double disqualification at 14:27

NWA @ Atlanta, GA - WTBS Studios - December 1988
World Championship Wrestling taping:
12/10/88:
Tommy Rogers & Bobby Fulton vs. Allen & Jones
Russian Assassin #1 & #2 vs. Holiday & Sweat

NWA Tag Team Champions the Road Warriors vs. Reno Riggins & Casey
Dustin Rhodes & Kendall Windham vs. Cruel Connection
Eddie Gilbert & Ron Simmons vs. Collie & Justice
Bobby Eaton & Stan Lane vs. Thompson & El Negro
The Commandos vs. Keith Steinborn & Hogan
Bam Bam Bigelow vs. Craig Brown
Rick Steiner vs. JD Wolfe
NWA US Champion Barry Windham vs. Gary Royal
Dennis Condrey & Randy Rose vs. Price & Menace
NWA TV Champion Mike Rotundo vs. the Itallian Stallion

NWA @ Atlanta, GA - WTBS Studios - December 1988
World Championship Wrestling taping:
12/17/88:
Bobby Eaton & Stan Lane vs. Simani & Bob Emory
Russian Assassin #1 & #2 vs. the Italian Stallion & Jones
The Junkyard Dog vs. Trent Knight
Dennis Condrey & Randy Rose vs. Allen & Price
NWA US Champion Barry Windham vs. Ryan Wagner
Dustin Rhodes & Kendall Windham vs. Thompson & Bill Holiday
Eddie Gilbert vs. Mike Jackson
The Commandos vs. Mulkey & Sweat
Rick Steiner vs. George South
The Varsity Club vs. Royal & Hogan
Sting vs. Keith Steinborn
NWA Tag Team Champions the Road Warriors vs. Wilde & Miles

Worldwide - 12/3/88 - featured Tony Schiavone & David Crockett on commentary; included Jim Ross conducting an interview with NWA Tag Team Champions the Road Warriors, alongside Paul Ellering, regarding their recent attack on Dusty Rhodes, with Road Warrior Hawk calling Rhodes "Popeye" and saying they did to him what they did to Sting and Lex Luger; Ellering then said they didn't need anyone else, with Road Warrior Animal cutting a promo on Sting; featured Ross conducting an interview with NWA US Champion Barry Windham & JJ Dillon regarding Windham's title defense against Bam Bam Bigelow at Starrcade, during which footage was shown of Bigelow recently attacking Windham as Windham had the claw applied on Bobby Fulton; included a Starrcade 88 Update with Schiavone & Magnum TA, with Magnum saying he was looking for the right person to have on as a guest for Straight Talk with the Boss at Starrcade and it was announced the first Bunkhouse Stampede would be held featuring Abdullah the Butcher, Steve Williams, Dick Murdoch, and more, Bobby Fulton & Tommy Rogers would be on hand, NWA TV Champion Mike Rotundo would face Rick Steiner - with Kevin Sullivan suspended above the ring in a cage - and Sting & Dusty Rhodes would face NWA Tag Team Champions the Road Warriors; the two then discussed the upcoming Luger vs. Flair match, showing footage from their match in Baltimore at the Great American Bash and the controversial ending; it was then announced if Flair was to be disqualified in the match then Luger would win the title; featured a Straight Talk with the

Boss segment with Magnum TA showing footage from World Championship Wrestling in which the Road Warriors blinded Rhodes with one of their spikes; a black censor circle covered Rhodes' face throughout the replay and new commentary was provided by Ross & Schiavone; Magnum then brought out Sting as his guest, who cut a promo on the Road Warriors:
NWA TV Champion Mike Rotundo & Steve Williams (w/ Kevin Sullivan) defeated two unknowns at 3:54 when Williams scored the pin with the Oklahoma Stampede; during the bout, Sullivan joined the commentary team to comment on kicking Rick Steiner out of the Varsity Club and about Rotundo's title defense against Steiner at Starrcade; there were numerous chants of "Steiner" during the match
Dennis Condrey & Randy Rose (w/ Paul E. Dangerously) defeated the Italian Stallion & Joe Cruz at 2:59 when Condrey pinned Cruz with the Double Goozle; during the bout, Dangerously joined the commentary team to cut a promo on Jim Cornette, Bobby Eaton, & Stan Lane and their match as part of Starrcade; after the bout, Eaton & Lane attacked Condrey & Rose as Cornette ran after Dangerously, with the two teams eventually fighting their way to the interview platform
Rick Steiner pinned an unknown with the belly to belly suplex at 2:37; after the bout, David Crockett conducted a ringside interview with Steiner, during which Steiner said "Alex" tells him what to do sometimes, then repeatedly putting his hand up to his ear, before talking about Kevin Sullivan & NWA TV Champion Mike Rotundo (Alex's debut)
Nikita Koloff defeated the Russian Assassin #1 (w/ Paul Jones & Russian Assassin #2) via disqualification at 10:00 after Ivan and #2 began fighting in the ring; after the bout, Nikita unmasked #1 before referee Tommy Young raised his hand in victory; #1's face was not shown on camera before he escaped backstage

NWA @ Amarillo, TX - Civic Center - December 2, 1988
Bobby Eaton & Stan Lane fought Dennis Condrey & Randy Rose to a 20-minute time-limit draw

NWA @ Houston, TX - Sam Houston Coliseum - December 3, 1988 (1,200)
Tug Taylor pinned Tony Torres
Mike Rotunda pinned Ron Simmons
Dennis Condrey & Randy Rose defeated Stan Lane & Bobby Eaton via disqualification when Jim Cornette hit the referee
Rick Steiner defeated Steve Williams via disqualification
NWA World Champion Ric Flair & NWA US Champion Barry Windham defeated Eddie Gilbert & Bam Bam Bigelow
Sting & Lex Luger fought NWA Tag Team Champions the Road Warriors to a double count-out

NWA @ Lubbock, TX - December 4, 1988 (900)
Rick Steiner pinned Alvin Martinez
Eddie Gilbert pinned Ted Heath
Mike Rotunda pinned Ron Simmons
Dennis Condrey & Randy Rose defeated Stan Lane & Bobby

Eaton via disqualification
NWA US Champion Barry Windham defeated Bam Bam Bigelow via count-out
Sting & Lex Luger fought NWA Tag Team Champions the Road Warriors to a double count-out

NWA @ Atlanta, GA - WTBS Studios - December 5, 1988
12/10/88:
Tommy Rogers & Bobby Fulton vs. Allen & Jones
Russian Assassin #1 & #2 vs. Holiday & Sweat
NWA Tag Team Champions the Road Warriors vs. Reno Riggins & Casey
Dustin Rhodes & Kendall Windham vs. Cruel Connection
Eddie Gilbert & Ron Simmons vs. Collie & Justice
Bobby Eaton & Stan Lane vs. Thompson & El Negro
The Commandos vs. Keith Steinborn & Hogan
Bam Bam Bigelow vs. Craig Brown
Rick Steiner vs. JD Wolfe
NWA US Champion Barry Windham vs. Gary Royal
Dennis Condrey & Randy Rose vs. Price & Menace
NWA TV Champion Mike Rotundo vs. the Itallian Stallion

NWA @ Columbus, GA - December 6, 1988 (2,300)
Television taping:
Sting, Bam Bam Bigelow, Ron Simmons, Eddie Gilbert, and Steve Williams were all no shows
Dustin Rhodes vs. ? (Dustin's debut)
Kendall Windham vs. ? (Kendall's debut)
Lex Luger & Rick Steiner fought NWA Tag Team Champions the Road Warriors to a 15-minute time limit draw
Televised matches:
NWA World Champion Ric Flair defeated the Masked Maniac
Dennis Condrey & Randy Rose defeated Bobby Fulton & Tommy Rogers after Paul E Dangerously hit Tommy Rogers with his phone
Bobby Eaton & Stan Lane defeated Dennis Condrey & Randy Rose at 14:30 after Cornette hit Rose with the tennis racquet

Clash of the Champions IV "Seasons Beatings" - Chattanooga, TN - December 7, 1988
Shown live on TBS - featured Jim Ross & Bob Caudle on commentary; included Tony Schiavone & Lex Luger as the secondary announce team:
NWA US Tag Team Tournament Finals: Tommy Rogers & Bobby Fulton defeated Ron Simmons & Eddie Gilbert at 27:03 when Fulton pinned Gilbert with a roll up after Gilbert hit the ringpost shoulder-first; the finish happened within the last minute of the time-limit; Jason Hervey was the guest ring announcer for the bout
Steve Williams (w/ Kevin Sullivan) pinned the Italian Stallion at 15:35 with the Oklahoma Stampede after catching Stallion in mid-air
Ivan Koloff pinned Paul Jones at 8:21 after hitting Jones with his own foreign object; Koloff wrestled the bout with one hand tied behind his back; after the bout, the Russian Assassins attacked Koloff until the Junkyard Dog made the save and

cleared the ring with his chain

NWA Tag Team Champion & NWA Six-Man Tag Team Champion Road Warrior Animal (w/ Paul Ellering) defeated NWA Six-Man Tag Team Champion Dusty Rhodes via disqualification at 2:54 when Rhodes hit Animal with a chair as Sting battled an interfering NWA Tag Team Champion & NWA Six-Man Tag Team Champion Road Warrior Hawk on the floor; Rhodes wrestled the bout with a heavily bandaged eye following an attack from the Road Warriors; due to pre-match stipulations, Animal won the NWA Six-Man Tag Team Titles for himself, Hawk, and a partner of their choice; had Rhodes won, he would have chosen who would be his championship partners

NWA World Champion Ric Flair & NWA US Champion Barry Windham (w/ JJ Dillon) defeated Bobby Eaton & Stan Lane (w/ Jim Cornette) at 17:41 when Windham pinned Eaton after Flair hit Eaton in the back of the head with Dillon's shoe following Eaton's Alabama Jam on Windham; during the bout, Paul E. Dangerously cut an insert promo on his team of Dennis Condrey & Randy Rose facing Eaton & Lane at Starrcade (*The Best of Clash of the Champions* Blu-ray)

NWA @ Atlanta, GA - WTBS Studios - December 8, 1988

World Championship Wrestling - 12/17/88:
Bobby Eaton & Stan Lane vs. Simani & Bob Emory
Russian Assassin #1 & #2 vs. the Italian Stallion & Jones
The Junkyard Dog vs. Trent Knight
Dennis Condrey & Randy Rose vs. Allen & Price
NWA US Champion Barry Windham vs. Ryan Wagner
Dustin Rhodes & Kendall Windham vs. Thompson & Bill Holiday
Eddie Gilbert vs. Mike Jackson
The Commandos vs. Mulkey & Sweat
Rick Steiner vs. George South
The Varsity Club vs. Royal & Hogan
Sting vs. Keith Steinborn
NWA Tag Team Champions the Road Warriors vs. Wilde & Miles

NWA @ Hampton, VA - Coliseum - December 9, 1988

Worldwide - 12/10/88:
Rick Steiner vs. an unknown
NWA US Champion Barry Windham vs. George South
NWA TV Champion Mike Rotundo & Steve Williams vs. two unknowns
NWA Tag Team Champions the Road Warriors vs. two unknowns
Sting vs. an unknown

NWA @ Philadelphia, PA - Civic Center - December 10, 1988 (1,626) (the smallest Philadelphia wrestling crowd in decades)

Russian Assassin #1 pinned Italian Stallion
NWA US Tag Team Champions Tommy Rogers & Bobby Fulton defeated Jonathan Holiday & Rip Morgan

Dennis Condrey & Randy Rose defeated Dustin Rhodes & Kendall Windham
Ivan Koloff defeated Russian Assassin #2 at the 5-minute mark in a death match
NWA US Champion Barry Windham pinned Eddie Gilbert by using the ropes
Dusty Rhodes & Rick Steiner defeated Kevin Sullivan & Steve Williams
Sting & Lex Luger defeated NWA Tag Team Champions the Road Warriors in an elimination match; Sting fought Hawk to a double count-out; Animal was disqualified when Paul Ellering interfered as Animal was in the Torture Rack

NWA @ ? - December 1988

The Main Event - 12/11/88:
Curtis Thompson vs. Trent Knight
Larry Zbyszko vs. Mike Justice
Rick Steiner & Ron Simmons vs. NWA TV Champion Mike Rotunda & Steve Williams

NWA @ Richmond, VA - Coliseum - December 11, 1988 (the smallest Richmond wrestling crowd ever)

Dennis Condrey & Randy Rose defeated Dustin Rhodes & Kendall Windham when Dustin was pinned
NWA US Tag Team Champions Tommy Rogers & Bobby Fulton defeated Rip Morgan & Mark Fleming
Ivan Koloff defeated Russian Assassin #2
Bam Bam Bigelow pinned Russian Assassin #1
Steve Williams & Mike Rotunda defeated Rick Steiner & Eddie Gilbert when Sullivan held Gilbert's leg down as he was covered
Dusty Rhodes, Sting, & Lex Luger fought NWA US Champion Barry Windham & NWA Tag Team Champions the Road Warriors to a double disqualification

NWA @ Atlanta, GA - WTBS Studios - December 12, 1988

World Championship Wrestling taping:
12/24/88 - featured Jim Ross & Tony Schiavone on commentary; included Schiavone conducting an interview with Paul E. Dangerously, Dennis Condrey, & Randy Rose regarding their upcoming match at Starrcade against Bobby Eaton & Stan Lane, during which Dangerously said Starrcade would be the last night of Jim Cornette's career; featured Ross & Schiavone conducting an interview with Cornette, with Cornette noting Eaton & Lane's losses since losing the NWA Tag Team Titles to the Road Warriors, said his team didn't fit in with their old locker room and wasn't wanted in their new one, but said he and his team had a lot of fans they didn't realize they had and would take out Dangerously's team at Starrcade; included Schiavone conducting an interview with Lex Luger regarding his upcoming match at Starrcade against NWA World Champion Ric Flair, during which there were boos and chants of "We can't hear you;" featured Ross conducting an interview with Paul Ellering & NWA Tag Team Champions the Road Warriors regarding their upcoming title defense at Starrcade against Dusty Rhodes & Sting; included Schiavone

518

conducting an interview with Flair regarding his title defense at Starrcade against Luger.

Ladies Champion Misty Blue & Heidi Lee Morgan defeated Linda Dallas & Kat Leroux at around the 9-minute mark when Mad Dog Debbie, who came ringside mid-way through the match to be in the corner of Dallas & Leroux, assaulted Blue with a cane as Blue had Leroux covered following a splash off the top; no official decision was announced and it appeared as though it was a disqualification but in the post-match replay Jim Ross said referee Teddy Long did count to 3 during the cover, which he did not

Sting defeated Bill Holiday via submission with the Scorpion Deathlock at 1:50; after the bout, Jim Ross conducted an interview with Sting, during which Sting took a fan sign from the crowd that had a likeness of him and said he was ready for Starrcade

Russian Assassin #1 & #2 (w/ Paul Jones) defeated Max Miles & Tony Suber at 5:09 when Miles was pinned after the other Russian Assassin used a loaded headbutt; during the bout, Jones briefly joined the commentary team and said he had the money to make sure his team wins at Starrcade, and subtly implied he would buy the services of the Junkyard Dog to make sure Ivan Koloff doesn't win

Rick Steiner, Ivan Koloff, & the Junkyard Dog defeated Eddie Sweat, Randy Hogan, & Keith Steinborn at 6:38 when JYD pinned Sweat following the powerslam; prior to the bout, Steiner gave his dog to Jim Cornette, who was being interviewed at ringside, with Cornette having to hold the dog for the duration of the bout while also providing commentary; during the match, Cornette walked around ringside trying to hand off the dog to members of the TV crew; moments later, Cornette briefly let the dog run loose until Steiner went to the floor and put it back in Cornette's arms; late in the bout, Steiner had a young ringside fan get in the ring and aid Steiner in kicking one of the opponents; after the match, Steiner put the dog on Sweat's body

Steve Williams & Kevin Sullivan defeated Randy Mulkey & Ryan Wagner at 5:20 when Williams pinned Mulkey following the Oklahoma Stampede; during the bout, there was a chant of "We want Steiner" from the fans

NWA US Tag Team Champions Bobby Fulton & Tommy Rogers defeated Rick Allen & Jerry Price at 4:27 when Rogers scored the pin following the somersault off the top double team

Bobby Eaton & Stan Lane (w/ Jim Cornette) defeated Mike Jackson & Gary Royal at 6:37 when Eaton pinned Jackson following the Veg-O-Matic; Cornette briefly joined the commentary team for the match

Dustin Rhodes pinned Trent Knight with a powerslam and elbow drop at 5:04; during the bout, it was announced Misty Blue, Heidi Lee Morgan, and another female would face Linda Dallas, Mad Dog Debbie, & Kat Leroux the following week

NWA US Champion Barry Windham (w/ JJ Dillon) pinned Eddie Gilbert in a non-title match at around the 19-minute mark with an inside cradle after Dillon landed a knee to Gilbert behind the referee's back; during the bout, it was noted Al Perez and the Commandos would be in action later in the show; moments later, Bam Bam Bigelow briefly joined the commentary team to discuss his title shot against Windham at

Starrcade; Dillon briefly joined the commentary team during the match to discuss the match as well as Windham facing Bigelow; after the bout, Gilbert confronted Windham, Dillon, and NWA World Champion Ric Flair at the interview area; moments later, Gilbert slid in the ring with Bigelow then running out and helping him clear the Hrosemen from the ring

12/31/88 - hosted by Tony Schiavone & Jim Ross; featured Ross conducting an interview with Eddie Gilbert, who claimed had been been underestimated by NWA World Champion Ric Flair & NWA US Champion Barry Windham and that he was ready to become the US Champion; included Missy Hyatt conducting an interview with Sir Oliver Humperdink about participating in the Manager's Bunkhouse Battle Royals throughout January; featured the Rick Steiner vs. NWA TV Champion Mike Rotundo match from Starrcade; included Magnum TA conducting an interview with Flair & JJ Dillon backstage at Starrcade following Flair's title defense; featured highlights of all the Starrcade matches to close the show; included the announcement that the show would move to 7:05 pm EST the following week:

NWA US Women's Champion Misty Blue, Vula, & Heidi Lee Morgan defeated Linda Dallas, Mad Dog Debbie, & Kat Leroux at 8:00 when Blue pinned Debbie with a splash off the top

Eddie Gilbert pinned Trent Knight at 6:47 with the Hotshot

The Junkyard Dog pinned Todd Collins at 3:56 with the Big Thump

Curtis Thompson pinned Bob Emory at 5:08 with a powerslam

The Commandos defeated Max McGyver & Max Miles at 4:37 when Commando Boone pinned Miles with a splash

Dustin Rhodes & Kendall Windham defeated Randy Hogan & Mike Justice at 6:32 when Rhodes pinned Hogan with an elbow drop after Windham hit a bulldog

Dennis Condrey & Randy Rose (w/ Paul E. Dangerously) defeated Tony Suber & Bo Graham at 5:35 when Condrey pinned Graham following the clothesline / clip to the knee combo; after the match, Tony Schiavone interviewed Dangerously who claimed his team would dominate 1989

Tommy Rogers & Bobby Fulton defeated Mike Jackson & Randy Mulkey at 5:41 when Rogers pinned Mulkey with a splash off the back of Jackson, who was held in a fireman's carry by Fulton

NWA @ Gainesville, GA - Georgia Mountains Center - December 14, 1988
Television taping

NWA @ Raleigh, NC - Dorton Arena - December 15, 1988
TV taping:

Rick Steiner pinned Steve Williams with a belly to belly suplex

NWA US Champion Barry Windham & NWA Tag Team Champions the Road Warriors defeated Sting, Lex Luger, & Dusty Rhodes when Animal pinned Sting after Paul Ellering interfered and hit Sting with a chair

Worldwide - 12/31/88 - hosted by Tony Schiavone & David Crockett:

Tommy Rogers & Bobby Fulton defeated Dennis Condrey & Randy Rose (w/ Paul E. Dangerously) in a Best 2 out of 3 Falls

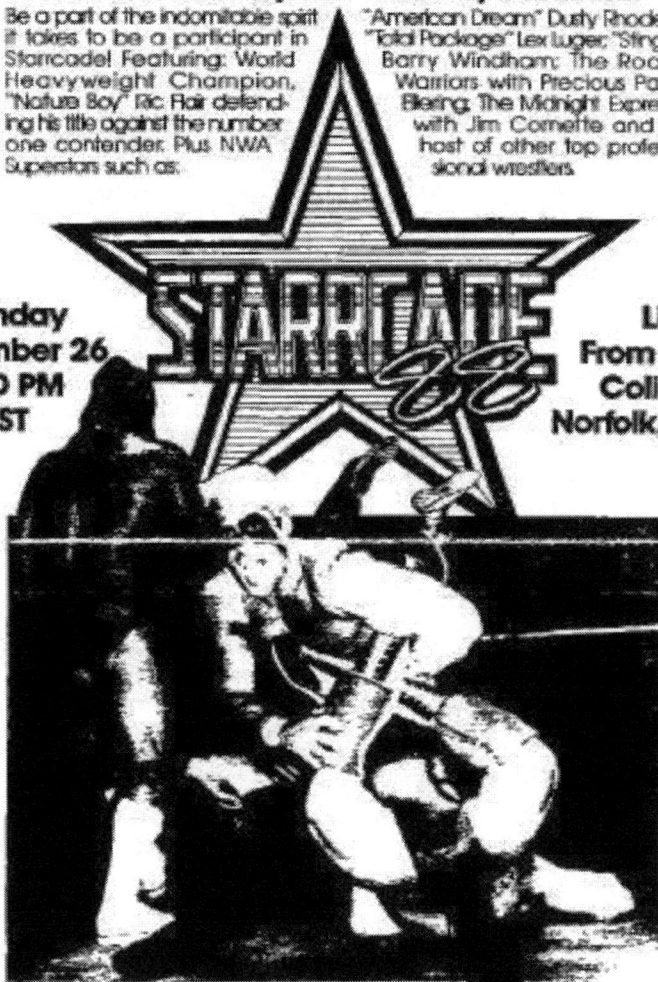

TURNER HOME
ENTERTAINMENT

Proudly presents

A Three Hour Pay-Per-View-Spectacular

Be a part of the indomitable spirit it takes to be a participant in Starrcade! Featuring: World Heavyweight Champion, "Nature Boy" Ric Flair defending his title against the number one contender. Plus NWA Superstars such as:

"American Dream" Dusty Rhodes; "Total Package" Lex Luger; "Sting"; Barry Windham; The Road Warriors with Precious Paul Ellering; The Midnight Express with Jim Cornette and a host of other top professional wrestlers.

Monday December 26 7-10 PM EST

Live From Scope Coliseum Norfolk, Virginia

True Grit

Call To Order 437-1401

Only $19⁹⁵

$24.95 DAY OF EVENT
OPERATOR ASSISTED ORDERS

NewChannels
Cable Television

match; fall #1: Condrey pinned Rogers at 13:51 with his feet on the bottom rope after rolling through Rogers' crossbody off the middle rope; fall #2: Fulton pinned Condrey with a sunset flip at 12:38; fall #3: Rogers pinned Rose at 8:18 after Jim Cornette interfered and hit Rose in the back with his tennis racquet, moments after Dangerously hit Rogers in the back with his phone; the bout was filmed when Rogers & Fulton were still NWA US Tag Team Champions and they were not shown with the titles; after the match, David Crockett interviewed Dangerously, along with Condrey & Rose, with Dangerously stating he would put Cornette in a coffin where his brain would be eaten by bugs before Dangerously was finished with the NWA, and he would step into the ring if he needed

NWA @ Winston-Salem, NC - December 16, 1988 (3,000)
Dustin Rhodes & Kendall Windham defeated the Cruel Connection
Bobby Fulton pinned the Italian Stallion
Tommy Rogers pinned Rip Morgan
Bobby Eaton & Stan Lane defeated the Commandos (Ray Candy & Grizzly Boone) after Jim Cornette hit Candy with the tennis racquet
Ivan Koloff defeated Russian Assassin #2 in a chain match
Steve Williams & NWA TV Champion Mike Rotundo fought Rick Steiner & Eddie Gilbert to a double count-out
Dusty Rhodes, Sting, & Lex Luger defeated NWA US Champion Barry Windham & NWA Tag Team Champions the Road Warriors when Rhodes pinned an interfering Paul Ellering

Worldwide - 12/17/88 - featured Tony Schiavone & David Crockett on commentary; included a Starrcade 88 segment which listed all the cable companies carrying the show in your particular state; featured a Starrcade 88 Update in which Schiavone & Crockett discussed the five title matches; included Jim Ross conducting an interview with NWA TV Champion Mike Rotundo & Kevin Sullivan regarding Rotundo's title defense against Rick Steiner at Starrcade; featured Dusty Rhodes, his eye taped up, as a guest of Magnum TA on Straight Talk with the Boss, with Rhodes saying his intentions for Starrcade was to hurt the Road Warriors and win the NWA Tag Team Titles; Rhodes went on to say the Road Warriors weren't really all that bad or scary:
Bobby Eaton & Stan Lane (w/ Jim Cornette) defeated Gary Royal & an unknown at 5:09 when Eaton pinned the unknown with one hand after the Veg-o-matic; during the bout, Paul E. Dangerously cut an insert promo saying Cornette was a joke and Eaton & Lane's flashy moves wouldn't work on Randy Rose & Dennis Condrey; Cornette briefly joined the commentary team to reply to Dangerously's comments; after the break, David Crockett conducted a ringside interview with Cornette about Dangerously, Rose, & Condrey
NWA TV Champion Mike Rotundo & Kevin Sullivan defeated JD Wolfe & an unknown at 4:22 when Rotundo pinned Wolfe with the butterfly suplex after Sullivan hit the double stomp to the chest; during the bout, Rick Steiner cut an insert promo on challenging Rotundo for the title at Starrcade, during which

Steiner talked with his hand "Alex" about the match and said he would get Alex a belt too when he wins his; during the match, the crowd chanted "We want Steiner"
NWA Tag Team Champions Road Warriors (w/ Paul Ellering) defeated Randy Hogan & an unknown at the 22-second mark when Road Warrior Hawk pinned the unknown with a running clothesline; after the bout, Crockett conducted a ringside interview with Ellering & the Road Warriors regarding their title defense at Starrcade against Sting & Dusty Rhodes
NWA US Tag Team Champions Bobby Fulton & Tommy Rogers defeated Curtis Thompson & Terry Jones at 4:32 when Rogers pinned Jones after a somersault off the top double team
Dustin Rhodes & Kendall Windham defeated Mike Jackson & an unknown at 3:51 when Rhodes pinned the unknown with the Bionic elbow after a bulldog from Windham; Rhodes & Windham were noticeably booed during the bout
NWA World Champion Ric Flair & NWA US Champion Barry Windham (w/ JJ Dillon) defeated the Italian Stallion & an unknown at 4:01 when Windham pinned the unknown with the lariat; during the bout, Lex Luger cut an insert promo on challenging Flair at Starrcade; after the bout, Crockett conducted a ringside interview with Dillon, Flair, & Windham regarding Flair facing Luger and Windham facing Bam Bam Bigelow at Starrcade

Worldwide - 12/24/88:
Bobby Eaton & Stan Lane vs. George South & an unknown
Rick Steiner vs. an unknown
Heidi Lee Morgan & Moolah vs. Linda Dallas & Kat LaRue
NWA TV Champion Mike Rotundo & Steve Williams vs. two unknowns
Dustin Rhodes & Kendall Windham vs. two unknowns
The Junkyard Dog vs. Max McGyver

NWA @ Greenville, SC - December 25, 1988 (matinee)
Bobby Eaton & Stan Lane defeated Dennis Condrey & Randy Rose
Also included a Bunkhouse Stampede match

NWA @ Charlotte, NC - Coliseum - December 25, 1988 (5,000)
Bobby Eaton & Stan Lane defeated Dennis Condrey & Randy Rose
NWA World Champion Ric Flair defeated Eddie Gilbert (sub. for Sting) (the first ever Flair-Gilbert match)
Also included a Bunkhouse Stampede match

Starrcade 88 "True Gritt" - Norfolk, VA - Scope - December 26, 1988 (10,000)
Pay-per-view bouts - featured Jim Ross & Bob Caudle on commentary and Tony Schiavone & Magnum TA serving as hosts; Gary Michael Cappetta served as the ring announcer for the show; included Magnum conducting a backstage interview with NWA TV Champion Mike Rotunda as well as the new NWA US Tag Team Champions Kevin Sullivan & Steve

Williams regarding the Varsity Club's tag team title win and Rotunda's title defense later in the show; featured Magnum conducting a backstage interview with Rick Steiner regarding his NWA TV Title win, during which the audio briefly went out; included Magnum conducting a backstage interview with NWA World Champion Ric Flair, during which Flair said his match against Lex Luger later in the show would be Luger's last title shot:

Steve Williams & Kevin Sullivan defeated NWA US Tag Team Champions Bobby Fulton & Tommy Rogers at 15:50 when Williams pinned Fulton to win the titles by dropping Fulton throat-first across the top rope as Fulton attempted a Thesz Press; during the bout, Jason Hervey of "The Wonder Years" was shown sitting in the front row

Bobby Eaton & Stan Lane (w/ Jim Cornette) defeated Dennis Condrey & Randy Rose (w/ Paul E. Dangerously) at 17:26 when Lane pinned Rose following the double goozle; both teams used the Midnight Express theme song; after the bout, Condrey, Rose, & Dangerously laid out Eaton, Lane, & Cornette with Cornette's tennis racquet and Dangerously's phone until Eaton eventually cleared the ring with the racquet

The Russian Assassins (w/ Paul Jones) defeated Ivan Koloff & the Junkyard Dog at 6:47 when Russian Assassin #1 pinned Koloff after Jones put a foreign object into the Assassin's mask, moments after Koloff hit the Russian Sickle on Russian Assassin #2 and made the cover; pre-match stipulations stated the Assassins would have had to unmask and Jones would have to leave the NWA if Koloff & JYD won

Rick Steiner pinned NWA TV Champion Mike Rotunda (w/ NWA US Tag Team Champion Kevin Sullivan) to win the title at 17:59 after Rotunda collided with Sullivan on the apron as Sullivan argued with head referee Tommy Young; Sullivan was placed in a shark cage for the duration of the bout, with the help of Klondike Bill; Sullivan was released late in the contest after NWA US Tag Team Champion Steve Williams appeared ringside and rang the timekeeper's bell, as Steiner had Rotunda covered following the belly to belly suplex, causing referee Teddy Long to believe the time limit had expired; moments later, Young came ringside to investigate who rang the bell

NWA US Champion Barry Windham (w/ JJ Dillon) defeated Bam Bam Bigelow (w/ Sir Oliver Humperdink) via count-out at 16:17 after Bigelow hit the steel ringpost while both men fought on the floor

Sting & Dusty Rhodes defeated NWA Tag Team Champions the Road Warriors (w/ Paul Ellering) via disqualification at 11:16 when Ellering prevented referee Tommy Young from making the count after Sting hit a crossbody off the top onto Road Warrior Animal; after the bout, Sting & Rhodes cleared the ring of the champions (*American Dream: The Dusty Rhodes Story, Starrcade: The Essential Collection*)

NWA World Champion Ric Flair (w/ JJ Dillon) pinned Lex Luger at 30:59 with his feet on the ropes for leverage after Luger's knee went out as he attempted the Torture Rack; pre-match stipulations stated Luger would win the title if Flair was disqualified (*Starrcade: The Essential Collection, Legends of Wrestling*)

Dark match after the pay-per-view: The Junkyard Dog won a $50,000 bunkhouse battle royal; other participants included Abdullah the Butcher, Ray Candy, Eddie Gilbert, Dick Murdoch, Dustin Rhodes, NWA US Tag Team Champion Steve Williams, and others

NWA @ Washington DC - Armory - December 27, 1988 (1,800)

Bobby Fulton fought Larry Zbyzsko to a draw
The Broncos defeated the Commandos
Lex Luger & Bam Bam Bigelow defeated NWA US Champion Barry Windham & Abdullah the Butcher when Bigelow pinned Abdullah
NWA World Champion Ric Flair fought NWA TV Champion Rick Steiner to a draw after the 30-minute mark
Sting & Dusty Rhodes defeated NWA Tag Team Champions the Road Warriors via disqualification; Rhodes was booed while the other three were cheered
Lex Luger won a Bunkhouse Stampede

NWA @ Chicago, IL - UIC Pavilion - December 28, 1988 (2,987)

Paul E. Dangerously, Jim Cornette, Eddie Gilbert, Ron Simmons, and Russian Assassin #2 did not appear as scheduled
The Broncos defeated the Commandos
Dennis Condrey & Randy Rose defeated Bobby Fulton & Tommy Rogers
Abdullah the Butcher pinned Bam Bam Bigelow after hitting him with a foreign object
NWA World Champion Ric Flair fought NWA TV Champion Rick Steiner to a draw at the 30-minute mark
Lex Luger, Sting, & Dusty Rhodes defeated NWA US Champion Barry Windham & NWA Tag Team Champions the Road Warriors when Luger pinned an interfering Paul Ellering
Larry Zbyzsko won a Bunkhouse Stampede by last eliminating Bobby Eaton

NWA @ Milwaukee, WI - Mecca - December 29, 1988

Bobby Fulton fought Randy Rose to a draw
The Junkyard Dog defeated Russian Assassin #1
Lex Luger & Bam Bam Bigelow defeated NWA US Champion Barry Windham & Abdullah the Butcher
NWA World Champion Ric Flair defeated NWA TV Champion Rick Steiner
NWA Tag Team Champions Road Warrior Animal defeated Dusty Rhodes via disqualification
Dick Murdoch won a Bunkhouse Stampede

NWA @ St. Louis, MO - Keil Auditorium - December 30, 1988 (4,500)

Randy Rose fought Bobby Fulton to a draw
The Broncos defeated the Commandos
Dick Murdoch defeated Russian Assassin #1
NWA US Champion Barry Windham & Abdullah the Butcher defeated Lex Luger & Bam Bam Bigelow when Abdullah pinned Bigelow

Dusty Rhodes & Sting defeated Larry Zbyzsko (sub. for NWA Tag Team Champion Road Warrior Hawk) & NWA Tag Team Champion Road Warrior Animal at the 4-minute mark when Rhodes pinned Zbyzsko

NWA World Champion Ric Flair pinned NWA TV Champion Rick Steiner at the 28-minute mark

The Junkyard Dog won a Bunkhouse Stampede at the 7-minute mark; stipulations stated the winner would face NWA World Champion Ric Flair at the following month's show

Feb. 20, 1989.

For some, it was like returning to the scene of the crime. Chicago's UIC Pavilion was host to Starrcade '87, Jim Crockett Promotions' disastrous pay-per-view debut. Where the Road Warriors were denied the tag team titles. Where Ric Flair and Dusty Rhodes, the cornerstones of Jim Crockett Promotions, emerged once again as the top stars of the night. Where the end result was the status quo.

But that was nearly 16 months ago.

JCP had been sold to Ted Turner, with the wrestling company now utilizing the National Wrestling Alliance name. Dusty was gone, but not before resigning as booker in a move forced by TBS executives.

The benefits of the Turner purchase were already evident by improvements in the production quality. And the absence of Rhodes and other longtime Crockett names plus the (temporary) dissolvement of the Four Horsemen created opportunities for new stars. Stars like Sting, Paul E. Dangerously, the Steiner Brothers, the Great Muta, and Brian Pillman. Plus returning names like Ricky Steamboat and Terry Funk.

The end of this night, hosted well outside the traditional Crockett market, saw Steamboat cleanly pin longtime rival Flair to win the NWA World Title when replacement referee Teddy Long counted 1-2-3. But like countless times before, the initial referee - knocked dizzy moments earlier - stepped in after the call. The "Dusty finish" was a trademark of Rhodes' booking. The challenger would appear to win the title only for the referee to call for a disqualification or other technicality ruling. It kept the challenger looking strong but kept the championship on the title holder.

Rhodes himself was a frequent victim of the call. As was Lex Luger in his infamous battle with Flair at the 1988 Great American Bash stop in Baltimore, where the match was stopped due to Luger bleeding as a helpless Flair was caught in the challenger's Torture Rack.

After years of "Dusty finishes" dating back to Starrcade '85, the audience had been conditioned to expect the call to be reversed and Flair to remain champion on a technicality. Steamboat would have to try again to unseat the champ.

But then a dazed Tommy Young did something few people expected. He joined in raising the challenger's hand in victory. Whether it was intended as a "Dusty finish" tease or not, it symbolized the death of the previous regime and birth of the new era.

The birth of World Championship Wrestling.

About the Author

Graham Cawthon is an award-winning journalist, columnist and newspaper editor. He grew up in a military family and spent much of his childhood traveling, from West Germany to Anchorage, Ak. His research on the wrestling industry has been cited by the Wrestling Observer Newsletter, Fighting Spirit Magazine, PWInsider.com and WWE publications. A graduate of Radford University, he lives in North Carolina with his wife, dog and cat. Follow him on Twitter at @GrahamCawthon or @TheHistoryofWWE.

About the Editor

Grant Sawyer is a lifelong sports fan and obsessive statistician who took his background in the film and video industry and went on to establish relationships with numerous independent wrestling organizations to tape, edit and produce their events. Today the majority of his production work can be seen at CWF Mid-Atlantic. Grant also enjoys comics, his smokin' hot wife & insane child, and NFL football where he obsessively loves and follows all things related to the Green Bay Packers. Follow him on Twitter at @Statmark

OTHER TITLES ALSO AVAILABLE IN THE
"HISTORY OF PROFESSIONAL WRESTLING" SERIES

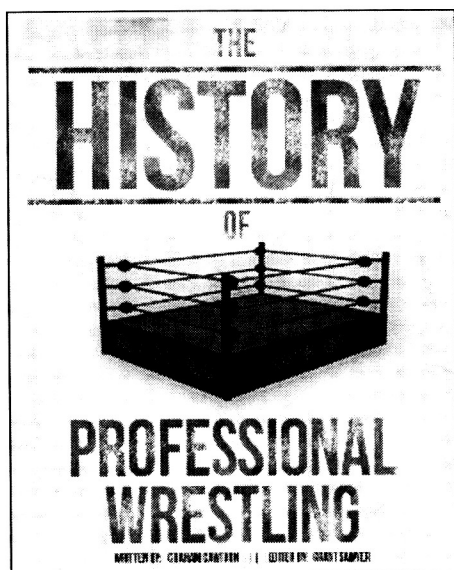

WWF 1963-1989

806 pages

ISBN-10: 1492825972

ISBN-13: 978-1492825975

WWF 1990-1999

594 pages

ISBN-10: 149356689X

ISBN-13: 978-1493566891

AVAILABLE AT AMAZON.COM AND
ALL FINE BOOK RETAILERS WORLDWIDE!

ALSO AVAILABLE ON KINDLE

Printed in Great Britain
by Amazon

19946982R00301